The Gospel according to John

A Theological Commentary

Herman N. Ridderbos

Translated by
John Vriend

WILLIAM B. EERDMANS PUBLISHING COMPANY
GRAND RAPIDS, MICHIGAN / CAMBRIDGE, U.K.

Dedicated to the

UNIVERSITY OF STELLENBOSCH

in gratitude for the
Graad D.Th. honoris causa,
bestowed on the author December 12, 1991

Originally published in two volumes as
Het Evangelie naar Johannes. Proeve van een theologische Exegese,
© 1987, 1992 Uitgeversmaatschappij J. H. Kok,
Kampen, the Netherlands

English translation © 1997
Wm. B. Eerdmans Publishing Co.
255 Jefferson Ave. S.E., Grand Rapids, Michigan 49503 /
P.O. Box 163, Cambridge CB3 9PU U.K.

Printed in the United States of America

02 01 00 99   7 6 5 4 3 2

Library of Congress Cataloging-in-Publication Data

Ridderbos, Herman N.
[Evangelie naar Johannes. English] The Gospel according to John :
a theological exegesis / Herman N. Ridderbos.
p.   cm.
Originally published: Kampen, Netherlands :
Uitgeversmaatschappij J.H. Kok, 1987
Includes bibliographical references and indexes.
ISBN 0-8028-0453-5 (pbk. : alk. paper)
1. Bible. N.t. John — Commentaries. I. Title.
BS2615.3.R4913   1997
226.5′07 — dc21   96-53632
CIP

Contents

Indexes

Preface

This book aims to present an exposition of the Fourth Gospel *as the Christian Church adopted it*. Among other things, this means that it proceeds from the canonical form in which the Gospel has come down to us from ancient times — taking into account, of course, the text-critical problems with which the multiplicity of manuscripts and textual witnesses confront us. And I am especially interested in presenting a *theological* exegesis of the Gospel, that is, in dealing with the significance of the gospel message that the Evangelist had in view as he wrote.

I have attempted to make this commentary readable for as wide a circle of readers as possible. Although in the nature of the case one can hardly do this without entering into dialogue with other commentaries and secondary works — of which I have made grateful and extensive use — I have not done so primarily to involve the reader in the scholarly enterprise, but only when it seemed of direct importance for gaining insight into certain passages.

For the same reason, in distinction from most, though not all, modern commentaries, I have not attempted a separate treatment of all the preliminary questions that have raised with regard to the origin of the Fourth Gospel, such as

- whether it was originally a single composition,
- the issue of the independence (or otherwise) of the sources and the way they were handled by the Evangelist,
- this Gospel's relationship to the Synoptic Gospels,
- whether we have the material in the Gospel in the original form and order (which is doubted by many scholars),
- the "phases" in the history of the Gospel's origination,

and the like. Opinions on all these questions are widely divergent and come to us in a body of literature almost impossible to survey, consisting as it does in a vast multitude of separate studies and monographs. I deal with these questions incidentally, but I regard a separate and systematic study of them as clearly outside the interpretive horizon of the gospel as it now reads.

For the commentator to stay as closely as possible to home, that is, to the text of the Gospel itself, there is much to be said in favor of the practice, followed by Bultmann in his famous commentary, of plunging immediately — without the typical "introduction" — into the text and dealing with disputed issues ad hoc, that is where particular passages occasion such discussion. In fact, this method has been followed in the present commentary, be it in a much more modest format and with less argumentation than Bultmann could permit himself.

On the other hand, it seemed to me meaningful, in view of the purpose of this commentary, to furnish the reader a *theological* introduction, one that explains how, gradually and in broad outline, the contours of what one might call the peculiar character of the Fourth Gospel, especially on the basis of its self-testimony, have emerged for me. I thus try to point out which road would seem to offer the best chance of enabling the reader to find the point of entry into this — at first blush, hardly accessible — book of the Bible. It might seem that what might be regarded as the outcome of this study is thus presented as the a priori interpretive key. But here, too, I can cite an example, be it one I can only follow from a much greater distance, namely that of the Evangelist himself, who also made the "last word" of his gospel narrative into the first word of his prologue (cf. 20:28; 1:1ff.). Having said that, I have at the same time arrived at "the peculiar character" of the Gospel.

Introduction

The Peculiar Character of the Fourth Gospel

The Evidence of the Gospel Itself

For our insight into the unique character of the Fourth Gospel the author's self-testimony is of decisive importance in more than one respect. Frequently this self-testimony is associated with the tradition of the ancient church, namely that the apostle John, the son of Zebedee, wrote the Gospel at an advanced age in Asia Minor. However, a sharp distinction needs to be made. The tradition can certainly not be derived directly from the Gospel itself, in which the name of John the apostle never occurs.

In the redactional conclusion of the Gospel, persons other than the author identify "the disciple whom Jesus loved" as the author (21:20, 24), but we are not given further information about this person either there or in other passages in which this person is mentioned. As a result the question of the identity of this disciple has become an important — and still unresolved — point of dispute among interpreters. Those who follow the ancient tradition recognize the apostle John in this disciple without any problem, but those who reject Johannine authorship — the large majority of modern interpreters — have, of course, greater difficulty with this identification. In the course of more recent scholarship a series of other candidates have been successively proposed to fill the vacancy, though none have found general acceptance. And some have expressed the notion that in the case of this disciple we are not dealing with a historical person but with an "ideal" figure (e.g., the Gentile Christian). Still others take a somewhat less radical but no less controversial intermediate position: The "disciple" in question was indeed a historical figure, but only symbolic significance — not historical reality — can be attributed to his conduct.

This array of hypotheses sometimes leaves the critical reader with the impression that almost anyone *except* the apostle John could have been "the

1

disciple whom Jesus loved." Nevertheless the fact remains that the Evangelist himself nowhere reveals the secret of this person's identity and apparently with great deliberateness allows this disciple, with whom he nowhere identifies himself, to figure in the Gospel as a person who remains anonymous throughout. Therefore, whatever one might think of the problem of "the disciple whom Jesus loved" — an issue that must be considered further in the exegesis of the pertinent passages — in any case the Evangelist himself apparently did not deem disclosure of that disciple's identity necessary for the proper understanding of his writing. In this regard, then, one cannot say that accepting or not accepting the ancient tradition is essential to an understanding of the unique character of the Fourth Gospel.

Matters stand quite differently with regard to the author's status as an eyewitness. The final redactor refers to this position by calling "the disciple whom Jesus loved" both the author and the "witness" of the things narrated in the Gospel (21:24; cf. 19:35). Furthermore, the Evangelist himself certainly has this in mind in the fundamental pronouncement in 1:14, where he includes himself among those who have seen the glory of the incarnate Word. Some interpreters, to be sure, believe that the Evangelist is speaking here on behalf of the church and is therefore referring more generally to spiritual contemplation of Jesus' glory. But the context clearly refers to beholding Jesus' glory in connection with the incarnation — Jesus dwelling among us — just as in what follows there is repeated reference to Jesus' disciples "seeing" as eyewitnesses of his glory in the flesh (2:11; 1:50, 51; 20:29, 30). Although in the same connection (cf. vs. 16) the Evangelist is also aware that he speaks on behalf of the church (which he is addressing) when he speaks of the fullness of grace from which ("we all)" (hence the readers included) "received," the "we" in 1:14 undoubtedly refers only to those who witnessed the *manifestation* of the glory of the only begotten of the Father; this is therefore corrrectly characterized as the "apostlic we" in distinction from the ("you)" of the church, as in 20:31, where it is said that the things Jesus did "in the presence of the disciples" were written in this book "that (you)may believe that Jesus is the Christ, the Son of God" (for this distinction between "we" and "you," see also 1 Jn. 1:1, 3; cf. Jn. 19:35).

The paramount importance for the Evangelist of this (apostolic) discipleship as foundational for the church's faith also appears in the calling of Jesus' first disciples (1:35f.) in direct conjunction with the witness of John the Baptist. This great witness to the Lord (1:6f.) and forerunner of the Lord (1:23) directs the disciples toward Jesus with the words "*Behold,* the Lamb of God" (1:35), and Jesus calls them to himself and they are led to him by the repeated "Come and *see*" (1:39, 46). Their meeting and "following" Jesus is not only the accession of the first *believers* to Jesus (which would have to be interpreted as such: see the commentary) but also very definitely the calling of Jesus' first *disciples (apostles)* in its redemptive-historical connection with, and transcending of, John's mission (1:6; see also under 1:33, 34 and 3:27ff.). To be sure, not all the particulars about the disciples — their number, names, and first mission (cf., e.g., Mt. 10:1ff.) — are reported. The readers are assumed to be familiar with these details (e.g., 6:70; 11:16), which are brought to their attention in the first part of the Gospel in their significance for the coming church in only a few — be it very important — incidents (cf. 4:35-38; 6:5f., 12, 13, 67f.; 9:2). But in the farewell discourses and after the resurrection, John's Gospel all the more emphatically and at length posits the mission of the disciples as the eyewitnesses chosen and empowered by Jesus, as those who "were with him from the beginning," as well as Jesus' promise that the Spirit will testify along with them and assist them in the fulfillment of their task (cf. 13:16, 20; 14:26; 15:16, 26, 27; 16:13f.; 17:18, 20; 20:21ff.; 21:20ff.)

The idea that the Evangelist wishes the readers to understand his own witness concerning the glory of God manifested and seen in the earthly life of Jesus in the light of that second reality seems hardly open to doubt, and so it is understood by most interpreters. One may therefore — correctly, we think — ask whether the opening pronouncement in 1:14 does not necessarily also carry the meaning that the Evangelist himself was one of those who was "with Jesus from the beginning" and even more concretely whether he was not the anonymous companion of Andrew who, together with him, at the suggestion of the Baptist, was the first to follow Jesus and who saw where he stayed (1:37). That he was cannot be affirmed with certainty or even less rejected as "a wish that is the father of the thought." But if we can be content with the view that the Evangelist, in speaking of himself, restricts himself to the "we" of the eyewitnesses, then by that very fact — taking it as it is apparently intended — a framework has been furnished that proves in more than one respect to be of decisive importance for an understanding of this Gospel and for a determination of its character.

The Evangelist as Tradent

This understanding casts light first of all on the unique and very special manner in which the author tells the story of Jesus and hence functions as a tradent. He does so with great independence and, in a way, with great freedom. Of the "many signs that Jesus did," the Evangelist chooses those he needed and deemed adequate for the goal that he sought (20:31). For this purpose he also uses stories that show a very close kinship with the tradition that was fixed in the Synoptic Gospels, for example the Synoptic tradition of the miracle of the loaves and of Jesus walking on the sea (though on close comparison there can be no question of dependence on those Gospels: see the commentary). From all this one may infer that it was not his aim, on the basis of his own knowledge of what happened, to re-record "from the beginning" everything that happened (cf. Lk. 1:4) and that in writing his Gospel he did not stand in the initial phase of the formation of the tradition. Rather, one discovers over and over that he assumes among his readers — the 'you' of 20:31; 19:35 — a more than superficial knowledge of the tradition and that he proceeded from the premise that he no longer had to inform them of the general course of Jesus' life. His narrative therefore often gives the impression that it is the woof woven in the warp of the existing and familiar tradition, for example, that of the "three days" in which the "witness of John" occurred (1:29, 35). All this points to a level of relating to the tradition and of building on it possible only for one who considered himself involved in its formation and authorized to work with it, one who therefore did not write as a spokesman for the later church, interpreting its faith, but who in his own way showed the church its own authentic tradition and who recorded it as the foundation on which that church — in the progression of time, certainly — could build its faith and expect its salvation (20:31).

On the other hand — and this brings out his independence no less — the Fourth Evangelist often displays a detailed knowledge of the events he narrates, events that we do not know about from elsewhere in the known tradition. This is true not only of the narrative materials themselves but also of the historical and geographical framework in which he places his materials. This framework constitutes an important departure from the limits within which events are generally placed in the Synoptic tradition. Our insight into the course of historical events is clarified and deepened to a considerable extent by that framework (specifically with regard to the duration of Jesus' ministry and his confrontation with the Jewish leaders in Jerusalem, which cannot be confined to the last week of Jesus' life on earth).

Thus, for example, though he "allows" Jesus' public ministry to begin in Galilee (2:1-12), the Evangelist immediately, already before the arrest and imprisonment of John the Baptist, transfers it to Jerusalem and Judea (2:13; 3:24). The Synoptic Gospels know, or at least relate, nothing of such an interim, and two of them have Jesus' ministry begin after John's imprisonment (cf. Mk. 1:14; Mt. 4:12). It is true that after this first Passover and Jesus' stay in Samaria (John 2–4), Jesus does return to Galilee (apparently to escape a premature conflict with the Pharisees: cf. 4:1), but in what follows almost all the events occur in Jerusalem at the great festivals. Jesus is in the city as a pilgrim and has long conversations with the Jewish leaders. It is true that he journeys to Jerusalem, each time starting out from Galilee as his base, but what transpires in Galilee after the events reported in 2:1-12 — events that form the main content of the Synoptic Gospels — are condensed in the Fourth Gospel into one grand summary in ch. 6, beginning with the miracle of the loaves and ending with the "separation of spirits," which occurs also in Galilee, and with Peter's confession. But after 7:1, the action again shifts to Jerusalem and Judea, and there is no longer any escape to Galilee (chs. 7–12).

Not only does this important measure of personal knowledge apply to the temporal and local "infrastructure" of John's Gospel but also, as we have noted, to the content of the narrative itself, in particular to the encounters between Jesus and certain persons (Nicodemus and the Samaritan woman, chs. 3 and 4), the lengthy conversations linked with specific miracles (chs. 6 and 10; cf. also ch. 9), and the repeated confrontations with "the Jews" who are hostile to Jesus, which take up a large part of the center section of the Gospel (chs. 5, 7, 8, and 10).

The scope of this material is such that the question of how the Evangelist came upon this knowledge repeatedly forces itself on the interpreter. In the case of those who reject the notion of any direct knowledge gained by the Fourth Evangelist being an eyewitness of Jesus' public ministry, this has led to extensive studies and discussions of the "sources" of this Gospel and the way in which the Evangelist presumably handled the traditions contained in the Gospel. Some posit written sources, whether a sayings source and a signs *(sēmeia)* source or only the latter. Others reject the notion of written sources because, among other reasons, the Gospel's language and style exhibit such a high degree of homogeneity and originality that source analysis has barely any foothold. They therefore infer the existence of *oral* tradition, to which they attribute the stories and sayings unique to this Gospel.

Now it is certainly not impossible but in fact rather likely that the Fourth Gospel, besides utilizing traditions that we also know from other documents, also used traditions that we cannot trace outside his Gospel; and it would be somewhat too simple to attribute such traditions solely to the direct knowledge of the eyewitness. But to push back, for instance, all of Jesus' activity outside Galilee, including all the encounters and miracles narrated as part of that activity, to a tradition utterly unfamiliar to us in any other way, though it relocates the problem, certainly does not solve it and rather creates a new problem involving pure unknowns. Moreover, there is the fact — and this is the principal objection to the theory — that the Fourth Gospel's unique structuring and special material show a highly *un*traditional character and rather give the impression of having been composed with a free hand and a high degree of independence from "the" tradition. It is quite possible, of course, that "the" tradition, however one may picture it, contains reminiscences of a much more frequent contact of Jesus with Jerusalem than can be deduced from the Synoptic Gospels (although indications of this are not lacking there either).

But such reminiscences are certainly not present in the detailed form we see in John: journeys to clearly identified feasts with indications as to where Jesus stayed in Jerusalem, conversations with his brothers about whether he was going, and the like. It is in this form that materials about pilgrimage to Jerusalem serve the Fourth Evangelist as ready-made structures for framing his stories. The autonomy and sureness with which he moves within these structures — mentioning particulars of each journey — reveal a much greater degree of independence from "the" tradition than could be explained on the basis of that tradition.

And this argument applies to an even greater degree to the content of the stories. One can accept without any difficulty that the recollection of certain encounters like those with Nicodemus and the Samaritan woman and the continual conflicts with "the Jews" might have persisted in one way or another in the early church. But it certainly did not persist in the manner and measure, the detailed elaboration and clarity, that it has in this Gospel. Here, too, it is the hand of the Evangelist as tradent and his independence with regard to what is supposed to have been "handed down" to him as tradition that determines the utterly unique character and stamp of the Fourth Gospel.

The real question confronting us here is, then: To whom can we, with the greatest probability, attribute this independence? Would it be an author who could write in this fashion because as a companion of Jesus, a disciple from the first hour (15:27), he "knew" what he was writing (19:35) and had witnessed Jesus in his encounters with people and in his painful conflicts with "the Jews"? Or would it be one who depended on the tradition for all he knew of Jesus' earthly life and hence derived the freedom with which he recorded it from the imaginative ability to create from the motifs of that tradition, unhindered by personal knowledge of what had actually happened, conversations, stories, and miracles that would endure throughout the centuries? Was it, in other words, one who worked on the basis of a charism that enabled him to link faith in the heavenly Lord with traditional motifs and reminiscences in such a way that it was no longer the historical Jesus who spoke in them and acted in virtue of his Sonship and his being sent by the Father, but the risen Lord who spoke and acted in virtue of the unlimited possibilities attributed to him by the faith of the church? That is the question.

Tradition and Interpretation

But even these alternatives, no matter how much conviction one might attach to one or the other of them, are not the last word about the unique character of the Fourth Gospel. For if one opts for the latter alternative — however one does this, for the modes in which this understanding is articulated are numerous — the problem remains that one still ascribes to the author of the Fourth Gospel a role in which what he himself testifies concerning it can no longer be recognized. After all, that which in his final declaration he says he is interpreting is not the faith of the church in its (risen) Lord, but rather — as we said earlier — *the apostolic witness concerning Jesus' historical self-disclosure* as the Christ, the Son of God, as the foundation on which that faith rests (what Jesus did in the presence of his disciples "*so that* you may believe," 20:30, 31). Of course these are not opposites. But what is at stake is the fundamental insight, which also applies to the Fourth Gospel, that it is not faith that produced the story but the story that produced the faith.

On the other hand, one would also fail to do justice to the uniqueness of the Fourth Gospel and even ignore it if one were to locate its significance in that which the author as eyewitness and tradent would be assumed to know of Jesus beyond what the Christian church (already) knew of him on the basis of the existing tradition, also beyond, say, what the Synoptic Evangelists knew. His interest definitely does not lie in having more information. Quite the contrary: What distinguishes the Fourth Gospel is precisely the vast reduction that he as tradent applies to the "*many other* things" that he could have written in the interest of the *one* thing to which he directs all his attention and that of his readers, namely, *the person and identity of Jesus as the Christ, the Son of God, and faith in his name* (20:30, 31). For that reason we may perhaps say that the Fourth Gospel, in the manner and to the degree in which it effects this reduction and concentration, represents the gospel genre in a unique way, modifying it in a way that can be characterized as the concluding phase of the phenomenon called "gospel."

And it is primarily on account of this single focus of the Fourth Gospel and its thus strongly interpretive character that many scholars no longer regard the author as an eyewitness but rather as a later "charismatic" or "theologian." It is true of all the Evangelists that they are not merely tradents but "Evangelists" in the full sense of the word — concerned not just to transmit historical information about Jesus but above all to initiate and strengthen "faith in his name" and each in his own way to shape the redaction of their materials with this in mind. But while it is precisely as Evangelists that they were devoted to the advancement and riches of the tradition in order to portray it to their readers in its saving content, for the Fourth Evangelist the primary goal consists in large measure in the direct and explicit *interpretation* of this knowledge, subordinating historiography to this goal much more deliberately than the other Evangelists do.

This comes out immediately in the prologue, in which, in a very fundamental way, he makes plain the light in which he understands "the life of Jesus" and wants his readers to understand it: Jesus is the incarnation of the Word who in the beginning was with God and was God. Thus what is advanced as primary in the prologue is not only the theological starting point but also that which governs the arrangement of the gospel story and serves as the criterion for what the Evangelist deems necessary and sufficient to bring the readers to and to strengthen them in: faith that Jesus is the Christ, the Son of God. Even if to that end the Evangelist can draw on a much larger fund of knowledge than he could assume to be familiar among his readers (e.g., the lengthy description of Jesus' activity outside Galilee), his interest is not to add items of information to the many things the readers already knew but is focused on the one thing around which everything, down to the finest details, is arranged.

The extent to which this is true may, because of its importance, be somewhat further illumined by comparison at some key points with the Synoptic Gospels. It is very striking and telling for this Gospel that, whereas in the Synoptics the coming of God's kingdom constitutes the great ("eschatological") issue at stake and the central content of Jesus' preaching, here the kingdom is referred to on only one occasion (3:3, 5) and then without any further explanation: It is a concept for which the readers require no explanation. This does not mean that in the Fourth Gospel this all-controlling "eschatological" background is missing. But here, too, it is *the person of Jesus* that provides the entire framework, that which in the Synoptic Gospels is provided by the kingdom of God. This is clear, characteristically, from the central place that Jesus' self-disclosure as "the Son of man" — the personal parallel to "the kingdom of God" concept — occupies in the Fourth Gospel; and it has this place particularly as the Gospel brings out, at key points in the story of Jesus' self-disclosure, the all-embracing and transcendent character of his messiahship (1:50, 51; 3:14f.; 5:27, etc.). But this is not to deny that there is in the Fourth Gospel only a small amount of material comparable to that in which we see the unfolding of the coming of the kingdom of God in its present and future significance in the Synoptics, that is, in the parables of the kingdom, the sermon on the mount in Matthew and Luke, and the soteriological depiction of the fatherhood of God and the forgiveness of sins in all sorts of sayings, stories, and parables. (The story in Jn. 7:53–8:11 is characteristic of this kind of material, but it is a later insertion.)

We can see the great difference between John and the Synoptics also in the place occupied in the Fourth Gospel by Jesus' miracles. Whereas the miracle chapters in the Synoptics (Mk. 1:23–2:12; 3:1ff.; Mt. 8 and 9) seem to hurry us along from one miracle to the next in order to depict in one grand tableau the overwhelming richness and diversity of Jesus' healings and acts of power (see esp. the frequent use of "immediately" in the beginning of Mark), the Fourth Gospel restricts itself to only a few miracles. It expatiates on them and allows the story of one miracle to expand into a separate chapter on Jesus' self-disclosure as the Son of God: The story in ch. 5 of the healing at Bethesda and the accompanying conflict with "the Jews" about the sabbath forms the introduction — through the transitional statement "My Father is working still, and I am working" (5:17) — to Jesus' foundational discourse on his relationship to the Father and on the power over life and death that flows from this relationship, thus going far beyond the opening miracle. The same applies, mutatis mutandis, to the interpretation of the miracle of the feeding of the five thousand in the next chapter. There, speaking to the multitude who now want to make him king, Jesus identifies *himself* as the bread come down from heaven, and that not only to satisfy their physical hunger and to provide for their earthly needs but as the enduring food that "the Son of man" will give as he offers his own flesh for the life of the world (6:27, 51, 53ff.). Both miracles are validating signs and pointers to the utterly unique character of Jesus' mission, both in the personal-christological sense of the word (ch. 5) and in the soteriological sense of the word (ch. 6). And they are therefore also criteria of faith and unbelief. The same is true, for each in its own way, of the miracles in chs. 9 and 11 (cf. 9:5, 35, 39f.; 11:25, 45, 46; see also the commentary).

Also to be mentioned in this connection are the many encounters and conversations in which again and again *the identity of Jesus in its all-embracing significance* is the subject applied in particular ways to each of "the people around Jesus": to the self-assured Nicodemus (3:2ff.), to a Samaritan woman with an eventful past (4:10), to the father of a dying child (4:47ff.), to a paralytic who risks continuing his old life without Jesus (5:14, 15), to a man born blind, who chose Jesus and was consequently thrown out of the synagogue (9:35), and to others. All of them, each in his or her own way and condition, come to stand for a moment in the all-embracing, healing, and critical light of the One, as an exemplification of the fact that in him is life and that that life is the light of humanity, the one that enlightens *every* person by coming into the world (1:4, 9).

What is demonstrated in these encounters and in the lives of these very different people returns in the collective exchanges with "the multitude" and especially with "the Jews" at Jerusalem. It returns as an answer to the recurring question "Who is this?" raised by people who "believed" in him on account of his miracles but were unable to fit him into the pattern of their messianic expectations. And it returns in his confrontation with "the Jews." In the Synoptics these opponents respond to Jesus' deviant teaching, conduct, and association with "tax collectors and sinners" by trying to catch him with trick questions. But in the Fourth Gospel they try, from the beginning, precisely because of his claim to be the Son of God, to kill him as a blasphemer (cf. 5:18). Therefore they ever more provocatively demand from him a clear and final answer concerning *his identity* (cf. 10:24). It is in particular in these conversations with "the Jews" in the large middle section of the Gospel (chs. 5–10) that Jesus' self-disclosure as the Son of God reaches a climax (e.g., in the "I am" sayings). These questions thus hasten and make irreversible the denouement of the conflict between him and the custodians of the Jewish religion (10:33).

If now we return to our starting point, two questions seem of paramount importance in determining the character of the Fourth Gospel:

- First, what led the Evangelist, as a tradent, to focus everything so exclusively on the person of Jesus as the Christ, the Son of God, putting aside the many other things that also belong to the core of the original gospel?
- Second, is this subordination of many other matters to one idea and the freedom with which this is done an indication that historical detail is, if not (from the vantage point of knowledge) the weak point in the Gospel,

then (from the vantage point of meaning and interpretation) no longer the essential point on which everything turns?

The Point of This Focus

The first of these questions has, in my view, everything to do with what we have already been said about the final phase of development in the description of the life of Jesus, which the Fourth Gospel seems to represent. Not only early church tradition but also the content of the Gospel itself clearly point to a historical development in which the Gospel has its *Sitz im Leben* and to which in a sense it responds. Especially relevant is the continual confrontation with "the Jews," a theme that completely governs the conversations about Jesus' identity in the long middle section (chs. 5–10), though it is present already in ch. 3. This subject will be dealt with more extensively in the comments on these chapters, especially ch. 8. If — in keeping with the scholarly attention that has been devoted to the Jewish background of the Fourth Gospel — my comments assume correctly that this sharp confrontation with "the Jews" has to be seen also in the context of the position of the later Christian church as it was confronted by the resurgent synagogue after the destruction of Jerusalem, then that could also help to explain the Fourth Gospel's focus on the person of Jesus as the Christ, the Son of God. For in that later confrontation people were divided — we may assume with increasing intensity — over the core question that kept (and keeps!) the church and the synagogue at arm's length: Was Jesus the Christ? And how could he be the Christ, he who, in his (supposed) descent, conduct, and death on the cross in no respect conformed to what the Jews pictured to themselves, and could picture to themselves, as the Messiah? And how could Christians honor and worship him as the Son of God? Other matters that were of great interest during Jesus' earthly life (such as his relationship to tax collectors and sinners) or of a more theological or ethical nature (his radicalization of the law, questions concerning divorce, the resurrection from the dead, etc.), though kept not entirely peripheral (e.g., the sabbath in chs. 5 and 7), do fall increasingly into the background. Jesus' self-disclosure as the Son of God in its central and deepest intent comes to the fore, not only in the controversy with "the Jews" but also for the benefit of the church. As already noted, this historical position of the church vis-à-vis the synagogue may have been one reason that the Evangelist focused his story entirely on the meaning of the person of Jesus, and it may have been for him an important criterion in the selection of his materials and the construction of his Gospel.

But there is every reason not to relate this christological concentration too much, as is done in some recent studies, to a specific situation in a specific

"Johannine community," as though the real interpretive key to the Fourth Gospel would lie there and as though even its "high christology" could be explained in terms of the church's need to defend itself against a threatening Judaism, or, as a result, to find this christological concentration no longer valid (at least without strong modification) for the church's present relationship to Judaism. This view, which we will repeatedly encounter in the commentary, is a narrowing of the Johannine purpose and a blurring of the historical portrayal of Jesus in favor of the later church's understanding of Jesus (the so-called "two-level theory"). For not only do we know too little of the situation of the first Christian community (let alone that of the "Johannine" community) but the flight of the eagle (the traditional symbol of John) among the Evangelists covers far too much distance for us to view it only from the perspective of the situation of one church or one phase in the history of the church.

The question on which the whole of the Fourth Gospel is focused is: Who is Jesus? This question does not arise out of a particular historical context. It is not just the real and final point of dispute between Christians and Jews. It is, rather, the question that every confrontation with Jesus ends with. It therefore had to become increasingly central as the preaching of the gospel progressed. For everything that Jesus gives, everything that one may expect of him, and everything that he asks in the way of faith, obedience, and love is finally determined by who he is. That is the meaning of the many "I am" statements in the Fourth Gospel, statements in which he is not only the bestower of benefits ("light," "life," "true food and drink") but also, in an absolute and exclusive sense, the benefits themselves: "the life of humanity," "the light of the world," "the way, the truth, and the life" (1:4; 8:12; 9:5; 14:6).

For that reason the church knew what it was doing when it accepted the Fourth Gospel, as different and peculiar as it seemed, as valid for the entire church (and world) and therewith applied the "you" of 20:31 to itself and to the entire church of the future. It did not choose among the four Gospels or in favor of three and against this one. It accepted all four into the canon of the New Testament and in the order we have them in. For the content of the Fourth Gospel does not ignore the first three or leave them behind (it presupposes them) any than they pronounce the last word on who Jesus was. Nor is the Fourth Gospel a superfluous and even "threatening" addition. In its own unique way it pulls together and identifies that toward which the others already more or less explicitly tend. It does this by focusing the entire coming and work of Jesus on what the prologue calls "the Word in the beginning," or, in the language of the gospel story, the presence of God in the Son of God's all-fulfilling love for the world.

History and Revelation

In a sense we have already answered the second question, but it does deserve separate attention. We might say that it is really the core question in the entire discussion of the "problem" — some call it the "riddle" — of the peculiar character of the Fourth Gospel. Already in the ancient church some were aware of the interpretive significance of the Johannine focus on the person of Jesus and therefore called him the "theologian" among the Evangelists (whence our old expression "St. John the Divine"). It could not remain hidden that this depth dimension of the Fourth Gospel exerted considerable influence on its presentation of the gospel story. Calvin, for example, explained the comparative brevity with which John describes the story of Jesus from the fact that John puts the soul in the foreground position, which is occupied in the Synoptics by the body, so that for Calvin the Gospel of John served as the key to the correct understanding of the Synoptics.

As long as Johannine authorship was assumed, the question of the historical character of the Jesus described in the Fourth Gospel hardly came up. Later, when scholars rejected as untrustworthy not only Johannine authorship but also any direct personal contact between the Evangelist and the historical events he described, they arrived at much more radical views concerning the relationship between interpretation and history. It was alleged that the great distance in time and space that separated the author from Jesus' historical appearance and ministry made it impossible for him to form a clear picture thereof and, going further, that his christology affected to a high degree his telling of the story, to the point where if he did not completely dissolve its historical character he at least weakened it.

We can, admittedly, observe a strong development and shift in modern interpretation of the background out of which the Fourth Gospel is supposed to have been written. For a long time, under the influence of the history of religions school, scholars sought to explain the Gospel against the background of syncretistic Hellenistic religiosity and placed it among the more idealistic movements or — increasingly — within gnosticism, with its dualistic conception of reality (see the comments below on the prologue). Interpreters sought in such a context the key not only to the "Johannine anthropology" ("flesh and spirit": see the commentary on 3:6ff.) but also to his christology, which they understood in light of the anthropology. Whether they proceeded from a more idealistic pattern of the higher and the lower or from a supposed "Johannine dualism" oriented to gnosticism, in both cases history is important in the Gospel only as a pointer to a higher or fundamentally different reality and hence, in its presentation, serves that reality.

Many, however, backed away from this one-sided "Hellenistic" interpretation of the Fourth Gospel and sought a base of interpretation closer to home, whether in the gospel tradition, the Old Testament, or especially the faith experience of the Jewish Christian community. Even so, the issue of history and interpretation generally continued to play a large role. Scholars felt that they could no longer recognize just the "historical" or "earthly" Jesus in the Fourth Gospel's portrayal of Jesus but also (or mainly) a projection of the church's experience of faith in the risen Lord. It was said that the Evangelist transferred this heavenly image to the earthly Jesus, portraying therein in earthly colors the all-embracing glory of the church's ascended Lord for the church's benefit. According to some interpreters, the Evangelist carries this to a point where the picture of Jesus' glory leaves the earthly reality completely behind and hence exhibits docetic traits.

Others view this projection rather as a blurring of the boundaries between the image of the earthly Lord and that of the heavenly Lord. Although the Evangelist proceeds from the "one and only" earthly Jesus, he at the same time makes him speak and act as the heavenly Lord present in the church, so that not only does John's portrayal of Jesus have a certain duality in which the earthly and the heavenly intersect, but the historical context in which the Evangelist supposedly makes Jesus act is said to show the characteristics of the later church. The conclusion is that in the Evangelist's representation of the gospel story we can see all sorts of anachronisms, that is, details not applicable to the life of the earthly Jesus. In our comments, much of this will come back for further discussion, in particular the supposed anachronisms (see particularly the comments on 9:22).

Here we have to restrict ourselves to what seems to be the essential point in this entire complex of problems, which is the meaning the Evangelist attributes, in his interpretation of the Christ-event, to *history*. And in this connection it seems that only one answer finally fits: The Evangelist views the real miracle of the coming and work of Jesus, the Christ, as the in-*carn*-ation of the Word or, as he states in a no less pivotal pronouncement, as the *descent* of the Son of man (3:14).

This is in total contradiction to any idea that in the development reflected in the Fourth Gospel the meaning of history is pushed back, blurred, spiritualized, or even simply fabricated. In 1:14 "flesh" refers precisely to that which is human, natural, and historical, and that neither as the unreal though visible world over against a real though invisible world nor as the concealment of the glory of the only begotten of the Father (in which case humanity and the world are supposed to be confronted with the great challenge to believe despite how things appear) but as the life in which and the means by which his glory was made visible to every eye and, as it were, palpable to every hand (cf. 1 Jn. 1:1ff.). Hence, to have "beheld" the revelation of that glory in the flesh and to witness to him who thus dwelled among us forms the foundation and content of the Fourth Gospel.

Accordingly, this glory is nowhere depicted more visibly and audibly than in John, as is evident particularly from the emphasis placed there on the irrefutability and reality of Jesus' miracles (9:18-34; 11:38-42; 20:27; also 2:9; 4:15ff.).

The miraculous is, to be sure, repeatedly fenced off against shallow interpretations that cannot see past the visible and that would see the thing itself contained in the sign. The referential character of the miracles ("the true bread," "the good wine," "seeing" in a spiritual sense, chs. 6, 2, and 9) is stressed (cf. 6:26, 27). But the historical reality of the miracles themselves does not thereby become a secondary or indifferent matter. When in his encounters with "the Jews" Jesus comes to the absolute and bitter end, he gives them as his last word the message that if they cannot or will not believe in him they should nevertheless still believe in his works as the indisputable signs of his mission and of his unity with the Father (10:37, 38). For that reason it is precisely the signs that Jesus performed that should persuade the readers and strengthen them in their belief that Jesus is the Christ, the Son of God — signs performed in the presence of witnesses duly appointed, selected, and recorded as such by the Evangelist (20:30, 31).

But it is no less clear that in this "flesh" in which Jesus "dwelled among us" there is a limitation that separates this earthly revelation of his glory from his future and heavenly glory (cf. 7:39; 9:5). The flesh is not consumed by the glory in such a way that he is no longer a man in the flesh and that the history dissolves into the revelation. He did not just "appear" to people in the flesh; rather, the Word "became" flesh: He dwelled among them as one of them. To that authenticity all sorts of people, situations, and encounters, which are graphically depicted, sometimes with striking precision as to time and place, bear witness. Nowhere is Jesus' glory more splendid than in the Fourth Gospel. Nor is his humanity more human anywhere else — right down to the account of his death and resurrection (19:34; 20:20, 27). And nowhere else does the Son of man, clothed by God with all power, descend more deeply, realistically, and scandalously into human flesh (cf. 6:27, 53).

The Witness of the Spirit

Here, too, however, the direct witness of the Evangelist himself speaks more clearly than what we might indirectly infer from the Gospel about (what in theological language we call) the relationship between history and revelation. For he himself very deliberately distinguishes the two. However much he appeals to the historical visibility of Jesus' glory in the flesh, he shows no less clearly that neither he nor anyone else who beheld this glory could, merely on the basis of eyewitness evidence, speak of that glory as that of the only begotten of the Father. And this applies not only to those who, though they did see Jesus' glory, either did not want to "see" it, as in the case of Jesus' enemies, or were unable to fit it into their theology, as in the case of Nicodemus (despite his "we know") or into the pattern of their future expectation, as with many of the people or "the Jews" who "believed" in him: It is also true of Jesus' closest disciples. With however much faith, at the direction of John the Baptist, they went to be with him, or like Nathanael were convinced of Jesus' messiahship in a way they found overwhelming, they were to see "greater things" than those for which their faith initially had room (cf. 1:50, 51; 4:31ff.; 6:6ff.).

All this comes up for discussion, directly and deliberately, in the farewell discourses. There, too, the disciples' inability to understand Jesus when he speaks of his Father and of going to the Father comes out (14:5ff., 8ff.). And there, too, Jesus promises those who have been with him "from the beginning" — and whom he designates as his witnesses *in that capacity* — the help of the Holy Spirit to "teach you all things and bring to your remembrance all that I have said to you" (14:25, 26; 15:26, 27). For the subject that engages us here these statements concerning the Spirit are of special importance, both negatively and positively.

They do not mean that in the end the Spirit takes the place of the eyewitnesses and, in that sense, of history. Nor do they mean that in that manner room is made for the spiritualization and sublimation of history. For it is precisely the Spirit who assists the disciples in their ministry as witnesses from the beginning and who holds them to that Jesus whom they have seen and heard and whose glory they have "beheld" in a way that was to them unforgettable. For that reason it is expressly said of the Spirit that "he will not speak on his own authority, but whatever he hears he will speak . . . and he will take what is mine and declare it to you" (16:12ff.). Although these verses present problems to the interpreter, one thing is clear: The Spirit will not push aside the word of Jesus or open a new source of revelation. The Spirit has nothing new to offer, nothing that Jesus has not brought. The Spirit will only enable the disciples to witness to Jesus as he really was, the one with whom they have been from the beginning (cf. 15:27).

Nor do these statements mean, secondly, that the disciples should make what they have seen and heard of Jesus' earthly glory into a vehicle for the expression of his heavenly glory and transfer the glory of the ascended Lord to the image of the earthly Jesus. It is true that the resurrection is the great presupposition of their "seeing" and understanding of Jesus' identity as they have known him and of his relationship to the Father of which he has repeatedly told them (cf. 14:19, 20). It is also true that the trajectory of his glory, which in him descended from heaven, does return to where it started (17:5). Nevertheless, the disciples are called and chosen to a "seeing" that finds in the resurrection not its beginning but its end (cf. 20:29). For that reason the Evangelist, who wants his Gospel viewed and understood in the light of these statements, does not testify to the glory of Jesus (if we may construe the issue in light of the central pronouncement of 3:13) in terms derived from the glory of the ascended One but from that of the descended One, he who said and did what he had "heard" and "seen" from the Father (3:11, 32; 5:19; 8:23, 28), who could say "Before Abraham was, I am" (8:58), whose glory radiated on him on earth not just from his "postexistent" exaltation but above all from his preexistent life as the Word from the beginning and the firstborn of the Father (17:4, 24).

But — and this positive dimension is of no less importance for insight into the uniqueness of the Fourth Gospel — it is also clear in light of chs. 14–17 that testimony concerning the true identity of the One who descended from heaven was possible only on the basis of both the experience of "witnessing" the risen One and the Spirit's co-witness. Therefore, also, the Evangelist is conscious (not only in the prologue but also in his record of Jesus' words) of being dependent not only on his own experience as an eyewitness but no less on the Spirit's co-witness, that is, the Spirit's teaching and bringing to remembrance all that Jesus said (14:26). Of course, what is "brought to remembrance" is not just what the Evangelist remembers, as if the Spirit enables him, infallibly and verbatim, to write down the words that Jesus uttered at some moment in the past. That which is expressed in the two concepts of teaching all things and bringing to remembrance all that Jesus said — two concepts formulated as a unity — is that the Spirit as fellow witness enabled the disciples to testify to Jesus as he wanted to be understood in his being sent by the Father, even though his witnesses had not understood him in that way when he was still with them.

In the promise that the Spirit would join its witness to that of the disciples, Jesus as it were hands them the substance of his self-disclosure. The witnesses repeat and confirm not only what he has said but, as independent spokespersons for Jesus, are incorporated into his self-testimony. Just as in obligations a servant is not greater than his master or an apostle than the one who sent him, so it is also true of the witnesses in regard to their authority to witness concerning him and in his behalf: "Whoever receives the one I send receives me, and whoever receives me receives the One who sent me" (13:16-20; cf. 20:21).

It is within this apostolic consciousness that the Evangelist writes his Gospel as he does and lets Jesus speak in the first person. But he does this in his own "Johannine" language and style, in an identification with the One who sent him, which also shines through in passages in which Jesus' speech concerning himself shifts from the first to the third person (cf. 3:11-21). This means that the boundaries between what is intended to be Jesus' own discourse and what the Evangelist says about him are not always clearly distinguishable (see esp. the epilogue to ch. 3 in vss. 31-36). The point at issue is always what Jesus said and did in his self-disclosure on earth, but it is transmitted in its lasting validity with the independence of an apostle who was authorized to speak by Jesus and endowed with the promise of the Spirit.

Finally, as was said earlier, all the above already anticipates the outcome of the — now following — interpretation of the Fourth Gospel. For that reason it will have to be explicated further and establish its validity in what follows.

1:1-18

The Prologue

The first chapter of John's Gospel falls into two parts: vss. 1-18 and vss. 19-51. The first part, the prologue, forms the introduction to the entire Gospel. Vs. 19 functions as a transition from the prologue to the gospel story.

The overall intent of the prologue is clear: to describe the background against which Jesus' historical self-disclosure must be understood. One can speak of the prologue as a splendidly constructed a priori introduction to the story, which is the gospel concerning Jesus of Nazareth. From the very start the person of Jesus and the significance of his work are placed in the context of the Word, which was in the beginning with God and to which all things that have been made owe their existence. It is the Word that in Jesus Christ came into the world, became flesh in him, dwelled among people, and was "beheld" in all its glory by those who saw him.

In the story that follows, certainly, the Word is no longer referred to in that separate sense, for the story speaks of the historical person of Jesus Christ, with whom the Word has been identified. But the entire story is full of the attributes that are ascribed to the Word in the prologue. For example, the story speaks of Jesus as "the Son" to whom the Father has granted to have "life in himself" (5:21, 24, 26; 6:51, 54, 57; cf. 1:4, 14, 18), who revealed his "glory" in the presence of his disciples (2:11; 17:22; cf. 1:14), who came into the world to be "the light of the world" (3:19; 8:12; 12:46, etc.; cf. 1:4, 5, 9), the light that shone in "the darkness" (12:35; 8:12) though the darkness did not receive it (3:19, 20; cf. 1:5, 10), who alone, as the one who was "with the Father," "has seen the Father" (6:46; cf. 1:1, 18), and who could speak of the glory he had with God before the world was made (17:5, 24; cf. 1:18).[1] Some interpreters

---

1. For this perspective, see the instructive article by M. D. Hooker, "John's Prologue and the Messianic Secret," *NTS* 21 (1974), pp. 40-58, esp. pp. 45ff.

have even believed that the structures of the prologue and of the gospel story are demonstrably parallel: 1:3 = 1:35–4:42 (Christ as re-creator), 1:4 = 4:43–6:71 (Christ as the life of the world), and 1:4ff. = 7:1–9:41 (Christ as the light of the world).[2] Although this division of 1:35 through ch. 9, taken as a whole, has some support in the key words of the prologue (1:1-4), it is too artificial to serve as a principle of division for the material in these chapters. But this is not to deny that the prologue and the gospel story form an intrinsic unity and have been "attuned" to each other. The story in several ways presupposes the prologue; in fact, in the elevated pronouncements Jesus makes concerning himself the story can hardly be understood apart from the thrust of the prologue; at least it would not have the context that the prologue gives to it. And, conversely, what is said in the prologue about the Word cannot be separated from the story's testimony concerning the historic self-disclosure of Jesus as the Christ as if it were simply free-standing. For the glory of the Word as that of the only begotten of the Father is "beheld" because the Word became flesh: The only Son who is in the bosom of the Father has made him known to us (1:18).[3]

For that reason the church has for a long time interpreted the prologue as an original and integral part of the Gospel. More recent research, however, has more or less radically backed away from that view. On the basis of the particular form of the prologue and the use of Logos ("Word") as a name, which we see only here in the Gospel, the distinctive character of the prologue has come to be strongly emphasized. Nowadays it is widely viewed as a separate hymn to the Logos. Some believe the Evangelist himself composed this hymn and afterwards inserted it as a preface to his Gospel,[4] but by far the majority of scholars who regard it as such a hymn see it as an existing church hymn that the Evangelist employed as the introduction to his Gospel.[5]

As indicated, scholars base this opinion on the distinct artistic form of

2. J. A. T. Robinson, "The Relation of the Prologue to the Gospel of St. John," *NTS* 9 (1963), p. 122.

3. Cf. C. K. Barrett: "The Prologue is necessary to the Gospel, as the Gospel is necessary to the Prologue; the history explicates the theology, and the theology interprets the history" ("The Prologue of St. John's Gospel," in his *New Testament Essays,* 1972, p. 48). See also my "The Structure and Scope of the Prologue to the Gospel of John," in *Placita Pleiadia* (in honor of G. Sevenster), 1966, pp. 191, 199f.; and my *Het Woord is vlees geworden. Beschouwingen over het eigen karakter van het Evangelie van Johannes,* 1979, p. 17.

4. As a substitute for an earlier and shorter preface, of which traces can still be found in the present prologue (vss. 6-8, 15); so Robinson, "Relation of the Prologue," p. 120f.

5. An exception to this is Bultmann's view of the "hymn" as pre-Christian, derived from the circle around John the Baptist. There use of Logos as a name is said to have been applied to John. The Evangelist, who came from this circle, is said to have transferred the name to Jesus, thus claiming for him the honor that John's disciples accorded to their teacher. This, says Bultmann, also explains the "negative" statements about John in vss. 6-8 and 15. Bultmann, *Comm.,* p. 17. This opinion has not found much acceptance.

certain parts of the prologue, in particular the progressive parallelism visible most clearly in vss. 1-5, with each line containing the key term of the next line, forming a stairstep pattern: a-b, b-c, and so on.[6] This gives to the prologue a certain regularity of diction that to some scholars suggests a poetic doxology devoted to the Logos, a hymn like those in Ep. 5:16 and Col. 3:16, with examples also in Ph. 2:6-11; Col. 1:15-20; and 1 Tm. 3:16.

Within this understanding of the prologue as a preexisting Logos hymn one does, of course, have to face the complication — no small one at that! — that the poetic form that emerges in vss. 1-5 (with the exception of vs. 2) is not continued. In vss. 6-8 and 15 we have prose statements about John the Baptist. In vss. 9-14 the poetic-hymnic style is resumed, but with increasing irregularities in the rhythm and in the length of the parallel parts (vss. 12c, 13). Also, as the prologue advances it contains an increasing number of elements and statements that in content no longer bear the hymnlike stamp of the beginning but increasingly change from a poetic to a polemic or kerygmatic mode of discourse. So, for example, vss. 16-18, which read more like added explanations than like parts of the hymn itself.

On the basis of all this scholars therefore assume that the original hymn was adapted by the Evangelist (or by a later redactor) by means of modifications, interruptions, and interpretive additions, in line with his intended purpose, that is, so that the hymn could function as an overture to his Gospel. But there are hardly two advocates of this general hypothesis who agree on what material is from the original hymn and what has to be attributed to the Evangelist.[7] Some are generous in their identification of material deriving from the original hymn, but others are inclined to attribute much more to the Evangelist. A consensus exists only with regard to vss. 1, 3, 4, 10, and 11, which are regarded as being clearly from the hymn.

But another matter makes things even more complicated. The exegete must continually ask not only where he or she is dealing with the hymn and where with the Evangelist, but also whether the Evangelist in his use of the "hymn" has left the original intent intact or in adapting it to his own purpose has given it another meaning. The clearest example of this is what happens to the hymn if one considers the prose material in vss. 6-8 an insertion or interruption from the Evangelist. It is clear, precisely because of these verses, which

---

6. Thus in vs. 1: "In the beginning was *the Word*. And *the Word* was with God." In vs. 3 the term is "was made." The pattern is clearest in vss. 4 and 5: "In him was *life*. The *life* was the *light* of humanity. The *light* shines in the *darkness*. The *darkness*. . . ." Note also "world" in vss. 9 and 10, "his own" in vs. 11a-b, "receive" in vss. 11b and 12a, "glory" in vs. 14a-b, and "fullness" in vss. 14b and 16.

7. See the comparative overview of the opinions of eight scholars in Brown, *Comm.* I, p. 22, each of whom has made a different choice. Brown himself, "with great hesitancy," adds his own as a ninth option, "emphasizing its tentative nature."

introduce John into the Gospel, that all that follows in vss. 9ff. (and perhaps even earlier, vs. 5) is immediately related by the Evangelist to the coming and the work of Jesus. John was the witness of the light that *Jesus* was and brought.

But if one disregards, for the purposes of the hymn, vss. 6-8 as an insertion, the person of Jesus Christ does not seem to appear on the scene till much later, namely when the incarnation of the Logos is mentioned in vs. 14. The preceding statements then seem — in the hymn — to refer to the Logos *asarkos,* that is, to his preexistence with God (vss. 1-4), to his "asarkic" penetration of the world in general and Israel in particular (vss. 5, 9-13), and then to arrive in vs. 14 at the final phase, the incarnate existence of the Word. The result is that then the section as a whole gets an entirely different structure and meaning. Much more than is the case in the prologue as it stands, the hymn's description of the Logos is thus central as a priori information, of which the incarnation is then the conclusion and climax.

But in the prologue, as is clear from vss. 6ff., everything is christological from the start, a circumstance that of course will be reflected in our exegesis of vss. 1-5. To express this in somewhat polarizing fashion: In the first instance Jesus Christ appears under the aspect of the Logos, and in the second the Logos under that of Jesus Christ.[8]

Some interpreters are so convinced of the precedence of the "original" hymn over the "secondary" prologue that they leave vss. 6-8 out of consideration in their exegesis as an inappropriate and disturbing late addition.[9] Others, like Bultmann, though they agree with this as far as the original hymn is concerned, nevertheless insist that the turn that the Evangelist gives to the sense of the hymn in vss. 6-8 must be examined on its own merits.[10] It cannot be denied, however, that in this manner the exegesis of Scripture is forced to labor under a heavy encumbrance. It has to assign to certain passages a meaning that it knows is alien, if not outright opposed, to their original intent.[11]

Although the hypothesis of the Logos hymn is advocated by many authoritative commentators[12] and is sometimes presented as a kind of exegetical

8. See also my "Structure and Scope," p. 191.
9. Cf. E. Haenchen, "Probleme des johanneïschen 'Prologs,' " in *Gott und Mensch. Gesammelte Aufsätze,* 1965, pp. 114f.; idem, *Comm.* I, pp. 125, 127. Cf. also Schnackenburg, *Comm.* I, pp. 254ff., on vss. 6-8, as also on vs. 5 ("a digression of the evangelist"). See also Schnackenburg's "Logos-Hymnos und johanneïscher Prolog," in *Biblische Zeitschrift* 1 (1957), pp. 66-109, esp. 103f.
10. Bultmann, *Comm.,* pp. 16f., 48.
11. Cf. C. K. Barrett's harsh judgment: "The analysts — Bultmann, Käsemann, Haenchen — have forgotten that exegesis must in the end concern itself with the entire text und contented themselves with reconstructing a primitive form, an *Urprolog,* of which the canonic text is an inferior, bowdlerized version, which can be safely consigned to the historical museum" (*New Testament Essays,* pp. 28, 29). This applies more to Haenchen than to Bultmann.
12. Such as Bultmann, Schnackenburg, Haenchen, and Wikenhauser in their commentaries, E. Käsemann, "Zur Johannes-Interpretation in England," in *Exegetische Versuche und Besinnun-*

dogma,[13] it is not surprising that others have resisted it. If this hypothesis can be maintained only if one contents oneself with a fragmented and vaguely contoured picture of this hypothetical hymn and is prepared to involve oneself in a maze of adaptations and interpretations of this hymn, then the question arises whether this hypothesis does not sink under its own weight. For a long time now, and seemingly in increasing measure, forceful arguments have been advanced that answer that question in the affirmative and that maintain the original unity of the prologue, though on very divergent grounds and in a variety of ways.[14]

First, in 1951 (and it continues to be of interest today) Ruckstuhl brought a stylistic argument against the views of Bultmann and others that 1:1-18 does not constitute an original Johannine unit.[15] If one nevertheless, like Schnackenburg, insists on maintaining the hypothesis of an antecedent Logos hymn (still recognizing the presence of these stylistic criteria also in the prologue), one will be forced to attribute ever more material to the Evangelist and will be less and less able to distinguish it from the peculiar features of the hypothetical hymn.[16]

Second, it has been pointed out from another direction that the inference of the existence of the hymn from the poetic character of the prologue passes too lightly over the criteria for such a poetic unit. In any case, the pertinent parts of the prologue do not stand up to evaluation in light of the precise rhythmic and metrical criteria of the Greek verse form:[17] The construction, for all the parallelism, is too diverse and free. If one thinks in terms of a more Semitic verse form and hymnic construction, in which meter does not play the same role as in the Greek forms, the literary unity of the prologue presents fewer problems because then there is more room for divergent forms. Of course, then the question arises whether the hypothesis of an antecedent hymn can stand.

---

gen II, 1960, 131-55; idem, "The Structure and Purpose of the Prologue to John's Gospel," in *New Testament Questions of Today,* 1969, pp. 138-67; J. Jeremias, *Der Prolog des Johannesevangeliums,* 1967, pp. 7ff.

13. So, e.g., S. Pancaro, *The Law in the Fourth Gospel,* 1975, p. 535.

14. See esp. E. Ruckstuhl, *Die literarische Einheit des Johannesevangeliums,* 1951; W. Eltester, "Der Logos und sein Prophet," in *Apophoreta* (Festschrift for E. Haenchen), 1964, pp. 109-34; M. D. Hooker, "John the Baptist and the Johannine Prologue," *NTS* 16 (1970), pp. 354-58; Barrett, "Prologue"; P. Borgen, *Logos Was the True Light,* 1983, pp. 13f.; see further the list of authors assembled by E. Loper in R. A. Culpepper, "The Pivot of John's Prologue," *NTS* 27 (1980), p. 1, n. 5.

15. Ruckstuhl, *Literarische Einheit.* Cf. his review after twenty-five years in "Johannine Language and Style," in *L'Évangile de Jean,* ed. M. de Jonge, 1977, pp. 126f. On stylistic criteria see also E. Schweizer, *Ego Eimi,* 1939, 1965, pp. 87f., later expanded and supplemented by R. Fortna in *The Gospel of Signs,* 1970, and W. Nicol, *The Sēmeia in the Fourth Gospel,* 1972.

16. Cf. Schnackenburg, "Logos-Hymnos und johanneïscher Prolog," pp. 78ff.

17. See esp. the penetrating criticism by Barrett, "Prologue."

Old Testament scholar H. Gese believes, for example, that in its form the prologue bears not a Greek but a Hebrew character rooted in the Old Testament. He has even translated it into Hebrew and has examined the literary structure of its parts with the aid of Hebraic stylistic criteria. His conclusion is that the original Logos hymn — which he also presupposes — was incorporated unchanged, without additions, into the prologue. He also finds that the freer style of vss. 15ff. can be explained very well from the perspective of the whole composition, thus viewed. Of vss. 6-8, 15 (about the Baptist) he states that while in content they seem to be clearly secondary, literarily they nevertheless fit completely into the framework of the original composition and are certainly not the product of a redaction alien to the original hymn. He says, finally, that the style of the hymn and that of the Gospel are quite congruent, so that the typically Johannine features in the prologue need not be regarded as secondary additions to the hymn.[18]

That being the case, one wonders how necessary it is to assume the existence of an antecedent Logos hymn. One certainly need not do so on form-critical grounds. If the boundaries between poetry and prose (as in vss. 6-8, 15) are fluid in the prologue[19] and if the transition between the hymnic beginning of the prologue and the later more kerygmatic or didactic pronouncements is by no means intrusive, then another conclusion seems much more obvious: In the prologue we are dealing not with a hymn adapted by the Evangelist but with a unit independently composed by him. In this connection he did not have before him a certain poetic model; rather, it was the content of what he intended to say to introduce his Gospel that was decisive, both for his composition as a whole and for the freedom of its poetic form.

This is not to deny either the special character of the prologue, particularly of its beginning, or that the remainder of the Gospel fails to reach the high level of harmonious form and poetic expression evident in some parts of the prologue. But from all this one can by no means conclude that the prologue must have its roots or setting in another religious context than the rest of the Gospel. Not only, as we have seen, do several central concepts and motifs of the prologue keep coming back in the Gospel, but in the sublime simplicity of language and expression that marks the entire Gospel one recognizes the hand of the author of the prologue. Some even believe that in the construction of the later discourses they can detect a structural similarity to that of the prologue.[20]

But even if this last point is farfetched, it can hardly be considered surprising that the Evangelist, when in order to explain the glory of the historical

18. H. Gese, "The Prologue to John's Gospel," in *Essays on Biblical Theology,* 1981, pp. 167-222, esp. pp. 170, 177ff.

19. Cf. also Barrett, "Prologue."

20. Cf. B. Lindars, "Traditions behind the Fourth Gospel," in *L'Évangile de Jean,* pp. 107-24, esp. p. 122, n. 51.

Jesus he refers back in a truly splendid manner to the Word that was in the beginning, he also knows how to raise his characteristic style to a lofty poetic level that does not recur in those forms later in his Gospel. The prologue is an introduction to the history of Jesus Christ, and it should not be surprising that its purpose is a factor in determining its line of thought and form and thus serves as the natural explanation for the fluid boundaries between what have been distinguished as "poetic" and "prosaic," "hymnic" and "kerygmatic."

For that reason the criteria for the form of a hypothetical hymn — which is said to have had a totally different function and origin than that of an overture to a gospel story — can by definition not serve as standards by which to judge what is original and appropriate in the prologue and what is secondary and disruptive. Admittedly, by making that assertion we have not proven the unity of the prologue. As we look at the prologue in detail, we will have to examine more closely the objections raised against its unity (esp. with reference to vss. 6-8 and 15). But we have cleared the way for an examination of the unity and structure of the prologue on their own merits, that is, in the form in which it lies before us, without making it dependent on a Logos hymn that was supposedly distinct from the prologue in origin, genre, and function.

The immediate gain of this approach is that the structure of the prologue suggests itself naturally. As the introduction to and background of the portrayal of Jesus as the Christ, the Son of God (cf. 20:31), the prologue speaks successively of:

- "the Word in the beginning" (1:1-5)
- the coming of the Word as the light of the world (1:6-13), and
- the glory of the Word in the flesh (1:14-18).

1:1-5

"The Word in the Beginning"

1, 2 The words "In the beginning," with which the prologue begin, also form the beginning of the book of Genesis and hence of the entire Torah. From this earlier occurrence they derive a solemn, perhaps even sacred, sound. Furthermore, the words that follow in John, the pronouncements concerning the Word, echo what in Genesis 1 constitutes the foundation of God's revelation in the Old Testament and of Israelite religion: God's creation of heaven and earth. All that now follows in the Gospel has to be understood from the perspective of that "beginning": It arises from that beginning, and that beginning is its deepest and most essential *Sitz im Leben.*

Some interpreters even believe that the opening lines of the prologue (vss.

1-5) can be explicated totally in light of Gn. 1:1ff. P. Borgen in particular[21] has argued that the prologue — in total divergence from the way the hymn hypothesis pictures it — forms an inner and independent unity that in its totality can be characterized as an "exposition" of Gn. 1:1ff. "Thus Jn 1:1-5 is the basic exposition of Gn 1:1-5, while Jn 1:6ff. elaborates upon terms and phrases from Jn 1:1-5." Borgen bases this view not only on the opening words of John 1 and Genesis 1 but also on the central terms "light" and "darkness" in Jn. 1:4, 5 (cf. Gn. 1:2-5). He also claims that the content of vs. 3 in the prologue is nothing other than a "midrashic" paraphrase of Gn. 1:1: God created "heaven and earth" (cf. vs. 10). Finally, the term "the Word" is probably, says Borgen, an interpretation of and substitution for the repeated "and God said" in Genesis 1, as in vs. 3 this divine speech hypostatizes itself into light ("and God *said* . . . and there *was*"), an identification present also in Jn. 1:10, where the "light" replaces the "Word." There is support in Jewish exegesis, says Borgen, for the existence of such an identification, namely in Philo, who in his interpretation of Gn. 1:1-3 "moves from the uttered word of God to the concept of Logos in an absolute sense," just as he sometimes attributes to the Logos quite personal features, similarly derived from the creation story, as "God's firstborn," "the beginning," "the Logos."[22] This interpretation not only has the merit that it views the prologue as an independent unit, unmixed with a Logos hymn derived from some other source, but also that it shows that the relationship between the prologue and Gn. 1:1ff. not only consists in the first words but continues verbally and materially with the terms "light" "darkness," and "life."

But it is another matter whether one can characterize the prologue (especially its beginning) as an "exposition" or midrash of Gn. 1:1-5. The purpose of Jn. 1:1-5 is not to provide a further exposition of Genesis 1 with an eye to the coming and work of Christ, by way of a "christological doctrine of creation," but rather the reverse: to give to the Christ-event the fundamental "setting" in which alone it can be understood. Therefore, John 1 does not, like Genesis 1, begin with the creation that came into being by the Word, nor does the hypostatization of the Word originate there (as, e.g., in Mt. 4:4), since before creation is even mentioned it is already said that the Word was with God and was God. In that sense one can say that the words "in the beginning" in John 1 have a broader meaning than they do in Genesis 1 and that they refer to something behind Genesis, so to speak. They refer to the Word and to the Word's existence with God "before the world was made" (cf. 17:5; 1 Jn. 1:2; 2:13) as a being distinct from God. Nor is the reference, as elsewhere, to a poetic personification or hypostatization of the mighty speech of God (cf. Pss.

---

21. P. Borgen, "Observations on the Targumic character of the Prologue of John," *NTS* 16 (1970), pp. 288-95; idem, *Logos Was the True Light,* 1983, pp. 13ff.
22. Borgen, "Observations," p. 290.

33:6; 107:20; Is. 40:8; 55:11) but to a unique existence of the Word with God, an existence that is not coextensive with God's actual speech.

Of the character of this relationship to God no further details are given.[23] The focus is entirely on the antecedent existence of the Word, that is, that it existed before all that is created, and on the Word's participation in the divine. This latter point is made in no uncertain terms by the emphatic positioning of the predicate noun: "And God was the Word." What we have here is not an exchange of subject, as if it were now being said of him who is called God in vs. 1b that *he* was *the Word*. What is at stake is the distinction of the subject, and hence the Word's own participation in the divine life, which is why the idea of a subordination of the Word or a "divinity" as a qualification in the sense of an attribute abstracted from God is excluded.

2 It is this fundamentally dual content of the preceding sentence that is repeated with great emphasis in vs. 2: *"He* was in the beginning with God" — he of whom it has just been said that he was God — he, no one else and no one less. It is stated so emphatically because "he" is also the great subject of all that follows and hence from the very start determines the Evangelist's discourse: the Word who has become *flesh* and dwelled among us. The thrice-repeated "he was" (vss. 1, 2) points in the same direction. Not, of course, that the content of these pronouncements about "the Word" is thus restricted to the past as something that once "was" and is no longer so. But from the viewpoint of the speaker (the Evangelist), that which was from the beginning is thus related to that which continued in the coming and the work of Jesus Christ in time and still continues, and is placed in the light in which alone it can be understood in its true nature.

This also implies, meanwhile, that the "in the beginning" of Jn. 1:1ff. transcends by far that of Gn. 1:1ff. and cannot be explained on the basis of Genesis 1. For between Genesis 1 and John 1 lies the Christ-event, and therein lies the "plus" (if one may call it that) of John over Genesis. Though the "score" of the prologue may be that of Genesis 1, the content is that of the gospel. Only the glory of the incarnate Word can enable us to understand the full thrust of God's speech in the beginning and can teach us to distinguish between God and the Word, between the Father and the Son (1:18).

For that reason one can say that the pronouncements concerning the Word "in the beginning" and those concerning the incarnation of the Word mutually condition and explicate each other. On the one hand, this referring back of the glory of God that appeared in the human existence of Jesus to that which was in the beginning makes it clear that the gospel in no way exceeds the boundaries

---

23. Apparently "with God" (πρός + accusative) is intended as an indication not only of place but also of disposition and orientation (cf. 1 Jn. 3:21; 5:14; see further the comments on 1:18).

of the monotheistic revelation of God of which Genesis 1 is the foundation. It has been said that one cannot understand from the Old Testament the fact that the prologue does not speak of "the Word of God" but refers, absolutely, to "the Word," and therefore that the proper name or title "the Word" is presupposed here, that is, as a name familiar from and borrowed from another source.[24] But that is to fail to do justice to the strong rootedness of the prologue in Genesis 1. This backward look to Genesis 1 is proof that the Evangelist did not wish to subsume the glory of Christ under some other heading and explain it in that other way. Instead, he sought to identify the presence of God in the advent and work of Jesus of Nazareth, on the basis of the Old Testament, as the presence of that God who from "the beginning" showed himself to be, not a self-sufficient, immutable, and silent God, but the God who "extended" himself and spoke: "Let there be light in the darkness." Of *that* beginning the "in the beginning" of the prologue is the continuation, and in that "beginning" it also has its most fundamental basis.

On the other hand, it is no less true that it is only on the basis of the incarnation of the Word and the revelation of the glory of the only begotten of the Father (vss. 14, 18) that the Evangelist can speak of the Word in the beginning as in fact he does in vss. 1ff., namely as the Word in his distinct mode of being.[25] It is the "seeing" of the glory of the Word in the flesh, the self-disclosure of Jesus in his words and works and in his utterly unique relationship of oneness with the Father, that enables the Evangelist to speak of Jesus as he does — not only of "that which" (1 Jn. 1:1) but also of "he who" was from the beginning. But that correlation between vss. 1-2 and vs. 14 also shows that there was no other way to speak about the Word of the beginning than with a view to the incarnation — to that which he was *for* and *in* the world. There is here no speculation about the Word that would betray the presence of an already existing Logos theology. All that is said about the Word as such is that it was in the beginning, that it was with God, and that it was God. It is hardly conceivable that a deeper issue could have been expressed with greater simplicity and in fewer words.

There could be no greater sobriety or more rigorous regard for the purpose that the Evangelist set himself in this reference to the beginning than he practices in the splendid and lapidary statement in vs. 2, a statement that serves no other end than to reinforce the preceding statement. The Evangelist cannot say a single word about either the concept of the Word or the glory of the Word, which was "before the world was made" (17:5; cf. 17:24), apart from the incarnation. The light that shines from "the beginning" and bathes the entire

24. Bultmann, *Comm.*, p. 21.
25. Cf. Brown, *Comm.* I, p. 253: "The Prologue has carried personification further than the OT did . . . , but that development *stems from the Incarnation*" (italics added).

gospel in the radiance of the divine glory does not come in from a "side window" but teaches us to understand the end in terms of the beginning, just as the beginning can only be understood in terms of the end. "No one has ever seen God. The only begotten Son, who was in the Father's bosom, has made him known." It is on the basis of this correlation that the splendid opening utterances of the prologue become intelligible in their redemptive-historical place and meaning — in the light of which also the rest of the prologue and the gospel story that follows should be understood and interpreted.

The History of Religions Approach

In contrast to the above, some exegetes have, in very different ways, looked for the background of the prologue in broad layers of Hellenistic syncretism. In this connection the "history of religions method" plays an important role. Within this method an effort is made to determine the "the locus of this hymn in the history of religions" as a "new task" confronting modern research.[26] It appears that Genesis 1, as also (according to the majority of the proponents of this method) the entire Old Testament, fails to provide an adequate explanation of this "locus," since personifying the speech of God (Gn. 1:3, 6f.) into a "person standing alongside God" (as with the Logos of Jn. 1:1) remained an alien idea for Jews.[27] Therefore, one who follows this method will have to look elsewhere in the history of religions for the background of this "hypostasis."[28]

There is all the more reason for this because both in Greek philosophical literature and in the literature of later Hellenistic syncretism the figure of a Logos as a metaphysical entity makes its appearance in a variety of ways. In philosophical literature (e.g., in Stoic writings) the Logos plays a large role as the essence of the divine world order and the principle that creates the world. Around the beginning of the first century Philo of Alexandria in particular, the most representative figure of Hellenistic Judaism, used the Logos concept to a great extent in his religious-philosophical writings. He fused various Old Testament influences, Judaism, and the popular Greek philosophy of his day, which incorporated both Stoic and Platonic elements. The Logos concept also functions in his work, particularly in his creation theology, as a divinely created intermediate being between God and the world, as a mediating principle in the creation of the world, and as the source of the meaning of the world and of humanity. Similar

---

26. So Haenchen, *Comm.* I, 135f.

27. Ibid., 136.

28. Cf. Bultmann's exegesis of 1:1f., especially his comments on the Logos in his *Comm.*, pp. 19-31. He seeks "what *possible forms of expression were open to the author; the possibilities being those he has inherited with the tradition in which he stands.* What the author intends to say here and now, is of course not simply to be deduced from these possibilities: but they have given a particular direction to what he intends to say, and have imposed particular limits . . ." (p. 20, italics original). The breadth of this "tradition" as Bultmann conceives it is evident from the scope of his investigation into the background of the prologue.

concepts occur in the equally syncretistic Hermetic literature, which was written in Greek in Egypt.[29]

It is against the background of such syncretistic religiosity that the prologue of the Fourth Gospel is to be understood, we are told. The author is said to have addressed himself not so much to Christians who needed a deeper theology as to non-Christians who in their desire to gain access to eternal life were said to be prepared to follow the Christian way if it were presented in terms intelligible to them and related to their own religious interests. Hence the beginning of the prologue. "It is clear that a reader who knew nothing at all about Christianity or its Founder could read that exordium intelligently, provided that the term 'logos,' and the idea of a 'man sent from God,' meant something to him. But these are ideas that are in no way distinctive of Christianity."[30]

It is certainly true that, with the advance in the comparative study of the pagan, Jewish, and Christian literature of the Hellenistic period, including the more recently discovered writings of the Qumran community and of Nag Hammadi, scholars have increasingly encountered commonality in the usage of religious language, speculative concepts, nomenclature, and the like. Particularly important for our purpose is the insight that the boundaries that existed in this respect between certain movements in later Judaism and syncretistic Hellenistic religiosity were much more fluid than scholars often thought. That there was reciprocal influence and that in this process Judaism was not only the receiving, but no less the contributing, party has been demonstrated in all sorts of ways.[31]

But what comes through no less clearly as the research advances is that precisely because of the commonality of similar usage one has to be extremely cautious before assuming direct connections of dependence and mutual influence. And this applies specifically to the Fourth Gospel, which, when it refers in the prologue to the Logos, the Son, the only begotten, though it certainly does not employ exclusively biblical terminology, is nevertheless far removed in content from the abstract idea of the Logos that pagan and syncretistic philosophy postulated as it considered the origin of the world and its (Logos-mediated) relationship to God. For how could such an idea, even though it is at times personified, be the background for the concrete person and work of Jesus as the Christ, the Son of God, as he is depicted in the Fourth Gospel?

In more recent research, not surprisingly, this history of religions field of exploration has been left behind, and the focus has shifted to what is called the Gnostic "redeemer myth." The advantage of this approach is especially said to be that in this myth the Logos does not just possess the abstract function of an idea or hypostatized principle that bridges the chasm between God and the world but assumes the concrete form of a revealer descending from heaven who at the same time is said to be a redeemer.

It was Bultmann who, from 1925 on, sought to understand the Gospel of John

---

29. For a comparison of the prologue with the Hermetic literature and Philo's writings, see C. H. Dodd, *The Interpretation of the Fourth Gospel*, 1953, pp. 10-73. For a critical response to Dodd, see G. D. Kilpatrick, "The Religious Background of the Fourth Gospel," in *Studies in the Fourth Gospel*, ed. F. L. Cross, 1957, pp. 36-44, and Bultmann, as noted below.

30. Dodd, *Interpretation*, pp. 8, 9.

31. See, e.g., already E. M. Sidebottom, *The Christ of the Fourth Gospel*, 1961, pp. 16ff. and passim.

against this particular history of religions background and who for a long time found a large measure of support for his view, especially in Germany.[32] In his view, the origin of this myth is no longer discoverable and its wide dissemination is hard to unravel on account of its entwinement with all sorts of mythological and philosophical motifs. Nonetheless, it occurs, he says, in John's prologue — in a form stamped by the cosmological thinking of Gnosticism.

In Gnosticism, God and cosmos are dualistically related to each other insofar as human souls, which originated in the supracosmic sphere and belong there, have become trapped in the material world as scattered sparks of light and must be liberated and gathered up from it. To that end the figure of the Logos, usually called *Nous*, descends from above. In him souls find their original unity. Apart from this cosmological function, however, the Logos also has a soteriological task as the divinely sent redeemer to gather the souls belonging to God and to bring them back to their heavenly home. Therefore, he disguises himself in a human body in order to deceive the demonic powers of darkness and thus descends. This — in the judgment of Bultmann and others — original Gnostic myth of the redeemer sent from heaven and disguised as a human being is said to have been taken over at an early stage by Christians and made fruitful for christology. Thus it is said to form the background of the Johannine prologue.[33]

For a long time this approach determined the options in discussion of the background of the Fourth Gospel. Some scholars believed that they could, with increasing self-assurance and elaborateness, demonstrate that this Gnostic "redeemer myth" is the starting point of Johannine christology. But skepticism about the existence of such a developed myth came to be on the rise.[34] As a result the correctness of this entire approach was increasingly discredited.

Admittedly, some new life was breathed into this rigid and polarized discussion by the discovery at Nag Hammadi of certain Gnostic writings. Of special interest for our subject in this collection is a revelatory discourse known as the *Trimorphic Protennoia*. In this document the Protennoia reveals itself in the first person as "the thought," "the voice," and "the word."[35] Especially with regard to "the word" there are statements that in diction and content are strongly reminiscent of John's prologue

32. "Die Bedeutung der neuerschlossenen mandäischen und manichäischen Quellen für das Verständnis des Johannesevangeliums," *ZNW* 24 (1925), pp. 100-146 = Bultmann, *Exegetica: Aufsätze zur Erforschung des Neuen Testaments,* ed. E. Dinkler, 1967, 55-104.

33. See the lengthy discussion of this background in Bultmann, *Comm.,* pp. 19-29. The conclusion is (pp. 30f.):

> The Prologue's source belongs to the sphere of a relatively early oriental Gnosticism, which has been developed under the influence of the O.T. faith in the Creator-God. This development has taken the following direction: the mythology has been severely pushed into the background; the Gnostic cosmology has been repressed and has given way to the belief in Creation; and the concern for the relation of man to the revelation of God, that is to say the soteriological concern, has become dominant.

34. Such, as early as 1961, was the view of C. Colpe in his influential work *Die Religionsgeschichtliche Schule. Darstellung und Kritik ihres Bildes vom gnostischen Erlösermythus,* 1961, p. 10; see also below.

35. Cf. *The Nag Hammadi Library in English,* revised edition, 1988, pp. 511-22.

and that are regarded by some scholars as clear confirmation of the prologue's dependence on the Gnostic redeemer concept.[36] Others explain these statements with no less cogency as proving dependence in the opposite direction.[37]

It has thus become evident that there must have been connections between John's prologue and certain Gnostic or gnosticizing writings of the early Christian centuries. But it is doubtful that anything more can be established from this material than that the Gospel of John, notably in its reference to the Word in the beginning and its sharp antithesis between Spirit and flesh, above and below, and light and darkness contained more points of contact with Gnostic thought than, say, any of the other Gospels and for that reason gained a certain reputation (and popularity?) in the circles that produced such writings.

Still, the objections that have regularly been advanced against the dependence of the Fourth Gospel on the so-called Gnostic redeemer myth have lost none of their validity. They can briefly be summarized as follows: First, the sources from which information about this myth has to be derived are of a later — in part much later — date than the Gospel of John. Hence these written sources could not have been utilized in the Gospel of John.

Second, even if we can assume that Gnosticism (which used to be understood mainly as a group of Christian heresies whose existence had to be deduced from the writings of the church fathers) was in vogue as a spiritual movement of a very specific character already in pre-Christian times, solid evidence that in this pre-Christian period the myth of the redeemed redeemer played anything like a typical role is far from present.[38]

Third and most decisive, the contexts in which Gnosticism and John's prologue speak of redemption do not coincide but rather exclude each other. In Gnosticism God and world are dualistic opposites. In the Johannine prologue all things — the "heaven and earth" of Gn. 1:1 — have been made by the Word that was with God and that was God. Jn. 1:14, 18 mentions the only begotten who made the Father known to us, and

36. See, e.g., the report of the Berliner Arbeitskreis für koptisch-gnostischen Schriften: "Die dreigestaltigen Protennoia," *TLZ* 99 (1974), 731-46, which compares the *Trimorphic Protennoia* with John's prologue and concludes that the substance of the third discourse of the *Protennoia*, on "the Word," is on the same level as the Logos hymn underlying John's prologue and that "it looks at first glance as if the light falls rather from the *Protennoia* on John's prologue than the reverse." See also H. M. Schenke in *Gnosis und Neues Testament*, ed. K. W. Tröger, 1973, p. 225.

37. Y. Janssens, "Une source du Prologue?" in *L'Évangile de Jean*, pp. 355-58, regards the Old Testament rather than the *Protennoia* as the interpretive key to the prologue. See also J. Helderman, "In Ihren Zelten," in *Miscellanea Neotestamentica* I, ed. T. Baarda, A. F. J. Klijn, and W. C. van Unnik, 1978, pp. 181-211. A mediating position is held by C. A. Evans in "On the Prologue and the Trimorphic Protennoia," *NTS* 27 (1981), pp. 395-401.

38. Colpe's *Religionsgeschichtliche Schule* cast much critical light on this fundamental thesis in Bultmann's position. Colpe especially emphasized the irresponsible generalization involved in speaking of the myth as if it were a single unified entity that can be found ready-made in the writings in question. On the contrary, the Gnostic concept of redemption is far too complicated and diverse for anyone to be able to reconstruct the model of a mythical redeemer figure from it (Colpe, pp. 203ff.; see also p. 171).

the reason for this mission of revelation is later found in the love with which God, in him, "loved the *world*" (3:16). Bultmann describes this difference as "a development" of Gnosticism "under the influence of the O.T. faith in the Creator-God." The mythology was pushed into the background, Gnostic cosmology had to "give way to the belief in Creation," and "the soteriological concern" became "dominant." But even this grand reduction does not solve the problem, for in what is called "the soteriological concern" we face the same enormous gap. It is true that in both the prologue and Gnosticism the light comes into the world to shine on the darkness, and also that in the Fourth Gospel the word "world" is used to express the break between God and humanity. But in John human souls are not, as in Gnosticism, imprisoned as preexistent particles of light in the darkness, and their salvation does not consist in their acknowledgment of their divine origin in the redeemer who comes to them and in their being led by him out of this prison of flesh and world. None of this can be related in any way to the redemption from the religious and moral estrangement of humanity from God that the Gospel identifies as the basic human problem or to faith in the saving love of God as the way of salvation (3:16), in which people escape from the judgment and wrath of God (3:18, 36). And none of it is compatible with what has been called the most pithy utterance of the prologue, namely that the Word became *flesh*. Here the descent of the Redeemer acquires a meaning that fundamentally distinguishes it from *all* pre-Christian notions of descent but most of all from the Gnostic world of thought. If one would want to posit a connection from the prologue to Gnostic speculation, it could only be as its antithesis.[39]

On the basis of all this it is hard to believe that "absolute" or "hypostatic" discourse about the Logos, which distinguishes John 1 from Genesis 1, should be explained on the basis of a Gnostic background.[40] For that reason it is not at all strange that an increasing number of scholars have become convinced of the untenability of this hypothesis and are inclined — to the extent that this is necessary — to look for such a background "closer to home," that is, in the Old Testament.[41]

The Logos and "Wisdom"

In the interest of shedding further light on the Logos figure in John 1 there has been fresh emphasis in recent exegesis on the Old Testament and Jewish wisdom poetry, in

39. Cf. E. Fascher, "Christologie und Gnosis im vierten Evangelium," *TLZ* 93 (1968), p. 726.

40. Others have pointed out that the idea of a descending and ascending divine messenger or redeemer was so widespread in the Mediterranean world, notably in Hellenistic Judaism, that it is impossible to see why, for such "hypostatic" discourse, Gnosticism should have to provide the material. E.g., C. H. Talbert, "The Myth of a Descending-Ascending Redeemer in Mediterranean Antiquity," *NTS* 22 (1976), pp. 418-40.

41. On "the search for the intellectual milieu of the Evangelist" see, e.g., the overview in R. Kysar, *The Fourth Evangelist and His Gospel: An Examination of Contemporary Scholarship*, 1975, pp. 106f. He concludes that "the Gnostic hypothesis for the background of the logos concept appears less tenable in the light both of the stronger evidence for an Old Testament-Jewish milieu and the effective refutations for a gnostic influence" (p. 111).

which *Wisdom* is celebrated in its involvement in creation and its world-embracing significance. At the high points in this wisdom literature Wisdom appears in a personified form, either, as in Proverbs 8 and Sirach 24, in the first person or, as in Job 28 and Wisdom of Solomon 7, in the third person. One of these high points occurs in Pr. 8:22ff., where Wisdom is introduced as saying:

> The LORD created me at the beginning of his work,
> the first of his acts of long ago.
> Ages ago I was set up,
> at the first, before the beginning of the earth.

> Before the mountains had been shaped,
> before the hills, I was brought forth —
> when he had not yet made earth and fields,
> or the world's first bits of soil.
> When he established the heavens, I was there. . . . (NRSV)

Another is Wis. 9:9, where God is addressed: "With you is wisdom, she who knows your works and was present when you made the world" (NRSV). Admittedly, it is nowhere said that Wisdom is God, nor in so many words that all things were made by Wisdom.[42] But the degree to which the attribute "divine" is applicable comes out in statements like Wis. 7:25f., where Wisdom is called "a breath of the power of God," "a pure emanation of the glory of the Almighty," "a reflection of eternal light," "a spotless mirror of the working of God," and "an image of his goodness."

In addition to these transcendent qualities of Wisdom some interpreters also place special emphasis on the several phases that Wisdom is said to have passed through in the course of its existence. This, then, is again said to be strikingly analagous to what in the "Logos hymn" (see above) is supposed to have been said about the fortunes of the Logos. Appeal is made particularly to Sir. 24:3-7, where it is said that Wisdom "came forth" from God's mouth and then inhabited heaven, after that seeking a lodging place on earth. "Then the Creator of all things gave me a command, and my Creator chose the place for my tent. He said, 'Make your dwelling in Jacob and in Israel receive your inheritance' " (vs. 8, NRSV). This is said to have happened because nowhere else in the world was Wisdom given a place to live. This is not stated in so many words in this passage (and vs. 6 may state the contrary), but grounds for the world's negative attitude toward Wisdom are clearly found in *1 Enoch* 42:1f., where it is stated that Wisdom returned to heaven because it found no dwelling place among humans.

On the basis of these — thus combined — passages picturing Wisdom as a transcendent person, scholars occasionally speak of the "Wisdom myth,"[43] with

---

42. But in Wis. 7:22[21] Wisdom is called ἡ πάντων τεχνῖτις, which some translate as "the fashioner of all things," others as "skilled in all things," which in this context seems more fitting. Cf., however, Pr. 3:19 and 3:34 (LXX!). Apparently the boundaries are fluid here. Cf. also my *Paul and Jesus*, 1957, pp. 124ff.

43. Thus, e.g., Bultmann, who also believes, however, that the Wisdom myth is only a variant on the pagan revealer myth and therefore that the similarity between Wisdom and the Logos is based not on the latter's dependence on the former but on their common rootage in this myth (Bultmann, *Comm.*, p. 23, n. 2).

which, according to some, the Johannine prologue (in its original form as a "Logos hymn")[44] is linked. For a long time, it has been said, the "disruptive insertion" in vss. 6-8[45] prevented interpreters from understanding that in the prologue, too, namely in vss. 9-12, there is a similar reference to the Logos's futile attempts, after the creation of the world, to gain a foothold among humans, as in the Wisdom myth. Thus the Wisdom myth was adopted in the first half of the prologue.[46] But there is this all-important difference: In the old Wisdom myth, Wisdom returns in desperation to heaven to resume its place among the angels, but the paean of praise sung by the Christian church was able to proclaim a different turn of events: The Logos "became flesh" and as a human being found a welcome among his people.[47] Hence the prologue is neither a vade mecum for Hellenistic readers nor a summary of the gospel; rather, it describes the history of redemption from its beginning in eternity and its progress in time before the incarnation in order to come to the climax of this development in vs. 14: the incarnation itself. In this way, the story of Jesus' words and deeds can then begin in vs. 19 as the historic sequel to that which is narrated in the prologue up to the coming of Jesus.

Regardless of what one might think of these "mythical" fortunes of Wisdom and their supposed adoption and elaboration in the "Logos hymn" (see below), this material does bring out that Wisdom, as it figures in the Old Testament and Jewish writings, in certain respects closely approximates the Logos in the Johannine prologue. At the very least we see here a common atmosphere of thought manifesting itself specifically in the fact that when the absolute significance either of Wisdom (and elsewhere, in connection with Wisdom, that of the Torah),[48] or of God's revelation in Jesus Christ is featured, they are in both cases referred back to, or derived from, "the beginning," that is, from the God of the beginning, the One who created heaven and earth. Wisdom and Torah belong to that God and in that beginning, as does the Logos, and they belong there as that which is antecedent to the creation of all things and involved in creation by God's design. In this respect there is a fundamental difference between them and the Gnostic cosmogony, in which God and world are dualistically opposed to each other — a difference that can hardly be understood as a late Old Testament interpretation or a repression of the original Gnostic conception, but rather demonstrates the different origins of the two systems of thought.[49]

Another matter is whether on the basis of all this one can find in these wisdom texts the tradition-historical "source" of the prologue.[50] Whereas the reference to Genesis 1 is very deliberate, given the opening words "in the beginning" and the

44. See above, pp. 18-19.

45. See above, pp. 19-20.

46. Haenchen, *Comm.* I, 138f.

47. Ibid., 139f.

48. Cf. Strack/Billerbeck II, pp. 353ff.

49. On this, see esp. Gese, "Prologue" (see n. 18 above), according to whom the post-exilic wisdom tradition, in contrast with the forms of wisdom developing outside Judaism in the direction of philosophy, is peculiar to Israel (190f.). With regard to the Old Testament background of the prologue, we are not just dealing here with "connections" but with "the real relationship of the entire text [of the prologue] to the whole Old Testament" (p. 169).

50. So Gese, "Prologue," 196f.

mention of light and darkness in vss. 4a and 5, any such reference to wisdom is lacking, not only here but in the Gospel as a whole. Nor is this surprising because, despite the analogy between "the Word" and "Wisdom," there remains an essential difference between them. In whatever noble and highly poetic language Wisdom may be celebrated, as in Wis. 7:25 (quoted above), Wisdom belongs, in distinction from "the Word" of John 1, to the created world. It was "created," "set up," and "brought forth" (cf. Pr. 8:22f.; Sir. 24:9). This sets a line of demarcation between the figure of Wisdom in the wisdom texts and the Logos in John 1, one that cannot be blurred, for example, by insisting that the reference to the Logos as God in Jn. 1:1 and the role as creator associated with it have their roots in, and indeed are "fully intelligible" in light of, Pr. 8:22f. and Sir. 24:1f.[51] The emphasis in Jn. 1:1 on the deity of the Logos and the role that he fulfills in creation is, in fact, intended to accentuate the line of demarcation that separates the Logos from that which has been created.

The same is true of hypostatizing personal references to Wisdom in its preexistence with God. Some of these references are very concrete: "I was beside him like a master worker; and I was daily his delight, rejoicing before him always, rejoicing in his inhabited world . . ." (Pr. 8:30f., NRSV). In this connection special reference is made to Job 28:20ff., where Wisdom is presented as hidden from the eyes of all creatures but "seen" by God when he created the world:[52] "He saw it, declared it, . . . and searched it out" (vs. 27) as an entity independent of himself but objectively present to him.[53]

But in my opinion all these personifications of Wisdom have a poetic character that can in no way be equated with the mode of existence of the Logos in John 1. Nor can they be called "mythical" in the sense of a story about God. When in Job 28 Wisdom is mentioned in a more or less hypostatizing sense, that is just as poetic as when in the same connection destruction and death are personified (vs. 22) and when it is said that wisdom is concealed even from the birds of the air (vs. 21). Also, passages like Pr. 8:30f. can hardly be characterized as anything other than poetic. The extent to which all this differs from the core pronouncements of Jn. 1:1f., which by saying "He was in the beginning with God" excludes all doubt about the utter uniqueness of the existence of the Logos, needs no demonstration. For that reason it can hardly be surprising that, whatever in John 1 may be reminiscent of the wisdom texts, there is not the slightest indication that the Evangelist would want what he has to say about the Logos understood in light of the figure of Wisdom.

The same applies to an even greater degree against the hypothesis that John 1 adopts the supposed myth of Wisdom's vain search for a dwelling place and provides it with a Christian meaning and outcome.[54] However ingenious such a construction may be, it consists, on closer scrutiny, of not just one but a series of unproven

---

51. So Gese, "Prologue," p. 197. This disparity of Wisdom and the Logos is also recognized by Schulz, *Comm.,* pp. 27f., when he asserts that the absolute personification of the Logos cannot be explained from the background in the wisdom literature. But for him this is proof that this absolute formulation of the prologue stems from Hellenistic Gnosticism.

52. So most interpreters.

53. Cf. Gese, "Prologue," p. 192.

54. Notably advanced by Haenchen; see above.

assumptions. After all, how can one possibly link together wisdom passages from very different periods, and in part of very different literary categories (cf. Pr. 8:31 and Wis. 24:6), in order to make up one mythological "story," especially when the essential point of this myth (wisdom's failure to find a dwelling place among the nations) stems not from the wisdom literature itself but from the much later apocalyptic book of *1 Enoch*?[55] And we are told it is precisely *that* form of the "myth" that was incorporated into the prologue and given its Christian meaning, not to be sure in the prologue as we now have it, but still visible as the intent of the underlying Logos hymn when it was not as yet "corrupted" by vss. 6-8. Indeed, there are as many gaps as links in this chain!

In summary, the following conclusions seem justified:

First, the "absolute" description of the Word that was with God and was God (1:1) is explained, at the deepest level, by the absoluteness of the historic self-disclosure of Jesus as the Christ, the Son of God. It is essentially nothing other than that which, at the close of the Gospel, brings the unbelieving Thomas to confess "my Lord and my God" as the ultimate human response in the confrontation with the glory of God in the coming, work, and, finally, the resurrection of Jesus Christ. In that sense, therefore, one can say that the first utterance of the prologue is not different from the last word of the gospel story. But the prologue places that glory where it belongs and in light of which alone it can be understood. And that place is not the great pantheon of gods and demigods of pagan mythology nor the conceptual teaching of philosophical cosmology in which the "crossings" of God to the cosmos were expressed, but — as the Evangelist himself says in so many words — the knowledge of that God of whom Israel had always known as the God of the beginning.

Second, the authors of Israel's wisdom books had this knowledge, and therein lies the reason that the similarity between John's prologue and these didactic wisdom poems is much deeper — and the result, after all, of a much closer kinship — than what we have from Hellenistic syncretism. Still, there remains a fundamental difference here. The "plus" of the "in the beginning" of John 1 over that of Genesis 1 cannot be explained by analogy from the pronouncements about wisdom. Nor can they serve as a link or intermediate stage for that explanation. For not even in the farthest reaches of the imagination with which they speak about wisdom can they cross the threshold that separates the beginning of the gospel from the Torah.

Third, one may ask whether and to what degree the absolute use of the name "the Word" with reference to the coming and work of Jesus Christ was already common property in the early Christian church. Some scholars believe that the manner in which the prologue posits the name "the Word" is itself an indication that the readers must have been familiar with it or at least did not need further explanation.[56]

---

55. Even though Gese also thinks that there is in *1 Enoch* 42 a striking parallel to vss. 10-13 of the prologue, he, too, believes that in tradition-historical interpretation of the prologue "it would be best not to begin with this late apocalyptic use of the wisdom motif," "since we have here, not a text from wisdom literature which fully represents a specific stage in this tradition, but only a borrowing of content that is then totally subordinated to the apocalyptic aspect of the document" ("Prologue," p. 202).

56. Cf., e.g., Bultmann, *Comm.*, p. 19.

In connection with this question, one often hears again about the supposed Logos hymn that is said to underlie the prologue. Even if one rejects that hypothesis, however, one can of course assume familiarity with the use of Logos as a name referring to the preexistence of Jesus as the Son of God among the members of that which is called the Johannine congregation or "school." On the other hand, there is no shred of proof that in the early church "the Word" already served as a title or name for the Son of God. The name Logos is not even used in those New Testament passages in which Christ's sonship is associated with the creation of all things (cf. 1 Co. 8:6; Col. 1:16f.; Hb. 1:2; Rv. 5:14). Our conclusion therefore can hardly be other than that the name, which is used in reference to Jesus' preexistence only in the opening lines of the Gospel and the first letter of John, has a unique, specific, and limited character that is conditioned by the rest of the Gospel, such that it can only be described as typically Johannine.

3 Vss. 3-5 form an immediate and natural sequel to vss. 1 and 2. "In the beginning" evokes the divine work of creation, when God called all things into being by his "word" (Gn. 1:1f.). Here all this is credited to "the Word" in an absolute sense, not only to qualify the creation, but in particular because it is this Word that has become flesh in the advent and work of Jesus Christ. *Because* the Word existed in the beginning with God and was God, it was *through him* that all things were created. The emphatic position that "all things" has in vs. 3 and the addition that *nothing* is excepted from what has been made by the Word[57] therefore intend to express — against all the speculations about the origin of the world that are in competition with this viewpoint — not only the absolute monotheistic idea of creation, but even more the all-embracing significance of the incarnation of the Word; in other words, the "christological" viewpoint presents itself here at the very outset.

The range of action of God-in-Christ at the creation coincides with the range of action of the Word in his incarnation. Therefore Christ is the light of the world (cf. 8:12) and by his coming into the world enlightens *every* person (1:9). The question arises whether in connection with the phrase "through him" anything more can be said about the relationship between "God" and "the Word." "Through" (διά) could imply mediation, and reference is made by some scholars to texts like 1 Co. 8:6; Col. 1:16; and Hb. 1:2, which are said to describe Christ as Mediator of creation. Whatever we think of these other passages,[58] in my opinion vs. 3 does not permit any conclusions in this regard beyond that which is already stated in vs. 1, namely that the Word was God[59] and that for that very

---

57. In this context πάντα is even stronger than τὰ πάντα; it denotes not only the totality of all things but also their diversity; cf. οὐδὲ ἕν.

58. On this cf. also my *Paul and Jesus*, pp. 128ff., and my *Paul: An Outline of His Theology*, 1975, pp. 79ff.

59. The preposition διά with the genitive, though specifically used elsewhere for the work

reason the coming and incarnation of the Word has this all-embracing significance. With regard to the nature of the distinction within God's being and the distinct role of the Word in creation, the prologue makes no further pronouncement. Here again (cf. the exegesis of vs. 2) it is clear that the prologue does not furnish us a theology of the Logos but seeks to convey the revelation of God in Jesus Christ in its absolute and comprehensive significance.

The old question whether the words "that was made" belong to vs. 3 or to what follows in vs. 4[60] should in my opinion be settled in favor of the former. Others opt for the latter from considerations of rhythm. These words are also said to be superfluous in vs. 3. But to combine them with vs. 4 also leads to difficulties: Would the meaning be "in what was made, therein was life," "therein he was the life," or "in him there was life (for it)"? The first is very unattractive, because then the second clause does not say much more than the first and no longer speaks of the Logos as the source of life. The third does, but without the added phrase "for it" the sentence would hardly flow. The second translation would, then, have to be preferred, but it is by no means clear on first reading that the Logos is the subject of the sentence. Another possible translation would be "what has come about in him was life," which would have to be understood in reference to the incarnation of the Logos. That which "was made" then has to mean something like "what has appeared in him." This translation is commended by the fact that it brings out "the thoroughly Johannine emphasis on the historical advent of salvific life and light in the person of Jesus."[61] Although I agree with this last point, it seems to me forced to interpret "what was made in him" (or "what has appeared in him") as a reference to the incarnation, in any case as the first announcement of it.

Nothing is more natural, however, than that the second "was made" should refer back to the beginning of vs. 3 and thus to that which was made[62] by the Logos at the creation, and not to what appeared in him at the incarnation. In my opinion, the difficulties all resolve themselves if one takes "that was made" as the somewhat stately — and certainly not discordant — conclusion of vs. 3 and continues in vs. 4 with "in him (the Logos) was life." The concepts then follow each other in logical sequence: "was made," "life," "light,"

---

of the Son in distinction from that of the Father (ἐκ; cf. 1 Co. 8:6), cannot be decisive here; διά with the genitive is also used elsewhere in a general sense of God (Gl. 4:7; Rm. 8:31).

60. Text-critically the issue cannot be settled with certainty, though some scholars think that the punctuation that adds ὁ γέγονεν to vs. 4 is the *lectio difficilior* and that the other reading may owe its existence to dogmatic considerations arising from the Arian conflict. The twenty-sixth edition of Nestle-Aland attaches ὁ γέγονεν to what follows in vs. 4. Cf., at length, also K. Aland, "Eine Untersuchung zu Joh. 1:3-4. Über die Bedeutung eines Punktes," *ZNW* 59 (1968), pp. 174f.

61. E. L. Miller, "The Logic of the Logos Hymn," *NTS* 29 (1983), pp. 552-61, here p. 553.

62. The perfect γέγονεν can be easily understood as the permanent effect of ἐγένετο.

"shines." It may be true that from a viewpoint of rhythm there is more to be said in favor of connecting "that was made" with what follows in vs. 4. But anyone wanting to bring the first five verses of the prologue completely into logical order has to perform all sorts of surgical operations.[63]

Verse **4a** now continues to speak of the Word as the source of life. The reference is not yet to life in its effect among people — that follows in vs. 4b — but to the Logos as the possessor and giver of life. Elsewhere this is conveyed by saying that the Father has life in himself and has granted the Son also to have life in himself (5:26). One can say that this is already implied in 1:3, but the life over which the Logos has control does not limit itself to the creation of all things but also extends itself in the power by which life is maintained, so that "life" has here its absolute meaning without further differentiation as to the forms in which it consists.

The past tense is consistently used (six times in vss.1-4), but this does not mean that the reference is to a state of affairs that is past. Rather, the tense is to be understood from the perspective of one who looks at the present in light of its origin, which is antecedent to all human experience.

Humans are first mentioned in vs. **4b**,[64] which says what the life that was in the Word meant for them: *light*. Everything is still totally qualitative: life in its absolute meaning, light as the gift that makes human life possible, and humans as such in their dependence on the light and without reference to place or time. The text does not explicitly refer to humanity before the fall, nor, I believe, is that meant.[65] We are dealing with neither the reception of the light nor who will and will not have a share in the light of life, but with the light that people need to live, whether they know it or not (cf. 8:12). Nor, for the same reason, are we to assume that in vs. 4 we are reading about the period between the creation and the incarnation and that this is one reason for the use of the past tense ("he was").[66] Of course one can ask whether the statement that the life was the light of humanity does not also apply to those who lived before the incarnation. This question must certainly not be answered in the negative. But the statement is too general to apply to one specific period in history. With both "the light" and the people that are spoken of, we are dealing with qualitative terms, not with something historical. This changes only in vs. 5.

5 This verse constitutes a further step in the development of the argu-

---

63. In order to achieve the desired parallelism in vss. 1-5 Miller, too, has to delete vss. 1c and 2 ("Logic," 555). On the whole issue of the poetic character of the prologue, see pp. 21-23.

64. τῶν ἀνθρώπων, objective genitive.

65. Cf. Aland, "Eine Untersuchung zu Joh. 1:3-4," p. 217.

66. Cf., e.g., E. Smilde, *Leven in de johanneïsche geschriften*, 1943, pp. 15, 16. On the speculations concerning light as λόγος σπερματικός and the like, see at length A. Wind, *Leven en dood in het Evangelie van Johannes en in de Serat Dewarutji*, 1956, pp. 42ff.

ment by speaking of the light in its actual effect, the source of illumination in its illuminating radiance. But what is the significance of the step made here? Are we dealing with:

- as before, a general qualification of the effect of the light, namely that it shines in the darkness and has never been apprehended by the darkness,
- a certain period in the revelation of the light, namely the period between the creation and the incarnation, which is then described further in vss. 9ff.,
- or a description in general terms of the situation that arose with the coming of Christ, that is, the situation on which the Evangelist and the community he addresses look back and in which they still find themselves?

Of these three possibilities, the second is improbable if not impossible. It clashes with vs. 7, where the reference is to the light attested by John and hence the light that came in Christ, so that then it becomes necessary to eliminate vss. 6-8 from the context. Further, there is mention here of "the darkness" without any mention (after vs. 4) of the fall, which in the theory of the "phases" or "periods" is inexplicable. And the strongest argument against this view is that present tense "shines" can hardly relate to a closed period in the past.[67]

There is then more to be said for the first view, namely that the verse is a timeless statement about the light. As a rule the second clause in the verse is then translated as "and the darkness has not overcome/extinguished it [i.e., the light, as the light of the Word, which was God]."[68] The greatest objection to this, however, is that the second clause of vs. 5 clearly corresponds to vss. 10b and 11b, which refer to the rejection of the Word as it appeared *in Jesus Christ*.

For that reason the present tense "the light shines . . ." is in all probability not a timeless statement but refers to the light that came when Christ entered the world and that now shines (cf. "the true light is already shining," 1 Jn. 2:8). Therefore, the second clause of vs. 5 must not be translated "the darkness

---

67. According to Bultmann, φαίνει already has to refer to the incarnation in the same way as in 1 Jn. 2:8. But this must then be viewed as an anticipation of vs. 14 whereas vs. 5b is said to describe the attitude of people from the creation of the world on. The identity of the light by which people were confronted from the beginning and the nature of the incomprehension of the darkness Bultmann then tries to articulate from within his existentialist view of humanity.

68. So, e.g., Barrett: "The light shines [simply because it is light — we are not yet, in vs. 5, dealing with the incarnation] in the darkness, and the darkness has never quenched it" (*New Testament Essays,* p. 45). He is more nuanced in *Comm.* (p. 158), where he believes he can combine the two meanings. Cf. also G. Delling, *TDNT* IV, p. 10: "to vanquish the power of His light"; Bernard, *Comm.* I, p. 6, thinks of the creation story, in which the light drives the darkness from the chaos.

has not vanquished it," but "the darkness has not *understood* it."[69] Therefore, though the first view described above cannot be totally excluded, the third certainly deserves preference. "The darkness has not understood it" also provides the best connection with vs. 7, where "the light" is unmistakably used of the coming of Christ. The same is true of vs. 9, where, in view of what follows in vs. 12, there can again be doubt about this point.[70]

All this means, then, that what is said about the Logos in vss. 1-4 is directly applied to what one can call the great content of this Gospel, that is, to Christ's appearance as the light of the world in its confrontation with the darkness (cf. 8:12; 3:19f.; 9:5; 12:35, all passages in which the core concepts of 1:4, 5 return). For that reason it is not permissible to end the first cycle of ideas, the Word in the beginning and so on, at vs. 4.[71] All the imperfect verbs in vss. 1-4 that describe the preexistence and essence of the Word that was antecedent to all existence and experience have their point and meaning in that they reveal the grand background of the actual situation of proclamation in which the Evangelist and the Christian community know themselves to be: "The light shines in the darkness, and the darkness has not understood it." For no other purpose did the Evangelist begin his Gospel with the Logos. He did not do so in order to place the coming and work of Christ in the context of an already existing universal Logos theology, of which his words would be the crown. His purpose was, rather, to trace the gospel story to its final and deepest origins and so — taking up the conflict between what he will refer to over and over as darkness and lies versus truth and light — to point out at the outset the importance and range of what he is about to narrate and the grounds on which he will call people to believe that Jesus is the Christ, the Son of God (20:31).

---

69. κατέλαβον. What is in view, according to Bultmann, is not intellectual understanding but, as in vss. 10 and 11, "the comprehension of faith"; for his reasoning here see his *Comm.*, p. 48, n. 1. Similar uses of καταλαμβάνω are in, e.g., Rm. 9:30; 1 Co. 9:24; Ph. 3:12; Ep. 3:18. Perhaps on this basis one can also translate it here as "appropriate," "absorb," or "grasp." To be sure, in Jn. 12:35 we read: ἵνα μὴ σκοτία ὑμᾶς καταλάβῃ, in which the verb has the meaning "overtake." But that is different from "vanquish." And "overtake" does not fit in 1:5. Therefore one must understand 1:5 in a way similar to vss. 10 and 11. See also H. Conzelmann's argument in *TDNT* IX, p. 352, n. 345.

70. For this exegesis see also Käsemann, "Structure and Purpose," pp. 142ff.

71. As does Käsemann, following Bultmann. Käsemann is concerned that the parallelism between vs. 5 and vss. 9ff. not be obscured (see n. 70 above). But the criterion for the prologue's structure is not its literary form but the Johannine pattern of thought, which is one of return and repetition of the same motifs and of progressive expansion of the field of thought. Thus also here: That which was provisionally concluded in vs. 5 is taken up again and continued in the new beginning in vss. 6ff.

1:6-13

The Coming of the Word as the Light of the World

Now begins a new cycle of thought that in a variety of ways elaborates what was said in vss. 1-5. In vs. 14 the third and last segment of the three-part cycle begins, and at the end (vs. 18) everything returns to the beginning.[72]

Verses **6** and **7** link up with the statement in vs. 5 by reporting on the ministry of John the Baptist, the man sent by God as a witness to the light mentioned in vs. 5. Here and in vs. 15 scholars have repeatedly found what they regard as conclusive evidence that the prologue is not an original unity. These intermezzi about John the Baptist are said to interrupt both the rhythm and the thought pattern of the Logos hymn. But as stated earlier, one cannot use rhythm and meter as criteria for the original hymn without getting stuck, and that for a number of reasons. The material about John is, it is true, more "prosaic" than the lofty opening lines about the Logos in vss. 1-5. But vss. 6-8 are by no means incongruous. They have been composed in a solemn, stately style on an Old Testament model (cf. Jg. 13:2; 17:1; 1 Sa. 1:1).[73] One can even arrange them in three parallel "couplets."[74]

In various ways some interpreters have forcefully maintained (against the long-dominant opinion) that these verses do not disturb the thought pattern of the prologue but rather constitute an essential contribution to it.[75] These pronouncements about John are picked up again later and elaborated in vss. 19ff. and 29ff., where the real gospel story begins. Although the prologue reaches past the "beginning" of the gospel (cf. Mk. 1:1; Ac. 10:37; 13:23; 1:22) to the "in the beginning" of Gn. 1:1, this does not mean that the salvation-historical role of John the Baptist as the herald of the coming One became of less importance to the Evangelist. On the contrary, the Fourth Gospel describes and identifies the purpose of John's mission and baptism (cf. 1:31), in a way different from that of the Synoptics, as that of a witness (1:7, 8, 15, 19 [cf. vs. 20], 32, 34; 3:26; 5:33). Therefore, the prologue's references to this witness are not distracting, "puzzling," "abrupt," or even "coarse" interruptions[76] but rather highly appropriate appeals to the witness of a man whose appearance and ministry belong integrally to the Christ-event.

One may add that these references to John's witness come at two strategic

---

72. Some scholars see a chiastic structure in the prologue; see at length and with references to targumic parallels Borgen, *Logos Was the True Light,* pp. 16f.; more carefully and with less force, Hooker, "John the Baptist and the Johannine Prologue," p. 357.

73. See, e.g., M. É. Boismard, *Le Prologue de Saint Jean,* 1953, p. 46.

74. So Barrett, *New Testament Essays,* p. 39.

75. See Barrett, *New Testament Essays,* pp. 45f.; even more convincingly, in my opinion, Hooker, "John the Baptist and the Johannine Prologue."

76. So also Hooker, "John the Baptist and the Johannine Prologue."

points in the prologue: first, after the thematic beginning in vss. 1-5, before it is further elaborated in vss. 9-13, and then after the pronouncements in vs. 14 about the revelation of the glory of God in the incarnation of the Word, before those pronouncements are explicated in vss. 16-18.[77] In both cases we are dealing with John's identifying witness concerning Jesus, first in regard to Jesus' unique significance as the light of the world, then in regard to Jesus' antecedent transcendent glory. The references to John thus do not break the thought pattern of the prologue but precisely reinforce what one may call its central content.

The unity of the prologue is particularly evident in that vs. 7 alludes to what has already been said in vs. 5 about the importance of the coming of the light. In the confrontation between the light and the darkness John is the great *witness,* a concept that here, and in general, has a forensic meaning. John appears as the divinely appointed spokesman on behalf of the light to put the darkness in the wrong. But at the same time that witness is also — and this, too, is divinely intended — one who recruits for the light (cf. 3:16). The purpose of his coming and mission is that through him all should come to believe (cf. also 5:33ff.). Here for the first time *faith* is referred to: The appearance of the light does not automatically bring with it acknowledgment and acceptance, though one might perhaps expect this. It is a light to which people may be blind (cf. 9:5, 39) and from whose illumination one can shield oneself because one prefers the darkness (cf. 3:19ff.). All that will come up at length later, but here already it is clear that the coming of the light demands a choice: People must want to leave behind the darkness in which they have been enclosed and imprisoned and "come to the light" (3:21; 8:12).

8 Before this line of thought is continued in vss. 9ff., vs. 8 first adds that John himself was not the light. This emphasis on John's subordination to the coming of the light returns in John's own words (vss. 15, 20f.; 3:28f.). Some scholars think that this emphasis is a polemic against a sect that considered John the Messiah. This is also said to be the explanation for the supposed insertion of vss. 6-8 into the prologue.[78] Regardless of whether such a tendency is at all present in the Fourth Gospel,[79] interpretation of vs. 8 does not make this hypothesis necessary. The thrust of vss. 6-8 is very positive with regard to John. That he himself was not the light does not diminish him in any way but rather serves to mark his unique place in salvation history as the one who pointed to the coming of the light but preceded the hour of fulfillment (cf. Mt. 11:11, 12).

9-13 After this first "Johannine intermezzo," vss. 9-13 return to the central opening theme, which was provisionally rounded off at vs. 5. One can

77. See especially ibid., p. 357.
78. Bultmann, *Comm.,* pp. 17f.
79. On this point see the comments on vs. 20 below.

perhaps speak of a second concentric cycle of thought, in which the categories of the first come back, but this time — after what has been said about John as witness — in their kerygmatic implications.

Verse **9** begins by saying that the light mentioned in vs. 5, to which John was the witness, was the true light that by its coming into the world enlightens every person.[80] "True" means *genuine,* that which is in fact what it claims to be, hence implying a contrast with what is falsely described or offered as the light. Here it also has a clearly exclusive meaning, referring as it does to the "uniqueness" of Jesus.[81]

Because of that uniqueness, it is also true of this light that it "enlightens every person" (cf. vs. 4b). This statement describes the light in its fullness and universality. It does not say that every individual is in fact enlightened by the light (cf. vss. 5, 10f.) but that by its coming into the world the light is for every human being that by which alone he or she can live (cf. 8:12). The light's "coming" is not of course just the moment of its arrival but the proximity and accessibility that result from that coming and by which every human being has come within reach of the light. The reference is to the coming of the Logos into flesh, even though this modality of its coming is not mentioned until vs. 14. In view here is only the coming as such.

Verse **10** again speaks (cf. vs. 5b) of the negative reaction of the world to the coming of the light. In order to bring out that contrast fully and vividly vs. 10a-b summarizes what has been said before. Though linked paratactically, these pronouncements essentially have a concessive meaning in relation to the last clause of the verse: "*Although* he. . . ." The "and" that introduces the third clause clearly (as in vs. 11) has an adversative meaning: "and yet, but."

80. The translation is difficult. Some scholars, claiming support in Hebrew usage (see Strack/Billerbeck II, p. 358; Schlatter, *Comm.,* p. 15), take that which was "coming into the world" (ἐρχόμενον εἰς τὸν κόσμον) as humankind. But after ἄνθρωπον this would be a pleonasm. Also that which is ἐν τῷ κόσμῳ in vs. 10 is the Logos (cf. 3:19; 6:14; 9:39; 11:27; 12:46; 16:28).

Others connect ἦν at the beginning of vs. 9 with ἐρχόμενον as a periphrastic verb with τὸ φῶς as the subject ("The true light was . . . coming. . . ."). But ἦν is too far removed from ἐρχόμενον for this, being separated from it by a relative clause, which would be very unusual. In this interpretation all the emphasis would lie on the light's *coming* into the world, which is already assumed in vs. 5.

The emphasis is rather on ἀληθινόν and πάντα ἄνθρωπον. We should take τὸ φῶς τὸ ἀληθινόν predicatively. The subject of ἦν is "it," the antecedent of which is φωτός in vs. 8b and vs. 7: "It was the true light."

Others take the Logos as the subject. But the Logos was last mentioned in vs. 4, so that here, too, the connection is very distant. It is, however, true that in vss. 10-12 αὐτόν refers to the Logos. Logos and light are identified such that "it" can easily become "he" (cf. also 1 Jn. 1:1; 2:13).

81. So correctly C. Maurer, "Der Exklusivanspruch des Christus nach Johannes," in *Studies in John* (Festschrift for J. N. Sevenster), 1970, p. 145: "ἀληθινός, which in John, in distinction from ἀληθής (= 'faithful, reliable'), consistently means 'unique, exclusive.' " For this distinction between ἀληθινόν and ἀληθής he refers to 1:9; 4:23; 6:32; 8:16; 17:3; 19:35a and to 3:33; 5:31f.; 6:55; 8:13f.; 19:35 respectively.

At this point the subject is no longer just the light but the Logos as well. Everything that has been said about the Logos to this point is cast into the scales against everything else to bring out the mysterious negative character of the world's "not knowing." Clearer proof that in the prologue and in the entire Gospel we are not dealing with a dualistic Gnostic world of thought is hardly possible.[82] The world to which the Logos came was his own creation. The world did not know him, not because he was a stranger but because it was estranged from him, from its origin. The world *should* have known him. The inner contradiction of this not knowing is not explained. The opposition simply posits itself in all its mysteriousness. It is not said that the world *could* have known him if only it had followed the clues provided by its own deepest being as created by him and its own deepest need of the light — of that which was made by him for it. All this is true, of course, but there is no mention here of an unsatisfied dormant sense or preunderstanding that needed only to be activated in order to acknowledge him. What is needed to bring about the suspension of this estrangement, the miracle of a new creation, will be named (cf. 1:13; 3:3ff.).

Connected with all this, finally, is that the term "world" is not unambiguous either here or elsewhere in the Gospel. As the world that came into being by the power of the Word it is the whole of creation (vs. 3), specifically the human world (vs. 10), that which belongs to God and alongside God, the object of God's love (cf. 3:16). At the same time, however, here and in several places in the Gospel "world" stands for the humanity that is estranged from and hostile to God — in that sense the world outside God. "Knowing" is not just intellectual but refers to total relatedness. It is rooted in a choice that embraces not only the intellect and not only the heart, but also the human will. Accordingly, *not* to know the Word is to reject a relationship with him (see also on 10:14).

Verse **11** has a similar thrust to vs. 10. The question is only whether "his own home" and "his own people" still refer to the world as that which came into being by the Word and hence as that which belongs to him — in the same sense as in vs. 10 — or to the special relationship between the Word and Israel as the people of God (cf. Ex. 19:5; Dt. 4:20). The choice is difficult because both make equally good sense.[83] But if one thinks of Israel in vs. 11, then one

---

82. See also H. Hegermann, "Er kam in sein Eigentum," in *Der Ruf Jesu und die Antwort der Gemeinde* (Festschrift for J. Jeremias), 1970, p. 131.

83. Schlatter, Bultmann, and Schnackenburg (at least in regard to the supposed original hymn; the Evangelist himself probably had Israel in mind) opt for the first view. Lindars opts for the first in regard to τὰ ἴδια but thinks of a "subtle transition" to Israel when it comes to οἱ ἴδιοι (*Comm.,* p. 90). Opting for the second in both clauses are, among others, Lagrange, Dodd (*Interpretation of the Fourth Gospel,* p. 402), Brown, Haenchen, and Barrett (though not with certainty).

gets two viewpoints in vss. 10 and 11, and a sort of climax: In Jesus Christ the Logos came not only to a world that had been made by him; he also came to a people adopted by God as his own possession. In the context of this "coming" of the Logos the Jewish people could hardly be left out of consideration. Throughout this Gospel there is reference to "the world," but that world manifests itself primarily in the confrontation between Jesus and Israel.

With this the negative reaction to the coming and work of the Logos, already referred to in vss. 5 and 10, the prologue has reached its low point. Those who from of old were called the people of God's possession (cf. Is. 43:21) did not receive him, that is, were unwilling to receive him as a welcome guest.[84] Again this does not apply to the experience of the Logos before the incarnation, whereupon there would follow an "evangelic turn" in vs. 14.[85] It is rather the actual historical situation that the Evangelist pictures to his readers, but he does it here against the all-determining background of the eternal Word. Therefore the rejection of the Word is the mysterious and culpable resistance of the creature against its creator, of humankind against its own redemption, and of the people of Israel against its God (cf. 8:54).

12   There is, however, another side to this, which is described in words that show that the transition to the revelation of Christ does not have to wait until vs. 14. After what we have heard of in vss. 5, 10, and 11 ("the darkness," "the world," "his own people"), "all who received him" are apparently those who went against the current, who broke with the general pattern by which the world thinks, lives, and acts. They are further described as those "who believed in his name" (see on vs. 7; cf. 20:31); that is, they accepted him for what he was and as he manifested himself.

Again the emphasis falls on what, in virtue of what he was from the beginning, he had to give them, namely the "power," that is, the right and the freedom "to become children of God." The ability to confer this right marks his exclusive relationship to God (cf. 3:35; 20:17) and his utterly unique position as the way to the Father (14:6). No one comes to the Father except through him, nor does anyone become a child of God except by the Son.[86] In John, unlike elsewhere in the New Testament, believers are not called "sons" (υἱοί) but exclusively "*children* (τέκνα) of God," while "son" is used only of Christ (cf. 11:52; 1 Jn. 3:1, 2, 10; 5:2).[87]

In John being a child is always rooted in a new birth "of God," "of the

---

84. Schlatter writes that the word translated "receive" is characteristic for the manner in which Jesus in his human presence was received and accorded hospitality or denied access into people's homes (*Comm.,* p. 18); see also G. Stählin, *TDNT* V, p. 28, n. 191.

85. For this view (held by, e.g., Haenchen), see above, pp. 32f.

86 On this see also M. de Jonge, *Jesus: Stranger from Heaven and Son of God,* 1977, pp. 151f.

87. See also A. Oepke, *TDNT* V, p. 653.

Spirit," or "from above" (cf. vs. 13; 3:3f.).[88] It denotes a totally new mode of existence, one that belongs to the "eschatological" renewal of all things by God, which as "eternal life" has already been initiated by the work of Christ; elsewhere in the New Testament it is as such also often linked with the future ("the revealing of the sons of God," Ro. 8:19; cf. Col 3:4 but also 1 Jn. 3:2). The privilege of being children of God is special and exclusive. It is not a natural quality that every human being has as a creature of God; nor is it the inalienable right of Israel as "his own" (cf. 8:42). It is, rather, the gift that is given only to those who believe in the Word.

Verse **13** concludes the train of thought begun in vs. 6. A reading occurs in some church fathers that continues in the singular: *(qui) non natus est,* which thus refers not to the rebirth of believers but to the virgin birth of Jesus. But this reading is hard to accept as original. Not only is the textual basis very weak, but a statement about the virgin birth of Jesus would not easily have been replaced by another about the rebirth of believers.[89] Also, such a statement about the Logos not being born of blood and so on would be very surprising after vss. 1-5 and 9-11 and before vs. 14.[90]

Some interpreters forcefully reject any idea that the relative clause with which vs. 13 begins ("who were born . . .") is a comment on the preceding clause ("who believed in his name")[91] since then faith would proceed from regeneration whereas, according to their view, a person must opt for rebirth as a possibility opened up to him or her in the call that comes from the Revealer. In the choice that faith makes a person can be "born again" and so change and come to his or

---

88. The linking of the juridical term ἐξουσία with γενέσθαι — which evidently refers here to being, not status — remains striking: "He gave power to become children of God." But Brown, with others, believes translating ἐξουσία thus ("power," "right") makes of the sentence "a semi-judicial pronouncement" alien to Johannine thought: "Sonship is based on divine begetting, not on any claim on man's part" (*Comm.* I, p. 11). For that reason some scholars explain ἐξουσία as a somewhat infelicitous rendering of a Semitic expression, "give" *(natan)* in the sense of "permit, grant." In any case ἐξουσία τέκνα θεοῦ γενέσθαι does not have a strictly juridical meaning such as comes to the fore in υἱοθεσία, *adoptio.* Perhaps one can best translate ἐξουσία as "privilege": τέκνα . . . γενέσθαι is not a description of the new birth (that does not come until vs. 13) but of the privilege of being children of God.

89. Tertullian asserts that we are dealing here with a falsification by the Valentinians who thus imported into the text their view about the class of the elect. But that is implausible simply because the Valentinians did not include "believers" among the elect. For the rejection of this reading see also the lengthy argument of Schnackenburg, *Comm.* I, pp. 264f.

90. So Barrett: "The Prologue reaches its climax in the assertion that Christians share the miraculous origin of the Lord" (*New Testament Essays,* p. 46). But then the question arises whether vs. 13 does not exclude every form of human participation in the birth intended here (not only that of a human father), and though that is true of the rebirth of believers, it would not apply to the virgin birth of Jesus.

91. So Bultmann: "Naturally οἱ ἐγενν. explains τέκνα θεοῦ and not πιστ." (*Comm.,* p. 59, n. 5; see also n. 4: "Naturally procreation by God is not the 'root and presupposition' of faith" [referring to Holtzmann's view]).

her real being.[92] However, against this it has to be asserted that the concluding statement in vs. 13 traces the entire gift of being a child of God, including the manner in which it is effected, to its deepest ground: "procreation" by God. The idea that faith as a human choice should precede that birth and therefore that in some sense a person should have this rebirth of God at his or her disposal not only seems absurd but is also at variance with statements like this in 1 Jn. 5:1: "Everyone who believes . . . is born of God."[93] By saying this one does not in any way detract from the call and invitation to believe so emphatically issued in John's Gospel, a call addressed to all without distinction (just as in 5:8 the lame man is asked to "rise"). The two-sidedness in the redemptive order consisting of God's gift and human responsibility, the secret of which the Fourth Gospel does not unravel,[94] will force itself on our attention again and again in the Gospel.[95]

Three opposites to birth from God are named in vs. 13a. The plural of "blood" is hard to explain. One thinks of the blood of two parents as bearer of the life that propagates itself, or something of that nature. The most probable solution seems to be something more general: "whose birth is not a question of blood" or the like. The double "of the will of" refers to sexual desire, first in general terms then in regard to a man's initiative in fathering offspring. In all three the reference is to the natural process of procreation — that which lies within human power (cf. Gl. 4:23, 29).

"Flesh" here denotes humanity in itself in its creaturely human potentials and limitations (cf. 1:14); but in this context "the will" of the flesh and of a man do not carry the connotation of something inherently inferior.[96] The "dualism" expressed in vs. 13 is not rooted in an anthropological opposition between the lower or the higher elements of a person or in a metaphysical contrast between a heavenly world and an evil world mired in matter. It is, rather, rooted in the distinction — characteristic also of Old Testament thought — between God as the all-controlling Spirit and the human person in his or her creaturely dependence (cf., e.g., Is. 31:5; Ps. 56:5).[97]

---

92. Cf. also Bultmann's *Theology of the New Testament* I, 1951, pp. 335f. On this complex of problems see at length R. Bergmeier, *Glaube als Gabe nach Johannes,* 1980, pp. 213f.

93. On this relationship see also Bergmeier, *Glaube als Gabe,* p. 219; de Jonge, *Jesus: Stranger from Heaven,* p. 153.

94. Cf., e.g., de Jonge: "We would like to know what is first and what comes later, and we like to think in terms of cause and effect, but the Fourth Gospel and the First Epistle also simply put things side-by-side, and they attribute all that is good, and all that is willed and given by God to his initiative" (*Jesus: Stranger from Heaven,* pp. 153f.).

95. The so-called "predestinarian problem" in the Fourth Gospel; see further on 6:44f.; 10:26.

96. Cf. Bergmeier, *Glaube als Gabe,* pp. 219f.: "not in the sense of late Hellenistic aversion to the body as that which is characterized by ἐπιθυμία or ἡδονή."

97. See also E. Schweizer, *TDNT* VII, pp. 138f., 109; Bergmeier, *Glaube als Gabe,* p. 221. See further under 3:6ff.

Therefore, the fact of being born of God does not cancel out the qualitative distinction between God and humanity. "Of God," "of the Spirit," "from above" qualifies the new life of the children of God as a participation, not in the divine being, but in God's imperishable gift. This gift does not lie within the range of possibilities granted a person in his or her natural birth. A person is entirely dependent for it on the Spirit of God (3:6f.), and all the more because the world made by God and the flesh in which he has given human beings their particular mode of existence have become the element in which, by human sin and self-will, people have alienated themselves from God and hence do not know and accept the light that comes to them in the Word.

It is this contrast that continues to shape vs. 13. That is, vs. 13 not only explains vs. 12 but also refers back to the negative statements in vss. 5, 10, and 11 to protect those statements from possible misunderstanding. The rejection of the Logos by the world and by his own people has been pointed out in its paradoxical and "unnatural" significance, but this does not mean that acceptance of the Word and faith in his name would be merely the obvious response to the revelation of the Word. In fact, the contrary is true because of what humanity has become in the world and in the flesh. Though human unbelief, viewed in the light of the creation of humanity by God, may be a riddle, faith is, in the light of human estrangement from God, a miracle, the fruit of new birth not from below but from above (cf. 3:3f.). However hard, accusatory, and humiliating the verdict against human unbelief may be, here and throughout the Gospel its intent is not to throw people back on themselves and to appeal to their "better" nature but to portray to them their radical lostness. But this is not done — and here lies the transition to the now following third cycle of the prologue — merely to place this dependence on God's grace in the context of the impotence and obstinacy of unbelief, but above all to illumine it from within the revelation of the Word in the beginning, the description of whose full glory is now about to begin.

1:14-18

"The Word Became Flesh"

14 This third and final cycle of the prologue is also the transition to the gospel story since here the figure of Jesus comes clearly to the fore, though he is not named until vs. 17. This further concretization of what so far has been credited to the Word — though from the very start the kerygmatic situation that came into being with the coming and work of Christ is aimed at — is first expressed in the statement "And the Word became flesh." Although the Word was repeatedly the subject in the preceding verses, after vs. 1 that name is mentioned expressly again only here. Whereas in what precedes all the emphasis lies on the divine presence of the Word as the light of the world, now the entire focus is on the self-identification of the Word with the man Jesus of Nazareth.

"Flesh" is not just the material side of human existence but, in the Old Testament sense, all of the human person in creaturely existence as distinct from God (cf., e.g., Ac. 2:17; Mt. 24:22; "flesh and blood" in Mt. 16:17). Also in view here is that which is human as such, apart from sin (which is sometimes referred to with "flesh," notably in Paul: Ro. 8:4, etc.). That the Word became flesh therefore does not implicitly mean that it also took upon itself the sin of the world. Although "flesh" as a term for the creaturely human in itself is also intended as a description of human weakness, perishability, dependence, and the like, one cannot say that the word is used here on account of the offense that the Logos, by appearing as a man and nothing more, occasions to the natural intellect — a notion strongly advocated by Bultmann.[98] For however much the incarnation of the Word in the man Jesus of Nazareth is also the occasion for human unbelief (cf. 1:45; 6:42; 7:27, etc.), this does not alter the fact that in 1:14a, as in 14b, "flesh" is clearly not the means by which the glory of God is concealed in the man Jesus but the means by which it is revealed before the eyes of all. The flesh is the medium of the glory and makes it visible to all people. By means of incarnation God has visibly appeared among humankind. And — we may immediately add — the entire Gospel of John is proof of it: proof of that abundant glory, a glory manifested before the eyes of all.[99]

If then we cannot interpret vs. 14a in isolation from vs. 14b, we also cannot lose sight of the expression "the Word *became* flesh." The Word remains the subject of that which follows. It did not cease to be the Word that was from the beginning, and "became" does not mean "changed into." It denotes an identification. However unfathomable this identification may be, it does not

---

98. So Bultmann, *Comm.,* pp. 63f., e.g.:

It is in his sheer humanity that he is the Revealer. True, his own also see his δόξα (v. 14b); indeed if it were not to be seen, there would be no grounds for speaking of revelation. But this is the paradox which runs through the whole gospel: the δόξα is not to be seen *alongside* the σάρξ, nor *through* the σάρξ as through a window; it is to be seen in the σάρξ and nowhere else. If man wishes to see the δόξα, then it is on the σάρξ that he must concentrate his attention, without allowing himself to fall a victim to appearances. The revelation is present in a peculiar *hiddenness.*

99. For a rebuttal of Bultmann's exegesis, see esp. E. Käsemann, *The Testament of Jesus according to John 17,* 1968, pp. 11-13. Käsemann goes in the opposite direction, to the thesis that the christology of the Fourth Gospel bears a (naive) docetic character, that is, that Jesus' humanity is regarded as little more than appearance, so that it is actually God who walks the earth in the guise of a human being (pp. 12-13, 16). For this entire discussion, see my *Het Woord is vlees geworden,* pp. 5f.; and in particular W. Nicol, *The Sēmeia in the Fourth Gospel,* 1972, pp. 130-37: "The Glory in the Flesh."

mean only that the Logos — that is, God to the degree that he reveals himself — "appeared" in the human sphere and that the Revealer, the one in and by whom God reveals himself, was a man and nothing but a man. Nor does it thus declare superfluous all questions concerning the "how" of that "became."[100] To "become flesh" is more than to "appear in the sphere of the flesh," that is, as Jesus of Nazareth. It is an identification that, though it is not further defined here or linked with the virgin birth, does mean that all the redemptive categories (the "life" and "the light of humanity") thus far attributed in the prologue to the Word now apply with the same absoluteness and exclusiveness to the man Jesus of Nazareth and, in his person as the possessor of that which belongs to God alone, completely transcend and exceed the possibilities of a mere man. One cannot (in "docetic" fashion) hide or even dissolve the reality of the flesh, the true humanity of Jesus, in the revelation of the glory of God any more than one can (in "kenotic" fashion) detach the glory of God from the humanity of the earthly Jesus. The Word did not become flesh by just assuming the form of the man Jesus as a garment in which God walked on earth or as an instrument that God used from time to time. Nor does "became flesh" only indicate the "place" or "sphere" where the revelation took place.[101] At stake here is the Word's act of being united with the man Jesus such that in his self-revelation in words and deeds the glory of the Word of the beginning manifested itself, visibly and audibly (cf. 1 Jn. 1:1f.), and is interpreted by him as such with a recurrent appeal to his Sonship and his having been sent by the Father (cf., e.g., 5:19f., 26f.).[102] Thus "became" refers to a mode of existence in which the deity of Christ can no more be abstracted from his humanity than the reverse.[103]

The words "and dwelled among us" further explicate the preceding words. One can take them to refer either to the beginning of the Word's residence among people or to the entire (past) period of that residence.[104] The verb means "pitch one's tent" and is reminiscent of numerous Old Testament statements in which mention is made of God dwelling in the midst of Israel, the fundamental motif being the tabernacle in the wilderness in which God's presence

---

100. Bultmann, *Comm.,* pp. 63ff.

101. See also E. Schweizer, *TDNT* VII, pp. 138f.

102. See the comments on ch. 5.

103. See also Nicol, *Sēmeia in the Fourth Gospel,* pp. 130-37. Although Nicol opposes Bultmann as well as Käsemann, he clearly prefers the latter. He believes the translation "the Word became flesh" is not entirely correct because then "become" would have to mean "changed into." He opts for Barrett's translation, "The Logos came on the human scene as flesh," and regards "flesh" as a description not of "the nature of the Logos" but of "his place, the human scene, where he had to come for the sake of manifesting himself to men" (Nicol, p. 131). In my opinion ἐγένετο says more than that.

104. Ingressive aorist (BDF §331) or "complexive" aorist (BDF §332: "for linear actions which [having been completed] are regarded as a whole").

in Israel and his glory were manifested (Ex. 25:8, 9; also, e.g., Ezk. 37:27; Jl. 3:17; Zc. 2:10; cf. also Rv. 21:3). In Sir. 24:8 Wisdom says, "The Creator of all things . . . assigned a place for my tent, saying 'Make your dwelling in Jacob . . . ,' " and to some this is a strong argument that the Johannine prologue is closely akin to wisdom literature.[105] I regard as unproven the view that the structure of the prologue was borrowed from, for instance, Sirach 24,[106] and there is no direct reference here to the tabernacle and temple as the place of God's dwelling in Israel[107] (cf., however, also 2:19-22!). Nonetheless, "pitch one's tent" in this context nevertheless has a clear salvation-historical connotation, which is reinforced by the connection in the following clause with "glory." The effulgence of God's glory is an aspect of his indwelling among his people (cf. Ex. 40:34, 35; Nu. 14:10; 1 K. 8:10, 11; Pss. 26:8; 102;16; Jr. 17:12; Ezk. 10:4, etc.; Rv. 15:8; 21:10, 11, 22, 23). Therefore, use of "pitch one's tent" does not emphasize the transience of the manifestation of the Logos in the human sphere but rather the act of taking up residence and then staying.[108]

The newness of this indwelling consists, of course, in the incarnation of the Word. It distinguishes itself from the divine indwelling operative up to that point by its totally different form of proximity — as that of one who permits himself to be seen and to be a member of society (cf. vss. 38, 39), to live among people as one of them.

It says that he took up residence "among us" and refers to the "we" who beheld his glory, that is, neither people in general nor the "we" of the Christian church, but the "we" with whom Jesus lived and who were with him as his witnesses from the beginning (15:27). This "we" is distinguished from the inclusive "we" of the church (vs. 16) just as 1 Jn 1:1f., in a very similar context,

---

105. Apart from the above-mentioned view of Haenchen (pp. 31-35) see in particular also Gese, "Prologue," p. 185: "The incarnation is called a *skēnōsai* (cf. *shkn*) and thereby brought into the great tradition of the revelation of God's having taken up his dwelling on Zion." See also Gese's paralleling of the content of Sir. 24:7f. with that of John 1 (pp. 202f.). In discussion of the alleged Gnostic background of the prologue, the term "tent" plays a large role, notably in the abovementioned (p. 30) comparison of the Nag Hammadi *Trimorphic Protennoia*. For this see esp. the long article by J. Helderman, "In Ihren Zelten," in *Miscellanea Neotestamentica* (*Novum Testamentum* Supplements 47), 1978, pp. 183-211, according to whom the use in *Protennoia* 47:13ff. of "tent" as a term for the manifestation of the Logos in the human sphere is a clearly recognizable reinterpretation of Jn. 1:14 on the basis of "a pure docetism" (pp. 206f.).

106. See above, pp. 34-35.

107. But whatever one makes of the close connection of vs. 14 with Exodus 33 and 34, the idea of God's dwelling in the tent of meeting lies close to hand (note also the comments on vs. 17).

108. So correctly Helderman, "In Ihren Zelten," p. 207, thus distinguishing the usage here from the reinterpretation that the term undergoes in the *Trimorphic Protennoia*; he appeals to C. Colpe, who writes that in this respect Johannine christology is distinguished from "the mere temporalization and historization of a mythological happening." "It is, first and foremost, something substantially and phenomenologically new" (quoted by Helderman, p. 207, n. 100).

distinguishes between the "we" who witnessed Jesus and the "you" of the church.[109] In this connection "beheld,"[110] more strongly than the word for merely "seeing," as is evident also from the climax in 1 Jn. 1:1, seems to point to the dramatic, spectacular, and totally absorbing nature of what is seen, which, after all, is the glory of God. Those who think the "we" means the church speak of "the sight of faith" that relates to the incarnation but is not restricted to eyewitnesses or contemporaries and can be transmitted to all future generations.[111] But that is to remove the specific connection between the incarnation and this sight. At stake is the glory of God in the flesh, which could only be seen and "beheld" by those who were the eyewitnesses of that flesh. Many contemplators of that glory were not moved to believe and could therefore be described as spiritually "not seeing" (cf. 9:39-41), just as others believe in that glory without having seen it in the flesh (20:29). But this is no proof that the glory of the revelation was visible only to the eye of faith. The reverse is much rather the case. The revelation of Jesus' glory, not just the weakness of the flesh, occasions the hostile reaction of "the Jews" (cf. 9:16, 24f.; 11:47). The plea they sometimes base on his human origins and the like (6:42; 7:27) is nothing but an attempt to hide from the power of that glory.[112]

For that reason it is not the function of the eyewitness to convey to every generation anew the offense that is said to lie in the incarnation of the Word,[113] but conversely to witness to the glory as in all the concrete visibility and tangibility that it manifested in their presence ("among us"). This is not to imply that for the witnesses in view here faith in Jesus as the Son of God kept pace from the beginning with the revelation of his glory. Much would still have to be made clear to them, and the witness of those who had been with Jesus from the beginning would not have led to the correct understanding of what they had heard and seen without the co-witness of the Paraclete (14:26; 15:26). But the issue in vs. 14 is, again, not faith but the revelation that underlies the understanding of faith. And not just the revelation of glory, of Jesus as the exalted and glorified Lord, but of his glory *in the flesh* — of his earthly, human existence (see also above, pp. 2-3, 12-14).

The Greek word δόξα, "glory," is a translation of the Old Testament word *kabōd* and refers to a visible and powerful manifestation of God. Though

---

109. Thus some writers distinguish the *pluralis apostolicus* from the *pluralis ecclesiasticus;* e.g., de Jonge, *Jesus: Stranger from Heaven,* pp. 27, 205, 212. Cf. Gese, who speaks of " 'we,' meaning the apostle [vs. 14] . . . which became in time the 'we' of the New Testament Church (vs. 16)" ("Prologue," p. 183).

110. θεᾶσθαι; see also Brown's discussion of the different words for seeing in John (*Comm.,* I, pp. 501f.).

111. E.g., Bultmann at length, *Comm.,* pp. 68ff.

112. See also Nicol, *Sēmeia in the Fourth Gospel,* pp. 132f.

113. So Bultmann on this passage.

the story of the transfiguration of Jesus offers various points of contact for this passage (cf. Lk. 9:32; 2 Pet. 1:16ff.), the idea that the reference here is solely or especially to that story is not likely. The transfiguration does not occur in John's Gospel, and the point here is not a single sensational event but that glory that is attendant on the dwelling, just as in the Old Testament there is a persistent connection between God's presence in tabernacle and temple and the divine *kabōd* revealing itself there. Accordingly, here as well we must think of the continuous glory in the earthly life of Jesus, notably in his miracles (cf. 2:11; 11:40; 17:4; 1:51, etc.). "Glory *as* of the Father's only begotten" does not imply a comparison but is explanatory: "in keeping with his nature as."

"Only begotten" is used as a term for Jesus' relationship to God only in John. Elsewhere it is used of a parent's only child (e.g., Lk. 7:12; 8:42), but also as an indication of the *value* of a certain child with no indication of how many children the parent has (cf. Hb. 11:17). Here the reference is clearly to oneness not in number but in being, the utter uniqueness of the Sonship of Christ. There is a difference of opinion on whether this is all it means or whether the "generation" of the Son by the Father is also included, so that the meaning is *unigenitus* (only begotten) and not just *unicus*. In the ancient Latin version the latter is used, but the later Vulgate has the former, possibly under the influence of the Arian controversy. Whereas some scholars believe that what is at stake here is no more than a quality, the uniqueness of Jesus as the Son of God, and not what in trinitarian theology is called his "procession" from the Father,[114] others advance strong arguments for the translation "only begotten" (and not just "only").[115] Although we will not pursue the issue further here, a text like 1 Jn. 5:18 proves that there is every reason to assume that here, too, "only begotten" means more than simply "only," and this is all the more true because here (as in vs. 18) it is meant to be read against the background of 1:1ff. and the glory rooted in that background. Also the preposition "from" ("from the Father") may point in that direction.[116]

The concluding words of vs. 14, "full of grace and truth," further qualify

---

114. So, e.g., Brown, *Comm.* I, p. 13. See also the lengthy treatment of this text by T. C. de Kruyf, "The Glory of the Only Son (John 1,14)," in *Studies in John*, pp. 111-23, who believes, esp. on the basis of 7:39, that the glory in 1:14 refers to the exaltation and glorification of Christ as God's only Son on the cross and in the event of his death. "Only Son" would be a reference to what God sacrificed, recalling Abraham's sacrifice of Isaac: "John uses the title of Isaac," and the use of μονογενής in this verse is soteriological more than it is christological (p. 123). However, in my opinion all this is based on an overly restricted view of the glory of the Word *in the flesh*, a view that is, moreover, not reconcilable with the entire thrust of the Gospel.

115. See esp. J. V. Dahms, "The Johannine Use of Monogenēs Reconsidered," *NTS* 29 (1983), pp. 222-32; F. Büchsel, *TDNT* IV, 737-41.

116. παρά + genitive; Lindars, *Comm.*, 96: "'of the Father' . . . is decisive for 'only-begotten.'"

him[117] who has just been called the only begotten from the Father (cf. vs. 16: "and from his fullness"). "Grace" and "truth" are used together frequently in the Old Testament of God's relationship to humankind and speak first of all ("grace") of God's favor, benevolence, and mercy.[118] In this combination grace is the supporting concept; in vs. 16 it therefore stands alone. The second term, "truth," adds to the first (in the traditional combination and therefore surely here also)[119] the element of trustworthiness, faithfulness, and unwaveringness and thus characterizes God's graciousness as a relationship in which he binds himself to his own and to which they can unconditionally entrust themselves.[120]

It is the fullness of that "grace and truth" that marks the revelation of glory in the incarnate Word. That revelation not only creates distance and radiates authority but is also powered by God's love for the world (3:16) and consists above all in the *descent* of the one who has power (3:13)[121] and his self-surrender for the life of the world (6:51) and for the sheep of his flock (10:11ff.); it is a "grace" that at the same time proves its "truth" and reliability by the fact that he loved to the end his own who were in the world (13:1) and that of those whom the Father gave him not one will be lost, but he gives them eternal life and no one will snatch them out of his hand (10:28, 29).

It is also clear from these last words of vs. 14 that, however much in the prologue and throughout the Gospel everything is focused on the glory of Christ as the Son of God, the soteriological significance of his coming is not thereby pushed into the background. Rather, it is the high glory of God's nearness "in the flesh" that determines the fullness of the grace and truth revealed in Christ (cf. 3:1-17). In vss. 16-18 these last words of vs. 14 are explicated further.

117. If one takes πλήρης as declinable, it is nominative and can strictly only go with ὁ λόγος, from which it is, however, far removed. But it can also be indeclinable, according to BAGD, s.v., though "almost only when it is used with a gen." In that case one could link it with δόξαν (cf. the variant reading πληρη in D) or, even better, with αὐτοῦ (so BAGD).

118. See the extensive discussion in Gese, "Prologue," 205-8.

119. Others think that here ἀλήθεια should be read against a Greek background, that it is above all an ontological concept distinguishing true reality from illusion, a contrast that — in distinction from dualistic Greek philosophy — is said to refer to the life lived genuinely under God versus the pseudolife in sin. See, e.g., G. Kittel, *Die Religionsgeschichte und des Urchristentum*, p. 87; so also Bultmann, *Comm.* and Bultmann in *TDNT* I, pp. 245f. But although elsewhere the element of faithfulness does not come to the fore in ἀλήθεια, in this traditional connection with grace, love, etc., it has just that meaning.

χάρις is not typically Johannine (it occurs in the Gospel only here and in vss. 16 and 17). For the conceptual linkage between love and faithfulness, see also 13:1. As to the rejoinder that the word translated by χάρις here *(hesed)* is normally translated by ἔλεος, see the contrary evidence in Gese, "Prologue," 205, and A. Hanson, "John I:14-18 and Exodus XXXIV," *NTS* 23 (1976), pp. 92f.

120. So Schlatter, *Comm.*, p. 28: "In John, therefore, love and truth are not contrasts, for in combination they are the powers that establish community."

121. For the central meaning of the motif of this descent in John's Gospel, see the comments under 3:13.

When we come to them there we will have to consider to what degree this qualification of the glory of the only begotten from the Father has its background in the story of the theophany at Sinai in Exodus 33 and 34.

15 First, however, comes the second reference to the "witness" of John,[122] this time in relation to the glory of the one coming after him. The Evangelist cites here a testimony — described more exactly as a proclamation ("cried")[123] that recurs more precisely localized in vss. 29ff. and also refers back ("of whom I said") to what John had told the Jews earlier (though it is recounted later, in vss. 23ff.). The manner in which John testified of the glory of "the coming one" is characteristic for his role as a forerunner, one who can speak of the coming one only in veiled and, in a sense, paradoxical language: "He who comes after me ranks before me, for he was before me." The translation is difficult because the temporal and the spatial are involved in a play on words.[124] But the intent is clear: "He who comes after me (i.e., whose forerunner I am) has left me behind," obviously in the metaphorical sense of "has surpassed me in importance, has put me in the shadows." "For" — and this in view of the first clause is the paradoxical part — "he was before me." This explains the superiority of him who came after John (elsewhere, too, chronological priority is considered proof of superiority, e.g., 1 Tm. 2:13).[125] What John had in mind with "before me" remains unclear ("mightier than I" in Mark and Matthew), but in the context of his witness it is limited to a general reference to the superiority of the coming one: "He was the point of it all" (see the comments below on vs. 30). In the context of the prologue these words certainly have a longer reach, namely, to the absolute beginning of all things (1:1). It is only the incarnation itself that enables us to understand the deep thrust of John's prophetic word.[126] In the later disputes over John's significance (see the comments on vss. 6-8), the fact that his ministry preceded that of Jesus played a role. Whether this polemic is also behind vss. 15 and 16[127] is another

122. Which we have already argued belongs to its context: see the comments on 1:6-8.

123. μαρτυρεῖ . . . καὶ κέκραγεν, a hendiadys in which the first verb describes the enduring significance (present tense) of John's testimony, the second the modality of that word once for all spoken (perfect tense) as a prophetic, Spirit-inspired proclamation intended for the ears of all (cf. Ro. 9:27); see also W. Grundmann, *TDNT* III, pp. 901f.; Bultmann, *Comm.,* p. 75, n. 1.

124. ὀπίσω is primarily spatial but is sometimes used temporally (BAGD, s.v.). ἔμπροσθεν is a spatial term but can refer metaphorically to rank. πρῶτος clearly refers to temporal priority (used here comparatively, not προτέρος as often in the koine). ὀπίσω may therefore be the opposite of either ἔμπροσθεν or πρῶτος.

125. See also Strack/Billerbeck III, pp. 256ff.

126. "The proposition [in 1:15] introduced by ὅτι [looks] at the matter from the standpoint of absolute chronology, which is that of the prologue," according to O. Cullmann, "Ὁ ὀπίσω μου ἐρχόμενος," in *The Early Church: Historical and Theological Studies,* 1956, pp. 177-82, here p. 181.

127. So already W. Baldensperger, *Der Prolog des vierten Evangeliums. Sein polemisch-apologetischer Zweck,* 1898. See further in Cullmann, "Ὁ ὀπίσω μου ἐρχόμενος," pp. 181f.

matter (see comments on vs. 20). Vs. 16 can be understood apart from the polemic.

Verse **16** no longer forms a part of John's testimony but (as is evident from the word "fullness") continues vs. 14. This obviously implies that vs. 15 is an intermezzo that the Evangelist may have inserted later. It does not, however, disturb the connection. Vs. 16 is intended as a confirmation of vs. 14, and its causal "for" (ὅτι) is not isolated by the insertion of vs. 15. Rather, it incorporates vs. 15 into what is explained.

The fullness of the Word that was from the beginning proves itself in that which "we all" have received from it: "grace upon grace." "We all" is now the appropriate expression because not only the "we" of vs. 14 is meant but the entire community of those who believe in Christ. Of the hendiadys "grace and truth" in vs. 14 only the first term is repeated in this hard-to-translate phrase: "grace upon grace."[128] Some interpret this occurrence of ἀντί, "upon," as referring to substitution: The grace of Christ takes the place of that of the Old Testament, the covenant given at Sinai (cf. vs. 17). In my view this is incorrect because John's Gospel does not understand the relation of the old and the new, Moses and Christ, in that way (cf., e.g., 5:39, 45f., and the comments below on vs. 17). Others read the "for" (ἀντί) as expressing the correspondence between grace and the giver of grace. This would, however, be a very difficult way to convey that idea.   *Accumulatively*

More appealing is the view that interprets that "grace for grace" accumulatively.[129] The phrase then serves to explicate "his fullness." This translation is all the more commendable if — as will be further discussed in the comments on vs. 17 — one may relate this double expression to the revelation of God's glory on Mt. Sinai according to Exodus 34. There "grace and truth" constitutes but one of the many designations by which Yahweh makes himself known in his glory: "Yahweh, Yahweh, a merciful and gracious God, slow to anger, abounding in steadfast love and faithfulness, keeping steadfast love for thousands, forgiving iniquity, transgression, and sin" (Ex. 34:6, 7). "Grace upon grace" then reflects the "fullness" in which Exodus 34 speaks of grace and then again more grace.[130]

The Evangelist says that this abundance of grace is "received." After all the elevated pronouncements about the Logos himself, the Evangelist thus now

---

128. For the different translations that have been proposed, see Hanson, "John I:14-18 and Exodus XXXIV," p. 97.

129. BDF §208, refers to Philo, *De Posteritate Caini:* τὰς πρώτας χάριτας . . . ἐτέρας ἀντ' ἐκείνων . . . καὶ ἀεὶ νέας ἀντὶ παλαιωτέρων, which would mean "an unbroken succession of grace."

130. A similar accumulative repetition is in Ro. 1:17: "through faith for faith," i.e., by faith alone.

makes himself the spokesman for the grateful church with its experience of this grace as an ever-accessible and inexhaustible fountain.[131]

Verse **17**, again as a further explanation ("for"), juxtaposes the "grace and truth" that came through Jesus Christ with the law that was given through Moses. This is the first and — apart from 17:3 — the only time that the full name "Jesus Christ" occurs in this Gospel. Thus the approaching story announces itself. Jesus was the focus from the beginning, and everything up to this point led to his story.

The contrast with Moses (if indeed that, rather than a simple juxtaposition, is what we have here) is not straightforward. We need to ask whether all of vss. 14-18 must be read against the background of the story of the giving of the law in Exodus 34. One can advance several arguments in support of this view.[132] Vs. 17 explicitly mentions the giving of the law. Exodus 34 mentions God's "grace and truth"[133] and explicates it as "slow to anger, abounding in steadfast love and faithfulness . . ." (vss. 6f.) and describes the revelation of God's glory to Moses (cf. Jn. 1:14). Exodus tells of Moses' desire to "see" God's face, just as Jn. 1:18 mentions "seeing" God. Though most interpreters acknowledge the connection with Exodus 33 and 34 at least in regard to the expression "grace and truth,"[134] only a few explore this link more deeply. That this link exists and that it illumines the comparison between Moses and Jesus is — in view of the striking points of resemblance — hard to deny.[135]

On this assumption it is clear that in vs. 17 we are not dealing with a Pauline contrast between law and grace. In the giving of the law God revealed himself to Moses, when "Yahweh passed before him" (Ex. 34:6) as the God of grace and truth, steadfast love, and faithfulness. But in that event Moses was not to see God's glory, even though he had prayed for it (33:20). Only after God had passed by would he remove from Moses the hand that covered him (33:18f.).

Therefore, the difference between Moses and Jesus Christ as it is described in Jn. 1:17 is not that Moses and the dispensation of which he was the great

---

131. The καί before χάριν can probably best be translated as "that is": "Of his fullness have we all received our share, that is, grace upon grace"; cf. BDF §442.9, on epexegetical/explicative καί: "that is to say."

132. For what follows see Hooker, "John the Baptist and the Johannine Prologue," pp. 53ff.

133. The LXX translates it as πολυέλεος καὶ ἀληθινός; in view of the entire context of the two passages, this is clearly no argument against the notion that John 1 refers back to Exodus 33–34; see above in the comments on vs. 14.

134. An exception is Bultmann, *Comm.*, p. 78 (see above). There is an extensive overview of the different opinions in Hanson, "John I:14-18 and Exodus XXXIV," p. 90.

135. Cf. Hanson, p. 95: "It would be impossible to find a scripture passage which contains more fundamental elements in common with John 1:14-18. I find it inevitable to conclude that the one is the basis of the other."

representative stood outside the grace and truth of which Jesus Christ was the personification. After all, it was just before the giving of the law that the Lord revealed himself to Moses in the "fullness" of his grace. Still, however un- equalled Moses' significance was as the mediator between God and the people of Israel, he could not see God's glory except from afar as the last rays of the sun, and even less could he be the bearer or dispenser of that glory in its fullness. But of Jesus Christ we are now told that grace and truth "came through him." That is, he not only proclaimed grace and truth but, as the one who was from above and into whose hand the Father had given all things (cf. 3:31, 35), he himself represented them in such a way that "from his fullness we have all been allowed to receive" (vs. 16). It is in this totally different background of God's revelation in Jesus Christ that everything ends in the last verse of the prologue, which is thus the summation and intensification of its entire content.

Some interpreters go further and are of the opinion that Moses and Jesus are not opposed here as representatives of two dispensations, the first of less value by comparison with the second. This is true of the law, to be sure, for it was temporary and antiquated, but what Moses saw of the revelation of Yahweh's glory was nothing other than the revelation of God in Jesus Christ (cf. Jn. 12:41). It differed from the revelation in the incarnate Word only in that it was temporary and restricted to Moses. For that reason "grace for grace" is not the substitution of one grace for the other but the continuation, renewal, and maintaining of the old.[136] It may be that neither here nor else- where does the Evangelist oppose Moses and Christ as bearers of two different "principles" or even of two different "kinds" of grace.[137] But this does not alter the fact that while Moses is the one whose significance is in the mediation of the giving of the law,[138] Christ is the one who has God's grace and truth at his disposal. Apart from this contrast the mention of Moses here is hard to make intelligible.

That is also true of vs. **18**. What has just been said about Moses resonates with the statement that "no one has ever seen God." Although the Old Testa- ment speaks in different ways concerning the vision of God (cf. Ex. 33:11, 20;

---

136. So Hanson, "John I:14-18 and Exodus XXXIV," pp. 96f., with an appeal to earlier authors such as H. J. Holtzmann and A. Loisy.

137. Against E. Grässer, who, following Bultmann, *Comm.,* pp. 78f., sees here an absolute contrast between Christ and the Torah, the latter typifying the Jewish and the (later) Christian *religion,* "in which 'Torah' stands for a certain synagogal dogmatics, just as ἀλήθεια or Jesus Christ is the quintessence of a certain churchly, not to say, dogmatic confession"; every form of salvation-historical thinking is foreign to the Fourth Evangelist ("Die anti-jüdische Polemik im Johannesevangelium," *NTS* 11 [1964], p. 79). This interpretation of the Fourth Gospel is mislead- ing, as is evident not only from the Old Testament background of vss. 16-18 as I have described it, but also from later passages (see the comments below on chs. 4 [esp. vs. 22], 5 [esp. vss. 39 and 45ff.], 6 [esp. vss. 31ff.], and 8 [the summary after vs. 47]).

138. διὰ Μωϋσέως ἐδόθη.

Nu. 12:8; Dt. 18:16),[139] the persistent view is that for no one, not even for Moses, can God be an object of direct observation and that the human person cannot even exist in God's unveiled presence.

In vs. 18b this divine presence is attributed to "God's only begotten Son,[140] who is in the bosom of the Father" (see the comments on vs. 14). The idea that already in Pr. 8:30 this last phrase referred to the transcendent Logos as one who "was enthroned before all time like a child on the lap of his father"[141] seems unacceptable on general grounds.[142] Also, the imagery is different here in John: It is not that of a child seated on his father's lap but that of two adults reclining next to each other at the same table, able to converse intimately (cf. 13:23). In this imagery there is also perhaps an allusion to the contrasting position of Moses ("you will see my back, but my face will not be seen," Ex. 33:18-23).

In any case, it is from this unique and direct communion with the Father, the immediacy of this "seeing" and "hearing," that the Son can speak (6:46; cf. 3:11, 32; 5:19f.). Therefore, the concluding statement of vs. 18 and of the entire prologue is: "He it is who has made God known (to us)."[143]

And thus the circle is completed. No one, of all the witnesses to God, has witnessed to God like the one who was from the beginning with God and was God. No one ascended to God but he who descended from him (3:13). He who comes from above is above all and bears witness to what he has seen and heard (3:31). That is the great thrust of the prologue, and it keeps returning in the Gospel. It is only in that light that we can understand what the Gospel will from this point say about the coming and the work of Jesus Christ.

139. See also Gese, "Prologue," pp. 207f.

140. Another important reading is μονογενὴς θεός (p[66], ℵ, B) or ὁ μονογενὴς θεός (p[75], ℵ[1], etc.). Although this reading is well attested and is not impossible in John (cf. 1:1; 20:28), "the only begotten God" or "God, the only begotten one" is very difficult ("θεός cannot be defended here, for it neither fits in with the preceding θεόν κτλ., nor can it take the appositional phrase ὁ ὤν κτλ.," Bultmann, *Comm.*, pp. 81-82, n. 2). The material grounds against this reading motivate us to choose the reading of the later Greek mss. and the Latin and Syriac versions (μονογενὴς υἱός).

141. So Gese, "Prologue," p. 208.

142. See p. 34 above.

143. ἐξηγήσατο, not in the sense of "explain" but "reveal," referring to communication of direct knowledge of God, here on the basis of having seen God (vs. 18a; cf. F. Büchsel, *TDNT* II, p. 908; Bultmann, *Comm.*; Schnackenburg, *Comm.*).

1:19-51

Preparation for Jesus' Public Ministry

The actual gospel *story* begins in 1:19. Up to the end of ch. 1 the story is limited to the account of the preparations leading to Jesus' public ministry, that is, to the witness of John the Baptist and the attendant calling of a number of disciples. Elsewhere, too, John's ministry is mentioned as the beginning of the gospel (cf. Mk. 1:1; Ac. 1:22; 10:37; 13:24); similarly, it is also said of the disciples that from the beginning, as Jesus' witnesses, they had been with him (cf. 15:27; Lk. 1:2). But as will appear from what follows, in his account of these two things the Evangelist John goes his own way, one that is most characteristic for his whole Gospel.

Accordingly, the second part of ch. 1 clearly falls into two parts. The first concerns John's witness, including, in vss. 19-28, his self-testimony to "the Jews" and, in vss. 29-34, his direct witness concerning Jesus. Then, as the immediate result of this witness, John's disciples come into the company of Jesus (vss. 35f.), and Peter, Philip, and Nathanael are called (vss. 41-51). The section as a whole clearly forms a unit. The last word of the Baptist prompts his disciples to go to the "coming one," who has now appeared. That John does this exemplifies his significance, not only in its salvation-historical "once-for-allness" but no less as the permanent starting point for the faith and formation of the coming church.

1:19-28

The Forerunner

19 The transition from the prologue to 1:19ff. is smooth, in regard to both the conjunction used (a simple "and") and the content: "This is the testimony of John," which picks up the theme begun in vss. 6-8 and 15. This again shows how closely the prologue and the gospel story are linked and how essential vss. 6-8 and 15 are for that connection. It also shows that the Evangelist's sole concern is the *testimony* of John concerning Jesus (cf. vs. 6).

What is said about John in vss. 19ff. does not relate to the beginning and course of his ministry but to a time when he had already become generally known and Jesus himself had already come to be baptized by him. This also shows that the Evangelist assumes that his readers know of John and his ministry; hence in writing his Gospel he does not have a primarily missionary purpose. He addresses himself, rather, to an already existing Christian community and seeks to bring it to a deeper insight into what it already knows as the gospel of Jesus Christ (cf. 20:31).

The first testimony of John relates to his own place and calling in the redemptive process, which began with his coming and is presented to a commission of inquiry consisting of priests and Levites sent by "the Jews" of Jerusalem.

"The Jews" in the Gospel of John

Here for the first time we encounter the term "the Jews," which recurs frequently in this Gospel. Although its meaning in John shows clear nuances, we will have to proceed exegetically from the general usage current in the post–Old Testament period, when both "Jew" and "Israelite" were used to indicate that a person belonged by ancestry to Israel both as a people and as a religious community. Increasingly "Jew" displaced "Israelite." Whereas "Israel" was still the people's self-designation, "Jew" was generally used by non-Jews for Jews, and Jews in the diaspora gradually adopted this designation.

As a rule this Evangelist adopts this usage; he rarely uses "Israel" or "Israelite," and only when he is citing statements made by Palestinian Jews among themselves (1:31, 47; 3:10) or when he is referring to standardized names or texts (1:49; 12:13). He himself lives and writes (as a Jew) in an environment in which the term "Jews" was used exclusively; and he writes for readers who, even if they are themselves Jews, live at a great distance — in time, place, and mind — from the events in Palestine recounted in the Gospel and who therefore need to be more precisely informed in many respects about the customs, etc., of "the Jews" (cf., e.g., 4:9; 19:40).

Obviously this does not mean that "Jew" had a negative connotation for them. The Evangelist speaks of Jesus himself as a Jew (4:9) just as Jesus can say to the Samaritan woman who addresses him as such that salvation is "from the Jews" (4:22). And the Evangelist mentions many Jews who believe in Jesus (8:31; cf. 11:45; 12:11). The feasts "of the Jews" are mentioned with no negative connotation (cf. 6:4; 2:13; 5:1; see also 19:40; 42; 3:1, etc.).

Nevertheless — and this is an important nuance in the Fourth Gospel — "the Jews" are frequently seen in dialogue with Jesus, and the term thereby acquires a strong connotation of "Jews who are hostile to Jesus," with special reference in many cases (a sharp line of demarcation is impossible here!) to the Jewish leaders and authorities. For instance, it is said that the feast pilgrims — themselves Jews! — dared not speak about Jesus "for fear of the Jews" (7:13; similarly 9:22; 19:38; 20:19), who in that case are those more specifically called "the Pharisees" elsewhere (12:42; cf. also 5:10 with 9:13).

Therefore, this specific sense of "the Jews" is not based on anything inherent in the word itself or on any desire of the Evangelist to give the term itself a denigrating overtone. It reflects, rather, the historical reality that in Jesus' confrontation with the Israel of his day the people generally and especially their religious leaders did not accept him as the Messiah and Son of God. The use of this designation neither implies a contrast between Jews and non-Jews nor, even less, reflects a racist or anti-Semitic tendency. It represents, rather, the dominant religious decision of the Jewish people themselves. Even then one will have to guard against a generalizing explanation that suggests that this nuance contains an exclusive tendency toward all Jews and everything that is Jewish. There is in this Gospel a spectrum of nuances, from "the Jews" as the people called and chosen by God to salvation (cf. 4:22) to "the Jews" as the leading aristocracy, those that sought Jesus' destruction (cf., e.g., 5:18; 7:1; 11:8, etc.).[1]

In ch. 1 there is no pressing reason to take "the Jews" to mean, already here, religious opponents of John and his testimony (cf. 5:33, 35). But Jewish *leaders* are meant here, and, considering the role they will play in this Gospel, one can say that from the start, in their conduct toward John and his witness to the Light (cf. vs. 7), the "darkness" (vs. 5) is casting its shadow forward.[2]

At first, the Jewish authorities limited themselves to gathering information, though they soon proceeded to asking critical questions. The use of priests and Levites as emissaries can be understood in light of the fact that John's ministry was characterized by the baptism to which he called people. In the sphere of "purification" (cf. 3:25) priests and Levites were the most expert and involved.

The core question in this first encounter is: "*You*, who are you?" The intent, of course, is not to inquire into John's personal background but into what and who in his ministry and baptism he claimed to be; specifically, as is evident from the questions that follow, what significance he believed he should attribute to himself within the context of the judgment that he was so emphatically announcing and the baptism he offered as a means of escaping that judgment (cf., e.g., Mt. 3:7). In other words, the question concerns John's

1. See the very balanced discussion by W. Gutbrod in *TDNT* III, pp. 375ff. (pp. 377-79 on the Fourth Gospel) and the extensive documentation in R. Leistner, *Antijudaismus im Johannesevangelium?* 1974. On the word "Israelite" see the comments below on 1:47.

2. On the structure of ch. 1 see also J. Willemse, *Het vierde Evangelie. Een onderzoek naar zijn structuur,* 1965, esp. p. 236.

"eschatological" or "salvation-historical" identity, which determines everything about his ministry.

20   The terms in which John's reaction is described characterize it as an answer in a legal examination (in keeping with the forensic meaning of "testimony"). "Confess" and "deny" therefore do not relate to faith but mean something like "clearly acknowledge." Both verbs are used absolutely: "He clearly stated it and did not hedge." Then the first verb returns with a dependent clause: "He declared openly '*I* am not the Christ.' " The emphasis thus put on the denial (partly by the initial position of "I") repeats forcefully what has been said in vs. 8 and will be repeated again in 3:28. Many interpreters regard this as polemically directed against the sect of John's adherents, who regarded him as the Messiah (see above, on vs. 15). It seems hard to determine whether and to what extent the Fourth Gospel would have wanted or would have been able to take a position against this notion — which can only be shown to have existed in a later period. In any case, the repeated emphasis on John's testimony that he is *not* the Messiah is not only or primarily to be explained in terms of polemical considerations but rather in terms of "the Evangelist's desire to portray John as *the ideal witness to Christ,*"[3] one who as much as possible diverted all attention away from himself and onto Christ. In his emphatic and repeated "I am not" he leaves no doubt that the question itself, namely that of the coming of the Messiah, was at issue in a most existential way. But one must not misidentify the person who is the Messiah.

21   This is confirmed by the fact that John not only disclaims all messianic dignity for himself but also rejects the notion suggested by the Jews that he might (believe himself to) be "Elijah" or "the prophet." To these questions as well John gives the negative answer that he gave to the first, apparently with the same intent.[4]

It is not easy to say precisely what the role of "the prophet" and of "Elijah" — expected on the basis of Dt. 18:15 and Ml. 3:23 — was thought to be, either in regard to their mutual relationship or their position in relation to the coming Messiah. Some scholars think that messianic significance was attributed especially to "the prophet," specifically in connection with Moses and his miracles.[5] The Qumran writings refer frequently to "the prophet,"

---

3. So correctly W. Wink, *John the Baptist in the Gospel Tradition,* 1968, p. 105. He continues: "John is made the normative image of the Christian preacher, apostle and missionary, the perfect prototype of the true evangelist, whose one goal is self-effacement before Christ: 'He must increase, but I must decrease' (3:30)." See also Wink's well-documented and careful views of the supposed anti-Baptist tendency in the Fourth Gospel.

4. Here in any case there can be no question of a polemic against the later adherents of John since there is no evidence that they identified John with Elijah or "the prophet."

5. On the combination "miracles," "a prophet like Moses," and "Messiah," see at length Nicol, *The Sēmeia in the Fourth Gospel,* 1972, pp. 81-90; see also the comments below on 6:14f.

sometimes in close conjunction with "the anointed one of Aaron" and "the anointed one of Israel" (1 QS 11). Some see in these three figures the three figures referred to here in vs. 25.[6] Still, especially in regard to "Elijah," a great deal remains uncertain here. In any case, at Qumran as here and in 7:40f., "the prophet" and the Messiah are clearly distinguished. Elsewhere in ancient Jewish writings Elijah plays a large eschatological role as the Messiah's forerunner, as the one whose task it is to prepare the people for the Messiah's coming and, to this end, to "restore all things" (as summarized in Mt. 17:11).[7]

However much his public conduct and the spirit and power of his preaching of repentance reminded people of Elijah, John himself rejected any notion that he would identify his coming with that of Elijah redivivus or of "the prophet," however that was understood. Evidently he knew himself to be the inferior of the coming one (cf. vs. 27) so well that he rejected as unbecoming to himself every claim to a role in which, according to Jewish eschatology, the glory of the coming bringer of salvation would also radiate from him.[8] In light of this, one can also understand that later, when John's ministry had lost its initial appeal among the masses, Jesus called him a prophet, even more than a prophet, and in fact, against all appearances ("if you are willing to accept it"), pointed him out as the Elijah who was to come (Mt. 11:9ff., 14).

22 The emissaries are not content with John's negative answers. If he is neither the Christ, nor Elijah, nor the prophet, then who is he? They add that they are asking him these questions as persons who have been "sent." He must be aware that his public conduct has attracted attention on the highest levels and therefore that there must be an answer. Therefore, "What do you say about yourself?"

---

6. Cf. G. Richter, " 'Bist du Elias?' Joh. 1,21,' *BZ* 6 (1962), pp. 79-92, 238-56; 7 (1963), pp. 63-80; A. S. van der Woude, *Die messianischen Vorstellungen der Gemeinde von Qumran*, 1957, pp. 80-89, against H. Braun, *Qumran und das Neue Testament* I, 1966, pp. 100f.

7. See Strack/Billerbeck IV/2, pp. 764-98; J. Jeremias, *TDNT* II, pp. 928-41: "No biblical figure so exercised the religious thinking of post-biblical Judaism as that of the prophet Elijah . . ." (p. 928).

In his *Dialogue with Trypho* Justin Martyr mentions the Jewish expectation that it was Elijah's task to anoint the coming Messiah to office. By this act he would not only make the previously hidden Messiah known to the people, but would also make the Messiah aware of his messianic calling. M. de Jonge defends the hypothesis that all this is implied in the question posed to John and that for that reason John gives a negative answer (*Jesus: Stranger from Heaven and Son of God*, 1977, pp. 87f.). But in the Jewish writings themselves there is at best indirect reference to Elijah's anointing of the Messiah and no evidence at all that the "hidden Messiah" was unfamiliar with his future task (Strack/Billerbeck IV/2, p. 797). So it is questionable whether de Jonge is right in saying that "John knows Jewish conceptions like that defended by Trypho and his colleagues" and that "in the view of the Fourth Gospel calling John Elijah did imply that" (p. 89). On whether the idea of the "hidden Messiah" plays any role in this connection, see below in the comments on vs. 26.

8. On this see also Jeremias, *TDNT* II, p. 937; see also Brown, *Comm.* in loc.

23 John's answer to this question consists of a direct reference to the prophecy in Isaiah 40. It is noteworthy that he refers the words of Is. 40:3 to himself quite explicitly: The last clause of vs. 23 apparently also belongs to what John said. In the Synoptics this reference to Isaiah 40 is an interpretation of the Evangelists or of the tradition they followed. One is inclined to think that the Johannine Evangelist put this (later) interpretation in John's own mouth. Obviously that is not an impossibility. But neither is the reverse, that is, that the Baptist identified himself with the herald of Isaiah 40. In this regard it may be pointed out that the Qumran sect, which was active in the same region and period as John, also related its existence "in the wilderness" to Isaiah 40. Hence it is certainly not inconceivable that John also made this connection and that the interpretation of the Synoptics is traceable to him and not vice versa.[9]

By basing his mission on Isaiah 40, John both places it in the light of the great prophecy and expectation of the coming kingdom of God and also clearly distinguishes himself from the one who is to bring salvation. His role is restricted to that of preparing the way for the Lord. He who is coming is near, but his "path" has not yet been made level. The region that he desires to pass through is still desolate and impassable. Therefore the forerunner's voice resounds "in the wilderness"; it is a cry for straight and level paths, for penitence and conversion, without which the people cannot receive the coming one. So John identifies himself, and in his self-identification, against the background of the great salvation motif of prophecy (cf. Is. 40:1ff.) and over against Israel's spiritual leaders, the light unmistakably falls on the desperate spiritual condition of the people under that leadership.

Verse **24** first tells the readers, for their further information, that the emissaries are in part also members of the Pharisaic party,[10] who in the remainder of the Gospel repeatedly act over against Jesus as the representatives of official Judaism, with or without the cooperation of the chief priests (cf. 4:1; 7:32, 45f.; 8:3, 13; 9:13f.; 11:46, 47, 57; 12:42; 18:3). That these Pharisaic emissaries are mentioned here separately as those who ask further questions in vs. 25 is probably intended to make clear that the most influential party stalwarts among the Jews were involved in this confrontation — which places in even sharper relief the critical element in the confrontation.

25 Their next question does not relate to John's self-testimony. Apparently their greatest concern was not that he acted as a preacher of penitence. What interested them most in his public conduct was baptism, which he linked

---

9. For this view see also H. Braun, *Qumran und das Neue Testament* I, p. 9.

10. ἀπεσταλμένοι without οἱ has the best textual support. But even then the translation is uncertain. Should one translate "and they were emissaries from the Pharisees," which would mean that the Pharisees were behind the delegation mentioned in vs. 19, or "and there were emissaries from the Pharisees"? It would seem in any case that there is no mention here of a second delegation.

with penitence within the context of the message of judgment, thus offering people a means of escape from judgment ("flee from the wrath to come," Mt. 3:7). Their repeated reference to the Messiah, Elijah, and the prophet does not imply that these figures were expected to baptize, but it does imply that one who baptized with a view to the judgment to come certainly had to possess "eschatological" authority such as these expected figures did. Therefore, "Why — and on whose authority — do you baptize?"

26, 27 John's answer is plain. In one sentence it describes precisely both his own situation and their involvement in it. Here we have the first half of the pronouncement that we know from the other Evangelists (cf. Mt. 3:11): "I baptize with water." The second half does not come until vs. 33. With "I baptize" John stands by his own ministry and authority as baptizer, but with "with water" he relativizes the significance of his ministry by immediately linking it with a reference to one "who comes after" him. The opening words thus acquire concessive meaning: "True, I baptize, but. . . ."[11] By stating the matter thus he informs his interrogators at the outset that any self-elevation of which they apparently suspect him is foreign to him. Whoever he himself may be, in comparison to the one who coming after him, even serving that person as a slave would be too great an honor for John.[12] This is what he has "to say about himself" (cf. vs. 22). When he baptized, his task consisted in nothing other than pointing away from himself and toward the coming one.

By introducing the coming one to his interrogators in this way John indicates that as long as they occupy themselves with him they do not realize what is really happening in the wilderness in which he preaches and baptizes. After all, the "one [who] stands among you whom you do not know" is he of whose superiority John is utterly convinced. This does not necessarily mean that on that day Jesus was personally present in John's audience (cf. vs. 29). But it does mean that he who was to come had arrived — his presence among them was an accomplished fact — and therefore that attention to him was a matter of the greatest relevance and urgency for them. Many interpreters think that in "whom you do not know" a theme is being struck that was already sounded in the prologue (vss. 10f.) and that makes itself felt with increasing force as an indictment against "the Jews," who inquire concerning one who is already among them, though they do not acknowledge him.[13] But this is questionable. In vss. 31 and 33 John also says of himself that he "did not know" the coming one before God pointed him out. In the same sense "the Jews" did not know him. They were still at the stage where they needed

---

11. Though μὲν . . . δέ is lacking in the most important manuscripts, the meaning of those particles is implied, as appears from their insertion in a great many other manuscripts.

12. Typically hyperbolic: unworthy to untie "the thong of his sandal"!

13. So Bultmann, *Comm.*, p. 91; see also, e.g., H. Seesemann, *TDNT* V, p. 118.

someone to point Jesus out and make him known to them, and it was John's task (vs. 31), by his baptism with water, to do just that, to make Jesus known to Israel. But here this point is not yet made in so many words. John ends his testimony to "the Jews" — very characteristically, to be sure! — with "whom you do not know" even while "he stands among you." If therefore they want to go home with an answer for those who have sent them, it is this: There is more at stake in John's baptism than they are apparently aware of.

In the repeated reference to "not knowing" and "being revealed" in vs. 31 some scholars see an allusion to the notion — current in certain Jewish circles — that before appearing in public the Messiah would first live a hidden life on earth. Occasionally also 7:27 is interpreted in that fashion.[14] Though there could be terminological affinities here, this repeated "not knowing" is intended to stress not correspondence with a certain Jewish pattern of expectation concerning the Messiah, but rather the special and undeniable revelational character of John's testimony. What drove John to his public action as forerunner of the coming one and to his baptizing "with water" was not his own initiative or his arrogant desire to be something special; it was solely the result of the prompting of the one who sent him to prepare for and identify the coming of him who would baptize with the Holy Spirit (see further the comments on vss. 31ff.). And it was *this* knowledge that "the Jews" from Jerusalem still lacked, knowledge needed to acknowledge as Messiah this one who stood among them.

The Evangelist restricts the words to "the Jews" to this general statement. The more specific nature and content of the glory of the coming one will not be expressed until "the next day," when Jesus himself will appear on the scene.

28 The topographical reference with which the pericope is concluded (as elsewhere, cf. 6:59; 8:20; 11:54) marks a division in the text and imparts to what follows its own weight, which leads to the climax of John's testimony. The reference also underscores the historic importance of John's conduct and the trustworthiness of the narrative as referring to what really happened in a real place. The actual location of this Bethany beyond the Jordan (cf. 3:26; 10:40) can no longer be ascertained with any certainty.[15] Although a symbolic interpretation of the name has been attempted, it has not been persuasive.

---

14. For this view see, e.g., Strack/Billerbeck II, pp. 488f., 339f.; S. Mowinckel, *He That Cometh,* 1954, pp. 304f.; Bultmann, *Comm.,* p. 91; Brown, *Comm.* I, pp. 53f. For the view of M. de Jonge, see above in the comments on vs. 21.

15. For the presumed location, see G. Dalman, *Orte und Wege Jesu,* 1924³, pp. 96, 98f. Other scholars identify it with the Bethany where Lazarus lived, which was much closer to Jerusalem (P. Parker, "Bethany beyond Jordan," *JBL* 74 [1955], pp. 257ff.). But in that case Βηθανία πέραν τοῦ Ἰορδάνου would have to mean "Bethany that lies across from the point of the Jordan where John had baptized," which seems rather forced, especially in view of 3:26; 10:40, where "beyond the Jordan" refers to the region east of the river. The reading Βηθαβαρα (e.g., Sinaitic Syriac, Origen) offers little support for a specific location and has a weaker textual basis.

1:29-34

"Behold, God's Lamb!"

29 In this pericope John's witness to Jesus reaches its climax, no longer as his response to questions from "the Jews" but as his reaction to the appearance of Jesus himself. Now — on "the next day" — there is no mention of "the Jews" or, indeed, of any audience, though an audience is of course assumed. Nor is there any further explanation of Jesus' coming to John. The readers' knowledge of the person of Jesus, who appears here for the first time, is assumed, as is knowledge that at a certain time he went from Galilee to the Jordan and answered the general call to be baptized (Mt. 3:13). We are not, therefore, dealing with Jesus' first encounter with John. Though it has not been described, John's baptizing activity has already been taking place (vs. 33). But all these historical details remain unmentioned.

What is at stake here is John's central witness that he gives about the coming one, as he stands face-to-face with him, in the solemn form of a revelational utterance:[16] "Behold, the Lamb of God, who takes away the sin of the world." The first part of this pronouncement is repeated in vs. 36. The pronouncement is clearly intended, both there and there, as the descriptive statement most characteristic of John's witness.[17]

What follows in vss. 30ff. provides a more detailed account of how John came to understand that Jesus was the coming bringer of salvation. While these explanatory statements clearly reflect traditions that we also find in the Synoptics, the opening pronouncement itself ("Behold, the Lamb of God . . .") is exclusively Johannine and on the face of it does not appear to find further explanation in vss. 30ff.

Many scholars even believe that this first pronouncement cannot be understood within the limits of the Baptist's message itself since, they assume, it refers directly to the expiatory power of Jesus' sacrificial death. John would thus, in his first witness to Jesus, be anticipating everything that was still to come and immediately saying "the last thing" about Jesus without giving any further explication of it. But even if one rejects this argument and ascribes such foreknowledge of Jesus' future sacrificial death to John's special inspiration as a prophet,[18] the objection remains that the pronouncement is still not clearly integrated into the context. And the same objection applies no less to the view that it is a later Christian interpretation of Jesus' coming and work, specifically of his

16. On this see esp. M. de Goedt, "Un Schème de Révélation dans le quatrième Evangile," *NTS* 8 (1962), pp. 142ff.

17. See also B. Olsson, *Structure and Meaning in the Fourth Gospel,* 1974, p. 51: "The heart of John the Baptist's revelation of Jesus is *that he is the Lamb of God who takes away the sin of the world.*" Later Olsson speaks of the Baptist's "chief message."

18. Cf. Grosheide, *Comm.* I, pp. 135f.

death, that the Evangelist put in the mouth of John the Baptist as basic to the understanding of the Gospel.[19] For with however much justification one can say that all historical gospel stories contain interpretive elements in their construction, this does not mean that the Evangelists put into the mouth of just anyone, at just any point in the narrative, all that the church gradually came to confess on the basis of the gospel narrative without the least concern about the historical context. Here, how should one view the idea that at the center of the Baptist's witness the Evangelist put into his mouth a pronouncement about Jesus for which the context contained not a single explanation or even a point of contact?[20]

It is not surprising, therefore, that many scholars have been unable to content themselves with explaining vs. 29 as something imported — an explanation that does not arise from the context — but have taken great pains to arrive at a solution within the framework of John's own witness.

Various attempts deserve mention:

a) According to one view, the pronouncement about the Lamb of God reflects the heavenly voice that John heard at the baptism of Jesus and by which, according to the Synoptic tradition, Jesus was designated (with an allusion to Is. 42:1) as God's beloved Son, in whom God was well pleased (cf. Mk. 1:11; Mt. 3:17). Hence, proceeding from this identification of Jesus with the Servant of the Lord in Isaiah 42, the Baptist is said to have referred here especially to the sequel of this prophecy in Isaiah 53, where the Servant vicariously takes the sins of others on himself and is compared, in his voiceless suffering, with a lamb (though not with a sacrificial lamb: cf. Is. 53:5f.). In favor of this view is that it moves in the direction indicated by John himself in vss. 30ff. Against it is that for his "knowledge" of Jesus John does not appeal to the voice that spoke at the baptism (about which he is completely silent) but to the descent of the Spirit onto Jesus. Also, even if one should insist on thinking of the voice, the objection remains that one cannot, certainly not directly, derive from the allusion to Is. 42:1 the proclamation of Jesus as the suffering Servant of the Lord who expiates the sin of the world.[21]

19. So, e.g., Schnackenburg, *Comm.* I, p. 301. About the Evangelists' method of weaving the "interpretatio Christiana" into the historical narrative he writes: "The evangelists were not interested in historicizing their narrative, they followed another literary genre in which the narrative was employed in the service of faith, by means of a presentation which developed more fully what was already contained in germ in the historical elements."

20. We may assume that all this is why Bultmann (who himself is not overscrupulous on this point!) believes that the pronouncement in vs. 30, which he characterizes as an "oracular utterance," cannot be original with the Evangelist himself but derives — at least as far as the first part is concerned — from the source that he used. "For the Evangelist the title must have seemed specifically Old Testament and Jewish, for he does not use it again" (*Comm.*, p. 96). However, though in this manner the Evangelist himself is no longer primarily the responsible party, it remains hard to accept that — from purely traditional motives — he makes the Baptist utter as a central pronouncement something that he himself felt to be more or less alien. Also, in this way "the problem" is merely shifted from the Evangelist to his source.

21. So, correctly, Schnackenburg, *Comm.* I, p. 301.

b) Other scholars believe that this last objection could be resolved if for this utterance ("Behold, the Lamb of God") one went back to the Aramaic. Ἀμνός is said to be the translation of *ṭalyâ,* which, besides "lamb," can also mean "servant" or "boy" (παῖς). The assumption then is that in the Greek tradition a shift took place from the originally intended "servant of God" to "Lamb of God." This change in the Greek is supposed to have arisen in connection with the concept — which later emerged in the church — of the Messiah as the sacrificial lamb.[22] But apart from the general objection (see above) that for this explanation one has to appeal to the voice at the baptism, to which the Baptist does not refer, there are other objections against this subtle hypothesis. *Ṭalyâ* is not the most obvious translation of *ʿebed* in Is. 42:1f. One would rather expect Aramaic *ʾabdāʾ* since *ṭalyâ* usually means "boy" and not "servant." Furthermore, τοῦ θεοῦ is not used of the Servant in Isaiah 42.[23]

c) Similar objections have to be advanced against Schlatter's view, which is that the Baptist's pronouncement is based on Jesus' willingness to be baptized by John and thus to put himself in the company of sinners.[24] It is just as true of the baptism as it is of the voice from heaven that it is not mentioned.

d) Dodd has suggested an entirely different background against which to understand John's pronouncement about the Lamb of God.[25] He points out that in the Old Testament the lamb is "not the characteristic sin-offering" and that the widely favored opinion that the reference here is to Christ as the true paschal lamb is highly improbable because that symbolism is nowhere mentioned in the story of Jesus' suffering and death and because the indirect evidences cited for it are weak.[26] Also the expression "take away sin" need not be understood in the sense of "vicariously bearing sin away" but can also very well refer to "removal," that is, more an act of power than one of expiation or atonement. Dodd also believes that in the expression "Lamb of God" we are dealing with an original messianic title of power, as it is in Revelation, where the lamb shares in the omnipotence of God (Rv. 22:1, 3) and battles against God's enemies (14:1-5; 17:14; cf. 5:6). This image is said to occur elsewhere in apocalyptic literature where the people of God is pictured as a flock and its leaders as horned sheep or rams,[27] as in Revelation, which mentions a many-horned lamb.

Others such as Barrett[28] and Brown[29] have followed Dodd partly in attributing this supposed apocalyptic understanding of the "Lamb of God" to John the Baptist. The church, they say, later associated John's pronouncement with the expiatory function

---

22. E.g., J. Jeremias, *TDNT* I, p. 338; O. Cullmann, *The Christology of the New Testament,* 1963[2], pp. 71f. A similar explanation in terms of ambivalent word use (Aramaic *ʾimmar* = "lamb," pronounced as *ʾimrâ* = "word") is offered by A. Negaitsa and C. Daniel in "L'Agneau de Dieu est la Verbe de Dieu," *NovT* 13 (1971), pp. 24-36. Against this, however, see, e.g., P. J. du Plessis, "Zie het Lam Gods," in *De Knechtsgestalte van Christus* (Festschrift for H. N. Ridderbos), 1978, pp. 120-38, here p. 125.

23. See also Bultmann, *Comm.,* p. 96, n. 3.

24. See Schlatter, *Comm.,* p. 51; see also below.

25. C. H. Dodd, *The Interpretation of the Fourth Gospel,* 1963, pp. 230ff.

26. Ibid., p. 233. See also the similar verdict in Bultmann, *Comm.,* pp. 96f., n. 4.

27. E.g., *1 Enoch* 89:46; *Testament of Joseph* 19:8.

28. C. K. Barrett, "The Lamb of God," *NTS* 1 (1954-55), pp. 210ff.

29. Brown, *Comm.,* in loc.

of the Lamb. According to Barrett, it was in reflection on the Lord's Supper that these different elements came together.[30] The expression then refers to Jesus as *the* eschatological, true, God-given Lamb in whom the paschal meal celebrated at the exodus finds its eschatological fulfillment. Thus, though in the Baptist's saying the title is said to have a historic point of connection, in later reflection it came to be joined with other elements, namely expiatory death, passover, and eucharist.

However weighty the objections that Dodd has advanced against the traditional interpretation and however much there is to be said for the view that in vs. 29 we are dealing with a title of power (see below), the basis for the apocalyptic significance of the lamb as an image of power and of messianic leadership of the people of God is weak. The material culled from a few scattered utterances in Jewish apocalyptic literature is certainly not adequate to support the conclusion that we are dealing with an existing messianic title of power.[31] And in the Revelation of John the horned lamb does serve as a representation of Christ's position of power, but it does so as the image of the crucified one, now exalted, whose violent death is determinative for our understanding of the figure ("a lamb standing as though it had been slain," Rv. 5:6, etc.).

e) The view of P. J. du Plessis is based on extensive and astute structural analysis and is affirmed against all "diachronic" explanations of ἀμνός. He, too, believes that John's pronouncement relates not to Jesus' future suffering and humiliation but rather to his power and glory. This is the case with the "taking away of sin," which is further described as the "baptism with the Holy Spirit" in vs. 33, that is, as the authority and power to take away sin. And it also applies to ἀμνός, a term that must be understood in the context — in terms of the glory of the coming one as the only begotten of the Father and as the Son of God — as a *terminus gloriae,* that is, as the expression of the tenderness, love, and glory that proceed from God to Jesus as his only begotten Son. "If one now asks," writes du Plessis, "precisely why he uses the word ἀμνος, it is not because the word itself *carries* the tenderness, love, and glory, but because, in and by his argumentation, the author *assigns* this meaning to the word."[32]

Although, as will be clear from what follows, we consider du Plessis's analysis of John 1 most illuminating, specifically in the manner in which he wants to see the pronouncement of vs. 29 explained as totally rooted and integrated in the context, this filling out of the word ἀμνός purely on the basis of the context and without clear points of contact in what the word means "as such" seems a bit forced. From a semantic point of view, the combination "lamb" and "sin" is too specific for the exegete to ignore the intrinsic connection between the two concepts; all the less because (see below) the idea of plenary authority inherent in this pronouncement, as correctly pointed out by du Plessis, thereby need not be abandoned.

30. Barrett, "Lamb of God," p. 217: "I suggest that there is the crucible in which the strange amalgam of John 1:29 was fused."

31. As Bultmann, *Comm.,* p. 95, n. 3, also concludes in connection with similar views advanced by Lohmeyer and Spitta.

32. Du Plessis, "Zie het Lam Gods," p. 130. Du Plessis appeals to the Afrikaans original of J. P. Louw, *Semantics of New Testament Greek,* 1982, and adds: "One of the great gains resulting from linguistic and semantic analysis is, in fact, the insight that a word does not simply *have* a meaning but that a word is *given* a meaning."

In light of the total picture, the pronouncement in vs. 29 can hardly be understood other than as John's pointing to Jesus as the Lamb of God because it is Jesus who will effect the reconciliation of the world to God. On closer scrutiny, the thesis that such a description of Jesus in the language of Israel's sacrificial cult would not fit in the context of John's preaching is hard to maintain, *at least as long as one guards against overinterpretation,*[33] that is, against any interpretation not based on the context here but on any of a variety of specific expiatory motifs derived from elsewhere, such as Isaiah 53, Christ as the true paschal lamb, or the institution of the Lord's Supper.

In general one can say, as does Schlatter, that where penitence and conversion are the issue, as in John's preaching, "the matter of sacrifice takes on the greatest importance." After all, in Israel the ministry of reconciliation was centered not on a ritual of baptism but in the temple service, and that not only incidentally at the high points of the liturgy but rather in the continual daily morning and evening sacrifice of a one-year-old lamb.[34] We do not know John's attitude toward the ministry of sacrifice practiced in Jerusalem. But it is clear that — though himself the son of a priest — he did not fulfill his mandate of calling people to faith and repentance from sin within the setting of the temple service but, like the Qumran sect, distanced himself from that setting. And his criticism of the official Judaism of the day is just as unmistakable from what else we know of him (cf. Mt. 3:7ff.) and of those who opposed his public ministry (cf. Jn. 1:19ff.), namely, that they included "priests and Levites."

This is not to say, of course, that the whole idea of the ministry of sacrifice as the foundation of communion between God and his people and of his indwelling in Israel was for John a strange or objectionable thing. When on the day after his meeting with the temple authorities he points to Jesus as the Lamb of God, there is rather implied in this most striking, absolute description that, in place of and as the fulfillment of the continual *(tāmîd)* sacrificial lamb in the temple service, God himself is now, once and for all, providing the true ("eschatological") Lamb (cf. Gn. 22:8) that takes away the sin of the world. The idea that in this statement John immediately, by implication, also refers to Jesus' death as the way in which God would vicariously take away the sin of the world is a conclusion for the support of which one can of course adduce all sorts of material from the outside ("diachronically"), but which is by no means prompted by the words of the text as it stands (or by the Gospel as a whole).[35] All that is said here in one

---

33. Against this, see also du Plessis, "Zie het Lam Gods," pp. 124ff. He speaks of "semantic overloading."

34. Cf. Ex. 29:38-46, where in connection with this daily *tāmîd* offering there is also mention of God "dwelling" with his people and revealing "his glory," words immediately reminiscent of Jn. 1:14. Schlatter, *Comm.,* p. 47.

35. Nor does the verb αἴρω carry the connotation of substitution in the sense of "taking on oneself" or "bearing," but means, here as elsewhere in John, "take away," "remove" (cf.

splendid and comprehensive pronouncement is that from now on Jesus acts and answers for the reconciliation and indwelling fellowship between God and his people symbolized till now by the lamb — and does so for the whole world. The pronouncement limits itself to that general and foundational thought: Jesus is the Lamb, as he is also the temple (2:19) and as the rituals of the great festivals in Jerusalem and the meaning of the sabbath find their fulfillment in him (see the comments on 7:37ff.; 8:12; 7:22ff.).[36]

Certainly in all this lies the continuity between the old and the new (see the comments on 1:17). But at the same time it is clear that in Jesus the boundaries of the old are absolutely transcended in regard to the place of worship, the manner of God's indwelling, the way of reconciliation (cf., e.g., 4:21ff.), and also the effect of all this for the whole world. It is — as is clearly apparent from the context (see the comments on vs. 30) — that wholly other and superior dimension in the effectuation of reconciliation between God and the world that the Lamb of God, as presently pointed out by John, provides, and that not only with a view to John's own mission but also with reference to the entire dispensation of salvation in force up to this point.

For that reason, those interpreters who speak here of a *terminus gloriae* or title of power (see above) are correct in substance. Jesus is the Lamb provided by God, but in this passage not in his capacity as one who will humble himself to death, but in his God-given power and authority to take away the sin of the world and thus to open the way to God for the whole world. That all this will also require him to give himself for the life of the world will emerge in ever clearer terms in what follows, that is, in the disclosure by Jesus himself of the deepest secret of his mission (see the comments on 3:13ff.; 6:51ff.; 10:15, 17f.; 13:8). But there, too, in keeping with the nature of this Gospel's soteriology, this will be constantly accompanied by an appeal to the "power" granted to Jesus by the Father. It will be depicted, that is, as the self-surrender of the Son

---

2:16; 5:18ff.; 10:18). In that more general sense of "taking away sin," it occurs also in 1 Jn. 3:5 in a statement using the same words as those used here. Elsewhere in 1 John there is mention of "the blood of Jesus his Son (that) cleanses us from all sin" (1:7) and of "the expiation (ἱλασμός) of our sins" (2:2; 4:10), which clearly refers to Jesus' death as an offering for sin. Although, as is evident from 1 Jn. 3:5, there is a close affinity between the pronouncements in the Gospel and those in the letter, there is in the expiation texts of the letter no mention anywhere of Christ as the Lamb of God, an indication, in my opinion, that in the Johannine line of thought "Lamb of God" is not specifically linked with Jesus' expiatory death.

36. Cf. also M. D. Hooker, "John's Prologue and the Messianic Secret," *NTS* 21 (1974), p. 43. On the "Lamb of God," etc., she writes:

The title is puzzling and no satisfactory explanation has ever been given. Perhaps it is best understood in relation to the Evangelist's arrangement of signs and discourses, by which he shows Jesus to be the one who is the fulfilment of all the Jewish festivals: in him are brought together all the functions of the old ritual — but now they are effective for the world.

of man who descended from heaven (see the comments on 3:13ff. and 6:53), "into whose hands" "the Father has given all things" (13:1, 3) and who has "power to lay down his life and to take it up again" (10:17f.).

But, as we have said, it was not in the nature of John's mission to anticipate all this in a single "cryptic saying" but rather, at the first appearance of the coming one to Israel, to point out, in its fundamental significance, the reversal in the divine dispensation of salvation that the Lamb was to accomplish (cf. 1:17); and that not only for the worshipers in the ceremonial temple service at Jerusalem but for all those in the world who worship God in spirit and truth (cf. 4:21-24).

30 All this is true all the more because, as stated earlier, the pronouncement in vs. 29 does not function *structurally* as an isolated foreign element in this context but has the form of an emphatically positioned revelational utterance that will be elaborated and further explained in what now follows[37] and will be echoed in vs. 36. In fact, closer inspection shows that vs. 29 constitutes a new beginning of the witness of John to the one greater than he — a witness that began in general terms in vss. 26 and 27.

In vs. 30 John repeats in slightly different terms the statement of vs. 27, but this time in direct reference to Jesus as he comes walking toward John and as John proclaims him as the Lamb of God. For — as John now says emphatically — he had Jesus in mind when he spoke of him as the one who came after him but was before him ("This is he of whom I said . . .").[38] Of that superiority — already articulated in vs. 29 — he provides further evidence in vss. 31ff.

The opening words of vs. **31**: "I myself did not know him," repeated in vs. 33 and with the same emphasis as here,[39] are also to be understood here as a pointer to the provisionality and subordination of John's own role in the history of salvation. He did not belong to or enter into the company of Jesus' disciples, not even as Jesus' least important slave (vs. 27; cf. Mt. 11:11). Instead, he came as the one who had to prepare for Jesus' coming. Hence: "I myself did not know him; but for this I came baptizing with water: so that he might be revealed to Israel." Equally typical is the expression, used already in vs. 26

---

37. On this see at greater length de Goedt, "Schème de Révélation."

38. Apparently he is referring to the situation recounted in vs. 27 even though he uses different words there. But already in vs. 15 the Evangelist cites the pronouncement in vs. 30. We are repeatedly dealing here with pronouncements of John known from tradition, not with precise points in time. For the exegesis of vs. 30 see further the comments on vs. 15, though the pronouncement does not function here exactly as it does there. In the prologue the superiority of Jesus over John is specifically mentioned in connection with the glory of the Word that was with God. But in vs. 30 we are dealing especially with Jesus' superiority over John in a salvation-historical sense. In the divine order, in which both had a place and a role, the Baptist is not first even though as forerunner he was first on the scene; he was first who came after John but around whom everything revolved.

39. See the comments on vs. 26.

and repeated in vs. 33, "baptize with water." There, too, we see the inferiority and provisionality of John's mission. His mission and power did not extend beyond cleansing with water those who, in response to his call for repentance, came to be baptized. He could not remove the sin itself. Still, for this purpose he did come and was sent so that by his baptism with water he might reveal the coming one to Israel, that is, make that one known in his true significance. That baptism was intended to get Israel on the right track, where the people could look for and, as it were, go out to meet the coming one, the one who — perhaps against their expectations — had to do above all with their sin, both in judging it and redeeming them from it; and not only with their sin but also with the sin of the whole world. That is why John's call to penitence and to conversion preceded the coming of Jesus. And when John saw Jesus coming toward him to receive the testimony of the forerunner in the hearing of all the people, John's prophetic proclamation was therefore also completely determined by the sin of the world: "Behold, the Lamb of God who takes away the sin of the world." For as such Jesus had to be "revealed": as the one who would take away sins (cf. 1 Jn. 3:5).[40] Accordingly, it is of that revelation that John gives a further account in vss. 32 and 33.

Verse **32** introduces this with the appropriate forensic terminology: "And John *bore witness: 'I saw* [cf. 1:14] the Spirit descend as a dove from heaven, and it remained on him.' " This is of course a reflection of the event recounted in the Synoptic Gospels and assumed to be familiar to the readers: the descent of the Spirit onto Jesus, permanently equipping him for his divine mission. But the whole historic sequence remains unmentioned here. All that matters is the revelational event — that which legitimated John's ministry and on which his witness concerning Jesus was based — and the accompanying voice of God, which enabled John to understand the event's redemptive significance.

This voice from heaven is described in vs. **33**. Again John says, "I myself did not know him" (see the comments on vs. 31). Here everything is focused on the divine designation of Jesus as "the coming one," the one on whom John would see the Spirit descend, the one who "baptizes with the Holy Spirit." By this God himself identifies Jesus as not only the bearer but also the dispenser of the Spirit.

The clause used to describe this, "baptize with the Spirit," is of special importance for the understanding of this entire pericope. In the nature of the case it functions as the — now finally disclosed — complement of John's repeated baptizing with water. The baptism with the Spirit makes clear again,

---

40. In similar-sounding words and clearly reflecting the present context: "He appeared to take away sins," ἐφανερώθη ἵνα τὰς ἁμαρτίας ἄρῃ. See also de Goedt, "Schème de Révélation": "We believe in effect that the final clause ἵνα ἐφανερωθῇ τῷ Ἰσραήλ defines the goal attained by the oracular designation 'the Lamb.' "

and now in its full significance, the absolute superiority of the coming one over his forerunner: Whereas John baptized with water, the coming one baptizes with the Holy Spirit as the possessor and dispenser of the reality to which John with his water baptism only pointed. And because the baptism with the Spirit is the fulfillment of what John did with water, the redemptive significance of the Spirit is revealed above all in its cleansing, sin-removing power,[41] and thus the proclamation in vs. 29 is also rooted in the revelation that was granted to John.[42]

The two utterances in vss. 29 and 33 determine, in their interrelationship, the content of the Baptist's great initial witness to Jesus. The second does so in the language of John's own mandate (baptism), the first in the language — so much more characteristic of Israel's religion — of the sacrificial cult. John thus puts all the emphasis on the redemptive significance of the coming one, on his identity as "the Lamb of God" and his "baptizing with the Holy Spirit," when in vs. **34** he concludes his testimony with "I have seen and have testified that *this one* is the Son of God." This "seeing" and the witness based on it refer again to the revelation granted to John — specifically, one suspects, to the voice that sounded from heaven at the time of the revelation (cf. Mt. 3:17; Mk. 1:11; Lk. 3:21).

"This one" and "the Son of God" are codeterminative, and both have, in a sense, predicative significance: On the one hand, the title "Son of God" is strongly emphasized as the divine identification of Jesus as the Christ.[43] John's witness in

---

41. Elsewhere, too, the purifying power of the Spirit is described as the gift of the messianic age. See, e.g., Schnackenburg, *Comm.* I, p. 304; apart from the Old Testament prophets see also 1 QS 4:20f.: "God, by his truth, will cleanse all human works . . . to banish the whole spirit of perversity from each person's members and to purify that person of all wicked deeds by the Spirit of holiness."

42. Cf. here also de Goedt, "Schème de Révélation": "This revelation [of Jesus as the one who baptizes with the Spirit] constitutes the very origin of the oracle of manifestation ['"behold, the Lamb of God"]." See also du Plessis, "Zie het Lam Gods," pp. 128, 132.

43. In vs. 34 many prefer the reading ὁ ἐκλεκτὸς τοῦ θεοῦ, "the elect one of God," also understood in connection with the voice from heaven (cf. Schnackenburg, *Comm.* I, pp. 305f. and the literature cited there). Not so Bultmann, who does not understand the title "Son of God" in a specifically messianic sense but thinks that it is intended to "outdo" the messianic titles. In his view, the μαρτυρία of John, "even if it is addressed in the first place specifically to the Jews, is nevertheless directed beyond them to the whole world. For the whole world shares the expectation and knows of the glorification of sons of God" (*Comm.*, p. 93). But the reading "Son of God," if it is original, must be interpreted in connection with the voice from heaven reported by the Synoptics, i.e., in a messianic sense, as referring to the bringer of salvation designated by God and placed in his service (cf. Is. 42:1, which also mentions the Spirit of the Lord). This is the meaning it must have had in John's mouth as in that of Nathanael and Martha (1:49; 11:27). This is not to deny that in the Fourth Gospel this title obtains a deepened significance in connection with what is said about the incarnation of the Word (cf. 1:14, 18). But this does not mean that thereby every use of the title "Son of God" by the Baptist, Nathanael, and others is wrenched from its historical connections.

this regard forms part of the foundation of what the Evangelist seeks to accomplish with his entire Gospel (20:31). On the other hand, "this one" is also emphatically positioned; it refers to the one who baptizes with the Holy Spirit and thus takes away the sin of the world. This summarizing conclusion of John's witness refers, then, to both the person and the redemptive significance of the one whose forerunner he is. Accordingly, it is that specific meaning implied in "this one" that in vs. 36 forms the link between vss. 29-34 and the following pericope, which speaks of what happened "the next day" (vs. 35).

At the same time this casts light on the peculiar and significant structure evidenced in the witness of John, which is once more continued in vs. 36, specifically in the way this witness is distributed over three days (cf. vss. 29 and 35) so that the whole of it acquires a clear salvation-historical meaning. The conversation with the Jews is on the first day. On the third day John directs his disciples toward Jesus. So the middle day — with John face-to-face with Jesus as he walks toward him, without any input from others and at the apex of John's mission as it were — marks the division between the old and the new, between what is past and what is to come. What lies behind John and belongs to "yesterday" is the ministry in the temple with the "continual" daily offering of the lamb, a ministry performed by priests and Levites and limited to the sanctuary of Israel. What lies behind is also the law given through Moses, with its interpreters and scribes. What is to come on the new day is that which God, in his Son, now and once for all time, puts in place, and not only for Israel's sin but for the whole world's sin.

It is for that reason that on the third day the proclamation of the Lamb of God is repeated, now as the pivotal issue of the new dispensation being inaugurated here. At the same time the proclamation thus becomes the Baptist's last word, the utterance by which he also expressly directs his disciples away from himself and into the company of the coming one. His greatest day was, in a sense, his last. He brought salvation history to a boundary that he himself was not allowed to cross (cf. Mt. 11:11). All that was left for him to do was make room, to "decrease," to leave the scene (cf. 3:30). But for his disciples his last word on the third day is the first and foundational reference to the new era inaugurated *for them* and to their new worldwide horizon as the future agents of the ministry of reconciliation (2 Co. 5:18ff.).

1:35-51

Jesus' First Disciples: "Come and See"

The section that now follows forms the transition from the public ministry of John the Baptist to that of Jesus. It still belongs to the introduction of the actual gospel story insofar as it first, before proceeding to the account of Jesus' first public action (2:1ff.), tells the story of a number of encounters between Jesus and persons who were prepared to join him and who were later called his "disciples."

These stories have no parallels in the Synoptic Gospels. Scholars have compared them with the "call" stories in Mk. 1:16-20 and Mt. 9:9, and in part this comparison is valid (cf. 1:43). In any case, we learn here how the Gospel can later refer to Jesus' "disciples" (2:1ff.). It does not mean that the Evangelist was either ignorant or critical of the Synoptic "call" stories. He assumed, rather, that his readers were familiar with the main lines of the tradition according to which Jesus was accompanied by disciples from the beginning and that there were not five or six but twelve (6:67; 20:24), though this Gospel never lists their names or tells how most of them were called. Hence the encounters described here, by which Andrew, Peter, and Philip became disciples, are not to be viewed as "call" stories competing with Mk. 1:16ff.; 3:16 par., but rather as a report that the Fourth Evangelist edited for his own purpose and that goes back behind the "call" stories known from elsewhere.[44] Only once does this Gospel mention Jesus calling someone (Philip in vs. 43), and we do read of the first two disciples "following" Jesus (vs. 38). For the most part the initiative does not come from Jesus; it comes either from the (future) disciples themselves or from those who themselves have already found Jesus and are now bringing others to him — Andrew bringing his brother Simon Peter and Philip bringing (his friend?) Nathanael.[45]

All this can give us a measure of insight into the Evangelist's purpose in giving these stories. We have three main points here: First, we see more clearly here than anywhere else the connections among John the Baptist, his disciples, and Jesus. Jesus' first followers are disciples of John and they follow Jesus at John's instigation. Here lies the confirmation of the datum — fixed and fundamental elsewhere in the New Testament but finding its historical clarification only here — that the apostolic tradition concerning Jesus Christ begins with the public ministry and baptizing activity of John (cf. Ac. 1:21, 22; 10:37, 39; 13:24, 26).

Second, it is of paramount importance that the ones brought on the scene here act not only as models of the later church's faith[46] but also as witnesses of the revelation in Jesus Christ. They are those who are with Jesus "from the beginning" and as such are his witnesses (15:26); they represent the "we" of

---

44. See also Bultmann, *Comm.,* p. 100; Schnackenburg, *Comm.* I, pp. 306f.

45. See also the extensive form and tradition-critical examination of the text by F. Hahn in "Die Jüngerberufung Joh 1:35-51," in *Neues Testament und Kirche,* ed. J. Gnilka (Festschrift for R. Schnackenburg), 1974, pp. 172-90, esp. pp. 177ff.

46. So Hahn, "Jüngerberufung," p. 182. See also below.

1:14 not only as the first members of the church but also as its founders. As such they also constitute the salvation-historical transition from John as forerunner to Jesus as the coming one (see above). John placed them "on track": "Behold, the Lamb of God!" (vs. 36), but while he had to stay behind, they crossed the threshold of "the kingdom of heaven" (cf. Lk. 16:16); in Mt. 11:11ff. they no longer belong to the sowers but are among the reapers (cf. Jn. 4:37ff.).

But all this does not yet come explicitly into view here. What is of greatest importance here and what makes their witness fundamental for the whole coming church is expressed three times (twice in vs. 39, once in vs. 46) in the invitation "come and see," an invitation to see for themselves who Jesus is (cf. 1 Jn. 1:1ff.). They accept this invitation and immediately confess — in a variety of ways but unanimously nonetheless — Jesus as "the Anointed" (vs. 41), "him of whom Moses in the law and also the prophets wrote" (vs. 45), "the Son of God and the King of Israel" (vs. 49). It is this remarkable and in a sense overwhelming messianic confession of Jesus by his disciples that the Evangelist lays down as the foundation of his entire Gospel. He thus bases his work unambiguously on the foundation — common to the entire church — of the apostolic tradition, a reality that finds its confirmation no less explicitly in his definition of his Gospel's aim in words identical with those of the first witnesses: "that you may believe that Jesus is the Christ, the Son of God, and that thus believing you may have life in his name" (20:31).[47]

And third, some have been astonished that in the Fourth Gospel, in distinction from other accounts, the disciples already at their first encounter come to make such positive and unrestrained pronouncements about Jesus' messiahship. That in turn has been viewed as proof that from the beginning the Evangelist put his christology into the disciples' mouths without taking account of the historical situation. One can, indeed, point to proleptic features (cf. vs. 42), but in these encounters what comes no less to expression — and is a recurrent and dominant motif in the entire Gospel — is that the messianic fulfillment in Jesus exceeds in a number of ways the expectation present in Israel. However immediately focused on Jesus as the Messiah the disciples' initial faith was — and that in response to the witness of John the Baptist — it was gradually and increasingly faced with a revelation of glory for which the traditional hope of salvation had neither adequate categories nor sufficient space beyond what is merely human. This comes out specifically in the pronouncement made to Nathanael at the close of ch. 1 and later extended to all the disciples — "You will see greater things than these" — and in the immediately following announcement of what they would see (vss. 50f.). It is the prospect

---

47. See also W. C. van Unnik, "The Purpose of St. John's Gospel," in *The Gospels Reconsidered,* 1960, pp. 166-96, esp. pp. 174ff.

of this glory, which was already described in the prologue as "that of the Father's only begotten," that was held out to the first witnesses and that was bound to shape their faith in Jesus as the Messiah further (cf. 2:11).

In this manner the Evangelist certainly also reflects what the church, in its ongoing struggle in relation to Jesus' messiahship, needed and would always need: a faith in Jesus as the Christ, the Son of God, a faith for which the standards could not be derived from traditional opinions or from ever-changing assumptions but only from the witness of the revelation of his glory in the flesh.

The story itself can best be divided into two parts: 1:35-42 and 1:43-51. The first part tells of the encounter of the two disciples of John with Jesus (vs. 37), immediately followed by the "winning" of Peter by his brother Andrew, one of the two. The second tells of the calling of Philip and, in close association with it, the "winning" of Nathanael. The harmony of the construction also appears from the striking similarity in diction between vss. 40f. and vs. 45. What we have here, then, is two stories of two encounters each, with the second of each pair (Peter and Nathanael) as the consequence of the first (Andrew and Philip).

Verses **35-37** mention first two disciples of John who at his direction follow Jesus. Their action "the next day" (see the comments on vss. 27-29) is shaped by their position as the link between John the Baptist and Jesus' circle of disciples. They are among those who heard John's repeated testimony, "Behold, the Lamb of God!" (vs. 36), and they are therefore expressly mentioned again in vs. 40 as "the two who heard John and followed Jesus." The report of their passing from John to Jesus is very graphic. That "next day" John again saw Jesus walking, not this time toward him, but still apparently for some reason spending time near him. John, then looking at Jesus, repeated his testimony of the day before, but this time obviously for the special benefit of the two disciples who were "standing" with him. And the two "heard him say this" and understood that he was not just repeating what he said earlier but was addressing them personally. And they "followed" Jesus, a statement full of content but at this point meaning simply that at John's direction they followed Jesus' walking.

38, 39 What follows is even more graphic. The encounter is described as a tentative and mutual examination ending with Jesus' invitation to accompany him to where he was staying and with a precise time indication. An eyewitness report could not be clearer in its description of what happened.

No less remarkable is that the entire story, however vivid, seems to confine itself totally to the "exterior" of the encounter. With some justification it has been said that it contains "all, apparently, facts of no particular importance; and yet the essential meaning of the narrative is hidden behind these events."[48] To be sure, interpreters have with varying degrees of validity sought to give

48. Bultmann, *Comm.*, p. 100.

deeper, at least more "loaded," meanings to certain components of the story: first to the word "follow" in vs. 37 (see above) and then to Jesus' question, "What do you seek?"[49] and the disciples' counterquestion, "Rabbi, where are you staying,"[50] or more inclusively to the combination "follow . . . seek . . stay."[51] These are attempts to give more content to the supposed exemplary character of this first encounter. But the question is whether the Evangelist wants to be understood in that fashion.

The most characteristic feature of the general character of these encounters seems to lie rather in the answer that Jesus gives to the question of the disciples: "Rabbi,[52] where are you staying?" — namely: *"Come and see"* (vs. 39a), which is immediately echoed in their action (vs. 39b) and then repeated by Philip in vs. 46.[53] By itself this combination of imperatives is not unusual, but here it functions as an invitation extended by Jesus himself to the two disciples to come and ascertain with their own eyes what they want to know about him. But it is striking that this "come and see" should at this point relate only to Jesus' place of residence and that the result of the entire encounter should twice be described in terms of "staying": "They came and saw where he was *staying,*[54] and they *stayed* [that is, "dwelled"][55] with him that day." The narrative of this first encounter is concluded with the statement that it was "about the tenth hour." "All, apparently, facts of no particular importance," only the "exterior" of the events!

Only apparently, however. In connection with the repeated and therefore emphatic "come and see" this thrice-mentioned "staying," that is, "dwelling" (vs. 38, twice in vs. 39), does in fact acquire an importance that is strongly reminiscent of an essential element in the core pronouncement of the prologue in 1:14: "He dwelled among us." The unforgettable beginning for Jesus' first followers is precisely dated — down to the hour: Not only did they see *that* he lived among them and *where* he lived among them, but at his invitation they also stayed *with him* that day, and he spent time with them as a human among

---

49. Bultmann, *Comm.,* p. 100: These "first words that Jesus speaks in the Gospel" constitute "the first question which must be addressed to anyone who comes to Jesus, the first thing about which he must be clear." Somewhat differently Schlatter: "For fellowship with him there is no other condition than that they seek him and come to him" (*Comm.,* p. 53).

50. Schnackenburg, *Comm.* I, p. 308: "The request probably indicates a desire to hear Jesus expounding the Scriptures on the all-decisive question of the Messiah (cf. v. 45)."

51. M. É. Boismard, *Du Baptême à Cana,* 1956, p. 75: "the type and model of every call to become a disciple of Christ . . . ; *to follow and to seek,* that is what Christ requires . . . , *to find and to remain,* that is the reward. . . ."

52. For the translation see below in the comments on vs. 42.

53. Cf. Strack/Billerbeck II, p. 371: "This unusually frequent use serves to call the readers' attention in advance to something new, weighty, serious, recognized. . . ."

54. ποῦ μένει.

55. παρ' αὐτῷ ἔμειναν.

humans. So this encounter becomes the basis of all subsequent encounters in the sense that Jesus, though he was so much greater than John, nevertheless accepted them into the fellowship of his life and teaching.

And there is more to be said. However much this pericope is focused on "dwelling," it is striking that it *ends* there and that about that first encounter in Jesus' dwelling place not another word is said, neither of Jesus' self-revelation to them nor of their confession of him as the Christ. All this differs from what we learn of the subsequent encounters. That there was further discussion about who Jesus was is not only inherent in the situation itself but also evident from what Andrew said later: "We have found the Messiah!" (vs. 41). But this is merely an indirect statement about that first meeting and is intended as the introduction to and theme of what follows.

Furthermore, and no less striking, in this first report the identity of the two, though they are the first to follow Jesus, is kept hidden from the reader. The anonymity of one, Andrew, is lifted after the narrative as a way of introducing the second encounter (vs. 40). It is therefore all the more striking that the only person whose name remains unmentioned in all these encounters is that of Andrew's companion. The idea that the Evangelist did not know this person is unacceptable. Therefore, we can hardly avoid the conclusion that the anonymity is intentional. From ancient times it has been viewed as a clue that this unidentified first disciple was none other than the Evangelist himself, who for reasons of modesty wished to remain in the shadows. But most recent interpreters want nothing to do with such a close bond between Evangelist and eyewitness.[56] Nevertheless, many are convinced that the Evangelist maintained the anonymity for a reason; and it is natural then to think of the likewise anonymous disciple "whom Jesus loved," who plays an important role in the Gospel from ch. 13 on.[57] Whether this provides a clue to the authorship of the Fourth Gospel (cf. 21:24) is a question that cannot be resolved here but will have to be addressed later.

The idea that in the anonymous disciple of vss. 35ff. we are in fact dealing with the disciple whom Jesus loved is also interesting because it rests not just on the anonymity of both but also on the relationship of both to Peter. In Peter's first appearance in the Gospel he clearly comes second and has to learn the message of the Messiah from his brother Andrew and from Andrew's anonymous companion ("we," vs. 41). But Jesus immediately assigns to Peter the prominent place that he holds in the entire tradition. By comparison with him

56. Bultmann, e.g., speaks of this identification as "purely wishful thinking" (*Comm.,* p. 101, n. 3). But the assumption that the author of the Gospel could not be an eyewitness is also hard to accept in this context.

57. So, e.g., Hahn, "Jüngerberufung," p. 184; H. Thyen, "Entwicklungen der johanneischen Theologie," in *L'Évangile de Jean,* ed. M. de Jonge, 1977, pp. 259-99, esp. pp. 274ff. and the literature cited there (n. 41).

the anonymous disciple remains completely in the shadows, though it was he and Andrew who were the first to hear the "news" from John and to follow Jesus. Similarly, the disciple whom Jesus loved is in some respects repeatedly "ahead" of Peter (cf. 13:23; 20:4, 8; 21:7) but much less in the foreground than Peter.

If this resemblance is not accidental, then both the anonymity of Andrew's companion and the great sobriety with which — for all its vividness! — this first encounter is described come to stand in another light and in a wider context, and that all the more if one relates this account to 21:24. That this unnamed disciple was, along with Andrew, the first to follow Jesus could explain the special relationship between him and Jesus that gave him the name of "the disciple whom Jesus loved," though of course this point cannot be derived from what we have said with absolute certainty.

40 By way of introduction to the second encounter (see above) Andrew is named as one of the two who heard John speak and who followed Jesus. The description of Andrew as "Simon Peter's brother" (cf. also 6:8) assumes that the readers are more familiar with Peter than with Andrew. Some interpreters relate Andrew's prominence in the Fourth Gospel with a supposed tendency in Asia Minor to accord him (likewise Philip, mentioned in 6:5ff. and 12:22) a certain priority.[58] But it is questionable whether, if he was such a familiar figure to the readers of the Gospel, Andrew would be introduced, and this more than once, as Simon Peter's brother. A more natural explanation would seem to be that the Evangelist himself was especially familiar with Andrew (and with Philip).

41 It is then further said of Andrew — without any time indication in order not to lose the connection with the preceding scene[59] — that he "first" found his brother Simon and told him: "We have found the Messiah!" "First"[60] has to be taken with the entire sentence and means that Andrew, before doing anything else,[61] informed his brother Simon of what he and the

---

58. This is said to be evident from the Papias fragment in Eusebius, *Historia Ecclesiae* 3.39.4, which has Andrew first in a list of the disciples, followed by Peter and Philip; see also C. H. Dodd, *Historical Tradition in the Fourth Gospel*, 1965, pp. 303ff.

59. So Brown, *Comm.* I, p. 79.

60. The text is uncertain. Some important witnesses read πρῶτος instead of the widely (and correctly) accepted reading πρῶτον. In connection with πρῶτος it is sometimes suggested that Andrew was the first to find his brother and that the other disciple later found his own brother (James?). But this seems far-fetched. Other scholars think that Andrew is still the subject in vs. 43a. In that case πρῶτον would indicate that Peter was found first and Philip second. But this view of vs. 43a also runs into difficulties. See further below.

61. Cf. Hahn, "Jüngerberufung," p. 186. He, too, opts for πρῶτον as an indication of the close connection between vss. 35-39 and vss. 40-42: "It serves then not to open a longer series but to emphasize an immediate consequence. It is assumed here that, immediately after being with Jesus, hence still on the evening of the same day, Andrew persuaded his brother Simon to become a disciple."

other disciple had experienced. That he immediately sought out[62] his brother can be considered natural and apparently assumes that Simon was in the neighborhood. Against this background we can perhaps also understand Andrew's enthusiastic exclamation, "We have found the Messiah!": He is communicating not a sudden discovery but an encounter with and the identification of the one whom John had already announced as being present among them (vs. 26). Therefore Andrew might expect his brother to give immediate credence to the exclamation.

Finally, special attention is called for by the way in which the Evangelist has Andrew describe Jesus with the Semitic term Messiah, which he then translates into Greek for his readers: "which means 'anointed.'" We find similar translations also in vss. 38 and 42. These Semitic terms make apparent both the Palestinian-Jewish background of the Gospel and that the Evangelist is addressing those among his Greek readers for whom this background still meant something, namely Hellenistic Jewish Christians (and Jews in general). This is true particularly of "Messiah," which the Evangelist — the only author in the New Testament to do so — uses here and in 4:25. Use of the term enables him to make clear to Hellenistic Christians — for whom "Christ" functioned simply as a proper name for Jesus — that this name was the translation of the Jewish title Messiah ("anointed one"), which played such a large role in Jewish eschatology as the designation for the one "of whom Moses in the law and also the prophets wrote," as Philip puts it in vs. 45.

It is *the* anointed one of whom Andrew speaks to Peter and toward whom the Evangelist wants to direct the faith of his readers (cf. 20:31). This is also evident from the large place the messianic king occupies in this Gospel (vs. 49; 12:13; 18:36f.; 19:19ff.), partly to resist nationalistic and this-worldly messianic expectations present in Israel (cf. 6:15). Hence, on the basis of 1:41, it has been correctly emphasized that when the Evangelist states as the aim of his Gospel that his readers may "believe that Jesus is the Christ, the Son of God" (20:31), he is not making the title "Christ" subordinate to "Son of God" but rather wants it understood in its full significance as referring to "the anointed one."[63]

42 Of Peter's reaction to Andrew's announcement we hear only that he let himself be brought to Jesus by his brother. The whole encounter is focused on the way in which Jesus approaches Peter and speaks to him. The pronouncement is very similar to the report of the giving of the same name in Mt. 16:17f. ("you are," and Simon's father's name is mentioned in both). It is striking here that, as in vs. 41, the Aramaic form of the name, Cephas, is used, which

62. εὑρίσκει (vss. 41a, 42) has the connotation not of an accidental but of purposeful finding.

63. See esp. van Unnik, "Purpose," pp. 174f.

emphasizes all the more the meaning of the name Peter,[64] and that Simon's father is called John here, not Jona as in Matthew. All this suggests that the Fourth Evangelist was using a separate early tradition.

The giving of the name means in this context primarily that, in virtue of his special knowledge of people (cf. vss. 47f.; 2:15, etc.), Jesus knew, when he saw Simon coming to him, what their relationship would be. There is no evidence that Jesus already knew Andrew and Simon. Like Philip, the two brothers came from Bethsaida, a city in Galilee (vs. 44). But that need not mean that Jesus knew them from earlier contacts. The words "looking at him" and the subsequent giving of the name mean not that Jesus recognized Simon but that he "read" him, so to speak.

The giving of the name involves not just a characterization of Simon as Peter, that is, as a rock of a man, a trustworthy person,[65] but also his significance as a future disciple and apostle of Jesus, even though no further explication like that in Mt. 16:18 is given. For that reason it is proper to ask whether this first giving of the name is to be understood as a prediction.[66] However this may be, the main thing is that here, at the very beginning of the Gospel, Peter is immediately presented as the "rock-man." Thus the Evangelist unmistakably brings out for the church the reliability of the apostolic witness — a reliability attested by Jesus — the historic foundations of which are laid bare here.

In vss. **43-50** we have the second pair of closely related encounters with Jesus, first that with Philip, then through Philip's mediation the one with Nathanael. Again there is mention of "the next day," apparently the day after the day introduced in vs. 35. Accordingly, the things narrated in vss. 35-39 and in vss. 40-42 must all have occurred on one day (see also the comments on vs. 41).

Verse **43** brings with it a number of problems. Who is the subject of vs. 43a: still Andrew, or Jesus? But Jesus is not mentioned until vs. 43c. Other scholars think that the text as we have it is based on changes made by the Evangelist and that originally the subject was either Andrew, who after "first" (vs. 41) finding Simon Peter then finds Philip, or Andrew's anonymous companion, who, after Andrew "as the first," finds Simon, then himself finds Philip.[67] According to this view vs. 43b is not original. Others go still further,

64. Cf. also Hahn, "Jüngerberufung," p. 184, n. 52: "The use of the name Simon Peter in vs. 40 shows, to be sure, that awareness of the titular character of Κηφᾶς/Πέτρος was already diminishing and therefore had to be expressly called back to mind."

65. So Lindars, *Comm.,* 116; he believes that this refers only to "Jesus' estimate of Simon's character" and that no allusion is made to Peter's symbolic significance for the founding of the church (as in Matthew 16).

66. Bultmann therefore takes future tense κληθήσῃ as predictive. Brown, however, refers to texts like Gn. 17:5, 15; 32:28, in which a new name not only indicates a future role the person is to play in salvation history but also responds to the situation of the moment, even though the future tense is used: "from now on you will be . . ." (*Comm.* I, p. 80).

67. Cf. Bultmann's analysis, *Comm.,* p. 101, n. 3.

considering all of vs. 43 secondary and identifying Philip, who is not mentioned until vs. 44, as himself the unnamed companion of Andrew from vs. 35.[68] But this is all very hypothetical,[69] and although not everything is equally clear, we will have to go by the text as it has been transmitted. The best evidence argues for thinking immediately of Jesus in vs. 43a.

The call of Philip is briefly described. It takes place on the following day, on which Jesus plans to leave for Galilee, though it is not altogether clear when and where Jesus encounters Philip. In view of vs. 44, it seems likely that Philip, Andrew, and Peter, all of them from Bethsaida, form one group, have gone together to John, and have become his disciples. When Jesus decides to go to Galilee (with his new followers: cf. 2:11), he sees in that grouping a good reason for inviting Philip also to join and follow him. That may also explain the plural Philip uses in speaking to Nathanael (vs. 45).

Like Andrew, Philip repeatedly comes to the fore in the Fourth Gospel (cf. 6:7; 12:21ff.; 14:8f.). The Evangelist here clearly draws his material from his own source, which enables him to write about these two in all this detail. But he does not pause to enlarge on the calling of Philip. Just as Andrew is important especially as a link to Peter (vs. 40), so Philip is important as a link to Nathanael.[70] The story of this connection forms the conclusion and, in a sense, the climax of the whole pericope of vss. 35-51.

45 The parallel roles of Andrew and Philip are also reflected in the sentence construction of vss. 44 and 45, which conforms entirely to that of vss. 40 and 43. Here again "finding" means more than accidental encounter;[71] rather, it represents a purposeful act of looking for and going to a person. It assumes a relationship of familiarity or friendship between the two as well as the desire of Philip to make Nathanael a fellow participant in that which possessed him ("we have found!").

Nathanael's name occurs only once more in the New Testament, in 21:2, where we learn that he came from Cana. It is not certain that he was one of the Twelve. In the course of time he has been identified with more than one of the men named in the lists of the apostles. The hypothesis most deserving of attention identifies him with Bartholomew, whose name follows that of Philip in all the lists except in Ac. 1:13. That would correspond with the present story,

---

68. So Thyen, "Entwicklungen der johanneischen Theologie," p. 275.

69. Cf. the criticism of Hahn, "Jüngerberufung," p. 176: "The alleged tensions are not enough for us to assume a division into two levels."

70. Again in 12:21ff. Andrew and Philip work together to bring others to Jesus.

71. Bultmann calls εὑίσκει in vss. 41, 43, and 45 "unintentional finding," in distinction from εὑρήκαμεν in vss. 41 and 45 (*Comm.*, p. 101, n. 4; cf. also H. Preisker, *TDNT* II, pp. 769f.). But the idea that Andrew's "finding" of his brother and Philip's calling by Jesus were coincidental is hard to accept and is not therefore likely in the case of Philip's "finding" of Nathanael either.

but is of course no proof.[72] But the special place that Nathanael's encounter with Jesus and Jesus' subsequent utterance (vss. 50f.) occupy in the story leads one to suspect that from that moment on Nathanael followed Jesus along with the other four mentioned here and that he belonged to the circle of those always around Jesus from this point on.

It is not clear when and where Philip found Nathanael — already before the departure to Galilee or later in Galilee itself. Considering Nathanael's divergent, initially negative, attitude, one does not get the impression that he also belonged to the disciples of John. In any case, Philip did not find him in their company (vs. 48). For that reason it is very well possible that Philip found Nathanael in Cana, Nathanael's home and the place where Jesus was to perform his first great miracle.

Philip announces to Nathanael the great news similarly to the way in which Andrew announced it to Peter. The idea that the words "him of whom Moses in the law and also the prophets wrote" convey something more than the title "Messiah" and that they demonstrate a gradual deepening of insight on the part of the disciples[73] is not persuasive. After all, with the one word "Messiah," that is, "anointed," Andrew had in mind no one other than he who was expected by Israel on the basis of Old Testament prediction.[74] It is true that here the repeated "we have found" clearly has the added value of the "we" of the eyewitnesses on which the entire Gospel is based (1:14; 1 Jn. 1:1ff.).

46 As already mentioned, Philip's words encounter no little resistance in the mind of Nathanael, resistance evoked by the presentation of the announced bringer of salvation as "Jesus of Nazareth, the son of Joseph." This is the first time that Jesus is described as such. In the nature of the case, Jesus' identity and place of origin could not remain unknown, certainly not to people from Galilee. But whereas this information presented no problems to the disciples who were called first, no doubt in part because of the testimony they had heard concerning Jesus from John, Nathanael apparently had to go by Philip's words alone. His objection concerned Nazareth as Jesus' place of origin (he does not mention Jesus' father); in this connection this suggests not that the town had a bad reputation but that it was considered totally insignificant. In raising the issue, Nathanael formulated what for many Jews was to remain an offense and a hindrance to the acknowledgment of Jesus as the Messiah. They not only did not generally expect a Messiah to come from Galilee (cf. 7:41, 52), but certainly least of all from Nazareth, a town mentioned nowhere in the Old Testament or in literature of Nathanael's time. "Can anything good

---

72. See also Brown, *Comm.* I, p. 82, and the literature cited there.

73. So apparently ibid., pp. 77, 86.

74. "The law and the prophets," in both Jewish and Christian usage, refer to the entire Old Testament (cf. Lk. 16:16, 29; Ro. 3:21).

be expected to come from such a place?" is Nathanael's condescending reaction to Philip's enthusiastic message.

Philip, undaunted, only answers: "Come and see." He does not engage Nathanael in discussion. Meeting Jesus himself would have to convince his friend. The expression "come and see" is characteristic for the entire pericope in vss. 35-51 (see the comments on vss. 39 and 51). Though this "seeing" does not by itself yield proof of Jesus' true identity, it is nevertheless the undeniable and unique privilege of those who were with Jesus "from the beginning." Reflected, above all, in this "seeing" is the manner in which the revelation of God in Jesus Christ has entered history in the "flesh." The seeing is, as such, part of the foundation of the later church. In that sense one can say that the "come and see" of vs. 39a, repeated in vs. 46, is of decisive importance as a motif for the thrust of the whole pericope.[75]

47 When Nathanael follows his friend and lets himself be taken to Jesus, we witness again what we saw in Jesus' encounter with Peter: At first "sight" (cf. vs. 42) Jesus "sees through" the person with whom he is meeting (cf. 2:25; 4:18ff.). This supernatural "knowing," which brings Nathanael to the confession that Jesus is the Son of God and prompts the Samaritan woman to acknowledge Jesus as a prophet, also occurs from time to time among "men of God" in the Old Testament (cf. 1 Sa. 9:19ff.). In the case of Jesus, however, it comes to the fore in all sorts of ways (cf., e.g., 11:4, 11-14), including with regard to his own future (cf. 3:14; 6:64, 70; 13:1, etc.). It constitutes a part of his plenary authority and his preparation as the one sent by the Father (cf., e.g., 3:34f.). Here, as in 4:18ff., it functions as a means to lead people who are still in the dark about Jesus to the discovery that before they knew him they themselves were already known by him: Their own attitude and life history or life secret were an open book to him. It is that discovery that pulls each of them up short and breaks through the wall that had been separating them from Jesus.

Jesus' statement about Nathanael, uttered as he sees Nathanael coming toward him, is very positive — despite Nathanael's initial skepticism: "Behold, truly an Israelite in whom there is no guile!" The adverb "truly," "in truth," goes with the entire statement and must not be taken, as so many interpreters do, as an adjective with "Israelite" ("Behold, a true Israelite").[76] Nathanael is

---

75. So Hahn, "Jüngerberufung," pp. 182, 187.

76. So, e.g., Bultmann: "one who is worthy of the name of Israel" (*Comm.,* p. 104, n. 4; cf. also Barrett, *Comm.,* p. 184). Such adjectival use of an adverb is very unusual, and if all the emphasis were laid on Nathanael being a true Israelite, then everything would be said, so that the relative clause that follows would be useless. Furthermore, such pregnant use of "Israel(-ite)" occurs nowhere else in the Gospel (F. Büchsel, *TDNT* III, 386: "We do not detect in John any extension of the name to the new people of God. The true Israelite is the man who is bound to the Law, and therewith to God"). See also J. Painter, "Christ and the Church in John 1:45-51," in *L'Évangile de Jean,* p. 360.

being described — on account of his faith — as a typical representative of the true ("spiritual," cf. Ro. 2:28ff.; 9:6, etc.) Israel.[77] So the uniqueness of Nathanael is not that he is, in distinction from other Israelites, a true Israelite, but that he is "an Israelite in whom there is no guile." It is unlikely that "no guile" refers by anticipation to Nathanael's faith, of which he has given no evidence. Nor can it be an allusion to his reaction to Philip's message, which required no special honesty or sincerity. It is, therefore, a reflection of texts like Ps. 32:2 in which uprightness is closely bound up with a person's relationship to God (cf., e.g., Is. 50:9; 1 Pt. 2:22; Rv. 14:5). Thus the reference is not primarily to the true Israel but to the inner disposition associated with the knowledge of the true God as this is found in Israel. By thus welcoming Nathanael, Jesus ignores Nathanael's initial rejection of Philip's announcement and lays bare the pure disposition that nevertheless animates Nathanael.

48 Nathanael, feeling that Jesus "sees through" him and knows him, asks in perplexity how that can be. Jesus informs Nathanael further about this precognition: Before Philip called Nathanael, Jesus already saw him sitting under the fig tree. Did Nathanael's sitting under the fig tree occasion Jesus' favorable opinion of Nathanael? A long list of explanations have been advanced.[78] All of them either (1) assume some special event under the fig tree not mentioned here but known to Jesus and Nathanael, (2) attribute a certain symbolic meaning to sitting under a fig tree (cf. Mi. 4:4; Zc. 3:10; Ho. 9:10), or (3) think of the fig tree as a place where a rabbi might study and teach.[79] But all this is highly uncertain. The important thing is that by mentioning this concrete situation, one that Nathanael could verify, Jesus gave evidence of knowing Nathanael in advance. The phrase "before Philip called you"[80] may mean that Jesus did not receive his knowledge from Philip. It seems more likely, however, that Jesus wants to convey that the calling of Nathanael was not just an act of Philip but that Jesus understood himself to be involved in Philip going to Nathanael (cf. 2 Ch. 5:26), who was thus one whose heart was upright before God, one of the "true worshipers" known and sought by God (cf. 4:24; 6:37, 45; 10:14, 27b).

49 For Nathanael the discovery that he was thus known by Jesus was

---

77. On this see at length S. Pancaro, " 'People of God' in St. John's Gospel," *NTS* 16 (1970), pp. 123ff.; idem, "The Relationship of the Church to Israel in the Gospel of St. John," *NTS* 21 (1975), pp. 398ff.; idem, *The Law in the Fourth Gospel,* 1975, pp. 293ff., 513.

78. See the overview in Hahn, "Jüngerberufung," pp. 187ff.

79. Strack/Billerbeck II, p. 371, mention a talmudic passage in which the learned are described as "those who occupy themselves with the Torah under the olive tree, the vine, and the fig tree." But can merely sitting under a fig tree be considered proof of Nathanael's disposition? Sometimes scholars try to prove too much (cf. Bultmann, *Comm.,* p. 104, n. 6). Against this explanation, see at length also C.-H. Hunzinger, *TDNT* VII, p. 753.

80. Described by Betz, *TDNT* IX, p. 303, as "the mighty [*bevollmächtigt* = "authoritative"] summons into the place of salvation."

so overwhelming that he gave up all resistance and, in the strongest language at his disposal, confessed Jesus as the Messiah. In that moment he understood that Philip had spoken the truth about Jesus. But we cannot regard his confession, "Rabbi, you are the Son of God! You are the King of Israel!" as proof of deeper insight by comparison with what Andrew and Philip had already asserted. But it is true that under the enormous impact of Jesus' knowledge, Nathanael uttered his confession with the greatest possible emphasis and assurance ("You are . . . you are . . . !").

Both "Son of God," with which he acknowledges Jesus (whom he addresses as "Rabbi": cf. vs. 38), and "King of Israel" are intended — in line with Old Testament predictions and Jewish expectations — as messianic titles (cf. 2 Sa. 7:14; Ps. 2:7; Mt. 16:16; Ro. 1:4, etc.).[81] The notion that here and elsewhere (cf. 20:31) "Son of God" completely overshadows "King/Messiah," thus proving that in Johannine christology the typically Jewish categories are blurred, is in conflict with all that has preceded in vss. 35ff. (see the comments on vs. 41), which in fact depicts all these initial encounters in colors derived from Old Testament and Jewish future expectation.[82] However much the fulfillment in the coming of Christ surpasses that expectation (see also the comments on vss. 50, 51) and, specifically, pushes the Sonship of Christ back to "the Beginning," this does not mean that in the Fourth Gospel "Son of God" has acquired an exclusively ontological significance abstracted from its "official" messianic meaning. Accordingly, in this connection "Son of God" and "King of Israel" have the same meaning, and the movement from the first to the second is not anticlimactic.[83]

Conversely, it is no less incorrect, on the basis of this second title, "King," to ascribe to Nathanael a national-political view and with that to think that Jesus has called Nathanael, in a deprecatory sense, a real and unadulterated Jew ("a blunt and guileless Israelite," vs. 47) and is about to correct rather than accept Nathanael's confession (vss. 50f.).[84] It is true that vis-à-vis the crowd in 6:15 and before Pilate in 18:15f. Jesus will reject every worldly understanding of his kingship, but this does not mean that the messianic title "King of Israel" or "King of the Jews" has in the Fourth Gospel an exclusively negative sound (cf. 12:13; 19:19ff.). The witness to Jesus as the messianic king is part of the inalienable content of the Fourth Gospel, just as faith in Jesus as the Christ, the Son of God, understood in that same sense, belongs to the undeniable goal of the Fourth Gospel (20:31).[85] It is this very content and faith that the story of these first encounters intends to undergird with its witness.

---

81. See also Strack/Billerbeck I, pp. 17ff.
82. Cf. van Unnik, "Purpose"; Barrett, *Comm.,* pp. 185f.
83. So, correctly, Barrett, *Comm.,* in loc.
84. So Painter, "Christ and the Church," pp. 360f.
85. Cf. van Unnik, "Purpose," pp. 177ff.

50, 51   Still, all that has been said till now and has been "seen" by each of these disciples in their first encounters with Jesus is only a beginning of what is to come. However persuaded they are in those first encounters that Jesus is the Messiah, the content of that confession will prove to be much greater than they have been able to comprehend. That is the essence of Jesus' reaction to Nathanael's confession. Whether vs. 50 is a question or an observation is uncertain but of little consequence. The main thing is that Nathanael will not be able to stop at what has impressed him thus far, which is that Jesus knew and understood him before he knew Jesus. He is to see greater things.

The promise of that greater future is made to Nathanael ("and he said to him"), but it is immediately extended in a solemn manner to all: "Truly, truly I say to you. . . ." In the New Testament the double "amen!" occurs only in John, and there only in the mouth of Jesus. For many scholars this unique use of "amen" constitutes proof that words thus introduced belong to the most authentic tradition.[86] The word thus uttered with great solemnity constitutes the conclusion of what precedes as well as the emphatic announcement of what is about to be realized. Some interpreters believe, and here the second introduction at the beginning of vs. 51 is taken as evidence, that the pronouncement in vs. 51 comes from another context.[87] However this might be, it cannot be denied that in the present context, in what follows as well as what precedes, the pronouncement is very appropriate. After all the testimonies and confessions concerning Jesus' messiahship from others, Jesus for the first time speaks about himself.[88]

And here it becomes evident that the belief that Jesus is the Christ, the Son of God, will acquire a content that can no longer be expressed in the traditional messianic terms but far surpasses them. Jesus gives expression to this by speaking of himself in the third person, and hence entirely in keeping with his use of this title "Son of man" both in this Gospel and in the Synoptics. He uses the title, in accord with its origin in Dn. 7:13ff., of him who, clothed by God with heavenly glory, is to exercise God's rule on earth. The use of this title at the beginning of Jesus' self-revelation is of special importance for the understanding of the entire Gospel. Together with "Christ" and "Son of God"

---

86. See, e.g., Lindars, *Comm.*, p. 48, who cites J. Jeremias and E. Käsemann. Elsewhere, "amen" is usually an affirming response to something said by others (e.g., 2 Co. 1:20). It sometimes occurs as such in the double form, whether as confirmation of a curse (Nu. 5:22) or of praise (Ne. 8:6; Pss. 41:13; 72:19).

87. See the overview in F. J. Moloney, *The Johannine Son of Man*, 1978[2], p. 246. The transition from singular (vs. 50) to plural (vs. 51) is also seen, with no change in address, in 3:7: "Do not marvel [singular] that I said to you [singular], 'You [plural] must. . . .' "

88. One finds a similar pattern in Peter's confession, which is followed by Jesus' testimony concerning himself (Mk. 8:29, 31ff. par.); cf. also Mk. 14:61f.; Mt. 26:63f., where a pronouncement concerning the Son of man follows, introduced by ἀπ' ἄρτι ὄψεσθε. Scholars therefore (probably correctly) consider the reading ἀπ' ἄρτι in Jn. 1:51 to be secondary (derived from Mt. 26:64).

it forms the foundation of that revelation. This self-designation is an expression of the utterly transcendent character of Jesus' messiahship and functions thus as an alternative to "Son of God." The two titles are used together repeatedly with no clear distinction or transition (cf. 3:13-15 with 3:16 and 3:31ff.; 5:26, 27; 6:62; 12:23 with 12:28; 17:1ff.).

In the vision in Daniel 7 the appearance of the Son of man is depicted as a theophany: The Son of man is to "come on the clouds of heaven," words used elsewhere only of God. The phrase "one like a son of man" does not point to human origin but rather suggests a humanly recognizable form in the manifestation of divine glory (cf. Ezk. 1:26b, 28b). At the same time this Son of man is he to whom is given (by "the Ancient of Days") divine glory and unlimited kingship. In this respect Daniel 7 reminds one of the divine characteristics attributed elsewhere in the Old Testament to the messianic king as coregent and son of God (cf. Is. 9:1-6; 2 Sa. 7:14; Pss. 2:7ff.; 110). But the way in which Daniel 7 speaks of the Son of man far surpasses those features. To be sure, the Son of man is also distinguished from God ("The Ancient of Days"), but his appearance on the clouds and his divine "glory" and possession of unlimited power impart to his kingship an absolutely transcendent character.[89]

Although the use of the title Son of man in the Fourth Gospel needs to be examined on its own merits[90] and though it evidently made an enigmatic impression on those who heard Jesus use it,[91] in this first announcement of Jesus to Nathanael its general thrust already comes significantly to the fore. As in 3:14f., the pronouncement about the Son of man is linked with a high point in the history of salvation, namely, Jacob's vision at Bethel, where both the continuity and the unanticipated progress and fulfillment of God's saving work in history find expression.

The opening words, "You will see heaven opened," cannot, to be sure, be traced back to an equivalent statement in the story of Jacob (though there is mention there of "the gate of heaven"); rather, they belong to the apocalyptic language in which use of "Son of man" is often clothed (cf. Ac. 7:56; Mt. 26:64 par.; Jn. 6:62, etc.). This "seeing," however, is bound up with images from Jacob's dream. The story of Jacob's dream describes a ladder set on earth and with its top reaching to heaven. At the top of the ladder stands the Lord, who in the uncertain situation in which Jacob finds himself confirms — by this vision and by the oracle associated with it — the promise made to Abraham,

---

89. On this see also W. Bittner, " 'Gott-Menschensohn-Davidssohn.' Eine Untersuchung zur Traditionsgeschichte von Daniel 7, 13ff.," *Freiburger Zeitschrift für Philosophie und Theologie* 32 (1985), pp. 343-72, and the literature cited there.

90. For extensive literature and discussion thereof see, e.g., the summarizing work of Moloney, *Johannine Son of Man.*

91. See also the comments on 9:35f.

and then promises Jacob divine protection on the way he must go (cf. Ps. 91:11). The pronouncement in Jn. 1:51 does not mention the ladder. It is, rather, the Son of man himself who links heaven and earth, while the angels who ascend and descend on him (as on the ladder in Jacob's vision)[92] represent the heavenly powers at his disposal. But whereas elsewhere angels are attributes of the *heavenly* existence of the Son of man (cf. Mt. 13:41, 49; 24:30, 31; 25:31ff.), the special character of their action here is that they maintain the link with heaven for the Son of man on earth (cf. Mt. 26:53; Mk. 1:13; Lk. 22:43). The author specifically has in mind here — as is evident also from the "greater things" promised to Nathanael — the divine glory manifest in his descent as that of the incarnate Word (1:14; 2:11; 11:40; 17:14). From now on the disciples will be witnesses of that glory and will become conscious, as they join and follow him, of being under the "opened" heaven. Accordingly, the statement is not related, as some interpreters would have it,[93] to one specific event in the life of Jesus (e.g., the transfiguration) but much more to the continuing — and from now on intermittently visible — glory present in Jesus' self-revelation in words and works and in his constant communion with the Father (cf. 8:29; 12:28ff.).

Our text clearly alludes to Jacob's vision, but it contains no explicit reference to Jacob himself. Nor does Jacob fulfill in his story in Genesis 28 the role attributed here to the Son of man.[94] The angels did not ascend and descend on him. He was not the bearer of the heavenly power but, like the disciples here, the one whose eyes were opened to that power in the vision granted him. Still, we are certainly not dealing here, any more than in similar allusions (cf. 3:14f.), with imagery arbitrarily borrowed from the Old Testament. Jacob received this vision, as we learn from the divine oracle associated with it in Genesis 28, as the bearer of the promise to Abraham and thus as one of the great witnesses to the God of the Old Testament. Hence, as we noted earlier, we see in the Fourth Gospel both salvation-historical continuity and subordination of the sacred past to the coming of Jesus Christ, which transcends that entire past. What Jacob saw and heard as Israel's patriarch and as the bearer of the divine promise is what from now on the disciples will see and hear in full bloom as witnesses called by Jesus and founders of the coming church — in the glory of the Son of man. In that "seeing" they will therefore be those whom Jesus elsewhere calls "blessed" because they have seen and heard what many prophets and righteous people longed to see and hear but did not (Mt.

---

92. ἐπὶ τὸν υἱὸν τοῦ ἀνθρώπου corresponds to *bô*. Ἐπί + accusative here has the same meaning as ἐπί + genitive in Gn. 28:12 LXX (ἐπὶ αὐτῆς [= κλῖμαξ, "ladder"]): It says not where the angels are going but where they are, as often in New Testament Greek (cf. BDF §233.1).

93. For this see Moloney, *Johannine Son of Man*, p. 38.

94. As assumed by some scholars at least with regard to the descent of the angels onto him (see below).

13:17) — and that not only for the edification of their own faith but as persons involved together in the ("eschatological") time of salvation now dawning.

Other interpreters see something very different underlying "the ascent and descent of the angels of God" here, namely, the ascent to the Son of man and the descent onto[95] the Son of man — two figures that need to be distinguished. The first is the Son of man in his heavenly glory; the second his appearance in the flesh. What Jesus promises his disciples is said to exist in seeing the connection between the two in their interaction with him, a "seeing" that is also a participation on their part in the heavenly world as a spiritual (mystical?) vision.[96]

But this view has two fundamental flaws. In the first place, there is no basis in the Fourth Gospel whatever for the simultaneous existence of a heavenly Son of man and an earthly Son of man. On the contrary, the motif that governs the entire Johannine view of the Son of man is precisely that the heavenly Son of man descended from the place "where he was before" (cf. 6:62) and that only by way of that descent could he later ascend and impart life to humanity (see the comments on 3:13f.; 6:27, 53, etc.). Secondly, as is evident from the entire context of which vs. 51 is the conclusion and climax, "you will see heaven opened" refers not to personal experiences of the heavenly world in which the disciples are to take part "in the spirit," but to their witnessing the glory of the descended Son of man as the glory of God *in the flesh*. In this respect one can say that "you will see" constitutes the climax of the motif that governs the coming of the disciples to Jesus in this entire pericope: "come and see"; and thus that the last word of the introduction to the gospel story brings to expression, in one all-embracing salvation-historical pronouncement, the theme of the story that now follows.

---

95. In which case ἐπί indicates not "where" but "where to" (cf. n. 92 above).

96. Cf. H. Odeberg, *The Fourth Gospel Interpreted in Relation to Contemporaneous Religious Currents in Palestine and the Hellenistic-Oriental World,* 1929, pp. 33-42. He goes back to a speculative Jewish distinction between the heavenly image of the true Israel and the earthly reflection of that image, and he applies that distinction to Jacob, who in his sleep receives a heavenly vision. According to this view, then, the angels do not descend on the ladder but on Jacob. Odeberg believes that Jn 1:51 should be interpreted in accordance with this pattern: The angels ascend to the heavenly Son of man and descend down onto the earthly Son of man.

According to G. Quispel the angels ascend on the exalted Son of man into heaven, but in their descent come on Nathanael, "the Israelite in the true sense of the word, in whom, unlike Jacob of old, there is no guile. It happens in his experience of faith in the exalted Christ." Quispel develops this explanation on the basis of certain ideas and speculations of Jewish mysticism (Quispel, "Nathanael und der Menschensohn [Joh I 51]," *ZNW* 47 [1956], pp. 281-83).

2–4

From Cana to Cana:
The Revelation of Jesus' Glory

Although various divisions of the Fourth Gospel are possible and have been used in the commentaries,[1] it seems to me proper, after what may be considered the introduction (1:1-18) and the preparation (1:19-51), to regard ch. 2 as the beginning of the real story of Jesus' self-revelation as it is described in the Fourth Gospel. A clear indication that this is so occurs in 2:11, which describes the miracle at Cana as "the beginning of the signs" that Jesus did. The main division that begins with 2:1 continues to the end of ch. 4, where a new break becomes visible. Important indications of the correctness of this division are that chs. 5 and 6 form a new unity and that the conclusion of ch. 4 returns to Cana (cf. 4:54), thus concluding this first great cycle, which begins at Cana, proceeds via Capernaum to Jerusalem, and thence returns via Samaria to Cana.

We are dealing here not only with an initial geographic outline of Jesus' public ministry but also with an important initial characterization of that ministry: The beginning lies in the inconsequential region of Galilee, where the glory of the Son of man takes shape in the miracle of the abundance of wine (2:1-12). From there the line runs to Jerusalem, the center of Israel's national and religious life, which Jesus as it were seizes at the heart in the cleansing of the temple, in the claim he lays on it as the house of his Father — and all this at one of the great feasts (2:13ff.) — and in his first encounter with Nicodemus. Nicodemus appears here as a representative of the Jewish government and scribal learning. Jesus confronts him with the necessity — which applies to everyone — of "being born from above" (3:1ff.). With this there is the first

---

1. See, e.g., M. Rissi, "Der Aufbau des vierten Evangeliums," *NTS* 29 (1983), pp. 48ff. and the literature cited there.

great testimony concerning the "heavenly things," that is, the descent of the Son of man (3:11, 13ff., 31ff.). In ch. 4 follows the story of a very different but no less characteristic encounter,[2] namely that with the Samaritan woman (4:4ff.). Then there is the conversation between Jesus and his disciples about the harvest time that has begun (4:31ff.) and the arrival of the people of Samaria who confess him as "the Savior of the world." This first great orienting cycle is then concluded with Jesus' return to Cana in Galilee and the second miracle there (4:43ff.; cf. vs. 54). This second miracle, as we shall see, at the same time forms the link with the following section in chs. 5 and 6.

Various attempts have been made to characterize chs. 2–4 more specifically. In discussion of the prologue we have already noted the view[3] according to which 1:35–4:42 is the elaboration of vs. 3 of the prologue (Christ as re-creator), while in chs. 4:43 through ch. 6 and chs. 7–9, respectively, vs. 4 and vss. 4f. of the prologue are further explicated. But however much the prologue manifests itself again and again in these chapters (cf., e.g., 3:19) — as in the entire Gospel — nevertheless such a schematic elaboration of its content in the text of chs. 2–4 (and 5–9) cannot be demonstrated.

Others look for the main line of 2:1–4:54 in the different reactions to Jesus' conduct seen there.[4] Although these reactions do furnish an important

2. See also Bultmann, *Comm.*, p. 111:

ch. 3 (for which the introduction is provided by 2.23-25) *and chap. 4 should be taken together;* in each of the two chs. (and only there) the central feature is provided by Jesus' conversation with a single person, with the διδάσκαλος τοῦ Ἰσραήλ and with the γυνὴ Σαμαρεῖτις, with the man and the woman, with the official orthodoxy and with heresy.

3. That of J. A. T. Robinson.

4. See F. J. Moloney, "From Cana to Cana (John 2:1–4:54) and the Fourth Evangelist's Concept of Correct (and Incorrect) Faith," *Studia Biblica* 2 (1978), p. 200; see also Brown, *Comm.* I, p. cxl ("Part Two: From Cana to Cana — Various Responses to Jesus' Ministry in the Different Sections of Palestine [chs. II–IV]"). Moloney then makes the following further distinctions:

perfect faith, 2:1-11
no faith, 2:12-22
partial faith, 3:1-21
perfect faith, 3:22-36
no faith, 4:1-15
partial faith, 4:16-26
perfect faith, 4:27-30
perfect faith, 4:43-54.

The three instances of perfect faith are further distinguished as occurring in Jewish, Samaritan, and non-Jewish contexts (the last in 4:43-54). This last classification, in any case, is based on conjecture: In the text — in distinction from the story in Mt. 8:15ff. and Lk. 7:2ff. — the Jewish or Gentile identity of the royal official is left completely open. In vs. 48 he is considered from the perspective of Galileans in general. Brown, more restrained and less schematic than Moloney, repeatedly and rightly warns: "We must beware of being more ingenious than the evangelist himself" (p. cxliv).

perspective for the intent of the whole (see the comments below on 3:1ff.), they do not provide the key to the understanding of the overall thrust of chs. 2–4. The (over)schematization of these reactions in this understanding of their significance is too artificial and forced to be credible, and the revelation of Jesus' glory itself and not the reactions to it constitutes the all-controlling viewpoint from which these chapters are to be understood.

Here, in the first great cycle of the story, the contours of all the great themes that dominate this entire Gospel become visible — namely, the focus *on the person* of Jesus and the ("eschatological") *"hour"* of the *promised time of salvation.* That hour has begun and has become present in him; it consists in the *breaking* of the boundaries established till now *in the law of Moses,* and it is revealed in the *transcendent glory* of the Messiah of Israel as *the Son of man descended* from heaven and as *the Son of God sent* by the Father. It is on the basis of this absolute significance of Jesus as the Christ and the Son of God that the *critical* and *imperishable* importance of the salvation granted by him comes to the fore in the words concerning the *birth from above* without which no one can enter the kingdom of God and of *eternal life,* which already in the present is possessed by those who believe in the Son. In this context, then, the various reactions of those who hear Jesus have their significance, though only in tentative fashion, while the antithesis that marks the later dialogues with "the Jews" still has not yet fully surfaced.

One can thus say that in chs. 2–4 the foundations are laid and the contours emerge that, ever more explicitly and intensively, determine the construction of all that follows.

2:1-11

The Wedding in Cana

This story ties in chronologically and materially with the preceding story, specifically with 1:50. The events occur "on the third day" (2:1) after the events narrated in 1:43-51 and make a start with what, in 1:50f., Jesus had offered in prospect as "greater things." The role of Jesus' disciples as witnesses of his glory (1:14, 51) and thus as founders of the coming church (cf. 20:31) is here initially but emphatically confirmed (2:11).

From the beginning the story of the wedding at Cana, partly as a result of its dominant place in the Gospel, has enjoyed special attention and been interpreted in the most divergent ways, often symbolically, sometimes allegorically.[5]

---

5. Apart from the commentaries see the overview and bibliography in A. Smitmans, *Das Wunder von Kana. Die Auslegung von Joh. 2:1-11 bei den Vätern und heute,* 1966.

Others have gone further and completely abstracted the miracle recounted here — as well as those to come — from history and viewed it as a story told to give expression to certain notions of faith. Still others believe that the Evangelist drew his miracle stories from a specific miracle *(sēmeia)* source in which all the emphasis lay on the value of the miracles as evidence, though he himself is said to have assumed a much more ambivalent attitude to miracles, a fact that is supposed to be manifest in the way in which he has edited or supplemented the miracle stories. He is said to have regarded only, or at least primarily, the spiritual significance that he ascribed to the miracles as valid.[6]

Whatever we think about the factuality of the miracles and however we spiritualize their significance, it is certain that by denying their historical significance or casting a shadow on them we do not do justice to the Evangelist's intention. This is immediately evident from the conclusion of the first story, where the Evangelist himself describes the miracle as the "revelation" of Jesus' glory. He thus echoes 1:14, where he described the glory of the only-begotten Son as having become visible in its existence as *flesh,* as human. Any suggestion that in the Fourth Gospel one can separate "flesh" and "glory," history and revelation, violates the most specific aspect of that Gospel's character. Miracle is neither parabolic story nor symbolic action. This will become evident in all sorts of ways, for example, when Jesus speaks of his "signs"[7] as proof and witness that he has been sent by the Father (5:31, 36ff.) and, at the end of his dialogue with the Jews, precisely with a view to his miracles, he says "If I am not doing my Father's works, then do not believe me. But if I do them (as you cannot deny), even though you do not believe me, believe the works" (10: 37f.). Thus it is far from the truth to say that the miracles Jesus did do not play a decisive role in the christology of the Fourth Gospel.

But this does not mean that exegesis can end with mere acknowledgment of miracle as such, as supernatural event. This Gospel itself explicitly opposes that notion (cf. 2:23ff.; 4:48, etc.), and does so so emphatically that by comparison with passages like 10:37ff. some scholars think they must speak of a certain ambivalence toward miracle in the Fourth Gospel. Whatever we think of this last point,[8] a distinctive of the Fourth Gospel is its repeated linking of miracles with lengthy conversations focused on the *meaning* of the miracles in the framework of Jesus' self-revelation as the Christ, the Son of God (so chs. 5, 6, 9, and 11). If one fails to see that connection and hence also the deeper spiritual significance of the miracles, then one has not "seen" the signs (6:26),

---

6. For this entire complex of problems see esp. W. Nicol, *The Sēmeia in the Fourth Gospel,* 1972 (e.g., p. 123), who assumes the existence of a *sēmeia* source but takes a much more positive view of the significance that the Evangelist attached to miracles.

7. For the meaning of σημεῖον see the comments on 2:11.

8. See below on 4:47.

and faith that rests solely on miracle "as such" has fundamentally forfeited its claim to that name (cf., e.g., 2:23ff.; 3:2 with 3:11f.; 4:48).

All this, in keeping with the Evangelist's intention, confronts the interpreter with a double demand: on the one hand, to explain the miracle within a specific historical context, on the other to explain its intent within the framework of Jesus' entire self-revelation. Scholars have often fallen short of this hermeneutical goal in interpreting this passage — where there is no interpreting dialogue, unlike most other miracle stories, and the interpretation of the miracle is thus on its own, so to speak.

The symbolic interpretation of this miracle has taken possession in such a way that the historical context of the miracle is either completely ignored or totally abandoned — for example, when scholars seek to understand it merely as a text form in which faith in the resurrection of Jesus is symbolically expressed.[9] It has been easy to exchange the identification of the form for interpretation of the text. To the degree that the "theological" or "symbolic" interpretation asserts itself, to that degree the form of the text (which presents itself as historical) must surrender more of its rights and must be interpreted ultimately as a distinct literary genre.

But the cure for this disease cannot consist in the total elimination of every kind of symbolic interpretation of Jn. 2:1-11 and in saying, for instance, that one must be satisfied with what is "natural" and seek the meaning of the miracle solely in Jesus' beneficent significance for daily life and in his power to bring about change in every situation of life.[10] By doing so one too radically isolates the miracle at Cana and runs the danger of succumbing to the error of those who became fixated on the bread in ch. 6 and were told by Jesus that they "had not seen the signs" and should not work for the food that perishes but for the food that endures to enternal life (6:26f.).

Undoubtedly it is not always easy to mark the boundaries here.[11] Exegesis will always have to defend itself before the text and in light of the character of the Fourth Gospel. The secret of the text and its explanation, then, prove to lie, not in the skill with which the author supposedly conceals all sorts of deeper truths, but rather in how in this fundamentally sober narrative he highlights certain details of the historical situation above other details — no less interest-

---

9. Cf., e.g., J. Breuss, *Das Kana-Wunder. Hermeneutische und pastorale Überlegungen aufgrund einer phänomenologischen Analyse von Joh. 2:1-12,* 1976, pp. 69ff.

10. Cf., e.g., H. van der Loos, *The Miracles of Jesus* (*NovT* Supplements), 1965, pp. 615ff.

11. Cf. also Nicol, *Sēmeia,* p. 107:

> It is not accidental that we doubt again and again. The interpretation is not given separately from the story so that we can be certain, but it is hinted at in the narrative. Literal meaning and deeper meaning cannot be clearly distinguished; the deed of Jesus and its meaning are not separated. . . . History and divine meaning are not on different levels.

ing to us — that remain in the shadows or are left unmentioned as apparently irrelevant to the thrust of the narrative.

1, 2 The dating, "and on the third day," with which the story begins, is a test case for all that we have said about the story so far. Some scholars believe that it is rooted in the confession that "Jesus is the Christ" in that "the third day" alludes to the day of resurrection and marks "salvation from the predicament of death."[12] But in two respects this interpretation ignores what may be considered especially characteristic of the Fourth Gospel. First, it apparently understands the "glory" of Christ as referring from the beginning to Jesus' future exaltation, whereas in this Gospel we are above all dealing with the glory of the incarnate Word, that is, with the revelation of the glory (brought "down" from heaven, as it were) of the only begotten of the Father. And second, it wrenches the words "on the third day" out of the retrospective historical context in which the Evangelist obviously intends them to be understood.

There is, therefore, more plausibility in the attempt to link the "days" of ch. 1 (vss. 29, 35, 43) with the "day" of 2:1 to form a connected whole by adding them up. But this, too, poses large problems.

The outcome is a period of six days in 1:29-42 (or seven if we assume an additional day distinct from that of vs. 35 in vss. 40-42[13]). Thus one comes in 2:1 to the seventh day and can thus speak of "the Johannine week of introduction."[14] And one can, of course, link this with a symbolic interpretation — according to some a parallel to the week of creation (cf. 1:1),[15] according to others a designation of the day in 2:1 as "the day of the Lord, the day of the Epiphany."[16]

Others, however, advance numerous objections to this notion of a creation week: "The sixth day, the high point of the days of creation in Genesis 1, is conspicuous by its absence. The seventh day . . . the day on which God 'rested,' now becomes a wedding day on which Jesus gives orders to fill six jars with five to seven hundred liters of water. . . ."[17] Furthermore, in 2:1 a new beginning is made, which can hardly be intended as the last day of the first week. And John 1 itself already embraces seven days, 1:1-18 being the first day, "the day on which light shone in the darkness." 2:1

---

12. Breuss, *Kana-Wunder,* p. 55; cf. also pp. 40ff. See also K. Hanhart, "The Structure of John I 35–IV 54," in *Studies on John* (Festschrift for J. N. Sevenster), 1970, pp. 38ff., who also regards "the third day" as an allusion to Jesus' resurrection and who, on the basis of the connection between Jn. 2:10 and Ac. 2:13 (translated as "they are full of new wine"), understands the whole story as an allegorical description of Pentecost.

13. With an appeal to a textual variant in vs. 41 where there is express mention of πρωΐ ("early in the morning").

14. Cf. B. Olsson, *Structure and Meaning in the Fourth Gospel,* 1974, pp. 103f.

15. So, e.g., M. É. Boismard, *Du Baptême à Cana,* 1956, pp. 75f.: "The second creation, that of grace, corresponds to that of nature in order to demonstrate that it is truly a creation."

16. Cf. Bultmann, *Comm.,* p. 114, n. 3.

17. So J. Willemse, *Het vierde evangelis. Een onderzoek naar zijn structuur,* 1965, p. 153.

thus speaks of the eighth day, the first day of a new week, the day of "the first of the signs." Thus one comes to a distinction between "the two first Sundays" in 1:1-18 and 2:1-11.[18]

But the artificiality of all this is obvious: 1:1-18 is clearly not a first week; it is the prologue that precedes the story, that is, the days. And we can hardly interpret as the first day of the new week what 2:1 calls "the third day." If on top of all this we also have to factor in the prescriptions of the Talmud according to which wedding days were restricted to certain days,[19] then the whole picture becomes even more complicated.

In view of these rather dubious constructions one has to face the question whether the Evangelist, if he in fact wanted us to engage in all this "counting," could not have furnished us with less ambiguity.[20] We therefore take the position that there is not sufficient ground to ascribe to "the third day" any other meaning than that it serves to establish a direct historical and material connection between the story that follows and what has taken place two days earlier between Jesus and Nathanael.

The same sort of questions arise in connection with the place indication, "Cana in Galilee." The name Cana has from ancient times been translated as "ownership, possession," and scholars have linked with this the idea that in the Fourth Gospel Jesus' disciples are called "his own" (cf. 1:10ff.; 4:44; 10:1ff.; 13:1ff.). In Cana, Jesus' possession, the true people of God, becomes manifest (cf. vs. 11). The addition "in Galilee" is said to confirm this because in John Galilee is the birthplace of the new people of God. What we are said to have here is a transition, one that is also visible in wine made of water from Jewish water jars.[21]

The text itself, however, furnishes not a single point of contact for such an explanation of "Cana." The case is rather that here — as with the time

---

18. Ibid., pp. 154ff.

19. Cf. Strack/Billerbeck II, pp. 398ff.

20. Cf. also Brown, *Comm.* I, p. 106:

The application of the theory of *seven* days to John i 19–ii 11 is very attractive, but how can we possibly be sure that we are not reading into the Gospel something that was never even thought of by the evangelist or the redactor? . . . The Gospel itself counts Cana as occurring on the *third* day, and the day that covers i 40-42 is only obliquely indicated. That the reference to seven days fits well with clear parallels to Genesis in the Prologue . . . is true, but this does no more than at most to make the theory of seven days a *possible* interpretation.

21. See Olsson, *Structure and Meaning,* pp. 26ff., 109ff. Even farther down this road, to the point of the fantastic, goes Hanhart, "Structure of John I 35–IV 54," pp. 43ff. He deems it likely that no real city is intended and that the name must therefore have a symbolic meaning. "Perhaps Κανά is simply a combination of Καφαρναούμ and Ναζαρέτ," a combination for which Hanhart then seeks an explanation.

indication — it is the narrative in 1:46-51 that gives to the place indication more than merely geographic significance. Like Nazareth, Cana is an insignificant place in Galilee, one from which, in Nathanael's opinion, nothing good can be expected. Still it is precisely this "Cana in Galilee" (which it is called again in vs. 11) — the place, moreover, where Nathanael himself came from! (21:2) — where the revelation of Jesus' glory begins. Undoubtedly this place indication bore considerable meaning for the Evangelist: the first main division of the gospel story begins and ends in Cana, and the end explicitly recalls the beginning and emphasizes Cana's location in Galilee (4:43ff., 54). This is clearly done not with any idea that in Cana Jesus' "possession," the true people of God, becomes visible (cf. 4:44) but rather that, against all expectation (cf. 7:52), the starting point of Jesus' public activity lay in the despised region of Galilee (see the comments below on 4:54).

As to the wedding that took place on the third day at Cana, at this point we learn only that the mother of Jesus was there and that Jesus and his disciples had also been invited. The extreme sobriety with which the situation is thus depicted at once discourages as irrelevant any attempt — no less frequently made for all that — to give it somewhat more historical, biographical, or psychological color. Nathanael came from Cana (cf. 21:2), and we may conjecture that that was the reason Jesus and his disciples came to the wedding.[22] The words "his disciples" obviously refer to the persons mentioned in ch. 1; here already we have the general expression that elsewhere in the Gospel refers to the twelve known from tradition (cf. 6:67; 20:19, 24). They play no role in the story, however important their presence as witnesses was both for themselves and for the later church (cf. vs. 11).

3   As a result of this lack of detail, the presence of Jesus' mother and the conversation she conducts with Jesus has received all the more attention. Her name is not mentioned; only her relationship to Jesus is important. What she says to Jesus, "they have no wine," is the first thing the Evangelist says about the wedding feast. It is evident from Jesus' negative response that Mary thus appeals to him for help. Her directions to the servants in vs. 5 shows that she has unlimited confidence in his capacity to provide that help. How she could entertain such confidence in her son's abilities is not explained. The Evangelist evidently assumes that his readers knew enough of Mary and her unique involvement in Jesus' person and work to be able to understand such an initiative on her part. In any case, it is that special relationship and that

---

22. According to a third-century Latin preface to the Gospel, the bridegroom was John the son of Zebedee. According to another tradition, John's mother was a sister of Jesus' mother, making John and Jesus cousins, which would explain why both Mary and Jesus were present at the wedding. But there is no trace of any of this in the text.

knowledge of Jesus' "secret" that enables Mary to fulfill a role in the story that emphasizes the nature of Jesus' action and self-revelation.[23]

4 But it does so negatively because Jesus — not without some sharpness — rejects her (indirect) appeal to him as invasive of his responsibility and hence as not pertinent: "Woman, what have I to do with you? My hour has not yet come." In the social context of the time the address "woman" was in itself certainly not hard or impolite (cf. Mt. 15:28; Lk. 13:12; Jn. 4:21; so also in other Greek writings). But as the address of a son to his mother it is not common and may seem distant and impersonal. It is true that on another occasion, when there could be no question of such distance, Jesus again addressed his mother as "woman" (19:26).

But here this form of address is accompanied by rejection: "What have I to do with you?" The expression is Semitic and occurs often in situations in which failing to mind one's own business, so to speak, is considered objectionable.[24] Although in itself it need not contain anything offensive, materially it has the intent of a sharp reprimand. The fact that Jesus addresses it to his mother serves to show therefore how much is at stake for him here. And it is precisely in regard to her that he had to observe sharply the boundaries of his authority (cf. Lk. 2:49f.).

In that connection "my hour has not yet come" is of special importance. The saying occurs over and over in John (cf. 7:30; 8:20; 12:23; 13:1; cf. 16:21; 17:1; cf. also 7:6, 8). As a rule the coming of this "hour" refers to the beginning of Jesus' suffering, his going to the Father, his glorification, and many interpreters understand it thus here. Some think particularly of the hour of Jesus' death and regard the subsequent miracle as a sign of the forgiveness of sin through Jesus' blood.[25] But Jesus' "hour," as a reference to the end of his earthly career, embraces the fullness of his glory, of which his death is only a part. Others, therefore, think that "the hour" in 2:4 refers to all this future glory.

23. Here, too, all kinds of historicizing suggestions have been made, though they divert attention from the matter itself. For example, the supply of wine was inadequate because so many new guests arrived suddenly, and that was the situation that Mary wanted to make Jesus aware of. On the other hand, in the story of Mary's attempt to "mediate," scholars have seen signs of an emerging mariology and have sought to relate Jesus' address "woman" to the woman in Revelation 12. Others have seen anti-mariological tendencies in the answer attributed to Jesus. See, e.g., Brown's criticism of all sorts of fanciful views and his attempt to arrive at a more responsible mariological interpretation (*Comm* I, in loc.): "Mary is the New Eve, the symbol of the Church; the Church has no role during the ministry of Jesus but only after the hour of his resurrection and ascension." On the meaning of "the hour" see below under vs. 4.

24. Here, too, from a mariological viewpoint interpreters have arrived at a number of explanations and refinements; see Brown, *Comm.* I, pp. 99, 102, who himself sees a connection between "woman" and Gn. 3:15 and Revelation 12 (pp. 108ff.). Others have inferred from the sharpness of Jesus' reply that Mary is a symbol here of a Judaism that is keen on miracles and signs. Both are fantastic in my opinion.

25. So, e.g., Strathmann, *Comm.,* pp. 58ff.

This hour never came during the life of Jesus, and in vs. 11b there is said to be only prophetic mention of Jesus' glory. In this way the Evangelist is said to have warned his readers that the full significance of Jesus' glory must be sought not in his miracles but in his subsequent glorification by the Father.[26]

But all this pays too little attention to the setting of the saying here. It is hard to see what a reference to the hour of Jesus' departure could mean as a reply to Mary's appeal for help. After all, she did not in fact have to wait that long before Jesus acted. The reference here is not to the hour of Jesus' departure but to the hour of the beginning, of the breakthrough of the revelation of his glory on earth and in the flesh, and it is therefore arbitrary, in my opinion, to speak of vs. 11 as an anticipation of Jesus' future exaltation. All that is at issue here is that Jesus cannot seize this hour, that is, this beginning, beforehand — even if his own mother urges him to do so.

This is not to say that for every deed Jesus had to wait, as it were, for a certain cue from God; rather, that he was conscious that the great moment at which the Father called him to this revelation of glory had not yet come. Hence what comes sharply to the fore here, precisely at the beginning of Jesus' ministry, is his awareness that his life was subject to a certain calling that he had to fulfill at God's direction (cf. 4:35), an awareness that one can describe in the entire framework of this Gospel both as Jesus' messianic self-consciousness and his consciousness of his divine sonship.[27] Meanwhile the "not yet" also implies that what Mary asked of him was not something that in itself lay outside that order[28] but was something for which she had to await the time.

5 Mary conducts herself in accordance with both realities. She understands that she must await his time, but also hears a promise in his negative answer. And in her own way she prepares the way for fulfillment of that promise by telling the servants: "Do whatever he tells you" (as Pharaoh told the Egyptians in relation to Joseph when the famine came in the land, Gn. 41:55).

By saying this Mary plays her exemplary role in the story. When it comes to the hour of the fulfillment everyone must stand back. No human being, not even Mary, enters into that hour. But that does not condemn faith to inactivity. When, sometime soon, the hour of fulfillment arrives, then everything will have to be at Jesus' disposal. Without the faith represented by Mary, Jesus "cannot" do any miracles (cf. 2 Kg. 4:3ff.).

---

26. So Nicol, *Sēmeia*, p. 129. He regards it as "nearly certain" that the hour in 2:4 is the hour of Jesus' departure, and he believes that 2:4 thus "implies an admittance of John that he has reinterpreted the miracles." See also Nicol, pp. 30, 110.

27. This is totally misjudged by Bultmann, who thinks here of the miracle worker of antiquity, the θεῖος ἀνήρ, who also had to wait for his hour and for the voice that called (*Comm.*, p. 117, n. 1).

28. And therefore not like the temptation to make arbitrary use of that miraculous power (cf. Mt. 4:7), as some interpreters believe.

6 This is evident from what now, suddenly, dominates the scene, the now-mentioned six stone water jars.[29] Stone jars were used especially for ritual purposes.[30] The capacity of these jars was very considerable: a *metrētēs* is almost 40 liters, so the six jars altogether would hold 480 to 720 liters. These jars had been placed there in accordance with the Jewish rules of purification, for example, for rinsing the hands before and after every meal. Others think here of the prescribed purification bath before conjugal intercourse. Whichever is correct, in the context of this miracle story only the general function of the jars and their enormous capacity are significant. What was lacking at the wedding was wine, not water, the water of the law. The jars needed at the wedding to meet the requirements of the law were requisitioned to remedy what threatened to turn the wedding feast into a big disappointment — the lack of wine. If there is a clear hint anywhere for the understanding of the meaning of a miracle, then surely it is here, in the manner in which the Evangelist quantifies the capacity of the "vessels of the law" in order to enable the reader to measure by that standard the abundance of what Jesus Christ provided.

7, 8 Meanwhile, the idea that it was the sight of these enormous water jars that suddenly prompted Jesus to think that "his hour had come" and drove him to his initiative is not expressed in so many words here. We are denied any psychological insight into Jesus' messianic consciousness. The Evangelist immediately brings us face-to-face with the miracle itself, which manifests itself first in the authority with which Jesus tells the servants to fill the jars. And only when that instruction has been strictly ("to the brim") complied with does his command ("now draw some out") become the announcement of the "hour" of the fulfillment, in which people can draw from the abundance as much as they want (cf. Is. 12:3). For *now* there is wine as plentiful as water, indeed as plentiful as all the water of purification, which has flowed continually but cannot take away the sin of the world (cf. 1:26f.).

From that point on the emphasis lies not so much on the quantity but on the special quality of the wine provided by Jesus. He has it confirmed by the steward of the feast, who is the most qualified person present. But because the steward does not know what has happened, he is also unsuspecting and hence the most objective judge and witness.

The parenthesis in vs. **9**, "he did not know where it came from, though the servants who had drawn the water knew," is not intended, as some interpreters suggest,[31] to pose a "spiritual" contrast between the steward, who does not know the secret and thus becomes a type of so many unbelieving

---

29. Wherever John uses periphrastic verbs, "ἦν exhibits a certain independence" (BDF §353.1): The jars were not (always) there but had been "put" there for the occasion.

30. Because it was believed that stone does not attract impurity. Cf. Strack/Billerbeck II, p. 406.

31. See at length Olsson, *Structure and Meaning,* p. 59.

Jews (cf. 1:48; 3:8; 4:11, etc.), and the servants, who supposedly have understood it. It is intended rather — as the context indicates — to highlight the
objectivity of his judgment of the wine. The statement that the servants who
had drawn the water did know the origin of the wine is intended only to
remove all misunderstanding or doubt about what they offered their "chief"
for his evaluation. The entire description is intended to render unquestionable
the genuineness of the miracle. It is on account of his unbiased ignorance that
the steward of the feast addresses not Jesus but the bridegroom as the person
solely responsible for the wine supply and makes known his astonishment at
the course of action that has been followed. He does this as one who knows
the customs followed at weddings, that the best wine is normally served first
and later, when the guests have had a few drinks and are in a good mood, the
lesser wine.

10 The steward's comment to the bridegroom is certainly not intended
as a reprimand. It is rather a compliment on the quality of the wine now being
served. The steward undoubtedly speaks out of ignorance, since he does not
know where the wine has come from. But in spite of himself, on the basis of
what he does know, he describes precisely what has happened. With this
statement — "You have kept the good wine until now" — the Evangelist ends
the story as a perfect characterization of the situation that has come into being
with Jesus' coming and work.

On the basis of the undeniable depth of this concluding statement, it does
not seem difficult to sketch, in its general significance, the place and intent of
the narrative as the opening story of the revelation of Jesus' glory — and to
distinguish it from all kinds of historicizing and psychologizing additions on
the one hand and allegorizing interpretations on the other. What seems dominant
is the salvation-historical perspective, the perspective of the divinely apppointed
"hour" of the revelation of Jesus' glory. All the emphasis comes to lie on that
divinely appointed time as a result of Mary's premature pressure. In this way
Mary herself represents the role of believing Israel, which impatiently awaits
the breakthrough of the promised salvation but must await the moment when
"the time is fulfilled," when the "fullness of time" has come (cf. Mk. 1:15;
Gl. 4:4). Corresponding with this is the pronouncement of the steward to the
bridegroom: "You have kept the good wine *until now*." The "now" is the
breakthrough initiated by Jesus, just as he himself, having first said "not yet"
to Mary, at the decisive moment says to the servants, "*Now* draw some out."
For at that moment the water has become wine and the hour has come (cf. 4:23;
5:25).

This transformation of water into wine also determines the *nature* of this
breakthrough in time. The motif of *abundance of wine* often occurs in prophecy
as characteristic for the glory of the coming kingdom of God (cf. Is. 25:6; Am.
9:13, 14; Jr. 31:12ff.; cf. also Gn. 49:11), as it does also in Jewish visions of

the future.[32] But also in Jesus' own preaching "new wine" is the symbol of the time of salvation that has come and is still to come (cf. Mk. 2:22 par.; Lk. 22:18, 30). Joy and a festive meal, specifically a wedding meal, are naturally associated with this motif of wine (cf. Mk. 2:19; Mt. 22:2).[33]

But we need to bear in mind the uniqueness of the salvation-historical (or "eschatological") character of the present narrative. This applies, notably, to the so-called messianic wedding motif, which is made central by some interpreters.[34] Although in John, too, Jesus is once depicted as a bridegroom (3:19), there is not a single hint in *this* wedding story that Jesus is acting as host or bridegroom (cf. Mk. 2:19; Rv. 19:7; 21:2, 9; Is. 62:4ff.). The events associated with the wedding remain completely in the background. Jesus is not the host here; he is the wine, more specifically the "good wine" reserved until now (vs. 10). In this regard there is here a striking resemblance with the multiplication of the loaves, surely also intended as an "eschatological" meal, where, according to the traditional story taken over by John, Jesus is the host (cf. 6:11), but where in the ensuing discussion with the Jews all the emphasis is shifted to Jesus as the bread, the true bread come down from heaven, as later he is the (divinely promised) "good Shepherd," "true vine," and "true light" (10:14; 15:1; 1:9; 8:12; see also 4:10ff.; 7:37ff.).[35]

All this serves the concentration on the person of Jesus as the Christ that is so characteristic for the Gospel of John. All that has been promised by God and held out in prospect in a profusion of images and concepts is fulfilled in Jesus,[36] it all lies enclosed in him, and it can therefore only be known in its realization and concretization from him — sometimes even in a totally unexpected way (cf., e.g., 6:51). Here, in the story of the first sign, which determines the shape of all that follows (see the comments on vs. 11) all the emphasis lies on the fact that in him is given the fullness of God's gifts in their joy-full, world-illuminating, and life-giving meaning, entirely in keeping with what was

32. See the passages cited in Strack/Billerbeck IV, pp. 951ff., specifically those relating to Gn. 49:11, with special attention to the wine (every grape will contain at least thirty jars of wine, etc.). *2 Baruch* 29:5 describes hyperbolically the abundance of wine and 29:8 the "supply of manna" that "will again come down from above."

33. Against this eschatological interpretation E. Linnemann, "Die Hochzeit zu Kana und Dionysos," *NTS* 20 (1974), p. 411, advances the objection that in Jewish eschatology the abundance of wine is never the result of a miracle done by the Messiah but is described as a marvelous "natural" growth. But this is based on an overly literal view of what the New Testament considers the fulfillment of prophecy and of Jewish future expectation. In the multiplication of the loaves in John 6 the participants also see evidence that Jesus is the prophet and the messianic king (6:14f.; cf. 7:31).

34. In the interpretation offered by Olsson, for example.

35. For the typically "Johannine" character of the miracle at Cana, see also Nicol, *Sēmeia*, p. 110.

36. For this point see also the predicative significance of "I" in the "I am" pronouncements, pp. 223-29.

said in the prologue of the glory of the light as a fullness of grace and truth from which the church may draw grace upon grace (1:14, 16). And all this is meant here, as a clear reflection of 1:17, as the new "good" and "true" that puts the old dispensation entirely in the shadow. In the place of the law given through Moses (the Jewish rites of purification) grace and truth in all their fullness have now come through Jesus Christ. In this light Mary's statement, "They have no wine," as a statement about the regime of the law, gains a still deeper meaning. At the same time, in this focus on the person of Jesus as "the good wine, kept until now" lies the criterion of what this fullness of joy and salvation holds and means for Israel and the entire world: the rejection of every manner of life and every kind of future expectation that does not have its all-sustaining foundation in his person and work (cf., e.g., 6:26f.).

With this exegesis we distance ourselves from other explanations that either (a) interpret the story of the miracle at Cana on the basis of a very different thought world, that of Hellenism, or (b) proceed from the assumption that the Old Testament background yields much more for the fundamental meaning of this miracle (as the opening story of the entire Gospel) than has been given above.

a) For the Hellenistic approach scholars refer to parallels in the Hellenistic religious world, whether more philosophical or more folkloristic. For instance, we are referred to Philo, who speaks of the Logos as "God's wine-pourer and feast-leader"[37] and says of Melchizedek, as the type of the Logos, that he gave to the souls "wine instead of water."[38] The more folkloristic "motif of the Dionysus legend" has been accorded more attention and support as the background and possible genesis of the miracle at Cana.[39] Thus, according to Bultmann, this miracle, which he calls "the miracle of the epiphany of God," is linked with the legend that on the day of the Dionysus feast, that is, January 5 and 6, the temple springs in Andros and Teos poured out wine instead of water, and empty jars set up elsewhere in the temple proved to be filled with wine the following morning. In the early church this link with the Syrian Dionysus cult can, according to Bultmann, still be seen in the dating of Jesus' baptism on January 6 and the reading of the pericope of the Cana miracle on the same day.

On religio-historical grounds alone serious objections have been advanced against this interpretation.[40] The reading of the story of the wedding at Cana on January 6 "cannot be documented before the second half of the fourth century."[41] The motif of *changing* of water into wine occurs nowhere in the Dionysus legend. Hence it is not

---

37. ὁ οἰνοχόος τοῦ θεοῦ καὶ συμποσίαρχος.

38. ἀντὶ ὕδατος οἶνον; see further Bauer, *Comm.*, p. 29; H. Seesemann, *TDNT* V, pp. 163f.

39. See, e.g., W. Bousset, *Kyrios Christos: A History of the Belief in Christ from the Beginnings of Christianity to Irenaeus*, 1970, pp. 102f.; Bultmann, *Comm.*, p. 119.

40. Esp. in H. Noetzel, *Christus und Dionesos*, 1960; see also Haenchen, *Comm.* I, p. 178.

41. Noetzel, *Christus und Dionesos*, pp. 33ff.

possible that the miracle of the Cana wedding was first ascribed to Dionysus and later attributed to Jesus, as Bultmann believes.

Some scholars have argued — not that the legend was transferred to Jesus, still less that Jesus was identified with Dionysus — but that the miracle story was an independent counterpart of the legend, born of dialogue between the Christian church and the Dionysus legend. "When the church presents Jesus, like Dionysus, as the wine-dispenser, it makes clear the claim that the fullness of life can only be found in the Crucified."[42]

But apart from the lack of any *historical* connection with a miracle performed by Jesus, the whole idea that the overture of the revelation of Jesus' glory in the Fourth Gospel is patterned on (the antithesis to) a pagan mystery story is irreconcilable with the entire construction and thrust of the Gospel itself. The story itself points in a totally different direction (see the exegesis above), and the thrust of what follows this opening story (the cleansing of the temple, the dialogue with Nicodemus, later the running confrontation with Judaism at the great feast in Jerusalem) is so clearly set against the background of the Jewish religion that the search for a starting point for all this in the adoption of or confrontation with purely pagan motifs seems a priori a method that cannot lead to the desired goal.

b) A totally opposite direction has been taken by those who have searched for the background of John 2 in the Old Testament, in, that is, the motif of the messianic wedding. The redaction of the story is said to show all sorts of striking points of resemblance with those of another opening story in the Israelite history of salvation, one in which the idea of the wedding is also said to be central, namely that of the establishment of the covenant on Mount Sinai as it is described in Exodus 19–24 and further explained in the Targum Pseudo-Jonathan. Following through on suggestions from A. M. Serra, B. Olsson, in a very extensive monograph on Jn. 2:1-11,[43] attempted to understand the entire story against what he calls the "Sinai Screen." He bases this link on various expressions and phrases in Jn 2:1-11 that occur more or less in the same form in Exodus:

Jn. 2:1: *on the third day*	Ex. 19:11, 16: *the third day*
Jn. 2:2: *Jesus was invited*	Ex. 19:20: *The LORD called Moses . . . and Moses went up*
Jn. 1:12: *Jesus went down to Capernaum*	Ex. 19:24f.: *Moses went down the mountain*
Jn. 2:5: *do whatever he tells you*	Ex. 19:8: *all that the LORD has spoken we will do* (cf. 24:3, 7)
Jn. 2:11: *he manifested his glory*	*These terms do not occur in the Masoretic Text or the Septuagint, but do in the Targum.*
Jn. 2:11: *his disciples believed in him*	Ex. 19:9: *so that the people may believe you forever*

---

42. So Linnemann, "Hochzeit," p. 411.
43. *Structure and Meaning,* pp. 18-114.

Olsson further refers to the purification motif, which plays an important role in the covenant establishment story (Ex. 19:14ff.) and is represented in Jn. 1:19ff. by the baptism of John, the revelation of Jesus as the Lamb of God, and the Jewish water jars.

The story of the wedding at Cana is to be understood, Olsson says, against this Sinaitic background. Jewish tradition often speaks of the Sinai tradition as the Lord's marriage to Israel. It would not be too "farfetched, from a Sinai perspective, to allow events at a village wedding to carry a message of something that, according to the narrator, replaces the old wedding at Sinai." On this basis Olsson believes he can uncover a number of hidden allusions in the story. For example, the wine does not function as an eschatological symbol but (in the light of the "Sinai Screen") stands for the law, which is now replaced by something new; the disciples are the people of the New Covenant, already manifest in the obedience of the servants; the miracle is therefore the fundamental "beginning" because the Son transforms the old into the new; and from this new perspective Mary's role can also be understood, etc. Olsson does not regard this as allegorical interpretation. What we have are "allusions" that reveal deeper backgrounds to the initiate. The story is "a symbolic narrative with many allusive elements."[44]

This lengthy citation of Olsson's views is motivated by the fact that in the more recent literature there is a clear tendency to find everywhere in the New Testament hidden allusions not only to the Old Testament but also to the Jewish Targums and the liturgical readings of the synagogue. Now there certainly is an important element of truth in this approach. In the Fourth Gospel we again and again encounter expressions that are clearly reminiscent of all kinds of Old Testament stories and statements, though they are not directly cited as such. Perhaps we may say that there is here a playing with the "sacred language" (in, e.g., vs. 5) to which the ears of the first readers were probably better attuned than those of today's church.

But it is something very different to find in these sometimes extremely vague allusions the real key to the understanding of the intent of the text. That 1:14-18 is shaped by the events on and around Sinai seems to me obvious (see my comments above). The reference to Moses and the giving of the law is explicit. But to say that the story of the Cana wedding can only be understood in light of a number of highly dubious allusions that one must discover by close comparison of the two texts would be to attribute to the Evangelist an artificial method of telling a story, a method that cannot be made plausible. Following B. Lindars one may ask:

> Is [the Evangelist's] intention lost if the supposed allusions to the Sinai narrative are missed? If they are essential, why has he not taken the trouble to make his point plain? . . . The text must be allowed to make its point for what it is in itself. In fact this kind of interpretation is far more likely to distort the author's meaning than to elucidate it. There is simply no firm evidence that the New Testament writers were accustomed to work in this way.[45]

---

44. Ibid., pp. 107ff., 114.
45. "The Place of the Old Testament in the Formation of New Testament Theology," *NTS* 23 (1976), pp. 59-66, here p. 65.

In a few general terms vs. **11** describes the meaning of the preceding narrative. By speaking of the "beginning" of the signs the author tells his readers not only that the miracle at Cana was the first in a series, but also that it was the opening act of a much larger work, the foundation and pattern for everything that follows.[46]

The word "sign"[47] which is characteristic for John (just once, in 4:48, linked with "wonders"[48]) has the meaning "miraculous act," in keeping with the use of the word in the Septuagint (especially in the combination "signs and wonders"), usually as a reference to the miracles and mighty deeds by which Israel was led out of Egypt and by which Moses was legitimized as one sent by God (e.g., Ex. 8:4ff.). Therefore, in distinction from both general use of the Greek word and our word "sign," use of this word in John does not refer primarily to a deeper or symbolic dimension of meaning but to miracle as a sign of authentication or legitimation. This is not to deny that the miracles that Jesus performed were also manifestations of his glory and that they materially disclosed the character of his coming and work (as was pointed out in the story) and sometimes served as symbols thereof. But even where that is the case, the sign is a miraculous event and not a parabolic story or a symbolic action in which the reference is *only* to a deeper or higher reality.[49]

Here the significance of the miraculous sign is that it is "the manifestation of his glory" (cf. 1:14), which had earlier been proclaimed to the disciples as "greater things" (1:50f.). Of that glory they now witnessed the first realization. Only the disciples are mentioned here even though Jesus' self-manifestation also extended itself to others who were present and also called them to believe. But the disciples are mentioned because they were those who had been with him from the beginning as officially appointed witnesses of his glory (cf. 15:27). Here at Cana, having seen his self-manifestation, they "believed in him," even though their faith has been mentioned earlier (cf. 1:50). "Believing" means here that more and more they learned to understand the person with whom they had to do; it was faith, therefore, that did not stop at astonishment over his power (cf. 2:23ff.) or at the expectation with which they had approached him. It is faith in Jesus as the Christ, the Son of God, in the sense in which the Evangelist meant to strengthen the church he was addressing (20:31). Of that church the disciples, as witnesses of Jesus' glory, came to be not only the founders but also the first representatives.

---

46. Cf. Olsson, *Structure and Meaning,* pp. 67f. ("somehow representative of the creative and transforming work of Jesus"); Nicol, *Sēmeia,* p. 114.

47. σημεῖον.

48. τέρατα.

49. See the extensive analysis in Nicol, *Sēmeia,* pp. 62-66, 113-16, and passim.

2:12-22

Jesus at Jerusalem, the Cleansing of the Temple

In vs. **12** we have a transitional passage in which Capernaum is mentioned as the new base of Jesus' activity. "After this" is not intended to make a direct connection with what happened in Cana. Mt. 4:13 and Lk. 4:31 also mention Jesus establishing himself in Capernaum. Apparently the Evangelist here refers back — briefly — to this precanonical tradition, in which it is a given that during his activity in Galilee Jesus operated — at least for a time — from a base in Capernaum (cf. Mt. 9:1).[50] It is striking that at this point also his mother and brothers are mentioned (see, however, texts like Mt. 12:46f.; Mk. 3:31f.; Lk. 8:19f.). Capernaum plays no special role in the Fourth Gospel (cf., besides 4:46, also 6:17, 24, 59). Jesus' mother is not mentioned again until 19:25-27, and his brothers are mentioned again only in 7:3ff. Besides furnishing general orientation, 2:12 also prepares for the remainder of the story. But everything is stated with the greatest possible brevity. The reader's attention is immediately directed to what follows, events foreshadowed in the concluding words: "and there they stayed for a few days." If the correct reading is "they" (and not "he," as some important manuscripts have it), the reference is, of course, to Jesus and his disciples.

In the extreme succinctness of the transition we again come to know the character and purpose of the Fourth Gospel. It does not aim to give a complete account of the life of Jesus. As a rule the chronological viewpoint has only marginal significance. The author assumes that the reader has sufficient general knowledge of the tradition as background for understanding the events that he has selected.

13   The introduction to the story that now follows explains Jesus' journey to Jerusalem: "the Passover of the Jews was at hand." "The Jews" are mentioned here (as in vs. 5; 5:1; 6:4; 7:2; 19:14) not to distinguish them from the nationality of the readers but to describe the Passover and other Jewish customs celebrated by Jews but now abandoned by the Evangelist and his readers. Jewish feasts are occasions for Jesus to go to Jerusalem several times in this Gospel (6:4; 7:2; 10:22; 11:55; 12:1). There, at the Jewish geographical center and at the high points of the religious life of the Jewish people, the great confrontation between Jesus and the Jewish leaders takes place.

What is primarily at stake in the story that now follows is the all-controlling significance of the temple. By placing the story of the "cleansing" of the temple immediately after the story of the first manifestation of Jesus' glory, the Evangelist now in a most fundamental way poses for the reader's

---

50. See also C. H. Dodd, *Historical Tradition in the Fourth Gospel,* 1965, pp. 235f.

consideration the critical significance of Jesus' coming and work. In conjunction with the conversation with Nicodemus, which follows in ch. 3, we have in this journey to the temple the first great confrontation with "the Jews," which is concerned with authority over the temple and the "knowledge" of the Jewish scribes (cf. 3:2, 11; see pp. 97ff. above).

The first question in regard to this passage is always where to place this event historically: as the Synoptics do, just before the last Passover before Jesus' death, or as John does, during a (much) earlier Passover? The idea that we are dealing here with a repetition of precisely the same action at the same location and with the same attendant question concerning Jesus' authority, though not intrinsically impossible, nevertheless seems highly improbable.

If, then, the event must go in one place or another, there are weighty arguments on both sides.[51] An argument for the Johannine version could be that the Synoptics mention only one Passover and one journey to Jerusalem, leaving no other place to put the story. John, by contrast, demonstrates that he has a much more differentiated knowledge of Jesus' conduct at the Jewish festivals. Another argument could be that a cleansing of the temple where John locates it would be Jesus' *initial* reaction to the "worldliness" of the activities around the temple rather than a reaction occurring the last time he was in Jerusalem.[52] Another matter of importance is the precise time indication, "the forty-sixth year," in vs. 20, which seems to argue more for the earlier Johannine dating than for the later Synoptic dating.[53] In any case the date shows that, however much John is guided in the selection and ordering of the events narrated by other concerns, he by no means loses sight of a chronological perspective.

It cannot be denied that Jesus' saying about the tearing down and building up of the temple (Jn. 1:19) plays a distinct role in the history of Jesus' trial before the Sanhedrin and his subsequent execution (Mk. 14:58; Mt. 26:61; cf. Mk. 15:29; Mt. 27:40). But the Synoptics neither mention this connection nor set the saying into the story of the cleansing. They say that there was no consensus among the witnesses with regard to the saying, which does not suggest that there had just recently been a serious conflict over the issue between Jesus and the Jewish authorities.

Though there is thus much that argues for the Johannine dating of the cleansing, with regard to this much disputed point it is not likely that we shall ever arrive at absolute certainty or a unanimous judgment.

14-16   What comes most prominently to the fore in this confrontation

---

51. For a summary of the arguments see Brown, *Comm.* I, pp. 117ff.

52. The argument is also taken the opposite direction: see Brown, *Comm.* I, in loc.; Grosheide, *Comm.* I, p. 183.

53. See also Schnackenburg, *Comm.* I, pp. 354ff.

between Jesus and the Jews is the absolute authority and attendant severity of Jesus' public action. He not only tells the merchants and the money changers whom he found in the temple to leave but with a hastily improvised whip he drives them all[54] — merchandise and everything — out of the temple. He spills out the money changers' money and turns their tables over and commands the pigeon merchants to take their merchandise and leave — all this with the message intended for them: "You shall not make my Father's house a house of trade!" In this description of the temple there is, of course, an implied legitimation of his action as well as an explanation of his anger and of the violence he uses. He acts and speaks as the Son, whose holy wrath and zeal are ignited at sight of what people have done with his Father's house.

It has been asked whether what the merchants did was really that great an evil. After all, they provided pilgrims what they needed for the sacrifices and enabled them to pay the obligatory temple tax in the prescribed currency. The merchants had to pay substantial rent for their spaces in the temple court to the temple authorities. But Jesus' fury and severity were not directed against the merchants' or money changers' profits but against the very fact of business being conducted in the precincts of the sanctuary. For him it was intolerable that the place of access to God's holy dwelling and to communion with God himself was made into a place of trade in animals and money, a business for which in the nature of the case the temple was not intended. That his criticism was not only directed against the merchants but also concerned the authorities in the temple and the pilgrims in general, all of whom apparently accepted such a combination of contradictory matters as natural, is obvious and, as the sequel shows, was clearly understood as such by the Jewish leaders. The real conflict was between him and them. And, as will appear in vs. 18, the dispute was ultimately not over what was permitted or prohibited in the temple but over βόας who wielded authority there.

17 In a parenthetical statement we learn that the disciples — whose presence as the regular companions and witnesses of Jesus is simply assumed here — remembered these words from Scripture: "Zeal for thy house has consumed me" (cf. Ps. 69:9). The idea that we have here a later reflection (as in vs. 22 and 12:16) is not suggested by the text itself. "Consume" does not refer to the intensity of the emotion that was manifest in Jesus' zeal for the house of God but, as is clear from Ps. 69:9b itself,[55] to the lethal hostility that his

---

54. Some scholars believe that πάντας in vs. 15 must refer to the sheep and cattle and that Jesus used the whip to drive them away, not the people ("since one cannot drive animals merely with one's hands," Haenchen, *Comm.* I, p. 183). But even if the whip was intended mostly for the animals, πάντας clearly refers primarily to the people. τε is unusual in the Fourth Gospel, and some therefore consider τὰ τε πρόβατα καὶ τοὺς βόας, a difficult apposition next to πάντας, a secondary addition. But one can see τε in the light of the preceding verse and take the partial repetition with πάντας in this verse in the sense of "sheep and cattle and all."

55. Future κατάφαγεται agrees with the LXX.

zeal was to evoke from his adversaries. The full manifestation of this hostility would undoubtedly not surface till later, and the scriptural proof[56] from Psalm 69 (cf. Ro. 15:3; Jn. 19:28) was therefore undoubtedly proleptic. But this is not to deny that in Jesus' violent and authoritative resistance against the misuse of the temple the disciples saw the spirit of prophecy moving in him — and that in that context they learned to understand his conduct also during his lifetime (cf. 14:25).

18 "The Jews" — a term that here as so often in the Fourth Gospel refers to the Jewish authorities in their hostile attitude toward Jesus[57] — react by asking Jesus for a sign of legitimation[58] — a supernatural demonstration of his authority. Such a sign was repeatedly demanded of Jesus (cf. Mt. 12:38, 39; 16:1ff.; Lk. 23:8) and was, indeed, characteristic of Jewish thinking (cf. 1 Co. 1:22; Jn. 4:48; 6:30). But Jesus never met such requests.

19 Jesus does respond with a pronouncement in which the prospect of such a "sign" is held out to them, but he does so in a way that for his adversaries (and for his disciples!) must have been a complete mystery: "Destroy this temple, and in three days I will raise it up."

20-22 "The Jews" took Jesus' words literally[59] and, in view of the long period of time already spent (and still being spent) in the construction of the temple,[60] could only view the "three days" as an absurdity, about which there could be no sensible discussion. The Evangelist explains that Jesus spoke of "the temple of his body" (vs. 21) and tells us that after his resurrection the disciples remembered Jesus' statement (vs. 22), and in both additions[61] it is clear that the Evangelist intends us to understand "tearing down" and "raising up" as referring to Jesus' death and resurrection. By his words in vs. 19, then, Jesus seems to be serving notice to his adversaries that his authority with regard to the temple would manifest itself when they would raise to the limit the hostility that they already felt toward him, by executing him. Then in three days he would build up again what they had broken down — his body — by rising from the dead. However much this explanation of Jesus' enigmatic saying — unintelligible alike to friend and foe when he spoke it — illumines the

---

56. γεγραμμένον ἐστιν.

57. See the comments on 1:19 above.

58. "What sign do you show us that you (have the right to) do these things"; cf. Mk. 11:28.

59. As always when such "misunderstandings" occur; see also the comments on 3:3ff.; 4:15, etc.

60. The reference of course is to the "second" temple, the construction of which, according to Josephus (*Antiquities* 15.380), began in the eighteenth year of Herod's reign, that is, in 20-19 B.C. "Forty-six years" would mean, therefore, that the conversation here took place around 27-28 A.D. The construction of the second temple was not completed until just before the outbreak of war in 66.

61. Cf. οὖν in vs. 22.

background of the dispute between Jesus and his adversaries that erupts with increasing force in the following chapters, it does not remove the fact that as an interpretation of Jesus' answer to the Jews it poses questions that are difficult to answer.

The first question is whether in the explanation every connection with the historic temple is excluded and Jesus, in total detachment from the situation in which he found himself, had in mind only his own body when he spoke of "this temple." We must ask this because elsewhere in the Gospels similar — at first sight — statements of Jesus occur (or at least are put in his mouth) that seem to have a very different thrust. We specifically have in mind the statements made during the trial before the Sanhedrin: "I will destroy this temple that is made with hands, and in three days I will build another, not made with hands" (Mk. 14:58), "I am able to destroy the temple of God, and to build it in three days" (Mt. 26:61; cf. Mk. 15:29; Mt. 27:40; Ac. 6:14). Scholars usually view these as eschatological sayings of judgment that Jesus uttered over the temple at Jerusalem, following it with a messianic announcement of another reality complete with a new temple "not made with hands." "Three days" is sometimes taken as an indication of a short perod or as an allusion to the rabbinic dating of the resurrection from the dead on the third day after the end of the world, in accordance with Ho. 6:2.[62] Jesus' answer in Jn 2:19 is said to have been understood in a similar sense by the spectators and to have been echoed in the charges made and the mockery expressed before Caiaphas and at the cross. The assumption is then that the Evangelist reinterpreted all this by taking "this temple" to mean not the temple in Jerusalem but the temple of Jesus' body.

But can the parallel utterances really help us understand Jn. 2:19ff.? They are, after all, related as false testimony. And here in John Jesus does not say "*I* will tear down this temple," but "Destroy this temple." The imperative has a much fiercer sound than a conditional — "*if* you destroy this temple" — would have. It has the character of an ironic provocation, as in prophetic utterances like Am. 4:4; Is. 8:9f.:[63] "Go ahead, destroy this temple — as you are already doing and apparently love to do — and in three days I will raise it up again." So tearing down the temple is not the judgment of God or Jesus on the temple (of which the violent cleansing would then be the prelude) but the manner in which the Jews themselves were disturbing God's dwelling among them. Jesus announces that what they are apparently consciously tearing down he will build up in three days in a way that is not conceivable to them ("in three days"). Viewed in this light the connection with the temple in which they are standing (and with Jesus' cleansing of it) is maintained — even given the

---

62. Cf. Strack/Billerbeck I, p. 747.
63. So correctly Bultmann, *Comm.*, p. 125, n. 4.

Evangelist's explanation. There lay the starting point of the entire confrontation. "This temple" the Jews, by their unspiritual "management" of the house of God, were in the process of tearing down. And, as is already clear now, Jesus himself, in his zeal for God's claims upon the temple, was to fall a victim to that attitude. But the sign that they demanded of him and Jesus held out to them would *not* consist, as the Jews thought and later charged, in a new building ("made with hands," Mk. 14:58) at Jerusalem, but — as the disciples, the church, and the Evangelist were to understand in retrospect — in the miracle of his resurrection, both as the proof of his authority and as the new way in which God would make his dwelling among people (cf. 4:21ff.). By way of this new focus, in which the entire dispute with the Jews is placed under the "heading" of *that* future, all the words about the temple in this context gain a new meaning and are placed on a new level, and "this temple" in vs. 19 is seen as a transition, the ambiguity of which only emerges later.

Interpreters are very divided in their opinions on this difficult passage. Some believe that vs. 19 should be explained by itself, apart from the temple at Jerusalem and the cleansing of the temple. In the words "this temple" Jesus is said to have had in mind only his own body, to which he perhaps pointed with his finger ("this"). Others believe that in vs. 19a the temple at Jerusalem is meant and in vs. 19b ("it") Jesus' body is meant. Brown, who reports all these ideas, calls the explanation of the Evangelist himself "a post-resurrectional amplification" of an original "eschatological proclamation referring to the Jerusalem temple."[64] But, as stated above, we do not know with any clarity of such a proclamation from the mouth of Jesus, considering the murky source (Jesus' accusers and opponents) we have to draw on. However, the idea that the words "this temple" are completely detached from the temple in Jerusalem where the disputants found themselves and which was at issue seems to me (as to Brown) equally hard to defend. Bultmann's judgment is very radical. According to him it is clear that vss. 20 and 21 are "a secondary interpretation" because "the temple referred to in vs. 19 is the real temple of Jerusalem as is shown by . . . τὸν ναὸν τοῦτον." And he regards it as a comical "way of getting out of the predicament" to say (as vs. 20 states) that with this τοῦτον Jesus pointed to his own body.[65] However much the starting point for the temple saying may have been "the real temple of Jerusalem," it is no less clear that (in the mouth of Jesus) the *object* of the "tearing down" and "building up" cannot be the temple in Jerusalem. Jesus is not referring to the destruction of the temple as the coming judgment of God, as in Mt. 24:2, but to the manner in which the Jews were guilty of violating their own temple. And there is even less ground for the notion that he is holding out the prospect of an eschatological reconstruction — and that by himself — of this "real temple of Jerusalem." The contrary is rather the case (cf. Jn. 4:21f.).

64. Brown, *Comm.* I, p. 123.
65. Bultmann, *Comm.,* p. 126, n. 2.

In addition, as far as the terms of the text are concerned, for "raising up" (again) the Evangelist uses a word[66] that can refer to "new construction" of a house or to "raising up" of a body — surely also with a view to the interpretation that is given. It is hard to say with certainty whether "in three days" is a direct prediction of the period between Jesus' death and resurrection (elsewhere usually described as "after three days" or "on the third day," cf. Mk. 8:31; 9:31; 10:34; Mt. 27:63; 16:21; 1 Co. 15:4) or an eschatological time indication (as it is used in the rabbinic literature; see above).

The most striking feature in the whole pronouncement is of course that in speaking of this marvelous construction Jesus is referring to his resurrection and in speaking of "this temple" he is referring to his body. Among the numerous explanations of this, it has been pointed out that elsewhere the body is called the temple of God or of the Holy Spirit (cf. 1 Co. 3:16; 6:19). But the point of departure for this idea does not lie in the body but in Christ himself, who in rising from the grave to which he has been consigned by people proves himself to be the one in whom the glory of God dwells among people. In Rv. 21:22 God and the Lamb are identified as the "temple" of the heavenly Jerusalem, and in Jn. 1:14 the indwelling of the glory of God in the flesh is described with as the "tabernacle"[67] (cf. also Mt. 12:6). But rather than seeking the explanation for Jesus' identification with the temple in proof texts, we should find it in the general conceptual framework of the Fourth Gospel: In Jesus Christ has become manifest the truth of what in all sorts of ways was foreshadowed and predicted in Israel's history, in the law of Moses, in the holy institutions of Israel as the people of God, and in the prophets' future expectation. In other words, just as Jesus is the Lamb of God (1:29), so he is also the temple that will replace the existing temple and in whom the indwelling of God among people will be truly and fully realized.

This last point explains why the Evangelist uses the story of the cleansing of the temple to lead into Jesus' confrontation with the Jewish leaders, which began with his appearance in Jerusalem. In that temple, in which all the privileges and pretensions of the religion they represented were concentrated, Jesus set himself as the Son of the Father with full power and authority over his house. And there he pronounced a devastating judgment over the havoc that the people had wreaked there. Over against that havoc he announced a new way of worshiping God that God would establish in him, a new way in which — as he was to tell the Samaritan woman — the true worshipers would worship the Father in Spirit and in truth (4:23).

For that reason the story of the temple-cleansing, together with that of the wedding at Cana, can also be viewed as the background of all that follows.

---

66. ἐγείρω.
67. With the verb ἐσκήνωσεν.

In both stories the presence of God among people becomes visible in Jesus' coming as a sign, in its salvific as well as in its critical significance. To his readers — in their struggle for the true religion — the Evangelist could hardly picture the radicality and exclusiveness of faith in Jesus as the Christ, the Son of God, with greater force than by the conjunction of these two introductory stories.

The last words of the pericope (vs. **22**) say that the disciples did not remember that he had said this until after the resurrection. They, too, were unable to understand the meaning of his words before that. But then "they believed the Scripture and the word that Jesus had spoken." That is, they understood, by the light of Scripture, the way Jesus had to go and where it led. Then the word Jesus had once uttered became for them (all the more) reason to believe in him.

For our insight into the origin of the faith of the Christian church and of the gospel, this concluding verse is of special importance. It does not say that the roots of the Christian faith and of the way the historical Jesus was described lay in the experience of the resurrection. The Fourth Gospel emphasizes the manifestation of the glory of Jesus as the Christ, the Son of God, during his *earthly* life. It is not just the glory of the resurrection that retroactively shines over his earthly life. It is the glory with which he "dwelled among us," the glory of the Word that became flesh, to which the Gospel consistently testifies.

But the disciples' understanding of that glory did not keep pace with the revelation. It was the resurrection, the witness of the Spirit (14:26; 15:26), and the Scriptures that "brought to their remembrance," that gave them the correct understanding of what Jesus had said and done. Thus they became aware of who he was and what he had said and meant. Neither the resurrection, nor the Spirit, nor the Scriptures, nor their faith was primary. What was and remained primary was the glory of the indwelling of God in Jesus. The gospel is not the story of the later faith of the Christian church; it is the report of the revelation of God in the flesh. But only the end, the resurrection, and the Spirit teach disciples to understand the beginning and offer faith a foothold in "the word that Jesus had spoken."

2:23–3:10

Jesus' Knowledge of Humankind, the Dialogue with Nicodemus

The purpose of vss. 23-25 is clearly to introduce a new perspective in relation to the revelation of the glory of Jesus Christ. Up to this point the revelation led to two opposing reactions: that of Jesus' disciples and that of "the Jews."

The disciples beheld his glory and believed in him (2:11). "The Jews" questioned the authority with which Jesus acted in the temple and thus began the opposition that in the end was to lead them to their total rejection of Jesus as the Christ, the Son of God. Now in 2:23ff. we learn of a third reaction, one more favorable than that of "the Jews": the "many" at Jerusalem were deeply impressed by Jesus' miraculous power and so "believed in his name." But Jesus adopted a very reserved posture toward this reaction.

All this constitutes a point of departure for the conversation with Nicodemus in ch. 3, where, in a profound way, the deficit of this faith on the part of the "many" — represented by Nicodemus — is stressed. This is done, first, on the basis of the "knowledge" (vs. 25) Jesus had of humanity (3:1-8), then in the light of a new and great exposition of Jesus' coming into the world and of a corresponding faith in his name (3:11-22).

23, 24   The manner in which the transition is made to this new perspective is characteristic for the way in which the author works: there is a historical link with the preceding, Jesus' stay in Jerusalem during the Passover, but there is no information whatever about any other action of Jesus at the feast, including the miracles he apparently performed repeatedly[68] in those days. The Evangelist considered Jesus' performance of miracles wherever he was staying sufficiently well known to be able to refer to them in connection with the reaction of the "many."

The Evangelist describes that reaction as "believing in Jesus' name," and we thus immediately encounter a problem that returns again and again in the Gospel and that surely played an important role in the later relationship between the church and the synagogue, namely what one can and should understand by "believing in Jesus." The expression also occurs in 1:12, just as elsewhere there is repeated mention of "faith" that later proved impermanent (7:31; 8:30; 10:42; 11:45; 12:42). The Evangelist does not say that they pretended to be believers or anything like that; he does not deny that they believed. They believed in Jesus as a man sent from God, as, expressing the conviction of many, Nicodemus put it ("we know" in 3:2), and they did this because, unlike many of the Jewish leaders, they did not question the genuineness of Jesus' miracles (cf. 9:16; Mt. 9:34; 10:25; 12:24, etc.). At the same time it is clear that not all "believing" or "believing in his name" could be equated with the faith mentioned in 1:12, where the link is made — as it will be in the conversation with Nicodemus — with "being born of God."

The Evangelist himself does not pronounce this judgment, but refers in vs. 24 to the posture Jesus adopted toward the many who believed in him because of his miracles. Jesus "did not trust himself to them," did not count on them as followers of whom he could be sure. We are not told in what way

---

68. Cf. imperfect ἐποίει in vs. 23; also 4:45, which alludes to the miracles.

Jesus maintained this reserve toward them. He apparently did not prevent them from following him as his disciples (cf., e.g., 6:66) but he knew that the impression made on them by his miracles did not offer a guarantee that in the end they would choose for him. It is on that "knowledge" of Jesus that all the emphasis falls here.

25   Bultmann speaks of the cumbersomeness ("Umständlichkeit") with which in vs. 25 Jesus' omniscience is emphasized as the ground for his reserve and calls it typical for this Evangelist. However, this copiousness not only serves to explain Jesus' restrained posture toward the people referred to in vss. 22-24 but is also meant to prepare for what will come up as the first decisive point of discussion in the dialogue with Nicodemus, which follows: "what was in the human person" (vs. 25b).

3:1   The conversation with Nicodemus offers a very specific elaboration of what was said in a more general sense in 2:23-25. In the figure of Nicodemus we are given an illustrative demonstration — perhaps we may say *par excellence* — of what in the preceding is called "the faith" of the many in Jerusalem who were impressed by the signs that Jesus did.

Nicodemus is introduced as "a man of the Pharisees." "A man" could simply mean "someone," but in light of the repeated ἄνθρωπος in 2:25 (and with a view to 3:4, 27), the use of the word is probably intentional. As a Pharisee Nicodemus was an adherent of a rigorously orthodox and nationalistic party and as such also a scribe (vs. 10). He was also "a ruler of the Jews," which means, as is evident from 7:26, 48 (as also from the usage in Luke and Acts), that he was a member of the Sanhedrin. Again, then, we have here a confrontation between Jesus and official Judaism, but one that is very different from that in 2:18ff. Nicodemus clearly did not belong to the leaders who were hostile to Jesus, and later in the Gospel he speaks on Jesus' behalf in the Sanhedrin (7:50) and joins with those who provide Jesus an honorable burial (19:39).

2   Nicodemus's motive for going to Jesus was certainly that he wanted to become better acquainted with him, and this comes out in the significant remark he later addresses to his colleagues (7:51). That he came to Jesus "by night" is interpreted variously. The inference that he wanted to speak with Jesus without being noticed is obvious. This does not necessarily mean, however, that he was motivated by fear, as is often assumed (with reference to the context in which "by night" comes up again in 19:39 [cf. vs. 38]). But although in this encounter by night the element of prudence may have been a factor, one can hardly, in light of all the facts, call Nicodemus a model of fear.[69] And we certainly cannot place him among the "many of the authorities" whose secret faith is disqualified in 12:42f. Therefore some scholars look for the motive of

---

69. On this see at greater length the comments on 7:52 below.

this nocturnal visit simply in a desire to talk with Jesus undisturbed, just as the rabbis made a habit of studying the Torah by night.[70]

The manner in which Nicodemus addressed Jesus and made known his view of him is typical for his role throughout this encounter. He comes to Jesus not with a question but with a statement ("we know"), one, indeed, that reflects what is said in 2:23 concerning the "many" in Jerusalem who believed in Jesus' name. His position as a scribe and a member of the Sanhedrin gives all the more relief to this "we know"; still he is speaking in the first place as representative of this "faith" in Jesus and not so much as an authoritative scribe. Nicodemus speaks in the plural, as others do later (4:24; 9:24, 29, 31; 16:30), to say what certain groups believe or do not believe about Jesus.[71]

Nicodemus's witness concerning Jesus is certainly not devoid of significant content. He not only addresses Jesus as "Rabbi" but expressly calls him "a teacher come from God," mentioning Jesus' signs as incontestable ground for this. He could base this on the general opinion of Jews that performance of miracles, and certainly miracles of the kind Jesus did, served as a clear indication that a person had been sent by God (cf., e.g., 9:31ff.).[72] Others, going farther, believe that Nicodemus was referring here to the prophet predicted in Dt. 18:15, 18.[73] He does not speak of a prophet, however, but of a teacher, and Deuteronomy 18 does not mention miracles. Also, the description is too general to serve as a reference to the expectation of one very specific prophet (or teacher; cf. 9:33).

The qualifications Nicodemus uses of Jesus ("come from God"; "God is with him") approximate or coincide with what Jesus says of himself (e.g., 8:29; 16:32). Therefore, we are faced with the question why Nicodemus is presented as one of those of whom it is said (2:24) that Jesus "did not trust himself to them," one of those who "do not receive our testimony" and "do not believe" (3:11f.).

3 Jesus' response is given with the great emphasis of "Amen, amen" (see the comments on 1:51) and is repeated in somewhat different language in vs. 5. It resembles (like 1:51) a revelational utterance that not only transcends human certainties ("we know") but also replaces them with something of another order and a higher priority. Nicodemus had spoken of Jesus' signs as proof that God was with him. Jesus himself reached beyond the signs and spoke

70. Cf. Strack/Billerbeck II, p. 420. Still others think symbolism is involved here. Nicodemus is said (by contrast with Judas, 13:30!) to come out of darkness to the light (cf. vss. 19, 21); see Brown, *Comm.* I, p. 130. But of course this says nothing about Nicodemus's preference for *meeting* Jesus by night!

71. See also M. de Jonge, *Jesus: Stranger from Heaven and Son of God,* 1977, p. 46.

72. Cf. Strack/Billerbeck I, p. 127; IV, pp. 313f.

73. See, e.g., J. L. Martyn, *History and Theology in the Fourth Gospel,* 1979[2], p. 116, with an appeal to G. Bornkamm.

of (seeing) the kingdom of God. He thereby placed his public conduct in a context in which God was with him in another, superior, more decisive way than Nicodemus and the "many" in Jerusalem were apparently aware of: by revealing in him God's salvation in its "eschatological" all-embracing significance.

Only here and in vs. 5 is the kingdom of God mentioned in the Fourth Gospel. This surely ties in with the fact that John focuses everything on the *person* of Christ. All the more prominent in the Fourth Gospel, therefore, is the "personal" concept[74] that corresponds to the concept of "the kingdom of God," that of "the Son of man" as the fully empowered Revealer and Bringer of the kingdom of God, as Daniel 7 speaks of him. In what follows, what is called the kingdom of God here will be referred to as the descent from heaven of the Son of man (vss. 13ff.). But to attribute such significance to Jesus and to *see* (that is, to be permitted to share in)[75] the kingdom represented by him, or to be allowed to *enter* it (so vs. 5), requires more than just being impressed by his miraculous power and ascribing to him a place of honor in the situation in which one finds oneself and considers oneself competent to judge. It requires a complete reversal in that situation, a reversal that Jesus describes as "being born from above."

There has been much controversy over whether we should translate ἄνωθεν as "from above" or "anew."[76] A clear argument for the first is that "from above" is the starting point of the pericope in vss. 31-36, one that is intimately tied in with vss. 1-21. Just as the Redeemer "comes from above" (3:31; see also 3:13), so also the redeemed must be born "from above." For the second meaning, "anew," one can appeal to the response of Nicodemus, who speaks of "a second time." Sometimes scholars speak of a play on words possible only in the Greek: Jesus had in mind "from above," but Nicodemus understood "anew." If, however, one goes back to the unquestionably Semitic origin of this pronouncement, then such a play on words is hard to construe, and one encounters an Aramaic word that can only mean "from above."[77] We are not, however, dealing with an essential difference. As is evident from vss. 5 and 8 Jesus had in mind a birth "of the Spirit," and it is "of God" in 1:13. Such a birth is both "from above" and "anew." Nicodemus takes it to mean "entering one's mother's womb a second time" and in any case does not

---

74. See on this at greater length my "Jezus van Nazaret," in *Bijbels Handboek* IV, 1987, pp. 59-125.

75. For "see" with the meaning "have personal experience of, participate in," see, e.g., 3:36; Ac. 2:27; 1 Pt. 3:17.

76. Latin *desuper* or *denuo;* for the first meaning see, e.g., Mt. 27:51; Jn. 3:31; 19:11, 23; Ja. 1:17; for the second Gl. 4:9.

77. Cf. Strack/Billerbeck II, p. 420, which mentions as the equivalent of ἄνωθεν Aramaic *millᵉ῾êlā'*, which is used spatially, not temporally.

understand Jesus' meaning. Therefore, although the translation "anew" is certainly not impossible, on the basis of the context I favor "from above."

Scholars have tried in various ways to delineate the theological meaning of this striking expression more precisely. But, with a view also to Nicodemus's answer in vs. 4, birth "from above" does not function in this specific Johannine form (which does not occur anywhere else)[78] as a fixed theological term adopted from some existing doctrinal system so that Jesus could expect an expert to understand it.[79] It has the character, rather, of one of those recurrent paradoxical sayings (e.g., 2:19; 6:41, 51) that were intended to produce some kind of shock. Although in vs. 5 Jesus will explain his meaning further, his primary intent is obviously not to refute or correct Nicodemus's theological certainties by means of scribal terms or arguments, but to impress him at a much deeper level, where his entire existence before God is at stake.

Some regard this pronouncement as another version of the saying in Mk. 10:15; Mt. 18:3: "Truly I say to you, whoever does not receive the kingdom of God like a child will not enter it." Others mention the reference to *being* a child of God, which is more than the comparison "like a child" and thus assumes a new beginning. Still others look for the background of this mode of speaking in Hellenistic religiosity. Dodd refers specifically to the Hermetic literature, which mentions rebirth.[80] Bultmann speaks of a Gnostic source that the Evangelist used and that supposedly mentioned "being begotten from above."[81] In rabbinic writings, too, one finds many expressions that denote rescue from death, the forgiveness of sins, and the like as a re-creation,[82] though this is different from what Jesus meant. All this may serve to show that Jesus was not speaking into a spiritual vacuum, but that does not remove the surprising (in this context) and paradoxical character of his emphatic revelational saying (cf., e.g., 6:53; also 1:51).

4 Accordingly, Nicodemus's answer is not that of one who is unfamiliar with a certain "theological" terminology or thought pattern, but that of a natural man, one for whom being "born from above" is the end of all human knowledge or scribal learning.[83] He gives realistic expression to his feelings with a question

78. For ἄνω-θεν see also 3:31; 8:23.

79. In vs. 9 Jesus does call into question Nicodemus's competence as a teacher (see also vs. 7: "Do not marvel"), but only after he has explained his meaning further. Therefore, he means only that, on closer scrutiny, his first utterance (vs. 3) was not as enigmatic as it might have seemed.

80. C. H. Dodd, *Interpretation of the Fourth Gospel,* 1963, pp. 49f., 304f.

81. *Comm.,* p. 136.

82. Cf. Strack/Billerbeck II, p. 421.

83. So Bultmann: "He makes not a typically Rabbinic, but a specifically human reply." Bultmann correctly rejects views like those of B. Weisz and Schlatter that attempt to impart to Nicodemus's answer a certain theological meaning (Bultmann, *Comm.,* p. 137).

calculated to show up the absurdity of what Jesus has said. One may call this rather primitive reply of Nicodemus a rhetorical form: John frequently has the conversation partners of Jesus — all responding to similar paradoxical statements — pose questions that show misunderstanding and incomprehension and that provide Jesus with an opportunity to explain himself further (e.g., 2:20; 4:11f.; chs. 8–9). But this sort of reaction also shows how great the distance is between Jesus' mode of thought and theirs and how time and again his words thus sound strange or even absurd to them (cf. 2:19; 4:10; 6:52; 8:58) — an effect that Jesus undoubtedly intended to stimulate them to reflection but whose background and actual cause lay in the fact that Jesus spoke and acted from another reality than his partners in dialogue.

5   To Nicodemus's question ("How can a person . . . ?") Jesus replies with a factual as well as formal repetition of his first pronouncement, using different words in place of the expression that had proven to be so puzzling and even absurd to Nicodemus, saying now not "from above" but "of water and the Spirit." The reference to "the Spirit" as the creator of life as promised eschatological gift should have made clear to Nicodemus what Jesus meant. But "water and Spirit" together are harder to understand.[84] Some see here in "born of water and the Spirit" a reflection of the later ecclesiastical doctrine of baptismal regeneration and accordingly regard "of water" as a later "sacramental" insertion. But it would then be more natural to reverse the argument and explain the later teaching (partly) in terms of this expression — and also to explain the use of the words "regeneration," "born anew" (cf. Tit. 3:5; 1 Pt. 1:3, 23), which display a much more fixed and hence later character, on the basis of this unusual "born from above"/"born of water and the Spirit."

The question remains what might have been meant by "water," which is governed by a single preposition with "Spirit,"[85] in the context of John 3. Some think that it need not refer to baptism but is a symbol for "Spirit," as in 7:38f. and that the conjunction "and" is epexegetical, meaning "that is to say."[86] But it is unlikely that "water" should mean no more than "Spirit," which follows in the same breath. Why then mention water first? On the other hand, it is not at all necessary to think in this connection of the church doctrine of baptism, of which Nicodemus could not have had any notion. And Jesus is

84. In some manuscripts it is repeated in vs. 8, presumably on the analogy of vs. 5.
85. ἐξ ὕδατος καὶ πνεύματος.
86. Cf. Calvin, *Comm.* I, p. 65: "Nor is it unusual to employ the word *and* explanatorily when the latter clause is an explanation of the former." For the entire question of ὕδατος καὶ πνεύματος, see X. Léon-Dufour, "Towards a Symbolic Reading of the Fourth Gospel," *NTS* 27 (1981), pp. 449ff., who asserts that an original nonsacramental symbolic meaning in 3:5 need not exclude a later sacramental interpretation: "It is not necessary to reconstruct two successive stages of the text. But it is necessary to perceive two times of revelation, that of Jesus to Nicodemus and that of the Spirit to me, the reader of the Gospel" (p. 450).

speaking not of access to the church but about entering the kingdom, with reference to which the connection between (baptismal) water and the Spirit was relevant from the start, as we have seen at length in the Baptist's testimony (1:26ff.), and it can hardly be accidental that the pericope that immediately follows the present one (3:22ff.) again mentions John's baptism.

Accordingly it is against *that* baptismal background that one must understand Jesus' pronouncement to Nicodemus. The message of the kingdom was bound up from the beginning not only with the call to repentance but also with water baptism, in close connection with which the baptism of the Holy Spirit had been held out as the gift of the Coming One (cf. 1:33). Therefore, "water and Spirit" can be used together of the birth needed to enter the kingdom: baptism as the putting off of the old, the Spirit as the creator and gift of the new life. It thus becomes clear why Jesus counters Nicodemus's seemingly positive and well-considered words with such a radical reply, one that shatters all human certainties. Where a person is actually confronted with the reality of the kingdom of God, that person's entire existence is at stake, and in this crisis something more is needed than what he or she claims to "know" on the basis of experience: only "water and Spirit," as the way and the gift of the new world of God, are relevant.

6 To demonstrate the necessity of such a new birth of the Spirit Jesus contrasts it with being "born of the flesh" as the mode of existence that belongs to humanity by nature and conditions all human thoughts and deeds. What is meant here by "flesh" can best be illumined with the aid of 1:13, where being "born of God" is opposed to being "born of blood, of the will of the flesh, of human will." Hence "flesh" denotes a person in his or her natural existence as begotten by a father and given birth to by a mother. It is that birth that both determines and limits the nature of human existence, which thus does not extend to the ability to see and enter the kingdom of God. This is not just a matter of "above" and "below" as two mutually exclusive modes of existence, since one, in virtue of its origin, is by definition inaccessible to the other. Being born of "water and Spirit" does not mean — and it is precisely the Fourth Gospel that is very emphatic about this — being released from the temporal and "fleshly" existence of this world; it means rather the subjection of the flesh to the reign of the Spirit, of reconciliation, forgiveness, and renewal, a reign that deeply enters the sphere of the flesh (see also the comments on 1:29-34 above).

Hence — according to vs. **7** — Nicodemus must not be too surprised[87] over the fact that Jesus spoke of the necessity of being "born from above." How could that which is born of flesh, on its own strength as it were, secure for itself a share in the kingdom of God? Conversely, how could the Spirit,

---

87. μὴ θαυμάσῃς (cf. 5:28; 1 Jn. 3:13) was a characteristic turn of speech in rabbinic discussions; see Schlatter, *Comm.,* p. 90; Bultmann, *Comm.,* p. 142, n. 1.

precisely as the Spirit of God and from above, not have the power to bring about this event, however puzzling and absurd it might seem to Nicodemus?

Verse **8** focuses on the *positive* side of Jesus' initial pronouncement and illumines it by means of the image of "wind." Both Hebrew and Greek have one word for "wind" and "spirit," and wind, in its power and effect, is a common image for the Spirit (e.g., Ac. 2:2; Ec. 11:5). Wind is observable,[88] but it goes sovereignly where it pleases[89] and is untraceable in its origin[90] and disappearance.[91]. Also free, mighty, and untraceable in its movements is the Spirit in a person who is born of the Spirit.[92]

In all this the divine possibilities are set over against the impossibilities of humankind ("flesh"), but not just negatively but precisely to cause people to look away from their own (im)possibilities and toward God for their salvation. For the freedom of the Spirit to go where he pleases is not capriciousness but power that nothing can hold back. And the Spirit's untraceability is not anonymous incalculability but possession of means that humans cannot have but are possible with God (cf. Ro. 11:33ff.). It is in that way, a way not only determined by God but now opened up by him, that humans become participants in that new existence and hence gain entrance into the kingdom, which in vs. 16 is called eternal life. Accordingly, it is *faith* in the salvation thus revealed in Christ on which the now following verses focus and in which the "dialogue" with Nicodemus achieves its real goal.

Flesh and Spirit

In contrast with the above, scholars have sought to understand Jesus' pronouncements concerning birth from above and the contrast between flesh and Spirit against the background of certain forms from the contemporary Greek world of thought and religion. In this pericope, according to this approach, we have been given an important hermeneutic key for the understanding of the Fourth Gospel: here the anthropological presuppositions that are determinative for Johannine soteriology and christology come to the surface. We are talking specifically of both C. H. Dodd's idealistic interpretation and R. Bultmann's Gnostic interpretation.

Dodd writes that in Jn. 3:1ff. we are very close to the widespread Hellenistic notion of the two levels of existence, "the upper world (τὰ ἄνω) which is the sphere

---

88. τὴν φωνὴν αὐτοῦ ἀκούεις.

89. ὅπου θέλει πνεῖ.

90. πόθεν ἔρχεται.

91. ποῦ ὑπάγει.

92. Strictly speaking it is not the Spirit but the one born of the Spirit that is compared with the wind. The one that does the work and the work are telescoped, so to speak (cf. Mt. 13:19, 20, 22, where what happens with the seed is transferred to the person in whom the seed either does or does not have its effect).

of the νοῦς [referred to as πνεῦμα in this passage] in which alone dwell light and immortality, and the lower world (τὰ κάτω) which is the sphere of the ὕλη or of darkness [σάρξ in this passage]." "The main theme of the discourse, then, is the passage of man out of the lower order of existence, the realm of the flesh, into the higher order of existence, the realm of spirit in which alone eternal life is his portion." Accordingly, we are told, we have here the (anthropological) key to the understanding of the nature of Jesus' public conduct: passage (or rebirth) into the higher order of existence underlies both the story of the wedding at Cana, where it is symbolized by the changing of water into wine, and the story of the cleansing of the temple.[93]

Bultmann rejects this idealistic understanding[94] and believes one must rather explain the contrast in a sense characteristic of Gnostic anthropology. In his view "flesh" and "spirit" denote not just the lower and higher levels in the human person but the radical opposition between two mutually exclusive metaphysical principles, which Bultmann, with the aid of terms derived from existentialist philosophy, then "demythologizes" and further interprets. "Flesh" refers to "the nothingness of man's whole existence; to the fact that man is ultimately a stranger to his fate as to his own acts; that, as he now is, he does not enjoy authentic existence, whether he makes himself aware of the fact or whether he conceals it from himself. Correspondingly, 'spirit' refers to the miracle of a mode of being in which man enjoys authentic existence in which he understands himself and knows that he is no longer threatened by nothingness." Once a person has understood this, Jesus' statement to Nicodemus (vs. 7: "Do not marvel . . .") applies to that person.[95]

All this should show how far-reaching and profound the influence of the "anthropological" key one uses is in exposition of Jn. 3:1-8. It not only radically shapes one's concept of rebirth but also one's entire understanding of the coming and work of the Redeemer. Thus, according to Bultmann, vss. 3-8, in which the necessity of rebirth is spoken of, form the "explanation for the coming of the Revealer."[96] Given this understanding, it is clear that the nature and goal of this coming are totally determined by one's anthropological "preunderstanding," one's understanding of what "flesh," "spirit," and "birth from above" presumably mean here.

However much these concepts and the opposition between flesh and spirit may function in a variety of forms in Hellenistic religion, this does not yet say anything about the background and meaning of this pair of opposites in the Fourth Gospel. Bultmann is surely correct when over against Dodd's interpretation he advances that the opposition between flesh and spirit in John is much more radical than that in the neo-Platonic idealism to which Dodd refers. But this is not yet to say that this opposition is rooted, as in Gnosticism, in an original and metaphysical dualism that, though in the gospel it has been stripped of its mythological and ontological character, nevertheless

---

93. Dodd, *Interpretation of the Fourth Gospel,* pp. 304f.

94. *Comm.,* p. 139, n. 1.

95. *Comm.,* p. 141, see n. 2: "What is decisive in each case [in both Paul and John] is the radical way in which the nullity of human existence is understood, whether it is more or less limited to the idea of transitoriness and death, or whether it is related to the radical perversity of man's will and of his understanding of the world and himself."

96. Ibid., p. 132.

continues to shape the radical opposition that occurs in the "anthropology" of this Gospel.

In my opinion the opposition between flesh and Spirit — though in this connection it is not elaborated: see below! — has to be understood against a very different background. However sharp it may be, in the Fourth Gospel it is clearly not determined by an original dualism. The Fourth Gospel is, rather, sustained from the very beginning by the idea of the creation of all things by the Word. The Word did not come to a world that was foreign to him but to one that he had made, granted that it did not know him, and to his own, granted that his own did not receive him (1:9ff.). The opposition between flesh and Spirit primarily relates therefore to the creatureliness and dependence of humanity in relation to God as Spirit, Source, and Ruler of all of life. In that connection "flesh" does not denote what is "lower" in humankind but the whole human person, physical as well as spiritual. Accordingly, what is opposed to humankind in its "authentic existence" and threatens us as our "fate" is not our existence as flesh but the radical disturbance that has arisen in that existence as a result of the self-direction that has brought us into a position of estrangement from God, of guilt and powerlessness, of transience, uncertainty, and meaninglessness. Hence when, as here, the "Spirit" is contrasted with this powerlessness of the flesh to enter the kingdom of God and to inherit the true life, "Spirit" does not denote the great ontological anti-flesh principle, but God himself as the source of life (cf. 1:13) and above all in his restorative and life-renewing power as the only possibility left to humans to save them from lostness and alienation from God and to give them eternal life.

The opposition between "flesh and Spirit" thus understood also shows, however, that the dialogue about the necessity of rebirth must not be understood as an "anthropological insertion" into the christocentric construction of the Gospel followed up to this point, made in order to determine, from within this preunderstanding of what is human, the nature of the salvation that people need in order to enter the kingdom of God. All that is said in the dialogue before vs. 11 is that as flesh, and from within the "fleshly" orientation and perspective concerning Jesus ("we know"), no person can see or enter the kingdom of God. The alternatives "flesh" and "Spirit" are not "anthropological" in the sense of humankind as it is and as it should become in order to rise from the inferiority or nothingness of one existence (flesh) to a higher or "authentic" existence (Spirit). The alternatives rather concern humankind in its (fleshly) powerlessness over against the sovereignty and omnipotence of God (the Spirit), who alone can transform humankind, that is, grant us the needed rebirth from above.[97] It is in that sense that vss. 1-10 constitute the introduction to what follows, an introduction that is significant not only because it so powerfully

97. See also de Jonge, *Jesus: Stranger from Heaven*, p. 40, where against Bultmann's thesis that "the coming of the Revealer is explained by the necessity of rebirth" de Jonge asserts that "the necessity of 'birth from above' rather follows from the 'coming from above' of the Revealer."

and rigorously poses the necessity of such a birth from above but because in precisely those terms it leads up to him who "is from above" and "comes from above" (cf. vss. 13, 31; 8:23) and who therefore can only be known and received by those who are "born from above."

9, 10   After Jesus' elucidation of his original pronouncement, Nicodemus still does not fathom the possibility of the things Jesus has spoken of, though he now no longer, as in vs. 2, attempts to demonstrate their absurdity. With "How can this be?"[98] he is primarily responding to what Jesus has said concerning the working of the Spirit, but his skepticism concerning the "birth from above" continues to be present as an undertone. Jesus' reply, accordingly, does not limit itself to an explanation of the words he uttered last but places all he has said in the grand context of his coming and work.

Jesus does find fault with Nicodemus, and more emphatically than he did in vs. 7: "Are you the teacher of Israel, and yet you do not understand this?" The emphatic "*the* teacher of Israel" means something like "the man who has to teach Israel the knowledge of God."[99] In Jesus' coming and work is manifest the breakthrough toward the absolutely new, which requires a new approach, one that can be received only "from above." But this is not to say that the background (the "preunderstanding") for that approach was lacking in Israel, the people of God's revelation, or that the knowledge of it could not reasonably be expected from Israel's teachers. The prophets of Israel repeatedly spoke of a fundamental inner change and of the promise of the Spirit to that end (Ezk. 11:19ff.; 36:26f.; Is. 44:3; 59:21; Jr. 31:31ff.; Ps. 51:10). As far as the hermeneutical key to or horizon of Jesus' words is concerned, he did not speak from within a thought world or "anthropology" foreign to Nicodemus or Israel. In that respect, too, Jesus came to his own (1:11).

But Jesus does not stop to discuss that background. For, as indicated earlier, all his words about the necessity of rebirth are only intended, from within the glory of God manifest in Christ, to cut off all "fleshly" knowledge of Jesus ("we know," vs. 2). Hence the entire dialogue with Nicodemus now culminates in the new "we know" (of heavenly things) — though without his further participation.[100]

---

98. For "How (can this be)?" see also 6:42; 8:33; 12:34.

99. The article before διδάσκαλος does not mean that Nicodemus is the teacher in Israel *par excellence* but has representative meaning (contra BDF §273.1).

100. See also the insightful characterization of ch. 3 in de Jonge's essay on "Nicodemus and Jesus," in his *Jesus: Stranger from Heaven,* pp. 29-47, esp. pp. 38ff.: John 3 "intends to give a deepening and correction of Nicodemus's Christology in vs 2," in which "vss 3-10 are no more than an intermezzo, though a very appropriate and necessary one." "We relegate the 'birth from above' theme to a secondary place within the whole discourse in chapter 3 and put the christological discussion in the centre."

3:11-21

The Descent of the Son of Man

Beginning with vs. 11 the "dialogue" changes into a monologue. Nicodemus, though he is addressed one more time, does not reply again. Jesus does still address an audience (vss. 11b, 12), still using the second person plural (as in vs. 7b). In vs. 13 the entire discourse seems to change in character. In keeping with the manner in which in vss. 13f. (as he does consistently elsewhere) Jesus speaks of the Son of man in the third person, in the succeeding verses of the pericope only the third person is used. Still, vss. 11-13 are still influenced by the encounter with Nicodemus, not only in the form of address ("you" singular, "you" plural) but also in the form of the pronouncements themselves.

Thus in vs. **11** it is said in the same emphatic tone as in vss. 3 and 5: "Truly, truly, I say to you [singular], we speak of what we know, and give witness to what we have seen. But you [plural] do not receive our testimony." This "we know" clearly echoes the "we know" of Nicodemus in vs. 2. In a sense one can say that the confrontation only really begins here: the reference is no longer (negatively) to the inadequacy of Nicodemus's knowledge but (positively) to another knowledge on the basis of which Jesus speaks. This discourse is further described as "bearing witness" on the basis of "what we have seen" and, therefore, as eyewitness testimony has judicially valid, faith-claiming force. Intended above all is the Son's nonmediated knowledge of the Father (cf. 1:18), which in vss. 31-36 is defined as knowledge on the part of him who "comes from above" and who "bears witness to what he has seen and heard" (vss. 31, 32f.; cf. 7:28f.). Elsewhere, too, Jesus bases his knowledge of God on what he has "seen" and "heard" (e.g., 5:19, 20, 30; 8:26, 28, 40, 50; 12:50), and that in contrast with those who have never heard his voice or seen him (5:37; cf. 6:46).

To be sure, 3:11, in distinction from 3:31 and other passages, speaks of "we," a fact that has given rise to divergent interpretations. Some think that Jesus here identifies himself with the prophets, but then one has to take "what we have seen" as referring to visions, which certainly does not fit Jesus (see above). Others think the reference is to Jesus and John, a view that in my opinion is no less improbable (in view of "have seen"). Nowadays many interpreters understand the "we" as the "we" of the church (the so-called *pluralis ecclesiasticus*).[101] But such a change of subject from Jesus to the church is hard to accept because vs. 11b is introduced with the emphatic "*I* say to you" and because in vs. 12 Jesus again speaks of himself in the first person.

---

101. So, e.g., H. Hegermann: "Seldom is it so clear as it is here that the Evangelist quite consciously formulated his own witness and that of the church out of the mouth of Jesus" ("Er kam in sein Eigentum," in *Der Ruf Jesu und die Antwort der Gemeinde* [Festschrift for J. Jeremias], 1970, p. 120).

"Bear witness," in the Johannine (forensic) sense, is used, apart from Jesus himself, especially of his disciples as those "who were with him from the beginning," who on that basis bore witness concerning him (cf. 15:27; 19:35; 21:24), and of whom it can therefore be said — though in another sense than of Jesus himself (cf. 1:18; 6:46; see, however, also 14:7, 9) — that they bear witness to what they have seen and heard (cf. 1 Jn. 1:1ff.; Jn. 1:14). Accordingly, in vs. 11b the plural presumably relates not only to Jesus but also to his disciples as those whom he brought into his mission from above from the beginning (cf. 6:69).

It is "this unique character of eyewitness and this superior knowledge" that "come to expression in the 'we' forms in vs. 11"[102] and in which the fundamental difference from the "we know" of Nicodemus consists. At the same time, we have here the reason that Nicodemus and those who are represented by him ("we") require a "birth from above" if they are to understand what is happening in Jesus' coming. As long, therefore, as Nicodemus persists in his incomprehension with respect to Jesus' coming, the statement "but you do not receive our testimony" (cf. vss. 31f.), which is true of the "natural" person in general, applies to him. In that respect those who speak (as charitably) as Nicodemus are no different from other people. They acknowledge Jesus as a man of God endowed with special gifts, but they do not acknowledge him in his unique significance as the Son of God sent into the world, or, therefore, the secret of the Christian witness that proceeds from him.

Verse **12** confirms this with an argument *a minori ad maius*. The "earthly things" apparently are the matters that have been discussed in the preceding dialogue and not believed by Nicodemus. To be sure, the subject matter then also concerned being born "from above," etc., but in that light it was restricted to humanity and the earth, things that one would assume a teacher in Israel could understand and believe. If they could not believe these earthly things made known to them by Jesus, then how would they believe heavenly things? Still, the question of the "how" of the earthly things cannot be resolved without faith and insight into the heavenly things of which Jesus is about to speak. For in light of the heavenly things it will become clear that being born from above, from "water and Spirit," is not an "anonymous" miracle from above but something that occurs only through faith in him who came from above or, as vs. 13 has it, "descended from heaven."

Verse **13** is the pivotal text for the entire context, but it is very hard to exegete. Echoing "the heavenly things" of vs. 12, it mentions "heaven" twice, both times in connection with (the ascent and descent of) the Son of man, the one whom God was to endow with all power as the Christ (see the comments

---

102. So E. Ruckstuhl, in *Jesus und der Menschensohn* (Festschrift for Anton Vögtle), 1975, pp. 314-41, here p. 319, though he does not delve any further into the problem of the "we."

on 1:51). But why does Jesus suddenly refer to this ascent and descent? Is it because the Son of man has at his disposal knowledge of the "heavenly things" and has brought it with him as the one who descended from heaven? But then how is the prior clause ("No one has ascended into heaven") to be understood? Knowledge concerning heavenly things cannot be based on the fact that the Son of man (first) ascended to heaven, but only on the fact that as the one sent by the Father, the incarnate Word, he came *from* heaven. In other words, his descent precedes his ascent and not vice versa.

Those who think the reference here is to knowledge of the heavenly things (the majority of interpreters) are therefore compelled either to construe "ascend" in the first clause in a wider sense ("no one has ever been in heaven" or the like) or to assume an elliptical construction here ("no one ascended to heaven — and has seen heavenly things there — only the Son of man who descended from heaven has seen them"). This last view is defended at length by E. Ruckstuhl, who assumes that the first clause in vs. 13 refers not to the Son of man but to "not any one, whoever that may be." The language is said to be that of wisdom, with special reference to Pr. 30:4, which also mentions ascent and descent. The idea is that no one has ever been able to ascend on high to bring down the hidden Wisdom. Only one was there — Wisdom itself, now incarnate in Jesus.[103] This entire view is implausible, however, not only because of the tortuous sentence construction one has to assume, but also because it subsumes everything under the category of wisdom (incarnate) simply on the basis of similarity of language with Pr. 30:4. However, not Wisdom (which is nowhere mentioned) but the Son of man is here the dominant figure (cf. vs. 14); his descent from heaven itself constitutes the core of "the heavenly things."

In my opinion the issue is not who brought knowledge of the heavenly things to earth; the reference is to the ascent and descent itself as the divine work of redemption to be accomplished by the Son of man.[104] Ascent to heaven is not acquisition of knowledge from heaven (cf. Dt. 30:12; Pr. 30:4, etc.). It should rather be understood in the same sense as "the ascent of the Son of man" in 6:62, namely as participation in the divine glory (cf. 20:17; 17:5), what in 3:14 is called the "lifting up" of the Son of man, which entails salvation for those who believe in him. All these contexts (cf. also 8:28; 12:32) refer to the Son of man — occasionally alternating with the Son of God (cf. vss. 16f.) — because in this Gospel (as in the Synoptics) that is the name that denotes the

103. Ibid., p. 327.
104. Bultmann, *Comm.*, pp. 150f., n. 2, cites Odeberg, according to whom "v. 13 is not intended as an answer to the question: 'Who can bring knowledge from the heavenly world?' but: 'Who can enter the heavenly world?' "

transcendent character of Jesus' messianic identity (and the kingdom of God represented by him; see the comments above on 1:51).

The staggering truth of what is said in vss. 13-16, however, is that there simply cannot be any talk of such a heavenly position of power ("no one") unless — as is true of the Son of man — a descent from heaven has preceded the ascent to heaven. In other words, the mystery of God's revelation in Christ consists in the incarnation of the Word as the gift from God of his only begotten Son, which is basic to the coming of the kingdom and the exercise of power by the Son of man. This is further explicated in vs. 14, which is simply joined with what precedes by the conjunction "and."

Even given this as the explanation (the only possible one, I believe) of the order (no ascent except by way of descent), the first clause remains somewhat problematic. One might get the impression that the ascent in question has already been accomplished ("has ascended"). This is sometimes explained by saying that the Evangelist is speaking from a postascension standpoint, one that is no longer related to the situation of the encounter with Nicodemus. But vs. 14, where the exaltation of the Son of man is presented as a future event, argues against this, as does the fact that Jesus speaks about the heavenly things not as one who ascended but as the descended one (vs. 11). For that reason one has to take the perfect in the first clause of vs. 13 not in the historic sense, as referring to a completed action, but in the gnomic sense of a general pronouncement;[105] or — and this seems no less probable — as a reflection of Dn. 7:13f., where we read of such an ascent and exaltation in a prophetic apocalyptic sense (cf. "where he was before," 6:62).[106]

Verses **14** and **15** speak with increasing clarity about the way this descent and ascent of the Son of man, as well as the salvation represented in those events, is effected. Vs. 14 does so by comparing the raising up of the Son of man with that of the serpent in the wilderness. The reference is to the story in Nu. 21:8f., where Moses raised a serpent up on a pole as a visible sign of salvation for all who thought they were about to die. Jesus speaks of the exaltation of the Son of man, so "lifted up" acquires a double meaning here (as also in 8:28; 12:32, 34): the exaltation of the Son of man (= his glorification) is effected by his being raised up on a cross. The comparison brings this last meaning to the fore as *tertium comparationis,* since the element of glorification cannot be applied to the serpent. In this connection the redemption-historical "necessity" ("must be") of this being "lifted up" is important, strongly reminiscent as it is of passages like Mt. 16:21; Lk. 9:22 in which the humiliation of the Son of man is described as the way of his exaltation and is related to

---

105. Cf. Bultmann, *Comm.,* p. 151, n. 2, citing BDF §344.

106. Namely as of one, as a Son of man who "came on the clouds of heaven" and "set himself before the Ancient of days." See the comments above on 1:51.

God's counsel of salvation. Still — and this is typical for the Fourth Gospel — the crucifixion is not presented as Jesus' humiliation but as the exaltation of the Son of man. The reason, obviously, is that Jesus' suffering and death were the way in which he would return to God and be glorified by him and that in that way he would grant eternal life to those who believed in him (vs. 15). This last point again ties in clearly with Numbers 21: Just as gazing at the serpent was the God-given means of life, a sign both of God's will to save and of his power over death, so Jesus as the Son of man in his suffering and death on the cross also embodies God's will to save and power over death. But it "had to" happen in the way of the descent from heaven, of the in*carn*ation of the Word, of his suffering and dying on the cross. Later, therefore, the living bread that came down from heaven and that "the Son of man will give" (6:27) will also be called his "flesh" that he gives for the life of the world, and only those who "eat the flesh of the Son of man and drink his blood" will have life in themselves (6:51, 53).

But all this is not further explicated, at least not in vss. 14 and 15. Here the reference is to "whoever believes in him."[107] The object of this faith is the Son of man as the crucified one as well as the crucified Son of man. The Son of man "must" go this way, which is inconceivable to the flesh. But he takes it as one destined by God to the highest glory, as one who enters death in order thus, like the serpent lifted up by Moses, to be the great sign that in him God has the will and the capacity to save from destruction everyone who believes. Faith receives its character from the one as well as from the other truth. It is faith in the powerful Messiah-King promised by God, the Son of man, but in him as the crucified one; it is faith in the power of him who is powerless in the flesh and in the eyes of the flesh. Therein, also, lies the difference from "belief in his name" (2:23), which rests exclusively on the manifestation of Jesus' power and which by itself need be no more than a conclusion of which the "flesh" is capable. But to be able to see and to believe in the heaven-descended, cross-exalted Son of man — that takes a different set of eyes, and for that one must be born from above.

Verse **16** reduces all this to its deepest underlying cause and to its ultimate simplicity with an explanatory statement: "For God so loved the world. . . ." What Moses did at God's instruction in the wilderness, lift up the serpent, was great and marvelous. But nowhere more clearly than here do we see the difference (described also in 1:17) between what God gave through Moses and the grace and truth that came through Jesus Christ (cf. 6:32).

---

107. The reading of certain important manuscripts is ἐν αὐτῷ. Others (e.g., p⁶⁶) have ἐπ' αὐτῷ; still others εἰς αὐτόν. This last reading looks like assimilation to vs. 16. ἐν αὐτῷ appears to be the most original. Several interpreters take it with ἐχῇ, partly on account of the distinction from εἰς in vs. 16. Still, the emphasis probably lies on the object of faith and in this connection there need not be a difference between ἐν and εἰς.

All the emphasis here lies on the "so": "in this manner," "in this measure." This word refers back to the "how" of the lifting up of the Son of man, but it also directs the reader's attention to the measure of God's love that underlies that lifting up. All the terminology is attuned to the latter. Here we read not of the Son of man but of God's only-begotten Son (cf. 1:18), so designated here as the highest gift God could give (cf. Ro. 8:32: "who did not spare his own Son"; Gn. 22:16). And we read "gave" in the sense of what is elsewhere called "giving up," "surrendering" (e.g., Ro. 4:25; 8:32; Mk. 9:31), namely to death on the cross.[108] All this shows how in the Fourth Gospel, as elsewhere in the New Testament, the God-given *sacrifice* of Christ is of central significance. This is surely the case also because in that surrender the glory of God manifested itself so clearly "in the flesh" of the man Jesus, but above all because it brought to its highest manifestation the measure of God's love for the world (cf. 13:1).

There is a close connection here with the utterance of John the Baptist in 1:29 (35): "Behold, the Lamb of God, who takes away the sin of the world!" That utterance includes no reflection on the death of Christ,[109] and 3:16 does not mention in so many words the sin of the world as that which makes necessary God's surrender of his Son. The common component in the two pronouncements is that it is God who makes the all-embracing sacrifice for the world. There is no further analysis of why God loves thus. The text's exclusive concern is the fact and the magnitude of God's love. It is love that not only manifests itself in God's power over death, the death into which the world (like Israel in the wilderness) would sink; in the death of Christ it also identifies with the world in its lostness and thus imparts the deepest meaning to the great statement in the prologue, "and the Word became flesh."

Again, as in vs. 15, we read: ". . . that whoever believes in him (the Son) . . . ," and again the essence of believing in his name becomes clear. The starting point of faith does not lie in the fact that the world returned to God in the ascent of the Son of man and so found its lost self, any more than the starting point of faith in the incarnation lies in the fact that in the man Jesus God again put the world on the track of true humanity ("not perish," "have eternal life"). The starting point is that God in his eternal love returned to the world as to his own, that he loved it in the surrender of his only-begotten Son (cf. 3:35), and that the Father loves the Son because he gave his own life (cf. 10:15) in a love that persisted to the end (cf. 13:1ff.). It is faith in a path that,

---

108. In other places in this Gospel "send" is used. It is only here that the sending is described as a giving. In place of the Son of man (vss. 13f.) we now read "the Son" because of the motif of surrender: "The Son" implies a (preexistent) personal relationship, while "the Son of man" implies a salvation-historical function. For a shift from "Son of God"/"Son" to "Son of man" see 5:25-27.

109. See the comments on 1:29.

before it ascended to the glory of heaven, first descended to the depth of the earth, that is not itself from below but from above as the sign of true sonship and of those who are born of God (cf. 1:12f.).

17-18 If thus, as the content of the heavenly things, vss. 13-16 refer above all to the great salvation-historical ("eschatological") events effected in the mission of Jesus as the Son of God, the consequence for humanity and the world is an all-determining final decision. Already vss. 15 and 16 mentioned "eternal life" twice as the presently inaugurated gift for one who believes (and thus "has" eternal life).[110] Vss. 17ff. refer to the decisive "critical" character of the mission of the Son of God. In close connection with vs. 16, but now *per negationem,* the divine will to save that is manifest in this mission is again confirmed, and any notion that the Father sent the Son into the world to judge the world is banished. The idea in itself is not foreign: throughout prophecy the coming of the kingdom of God is accompanied by the judgment of God over his enemies (cf. also Mt. 3:7f. par.), and judgment is part of the fullness of the divine powers of the Son of man (cf. 5:22, 27; Mt. 25:31ff.). But in the present passage everything is viewed from the perspective of the mission of the Son and the descent of the Son of man *from heaven*. And that mission and descent have no other purpose, as the Evangelist keeps saying (cf. 12:47; 8:15), than to open a way, in him, for faith and for the world's salvation.

This is not (vs. 18) to delay the decision; on the contrary, it is to bring it closer. For he who descended is God's only-begotten Son, and God has put "all things into his hand" (vs. 35). For that reason the Son has the power even now to release people from their guilt ("authority on earth to forgive sins," Mt. 9:6), and one who believes in him does not come under judgment. In the fellowship of faith with him judgment is suspended. And conversely, one who does not believe in him is already under judgment. The judgment to come in the confrontation with the coming judge of the world has become for that person an issue of great present relevance. The perfect tense ("are condemned") refers to the situation in which that person has placed himself or herself, not on account of the verdict already pronounced by the Son, but "because he (or she) has not believed in the name of the only Son of God." That person has not acknowledged the saving love of God manifest in his Son; and that does not only mean not to know God's love but to live under the doom of its absence, the *privatio*

---

110. Surely also in close association with the "seeing" and "entering" of the kingdom of God mentioned in vss. 3 and 5. "Eternal life" and "the kingdom of God" are also used synonymously in the Synoptics (cf. Mk. 10:17; Mt. 7:14; 18:8f.; Lk. 10:25). In John (except in 3:3, 5) the reference is consistently to "eternal life" or "life" (3:36; 5:24, etc.). Bultmann distinguishes the two: "However a distinction is made, inasmuch as ζωή, when characterised as αἰώνιος, always refers to the life as a *condition* of man, while ζωή by itself may also refer to the *power* which creates life. . . . Thus ζωή αἰώνιος is never predicated of God or the Revealer, whose ζωή is the power which creates life (1.4; 5.26; 11.25; 14.6)" (*Comm.*, p. 152, n. 2).

actuosa. Still for that person, too, the truth is that the coming of the Son is not aimed at condemnation. That person still has to deal, not with the judge of the world in his heavenly glory, but with the Son who has descended into the world and who continues to woo people with the love of God, yet even now with no other purpose than to save the world, even those in the world who do not believe in him (cf. 5:34).

A striking feature of this passage, finally, is the degree to which everything is concentrated on the importance of believing. Whereas in vss. 1-8 the birth from above is posed above all else as the indispensable condition for entry into the kingdom of God, in vs. 12 and especially in vss. 15ff. the crucial importance of believing comes increasingly to the fore. It is clear that the one cannot do without the other: the birth from above, however much it is a miracle of the Spirit, is not effected without the call to faith and the response of faith. Nor is faith simply a stage in the salvation-order transformation of a person; it rather describes the totality of transformation as the work of the Spirit. And in this connection faith is always the way in which and the means by which the new life comes into being. It is for this reason that all the emphasis falls on believing.

On the other hand, it is no less true that the new birth does not rest on an antecedent human decision. Faith is not the response of the higher or the better self to the message of the gospel. Nor is it an enlivening in the prisonhouse of the flesh by a voice in which a person recognizes himself in his divine origin, his deepest "disposition," his "authentic existence," or the like, for as we read in 5:25: "The hour is coming, *and now is,* when *the dead* will hear the voice of the Son of God, and those who hear will live" (cf. vs. 24). In other words, faith belongs to the ministry and miracle of the Spirit. It is not a predisposition that is already present but a decision that is realized in the address of the Word and that is subject to the moral power that proceeds from that Word. There can be a "hearing" and a "seeing" only when the Word is understood and followed in accordance with its meaning (cf. 5:25; 6:26).

In this connection much has been, and is being, written about the Johannine idea of predestination,[111] and the reference to texts like 6:37, 39, 44; 10:29; 17:2ff. is self-evident. And, in contrast, when it comes to faith or the call to faith the Evangelist obviously does not think of a preestablished divine decision,

---

111. H. Hegermann speaks of a conjunction made by the Evangelist of "two almost disparate messages," "a message of a new creation and one of predestination," in vss. 6-8 as well as in vss. 19-21. In this connection the latter message is said to have been made subject to the former: "The pronouncements oriented to predestination stand in the service of this concept of salvation," namely that of an "inconceivable divine miracle of a new creation" ("Er kam in sein Eigentum," in *Der Ruf und die Antwort der Gemeinde,* 1970, pp. 119-21). But if one wishes to speak of the idea of predestination, is that not precisely in the idea of the new creation as a miraculous work of God unattainable for the flesh? For this entire complex of problems see the extensive work of R. Bergmeier, *Glaube als Gabe nach Johannes,* 1980.

for his entire Gospel is a continuing struggle on behalf of faith and a continual indictment of the culpable and mysterious character of unbelief. Especially in the dialogue with Nicodemus, where the necessity of birth from above is so clearly asserted, not believing and not accepting (vss. 12, 13, 18ff.) are not attributed to the flesh, and the situation of Nicodemus himself is viewed not as closed but as clearly kept open.[112] The Spirit is like the wind, blowing where it wills. Hence one must inevitably conclude that every deterministic schematism is as alien to the gospel as is any dogma of inviolable human freedom. Faith will always bear on its face the sign of the grace of being a child of God, just as unbelief bears the sign of disobedience to the summons of the gospel (cf. vs. 36; see also the comments on 1:12f.).

Finally, in vss. 19-21, the background and significance of the faith and unbelief mentioned in vs. 18 are further elucidated. The beginning of vs. **19**, "and this is the judgment" (*krisis* in vs. 19, as in vs. 18, means "judgment" and not just "separation") means something like: And, this is the reason — despite the contrary intention of God — the coming of the Son has turned into a judgment for unbelievers: "People" have not been able to bear the light of his coming, which arose over their darkness, and therefore have turned away from him.[113] "People" refers to the world as a whole. The passage is strongly reminiscent of 1:4f., 9-11. But now this not knowing and nonacceptance are explained: people have loved darkness more[114] than the light. The reason is that "their deeds were evil." In the nature of the case, the author's concern is not just with evil deeds but with people. But here and in vss. 20f. the emphasis, in connection with the image of the light, is on the deeds. When the light appears, people become manifest first of all in their *deeds*.

The fact that evildoers are averse to the light is repeated, as a kind of rule of experience, in vs. **20**: "Everyone who occupies himself/herself in doing[115] worthless/reprehensible things hates the light." That person does not come to the light so that his or her work will not be manifest in its true nature, unmasked as evil and worthless.[116]

Verse **21**, by contrast, speaks of the one who "does what is true," an expression that, like others in this context, has a strong Semitic flavor.[117] It is

112. See also the comments on 7:50ff.
113. Taken strictly the content of the ὅτι clause falls into two parts, which of course have to be taken as a unity. The judgment did not consist in the coming of the light as such.
114. μᾶλλον refers not to a relative choice but to an absolute choice: *potius*, not *magis*.
115. πράσσων, present participle.
116. ἐλέγχειν, not φανεροῦσθαι, which appears in vs. 21. The idea is to bring to light the truth, and in vs. 19, of course, *in malam partem*. It can also have a forensic meaning. It doubtlessly has the more general sense here of: "prove in error, expose, find culpable." For the whole idea, cf. Jb. 24:13-17.
117. See Schnackenburg, *Comm.*, I, p. 407, who refers regularly to the resemblance with Qumran documents.

literally "act in such a way that truth comes into being,"[118] "truth" being that which is trustworthy, genuine, and nondeceptive. One who so acts "comes toward the light," and here we have the question whether this statement refers to experience in general or specifically to the coming of the Son of God as light. The conclusion of the sentence might suggest the latter, though the idea expressed can have a broader meaning. The idea is not that he who does what is true comes to the light to bring his deeds as much as possible into public view — to "show them off" as it were — but to make them cognizable as having been done "in God" (that is, in communion with him and in keeping with his will) and thus to identify himself in his deepest intentions. The fact that in the conflict between truth and error, uprightness and deception, reality and illusion one person shuns the light and another is attracted to the light is not just a matter of psychology or of a good or a bad conscience. At its root it is a matter of "being" of God or not of God, that is, of the devil (8:44; 1 Jn. 2:21). For that reason one hates the light not only out of fear that he will be unmasked by it but because the darkness is his or her natural element; and the other comes to the light out of knowledge that he or she is profoundly understood there.

One may still ask whether in this way everything — faith and unbelief, being saved or being lost — is not reduced merely to the "moral issue" of doing evil or doing good deeds. But after all that has been said about the descent of the Son of man and the birth from above as a birth of the Spirit, that can hardly be the conclusion or intent. The repeated and emphatic mention of "deeds" is due not to the idea that in the end it is works and not faith that is decisive for entry into the kingdom of God; it is based rather on the idea (deeply rooted in the Old Testament and the religion based on it) that the truth is practical, that something must be done, and that what most deeply motivates a person becomes cognizable in his or her deeds (cf. Mt. 7:16ff.). Accordingly, that is what the light of Christ brings into the open either as evil and worthless or as true and done "in God" and hence as coming from him. The antithesis is posed in such absolute terms because the light in view here is the light of the Word, which was in the beginning with God and was God, and because "in him was life, and the life was the light of humanity" (1:4). What light and darkness, life and nonlife, "evil and worthless" and "doing the truth" are, therefore, is determined by whether or not one knows and accepts the light (cf. 1:4, 5, 9ff.). "Because their deeds were evil" extends, therefore, beyond a merely moral judgment. It concerns the nature of the darkness of life outside God and of the evil works done outside of God.

All this does not mean, meanwhile, that the light that came with the sending of God's Son into the world has no other purpose than to make visible this difference between the two kinds of people. It undeniably has this effect. Still, it is the *descent* of the Son of man and the *incarnation* of the Word that should banish

---

118. See also Schlatter, *Comm.*, p. 101.

from our minds any notion that this effect is what is primarily at stake. The light that comes into the world and penetrates it, however true it is that it absolutely unmasks the darkness and everything that is done outside of God, has no other aim than to attract the world to the light of God's love, in order that everyone who believes in the Son should not perish in darkness (cf. 8:12).

3:22-30
John the Baptist's Final Testimony

Verses 22 and 23 depict the situation of the continuing activity of Jesus and John the Baptist. "After this" in vs. **22** is very general but apparently means "after Jesus' stay in Jerusalem as described in the preceding section." There is no mention of a place where Jesus and his disciples stayed in "the land of Judea."

As to Jesus' activity we are told only that he "baptized," and this we are told clearly in preparation for what follows (cf. vs. 26). This striking statement — nowhere else in the tradition are we told of Jesus baptizing — is restricted in 4:2 to Jesus' disciples. The idea that here the Evangelist uses another tradition (according to which Jesus himself baptized) so as to contrast Jesus' baptism, as a baptism with the Holy Spirit, with John's baptism[119] is fraught with difficulties. Not only does the correction in 4:2 then have to be from a later author (or editor) who directly opposed the Evangelist's intent (see the comments below on 4:2), but the whole idea that in the dialogue between John and his disciples the issue was one of concern over *this kind* of superiority of Jesus' baptism over that of John can in no way be derived from the text. All the emphasis, in this view, would then lie on vs. 34, where alone the Spirit is mentioned. But vs. 34 belongs to another context (see below), and what occasioned John to speak of Jesus as he does in vss. 27ff. was his disciples' complaint that "all" were going to Jesus to be baptized (vs. 26). There is no question that "all" received the baptism of the Spirit, and according to the Evangelist's own estimate (cf. 7:39) that was simply not yet a possibility.

Hence the activity of Jesus described in 3:22 can, in my opinion, only be interpreted to mean that, just as John for a time continued his activity even after Jesus' appearance, so Jesus and the disciples who followed him did not immediately abandon the pattern of John's preaching of an approaching kingdom and the baptism of repentance that went with it. This is apparent, with regard to Jesus' preaching, from Mt. 4:17; 3:2, where Jesus' message ("Repent, for the kingdom of God is at hand") is identical to that of John. That this call

---

119. So, at length, Dodd, *Interpretation of the Fourth Gospel,* pp. 309ff., further developed in his *Historical Tradition in the Fourth Gospel,* 1965, pp. 285ff.

to repentance with a view to entry into the kingdom was accompanied also in Jesus' ministry by the "baptism of repentance" is not hard to understand (cf. 3:5), even if it should eventually become evident that Jesus' ministry and baptism embraced far more than that of John. Still, this link with John's baptism means that the turning point in the history of salvation represented by Jesus, a turning point to which John had borne witness, precisely in relation to the baptisms of both, did not manifest itself in Jesus' public ministry as a sharply demarcated break but rather as an increasingly more manifest fulfillment of the preparatory work of the Baptist.

But from the outset it could escape no one that Jesus was very different from John and that in his preaching and baptism he had much more to offer than his predecessor. The difference manifested itself not only in their outer appearance and public conduct (cf. Mt. 11:18ff.) but above all in the authority with which, both in words and miraculous deeds, Jesus proclaimed the richly salvific significance of the kingdom that was at hand — which was undoubtedly why so many more people came to him than to John (vs. 26; cf. 4:1). In this connection perhaps some light is cast on the remarkable statement in 4:2 that not Jesus himself but his disciples baptized: by not baptizing Jesus immediately distinguished himself from John, even while he sought to maintain continuity with his forerunner through his disciples' baptizing. But for them as well their activity as disciples of Jesus would in time not be linked with the forerunner's baptism but would rather become *their* baptism — mandated to them by Jesus on the basis of his universal authority — in the name of the Father, the Son, and Holy Spirit (Mt. 28:16-20).

23 The (new) place where John's baptized ("Aenon near Salim") cannot be identified with certainty, though it is clear from vs. 26 that it was on the west side of the Jordan. According to an ancient Greek tradition the Salim referred to here was in the northern part of the Jordan valley, in the watery plain of Beth Shean (Scythopolis).[120] But other locations to the south have been considered.[121] Some believe the reference is symbolic: Aenon (= "spring") near Salim ("salvation"), with Aenon understood as the place where Jesus lived. But though the Evangelist sometimes refers to the symbolic meaning of the name of an actual place (cf. 9:7), there is no such allusion here, nor is the name fictitious, since such symbolism would have been attached to the place where Jesus baptized. And the symbolic interpretation that has been suggested is too far-fetched for us to attribute it to the Evangelist.

24 Of more importance to us is the parenthetical statement that John had not yet been put in prison. The Evangelist clearly alludes here to the violent ending — assumed to be familiar to the original readers — of John's activity, without, however, relating the story of how it occurred (which we find in the

---

120. See G. Dalman, *Orte und Wege Jesus,* 1924[3], p. 250.
121. See, e.g., Brown, *Comm.* I, p. 151.

Synoptics). We find a reference to the brevity of John's ministry only in 5:35. The seemingly superfluous insertion here in 3:24 is linked perhaps with the Synoptic tradition according to which Jesus' ministry in Galilee occurred after the arrest of John (Mk. 1:14; Mt. 4:12), the Evangelist explicitly indicating here that John and Jesus acted and worked side by side in Israel for a time. Although the Synoptics, especially Luke (cf. 4:14), suggest that, immediately after his baptism by John and the temptation in the wilderness, Jesus returned to Galilee and began his public ministry there, the chronological order of events remains murky. Must we conclude from Luke that John, after he baptized Jesus, was immediately imprisoned by Herod? In Matthew (4:12) Jesus' going to Galilee is immediately described as a "withdrawal," which suggests that he retreated from the center of Jewish life for reasons of security (cf. Jn. 4:1, 44). That assumes that he had become known among the people.

So, although the Synoptics — Matthew and Luke following Mark in this — place the beginning of Jesus' activity in Galilee, the portrayal in Jn. 3:22ff. is not for that reason less trustworthy. It rather provides more historical perspective on the beginning of Jesus' ministry and hence more insight into his "withdrawal" to Galilee: his spectacular conduct in Jerusalem and Judea led to this development.[122]

The description of John's "final" testimony concerning Jesus at this point in the Fourth Gospel also finds a ready explanation in this development. It clearly assumes that Jesus has become known and popular among the people and can therefore hardly be viewed, as some authors wish,[123] as an alternative to John's testimony, reported earlier. It may be true that the Evangelist had no concern to "correct" the historical situation (as compared with that of Synoptics?). His interest clearly lies in the material thrust of the story. But this does not remove the fact that the latter in its very "intentionality" represents a tradition that lifts the edge of the curtain on a period in the life of Jesus into which we would otherwise have no insight at all.

25 John's testimony was occasioned by a dispute of John's disciples[124] with a certain Jew[125] about "purification." It is not clear precisely what started

122. See also the treatment of this passage in Dodd, *Historical Tradition,* pp. 291ff.

123. See the critical discussion of the views of Wellhausen and Boismard in Brown, *Comm.* I, p. 154; his own view is that "this scene has been transposed from the beginning of the Gospel to its present site and adapted (in vss. 26 and 28) to make it fit" (p. 155).

124. ἐκ τῶν μαθητῶν.

125. "Certain" (τινος) is not present in the text even though with singular "Jew" one would expect it. Some important manuscripts have the plural (with no article!), which has to be considered a change from the (strikingly indefinite) singular (rather than the reverse). Some interpreters, assuming textual corruption, have proposed that the original reading was "Jesus." But the text as we have it is not so incomprehensible that one has to resort to such a drastic correction; cf. also the comments on vs. 26. See also Dodd, *Historical Tradition,* p. 280, n. 2, though he opts for the plural.

the dispute. The purification in question presumably refers to the baptism (cf. vs. 26), although this designation for baptism is unusual. But what was the point of the dispute, who was this Jew, and what did he advocate over against John's disciples? Was John's baptism the subject of discussion — possibly in relation to Jewish practices of the day?[126] To judge by vs. 26, the baptism now administered by Jesus and his disciples was also drawn into the dispute. This naturally led to the question by whom one should be baptized, John or Jesus, and whose baptism was more effective.

26   Whatever may have been involved in this dispute for John's disciples, it prompted their need to speak to their master. And what played a no less important role was that the number of people who went to Jesus began completely to overshadow the number of those who came to John.

One is struck by the impersonal way in which John's disciples refer to Jesus: "he who was with you beyond the Jordan, the one to whom you bore witness." Apparently they had been present on the occasion or at least had heard of it. It had not, however, prompted them to join others in following Jesus. On the contrary, they witnessed with displeasure how Jesus' influence grew and that of their master declined, and now they express their feelings in a way ("all") that betrays their envy and unhappiness. It is hard to say with any certainty whether there is an allusion here to a continuing controversy between the disciples of John and the later Christian church — especially because there is a lack of clear data on that controversy. In any case, one gets a very one-sided picture here if one tries to interpret this pericope totally or primarily from the vantage point of a polemic against the "Baptist sect" of the time of the Evangelist in which John is supposedly brought in as the main witness against his own later followers.[127] Rather, this final testimony of John shows positively the extent to which he — as a model to all other witnesses of Jesus — fulfilled to the end, and in keeping with its nature, the mission mandated to him by God (cf. 1:6).

27   In his more or less aphoristic reply John reminds his disciples first of all of the principle that no one can "receive" (in the sense of "appropriate," "have") anything "except what is given[128] to him from heaven."[129] This does not mean that everything a person manages to lay claim to has come to him as

---

126. On this pericope see at length Dodd, *Historical Tradition,* pp. 279ff., esp. p. 281.

127. See, e.g., Bultmann, *Comm.,* p. 172; see also his *History of the Synoptic Tradition,* 1963, p. 165. Cf. the comments on 1:20 above and the work by W. Wink cited there.

128. It is better not to take δεδομένον ἐκ as the opposite of λαμβάνειν but as meaning "allowed [to do something]." Thus one avoids the notion rejected above, which is undoubtedly not intended here; see also Schnackenburg, *Comm.* I, p. 415.

129. Here and elsewhere "from heaven" means "from (the side of) God" (Mk. 11:34; Lk. 15:18), also indicated by "from above" (cf. 19:11), in keeping with Jewish usage (to avoid using the name of God).

a gift from God (cf. 19:11); it means rather that a person has a thing at his disposal only if and to the extent that God permits. One could take this statement in both negative and positive senses, that is, with reference to both John's "decrease" and Jesus' "increase." But that understanding does not fit very well with vs. 26. Undoubtedly the point here is that Jesus "received" more people than his forerunner in accord with God's plan.[130]

28 And that more people went to Jesus was also in keeping with John's earlier witness concerning Jesus. John does not merely acknowledge this because events force him to. He calls his disciples to witness that from the beginning he has referred to himself not as the Messiah but as the Messiah's forerunner (cf. 1:20, 23, 27).

29, 30 This relationship between John and Jesus is now elaborated with the aid of a wedding metaphor. The point of comparison is the difference between the bridegroom and "the friend of the bridegroom." The bridegroom is the principal person because "he has the bride."[131] The "friend," familiar from the Jewish life of the day, is the one who both before and during the wedding assists the bridegroom in everything having to do with the wedding. His goal is achieved and his happiness is complete[132] only, when at the feast, standing by the bridegroom,[133] he can witness the bridegroom's unconcealed joy.

It is not merely with resignation therefore that John witnesses Jesus' success among the people; it is rather a sense of full and unmixed joy that fills him when he sees that his work of preparation has reached its intended goal. All that is now left for him to do is to withdraw like the friend of the bridegroom. By way of conclusion that is now succinctly expressed: "He must increase, but I must decrease." This is the divinely ordered, salvation-historical "must" to which John refers (see the comments above on 3:14). John stands at the border of two worlds, two dispensations (cf. Mt. 11:11-13).[134] The old has run its course; the time of fulfillment has come, in which, the more radiantly the rising

---

130. One could also take the receiver (the "him" of vs. 27) to be the believer; cf. "no one can come to me unless it is granted him by the Father" (6:65). But the reference here is more directly to Jesus as receiver than to those who follow him (cf. 6:37, 44).

131. The reference of the metaphor is restricted to the role of the bridegroom and his friend (cf. Mk. 2:18f. par.). That the church is the bride of Christ (cf. Rv. 7:7; 21:2; cf. also Ho. 1:2; Jr. 2:2; Is. 41:10) does not play a distinct role in this text, and it is questionable whether it is assumed in the metaphor. It would seem that one has to keep the two images separate and not unite them into one (allegorical) complex.

132. χαρᾷ χαίρει is a Hebraism: Adding the cognate noun to the verb is meant as an intensive ("greatly").

133. ὁ ἑστηκὼς καὶ ἀκούων αὐτοῦ. . . . "His standing there is not without meaning. He stands and waits in front of the bridal chamber for the jubilant cry of the bridegroom" (Schlatter, *Comm.*, p. 108).

134. See the comments on 1:29, 34 above.

sun begins to shine, the more John's star will grow dim (his words here are often understood in the sense of the increase and decrease of the light of celestial bodies).[135]

With this last statement the witness of John to Jesus, which already in the prologue (1:6ff., 15) plays such an important role in the Fourth Gospel, is pithily concluded. In what follows there is more than one reference to him as the great witness to the truth (5:33; 10:41). But from now on the light of the lamp, in which people had occasion to rejoice for a while (5:35), will pale, and the entire focus will steadily be on the greater one, the one to whom John had witnessed so forcefully. The pericope that now follows provides, as it were, an interim epilogue that sums up that superior greatness.

3:31-36

Epilogue

Verses 31-36 are joined to what precedes without explanation or attribution. It is more or less natural to take them as a continuation of the words of John the Baptist, who would thus continue to speak of Jesus' superior greatness, though no longer in relation to himself, as in the preceding verses. The reference to the gift of the Spirit (vs. 34) is said to fit very well among the words of the Baptist (cf. 1:26, 31). For that reason there have always been scholars who accept the traditional view that vss. 31-36 belong to John's response — which began in vs. 26 — to the words of his disciples.[136]

It has been correctly noted, however, that the content of vss. 31-36 has many more points of contact with the dialogue with Nicodemus: "from above" (vs. 31; cf. vss. 3, 7), "comes from heaven" (vs. 31b; cf. vs. 13), "is of the earth/speaks of the earth" (vs. 31; cf. vss. 6, 12), "bears witness to what he has seen and heard" (vs. 32; cf. vs. 11), "(not) receive his testimony" (vss. 32f.; cf. vs. 11), "the gift of the Spirit" (vs. 34; cf. vss. 5f.), and "believe in the Son" and "have eternal life" (vs. 36; cf. vss. 15f.). This parallelism is so strong that a number of commentators even believe that we have here a displaced part of the dialogue with Nicodemus, which they would insert after vs. 21.

But as Dodd has noted, vs. 31 does not naturally follow vs. 21,[137] though it does form a good transition after vs. 30. There is more to be said, therefore,

---

135. See also BAGD, s.v., which points out that in 3:19, 21 there are five uses of φῶς and that this meaning, at least of ἐλαττοῦσθαι, occurs elsewhere as well.

136. See Barrett, *Comm.*, p. 224.

137. Dodd, *Interpretation*, p. 309.

for viewing vss. 31-36 as a sort of meditation on everything that precedes. Some consider it an epilogue written by the Evangelist himself, while others view the material as words of Jesus inserted here by the Evangelist. An obvious argument for the first is that throughout the passage Jesus is spoken of in the third person, though the same is true of vss. 13ff., for which reason those verses are sometimes viewed as a gradual transition from Jesus' words to the Evangelist's commentary. But others have pointed out that what is said there about Jesus has strong affinities with what Jesus says in the first person about himself in 12:46-48.[138]

From all this it may be inferred that what is said in ch. 3 about Jesus in the third person (vss. 13ff., 31ff.) is intended by the Evangelist to be understood *materially* as the words of Jesus, but the boundaries between Jesus' self-testimony and the Evangelist's witness to Jesus seem to be indefinite, at least in this chapter (cf. 14:26; 15:26ff.).

In that sense, then, we may view vss. 31-36 as a recapitulating epilogue subjoined by the Evangelist to the dialogues reported in vss. 1-30, but derived from what Jesus revealed concerning himself.[139] The subject of this epilogue is the surpassing significance of Jesus Christ as the one sent from God, which was fundamentally also the content both of the preceding self-definition of John in relation to Jesus and especially of the dialogue with Nicodemus, in which Jesus is described as the Son of man come down from heaven and as the only-begotten Son of God sent into the world (vss. 13ff.).

Verses **31** and **32** again put all the emphasis on this heavenly origin of Jesus: "He who comes from above is above all." "From above" alternates here with "from heaven" as a conventional reference to the world of God, to which no one can ascend (cf., e.g., Dt. 30:12). The specific meaning of this pronouncement emerges from the contrast with what is said of the one "who is of the earth" — again a reference to humankind in its natural existence as those "born of the flesh" (vss. 6b, 7; 1:13). The human person "is of the earth," that is, is characterized and shaped in his or her entire existence and possibilities by the earth[140] and "speaks of the earth." Therefore, he who comes from above is qualitatively distinct from and above all.[141] What he, as the one come down

---

138. See, e.g., Brown, *Comm.* I, pp. 147ff.

139. For this complex of problems, see also Schnackenburg, *Comm.* I, pp. 380ff., who does not regard vss. 31-36 as an epilogue to the whole chapter, however, but as "a connected and complete discourse" that should precede vss. 13-21. For the composition of ch. 3 see also D. M. Smith, *The Composition and Order of the Fourth Gospel,* 1965, pp. 125-27.

140. "The expression εἶναι ἐκ is not tautological, but brings out the two meanings of ἐκ, origin and type, with the origin determining the type (cf. v. 6)" (Schnackenburg, *Comm.* I, p. 382).

141. One can also relate "he who comes from heaven" (vs. 31b) directly to vs. 32, as some important manuscripts do by omitting "is above all" and in some cases τοῦτο in vs. 32 as well. This reading seems attractive because then the repetition "is above all" is avoided and one

from heaven, has seen and heard (vs. 32), that he bears witness to. So again we hear of the contrast of both "knowledge" and "speech" (which also dominated the beginning of the dialogue with Nicodemus: cf. vss. 2, 11) and of the testimony of and to Jesus as one who heard and saw heavenly things (see the comments on vs. 11). Of that testimony we are told that "no one receives his testimony" (cf. 1:10f.). That general judgment corresponds with what is said in vs. 31 about the one who is "of the earth." That person is so totally conditioned by the earth that he or she does not recognize the one who comes from above and does not accept his testimony, even if on the basis of earthly knowledge he or she comes to Jesus with ever so much respect. Hence the absolute "no one."

33-35   As in 1:10-12, universal rejection is immediately followed by "[but] whoever *does* receive his testimony." That this can only occur in virtue of new birth "from above," "from the Spirit," "from God" (3:3, 5; 1:13) is not mentioned again. The focus is rather on the effect of acceptance or rejection of the testimony. To receive Jesus' testimony is to "seal [confirm, validate] that God is true" (just as one who does not believe makes God a liar; cf. 1 Jn 5:9f.). That and nothing less is at stake: not just the truthfulness and trustworthiness of him who was sent but also that of the Sender. For the Father identifies himself with the one he has sent to such an extent that the words that one speaks are "the words of God." "For it is not by measure that he [the Father] gives [Jesus] the Spirit."[142] Jesus is not merely a prophet who speaks the word of God on occasion, when called on to do so. His authority to speak as God is unlimited, or as vs. 35 has it: "The Father loves the Son and has given all things into his hand."

With mounting urgency and increasing simplicity the "above all" of him who "came from above" is made personal and identified as divine, a pattern that culminates in the statement that distills the essence of it all: "The Father loves the Son," which refers back to 1:18 and recurs in the Gospel (5:20; 10:17; 15:9; 17:23ff.). As is evident from vs. 35b (and the other passages just cited), this means that the love that proceeds from God is directed toward and concentrated in the Son, who as the bearer of God's love can be called God's Son and is, in fact, God's Son. The reference is not just to the relationship between

---

arrives immediately at "the matter" itself: The one who comes from heaven bears witness to what he has seen and heard. But Johannine style is sometimes circuitous. One can hardly make a choice on the basis of the importance of the different manuscripts. However, the thought pattern is the same in both cases.

142. Other scholars believe that it is Jesus here who gives the Spirit (on the basis, e.g., of 6:63; cf., e.g., I. de la Potterie, "l'Esprit saint dans l'Évangile de Jean," *NTS* 28 [1972], pp. 448f.). But in this connection (with γάρ as introducing explanation of the preceding and vs. 35 as parallel) the above view that God is the subject (a view shared by Barrett and Bultmann) seems preferable. Many ancient textual witnesses also reflect this preference.

the Father and the Son as such but to the fact that God is manifest in his Son as the God of love.

Therefore, "the Father loves the Son" is a pronouncement about both the nature and the authority of Jesus' mission. With regard to the nature of that mission, as the Son he represents the love of God. In him and in his mission God is present in the world as the God of love. For that reason the same truth can be expressed in the words of 3:16: "God so loved the world that he gave his only-begotten Son." With regard to Jesus' authority, it is he in whom the victorious fullness of God's love makes its way and into whose hand, for the sake of that revelation, all things have been given (cf. 13:3). This reality is explicated in various ways in what is to follow in the Gospel (cf. 5:20, 26f., 36; 10:17f.; 17:2, etc.), not infrequently where the Son is described as "the Son of man" (cf. 5:27; 6:27; 8:28). It is on account of this concentration of the Father's love in the Son, the Son's authority over all things, and his being endowed with the Spirit ("not by measure") that the revelation of God in Jesus Christ is absolute, all-embracing, and all-sufficient and that "outside him salvation is not to be sought or found."

36 It is also for that reason that in believing or not believing the Son the disjunction between having and not having "eternal life" is realized. Here, in other words, the truth of vs. 18 is repeated (cf. vs. 15). Because he is the Son, believing in him means eternal life; it is the power of his word, by which the dead hear his voice and live, now and on the last day (5:28f.). "He who does not obey the Son will not see life."[143] "Disobeys"[144] serves as a description of "unbelief" because the crucial decision lies in "hearing" the word that issues from the Son of God. Because he is the Son, no one can ignore his word with impunity. Such a person is already condemned (vs. 18), or as the final clause of the pericope reads, "God's wrath remains on him (or her)." God's wrath is his judgment (cf. Ro. 2:5; Mt. 3:7). "Remains" implies that this judgment is a present reality (cf. Ro. 1:18). In the estrangement of unbelief judgment is already present. But to save the world from that judgment God has sent his Son (vs. 16). As the conclusion of all that has been said up to this point, here, too (see the comments on vs. 21), all the emphasis comes to lie on the definitive eschatological decision confronting the world in the coming of Christ. "The conclusion is less a promise than a warning" (Bultmann). The warning is there, however, not to condemn the world but to save it (vs. 17).

---

143. For "see" see the comments on vs. 3.

144. ἀπειθέω, disobey, appears here alone in the Fourth Gospel, though it is common elsewhere in the New Testament (e.g., Ro. 11:30f.). The noun ἀπείθεια has the same sense in, e.g., Ro. 11:30; Col. 3:6.

4:1-26

The Woman of Samaria: The Well and the Mountain

This long and graphic story is another in the series of images and encounters
by means of which the Evangelist seeks to demonstrate the significance of
Jesus as the Christ, the Son of God. The persons who appear briefly on center
stage in this process represent, for the Evangelist, a certain "christological" (or
"evangelical") interest: in their uniqueness and reaction to the encounter with
Jesus they serve as mirrors in which, each time in a different way, the image
of Christ is reflected. One can speak of the "people around Jesus" since in
these encounters not only Jesus' image but also that of each of these people
emerges more clearly — but hardly in a personalistic sense. The focus is not
on their histories or their psychological makeup. They appear on stage too
briefly and too fragmentarily for that. Their stories have quite another focus.
It is not the task of the exegete — as has been all too often attempted with
much imagination and skill — to supplement the profile sketched by the Evangelist with historical and psychological detail.

All this applies to the story of the Samaritan woman. The scene by the
well — like other such scenes in the Bible (cf. Gn. 24:11ff.; 29:2ff., 9ff.; Ex.
2:16ff.) — is picturesque enough, and the dialogue here is much more "personal" than that between Jesus and Nicodemus. Still this encounter represents
more than an individual event, however it was essential to the woman herself
and in that way is a model for others. Here, too, it is the great salvation-historical
eschatological motif of the breakthrough, in Christ's coming, of the promised
time of salvation that shapes and transforms everything (cf. vss. 21ff., 35ff.).

The story has been composed with great care, and its structure is transparent. After the historical transition in 4:1-3 comes the first major part of the
story, the dialogue between Jesus and a woman of Samaria in vss. 4-26. The
second half of the story, vss. 27-42, is a report of the woman's return to her
village and the ensuing arrival of other Samaritans and, while she is gone, Jesus'
conversation with his noncomprehending disciples about the meaning of what
is happening. The story ends with the meeting between the Samaritans and
Jesus and their confession that Jesus is the Savior of the world.

Verses **1-3** place the following event in the broader context of Jesus' return
(cf. 2:2, 13) from Judea to Galilee. Hence what is about to take place in Samaria
is not the purpose of the journey. Jesus saw himself forced to return to Galilee
when he learned of the hostility of the Pharisees, hostility occasioned by the
large numbers of people coming to him to be baptized and to be his disciples,
even more than had come to John (cf. 3:26ff.). This probably means not that
the Pharisees sided with John against Jesus but that they regarded Jesus as even
more dangerous to their authority than John. We may therefore assume that

Jesus' departure was motivated by concern for his own safety (cf. 7:1). A striking feature is the correction or clarification (by a later hand?) in vs. 2 with regard to Jesus' baptizing. It is not altogether clear why this note occurs here and not in 3:22, 26, to which 4:1 is evidently related.[145]

The story begins with verse **4**. It is unclear how much weight one should give "had to." One instinctively thinks of the "must" — frequent in the Synoptics but occurring in John also (cf. 3:14) — of the divine plan of salvation that Jesus came to carry out. But here the expression has primarily a geographical focus. The main road from Judea to Galilee ran through Samaria. It was possible to avoid this road, but Jesus chose otherwise (cf. Lk. 9:52; 17:11), and that choice brought him by necessity into the country of the Samaritans. But this does not exclude (a point one must always add in John!) that for the understanding reader the other "necessity," the deeper necessity, is also present tacitly (cf. the comments on vs. 42).

5-6 For the time being all the emphasis lies on the "natural" course of events. There is some uncertainty about the location of the place (called "Sychar" in most manuscripts) to which Jesus went. Some scholars identify it with Tell ʿAskar, but that is located more than a kilometer from the well of Jacob. The Syriac version has "Sychem," the name of a village known from other sources and located much closer to the well, but that makes a scribal change from "Sychar" to "Sychem" much more likely than the reverse. But the history of Jacob, to which vs. 5 refers, explicitly mentions Shechem (Gn. 33:18; 35:4; 37:12f.), and the same name comes up in connection with the land that the descendants of Joseph inherited from Jacob (Josh. 24:32; Gn. 48:22). Jacob's well itself is not mentioned in the Old Testament. It is mentioned first in pilgrim stories from the fourth century A.D.; to this day it is pointed out alongside the road to Galilee by the city of Shechem. Jesus apparently knew the site and chose it as a place of rest from the journey. "And so," as a tired traveler, Jesus sat down by the well. The time indication, high noon, the hottest time of the day, is part of this description of the setting. The whole account is designed to give as natural and human a picture of Jesus' presence at the well as possible, one that should eliminate from the outset any idea that John's christology has some degree of "docetic" character.[146]

145. Many exegetes believe that 2:2 is the work of a later editor. Brown regards it as "almost indisputable evidence of the presence of several hands in the composition in John." The unusual expression meaning "however" in vs. 2 (καίτοιγε) is also said to point to this (Brown, *Comm.* I, p. 164). Dodd, too, believed that the correction could not be from the Evangelist himself and that the parenthesis in vs. 2 "has a better claim to be regarded as an 'editorial note' by a redactor than anything else in the gospel except the colophon XXI, 24, 25" (*Interpretation*, p. 311, n. 1; cf. idem, *Historical Tradition*, p. 285). But one can regard the parenthesis as a clarification by the Evangelist himself if one accepts that he omitted it in 3:22ff. because there the baptizing by (or, as now appears, under auspices of) Jesus was the crucial point that John's disciples took to their master. See also the comments on 3:22.

146. See also my *Het Woord is vlees geworden,* 1979, pp. 10ff.

7-8   The description of the appearance of the woman is extremely concise, but — and this can hardly be an accident — it contains precisely those words that will dominate the conversation that now follows: "woman," "Samaria," and "water." Not a word is said about the encounter itself. The request for water with which Jesus opens the dialogue elicits from the Evangelist no other comment than that the disciples had gone to the city to buy food. So to quench his thirst Jesus had to rely on the good will of the woman. He — and this is of course deliberate — makes no distinction. He does not hesitate, a Jewish man sitting thirsty by a well, to ask a Samaritan woman for the favor of a drink. It is as though he were oblivious of the boundaries and barriers that alienate and separate people from each other.

9   But the woman is not so ready to comply with Jesus' request. She immediately recognizes this stranger as a Jew. And although she does not directly refuse to give him a drink, she does want first to express to him the surprise that his blunt request has occasioned in her. She minces no words. She does not say, "How can I, a Samaritan woman, give you water?" She says, rather, "How is it that you, a Jew, can ask this of me?" Surely no right-minded Jew would do that even if he were dying of thirst![147]

To explain this reaction, the Evangelist inserts in vs. 9b (at least according to some important manuscripts) the statement "For Jews have no dealings with Samaritans," referring to the deep-rooted hostility and even contempt that Jews felt for the Samaritan people (cf. 2 Kg. 17:33ff.; Jn. 8:48), an attitude that Samaritans reciprocated (cf. Lk. 9:53). The Samaritans were descendants of Israelites from the ten tribes who were left behind after the destruction of Samaria in 722 B.C. and colonists from the East imported by the Assyrian kings (cf. 2 Kg. 17:24ff.). They accepted as authoritative only the five books of Moses and worshiped the God of Israel on Mount Gerizim, rejecting Jerusalem as the place of worship (cf. vs. 20; Lk. 9:51ff.). Along with these religious differences were a number of political conflicts between Jews and Samaritans over the centuries. All this led to what the Evangelist calls, speaking in general terms, "no dealings."[148]

10   Although the woman's question in vs. 9 touches one of the main motifs of the entire story, Jesus refrains from commenting directly on the

---

147. On this request of Jesus to a Samaritan woman see at length E. Leidig, *Jesu Gespräch mit der Samaritanerin,* 1981[2], pp. 84ff. In this connection Leidig discusses at length the Jewish laws of purification, about which the Evangelist, however, does not breathe a word.

148. The translation of συγχρᾶσθαι is not certain. Some translate it more literally by "use together" (cf. NRSV "share things in common"). If this were correct, one would have to think in this case of the water jar mentioned in vs. 28 and the reference would be to Jewish laws of purification (see, e.g., Brown, *Comm.* I, p. 170; Olsson, *Structure and Meaning,* pp. 154ff., following D. Daube, "Jesus and the Samaritan Woman: The meaning of συγχράομαι," *JBL* 69 (1950), pp. 137ff. The problem is that vs. 9b does not mention any common utensil.

polarity she refers to. As with Nicodemus (3:13), Jesus answers her by referring to another world and reality than the one in terms of which she lives, one in which the barrier she has mentioned plays no role, though he does speak in terms entirely derived from the situation at hand. The "gift of God" is the well from which Jesus draws and gives living water. It is called that to distinguish it from the well that Jacob had once "given" (vs. 12) and from which the woman was accustomed to draw water. If she knew the gift of God and, in that connection, who the stranger was who was speaking with her, she would no longer trouble herself about problems between Jews and Samaritans but would ask him for water and he would give it to her: living, running, water (again, whether she was a Samaritan or not). Essentially it is the same set of alternatives we encountered in the dialogue with Nicodemus: By what is a human being to live — by what is at hand, by what she knows and what lies within her reach, or by what is from above and she does not have at her disposal but must be given to her by him who "came down from heaven"?

In verses **11** and **12** the woman shows no sign of understanding what Jesus is talking about and, like Nicodemus (3:4) and the disciples later (vs. 32f.), clings to the literal meaning of Jesus' words.[149] After all, "living" water was what one called *running* water, such as flows from the spring that feeds the well of Jacob and makes it so important for the people living near it. The woman's answer, though couched in respectful terms ("Sir") and in the form of a question, shows some annoyance. How can he give her water from the well, which is very deep,[150] with nothing to draw the water up with? Or — and this seems even more absurd to her — does he think perhaps he can get running water from some other source than this well? The first possibility simply does not make sense to her (vs. 11), and her self-awareness as a Samaritan rebels against the second (vs. 12). Does Jesus, a stranger, imagine that he is greater than "our father Jacob, who gave us the well and drank from it himself, and his sons, and his cattle"?

Emerging ever more clearly is the extent to which the entire encounter derives its meaning from this background, which vss. 5 and 6, by twice referring to the patriarch Jacob, already anticipate. It is also becoming more and more apparent that Jesus' request for a drink and the theme of living water that he broached immediately after, however general in thrust, are related from the start to the contrast beween Jews and Samaritans. Here in vs. 12, however, this emerges for the first time in the woman's critical questioning of Jesus: "Certainly[151] you are not greater than our father Jacob?"

---

149. On this stereotypical reaction as a rhetorical form, see the comments above on 3:3.

150. The deepest well in Palestine according to R. D. Potter, "Topography and Archaeology in the Fourth Gospel," *Studia Evangelica* I, 1959, pp. 329-37, here p. 331. See also Dalman, *Orte und Wege*, p. 176.

151. The question begins with μή and so is a rhetorical question expecting a negative answer.

13, 14   Although in a sense this posed the central issue of the dialogue (see below), in his answer Jesus limits himself to the superiority of what he had to give and does not yet speak about himself. He therefore contrasts the water from Jacob's well ("this water") with his gift. He does not condemn the first as though there was something wrong with it. He had, indeed, begun by asking for it. But it has only a limited effect. It only temporarily quenches one's thirst. In the nature of the case, this is as far as the gift of father Jacob goes. Over against it Jesus sets the water — described with repeated emphasis as *his* gift — that will forever assuage a person's thirst, water one does not over and over have to go and get but that becomes a spring of living, self-replenishing water *within*. Not that a single drink will satisfy, but as the gift of God it is an everlasting,[152] self-renewing spring of refreshment and life.

Much has been written about this pronouncement, and its explication is decisive for the interpretation of the entire Fourth Gospel. As with the contrast between flesh and Spirit in 3:6ff., here, too, scholars have looked for the background in the dualistic thought of contemporary Hellenistic religiosity,[153] whether in an idealistic sense (the material and earthly as the lower over against the spiritual and heavenly as the higher)[154] or in that of Gnosticism (the earthly as the unreal over against the immaterial, which comes from above).[155] Within this approach, the history of salvation recedes completely into the background. Everything — not only soteriology but also christology — is then governed by a strongly individualistic view of humankind.[156]

However, as a reaction to the statement by the Samaritan woman ("Certainly you are not greater than our father Jacob") Jesus' answer certainly has a very different background. At stake is the contrast between what Jacob, patriarch of the Samaritans, gave his children and descendants and the water that Jesus will give. One thinks instinctively of ch. 6, where the bread from heaven that Jesus gives and *is* (6:32f., 48ff.) is contrasted with the manna that Moses gave the fathers in the wilderness. There, too, we find the motif of the inadequacy of what was given in the past (vs. 49) and of the fact that those who partake of what Jesus gives and is will never lack (vs. 35); there too we encounter a request for "this bread" (6:34) paralleling the Samaritan woman's request for "this water" (4:15). It is said by Bultmann and his followers, to be sure, that when the Jews or the

---

152. The words "to eternal life" go with "welling up," not with "will become," and thus indicate the imperishability of the water that Jesus will give (cf. 6:27). The future tense (twice) is not explained but must presumably be understood in keeping with the parallel pronouncement in 7:38.

153. See on 3:6-8 above.

154. See, e.g., Dodd, *Interpretation,* p. 314.

155. Cf. Bultmann, *Comm.,* pp. 181ff., and the history-of-religions material given there.

156. Against this view, cf. also Leidig, *Jesu Gespräch mit der Samaritanerin,* pp. ixff., with a strong appeal to "salvation-historical exegesis" (pp. xi-xvii, and in connection with vs. 11, pp. 45ff.).

Samaritan woman makes these requests they represent only "the world" in its unbelief, which views illusion as though it were real.[157] In this fashion the Jewish and Samaritan historical background becomes unimportant. All we find here then is the universally valid antithesis between the understanding of the human situation from within the revelation in Jesus (the Christian faith) and the world, represented by Judaism or Samaritanism.[158]

Still, however true it is that Jesus is "the way, the truth, and the life" for all people without distinction, this does not remove the fact that he is this — especially in the Fourth Gospel — as Israel's Messiah. That is why the point of this story and the way by which Jesus leads the woman to faith can only be understood against the salvation-historical background of God's revelation to Israel. The gift of water from the well of Jacob was for the Samaritans, like the manna in the wilderness to Israel, a reminder of the sacred tradition — continuing evidence of God's richly salvific involvement with his people through history. When Jesus describes the gift of God in terms from tradition, such as "living water" and "bread from heaven," the adjectives "living," "true," "good," and the like are rooted theologically not in an ontological contrast between illusion and reality but in a salvation-historical contrast. What Jesus brings is the fulfillment, the "truth" and the "fullness" of the gift of God. Everything that preceded had reference to that fullness, but could not provide it. None of this is opposed to the past, therefore, but it brings the past into the future (cf. 8:56ff.; see also the comments on 1:17). What is referred to here as "living water" is already present in the Old Testament portrayal of what the people in their distress desired from God, and that not only in a physical sense (cf. Pss. 23:2ff.; 36:8; Is. 12:3, etc.): one reads of "thirst for God" (Ps. 42:1) and of God as the "fountain of life" (Ps. 36:9; Jr. 2:13: "the fountain of living waters"); the salvation of the Lord is offered as waters for those who are thirsty (Is. 55:1ff.) as contrasted with that which only temporarily quenches thirst.

Vs. 14 does not define how Jesus is the fulfiller of all this. In 7:37ff., where he speaks in the same sense of "rivers of living water," this is explained as referring to the coming outpouring of the Spirit, just as in ch. 6 the living bread of Jesus' flesh and blood, which give eternal life (cf. 6:35, 51, 53ff.), is understood. Some interpreters try to find a more specific meaning here also[159] — but mistakenly in my opinion. What is central here is not a specific meaning

157. "To confuse the inauthentic with the authentic" (*Comm.*, pp. 186, 223ff.).

158. Bultmann, *Comm.*, p. 86.

159. See, e.g., Brown, *Comm.* I, pp. 178ff. Also Leidig, *Jesu Gespräch mit der Samaritanerin*, pp. 46ff., who makes much of the distinction between the water from Jacob's well, for which one needed an ἄντλημα, and the water that Jesus gives and of which the wellspring that (in accordance with rabbinic tradition) went with Israel in the wilderness is said to have been the historical prefiguration. In my opinion this explanation is far-fetched.

of "living water" but the proclamation that in Jesus as the divinely sent Messiah the gift of God is present, the gift, namely, to which prophets and psalmists ever and again testified and for which people in their thirst for God were always looking. In the messianic context of "him who speaks to you is he," of what he reveals and does, the gift he confers on those who thus believe in him will be increasingly understood, as will appear from the dialogue as it now continues.

15   But the woman has not yet reached that point, though her tone has changed. What at first seemed utterly absurd to her is now beginning to assume the form of something miraculous, of which the stranger apparently knows the secret and that might perhaps be useful to her. In any case, her request, again couched in respectful terms ("Sir, give me this water that I may not thirst"), seems sincere (and not ironic or playful, as some interpreters think; cf. also 6:34). But to judge by what else she says ("so that I do not have to come here repeatedly[160] to draw water") she seems still not to understand what Jesus wants to give her. Or is it that things are beginning to dawn on her and she is only repeating Jesus' words in order to prompt him to explain himself?

16-19   Things only change when Jesus suddenly shifts the conversation to something seemingly unrelated to the subject at issue: "Go, call your husband, and come back here." Scholars differ greatly on the meaning of this shift. Some think that there is no connection with what preceded and that therefore the transition from vss. 10-15 to vss. 16-19 cannot be original. The idea is that vss. 10-15 were taken by the Evangelist from another source and inserted after vs. 9, with the implication that vss. 16-19 originally followed vs. 9.[161] Even ignoring the fact that scholars thus have the Evangelist deal most awkwardly with his "sources," it is very questionable whether linking vss. 16-19 with vs. 9 furnishes a clearer sequence than the present one.[162]

Admittedly, the linkage is not devoid of problems. What could have been Jesus' motive for having the woman call her husband? All kinds of explanations have been proposed.

It is suggested that Jesus wanted to involve the woman's husband in what he had discussed with her since his gift was not intended only for her. Or that Jesus wanted to test the confidence the woman had expressed. Or that he wanted to make her understand that he knew her life history in order thus to create in her a better understanding for what he wanted to give her. And the allegorical interpretation is back in circulation: The "marriage" relationship(s) of the woman are said to refer here to the religion of the Samaritans. For this, reference is made to symbolism also to be found in Ho. 2:2, 7, 16. The "five husbands" (vs. 18) are said to be the five gods of the

---

160. δι-έρχομαι.
161. Cf. Bultmann, *Comm.,* pp. 175f., 187.
162. Cf. also Leidig, *Jesu Gespräch mit der Samaritanerin,* p. 8.

nations that had gone from Assyria to settle Samaria (cf. 2 Kg. 17:24ff.), while the present husband of the woman (who was not her husband, vs. 18) is said to refer to the illicit worship of Yahweh by the Samaritans.[163] But surely this intepretation is too fantastic. Not only does the Evangelist not "use allegorisation but rather symbolic representation as his main literary device"[164] but in Samaria there were not five but seven nations that worshiped their gods, and they did so simultaneously, not successively (cf. 2 Kg. 17:29ff.). And could Yahweh be called the illicit husband of the Samaritans? The woman's own explanation in vs. 29 in no way points to an allegorical interpretation, any more than one can interpret the later dialogue concerning true worship as a further application of this "allegory." Hence we shall have to take the command of Jesus to the woman to call her husband in a literal sense.

In view of what follows the intent can hardly be other than that, by bringing up the subject of her husband, Jesus wanted to lead the woman to the realization that he knew her past and present life and thus to make her more open to the meaning of his words.

In the history of exegesis (and of preaching) this interpretation has often been given a religio-psychological twist, according to which Jesus sought to lead the woman to repentance and conversion by way of increased self-knowledge. The command "Go, call your husband" is said to have been the first step toward getting her to realize how sinful her life was. The woman's answer in vs. 17a would then be ambiguous, even misleading, as an instinctive reaction to escape further interrogation at this point. Jesus then used her answer, so the argument goes, to unmask her sinful life further (vss. 17b, 18). Although the woman has to acknowledge Jesus' prophetic knowledge concerning her life, she next tries (vss. 17, 19f.) to divert attention from herself to a more impersonal "subject," the nature of true worship, as a kind of confessional diversionary tactic.[165]

163. Cf. the remarkable interpretation of C. M. Carmichael, "Marriage and the Samaritan Woman," *NTS* 26 (1980), pp. 332-46, according to whom the whole discussion about water is determined by sexual imagery. Jesus' offer of water to the woman "has a deliberately intended conjugal association." Carmichael refers to 4:15 as well as to Jacob's encounter with Rachel at the well (Gn. 29:7). Jesus woos the woman in the way Hosea was instructed to take a prostitute as wife to give expression to the relationship between God and Israel. The shift in the dialogue in vs. 16 "would be inexplicable if it were not for the underlying marital theme." Hence when the woman asks Jesus for "water" it has to be made clear first that she has no husband and that only Jesus can give her water that will never let her be thirsty again. Hence: "Go, call your husband." In the woman Jesus weds Samaria to the true worship of God, and so forth. In my opinion there is not a single point of contact for this interpretation in the text itself.

164. Bultmann, *Comm.*, p. 188 n. 3.

165. For this pastoral-psychological approach to Jesus and the woman's attempt to divert the conversation see at length F. Pfau, *Normen für die Seelsorge aus Joh. 4,1-42,* 1889, pp. 161-87. For the above analysis, cf. esp. Brown, *Comm.* I, p. 177, who closely follows F. Roustang, "Les moments de l'acte de foi et ses conditions de possibilité. Essay d'interprétation du dialogue avec la Samaritaine," *Recherches de science religieuse* 46 (1958), pp. 344-78. Brown speaks of "the drama of a soul struggling to rise from the things of this world to belief in Jesus" (p. 178).

This interpretation undoubtedly contains the truth that Jesus led the woman to this acknowledgment, not by an arbitrary manifestation of his supernatural knowledge, but by focusing this knowledge on her own life. And what he thus brought to the fore was certainly not flattering for her. The words "you are right" — echoed in vs. 18 with "this you have said truly" — must have sounded in her ears as a judicial verdict that, by saying "I have no husband," she herself had pronounced. And the explanation of this verdict made this "truth" all the more unambiguous and revealing: by Jewish standards[166] and in the general Near Eastern view, it was an indecent extravagance for a woman to have been married successively to five men. And if that was followed by "living with" another man, any claim to the honor of being a married woman had been totally abandoned. There can be no doubt, therefore, that by thus revealing to the woman his knowledge of her life, Jesus sought to give his conversation with her a dimension of depth for which until now she had shown no understanding. It is not difficult, therefore, to find material points of connection between this and what has been said in the preceding conversation about a thirst that ever returns and water that cannot quench it.

Still, it is questionable whether the text permits a psychological-pastoral interpretation ending with a deepening of the woman's sense of sin and her repentance. In any case, her answers do not show this. The idea that she lacked the self-knowledge that Jesus is presumably now imparting to her is nowhere evident. When he says to her, "Go, call your husband," her reply tersely and radically reflects her real situation: "I have no husband." That she does not immediately reveal her entire situation to him can hardly be interpreted against her. In any case, Jesus does not reproach her for this but rather commends her for saying she does not have a husband. And when he then proceeds to confront her with a picture of her life, she does not act like this were the first time she realized the seriousness of it or finally arrived at self-knowledge and a sense of sin. At least she shows no sign of this.

Her only reaction to Jesus' unveiling of her life is: "Sir, I perceive that you are a prophet." Hence her answer relates more to Jesus than to herself, though of course it implies the acknowledgment that he has spoken the truth about her. And that also is the viewpoint from which the Evangelist would have us regard this decisive shift in the conversation: Jesus knew with whom he had to do when he sought contact with *this* woman by asking *her* for a drink and then offering *her* the living water. It is that knowledge that over and over illumined the authority and nature of Jesus' messianic mission. On the basis of this knowledge he called Nathanael, as a true Israelite, to follow him (1:47), kept Nicodemus and the "many" represented by him at a distance (2:25; 3:3), and, through this woman with her dubious past and reputation (cf. vss. 29, 39),

166. Cf. Strack/Billerbeck II, p. 437.

sought entrance among the despised and hostile people of Samaria. What therefore determines the goal and progress of Jesus' conversation with the Samaritan woman is not that she — in four steps or stages[167] — arrived at ever deeper self-knowledge but began, in the face of all her personal and shared prejudices, to understand who the Messiah of Israel was and what "the salvation from the Jews" represented by him amounted to (vss. 22, 29, 39).

But the faith that reaches that goal is not achieved all at once. She has come closer to Jesus than she did in vs. 15, but still no closer than the admission that he is a prophet. She insists on the indefinite article: *a* prophet. Still, this was a step that, as the developing conversation shows, arose not from a general sense that she was dealing with a kind of miracle-worker,[168] but rather from the Old Testament image of the prophet as one who is endowed with supernatural knowledge (cf., e.g., 1 Sa. 9:19; 2 Kg. 4:27; Lk. 7:39) and to whom one could turn to hear the Word of God.[169]

20 It is in the light of that discovery that the woman now brings up the heart of the issue that has from the beginning made her reserved toward the stranger but that she now poses to him, now understanding him as a prophet and hence as expert on that issue: What did he think about the great stumbling block between the Samaritans ("our fathers") and the Jews ("you," plural), namely "where people ought to worship"?

From of old the Samaritans had worshiped Yahweh alongside their idols (2 Kg. 17:26f., 32, 41). In distinction from the Jews who, according to Dt. 27:4 (Masoretic Text), brought their sacrifices to Mount Ebal, the Samaritans, in their Pentateuch, gave this significance to Mount Gerizim, which was situated adjacent to Jacob's well (*"this mountain"*) and worshiped Yahweh there. In the course of time they built a temple there (with permission from Alexander the Great, according to Josephus), but it was destroyed by John Hyrcanus I, a Jewish king, in 128 B.C. But the Samaritan worship of Yahweh was continued on Mount Gerizim[170] and remained the great religious bone of contention (cf. Lk. 9:53).

Here, too, the "psychological" interpretation, which views this shift in the conversation as a diversionary tactic of a "confessional" nature (see above),

---

167. On these "four cognitive stages of the Samaritan woman," see at length Leidig, *Jesu Gespräch mit der Samaritanerin,* pp. 154f.

168. Cf., e.g., Bultmann, who thinks that "prophet" here represents the Hellenistic θεῖος ἄνθρωπος (*Comm.,* pp. 187f.; see also pp. 101f. and the literature cited there).

169. See also Nicol, *Sēmeia,* p. 61; Leidig, *Jesu Gespräch mit der Samaritanerin,* pp. 11f., 271, n. 41. The idea that she is referring to the prophet like Moses (Dt. 18:15-22; so Leidig, p. 13) seems to anticipate the following "phase" (vs. 25).

170. And continues now. See also J. Jeremias, *Die Passahfeier der Samaritaner,* 1932.

takes us into the wrong direction. According to this interpretation one not only faces the question why Jesus did not cut her off but in fact followed her when she took this track but also thus disregards the christological viewpoint that dominates the entire conversation. What follows does not have a "theoretical" character.

The situation is rather — and this is the strategy of the Evangelist in all these conversations — that the "case" of the woman herself illustrates the relevance of the controversy in a highly personal way. After the conversation about the well has taken this turn, how could conversation about the mountain be avoided? The woman's first question was: "How can you, a Jew, ask a drink of me, a woman of Samaria?" But at this point another question urges itself on her even, and more forcefully: "How can you, a Jew (in fact, a Jewish prophet), speak about the *gift* of God and of living water to me, a woman of Samaria (and what a woman), as if 'this mountain' were not an enormous stumbling block between us?"[171] She does state the issue in more general terms. But what drove her to do this was not a theological attempt at diversion but the awareness that the issue between Jews and Samaritans had never been more personally important to her than it was at this point in her conversation with this Jewish prophet.

21-22 Accordingly, Jesus reacts to her pronouncement without any deviation. He, too, feels no need to return to the personal life of the woman but addresses her as representative of her people ("you," plural). For, however much in all his words he kept the woman in mind, now that he has gained her attention for who he is, it had to be made clear to her that the issue between him and her was not just the shift in *her* history but a breakthrough that concerned her entire people, indeed, the whole world. With solemn emphasis ("Believe me, woman")[172] Jesus announces the hour when they (she and her fellow Samaritans) would worship the Father "neither on this mountain (Gerizim) nor in Jerusalem." That is, they would no longer have to choose between these two cult locations. This is not to say that Jesus made no distinction between the two existing places of worship. He describes the worship of Samaritans as based on ignorance of what they are doing. For, in virtue of the revelation given to Israel, salvation is "from the Jews," and all worship that puts itself in opposition to that revelation or separates itself from it is worship of one's own choosing.

Much recent scholarship regards this verse as a later insertion because the Jesus of the Fourth Gospel, it is thought, could not have said anything of

---

171. The mountain was in full view from the well (see Potter, "Topography and Archeology in the Fourth Gospel," p. 331).

172. Bultmann: "It is introduced by the singular πίστευέ μοι, which clearly stands in place of ἀμὴν ἀμ. λέγω σοι (the latter occurs nowhere in ch. 4)" (*Comm.,* p. 189).

the sort.[173] Reference is made to texts (such as 8:41ff., 17; 10:34; 13:33) in which Jesus either sharply attacks "the Jews" or clearly distances himself from "their" law. But however often "the Jews" is the term by which the leaders of the Jews who are hostile toward Jesus are described, that does not mean that the designation can have only this antithetical sound or meaning in the Fourth Gospel (cf. 2:13; 5:1; 7:11; 11:19ff., etc.).[174] Much less can it be maintained that in so-called dualistic thought, with "the world" on one side and believers on the other, "the Jews" and their tradition (Moses!) always represent "the world." It has been correctly noted by some that one who approaches and interprets the Fourth Gospel in this way totally misunderstands it and in fact even runs the danger of attributing anti-Semitic tendencies to the Gospel. However true it is that Jesus, in his conversations with Jews who are hostile to him, dissociates himself entirely from their spiritual motives and their handling of the Torah and makes very strong statements, it is no less true that his entire mission, even according to John, is rooted in the revelation granted to Israel (cf., e.g., 5:45ff.; 7:19ff.; 8:39ff., 53ff.; 10:34). Hence one must not for that reason, any more than on that of the textual witness, question for a moment the genuineness of either part of vs. 22.[175]

23-24 The "but" with which vs. 23 begins also points to the authenticity of vs. 22: However much the Jews may have been right in their dispute with the Samaritans, now other criteria for true worship are going to apply. Again Jesus announces "the hour is coming" (cf. vs. 21), referring thus to *the* great time of salvation, and follows this, as in 5:25, with "and is now." The breakthrough has come and the future has become present tense, but without losing its future character.

The mark of that future is worship "in Spirit and truth," as contrasted with worship that is bound to a specific place. This is not to be understood as saying that true worship is realized totally in the sphere of the supersensuous and elevated above the visible temporal world or any cultic form.[176] "Spirit" — here linked with "truth" in a hendiadys as with "grace and truth" in 1:17 — refers to the time of salvation that has come with Christ and to the concomitant new way in which God wants to relate to human beings. Whereas "grace and truth" above all describe the compassion and love God displayed in the

173. In this regard one finds strongly categorical pronouncements, especially in Bultmann, *Comm.*, pp. 189f. Cf. on 1:11: "It is impossible in the Prologue . . . to take τὰ ἴδια (or οἱ ἴδιοι) to mean Israel or the Jewish people" (p. 56, n. 1).

174. See the comments on 1:19 above.

175. For the polemics concerning the genuineness of vs. 22 see at length Leidig, *Jesu Gespräch mit der Samaritanerin,* which is devoted to a large extent to defense of the verse (p. xvii: "We have made it our task to show how John's statement in 4:22 can be understood in relation to his positive utterances about the Jews"; see esp. pp. 49-63).

176. See also E. Schweizer, *TDNT* VI, p. 439: "πνεῦμα, then, does not mean man's soul or understanding, that which is most like God in him, his immaterial or purely inward part."

sending of his Son (cf. 3:16), "Spirit and truth" refer to the fellowship thus established in its life-creating and life-giving power, as leading to the fullness of God's gifts (cf. 1:16) that is no longer mediated by all sorts of provisional and symbolic forms, but by the Spirit of God himself, which is why it is repeatedly called worship of the "Father."

And all this takes place "from now on" because in Christ the way to the Father is being opened in a totally new manner (14:6), the limits of the old patterns of worship are being broken through (see comments on 1:29), and the true worshipers are being brought together in a single fellowship. They, accordingly, are such (vs. 23b) as God "seeks," that is, desires, as his worshipers. Therein lie both the condition (cf. "must" in vs. 24) for true worship and the desire of God to attract such. For (vs. 24) "God is Spirit," not a statement intended to emphasize God's inaccessibility to earthly, material beings (so that they would have to draw near to God by way of interiorization and spiritual self-emptying), but the description, rather, of God as the Foundation and Giver of the true life (14:16), he to whom, therefore, one can come only in the way he has opened for that purpose in Jesus Christ.[177]

25 The woman does not respond to the specific content of Jesus' words. But she does reveal her awareness that they relate to the great future — matters that suggest to her mind the thought of the[178] Messiah, of whose coming she as a Samaritan knew. Hence she comes increasingly closer to Jesus' way of thinking. She names the Messiah, but still (cf. vs. 29) distances herself from the relevance of what she has heard ("the hour is now"). She prefers to appeal to the *coming* Messiah, an expectation she shared with her people: "When he comes, he will show us all things."

Just what kind of Messiah was this woman looking for? And in what respect did Jesus identify with her expectation. She refers to "Messiah," but the eschatological figure expected by the Samaritans was called Taheb, not Messiah.[179] The fact that the woman nevertheless calls him Messiah seems to be based on a certain accommodation or generalization in the designation of the future bringer of salvation.[180] Although, on the basis of the available his-

---

177. Cf. also ibid., p. 439: "Hence ἐν πνεύματι corresponds materially to the Pauline ἐν Χριστῷ. God's sovereign act of revelation in Jesus has marked out the sphere in which there is true worship. Hence any cultus, however spiritual, is judged as not in the πνεῦμα if it is not based on this divine act."

178. Without an article but not meant indefinitely.

179. On the Evangelist's parenthetical addition ("he who is called Christ"), see the comments on 1:41. Other scholars think that in the tradition that John followed this addition was attributed to the woman. She is supposed to have said: "Taheb, the one that you Jews call Messiah" (see Bultmann, *Comm.*, p. 192, n. 2). But for one to understand the text as handed down it is not necessary to resort to this (ingenious) reconstruction.

180. "The conversation in John IV 19-25 fits the Samaritan concept of the Taheb as a teacher of the Law . . . even though the more familiar Jewish designation of Messiah is placed

torical material one cannot form a clear picture of this Taheb, at least not for the time of Jesus, as background one will in any case also have to consider the Pentateuch held in honor by the Samaritans and the prophetic figure predicted there: "I will raise up . . . a prophet like you. . . . I will put my words in his mouth, and he shall speak to them all that I command him" (Dt. 18:18). The woman speaks of this prophet as the one who "will show us all things."

26   With this last statement the woman has come very close to the truth, so close that for his self-revelation Jesus needs no other description of his identity. Still, the real truth must come from Jesus himself: "I who speak to you am he." These words return in the Fourth Gospel in a variety of ways, and each time "he" has a different content (e.g., 6:35; 9:37). But they all give expression to one and the same thing: all the adjectives with which divine salvation can be described, all the predictions of the prophets, and all the expectations based on them find in him their only subject, their fulfillment, their "truth." Here, too, this pronouncement is, as it were, the terminal point to which the woman is led step by step. He it is, not only for the Jews but also for the Samaritans; and he it is not only in the future (as the coming Messiah, who "will show us all things") but here and now ("I who speak to you").

Over and over, wherever that is possible, this is where the conversations climax (cf. 9:37) throughout the entire Gospel (20:31). What is constantly at stake in this connection is the unity of two focal points: Jesus is the *Messiah* and the Messiah is *Jesus*, though now one and now the other is predominant. In the nature of the case, one is determined by the other. Nevertheless, materially the identity of the person precedes that of the salvation in question. The identity of the Messiah, the one sent by the Father, and the way messianic salvation comes into being — in short, the entire soteriological process of events and its effect — is manifest in *Jesus* and fulfilled in him; and one cannot, conversely, fill in the christological identity of the person with what people expect of him or desire of him on the basis of their "existential understanding" or tradition. But there is definitely also continuity in the history of salvation because salvation is "from the Jews." Therefore the true outlook on the coming Messiah is revealed, as with the Samaritan woman, in the context of the expectation that is oriented to Israel. For that reason Jesus does not at this point react to the content of the woman's messianic expectation but focuses in his final statement on the fact that it is *he* who is speaking to her.

---

on the woman's lips" (Brown, *Comm.* I, p. 172). See also, W. A. Meeks, *The Prophet-King: Moses Traditions and Johannine Christology,* 1967, p. 318, who speaks of a "levelling of different terminologies."

4:27-42

Fields White for Harvest

In verse **27** the conversation is suddenly broken off by the return of the disciples. The Evangelist skillfully relates the story of what follows along two tracks, with both Jesus and the woman returning to their "natural associates," he to his disciples and she to her fellow citizens in the Samaritan town. But the story is continued on both tracks. Now both the disciples and the Samaritans, each in their own way, are involved in the story. And then the story again flows through a single channel when the woman returns to Jesus through the fields with her people and meets his disciples, who have meanwhile been informed of what was happening.

The change of situation is sketched with just a few striking brush strokes. The coming of the disciples not only interrupts the conversation at its climax but brings with it a disturbance of the atmosphere. They are clearly astonished to find Jesus thus engaged in conversation.[181] The mere fact that he has been talking with a woman is bad enough, by the conventions of the day,[182] but how much more with a Samaritan woman! Still none of the disciples ventures to ask, "What do you want of her?"[183] or "Why are you speaking with her?" They somehow sense that their "why?" is not his and that he is acting from motives they dare not encroach on.

28-30   But to the woman this whole change was a sign for her to return in haste — leaving her jar behind — to the city and to her people. The picturesque detail of the jar has been given a range of all too profound explanations,[184] but it does of course mark the change of mood that has occurred in the woman — she has forgotten the real object of her journey — as also her eagerness to share with her fellow townspeople what has happened to her at the well.

It is clear how deeply she has been struck not only by Jesus' knowledge of her life but also by his statement that he is the Messiah. Now she no longer refers to a prophet, and for a chance to see a prophet she would probably not have attempted to mobilize the whole city ("Come, see . . ."). Her appeal is couched in the form of a question, as though she herself was not at all sure of the answer ("Can this man perhaps be the Christ?").[185] But the way she involved herself

---

181. ἐλάλει, imperfect.

182. Cf., e.g., Strack/Billerbeck II, pp. 155f.

183. The question was undoubtedly addressed to Jesus, not to the woman.

184. "The symbol of her old life and religion." So, e.g., Olsson, *Structure and Meaning,* pp. 155f.

185. "The μήτι does not demand absolutely a negative answer, but can express a cautious opinion" (Schnackenburg, *Comm.* I, p. 444).

sounded to the Samaritans who heard her like a strong motive not for immediately suspecting her of credulity or a desire for sensation but for determining for themselves what could possibly be happening. And so, on the basis of this woman's witness, despite or perhaps precisely because of her notorious past, "they went out of the city." Could Jesus have sent a better witness?

31 While the Samaritans were on their way to Jesus, a most remarkable conversation ensued between Jesus and his disciples, one which was to prepare them for the coming of the Samaritans. Although there are difficult exegetical problems, which have occasioned a wide variety of views of the text,[186] the general thrust of this pericope is not unclear: The harvest of the world has begun! And in this connection the entire focus is on persuading Jesus' disciples of the relevance of this event and on involving them in God's "work." After the woman had left, the disciples, in their silent astonishment at Jesus' conduct (cf. vs. 27), could only think of urging him to eat: "Rabbi,[187] eat!" After all, it was so that he (and they) could eat that they had gone to this city.

32, 33 Jesus' reply to their invitation and their subsequent reaction are strongly reminiscent of the beginning of Jesus' conversation with the woman (vss. 11, 12). Just as in that conversation the water, so here the food, has a different meaning for him than for them. He speaks the same language but uses it, as it were, from within another world. And although he points this difference out to them clearly enough ("I have food to eat of which you do not know"), they, like the woman, continue to cling to their one understanding of food and eating. They can do no better than to ask — each other! — a dull-witted and improbable question:[188] "Surely, no one else has brought him food?" In the Fourth Gospel, the disciples' incomprehension, though it is not cited as proof of a lack of faith or loyalty to Jesus (cf. 1:41ff.; 2:11; 6:66ff., etc.), continues to the end to be a factor in their conduct (cf. 6:7f.; 11:12; 13:6, 37; 14:8, etc.). Not until after his resurrection do they fully learn to understand his words (cf. 14:20; 16:25ff.). That is not to deny that, as we see it here, their time with Jesus on earth was for them a continuing school in which Jesus taught them to see with different eyes what till now had only had one valid meaning for them (cf. vs. 35ff.).

34 To that end Jesus gives them a further reply. His food — apparently in distinction from theirs[189] — as a means of life and the fulfillment of his deepest need, lay in the fulfillment of his divine mission. For the first time here

---

186. See, e.g., Olsson, *Structure and Meaning,* pp. 218ff.; W. Thüsing, *Die Erhöhung und Verherrlichung Jesu im Johannesevangelium,* 1970², pp. 56ff.; Schnackenburg, *Comm.* I, pp. 444ff.

187. Although Jesus did not have the schooling that the scribes had (cf. 7:15), he did act publicly as a teacher (e.g., in the synagogue, 6:59), he called disciples to follow him (1:43), and he was respectfully called "rabbi" by both his disciples and others (1:38, 49; 9:2; 13:13; 3:2, 26).

188. For this reaction as a rhetorical form, see the comments on 3:4 above.

189. ἐμόν, "my," the emphatic form.

we encounter the designation — one that occurs more than twenty times in the Fourth Gospel on Jesus' lips — of God as "he who sent me," sometimes (as in 5:23; 6:39f.) with "the Father" (cf. also 3:34f.). It is that mission, that is, the authority given to Jesus by God and the gift of God comprehended in it, that determines his entire existence. He describes it further as "the will," that is, the plan of salvation, that it is his task to realize and "the work" that he must accomplish.[190] In this one word "work" — elsewhere called "works" (9:4) — here and repeatedly in the Gospel, Jesus' entire mission, both in words and in deeds, is summed up (cf. 17:4).[191]

35 All this not only applies to Jesus but must also govern the disciples' outlook on the present. To make that clear, Jesus uses a common saying ("Do you not say . . . ?" "Is it not your way of speaking . . . ?") about the harvest: "There are yet four months, then comes the harvest." Although we know of no such saying from other sources, it is rather generally assumed that such a saying is being referred to here.[192] It is thought to have meant that just as there are (at least)[193] four months between sowing and harvesting, things cannot be expected at once but take time and must be given time.[194] However true this may be in itself, it is not the wisdom by which the disciples could live now so that they could direct their energies to all sorts of other things than those for which Jesus had called them. Therefore he exhorts them with great emphasis and authority — "I tell you!" — to lift up their eyes and focus on what must now be their highest priority: "See how the fields are already white for harvest!" He is evidently referring to what is literally taking place in the field in front of them,[195] namely the exodus from their city of the Samaritans who at the woman's saying, "Come and see," have started out to go to Jesus. For Jesus that scene is a sign and proof of the breakthrough in time: people in a strange country have heard of him and cross ancient boundaries to ascertain for themselves the possible fulfillment of their long-cherished hope.

190. Some wish to distinguish between "will" and "work" by saying that the first relates more to the present and the second more specifically to the completion of Jesus' mission in the future in his death and resurrection. This is partly based on the future tense of τελειώσω (cf. Olsson, *Structure and Meaning*, pp. 224ff.). But in my opinion both refer to the present as well as to that which is still to come; hence: "accomplish."

191. For ἔργον (in connection with σημεῖον and δόξα) see the lengthy exposition in Nicol, *Sēmeia*, pp. 116ff.

192. Scholars have also often believed that Jesus is speaking here of the season that at that moment still separated them from the time of harvest (so that the matter related here must have taken place around December), a view that has played an important role in the "chronology" of Jesus. But for that the introduction ("Do you not say . . .") would not quite fit. It seems rather artificial to thus attach the coming of the Samaritans to a time four months before the harvest season.

193. The latest one could sow was in December, and the harvest came in April.

194. "Rome was not built in a day."

195. Cf. Potter, *Topography and Archeology*, in loc.

36 Jesus continues to speak in terms of the harvest: *already* the time of the harvest has begun and the reaper can gather in the fruit of labor. This to be understood in the salvation-historical ("eschatological") sense of the harvest of people for eternal life.[196] All the emphasis falls on the word "already"[197] because that is what the disciples need to understand. Sowing is no longer only a time of expectant waiting: sowing, harvest, and the time in between all now coincide, since while the sower is still going out to sow the harvest is already coming in. In other words: the sower and the reaper meet each other, "rejoicing together" at the same time. This is the paradoxical new wisdom about the "sower" and the "reaper" that replaces the old and leaves it behind.

37, 38 These verses, with a view to the disciples, express this truth in still another way, "for" that which was said in general terms above applies in still another sense to them. Jesus here bases himself on yet another saying about harvest: "One sows and another reaps" (cf. Mi. 6:15; Jb. 31:8). It probably owed its origin to the experience of disappointment in the life of many a sower who was unable to pluck the fruit of his or her labor but had to leave it to others to enjoy. In the case of Jesus' disciples, however, the reverse is the case; it is their privilege, as those involved in his work, to live in the time of harvest and to reap what they themselves have not sown. Many before them labored for the day of the harvest but were not permitted to see it. The disciples have entered into the labor of the others. While those others never saw the day of the harvest, the disciples are now permitted to see with their own eyes that the fields are white for harvest. It is this awareness of being allowed to participate in the time of fulfillment that Jesus wants to bring home to them now that the Samaritans are at the point of coming to him. Otherwise they might be superseded by the Samaritans when moments later the Samaritans confess Jesus as the Savior of the world.

This interpretation differs from most others in that it makes no attempt to identify the sower, the reaper, and the "others." This concern to identify these figures has led to great difficulties and consequently to many hard-to-swallow "solutions." In vs. 36 many interpreters correctly refrain from making such identifications. That sower and reaper rejoice together means simply that sowing and harvesting coincide.[198] For this idea one can also refer to Old Testament salvation prophecies such as Lv. 26:5 and Am. 9:13.[199]

196. In other places, too, "harvest" as an image of the consummation plays a large role in Jesus' teaching, specifically in connection with the work his disciples had to do (e.g., Mt. 9:37) and as a reference to the judgment, in which the good and the evil will be brought together (Mt. 13:30); so also "the gathering for eternal life."

197. ἤδη should be read as the first word of vs. 36, not as the last word of the preceding sentence (so some manuscripts).

198. Cf. Bultmann, *Comm.,* p. 197.

199. Cf. Brown, *Comm.* I, p. 182; Olsson, *Structure and Meaning,* pp. 227ff., 232.

But some think that in vs. 36 the sower is God and the reaper is Jesus.[200] Once this has been laid down, the difficulties arise in interpreting vss. 37 and 38, where the reapers are the disciples and the "others" are the sowers. The assumption then is that vs. 36 speaks of the time before the resurrection and vss. 37 and 38 to the time after the resurrection, when the disciples take over reaping. Jesus himself might then belong among the "others," a very difficult line of thought and one not supported by the text.[201]

However, the reference in vss. 37 and 38 is not to something other than or to another time than vs. 36. In both cases the focus is the one great fact that the time of harvest has come, that the disciples are now in that time and, as his disciples, involved in it, and that this privilege should determine their view of their surrounding world. If one neglects this point of view, one cannot avoid the question of who the "others" are. But it is obvious, in any case, that in vs. 38 the disciples are the reapers. The words "I sent you to reap that for which you did not labor" raise questions because what has come before makes no explicit mention of any such mission. But the Evangelist assumes much more knowledge of Jesus' disciples among his readers than what he tells them. The idea that the Fourth Gospel could describe the disciples (apostles) in this fashion only after the resurrection (cf. 20:21ff.) is, in light of what Jesus tells them in the farewell discourses, entirely incredible (cf. 13:16; 15:27; 17:18; cf. 9:4; 6:5ff.).

In this "mission" ("I sent you") the paramount idea is that in the time of fulfillment, the time of harvest, they have their task — and that in distinction from those who (in connection with vs. 37) are called "others" and are defined by the fact that they had their task in sowing time, the time of hard preparatory work. There is no indication that one should think here of particular "others" like the prophets or John the Baptist and his disciples. Still less should one think of others who presumably preceded the disciples in preaching the gospel, such as the Samaritan woman, or other (previously unreported) predecessors who are presumed to have been working among the Samaritans before this, or even Jesus and the Father himself.[202] All of those no longer belong to the time of sowing but, like the disciples, to the time of the harvest.

For that same reason there is no help in the solution that many contemporary interpreters finally adopt, namely that "I sent you" refers not to the disciples who are present in the narrative but was "spoken from the standpoint of later missionary work where every missionary could look back on some predecessor in his field"[203] or was meant specifically of Peter and John, who went to Samaria to continue the work of the "sower" Philip and impart the Holy Spirit to the Samaritans (Acts 8).[204] For this totally

200. So, e.g., Olsson in his lengthy exposition of Jn. 4:31-38 in *Structure and Meaning,* pp. 218-41, esp. pp. 227f., 232; see also Schnackenburg, *Comm.* I, pp. 451, 453ff.

201. Schnackenburg, who holds this view, has to acknowledge (*Comm.* I, p. 444): "The transition from the time of Jesus' labor to that of the Apostles is made, not very smoothly, by the rather awkward parenthesis of vs. 37."

202. So Thüsing, *Erhöhung und Verherrlichung,* pp. 54ff.

203. Bultmann, *Comm.,* p. 200.

204. See, e.g., Brown, *Comm.* I, p. 184. Schnackenburg, on the other hand, who wants to interpret ἀπέστειλα from the historical situation by Jacob's well, says of Jesus that he is "fully conscious of his future exaltation and of the salvation which he will effect through his disciples" (*Comm.* I, p. 453). ἀπέστειλα (aorist) then has to be interpreted "in terms of prophetic prevision"

ignores what must be regarded as the real point, namely that as followers of Jesus the disciples were permitted to do their work in the joy of harvest time and in that respect were distinguished and privileged above all those who preceded them in the work of God.

Should one look for a comparable utterance in the Synoptics, one might consider a passage like Mt. 13:16f.: "Your eyes are blessed because they see and your ears because they hear. Truly, I say to you, many prophets and righteous people wanted to see what you see, but did not, and to hear what you hear, but did not" (cf. also Mt. 11:11f.). In this light it is not hard, precisely because of the generality of the contrast, to understand the statement that Jesus sent out his disciples to reap that for which they did not labor and that they thus "entered into the labor of the 'others.' " The statement indicates the difference between the time before and the time after the fulfillment, especially for those who with intense longing looked forward to that time of harvest.

39-42   The conclusion of the story — the arrival of the Samaritans and their confession concerning Jesus — links up with vs. 30 but can only be read in the light in which the Evangelist wants to have it understood after vss. 31-38: that of the visible breakthrough of the time of the harvest, climaxing in the confession of Jesus as the Savior of the world. At their request Jesus spends two days among them. It is a visit "in passing." It is not certain, however, that it was the Evangelist's intention to stress the brevity of the visit. In any case, the time was long enough to lead still many more people to faith in Jesus and to move the people from the testimony of the woman to the word of Jesus himself as the basis for their faith. Although they give somewhat negative expression to this vis-à-vis the woman ("no longer"), the statement is not intended to minimize her importance in the whole episode. It was "the word" of her "testimony" (vs. 39) that had awakened faith in Jesus in their hearts.[205] Still it was not her story but what her fellow townspeople now heard with their own ears that led them to the conviction ("we have heard for ourselves, and we know . . .") that Jesus was truly what the woman had so tentatively proposed to them: the Savior of the world.

Here one senses anew the power and significance of the cry "come and see" (cf. 1:39, 46) with which now the woman has exhorted her fellow townspeople to ascertain for themselves what she has found in Jesus (cf. vs. 29). This repeated exhortation and the emphasis on the fact that the Samaritan

---

(p. 452). But this grammatically difficult interpretation is superfluous if one regards the element of mission as included from the very beginning in the calling of the disciples as Jesus' special followers (cf. 1:43, 51). According to the Gospel they already baptized during Jesus' time on earth (3:22; 4:2)!

205. There is therefore no reason to take λαλιά in vs. 42, though the word could also be used in a denigrating sense ("chatter," "prattle"), as inferior in importance to the "word" (here διὰ τὸν λόγον) of Jesus.

population "heard for themselves" obviously do not mean — as many interpreters think — that no one should be content with what others witness concerning Jesus and that therefore everyone should seek a personal encounter with Jesus. The point of this "come and see" is the position of eyewitness, which intrinsically cannot be the privilege of all and which does not keep Jesus from calling those blessed who have not seen and yet have believed (20:29). The Samaritans' pronouncement rather proves how powerful and all-embracing Jesus' self-revelation "in the flesh" actually was. It did not limit itself merely to the the woman and her life story but communicated itself in its saving significance (crossing all traditional boundaries) also to those who had come in response to the woman's testimony and that of many in the city who met him themselves. For when they heard him himself, they understood that they were in fact dealing not just with a clairvoyant or miracle worker but with the Savior of the world.

These words with which the whole story ends unmistakably convey the thrust of the story: salvation is not only for Jews. The Samaritans understood this from the manner in which Jesus had made himself known to the woman (*this* woman) and had spent two days with them. They do not call him by the name which was typical for the future expectation of the Jews, "Messiah," or by that of their own, Taheb, but by a name in accord with universal salvation.[206] The theme of the universal redemptive significance of Jesus' coming keeps returning in the Fourth Gospel (e.g., 1:29; 3:16; 6:33; 12:47; see also 1 Jn. 4:14; 2:2). Still, the story in ch. 4 is the only place where that salvation is actually effected — and that only among the Samaritans, Israel's nearest neighbors, perhaps also the neighboring people most hated by the Jews (cf. 8:48). The gospel was to go to Gentiles only later (cf. 12:20-23), when Jesus' glorification, his return to the Father, had begun (cf. 12:32). But now already, in his lifetime, Jesus could not, as it were, go beyond the Samaritans. He "had to" pass through Samaria. And by that token the geographical "had to" (see the comments on vs. 11) acquires in retrospect a deeper meaning. And wherever he had to go he was the Savior, even among the Samaritans, and that in consequence of his encounter with this one woman. The fact that God loved the world in him could hardly be more clearly evident than here; and this was undoubtedly the compelling reason that the Evangelist took so much care to include among the deliberately selected encounters between Jesus and people this encounter with a Samaritan woman.

---

206. It must be granted that salvation for Israel was also called σωτηρία (cf. vs. 22; Lk. 1:47, etc.).

4:43-54

Back to Cana: The Healing of the Royal Official's Son; Faith and Miracles

43-45 These verses constitute the transition to the following story. After the two-day stay in Samaria the journey to Galilee (cf. 4:3) is continued. Vs. 44 immediately confronts us with a seemingly insoluble difficulty. Apparently to explain ("for") Jesus' journey to Galilee, the Evangelist cites the familiar saying of Jesus that "a prophet has no honor in his own country" (cf. Mt. 13:57; Mk. 6:4; Lk. 4:24). But this involves a double problem: First, how could this be a reason for Jesus to go to Galilee? Second, is this not immediately contradicted by vs. 45, which describes the welcome extended to Jesus by Galileans who had seen what he had done at the feast in Jerusalem?

From ancient times[207] scholars have sought a way out by saying that by "his country" not Galilee but Judea is meant, and this view has maintained itself to the present day.[208] But this goes against what is meant elsewhere by the same saying (cf. Lk. 4:24, also speaking of Jesus' initial public ministry in Galilee!). Furthermore, in John Galilee could hardly function as a place of refuge from Jesus' country since "for Jesus himself testified . . ." explains not only why he departed from Judea but also why he went to Galilee instead (cf. vs. 3). Assuming that one could argue that Jerusalem was Jesus' city or country, that could hardly be true in explicit contrast with Galilee.

Most recent scholarship therefore maintains that Galilee was Jesus' country referred to in the saying. The "for" of vs. 44, it is said, is an a priori allusion to the resistance Jesus was to encounter there. In consequence vs. 45 has to be understood in an exclusively negative sense: people only welcomed Jesus for his miracles, as Jesus himself expressly says in vs. 48.[209] Still, one cannot be content with this view either. With it the "for" in vs. 44 remains very difficult, and above all the story of the royal official contradicts the idea that in Galilee Jesus would encounter exclusively negative reactions (cf. vss. 50, 53).

The "for" in vs. 44 explains, rather, Jesus' escape to Galilee in connection with his reason for leaving Judea, namely his own security (cf. 7:1). There, in

207. Cf. Origen, *In Joh.* 13.54 (quoted by Brown, *Comm.* I, p. 187).

208. See the extensive treatment of this issue by J. Willemse, "La Patrie de Jésus selon Saint Jean IV,44," *NTS* 11 (1965), pp. 349ff. Among Willemse's conclusions is that πατρίς represented Judea/Jerusalem specifically because Jerusalem was the city where the house of Jesus' Father was located and could therefore be called "his Father's city" (pp. 359ff.). See also M. Rissi, "Der Aufbau des vierten Evangeliums," *NTS* 29 (1983), p. 48. Other advocates of this view (Jerusalem/Judea = πατρίς) include Barrett, *Comm.*, p. 246; Dodd, *Interpretation*, p. 352; de Jonge, *Jesus, Stranger from Heaven*, p. 64 ("clearly Judea for the Fourth Gospel").

209. See, e.g., Bultmann, *Comm.*, p. 204.

his own country of Galilee, he did not have to fear the attendance of large crowds, which in the eyes of the Jewish authorities made him so dangerous. Being "held in honor" was to run the risk of universal adoration, of being viewed as something more than "one of our own." This is not in conflict with vs. 45. The Galileans welcomed him on account of what they had seen him do in Jerusalem. But that was all. People there, by contrast with Judea, did not regard his coming as a threat to their own authority or power but as a chance that, being one of them, he would demonstrate his miraculous power also in his fatherland (cf. Lk. 4:22f.).[210]

46 Jesus went again to Cana in Galilee. The verse explicitly mentions the miracle he performed there before. Two things are striking here: first, the special significance thus attributed to Cana as the place where a miracle again takes place and, second, that Cana is again identified as being *in Galilee* (2:1, 11; 4:45; also 21:2, cf. comments on 2:1 above). In vs. 54 the Evangelist returns to the fact of the second miracle (see comments there).

The view that the story that now follows is a variant of the healing narrated in Mt. 8:5-13 and Lk. 7:1-10 is widespread.[211] The *basilikos* in Jn. 4:46 is then said to be the same person as the centurion of Mt. 8:5; Lk. 7:2. This identification is not in itself impossible because in vs. 46b the *basilikos* is said to be someone in the service of King Herod Antipas (really a tetrarch but popularly called a king). Hence he could be a military man, though *basilikos* rather suggests a court official.[212] But there are other more striking similarities between the two stories: Capernaum as the place of residence of the official, healing from a distance, the father's pleading for his child (in Matthew the παῖς could also be a son, though in Luke he is clearly a slave).

But there are also conspicuous differences. In John, in contrast with the Synoptics, Jesus is in Cana, and the view (partly based on that fact) that vs. 46 is a later addition and that the story originally began with "Now there was a royal official at Capernaum" (cf. 3:1) lacks all textual support and runs into conflict in vs. 52 ("yesterday"). Furthermore, the thrust of the two stories differs to a considerable degree. In the Synoptics the central subject is a Gentile centurion, whom Jesus praises as a model of faith such as is not found in Israel. In John we are told nothing of a *Gentile* official. In response to his first request Jesus answers the official very critically and places him

---

210. For this view, cf. also Strathmann, *Comm.,* p. 93.

211. For lengthy considerations of this question see Schnackenburg, *Comm.* I, pp. 471ff.; Nicol, *Sēmeia,* pp. 41ff. Schnackenburg, p. 474: "Similarities and divergencies [in John 4 as compared to Matthew 8 and Luke 7] are equally apparent and the verdict as to whether one or more events are involved seems to be left to the judgment of the individual commentator." Schnackenburg is inclined to the view that one event is referred to (p. 475). Nicol speaks of "possible parallels" (p. 55; cf. pp. 41f.), but also has difficulties with the theological differences (pp. 55ff.).

212. οἱ βασιλικοί is sometimes used of soldiers in the king's service (see BAGD s.v.), but here the singular probably refers to a civilian official.

among the Jewish population (note the plural in vs. 48).[213] His faith is mentioned only in the second place (vss. 50 and 53, after the fact). If one wishes to trace the two stories back to a single event, one has to assume that the Evangelist regarded the father's conduct from a totally different theological viewpoint and reshaped the entire story in terms of that viewpoint.[214] This constitutes an identification, therefore — one that is not very persuasive — of two traditions with two sharply divergent theological profiles.

47 This brings us to the story's most conspicuous feature, the ambivalent way in which the relationship between faith and miracle is referred to. This verse clearly evidences the father's faith in Jesus' power to do miracles. When he heard that Jesus was coming to Galilee, he went to Cana and made an urgent[215] request to him to come down[216] to Capernaum with him and to heal his child, who was deathly ill.

48 At first blush Jesus' response in vs. 48 seems to be hard and to ignore the true faith that the father placed in his miraculous power. Some interpreters therefore regard vs. 48 as a *corpus alienum* that was not in the original story but was added by the Evangelist as part of his criticism of mere faith in miracles.[217] But this ignores the real point at issue: Jesus does not charge the father of the sick child with wanting to see a miracle as legitimation of Jesus' claims (as, e.g., in Mk. 8:11ff.). His complaint is, rather, that all that moved the man to come to Jesus was Jesus' miracles: "If I did not perform miracles, you would have no interest in me," you would not "believe" in me.[218]

Accordingly, the special character of our text remains that this critical approach to a miracle-oriented faith is directed to someone who is not, in fact, out to see miracles of Jesus in general but who is appealing to Jesus out of his own distress. This difference may be explained by Jesus' use of the plural: He

213. "Very probably representative of Galilee" (de Jonge, *Jesus, Stranger from Heaven,* p. 63.

214. This is argued at great length by E. Schweizer in "Die Heilung des Königlichen: Joh. 4.46-54," in *Neotestamentica,* 1963, pp. 409ff. Cf. p. 207 of the same book, where, in relation to Jn. 4:46f., Schweizer writes: "The changing situation of the hearers changed the message of this story," which he regards as a pointer also for modern interpretation. But is it really conceivable that an Evangelist dealt with historical tradition as though it were a pile of Lego blocks from which one could make new figures at will by rearranging the pieces and adding new pieces?

215. ἠρώτα, imperfect to indicate the persistence of the request.

216. καταβῇ.

217. See, e.g., Nicol, *Sēmeia,* pp. 28ff.

218. Cf. ibid., p. 100; see also Schweizer, *Neotestamentica,* p. 413: "Hence the false component here does not consist in that he will recognize Jesus only on the basis of a sign (cf. Mark 8, 11, etc.), but in that he is not at all interested in Jesus himself, only in something to be obtained through him" (cf. 4:15; 6:34). Vs. 48 is strongly reminiscent of Lk. 4:23 (together with 4:24!), where at his first public appearance in Galilee (Nazareth) Jesus also sharply rejects, as being oriented solely to miracles, the acclaim of his countrymen. Hence vs. 48 does not just represent a Johannine feature but is deeply rooted in the tradition.

is not addressing the official personally but in light of the general mood that arose around Jesus, in Galilee as in Jerusalem, and that Jesus "knew" (cf. 2:23ff.). On the other hand, for Jesus to make an issue of the inadequacy of miracle-oriented faith precisely vis-à-vis the father of a critically ill child shows how serious Jesus was in not wanting to be misunderstood in his miraculous power both for the sake of his mission and for the sake of this man himself. Even in the heart-rending situation in which the royal official came to him, Jesus was not content simply to heal the man's son: his seeming harshness was aimed at not letting the man (and his entire household) remain stuck halfway on the road of faith. It has therefore been correctly remarked that Jesus' answer in vs. 48 was not so much an accusation as a challenge.[219] In other words, Jesus did not only want to give the son back to his father: he wanted to give himself (cf. also 6:27-29).

49, 50   This is also evident from what follows. The father, motivated by the critical condition of his son, persists — now with a passionate appeal to Jesus for help: "Sir, come with me before my child dies!"[220] He urges himself upon Jesus all the more intensely just as Jesus seems to withdraw himself from him (cf. Mt. 15:25ff.). Hence he presents the picture Jesus elsewhere describes as "entering the kingdom violently" (Lk. 16:16; Mt. 11:12).

And then, as in Mt. 15:28, Jesus succumbs — but only in part. He says: "Go; your son will live." With increasing[221] urgency the man has asked Jesus to go down to his house with him, which to him seemed indispensable if his son was to have a chance. But Jesus sends him away — with his word of power "your son will live,"[222] to be sure, but that *word* had to be enough for the man. Hence the Evangelist puts all emphasis on that fact when he describes the man's positive reaction: "the man believed the word that Jesus spoke to him and went his way."

51-53   The outcome of the story confirms both Jesus' word and the father's faith. The servants who come out to meet him are unbiased witnesses because they know "nothing." Also, the determination of the hour of the healing excluded all doubt. When Jesus spoke, at a great distance, the condition of the

---

219. See de Jonge, *Jesus, Stranger from Heaven,* p. 123.

220. Here παιδίον μου in place of υἱός, which appears in vs. 47.

221. See also C. H. Giblin, "Suggestion, Negative Response, and Positive Action in St. John's Portrayal of Jesus," *NTS* 26 (1980), p. 204: "V. 49 not only reiterates the request to 'come down,' but more obviously presents that 'coming down' as the supposedly indispensable condition for saving the boy's life (aor. imv. immediately followed by πρίν w. inf.)."

222. These words recall 1 Kg. 17:23: "Live" in this connection is a typically Jewish word for "become well," "remain alive" (cf. Nu. 21:8; 2 Kg. 1:2; 8:8) and need have no deeper meaning. Cf. Nicol, *Sēmeia,* p. 107: "John narrates the healing of the boy without any conscious allusion to deeper meaning, but he would not have objected to anyone (such as Dodd, p. 324) who saw in the thrice repeated 'your boy lives' (4:50, 51, 53) a reference to the spiritual ζωοποιεῖν of Jesus discussed in the next chapter. . . ."

sick boy changed, "yesterday at the seventh hour."[223] The statement at the end, "and he himself believed and all his household," speaks in contemporary terms (cf. Ac. 11:14; 16:15, 31f.; 18:8) of the reversal that from that moment occurred in the life of this father and his family. The "absolute" statement "he believed" (without an object) no longer denotes a single act of faith, as in vs. 50, but conversion to a life of faith: "they became believing," adherents of Jesus in the deeper sense of the word. The miracle of healing had paved the way for this. It is precisely these last words that express the change that occurred since the father had hastened to Cana to ask for Jesus' help. He already "believed" in Jesus, that is, that Jesus could heal his son. But by the way in which Jesus had countered and tested him, Jesus had made him believe *at his word* and thus related him entirely to himself.

It is from this latter point that this "miracle story" derives its meaning in the series of encounters described by the Evangelist. Miracle belongs inseparably to Jesus' mission, as his witness to the Father (cf. 5:36; 10:25), as the sign of the salvation represented by him (cf. 9:1, 39; 6:32), and hence as a means of leading people to faith (10:38; 12:37; 20:30). But Jesus is more than the miracles he performs, more than the bread he distributes, and more than the child he restores to its father (and mother and whole family, vs. 53). He is himself the miracle from above; it is therefore also himself he imparts in his miracles, the bread of life (6:35), the resurrection and the life (11:25), the light of the world (9:35). The faith he demands is therefore more than faith in (his power to do) miracles; it is faith in him as the gift of God come down from heaven (4:10; 6:29, 33). *For that reason* the mere fact of being allowed to participate in a miracle does not yet by itself mean that the recipients have participated in the gift of God in Jesus (cf. 6:27; 5:14). The opposite rather is the case: only one who believes *in him* participates in the miracle he grants and is (11:25). Miracles not only precede faith as a means of coming to Jesus; they also come after as the ever-remaining "benefit" of faith in him.

Of this the royal official is an example. He came to Jesus on account of the miracle he desired, but Jesus placed himself between the father and his child. Only when he allowed himself to be sent on his way by Jesus' word did the father find that the miracle he wanted was, as it were, already waiting for him. There is in this story of Jesus' miracle-at-a-distance, among "the many other signs he did," a unique motive for believing that "Jesus is the Christ, the Son of God, and that believing one may have life in his name" (20:30f.). The

223. According to Dalman, *Orte und Wege Jesu,* the shortest road between Capernaum and Cana was twenty-six kilometers long ("a truly wearisome road"): "If the father left at sunrise he could be at his destination by noon and hear Jesus' comforting word at 'the seventh hour' (Jn. 4:52); but on this day he could at most travel half the distance to Mammela, so that on the following day the servants, who were rushing toward him, could meet him in the plain of Gennesareth" (pp. 113f.).

readers of this Gospel also lacked, and still lack, the chance to see first and then believe. But anyone who, like this anonymous official from Capernaum, lets himself be sent on his way in faith without first having seen, will see that the miracle is already there waiting for him. It is that order that governs the key statement of this entire story: "Go, behold your son will live" (cf. also 20:29).

Verse **54** concludes the pericope. It presents a problem in that while it speaks of "the second sign," apparently with reference to "the first of his signs" in 2:11, it seems to ignore 2:23 and 4:45, which mention signs Jesus had performed between this "first" and "second." Moreover, this enumeration is not continued and as such seems rather senseless in the Gospel as we now have it. All this has led to the hypothesis that this enumeration stems from another source,[224] one in which these two miracles are, in fact, the first and the second. In drawing from this source the Evangelist is then said to have adopted also its enumeration, ignoring the miracles that he has reported in the meantime.[225] Although many commentators place much emphasis on this assumed inconsistency ("aporia") in the text as we have it and make it one of the pillars of the hypothesis of the "*sēmeia* source,"[226] it seems to me that the Evangelist is, here again,[227] being too readily charged with disturbing his own narrative — not this time, as in vs. 48, on "theological" grounds, but on account of his careless handling of his source.

But two things are being overlooked: First, the Evangelist does not just mention the miracles Jesus performed in Jerusalem in passing in 2:23, that is, in such a way that he could easily miss them in the enumeration, and he brings them up again in 3:2 and in the present pericope (vs. 45; cf. vs. 48) as an important datum in these chapters. Second, the connection between 4:54 and 2:11 is much too organically integrated in the text for one to regard it as an "alien body" inappropriately taken over from another context. In vs. 46 also, as soon as Cana in Galilee is mentioned, there is immediate reference to the miracle Jesus performed there (just as in 2:11, Cana in Galilee is again expressly mentioned as the place of "the first of the signs"). When, therefore, in 4:54, following the mention of "the second sign," there recurs the seemingly redun-

---

224. Usually thought of as a "*sēmeia* source" (see the comments on 2:1-11 above). On this source there exists an extensive body of literature; see, e.g., J. L. Martyn, *History and Theology in the Fourth Gospel,* 1979[2], pp. 164-68.

225. See, e.g., Nicol, *Sēmeia,* who also infers the existence of a sēmeia source.

226. Brown speaks of "the backbone of the theory of a collection of signs" (*Comm.* I, p. 195). Brown himself does not hold to this theory but does believe that the two "closely related" Cana miracles were borrowed from a single source and separated to form the beginning and the end of the second main division of the Gospel (chs. 2-11), which Brown entitles "From Cana to Cana."

227. See the comments above on vs. 48.

dant (after vss. 43, 45, and 46) reference to time and place "when Jesus had come from Judea to Galilee," it is clear that the Evangelist very specifically wants to direct the attention of the reader to the *second sign in Galilee.* Grammatically there is no objection to taking vs. 54b as a qualification of "second" in vs. 54a ("As the second miracle that Jesus peformed after his arrival").[228] Therefore, "again" in vs. 54a is not to be taken as a pleonastic apposition[229] alongside "second" but rather, as in vs. 45, as an indication that there was an "encore" in the same place (cf. also 4:36).[230]

The question then becomes: Why did the Evangelist expressly link the two Galilean miracles? It is unlikely that we are dealing merely with a geographic coincidence. In all kinds of ways scholars have attempted to bring out points of correspondence between the two miracles that are assumed to explain this connection.[231] Nor can it be denied that — as far as the construction of the two stories is concerned — such points are clearly present.[232] But in 4:54 that is obviously not the point.[233]

It seems to me more important that with this second miracle the story returns, as it were, to the location of the first, where everything began, forming an *inclusio*[234] and giving the intervening cycle of stories a kind of conclusion. As a result Galilee attains a certain strategic significance as the base for the manifestation of Jesus' messianic glory (against all human expectations and prejudices: cf. 1:46; 7:41). The road to Jerusalem and the temple ran from there (2:13) and not the other way. Each time he returned to Galilee, it was as to his own country. It was also a place of refuge from dangers present in Judea (4:1ff.; 7:1, 9).

228. As Bultmann also recognizes (*Comm.,* p. 209, n. 2). But he thinks this is impossible "because in that case the first miracle would have had to be recorded." However, though the entire sentence is also applicable to the first miracle (cf. 1:43!), the Evangelist's focus is clearly not the *time* but the *place* of the miracle.

229. Though by itself not uncommon (cf. 21:16; see also BDF §484).

230. So Giblin, "Suggestion, Negative Response, and Positive Action," p. 198, n. 7:

The evangelist is not numbering signs consecutively ("first," "second," etc.). He begins with an inaugural sign in Cana of Galilee ("This beginning . . . ," ταύτην . . . ἀρχήν . . . , 2,11), mentions other signs (2,23; 3,2), and then returns to "this second" sign (τοῦτο . . . δεύτερον) on his return to Galilee — omitting the definite article after τοῦτο and imposing πάλιν between τοῦτο and δεύτερον, etc. . . . In 4,54 as in 4,46 πάλιν helps correlate this Galilean sign with that Galilean sign that was already mentioned.

231. E.g., F. J. Moloney, "From Cana to Cana (John 2:1–4:54)," in *Studia Biblica (Sixth International Congress on Biblical Studies, Oxford 1978),* 1980, p. 190; Brown, *Comm.* I, pp. 194ff.

232. Cf. Brown, *Comm.,* ad loc.: "Someone comes with a request; indirectly Jesus seems to refuse the request; the questioner persists; Jesus grants the request; this leads another group of people (the disciples; the household) to believe in him."

233. The same structural pattern occurs elsewhere also; see Giblin, "Suggestion, Negative Response, and Positive Action," p. 200.

234. So also Brown, *Comm.* I, p. 198.

Furthermore, the "second" miracle in Galilee also constitutes a new beginning of Jesus' self-manifestation *in* and *from within* Galilee — not, like the first time, to manifest his glory before the eyes of his disciples (cf. 1:11) but rather to take an unambiguous position against the chauvinism and craving for miracles of his compatriots and to bring to light the true "faith in his word." That struggle for the recognition of his true identity will continue in Galilee in a decisive way (cf. ch. 6) but will also from now on be the great issue in all those journeys he will make from Galilee to Jerusalem in the confrontation with "the Jews," who are increasingly hostile to him. In view of all this 4:43-54 serves as a hinge[235] in the construction of the narrative, being the conclusion of the preceding and a bridge to what follows, where the relationship between faith and miracle (which is so fundamental in this pericope) will increasingly prove to be of cardinal significance (especially in chs. 5–10: note 5:14ff.; 6:26ff.; 7:2ff.; 9:35ff.; 10:37f.).

235. Most interpreters believe it belongs to what precedes. Others (e.g., Dodd, *Interpretation,* pp. 318f.; A. Feuillet, "La signification théologique du second miracle de Cana [Jn IV, 46-54]," in *Études Johanniques,* 1962, pp. 34-36) view it as a preparation for ch. 5. One does not really have to choose, though it may be most natural to think of it as primarily the conclusion of chs. 2–4 (see also Brown, *Comm.* I, p. 198).

5–6

Jesus' Self-Revelation as
Son of God and Bread of Life,
Resistance from "the Jews"

Starting with ch. 5 there is a clear shift in the Gospel's story. The report of
Jesus' self-revelation in chs. 2–4 continues with an ever-increasing and deepening wealth of topics and motifs. But there is now a new element in the
construction of the Gospel: the portrayal of the radical resistance that Jesus'
public conduct evoked in the leaders of the Jewish people, who are often simply
called "the Jews." In that confrontation the Jewish people, called "the multitude," is repeatedly in conflict with itself: one moment it is deeply impressed
by Jesus' authority in words and deeds, as is indicated by the repeated statement
"and many believed in him"; then it is profoundly uncertain about Jesus'
identity ("Who is this?") and afraid of "the Jews," who are increasingly
opposed to Jesus. This picture continues to the end of ch. 10, where the disputes
between Jesus and "the Jews" that mark chs. 5–10 come to a decisive end,
after which the last phase of Jesus' associations with people begins.

Chapters 5 and 6 occupy an important place of their own in this structure:
they contain the central issue of the conflict, which will manifest itself from now
on in all of its intensity, between Jesus and "the Jews," and bring out its
fundamental cause. To this end both chapters are constructed in the same pattern,
each starting with a miracle of Jesus, then continuing with the ensuing reaction of
"the Jews" (ch. 5) or "the multitude" (ch. 6; see, however, 6:41, 52), and
culminating in a lengthy and largely monologic discourse of Jesus. Pivotal in both
is the absoluteness of Jesus' self-revelation and Jewish resistance to that revelation. In ch. 5 we see — over against the accusations of "the Jews" — *Jesus'
self-identification as the Son of God,* in an unfolding of the authority given him
by God, in such a manner that hardly has its equal anywhere else in the Gospel

181

(see the comments on 5:19-29 below). Then in ch. 6, after the miracle of the loaves and Jesus' walking on the Sea of Tiberias, follows the long discourse in the synagogue of Capernaum, in which Jesus, in a most exclusive and highly offensive (to the flesh) manner, describes himself as the bread that has come down from heaven, which he gives for the life of the world. Both of these chapters' central perspectives, both the christological perspective of ch. 5 and ch. 6's related perspective of the salvific significance of his descent from heaven, will return, more fragmentarily and in more of a swirl of dialogues and intermezzos, in chs. 7–10, but always against the full background of chs. 5 and 6.

Of no less importance for insight into the construction of the Gospel is the locale in these chapters, Jerusalem in ch. 5 and Galilee in ch. 6. The dominant interest of these chapters is thus "allotted" equally to the two places. Jerusalem, to be sure, will increasingly prove to be the place where the denouement of the conflict will occur and where the great spiritual struggle of Jesus with "the Jews" takes place with ever increasing intensity. After ch. 6 (and the beginning of ch. 7) we do not find Jesus back in Galilee. But that does not mean that the Galilean "contribution" to the content of the Gospel is less essential. For the Evangelist "knows" that not Jerusalem and Judea but Galilee is Jesus' home and the base of his activity (see comments on 4:1ff., 54). Jesus' stays in Jerusalem are restricted to the great feasts to which he as a pilgrim from Galilee "went up." But also in terms of content Galilee is given full measure; this is the case in chs. 2–4 (see comments on 4:54) but especially in ch. 6, where the Evangelist summarizes Jesus' self-revelation in Galilee and "the divergence of minds" taking place also there and brings them together at a point in his Gospel that is most pivotal for the construction of the whole.

All this, however, does not alter the fact that the big decision is made, not in Galilee, but in the center of Jewish life — in Jerusalem and specifically in the temple, the heart of Jewish religion. There is good reason that already in the first cycle (chs. 2–4) the first confrontation with "the Jews" takes place in the temple, the temple itself being an issue as the place where God dwells and as the house of Jesus' father. One could even say that the saying of Jesus, "destroy this temple," finds its sinister fulfillment in the rising resistance of the Jews to Jesus' self-revelation as the Son of God.

In this light, finally, one may regard also the long-standing literary-critical contention over the original order of chs. 5 and 6. Many commentators believe that, for whatever reason, these chapters have traded places. The main argument for this is that 6:1 links up much better with the conclusion of ch. 4 than with that of ch. 5; 6:1 mentions Jesus going "to the other side of the sea," which would presuppose a stay on the western side of the Sea of Galilee, as at the end of ch. 4. By contrast there is no local connection between 6:1 and the end of ch. 5, where, to the end, Jesus is in dialogue with "the Jews" in Jerusalem. Moreover, with the order reversed, the nonspecified "feast of the Jews" of 5:1

turns out to be the approaching Passover mentioned in 6:4. If one further assumes that the geographic reference in 7:1 ("Jesus went about in Galilee") concerns not a continued but a new stay of Jesus in Galilee, that would also tie in better with ch. 5 than with ch. 6, where Jesus already is in Galilee.

There is much to be said against this explanation of 7:1, as we will see when we get there. If one focuses, therefore, chiefly on the lack of a proper transition between chs. 5 and 6, it cannot be denied that the hypothesis of their reversal has some appeal. And scholars who as a rule make sparing use of such reconstructions of the traditional sequence of the Fourth Gospel do adopt this hypothesis.[1] One may question, however, to what degree the Evangelist felt it necessary to give the reader detailed insight into the chronological sequence of the events narrated; it is clear that the kerygmatic content of these events was of more importance to him. The repeated "after this" in 5:1; 6:1; and 7:1 is very general; it allows room for intervening occurrences and offers only a very general indication of the chronological connection between the conceptual sequences thus woven together. If in this connection one bears in mind that for John Galilee was Jesus' real and ongoing place of residence, then the absence of a clear chronological and local transition between chs. 5 and 6 is not as strange or striking as it may seem at first sight. In that case the journey to and stay at Jerusalem in ch. 5 would constitute a temporary break — motivated by one of the great feasts — in Jesus' ongoing residence in Galilee. Then ch. 6 simply continues the story of this residence, one that is quite intelligible even apart from any mention of Jesus' return from the feast. If one further accepts (as we will explain) that the opening words of 7:1 ("after this") refer to the continuation (and not a resumption) of Jesus' going about in Galilee, then, from the perspective of geographical clarity, there is no longer any compelling reason to deviate from the traditional sequence of chs. 5 and 6. The case is rather that then the "infrastructure" of chs. 4–7 will thus become clearer to us.

What seems more important, however, is the content of these chapters. From the vantage point of the construction of the Gospel, as we have seen, the new start *at Jerusalem* and the self-revelation of Jesus as the Son of God as the central content in ch. 5 are most meaningful. If one reverses the order of chs. 5 and 6, the most crucial issues are already settled in Galilee before there has occurred even an initial great confrontation in Jerusalem over Jesus' sonship like the one in ch. 5. Moreover, from the perspective of content ch. 6 presupposes ch. 5 rather than vice versa. It is only against the christological background of Jesus' self-revelation as the Son that the soteriological discourse about the bread that has come down from heaven, along with Jesus' calling his flesh the true food and his blood the true drink, get their true meaning. This will constantly be in evidence in the exposition of ch. 6. Accordingly, it is

---

1. So, e.g., Schnackenburg.

specifically with a view to the material construction of the Johannine kerygma that we shall adhere to the traditional sequence of chs. 5 and 6, which also has no manuscript witness against it.

5:1-18

The Healing of a Paralytic at Bethesda, Conflict over the Sabbath

1 The transition from ch. 4 to ch. 5 follows a standard form (cf. 6:1; 7:1). If one does not accept the transposition of chs. 5 and 6 (see above), one may be surprised at first that, whereas in ch. 4 — to escape the threatening hostility of the Pharisees — Jesus left Judea and went to Galilee, the setting of the narrative that now follows is again Jerusalem. But the formula "after this" is very general; it says nothing about the duration of the intervening time and indicates little more than a change of subject. Moreover, the return to Galilee, the (permanent) place of residence, does not mean that Jesus will no longer go as a pilgrim to the great feasts at Jerusalem. Also "*a* feast"[2] is very general. If one follows the transposition hypothesis, 5:1 might refer back to 6:4. But the striking reference to "*a* feast of the Jews" (see the comments on 2:13) does not so much assume a non-Jewish readership as the temporal and material distance that had developed at the time of this Gospel between the Christian church and the situation to which the story takes us. The character of the feast remains obscure throughout the story and all efforts to identify it and to establish a material connection between the feast and the story lack a solid foundation. At stake in what follows is rather the issue of the sabbath (cf. comments on vs. 9b), an issue that was undoubtedly still relevant to the first readers.

2-4 The miracle story that now follows has the traditional form also familiar from the Synoptic Gospels: depiction of the situation and of the seriousness of the illness ("thirty-eight years"), dialogue between Jesus and the sick person, and the immediate marvelous effect. One is struck by the detailed depiction of the situation, which assumes precise topographical knowledge (confirmed by excavations).[3] There is mention of a pool situated by the Sheep Gate[4]

---

2. At least if one follows most (and the most important) manuscripts.

3. Cf. J. Jeremias, *Die Wiederentdeckung von Bethesda,* 1949.

4. Actually the text only mentions a "sheep place." Some scholars connect it with the following word: "Sheep pool," following a reading in which "sheep" is not connected with a preposition and occurs in the nominative. In that case the pool took its name from the Sheep Gate, which in Jesus' day and still now is a familiar gate in the northern part of Jerusalem, northeast of the temple square. But the pool also has another name, so we assume that "sheep" refers to the well-known gate.

that in "Hebrew" (i.e., Aramaic) is called Bethesda or, according to other readings, Bethzatha.[5] The porticoes mentioned have also been uncovered by excavations, so that speculations about the number five (relating it to the number of the books of Moses, for example) have become even more incredible than they already were.

Many invalids sought healing at this place: the blind, the lame, and the paralyzed.[6] Vs. 7 shows that therapeutic significance was attributed to the periodic "troubling" of the water, and some translations have in vs. 3 the words "waiting for the moving of the water," which, though they agree with the intent of the author, because of the weaker textual witness and because addition is more likely than omission, are to be regarded as a later gloss. This is even more true in vs. 4 in the mention of "an angel of the Lord who at certain times went down into the pool and troubled the water; whoever stepped in first after the troubling of the water was healed of whatever disease he had," a reading universally regarded as inauthentic. This insertion probably expresses a folk belief, associated with certain therapeutic springs, that angels from time to time made the water of the pool bubble or spout up. It is not clear that the words of the paralytic in vs. 7 were also so intended. Apparently for him, too, the moment when the water was "troubled" was important.

5 It is further said of this man that he had been sick for thirty-eight years. We do not know what was wrong, but the manner of his healing clearly indicates paralysis (cf. Mt. 9:6 par.). The length of time is mentioned in order to highlight the seriousness of the ailment and the hopeless condition of the man.

6 A special motif is that the initiative for the healing proceeds from Jesus. Jesus "saw him" here, and as elsewhere this is an introduction to action (cf. 9:1; Lk. 7:13, etc.). That Jesus knew (cf. 9:1, 2) that the man had been sick for a long time shows that Jesus not only caught sight of him among the many others but saw him in the depth of his misery. Hence the words with which Jesus addresses him ("Do you want to be healed?") are not just a way of starting a conversation but an indirect offer, based on the power and authority at Jesus' disposal, to which he called the sick man's attention as a new possibility.

7 But this man, who did not know Jesus (vs. 13), saw no other possibility than the therapeutic power of the water for his healing. He therefore politely

---

5. There is a wide diversity of readings and opinions about the name of the pool. The reading "Bethesda" is ancient, perhaps supported by its meaning: "House of Mercy." A stronger textual witness has "Bethzatha," which is assumed to be identical with "Bezetha," the name of a northern part of Jerusalem, which, it is assumed, gave its name to the pool. However, there is also an opinion that the name intended here is identical with one found in the Qumran writings in a reference to the same place, which is said to have led to the name Beth-eshda (see, e.g., Brown, *Comm.*, in loc.).

6. The verb related to the third of these words occurs in Mk. 3:1. They are used of those who are unable to walk.

answered that he had "no one" to help him and hence always came too late. This raises all kinds of questions: In all the time that the man had been sick had there never been a person willing to help him? And had none of the other patients ever been willing to let him go first? One can infer — correctly — from this that, even if the water had therapeutic qualities, this was undoubtedly a matter of trying to reach it not just once but over and over, and even then it was not enough to heal. Proceeding along that line one can then assume that Jesus' question was intended to make the man aware of the hopelessness of seeking healing in this manner. But for all such reflections there is no place within the framework of this story (as in so many others). What we have here is a snapshot of a man doomed for years to powerlessness on account of an incurable illness, looking in vain for a miracle to happen, who had no one (or no one left?) to assist him in this predicament. To such a person Jesus comes with his question, a question full of power and promise: "Do you want to be healed?"

8, 9a The account of the miracle is as restricted to essentials as the description of the man's misery has been.[7] The striking similarity between this passage and Mt. 9:6 par. shows how utterances like this were fixed in the tradition. The word "rise"[8] is going to play a very essential role in what follows (cf. vs. 21). For the paralytic to carry his pallet[9] home manifested the reversal in his fortunes: no longer does the bed carry a powerless man but, with vitality to spare, he (triumphantly) carries the bed. For now there is no mention of any other reaction. The entire focus is on the manifestation of Jesus' glory.

The statement in vs. **9b** that all this took place on a sabbath comes after the action has been described, as in ch. 9, and has occasioned the hypothesis that what now follows — with the exception perhaps of vs. 14 — is an expansion of the healing story that the Evangelist is supposed to have used as a fitting introduction to his real topic: Jesus' self-witness as the Son of God.[10] Others even believe that the sabbath issue has been imported into the story and, in fact, works there as a disturbing factor.[11] But in whatever way one imagines the combination of the different elements — the miracle, the sabbath, Jesus' dispute with "the Jews" — it cannot be denied that in the text as we

---

7. For that reason the passage does not lend itself to explanation — as is often attempted — by the introduction of all kinds of elements that the text itself does not contain (such as the paralytic's desire to be healed, his "faith," or Jesus' "challenge" of that faith); see, e.g., C. H. Dodd, *Historical Tradition in the Fourth Gospel,* 1965, pp. 174ff. For a survey of a variety of older interpretations of vss. 1-9, see Haenchen, *Comm.* I, pp. 255-57.

8. ἔγειρε.

9. The word used here (κράβατος), as in Mk. 2:11, is more colloquial than the word used in the same connection in Matthew and Luke (κλίνη).

10. Cf. Haenchen, *Comm.,* in his extended reflections on Jn. 5:1-30 (I, pp. 255-57).

11. Loisy spoke of the sabbath issue as an "accessory complication" and believed that the healing miracle had to be interpreted by itself apart from the sabbath issue (*Comm.,* p. 393).

have it they constitute an organic unity and cannot do without each other as the story stands.

First, the story as such can hardly be cut in two. It clearly functions, as we shall see later, as the counterpart to the story in ch. 9 of the man born blind. The point here is not just the healing but, as in ch. 9, the reaction to the healing. It is also hard to detach vs. 14 from its context in order to let it serve as the conclusion of the story in vss. 1-9a (which would in that case come to a very abrupt end). The shift from Bethesda to the temple is not explained until vs. 13, and the meaning of Jesus' statement in vs. 14 ("See, you are well! Sin no more that nothing worse befall you") can only be understood in the broader context of the story as it involves the man (see the comments).

Second, the subsequent dialogue about Jesus' "works" presupposes an antecedent miracle (cf. vs. 20; see also vss. 36ff.), and, as indicated, the character of the "works" has a significant point of connection with the "rising" of the paralytic (vs. 21).

Third, while it is true that the story of the healing can also be understood by itself without the fact of the sabbath (cf. Mt. 9:2-8), the same cannot be said about the point of Jesus' discourse in vs. 19. This discourse is framed apologetically as a response to an apparently antecedent indictment, and its argumentation is totally shaped by the sabbath pronouncement in vs. 17.

On balance, therefore, it is hard to see why the profound and harmonious integration of all these elements has to be explained as secondary simply because "the element of the sabbath" does not come up from the very start but only in vs. 9b — a construction that returns in precisely the same way in 9:14 but apparently does not occasion the same problems there.

10 It has been correctly said that in order to understand a story like this one must know the enormous significance of the sanctity of the sabbath for the Judaism of that day (and thereafter).[12] In whatever respect Pharisaism may have been tolerant, in regard to the sabbath it was uncompromising. The casuistry as to what was and was not allowed on the sabbath had been refined to the smallest details. In the Mishnaic tractate on the sabbath carrying objects from one domain to another was expressly forbidden.[13] Accordingly, it is not surprising that — after the dispute between Jesus and the Jews about the temple (2:14-22) — the Evangelist now gives such a prominent place to the Jewish application of the sabbath commandment as a critical point of departure for Jesus' confrontation with the Jewish leaders. That the conflict broke out over the seemingly innocuous detail of a man carrying his mat does not detract from the importance of the matter. One may infer from the way the Jews addressed

---

12. Cf. K. Bornhaüser, *Das Johannesevangelium eine Missionschrift für Israel,* 1928, pp. 34, 39ff.

13. Cf. Strack/Billerbeck II, pp. 459ff.

the man that they were aware of what moved him to carry his mat on the sabbath. He did not just carry "a" mat, but "his" mat (vss. 9-11), that is, the mat on which he had lain so long as a powerless person. And he carried it not because of any urgency to stow it away, but as a demonstration of his healing. Which was how Jesus intended it: not as a challenge to the sabbath commandment but as a sign of victory over suffering and death and thus of the glory of God. That all this did not count in the judgment of the Jews shows that at issue between Jesus and them was not merely a stricter or more relaxed view of the sabbath but — as is also evident from the continuing dispute over the sabbath in 7:19ff. — the nature of the law as the expression of the will of God and hence Jesus' authority as the one sent by the Father. It is this "theocentric" viewpoint that dominates in what follows (vss. 17, 19-30) and that makes this seemingly banal conflict over carrying a mat on the sabbath the occasion for the self-revelation of Jesus as the Son of God (here, perhaps, in the whole Gospel at its most central and fundamental).

11-13 But first the Evangelist still focuses on the healed man himself. It has correctly been pointed out that the role he plays in the story is very different from that of the man born blind in ch. 9. This man remains totally out of harm's way. Responding to the verdict of "the Jews," he refers them to the one who has healed him and instructed him to carry away his mat. When they continue to question him he has nothing to say (vs. 13) because he does not know who has healed him and because, with the crowd around, Jesus has gotten away. Having thus transferred responsibility for his conduct to Jesus, whom he does not know, he evidently sees a chance to dispose of his interrogators with impunity and proceed, as vs. 14 indicates, to the temple (i.e., the temple courtyard), a privilege he had long had to forgo and a place where, in the midst of many pilgrims, he could rejoice as nowhere else in his newfound health.

14 But though Jesus had thus gone on his way, he was not finished talking with the healed man. When he "found" (cf. comments on 1:41ff.) the man in the temple courtyard near where he had been healed, he also spoke to him (as did "the Jews," vs. 10) about his healing, but with a warning: "See, you are well! Sin no more, that nothing worse befall you." Commentators have often viewed this utterance as contradicting the answer Jesus gave his disciples with regard to the man born blind, where he rejects the notion of any causal connection between congenital blindness and antecedent sin (9:2).

But the connection he suggests here is of a more general kind and reminds one of the statement in Mt. 9:2 par.: Jesus' works of healing do not occur outside the circle of forgiveness of sin. Rather, they are the outflow of it, proof that in Jesus God reaches out to humankind in its totality, which means, above all, in its estrangement from God. That which Jesus gives is more than healing and relief from suffering (see the comments on 4:48ff.). Accordingly the warning addressed to the healed man ("Sin no more . . .")[14] does not relate to a specific sin by which the man might bring a worse illness or handicap upon his head but to the threatening danger of being content with the cure he has received without becoming conscious of his much deeper lostness as a sinner before God and rising from *it*. The "worse thing" that would then befall him would be not just a worse illness or accident but nothing less than the judgment of God (cf. Lk. 13:1-5). It is in that sense that the statement "you are well" echoes the question "do you want to be healed?"; it is related not only to rising from the sickbed but also to what Jesus was to call later "the greater works" of "rising" and "making alive," for which the Father had given him all power (vs. 20). As he now addresses this man on the point of his sin, Jesus wants to open the eyes and the life of the man to that greater experience, indispensable also to him, lest it also be true of him that his last state should be "worse" than the first (cf. Mt. 12:45).

15 Of the healed paralytic, as his only reaction to this second encounter with Jesus, it is only reported that he went to the Jewish authorities and told them who had healed him. With that he disappears from the account. All that follows is the action of "the Jews" against Jesus, for which the man has provided them with the necessary evidence (vs. 16).

It is true that the Evangelist thus proceeds directly to the essential point of the narrative, but one cannot help asking whether precisely the austerity with which he depicts the role of the healed man and the abruptness with which he ends it do not have a deeper meaning. Interpreters deal with it in various ways. Schlatter "historicizes": by making Jesus known to the Jews the man wanted to free himself from the suspicion that he opposed the validity of the sabbath commandment.[15] Bultmann recognizes that this could be a motive but thinks that thereby one goes outside the purpose of the narrative.[16] Brown believes that the story portrays a true-to-life character but serves no theological purpose. Brown argues for the originality of the tradition (over against later literary invention). He then describes the character of the man as "unimaginative," as marked by "a chronic inability to seize opportunity," an example of "real dullness" (letting his benefactor slip away without asking his name). That he repays Jesus by reporting him to the Jews is, according to Brown, to be viewed less as "an example of treachery" (as Theodore of Mopsuestia urges in his commentary on John) than of "persistent naiveté."[17] It is questionable, however, whether, alongside all the marks of genuineness the tradition displays, one may also attribute to it such psychological

14. μηκέτι ἁμάρτανε, present imperfect: Do not continue what you are doing, in this case, sinning.

15. Schlatter, *Comm.*, p. 145.

16. "The reader is clearly not required to pass judgment on the behaviour of the healed man; all interest in him ceases after v. 15" (Bultmann, *Comm.*, p. 243).

17. Brown, *Comm.* I, p. 209.

finesse in the portrayal of characters. Generally speaking, one can certainly not rank this as one of its marks.

Another approach, one that involves the role of the healed man in the kerygmatic thrust of the story, seems more acceptable. For this a compromise with the story of the man born blind (ch. 9), which in many respects runs parallel, offers the key. Not only are both stories governed from the start by the purpose of the healings (cf. 5:14 and 9:1-4), but their details also show a striking resemblance. In both Jesus "saw a man" (9:1; cf. 5:5, 6), the healed man is called to give account (5:10; 9:13), the man does not know where Jesus is (5:13; 9:12), and Jesus later encounters him and speaks with him (5:14; 9:35ff.). But while the healed paralytic here places all responsibility for the violation of the sabbath on Jesus' shoulders (5:12), the blind man increasingly defends Jesus and even takes his side to the degree that the Jews excommunicate him (9:24-34). And when Jesus then "finds" him and reveals himself to him, he falls down at Jesus' feet and acknowledges him as the Son of man (9:38). But the healed paralytic returns to "the Jews" (5:15). He takes their side, remains in his old world, and does not let himself be led out of it by Jesus, neither by his healing nor by the warning word of farewell. This involves more than weakness of character. It is a portrayal of people who will not let themselves be moved to enter the kingdom of God by Jesus' power and words, no matter how liberating the effect of those words. This story thus represents a particular response to the gospel, one with which, without any further explanation, the Evangelist unmistakably confronts his readers.[18]

Verse **16** takes us to the actual core of the story: the conflict between "the Jews" and Jesus. That they *persecuted* him (because he did "these things"[19] on the sabbath) indicates the seriousness of the matter. Some scholars assume this entailed a formal judicial process, even a trial before a sanhedrin. Vss. 17-47 would then represent Jesus' defense.[20] But the further course of the narrative does not point in that direction. In vss. 19-47 Jesus alone is the speaker and there is nothing about a trial — no verdict or adjournment. The "persecution" was a conspiracy against Jesus' life (vs. 18; cf. also Mt. 12:14; Mk. 3:6). The imperfect tense verbs in vss. 16 and 18 speak not just of the immediate reaction to what has happened in vs. 15 but of the continuing position of "the Jews" vis-à-vis Jesus, arising from that reaction.

18. See also J. L. Martyn, *History and Theology in the Fourth Gospel,* 1979[2], p. 71, who in keeping with his "two-level" theory goes much further. He sees in Jesus' miracle the action of Christian healers in the later church, and in the reaction of the paralytic in ch. 5 and the blind man in ch. 9 he sees the different attitudes of their potential converts vis-à-vis the later (Jewish) authority, the Gerousia.

19. This indicates that not only Jesus' command to the paralytic, but also Jesus' attitude toward the sabbath manifest in the healing, prompted "the Jews" to act.

20. Cf. Bornhäuser, *Johannesevangelium eine Missionschrift,* p. 35.

Verse **17** contains Jesus' fundamental answer and the basis for the entire discourse that begins in vs. 19. In this answer Jesus raises the conflict over the sabbath to the level on which he wants people to understand both the sabbath and his own "work" on the sabbath: "My Father is still working, and I am working." Just what is meant by the Father's work and his own concurrent work will become clearer in what follows. But with this statement the difference between him and those who are against him is established. No more than in the conflict over the temple (2:18ff.) does the dispute concern the manner of worshiping God or the measure of strictness to be applied in the observance of the law. The lines are, rather, drawn over God in the temple and over Jesus' authority to act and to speak with regard to temple and sabbath as the One sent by the Father.

18 "The Jews" do not see the underlying unity between the two issues: they speak in terms of "not only, but also." But they do understand where the radical break between them and Jesus is located. In their own words: he not only makes (the law of) the sabbath non-binding, thus "breaking" it, but also, by calling God his Father, makes "himself equal with God" — for them the most direct kind of blasphemy. Jesus' reply, which begins in vs. 19, is a response to both charges.

5:19-30

The Self-Witness of God's Son[21]

19-20a The discourse that now follows is very important for the entire construction of the Gospel (see the Introduction). The first part contains Jesus' real defense against this double charge spelled out in vs. 18: Vss. 19 and 20 are closely related to vs. 17 and therefore echo the conflict over the sabbath. At the same time this beginning of the reply also takes up the charge that Jesus would make himself equal with God. With great emphasis ("Truly, truly . . .") Jesus rejects any idea that he would ascribe to himself the authority and freedom that belong only to God and thus put himself next to God. He appeals to the fact that as Son he is not able to do anything of his own accord if he does not see the Father do it (vs. 19). And that is again (vs. 20) because the love of the Father goes out to him (cf. 3:35) and makes him a participant in all that he does. Hence this entire passage places Jesus' "working" on the sabbath — absolutely excluding every form of presumption — on the basis of his relationship to the Father (cf. 2:16).

In this connection, some interpreters speak of a parable that expresses, in general terms, a son's dependence vis-à-vis his father and that is used here to

---

21. Much has been written about this passage. See the discussion of the literature in F. J. Moloney, *The Johannine Son of Man,* 1978[2], pp. 71ff.

illustrate Jesus' relationship to God: "if we read Son and Father without the capital letters . . . , we have a little picture of an apprenticed son, learning his trade in his father's shop, as Jesus himself did at Nazareth."[22] However attractive at first sight this view may be, there are significant objections against it. In the first place one has to assume that the absolute reference to "the" father and "the" son first occurs parabolically and then, without no indication, passes directly to God as "the Father" and Christ as "the Son" in vs. 20b, and that the father and the son occur first as subjects in the parable (vs. 20a) and then (vs. 20b) in divine reality — a rhetorical form that is hard to place.

Furthermore, the Fourth Gospel repeatedly traces Jesus' speech and action to what he "saw" and "heard" (while with the Father), and in that connection there is no reason to think of a parable. Vs. 30 mentions "hearing," which is parallel to "seeing" in vs. 19. In 3:32 "seeing" and "hearing" occur together, while 8:26, 40; 15:15 mention only "hearing." These texts expressly associate this "seeing" and "hearing" with Jesus' relationship to the Father, clearly not by means of a parable, but by direct reference to God as the Father (cf. 1:18; 6:46; 8:26, 38, 40). There is no reason to interpret 5:19ff. differently. Here the Son's "seeing," the Father's "love" for the Son, and the Father's "showing" the Son all that the Father does have the surplus value of the unique relationship between Christ as Son and God as Father, extending right into preexistence (see the comments on 3:11, 32). Vs. 19 does, to be sure, mention "seeing" in the present (by contrast with the other texts mentioned), whereas vs. 25 has "hearing" in the future. From this alternation it is clear that in "seeing" and "hearing" we are dealing with neither just a "program" that the Father has given the Son once for all to carry out nor with incidental ad hoc instructions, but with the continuing agreement of the Son's speech and action with the Father, agreement rooted in his oneness with the Father (cf. 1:1a) and in the absolute authority bestowed on him as the beloved Son (cf. 3:35; 5:21ff.). Hence it can be said that the Son speaks and acts in accord both with what he *has* seen and heard from the Father and with what the Father *will* show him.

Furthermore, there should be no misunderstanding with regard to the thrust of the statement "the Son can do nothing of his own accord but only. . . ." These words have often been understood as an expression of Jesus' modesty and sense of subordination to the Father by means of which he is said to have defended himself against the accusation of "the Jews" that he made himself equal with God. Jesus does not reject equality with God, however, but the idea that he *made* himself equal with God. "Of his own accord" means apart from the Father, on his own authority. Over against this

---

22. Lindars, *Comm.*, p. 221, referring to articles by C. H. Dodd and P. Gächter; see also Brown, *Comm.* I, pp. 218f.

vss. 19 and 20 place all the emphasis on Jesus' fellowship and unity with the Father. That the Son "can do nothing of his own accord but only what he sees the Father doing" is explained not by subordination to the Father but by Sonship: "For whatever he [the Father] does, that the Son does likewise" (vs. 19c).[23] That is what makes him the Son. Similarly vs. 20a: "For the Father loves the Son and shows him all that he himself is doing." That is what makes him the Father.

So-called liberal exegesis of the turn of the twentieth century attempted to understand this unity of Jesus with God in a moral sense, as a unity realized in Jesus' decisions and action, a unity that could and should be the final outcome of every person's relationship with God. But, as Bultmann correctly remarks, vs. 19 "seeks to guard against just a way of looking at him."[24] The "not of his own accord" that runs through this whole Gospel (neither "acting" of his own accord [5:19; 8:28], "speaking" on his own [7:17; 12:49; 14:10], nor "coming" of his own accord [7:28; 8:42, etc.]) is the negative counterpart of all the statements that say that the Son does what the Father does, does the will of the Father, acts on the authority of the Father, that those who see him see the Father, and that he and the Father are one (e.g., 4:34; 8:16, 29; 14:9; 17:2, 23).[25]

All this brings to expression, in a variety of phrases and innumerable variations, the great themes of the prologue: the Word became flesh and the Word was God, that is, both the identity of action and speech of the Father and the Son, an identity proceeding from the deity of the Word, *and* the distinctive discourse about Father and Son. Because the *Word* became flesh, the Father, by sending the Son and putting all things into his hand, so far from remaining behind in heaven, makes himself present in all that the Son does, so that he that has seen the Son has also seen the Father. But in the incarnation of the Word the Son reveals himself as distinct from the Father, as the one who was sent by the Father and who does what he sees the Father doing and what the Father "will show him." Hence the unity of the Father and the Son cannot be expressed apart from the distinctive discourse about both; and, on the other hand, this distinctiveness never detracts from the unity.

In his commentary Bultmann deals at length with this relationship, upholding its utter uniqueness against all ethicizing interpretations and interpreting the unity of Father and Son only partially on the analogy of the relationship to God of the Old Testament messengers from God and prophets. But he argues that the Fourth Gospel does not

---

23. ὁμοίως does not mean "in the same manner" (imitation) but "also," "likewise," "in agreement with."

24. "The μὴ ἀφ' ἑαυτοῦ gives expression, not to his humility, but to his claim as the Revealer" (Bultmann, *Comm.,* p. 249).

25. Cf. Bultmann, *Comm.,* p. 250.

present this unity "in order to provide the basis for a speculative Christology."[26] When it is said that the Son does not act "of his own accord," that he has been sent and acts on behalf of his Father, this reference to his origin only attests and grounds his significance to those who see and hear him. According to Bultmann, the statements about Jesus' equality with God (one that hears him hears God; one that sees him sees God; cf. 3:34; 17:8; 14:9) mark the situation of those who hear and see Jesus and do not define the "metaphysical nature" of the Revealer himself. In this regard Bultmann cites Calvin, who wrote that in the Arian conflict both sides mistakenly appealed to Jn. 5:19 because "this discourse is not concerned with the naked divinity of Christ" but with "the Son of God as He was manifested in the flesh."[27]

Bultmann further believes that in the Fourth Gospel this wholly unique relationship of the Son and the Father and the discourse of Jesus authorized by it are expressed in the terminology of the Gnostic myth. "The latter speaks of the sending of a preexistent divine being that in its metaphysical mode of being is equal to God and was sent by him to carry out his work of revelation." While John distanced himself from the content of this mythology, he is said to have used its images and concepts to describe the nonmythological historical reality and validity of Jesus' words and works as the words and works of God.[28]

Undoubtedly all this contains the important truth — mentioned in our discussion of the prologue (see on ch. 1 above) — that in the Fourth Gospel Jesus' Sonship, deity, and preexistence are always referred to in close connection with his work as man, as the incarnate Word, and hence always "on two levels."[29] It is also clear that the basis — and "background" — of this discourse about his unique relationship to God does not lie in an ontological christology, into which and against which the significance of the historic self-revelation of Jesus as the Son of God could be fitted and understood, but that, conversely, it is precisely this historic self-revelation that is fundamental for the Fourth Gospel's "christology."

But that does not mean, as Bultmann thinks,[30] that everything the Fourth Gospel says about Jesus' unique relationship to God as that of the Son to the Father is there only to bring out the meaning that his words and actions have for those who see and hear him and that this meaning could be abstracted from the identity of his person. Other commentators also want to distinguish between a "functional" and an "ontological" christology: the latter is only the "mythological" or "ideological" expression of the meaning of the work of Jesus of Nazareth. But it has been correctly noted, for example by de Jonge, that in order to bring out the distinctive and unique character of Jesus' discourse and actions John had to go back to the origin of him who spoke and acted thus; and therefore that it does not make sense to play "action" off against "being," "function" against "nature." And in texts that some characterize as using "mythological" language, such as the descent of the Son "from heaven" or "from

26. Ibid., p. 249.

27. Calvin, *Comm.* I, p. 125.

28. Bultmann, *Comm.*, pp. 250-52.

29. See also my *Het Woord is vlees geworden,* 1979, p. 17.

30. One can undoubtedly appeal to Calvin for this, but not for the conclusion that Bultmann draws from it; see the comments below on 8:58.

above," even there one would have to say that the Evangelist is dealing with the "nature" of the Son in his relationship with the Father.[31]

Hence, while one can correctly say that the Fourth Gospel refers repeatedly to Jesus' origin, Sonship, and preexistence in close connection with and as grounding for the meaning of his work,[32] such reference makes sense only if it is meant, not in an ideological or mythological sense, but ontologically. For however true it is that "to know Christ" is "to know his benefits," that does not mean that as the Son of God Christ *derives* his existence (his "nature") from what he *means* to those who see and hear him. Rather, it is the grand goal of the Fourth Gospel to trace the miracle of Jesus' work to the miracle of his person and to bring out that *because* he is the Christ, the Son of God, he gives life to everyone who believes in him.

This implies that it is extremely unlikely that, for his readers in their confrontation with the synagogue, John, and Jesus himself in his dialogue with the Jews, spoke of this origin and "nature" in the language and imagery of a Gentile-syncretistic mythology and not from the knowledge of that God whom Jesus called his Father and whom Israel had always known, the God of "the beginning." It is of the Word of this God, who in the beginning created life and light, that the Evangelist speaks when in his prologue he mainly traces the "meaning" of Jesus' words and works to his origin and "nature." It is also the nature of the incarnate Word that forms the basis for the pronouncements in ch. 5, which are pivotal for the entire Gospel, to the effect that "the Son can do nothing of his own accord but only what he sees the Father doing" because "the Father loves the Son and shows him all that he himself is doing."

Verses **20b-23** refer to the nature of these works, still in connection with Jesus' appeal to the works of his Father (vs. 17). The idea that though God rested from his work of creation (Gn. 2:2ff.; Ex. 20:11; 31:17) nevertheless continues to work was not disputed among the Jews. The rabbinic literature does reflect on the nature of God's work, specifically in regard to what he did, and did not, continue to do after creation.[33]

But the Johannine text does not allude to any of this; Jesus simply assumes the continuity of the divine work, and what he understands by it becomes clear enough: It is the works that are now becoming manifest in what the Son is doing, the works of divine love that are making their way into the world in the work of the Son (vs. 20; cf. 3:35). These include the healing of the cripple, and other works;[34] but they will be even "greater than these": raising the dead,

---

31. M. de Jonge, *Jesus: Stranger from Heaven and Son of God,* 1977, p. 150: "In its 'mythical' discourse the Fourth Gospel is also dealing with the nature of the Son in his relationship with the Father"; see also de Jonge, p. 166.

32. So Bultmann: "because his origin is grounded in *what he means for us*" (*Comm.,* p. 249).

33. Cf. Strack/Billerbeck II, pp. 641ff. Philo also devoted much thought to this question; see, e.g., C. H. Dodd, *Interpretation of the Fourth Gospel,* 1963, pp. 320ff.

34. Cf. the plural in vs. 20b: τούτων.

giving them life, and the exercise of judgment (vss. 21, 22). In other words, they are the works that usher in the great future, the coming of the kingdom of God, and that therefore are to give Jesus' opponents even more reason to marvel at him than they did now in their perplexity and unbelief (cf. 7:21).

There is now no further mention of the sabbath. The conflict over the sabbath serves as the occasion and basis for the grand self-revelation and self-legitimation of Jesus as the Son of God. But, it is implied, that is all that needs to be said about the sabbath. The issue does not sink out of sight in this mighty christology as an insignificant minor matter but is rather incorporated into, and made serviceable to, the consummating and saving work of God in the Son — even on the sabbath. Thus the christological understanding of the sabbath in the Fourth Gospel is combined with the soteriological and anthro-pological approach of the Synoptic Gospels (e.g., Lk. 13:15). Conversely, the condemnation of the healing of a paralytic on the sabbath is an abstraction of the sabbath law from the whole of redemptive revelation and hence a reversal of the meaning of the law, an idea developed further in 7:19-24.[35] Jesus' warning to the healed man (vs. 14) now becomes fully clear. The healing is not an incidental case occurring within the confining context of the old life; it is rather an announcement of the "greater works" of God with which everyone who meets Jesus is confronted and by which the door to a new life and another world is opened (cf. also 9:3).[36]

For the Father also performs those greater works of the consummation and the future only in and through the Son (vss. 21, 22). The Son, too, like the Father, gives life "to whom he will," not of course as an act of self-willed, much less arbitrary, conduct apart from the Father, but precisely in virtue of the unlimited power and authority given to him by the Father (cf. 3:35). So also "the Father judges no one but has given all judgment to the Son" (cf. Dn. 7:10; 13f.; see also comments on vs. 27) must be understood in the sense of 3:17ff., namely as the inseparable obverse of the saving and life-giving mission of the Son, for those who reject him in unbelief. And all that (vs. 23) in order that the Son, as he does in all the work of the Father, might share in the honor extended by all who honor the Father. For the one is not possible without the other.

This last assertion of course again touches upon the great breaking point between church and synagogue, in connection with which the Evangelist doubt-lessly gave the statement this pointed form: "does not honor the Father." Not as if by this statement the whole of Israelite religion and worship was called

---

35. On this see at length S. Pancaro, *The Law in the Fourth Gospel,* 1975, pp. 158-169 and passim.

36. For the link between this miracle of healing and "the greater works," see also W. Nicol, *The Sēmeia in the Fourth Gospel,* 1972, p. 117.

into question, for its very ground rule was that the Lord God is one. The point at issue is that the one God can be known and honored in no other way than in the Son and that only in the revelation of the Son is the oneness of God manifest in its utter uniqueness. The inseparability of the adoration of the Father from that of the Son prohibits any notion that "next to" and "besides" God as Father, the Son as "a second party" must be honored as God. For by giving all things into the hands of the Son, the Father does not retreat to a position behind the Son, but posits himself as present in the Son. God is not two but one. But at the same time and for the same reason he can and will be known in no way other than in the Son and thus honored by all who know and honor him as God and Father.[37] Again from this pronouncement it is clear how the oneness of the Son with the Father, of Christ with God, is the fundamental motif of Jesus' entire self-revelation.

24 No less grand and striking, however, is the soteriological conclusion that, with the same emphasis and authority as that with which Jesus spoke about himself (cf. vs. 19), is drawn from this self-revelation: that for one who hears his word and believes God who sent him[38] eternal life has already begun, the judgment of God has lost its fearsomeness, and death has been superseded. What makes this pronouncement special is, of course, that the final decision that determines the life and future of human beings and that is spoken of here and in what follows in eschatological language is transferred from the future to the present, in accordance with the word that Jesus speaks as the one sent by the Father and with the answer people give to it. The distinction between present and future is not thereby canceled out (see below), but eternal life does begin qualitatively in the present. Death also gains a different content than what it usually has for humans: already in this life it is experienced as a passage to true eternal life and thus loses its all-threatening, ultimately critical character for the future. It is no longer ahead of a person but behind him or her.

25 This is confirmed in a new and most emphatic statement. As an expression of Jesus' messianic consciousness, it may perhaps be considered the most powerful pronouncement in John's Gospel, one in which what was said in vs. 24 is concretized in an extreme and almost paradoxical way: "The hour is coming, and now is [as in 4:23!] that the dead will hear the Son of God's

---

37. Calvin's comments on Jn. 5:23 are of lasting importance and are also set in the context of the relationship between the church and Israel (*Comm.* I, p. 128): "All admit that we should worship God, and this sentiment, naturally inborn in us, has deep roots in our hearts, so that none dares absolutely to deny honour to God. Yet men's minds fade away in seeking God out of the way. Hence so many pretended deities; hence so much perverse worship." And concerning Israel: "Nor was the state of the Fathers under the Law different; for though they beheld Christ obscurely under shadows, God never revealed Himself without Christ. But now since Christ has been manifested in the flesh and appointed King over us, the whole world must bow to Him in order to obey God."

38. The two clauses of vs. 24a constitute a hendiadys.

voice, and those who hear will live." The reference here is not only to the dead in the great future. For the voice of the Son of God that calls the dead to life resounds now. Those who hear this voice will not just live in the future, therefore, but now already they will "pass out of death into life," delivered from the power of death by the voice that calls them to rise (cf. 1 Jn. 3:14).

26 All this is again motivated (cf. vs. 21) by means of an appeal to Jesus' Sonship. The expression "to have life in oneself" is not intended as a general description of the divine "being" but as a reference to the fact that, just as the Father as Creator and Consummator possesses life, he has given that possession also to the Son, not merely as the executor of incidental assignments but in the absolute sense of sharing in the Father's power. And it is on account of that power and authority (see also vss. 27ff.) that the great decisive "hour" of God is not only *coming* but *here.* The second does not suspend the first. The hour that *is* continues to *come,* just as he who has come can still be called the Coming One (cf. 1 Jn. 2:28; 3:2). But the central point in this context is that both the "coming" and "the having come" of the hour — both future and present, salvation and judgment — have their ground in Jesus as the one sent by the Father, the Son of God clothed with all authority. For that reason all the questions one might wish to ask here can only be answered in terms of him, the nature of his mission and sonship.

We are not expressly told what it means to "have eternal life" or to "pass out of death into life." The same thing is described elsewhere in soteriological terms like "light" (cf. 1:4), as not "remaining under the wrath of God" (3:36), as becoming "children of God" (1:12f.). It does not consist in a temporary or incidental anticipation of the heavenly life, an ecstatic state, being temporarily lifted up out of time, or the like. Nor does the death from which those who hear the voice of the Son of God rise to life consist only of the experience or fear of death, in which a person shrinks back from the limit of his possibilities and "existence" — for one of the marks of this state is that one can think himself alive (e.g., 9:40, 41). The criterion of what "life" or "death" means and of what a person should or should not desire, fear, or not fear does not lie in what he understands of them from within himself, but in hearing the word of the Son of God, that is, in what the Son of God promises to and demands from him in the way of faith. As for life, it is life, light, and freedom *in him* (3:16; 20:31; 16:33, etc.); and as for death, it is the death of which the Son makes one aware and from which *he* wants a person to arise.

But, as already indicated, all that is not summed up at once here. The issue here is, above all, the *that:* that it is *he,* that life is in *his* name, and in the path he travels as the one sent for that purpose by God (see also on 8:12). It is this *that* that was and remained the core issue in the continuing confrontation between church and synagogue and (we may add) between church and world and between a person and himself or herself.

In verse **27** this self-legitimation of Jesus as the one who, like God, "has life in himself" is continued, but now from the perspective of the coming "hour." On the meaning of this verse, especially as the transition to vss. 28 and 29, there is great diversity of opinion.

Some interpret the striking transition from the "realized" eschatology of vss. 25 and 26 to the future in vss. 28 and 29 as a later insertion. So specifically Bultmann,[39] according to whom a later redactor reintroduced, by way of a simple addition, "the popular eschatology . . . so radically swept aside" by the Evangelist in vss. 24 and 25. In this way, the bringing into the present of the great future (which Bultmann so much values as the Evangelist's "demythologizing") in the word of the Son of God that acquits and judges now is said to have been neutralized by the redactor on account of the heresy it might yield (cf. 2 Tm. 2:18). Others, who reject the notion of a material set of opposites, nevertheless posit a theological *development* in the Evangelist in which the conception embodied in vss. 19-25 is said to represent another (probably later) phase of Johannine theology than that of vss. 26-30.[40]

Still, however great the emphasis with which this Gospel stresses that salvation has already come and that eternal life has begun in the present, the idea that this realized eschatology is incompatible with the futuristic pronouncements of vss. 28 and 29 seems to me totally unacceptable. Already in the very statement that "the hour is coming and now is," the future is included in so many words. If one surveys the entire Gospel,[41] this becomes even clearer. One can hardly dismiss as incidental "corrections" or "accommodations"[42] to "popular images," the emphatically repeated pronouncements Jesus makes about raising believers up at the last day (6:39, 40ff.; cf. 12:48; together with

---

39. So Bultmann, *Comm.,* pp. 260ff., in agreement with earlier writers (p. 262, n. 1). See also Moloney, *Johannine Son of Man,* p. 73, n. 27. Haenchen, *Comm.* I, p. 259, expresses himself even much more sharply. He speaks of a redactor with a totally different understanding of God from that of the Evangelist:

> For this Father, whom Jesus, as the son of man, will make evident, has become unlike the Father proclaimed by the Evangelist. Jesus himself has become like the Jesus in the Sistine Chapel. Before him those condemned, those who have done evil, will be cast into hell. With this doctrine of judgment the moral demand has been inserted into the Gospel of John as what is really essential. And there arises a furtive struggle between the Johannine picture of Jesus and God and that of the redactor. The reader, as well as the learned exegete, will therefore easily become bewildered and will often not know how he or she is to forge a unity out of everything that nevertheless appears in this Gospel.

40. So, e.g., M. É. Boismard, "L'évolution du thème eschatologique dans les traditions johanniques," *Revue Biblique* 68 (1961), pp. 514-18. See also the commentaries of Brown and Schnackenburg.

41. See also L. van Hartingsveld, *Die Eschatologie des Johannesevangeliums. Eine Auseinandersetzung mit Rudolf Bultmann,* 1962.

42. So, e.g., Bauer, *Comm.,* p. 38.

5:27-29!), given their content and the prominent place they occupy in ch. 6.[43] And even more, the entire basic structure of the Gospel (both "christological" and "soteriological") is opposed to such a procedure. That believers "have" eternal life already in the present and have "passed out of death into life" (vss. 14-16, 24) does not exclude the idea that death also continues and that life is still full of threat and awaits a final redemption and glorification (cf. 11:25; 12:26; 14:2f.; 17:24). This is so partly because the mission of the Son, not finding its fulfillment in the present world, offers to his own, in his exaltation and glorification, a future that transcends the present world (cf. 16:33; 17:5, 24; 21:22). It is inconceivable, therefore, that the Evangelist, though his Gospel lacks lengthy prophecies like those in Mark 13 par., wanted to eliminate this future expectation in favor of a radically present "eschatology" whose only future consisted in being placed over and over before a decision and in freedom (an eschatology "in the Word").

This salvation-historical unity of present and future, in which the two are inseparably bound up with, and determine, each other, can be maintained in this passage not only on the basis of general considerations but is no less present in the passage itself, specifically in the manner in which "the Son of man" occurs in the transitional verse, v. 27. There the pronouncement of vs. 22 that the Father "has given all judgment to the Son" is explained: *"because he is the Son of man."* At first blush it may seem strange that to support the powers of the Son reference is made to the fact that he is "the Son of man." But by this argument a line is being extended that is visible from the beginning (cf. 1:51; 3:13f.) and that continues in what follows (see on 6:27, 62; 12:23, 28), where in each instance the figure of the Son of man is advanced to express the transcendent character of Jesus' messiahship and the all-embracing, present-and-future-encompassing mission of Jesus as the Son of God (on this see at length the comments on 1:51).

But nowhere more clearly than here do we learn that this title refers to "the Son of man" of Dn 7:13f., the one who comes on the clouds of heaven and is clothed with divine glory and unlimited power.[44] It is from within his

---

43. See C. K. Barrett, *The Gospel of John and Judaism,* 1975, pp. 73f., 91f.:

John contains apocalyptic with non-apocalyptic material. In this regard the gospel is very often oversimplified. . . . For him eschatology is realised in the present, but not so completely that the future is no longer of any significance. . . . Precisely the coexistence of both is important for Johannine Theology. To set out to dissolve this coexistence through source or redaction hypotheses is methodologically false.

It is not a matter of maintaining that any source or redaction hypothesis must be wrong. . . . I maintain only that the redactor was a theologian, not a fool.

44. LXX: καὶ ἐδόθη αὐτῷ ἐξουσία; cf. also Dn. 12:2 with vss. 28f. See also C. Colpe, *TDNT* VII, pp. 464f., who refers to the "plain use" of Dn. 12:2 in Jn 5:28f. (n. 441) and further remarks: "There is agreement even to the indefinite ἀνθρώπου" (n. 437), which also proves that

self-identification with this "eschatological" figure and the divine qualities attributed to him that Jesus not only speaks of the transcendent (surpassing all human measure and power) meaning of his coming into the world already in 1:51 and 3:13, but here also traces his authority as the Son to call the dead to life *now* to the power given the Son of man to execute judgment (cf. also Mt. 19:28; 24:30f.; 25:31f.; 26:64; Mk. 8:38; 13:26f.; Lk. 21:27).

28, 29 For that reason those to whom Jesus is speaking should not "marvel"[45] at what has been said about the "voice" that calls the dead to life. What they should understand — but do not because of their unbelief (vs. 18) — is that in Jesus as the Son sent by the Father they are confronted with the great future that they themselves expect and are thus placed in the presence of him whose voice will one day be heard (not only by those who are listening now but) by all who are in the graves and who on hearing it will rise — those who have done good to the resurrection of life and those who have done evil to the resurrection of judgment (see the comments on 3:20f.).

Hence in vss. 24-29 there is no question of two mutually exclusive eschatologies or of an "apocalyptic compensation" in vss. 28 and 29 for the "now" in vs. 25. We see, rather, the inseparable connection between the present and the future.[46] What is most prominent is the utterly unique relevance of this great future, as a result of which decisions are already being made now with regard to what will one day come to pass. On the other hand it is no less true that the relevance of the coming hour ("the hour is coming, and now is") derives its basis and urgency from the fact that he who thus speaks ("on earth," cf. Mt. 9:6) is the one who descended from heaven and who possesses *eternal* life in virtue of an authority that encompasses earth and heaven, present and future, and thus represents the salvation and judgment of God in its all-inclusive significance.

30 Here Jesus repeats what he said at the beginning of the pericope (cf. vs. 19: by thus speaking Jesus is not acting of his own accord but on behalf of and in fellowship with the Father) and applies it to the authority with which he judges: "as I hear, I judge." Here again "hearing" is equivalent to "seeing" (see the comments on vs. 19). And "judging" presumably refers to the acquittal and judgment that are realized already now in his preaching. On account of his

---

the lack of an article in vs. 27b cannot be an indication, as some think, that "Son of man" here refers to Jesus' humanity and not to the title from Daniel 7; see the extensive treatment in Moloney, *Johannine Son of Man*, pp. 80f.

45. A typical rabbinical expression; cf., e.g., 3:7.

46. The view advanced by Schulz (*Comm.,* p. 91) that also in vss. 27-29, regardless of whether these verses are original in this context, one must presuppose "a tacit reinterpretation by John in the sense of 5:24f. and 11:25ff." therefore not only fails to appreciate the clearly future-oriented thrust of these verses (cf. Colpe, *TDNT* VII, p. 465, n. 441) but also the meaning of the passage as a whole.

"hearing," his fellowship with his Father, he does nothing "on his own authority," on the basis of which they might charge him with blasphemy. Therefore his judgment is just, in accord with the standards of God. Nor is it his own *will* that he seeks to effect but the will of the one who sent him (cf. 4:34). And herein lies the transition to what follows, where the "witness," that is, the legitimation of what has so far been said, becomes a separate topic of discussion.

5:31-47
Jesus' "Witnesses," the Unbelief of "the Jews"

31 In vss. 31-40 the concept of "witness" is central. The reference is to the witness in the judicial sphere. How can Jesus legitimate himself vis-à-vis these powerful pronouncements about himself? Even though in vs. 16 the word "persecute" is not meant in a formal juridical sense (see comments on vs. 16 and 8:14ff.), nevertheless there is between the Jewish authorities and Jesus a "case" in which he has to justify himself before his accusers in a way that is also valid for them. Therefore, what witnesses can he summon to testify on his behalf? In a way vs. 31 acknowledges the validity of such a demand. Here Jesus reacts to a judicial rule according to which, in an indictment, one cannot be exculpated on the basis of one's own testimony.[47] Hence if Jesus were to appeal solely to himself ("bear witness to myself"), such testimony would not be "true," that is, judicially valid.

32-35 The "other" who "bears witness to him" (vs. 32) is God (not John the Baptist, as is evident from vs. 34). Jesus' comment that he "knows" that God's testimony is "true" (i.e., valid) means something like: this testimony is conclusive for him even if his opponents do not want to acknowledge it (cf., e.g., 7:28). But they, too, had already received clear testimony concerning Jesus from John the Baptist (vs. 33). For this Jesus refers to their own delegation and the testimony it had furnished them (cf. 1:19ff.). It is not (vs. 34) as if he himself[48] were dependent on this testimony for the truth concerning himself. He does not depend for this knowledge on any human testimony. He mentions John because John was the great witness sent from God to lead Israel to faith (cf. 1:7, 31). Therefore, in order still to "save" his adversaries, Jesus confronts them even now with John's testimony.

When he further calls John (vs. 35) "the burning and shining light," he

---

47. Cf. Strack/Billerbeck II, p. 466. In 8:17f. Jesus appeals to another legal rule according to which his own testimony concerning himself did have evidential validity, namely, in conjunction with that of others (the Father); see the comments there.

48. See the contrast between ἐγὼ δέ in vs. 34 and emphatic ὑμεῖς in vs. 33.

thus reminds them of the enormous impression John made at the time, in comparison with which the "light" emitted by all other teachers and preachers was dimmed (even though John was not "the" light that was to come into the world: 1:8; Lk. 1:78f.; cf. Mt. 11:7ff.; 21:25ff.). For John was the herald of the kingdom of heaven that Israel had so long awaited. The fact that even Jesus' opponents had been "willing to rejoice for a while in [John's] light" proves on the one hand that their own past testifies against them when they now pretend that for his claim to have been sent by God Jesus had no other witness than himself; but it also shows the superficiality with which they treated those who on behalf of God bore witness to the truth among them: "for a while" they had been pleased to let themselves be mesmerized by the power with which John announced the arrival of a new dawn for Israel. But in their fickleness they had soon turned away from him again (cf. Mt. 11:17, 18): they did not (and do not) have the word of God abiding in them (vs. 38; cf. Mt. 13:21).

36 Jesus himself — "I, however" in the emphatic position — is not dependent on John's witness; he has a testimony greater than that of John. For this Jesus bases himself on the "works" that the Father "granted" him "to accomplish" (cf. the comments on 4:34). As is evident from the preceding mention of Jesus' "works" (cf. vss. 17, 19-20),[49] this term refers to the content of Jesus' entire mission, his miracles *and his words;* for the words, Jesus' speaking with the authority of God's Son "to make alive" and "to judge," also belong to that which the Father has "granted" Jesus (cf. vss. 22, 26, 27). Implied in this, however, is that Jesus' legitimation does not consist only in something outside his own actions, or in some additional verification from without, as the Jews desired (cf. Mt. 12:38ff.; 16:1ff.; 1 Co. 1:22), something that would furnish to everyone an "objective" proof of his heavenly origin. No person who cannot recognize the work, voice, and revelation of God *in Jesus' work itself* will be persuaded of it by some other independent means.

37-38 Finally, in vs. 37, this is asserted one more time with all possible clarity and emphasis: "[accordingly] the Father who sent me — he it is who has borne witness to me," namely in that which Jesus accomplished and said in virtue of the Father's mandate and authorization. Noteworthy in that connection is the perfect tense: "has borne witness." Although this may relate exclusively to Jesus' works,[50] it may also mean that this witness began before the coming and work of Jesus (cf. vs. 39).

However this may be, starting with vs. 37b Jesus charges that his accusers, despite the many reasons for them to accept the testimony concerning him, persisted in their unbelief. The point of vs. 37b in the argumentation is some-

---

49. See also the precise analyses in Nicol, *Sēmeia,* pp. 117ff.

50. In that case the perfect means that it is the Father who bore witness and still bears witness to Jesus (by Jesus' "works").

what unclear. The statement has some affinity with Dt. 4:12, where God's "voice" and "form" are also referred to, though there, in the Sinai theophany, it is said that God's voice was heard. If, as some interpreters now think,[51] one reads in the present verse that already at Sinai the Jews evinced the attitude they now assume toward Jesus, then we are told here that the "hearing" at Sinai was not the genuine hearing of faith. But then again in vs. 38 God's word is referred to as something they *had* received. It is questionable, therefore, that vs. 37b carries such a direct echo of Deuteronomy 4 as proof of the unbelief — manifesting itself even then — of the Jews. It seems rather that here again the reference is to "seeing" and "hearing" that are attributable only to the Son of God, and from the vantage point of which *he* speaks (cf. 1:18; 3:11; 5:19, 20; 6:46; 7:29). Jesus, then, is telling the Jews that, however much they as the people of the law pride themselves on their knowledge of God, they are barred from every form of direct access to God and that they are dependent on the testimony of others. And if, in keeping with this, Jesus then adds "and you do not have his word abiding in you," that implies both that the word of God had nevertheless come to them (above all, of course, in the law that had been given them [cf. vss. 39ff., 45ff.], but also in John's testimony) and that it had done them no good. For they did not have this word in them as something "abiding" (cf. vs. 35: "for a while"; 15:17; 1 Jn. 2:14, 24) as a guiding, life-directing word from God. Otherwise they would not, as now, react in unbelief toward him whom the God of that word had sent to them.[52] They would have acknowledged him and not asked him for a testimony, for legitimation of his mission.

Verses **39** and **40** furnish further concretization of this point. Jesus refers his audience to the Scriptures, which did contain the word of God for them, and to their claim that they were students of it. The word used here for "search" or "explore" corresponds to a rabbinic term — *daraš*, cf. "midrash" — which denoted professional study and exposition of the law. It was Israel's privilege to possess these Scriptures (cf. Ro. 3:1), the fountain of all salvation and life, hence Israel's boast and glory (cf. Ro. 2:18ff.). The Jews believed that in the Scriptures they had, unlike other nations, received the divinely given means by which to acquire righteousness unto life, the means of "making alive" (cf. Gl. 3:21; Lv. 18:5). It is to this belief that Jesus refers with "You search[53] the Scriptures because you think that in them you have eternal life." The intent of "you think" — also in light of vs. 39b and vss. 45ff. — is not to discredit the

---

51. For this view that there is a direct material connection between vs. 37b and Dt. 4:12, see the lengthy treatment of this text by Pancaro, in *The Law in the Fourth Gospel,* pp. 220-31; also P. Borgen in *NTS* 23 (1976), pp. 72f.

52. ὅτι in vs. 38 means something like "for," "which is evident from the fact that."

53. Some take this as an imperative. The word "for" that follows the indicative in vs. 40, however, makes this translation less likely. There is a somewhat divergent tradition of these verses in Papyrus Egerton. Some believe that the imperative would be more natural there.

Scriptures as the source of light and life or, even less, to reject them altogether,[54] but to persuade Jesus' hearers to distance themselves from the manner in which the Jews "searched" the Scriptures and believed they "had" life in that pursuit. For despite all their scrupulous examination of and boasting in the Scriptures, it escaped them that precisely those Scriptures could provide them with the evidence that they demanded from Jesus and could show them the way to eternal life. Jesus is not speaking here of specific Scripture passages but of the Scriptures as a whole, although, in view of vs. 45ff., we should probably think in particular of the books of Moses (cf. 1:45). Where and how these Scriptures testify of Jesus is not stated. Involved here is not just lack of insight into the Scriptures on the part of Jesus' opponents but (vs. 40) their ill-will, which prevented them from coming to Jesus to have the life that he wanted to bestow on them. It was this inner resistance that obscured for them the true meaning of the Scriptures (cf. 2 Co. 3:14).

41-44 What constituted the real cause of this resistance and would, as long as there was no change, permanently block the road to faith is further now analyzed from a new vantage point (vss. 41-44), again with an appeal to Moses (vss. 45-47). Central here is the concept of "honor" or "glory" (see also 7:18; 8:50, 54), which is linked here with the verbs "receive" (vss. 41 and 44a) and "seek" (vs. 44b), meaning: "gain honor, status for oneself," "vie for the favor of." In this connection everything depends on *from whom* one "receives" honor and tries to obtain favor. Whereas Jesus (vs. 41) testifies of himself that he does not seek "glory from people,"[55] he states, in a very sharp declaration, that he has come to know[56] his opponents as people who do not "have the love of God within them" (cf. vs. 38).

The reasoning in vs. 42 is somewhat proleptic insofar as it states a priori the reason for what is said in vs. 43a, namely that Jesus came in his Father's name but his opponents did not receive him. The reality of "coming in the name of the Father" as the one from whom Jesus derives his authority and credibility stands opposed here to seeking "glory from people" (vs. 41). But his opponents did not receive him because they did not have the love of God in them. What motivated them is that which counts and is considered "honorable" among humankind. For "if another comes in his own name, him you will receive" (vs. 43). "In his own name," in contrast with vs. 43a, means "on his own authority" (cf. 7:18), deriving, that is, his credibility from that which he has to offer out of his own resources. They "receive," that is, make

---

54. Against this view (an anti-Jewish bias on the part of the "revelational sayings source" — so Bultmann, *Comm.*, p. 268) see, e.g., Günter Reim, *Studien zum alttestamentlichen Hintergrund des Johannesevangeliums,* 1974, pp. 278ff.

55. οὐ λαμβάνω, probably to be taken as conative present: "I do not attempt to obtain."

56. Literally "I know you that you . . ."; perhaps to be taken as a Semitic construction in which the subject of the subordinate clause becomes the object of the main clause.

room for, regard as trustworthy, the "other" when he "comes," that is, when he plays his role among them, imposes his authority on them, and shares his favors with them. For in his coming he represents precisely that which counts as "glorious" and admirable among people. From patristic times there have been those who believed that this "other" is the devil or the Antichrist. It is more plausible that Jesus is referring to the false prophets or pseudo-messiahs who kept coming up in the history of the Jewish people (cf. Ac. 5:36f.) and would continue to do so (cf. Mt. 24:24 par.; 1 Jn. 2:18, etc.). But evidence for this is also lacking, nor is it implied in the context. Jesus is in fact speaking in very general terms about the way things are among people, how they try to impress each other and how they let themselves be impressed by each other.

But therein lies (vs. 44) the explanation for their lack of faith in him: "How would you be able to believe — you who [or "as long as you"]. . . ." "Believe" occurs absolutely here, but what is meant is that which is at stake over and over throughout this entire Gospel: faith in Jesus as the Christ, the Son of God. We may assume that part of the background for this absolute formulation is found in the continuing confrontation between church and syn-agogue at the time this Gospel was written. In that context "the estimation of people" must have played a large role, especially on the part of Jews who out of fear of excommunication from the Jewish community could not persuade themselves to take the big step[57] to Christian faith (cf. 12:43). At the same time the culpable and objectionable character of this "inability" to believe is laid utterly bare, specifically in the case of those who, in virtue of their own spiritual background, should have known better.

To the glory people "receive from one another" Jesus opposes the seeking of glory (approval, favor) from the only God.[58] With "the only God" Jesus alludes to the great principle on which Israel's religion was founded, namely that the LORD, Israel's God, was one and as such commanded the people to love him with undivided love (cf. Dt. 6:4ff.). For that reason "honor" and glory are to be sought and found only in him — the glory of "the life" he wants to bestow on them (vs. 40). Here, too, Jesus confronts the Jews who contradict him with the choice for or against him in its absolute significance: it is a choice for the honor of God or for that which comes from humans. Again it is clear how in this connection he is not (as they think, vs. 18) seeking his "own glory" or advancing his "own name" but the glory of his Father, who, of course, they claim to honor as the only God (cf. 8:54).

45-47 Jesus' repeated appeal to Moses has the same intent. When he asks them to believe and they refuse, they must not think that this is merely a matter between themselves and him or that he is therefore their accuser

---

57. πιστεῦσαι is probably to be taken inchoatively here.
58. τὴν δόξαν τὴν παρὰ μονοῦ θεοῦ.

before the Father. Rather, their unbelief relates to their own sacred tradition, and thus the one who will accuse them is not Jesus but Moses, "on whom you set your hope." Therefore they are, by their unbelief, undermining their own position. Some think "hope" here refers to the personal role ascribed to Moses as intercessor with God.[59] The contrast with "accuser" thereby becomes all the more striking. Still, what is presented here is primarily something other than the picture of Moses as the personal accuser before God in heaven.[60] For in vss. 46 and 47 the reference is expressly to Moses' *writings,* in which Jesus' opponents have to do with Moses and from the possession of which they derive their hope and assurance (cf. vs. 39). Accordingly, Moses is above all their accuser on account of and in those writings: "he wrote of me." Therefore, Jesus can trace their unbelief in him to unbelief in Moses[61] and can refer to Moses, on whom they placed their hope as intercessor and advocate, as their accuser.

Here again, as in vs. 39, the question is whether the reference is to a specific prophecy of Moses (Deuteromony 18?) or in a broader sense to the character of all of Moses' writings as witnessing to Christ (cf. 1:45; 8:56). The latter might be suggested by the plural: his "writings" (vs. 47).[62] In any case, if the Jews had "believed Moses" and had understood in its true meaning Moses' reference to the one who was to come after him, they would not have rejected Jesus as a blasphemer. They would have recognized in Jesus the bringer of salvation predicted by Moses. But precisely this faith in Moses is what they lacked. They were unable to view "the law given through Moses" in its reference to the "grace and truth" that came "through Jesus Christ" (1:17). And therefore the issue between Jesus and them is irresolvable. For "if you do not believe his writings, how will you believe my words?" If they did not follow the course that Moses had pointed out to them for their faith, how could they ever come out in the vicinity of Jesus?

The distinction between "his writings" and "my words" seems at first to contain a *conclusio a maiori ad minus* ("if not his writings, how much less my words").[63] But the intent is not to indicate a difference in importance or intelligibility between (Moses') *writings* and (Jesus') *words* but rather the unchangeable correspondence between the two. As long as the Jews did not understand that the Scriptures of Moses taught the same faith that Jesus demanded from them, he would always remain for them a stranger.

59. Cf. Strack/Billerbeck II, p. 561.

60. As Pancaro argues at length in *The Law in the Fourth Gospel,* pp. 254ff.

61. "Believing Moses" (cf. Ex. 4:1-9, 27, 31) apparently means believing him as a witness to the coming Messiah (cf. vs. 39).

62. See also G. Schrenk, *TDNT* I, p. 765.

63. Cf. Schnackenburg: "What is written, being fixed, is easier to comprehend than the spoken Word" (*Comm.,* II, p. 129).

As in vs. 44 so here, the sentence, and now the chapter, ends with a rhetorical question: "how will you believe . . . ?" The question could hardly be posed in a more pointed fashion. For by again involving Moses in the dispute and by designating him as the great accuser of the unbelief of the Jews, Jesus brought into the open the deepening background of conflict between himself and the Jews who rejected him. We are dealing not just with a divergence of roads within one and the same Israelite faith, but with the now-visible break in the essence of this faith itself.

6:1-25

The Feeding of the Five Thousand, Jesus Walks on the Sea

As stated earlier, chs. 5 and 6 constitute the thematic beginning of the great middle section of the Gospel, which ends with ch. 10. In broad outline ch. 6 has the same construction as ch. 5: a miracle performed by Jesus (here a double miracle, vss. 1-25) is the point of departure for a lengthy discourse or didactic dialogue in continuing confrontation with the hearers — first with "the people," then also with the Jews — with regard to Jesus' identity and the significance of his coming (vss. 26-58).

In vss. 1-25, two questions deserve priority: First, how is this section connected with what precedes? Second, how should we evaluate the relationship between the narrative of the two miracles and the corresponding material in the Synoptics? For the first question, see the introduction to 5:1–6:71 above. In my opinion, the narrative in ch. 5 constitutes an intermezzo in Jesus' stay — mentioned in 4:1ff., 44 and further described in 6:1 — in Galilee. Hence, although any geographic link with ch. 5 is lacking, in many respects ch. 5 is basic to the theme that dominates ch. 6 ("bread from heaven"), as regards both the work Jesus had come to accomplish (cf. 6:38ff.) and the life-giving and division-causing effect of that work (cf. 6:47ff., 53ff., 66ff.). With regard to Galilee, this discourse leads to a climax and conclusion with the departure of some disciples and Peter's confession (6:66ff.).

As for the second question, quite apart from the story of the feeding of the five thousand itself one can point to the combination of that story with that of Jesus' walking on the sea, which occurs in both John 6 and Mt. 14:13-32; Mk. 6:32-51 (Luke lacks the latter story). Moreover, the contexts of the story in John and Mark (with Matthew) exhibit a variety of analogous components: the request for a sign (Jn. 6:25-34; cf. Mk. 8:11-13), Peter's confession (Jn. 6:60-69; cf. Mk. 8:27-30), and the prediction of suffering (Jn. 6:70, 71; cf. Mk. 8:31-33). To this one may perhaps add Jesus' warning against the leaven of the Pharisees in Mk. 8:14ff. in contrast with the true bread that Jesus offers (Jn.

6:35-39), and that as a possible allusion to the time of Passover (cf. Jn. 6:4). All these motifs and themes, though they diverge somewhat and are expressed in different ways, somehow belong together in the tradition, whether historically or thematically or both. At the same time the differences are such that it must be deemed almost impossible to trace the story of John 6 to (one of) the Synoptic Gospels. That Matthew and Mark record two feedings and that the themes of a request for a sign, the leaven of the Pharisees, and Peter's confession do not come up until after the second show that there can be no question of direct dependence, unless one assumes a most fragmentary and arbitrary use by John of his fellow Evangelists.

The same is true of the reproduction of the two main events — the multiplication of loaves and Jesus' walking on the sea. Brown's detailed comparison of the story of the loaves in John and Luke and the two stories in Matthew and Mark shows the following: First, though there are several far-reaching similarities between John and the (five!) stories in the Synoptics, none of the Synoptic versions can be identified as John's model or starting point. Second, John has a number of details that can be found in none of the Synoptics — for example, the crossing of the sea (vs. 1), the Passover season (vs. 6), the identification of Philip and Andrew (vss. 7, 8), the lad with five *barley* loaves (vs. 9), and Jesus' command to gather the fragments so that nothing would be wasted (vs. 12). Third, John lacks all sorts of details present in the Synoptic versions, which would be hard to explain if he used (one of) these stories. Brown's conclusion seems justified: "There is one logical explanation for all these features, omissions, additions, and parallels, namely, that the Evangelist did not copy from the Synoptics but had an independent tradition of the multiplication that was like, but not the same as, the Synoptic traditions."[64]

The conclusion from both these questions leads us to adhere to the traditional sequence of chs. 5 and 6 and to evaluate the text of the narrated material on its own merits and not as dependent on the Synoptic stories.

1-4 The opening of the story takes us to the region — characteristic of the Synoptic Gospels — around "the Sea of Galilee," which is "the Sea of Tiberias."[65] It is not stated precisely from where to where the crossing took place but the destination was clearly the eastern shore (cf. vs. 16). The "multitude" (vs. 2) that constantly[66] followed Jesus apparently traveled on foot along

---

64. Brown, *Comm.* I, pp. 236-44, here quoting p. 239; cf. p. 244. Lindars reaches similar conclusions (*Comm.,* p. 236).

65. The two genitives, "of Galilee of Tiberias," are difficult and led to all sorts of variations in the manuscripts. Matthew and Mark call it the Sea of Galilee. Luke speaks of the Lake of Gennesaret (5:1), and John refers in 21:1 to the Sea of Tiberias. Since Tiberias was founded by Herod Antipas, this last designation was from later than Jesus. It is apparently used in Jn. 6:1 to explain the older name, Sea of Galilee.

66. ἠκολούθει, imperfect.

the northeastern side of the lake. The signs that caused them to do so are not the specific miracles reported earlier; this assumes, rather, as in 2:23, that the reader knew of Jesus' miraculous power in general. That the crowd's aim was to see miracles is not presented as a positive assessment of their interest (cf. 2:24; 4:45, 48). Vss. 1 and 2 are strongly reminiscent of Mt. 15:29, 31, but are intended to furnish only a general depiction of the setting, of which "the hills" in vs. 3 also speak (cf. Mt. 5:1; Mk. 3:13). The mention of the approaching Passover in vs. 4 is striking. This is apparently not just a time indication but is also intended to evoke the content of the story that follows (see below). This is the second Passover reported in John (cf. 2:13, 23). For the expression "the feast of the Jews," see the comments on 2:13.

5-9 Jesus "lifting up his eyes" and "seeing a large crowd coming toward him" (vs. 5) is reminiscent of 4:35. As an introduction to Jesus' question to Philip it evokes (as in 4:35) the image of the messianic age, in which (as the harvester: cf. again 4:35; as the shepherd: cf. Mk. 6:34; as the king: cf. Jn. 6:15) Jesus sees the people come to him with all their needs and hopes — a situation in which, by way of a pertinent question, he also immediately involves his disciples ("From where shall *we* . . . ?"). But the question does seem totally inspired by perplexity or even meant as a rhetorical question rather than intended seriously to inquire from Philip where the bread could possibly come from to feed that many people. But, as the Evangelist immediately adds, the question served to test Philip, to see whether, as a follower and confessor of the Messiah, he understood the challenge inherent in this situation and how he would react to it. For — says the Evangelist — "Jesus himself knew what he would do."

By thus having Jesus ask the first question (unlike the Synoptics; cf. Mk. 6:35ff.) and therefore immediately giving him the initiative, the Evangelist again focuses the entire narrative on Jesus and from the beginning gives to this question to his disciple a certain slant that, initially at least, the disciple does not understand. As the shift in the story will show with unmistakable clarity (cf. vss. 26ff.), Jesus is not simply or primarily interested in providing for a momentary need for food (cf. Mk. 6:35ff.) but no less to give to his disciples an answer to the question "from where?" of the "bread for so many" in which they were soon to be involved as his servants. He himself, as the one in whose hand "the Father has given all things" (3:35; cf. 5:20ff.), knew what he would do, but would they also know the "whence"?

For the time being Philip offers his answer, as people have answered over and over, even those who ought to have known better and were to know better (cf. 4:11b, 33). He clings to the literal sense of Jesus' words: "Where are we to buy?" and tells Jesus in round figures that the whole idea is unthinkable. Even if they had at their disposal an enormous amount of money like two hundred denarii (i.e., two hundred times the amount a day laborer could earn in a day; cf. Mt. 20:2),[67] even this would not be enough to furnish a mouthful of food to every person in this crowd. Nor is Philip alone in his calculations. He gets support from Andrew (with whom he is also linked in 12:21f.; 1:44),[68] who, without bothering himself about imagined amounts of money, limits himself to the actual supply of bread on hand: five loaves and two (dried) fish. But what could one do with that, given so many mouths?

Although some of the details of the story correspond completely with those of the Synoptics — there, too, we read of five loaves and three fishes! — John's version is conspicuously his own. Apart from the roles he assigns to Philip and Andrew, there are in Andrew's mention of a boy[69] and of *barley* loaves two special features that occur also in the story of the miraculous feeding in 2 Kg. 4:42ff. There "the boy"[70] is Elisha's servant. In John the boy is also undoubtedly a helper or servant (of the disciples); Andrew would of course not make an inventory of what food the whole crowd had but of what they themselves had on hand (cf. Mk. 6:38). The servant's question in 2 Kg. 4:43 ("How am I to set this before a hundred men?") strongly resembles Andrew's question in John: "But what are they among so many?" Although this last point of correspondence is natural and cannot by itself be considered striking, the combination of these three links — the boy, the barley, and the question — can hardly be regarded as accidental.[71] Elsewhere in the Gospel we encounter expressions that bear a striking resemblance to certain features or statements in Old Testament miracle stories; cf. Jn. 4:50 with 1 Kg. 17:23; Jn. 9:7 with 2 Kg. 5:10; Jn. 2:6 with Gn. 4:55 (and possibly Jn. 1:29 with Gn. 22:8). Some scholars go even further and also see a clear resemblance in character between Jesus' miracles and those of Elijah (and Elisha) and Moses.[72] It is said that in

---

67. Mk. 6:37 also names this amount, but as enough to buy the bread, while here it is considered inadequate for the same purpose. This is a clear illustration of how details can be fixed in tradition but function differently depending on the context.

68. It is striking that Andrew here — as though, by contrast with Philip, he were still unknown to the reader — is again introduced as "one of [Jesus'] disciples" and — as already in 1:40 — as "the brother of Simon Peter," who was, of course, well known. Apparently not all the details in the Gospel are carefully attuned to each other.

69. παιδάριον.

70. In 2 Kg. 4:43 the LXX has λειτουργός but in vs. 38 (and elsewhere) παιδάριον.

71. So, e.g., Reim, *Studien zum alttestamentlichen Hintergrund des Johannesevangelium,* p. 157: "an obvious allusion."

72. This is said to be true specifically of the "signs source" ("S," from *sēmeia*) from which John is supposed to have drawn his miracle stories. For this see Nicol, *Sēmeia,* pp. 89ff. In his opinion it cannot be accidental that

> the kind of miracles which S describes agree with those of Elijah and Elisha: the multi-
> plication of bread (2 Kgs. 4:42-4; cf. the multiplication of oil, 4:1-7); raising from the dead
> (1 Kgs. 17; 2 Kgs. 4 — both concern a *boy;* cf. Jn. 4:46ff.); changing of bad water to good
> water (2 Kgs. 2:19-25 — cf. changing water to wine); washing oneself to be healed (2 Kgs.
> 5:10 — the closest parallel to Jn. 9:7, cf. Jn. 5:3). . . . If the kinds of miracles in S are

Jesus' miracles those of the great figures of the Old Testament return, a powerful proof for his messiahship.[73]

Still, the direct allusions, insofar as one can speak of them, are few, and where they are most clear — as in this chapter — they are marginal. The Johannine miracle stories themselves, even where one might speak of a certain similarity in character with those of Elijah and Elisha, are, in both construction and redaction, absolutely independent over against those in 1 and 2 Kings, and the corresponding features we have noted are no more than hints for the perceptive reader. Of course this does not remove the fact that these hints are of fundamental importance, because therein emerges the salvation-historical continuity between God's work of redemption in the past and that which transpires in the coming and ministry of the Messiah — a continuity that underlies the entire Fourth Gospel. That is not to say that the christology of the Fourth Gospel bears a character derived from the Mosaic "prophet" or even from the figures of Elijah and Elisha. Elijah and Elisha are not mentioned in this connection, and one would therefore have to subsume their significance under that of Moses. And admittedly, as we learned already from 5:39ff., 45ff., Moses is cited repeatedly in the Fourth Gospel as the great "witness" to Jesus as the Christ in virtue of the "Scriptures" he represents, but not, as himself a prophet and miracle-worker, as a "model" for Jesus' messiahship. It is rather the case that he serves as the example that shows how the messianic character of Jesus' coming and work totally transcends the Old Testament framework of salvation. This is true even of the miracles performed by Moses, as will become apparent in what follows in this chapter when the bread from heaven given through Moses, in its insufficiency for life, is contrasted with the bread that Jesus, as the Son of man, gives and is (cf. vss. 27ff., 32ff., 58).

10-13   After the two disciples have thus said their piece, Jesus carries out his intent (vs. 6; vss. 10ff.). At his command all must sit down. The abundant grass (in this season, cf. vs. 4) made this opportune (Mk. 6:39). Immediately, as in Luke (but unlike Matthew and Mark), the number of about five thousand men is mentioned. As a result, from the very beginning the emphasis comes to lie on the immense crowd for which Jesus prepares the meal. As host, he gives

---

paralleled by those of Kings, they agree nearly as much with those of Moses because Kings already shows many parallels to Moses.

See also the essay by J. Louis Martyn, "We Have Found Elia," in his *The Gospel of John in Christian History*, 1979, pp. 13ff., according to which the Johannine Jesus resembles Elijah.

73. Nicol, who deals with all this in his analysis of the signs source, speaks of a typology "beneath the surface; it is the barely visible foundation of the whole Christology of S., namely the expectation that there would be a correspondence between the final salvation and the salvation of Israel of old, between the Messianic time and the Mosaic era — including the 'Mosaic figure of Elijah.'"

thanks and distributes the bread and the fish, then the miracle is realized in the abundance he sets before these thousands of people (cf. 10:10). The fact that this is the great vantage point from which the meal has to be viewed is clear from vss. 12 and 13. The disciples, undoubtedly already involved in the distribution (as the Synoptics explicitly report), are told to gather up not only the remnants but the surplus, the overflow[74] of the meal. It then turns out that of the five barley loaves *twelve* baskets can be filled with the fragments that those who had eaten and were satisfied had to spare, for they were not allowed to "waste" any part of this abundance. For this practice scholars refer to the Jewish custom of gathering the fragments after a meal. This is correct and — within the context of the narrative — certainly in the sense that of the gift for which the father in the home thanks God nothing should be lost. How much less, then, of *these* gifts! Not as sacred miracle bread but as evidence of the power and authority with which the Father had clothed his Son. Of this reality especially the disciples, as fellow participants in the work of the Lord (cf. also 4:35ff.), and in spite of their initial inability to follow him in it, had to be witnesses, individually and collectively as the twelve. For only as they trust the fullness of God's gift in the sending of his Son could they be his disciples and continue his work in the world.

The intent of this picture of Jesus — one that is presented with so much emphasis in all four Gospels — was to make visible the great future inaugurated in Jesus' coming and work as that had been repeatedly prefigured in prophecy under the image of the host presiding over and providing an abundant meal and that had a prominent place in the parables and predictions of Jesus himself (e.g., Is. 25:6ff.; 49:9ff.; Mt. 22:1-14; Lk. 22:16, 29, 30). In this regard there is a clear resemblance between this meal and the wedding in Cana: here an abundance of bread, there an abundance of wine. But while in that revelational miracle in ch. 2 everything is still focused on the (first) disclosure of Jesus' glory and while the meal itself and the guests receive no special attention there and the disciples only fulfill the role of spectators, here the dominant motif is the great multitude for which Jesus is the host and for which his disciples, already serving as the executors of his work, are directly involved. In this respect the presentation of the miracle of the feeding of the five thousand in the Fourth Gospel forms a clear parallel to that in the Synoptics.

Still, it cannot be denied that in the dialogue and teaching in the synagogue that follow the significance of the miracle of the loaves is given a typically Johannine twist in that it is not (as in the Synoptics) the coming of the kingdom that constitutes the central theme but the identification of the miracle with Jesus himself in which everything culminates. This bread discourse in the synagogue

---

74. τὰ περισσεύσαντα κλάσματα. So Brown, *Comm.* I, p. 234, appealing to Léon-Dufour.

is, in fact, the great example of this identification, for here in constantly new forms and phrases Jesus calls himself "the bread that has come down from heaven" and even refers to his own "flesh" as the bread that he will give for the life of the world (cf. vss. 32ff., 48ff., 51ff.; see, however, the comments already on 2:10b; 4:10).

Many (both earlier and more recent) exegetes are even of the opinion that the story of the bread miracle in John was redacted under the influence of the bread discourse so that the point of the multiplication comes to lie in its reference to the Last Supper. In the exegesis below we shall consider in greater detail the sacramental interpretation of the bread discourse. Here the question is whether eucharistic tendencies are already shaping the account of the miracle of the loaves itself. According to some commentators, this is indeed the case. Brown, for example, writes at length about the "eucharistic features" that mark the miracle story itself, finding them in the first place in that which the Synoptic and the Johannine accounts of the multiplication have in common with the reports of the institution of the Lord's Supper, where Jesus also takes the bread, pronounces the blessing or thanksgiving, and breaks and distributes the bread.[75] Scholars also appeal in this regard to the eucharistic prayer in the *Didache,* in which God is petitioned that "as this fragmented bread was scattered on the mountains [like grain] but was gathered up *[synagein]* . . . so let the church be gathered up from the four corners of the earth into your kingdom."[76]

But these arguments are not very persuasive. All that the reports of the institution of the Lord's Supper and of the multiplication of loaves have in common is what, according to Jewish custom, every father or host did at the beginning of a meal. This qualifies both the feeding miracle and Jesus' last meeting with his disciples as *meals,* and it is not at all obvious why the (naturally) close agreement in the description of Jesus' action as host at both occasions should impart "eucharistic features" to the miracle of the multiplication. The great theme of the miracle story is the eschatological abundance that Jesus supplies and the messianic authority given him by the Father. It is true that in the course of the subsequent discourse Jesus will increasingly relate the significance of the bread to himself and (in 6:51ff.) arrive at the pronouncement that the bread he will give "for the life of the world" is his "flesh." But this symbolic interpretation in the bread discourse does not allow us to project it back into the redaction of the miracle story, thus making the entire account into an allegorical presentation of the Last Supper. It is even disputed whether in the bread discourse itself Jesus, in speaking of eating the bread descended from heaven (explicated as his flesh), refers to the eating of the communion bread and not to the believing appropriation of

75. Brown, *Comm.* I, pp. 246ff., with repeated reference to his extensive comparison of the Synoptic and Johannine versions of the multiplication of the loaves (see above).

76. Following C. F. D. Moule, "A Note on Didache IX 4," *JTS* 6 (1955) pp. 240-43, in which Moule attempts to explain the *Didache* passage in terms of John 6. However, this would not constitute proof that, conversely, the passage in John 6 exhibits the features of the Eucharistic prayer. See also Lindars, *Comm.,* p. 243, who endorses Moule's argument but interprets the "gathering up" of the fragments as an allusion to Ex. 16:16 (the gathering of the manna).

his self-offering in death.[77] And there is no more sign of or allusion to such sacramental eating in the redaction of the bread miracle in John than in the Synoptics. The remarkable fact is that John, though his interpretation of the bread given and presented by Jesus goes beyond that of the Synoptics and is very much his own, leaves the general eschatological character of the traditional story intact.

Nor, in my opinion, can the appeal to *Didache* 9:4 detract from this. In the *Didache* the image of the harvest gathered from all the mountains dominates everything; in John 6 the dominant image is that of the plentiful meal. Therefore, in John the "gathered" bread is not an image of the church gathered from the four corners of the earth, as in the prayer in the *Didache,* but of the abundant gift of God in Christ of which the church, in this case the disciples called by Jesus, is the witness and of which they may not let anything "perish." To project the former into the latter is a contamination of heterogeneous matters.

14, 15   The first reaction of "the people" shows that they, too, understand this miracle of the loaves in an "eschatological" sense, namely as the evidence of the expected coming into the world of "the prophet" (see the comments on 1:19; cf. 7:40). Many interpreters take "the prophet" to be the prophet promised by Moses in Dt. 18:15: "a prophet like me." Moses was known as the great miracle worker (e.g., Dt. 34:10, 11), as was Elijah, and Jesus' miracles evoked the thought of the coming of the Mosaic prophet (as of Elijah; cf. Mk. 6:14ff. par.; 8:27ff. par.). What is remarkable is that in the present passage the coming of "the" prophet is apparently associated with the *royal* function (cf. vs. 15) generally attributed to the *Messiah* as the one who would restore the Davidic kingship, but who, in the pertinent Jewish literature, did not act as miracle worker (see, however, the comments on 7:31).[78] Some interpreters therefore believe that the reference here cannot be to the prophet of Deuteronomy 18 because the latter is not said to be a king; others think, however, that in Jewish (and Samaritan) future expectation the Mosaic "prophet" does exhibit royal features and that in vs. 15, therefore, the reference is not to the Messiah.[79] It is questionable, however, whether in Jewish future expectation, which is not always transparent to us, one can make such sharp distinctions among the functions of the figures expected in the messianic age. In this connection John does clearly make a distinction between "the prophet" and "the Messiah"

77. On this see the longer discussion below.

78. On this material see de Jonge, *Jesus: Stranger from Heaven and Son of God,* chs. 3 and 4.

79. For this interpretation see W. A. Meeks, *The Prophet-King: Moses Traditions and Johannine Christology,* 1967, who regards Jn. 6:15 as the basis for understanding that in the christology of the Fourth Gospel the kingship of Christ was redefined in terms of the Mosaic "prophet" (p. 67). Against this entire view see de Jonge, *Jesus: Stranger from Heaven and Son of God,* pp. 51ff.; Nicol, *Sēmeia,* p. 88.

(1:21; 7:40, 41); from the Messiah, however, miracles were also expected (see comments on 7:31; cf. also Mt. 24:24; Mk. 13:22) and there are clear associations throughout the New Testament between messiahship and prophecy.[80] It is clear that John the Evangelist does not aim to characterize or define Jesus' messiahship from the perspective of specific Jewish expectations. However much scholars think they can illumine the connection between prophet and king in vss. 14 and 15 from Jewish expectations, it is presumably well established, first, that, in connection with the kingship of Jesus as the Christ, the Evangelist takes his starting point in the promised *messianic* (Davidic) king (cf. 1:49; 12:13ff.; 20:31), and, second, that on the basis of Jesus' self-revelation the Evangelist redefines this kingship in a way that transcends all existing expectations (cf. 1:50, 51; 20:31: Son of man and Son of God; see also the comments on vs. 27). This is also evident from how, in the present context, Jesus withdraws from what he perceives to be the intent of the multitude, namely "to make him king."

The situation here is not depicted very clearly. Are "the hills" of vs. 15 identical with those in vs. 3? Or is the idea that Jesus merely withdrew to one of the surrounding hills? And what is meant by "again"? That this was his practice (cf. Mk. 6:46)? But the intent is clear. Jesus does not give the multitude a chance to put their conceptions concerning him into effect. He rejects a priori any notion of kingship as they conceived it. And the reason is not that he wanted no part of the messianic kingship for himself (cf. 1:49; 12:13ff.) or that he objected to the application to himself of the prophecy of a prophet like Moses (cf. 1:45; 4:25, 26). But he wanted no part of kingship in the way the people understood it, something he would later describe as a "kingship of this world" (18:36). What the multitude envisioned was that *they* would *make* him king and that he would exercise a worldly kingship over them. Throughout this discussion of Jesus' true identity, even with those who were disposed on the basis of his messianic self-disclosure to accept him as the (or a) divinely sent prophet or messiah, one must undoubtedly also read the Fourth Gospel against the background of the continuing conflict over Jesus' messiahship between church and synagogue.

16-19 In his description of the miracle of "Jesus walking on the sea" (cf. Mt. 14:22; Mk. 6:45), a miracle that follows at the heels of that of the loaves, the Evangelist clearly follows his own course. In his version the disciples take the initiative (cf. Mk. 6:45). When evening falls and the time has come to return, they go down to the sea (vs. 16) and embark to go to Capernaum (vs. 17). We are not told why they go without Jesus. Jesus had earlier withdrawn from them to go to "the hills" (vs. 15) and is therefore for a time the great Absent One in the story. For now the disciples are on their own. The statement

---

80. For the argumentation see Nicol, *Sēmeia,* pp. 84ff.

that after nightfall[81] Jesus had still not come to them does not, therefore, refer to their expectation or to an arrangement between him and them but, anticipating the sequel, calls attention to the fact that now also the darkness separated them from him and he therefore had to come to them in the dark. Moreover[82] (vs. 18), in the meantime, as a result of a fierce wind, the sea had become very agitated. Still, the emphasis does not come to lie so much on the disciples' predicament but on the inconceivability of Jesus' coming to them — in the darkness and over the high waves. To this vs. 19 adds the new element of distance: "the twenty-five or thirty stadia," that is, some three or four miles, about half of the width of the sea at its widest point. Then when the disciples had come thus far and found themselves in the midst of the sea, they saw coming toward them the figure of Jesus "walking" on the tumultuous sea. "Walking" (the current and literal translation of the Greek word)[83] suggests the effortlessness of Jesus going over the sea. They "saw" Jesus: a "seeing" reminiscent of that of 1:14.[84] That the sight frightened them is consistent with the nature of this "seeing." It is the fear that fills a person confronted with the revelation of God or the divine (cf. Lk. 1:12; 2:19) or, in general, with the supernatural (cf. Mt. 14:26), a fear that apparently also prevented the disciples from immediately recognizing Jesus in the approaching figure. For they had never learned to know him in that way and thus, in that place and horrendous situation, had not expected him at all.

20 The austere, nondramatic way in which everything is told climaxes in the simple saying of Jesus: "It is I; do not be afraid." In its literal sense this is only a self-identification intended to soothe the disciples' fear (cf. Mk. 6:50). But by saying this Jesus also describes his coming and appearance as a divine epiphany;[85] and this occurs in a context — and that is where the emphasis lies in this self-revelation — that should convince them that, in virtue of the glory given him by God, no darkness was too deep, waves too high, or sea too wide for him to find them and be with them in the midst of that tumult.

21 The conclusion in vs. 21 is as succinct in form as the whole story itself. "They wanted to take him into the boat" has an indefinite air but presumably means that the disciples expressed the wish — urged him — that

---

81. Some manuscripts have "darkness had fallen on them" (κατέλαβεν; cf. 1:5; 12:35), which accentuates the situation even more without implying any "deeper" meaning.

82. τε makes the addition emphatic.

83. περιπατοῦτα.

84. θεωροῦσιν, historical present ("a reflection of eyewitness traditions?" asks Brown, *Comm.* I, p. 252).

85. See, also in combination with "do not be afraid," Gn. 26:24; Rv. 1:17. For the absolute meaning of the "I am" statements and the connection with texts like Is. 41:1; 43:10, etc., see at greater length the comments on 8:24.

he should come aboard with them, as the direct and natural consequence of their recognition of Jesus and the change in their outlook. That he complied, though it is not expressed, is assumed. The concluding statement, "and immediately the boat was at the land to which they were going," apparently only means that once Jesus was with them there were no further problems and they soon reached the other side of the lake. There is no explicit mention here, as in the other Gospels, of "a stilling of the storm." Some commentators see here instead a "miraculous landing."[86] But this seems extremely far-fetched. What is undoubtedly meant is that as a result of Jesus' presence, they soon reached their destination. That this was due not to the fact that the sea had become level but to a new miracle seems, in the context of the entire story and of the knowledge of the tradition constantly assumed among the readers, an entirely unmotivated hypothesis (cf. also Ps. 107:29, 30).

One can, finally, inquire about the specific significance of this miracle in the whole context of ch. 6.[87] The manner in which the Evangelist edited the story shows that he did not incorporate this "sequel" to the miracle of the loaves in his Gospel on purely traditional grounds. This is also evident from the fact that the multitude groped in vain for the time and manner in which he had come to Capernaum (vs. 25). We may say perhaps that in the statement "It is I" — in which the second miracle culminates — Jesus reveals himself to his disciples as wholly other than the multitude pictured him and wanted him to be. He withdrew from the crowd in order to reveal himself to the disciples. But this did not occur until there had also been a substantial change in the role of the disciples. In the miracle of the loaves they share in his glory. Then he lets them go away in a boat alone — here, in John, by withdrawing himself from them, in the Synoptics, by expressly making them go (Mt. 14:22; Mk. 6:45). Do they perhaps need to be safeguarded against an all-too-human, "worldly" conception of his kingship and their own role in it? In any case, once they have arrived on the sea they are confronted by another reality, one in which all glory departs from them; darkness and waves tower over them while the safe shore of the other side is still at a great distance. In that situation Jesus reveals himself to them in the absoluteness of his messianic power and authority. It is in this way that he wants to be known as the one sent by the Father over against all that human beings want to make of him and use him for. And it is faith in that identity to which he wants to lead his disciples, even when they might have to follow him not in the light of his glory but along other roads and under the threat of other powers.

22-25 The next segment of the story occurs on the following day. The

---

86. So, e.g., Bultmann, *Comm.,* p. 211; Nicol, *Sēmeia,* p. 59.

87. According to Moloney (*Johannine Son of Man,* p. 108), it is "difficult to explain the present position of the miracle story" (in vss. 16-21).

Evangelist positions this time indication, which he often uses, at the head of this unit, although what follows in vss. 22ff. still relates to the previous day, and he does not get to the intended continuation of the events on the next day until vss. 24b and 25. The resulting incongruency in the sentence structure cannot be resolved in translation. However, the intent is not unclear.[88] The people who, after the miracle, had remained on the other side noticed that the disciples had embarked without Jesus, although there was no other boat available to him (vs. 22). In the meantime (vs. 23) other boats had arrived from Tiberias, close to where the miracle had occurred. When the people (vs. 24) again ascertained for themselves that neither Jesus nor his disciples were still present, they set out for Capernaum in search of Jesus. And when they found him there a day later, they came to him with the question, "Rabbi, when did you come here?" (vs. 25). This question is the starting point for Jesus' great discourse on the true bread from heaven.

6:26-59

Bread from Heaven, the Synagogue at Capernaum

This lengthy discourse — which can also be called a didactic dialogue — in the synagogue at Capernaum (vs. 59) is one of the most controversial topics in the study of the Fourth Gospel, not only in commentaries but also in a multitude of monographs.[89] The questions most at issue are the "sacramental" character of the discourse (see above on the bread miracle), the unity of vss. 26-58 in the text transmitted, and, therewith, the composition and division of the material. One commentator has been said of chapter 6 that it "has such a clear internal unity and self-consistency, it is so well balanced and articulated,

---

88. Although all sorts of historical questions remain unanswered. The continuation of the story (in Capernaum) is very different from what is in Matthew and Mark (cf. Mt. 14:34; Mk. 6:53 [in Gennesareth]). In addition, the embarkation of the people cannot possibly relate to all who ate the bread. The Evangelist moves directly to the discourse about the bread of life in the synagogue at Capernaum as the material sequel to the miracle of the loaves, without involving himself in questions that the transition from one situation to another (very different) situation would raise in the minds of readers concerned about historical sequence. The highly succinct, stylistically even deficient, transitional passage furnishes (even taking account of corruptions of the text) a certain insight into what he deemed important for his readers' understanding of his Gospel.

89. Brown, *Comm.* I, p. 293, refers to a bibliography composed in 1935 by Gärtner and supplements it up to 1966; Moloney (*Johannine Son of Man*, pp. 89f.) "adapted and supplemented" it up to 1978. See also H. Leroy, "Rätsel und Mißverständnis," *Bonner Biblische Beiträge* 30 (1968), pp. 108f.; H. Thyen, "Aus der Literatur zum Johannesevangelium," *Theologische Rundschau* 43 (1978), pp. 328f.

that it ranks as one of the finest products of John's pen,"[90] but others are convinced of the opposite. Here again[91] it is especially Bultmann who believes that almost everything is lacking to this unity. He himself attempts to reorder a "disordered" text and considers vss. 51b-58 so contradictory of what precedes that he regards these verses as an addition by a later "churchly" redactor.[92]

However, as has been remarked, such an approach to the text, which was in vogue with some commentators for a long time and carried to its limit in Bultmann's commentary, is finding less and less acceptance. Not only are the results of these reconstructions usually no less problematic than the difficulties they are intended to resolve,[93] but the insight is growing that the author of this Gospel must have moved along very different conceptual lines of thought than those that characterize a modern, systematically constructed discourse.

More plausible, therefore, are more recent attempts to explain the construction of the "teaching" in the synagogue at Capernaum in the light of Jewish liturgical or homiletical models said to be governed by a similar structure. Some interpreters, proceeding on the basis of vss. 4 and 59, have attempted to posit a direct link between Jesus' discourse and the Passover[94] or selected Passover.[95] The attempt is made to show that during Passover, when the history of the exodus is central, the eating of manna in the wilderness was given special attention. Accordingly, the miracle of the loaves is said to have been very closely tied in with the eating of the manna. In that connection the construction of Jesus' discourse in the synagogue is said to have been reminiscent, in more than one respect, of the Passover haggadah — for example, in the questions that the multitude directs to Jesus (vss. 28, 30f., 41f., 52), which are said to correspond with the sort of questions that were raised with respect to the meaning of the meal during the Passover celebration by four children.[96]

This view has not found much acceptance, however. For however attrac-

---

90. So Lindars, *Comm.*, p. 234. See also H. Schürmann, *Ursprung und Gestalt*, 1970, pp. 13ff. L. Schenke, "Die formale und gedankliche Struktur von Joh. 6,26-58," *BZ* 24 (1980), concludes (p. 38): "The text in its *present* condition is a consciously constructed literary entity with a clearly conceived theological line of thought. It is not possible to divide it between two authors, each with a different theological objective."

91. See also the introduction to ch. 5 above.

92. He already regards the transition from the feeding to the discourse as artificial, the dialogue in vss. 27ff. as originally related to another situation than that underlying vss. 1-25, and vss. 27-50a as in such "a state of disorder or at least of a very poor order" that it can only be explained "by suggesting that it is the work of an editor who, having found a text which for external reasons had been completely destroyed and so disordered, attempted himself to reconstruct the original order." In his opinion, the original order was vss. 27, 34, 35, 30-33, 47-51a, 41-46, and 36-40.

93. Cf. also Dodd, *Interpretation*, p. 290; see the comments on ch. 5 above.

94. B. Gärtner, *John 6 and the Jewish Passover*, 1959.

95. A. Guilding, *The Fourth Gospel and Jewish Worship*, 1960.

96. Gärtner, *John 6*, pp. 25ff.

tive it may seem, at first blush, to forge a connection between, on the one hand, Passover (6:4) as the celebration of the great salvation event of the exodus from Egypt and the associated miracle of manna and, on the other, the miracle of the loaves as a portrayal of the messianic time of salvation, it is quite another matter whether these connections can be persuasively shown to exist in the miracle story itself and in the subsequent discourse in the synagogue. That which is supposed to serve as proof is too general and forced — like the questions asked by the four children, which are supposed to be "parallels" — to serve as the interpretive key to the construction of John 6.

More deserving of credit in this respect is the view — initiated by P. Borgen[97] and adopted by others[98] — that ch. 6 contains evidence of a certain homiletic "model" or "pattern" of Scripture exposition that one also encounters in the writings of Philo and in later rabbinic literature. These scholars have in mind specifically a form of midrash in which, from a given statement in Scripture (usually from the Pentateuch), individual words are taken as starting point for an extensive paraphrase ending in a summary conclusion. In the course of such a teaching a fitting saying from another part of Scripture is then usually taken to support the argumentation. This pattern is said to be present in the discourse here, and vs. 31 is taken to be the central text, later supported by the quotation from Isaiah in vs. 45. The quotation in vs. 31, the words "bread" and "from heaven" in particular, is said to be explained in vss. 32-48, while the "eating" of the bread comes up first in vss. 49-51 and again after the question in vs. 52, thus demonstrating the original unity of vss. 52-58 with what comes before.

The general importance of these studies seems to lie in the fact that, for the evaluation of the structure and construction of (not always transparent) units like the bread discourse in John 6, they uncover broader criteria than those that have usually been applied by literary criticism with a strictly "Western" orientation. And this is all the more true when the intent of scholars is not strictly to evaluate the construction of the text by a fixed pattern of midrash, but to make visible, in a more general sense, contemporary backgrounds of homiletical or expository forms.[99] In particular, this approach to the discourse here has the merit that, for the mode of argumentation followed there, it can point to clear

---

97. P. Borgen, *Bread from Heaven: An Exegetical Study of the Concept of Man in the Gospel of John and the Writings of Philo* (*NovT* Supplements 10), 1965; further defended and explained in idem, *Logos Was the True Light*, 1983, pp. 21-46.

98. See, e.g., the commentaries of Brown, Barrett, Lindars, and Schnackenburg. An overview of the continuing discussion can also be found in Moloney, *Johannine Son of Man*, pp. 94ff.

99. See also Borgen's own rejection of an excessively strict application of the midrashic "pattern" in his later book, *Logos Was the True Light*, p. 35: "The Evangelist expressed the ideas in traditional forms, and had hardly any independent interest in form as such. Therefore, the forms were not applied in a mechanical way."

features of correspondence in contemporary Jewish literature[100] and that it can advance forceful arguments for the unity of the discourse, in particular that vss. 51c-58 belong integrally to what comes before.

Another matter, however, is whether one can go so far as to qualify vss. 31-58 as a running paraphrase — constructed in the manner of a midrash — of the citation in vs. 31. It has been correctly remarked by others that one cannot really consider John 6 a coherent discourse or didactic address, since it is repeatedly interrupted by questions and objections from the hearers. In the light of vs. 59 it should rather be referred to as a didactic dialogue.[101] This distinction not only has formal value but also and especially material significance because the construction of the whole is thus seen to be clearly shaped not only by the citation in vs. 31 but no less by the repeated interjections of Jesus' hearers. The result is that one can certainly not say (with Borgen) that the discourse is composed of two parts, of which the first (vss. 32-48) paraphrases "bread from heaven" and "give" and the second (vss. 49-58) "eat." Borgen thus isolates vss. 26-30 from the discourse proper, whereas they are organically bound up with it (note the links between vss. 30 and 31 and vss. 27 and 28). But it is of no less importance that in vss. 31ff. Jesus, because he responds each time to questions and objections from his hearers, deviates, as it were, from "the text" and pursues a line of thought that one can hardly describe as a paraphrase of the text. This happens specifically in vss. 36ff., where, before picking up in vs. 47 the thread of vs. 35, he first reacts at great length to the unbelief of his hearers, and "bread from heaven" is no longer the dominant motif in this section (cf. vss. 37ff., 44ff.). This is not to say that these verses break up the unity of the discourse, for the connection with what precedes is still clearly evident (indirectly, e.g., in "come down from heaven" in vs. 38; very directly in vss. 41ff.). But this does, to my mind, constitute a clear hindrance to bringing the entire discourse (beginning in vs. 26) about the bread from heaven that Jesus *gives* and *is,* under the heading of a homily or midrash on the citation in vs. 31. Therefore, the division of the whole cannot be derived from the sequence of the terms in the citation in vs. 31 but needs to be seen as also determined by the course of the dialogue between Jesus and his hearers. With others,[102] therefore, I opt for a division in which vss. 26ff. are seen as integrated into the whole of the dialogue and vss. 36-46, though taken as an integral part of the

100. For this, too, see *Logos Was the True Light,* pp. 24ff.

101. Cf. W. Weren in W. Beuken et al., *Brood uit de hemel. Lijnen van Exodus 16 naar Johannes 6 tegen de achtergrond van de rabbijnse litteratuur,* 1985, p. 45.

102. E.g., Weren, in *Brood uit de hemel,* p. 49. As far as I can tell, he leaves out of consideration the background of Borgen's division but arrives, on the basis of his own "synchronic" structural analysis (cf. p. 60), at the following: vss. 25c-34; vss. 35-47; vss. 48-56. He points out the parallelism in vss. 35-47 and 48-58 and thus does justice to the distinctive character as well as the integrity of these passages.

text, nevertheless occupy a place of their own as an intermezzo between vss. 26-35 and vss. 48-58. Briefly, then, the passage can be outlined as follows:

a. Verses 26-35: "I am the bread of life." On the basis of the question in vs. 25, Jesus begins to speak of the food that does not perish. In the resulting dialogue, the appeal to Moses and to the bread from heaven that Moses gave the people to eat acquires an important thematic significance. This leads to Jesus' pronouncement — a provisional high point in the discourse: "I am the bread of life."

b. Verses 36-47: God's saving will is realized in people coming to Jesus. Over against the unbelief of those who desire the heavenly bread but do not believe in Jesus himself as the one sent from heaven, Jesus — before again picking up in vs. 47 the theme of vs. 35 — maintains that his mission is the fulfillment of God's saving will with regard to those whom the Father has given him. For this he specifically appeals to the words "And they will all be taught by God" (Isaiah 54).

c. Verses 48-58: "The bread that I will give is my flesh." Vs. 48 again takes up the pronouncement of vs. 35a and explicates why and in what respect Jesus, in distinction from the bread in the wilderness, is the bread of life. He is because he gives his *flesh* for the life of the world. Despite the paradoxical and offensive character of this utterance (vs. 52), his flesh is truly food and his blood truly drink, and only they who *eat* his flesh and *drink* his blood have eternal life. Vs. 58 summarizes and concludes.

6:26-35

"I Am the Bread of Life"

26 The emphatic pronouncement in vs. 26, which functions as a new beginning, above all echoes what happened the day before and the reaction of the people. Jesus' statement is not a real answer to their question in vs. 25. With that question they touched on the secret of Jesus' identity — the miraculous way he had come across the lake! — but without realizing it. Still their question evinces more than mere curiosity. Implied in it is puzzlement over his conduct: Why had he withdrawn himself from them? Why had he left them in a state of uncertainty so that they had to go out in search of him?

Jesus' answer is striking in its utter negativity.[103] It is also striking that he charges the people that they do not seek him because they had seen the

---

103. Cf. de Jonge (*Jesus: Stranger from Heaven and Son of God,* p. 57): "Jesus' reaction towards the ideas of the crowd in the following discourse is entirely negative. In that Chapter [6] not the similarities but the dissimilarities receive all emphasis."

signs, even though it was seeing the sign that led them to say, "This is indeed
the prophet" (vs. 14). This fact, as also their request for a sign in vs. 30, has
occasioned the question whether the situation of the miracle story and that of
the subsequent dialogue are really in sync and whether the Evangelist has not
brought together here materials that do not belong together (see the Introduction
above). But vs. 26 clearly echoes the preceding, not only in the second part but
also in the word "signs." The point of the pronouncement consists in the
charged way Jesus uses the expression "seeing signs," as distinct from its
meaning in vs. 14 (cf. vs. 2; 2:23). In John the word translated "sign"[104] often
means no more than "miracle." Still, the word in Greek also (and as a rule)
has the meaning of our word "sign." In the context of the miracle stories it
then means something like: miracle as symbol, miracle with a meaning inherent
in and depicted by the miracle. Accordingly, some scholars translate vs. 26
". . . not because you have *understood* the signs. . . ." Still it is questionable
whether in the word "sign" the symbolic significance of the bread is referred
to.[105] True, later in the discourse Jesus will explain the meaning of the miracle,
but what is at stake here is not primarily the (noetic) act of understanding a
symbolic miracle but the (visual) act of seeing the miraculous event as the
authenticating sign of another heavenly reality, a sign designed to awaken in
the people a corresponding "faith" (cf. vss. 29, 30, 36). However, all that they
"saw" (vs. 14) and that aroused their attention and enthusiasm were the loaves
that had stilled their hunger. For that reason their "seeking" of Jesus had been
inspired by desire, not for the heavenly and permanent, but for the earthly and
perishable. And insofar as they saw in Jesus, on the basis of the miracle he
performed, "the prophet who was to come into the world" and were prepared
to enthrone him as king (vss. 14 and 15), to that degree they gave proof that
they had not "seen" the "sign."

27 Over against this intense focus on the food that perishes (cf. Is. 55:2;
as elsewhere on earthly riches, cf. Mt. 6:19ff.), Jesus now poses as an absolute
contrast — and hence in the manner of a *mašāl*[106] — labor for the bread that
endures to eternal life. The parallel with what is said in ch. 4 about living water
is striking (cf. 4:9, 13ff.; see also the comments below on 6:34). In what follows
what Jesus means by the food will be identified ever more closely with his

104. σημεῖον.

105. See also the analysis of this text in Nicol, *Sēmeia,* pp. 113f.

106. A rhetorical device by which, e.g., by posing an absolute contrast, the writer emphatically brings to the fore a specific aspect of the truth without intending thereby to reject every
other consideration (e.g., Pr. 8:10a-b; Jl. 2:13; Ho. 6:6; Mt. 6:1). Obviously the verse here does
not mean that one should not work for perishable food or that Jesus was indifferent to the material
needs of people, especially of the poor. Conversely, Jn. 6:27 does furnish proof that the current
tendency of many people to view Jesus' kingdom above all from the vantage point of the material
and social needs of people is far removed from the center of Jesus' message.

person and work (vss. 35, 48, 51, 55). Here it is primarily described as "the gift of the Son of man" (cf. vs. 53), an expression that also denotes the transcendent character of the gift (see the comments on 1:51; 5:27). Although he is still speaking in the third person, it is clear that Jesus is also referring to his own powers as the one sent by the Father (cf. vs. 29), and that especially to indicate the heavenly and imperishable character of the gift at his disposal: eternal life (cf. vs. 53). The clause "for on him has God the Father set his seal" speaks of the exclusive ("on *him*") appointment and authorization of the Son of man as the bringer of salvation. The idea that this sealing refers to a specific event in Jesus' life, specifically to his baptism (as some interpreters think), is not likely. This Gospel never mentions Jesus' baptism. The reference is rather to the divine authorization of the Son of man as such. It is for that reason that one should zealously labor for the food that he gives and not labor merely for earthly bread (see also the comments on vs. 53).

28, 29 The people, however, do not respond to this clear reference to the Son of man, perhaps because they were not familiar with this figure (cf. 9:35, 36; 12:34). But they do understand that Jesus is urging them to seek "something higher" than what has up to this point motivated them to follow him. They therefore ask him what they must *do* (picking up the cue from Jesus' words) "to be doing the works of God."[107]

Jesus' answer (vs. 29) tersely expresses the issue at stake here as in all the conversations and encounters of the Fourth Gospel: "This is the work of God, that you believe in him whom he has sent." The idea is not to elucidate the concepts "works" and "faith" in their mutual relations, as in Paul. All that is at stake here — which also governed the preceding — is that Jesus, including by means of the preceding miracle, pursues but one goal with the people: to open their eyes to the fact that in his coming and work God is in the process of addressing himself to them with his redeeming action, of introducing his kingdom, and of fulfilling his promise. In that connection the continual reference to the Son of man serves, over against all earthly and temporal patterns of expectation, to maintain the divine character and content of his messianic mission. For it is the person of the sent one and the way to which God will hold *him* that imparts to the food he gives its imperishable character (cf. vss. 51ff.). And the appropriate attitude on the part of those for whom this is intended is openness for what God gives and does, not works as a human achievement. That this "believing in him" is nevertheless called "the work of God"[108] has its roots in the pronouncement in vs. 27. All the labor and effort the people are investing to remain near Jesus is vain and unprofitable — a dead work — as

---

107. Cf. 3:21; 9:4, a Semitic manner of speech (cf. Nu. 8:11); the reference is to human work, to that which God *asks* of a person.

108. Which still refers to the work that God requires; cf. vss. 27, 28.

long as they follow him on the basis of human expectations and not on the basis of faith.

30   The answer the people give may at first sight take us completely by surprise in view of what Jesus has done the previous day. But here, too, as in vs. 26, everything depends on who uses the words "sign" and "see": Jesus or the people. What the people had "seen" as a "sign" was bread, and for that they were prepared to recognize Jesus as "the prophet" (vs. 14). But what he now claimed to be able to give them — eternal life — *that* they had not seen in him; and before believing *that* they would like to see a "sign" corresponding to the claim. Hence their answer, in which, in a somewhat parodying retort, they return the demand he made to them: "Then what sign *do* you do that we may see and believe you? What work do you yourself perform?"

31   Here an important shift occurs in the dialogue: from here on the discourse is dominated by the terminology of the manna miracle that occurred after the exodus from Egypt. The people bring this up to oppose Jesus' claim that he had imperishable food at his disposal and hence had a superior claim to their faith. Over against this they appeal to the great wilderness experience of their fathers, expressed in the words of Scripture: "He gave them bread from heaven to eat." The citation cannot be found in this precise version in the Old Testament; we are dealing, rather, with a combination of a number of terms that are central to this whole context (cf. Ex. 16:4 and 15).[109] One can also refer to Ps. 78:23, 24, which also mentions the heavenly character of the bread that God, through Moses, gave to Israel in the wilderness ("he . . . opened the doors of heaven . . . and gave them grain from heaven. Humans ate the bread of angels").

Jesus' bread miracle was associated with the manna in the wilderness for more than one reason. It was the time of the Passover (vs. 4), the feast of the exodus. But of more importance is the connection that the people had already made (vs. 14) between Jesus and "the prophet" promised by Moses, along with the understanding in later Jewish writings of manna as a gift of the eschaton: the ancient miracle in the wilderness, it was said, would be repeated; thus the Messiah, the "second Redeemer," would do what Moses, the "first Redeemer," had done.[110] We do not know how much this played a

---

109. R. Bergmeier, *Glaube als Gabe nach Johannes,* 1980, speaks of the "deliberately contaminated Scriptural citation from Ex. 16:4 ἄρτους ἐκ τοῦ οὐρανοῦ and 16:15 Οὗτος ὁ ἄρτος, ὃν ἔδωκεν κύριος ὑμῖν φαγεῖν" (p. 215). On the connection with Exodus 16 see specifically Beuken et al., *Brood uit de hemel.*

110. Cf., e.g., Strack/Billerbeck II, pp. 481ff.; Schlatter, *Comm.,* p. 172:

The Galileans were not yielding to an arbitrary impulse when they asked Jesus whether he was crediting himself with feeding the people with manna. The same was expected of

role in the dialogue described here because there is no explicit reference to it. But in the conflict over Jesus' identity and the nature of his messiahship, both during his life and later in the conflict between church and synagogue, it was inevitable that his place in the history of redemption and comparison with the great figures of the past would come up again and again. Just as the Samaritan woman asked Jesus whether he was greater than "our father Jacob," so now these Jews appeal to the heavenly bread that God, through Moses, gave the fathers to eat in the wilderness. In view of how he has spoken of the imperishable food "that endures to eternal life," does he think he is greater than Moses and able to give more than the manna, the bread from heaven, that God gave through Moses?

32 Jesus responds at length to this statement, which is intended as an objection. He begins by denying with great emphasis — with the "truly, truly" with which he regularly introduces a pronouncement relating to his mission — that it was Moses who gave Israel ("you") the bread from heaven. Then he says that it is his Father who now gives them "the true bread from heaven." The second part of this argument makes clear the meaning of the first. The issue is not "bread," not even "bread from heaven," but the "true" bread from heaven. Nor is it Jesus' intent to say that the bread Moses gave was illusory, bread only in appearance.[111] For by this bread God upheld his people in the wilderness and brought it to Canaan: a revelation-event! (cf. also the comments on 4:12). Nevertheless it was not the *true* bread,[112] in the sense in which, over against Moses, Jesus Christ is "the truth" (1:18) and in which the "true" worshipers worship the Father in Spirit and "in truth" (4:23). It was not the bread of the fulfillment, of the full revelation of God in his Son. Admittedly, this bread was also "word, deed, power, proceeding from the mouth of God" (Dt. 8:3; Mt. 4:4)[113] and in that sense also bread from heaven, but it was not the Word incarnate in the Son.

---

the Messiah in the eschaton in rabbinic writings. John shows himself exactly as knowledgeable here as when he says of the Jerusalem priests that they regarded their temple as irreplaceable, or of the Samaritan woman that she laid before Jesus the question concerning the right of her place of worship, or when he attributes to the people of Jerusalem the conviction that to think of divine sonship was ungodly arrogance.

For the *positive* connection between manna and the bread given by Jesus, see also W. Weren, "Jezus en de manna," in Beuken et al., *Brood uit de hemel,* pp. 74ff. Weren, however, goes so far that little is left of the contrast emphatically made here by Jesus.

111. Cf. Bultmann, *Comm.,* p. 228: "The emphatic τὸν ἀληθινόν makes it clear that all earthly goods are mere appearances in relation to the revelation." For the opposite and correct view see Weren, "Jezus en de manna."

112. See also Strack/Billerbeck II, p. 482.

113. In Dt. 8:3 and Mt. 4:4 the point at issue is not — as is often thought — an antithesis between material and spiritual bread but between normal bread from the bakery and bread called into being by God's word of power — in Dt. 8:3 the manna, in Mt. 4:4 the bread Jesus could

33   For the true bread is he who comes down from heaven and gives life to the world.[114] At this point the words "from heaven" (describing the bread) flow together with the repeated description of the one sent by the Father as "he who descended from heaven" (the Son of man in 3:13), "he who comes from above" (3:31, etc.). He is the true bread of God because he gives life to the whole world (vs. 51; cf. 3:10). Thus he absolutely distinguishes himself from Moses (cf. the comments on 3:13), and thus the bread from heaven that Moses was able to give was not the true bread from God.

34   Evidently the Jews do not understand Jesus' indirect (third-person) self-identification.[115] But they have heard of bread — descended from heaven — that gives eternal life. And again their reaction recalls that of the Samaritan woman (cf. 4:15) when they ask him to give them this bread always.[116] They say it respectfully ("Lord"), not sarcastically or provocatively. Over and over, in their encounter with Jesus, the people reach a point at which they approach Jesus in terms of their pattern of expectation, groping as it were, for his secret. But what lures them is the gift of present temporal life, the resolution of the bread issue (cf. 4:15b). It is the desire to have such bread at their disposal, not faith in Jesus as the giver of God's imperishable, heavenly gift, that makes them speak thus (cf. vs. 36).

35   The discourse reaches a provisional conclusion in Jesus' answer. He

---

create from the stones. The bread that God calls into being is also material and perishable (cf. Jn. 6:32, 49), as is the bread that Jesus has distributed. It did relieve the physical hunger of the five thousand. But in the subsequent discourse Jesus shows that one who stops there is concerned only about perishable food (however miraculously obtained) but has no part in the food that endures to eternal life. And in that respect the latter food is greater than the manna Moses gave to Israel.

Weren denies all this in his essay "Jezus en de manna." He believes that the manna, no less than the bread Jesus gives, entails eternal life, namely "when, in accordance with its intent, it is linked with the laws God gave to Israel through Moses" (p. 107), and that it only lost this function on account of the obduracy of the fathers and thus became perishable. He acknowledges that this last point cannot be deduced from John 6 and therefore regards it as "an open question" (p. 103). But Jesus locates the antithesis between that which gives life and that which does not give life not in what people do with the bread but in the bread itself. The bread he gives — his flesh — is not bread Moses was able to give!

114. Many interpreters believe that "who (which) comes down from heaven" should not be taken predicatively but understood attributively of the bread ("this is the bread of God that comes down from heaven"). Because both translations are grammatically possible, other interpreters also speak of "intentional ambiguity" as a possibility (cf., e.g., the comments on vs. 34); so, e.g., Brown, Dodd, and Lindars. But the attributive view labors under the disadvantages that vs. 33a would then be a repetition of what was already said in vs. 32 and that the "for" clause would not explain anything.

115. See n. 114.

116. Another proof, in my opinion, that the question-and-answer pattern of vss. 25ff. is not analogous to the questions and answers of the Passover meal; on this issue, see also Brown, *Comm.* I, pp. 266f.

now states unambiguously that he is the life-giving bread[117] and thus brings the dialogue to the point — always decisive in the great contest between faith and unbelief — of not only what he teaches and does but of who he is. To that end he makes one of the many "I am" pronouncements in which his "I" is the real predicate.[118] Over and over the question is what really is the bread for which a person should "labor" — the bread that does not perish — and where it comes from. Now Jesus says that *he* is that bread. The intent is not primarily to describe the salvation granted by Jesus (as, e.g., in 14:6), namely that aside from other things he is and gives also the bread of life, but rather that anyone — as those in vs. 34 apparently were — in search of bread that does not perish should accept *Jesus*. He not only grants that bread but *is* that bread. For that reason it is decisive whether or not (vs. 36) a person "comes to him" (a recurrent expression: cf. vss. 37, 44, and 45) and "believes in him." Then the hunger ends forever. The question of faith is decisive for the bread question and not — as the multitude thought — the reverse (Mt. 6:33).

Thirst is mentioned along with hunger here (cf. 4:14). Some interpreters think that here one should think, on the analogy of the manna, of the water from the rock, as constantly associated themes. But elsewhere, too, the stilling of hunger and the assuaging of thirst as primary needs and therefore as images of salvation and fulfillment, often go together (cf. Pr. 9:5; Is. 55:1ff.). At the same time it is already clear at this point how eating Jesus' flesh as the true food and drinking his blood as the true drink have to be understood from the semantics of the bread discourse.

6:36-47

God's Saving Will Is Realized in People Coming to Jesus

Before Jesus further explicates (in vss. 48ff.) the revelation that he is the bread of life (vs. 35), he first takes a stand against those who, though they have seen him act in the fullness of his messianic power and authority, still do not believe in him. Although the actual subject of this discourse is at no time lost sight of (cf. vs. 41), these verses do nevertheless form a kind of intermezzo or interruption in the flow of the argument.[119] What needs to come first is an extensive

---

117. ὁ ἄρτος τῆς ζωῆς, like the "living bread" (ὁ ἄρτος ὁ ζῶν) in vs. 51 and the "living water" (i.e., life-giving water) in 4:10. For parallels in the history of religions, see the extensive material in Bultmann, *Comm.,* pp. 222ff.; Schnackenburg, *Comm.* II, p. 44 (with special reference to the apocryphal Jewish writing *Joseph and Asenath*).

118. This is clear from the great emphasis resting on the "I," as also from the entire context. See also p. 292, n. 121.

119. See the introductory comments on chs. 5 and 6, above.

further explanation of what is called "coming to God" and faith in him (vs. 35) as the only way in which God's saving will with regard to the bread from heaven as the food that endures is realized.

Verse **36** reflects back on vs. 34, as vs. 37 does on vs. 35. The people are desirous of the bread that imparts (eternal) life, but they do not believe that Jesus is the one who gives, and *is*, this bread. He confronts them with this as something he has already said earlier: "you have seen me, yet do not believe." It is most natural to link this saying (a "self-quotation") with vs. 26, though there the reference is not to "seeing me" but to "seeing the signs" (in close association, however, with "seeking me"). In any case, "seeing me" materially reproduces the content of vs. 26 (cf. also vs. 40).[120] Here again the ambivalence — perhaps one may say the wordplay — in the word "see" asserts itself. They have seen him act in power but not in such a way as to arrive at true insight into and the full consequence of Jesus' mission (as the Son, vs. 40) and at true faith in him.[121]

37 Over against that failure Jesus posits that nevertheless people who "come to him," that is, believe in him (as described in vs. 35), will not be lacking. He bases that belief on "all that the Father gives me," an expression that recurs in the Gospel and describes those who have "received" Jesus (cf. vs. 39; 10:29; 17:2ff.; 18:9) and denotes the close fellowship that exists between the Father and the Son in the fulfillment of God's saving will. The Father does not place all things into the hands of the Son at once (3:35) but accompanies the Son in the execution of his mission from step to step, as it were, ever and again bringing to the Son those who are his.[122] This is even more sharply formulated in vs. 44; there the background against which "all that the Father gives me" is to be understood is further clarified (see below). In the present context, however, the emphasis is on the positive: whatever Jesus' hearers may think of him, there are others who will "come to him," namely those whom God will bring to him as his own. And if

---

120. The text of 6:36 is uncertain. The most important manuscripts have με; other important manuscripts omit με, perhaps with an eye to vs. 26. If one reads "see" without με and hence without an object, there remains a certain incongruency with vs. 26, which mentions "seeing the signs." In light of vs. 40, however, the focus on "seeing" the person of Jesus corresponds to the Evangelist's whole line of thought. Therefore, I opt for the reading most often followed and hear in it an echo of vs. 26.

121. "They misunderstand: the bread from heaven is not a gift that can be abstracted from the one sent by God, a gift that is given from time to time (πάντοτε), but is Jesus as the sent one himself." So Schenke, "Formale und gedankliche Struktur von Joh. 6,26-58," p. 32.

122. Cf. J. P. Miranda, *Der Vater, der mich gesandt hat,* 1972, p. 124:

The relationship of God to Jesus is described as a transfer of power, in connection with which the objects of divine giving are specified in detail: God's name (Jn. 17:11), the δόξα (17:22, 24), the ἐξουσία πάσης σαρκός (17:2), ζωὴν ἔχειν ἐν ἑαυτοῦ (5:26), the works or work (5:36; 17:4), the words (17:8), the κρίσις or ἐξουσία for κρίσις (5:22, 27), believers (6:37, 39; 10:29; 17:2, 6, 9, 12, 24; 18:9), the cup (18:11), and, more simply, everything (3:35; 13:3; 17:7) or all he asks (11:22). But these objects are not external gifts but expressions of the unity and fellowship of the Father with the Son.

they desire the heavenly gift from him (cf. vs. 39), he will by no means reject[123] the ones who thus come to him.

Verses **38-40** confirm this with a continual appeal to the "will" of him who sent Jesus. Again he describes himself as the one who descended from heaven, but now in the first person so that there can no longer be any uncertainty about what he meant when he used the third person. He now denies that, by thus speaking of himself, he is seeking the execution of his own will, that is, the exercise of his own authority (cf. 5:30b). He does not place himself in God's way, or put himself in the place of God, as a hindrance for people seeking the true bread from heaven, which is eternal life. For he came down from heaven for no other reason than to carry out the will of the Father. And this will, which is twice emphatically referred to as such in vss. 39 and 40 ("and this," "for this") and is explicated in two parallel sentences, consists precisely in the fact that "he will lose nothing" of "that which the Father gives him" (cf. vs. 37) "but raise it up at the last day." These last words return like a refrain in the following verses (vss. 39, 40, 44, and 54), not as a later addition (to offset a one-sided "realized eschatology") but to bring to full expression the heavenly, transcendent character (expressed in the title "Son of man," vss. 27, 53; cf. 3:13; 5:27ff.) of Jesus' mission. That mission is not limited to a gift that, like the manna, was only of temporal significance (cf. vs. 49). What he gives has validity that "endures unto eternal life" (vs. 27). For (vs. 40) it is the will of God in the sending of his Son that everyone who sees the Son and believes in him should have eternal life and be raised on the last day — that and nothing else. Here again "seeing" occurs in its pregnant meaning, as in vs. 26, namely as the seeing of the Son in whom the Father fulfills his saving will in its all-embracing eschatological gift for humankind and world.

41, 42 It is precisely at this point that Jesus' hearers react anew. They are now described as "the Jews," the name that John often uses for Jewish leaders and spokesmen hostile to Jesus. The idea that a historical situation other than what the passage explicitly refers to should be inferred from this title is an unnecessary hypothesis. The speakers here are obviously Galileans (vs. 42).[124] When Jesus now describes himself without restraint as the one who came down from heaven, they rebel, "murmur" (cf. vs. 61), probably an allusion to what their ancestors had done in the wilderness in their unbelief toward Moses (cf. Ex. 16:2, 7ff.).[125] And they do so (vs. 42) by telling each

123. Literally "cast out," in the sense of "not recognize as his own," "eject from his fellowship."

124. The use of the name here is proof that Ἰουδαῖοι does not refer in the Fourth Gospel just to "Judeans," as M. Lowe argues in "Who Were the Ἰουδαῖοι?" *NovT* 18 (1976), pp. 101ff. On this matter see at length J. Ashton, "The Identity and Function of the ΙΟΥΔΑΙΟΙ in the Fourth Gospel," *NovT* 27 (1985), pp. 40ff.

125. Cf. also Weren, "Jezus en de manna," p. 90.

other that as Galileans they certainly knew who he was and where he came from. For was this Jesus — the man who was so emphatically talking about himself — not the son of Joseph? We find the same sort of comment in 1:45, 46 and in Mt. 13:55. The Fourth Evangelist goes his own way, but over and over we discover that he is speaking about the same Jesus and the same history as his fellow Evangelists. Still the reference to Jesus' earthly origin does not always have the same intent. In Matthew the people are astonished and wonder how someone whose background they thought they knew could exhibit so much wisdom and power. Here the situation is reversed: how could someone whom they knew as the son of Joseph say, "I have come down from heaven"? As long as people kept their attention on Jesus' earthly origins, insight into the true secret of Jesus' coming into the world — that is, faith in the descent of the Son of God, the incarnation of the Word — always suffered shipwreck, and offense at this always triumphed over astonishment (cf. Mt. 13:57). That is the message of the Gospel of John, and Jesus' answer in vss. 43ff. also concerns this issue.

43-45   Although "the Jews" do not address Jesus directly but express their displeasure and unbelief with regard to his claims to heavenly descent "among themselves" (vs. 43), he is by no means unaware of their reaction. His answer is first of all sharply negative: "Stop murmuring among yourselves!" Nor does he respond to the objection expressed in the words "Is not this . . . ?" What they regard as possible or impossible by their human standards (cf. 5:43ff.) will never bring them to faith in his name or make them participants in his imperishable gift. This demonstrates the powerlessness of the natural person ("no one") to come to the salvation disclosed in Christ unless the Father who sent him "draws" that person, that is, moves him or her toward it (for this "drawing" see also 12:32 and Jr. 31:3;[126] Ho. 11:14). It may seem that by this statement Jesus wants to bring out the fruitlessness of any dialogue with Jews. Some speak of a concept of predestination in John: that the Jews do not want to come to Jesus shows that they have not been drawn by God and therefore that for them salvation is not a possibility.

But as vs. 45 shows, the intent is clearly otherwise. Jesus bases the negative pronouncement of vs. 44a on a divine promise of *salvation*, "as it is written in the prophets,"[127] namely, "They shall all be taught by God." Although not cited verbatim, the reference is apparently to the statement in Is. 54:13, where to a confused and needy Israel the promise is given that God himself will impart to them the true knowledge of salvation that they so direly

126. εἵλκυσά σε εἰς οἰκτίρημα, Jr. 38(31):3 LXX; see also Schlatter, *Comm.,* on Jn. 6:44.
127. ἐν τοῖς προφήταις. Although the words refer to only one specific text (Is. 54:13), the reference to "the prophets" indicates that the content of the pronouncement is true of the prophets in general: "So prophecy speaks of the great future" (cf. Ac. 8:42).

lack: "All your children will be taught by the LORD," a promise also extended elsewhere with regard to a future salvation (cf. Jr. 31:33, 34) as the gift of the new covenant between God and his people by which they all come to know the Lord, "from the least of them to the greatest" (cf. 1 Th. 4:9; 1 Jn. 2:20, 27ff.). By appealing to this promise of salvation vis-à-vis Jews, Jesus therefore does not a priori exclude Jews: in the "all" of prophecy the universal character of God's redemptive will is implied.

But Jesus does confront these Jews with the reverse side of this promise, namely that no one will share in this salvation on the basis of his or her own insight and knowledge (cf. "we know," vs. 42 and 3:2). What prevents "the Jews" from coming to Jesus and believing in him, therefore, is not that salvation is not intended for them but that they do not want to receive it in the manner in which God would give it to them, namely by their coming to Jesus. For "everyone who has heard and learned from the Father comes to me." Hence the remarkable fact is that Jesus would have the Jews understand their unbelief and powerlessness ("no one can . . .") in light of a divine prophecy of *salvation.* The very thing that they reject in him as self-willed conceit is what God wants to give them in him. "Unless the Father draws him" (vs. 44) therefore applies to them, not only negatively but also positively.

Of course, this does not make rationally transparent the relationship between coming to Jesus as a consequence of the divine drawing and as a voluntary and responsible act. On the basis of "everyone," Bultmann concludes that "any man is free to be among those drawn by the Father."[128] "Draw" is said to mean only "let oneself be drawn." But this exegesis has correctly been rejected by others as not in keeping with "hearing" and "learning"[129] totally determined by the divine will to save. "No one can come to me" is intended to take away the illusion that "coming to Jesus" is a matter about which one can freely decide on the basis of one's own "knowledge" and possibilities. This observation keeps coming back in the Gospel (cf. 1:12, 13; 3:3ff.; 5:44); one might call it one of its fundamental thoughts. On the other hand, however, it is no less typical for the Fourth Gospel that *in* (not despite) its radical reference to God it calls a person to do what he or she cannot do of himself or herself, just as the lame man is told to arise and the dead to become alive again.[130] Even the present pericope ends with an implied

---

128. *Comm.*, p. 231.

129. ὁ ἀκούσας παρὰ τοῦ πατρός, etc. — not "listen to the Father" (as Bultmann explains it) but "hear and learn from the Father" (as Bergmeier correctly has it: *Glaube als Gabe nach Johannes*, p. 216). Bultmann does acknowledge that "ἀκούσας is qualified by μαθών as the true hearer as opposed to the mere casual listener" (cf. 5:25). But is "true hearing" something that "any person" can do?

130. Bultmann, too, acknowledges this: "So if faith is such a surrender of one's own self-assertion, then the believer can understand his faith not as the accomplishment of his own

appeal to believe (vs. 47). No attempt is made to explain faith's involvement in the vivifying power of God.[131] The Bible speaks in two ways about a reality that as a miracle from God is not transparent to the intellect but to which the gospel seeks to open the eyes and hearts of people.

46, 47 The end of the pericope stipulates anew that God's turning to people and "being taught" of all are realized exclusively in him who is sent from God: "Not that anyone has seen the Father except him who is from God;[132] he has seen the Father." The content of the first clause is true also of those who have "heard and learned from the Father." That which God has caused them to hear and understand is not realized in the immediacy of "seeing" God, but only through the mediation of him who is from God and who descended from heaven. For "seeing" the Father, as the ultimate source of the knowledge and certainty of God's saving will for all, is the experience only of him who has come from God (cf. 1:18; 3:11, 32; 5:37; 7:29). Admittedly, it seems that preceding "coming to me" (vs. 45c) there is a "hearing and a learning" from the Father (cf. vs. 44). But we are dealing here not with a number of steps or phases set out in salvation-order but with an attempt to analyze conceptually the indivisible unity of the work of the Father and the Son. No one comes to the Son unless drawn by the Father. But, along with that, no one hears the vivifying voice of God except in the Son, and those who hear *his* voice will live and be raised on the last day (cf. 5:25).

Accordingly, everything issues in that believing "hearing" in the great emphatic conclusion for all — at the same time the transition to what follows: "Truly, truly, I say to you that he who believes has eternal life." "Believing" is now referred to absolutely, without an indicated object. Many manuscripts add the words "in me"; some "in God." But one cannot make such distinctions here. Indicated in the absolute "believe" is rather that God does not want to be believed in in any other way than in him whom he has sent (cf. 1:18; 14:1). With that the end of the pericope returns to the beginning (vss. 36ff.) and the way has been cleared, in direct connection with vss. 26-35, for the unfolding of the vivifying power of the bread that has come down from heaven.

---

purposeful act, but only as God's working upon him." So *Theology of the New Testament* II (1953), p. 23; see also p. 77:

> Admittedly, [the decision of faith] is wrought by God, but not as if the working of God took place before faith or, so to speak, behind it; rather, God's working takes place exactly in it. For when the Revelation encounters faith, the reply which faith makes to the Revelation's question feels itself to have been wrought by the question itself. In making its decision, faith understands itself as a gift. The disciples did not choose Jesus; he chose them (15:16).

131. See also de Jonge, *Jesus: Stranger from Heaven and Son of God*, pp. 17ff.; 151ff.
132. ὁ ὢν παρὰ τοῦ θεοῦ.

6:48-59

"The Bread That I Will Give Is My Flesh"

48-51b   As already stated, vss. 48ff. refer back to what was initially said with regard to the Scripture citation in vs. 31 and pursue that line of thought. Again Jesus posits what can be regarded as the main theme of the entire discourse (or dialogue), namely that *he* is the life-giving bread, and now in contrast with what the Jews considered that bread to be: the manna given by Moses. To this Jesus adds as a new argument that the fathers, to whom the Jews have appealed ("your fathers," alluding to "our fathers" in vs. 31), though they ate the manna given them through Moses, died. In contrast Jesus states (vs. 50) that the true bread (cf. vs. 32) from heaven can only be that which, if a person eats it, he or she will *not* die. And in vs. 51a he repeats that statement, this time directly applying it to himself: "I am the living bread that came down from heaven; if anyone eats of this bread, he will live forever." However wonderful the descent of manna from heaven was, however much it was a fruit of God's creative word (cf. Dt. 8:3; Mt. 4:4), as "food that perishes" (vs. 27) it had only temporary life-giving power. By contrast, the bread that Jesus is and gives to eat has an effect not bounded by death but continuing into eternal life.

It is important to note that the figurative language about Jesus as the bread of life has become somewhat more specific in these verses. Now "eating" is included. That which has been expressed without imagery in the words "believe" and "come to me" (vss. 35, 47) is now, in connection with Jesus' self-identification as "the bread," metaphorically called "eating this bread" or (vs. 57) even more directly "eating me." Hence it is clear that "eating" is a metaphor that flows directly from the semantics of the preceding and does not suddenly emerge from another (sacramental) semantic context.[133]

51c   The general pronouncement about the life-giving power of the bread that Jesus *is* and *gives* now takes a most remarkable turn, and at the same time the secret of the preceding words is laid bare. In a single stroke Jesus adds to the clause about "eating the bread" the following: "and the bread that I shall give is my flesh — for the life of the world."[134]

---

133. If anywhere, the basic principle of structural-analytic exegesis applies here, namely that of the synchronic approach: We should explain the text from within its own semantic frame of reference (here that of the bread discourse) and not derive its meaning (diachronically) from an externally adduced semantic context (sacramental language). Cf., e.g., W. S. Vorster, "De structuuranalyse," in *Inleiding tot de studie van het Nieuwe Testament,* ed. A. F. J. Klijn, 1982, pp. 127ff.

134. The last five words come somewhat lamely at the end. There are textual variants that obviously correct this by putting the words earlier, where one should expect them (after "give"; cf. RSV), or by inserting a second relative clause ("that I will give") after "flesh." But as the text now reads, all the emphasis lies on "is my flesh." That is the intent. What follows is a further

At this point opinions about the meaning of the rest of this pericope strongly diverge, especially over whether and to what degree vss. 51c-58 or even the entire bread discourse (with or apart from the preceding bread miracle) are to be understood sacramentally (see comments on vs. 15 above). One can list the different views as follows:[135]

a) The most extreme view is that of those who not only understand "my flesh" in vs. 41c and "eat my flesh" in vss. 53ff. as sacramental, but also, partly on that basis, consider the entire bread discourse and the preceding feeding miracle "eucharistic." So many Catholic exegetes (early and recent) and many others — Cullmann, for example.[136] The bread about which Jesus is speaking throughout the discourse is that which he distributes to believers at the Lord's Supper. Because of this total orientation of the content to the eucharist, the unity of the discourse is not a problem to these authors.

b) Others argue with no less emphasis that there is no discernible trace of sacramentalism either in vss. 27-50 or in the account of the bread miracle, but that in vs. 51c (others say in vs. 53) a shift occurs from the symbolic and metaphorical reference to Jesus as bread to a very different sacramental use of words, in which "eating" and "drinking" are to be understood realistically. For some interpreters this shift constitutes the (decisive) argument that vss. 51c-58 (or 53-58) are later than what precedes, either inserted by a redactor who sought in this way to compensate for the lack of the Lord's Supper in the Fourth Gospel in order to make the Gospel more acceptable to the church community[137] or, less radically, a development within the process of tradition in which eucharistic undertones present in the first part of the chapter became more pronounced.[138] Interpreters sometimes also base the alleged nonoriginality of vss. 51c-58 on the reactions that follow the discourse in vss. 60ff. They regard vss. 63ff. as especially hard to reconcile with vss. 51ff., whereas vss. 60ff. harmonize well with vss. 27-50. This sequence is said to have been disturbed by the insertion of vss. 51c-58.

c) Many contemporary interpreters distance themselves clearly from this basic sacramental ("eucharistic") exposition of vss. 51c-58 and a fortiori of the entire chapter. Admittedly, many also remain convinced that in vss. 53ff. — specifically on the basis of the expressions "eat my flesh" and "drink my blood" — we are dealing with sacramental *language*. This is not to say, however, that vss. 51c (53)-58 refer *materially* to eating and drinking in the Lord's Supper, thus imparting a "eucharistic" meaning to the conclusion. The *Evangelist* (not, of course, Jesus) is said to have derived the imagery or the terminology from the eucharistic meal in order to bring out forcefully Jesus' significance as the bread of life — a significance variously described: as the

---

qualification alluding to vs. 33. One might place a semicolon after flesh and then continue the sentence with "and that for the life of the world."

135. For more extensive overviews see, e.g., Moloney, *Johannine Son of Man,* pp. 93ff., 98ff.; Brown, *Comm.* I, p. 272. For a clear and succinct overview, see Schnackenburg, *Comm.* II, pp. 56ff.; also his lengthier discussion "Changing Interpretations of the Bread Discourse," *Comm.* II, pp. 65-69.

136. O. Cullmann, *Early Christian Worship,* 1953; and especially idem, *Les Sacraments dans l'Évangile johannique,* 1951. See also Bauer, *Comm.;* Lightfoot, *Comm.*

137. So Bultmann, *Comm.,* pp. 234ff.

138. Cf. Brown, *Comm.* I, p. 286.

offense of Jesus' death on the cross,[139] as the unity between Jesus and believers,[140] as the reality of the incarnation;[141] in other words, in all this we are dealing not with the mystery of the sacrament but with the mystery of christology. Others, especially Roman Catholic interpreters, though maintaining the basically eucharistic interpretation of vss. 51-58, point out that in these verses the reference is more generally to fellowship in Christ's flesh and blood than to fellowship only in the eucharist; as a result both the sacramental and hence proper "eating and drinking" at the Lord's Supper and the symbolic eating of Christ's self-surrender in death prove to be more "tightly connected . . . than first appears."[142] At any rate, in such ways attempts are made to maintain the unmistakable unity of the entire discourse in John 6. On the other hand, in this movement between the sacramental-realistic and the symbolic-metaphorical interpretation of Jesus' words[143] there is such ambivalence that one cannot avoid asking whether the ambivalence is not rather to be attributed to the interpreter than to the text.

d) Calvin, with an appeal to Augustine, articulated clearly and consistently a rejection of this sacramental interpretation of vss. 51c-58: the discourse speaks not of the Lord's Supper but of uninterrupted fellowship with Christ, even apart from observance of the Supper.[144] He regarded the first alternative, identification of the whole discourse and miracle story as sacramental, as in conflict not only with the historical situation in which the words were spoken but also with the significance of the Lord's Supper itself, since, according to vs. 54, this sacramental eating and drinking would guarantee eternal life and resurrection from the dead. He therefore considered it certain that Jesus is speaking here of "the perpetual eating of faith" *(Ideo de perpetua fidei manducatione eum tractare certum est),* which is not restricted to the Lord's Supper. On the other hand, he acknowledged that

> there is nothing said here that is not figured and actually presented to believers in the Lord's Supper. Indeed, we might say that Christ intended the holy Supper to be a seal of this discourse. This is also the reason why John makes no mention of the Lord's Supper. And therefore Augustine follows the proper order when, in expounding this chapter, he does not touch on the Lord's Supper until he comes to the end. And then he shows that this mystery is represented in a symbol whenever the Churches celebrate the sacred Supper. . . .[145]

More recent exegetes have given important arguments in support of Calvin's view.[146] Most recent interpreters, however, still cling to the so-called sacramental

---

139. So, e.g., Strathmann, *Comm.,* p. 126.

140. So de Jonge, *Jesus: Stranger from Heaven and Son of God,* p. 208.

141. So Borgen, *Bread from Heaven,* p. 166.

142. So Schnackenburg, *Comm.* II, p. 61.

143. See, e.g., Moloney, *Johannine Son of Man,* pp. 103ff., who speaks of "two levels" (p. 106).

144. "Neque enim de Coena habetur concio, sed de perpetua communicatione, quae extra Coenae usum nobis constat." Cf. Calvin, *Comm.* I, p. 169.

145. *Comm.* I, p. 170.

146. See, e.g., Grosheide, *Comm.* I, pp. 464f.; Godet, *Comm.* Materially these authors agree with Augustine's view (already commended by Calvin) that John 6 can only be applied to the

terminology (see under c), though it seems that the tendency to distance oneself even from this approach is growing.[147]

However one construes the sequel, there is in any case no reason to interpret vs. 51c in a sacramental sense.[148] What is remarkable about the shift in vs. 51c is that now Jesus suddenly speaks of his *flesh* as the bread that he will give for the life of the world. But this only means, in keeping with the line of thought followed in the discourse thus far (and in the entire Gospel), that the vivifying power of the bread (that he both *is* and *gives*) consists in that he gives *himself* for the world, by his self-surrender in death.[149] The idea that this self-surrender should occur especially in the sacrament is, in general, totally foreign to the Fourth Gospel (cf. 10:11, 15; 11:51-52; 15:13; 18:14, where each time the reference is to Jesus' *death*); nor is it in any way expressed or suggested in vs. 51c. The words "bread," "give," and "for the life of the world" all echo what has been said earlier (cf. vss. 27, 32, 33) and have nothing to do there with the Eucharist. And as far as the core word "flesh" is concerned, in the argument that has been followed until now there is no reason to understand it any differently from the way it is used elsewhere in the Gospel, namely, as a reference to the human as such (sometimes in combination with "blood" [cf. 1:13; 3:6]) — above all, as the most characteristic christological qualification of the earthly-human existence of the one who descended from heaven.[150] Accordingly, what comes to expression in the shift in vs. 51c is nothing other and nothing less than that he who is true bread given by God not only descended from heaven and became flesh but also surrendered himself to death in that flesh, that is, in the totality of his earthly-human existence, in order thus to give his life to the world. In vs. 53 this flesh is referred to as "the flesh (and blood) of the Son of man" (cf. vs. 27!), which makes it all the more clear that in this expression we are not dealing with a "shift to the sacramental" but with a new

---

Lord's Supper indirectly. Godet (II, 536): "It must not be said, then, that the discourse alludes to the Holy Supper; but it does have to be said that both the Holy Supper *and* the discourse refer to one and the same divine reality, expressed here by a metaphor and there by an emblem."

147. See, e.g., H. Schürmann, "John VI 51c — ein Schlüssel zur großen johanneïschen Brotrede," *BZ* 11 (1958); J. D. G. Dunn, "John VI — A Eucharistic Discourse?" *NTS* 17 (1971), pp. 328ff.; W. Weren, "Structuur en samenhang in Johannes 6," in Beuken et al., *Brood uit de hemel*, pp. 44ff.

148. As Schnackenburg believes. He speaks of a "discernible change in the wording" related to "the reception of the Eucharist" (*Comm.* II, pp. 54ff.).

149. Cf. Bultmann: "If this flesh is described as the flesh which was given for the life of the world, clearly this has Jesus' submission unto death in mind, which in the early Christian view was a death ὑπέρ . . ." (*Comm.*, pp. 234f.).

150. For this "incarnational" sense of σάρξ in vss. 51ff. see also E. Schweizer, *TDNT* VII, p. 140 (though he also follows the sacramental interpretation!). See also Weren, "Structuur en samenhang in Johannes 6," p. 47; Dunn, "John VI — A Eucharistic Discourse?" p. 331.

explication of the pregnant pronouncement in 3:13: only by "descending" will the Son of man "be exalted." What is described there (3:14), on the analogy of Nu. 21:8ff., as the necessity that "the Son of man be lifted up, as Moses lifted up the serpent in the wilderness," namely on the cross, is here referred to in the language of the bread discourse as the gift of Jesus' flesh: the true bread descended from heaven for the life of the world. In the increasing clarity with which — in this last great dialogue in Galilee — Jesus announces his death, we have before us the Johannine version of the same paradoxical shift in Jesus' self-revelation as occurs in the Synoptics, where Jesus announces to his disciples that the Son of man "must suffer many things" (Mk. 8:31; 9:31 par.).

52   To the Jews Jesus' statement was not only totally obscure but also highly offensive. Again, as in vss. 41ff., they avoid a direct confrontation with Jesus himself. It seemed to them increasingly clear that common ground for conversation with him was lacking. That they "disputed among themselves" (cf. vs. 43) does not mean that some were for and others against Jesus but that in vehement mutual discussion they gave vent to their astonishment and displeasure. Earlier already they had expressed these feelings when he called himself the bread descended from heaven (vs. 41), adding that only those who ate of that bread would never die but have life (vss. 50, 51a); now they had to hear that this bread consisted in his flesh. As so often in the Fourth Gospel (cf. 3:3; 4:11; 6:7), so here, the natural person's utter incomprehension is expressed in questions that disregard the deeper meaning of Jesus' words but cling to the sound, here in a question calculated to bring out as clearly as possible the absurdity of Jesus' pronouncements: "How can this man give us his flesh to eat?" After all, they were not cannibals!

53   Jesus' reply makes no concession to their misunderstanding. Rather, he takes over their own words in all their offensiveness, making them his own with all the authority at his disposal and posing what they repudiate among themselves as utterly offensive and foolish as the absolute and exclusive condition ("Truly, truly, I say to you, that unless . . .") for receiving eternal life. Here that life is called "to have life in you," a phrase that is not of course meant in the sense of 5:26 but of 6:57 (cf. 4:14; 7:37). Nor does he tone down their words as though they were too strong. He does introduce some new nuances by speaking not only of "eating the flesh" but also of "drinking the blood" — as though to accentuate the "hardness" (vs. 60) of the whole even more — and by referring not to "my" flesh but to the flesh and blood "of the Son of man." Thus, in continuing agreement with what he has already said about the Son of man (cf. vs. 27 and the comments on vs. 51c), he again and now even more dramatically brings out the paradoxical unity of the highest authority with the deepest self-surrender. Here, too, it is evident that the sacramental interpretation of this pericope bypasses the actual point at issue,

namely, that which is unintelligible and offensive for those who judge "according to the flesh" (the "skandalon," vs. 61) of Jesus' pronouncements. This *skandalon,* after all, is not that Jesus gives his flesh to eat and blood to drink in a *figurative* sense, as in the Lord's Supper. If that were the case, the whole misunderstanding would only arise from the fact that the Jews did not (yet!) understand sacramental language[151] and the entire issue could have been cleared up with a word! What Jesus maintains here with the greatest possible force, both vis-à-vis "the Jews" and somewhat later vis-à-vis the disciples who can no longer follow him in this respect (vss. 60ff.), is nothing less than the surrender to death of the flesh and blood of the Son of man and the (believing) "eating" and "drinking" of it as the bread that came down from heaven by which alone a human being can live (vs. 50).

It is precisely to these pronouncements, however, that the advocates of the eucharistic interpretation always appeal. The argument goes like this: whereas one could still understand "my flesh" in vs. 51c to refer to Jesus' self-offering in death, the addition "his (my) blood" in vss. 53 and 54 makes it undeniably clear that the reference is to the Lord's Supper.[152] Moreover, in this context the words "eat flesh" and "drink blood" are totally unintelligible — except in a sacramental sense. When these expressions occur elsewhere, they either describe bitter hostility (cf. Ps. 27:2; Zc. 11:9) or "some horrendous thing forbidden in God's law" (cf. Gn. 9:4; Lv. 17:10; Dt. 12:23; Ac. 15:20, etc.). "Thus, if Jesus' words in VI 53 are to have a favorable meaning, they must refer to the Eucharist."[153]

However, this argument cannot be maintained on either terminological or material grounds. As for terminology, however much at first sight these words remind one of the words of the institution of the Lord's Supper, on closer scrutiny they deviate from them in a way that is very characteristic for John: "Flesh" does not occur anywhere in the New Testament terminology of the eucharist and, as stated earlier in connection with vs. 51c, must rather be understood in terms of the incarnation. Accordingly, the addition in vs. 53 of "blood" must not be understood, as it would be with "body," as sacrifice language ("my blood of the covenant, poured out for many," Mt. 26:28 par.); with "flesh," as here, it constitutes the usual designation of that which is human per se (cf. Mt. 16:17; 1 Co. 15:50; Jn. 1:13) and thus reinforces the incarnation motif here.

---

151. Bultmann, who regards vss. 51c-58 as a later sacramentalist addition, believes that in fact this is the intent of the later redactor who was responsible for this addition. Hence he speaks of the "externalizing" of the concept of *skandalon.* "The idea of the sacrament is not as such a *skandalon* and cannot be so. By this the real *skandalon* was made into a 'literary motif.' " "The hearers cannot understand that Jesus is speaking of the Lord's Supper" (*Comm.,* p. 237). This criticism would be entirely on target *if* the reference here was to a sacramental eating and drinking!

152. This is the view not only of traditional Roman Catholic exegetes but also of Bultmann: "Jesus' reply (v. 53) . . . unmistakably refers to the Lord's Supper, since now the drinking of the blood is added to the eating of the flesh" (*Comm.,* p. 235).

153. So Brown, *Comm.* I, p. 284.

Therefore it cannot be accidental[154] that mention is made here of "the flesh and blood" of "the Son of man," a combination that occurs nowhere in the communion texts[155] and is not intrinsically connected with them, whereas here it clearly links up both with what has already been said about the Son of man's authority over the food that endures (vs. 27) and with the full meaning of his "descent from heaven" (see the comments on vs. 51c). Furthermore, the argument that the "hard" expressions ("eat his flesh" and "drink his blood") can only have a favorable meaning if this eating and drinking is understood sacramentally completely disregards the *skandalon* expressed in the passage (see the comments on vss. 52, 53).[156]

If from this it may be evident that even on terminological grounds vss. 51cff. must be understood completely within the context of the preceding bread discourse and that there is no transition to a sacramental semantics, much more serious are the material objections, advanced from of old — see Calvin, above! — and increasingly in more recent schoalarship, against the sacramental interpretation of vss. 51c-58 (and, in consequence, of the whole of ch. 6). At issue specifically is the absolute salvific significance accorded in these verses to "eating the flesh" and "drinking the blood" of the Son of man. This absolute and exclusive meaning cannot have been intended for the — still to be instituted — sacrament and participation in it, but only for Jesus' self-offering in death as the food and drink of eternal life given by Jesus for the life of the world and taken with the mouth of faith. At no point in this Gospel or any part of the New Testament is such an absolute value accorded to the sacrament — however important it is — as though in it the great redemptive event of Jesus' self-sacrifice was realized; and nowhere is there such an unbreakable and exclusive link between the eating and drinking of the eucharist and participation in eternal life, as there would have to be in vs. 54 in the sacramental interpretation, as though only those who received the eucharist had the guarantee of eternal life. It is therefore correct to say, with Schlatter, for example, that John does not describe Jesus as the founder of a sacrament but as the one who feeds his church with life by means of his body offered up in death.[157] Or in the words of Strathmann: "He [the Evangelist] linked the acquisition of life, which occupies him throughout his entire Gospel, not to a — here, once, ambiguously treated — ritual act but to the act of coming to Jesus, the crucified Son of God, and believing in him."[158]

Authors such as Schnackenburg and Bultmann who proceed from the sacramental view have encountered the difficulty that such exclusive significance is apparently

---

154. As is apparently assumed by most adherents of the sacramental view; cf. Bultmann, who says the identity of Jesus with the Son of man "was obviously assumed without further thought" (*Comm.*, p. 125).

155. Some scholars assume that the title "Son of man" comes from the eucharistic liturgy of the Johannine community (e.g., Bultmann, *Comm.*, p. 235), but evidence is lacking, as Schnackenburg acknowledges (*Comm.* II, p. 454, n. 174).

156. This is undoubtedly the reason why this "hard" expression ("eat the flesh and drink the blood of the Son of man") occurs nowhere as a sacramental expression. Schnackenburg asks, from within his eucharistic interpretation (*Comm.* II, p. 61), "Why the sharp wording. . . ?" He then looks for an explanation in John's attack on a Gnostic-docetic group that rejected the eucharist. I find this interpretation forced.

157. *Comm.*, p. 182.

158. *Comm.*, p. 126.

attributed here to the eucharist. Schnackenburg sees a possible explanation in the idea that the Evangelist was opposing a Gnostic-docetic group that rejected the reception of the eucharist. Accordingly, the audience of the bread-discourse is said to shift here from "unbelieving Judaism" to a much later sect in the church.[159] Even apart from the forced character of such a "digression" in the discourse, there is the remaining objection that the Fourth Gospel, which otherwise does not mention the institution of the Lord's Supper, should suddenly proclaim here with the greatest possible emphasis that participation in it is the indispensable condition for, and infallible guarantee of, eternal life.

Bultmann, therefore, wants to see in the connection made here between the Supper and eternal life a later view of the Lord's Supper as "the medicine of immortality" *(pharmakon athanasias)*. According to this view, "those who participate in the sacramental meal bear within them the power that guarantees their resurrection."[160] For Bultmann this is just one more argument for the utter strangeness of this pericope in the Gospel. He therefore attributes the pericope to a later ecclesiastical editor.

Still somewhat different is the explanation that Brown offers for the absolutizing of the sacramental eating and drinking. In his opinion, we are dealing here with a typically Johannine "contribution to eucharistic theology." Whereas the Synoptics and Paul still link the words of institution tightly to the remembrance of Jesus' death, John is said to have detached the eucharist from the context of the Last Supper and its interpretation as food and drink that imparts eternal life. John "has launched Christianity on the road to a distinctive sacramental theology whereby visible elements are signs communicating divine realities."[161] Here too — in order to interpret the absoluteness of the statements in vss. 53 and 54 "eucharistically" — a search is made for a link with later ecclesiastical developments or deviations in the doctrine of the sacraments.

But these forced solutions are the — perhaps inevitable — result of the sacramental interpretation of this pericope. They become irrelevant the moment one sees that "eating Jesus' flesh" and "drinking his blood" are the specific description not of the physical eating and drinking that take place at the Lord's Supper but of the believing appropriation — by the mouth of faith — of Jesus' self-offering in death.[162]

54, 55 Vs. 54 repeats the content of vs. 53 in almost the same words,[163] but now in a positive sense and in the first person as relating to Jesus himself. It

159. *Comm.* II, p. 61.

160. *Comm.*, pp. 235f.

161. R. E. Brown, *The Community of the Beloved Disciple,* 1979, pp. 78f.

162. What Calvin in his comments on 6:53 calls the "perpetua fidei manducatio," which "extra Coenae usum nobis constat." Cf. *Comm.* I, p. 169.

163. One is struck by the use of τρώγειν for eating; the same word occurs in vss. 54, 56f. in alternation with the more general φαγεῖν, which occurs five times in vss. 49-53 (in John only there and in 13:18). τρώγειν is a very "realistic" word for eating and is therefore used in the more vulgar sense of "biting," "chewing," and the like. Some interpreters believe that it is precisely for this reason that it is used for the physical eating of the eucharist (so, e.g., L. Goppelt, *TDNT* VIII, p. 237; cf. also C. Spicq, *NTS* 26 [1980], p. 416: the word is used "to insist on the realism of the eating"; it has a nuance of "savoring, appreciating" food, a nuance that "St. John has

is the descent of the Son of man, his "exaltation" on the cross, the "must" of
3:14, that determine the course of Jesus' life and bring it about that those who
thus eat him in his self-offering in death as the bread that came down from
heaven already now receive the life-giving power of that food and drink ("have
eternal life") and will be raised up by him on the last day (cf. vss. 39, 41, 44).
For the authority to do this is given to him as the Son of man (vs. 27; cf. 5:27).
Vs. 55 then again stresses that there is life for the world only in the way of
Jesus' self-offering to death: "For my flesh is food indeed," namely "the food
that endures to eternal life" (vs. 27), and "my blood is drink indeed," namely
a drink that takes away one's thirst, not temporarily but forever (vs. 35; cf.
4:14).

56 In this eating and drinking of his flesh and blood lies the secret of
the enduring fellowship between Jesus and his own, which is here described
as a mutual "remaining in" one another, an expression that recurs in the Gospel
in a variety of ways.[164] For this "eating" and "drinking" are not a one-time
event but a repeated activity of faith.[165] It remains an eating of his flesh and
drinking of his blood, for the spring of all life continues to be his self-offering
in death. But it works itself out as a lasting fellowship between him and those
who believe in him — on their part as a continual centering on him who gave
himself for them, on his part as his indwelling in them with all his gifts and
power (cf., e.g., 7:37, 38).

57 Accordingly, this eating can also reflect Jesus' relationship with God
and can be traced back to the way he himself lives "because of the Father" (διὰ
τὸν πατέρα). "The living Father," from whom all life springs, has sent him, and
Jesus lives "because of him," namely in virtue of that mission and the living
fellowship with the Father (of whom he says elsewhere that it is his "food to do
the will of him who sent me," 4:34). So it is also with the relationship between
Jesus and his own: "so he who eats me will live because of me." The focus is the
continual exercise of fellowship. Believers live "because of him"; "having
eternal life in oneself" is not automatic. It is remaining in him, the living Lord,
that here, in close association with vs. 50, is called "eating me." It is not only
directed to the one-time act of his self-offering into death ("eat my flesh," etc.)
but to himself, the one who once performed this act ("eating me").

---

retained for the Eucharist"). But the idea that such a more or less colloquial word should function
in John 6 specifically as *liturgical* language seems most implausible ("Never, until St. John, was
τρώγειν utilized in a religious text" — so even Spicq). This realism seems rather to belong to the
"hard" language of "eating and drinking Jesus' body and blood." But it remains an open question
whether one has to ascribe a deeper significance to the use of τρώγειν in place of φαγεῖν.

164. Cf., e.g., 5:38 (of the Word of God); 6:27 (of the food that abides); 15:4, 7 (of
remaining in Jesus); 8:31 (of remaining in his word); 15:9, 10 (in his love); 15:4, 5 (of Jesus in
his own); 14:10 (of the Father in the Son); 14:17 (of the Spirit's indwelling of the disciples).

165. As is also evident from present tense ὁ τρώγων . . . καὶ πίνων in vss. 54, 55, 57, 58.

58 Here at the end everything returns to the beginning in the form of a recapitulation *(inclusio)* in which the heaven-descended bread, its life-giving power, and its total superiority over what the fathers ate in the wilderness are pointed out one more time. But this time the key word is added: "He who *eats this bread* will live forever," with all the connotative power that "this bread" acquired in the course of the dialogue and with all the emphasis on "eating," not as a legal condition but in accord with what "eating and drinking" means for "life": only the one who eats and drinks will live.

59 As elsewhere (cf. 8:20), Jesus' teaching is followed by a reference to its setting, here the synagogue at Capernaum. Jesus' discourse is called "teaching," which in the Fourth Gospel is a rarely occurring qualification of what Jesus did (see further the comments on 7:14). There is no clearly marked transition between Jesus' first encounter with the people on the day after the bread miracle and this meeting in the synagogue. This proves that the Evangelist's aim was not to furnish insight into the precise course of events, and it indicates that this discourse (or dialogue) about the bread of life formed a historically and locally demarcated climax — and at the same time a decisive turning point — in Jesus' public ministry in Galilee, as the following pericope shows.

6:60-71

Division among the Disciples

Verse **60**, coming after the conclusive vs. 59, no longer belongs to that which occurred in the synagogue at Capernaum but speaks of the reaction that Jesus' discourse prompted, especially among his disciples. The reference is not to the Twelve (cf. vs. 70) but to a wider circle of people who had joined him as pupils and followed him (cf. also 7:3, and for Judea also 3:22; 4:1). The idea that such people, since they are not mentioned in the preceding, cannot be the respondents here to what was said there, imposes demands on the historical completeness of the Fourth Gospel that it was obviously not at all designed to meet. The point, rather, is to make it clear that this discourse was not only misunderstood by "the Jews" (vss. 41, 51) but also formed a turning point for many of Jesus' followers. To what they had heard many of them responded by saying: "This is a hard saying; who can listen to it?" With this they were not rebelling against what Jesus had said. The phrase "this saying" is not specifically identified but presumably relates to the conclusion of the discourse. The argument that vs. 60 ties in better with vs. 50 than with vs. 58 and that vss. 51-58 therefore have to be viewed as a later insertion is hard to accept. Especially for Jesus' disciples the offensiveness of his words certainly derived not from the fact that they had to accept him as the one sent by God from heaven, but from the idea that their salvation should be bound up with his self-offering into death. This is also clear from Jesus' answer in what follows.

61, 62 Although their words were not addressed to him, Jesus does respond (cf. 4:34; 6:43; 7:16, 28, etc.). The Semitic expression "knowing in himself that . . ." means not only that Jesus knew what people were thinking (see the comments on 2:24ff.; cf. Mk. 2:8) but also that he was aware of the offensive nature of his words. Here again they "murmur" or "grumble," as did "the Jews" in vss. 41, 43. Jesus then speaks of "taking offense," "causing to stumble," "making someone fall," an expression that recurs in the New Testament in connection with the humanly unacceptable road Jesus had to go, ending in his death on the cross (cf. 16:1; 1 Co. 1:23; Gl. 5:1; Mt. 11:6).

His question, "Do you take offense at this?" is followed in vs. 62 by a second question in which he apparently seeks to confront his apostate disciples with the prematurity and serious consequence of their reaction. This question, in keeping with a rhetorical device,[166] is incomplete: "[But what] if you should see the Son of man ascend to where he was before?" The apodosis apparently intended is: "Would you also then [or still][167] take offense?" Still, the intent of the question is not easy to discern. The idea that with "see . . . ascending" Jesus had in mind that his disciples were to witness his ascension (cf. Lk. 24:51) is, because of the "many" (vs. 60) he was addressing, hard to accept. The story of the ascension is lacking in the Fourth Gospel, though the statement in 20:17 apparently refers to this event. It is much more natural to take the ascent here as parallel to the descent mentioned in the preceding discourse (cf. vss. 33, 38, 41; see also both in 3:13).

Many interpreters take this "ascent" in the sense elsewhere implied in "exaltation," that is, as a reference to Jesus' crucifixion (so "exaltation" in 3:14 [associated with "ascend" in vs. 14]; 8:12; 12:32, 34), and conclude that Jesus here meant that the offense that the disciples take at his preceding words will come over them fully only when they witness his "exaltation" on the cross. But then it might be too late for them. For then they would also be confronted with the glory of the Son of man as judge, a glory that after all he was to receive in the way of his "exaltation" on the cross (cf. 8:28). But it is questionable whether such a future climax of the *skandalon* can be intended here. "Ascend" does not have as ambivalent a meaning as "exalt." The entire focus in Jesus' question is the future glory of the Son of man, with an implied reference to the glory with which he, precisely as the Son of man, was clothed "before" as the one sealed by the Father (cf. vs. 27; 17:5, 24) and thus to the unity of "de-

---

166. Called "aposiopesis," i.e., omission of the apodosis. The protasis ἐὰν οὖν θεωρῆτε expresses a potential condition (see BDF §§373.1; 483).

167. So BDF: "Would you then still take offense?" (§482).

scending" and "ascending" as the great mystery of the gospel (cf. 3:13ff.).
Whereas in the preceding discourse the descent has been brought to the limit
of its implications ("eating the flesh of the Son of man and drinking his blood"),
here Jesus confronts his disciples, who are "offended" by what he says, with
his full identity as the Son of man descended from heaven. On that basis, do
they realize what they are doing? If it is *he* who gives them his flesh to eat and
blood to drink (cf. vs. 27), what then[168] if they should one day see this Son of
man ascend again to where he was before? Where then would they be with
their unbelief and *skandalon*?

Where and how they would "see" this ascent is not made explicit. One
cannot even say that Jesus predicts that "seeing" — whether as an experience
of salvation that will one day shame them or as a judgment awaiting them (as
in 8:28; cf. also Mt. 26:64). Jesus speaks — less specifically — of the "if" (if
it should one day happen that they would "see" him thus),[169] not, of course,
as though that exaltation is only a possibility, but to confront his disciples in a
very telling way with the possibility that, as long as they measure the way and
salvation of the Son of man by their human standards, they might be terribly
wrong, even if they still cannot conceive of that. (See the comments on 3:3,
5ff. Here, too, lies the transition to vs. 63.)

63   Just as in his conversation with Nicodemus, Jesus speaks of what is,
or is not, acceptable to human thought (vs. 61: "Who can listen to this?") and
divine reality in the light of the contrast between "Spirit" and "flesh." Only
the Spirit, as the author of God's renewing and redeeming work, makes alive,
creates and imparts life. But the Spirit does so in the way and manner of the
Spirit (cf. 3:8). The flesh cannot touch it! The words Jesus has spoken "are
Spirit and life"; they are from God, hence life-giving for whoever believes.
But the flesh — in its reflections and powerlessness — is of no avail here; it
cannot hear that word, it takes offense at it, and it lapses into unbelief (vss. 64,
65).[170]

With this interpretation of the opposites "Spirit" and "flesh," I am rejecting the view that "flesh" here is an echo of what Jesus said earlier (vss.
50ff.) about *his* flesh. In this connection one must again distinguish between
those who regard vss. 50cff. as referring to the "sacramental" flesh and blood
of Jesus and those who (correctly, I think) understand by his "flesh" (and blood)
Jesus' self-offering to death (see above). Noteworthy among the former is
Zwingli, who, in the conflict over the Lord's Supper, based his opposition to
the real presence of Jesus' body and blood in the Lord's Supper on vs. 63. In

---

168. οὖν is inferential.
169. ἐάν designates that which, given the circumstances, may be expected, what will
eventually occur (cf. BDF §373).
170. For this interpretation of vss. 63f. see also I. de Potterie, "L'Esprit Saint dans l'Évangile de Jean," *NTS* 18 (1972), p. 449.

vs. 63, he thought, Jesus clearly indicated that, in the signs of his body and blood with which he nourishes his disciples at the Lord's Supper, he is only present in a spiritual manner. Thus, in the Lord's Supper "it is the Spirit that gives life, the flesh (the material) is of no use."

Many more recent commentators who reject the sacramental view of "flesh and blood" nevertheless believe that "flesh" in vs. 63 does relate to "flesh" in vs. 51c, and then in the sense that, over against his flesh (and blood), which he gives for the life of the world, Jesus here posits the vivifying Spirit that he would acquire and have at his disposal through his ascension. In this manner, then, Jesus is said to make known that, although his self-offering into death is the way in which he would fulfill his promise to those who would "eat" this flesh (and "drink" his blood; i.e., believe), *taken by itself* it would be of no avail.[171] But this view is not acceptable because it is hard to think that, after speaking (in vss. 50ff.) of his "flesh" as the heaven-descended, life-giving bread, which to eat is the absolute and exclusive condition for "having life in oneself" (vs. 53), Jesus would now in vs. 63 describe it as "of no avail." Furthermore, if one thus sets the vivifying Spirit of the exalted Son of man over against his flesh, one thus fails to appreciate the peculiar salvific import that Jesus' death itself has for his own and dissolves it, as it were, in the Spirit.

This by no means warrants the conclusion, however, that vss. 60ff. cannot be the original continuation of vss. 50ff. but link up immediately with vss. 35-50.[172] Those who hold this view state correctly that by "flesh" (vs. 63) is meant human flesh in general in its opposition to Spirit, as in 3:6f. But they add that the offense that the "flesh" takes at Jesus' preceding words cannot be reconciled with the way in which, in vss. 50ff., Jesus speaks of *his* flesh. On the contrary: the great *skandalon* for the natural person (cf. Mt. 16:23b!) present in the descent of the Son of man consists in the fact that he must be lifted up on the cross and enter into death; and that the food that he will give and that

---

171. E.g., Dunn, "John VI — A Eucharistic Discourse?" p. 338:

However essential was the incarnation to the work of redemption, for John it is not merely Jesus descended who gives life, merely as σάρξ, but rather as also ascended, when he gives himself through and in the Spirit. It is in the believing reception of the Spirit of Christ, the ἄλλος παράκλητος, that we eat the flesh and drink the blood of the incarnate Christ.

Weren now argues along the same lines ("Structuur en samenhang in Johannes 6," p. 60):

Only when the Son of man has ascended can he follow through on what he promised in the dialogue, namely, giving his flesh to eat for the life of the world. By the gift of the Spirit the believer can participate in that life. In that sense the flesh, considered by itself, is of no use.

172. Bornkamm asserts this and, following him, also such an influential interpreter as Brown (*Comm.* I, pp. 299-302).

endures to eternal life (vs. 27) consists in his flesh and blood offered up into death as the flesh that is food indeed and the blood that is drink indeed (vs. 55).

Verse **64** directly applies the contrasting alternatives in vs. 63 to the break now becoming manifest among the disciples. Over against the life-giving power of Jesus' words as Spirit the flesh now asserts itself as unbelief that takes offense at those words. Jesus speaks of "some of you," whereas in vss. 60 and 66 the reference is to "many." His statement, "there are some of you who do not believe," is not meant as a direct portrayal of the state of affairs but rather as a revealing description of what was beginning to manifest itself among the disciples: "unbelief" as, fundamentally, the inability and refusal to accept Jesus for who he is. Those whom Jesus is referring to had indeed followed him, were impressed by his words and works, and in that sense had begun to believe in him (cf. 2:23; 7:31; 8:30). But that faith was to suffer shipwreck and would be manifest as nonbelief, because they were unable to overcome the offense felt by the flesh at the increasing visibility of the cross. Jesus — according to the Evangelist — knew from the beginning (from the beginning of his ministry and his choosing of his disciples; cf. vs. 70; see also 13:11, 18, 21ff.) that he would be betrayed and who would betray him. This says something both about Jesus' knowledge of people (cf. the comments on 2:24, 25) and about the outcome of his life. It is clear, nowhere more than here, that the cross has a dominant place in the Fourth Gospel.

65 The words "This is why I told you" connect with vs. 64a and obviously refer back to vs. 44 (cf. vss. 37ff.). Faith, here described as "coming to me" (as in vss. 35, 37, etc.), does not lie within the domain of "the flesh"; it is only possible as a gift from God (see the comments on vss. 44ff. above), namely as being "taught by God" and being "born of God," or "from above" (1:13; 3:3ff.). By saying this Jesus does not separate faith from his own words, which call people to believe and confront them with the need to make a decision. But when a person obeys this summons, that happens not on account of that person's reflections and wisdom but on account of the power of the word itself, which "draws" that person and overcomes his or her powerlessness.

66, 67 The phrase "after this" or "from then on" marks the moment of an important break[173] among Jesus' disciples that resulted in many of his followers no longer staying with him.[174] This break was apparently such that Jesus also placed before the Twelve the choice of remaining or leaving.[175] For the first time they are here called the Twelve (otherwise only in 20:24; see the

173. ἀπερχέσθαι εἰς τὰ ὀπίσω, "go away, leave."
174. περιπατεῖν, here in the more general sense of "spend time with," "go about with."
175. The question that begins with μή expects a negative answer: "Certainly you do not also want to go away?"

comments on 1:35ff.). Here again knowledge of what the Synoptics say at much greater length about the choice and number of the disciples is presupposed.

68, 69 In fact, the whole scene here runs parallel with the story of Peter's confession in Mt. 16:15ff.; Mk. 8:29; Lk. 9:20. In both a confession occurs in response to a question asked by Jesus and in contrast with what others say of him, and Jesus' passion announcement is directly connected with a turning point in his relationship with his disciples (cf. also Mt. 16:24ff.; Mk. 8:34ff.; Lk. 9:23ff.).[176] In John Jesus' question and Peter's answer bear a clearer stamp of the crisis among those who followed Jesus. Peter's resistance to Jesus' passion announcement (Mt. 16:22) is not mentioned here (see also the comments on vs. 70). Peter clearly represents ("we") true discipleship (and the true confessors: cf. 4:23) over against unbelief and apostasy, in the midst of which this confession is elicited; and he functions as such — over against Judas (vss. 70, 71) — as the great example and foundation of the Christian community (cf. Mt. 16:17ff.; see also there, as here in vs. 63, the contrast with "flesh and blood," as also being "on God's side" versus "on the side of people," Mt. 16:17, 23).

Peter's answer is a genuine confession not only because in it he adopts Jesus' words as his own (cf. vs. 63b) but also because the faith that comes to expression in it reveals the awareness that Peter is confronting a radical choice: when life is at stake there is no other way to go than that of following Jesus ("to whom else . . . ?" cf. 14:6). Vs. 69 brings out the most basic component in the answer. It is not merely a spontaneous reaction of fidelity and attachment to Jesus' challenging question; it reveals a deepened insight[177] on the part of the disciples into the identity of the person in whom they have believed: "We have believed and are convinced that you are the Holy One of God." The certainty of faith consists and rests in what it has grown to understand as its object: "The believer does not speak of himself but of him on whom he believes."[178]

This developed understanding of faith also comes to expression in the title with which Peter refers to Jesus. From the beginning the disciples have acknowledged and confessed Jesus as the Messiah (cf. 1:41, 45, 49). But the manner in which Peter now voices this conviction gives evidence of the totally new content this traditional title had acquired for the disciples (see the comments on 1:50, 51). With "you are" the authority and glory of Jesus' "I am" pronouncements — a glory that exceeds all human expectations — is reflected. Accordingly "the Holy One of God" is not intended as a new messianic title alongside others but as a further description of this messianic identity (cf. also Mt. 16:16: "You are the Christ, the Son of the living God"). In this pronounce-

---

176. In some manuscripts certain elements from the Synoptic tradition of Peter's confession also occur in John, presumably by adoption.

177. Note the double perfect: "We have believed and have acknowledged," a hendiadys (cf. Is. 43:10f.).

178. Bultmann, *Comm.,* p. 448.

ment Peter refers to Jesus as the one whom God placed at his own side before all others and destined and separated for his service (cf. 10:36; 17:19).[179] It is this wholly unique relationship of Jesus to God that has increasingly begun to shape the faith of Jesus' disciples and has made them aware that in Jesus they are dealing in the most direct way with the reality of God.

70, 71   Just as Peter has spoken on behalf of the Twelve, so Jesus' answer is also directed to them all. He does not respond specifically to Peter's confession. Although Peter's confession shows that it was inspired by the Spirit and not by the flesh (Mt. 16:17; vs. 63 above), now something else comes to the fore that ties in with vs. 69 and will be continued later: in the circle of the disciples, even of the Twelve, from which such an exalted confession sounded, the devil also did his work. In fact, a devil was present there. Jesus very sharply voices this in one concluding sentence. He reminds them that he had chosen them as "the Twelve" (cf. Mk. 3:14; Mt. 10:1; Lk. 6:13). Then in the same breath and as a profound complaint and indictment he adds: "and one of you is a devil." The construction of the sentence marks the antithesis in all its sharpness. On the one hand, there was Jesus' salvific election of the Twelve that he called to follow him as the numerically complete representation of Israel; on the other, precisely in this circle, there was the devil who would betray him and break that sacred number.

The sharp turn that, immediately after Peter's confession, Jesus here gives to the conversation is most remarkable especially when one compares it with the shift in the parallel conversation in Matthew, where not Judas but Peter is rebuked by Jesus as Satan because of his opposition to Jesus' announcement of his suffering and death (Mt. 16:23). We cannot say with any certainty whether John was familiar with this tradition preserved in Matthew. But if he was, this need not yet mean that he deliberately omitted it to spare Peter and that he therefore substituted Judas in the role of Satan. There is no evidence in the Fourth Gospel of any tendency to favor Peter (cf. 13:6ff., 36ff.; 18:5ff.; 20:4).

Something is at stake here on a totally different level than any supposed tendency on the part of the Evangelist or a later redactor to favor one disciple.[180]

---

179. "Holy" is above all a term for what belongs to the divine sphere and to the service of God, that which is consecrated to God. Jesus is also described as the Holy One in 1 Jn. 2:20; Ac. 3:14; 4:27, 30 ("thy holy servant"); Rv. 3:7 and as "the Holy One of God" in Mk. 1:24; Lk. 4:34.

180. Others regard the fact that Peter's confession is not followed here, as in Matthew, by Jesus' pronouncement about Peter's special position in relation to the coming church (Mt. 16:18, 19) as a Johannine depreciation of the role ascribed to Peter in the Synoptic Gospels (see A. H. Maynard, "Peter in the Fourth Gospel," *NTS* 30 [1984], p. 543). That depreciation is also said to be discernible in the name, "Holy One of God," that Peter ascribes to Jesus, the same name with which the *demons* address Jesus in Mk. 1:24; Lk. 4:34! This, then, is the converse of the suggestion that John transferred the role of Satan from Peter to Judas. Obviously, the Evangelists are occupied with something other than such assigning of roles.

What the Evangelist (again; cf. vs. 64) brings out here is rather the extent of Jesus' awareness of the radicalness of the separation that he, by placing the prospect of his death before his disciples, was causing and of the offense he was thereby unleashing. Hence *this* reaction to Peter's sublime confession! — certainly not, in contrast with Matthew 16, to put a damper on it but because he knew that the "nature" of the death with which he would glorify God and draw many people to himself (cf. 12:33, 34) was also a great stumbling block that the devil would use with force and cunning and with which he would even violate the sacred number of the circle that Jesus had gathered about him as the firstfruits of his church. His heartfelt complaint is not only intended, therefore, to give voice to the painful certainty that he would have to pursue his way in the company of his betrayer but also to impress on his disciples that even their — as yet unshaken — loyalty to him would not save them from being sifted by Satan (cf. Lk. 22:31).

It is undoubtedly for that reason that the Evangelist places the story of these two core motifs from the tradition (Peter's confession and Jesus' foreknowledge of Judas's betrayal) in the same context at this critical juncture in Jesus' history. Accordingly, the added comment that Jesus' reference was to Judas is not meant to stigmatize Judas by name[181] or to inform the reader assumed to be unfamiliar with the tradition, but rather to picture to the church, in the concrete figure of Judas, the offense of the gospel of the cross in its permanent actuality and relevance, an offense that cannot be overcome from within the "flesh." It can hardly be an accident that this grand chapter about the bread of life — at the same time the conclusion and summary of Jesus' continuing miraculous work in word and deed in Galilee — ends with the reference to Judas — with the telling addition: "one of the Twelve."

---

181. The name of Judas's father, Simon, is only reported in the Fourth Gospel, here and in 13:2, 26. This Simon is called, here and in ch. 13, "the Iscariot," a surname given in 12:4, as in the Synoptics, to Judas himself, which has occasioned the many changes in the manuscripts at this point. The meaning of "the Iscariot" is uncertain but is often interpreted as "the man from Kerioth," i.e., from the town in southern Judea called Kerioth Herzon. However, there are many other explanations, none of which has led to a consensus (see, e.g., Schnackenburg, *Comm.* II, p. 78).

7–10

Who Is Jesus?

Starting with ch. 7, the story shifts to Judea, specifically Jerusalem. Jesus leaves Galilee and does not — at least in the account given here — return. Apparently his great discourse in ch. 6 and the separation that thereupon took place among his disciples (6:60-71) are meant to round off Jesus' work in Galilee. True, ch. 7 does speak of a continued stay in Galilee, but we are not given any particulars. The Evangelist demonstrates how Jesus' ministry in Galilee, which was initially welcomed with so much enthusiasm (cf. 4:45), ended in a divergence of minds. From this point on everything takes place in the center of Jewish life.

In consequence, the buildup to the Passion narrative is very different and much broader in John than in the Synoptics. Jesus' departure from Galilee took place about the time of the Feast of Tabernacles, that is, in the fall (September-October, 7:1-2). After that the Feast of the Dedication, which fell in the winter, is mentioned (10:22). If, as is apparently intended, one draws the chronological line through to Jesus' "last" Passover (13:1ff.), then this period in Jesus' life covers at least half a year. It is marked by all sorts of encounters, conversations, and confrontations between Jesus and Jew, especially with leaders of the Jews, and hence gives us deeper insight into the cause and development of the growing conflict than does the Synoptic account of what took place just a few days before Jesus' death at Jerusalem.[1]

In this development chs. 7–10 have a place of their own; here the dialogue-pattern is predominant and the effective break between the Jews and Jesus comes to some kind of conclusion. The historical and local contours by and large remain vague. Not until ch. 11 is there a clear change. The events of

1. This applies specifically to the *blasphemy* attributed to Jesus as the real cause (so also in the Synoptics) of his condemnation; see also, at length, S. Pancaro, *The Law in the Fourth Gospel,* 1975, pp. 506ff.

ch. 7 occur against the background of the Feast of Tabernacles (especially vss. 37ff.). The extent to which this is still the case in chs. 8 and 9 (see the comments on 9:7) is uncertain. The dialogues in ch. 8 are best understood as the escalation of those of ch. 7 (cf. 8:12 with 7:37; 8:14 with 7:27, 28; 8:15 with 7:24; 8:21ff. with 7:33ff.). Ch. 9, the story of the man born blind, forms a new unit and clearly distinguishes itself from what precedes in that it is no longer Jesus himself but the healed man who is the partner in dialogue with "the Jews." In the connected but antithetic parable of the good shepherd, followed by the dialogue on the Feast of Dedication (ch. 10), Jesus again speaks at length. But with that the conversations with "the Jews" are definitely coming to a close (cf. 10:31, 39). From that point Jesus withdraws himself from every contact with them (11:40, 54). Beginning with the story of the raising of Lazarus (ch. 11), we now witness the events that form the immediate prelude to Jesus' death (11:55ff.). For that reason, in distinction from most other commentators, we assume, in marking the divisions of this Gospel, that the division between the middle and the end of the Gospel should be found, not between chs. 12 and 13, but between chs. 10 and 11.[2] The conclusion of ch. 10 also points in that direction. There (10:40) Jesus returns to the other side of the Jordan, to the place where John first baptized, hence to the starting point of his own ministry. Thus the circle, as it were, completes itself. There we also encounter the summarizing testimony of the many who followed him there: "Everything John said about this man was true" (10:41). Jesus had completed everything that, according to his herald (1:6ff.), could have been expected of him.

Chapters 7–10 are unlike chs. 5 and 6 in content and composition in that, with the exception of ch. 9, they can be less easily understood as coherent units and hence less easily summarized. It has been remarked that in these chapters the Evangelist brings together the major part of what he has to say in response to Jewish objections to Jesus' messiahship.[3] Many voices are heard here and all sorts of criticisms that, on the basis of current expectations with regard to the coming of the Messiah, could be advanced against Jesus.

Some scholars believe that one can discern here the voices of the many groups in and outside the later Christian community for which the Evangelist wrote, and on that basis attempt to reconstruct a picture of such groups in the period and in "the city" in which he lived.[4] Undoubtedly this view contains the truth that in the selection and redaction of these dialogues the Evangelist especially brings to the fore that which was pivotal in the relationship between

2. On this issue see also the argument of M. Rissi, "Der Aufbau des vierten Evangeliums," *NTS* 29 (1983), pp. 50, 51.

3. Cf. C. H. Dodd, *The Interpretation of the Fourth Gospel,* 1953, p. 346; see also M. de Jonge, *Jesus: Stranger from Heaven and Son of God,* 1977, pp. 34ff., 79.

4. Especially J. L. Martyn, *History and Theology in the Fourth Gospel,*1979[1].

Jews and Christians in his day and that he therefore viewed the historical tradition "through the situation he and his community were living in."[5] But it is going too far in analysis of the material to make such a reconstruction the controlling viewpoint, using it as the hermeneutical key in exegesis.

This is so because the overall image of those who are here voicing their questions and objections, as also of their messianic expectations, is too indefinite for that purpose. One can hardly speak of genuine "discussions" between Jesus and "the people," "some men from Jerusalem," and others. Jesus does not justify himself by responding to all their criticisms (cf., e.g., 7:27, 36, 41, 42). He speaks rather from within his — to his hearers, incomprehensible — messianic authority. That offends them because they cannot verify his words and because he does not fit their messianic expectations. Accordingly, it is undoubtedly not the intention of the Evangelist to furnish his readers with arguments in their confrontation with Jewish criticism; but rather, positively, to bring out how from the beginning, in his unique relationship with God and his mission from the Father, Jesus was utterly different from, indeed other than, what Jews expected and desired of him — and, more generally, other than what human beings can conceive another human being to be. The figure of this Jesus rises far above all discussions about his person. He leaves that, as it were, behind him. Accordingly, it is the utterly unique significance of Jesus' person and work and the radical choice with which he confronts his hearers that constitute the all-controlling aim of these dialogues and that at the same time, as his "hour" approaches, brings him into ever more intense conflict with the Jewish leaders.[6]

The very diverse and partly also fragmentary character of the content of these chapters has also given rise to the idea that the sequence and composition of the various parts can hardly be understood as an original whole and that they show signs of disorder, especially chs. 7 and 8 and also ch. 10. This has led to all kinds of attempts to reconstruct what the author originally had in mind.[7] However, most interpreters have abandoned this method,[8] especially because:

---

5. So Pancaro, *Law in the Fourth Gospel,* p. 513.

6. See the valuable discussion of these chapters in de Jonge, *Jesus: Stranger from Heaven and Son of God,* pp. 34ff., 80ff., 96ff.; see also his cautious judgment regarding attempts to see in these chapters a reflection of later conditions in the church: "The way from a literary document like the Gospel of John to a reconstruction of the actual situation in which it was written is much longer and much more difficult than some authors seem to realize" (p. 114, n. 70; cf. also Pancaro, *Law in the Fourth Gospel,* pp. 512ff.).

7. Cf. pp. 10-11 above. On these chapters see also Bultmann, *Comm.,* pp. 285ff.; see also pp. 238f., n. 4, where Bultmann calls ch. 8 "a collection of isolated fragments which have been put together without much plan." For his reconstructed order of the entire Gospel, see pp. 10f.

8. Even an author like Haenchen, whom one cannot charge with a lack of appreciation for Bultmann's (in many respects hardly surpassable) commentary, writes: "The time of theories of displacement is gone" (*Comm.* I, p. 51).

these regroupings have no support in the text as handed down; the proffered reconstructions always raise new problems; the person (or persons) responsible for the redaction of the Gospel in its present form has (have) apparently regarded what we now have before us as sufficiently unified, and it is the primary task of exegesis to give a more detailed account of this unity; it is inappropriate to apply to the Gospel standards that its author probably had neither the intention nor the ability to meet;[9] and upon closer scrutiny it frequently turns out that there are connections in the text even where interpreters have found none.

It is true that this does not solve all problems or — conversely — that we need to be critical toward attempts to illumine the inner unity of the various chapters.[10] Therefore, we will adhere to the traditional chapter divisions, but will have to consider possibilities for arriving at acceptable subdivisions.

7:1-13
Jesus' Delayed Departure for Jerusalem
for the Feast of Tabernacles

1   About the transitional phrase ("after this") there is a difference of opinion. Some scholars infer a change of locale from vs. 1a, namely from Judea (Jerusalem) to Galilee; in that case 7:1 does not link up with ch. 6, because there Jesus is already in Galilee. This is one of the arguments for reversing the order of chs. 5 and 6 (see introduction to ch. 5 above). But aside from the objections against this hypothesis mentioned earlier, it would be striking if of this new stay in Galilee we are only told that Jesus then again returned from there to Judea (vss. 2-10) and if Jesus' brothers thought they had to urge him to do something that he had already done (in ch. 5). Furthermore, there is no reason not to take vs. 1a as a continuation of Jesus' stay in Galilee in ch. 6, explained by the reason already given in 4:1f. (cf. vs. 44), which had become even more urgent during his stay in Jerusalem recorded in ch. 5 (5:18). Nor do we read that Jesus "withdrew" to Galilee, as we should expect if ch. 7 immediately followed ch. 5, but that he "went about in Galilee." Also the imperfect tense in vs. 1a does not point to a change.[11] So one can for good reason ask whether

---

9. Haenchen, *Comm.* I, p. 80: "We thus have no right to reorder the Gospel arbitrarily, as, for example, Bacon, Macgregor, Bultmann, and Hoare have done, and then to represent this new sequence as the true outline, the original composition of the Gospel, and to interpret everything in accordance with it."

10. See on ch. 8 the overview in F. J. Moloney, *The Johannine Son of Man,* 1978[2], pp. 125f.

11. Cf. Barrett (*Comm.,* p. 309): "imperfect of customary action." He also writes: "It is not implied that the sequence of events is immediate"; in his view, too, therefore, there is no support here for the reversal of chs. 5 and 6.

the first words here should not be translated *"also* after this." Usually scholars translate "and"; but in the usual formula for "after this" this "and" is normally lacking (cf. 2:12; 3:22; 5:1, 14; 6:1; 19:38; 2:1 — probably why it is omitted here in many important manuscripts), which may suggest that an emphatic "also" is intended.

After what was reported in the preceding, namely that people turned away from him, Jesus nevertheless remained in Galilee because being in Judea was too dangerous.[12] "The Jews" are not the inhabitants of Judea here but the authorities in Jerusalem.

2 Again we read that "the feast of the Jews" is "at hand" (see comments on 2:13; 5:1; 6:4), in this case the Feast of Tabernacles. It was celebrated for seven days, from the fifteenth to the twenty-first of Tishri (September- October). Then followed an eighth day on which the feast was concluded with a holy convocation (cf. Lv. 23:34ff.; Nu. 29:35; see also the comments below on vs. 37). Originally the feast was a harvest festival celebrated with great exuberance, which became associated, specifically in connection with the daily solemn outpouring of water during this feast, with eschatological hopes (and "the wells of salvation" predicted in them; cf. Zc. 14:16ff.; Is. 12:3).[13]

3, 4 The nearness of the feast prompted Jesus' brothers (cf. 2:12; 20:17 [?]) to urge him to go to Judea. The word translated "leave here"[14] has a broader meaning than the usual word for the pilgrimage to Jerusalem ("go up").[15] This might indicate that they had in mind not just a journey for the feast but a longer stay, perhaps a change of residence from Galilee to Judea. Thus Jesus' brothers pressure him to seek more publicity, especially among his "disciples": "that your disciples may see the works you are doing." "Your disciples" may mean the followers Jesus had already won in Judea (cf. 2:23ff.; 3:23; 4:1). If Jesus should permanently withdraw into Galilee, they might become estranged from him. But in what follows we do not hear of them as an existing group of adherents. It is more likely that "your disciples" has a more general meaning here (and elsewhere in the Gospel).[16] In 6:60, 66 we are told that "many of his disciples" turned away from him in disappointment. It is natural that Jesus' brothers should have in mind this disappointing — also for them — course of events and hence urge him to go to the center of the land

---

12. For "he would not" in vs. 1b there exists the striking variant: (οὐκ) εἶχεν ἐξουσίαν, "he was unable," which as *lectio difficilior* is regarded by some as original (e.g., Barrett, *Comm.*, pp. 309f.; Lindars, *Comm.,* p. 281).

13. On the Feast of Tabernacles, see, e.g., Strack/Billerbeck II, pp. 774-812 (on the pouring of water, pp. 799ff.); W. Michaelis, *TDNT* VII, pp. 390-92 and the literature cited there.

14. μεταβαίνειν (ἐντεῦθεν).

15. ἀναβαίνειν (cf. vss. 8ff.).

16. On this passage see also J. R. Michaels, "The Temple Discourse in John," in *New Dimensions in New Testament Study,* ed. R. N. Longenecker and M. C. Tenney, 1974, pp. 200-213; esp. pp. 203f.

to manifest himself there with the miracle-working power given him ("the works you are able to do"). In this connection they hold before him as a matter of common sense that certainly "no one works in secret if (at the same time) he seeks public recognition for himself."[17] By this last statement the brothers evidently mean that, as would appear from all of Jesus' public activity, Jesus' aim must certainly be to become known as a person and to gain a hearing. But how then could he keep his works concealed? Therefore: "If you do these things" — that they do not deny; on the contrary, it is the basis of their argument[18] — "then show yourself to the world!" The passage as a whole is reminiscent of the first miracle in Cana, where Jesus "manifested" his glory (2:10), "the Passover" (as here the Feast of Tabernacles) was "at hand" (2:13), Jesus had gone to Jerusalem, and his brothers are mentioned (2:12). From nearby or from some distance, they had witnessed that first great manifestation and knew what had followed in Jerusalem when Jesus had "gone public" there and had impressed people with his power (2:23ff.; cf. 4:45). Apparently it was the impact Jesus had then that they again now want to see continued.

5 But the Evangelist advances this information as proof ("for") that Jesus' brothers "did not believe in him." Their attitude was like that of the people who took offense at Jesus when he, in language incomprehensible to them, began to speak of his death (6:60ff.). Hence their urging Jesus to go public, rather than being proof of cynicism with respect to Jesus' claims (vs. 4), is evidence of regret, of "worldly" (cf. vs. 6) expectations that they still had of him and that they saw go up in flames in the retiring attitude he adopted.

6-8 Jesus' answer speaks of "his time," elsewhere called "his hour" (cf. 2:4; 7:30; 8:20; 13:1; 17:1). The fixing of that "time," that is, the moment for action, is for him always related to God's commission and plan for his life, specifically also the great hour of his death and departure from the world (cf. vs. 30; 13:1, etc.). Therefore that time must be "fulfilled" (vs. 8). That is, it must be in accord with the eschatological action of God being realized in him.

Here that determination of that "time" has to do with the rising opposition of the Jews who were threatening his life. Therein lies the difference between his time and his brothers' time. They do not understand that difference because they do not understand the depth of the opposition to Jesus. It is not a problem for them directly, and they apparently do not take it seriously as it relates to Jesus. Therefore, "your time is always here." They can go where they please. For (vs. 7) "the world cannot hate you." They do not do anything that displeases the world, so they can speak optimistically about the world (vs. 4). But Jesus ("me" in the emphatic position) it hates. Awaiting Jesus in Jerusalem is not

---

17. ζητεῖ ("has aspirations to," "makes an effort to"), αὐτός (other manuscripts have αὐτό or αὐτόν or omit the pronoun altogether) ἐν παρρησίᾳ εἶναι. Here παρρησία means "publicity."
18. εἰ in vs. 4b is *siquidem,* "if indeed."

festively attired Israel prepared to meet the one sent by God, in the manner of the feast, to receive living water from the wells of salvation (Is. 12:3), but "the world," those who, despite all their religiosity, are estranged from God, who do not recognize him for who he is because they do not recognize God (vs. 28) and therefore do not believe in Jesus, but indeed hate him. And why do they hate him? Because he does not come to them as they would have him come and as they would love to lift him up on their shoulders (cf. 6:14, 15); because he testifies of it "that its works are evil." These last words are strongly reminiscent of 3:19, 20. They do not describe Jesus as a prophet of misfortune who has come to indict people before God on account of their corruption and immorality but as the one who in his effort to win the world brings to the light what is of God and what is of the world; and hence which works — having been done in God and directed toward him — are good, and which are "evil," that is, done in accord with what the world itself thinks fit and with the standards it applies. It is that crisis, that disturbance of the world's desire to be itself, that offends the world and arouses its hatred. For that reason (vs. 8) Jesus is not willing to go along with his brothers. He is not going to "this feast" with them because his hour has "not yet fully come." It is determined by very different considerations than what makes them go up to the feast.

9, 10 "Having said this," Jesus remained in Galilee. And not until after his brothers had gone up to the feast did he also go. But not like them. Not "publicly" or "openly" so that it was clear to everyone that he went to Jerusalem as a pilgrim, but "privately," as someone who wanted to remain unnoticed and went his own way. He apparently did not observe the time of the feast either, since not until about the middle of the feast and after people had looked for him in vain (vs. 11) did he appear (see the comments on vs. 14). Then his time was fulfilled, the time for him to do and say that for which the Father had sent him.

There is great divergence among interpreters about the contradiction between vss. 8 and 10 if one takes the words in vs. 8 ("I am not going up to this feast") absolutely. There is a reading (in very important textual witnesses) that has "not yet" in place of "not" here, as in vs. 6. However, this reading strongly appears to be an attempt to reconcile vs. 8 with vs. 10. Some interpret vs. 8 with a tacit restriction: "I am not going with the other pilgrims," or assume a provisional intention that was later modified under divine inspiration. Others place all the emphasis on *"this"* feast, with the idea that the real feast to which Jesus would go was still to come: namely, his last Passover. Moreover, his "going up" is sometimes understood in a deeper sense: namely, of his "ascent" to the Father (cf. 20:17).[19] But all these suggestions are forced and artificial.

19. For this view see, e.g., Brown, *Comm.* I, p. 308: He speaks of "a classic instance of the two levels of meaning found in John."

Bultmann believes that, suitable as the general idea of vss. 1-13 is as an introduction
to what follows, "nevertheless the form in which the idea is expressed raises grave
difficulties, for Jesus' actions contradict his own words."[20]

Over against this C. H. Giblin argues in a lengthy essay that in 7:1-13 we are
dealing with a fixed pattern that he describes as "Suggestion, Negative Response,
and Positive Action in St. John's Portrayal of Jesus" and that, aside from 7:10, also
occurs in 2:1-11; 4:46-54; and 11:1-44. According to him, in none of these four
examples of this "literary pattern" is there any inconsistency or change of mind on
the part of Jesus. He cites as typical for this narrative pattern the manner in which
Jesus distances himself each time from people, even from those who, by purely human
standards, should be very close to him: his mother (2:1ff.), a royal official (4:46ff.),
his brothers (7:1-13), and his disciples (11:1ff.). Still, Jesus consistently acts radically
"on his own terms."[21]

This undoubtedly gets to the heart of the issue. But it still does not furnish an
answer to the contradiction insisted on by Bultmann: "What Jesus refuses to do and
then does is simply ἀναβαίνειν — vv. 8, 10."[22] Without meaning to harmonize the
irreconcilable at any price, it must still be said that the Evangelist, by combining Jesus'
ἀναβαίνειν not (as three times earlier) with "to the feast" but with "not publicly but
in private," emphasizes the "wholly other" character of this "going up" compared to
what Jesus' brothers wanted him to do and themselves did, namely as pilgrims.[23]

In vss. **11-13** the situation is pictured "from the other side," namely from
Jerusalem. From this, too, it is evident that the tensions around Jesus are
growing and that the entire story is increasingly dominated by Jesus' conflict
with the Jewish authorities and the outcome of that conflict. In vs. 11 "the
Jews" apparently means those authorities, in distinction from "the people" (vs.
12; cf. also vs. 13). They expected Jesus at the feast and "sought" him, with
hostile intentions (cf. vs. 1; 5:16, 18, etc.), among the pilgrims and inquired
after him. Among "the people" as well there was much suppressed talk, "muttering," about Jesus, in which their uncertainty and differences of opinion were
clear. Some chose Jesus' side — in a general way, by saying "he is a good
man," "he cannot be charged with anything." Others denied this and called
him "one who leads people astray" (cf. Mt. 27:63), a serious accusation by
Jewish standards because it implied a violation of the true religion, whether

20. Bultmann, *Comm.,* p. 216.

21. C. H. Giblin, "Suggestion, Negative Response, and Positive Action in St. John's Portrait
of Jesus (John 2.1-11.; 4.46-54.; 7.2-14.; 11.1-44.)," *NTS* 26 (1980), pp. 197-211.

22. Bultmann, *Comm.,* p. 288, n. 3.

23. So also Giblin, "Suggestion, Negative Response," p. 208: "The evangelist does not
say that Jesus goes up for the feast, much less for *this* feast. As events work out, Jesus . . . arrives
when the feast is already half-over (v. 14a), even unexpectedly. . . . When he does arrive he goes
up to the temple to teach. Thus, he does not celebrate the feast or 'go up for it' as others would
— and would expect him to do."

against sound interpretation of the law[24] or even against monotheism itself.[25] But (vs. 13) no one dared to speak out either for or against him. People knew how intensely opposed the authorities were to Jesus and were afraid to become entangled in any legal action that might be taken against him.

7:14-24

Jesus Teaches in the Temple: Who Fulfills the Law?

14 That Jesus did not appear at the feast until it was halfway over, that is, on the fourth day, is to be viewed, of course, in light of his earlier refusal to go up to the feast. By going he ceased to be "private" (vs. 10; cf. vs. 26), and he even went to the temple, the great meeting place of the people. He did so, however, in a very different manner and for a very different purpose than his brothers wanted: not to manifest his miraculous power there but "to teach." The significance of this term, used absolutely, is evident in part from the (few) other places in the Fourth Gospel where mention is made of Jesus' teaching activity (cf. 6:59; 8:20): he thus made known to the people, on the basis of his messianic authority, the words of God, the import of his mission. But to the people such activity — and that at that location! — above all meant to exercise the office of the rabbi who in virtue of his training and ordination was authorized to teach there. And it was from that perspective that they immediately raised questions (vs. 15).

Some scholars say that already here, beginning with vs. 15, is a clear case where the original order of the material has been disturbed: vss. 15-24 should be transposed to the end of ch. 5 because their content links up closely, both historically and in content, with ch. 5 and because vs. 25 would function much better as the continuation of vs. 14 than of vss. 15ff.[26] This line of thought, in

---

24. On this see, at length, Pancaro, *Law in the Fourth Gospel,* pp. 96ff.

25. Cf. Martyn, *History and Theology,* pp. 74-81. He does not think here (in 7:12; cf. 7:47ff.) of the "Jesus-tradition," but of situations reconstructed (with the help of extrabiblical data) in "the city" where the Evangelist wrote this Gospel and where "to lead astray" amounted to a crime against monotheism (attributed to Christians) against which the Jewish athorities acted with legal means. However, for this meaning of "leading astray" one need not, in my opinion, refer to this later situation. It was in the first instance against Jesus himself that the charge of "blasphemy" was directed. In this use of "leading astray," the issue in any case is the significance that Jesus attributed to himself (cf. Mt. 24:4; 27:63); see also H. Braun, *TDNT,* s.v. πλανάω.

26. See also Schnackenburg, *Comm.* II, pp. 130f., though in general he distances himself from these reconstructions. In his judgment, the transposition of vss. 15-24 is a simple operation that "renders superfluous any extensive displacement hypotheses [like, e.g., Bultmann's] in Chapter 7." How then did these verses land in ch. 7? To that question Schnackenburg has no other answer than the all-too-easy hypothesis of "a detached sheet."

my opinion, immediately betrays with how little justification such radical operations are undertaken. First of all, vss. 15ff. fit very well after vs. 14, where the clause "and he taught" furnishes the theme for what follows, a theme to which, from the viewpoint of Jesus' "boldness" (παρρησία), vss. 25ff. refer back. Admittedly, vss. 19ff. clearly reflect the story of the healing on the sabbath told in ch. 5 and also again bring up Moses, as does the conclusion of ch. 5. But everything here in ch. 7 is different from ch. 5, in regard to both the setting of the dialogue and the viewpoint from which appeal is made to Moses. In ch. 5, at a location that is not further described, Jesus addresses himself to "the Jews" who on account of violation of the sabbath and blasphemy want to kill him (cf. 5:18). Here, in ch. 7, he appears in the temple as a teacher, and, during the discussion of that fact, the people tell him that he is possessed by a demon when he mentions their intent to kill him (vs. 20). And as for the dialogue itself: whereas in ch. 5 the entire focus is on Jesus' sonship and Moses is appealed to as a witness (5:39, 45ff.), the question here (in vss. 19ff.), in direct connection with what in vss. 15ff. is said about Jesus' authority to teach, is, Who can most justifiably appeal to Moses as lawgiver both for their teaching and conduct — Jesus, who healed a man on the sabbath, or his adversaries, who for that reason wanted to kill him? In all these dialogues, to be sure, the one great issue is that Jesus was sent by the Father. But each time the perspective from which this issue comes up is different. A reference back to earlier dialogues is no proof of displacement of materials originally belonging together. It rather suggests the modus operandi that characterizes the Evangelist (cf., e.g., 8:14ff. with 5:31ff.; 9:5 with 8:12, etc.).[27]

15 Jesus' teaching produced critical amazement and bewilderment among those who heard him in the temple,[28] not astonishment over his knowledge (as in Lk. 4:20), but offense (cf. 3:7; 4:27; 5:28; 7:21). How could this man, who had never received the appropriate training, act as one instructed in the Scriptures?[29] Moreover, the fact that he chose to teach in the temple undoubtedly reinforced this mood.

---

27. Against the displacement of vss. 15-24 see also the extensive argument of D. M. Smith, *The Composition and Order of the Fourth Gospel,* 1965, pp. 132ff. C. H. Dodd writes about this repeated reference back to themes treated in chs. 2–12: "A continuous argument runs through them. It does not move along the direct line of a logical process. Its movement is more like that of a musical fugue. A theme is introduced and developed up to a point; then a second theme is introduced and the two are interwoven; then a third, and so on. A theme may be dropped, and later resumed and differently combined, in all manner of harmonious variations" (*The Interpretation of the Fourth Gospel,* 1963, p. 383; see also pp. 289-91).

28. "The Jews" here are the people in general, not just the authorities (cf. vs. 19).

29. γράμματα εἰδέναι is a general term for one who has learned to read and write. Since, however, instruction in reading and writing took place with the aid of the Scriptures, it can, as here, also acquire the added meaning of "being instructed in the Scriptures"; see also G. Schrenk, *TDNT* I, pp. 764ff.

16   Over against this charge of presumption — though it is not personally addressed to him — Jesus appeals to the One who sent him. His authority as teacher was not rooted in study and human learning, still less in presumption, but in being sent by God. In saying this Jesus does not disown his own responsibility, as if he did not want to answer for his own teaching, but is rejecting any notion that he was either introducing a doctrine or building an authoritative position for himself apart from the One who sent him (see the comments on 5:19-23).

17-18   With this assertion Jesus now links the demand that everyone who — as was apparently the case with his hearers — really wants to take the will of God to heart should not pose the formal question of authority but rather form a material judgment[30] about Jesus' teaching, namely whether it bore the marks of being from God or was based on usurpation. For what is it that distinguishes the real emissary from the false emissary? The true one does not seek "his own glory" but that of the one who sent him (cf. 5:41, 44; 8:50, 54). By this statement Jesus is disavowing his questioners' shallow formalistic criteria of authority (vs. 15). He forces them to make a decision with regard to the intent that shows in his words and works. Can they, and dare they, brand them as evidence that he is seeking his own glory? Or must they acknowledge that all his words and works are designed to heighten the glory of him who (in Jesus) loves and seeks out the world and calls it to repentance and faith? Those are the questions in terms of which the people have to come to a decision with regard to his mission. Everything is at stake here. For if he is truly seeking the glory of the One who sent him, then he is true and trustworthy and "there is no unrighteousness in him"; in other words, then what applies to God (Ps. 92:15) applies to Jesus, and to accept his teaching is to "set his seal to this, that God is true" (Jn. 3:33).

19   To demonstrate the propriety of his action as a teacher and the error of his hearers' criticism, Jesus now refers back to his conflict with the Jews over the healing of the paralytic on the sabbath — a very clear example by which to illustrate and measure the difference between holding to formal authority (as the people do) and the material discernment (as Jesus requires) of what the teaching of God is. In this connection Jesus appeals to Moses himself. The question "Did not Moses give you the law?" indicates that the people did not lack insight into the true will and teaching of God and that Jesus asked them for nothing other than what Moses had already taught them. However, for all their supposed respect for and appeal to the authority of the law they were lacking in the *doing:* "but none of you keeps the law. Why else do you seek to kill me?"

20   With this statement, however, Jesus said something that the people

---

30. γινώσκειν περί, literally "gain knowledge of a thing," "form a judgment concerning."

not only rejected in utter astonishment but also with extreme indignation. They called him — who attributed to them such an intention — "possessed," a very strong expression that, even if it was not intended literally (as it is in Mk. 3:22), rejected Jesus' indictment of them as the greatest folly. Here we encounter a very different situation (as we have noted) from that of ch. 5. Whereas Jesus is obviously referring to what the leaders of the people, as he had come to know them in the conflict on the sabbath, had in mind to do against him (cf. 5:18), the people with whom he had to deal here were apparently still unaware of any wrong, either in themselves or in others ("Who is seeking to kill you?"). In vs. 25 the situation is different. There the people sought the intervention of the authorities. Some scholars have regarded that as additional proof of the disorder in which this part of the Gospel is supposed to be and an argument for transposing vss. 14-24 (see above). An interesting attempt to maintain vss. 14ff. in continuity with vss. 25ff. is the view that in the dialogue in vss. 14ff. the people were not aware that they were talking with Jesus and only gradually made that discovery.[31] However, support for this explanation is lacking in this pericope itself. Vs. 15 seems rather to indicate that they did know with whom they were dealing. In distinction from the speakers in vs. 25 ("some of the people of Jerusalem"), the large majority of the pilgrims did not know, however, how far things had gone between the authorities and Jesus. Accordingly, their indignation over Jesus' question "Why do you seek to kill me?" was undoubtedly not hypocritical or incomprehensible. That Jesus nevertheless made the accusation (vs. 19) again shows the degree to which he saw through the situation and how he assessed the — still unwary — crowd (cf. vs. 7). What they reject as an absurdity and proof of a demented mind, they would later, under the continuing and organized pressure of "the Jews," not only not prevent but even help to bring about.

21-22   Jesus offers no direct reply to their question. However, the following verses do serve as a further explanation of vs. 19a: their failure actually to keep the law of Moses that they regarded so highly! To that end Jesus reminds them of "the one deed" he performed and the general perplexity and offense it has caused among them. He speaks of "*one* deed," not to minimize it or to censure their narrow-mindedness with regard to just this "one instance" (of transgression) but rather to bring out clearly the basic and radical difference between him and them with regard to the law of Moses: "I need only do one deed, and all of you without exception turn against me!" This showed (vs. 22) how little they understood of the much-lauded law of Moses, and that none of them kept it; "for . . . ,"[32] and then follows the appeal to Moses' law on circumcision.

31. So, at length, Michaels, "Temple Discourse in John," §25, n. 6.
32. διὰ τοῦτο can also be taken with vs. 21, but would be more or less superfluous there. Hence as a rule it is taken with what follows in order to confirm the preceding line of thought.

In that connection Jesus states emphatically that *Moses* gave them circumcision; that is, he prescribed it as law (cf. Lv. 12:3), though he had not instituted it himself since it came from the patriarchs before Moses (cf. Gn. 17:10ff.; 21:4). This qualification is not only of "academic interest"[33] but accentuates the importance Moses attached to the ancient institution by incorporating it, unabbreviated and unconditionally, into his law. Accordingly, circumcision on the sabbath was entirely in keeping with *Moses'* law.

23 If then circumcision took place on the sabbath — precisely in order not to "undo"[34] the law of Moses — how could they, the Jews, then be angry with Jesus because he had healed "a whole man" on the sabbath? Of paramount importance in this pronouncement is the insertion "so that the law of Moses may not be broken." For Jesus the circumcision law did not mean that the sabbath law had to yield when the eighth day fell on a sabbath or, as it was stated in the oral Jewish tradition, that it had to be supplanted by circumcision.[35] It is characteristic for his approach rather that he nowhere mentions such a casuistic conflict of duties or precepts. For him circumcision on the sabbath is fulfillment of "the law of Moses" as such. Therefore Jesus does not ask the Jews to give him room (in accord with the analogy of circumcision) to consider himself free from his sabbath obligations. He reproaches them not for narrowness in their interpretation of the sabbath law but for not "keeping the law" (vs. 19), indeed with "breaking the law of Moses" (vs. 23), precisely on the point of the sabbath.[36]

This gains even more force in view of the reasoning Jesus employs, namely from the lesser to the greater *(a minori ad maius = qal wāḥômer)*,[37] contrasting, that is, (the healing of) the whole man with circumcision.[38] Undoubtedly the word "healing" contains an allusion to the so-called "humanitarian" purpose of the sabbath as that comes even more to the fore in the disputes over the sabbath in the Synoptics (cf. Mk. 2:27; Mt. 12:3 par.; see also Ex. 23:12; Dt. 5:14, 15). Although we have no evidence that circumcision was

---

Then, however, it relates to the whole line of reasoning that follows and not just to vs. 22. Therefore, it constitutes a somewhat elliptical transition, one that needs supplementation: "Therefore I say to you" or "Therefore you should rather first consider," or the like. For still other views of the connection see the extensive analyses of Pancaro, *Law in the Fourth Gospel,* pp. 163f.

33. So Bultmann, *Comm.,* p. 278, n. 3.

34. Fixed Jewish terminology for breaking or invalidating the Torah (cf., e.g., Mt. 5:17).

35. See, e.g., R. Meyer, *TDNT* VI, p. 82.

36. See also Pancaro, *Law in the Fourth Gospel,* pp. 161, 164.

37. On this see, e.g., Strack/Billerbeck III, pp. 223ff.

38. The same reasoning is followed by Rabbi Eleazar b. Azariah (ca. A.D. 100): "If circumcision, which affects only one of a man's members, supplants the sabbath, how much more saving a life supplants the sabbath" (cf. R. Meyer, *TDNT* VI, p. 82, n. 74). See also H. Seesemann, *TDNT* V, pp. 174ff.

viewed as a "healing" act,[39] it had to be clear to everyone that Jesus' act of healing the paralytic with comprehensive, life-renewing force represented a greater benefit than the merely partial operation of circumcision could ever yield. Accordingly, the conclusion could only be that if even circumcision in its limited importance had to take place on the sabbath in order not to invalidate the law of Moses, the healing of a whole man had to contribute much more to the fulfillment of this law. If the Jews were nevertheless angry at Jesus over this, that could only mean that, rather than he being a violator of the sabbath, *they* were opposing the law of Moses in its clear intent and robbing it of its force.

24   Jesus brings this to expression in a very general pronouncement in which the pericope reaches its summation and conclusion. He uses the verb "judge" twice and the noun "judgment" once in a short sentence: "Do not judge by appearances, but judge with righteous judgment."[40] He thus speaks not only to those who as judges or rulers of the people are called to judge but to all who, in their conversations, discussions, and criticisms, set themselves up as judges over him. The Evangelist clearly intends this as a general warning and exhortation, including for the people he had primarily in mind as he wrote his Gospel. Judgment by what is visible, by the appearance of things, is what largely governs the attitude of the people vis-à-vis Jesus. For "the Jews" this meant that Jesus could only be regarded as a teacher who set himself up as an authority, as a violator of the sabbath, as an "undoer" of the law of Moses. If they had delved deeper, they would be interested not just in a superficial conformity with the rules that had been handed down to them but in the will of God (vs. 17), in the law of Moses in its evident intent (vss. 19, 23); then they would pass "a righteous judgment." They would understand that he did not speak "on his own authority," that his teaching was of God. Jesus not only asserts his authority as the one sent by God. He also wants them to test his works by the will of God revealed by God himself, by the law of Moses in terms of its own import. Thus they would see that — by healing on the sabbath — he fulfilled the sabbath law of Moses in a manner to which the law indeed pointed but that the law itself could not effectuate. What was said earlier about the temple (cf. 2:18ff.) applies here to the sabbath and will soon also prove to be true of the feast (cf. vss. 37ff.), namely that the law for it was given by Moses but the grace and truth of it came only through Jesus Christ (1:17).

---

39. Cf. Seesemann, *TDNT* V, pp. 174f.

40. τὴν δικαίαν κρίσιν κρίνετε, cognate accusative. "John says τὴν δικαίαν κρίσιν; there are not several right judgments: only one is the right one" (Schlatter, *Comm.,* p. 196).

7:25-39

Jesus among the Pilgrims: "Whence" and "Whither"

This section bears a somewhat fragmentary character. It contains a number of sharply profiled pronouncements that Jesus made about himself during the Feast of Tabernacles in response to the growing hostility to him among both the people of Jerusalem and the authorities there (vss. 28ff., 37ff.). It is repeatedly clear that Jesus' public actions in no way fulfilled the messianic expectations current among the people (vss. 27, 35; see also vss. 41ff.), although others considered him trustworthy on account of his many miracles (vs. 31). In these differing, largely negative reactions interpreters have seen a reflection of later discussions about Jesus' identity between church and synagogue (see also the introduction to 7:1ff. above). But there is no real discussion here, nor anything resembling a defense against or refutation of the objections advanced against Jesus. What stands out, rather, is the sovereign manner in which Jesus asserts himself in the temple as the one sent by the Father (vs. 28), his warning to the Pharisees to change their minds before it is too late (vss. 34ff.), and the authority with which at the end of the feast he points to himself as the one in whom the Feast of Tabernacles will be fulfilled (vss. 37ff.). All this prompts Jesus' adversaries, who fear his influence among the people, to act against him with increasing hostility. But for the time being they are powerless, for "his hour had not yet come" (vss. 30, 32ff.).

Verses **25-27** still presuppose vs. 14 as the scene of action (cf. vs. 28) and thus form the direct continuation of vss. 15-24. In both pericopes Jesus' authoritative conduct in the temple is the subject. But whereas in vss. 15ff. his authority to teach is in dispute, in vs. 25 it is the unconcealed nature[41] of his conduct itself that arouses astonishment and offense among "some of the people of Jerusalem." That the latter are mentioned separately, after "the people" in vs. 20, is not strange (see above). While these people — undoubtedly largely people attending the feast from outside the city — apparently relate to Jesus less suspiciously, among the inhabitants of Jerusalem were people who appear to have been privy to what was going on in relation to Jesus and for whom, therefore, this entire manifestation of Jesus in the temple (and doubtlessly specifically the manner in which he asserted his authority there vis-à-vis the people in power) was totally inexplicable. Their question ("Is not this the man whom they seek to kill? . . . Certainly the authorities do not really think that this is the Christ?") brings to expression, if not real doubt whether the rulers had changed their minds about Jesus, then certainly some impatience that as

---

41. παρρησίᾳ, "openly," "not hiding anything" (as in vs. 4). See W. C. van Unnik, *The Christian Freedom of Speech in the New Testament,* 1962, p. 483.

members of the Sanhedrin and hence as the proper authorities they had not intervened.[42]

The people speaking in these verses did not shrink from mentioning specifically the issue about which all Jerusalem was talking under its breath (cf. vss. 12, 13): namely, who Jesus could be and whether he was perhaps the Christ (cf. vss. 31ff., 41ff.). And they spoke all the more boldly because, whatever others might think, they themselves had no problem with Jesus' identity. They repeatedly call Jesus "this man" — with obvious disdain. People should not expect them, the inhabitants of Jerusalem, to view him as the Messiah promised to Israel. After all, everybody (vs. 27) knew much too well "where he came from" (cf. vs. 41; 6:42). But when the Messiah came, things would be very different. No one would know where he came from; his origins would be shrouded in mystery. They are referring to the expectation that the Messiah would appear on the scene all at once (cf. Mt. 24:26; Lk. 17:23) so that no one would be able to tell what his background and origins were.[43]

28, 29 Here again (cf. 6:43, 61, etc.), although people do not speak to him directly, Jesus intervenes — most emphatically. To describe Jesus' action the Evangelist uses a word translated "cry out" that appears also in vs. 37 and 12:44 and refers to proclamatory, prophetic speech (cf. 1:15; Ro. 9:27). The addition "as he taught in the temple" adds all the more weight. In his reply Jesus first repeats their own words and in a sense endorses them, giving them a peculiar, somewhat tendentious, emphasis:[44] "Yes, you could say that you know me and also know where I come from." Jesus' appearance is not a miraculous phenomenon. People could trace his origins and knew his hometown (cf. 6:42). In that regard his appearance did not meet the specifications of their messianic theology. Still,[45] this kind of knowing does not cover everything. Even as they knew him, he had not come of his own accord. His "coming," that is, his public appearance with authority,[46] derived its authenticity and trustworthiness from the fact that "he who sent me is true." *Him,* however, they do not know and therefore all they know, or think they know, about Jesus is not real knowledge of him.

---

42. Literally, "and they say nothing to him" (cf. Mt. 22:3). The verbal clause means "raise objections against someone," "let him go his own way," a conventional Jewish way of speaking (see Schlatter, *Comm.,* in loc.).

43. See, e.g., Strack/Billerbeck II, pp. 488ff. At issue here is not the Messiah's Davidic descent or his birth at Bethlehem (cf. vs. 42). "Underlying the words of Jn. 7:27 is, rather, the idea that before his public emergence the Messiah will dwell unrecognized in secrecy so that beforehand no one could know who had been called to the messianic office and where the person concerned would suddenly appear" (p. 489).

44. Note καὶ . . . καί. Others take vs. 28a as a question (cf. de Jonge, *Jesus: Stranger from Heaven and Son of God,* p. 55).

45. The καί before ἀπ' ἐμαυτοῦ in vs. 28 is adversative.

46. For this expression in its different variations, see also Bultmann, *Comm.,* p. 298, n. 1; p. 50, n. 3.

What is at stake here is not just an issue of doctrine or law or tradition within one and the same theological horizon. It is, rather, nothing less than the knowledge of God himself, namely as God really is. One can hardly speak of a dispute here, nor of a defense or apologia from the side of Jesus. Over against their not knowing God, Jesus sets himself (vs. 29) as the one who knows God. For "I come from him, and he sent me." Nevertheless, such an appeal to God is something other than the mere assertion of God's authority behind his words and deeds, an authority of which his hearers, as noninitiates, had no knowledge, for which reason they did not (and could not) know God's purpose in the sending of Jesus. For in sending his Son God was in fact revealing himself to them and making himself known as he really was. Therefore Jesus' verdict ("him you do not know") is not just an observation that closes every prospect of further dialogue but a final and all-decisive call to them to come to the true knowledge of that God whose people they claimed to be and whom they claimed to know. It is thus a call to believe in God — but in the sense of opening themselves up to the gracious disposition that prompted God to send his Son into the world, revealing himself as he truly is.

30   Those whom Jesus thus addressed saw what he said as grounds for getting rid of him: "So they sought to arrest him." This absoluteness of his claims was what made his conduct in the temple intolerable and made their decision to kill him as a blasphemer (cf. 5:18) irrevocable. But still it is clearly not human beings who determine his lot. For despite all their scheming they are kept from striking out at him. For all sorts of reasons not mentioned here (cf. vss. 45ff.) they could not act. But the real reason they could not was that the divinely appointed "hour," the hour of Jesus' suffering and death, had not yet come. His lot did not lie in human hands but was determined by the progress of God's counsel.

Verses **31-32** provide further information on what is described in general in vs. 30. It was not only Jesus' conduct as such but also and especially its impact on many of the people that made the authorities look for means to get rid of him. "Many of the people came to faith in him," a faith that bore an immediate relationship to Jesus' messiahship. These people ask whether the Christ at his appearance would do more signs than Jesus had done, obviously meaning that Jesus' many miracles were reason enough for them to believe in him as the Messiah. The Fourth Gospel itself does not report many miracles, but this and other references to his "many miracles" (2:23; 3:1; 4:45) are indications that the Evangelist assumes that his readers know more about Jesus' words and works than he tells of. But the statement of the people here is remarkable because Jewish messianic expectation did not especially attribute performance of miracles to the Messiah.[47] Some scholars therefore think that

47. See, e.g., Martyn, *History and Theology,* pp. 95ff.

we are dealing here not with a Jewish but with a Christian proof of Jesus'
messiahship[48] and therefore that the Evangelist has in mind a later situation,
one in which Jewish sympathizers with the Christian church are speaking.[49]
However, not only here but throughout the New Testament Jesus' miracles play
an important role in the conflict over Jesus' credibility as the divinely sent
Messiah, specifically in relation to Jews and not only as an element in Christian
argumentation (20:31; cf. Mt. 11:2-6 [cf. vs. 1]; 12:38; cf. also Mk. 3:22; 2 Th.
2:9) but also in regard to signs demanded over and over by the Jews themselves
(cf. 6:30; 7:3; Mt. 12:28; Mk. 8:11; 1 Co. 1:22). The idea that what was
ultimately at stake was not Jesus' messiahship but whether he was "the prophet"
(from whom the Jews did expect miracles) is hard to maintain in view of 6:30
(cf. vs. 27, "the Son of man") and 1 Co. 1:22.

In any case Jesus' miracles were of such a nature that they had to arouse
in many people the hope of the time of salvation promised by God and the
great reversal that was a part of it. That hope, that pro-Jesus movement among
the people, was what, along with his blasphemous claims, most occupied the
rulers. The Pharisees were prominent in that resistance right from the beginning
(cf. 4:1) and will be mentioned frequently as such in what follows (vss. 45, 48;
8:3, 13; 9:13ff., 40, etc.). They are also the first and best informed of the covert
but perceptible whispering ("muttering") among the people about Jesus as
Messiah, and those who will persuade the proper authorities — the Sanhedrin,
of which together with the chief priests they are members[50] — to order the
officers[51] to arrest Jesus. The intention to do this, long entertained (cf. vs. 30;
5:18), was now at last to be carried out.

33 The words of Jesus that now follow are clearly intended not as a
reaction to vs. 31 but to vs. 32. Jesus is aware of what is happening around
him, and his time is therefore short. He gives expression to his awareness in a
fashion that again brings into the open the difference in understanding between
him and the Jews. This time it is not his origin (vss. 27ff.) but his future (vss.
35f.) that is in discussion. The crucial point is that Jesus not only speaks of the

48. So, e.g., Schnackenburg, *Comm.* II, pp. 148f.

49. Cf. de Jonge, *Jesus: Stranger from Heaven and Son of God,* p. 92.

50. The Pharisees belonged to the Sanhedrin not as a party but as members of a class of
men who know Scripture. That the Evangelist mentions them as leaders of the people par excellence
is perhaps explained in part by the fact that after the destruction of Jerusalem they increasingly
gained control of the spiritual leadership. Still, in the whole tradition concerning the life of Jesus
they play a dominant role.

51. Some scholars regard the "officers" not as the law-enforcing employees of the Sanhedrin in the time of Jesus (which would include the temple police) but as the court's officers in
the time of the Evangelist, that is, after the destruction of Jerusalem (cf. Martyn, *History and
Theology,* pp. 73ff.). It is this (supposedly inevitable) gradual transposition of the history of Jesus
to that of the later church that makes this entire hypothesis of the Fourth Gospel as a "two-level
drama" most dubious in its implementation.

short time ("a little longer") he will still be with them but also announces his going "to him who sent me," an expression the Evangelist will use from now on with regularity (8:13, 21, 22; 13:3, 33, 36; chs. 14 and 15 passim). What Jesus means by this expression is clear in the light of what he has just said about his origin, but for those who had their own self-assured knowledge (cf. vs. 27) it had to be totally puzzling.

34 This is all the more true because Jesus also predicts that this "going away" will deprive them of every possibility of ever finding him if they should look for him. For where he will be they cannot come. Jesus is of course speaking here of going to the Father, "where he was before" (6:62). He does not thereby bypass the suffering and death that await him since that is *how* he will go from this world to the Father (13:1). This language of departure is highly characteristic of the Gospel of John, in which Jesus, far from being a passive object in his suffering and death, is active. From this perspective one can also begin to understand what is meant by "and you will seek me." At first sight one might think that Jesus is here speaking of becoming unfindable and therefore invulnerable to the attacks they now undertake against him (cf. vss. 11, 30). But the idea that they would "seek" him in that hostile sense after he had gone to the Father is not very natural (see, however, Ac. 9:4, 5). The idea is rather that he would be inaccessible to them when, to escape the judgment awaiting them, they would seek his help (cf. 3:36; 8:21; Pr. 1:27, 28). The idea that this refers to a concrete event such as the destruction of Jerusalem is hard to prove, and no such event is referred to in the text. It is more likely that we are dealing with a general description of Jesus' inaccessibility as it is later predicted also to Jesus' disciples. But whereas for the disciples this inaccessibility would only imply a temporary separation (14:1ff.; 16:16ff.), for "the Jews" it meant it would become too late to retrace their steps.

35-36 Again, as in, for example, 6:41, 52, the Jews do not respond to Jesus directly but discuss among themselves what he could have meant by this — to their minds — enigmatic pronouncement. Again they go merely by the sound of his words and entertain various possible solutions that appear absurd even to themselves, thus miring themselves in questions (vs. 36). The "diaspora of the Greeks" probably refers here to the Greek-speaking Jews in the dispersion who are, under this assumption, called "the Greeks" here (cf. 12:20; Ac. 11:20).[52] It is often thought that, without realizing it, the Jews are thus prophesying future Christian missions among the Gentiles. What seemed to them an

---

52. The meaning is uncertain; cf. K. L. Schmidt, *TDNT* II, pp. 101f. Schlatter (*Comm.,* p. 198) thinks the reference is to the non-Jews among whom diaspora Jews lived. But, according to vs. 35b, that would mean that in the diaspora Jesus addressed himself especially to non-Jews. But then why is the diaspora mentioned here?

absurdity would prove to contain a grand truth. But in my opinion the reference here is just to diaspora Jews as a possible place of escape for Jesus. What the Evangelist wants to demonstrate is how utterly irreconcilable Jesus' self-revelation as the Christ is with everything the Jews in Jesus' day (and that of his own) could conceive or were inclined to accept.

In vss. **37** and **38** Jesus' activity on the Feast of Tabernacles reaches its high point. The "last day of the feast, the great day" is probably the seventh day, on which the celebration came to a climax. Elsewhere (see the comments on vs. 2) there is also mention of an eighth day, but that was apparently more a closing day, certainly not "the great day." Jesus' activity here is clearly bound up with what was done as part of the feast. What gave Tabernacles its special character, aside from living in booths during the celebration of this ancient and joyful harvest festival, was the daily procession to Siloam, where water was dipped to be brought to the temple to the accompaniment of music and the recitation of texts like Is. 12:3. After the procession around the altar (repeated six times on the seventh day of the feast), the water was poured out on the altar of burnt offering in the temple. The libation of water played a particularly great role in the people's imagination. It symbolized not only, as a harvest ritual, the hope and prayer for rain and fruitfulness (cf., e.g., Zc. 14:16, 17), but also, in connection with this, the eschatological hope of wells of salvation overflowing with abundance.[53]

It is against this background that Jesus, at the high point of the feast, stood up (no doubt in the temple)[54] and raised his voice (see the comments on vs. 28) and thus with great emphasis and authority offered himself to everyone who was thirsty. Although the water of the feast was poured out on the altar and not drunk and there is no mention here in John of pouring out water, it is generally assumed that Jesus' invitation to come and drink was prompted by the water ceremonies of the feast. Living, that is, running, water was the image of refreshment and revitalization, and this was symbolized by the pouring out of water during Tabernacles. Hence by inviting the thirsty to himself Jesus clearly indicated that what was sought and celebrated during the feast found its fulfillment in him. He was not only the temple (2:20ff.) but also the feast, the dispenser of refreshing and life-giving water as the great eschatological gift of God.

While this is the generally recognized meaning of Jesus' messianic pronouncement, there is great divergence of opinion whether vs. 38a ("He who believes in me") should be taken with what precedes or with what follows. If

---

53. On the Feast of Tabernacles, see, at length, e.g., Strack/Billerbeck II, pp. 774ff.; J. Jeremias, *TDNT* IV, pp. 277f.

54. "Jesus εἱστήκει in the bustle and surge of the temple procession. Jn 7:37" (W. Grundmann, *TDNT* VII, p. 647).

it is taken with what follows (so NRSV), then it is the last member of a chiastic invitation:

> If anyone thirst,
>> let him come to me,
>> and let him drink,
> who believes in me.

The rest of vs. 38 is in that case a pronouncement of Scripture in which such power to dispense living water is symbolically attributed to Jesus.

But some (e.g., RSV, NIV) put a period at the end of vs. 37 and thus take the first clause of vs. 38 ("he who believes in me") as a pendent subject with the rest of the verse:[55] "If any one thirst, let him come to me and drink. He who believes in me — as the Scripture says — out of his belly will flow streams of living water." In that case, not Jesus but the believer is the one Scripture is said to speak of.[56]

This second view, in my opinion, certainly deserves preference. In the first place, the parallelism on which the first view is based is not very obvious. The supposed use of chiasm would be unique in John,[57] and "he who thirsts" is not synonymous with "he who believes in me," which is, rather, paralleled by "come to me." The point here is clearly a call to faith, not an invitation to people who already believe. We therefore get a much better construction — structurally as well as materially — when "the one who believes in me" is taken as the beginning of a new sentence, as often in John, and not the unemphasized conclusion (most unusual!) of a sentence. Thus in a new opening vs. 38 advances the thought of vs. 37 by articulating the salvific result of the invitation it has given with reference to Scripture. Vs. 38 refers, then, to one person: "the one who believes . . . out of that person's belly." The Scripture quotation does not refer, as proponents of the first interpretation generally assume,[58] to Jesus, a construction that not only yields an unexplained change of person but a much more difficult idea.

---

55. The so-called *casus pendens,* which occurs repeatedly in the Fourth Gospel.

56. A third solution is to take "the one who believes in me" separately as the Evangelist's interpretation or "pesher" of what precedes. These words are said to have been derived from the interpretation in vs. 39 and placed as a clarifying gloss after the invitation in vs. 38. So J. Blenkinsopp: "John VII, 37-9: Another Note on a Notorious Crux," *NTS* 6 (1959-60), pp. 97f. This removes the difficulty of the *casus pendens* and the unconvincing parallelism disappears. Who is meant by αὐτοῦ in vs. 38b remains in this view an open question. On this understanding of "he who believes in me" see also K. H. Kuhn's reference to a Sahidic citation in "St. John VII, 37-8," *NTS* 4 (1957-58), p. 64. But in my opinion there is no objection to taking vs. 38 as a unit, so that then this rather implausible hypothesis, which, as Kuhn grants, has very little textual support, becomes superfluous as a "solution."

57. So Schnackenburg, *Comm.* II, p. 154, though he himself opts for the first view.

58. So ibid.: "surely Jesus."

Admittedly, the view we are endorsing "would produce the grotesque picture of streams of water flowing out of the body of the man who is drinking to quench his thirst."[59] But if we proceed from this degree of literalness, the idea that those invited to drink should have to drink from Jesus' body is no less strange. The idea that there is an allusion here to 19:34[60] is intrinsically most unlikely and cannot, at any rate, illumine the image. For the idea of drinking is entirely alien to what is said there of Jesus' "side." Strange speculations about Jesus' "belly" are superfluous if one explains vs. 38 on the analogy of the closely related pronouncement in 4:14, where it is said of the water that Jesus will give that the one who drinks of it will never thirst again because it "will become *in that person* a spring of water welling up to eternal life." In both cases the reference is to the Spirit as a forceful and never failing source of gifts in those who believe in Jesus.[61] "From his belly" in vs. 38 then has the same meaning as "in him" in 4:14, just as in Old Testament usage "belly" can refer to the inner person, as the equivalent of one's "heart."[62] Whether "*from* his belly" refers to the effect of spiritual gifts on others seems doubtful; in any case, "from" does not cancel out the correspondence with 4:14.[63]

What Scripture passage is meant here is hard to say within either interpretation. Nowhere can we pinpoint a text that bears any resemblance to the words quoted here.[64] Nonetheless, the words "from his belly" make it much more difficult to find support in Scripture for the first view than for the second. For wherever the Old Testament mentions "streams of salvation" that in the new age will issue from the temple or from Jerusalem, any idea that these would flow from God or the Messiah is lacking. On the other hand, where the gift of the Spirit is referred to under the image of water, the reference is to the refreshment and renewal of "the inner person" and is described, aside from Jn. 4:14, as a flowing fountain in the person (cf. Is. 58:11; Pr. 18:4). All this does not alter the fact that, just as in 4:14, Christ is the giver of the spring of living water. As such, and as bringer of salvation, he also invites everyone who thirsts to come to him (cf. Pr. 9:4; Mt. 11:28; Is. 55:1, etc.).

39 The Evangelist then proceeds to explain this as having been said with an eye to the Spirit. This makes it all the more plain that Jesus concentrates

---

59. Bultmann, *Comm.*, p. 303, n. 2. But see the reply of Blenkinsopp, "John VII, 37-9: Another Note."

60. Bultmann is cautious: "could"; Schnackenburg is more positive: "probable" (p. 154); so Brown also at least in his theological explication (*Comm.* I, p. 328).

61. Cf., e.g., Calvin, *Comm.* I, p. 198: "The meaning is that the Holy Spirit is like a living and ever-flowing fountain in believers."

62. Cf. J. Behm, *TDNT* III, pp. 786ff., and his explanation of Jn. 7:38 (pp. 788f.).

63. As Schnackenburg thinks (*Comm.* II, p. 154).

64. Calvin, *Comm.* I, pp. 198-99: "Christ is not pointing to any particular passage of Scripture, but takes a testimony from the common teaching of the prophets."

all the attention given the Feast of Tabernacles on himself. The entire ceremony of pouring out of water was taken as a picture of the grand future in which the people of God would share in abundant measure in the Spirit of God, and that future age was repeatedly represented under the image of water (cf. Is. 43:20; 44:3; Ezk. 47:1ff.; Jl. 3:18). Therefore, while in 2:19ff.; 4:23; 7:23; 1:17 Jesus acts as the one in whom the Old Testament cult finds its end and fulfillment, the Evangelist nevertheless makes a clear distinction between the time of Jesus and that of the Spirit. For that reason what Jesus promises here to those who believe in him cannot be immediately realized. "For as yet the Spirit had not been given."

In the transmission of the text these remarkable words have been supplemented in all kinds of ways. But even without the supplements the intent is clear enough. In the nature of the case the Spirit was already in existence. But the profuse outpouring of the Spirit's gifts still waited until Jesus was "glorified," that is, until he had gone to the Father. The statement here in vs. 38 anticipates, therefore, that which will be treated at length in the farewell discourses (cf. 14:26; 16:7), where we read of the Paraclete, "the Holy Spirit, whom the Father will send in my name," who will not come unless Jesus goes away; but "if I go, I will send him."

This does not mean, of course, that Jesus will give way, basically and definitively, to the Spirit. For as is evident also from vs. 38, Jesus himself is the giver and sender of the Spirit (cf. 1:33; 4:17). Admittedly there is a direct connection between Jesus' glorification and the sending of the Spirit. For not until Jesus is glorified can the Spirit draw the abundance mentioned here ("streams of living water") from the fullness of Jesus' finished work (cf. 16:13ff.). Not until then, when the Spirit will teach and proclaim it to them in the light of Jesus' glorification, will the disciples understand what at this point they cannot bear. But that is not to say that true faith, the birth "from above" (3:2), could not be a reality before the coming of the Spirit, for it is precisely to those who already at this feast come to Jesus and believe in him that the Spirit is promised. True faith, knowing oneself bound to the person of Jesus "for better or worse," as that comes to expression, for example, in 6:68, dates not just from the day of Jesus' resurrection,[65] however much before that day it was exposed to great attacks ("the sifting of Satan"; cf. 16:20; Lk. 22:31, 32). Attacks will continue later as well (2 Co 12:7, 8). The abundance of the gifts of the Spirit, referred to here, therefore does not mean that the believer will be transferred from a struggling faith to a purely triumphant faith but that the

65. True, John repeatedly mentions faith that proves to be ungenuine (cf. 2:23; 8:30f.), and in 14:10 Philip is accusingly asked, "Do you not believe. . . ?" But that is not to say that where faith and confession are mentioned before the cross and the resurrection, as, e.g., in 2:11; 4:53, it is not true faith and that the true confession of Jesus as the Christ could not begin yet (as thought by, e.g., E. Haenchen, *Gott und Mensch*, 1965, p. 73).

believer will become a participant, by the Spirit, in the glorification of Christ, that the believer will drink from a spring whose fullness for everyone who believes will never be exhausted.[66]

7:40-52

Division among the Jews, Nicodemus's Judgment

In what follows Jesus does not speak until 8:12, and then again with a proclamatory pronouncement. 7:40-52 describes the confusion and conflict occasioned by Jesus, ending in a "schism" (vs. 43) among the people and a fierce exchange of words in the Sanhedrin. Evidently the intent is to show that, despite all the hostility and contradiction of the Jewish authorities, Jesus' influence on the people was unstoppable, arousing strong messianic feelings. The members of the Sanhedrin, in response, took an increasingly stronger position against him, though without much success and in violation of their own law. And this passage also shows that, despite their groping for Jesus' true identity, the people do not really come to a clear decision. They try to fit him into their traditional messianic notions and fail.

40-44   Vs. 40 ties in with the preceding words of Jesus. His powerfully proclaimed messianic utterance prompts some people (other manuscripts have "many") to recognize him ("really," ἀληθῶς) as "the prophet" (see comments on 1:21; 6:14). Some expositors believe that it was specifically Jesus' utterance about "living water" that led people to identify him as "the prophet" (like Moses) in Deuteronomy 18, because this "second redeemer" was expected to do the same miracles as Moses (the "first redeemer"), namely the miraculous provision of water and bread. Others among the people (vs. 41a) are said to have gone a step further, concluding that this Mosaic prophet was the Messiah

---

66. Cf. Calvin, *Comm.* I, p. 199:

For the Spirit was not yet. The Spirit is eternal, as we know. But the Evangelist is saying that, so long as Christ dwelt in the world in the lowly form of a Servant, that grace of the Spirit which was poured out on men after the resurrection of Christ, had not come forth openly. And indeed he is speaking comparatively, as when the New Testament is compared to the Old. God promises His Spirit to believers as if He had never given Him to the Fathers. At that time the disciples had undoubtedly already received the firstfruits of the Spirit. For where does faith come from if not from the Spirit? The Evangelist then does not simply deny that the grace of the Spirit was revealed to believers before the death of Christ, but that it was not yet so bright and clear as it would be afterwards. For the chief glory of Christ's Kingdom is that he governs the Church by His Spirit. But He entered into the lawful and, as it were, ceremonial possession of His Kingdom when He was exalted to the right hand of the Father. So there is nothing surprising in His delaying the full manifestation of the Spirit until then.

himself. A third group (vss. 41c-42) are said to have argued against this entire identification that Jesus could not possibly be the Messiah since the Messiah would be of Davidic origin and would come from Bethlehem. Some have regarded this whole discussion as representing a phase in the disputes about the person of Jesus in the "Johannine community."[67]

It is doubtful, however, whether such a reconstruction of later disputes can be rightly inferred from the words of this text. That those who call Jesus "the prophet" do so on the basis of Jesus' miraculous power to produce "living water" does not agree with what the text says about the impression that Jesus' "words" made on his hearers. Nor does vs. 40 mention a miracle, unlike the reaction to the bread miracle in ch. 6. Nor is it by any means clear that those who say "This is the Christ" are merely injecting a nuance into the words of the first group, referring to the Mosaic prophet-messiah. It seems, rather, that, as in 1:20, 21, a clear distinction is being made between "the prophet" and "the Christ." All the Evangelist has in mind with this reproduction of internal discussions is to point out the confusion and division among Jesus' hearers, despite the impression he obviously made on them. They could not arrive at a correct insight into Jesus' identity because they reasoned from within their traditional conceptions (whatever they were), which, because of his origin, future, and relationship to God, Jesus did not fit.

It is remarkable, however, that neither the Evangelist nor Jesus himself responds to the appeal to Scripture advanced by some against his messiahship, namely to the Messiah's origin from "the seed of David" and Bethlehem, "the village where David was" (vs. 42). Many interpreters regard this as a typical example of Johannine irony: in their ignorance the Jews confirm precisely what they seek to oppose.[68] Others believe, however, that this shows that the Evangelist knew nothing of Jesus' birth in Bethlehem.[69]

But it is most unlikely that the Evangelist was completely ignorant of the Christian traditions concerning Jesus' birth in Bethlehem and his Davidic origin in view of the important role assigned from the beginning to the Davidic origin (Ro. 1:3; Rv. 22:16; Mt. 1:1, etc.) and the abundance of Scripture pointing to that tradition (2 Sa. 7:12ff.; Is. 11:1; Ps. 84:4f., etc.). Admittedly, the expected birth of the Messiah in Bethlehem (Mi. 5:1) apparently played no role in Jewish writings.[70] Nevertheless, not only here but also in Mt. 2:5 such an expectation

67. So, e.g., Martyn, *History and Theology,* p. 114.

68. So, e.g., Morris, *Comm.,* p. 429.

69. So Bultmann, *Comm.,* p. 306, n. 6: "The Jews, of course, are as little mistaken in this as they were in 6.42; 7.27. That is to say, the Evangelist knows nothing, or wants to know nothing, of the birth in Bethlehem."

70. See Strack/Billerbeck I, pp. 82f.; cf. also J. C. de Moor, " 'Van wie zegt de Profeet dit?' Messiaanse apologetiek in de Targumim," in *De Knechtsgestalte van Christus* (Festschrift H. N. Ridderbos), 1978, p. 103.

is assumed to be present among the people and specifically among the scribes; and conversely, the offense people took at Jesus' supposed Galilean origin comes up more than once in the Fourth Gospel (1:46; 7:27, 41, 52). The fact that the Evangelist never reacts to this recurrent complaint seems, therefore, to have a deeper reason than that he had no better information about Jesus' earthly origins. To refer in every instance to irony seems forced. The explanation for this silence is rather that what was of decisive importance for the Evangelist was not Jesus' earthly descent from the family of David and his origin in Bethlehem but his heavenly origin and mission. That is, in fact, the "answer" that the Gospel gives when the Galilean origin of Jesus is brought up. Hence "Come and see!" "Convince yourself!" in 1:46. Hence Jesus' persistent refusal in dialogue with the Jews to discuss his earthly origin (cf. 6:42ff.; 7:28f.). What is decisive for the "who" and "whence" of Jesus is not what can be established genealogically and geographically but only whether what he said and did was of God (cf. 6:44f.; 7:28, 29).[71] For that reason the Evangelist confines himself to the observation that there was "a schism" on this point among the people over Jesus[72] (cf. Lk. 12:49f.).

Meanwhile (vs. 44) attempts to arrest him are continued by those whose choice against Jesus has become fixed. This statement runs like a dark thread through these chapters (cf. 7:1, 13, 30, 32, 45) and is accompanied, as here, by an equally recurrent statement that no one laid hands on him (cf. 8:59; 10:39).

45, 46 In vss. 45ff. this last point is given a telling explanation that brings us into the circles of the Sanhedrin. The occasion is the report of the officers (cf. vs. 32) sent out to arrest Jesus. Asked why they came back empty-handed, these men say that the power of Jesus' words was too strong for them to arrest him: "No one ever spoke like this man!" Some expositors see proof,

---

71. De Jonge, in his chapter on "Jewish Expectations about the 'Messiah' according to the Fourth Gospel" (*Jesus: Stranger from Heaven and Son of God,* pp. 77-116), concludes that Jesus' Davidic origin and the question of his place of birth are not really important to the Evangelist and therefore that the Evangelist is critical of the way that these matters are dealt with in the nativity stories in Matthew and Luke (pp. 93f.). This conclusion is questionable. John sometimes places much emphasis on the literal fulfillment of prophecy in Jesus' coming and work (e.g., 19:36, 37), and Jesus' appeal to Moses is of great importance to John — and de Jonge admits this. Furthermore, Jesus is also for John the King of Israel (cf. 1:49; 12:13, 15), even if in that connection Jesus' Davidic descent is not expressly mentioned (though it is certainly implied). De Jonge rightly posits: "And yet, if Scripture is not read and interpreted with the center of Johannine theology as starting point, one will never discover the truth revealed by God." But, one has to ask, does the starting point of the nativity stories of Matthew and Luke not also lie in Jesus' heavenly origin (cf. Mt. 1:20; Lk. 1:31ff.; 2:9ff.; 3:23) and not just in the literal fulfillment of the prophecy concerning David and Bethlehem? Undoubtedly the approaches of the three Evangelists differ. But is the approach that can be considered characteristic for John *materially* and actually critical of those of Matthew and Luke? See also P. Pokorny, "Der irdische Jesus im Johannesevangelium," *NTS* 30 (1984), pp. 223ff.

72. δι' αὐτόν, "on account of him."

here again in this answer, that the Evangelist wanted to present Jesus as "the prophet" whose authority even impressed the court's officers.[73] But the problem between the members of the Sanhedrin and their employees was obviously something more than the identification of Jesus as "the prophet." What prevented the officers from arresting Jesus was not some "theological" identification of the person of Jesus but their own consciousness that they were faced with a power greater than what could be attributed to a mere human being, a power for which, as ordinary people, they had no words, but which made it impossible for them to carry out the instructions they had been given.

47-49 Having said this, the officers thus defined exactly what the opposition and hostility of the Jewish leaders were directed against: the impression of unassailability Jesus made on people. The Pharisees among the members of the Sanhedrin react to the officers' statement with anger and contempt: "Have you also [already] been led astray [by him]?" Certainly, as persons directly involved in the enforcement of the will of the highest authority, something different might have been expected of them.[74] The Pharisees use the word "deceived," a loaded expression that some expositors take even here as a technical juridical term that accuses Jesus of "tempting someone into idolatry or blasphemy" (cf. Dt. 13:6), which carried the death penalty.[75] But in this context the emphasis is on the despicable nature of letting oneself be "led astray."

After all (vs. 48), "Have any of the authorities or the Pharisees believed in him?" Instead of taking such people as their models, the officers had lowered themselves to the level of "the crowd who do not know the law," for whom the members of the Sanhedrin had no better word than "accursed" (vs. 49). "This crowd which does not know the law" is generally taken as equivalent to a phrase familiar from Jewish literature, ʿam ha-ʾāreṣ ("people of the land"), which in the course of time had varying implications but functions here, as in the usage of the day, as a pejorative term for those who cared little or nothing about the prescriptions of the scribes, especially of the Pharisees.[76] Some scholars think that because study of the law also brought with it a certain level of educational attainment, this expression also served to denote the lower social class of this "crowd." But even if this is the case, that element does not play a role here. The Pharisees' contempt responds not to Jesus associating with what they regarded as "a lower class of people" but to the lack of knowledge of the law and of respect for lawful authority that made these people an easy prey for all sorts of popular leaders, who (mis)led

---

73. Cf. G. Reim, *Studien zum alttestamentlichen Hintergrund des Johannesevangeliums,* 1974, p. 123.

74. That the question begins with μή gives expression to this feeling of enraged frustration.

75. See Martyn, *History and Theology,* pp. 73-81, 158-60.

76. E.g., R. Meyer, *TDNT* V, pp. 588ff.; Strack/Billerbeck II, pp. 494f.; at length also Pancaro, *Law in the Fourth Gospel,* pp. 101-5.

them out of the true service of God represented by the Jewish leaders. For that reason "this crowd" was in their eyes "accursed," estranged and excluded from the privileges of the people of God — a statement that in its intensity again shows how far the hostility of the Jewish leaders against Jesus and against his influence on the people had progressed.

50, 51 It is at this low point in the relations between "the Jews" and Jesus that the Evangelist suddenly again brings Nicodemus on the scene. As he does so, he recalls Nicodemus's earlier visit with Jesus (3:1ff.) and describes him as "one of them," that is, as a Pharisee. That a permanently negative judgment on Nicodemus is thus implied[77] is still to be considered (see below). In any case, at this moment Nicodemus clearly takes up the cudgels for Jesus with an appeal to the law itself, on the knowledge of which the Pharisees so much prided themselves over against "the crowd who do not know the law." Nicodemus thus argued his case on the basis of what bound him together with his fellow members of the Sanhedrin, namely "our law," and not as a confessor of Jesus or defender of Jesus' teaching. What he asks is that justice be done to Jesus in accordance with the law, which was valid for all and which allowed no one to be condemned unheard and without a careful examination (cf. Dt. 1:16; 17:4; 19:18).[78] That Nicodemus could have said the same for a thief or a murderer,[79] though true of course, is not relevant to the Evangelist's purpose. Rather, in the way the Evangelist brings in Nicodemus and lets him speak he shows that the man had all the more right to speak that way because by his visit with Jesus he had observed the rule that one must hear before judging. Perhaps Nicodemus thinks that if those he addresses had taken the trouble to listen first they would now be judging Jesus differently.[80] But that is not in the text and says more than the Evangelist apparently intended here. Nevertheless, it can hardly be accidental that it is Nicodemus, apparently as the only person to do so, who here exposes the hypocrisy of the Sanhedrin, especially in view of the way in which he reappears later (19:39).

77. Cf. de Jonge (*Jesus: Stranger from Heaven and Son of God*, p. 36): "one of them" "refers the reader to chapter 3, and there is no indication of a development in Nicodemus' attitude since this rather unsatisfactory discussion with Jesus. Nicodemus is, and obviously remains, εἰς . . . ἐξ αὐτῶν (vs. 50)." See also Barrett: "Possibly John means, that for all his good will and fairmindedness Nicodemus remains one of the Jews, not one of the disciples" (*Comm.*, p. 332).

78. The law is personified here in the Jewish manner; Schlatter, *Comm.*, p. 205: "It does not judge a man without first hearing him (παρ' αὐτοῦ, apparently out of his own mouth) and learning what he does."

79. So Calvin, *Comm.* I, p. 204.

80. Pancaro (*Law in the Fourth Gospel*, pp. 143-57) goes much further: Nicodemus, in saying ἀκούσῃ πρῶτον παρ' αὐτοῦ καὶ γνῷ τί ποιεῖ refers to hearing Jesus *in faith* and taking *believing* notice of his miracles as that which the law requires. But that, it seems to me, is hard to prove. Nicodemus appealed to "our law" as the members of the Sanhedrin should apply it, regardless of who they thought Jesus was.

52   The rulers' answer shows profound annoyance. Instead of responding to Nicodemus's irrefutable objection, they brusquely put him down. Again "Galilee" is the reason for their unbelief. "Certainly you, Nicodemus, did not yourself come from there, did you?"[81] No one mentions Jesus. But the intent of their sarcastic remarks is clear enough. If Nicodemus should identify himself with those who had their origins in Galilee (Jesus and the numerous *'am ha-'āreṣ* of Galilee), he would do well to make sure first of what the Scripture says in this respect.[82] He would then have to come to the conclusion that no prophet ever "arises" from Galilee. That at least is the import of the most accepted reading ("prophet" without the article). In that case the statement relates not only to Jesus but — ad hominem! — also to Nicodemus himself. Many more recent scholars, however, are inclined to follow the important manuscripts in reading "*the* prophet," which would be a reference to "the prophet" mentioned in vs. 40. In support of this, 2 Kg. 14:25 mentions a prophet from Galilee. But the validity of this argument is open to question. The present tense ("arises") does not make a historical or statistical pronouncement but indicates a general rule:[83] from Galilee one expects no prophets.[84] That rule applies even if at some time in the past a prophet had come from Galilee. If one considers "the prophet" original, the question remains why the members of the Sanhedrin speak of that figure as distinct from the Messiah, and not of the Messiah himself. Also, the question of vs. 52a would then lose its caustic force, which is so characteristic of the dispute here.

However this point is resolved, this last provocative pronouncement from the Jewish council not only demonstrates how the opposition to Jesus deepened, but also — and undoubtedly the Evangelist intended this effect as he abruptly ended the story here — the permanent hopelessness of the appeal to the law when it is not understood in the light of the gospel (cf. 1:17). The law is invalidated in its requirement that one be open to what a man (here Jesus) has to say about himself[85] and "recognize (learn) what he does."[86] Furthermore, the witness of the Scriptures concerning Jesus is then turned into its opposite. For over against Jesus' "Search the Scriptures because . . . it is they that bear

---

81. Again (see the comments on vs. 47) μή introduces the question — here, of course, intended as ridicule.

82. ἐραύνησον ("search") is the usual term for consulting the Scriptures (cf. 5:39).

83. The idea that the Evangelist intentionally put an error (with a view to 2 Kg. 14:25) in the mouths of the members of the Sanhedrin as a fresh example of their lack of respect for the Scriptures seems too far-fetched.

84. Timeless present; other textual witnesses have the perfect, which, however, even if it were original, would also "carry the dogmatic sense that it is impossible for a prophet to come from Galilee" (Bultmann, *Comm.*, pp. 311f., n. 5).

85. ἀκούσῃ παρ' αὐτοῦ, vs. 51.

86. γνῷ τί ποιεῖ, vs. 51.

witness to me" (5:39), one here, with the same word, reads: "Search and you will see that no prophet is to arise from Galilee."

Nicodemus

Various opinions are held, as already indicated, about the role of Nicodemus, depending in part on the meaning one assigns to his conduct in 3:1ff. and 19:39.

According to some expositors, Nicodemus projects the image of those among the Jewish people and their leaders who sympathized with Jesus but remained on the wrong side of the dividing line. This is said to be clear not only from his encounter in ch. 3 but also from his conduct on behalf of Jesus in ch. 7. He champions the cause of justice here but evinces no faith in Jesus. De Jonge pursues this line of thought into 19:39.[87] He deems it clear that in John 19 Nicodemus and Joseph of Arimathea are presented "as having come to a dead end." They saw, de Jonge argues, the burial of Jesus as final and were unable to look past the grave.[88] Others, however, believe that a gradual change took place in the life of Nicodemus and consider his conduct at Jesus' burial as proof of that. For example, Calvin, in his comments on 7:50f., still describes Nicodemus as a "neutral" man,[89] one in whom "the seed of the Gospel, which afterwards bore fruit, still lay choked in him."[90] In connection with 19:38 he speaks, however, of "heroic courage" such that "in the last straits they boldly come out into the open" — an attitude Calvin attributes to "a heavenly impulse, so that those who were afraid to give Him due honour while He was alive now hasten to His dead body as if they were new men."[91] In that turnabout Calvin sees a fulfillment of 12:24. Brown similarly thinks it possible that in 19:37ff. the Evangelist has in mind Jesus' pronouncement in 12:32 that "when I am lifted up from the earth I will draw all people to myself." This then, Brown writes, is true of those who until now had concealed themselves. Thus the Evangelist might be encouraging the crypto-believers in the synagogue to follow the example of Nicodemus and Joseph.[92]

A particular understanding of Nicodemus is that he is one of the pillars in the "two-level" hypothesis presented by J. L. Martyn[93] and followed to varying degrees by others. Nicodemus is at the beginning (3:2) the representative of the "secret believ-

---

87. He argues, correctly, I believe, against B. Hemelsoet, "L'Ensévelissement selon Saint Jean," in *Studies in John* (Festschrift for J. N. Sevenster), 1970, pp. 47-65, who draws far-reaching conclusions from the words ἔλαβον τὸ σῶμα τοῦ Ἰησοῦ in 19:38, 39 (and partly from 1:12) with regard to the faith of Nicodemus (and of Joseph of Arimathea).

88. De Jonge, *Jesus: Stranger from Heaven and Son of God*, p. 34 (see also p. 32).

89. Calvin, *Comm.* I, p. 203: A *homo medius* "not venturing on a serious defence of godly doctrine" but who "cannot bear to have the truth oppressed," a posture on which Calvin comments with much relevance for his own time.

90. *Comm.* I, p. 204 ("Semen Evangelii, quod postea fructum tulit, adhuc suffocatum in eo latebat").

91. Calvin, *Comm.* II, p. 188. So also Lindars, *Comm.*, p. 592: "The secret believers now come out into the open, carrying forward the idea of faith latent in the piercing episode."

92. Brown, *Comm.* II, pp. 959f.

93. In *History and Theology* (see also the comments above on 5:15).

ers" in the synagogue in "the city" of the Evangelist or at the time of the Evangelist. He symbolizes both their belief that Jesus could be the Mosaic prophet and their fear of being cast out of the synagogue for that belief (cf. 9:22, 34; 12:42; 16:2). Martyn appeals to 7:52, where the Pharisees (who represent "Jamnia loyalists" after the destruction of Jerusalem)[94] attribute to Nicodemus the opinion that Jesus was "the (Mosaic) Prophet," an opinion Nicodemus does not reject. Hence their demand (says Martyn): "Search the Scriptures and you will see that no prophet arises from Galilee." All this, Martyn says, sheds light on 3:2ff. This secret ("and, to be sure, embryonic") faith was confirmed when Nicodemus visited Jesus by night ("Jesus," in the two-level theory, is to be understood as he manifested himself in the Christian community that was separate from the synagogue; cf. "we" in 3:11) to secure "data sufficient to mount a midrashic defense" for the conviction that Jesus was the prophet (cf. 3:2: "we know"). In this secret dialogue between "Nicodemus" and the later church, in which the "midrashic" (theological) approach to Jesus' identity is rejected, the "dreadful dualism" between the divergent church and synagogue is said to have been concretized.[95]

One must guard against inferring from the fact that Nicodemus went to Jesus by night that he represents a certain type of faith, namely that of the "secret believers," a typology that is supposed to govern unfavorably his conduct from one end of the Gospel to the other. In the "two-level" theory the "figure" of Nicodemus even develops into an entire class of secret believers in the later synagogue with a "midrashic" christology of their own. Against this view we must advance the objection raised earlier[96] that in this way the historical background against which the gospel story is staged and the horizon within which it is interpreted is progressively transposed from the first "level" (that of the historical Jesus) to the second (that of the Johannine community). The result is that all the people and dialogues in the Gospel increasingly lose not only their distinctiveness but also their historical character and become symbolic figures and symbolic dialogues that are then joined with great resourcefulness and imagination into a new historical structure, to which, by studying the Gospel from this perspective, scholars then skillfully add ever new features and details.[97] This is a method — we daresay — that in its historicizing and reconstructive power yields in nothing to, and is also no less hypothetical than, that which was applied in the earlier "Lives of Jesus" to the story of the "historical" Jesus himself, but which in the course of time was increasingly (and correctly!) rejected as an inadequate approach to the kerygmatic character of the Gospels.

However, quite aside from this general objection, the entire notion that in the Fourth Gospel Nicodemus represents the model of the crypto-believer in which the definitive break between synagogue and church is mirrored lacks support in the texts. Whatever moved Nicodemus to come to Jesus by night (see the comments on 3:1ff.), it was certainly not that in secret he had already in some way committed himself to faith in Jesus as the Messiah. The hypothesis that he regarded Jesus as "the Mosaic

---

94. *History and Theology,* pp. 107, 110, 155.

95. See *History and Theology,* pp. 87, 116ff., 121ff.

96. In the discussion of the "figure" of the cured paralytic in 5:1ff.

97. E.g., R. E. Brown, *The Community of the Beloved Disciple: The Life, Loves, and Hates of an Individual Church in New Testament Times,* 1979.

prophet-Messiah" and secretly sought to secure from Jesus support for that belief so he could better defend himself over against Jewish orthodoxy can in no way be verified from the texts (see the comments on 3:2 and 7:52). Moreover, the motif of the crypto-believer nowhere has any point of contact in Jesus' reaction to Nicodemus's nocturnal visit. Jesus did not fault the "faith" that Nicodemus obviously represented (cf. 2:23) or the "we know" with which Nicodemus approached him (3:2) on the grounds that he and those he spoke for lacked the courage to acknowledge their faith in him (cf. also 2:23ff., where there is no notion of "a secret faith" in the case of the many either). He did so, rather, because this "faith" and this "knowing" were entirely alien to the self-witness and "knowing" of Jesus and his followers (3:11) and were therefore the same as not believing (3:12; cf. 1:11). On that issue the "dialogue," as far as Nicodemus is concerned, comes to no conclusion. Nicodemus disappears into the night exactly as he came, not as a model of the "secret believer" but of the scribe in Israel who for all his "knowing" hears from Jesus that no one can see the kingdom of God without being born from above.

But the Gospel does not thus write Nicodemus off. Because the Evangelist is silent about Nicodemus's departure and reaction, this first appearance in ch. 3 is open-ended, which becomes clear from his return in 7:52. Even then the Evangelist makes no judgment concerning Nicodemus's faith. Admittedly, there is an indisputable and very significant connection between these two appearances (cf. 7:50). Again Nicodemus is on the stage as a leader in Israel, this time not just as a scribe but also as a member of the highest court. The idea that with "being one of them" he is described as one of the secretly believing members of the Sanhedrin,[98] or even as the man who was *and remained* one of them (see the exposition above), fails to appreciate the entire thrust of the dialogue in the Sanhedrin and Nicodemus's part in it. It is clear that the Evangelist's aim is above all to expose the hypocrisy of the members of the Sanhedrin, who as the designated upholders of the law and of justice trampled on one of the most rudimentary principles of the law: judge no one unheard. In that conflict Nicodemus was the one who, as "one of them" and hence as one who was responsible for the administration of justice, became an advocate of Jesus' rights at the place where justice was to be administered. In that position and on that issue he appealed to universally valid law and not to his personal relationship to Jesus, which can hardly be explained by lack of courage, that of the crypto-believer, supposedly attributed to him by the Evangelist. The issue was not faith, but justice.

Nicodemus's appeal to the principle of legal procedure ("Does our law judge a man without first giving him a hearing[99] and learning what he does") obviously alludes to his own earlier meeting with Jesus. Therefore, if we view Nicodemus's appearance in ch. 7 against the background of ch. 3 — for which the Evangelist offers ready justification — then the sense can hardly be other than that (however much Jesus had faulted him as a teacher in Israel), now that Nicodemus has been called on to make a judgment concerning Jesus, his earlier meeting with Jesus prevented him from quietly standing by as his fellow judges denounced Jesus as a deceiver of the people and a blasphemer without first hearing

---

98. Martyn, *History and Theology,* p. 161.

99. ἀκούσῃ ... παρ' αὐτοῦ.

him (as Nicodemus himself had "heard" Jesus). That the Evangelist refrains from giving a further description of this action of Nicodemus is not surprising. His purpose is not, as was said earlier (see the comments on ch. 4), to sketch the spiritual history of the people around Jesus but much more to demonstrate the power of Jesus' word and the choice with which he confronted the people in their encounter with him. When it is viewed in that light, one can hardly, in my opinion, characterize Nicodemus's second appearance — now not at night but in the public light of the highest Jewish court — as the model of a frightened "secret believer" but rather as proof of the lasting impression Jesus had made on him. To say more about Nicodemus's motives and faith in this situation was evidently deemed superfluous by the Evangelist.

All this stands out all the more clearly if one also considers Nicodemus's third appearance, now with Joseph of Arimathea (19:38ff.). That Joseph is described as "a disciple of Jesus but secretly,[100] for fear of the Jews" and Nicodemus as the one "who had at first come to [Jesus] by night" is doubtlessly intended to place the initiative they now take (to give Jesus an honorable burial) in a certain light. But that the Evangelist thus sought to depict their care for Jesus' body as typical of people who had stayed on the wrong side and had come to a "dead end" with Jesus must rank as the least likely conclusion one could attach to their intervention with Pilate and the last respects they paid Jesus. Nicodemus's return in ch. 19 corresponds totally with that in ch. 7. Again he comes to the fore, this time together with the — till now — "fearful" Joseph, when only some powerless women are left on the scene to provide for the honor of the now dead Jesus. With that Nicodemus disappears from history, not with the image of the crypto-believer who opts out whenever things come to a head, but as the man who, however much he failed at the beginning to appreciate Jesus at his true worth (and was unambiguously told so by Jesus), later could not resist choosing the side of Jesus in the most critical situations. It is certainly a picture that the Evangelist draws as an example to be followed, not as a warning against what not to do. And that is how it has been understood over and over again in the church.

7:53–8:11

Jesus and the Adulterous Woman

The now following passage — often described as the *pericope de adultera* — is generally regarded as a later insertion, not belonging to the original Gospel. The arguments for this view are not only that it constitutes a clear interruption of the text (between 7:53 and 8:12) and differs sharply in language and style from John, but above all that the textual evidence strongly argues against the idea that originally this pericope belonged to the Fourth Gospel. In the uncials it occurs first in Codex Bezae (D, fifth century) and after that only in manuscripts like E (eighth century), G (ninth century), H (ninth century), K (ninth

---

100. κεκρυμμένος.

century), and M (ninth century). The most ancient textual evidence is found in the Western church (some Old Latin manuscripts, the Vulgate), and Western church fathers like Augustine defend its genuineness. But in the Eastern church there are also traces of this story.[101] It is undoubtedly of ancient date and in content evinces the character of an authentic tradition, not that of a fictitious story. But the many variants in which the text comes down to us and the fact that in some minuscules it is introduced into the text after 7:36 or 21:24 or in the Gospel of Luke after 21:38,[102] point to an unstable tradition that was not originally part of a ecclesiastically accepted text.

How did this textual state of affairs come about? No conclusive answer has been given. An explanation that has found support is that the manner in which Jesus sends the adulterous woman away with only a word and without condemning her was "hard to reconcile with the stern penitential discipline in vogue in the early church."[103] This interpretation is in keeping with Augustine's view that the pericope, though included in the original text, was later omitted because some feared that it might help defenders of adultery.[104] Only later, when a more liberal penitential practice had been adopted, did the pericope find acceptance, first in the liturgical reading of the church and then also in the text of the New Testament.

But why did it find a place in the Gospel of John, and why here in the Gospel? This is the more striking because the attempt to incorporate it in the Gospel of Luke had no permanent effect, although it would seem, because of its general character and the mention in 7:53 of the Mount of Olives as the place were Jesus would spend the night, to fit better in Luke than after John 7 (cf. Lk. 21:37). On the other hand, expositors have pointed out that John 7 and 8 with their frequent reference to "judging" and "witness" (cf. 7:49ff.; 8:14ff.) and especially Jesus' pronouncement in 8:15 could have furnished the point of contact for inclusion of the story here. That is undoubtedly an important point. But it cannot be denied that the story is in this context an interruption rather than an integrated part of the text. Despite the important and insightful studies that have been and continue to be devoted to the text-critical, church-historical, and material aspects of this pericope,[105] various questions remain that are not, and probably cannot be, definitely answered, as to the separate life of the

101. For the evidence see, e.g., Lindars, *Comm.,* pp. 306-7.

102. In the so-called Ferrar group.

103. So Brown, *Comm.* II, p. 335, who refers to H. Riesenfeld, "Die Perikope von der Ehebrecherin in der frühkirchlichen Tradition," *Svensk Exegetisk Årsbok* 17 (1952), pp. 106-11.

104. Grosheide, *Comm.* I, p. 547, though he believes the case for interpolation of this pericope is stronger than the case for its originality, would nevertheless grant "some value" to this testimony of Augustine.

105. For the literature see Grosheide, *Comm.* I, pp. 546ff.; Haenchen, *Comm.* II, pp. 21f. On the history of the transmission of the text see especially U. Becker, *Jesus und die Ehebrecherin,* 1963; Riesenfeld, "Perikope von der Ehebrecherin."

pericope, its late acceptance in the canonical writings, and its place in the Gospel of John. A return to the originality of the pericope at this location does not seem possible. But still we have here such a precious and — in the judgment of many — historically authentic tradition from the life of Jesus that not only does its place in the Fourth Gospel have to be maintained[106] but also exposition of it rightly remains in most commentaries on John.[107]

If one reads the text as a continuation of what preceded, then "each" refers to the members of the Sanhedrin. However, though it is lacking in some manuscripts, **7:53** belongs with the interpolated pericope. It is doubtful that it is meant as a transitional formula and therefore as connected with what precedes. If it is not, then it relates to a situation that is unknown to us; for example, to an earlier conversation with Jesus in the temple, of which 8:2 ("again") is then the continuation. In any case 8:1 refers to a historical situation, as in Luke, of Jesus' last week in Jerusalem, during which he taught in the temple during the day (19:47; 20:1; 21:37) and was outside the city on the Mount of Olives at night. Vs. **2** reflects the same kind of situation, even mentioning the time ("early in the morning") at which Jesus and the people met in the temple (cf. Lk. 21:38).

3-6a In vs. 3 the actual story begins. "The scribes and Pharisees" is common in the Synoptics; John does not have it and in such contexts speaks rather of "the Pharisees." "Scribes" refers to a class; "Pharisees" to a party. Hence, though the two groupings are not identical (not all scribes belonged to the party of the Pharisees and not all Pharisees were scribes), the combination undoubtedly related to a common mentality, that of the Pharisaic zealots for the Jewish tradition as that was manifest especially among the scribal leaders of that party.

Here, too, the issue is one of law, but in a very concrete way. The woman has been caught committing adultery and stands accused in the midst of her accusers. Those who ask Jesus for his opinion on what to do with the woman place all the emphasis on her having been caught in the act (vs. 4). Not that they were in any doubt about what the law of Moses prescribed for such a case (vs. 5). The penalty for adultery was death for both the man and the woman (Lv. 20:10; Dt. 22:22ff.). That the death penalty had to be carried out by stoning is not stated in the texts, but stoning was in fact the most common way in which the death penalty was carried out in Israel. Hence the question that the

106. The 25th edition of the Nestle-Aland *Novum Testamentum Graece* (1963) put it in the apparatus, but the 26th and 27th editions (1981, 1993) include it in the main text, but in double brackets (readings "known not to be a part of the original text" and "printed in their traditional place instead of in the apparatus only because of their incontestable age . . . , their tradition, and their dignity" [26th edition, p. 44]).

107. Others, such as Haenchen, furnish the text but no commentary, or, like Bultmann, omit both.

Pharisees and scribes posed to Jesus ("Teacher . . . what do *you* say?" — the "you" has the emphatic position) did not arise from any perplexity on their part over whether they should apply this cruel punishment or from any need for advice, but because they wanted to hear from him an opinion that did not accord with the law. They questioned him on account of his deviant attitude toward people like this woman and because of their own annoyance that such people listened to Jesus (cf., e.g., Lk. 7:36ff.; 15:1; 5:29ff.). This intention is expressly brought out in vs. 6a:[108] they asked him so that they might have some charge to bring against him before the Jewish court. If he would take a stand for the woman, he would thus, in their opinion, be in open conflict with Moses.

Meanwhile, all sorts of questions arise in the exegesis. Had the woman already been condemned when she was brought to Jesus? Some expositors are inclined to assume this; others, however, point — correctly, I think — to vs. 10.[109] Furthermore, death by stoning is stipulated in the law only for adultery with a still unmarried but betrothed woman (Dt. 22:23); a married woman who commits adultery is to be executed, but the method is not specified. For that reason some interpreters believe that in the present story also we are dealing with a woman who was engaged to be married.[110] However, against this it has been remarked by Blinzler and others, first, that if such a distinction were intended in vs. 5, it would have been indicated more clearly (as in Dt. 22:23ff.); in this context "woman" can hardly mean anything other than married woman. Second, in vs. 3 the woman's sin is called "adultery" and she herself "adulteress," words used in Greek, if not exclusively, then predominantly and certainly in lawsuits, for adultery, that is, for violation of one's own marriage. And, third, where the Mosaic law mentions the death penalty, death by stoning is usually meant and that, as may appear also from passages like Ezk. 16:38-41; 23:45-48, this is undoubtedly the case in Dt. 22:22.[111]

To all this must be added the question whether in the days of Jesus the Jews, under Roman domination, could still execute a person. The question addressed to Jesus could be intended to embarrass Jesus if he should express himself as being in favor of the death penalty for the woman, because in that case he would be turning against the Roman government (cf. Mt. 22:15ff.). But the text does not allude to such a complication. As is evident from vs. 5, when charges are mentioned, the ground for them would be a departure from the

---

108. In some manuscripts this half verse is missing.

109. E.g., Brown, *Comm.* II, p. 337.

110. So, e.g., Strack/Billerbeck, II, pp. 519f. In that connection John bases himself on the Jewish tradition according to which "adultery with a married woman was to be punished by strangulation." For additional arguments see J. Blinzler, "Die Strafe für Ehebruch in Bibel und Halacha. Zur Auslegung von Joh. VIII.5," *NTS* 4 (1957-58), pp. 32-47.

111. This is also the predominant interpretation in Old Testament studies; cf. Blinzler, "Strafe für Ehebruch," p. 45, n. 1.

Mosaic law and not the Roman law. And the entire context suggests that the threat facing the woman was not that people would report her to the Roman government but that they would execute her.

6b   Jesus' reaction is very unusual and has given rise to all kinds of explanations and speculations.[112] Expositors have attempted to reconstruct what, in his stooped posture, Jesus wrote on the ground. An ancient interpretation advocated by Ambrose and Augustine and considered acceptable by more recent interpreters refers to Jr. 17:13, where it is said of those who turn away from the Lord that "they will be written in the earth, for they have forsaken the Lord, the fountain of living water."[113] In a "parabolic action" Jesus sought, according to this view, to remind the men of this Scripture by writing on the ground, without attacking them openly, then said "You are those who have turned away," and warned them against their own judgment.[114] Others refer to the custom in Roman jurisprudence according to which the judge wrote down his verdict before making it known. In that case, then, it would be a judgment of acquittal.[115] But both of these interpretations remain far-fetched. One does not expect from Jesus, in the midst of Jewish country and certainly under the given circumstances, allusions to the internal customs of Roman jurisprudence. And that in what must be regarded as an extremely subtle way Jesus sought to remind the scribes of the word of judgment in Jr. 17:13, though not impossible, also remains very doubtful. We do not get the impression that any of those present read what Jesus wrote on the ground.

It was apparently not so much the content as the act of writing itself that was at stake. And that, too, however, can be interpreted in various ways. Did Jesus want to make plain to the scribes and Pharisees, who wished to see the letter of the law upheld and enforced at any price, that there are also situations in which it is better to "write in the sand," to make evil erasable, to let the punishment "blow away"? If that explanation is viewed as overloaded with symbolism, then all that remains is that with this silent act Jesus intended no more than to initiate a kind of delaying or cooling-off process. He attracted attention away from the woman. He did something strange, unusual, in fact trivial. While all around him anxiously awaited his answer, with the woman standing in their midst as the sinner "caught in the act," he turned away from all the commotion and stooped toward the ground, silently drawing letters or

---

112. E.g., the far-fetched hypothesis of J. D. M. Derrett, who, proceeding from the hypothesis that the case was staged by the jealous husband (or his accomplice), has Jesus first write on the ground words from Ex. 23:1, then words from Ex. 23:7 ("Law in the New Testament: The Story of the Woman Taken in Adultery," *NTS* 10 [1963-64], pp. 1-26).

113. E.g., Schnackenburg, *Comm.* II, pp. 165f.

114. So also J. Jeremias, *The Parables of Jesus,* 1955, p. 158.

115. Cf. T. W. Manson, "The *Pericope de Adultera* (Joh. 7,53–8,11)," *ZNW* 44 (1952-53), pp. 255f.

figures as if to keep himself occupied. However one might interpret this writing on the ground, it functions in any case in this dramatic situation as an anticlimax. Jesus seems to have been completely disregarding the urgency of the question and the case.

7 His interrogators, however, refused to accept such a delay and pressed him for an answer.[116] In response to this display of impatience Jesus straightened up. For only a moment he interrupted his work of writing on the ground in order, with a word, to bring home to them the disgraceful and precarious nature of their conduct. All right, then, you zealots for the law, "let him who is without sin among you be the first to throw a stone at her." There lies the challenge. Jesus continues to use the language of the law. For there it was stipulated (cf. Dt. 13:9; 17:7) that the witnesses of a capital crime were to be first to turn their hand against the guilty person. But by designating as the first the one "who is without sin," Jesus faces them with the full and final seriousness of the law, not so as to lay down conditions that would make all human administration of justice impossible, but in order to confront all who, ignoring their own sin, want to judge and condemn others without mercy, to confront such judges with what awaits them if the heavenly judge should some day judge them by the same standard (cf. Mt. 7:1ff.).

8-11 After this one statement Jesus "again stooped down and wrote with his finger on the ground." The answer to their question was now no longer for him but for them to give. Then they understood his word (vs. 9a), but also his continued silence and writing, as an opportunity to arrive at different thoughts, as time in which to repent. He did not so much as look up until they had left, beginning with the oldest, who understood that they had to be the first by giving an example. Jesus then was left with the woman, who still stood there as the accused — or in the famous words of Augustine: *relicti sunt duo, misera et misericordia.* Only then (vs. 10) did Jesus straighten up and turn — for the first time — toward the woman. And acting as if he himself had remained totally uninvolved and had not even noticed the departure of those who had come to trap him, he asked her, "Where are they? Has no one condemned you?" The question seems needless; still it is without a trace of irony or gloating; it serves only to bring home to the woman the full reality of the fact that she no longer had to fear anything from those who had threatened her life. Her answer (vs. 11) is no more than an echo of his words: "No one, Lord." That is all she says in the whole story. Of her state of mind not a word is said. She seems not the contrite sinner (cf. Lk. 7:36-50) but the object of God's seeking and freeing love in Jesus Christ. To her could be applied the Pauline word: "It is God who justifies; who is to condemn?" (Ro. 8:33, 34).

To this reality in particular Jesus' word of farewell to the woman testifies:

---

116. ἐπέμενον ἐρωτῶντες.

"Neither do I condemn you." Here, as in vs. 10, "condemn" is used in the legal sense of "sentence." Only now does Jesus answer the question put to him at the beginning: "Teacher . . . what do *you* say?" But he speaks not as a rabbi giving an opinion in a matter concerning the law but as one who has power "on earth to forgive sins" (Lk. 5:24) and "to set at liberty those who are oppressed" (Lk. 4:19). He sends the woman away free, but not without saying to her with the same messianic authority: "and from now on do not sin again." That Jesus does not condemn her does not mean that he does not disapprove of her adultery or, since no one is "without sin," that he ignores it. "From now on" may seem redundant before "again" and is missing from some manuscripts. But it takes its meaning for the woman from the event that has just occurred, not only because by sinning again she would again expose herself to the danger she has just escaped but also because of the new life on the road of forgiveness and deliverance that Jesus has opened for her (cf. 5:14).

With good reason, despite its uncertain provenance, this story has been called a pearl of great price. The masterful simplicity[117] of the story reflects the unique manner in which the gospel is brought to expression by Jesus: by silencing with a word or a gesture the curse of a law torn from its base and by (re-)establishing justice on the foundation of his grace.

8:12-20

Jesus' Self-Witness Again under Attack

12 As already stated in the introduction to chs. 7–10, 8:13-59 can best be understood as the continuation of ch. 7. Not only does the scene of the action — the temple — remain the same (cf. vss. 20, 59) but the subject of the dialogues ties in closely with what had already come up in the preceding chapters, specifically in ch. 7 (cf. 8:12 with 7:37; 8:14 with 7:27, 28; 8:15 with 7:24; 8:21ff. with 7:33), in keeping with the author's method of resuming earlier themes and developing them.[118] Again and repeatedly the main focus is the conflict over Jesus' true identity, an identity confirmed by Jesus himself in ever new pronouncements and misunderstood, doubted, and opposed by his hearers. This applies immediately to vss. 12ff., which are introduced by a very general transitional formula ("again Jesus spoke to them") and clearly linked with the solemn final pronouncement in 7:37 about the living water, which was uttered

---

117. A simplicity that maintains itself in all the variants and needless additions (e.g., in vs. 9: "and convicted in conscience").

118. See p. 262, n. 27, above.

in close association with the ritual of the feast on "the last day of the feast, the great day."

Similarly Jesus now proclaims himself (vs. 12b) the light of the world. This is sometimes linked with the great illumination of the Court of the Women on the eve of the morning on which water was drawn from the spring of Siloam.[119] There was so much light then that, according to Jewish tradition, "there was not a courtyard in Jerusalem that was not illumined by the light of the place of the water-drawing."[120] The reference to "the treasury of the temple" in vs. 20 may support this link (see the comments there). But after the reference to "the last day of the festival" in 7:37 it has to remain an open question whether the saying in 8:12 was uttered still during the Feast of Tabernacles itself or later but under the fresh impact of it. In any case, as in 7:37ff., the ritual of the feast would serve as the contrasting backdrop for what Jesus proclaims in this revelational utterance. What was symbolized at the feast, God's salvation, Jesus *is* and *gives,* as both "living water" and "the light of life." And aside from any link with the festal liturgy, the parallelism between the two pronouncements is undeniable:

7:37: If any one thirst, let him come to me
8:12: I am the light of the world

7:38: the one who believes in me
8:12: the one who follows me

7:38: out of his heart will flow rivers of living water
8:12: will not walk in darkness but will have the light of life.

In 8:12 we have one of the familiar "I am" sayings of Jesus. In these sayings the "I" receives so much emphasis that it no longer functions as the subject of the sentence (with, say, "light" as predicate) but, conversely, is itself the predicate with "light" as subject: "The light of the world am *I.*"[121] There-

---

119. Or the first such illumnation. It is not certain whether this illumination was continued on the following days.

120. Mishnah Sukkah 5:3 (cf. Strack/Billerbeck II, p. 806).

121. Cf. Bultmann, *Comm.,* p. 342, n. 4. Bultmann makes illuminating distinctions among four forms of "I am" sayings (pp. 225-26, n. 3):

1. *The "presentation formula,"* which replies to the question: "Who are you?" . . . 2. *The "qualificatory formula,"* which answers the question: "What are you?" . . . 3. *The "identification formula,"* in which the speaker identifies himself with another person or object. . . . 4. *The "recognition formula,"* which is to be distinguished from the others by the fact that here ἐγώ is the predicate. For it answers the question "Who is the one who is expected, asked for, spoken to?" to which the reply is: "I am he."

In the first three forms, "I" is the subject and is described in the predicate. In the fourth "I" is the predicate and identifies that which (or the one who) is the expected *real* light, *true* vine, or

fore the point is not primarily to analyze what "light" means here — understanding of that concept is assumed — but that the light that the world needs and by which alone a person can escape the darkness is *Jesus,* and therefore that whoever follows *him* will not walk in darkness. In this focus of the revelational utterance everything is concentrated on the person of Jesus, which explains why, in the Pharisees' reaction (vs. 13), the issue is not light but Jesus' claim to be the light.

That Jesus is the true light "of the world" refers primarily not to the universal significance of the light but the existential significance of what in 1:4 is called "the light of people" (cf. vs. 9: "every person"), the light that humanity and the world need to exist, what is therefore called here "the light of life," that is, the life-giving light. We are not expressly told in what that "life" consists; it is contrasted with "walking in darkness," which refers not primarily to the moral dimension of human conduct (as in Paul: Ro. 13:13 etc.) but to the conduct of life in a more comprehensive sense (cf. 12:35; Mt. 6:22, 23). The contrast with darkness is inherent in the word "light" but also typical of the Johannine use of sharp contrasts: light versus darkness, life versus death, truth versus untruth, and the like.[122] The significance of "light" is determined by that antithesis. The light does not merely bring about a degree of clarification by which human beings are raised to a higher level, say, of knowledge or conduct, but rather rescues them from the life-threatening forces of darkness. This absolute character of the light can then, because it is the light of *life,* be applied to all sorts of forms and facets of life. But again the focus is not on what is brought out by this kind of analysis but on the fact that *Jesus* is the light of the world and that the person who follows him as disciple will not walk in darkness.

13 In response to these claims of absoluteness the Pharisees again react sharply (cf. the comments on 7:32, 47). What offends them is not that Jesus can bring light, comfort, and happiness to people but that he says that he is *the* light of the world. And again the question concerning the legitimacy of such "testimony" arises, as in 5:31-40 (but there Jesus brought up the issue). As there, so also here, though figuratively (see below), the issue is the forensic meaning of "testimony." Since in court only the testimony of two had legal

---

good shepherd. Bultmann has assembled much religio-historical material representing these different forms of the formula and judges that in most cases where John uses it (he mentions 6:35, 41, 48, 51; 8:12; 10:7, 9, 11, 14; 15:1, 5) we have the fourth form, the "recognition formula," in view of the strong emphasis that Jesus' "I" has, always in contrast with what is not "real," "true," or "good" ("always contrasted with false or pretended revelation"). "On the other hand 11.25, and perhaps too 14.6, are probably identification formulae," while elsewhere (as in 4:26; 8:18, 23; 18:5f., 8) the "I am" does not have the character of such a ("sacred") revelational formula.

122. Often this so-called "dualism" is related to similar absolute contrasts in the Qumran literature; e.g., H. Braun, *Qumran und das Neue Testament* II, 1966, pp. 119ff.; on light and darkness see Braun II, pp. 120ff. and I, pp. 122ff., where Braun also discusses the expression "light of life" as used in 1QS 3:7.

force (cf. vs. 17), the Pharisees argued that Jesus could not claim credibility
on the basis of his own testimony alone. "You are bearing witness to yourself."
That is, you are attributing to yourself and on your own authority this absolute
significance of being the light of the world. But for that reason your testimony
is not true, that is, not valid for the purpose of legitimating yourself as such.

14 Jesus' answer to this objection and challenge takes a somewhat
different form than his argument in 5:31ff. There he follows the rule put to him
here by the Pharisees and says that if he alone bore witness to himself, his
testimony would not be valid. He refers to his works, and in those works to
his Father as his fellow witness. Here, however, he begins by emphasizing the
validity of his own testimony — though he does not stop there and in vs. 17
again concludes with his own conformity to the ("your") law.

He explains that his testimony (that he is the light of the world) is true
and valid, even though he bears this witness to himself, by referring to his
origin and destination. Because he knows himself to be incorporated in God's
work of salvation (cf. 13:1; 19:28), his testimony is not presumptuous but has
inner validity. He appeals repeatedly to this knowledge (cf. 7:29; 8:14, 55). His
opponents ask him for legitimation because *they* do not know either where he
is from or where he is going (vs. 14b), and they repeatedly manifest this
ignorance in their questions (cf. 7:28; 8:19, 54ff.; 9:29).

15, 16[123]   The Pharisees disbelieve Jesus' self-testimony and ask him for
further legitimation because they judge "according to the flesh," the appearance
of things, and therefore — as 7:24 states — cannot judge rightly. In antithesis
Jesus says, "I judge no one." The import of these words is not entirely clear.
Some expositors think that one should add the implied words "according to
the flesh." But the negation apparently concerns not only the manner of judging
but judging itself. Jesus stresses that, unlike the Pharisees (cf. 8:1-11!), his
aim is not to judge; judging is not his business (cf. 3:17; 12:47). Yet if he judges
(vs. 16, indicative, not subjunctive; cf. comments on 3:18, 19; 9:39), his judgment is true, that is, just.[124] It is because he is "not alone" but with "the one
who sent me." "Not alone" returns in vs. 29, where we read that the Father is
"with me" and "has not left me alone" (cf. 16:32). Therefore, "I and the one
who sent me" applies to all that Jesus says and does; he does nothing "of

123. According to some commentators these verses disturb the sequence because they
introduce another concept, namely "to judge," and thus interrupt the theme "to bear witness,"
which is picked up again in vs. 17. These commentators therefore speak of an interpolation or
later addition; so Brown, *Comm.* II, pp. 343, 345; cf. also Bultmann, *Comm.,* p. 280, n. 4. But
even though vs. 15b is striking, vs. 15a clearly constitutes a comment on vs. 14, and "not I alone"
in vs. 16 is a no less clear lead-in to vs. 17. See also the critical discussion of these views by
Pancaro in *Law in the Fourth Gospel*, p. 264.

124. ἀληθινός, in distinction from ἀληθής in vs. 13, where the validity of the law is the
issue. Here in vs. 16, "intrinsic" truth, the justness of a judgment, is in view.

himself" and judges no one "alone" and "of himself." He would certainly be able to judge "of himself" and "alone," and have good reason to do so over against his Jewish opponents (cf. vs. 26). But he does not do it. For he was not sent for that purpose; therefore, when he speaks and judges he does so in keeping with "what I have heard from him" (vs. 26).

The words "but I and the one who sent me," unlinked with any verb, are striking. They have sometimes been associated with a certain (later) Jewish tradition according to which at the Feast of Tabernacles, as the priests processed around the altar and sang the Hosanna of Ps. 118:25, they sang, instead of "O Lord" *('ānnā yhwh)*, "I and he" *('ᵃnî wāhû)* to avoid using the name of God.[125] By means of this phrase ("I and he") they brought to expression the fellowship existing between Israel and Yahweh. "I and he who sent me" is said to be the Christian equivalent, in which Christ has replaced Israel.[126] The connection with the Feast of Tabernacles is inherently attractive, but the identification with the text of the Hosanna thus sung (with which John might have been familiar)[127] remains highly uncertain, especially if one follows the reading "I and the *Father* who sent me."[128]

17, 18 "Not I alone . . . but I and the one who sent me" also explains why Jesus' self-witness (vss. 13ff.) is not only true in itself and traceable to himself. And they also meet the condition that the law sets for a legally valid testimony: that it be given by two persons.[129] This, then, is fully expressed in a chiastic pronouncement in vs. 18, literally, "I am he who bears witness to myself,[130] and concerning me witnesses the Father who sent me." And with that the argument recalls the argument in 5:31ff.

Here and elsewhere (cf. 10:34; 15:25; see also 7:19) Jesus refers very conspicuously to "your law." All sorts of explanations have been given for this.[131] It is clear, in any case, that by thus speaking Jesus is distancing himself from the law. Still, one cannot say that he does so in a derogatory fashion as if he were positioning himself over against the law. He appeals to the law as

125. Mishnah Sukkah 4:5 (see Strack/Billerbeck, II, p. 797).
126. Cf. Dodd, *Interpretation,* p. 96.
127. "It seems not impossible" (Dodd, *Interpretation,* p. 96).
128. "Father" is lacking in ℵ* D sy^s.c., but is supported by other important manuscripts like p39, p66, and p75 and is followed in Nestle-Aland26 and NRSV.
129. The text here says "two humans" (vs. 17: δύο ἀνθρώπων). Some expositors think this is intentional and that it carries the implication of "how much more" since Jesus is referring to God. But in vs. 18, which is carefully formulated, there is no allusion to this. Apparently in vs. 17 the reference is simply to two persons.
130. "'Ἐγώ εἰμι ὁ μαρτυρῶν is not, of course, one of the great ἐγώ-εἰμι sayings. . . . The sentence is not a revelation saying but part of a discussion" (Bultmann, *Comm.,* p. 282, n. 5).
131. See, at length, Pancaro, *Law in the Fourth Gospel,* pp. 517ff.

the authority for Jews (here and in 10:34), but he also appeals to "the Word" that "is written" ("is Scripture") and is fulfilled in his own life (15:25). He never speaks of "your Scriptures," though both "law" and "Scripture" go back to Moses and are simply referred to as "Moses" (cf. 1:17; 5:39, 45-47; 7:19-23). "Law" refers to what is in Scripture and what, with the coming of Jesus Christ, has been replaced by something else, or at least overshadowed as provisional and lesser (1:17), and fulfilled (15:25). When Jesus appeals to "your law," he distances himself from what for them was the highest and final authority, and he also thus indicates, here and in 10:34, that in their opposition to him their law testifies against them, not against him (cf. also 7:19ff.).

Although it is not quoted word-for-word, "that which is written in your law" probably refers here to Dt. 19:15, which states, as a general rule of law, that "only on the evidence of two or three witnesses shall a charge be sustained." This was a fixed rule in Jewish jurisprudence.[132]

It has been asked whether, from a formal point of view, Jesus was actually in a position to make such an appeal to the law. For, it is said, if to the Jews Jesus' testimony was invalid, then he would need at least two *other* witnesses to uphold his pronouncement. All kinds of attempts have been made to resolve this. Reference has been made to the stipulation in Jewish law that in exceptional cases the testimony of one person was sufficient (e.g., that of a father in identifying his son), which is said to apply here in the case of Jesus.[133] That seems too far-fetched.[134] We are dealing here, not with witnesses for the prosecution in a criminal case, of which there always had to be two (Nu. 35:30; Dt. 17:6; 19:15, etc.), but with the general legal principle that a case could be settled on the basis of the congruent testimony of two persons.

But what could Jesus mean by this appeal to the law? What judge could possibly declare on the evidence however many witnesses — and what witnesses could testify — that Jesus was in fact the light of the world? Bultmann thinks that this whole appeal to the law is "not an argument at all." After all, it would be an absurdity to attempt to summon God to appear in court. Rather, we are dealing with "an expression of scorn," a mockery of Jewish legalism. Bultmann thinks that Jesus meant, ironically, "The requirements of your law have been satisfied, indeed radically so, for here the two witnesses really are in unity, for the two witnesses *are* one!"[135]

---

132. See Strack/Billerbeck I, pp. 1001f.

133. See H. van Vliet, *No Single Testimony: A Study on the Adoption of the Law of Deut. 19:15 par. into the New Testament,* 1958, p. 88.

134. Schnackenburg, *Comm.* II, p. 487, n. 26, speaking of a similar explanation by J. D. Charlier, calls it "forced."

135. Bultmann, *Comm.,* p. 282. He concludes: "This pushes the satirical treatment of Jewish legalism to its extreme" — that is, by presenting the matter as if God's revelation had to answer for itself by way of a lawsuit in order to satisfy their legalism.

Still, however true it may be that there can be no question here of a lawsuit as would be ordinarily settled before a human tribunal, that does not mean that Jesus' appeal to the law here can only be meaningful as satire and not as argument. For, in the first place, we are in fact dealing here, in the figurative and deepest sense of the word, with a lawsuit,[136] as is evident from the repeated use of the word "witness" and the many witnesses mentioned earlier in the case: John the Baptist (5:31ff.; cf. 1:7; 3:27), "the Father, who sent me" (5:37), the Scriptures (vs. 39), and Moses (as accuser, vss. 45f.). It is in this legal sense that the Jews are also repeatedly faulted for their failure in "judgment" (vs. 15; cf. 7:24). When Jesus appeals to the law and its principle of what constitutes valid testimony, that is not sarcastic mockery of Jewish legalism, but rather an appeal to what the law intends: not merely external conformity to binding prescriptions but the maintenance and confirmation of the truth over against the lie, presumption, and the like. Here, too, the law, to which the Jews think they can appeal as their charter and the basis for their argument, is not, as so often (cf. 7:19ff.), on their side but on Jesus' side. If only they were a different kind of people and understood with whom in his self-witness they were dealing, they would not aim the law against him but understand that precisely in him they are confronted, in an unprecedented and most unexpected way, with the law's demand for truth and justice; and then not reject him but accept him.

19 But they were lacking precisely in the conditions for that kind of understanding. When Jesus appeals to his Father, they ask, "Where is your Father?" This question, far from reflecting naive incomprehension of what and whom Jesus had in mind, suggests the opposite (cf. 5:18). In raising the question they are assuming a formal legal position: if a person appeals to the testimony of a witness, that person should be able to produce the witness! Again, therefore, they are presenting a demand for legitimation and an indirect challenge: if the Father is going to be your witness, bring him forward!

Jesus' reply is direct and radical. It is not a simple misunderstanding needing to be cleared up that is at issue. What prevents them from accepting Jesus' word as true and legally valid is that they "know neither me nor my Father." That is, they are inwardly strangers to and outside the fellowship of both Jesus and his Father. And the two are inseparable. If they really knew Jesus and if his words did not sound strange and presumptuous in their ears, they would not ask, "Where is your Father?" They would know that what he says is of God and that the Father is his witness. But by rejecting him in unbelief they show that they do not know his Father either, the Father with whom and on whose authority he speaks.

With this statement the pericope ends. This connection of knowing Jesus with knowing the Father has been made earlier already (see the comments on

136. Cf. also Mi. 6:1ff.

7:28, 29). It is the underlying presupposition of this entire Gospel. But together with "I am the light of the world" and the repeated conjunction of "I and the Father" (vss. 12, 16, 18), it is now said in such a way that with the decision for or against Jesus everything has come to be at stake: not only he himself but with him everything the Jews, the world, all people believe they know of God and possess in the way of life-giving light.

For the person who does not know Jesus this "argument" is, of course, not convincing. On the contrary, that person will say that Jesus' "evidence" consists precisely in what needs to be proved: that the Father is with him as the great "witness" of what he says and does. This short circuit is inherent in the issue itself. God's revelation does not subject itself to human control and cannot be required to legitimate itself by human standards. It can only be "known" and assented to by those who "know" him, that is, by those who, as children of God, are born not of flesh and blood but of God (1:13; 3:3ff.). But this a priori is not a demand for a blind faith in the one sent by God. It is a "knowing" in the light of Jesus' words and works. If, therefore, Jesus bears witness to himself as the light of the world, this does not call for "unknowing" acceptance (cf. 6:69). Rather, it is a coming to know, by the content of Jesus' words and the power of his deeds, the claim and irrefutability of the love of God extended to the world in him. It is to that decision of faith that all these dialogues lead and in the confrontation with which they all find their conclusion and climax.

20 As elsewhere (cf. 1:28; 6:59), so here also the Evangelist postpones to the end saying where all this took place: "by the treasury."[137] This reference to the place where Jesus made these pronouncements[138] "when he taught in the temple" apparently has a certain significance.[139] Some expositors regard it as no more than one of the many brief indications of place and time in the Gospel that betray a precise knowledge of circumstances and heighten the vividness of the story. Some suggest a link with Jesus' pronouncement in vs. 12 because, if "the treasury" refers to the place where the alms boxes were located (mentioned elsewhere as a place where Jesus spent time when he was in the temple: Mk. 12:43; Lk. 21:1), then Jesus must have been in the Court of the Women, where the alms boxes were located and where, during the Feast of Tabernacles, the celebration of lights took place (see the comments on vs. 12 above). But if that is the intent of the reference, one would expect the place indication at the beginning rather than the end of the pericope. It seems more

---

137. The preposition ἐν used here must be translated "at," "near," or "by" if it refers to the (or a) treasury itself since the treasury would naturally not be open to all. But there was more than one "treasury."

138. ῥήματα.

139. So also Bultmann, who adds, however, "It is not possible to be sure" (*Comm.,* p. 283, n. 2).

natural to link the place indication with the immediately following statement that "no one arrested him," translating "and" as "and yet." The place reference is undoubtedly intended to make the contrast even sharper: Even though Jesus made his pronouncements in a crowded place that was accessible to all, no one seized him. This is all the more reason for the Evangelist to add again: "because his hour had not yet come" (see the comments on 7:30).

8:21-29

"I Am He"

In vs. **21** the dialogue between Jesus and "the Jews" continues. As in vs. 12, the transitional formula yields no information concerning time and place. But the scene seems to be the same. Not until vs. 59 do we read that Jesus has left the temple. Pharisees are no longer mentioned, only "the Jews." But the incomprehension of Jesus and resistance to him are no less intense (cf. vss. 20, 25, 27; but see also vs. 30). And the great theme of the dialogue remains that of Jesus' identity: "Who are you?" (vs. 25).

The dialogue begins with a statement Jesus also made earlier (7:33f.) concerning his going away and the futile attempts his partners in dialogue would make to find him. Where he will go they cannot go. The intent of the announcement is clarified by "and in your sin you will die." The implication is that when he has gone it will be too late for them to invoke his help and to be saved by him. His announcement that he is going away is intended to press them toward a decision. The expression "die in your sin" occurs repeatedly in the Old Testament (e.g., Ezk. 3:19). It refers not only to the desolate condition in which such a death takes place but also to the guilt of the person who dies thus.[140] The expression is repeated twice in vs. 24, but with the plural "sins." Although it describes the fallen condition of humanity and the world in general terms as subject to sin and judgment (cf. 1 Co. 15:17), the expression is closely related in John, here and elsewhere, to disbelief in Jesus as the one sent by the Father (cf. vs. 24; 9:41; 16:9) and to the human continuation in darkness and clinging to "evil works" (cf. 3:19ff.) that result from that disbelief — a condition of lostness and liability to punishment from which God wants to save the world in Christ (3:16ff.). Jesus is the light of the world (8:12) because it is he who takes away the world's sin (1:29, 36).

22 "The Jews" do not react to this threat. As in 7:35, all that occupies them is wondering what Jesus means by this "going to where you cannot come." More or less in mockery and not without malice they pose as a possi-

---

140. The phrase is also translated "to die of one's sin."

bility: "Certainly he is not planning to kill himself?" They would certainly not follow him to the place where those who commit suicide go.[141] Some expositors think that they thus (as in 7:35) unwittingly speak as prophets.[142] But since Jesus points in vs. 28 to them as those who will bring about his death, that there is any allusion here to his self-offering in death is questionable. In any case, his self-offering is something other than suicide!

23 At the moment, however, Jesus gives no further reply on the matter of his going away. In two short parallel pronouncements he indicates, with a certain solemnity, what distinguishes them from him, which at the same time explains why they can neither follow him nor understand what he is speaking about. That difference is rooted in their origin and his origin: they are from below, he is from above; they are of this world, he is not of this world. The same antithesis underlies 3:3ff., 31. It does not distinguish (idealistically) between a lower and a higher mode of existence or (dualistically) between two mutually exclusive modes of existence. It refers, rather, to the contrast between the world of God and God's Spirit, in which light and life are created, and the world of humankind in its creaturely dependence and fallen existence.

24 Here Jesus gives the reason for his pronouncement in vs. 21 that they would "die in their sin(s)." Such a death would not descend upon them as an inescapable fate. Rather, "unless you believe that I am he." He was sent into the world so that they and all the world should *not* perish (see the comments on vs. 21).

Very striking — and hence much discussed — is the expression "that I am (he)." It is striking, of course, because "I am" has no predicate. According to some expositors it is a mistake to supply the pronoun "he," as we have here and as many translations do; it is precisely the absence of any predicate that indicates, they say, the absoluteness of Jesus' existence, or, more precisely, his self-identification with God.

The explanation for this expression was formerly usually sought in Ex. 3:14 ("I am who I am"). But now it is sought in a great number of Old Testament pronouncements in which Yahweh reveals himself as the one and only God, the reliable Redeemer of his people (cf. Is. 43:10: "that you may know and believe me and understand that I am He") and similar utterances especially in Isaiah (e.g., 41:4; 46:4; 48:12) but also in texts like Dt. 32:39.[143] According to some scholars the absolute use of "I am," specifically in the Septuagint, became the equivalent of a divine name.[144] This would explain the many Johannine references to Jesus' name (e.g., 17:6, 26; 5:43; 10:25;

---

141. On the Jewish assessment of suicide, see, e.g., Strack/Billerbeck II, pp. 1027ff.

142. So, e.g., Bultmann, *Comm.,* p. 348: "He will indeed lay down his life (10.17f.) — but not in the way they think; for they themselves will kill him (v. 28)."

143. On the treatment of these texts see esp. H. Zimmerman, "Das absolute Ego Eimi als die neutestamentliche Offenbarungsformel," *BZ* 4 (1960), pp. 54-69, 266-76.

144. See Dodd, *Interpretation,* pp. 94ff.; Brown, *Comm.* II, p. 536.

17:11, 12).[145] The "I am" is said to confirm "the mystery of his own eternal being, in unity with the Father."[146] With this formula, it is said, Jesus reveals his unique claim to divinity, "his unity with the Father."[147]

But one may well ask whether the words "I am" are intended here as a divine name and whether the text implies such a self-identification of Jesus with God. If "I am" should function here as a name of God, it can hardly be itself the object of belief.[148] But apart from that formal objection there is obviously no question here of a self-identification of Jesus with God or a self-designation of him as divine being. Specifically opposed to this is vs. 28, where "that I am he" is joined in one clause with "and do nothing on my own authority but speak thus as the Father taught me."[149] Hence in the "I am" we are in fact dealing with (faith in) the authority, the messianic power, that Jesus represents. But Jesus does not infer this authority from his own deity but, relinquishing all reference to self, points to what the Father has taught him (cf. 5:19ff.). That this "I am" presupposes a unique relationship with the Father, a Father-Son relationship that embraces more than a union of will and disposition, emerged unmistakably in our discussion of 5:19ff. Still, as 8:28 shows, the words "(believe) that I am (he)" do not refer to the ontological relationship of the Son with the Father but to his action as the one sent by the Father. Or, in Calvin's words, "I am he" does not relate to Christ's divine being but to his office.[150]

But still it is striking that this "I am" is not accorded any further description. Calvin says that an undertone in it is "all that the Scripture ascribes to the Messiah and all that it tells us to expect from Him."[151] Other expositors also explain the "I am" as the "I am of the Messianic presence."[152] But this makes specific what was deliberately left indefinite in the words "that I am (he)." Also, when Jesus uses the term "Son of man" in vs. 28, this is not intended as a further description of *who* Jesus is.

Therefore it would seem that we must see in this remarkable pronouncement ("that I am [he]") some connection with the similar manner in which God is introduced as speaking in texts like Is. 43:10. Just as there Israel is

145. Brown, *Comm.* II, pp. 350, 537.
146. So Dodd, *Interpretation,* p. 351.
147. So Moloney, *Johannine Son of Man,* p. 132.
148. In that case one would expect "that I am 'I am'" (cf. Is. 43:25; 44:19 LXX — texts in which the name of God is thought to be thus referred to).
149. Without the repetition of ἐγώ.
150. Cf. Calvin on vs. 24 (*Comm.* I, p. 216): "Some of the ancients have misapplied this to the divine essence of Christ. He is in fact speaking of His office towards us." And on vs. 28 (p. 219): "*That I am.* I have already said that this does not refer to Christ's divine essence, but to His office. This appears still more clearly from the context, where He affirms that He does nothing but at the command of His Father. For this was as good as saying that He was sent by God and performs His office faithfully."
151. Calvin, *Comm.* I, p. 216.
152. See D. Daube, "The 'I Am' of the Messianic Presence," in his *The New Testament and Rabbinic Judaism,* 1956, pp. 325-29.

exhorted to believe in God and to know that "it is he," namely God, he and no other, before whom no god was formed and after whom no god will be, the LORD, besides whom there is no savior, so for those to whom Jesus is speaking there is no salvation unless they believe that it is he, the one who has revealed himself to them as the one sent by God, besides whom there was and after whom there will be no other, the eternal Savior.

With this "I am," therefore, Jesus is not identifying himself with God but revealing himself as the one sent by God in his uniqueness and exclusivity. That, of course, presupposes his unique relationship, his unity with the one who sent him. He and he alone represents God as God for the world and for people. Still one cannot say that when Jesus utters the "I am (he)" he primarily reveals not himself but the Father.[153] What in Isaiah 43 God reveals of himself as God, that Jesus reveals concerning himself as the Son of God, the one sent by the Father. As the "I am" he does not identify himself more precisely (neither as Messiah nor as Son of God) because he is referring not primarily to the *what* (what he is) but to the exclusivity and hence the absolute validity and trust-worthiness of the *that* (that he is) in his unity with the Father, but also in his distinction from the Father.

Verses **25-27** can be explained along this line, however difficult vs. 25b is to translate and understand in its context.[154] The question of "the Jews," "Who are you?" (vs. 25a), is clear. They do not understand what Jesus means by his indefinite "that I am (he)." Apparently they do not regard it as presumptuous or think that Jesus is applying the name of God to himself (unlike the situation in 5:18).[155] Their question shows how far they were from understanding what was most essential in Jesus' public ministry and how absurd it seemed to them that he held out faith in him as the only way in which they could be saved. Jesus' reply in vs. 25b can probably be best translated as a rhetorical question: "Why am I still speaking to you?"[156] a question in which he brings out the hopelessness of continuing the dialogue with them.

The first words of vs. 26, "I have much to say about you and much to

---

153. As Zimmermann ("Das absolute Ego Eimi," p. 270) explains Jn. 8:24f.

154. Bultmann, after an extensive analysis, declares a *non liquet* (*Comm.*, pp. 350-53).

155. Cf. Bultmann, *Comm.*, p. 349, n. 3.

156. The difficulty lies especially in the adverbial phrase τὴν ἀρχήν in its connection with λαλῶ. If one takes τὴν ἀρχήν to mean "earlier" or "in the beginning," then all kinds of additions have to be made to harmonize it with present tense λαλῶ. Some translate: "What I have been saying from the beginning and still say." But τὴν ἀρχήν seldom has that sense ("*from the* beginning"), if ever. The translation I have followed (taking the clause as a question), though not beyond criticism, is probably the least objectionable. See the lengthy discussions of Brown, who follows the affirmative translation, mentioned above ("a slight edge to the likelihood," *Comm.* I, p. 348), and of Bultmann, who, after rejecting all other translations, writes: "At best one could translate: 'Why on earth am I still speaking to you at all?' " (*Comm.*, p. 353). For the translation of τὴν ἀρχήν as "at all" (in the same sense as ὅλως), see BAGD, p. 112.

judge," lead in to what follows, "but he who sent me is true," but are hard to explain as such. The meaning is something like: for himself Jesus has every reason to speak (with them) about them and much to judge, namely about their negative attitude toward him, and to justify himself in his pronouncements with regard to them. But he refrains from doing so. His identity is not dependent on their judgment and consent; it depends, rather, on the fact that the one who sent him is true, the true and only God. And he utters as God's message in the world what he "has heard" from God (cf. the comments on 3:11; 5:19ff.). Thus understood, these words confirm — despite the Jews' incomprehension — that only belief that "it is he" can save them and the whole world from dying in their sins (cf. 3:16ff.).

That "they did not understand that he spoke to them of the Father" (vs. 27) can mean that even after what was said in vss. 25 and 26 they still did not understand. If so, then this comment is meant as evidence of their continuing incomprehension and unbelief. But perhaps it is better, with a view to vs. 30, to translate: "They *had* not understood." Then the statement refers to vs. 24b, especially to the words "that I am (he)." They had not understood Jesus when he spoke of himself as the one sent by the Father. Hence their question in vs. 25 and Jesus' reply in vs. 26.

This also makes the transition to vs. **28** clearer. There will come a time when, unlike now, they will understand that it is he, namely "when they have lifted up the Son of man." The striking expression "lift up" appeared earlier in 3:14 (cf. 12:32). But there the expression is in the passive voice and is used of Jesus' exaltation on the cross as an event in God's plan of redemption ("must"). Here it is active and refers to the role of the Jews in Jesus' death. By killing him they will, without knowing it, serve the counsel of God. This makes it all the more clear that in 3:14 "lift up" had a double meaning: Jesus' being lifted up on the cross is how he will be glorified as the Son of man, to whom all power will be given and who will sit in judgment of all (cf. 5:27). Thus the Jews' own action will lead them to the insight that Jesus arrogated nothing to himself when he said "I am he," that someday they will be confronted with him as the divinely exalted Son of man (cf. 6:62; Mk. 14:62 par.).

Does "you will know" refer to judgment or salvation (or to both)? There is more in the entire context that favors the first than the second.[157] The whole pericope, from vs. 21 on, is a warning. Time is pressing. When Jesus has gone away, those who now reject him will try in vain to find him. If they are not to die in their sins, they must, before it is too late, believe that "I am he" (vss. 21-24). Moreover, the double meaning in "lifting up" seems to presage judg-

---

157. For both views see the extensive discussion in Moloney, *Johannine Son of Man,* pp. 136ff.; Schnackenburg, *Comm.* II, p. 256.

ment rather than salvation: their victim will prove to be their judge. The idea that we must understand "then you will know" in the light of 12:32[158] seems too forced. "All" in 12:32 certainly does not include all who have first rejected Jesus in unbelief. And the "then" in "then you will know," if it implies a prediction of salvation, cannot be made specific. Where and when are all those who now reject Jesus to arrive at such salvific knowledge and acknowledgment of him? If we take the pronouncement as a prediction of judgment, then "then" refers not to a historical event (e.g., the destruction of Jerusalem) but the coming judgment by the Son of man (cf. 5:27). It is also hard to see how the pronouncement in vs. 28 could be presaging neither salvation nor condemnation but rather the possibility of both, presented both to the Jews in Jesus' time and in the time of the Johannine church.[159] The pronouncement rather contains an announcement of judgment for those who reject Jesus in his self-revelation as the one sent by the Father. By this statement Jesus draws a sharp line of demarcation but does not exclude the possibility that people who have rejected him or still reject him as the "I am" should yet be able to come to faith and repentance. Central in these chapters is the confrontation with the Jewish leaders and the later Jewish synagogue in their steadfast rejection of Jesus as the Christ, the Son of God. Should they persevere in this rejection they will have no other prospect but to meet him as judge.

Verse **29** continues the thought of vs. 28b and therefore still belongs to the explication of "I am (he)." Jesus is that "I am," not only because he adheres totally to what he has heard from the Father (vs. 28) but also because the one who sent him is with him and has not left him alone.[160] The thought is the same as that of 8:16, 18, which includes the formula "I and he who sent me." It is that unity with the Father that constitutes the basis both of the "I am he" and of the fact that, as the Son, Jesus always does what is pleasing to the Father (see the comments on 5:19; 6:38).[161]

The significance of this pericope is much like that of the preceding (vss. 12-20). Their starting points are different (vss. 12, 21), but the focus of both is Jesus' identity as the one sent by the Father, specifically that identity as the object

---

158. So, e.g., W. Thüsing, *Die Erhöhung und Verherrlichung Jesu im Johannesevangelium*, 1970², pp. 15ff.

159. So Moloney, *Johannine Son of Man*, p. 138; see the overview of similar views presented there.

160. The aorist tense of ἀφῆκεν does not relate to the moment of the incarnation (cf. Moloney, *Johannine Son of Man*, p. 138) but means something like "has never left me even for a moment."

161. The ὅτι clause in vs. 29 can better be construed as indicating the consequence than the cause of what precedes.

both of his self-revelation and of the opposition and incomprehension of the Jewish leaders, the Pharisees. Jesus makes ever sharper and more urgent pronouncements: "I and he who sent me," "I am he" (vss. 16, 18, 24, 28), and "the Jews' " questions become stronger: "Where is your Father?" "Who are you?" (vss. 19, 25). Jesus presses them to take a stand in view of his approaching departure, speaks in increasingly explicit language of the consequences of their unbelief (vss. 21ff., 28), and wonders out loud whether it still makes sense to continue the dialogue (vs. 25b), since all the conditions for fruitful exchange are lacking (vss. 19b, 23, 27). All these components of the dialogue point to the fact that time was running out. The cross is becoming visible in the attitude of the Jews and in Jesus' words to them (vs. 28). What follows will bring out these motifs even more vividly.

8:30-47

The Seed of Abraham and the Identity of the Father

30, 31 Some expositors think it is better to take vs. 30 with what precedes and to understand "the Jews who believed" of vs. 31 as referring to different people than the "many" who believed according to vs. 30. The reason for this is that after the positive statement about the "many" who believed after Jesus spoke "these words" one does not expect him to address them with harsh words like those in vss. 37, 39-47, 50, 55, nor does one expect such people to make plans to kill him (vs. 59). Those who assume a break between vs. 30 and vs. 31 have attempted to make credible the notion that those Jesus speaks to in vss. 21-29(-30) were much less hostile than those in vss. 31ff.[162] They also think, then, that this difference comes out in the distinction between those who "believe in" Jesus in vs. 30 and those who "believe" him (dative) in vs. 31.[163]

It is questionable, however, whether one can attach to these differences such decisive significance, if any at all. Generally speaking, the incomprehension in relation to Jesus in vss. 13-29 is not less than in vss. 31-59, though it is true that the conflict between Jesus and "the Jews" is assuming ever more serious forms. Whether one should, on the basis of the different ways "believe" is used, distinguish between "believers" and "sympathizers" is strongly questioned by most exegetes.[164]

162. See, e.g., Moloney, *Johannine Son of Man,* pp. 126ff., and his overview of the different views.

163. On this distinction see Brown, *Comm.* I, p. 513 (though with a question mark in regard to 8:31).

164. See R. Bultmann, *TDNT* VII, p. 222; Schnackenburg, *Comm.* II, pp. 204f.; Brown, *Comm.* I, pp. 354 (referring to Dodd), 513.

But not much is gained by that question for an understanding of the real problem, which is how we get from this belief to the statements that follow in vss. 33ff., which are striking even if addressed just to "sympathizers." If we avoid forced solutions,[165] we still have to assume that what at first seems to be a problem really brings us to the focus of the entire passage by showing that "the Jews" in conflict with Jesus are not just his obvious enemies but also, as time progresses, those who earlier "believed" in him and joined him as disciples. This reversal did not occur in a single dialogue situation — from one day to the next, so to speak. The conspicuous perfect tense in vs. 31, "those among the Jews who had believed in him,"[166] though it does refer back to vs. 30 and the believers mentioned there, certainly does not refer to those people alone. Vs. 30 reflects one (or more) specific situations(s): "As Jesus said these things to them" or — as the present participle[167] may indicate — "When he spoke to them in this manner, many believed in him." But vs. 31 speaks of such people more in general: Jews who over time had begun to follow Jesus as "disciples." It does so in order to indicate the reason that they ultimately turned away from him and against him, which was his absolute claim that faith in him was the only means by which they could become "free." This so struck at the root of their self-awareness as the "seed of Abraham" that their faith in Jesus changed into hostility. Vss. 30 and 31 are therefore not intended as a snapshot of a particular moment in time. They serve, rather, to show why many among the Jews who first believed in Jesus nevertheless finally turned against him (cf. also 6:60, 66).

I fail to see why this picture should not be applicable to developments occurring during Jesus' ministry but must rather be assigned to the Evangelist's concern only for what was taking place in and around the later church. Expositors who favor this opinion base it in part on the perfect tense in vs. 31a, which is said to refer to people who had long been considered believers and disciples (cf. Ac. 15:5; 21:20) and who should therefore be located among the Jewish Christians in John's own time (and "community"), people who, perhaps because of Jewish counterpropaganda, were in danger of lapsing from their faith in Christ.[168] Others think here of Jews who believed in Jesus but had not joined the Christian community (not Jewish Christians, therefore, but Christian Jews) and who were not prepared to accept the implications of the absolute significance of Christ — specifically with regard to their Abrahamic descent.[169]

165. See, e.g., Brown, *Comm.* I, pp. 351, 354. See also, however, his *Community of the Beloved Disciple,* pp. 76ff.

166. τοὺς πεπιστευκότας αὐτῷ.

167. ταῦτα αὐτοῦ λαλοῦντος.

168. So, e.g., Schnackenburg, *Comm.* II, pp. 258ff., partly following C. H. Dodd, "A l'arrière-plan d'un dialogue Johannique," *Revue d'Histoire et de Philosophie Religieuses* 37 (1957), pp. 5-17.

169. So J. L. Martyn, "Glimpses into the History of the Johannine Community," in *L'Évangile de Jean,* ed. M. de Jonge, 1977, pp. 166ff. Martyn mentions specifically σπέρμα

As the Evangelist wrote, he undoubtedly had in mind the situation of the Christians for whom he wrote (20:31), and that situation was shaped in large measure by the conflict between church and synagogue, a conflict focused on the absolute significance of Jesus as the Christ. But it is quite another matter to say that the discussion with believing Jews referred to in the present pericope can only be understood against that later historical background. If it did, the Evangelist's entire presentation would have a schizophrenic character. How could he ascribe to the Jews of the pericope things that apply only to Jews of Jesus' day, such as "you seek to kill me" (vss. 37, 40)? In other words, how can the "two levels" in the Gospel run through each other without repeatedly incurring anachronisms and incongruities?[170] Furthermore, what are regarded as descriptions of groups and relationships inside and outside the later church community are so vague and so open to a variety of interpretations that attempts on that basis to construe a somewhat plausible picture of the later church have hardly any support in the text, with however much acuteness and resourcefulness they are undertaken.[171]

On the basis of the text before us one can, in my opinion, draw no other conclusion with regard to the intent of the Evangelist than that the actual and deepest reason for the rejection of Jesus by the Jewish leaders and large groups of Jewish people lay in the absolute character of Jesus' self-revelation as the Christ and the Son of God. It is self-evident that this antithesis retained its permanent relevance in the preaching of the gospel, not only to Israel but to the entire world, but that does not mean that it arose only in the later development between church and synagogue and did not have its decisive beginning for all later time in the confrontation between the historical Jesus and the Israel of his day.

31b Jesus' exhortation to those who had evidenced their faith in him in the first place concerns the necessity of perseverance: "if you continue in my word." The expression "continue in" is characteristic of the Fourth Gospel and occurs there in all sorts of combinations and meanings. What is meant by "continuing in Jesus' word" is expressed elsewhere by "his word abiding in you" (5:38), the first referring of course to the activity, perseverance, and faithfulness of believers, the second to the reciprocal effect that the word has on them. See also the comments on 6:56, where the reciprocal "abides in me, and I in him" occurs in one and the same utterance.

Only by thus persevering will they "truly" be Jesus' disciples. The em-

---

Άβραάμ because of its "ambiguity," describing "loyal Jews" on the one hand and being "a secret expression of their Christian inclinations" on the other (p. 167). This, in my opinion, is a very weak argument since there is no evidence anywhere that Christian Jews used the expression "seed of Abraham" of themselves. The Pauline texts cited as proof (2 Co. 11:2; Gl. 3:6-29) certainly cannot serve that purpose.

170. See pp. 282-85 above on Nicodemus.

171. This applies to the development of Martyn's "two-level" hypothesis. See also Brown, *Community of the Beloved Disciple.*

phasis lies on "truly" (RSV, NRSV) or "really" (NIV). The genuineness of
their discipleship must prove itself in persevering continuance in the word of
Jesus and in doing his word (cf. 13:35; 15:8).[172] The emphasis that Jesus places
on this continuance in his word and the dependence of the reality of discipleship
that he places on it are in accord with what we read elsewhere of his distancing
himself from the large numbers of people who counted themselves among his
followers (cf. 2:24ff.) and with the experience he had already had with such
people (6:60). After all, "he himself knew what was in humankind" (2:25), as
he also "knew from the first who did not believe" (6:64). The warning in vs.
31 thus constitutes a significant, one would almost say ominous, introduction
to the reversal that happens immediately after in the attitude of those to whom
Jesus speaks here (vs. 33) and to the sharp reaction with which he responds to
it (vss. 37ff.).

32, 33 But awaiting Jesus' "true" disciples is the promise that they "will
know the truth." "Truth" here is not general or philosophical truth but the
trustworthy knowledge of God that is realized in its fullness in the coming of
Jesus Christ (cf. the comments on 1:14, 17; 3:21; 5:33).[173] It is the truth that
"came" through Jesus Christ, that became flesh and blood in him (1:14, 17),
that he therefore *is* (14:6), and that is referred to again and again in the rest of
this chapter (vss. 40, 44, 45). It is based on what Jesus himself "heard from
God" (vs. 40) and as such is God's gift to humanity. Corresponding with it is
"knowledge" of the truth, not merely theoretical insight but understanding,
gained by experience, of who God wants to be for people in Jesus; hence also
insight (and not only an indefinite or emotional experience) into the how and
what of the truth, how it is obtained and what it implies; a "knowledge"
therefore that also consists in observing and doing the truth (cf. 3:21).

The salvific power of the truth is further described here as *liberating* (the
only time this concept occurs in the Gospel of John).[174] The freedom meant is
not that of a person to manage his life free of all the ties that might hinder him
in the development of his own "identity" or "authority." That, after all, would
mean no more than that such a person has within himself a freedom that he
merely needs to discover and maintain against everything and everyone who
would hinder him in the exercise of this selfhood. The reference is rather to a
freedom that a person does not possess within himself, even if he thinks

---

172. In the Fourth Gospel, "disciple" (μαθητής), like "believe," sometimes refers to a
provisional, not permanent, decision for Jesus (cf. 6:60, 66).

173. See, e.g., the clear exposition of the Johannine concept of truth in G. E. Ladd, *A
Theology of the New Testament*, 1993[2], pp. 298ff.

174. Schnackenburg *(Comm.* II, p. 206) says of this statement: "This is one of the magnificent Johannine phrases which to this day have lost nothing of their radiance." However, he
rightly adds: "But it also shares the fate of other great sayings in being misunderstood and
misapplied."

otherwise and attempts to live by that illusion. It must be granted to him as a reality coming from the outside, in which he participates by "birth from above" and that thus makes him free. In vss. 34ff. Jesus explains this freedom further.

That does not happen, however, before (vs. 33) the Jews, on hearing Jesus say that freedom still has to be granted to them, erupt in lively protest. With great emphasis they object that as the seed of Abraham they have never been anyone's slaves. It becomes immediately clear, as a result, what is lacking in their faith in Jesus. They were prepared to accept him and grant him credence when he spoke to them of God (cf. 3:2). But that faith had to fit into the framework of their Jewishness and could not be allowed to violate what was fundamental for them in that Jewishness. And such a violation occurred, to their way of thinking, when they heard from Jesus that they still had to become free. The freedom of which they speak cannot be construed politically.[175] For they could hardly say that as a nation they had never sighed under foreign bondage. Their protest rather arose from a sense of spiritual superiority as children of Abraham chosen by God out of all the nations, and thus a sense of being exempt from any servant relationship to others (cf. Mt. 3:9; Ro. 2:17-20).[176] They rightly sensed that, by the way Jesus made their freedom contingent on faith in him, he was calling into question this inalienable privilege. Therefore, there they met the boundary of faith in him — a boundary they were not prepared to cross.

34 Over against this Jewish self-awareness, Jesus, with great authority ("truly, truly"), poses another point of departure: whoever commits sin is a slave (to sin)[177] and therefore cannot boast of freedom. The point is, of course,

---

175. For this see, at length, H. E. Lona, *Abraham in Johannes 8,* 1976, pp. 254ff. The concept of freedom based on the relationship to Abraham is seldom mentioned in Jewish literature (cf. Lona, pp. 254f.; for the Zealots' concept of freedom in distinction from that of the Pharisees, see pp. 256f.). According to Lona the controversy in 8:33 does not relate to freedom "that can be traced back to a certain historical situation" (p. 261). The Jews' protest against Jesus' message of freedom has a more general character.

176. Cf. Strack/Billerbeck, I, pp. 116ff., 523f.; Schlatter, *Comm.,* p. 212. Ro. 2:17-20, though it does not mention the seed of Abraham, may be considered the locus classicus of Jewish self-consciousness as the people of the law (cf. Strack/Billerbeck, III, pp. 96-105). The idea that John, like Paul in Gl. 3:16, by speaking of a singular σπέρμα, possibly alludes to Jesus as the real descendant of Abraham, the one who as the Son (vss. 35, 36) alone can make people free, as Brown suspects (*Comm.* I, pp. 355, 363), is in no way indicated in the text and is most unlikely in view of the highly individual character of Paul's exposition of σπέρμα in Gl. 3:16.

177. The two last words, τῆς ἁμαρτίας, "of sin," are lacking in a number of textual witnesses and are not, according to some interpreters, original since the term "slave" or "servant," on which everything depends here, is otherwise much less sharply limited (so, e.g., Bultmann, *Comm.,* p. 438, n. 2). Others think we have here an adaptation to Ro. 6:17. Apart from this last consideration, there is much to be said for this argument. The addition of τῆς ἁμαρτίας could be explained from the need to further qualify the absolute clause "is a slave," but then it dulls the point of the argument. The argument against omitting τῆς ἁμαρτίας is that these words have strong manuscript support. The overall meaning, of course, remains the same. We are dealing with a nuance that, in the context, should not be totally overlooked.

that this rule is valid also for Jews, and, as will become evident, that determines the nature of the sonship on which they base themselves. We can ignore here to what degree Jesus found points of contact for this statement in the Jewish views of sin and its power over humans.[178] He was not participating in a theological dispute over the freedom of the will. He positioned himself, rather, in the fullness of his messianic consciousness, against the illusion that as children of Abraham they had no need of the freedom he offered and were fundamentally different from all others in this regard. Accordingly, his pronouncement in vs. 34 agrees much more with what Paul says (Ro. 6:16ff.; 7:7ff.) about the superior power of sin and the insufficiency of the law in the face of it. Still, the angle here is different, not that of the powerlessness of the law (cf. Ro 8:3) but of the misplaced appeal to being the seed of Abraham, as though that by itself guaranteed freedom from the bondage of sin.

35, 36 Before proceeding to discuss the groundlessness of this appeal, Jesus develops the metaphor further, speaking of the hopeless situation of slaves unless they are given freedom from above. To that end he compares the position of the domestic slave with that of the son of the house. The slave does not remain in the house "forever." He cannot assert permanently valid claims to the privileges the house affords him (cf. Gl. 4:30). The son can. The son has permanent and unique rights, and he has disposal over the slave's freedom, which Jesus refers to in vs. 36. There Jesus proceeds directly from the metaphor to its referent by saying "you." Thus he identifies the position of his hearers with that of slaves and points them to himself as the only one who can make them free: "If the Son makes you free, you will be free indeed." Hence the point of the metaphor in vss. 35 and 36 is not that the Jews were only provisionally incorporated into the divine dispensation of grace or that Jesus is "the one seed of Abraham."[179] It is, rather, that freedom can only be received as a gift and that the (divinely appointed) Son is the only one with power to dispense the gift.

Verses **37** and **38** refer back to vs. 33, where the Jews claim that as the seed of Abraham they are free. Jesus begins his words on this subject in a radical way. He acknowledges the essential connection between fatherhood and sonship. But whereas the Jews, on the basis of their descent from Abraham, believe they can infer their freedom as his children, Jesus reverses this logic and turns it against the Jews: what the children "do" (cf. vs. 34) points to who their father is. Step by step through a long line of reasoning, he moves toward his conclusion.

178. The Jewish concept of the conflict between the evil and good impulses in the human person is familiar. The law was regarded as the God-given means for restraining the evil impulse and for bringing the good impulse to victory. On this see, at greater length, my *Paul: An Outline of His Theology,* 1975, pp. 130ff., and the literature cited there.

179. Cf. n. 176 above.

The beginning of vs. 37 is concessive: "I know. . . ." Of course Jesus acknowledges that as Jews his opponents are descendants of Abraham. But in the same breath he adds: "yet you seek to kill me." And he explains their wanting to kill him by saying "because my word finds no place in you."[180] That Jesus attributes to all of them indiscriminately the intent to kill him is (in connection with vs. 31) certainly striking and hard to explain satisfactorily.[181] The same thing occurs in 7:19, but there, unlike here, it is vehemently contradicted. Nonetheless, "seek to kill me" is heard again and again through these chapters (cf. 7:1, 19, 25 [30]; 8:40) and goes back to 5:18, the starting point for the entire confrontation between Jesus and "the Jews." It constitutes the ever more clearly visible background of these dialogues and thus anticipates the outcome of the conflict and shows its already lethal character.

It is against that background that we must understand Jesus' identification — in their fundamental choice — of the many who have followed him but are presently turning against him with those who have sought his death and in what follows emerge as his real dialogue partners ("the Jews," vss. 48, 51ff.). Of course, this does not mean that all who earlier or later turned away from Jesus did this partly with the intent to kill him. Nevertheless, in this dialogue, in which their privileged position as seed of Abraham and people of God is fundamentally at stake, those who have followed him choose, not his side, but that of his implacable adversaries. It is also in this context that Jesus again picks up, and takes to the limit of its logic, the question of "fatherhood" as that which at bottom separates him from them.

In two parallel sentences (vs. 38) Jesus begins to point out, by reference to his Father and theirs, the source of his and their speech and action: "I speak of what I have seen with the Father" (cf. comments on 3:11); "you also [evidently] do what you have heard from the father." Although the reference is to two different fathers, that is not brought out and — remarkably enough — in both sentences the possessive pronoun ("my," "your") is lacking.[182] As a result all the emphasis falls on fatherhood as such, namely as the decisive origin and background and hence also as the standard both for Jesus' speech and for what, in response, the Jews "do": "Only when the essence of the Father

180. χωρεῖν is also translated "go forward," but in connection with vs. 31 it probably means "find a (permanent) place," "gain a (firm) foothold."

181. See the trouble to which almost all commentaries go to offer a plausible explanation of this seeming discrepancy.

182. At least in the manuscripts most often followed. Consequently, the emphasis does not yet lie on the different paternity of each but on the fact that both act in accord with their father and that the identities of their fathers therefore emerges in their action and speech. The words "seeing" and "hearing" are used here interchangeably and without distinction (cf. the comments above on 3:11; 5:11ff.); the same is true of παρά with the dative and παρά with the genitive, though the former tends to assume an antecedent existence with the Father (cf. 17:5) more than the latter.

is disclosed will the character of the action manifest itself. Hence the relationship to the Father determines the action. That applies both to the Jews and to Jesus (5:19)."[183]

Obviously, considering the nature of their action (vs. 37), this was calculated to make the Jews think. Still, Jesus only arrives step by step at the final, inescapable conclusion concerning their "father." Before saying what he says in vs. 44, he offers the Jews an opportunity to draw that conclusion on their own.

39, 40 Their reply reflects irritation rather than reflection. They make no protest against his accusation. Whatever he thought he could say about his father and whatever consequences he thought he had to attach to their not continuing in his word, for them one thing was beyond and above all dispute: that their father was Abraham and no one else.

However, Jesus persists in asserting a connection between "fatherhood" and "works" and now declares openly that their appeal to Abraham would be valid only if they did "the works of Abraham."[184] Hence his opposition is not to Abraham, nor to an appeal to Abraham, but to a supposed sonship[185] of Abraham that no longer displays the spiritual characteristics of Abraham. But (vs. 40) "now" — where are they? Instead of doing the works of Abraham they try to kill Jesus, "a man who has told you the truth that I heard from God." "Man" (ἄνθρωπος) has no special emphasis here; it is used rather in the general sense of "someone" (but cf. "murderer," ἀνθρωποκτόνος, in vs. 44). Jesus speaks here openly of God as the Father from whom he "heard" the truth (see the comments on 5:19; 3:11). But having said that, he has thereby indicated to them the depth of the chasm that separates them from Abraham: "this is not what Abraham did." For Abraham's "work" consisted in attending to the voice of God and so becoming the father of Israel and of many nations (cf. Gn. 15:6; 17:5; Ro. 9:16ff.; Gl. 3:7, 29).

41 Therefore, in view of the works they do, only one conclusion is possible: they must have another, a "distinct," father of their own: "You do the works of *your* father!" Jesus still does not name that father, but from the emphasis with which he speaks of "your" father and after what in vs. 40 was

---

183. Lona, *Abraham in Johannes 8,* p. 219.

184. An expression that also occurs in the Talmud, though not as a stereotypical description of Abraham's conduct (Strack/Billerbeck, III, p. 514).

185. The view that a distinction is made here between σπέρμα and τέκνα, the first conceded and the second denied (so Lona, *Abraham in Johannes 8,* pp. 218, 272, appealing to Ro. 9:7), is most dubious. Paul also uses σπέρμα in a spiritual sense (cf. Gl. 3:16, 29), though it is doubtful that the way in which Paul discriminates between "seed" and "children" has any influence here. The case is rather that σπέρμα and τέκνα are used interchangeably and that being Abraham's seed is here attributed to the Jews in the natural sense (vs. 37) and denied to them in the spiritual sense (vs. 39), though in the latter with the term "children."

said of Abraham it is clear what he has in mind: their works betray a father whose "work" is to do what they are now doing: to kill (vss. 40, 44).

The Jews' offended response shows that they are beginning to grasp Jesus' intent. Still, even now they do not react to his continued reference to their works as the criterion for the identity of their father. But their reaction to the implication that they must have another father, a strange father, is all the more vehement: "We were not born of fornication."[186] Their spiritual descent is in no way as suspect or obscure as he apparently assumes and suggests. They are not pagans! For that reason they now reach out beyond Abraham: "We have one Father, even God." With the word "one" they point to the monotheistic basis of their religion and national existence (Dt. 6:4). Not that they thus relinquish the claim to descent from Abraham, but behind Abraham was God who called Abraham and made Abraham's descendants his own children, the children of one God. God was, therefore, their "one Father," Israel's highest defender and final court of appeal, even when Abraham could no longer help them (cf. Is. 63:16).

Although in ancient times the relationship between God and Israel was relatively infrequently described as that of a father and his children,[187] still already in the Old Testament we see repeated appeal to it under certain circumstances, in words of both God and the people. This portrayal of the relationship is not especially related to Abraham but more generally to Israel as God's creation (Dt. 32:6; Is. 64:8; Jr. 3:4), to God's covenant with Israel (Jr. 3:19; Ml. 2:10), and to God's rule and kingship over Israel (Is. 63:16; Ps. 89:27; 2 Sa. 7:14). Jesus' description of his adversaries as children of an alien father would be to their minds the most offensive accusation he could advance against them.

42 In the same manner in which in vs. 39 Jesus rejected their appeal to being children of Abraham, he now rejects their claim that God is their father. If God were their father, that, too, would be evident in that their works would be God's works (cf. 6:28, 29): "If God were your Father, you would love me." Jesus mentions "love" as the absolute opposite of what they in fact did, which

186. Some expositors believe that there may be in this statement an ad hominem insinuation directed against Jesus himself in view of later Jewish charges concerning his illegitimate birth. The emphasis on "we" in vs. 41b would then mean: "*We* were not born illegitimately (but you were)" (so, e.g., Brown, *Comm.* I, p. 357). Barrett is firmer: "The implication (especially of the emphatic ἡμεῖς) is that Jesus was born of πορνεία" (*Comm.*, p. 348). Barrett also thinks it likely that the Evangelist seeks thus to inform his readers that what appeared, in the case of Jesus, to be a birth out of a nonmarital relationship was in fact a supernatural birth. But the emphatic ὑμεῖς does not require this explanation. It may very well reflect the emphatic ἡμεῖς in vs. 41a. And there is nothing else in the context to suggest such an insinuation. See also the refutation by Schnackenburg, *Comm.* II, p. 212.

187. Rather seldom in the Old Testament, more frequently in later Jewish writings; see, e.g., W. Bousset, *Die Religion des Judentums,* 1926³, pp. 377ff.

was to hate and to seek to kill him. "Love" does not always have to refer to emotional or personal affection but can also be used of taking someone's side or opting in favor of something (cf. 3:19; 1 Jn. 3:14b). The idea here is recognition on the basis of spiritual kinship (cf. 1 Jn 5:1; Jn. 7:17). If God were their Father, they would, acting from within that relationship of kinship, not oppose Jesus but of course accept him: "For I proceeded and came forth from God."

This "proceeding from God,"[188] as the conclusion of vs. 42 shows (cf. also 17:8, "thou didst send me," parallel to "I came from you"), does not refer to what in systematic theology is called the intertrinitarian relationship (the "eternal procession of the Son from the Father"). Nevertheless this procession does presuppose an antecedent existence with God (see the comments on 5:19) and a "descent from heaven" (cf. 6:38). Hence "proceeded" comes before "came forth."

The word translated "came forth" has a certain solemn sound and is often used for the "dawning" of great events, the appearance of important personages and the like, in the New Testament often in an eschatological connection.[189] If God, therefore, were the father of the Jews who deny Jesus' claims, this would not have escaped them, and the plan to get rid of him would be the last thing to occur to them. Hence, again, "I came not of my own accord," which comes back in these dialogues like a refrain and serves as Jesus' defense against the notion that he arrogated to himself the authority with which he spoke (cf. 5:17; 6:41ff.; 7:27ff.).

Verse **43** pursues in still another way the idea that the Jews have a father other than God and thus constitutes a transition to the high point of the conflict in vs. 44: Jesus asks: "Why do you not understand my language?" Jesus himself answers: "because you cannot bear to hear my word." This somewhat tautological-sounding argument becomes clear if one understands the word translated here by "language" as referring to the unique way in which Jesus keeps speaking of "having come," "proceeding from the Father," having been "sent by the Father," and the like. That "language" or "manner of speaking"[190] confused or offended his opponents over and over (cf. 8:19, 22, 25; cf. also 6:41; 7:35; 3:9, 10). Jesus' answer is also stated in loaded language: they heard the sounds but lacked the ability to "hear." They did not hear with faith in their hearts (cf. 5:24). And for that reason they could not understand his word in its true meaning. It was for them like a strange language because the world from which and the Father from whom Jesus spoke were not theirs.

44 This last point is driven home with utter clarity and sharpness: "You

---

188. ἐξερχέσθαι, here with ἐκ, usually occurs with ἀπό or παρά (cf. 13:3; 16:27ff.; 17:8).

189. ἥκω; cf. J. Schneider, *TDNT* II, p. 928: "used predominantly of the eschatological coming to salvation and judgment. . . . In John's gospel ἥκειν is used . . . to express the epiphany."

190. λαλία, which occurs only here and at 4:42 in the Fourth Gospel. In Mt. 26:73 it means "language," "dialect."

are of the father the devil." Again, as in vs. 38, Jesus speaks of "the father" without the possessive pronoun, to indicate the background and dynamic out of which they speak and act. Now, however, abandoning his previous reserve, he adds (epexegetically): "the devil."[191] He uses the word, not as invective (the way they declared him demon-possessed), but to open their eyes to the actual source of their impulses, the real father of their works. That cannot be Abraham (vs. 39) or God (vs. 42); it is "your father's desires" that they plan to carry out. For from the beginning of the world he was a murderer, and it was he who from then on perverted the truth. This refers, of course, to the event in paradise in which the devil brought death on humankind by falsehood and deception (cf. 1 Jn. 3:8; Ro. 7:11). His desires consist in murder and falsehood.

From this point on, in connection with vs. 32 (cf. vs. 40), the emphasis falls on that perversion of the truth. The expression (literally) "he has not stood in the truth" means that the truth was not his starting point or standpoint[192] and must also be understood in connection with the Genesis story. For when the devil approached humankind he held out, not the truth (of the word of God), but the lie, thus deceiving and destroying humans (Gn. 3:1ff.). The conclusion of vs. 44 shows that when he did that the devil did not just incidentally deviate from the truth but was being himself: "For there is no truth in him. When he lies he speaks his native language" (NIV). His speech is by definition false. For his name is "liar," and he is the father of falsehood. In that connection one must not just think of dishonesty or mendacity in a moral sense, for the lie here is the antithesis of what in vs. 32 is called the truth. It is the contradiction of the word of God and therefore by implication enslaving and deadly (Gn. 3:3, 4). Therefore "lie" does not refer here to a distinct act that can be immediately rectified but to a transindividual power of deception with paternity of its own, not from God the Father but from the father, the devil.

On the meaning of ὑμεῖς ἐκ τοῦ πατρὸς τοῦ διαβόλου ἐστέ there is much divergence of opinion among expositors. Some think that grammatically these words can only be translated, "You are of the father of the devil." And even if there should be a grammatical error here, the conclusion of the verse, ὅτι ψεύστης ἐστὶν καὶ ὁ πατὴρ αὐτοῦ, can only mean: "for his (the devil's) father is also a liar." However, though in other literature speculation exists concerning the origin (and the father) of the devil,[193] in the present context, as in the entire New Testament, the notion of such a father is totally foreign. The reference here is obviously to the devil himself. The apparently difficult textual

191. See further below.

192. ἔστηκεν, imperfect of στήκω. One can also take it as the perfect of ἵστημι (ἔστηκεν), but in view of the preceding ἦν the imperfect is more probable.

193. For references to Gnostic literature see Bultmann, *Comm.,* p. 318, n. 2. Bultmann admits that the reference to the father of the devil makes no sense here since the one characterized as murderer and liar in our text is, of course, the devil himself.

construction presents no problems if it is viewed not in isolation but as the endpoint of a line of thought that began earlier. The words τοῦ πατρός occur here deliberately, as in vs. 38, without the possessive pronoun ("your") and therefore as a denotation of fatherhood as such, which is (finally, as the only possible conclusion of the preceding line of thought) identified as that of the devil; τοῦ διαβόλου is appositional:[194] "you are of the father, the devil." That is, the father of whom you give proof of being children is the devil. Finally, καὶ ὁ πατὴρ αὐτοῦ at the end of vs. 44 need present no problem if one understands them to refer to the devil himself as father of the ψεῦδος mentioned in the same sentence.[195]

One arrives at totally different conclusions if, following Dahl,[196] one takes the "murderer from the beginning" to be Cain, the first murderer. According to Dahl, there is in the background here an ancient legend to the effect that Cain was not the son of Adam, but of Eve and a fallen angel. This is said to explain why Jesus here calls the Jews who seek to kill him the children of the devil, just as Cain, the devil's son, killed Abel. Some leave the text intact, in which case the devil remains the "murderer from the beginning," not because of his temptation of the first people in Paradise but because of (the devil's child) Cain.[197] But others, including Dahl and Reim,[198] modify the text so that "the murderer from the beginning" is not the devil but Cain. The original idea here (and already in vss. 38, 41) is said to be that not the devil but Cain was the father of the Jews. Reim appeals specifically to τὰς ἐπιθυμίας ("the desires" of your father), which in Gn. 4:7 is used of Cain, and to vs. 48, where Jesus is made out to be a Samaritan, because the theory of Israel's descent from Cain was advocated by the Samaritans.

But even apart from the radical textual modifications one has to effect to support this view, the notion that throughout this passage the "father" of the Jews Jesus had in mind was Cain seems to me to be alien to the text and too lacking in support there to be credible. Furthermore, the text as we have it is clear enough, all the more so if one also takes into consideration the pronouncement in 1 Jn. 3:8 (cf. also 1 Jn. 3:15).

45 What follows from this is that where the devil exercises his fatherhood there is no room for truth: "but I" — "I" is in the emphatic position, referring to the one who speaks with God as his father[199] — "because *I* tell the truth, you do not believe me." Jesus does not say "in spite of the fact that" but "because" — the ultimate absurdity, it seems. For what else would a person wish (and claim) to believe than the truth? Still, what he says is intended precisely as it is stated. Because they are children of the devil, who is false,

---

194. See also BDF §268.2.

195. See also BDF §282.3.

196. N. A. Dahl, "Der Erstgeborene des Satans und der Vater des Teufels," in *Apophoreta* (Festschrift for E. Haenchen), 1964, pp. 70ff.

197. Cf. Brown, *Comm.* I, p. 358; Lona, *Abraham in Johannes 8*, pp. 285f.

198. G. Reim, "Joh. 8,44 — Gotteskinder/Teufelskinder," *NTS* 30 (1984), pp. 619ff.

199. ἐγὼ δὲ ὅτι, probably pendent nominative.

therefore it is precisely the truth in Jesus that makes them so averse to his word and hinders them from believing. What is at stake is not something more or less within one truth, not two separate roads of faith finally leading to the same destination, but the absolute either-or of truth and falsehood.

The two questions in vs. **46** say all this in still another way:[200] The first asks not just whether there is something in Jesus' conduct that makes him unbelievable in their eyes. Here "sin" is the proper work of the devil (cf. 1 Jn. 3:8: "He who commits sin is of the devil; for the devil has sinned from the beginning"). Things having come to such a pass between Jesus and the Jews, who among them is able to demonstrate that he is on "the wrong side," that in this contest he represents sin, contradicts God, and incites others to do evil as the devil did and still does? One might perhaps say that, after vs. 45, this is a question that can hardly be posed to the Jews and that the answer to it is obvious only to faith. But by stating the issue in such sharp terms (namely that he is possibly the great deceiver, the advocate of sin, and hence worthy of death) Jesus once more lays on them the full burden of proof. They can do no less than furnish that proof if they would own their responsibility toward him and toward the God to whom they appeal. Hence the challenge comes to them: "Which of you?" And hence once more the alternative is put to them: "If (however) I tell the truth, why do you not believe me?"

47 After all that has preceded, the posing of this last question (vs. 46b) is its own answer. And with that Jesus draws the awesome, and only possible, conclusion from the entire dispute: "He who is of God hears the words of God." The fatherhood out of which a person lives determines how that person "hears." To be "of God," that is, to be "born" of God, to be born "from above" (1:13; 3:3), is to hear, understand, and believe the words that God has spoken in this world. Therefore, despite all the words extended to them, Jesus' disputants do not "hear" because they are not of God. A clearer or more severe conclusion is hardly conceivable.

8:48-59

"Before Abraham Was, I Am"

48 The pericope that now follows is linked closely with the preceding. Again the fundamental position of Abraham surfaces, but now from a different viewpoint. Vs. 48 ties in with Jesus' concluding statement in the preceding dispute. To the Jews this means the end of every meaningful continuation of the dia-

---

200. Vs. 46 is missing in some manuscripts, obviously on account of the homoioteleuton of vss. 45 and 46 (οὐ πιστεύετε μοι).

logue. They do not respond further to Jesus' words. Could he not understand that, by speaking as he did, he was in their eyes nothing but a Samaritan and demon-possessed?[201] As a "Samaritan" he would be one with whom fellowship was impossible (cf. comments on 4:22). Because of his refusal to acknowledge his Jewish audience as the seed of Abraham, Jesus was in their eyes no better than the Samaritans, who, on account of their worship on Mount Gerizim and their encroachment on Israel's national existence, were avoided by Jews as despisers of true religion and as enemies. With "you are possessed" they asserted that for his — to their minds — boundless arrogance they had no other explanation than that he — not they! — was under the sway of the devil.

49, 50   Jesus' answer, "I am not possessed, but honor my father," indicates that they continue to misunderstand him if they think that he is out to advance his own honor and that the authority with which he speaks to them is based on (diabolical) conceit. He is doing nothing other than "honoring his father," that is, doing justice to God in the world. They call him names and spurn him for it: "and *you* dishonor me." But he ("Yet I," vs. 50) will not follow them in that and attempt to defend his honor against them. *That* he would do if he were seeking his own honor, which is precisely what they think he is doing. For that he again appeals to God: "there is One who seeks it and he will be the judge." He himself will not have to defend his honor; he can leave that to the Father (cf. 8:26). And judgment issuing from that tribunal will answer to what people, including Jesus' disputants, have done with his words, which are words spoken by one sent by the Father. That judgment is already being realized now (cf. 3:18; 5:32) and will be fully realized in the glorification of the Son by the Father (cf. vs. 54; 12:28; 17:4).

51   However, just as now Jesus' word will prove powerful in relation to those who reject and dishonor him, so it will demonstrate its validity also to those who keep it. With great authority, totally in accord with the opening statement in vs. 31, this is once more expressed and confirmed here. Instead of saying "continue in my word" (vs. 31) here, Jesus says, "keep my word." In both cases the reference is to perseverance in and observance of Jesus' word (cf. 15:20; 17:6, etc.). In vs. 32 the promised fruit of this is knowledge of the truth, while here it is never undergoing death ("see"; cf. vs. 52: "taste death"). The reference is to what is said in 5:24ff., there also with solemn emphasis and at great length, about receiving eternal life. Those who believe in Jesus' word already *have* eternal life; death is no longer facing them but behind them; when they pass away, they will not be handed over to death (see the comments on 5:24ff.). It is remarkable that in this connection Jesus makes this statement with so much emphasis. He lays bare, in all its radicalness and quite forcefully, the

---

201. οὐ καλῶς λέγομεν need not mean that they have used such language earlier to describe Jesus but only that they have every reason to call him what they now call him.

conflict between the Jews and himself and thus casts many of them into a crisis of faith (vss. 30, 31). But still the strong appeal that he here, as in vss. 31, 32, and 36, permanently extends to them is undeniable and unmistakable. One cannot say, therefore, that he is speaking here only to those who have already been won by him and that "the Jews" here and elsewhere in the Gospel merely represent the *massa perditionis* who die in their sins and from whom no one can any longer be won for Jesus.[202] The case is rather that even now no one remains excluded, but to the last the "Truly, truly, I say to you" remains in effect also in its salvific significance.

52, 53 To the Jews, however, this pronouncement is just one more proof of Jesus' boundless arrogance. They say that they are now completely persuaded[203] that he is possessed. Again they appeal to Abraham as the person by whom they measure all things. They now add "the prophets" as the great emissaries of God in the past. If Abraham died — according to Jewish pronouncements the most cogent proof of the inevitability of death[204] — as also the prophets, how could Jesus' word safeguard anyone from the bitterness of death?[205]

Again they attack Jesus (vs. 53) on the point of what most arouses their opposition: "Certainly you do not claim to be more than our father Abraham, who[206] after all died, as did also the prophets?" In a way this reaction is the same as that of the Samaritan woman (4:12) with regard to "our father Jacob." That Jesus goes beyond all that which is holy and inviolable to the Jews in their past and that forms the basis of their religion and existence as a nation is intolerable for them; that he does not wipe out that past or position himself *against* it but is its secret and its fulfillment (cf. vss. 56ff.) remains totally outside their purview. All they can ascertain in him is arrogance and self-conceit: "Who really do you claim to be?" The language of this question was used earlier in a directly accusing sense (5:18) and will come back in what follows (cf. 10:33; 19:7). The question expresses indirectly what constituted and re-

---

202. So E. Grässer, who poses an antithesis here between Paul, who became all things to all people in order to save some for Christ, and the "Johannine Christ," who no longer extends "the outward call" but for whom the issue whether one is of God or of the devil is settled by "continuing in the word" ("Die antijüdische Polemik im Johannesevangelium," *NTS* 9 [1963], pp. 74-90, esp. 87f.). Not so Bultmann, who writes on vs. 51: "In the presence of 'the Jews,' who as children of the Devil are in death, Jesus issues the solemn promise: 'He who keeps my word, will never see death.' Will the 'dead' hear the voice of the Son of God?" (*Comm.*, p. 324).

203. νῦν ἐγνώκαμεν.

204. So Schlatter, to illustrate the high esteem in which Abraham was held by Jews (*Comm.*, p. 218).

205. "Taste death," θανάτου γεύεσθαι (cf. Mk. 9:1; Hb. 2:9), a phrase occurring in Semitic languages especially for "experiencing death as what it is," "a graphic expression of the hard and painful reality of dying" (J. Behm, *TDNT* I, p. 677); cf. "see" in vs. 51.

206. ὅστις.

mained the real basis of the conflict between Jesus and "the Jews," namely their accusation that he made himself equal with God. For who can safeguard a person from death but God alone?

54, 55   Again (cf. vs. 50) Jesus rejects their accusation of self-glorification, again with an appeal to the Father. If he glorified himself, his glory would not mean anything: "It is *my Father* who glorifies me." Jesus' opponents should realize this, since it is the Father "of whom you say that he is your God." If they really knew that God, then they would hear his voice in Jesus' words and deeds.

But[207] (vs. 55) they do not know God, a statement we have heard before (7:28; 8:19), followed here (as in 7:28-29) by "but I know him." Jesus does not say that they serve another God but that they do not know the one they call their God. For that very reason he cannot ignore their accusation of self-glorification, but (again) must pose in all its rigor the antithesis between them and him: "If I said I do not know him, I would be like you: a liar." But he will not yield to that (diabolical) temptation, whatever the cost: "but I do know him and I keep his word." That word includes the charge the Father has given him (cf. 10:18; 12:49; 15:10). It is not self-glorification that impels him to act but obedience to the one who sent him.

56   On this basis Jesus now also rejects the idea that they could bring Abraham into the lists against him. The opposite is true. Jesus' statement about Abraham here, though most remarkable, is not entirely clear. "Abraham your father rejoiced that he was to see my day; he saw it and was glad." The word translated "rejoice" is often used in a religious sense for joy in God, especially for eschatological salvation.[208] The first part of the statement is to be understood then as a general characterization of Abraham's significance as the receiver of God's promise of descendants and as the father of believers. The expectation of fulfillment of that promise is then characterized by Jesus as a rejoicing in that Abraham would see *"my day."* What, therefore, God promised Abraham in his descendants, *that* Jesus draws into the light of the messianic-eschatological future, which in his coming has begun its fulfillment ("my day").[209]

The question remains, however, what is meant by the concluding words: "and he saw it and was glad." Some believe these words refer to the fulfillment

---

207. Adversative καί.

208. Cf. R. Bultmann, *TDNT* I, pp. 19ff.; here constructed with ἵνα: "rejoiced with a view to the fact that he. . . ."

209. See, e.g., W. Michaelis, *TDNT* V, p. 343, n. 147. So also Lona, *Abraham in Johannes 8,* 327f.: "The hope of Abraham enters its final fulfillment with the appearance of Jesus. . . . The traditional data concerning Abraham in no way coincide with the pronouncement of 8:56. Here one encounters a feature of the figure of Abraham determined from christology, not from tradition." Others think (incorrectly, I believe) that "my day" means "the day of the definitive revelation of His glory" (G. Delling, *TDNT* II, p. 951).

of God's promise already during Abraham's life, namely in the birth of Isaac. "When Isaac was born, Abraham prophetically and in faith already saw in the day of his birth the birth of the Messiah . . . whose coming was heralded by the birth of Isaac."[210] "Rejoicing" could then be linked to Abraham's "laughter" when Isaac's birth was announced (Gn. 17:17). But the significance of this "laughter" remains somewhat enigmatic, though the rabbis (and Philo) saw in it the joy of Abraham's faith.[211] Others refer to ancient Jewish traditions according to which, when God made a covenant with Abraham ("between the halves," Gn. 15:9ff.), he revealed to him the most distant future.[212] However, there is no evidence in those traditions of rejoicing on Abraham's part.

Many other expositors are of the opinion, therefore, that it is hard to find a point in Abraham's earthly life at which "and he saw that day and was glad" is applicable as (the beginning of) the fulfillment of God's promise. They therefore would read this last statement (vs. 56b) as referring to Abraham's *anticipation* of the coming of the Messiah (cf. 12:41).[213] But then it becomes hard (in vs. 56a and 56b) still to distinguish between "was to see" and "saw," which does seem to be intentional. Accordingly, others think that the "seeing" and "rejoicing" in vs. 56b occur *after* the advent of Jesus in the heavenly Paradise, where Abraham empathizes with the fortunes of his people on earth.[214] But the idea that here, without any further qualification, the reference is to Abraham's "seeing" in Paradise seems somewhat hazardous. It is improbable because in what follows the focus is on Jesus' contemporaneity with the *historical* Abraham, not on that of the *heavenly* Abraham with the historical Jesus (vs. 58). For that reason, though the choice is difficult, there is more to be said for the view that Abraham's joyful anticipation of the promise made to him and of its (provisional) fulfillment in the birth of Isaac is placed here in the perspective of the eschatological salvation that has dawned with the coming (the "day") of Jesus.[215]

The main thing, however, is that here Jesus again turns the Jews' appeal to Abraham on its head. Not only does he demonstrate what bad children of Abraham they have been: what they now consistently reject in cynicism and unbelief Abraham long ago fervently longed for and "saw" with "rejoicing." In his overpowering messianic consciousness, Jesus thus points out anew the salvation-historical background against which his coming and work must be

---

210. C. Brown, *Het Evangelie naar Johannes* (Korte Verklaring) I, 1950³, p. 231.

211. See, e.g., Schnackenburg, *Comm.* II, pp. 221f. At greater length also Lona, *Abraham in Johannes 8,* pp. 305f.

212. See Strack/Billerbeck III, pp. 525f.; Lona, *Abraham in Johannes 8,* pp. 296ff., 312ff.

213. So the majority of the older commentaries.

214. So many recent commentators such as Bultmann, Lindars, and Haenchen, and W. Michaelis, *TDNT* V, p. 343, n. 147.

215. So, e.g., Schnackenburg and Brown.

viewed and understood. His appearance is not an isolated, incidental event that, whatever greatness it may display, still has to be believed and understood solely for and by itself. Still less is it a display of demonic conceit or perverted messianism; rather, it announced itself in the earliest history of the people who heard God's voice and believed it. It is the point of intersection at which all the lines of God's speaking up to that point and of human believing response thereto come together and which must be understood and believed as their fulfillment. This is not a failure to do justice to Abraham but rather a vindication of Abraham's believing anticipation. What was true of Jacob, Moses, and all "others" who have "sowed" and "labored" was also true of Abraham (see the comments on 4:12, 37, 38; 5:46; 6:31ff.), namely that the "law" — in which all of these have their place — was given through Moses but that "grace and truth came through Jesus Christ" (1:17).

57   For the Jews, who again cannot get past the mere sound of the words (cf. vs. 22; 7:35; 6:42, 52; 4:11; 3:4), Jesus' pronouncement is an instance not just of conceit but also of the ultimate absurdity. How can a person not yet fifty years old have seen Abraham? It is striking that — unlike Jesus in vs. 56 — they speak of Jesus' seeing Abraham and not the reverse.[216] "Fifty years" is apparently a (generously estimated) round number for an age that Jesus has not yet reached.[217] Although other explanations of this number have been attempted, the most obvious (and least artificial) is that by naming this number the Jews only intended to expose the absurdity of Jesus' statement: how could he, who was less than half a century old, embrace the many centuries that separated him from Abraham?

58   It is, however, precisely with this seeming absurdity that Jesus' answer connects (cf. 6:52, 53). Once more — and now to conclude the entire dispute — he uses the assertion formula ("Truly, truly, I say to you") to emphasize that what his adversaries hold to be the height of folly is in fact the final and deepest reality underlying their conflict over Abraham: "before Abraham was [born], I am." It is, of course, most striking that over against Abraham's birth stands the absolute "I am," which is not bound to a specific time. Here also, as in vs. 24, many expositors think that the "I am" reflects Ex. 3:14 or texts like Is. 43:10. This would imply Jesus' self-identification with the divine "I." But the objections mentioned in our comments on vs. 24 also apply here.[218] Bultmann points to the Logos: "The ἐγώ of which Jesus speaks as the Revealer is the 'I' of the eternal Logos, which was in the beginning, the

216. Some manuscripts, instead of ἑώρακας, read: ἑώρακέν σε, an apparent adaptation to vs. 56.

217. The idea that it could serve as an indication of Jesus' age at the time of his public ministry is not necessary, therefore, and in view of Lk. 3:23 highly improbable.

218. See also Bultmann, *Comm.*, pp. 327-28, n. 5.

'I' of the eternal God himself."[219] It is questionable, however, whether the reference in the "I am" here is to the ontological category of divine being.

Calvin refers to Hb. 13:8 ("Christ the same yesterday, today, and forever"). He also knows of expositors who think that the "I am" here "simply applies to Christ's eternal divinity and compare it to that passage of Moses, 'I am that I am' (Exod. 3.14)." But Calvin himself wants to give the words a much broader meaning[220] "in that Christ's power and grace, inasmuch as He is the Redeemer of the world, were common to all ages."[221] After all, Abraham already delighted in just that, as vs. 56 has indicated. And it is also with a view to that that Jesus answered the unbelieving Jews: "Before Abraham was, I am." Calvin then adds: "Yet that the grace of the Mediator flourished in all ages depended on His eternal Divinity." Therefore, he continues, "this saying of Christ contains a remarkable statement of His divine essence."[222]

If one is to do justice to the context of this characteristic pronouncement, then the "I am" will indeed have to be understood with this distinction in mind. Christ's "mediatorship" is not explicitly referred to here; but the reference to "his day" is all the more clear as that of the eschatological Redeemer promised and sent by God. It is *that* reality that is denoted by the "I am" and from which it derives its specific meaning. The "I am" is uttered by Jesus, not by a divine person abstracted from the human Jesus; that is — in the language of the prologue — it was uttered by the *incarnate* Word. It is undoubtedly a statement made by the Word who in the beginning was with God and was God and in the strength of whom Jesus can now say: "before Abraham was I am." But even so he does not say "I was (there as God)," but present tense "I *am*," because in connection with what Abraham "desired to see" and in principle already "saw," this "I" can be spoken of in no other way than as it became incarnate in Jesus Christ.[223] And in that sense the "I am" also contains the answer to the Jews' question: "Are you then greater than our father Abraham?" (vs. 53).

59 For the Jews Jesus' words were not merely absurd but a reason for stoning him. However they understood Jesus' statement, it sounded blasphemous to them, like grounds for execution (cf. Lv. 24:11-26).[224] The reference here is not to a judicial act, however, but to an eruption of fury that took the form of an attempt (or threat) to stone Jesus (cf. 10:31). It did not come to that, however,

---

219. Bultmann, *Comm.*, p. 327. He again brings up "the meaning of 'pre-existence,'" on which I have commented at some length in connection with 5:19ff.

220. *"Ego vero longius extendo."*

221. *"Virtus et gratia Christi, quatenus mundi Redemptor est, omnium aetatum communis fuit." Comm.* I, p. 235.

222. *"Quod tamen saeculis omnibus viguit mediatoris gratia, hoc ab aeterna eius divinitate pendebat. Itaque hoc dictum Christi insigne divinae essentiae elogium continet." Comm.* I, p. 235.

223. See my *Het Woord is vlees geworden,* 1979, p. 17.

224. See also Strack/Billerbeck, I, pp. 1008-19.

because Jesus left the temple and so eluded them (cf. 12:36).[225] What follows in chs. 9 and 10 tells of Jesus' continued actions in Jerusalem (cf. also 10:22). Not until 10:42 do we read of Jesus going across the Jordan, and not until 11:54 do we find that Jesus "no longer went about openly among the Jews." What we have here is the first mention of an attempt to stone him. The conflict was assuming ever sharper forms. But here, too, the truth was that "his hour had not yet come" (7:30).

Reflections on Chapter 8

In ch. 8 Jesus' confrontation with "the Jews" reaches a stage that it has not yet reached in Gospel and that will not be exceeded in the later dialogues. For good reason this chapter has been described as "a classic summary of the true grounds of the clash between Jesus and the Jews,"[226] and it is especially with reference to the radical pronouncements in ch. 8 that a variety of views have emerged as to the alleged anti-Jewish character of the Fourth Gospel. The discussion of this issue has in recent decades usually been pursued in reference to Johannine "theology." That is, the object of the research is not "the historical Jesus" or the situation in which he acted and spoke, but rather the aim and motives that prompted the author of the Fourth Gospel to give the dialogues between Jesus and the Jews such a sharply antithetical thrust. In this connection two sorts of conceptions come to the fore.[227]

    1. According to the first,[228] the Fourth Gospel is a polemical or apologetic pamphlet against Judaism written when Christians and Jews had come to oppose each other as two mutually independent and exclusive groups. The focus was no longer, as with the Synoptic Gospels, on common issues such as those relating to the law (fasting, purity, divorce, and the like) but on the great question of the identity of Jesus. Was he really the Messiah — and that to be understood as the Son of God and the Son of man clothed with all power? Or was his claim unworthy of belief and in effect blasphemous? In that struggle the church was the embattled and threatened party, and the Fourth Gospel sought to shore up the church. To that end it not only placed the divine glory of Christ prominently in the foreground but also contained a sharp refutation of Judaism, or at least of the most representative groups within Judaism. The Gospel's argument is no longer, as in the Synoptics, against Pharisaic legal formalism (Matthew 23) or, as with Paul, against a teaching of justification on the basis of works of the law. It is, rather, against Jewish disbelief in Jesus as the divinely sent Messiah. That disbelief

---

    225. ἐκρύβη καὶ ἐξῆλθεν ἐκ τοῦ ἱεροῦ. The meanings of the two coordinate verbs mutually determine each other (see BDF §471.4: "He hid himself among the people and so escaped").

    226. So W. Beilner, *Christus und die Pharisäer. Exegetische Untersuchungen über Grund und Verlauf der Auseinandersetzungen,* 1959, p. 150.

    227. For what follows see the historic overview in R. Leistner, *Antijudaismus im Johannesevangelium?* 1974. See also E. Grässer, "Die antijüdische Polemik im Johannesevangelium," *NTS* 11 (1964), p. 74.

    228. For which, to this day, W. Wrede's *Charakter und Tendenz des Johannesevangeliums,* 1912[2], 1933, is representative.

constitutes the real break between Jews and Christians. In it the Jews demonstrate that they are no longer God's elect people, the seed of Abraham. In their zeal to kill Jesus they rather manifest themselves to be children of the devil.

In this conception, therefore, the Fourth Gospel is a clear forerunner of later Christian apologies directed against the Jews, such as the dialogue of Justin Martyr with Trypho the Jew. Although in the later (and still continuing) struggle against anti-Semitism some found in the Gospel of John the seeds of later Christian hostility and hatred against the Jews, such a conclusion is certainly not inherent in this understanding of the Fourth Gospel. In all probability the author of the Fourth Gospel was himself a Jew, and the frame of reference of his Gospel makes it likely that those for whom he wrote were mostly Jews. He did in a sense write against "the Jews," as he often, without making distinctions, called Jesus' opponents. But he wrote against them as those who had rejected and killed Jesus and who, in their later synagogal communities, adopted an increasingly hostile and aggressive (cf. 16:2) attitude toward the Christian community, which had separated from them. In this connection some expositors believe that it was precisely this bond with, and love for, the Jewish people that prompted the Evangelist to make such harsh pronouncements against its leaders, out of anger that they had so culpably and tragically led his own people astray.[229] Therefore, to call the Fourth Gospel a polemical pamphlet against the Jews is certainly a misconstrual of the goal the Evangelist set for himself.

2. Partly with a view to this problem, others have arrived at a totally different assessment of the so-called anti-Judaism of the Fourth Gospel.[230] In their opinion "the Jews" are in this Gospel representatives, not of their own law-bound religion, but much more of unbelief in general. Some scholars believe that the whole "historical" setting in which the discussions between Jesus and the Jews are set is totally unrealistic, on the one hand, and cannot, on the other hand, be identified with later disputes between church and synagogue. There is hardly any question here, they say, of real "conversations," or "dialogues." All that happens is that Jesus witnesses concerning himself; in response "the Jews" do not act as the empirical Jewish nation but as representatives of the "world"; their hostility toward Jesus stands for the "world's" hatred. The sharpness of the confrontation that marks the relationship between Jesus and "the Jews" in the Fourth Gospel and that culminates in ch. 8 is not, therefore, anti-Judaistic, much less anti-Semitic in the modern racist sense. It is, rather, to be explained in terms of the Fourth Gospel's radically "dualistic" concept of revelation, the background of which must be located in certain forms of Hellenistic syncretism, specifically in Gnosticism with its absolute dualism in both cosmology and anthropology. That dualism comes to expression at least terminologically in John's absolute antitheses between "truth and falsehood," "light and darkness," "above and below," "flesh and Spirit," and "God and devil." The conversations between Jesus and the Jews are not historical but only "exemplary" representations of that dualism.[231]

---

229. So, e.g., G. Baum, *The Jews and the Gospel: A Reexamination of the New Testament,* 1961, pp. 126f.

230. See Grässer, "Die antijüdische Polemik im Johannesevangelium."

231. So specifically and consistently Bultmann, *Comm.,* but see also quotations from Käsemann in Grässer, "Die antijüdische Polemik."

For the evaluation of the confrontation between Jesus and "the Jews" that has reached its culmination, at least for the time being, in ch. 8, both the *historical* and the *spiritual* aspects are, it seems to me, of paramount importance.

1. However difficult it will always be to assess, both as literature and as history, the lengthy dialogues between Jesus and the Jews, especially those in chs. 5–8, we must first say that within the framework of the entire Gospel they not only have symbolic meaning but also constitute a specific expression of the historic conflict between Jesus and the Jewish leaders over his identity as the divinely sent Messiah — a conflict that in the end led, and in a sense had to lead, to his violent death. To be sure, this concentration on Jesus' identity has, with reason, been associated with the continuing confrontation between church and synagogue, which was increasingly focused on that central point, while all sorts of secondary matters at issue between the church and official Judaism were relegated to less important positions. But this does not mean that the real historical background of the dialogues described in the Fourth Gospel should not be located in the life of Jesus himself but only in that of the later church in its threatened existence.

It is clear enough from the other Gospels that during Jesus' life his mission and identity increasingly called forth questions among Jews (e.g., Mk. 8:27ff. par.; 12:35-37 par.; 14:61ff. par.; Mt. 12:23ff.), though less frequently and directly than in John. There is, therefore, no reason whatever to think that the precisely situated dialogues at Jewish festivals, in or close to the temple, should be based merely on the historicizing of concerns that came up only later. It would be unnatural and incomprehensible if the power with which Jesus spoke and the authority with which (also according to the Synoptics) he acted with regard to the Jewish authorities should not have prompted people repeatedly to call him to account on this point and to ask him, "Who are you?" and "With what authority do you do these things?" (cf. Mk. 11:28ff. and see the comments on vss. 30, 31 above).

2. But that is not the most important thing to be said here. John traces all he has to say concerning Jesus back to the "historical Jesus," that is, to who Jesus was and not merely to what he became for the faith of the church after his resurrection and under the influence of all sorts of later antithetical developments. But this does not alter the fact that, by centering everything on the person and identity of Jesus as the Christ, the Son of God, the Evangelist in his record of the apostolic witness and the tradition that arose from it went strictly his own way. He was less "historical" than the other Evangelists in that he did not set out to repeat and thereby extend and complete his readers' knowledge of that tradition, but rather to say what was the great center and sustaining ground in that tradition, namely the divine Sonship of Jesus the Christ.

Most closely associated with all this is the whole character of the Johannine witness, specifically as this takes form in Jesus' words and dialogues, which function as revelation discourses. Nowhere more impressively than in this chapter does Jesus speak concerning himself, in, for example, the "I am" sayings and in the assertion formula ("Truly, truly, I say to you") of the one sent by the Father. This discourse does not bear the character of the testimony of the exalted Lord speaking by the mouth of "his servant John," as in the letters to the seven churches (Revelation 1–4); it has, rather, the character of gospel story. It presents itself as a report concerning the incarnate

Word and relates the story of who Jesus was, how he once dwelt among people and revealed his glory, with precise references to place and time. But it is no less clear that the Evangelist does not merely play the role of reporter. He also acts as a witness, as one who is himself involved in the mission of the Messiah (cf. 17:18, 20), who shares in his Sender's knowledge of himself (15:5; cf. 3:11) and derives from it the mandate and power to articulate this witness in its continuing significance and to shape it in the service of the community of faith in its critical situation. He carries out this task as one who not only knows himself guided and bound by what he himself has seen and heard as an eyewitness and has learned from others (cf. 1:14) but also by the assistance and teaching of the Spirit, whom Jesus promised to those who "were with him from the beginning" so that it could witness with them concerning him (cf. 15:26, 27; 14:26). It is clear that, viewed in this light, the "dialogues" of Jesus with the Jews differ in character and content from verbatim reports and have, instead, the character of apostolic witness and explication concerning Jesus' self-revelation as the Son of God (cf. 20:21ff.).[232]

3. This is evident from the analysis given above of these dialogues. We have seen that the Jews' questions, objections, and expressions of amazement, unbelief, or belief in these dialogues do not function as "points of discussion" or "themes" of a continuing discussion. They rather give Jesus occasion to posit himself, totally in his own way and for his part as the one sent by the Father ("from above").

Attempts have been made to reconstruct from the objections that the Jews advance against Jesus' messiahship (e.g., 6:42; 7:27, 41ff.) the core issues in later dialogues between church and synagogue.[233] But although these "objections" certainly show (see below) that what is at stake is the antithesis between Jesus and the Jews, they are nevertheless too incidental and of too little importance for the course of the dialogues to furnish us with a clear image of trends and ideas current among Jews either at the time of Jesus or in the period of the community to which John addressed himself. Jesus' "conversations" with the Jews are not real dialogues developed on a common basis, in which speakers and listeners alternate, in which right and wrong are argued, and where in the end conclusions are drawn. The antithesis is that between "from above" and "from below." In fact, the Jews only come to the fore in their inability and refusal to believe.[234] There is no common basis for discussion and no genuine communication.[235] The Evangelist's aim is not to furnish the Christian community with a polemical pamphlet or apology against Jews but rather — against both external and internal threats of ideas "from below" and from "the world" — to reinforce its faith in Jesus' glory as that of the incarnate Word and in his absolute authority and power as that of the Son of God, the one sent by the Father (20:31), although the call to believe directed also

232. On this see at greater length pp. 12ff. above.

233. See pp. 253-56 above.

234. On the character of the "dialogues" in the Fourth Gospel see also C. H. Dodd, *Historical Tradition in the Fourth Gospel,* 1965, pp. 317ff.

235. See also Lona, *Abraham in Johannes 8,* p. 249. He refers to the important essay of H. Windisch on the subject: "Der johanneïsche Erzählungsstil," in ΕΥΧΑΡΙΣΤΗΡΙΟΝ (Festschrift for H. Gunkel), 1923, pp. 174-213.

to those who do not believe remains consistently and forcefully present (see, e.g., the comments on 6:44f., 47).

4. This is by no means to say, however, that these "dialogues" and their Jewish historical setting only have "symbolic value" and are compositions in which "Jews" are no longer an "empirical people" but merely representatives of the "world" that contradicts God's revelation.[236] The Jews certainly give repeated proof of having the mind of "this world" and, because of their unbelief, are equated with "the world" (cf. 7:7; 8:23; 15:18; 16:2). But the questions they pose are nevertheless Jewish questions, and the protest they utter is above all Judaism's protest. They asked these questions because Jesus did not meet their messianic conceptions (cf. 6:42, 60ff.; 7:27, 35, 42, 52; 8:22), and their protest was directed against the fact that Jesus apparently left Moses behind (6:31), did not recognize their privileged position as Abraham's children and as those who had God for their Father (8:39, 42), considered himself higher than Abraham and the prophets (8:52, 53, 57, 58), and indeed made himself equal with God (5:18; cf. 8:53b). All this is as Jewish as Jewish can be.

And the same thing applies to Jesus' response in self-witness. We need not appeal just to Jesus' response to the Samaritan woman that "salvation is from the Jews" (4:22), a saying that some scholars contend cannot possibly be attributed to Jesus in light of his dialogues with the Jews (e.g., 8:44).[237] The dialogues themselves prove the contrary. When, in opposing Jesus, the Jews appeal to their history, to Moses in the wilderness and to Abraham their father, Jesus does not reject the appeal on the ground that it no longer has any validity for him, but instead shows that precisely against this salvation-historical background the divine purpose of his coming and work becomes visible and should be believed. Thus in ch. 6, over against their appeal to Moses, he calls himself "bread from heaven"; in ch. 5 he points out Moses as his great witness (5:39ff., 45ff.; cf. 7:19ff.); and in ch. 8, where the conflict seems to come to its culmination, he calls Abraham the one who rejoiced to see "his day." In the Fourth Gospel — it is necessary to keep repeating this! — Jesus' self-witness is totally intertwined with the Old Testament; to no small degree it derives its form from the Old Testament and refers back to it in all kinds of ways. This is so however much Jesus himself — as "the *good* wine kept until now," the "*true* bread from heaven," the "*good* Shepherd," the "*true* vine," etc. — transcends, in all its references and stipulations, the law given through Moses (1:17).

5. It is in this light that we must understand the argument between Jesus and "the Jews" in the chapters we have discussed — and understand it in all its intensity. It is not what one could describe even for a moment as aversion and hostility to "Judaism," as anti-Judaism that, if not traceable to Jesus himself, certainly gives evidence of incipient anti-Jewish sentiment in the Christian community. It is of a very different nature and order than that. The argument described in these chapters is not only not in conflict with the acknowledgment that "salvation is from the Jews" and that they are "the descendants of Abraham" ("I know," 8:37), but is, in fact, the converse of that faith and that acknowledgment.

236. Cf. Grässer, "Die antijüdische Polemik," pp. 82f.
237. See the comments on 4:22 above.

Nor can one trace the sharpness of this antithesis to the "dualism" that marked certain trends — Gnosticism, for instance — of Hellenistic syncretism, a dualism that in Christianized form is said to constitute the spiritual background of the Fourth Gospel.[238] At least the root of Johannine dualism is not of pagan or syncretistic origin;[239] it is rather grounded in the absolute manner in which Jesus in his self-revelation represents the salvation that is from the Jews, which Abraham longed to see and to which Moses witnessed.

It is against that consciousness of messianic authority, that absoluteness, that the Jews protest. Their rejection of Jesus in the Fourth Gospel is not "symbolic" or "ahistorical," nor was the Jesus of the Fourth Gospel so un-Jewish, posing alternatives that lay outside the Jewish horizon and proclaiming a dualism foreign to real Jews.[240] What they rejected in him was that in his person ("I am he") he claimed to embody in all its fullness the salvation that God had promised to them, promised to bring to light "greater things" than even true Israelites expected of the Messiah (1:50), and thus professed to give actual content and truth to the redemptive revelation granted to Israel. It is his "I am he," thus understood, that returns as a fundamental motif in every dialogue with the Jews, whether the subject is the temple, the serpent in the wilderness, manna from heaven, the fulfillment of the sabbath, the living water at the Feast of Tabernacles, or the good shepherd (chs. 2, 3, 5, 6, 7, 8, and 10). It is against this all-transcending consciousness of messianic authority over against their *own* religion and spiritual heritage that the Jews register their final and deepest protest. They will not let him call into question their prerogatives as the people of God, still less make them contingent on faith in him.

Finally, as the conflict moves toward its climax the issue is truth versus falsehood, freedom versus slavery. But this dualism is not at bottom non-Jewish. The question was who could rightly appeal, for this truth and this freedom, to the God of Israel, who represents him as "the Father," the Jews or Jesus. When Jesus appeals to God as his Father, they say they do not know where and who his Father is (8:19) and appeal against him to *their* father, first to Abraham and then, when he rejects that appeal, to God (8:41). They know where *they* have come from; they are not born of fornication (8:41), but who is he (8:25)? And when he rejects their claim, because their "works" (their

---

238. This antithesis in the Gospel of John is expressed in the same language that we find in passages in the Gnostic literature, and this has contributed much to the idea. But the Qumran literature as well makes such absolute reference to "truth and falsehood" and "light and darkness" and attributes the power of deception and darkness to the "rule of Belial," "the angel of darkness," and the like. This is an important indication that such a way of thinking and speaking was not alien to Judaism contemporary with Jesus, which is why most recent scholars are more reserved in speaking at least of direct influences of Gnosticism on the Fourth Gospel (on John 8, e.g., see the extensive Qumran references in Schnackenburg, *Comm.* II, p. 289, though others also point to the important differences between John and Qumran, specifically in "satanology"). Obviously the expression "(children of) the father, the devil" can be explained from the context of John 8 itself; on Jn. 8:37-44 see, e.g., Braun, *Qumran und das Neue Testament* I, p. 124; II, pp. 121, 124.

239. Not even in the more general sense that the Evangelist inwardly distanced himself from the Jewish nation and its religious values and adopted the widespread anti-Jewish mood of his day; cf. Bauer, *Comm.* (1933[3]), p. 31.

240. Cf. Grässer, "Die antijüdische Polemik."

plan to kill him) agree with neither Abraham nor God, and says that God is his father, then in their eyes he is a blasphemer, one who ought not to be allowed to live. It is in the context of the choice between father and father that Jesus asserts that not God but the devil is their father. They call him possessed. He goes further than they. Not because he is more "against" them than they are against him — for he came not to judge but to save (3:17) — but because from within his knowledge of the Father and the consciousness of his mission he saw, in their resistance and desire to kill him, his real adversary, the devil (cf. 13:2).

The antithesis so stated is not an extreme extension of Johannine "theology" or Johannine "dualism," against whatever background it is viewed. Though in John everything is concentrated on the person of Christ, this antithesis also repeatedly surfaces in the other Gospels — for example, when Jesus, immediately after the Father has proclaimed him Son, is tempted in this Sonship by the devil (Mk. 1:12 par.), when, as he sends out the disciples, he sees Satan fall like lightning from heaven (Lk. 10:18), when the Jewish leaders say that he casts out demons by Beelzebub, he speaks of the strong man whose house he plunders (Mt. 12:24ff.), and, the the clearest example, when at Caesarea Philippi, after Jesus' first passion announcement, Simon Peter tries to dissuade Jesus from taking that road, Peter is the target of that severe rebuke from his Master: "Get behind me, Satan! You are a hindrance to me, for you are not on the side of God but of humans" (Mt. 16:23).

This is not to say, of course, that Matthew's picture of Peter is the same as John's picture of "the Jews." But it does show that at a given moment Jesus could speak as revealingly about his first disciple and apostle as about the Jews who planned to kill him and about Judas the betrayer (6:70; 13:2, 27; Lk. 22:3). In each case the antithesis is so absolute because it is the converse of the unique — and thereby exclusive — significance of Jesus' mission and of the way that, to fulfill that mission, he had to go (14:6). Otherwise, the other great Johannine salvation sayings, "I am . . . the light of the world" and so many others, lose their absolute validity. It will always remain a question whether and to what degree all these utterances go back to the "historical Jesus" or constitute the expression of apostolic interpretation, the "the Spirit's co-witness." However difficult the discussion of this topic will remain, one will always have to conclude nevertheless that the absolute character of Jesus' self-revelation and of the choice with which he thereby confronts humans, in whatever way it is expressed, is not the *product* of the later Christian community but is basic to its existence as a community of faith. And that is at the same time to say that the radical antithesis that the Fourth Gospel evidences is — within the framework of the entire New Testament kerygma — in the last analysis of a different nature and order than what could be traced to "theological" motives (whether "Christian" anti-Semitism or Hellenistic dualism) or could be abstracted from the essential content of the Johannine kerygma.

9:1-41

The Healing of a Man Born Blind

Ch. 9 displays a clear, well-constructed, inner unity. The connection with what preceded is very loose (if one can even speak of it; see the comments on vs. 1). Apparently beggars (vs. 8) often sat near the temple (cf. Ac. 3:2), the place from which Jesus had withdrawn (8:59). The pool of Siloam (vs. 7) and Jesus' continued reference to himself as the light of the world (vs. 5) are clearly reminiscent of the Feast of Tabernacles and of Jesus' pronouncement in 8:12.

One expositor calls ch. 9 "a pleasant interlude" after "the long and involved dialogues" in chs. 7 and 8. In any case it offers us a very lively picture, is written with great narrative skill, and demonstrates in a concrete case what ch. 8 dealt with: the refusal of the Jewish leaders to acknowledge Jesus for who he was, despite the clear witness of his miracles. The story's development recalls that of the story in 5:1ff.,[241] but with the important difference that the dialogue linked with the miracle includes not Jesus but the healed man. Here, too, especially in the increasingly passionate discussion in 9:18-34, many expositors see a reflection of what took place in the later confrontation between the church and the synagogue. In this connection the different reactions of the two healed men in chs. 5 and 9 are said to symbolize the way in which in that later period the (dangerous) choice for faith in Jesus was avoided by some and accepted with all its risks by others.[242] The question is, then, of course how to understand the transfer of the miracle as an event to the later community, especially when its dramatic outcome, the expulsion of the healed man from the synagogue, could not occur until that later period.[243]

As to the structure of the story, one can only admire the skill with which event and meaning have been fused. An example of this is the exchange between Jesus and his disciples before the healing (vss. 1-5), in which, in connection with the blindness of the beggar, Jesus' saying about the light of the world is repeated (8:12); and this motif and its divisiveness (separating "the blind" from "those who see") form the conclusion of the entire story (vss. 35-41; cf.

---

241. See the comments on 5:15 above.

242. The theory of the "two levels" is primarily based, apart from ch. 5 (see p. 190, n. 18 above), on ch. 9 and in particular on the "expulsion from the synagogue" (vs. 22), which could not yet have happened in Jesus' day, according to Martyn, *History and Theology*, pp. 24-62.

243. Martyn attributes this miracle in the later community to "a faithful witness in the Johannine Church" through whom "the healing power of Jesus touches a poor Jew, afflicted by many years of blindness"; he says that it is not clear whether the reference is to physical or spiritual blindness (*History and Theology*, p. 30). He later refers to this hypothetical healer as "the Christian preacher who was instrumental in the man's healing," "the Christian herald" (p. 35). Martyn explains vss. 8-41 as "a *dramatic expansion* of the original miracle story," which is said to be located in vss. 1-7 (pp. 24-26). See further the comments on vss. 4, 22, and 34 below.

5:19-30).[244] The miracle itself (vss. 6, 7) is described with great restraint, but the translation of "Siloam" places it in a specific perspective. Then follow four clearly distinguishable conversations: in vss. 8-12, between the healed man and his neighbors and acquaintances, in which the indisputable fact of the miracle is established ("I am the man"); in vss. 13-17, a hearing held with the former blind man by the Pharisees, which does not lead to consensus on what actually happened; in vss. 18-23, a hearing with the man's parents with the clear but unattained purpose of getting them to deny that their son had experienced a miraculous healing; and in vss. 24-34, a second and decisive conversation between "the Jews" and the man himself.

These successive conversations depict the hardening attitude of "the Jews," who, in the face of obvious evidence, adopt an increasingly hostile position over against Jesus and the healed man. They also depict the increasing vigor and decisiveness with which the healed man defends himself and takes his stand for Jesus.[245] When all this finally ends with the man's expulsion by the Pharisees, his second encounter with Jesus follows (vss. 35-38), in which he confesses Jesus as the Son of man and falls at his feet. The entire section is concluded in vss. 39-41 by Jesus' pronouncement about blind people who gain their sight and seeing people who remain blind. We will follow the division that flows from the text itself.

9:1-7

The Miracle and Its Background

1, 2 For the context, see above; "pass by" can also simply mean "move on" (cf. Mt. 9:9, where Jesus also "saw a man"). "Seeing" does not simply refer to observation but serves to introduce what follows (vs. 3b); it is a seeing that evoked a certain reaction in Jesus. That the man was blind from birth is not directly visible, but is assumed to be familiar to Jesus and his disciples (vs. 2b). "His disciples," mentioned for the first time since 6:70, are probably, as there, "the Twelve," Jesus' usual (though not always mentioned) companions. They, too, though the figure of the blind beggar is apparently not unfamiliar to them (cf. vs. 8), are touched by his plight. Their reaction is a question of theodicy that assumes the dogma of direct relationship between sin and sickness (and misfortune in general).[246] Naturally, in the case of a man *born* blind, that

---

244. See also de Jonge, *Jesus: Stranger from Heaven and Son of God,* p. 61.

245. "The blind man's confutation of the Pharisees in vss. 24-34 is one of the most cleverly written dialogues in the NT" (Brown, *Comm.* I, p. 377).

246. Of course ἵνα is consecutive here.

belief was problematic. For who then had to be the guilty party? Was there a way in which the man himself could be responsible? Just how that could be the disciples do not say.[247] Perhaps that is precisely the subject on which they wanted Jesus' opinion. Or were the parents guilty of sin and hence punished in their son? Apparently both possible assumptions produced problems in the minds of the disciples. Whether with these questions they intended to challenge the entire manner in which the rabbis made a direct connection between sin and sickness (and the like) is something we cannot say. But for disciples of Jesus that would not be so strange.

3   Jesus himself flatly rejects such a direct connection. In Lk. 13:2-5 and Jn. 5:14 Jesus does not reject the connection between sin and suffering but instead warns against a superficial application of it. But here he subsumes suffering under a totally different viewpoint, namely that of God's purpose: "so that the works of God might be made manifest in him" (cf. 11:4). The clause beginning with "so that" is elliptical. Materially it refers back to the blindness of the man about whom the disciples have asked. Still we do not explicitly read: "This man was born blind so that. . . ." Hence, as far as God's hand and works are concerned, the emphasis is not on what caused the blindness but on what will happen to the blind man now (cf. vs. 4). This does not answer all questions about God's involvement with the blindness of people born blind; but for Jesus' disciples it opens a perspective from which they may and must view people born blind: the perspective of the manifestation of the works of God, which are the works that the Father has charged Jesus to accomplish (5:19f., 36). For in those works God is made manifest in his glory (11:4).

4   The obligation to do these works is extended to Jesus' disciples. It is not just a necessity laid on them as a task; it is also the "necessity" of the divine plan of redemption in which they have been taken up. These works are the works of him who sent Jesus into the world to accomplish them (cf. 4:34; 5:17; 10:32). That, according to the most likely reading,[248] Jesus involves his disciples in these works is not surprising. This also happens in other places

247. On this point there was apparently no consensus among rabbis; see, however, Schlatter, *Comm.*, p. 222: even at the sight of a person mutilated or handicapped from birth God was praised as righteous judge. The idea of the preexistence of the soul and the concomitant possibility of sinning before birth, or of the transmigration of souls from an earlier existence, is certainly not present here, though under alien influences such notions played a role in Judaism after the time of Jesus (cf. Strack/Billerbeck II, pp. 346ff.).

248. There is considerable difference of opinion about the reading "us" ("It is necessary for us") at the beginning of vs. 4. Many manuscripts have "me" instead of "us," while the most important have "me" and then "the one who sent us," not "the one who sent me," later in the sentence. It would seem that where the same word occurs in both places ("us" or "me") adaptation has occurred and that the dissimilar reading ("us," then "me") is original, as in fact in a third group of manuscripts. It would also seem more natural for "me" to have replaced "us" at the beginning than the reverse.

where the disciples are reported to be in Jesus' company (cf. 3:11; 4:38; 6:5, 10ff.).[249] And the fact that "us" occupies such an emphatic position apparently means that — whatever may occupy others and whatever questions the disciples themselves may have with respect to God's governance of the world — for them doing the works of him who sent Jesus is the great command of the hour. It is because time is pressing: "while it is day"; "night comes when no one can work." Some expositors think that underlying this last utterance is a wisdom saying (cf. also 11:9f.).[250] Of course, this is very well possible (cf. 4:35). But more than such general wisdom is at stake here. What puts pressure on Jesus and what his disciples have to realize is that *his* available time is limited (cf. vs. 5; 12:35). All the events narrated here and in the following chapters are under pressure from his approaching end.

5   That is also the meaning of "As long as I am in the world, I am the light of the world." "As long as" has a primarily positive meaning.[251] As long as Jesus is in the world, it is "day" for him: time and opportunity to work. He will also use that time to the very end, whatever may threaten (also perhaps meaning: sabbath or no sabbath).[252] But — negatively — therein also lies the *limitation* of his time for work and for being the light of the world, which is a motive not only for the world but also for himself to use that time to the full (cf. 12:35).

That is in a sense also the problematic nature of this utterance: "It is surprising enough that the time limit on the revelation should be the occasion for a warning not only to the world, but to the Revealer to use the time aright; but it is even more surprising that he, who according to v. 5 is the light of the world, and whose departure from the world brings night to it, should, according to v. 4, be dependent on day and night."[253] Because the same idea returns in 11:9f. and 12:35f., one cannot explain the utterance merely by referring to sources used here by the Evangelist.[254] It is clear from Jesus' dependence on "the day" and "the night" that follows the day how, even in the Fourth Gospel, the situation from which Jesus speaks and acts is not that of the ascended Lord but of the earthly Jesus, how the boundaries between one mode of existence and the other are not so fluid — not to say invisible — for the Evangelist as

---

249. Martyn (see n. 243 above) regards the plural "us" as a reference not only to the continuation of Jesus' works (as an activity of the risen Lord) in the acts of Christian witnesses but also to "the 'doubling' of Jesus with an early Christian preacher," who is then said to be active in vss. 8-41. In fact this exegesis of vs. 4 (along with that of vs. 22; see the comments below) is the main argument he adduces to support the hypothesis of this "doubling" — which, he says, may strike some readers "as a bold step indeed" (*History and Theology*, pp. 28ff.). But most of Martyn's readers will find this argument no less "bold" than his entire thesis.

250. Cf. Dodd, *Historical Tradition*, p. 186.

251. ὅταν, like ἕως in vs. 4, has a limiting sense here (see BDF §455.3).

252. Some think this already plays a role here. Others deny it.

253. Bultmann, *Comm.*, p. 332, n. 1.

254. So Bultmann, *Comm.*, in loc.

for some of his expositors,[255] and how the world (and the church) must live from what Jesus has "once" said and done and was. That this work finds its continuation in the word and Spirit of the exalted Lord is beyond dispute (cf. 13:1; chs. 14–17). But this does not alter the fact that Jesus' mode of existence in this world is not that of God or of the ascended Son of man, but that of a human being whose "day" would end in (the darkness of) the night in which no one can work. There is a caesura as a result of which his work was not merely transferred from earth to heaven in order simply to continue. In the coming of the Spirit and the working of his word "the light of the world" received another form than that of the Son of man. All this, though it is not explicated in this context, is implicit in the fact that the Word became flesh and as such once dwelled among us and that to him applies: "on this earth thou hast never more been seen." The sequel to this will — in this very Gospel — be still impressively articulated, especially in Jesus' farewell discourses. But the continuity does not wipe out all boundaries, not between cross and resurrection or between Easter and Pentecost, much less between Jesus and the church (or its charismatic "preacher-disciples").

It is not by accident, therefore, that the disciples join Jesus in the "us" of vs. 4 and that Jesus then continues with "me." For the reference at that point is to *him* above all and to the way *he* must go. Without the distinct segments and dispensations and deep discontinuities between "us" and "me," the oneness of salvation cannot be understood according to the Scriptures. The gospel, including the Gospel according to John, bears a salvation-historical character.

6, 7 Immediately after this follows the description of the miracle. Jesus takes the initiative. There is no evidence that a conversation between him and the blind beggar took place earlier (cf. 5:6), nor are there any other preliminaries. The application of saliva to blind eyes was considered curative (cf. Mk. 8:23; 7:33), though the texts cited for this do not mention the mixing of saliva and earth.[256] This procedure undoubtedly receives this detailed description because Jesus was later accused of violating the sabbath (vss. 15, 16). Kneading dough was expressly listed among the thirty-nine forms of work forbidden on the sabbath.[257] Jesus applied the resulting paste to the eyes of the blind man[258] and

---

255. See, e.g., Martyn on vss. 39-41: "Through his preacher-disciple [in the Johannine church] Jesus Christ speaks: For judgment came I into the world." When the Pharisees then ask, "Are we also blind? the voice of the Risen Lord continues: If you were blind you would have no guilt" (*History and Theology*, p. 36).

256. See Schlatter, *Comm.*, p. 225; Strack/Billerbeck II, pp. 15ff.

257. Strack/Billerbeck I, pp. 615f. Hence πηλός ("dough") refers to the mixture of earth and saliva.

258. αὐτοῦ is separated by τὸν πηλόν from ἐπὶ τοὺς ὀφθαλμούς. According to Schlatter one has to take it with τὸν πηλόν to emphasize "that the 'dough' had curative power because it came from Jesus" (*Comm.*, p. 225). As a rule, however, αὐτοῦ is thought to refer to the blind man.

instructed him to wash himself in the pool (or spring) of Siloam. According to Schlatter, the reference is not to the pool but to the spring that fed the pool by way of an underground channel constructed for that purpose. But generally the source of the water in the pool is thought to be the Gihon spring, and Siloam is understood to be the name of just the pool.[259] The name itself might point in this direction since it relates to the conducting of the water through the channel or to the water thus conducted ("sent out"). It is evidently understood in that sense by the Evangelist, who thus establishes an allegorical connection between the precious water of the spring and Jesus himself as the one sent by the Father. The miracle has its background here: not only is it (in its beneficient illuminating effect) a sign of Jesus' coming as the *light* of the world, it also symbolizes the sending of the Son of God himself, proceeding as it did from the ever-flowing spring of God's love to the world.

Why Jesus sent the blind man for his healing to the pool of Siloam and why the man was not healed until he had washed himself there cannot be answered with certainty. The man did, of course, need to wash the mud out of his eyes. That the healing did not occur before Jesus sent him off (cf. Mt. 8:4) can be taken as indicative of an initiative on the part of Jesus to arouse faith in the blind man (cf. vs. 35). Other miraculous healings happen after the person(s) in question has (or have) carried out a certain order (cf. 4:50; Lk. 17:14), at times not without resistance on their part (cf. 2 Kg. 5:10f.). But why was the blind man sent specifically to Siloam? There are hints that the water of Siloam was used for ritual purification.[260] So one might regard the sending of the blind man to Siloam as analogous to the sending of the ten lepers to the priests (Lk. 17:14). But there is in the text no sign of such a ritual element (see also below). Reference is also often made to Is. 8:6, where a prophecy of judgment mentions Israel's contempt for "the waters of Shiloah that flow gently." This then would be repeated in the lack of respect the Jews displayed toward this healing. But this connection is far-fetched. It seems better to think of the role (discussed above under 7:37ff.) that the water of Siloam played in the Feast of Tabernacles. Just as vs. 5 clearly refers back to what in 8:12 — also very likely in connection with the Feast of Tabernacles — Jesus says of himself as the light of the world, so in the sending of the blind man Jesus is revealed as the one who grants the living water, of which the name of the pool had become symbolic (cf. 7:37ff.).

259. The Qumran scrolls also mention Siloah as a bathing pool; see, e.g., Schnackenburg, *Comm.* II, p. 308 and the literature cited there.
260. Cf. Strack/Billerbeck II, p. 583.

Others regard the washing in Siloam as a prefiguration of baptism.[261] Already early in the history of the church John 9 played an important role in the practice of baptism.[262] The question is, however, whether the Evangelist himself had any sacramental intent in his redaction of the story. The arguments in support of this view seem weak. That the man was healed only after he had washed himself can, of course, be interpreted sacramentally in retrospect, but in the story the washing clearly relates, not to sin, but to the earth and saliva that Jesus applied to the man's eyes. Also, the word used for this washing offers no support for understanding it as a reference to baptism as a ritual purification. Still less can the idea (first raised by the disciples as a question, later expressed in invective by the Pharisees) that the man was born in sin (vss. 2, 34) serve as an argument that the washing was related to (original?) sin. Jesus distances himself from that explanation of the man's blindness. Moreover, the word for Jesus' applying the "dough" (ἐπιχρίειν, vss. 6, 11) can hardly, on the basis of the root χρι, be an allusion to the anointing (associated with baptism?) mentioned in 1 Jn. 2:20, 27; 2 Co. 1:21, 22. More significant, to my mind, is the appeal to the dialogue between Jesus and the healed man (vss. 35ff.), which might echo the liturgical questions and answers used in the admission of a candidate to baptism. Still, any allusion to baptism is lacking; if there is a connection with later baptismal liturgy, one would rather have to believe the lines of influence ran in the opposite direction. Even so, the question "Do you believe in the Son of man?" did not belong to later baptismal terminology.

Here again (see also the comments on 6:52ff.) my conclusion is that one can only attribute liturgical motives to the Evangelist in a forced way. After the baptism of John, everything is stated in the Fourth Gospel in the light of the one great testimony that answers the question: Who was Jesus? Liturgical motives, if present, are not explicit.

9:8-23

Preliminary Hearings

8-13 The remainder of the story consists of conversations, some of them interrogations (see the introductory comments on this chapter above). The first three are preparatory in relation to the fourth, the decisive interrogation of the man born blind. The first conversation is between the healed man and his neighbors and others who knew him as a blind beggar. At the sight of the healed

---

261. So O. Cullmann, *Urchristentum und Gottesdienst,* 1950,[2] who sees strong sacramental motifs in the Gospel of John (pp. 99ff.). For the older discussion of Cullmann's work, see W. Michaelis, *Die Sacramente in Johannesevangelium,* 1946. More recent advocates of this view ("a baptismal lesson" in John 9) include Brown, in a lengthy argument (*Comm.* I, pp. 380-82). Against this view, cf. Schnackenburg, *Comm.* II, pp. 257f., who concludes: "There is no really convincing basis in the text for crediting the evangelist with the intention of employing baptismal symbolism."

262. See the summary in Brown, *Comm.* I, pp. 380-82.

man it is as if suddenly they could no longer believe their eyes, as is evident
from the utterly astonished question they pose to each other: "Isn't this man
the one who used to sit and beg?"[263] That is, the blind man known to all. While
(vs. 9) some immediately realize the truth and exclaim, "No doubt it is he!"
for others the reality was too much, adding "no" ("it is not he"), "but he
strongly resembles him."[264] At that point, however, the healed man joins the
conversation and puts an end to all uncertainty: "I am the man." Of course all
three answers to this initial question serve, for the benefit of the reader, to let
the most "qualified" witnesses establish that the man in question was no one
other than the man born blind.

The conversation continues in vss. 10-12, and the neighbors and acquaintances now want to know precisely what happened. The former blind man
himself offers a brief account that shows first of all that he knows Jesus. His
words are striking: "the man called Jesus."[265] For now that is all he knows to
say about Jesus. Gradually that will change (vss. 17, 33, 38). And he does not
know where Jesus has gone (vs. 12). It all ends, therefore, with the people
taking the man — emphatically described as "the formerly blind man" — to
"the Pharisees" (vs. 13), a general term for the Jewish authorities with whom
Jesus had to deal. Such a sensational event, which raised all kinds of unanswered
questions, apparently could not pass without the involvement of expert authority. Further, the name of Jesus had been mentioned and "it was a sabbath day"
(vs. 14).

The whole narrative is strongly reminiscent of the story in ch. 5. But there
Jesus, having been pointed out by the healed man, must answer for himself.
His self-witness is central. Here Jesus remains entirely in the background until
vs. 35; up to that point everything transpires in dialogue between the Pharisees
and the man born blind (and his parents). This twofold presentation is, of course,
not arbitrary. Whereas in ch. 5 Jesus gives his foundational self-revelation as
the Son of God (5:17ff.), now, after everything that has taken place, in a no
less characteristic and fundamental way, the healed man himself takes the floor.
His testimony cannot be muzzled any longer but gains in forcefulness as
opposition to him increases. In the now following phases of the story this comes
to expression with dramatic vitality and psychological deftness.

14-17   Before the first interrogation of the healed man by the Pharisees

263. οὐχ οὗτος? The answer is Yes. In this form (with οὐχ) the question brings to expression
the undeniable reality of what they saw.

264. ὅμοιος implies more than a degree of resemblance; rather: "the exact image."

265. How this — and vs. 11 — is to be understood if vss. 8-41 are "a dramatic expansion
of the original miracle story [in vss. 6-7] in the situation of the Johannine church" is hard to
understand despite the efforts of Martyn and others (*History and Theology,* p. 31, n. 26). The
reference, as a statement of the healed beggar (who has no answer to the question "Where is
he?"), is all too clearly to "the historical Jesus."

begins in vs. 15, we are told that "it was a sabbath day when Jesus made the clay" and thus performed a prohibited act (see the comments on vs. 6). As in 5:9, this circumstance is mentioned after the story of the healing itself because it does not become relevant until now, in the confrontation with the Pharisees. They start by asking how the healing occurred. The man born blind gives his story without mentioning Jesus' name. Jesus is the great absent and unmentioned one, his name unmentioned in all the interrogations, but still the one around whom the story revolves.

Again the clay and the washing are mentioned. What interests the man's interrogators is that all this took place on the sabbath. Still their reactions vary (vs. 16). Some stand ready to judge, saying that, on the basis of this violation of the sabbath, Jesus, "this man," proved that he was "not from God," that is, that there could be no question of a divine miracle. Others are less sure and ask how a "sinful man" — that is, the sabbath breaker that they agreed Jesus was — could nevertheless do such signs.[266] Again (cf. 7:43; 10:19) the Evangelist explicitly mentions their division over Jesus. He is not thus aiming to say something in favor of "the Jews," since unbelief remains in control and the gainsayers do not get a chance to speak again (cf. vss. 18ff.), but does thus stress that even Jesus' most resolute opponents could not get around the factuality of his miracles.

In this predicament they once more ask the blind man what he has to say about the person who opened his eyes — at least according to his story (vs. 17).[267] Apparently, the object is to confront him with the incredibility of his story, namely that a sabbath breaker has opened his eyes. But he refuses to be put off. That he could now see was more important than any legal objections that could be brought against the miracle. His answer is short and sound: "he is a prophet," the same answer that a Samaritan woman has given (cf. 4:19). This is not everything that he (like that woman) is to confess concerning Jesus

266. Some expositors think that lurking behind this discussion is the antithesis between true and false prophets — those "from God" and those "not from God" — from Dt. 13:1-5; 18:5-22. This is said to be supported by what the healed man says about Jesus in vs. 17. So de Jonge, *Jesus: Stranger from Heaven and Son of God,* pp. 62ff. (see the comments above on 7:16, 18). But de Jonge correctly rejects the view of Meeks that whether Jesus is the true prophet or the false prophet, as predicted in Deuteronomy 18, is the central point of ch. 9, as also already of 5:19-47. The dispute about Jesus as true or false prophet in any case merely forms the transition to the much more essential question of his messiahship, since that is already referred to in vs. 22 though it is not posed to the healed man in its full significance until vs. 35 (again entirely in keeping with the theme of ch. 5; cf. vss. 27ff.). On the repeated identification by the people of Jesus as "the prophet" (6:14; 7:40ff.) and on the relationship between "the prophet" and the Messiah in the Fourth Gospel, see the extensive analysis of W. Nicol, *The Sēmeia in the Fourth Gospel,* 1972, pp. 87ff.

267. Literally, "What do you say about him that he has opened your eyes?" The ὅτι does not refer back to the *fact* of the healing (which they do not believe, vs. 18) and therefore cannot be intended causally (RSV: "*since* he . . .") but refers to the blind man's story.

(cf. vss. 33f., 36f.), but it is what a person whose eyes "have been opened" begins to notice as the first and crucial thing about Jesus: that the power of his word proceeds not from humanness but from God.[268] In that regard the former blind man differs from the paralytic in ch. 5, who after his healing and despite Jesus' warning (5:14) immediately fell back under the sway of the old. But this blind man not only chooses the side of Jesus, but against the verdict of the Jewish authorities ("this man is not from God") gives his own testimony: "he is a prophet." His disagreement with them will gradually deepen, but from the start it gives form to what Jesus will call the "judgment" for which he "came into the world" (vs. 39).

18-23 The third phase of the dialogue is the interrogation of the man's parents. Vs. 18 refers no longer to "the Pharisees," as in vss. 13-17, but, as several times earlier, to "the Jews," a designation of Jewish authorities hostile to Jesus. There is no further mention of the disagreement among these questioners described in vs. 16. The development of the case is now totally in the hands of those who do not believe they are dealing with a former blind man[269] as long as they have not first interrogated his parents. However, the questions they pose to the parents (vs. 19) are not designed to get more information from them but rather to confront them from the start with the incredibility of their assertion that the man standing in front of them was their son who was born blind: "How is it (possible then) that he now sees?" Their aim is clearly to embarrass the parents and to corner them as unreliable and deceptive witnesses. They apparently do not reckon with the possibility that the parents will also point to Jesus, undoubtedly because they do not believe Jesus performed this miracle and because everyone who before the forum of the Jewish authorities dares to attribute such power to Jesus knows what awaits him or her.

The parents allow themselves to be neither intimidated nor trapped. They insist that the man standing before them is indeed their son and that he has been blind from birth. They feign total ignorance as to the circumstances and explanation of his healing (vs. 21). They do not know "how he now sees" (vs. 19) and also — although the question has not been put to them — who has opened his eyes, though undoubtedly they really do (cf. vss. 22, 23). They cover themselves in advance and refer the authorities, with feigned innocence, to their son, who is old enough, after all, to answer for himself. The Evangelist (vss.

---

268. Other expositors consider (as in 4:19: see the comments there) a more specific explanation likely, namely that by "a prophet" (as in 6:14) *the* prophet is meant or, in any case, that "a prophet" "was possibly used somewhat pregnantly" (see Nicol, *Sēmeia in the Fourth Gospel*, p. 87). In 4:19 there is more reason for this than there is here, where the confession of the man born blind stands in contrast with the Pharisees' verdict, which is stated in general terms: "This man is not from God" (vs. 16).

269. The repeated ἀναβλέπειν in vs. 18 means "see again," which here of course means "regain sight."

22, 23) explains this attitude of the parents from their fear of the Jews. They avoid all allusion to Jesus since that might bring them under suspicion of confessing Jesus as the Christ. For "the Jews had already agreed that if anyone should confess him to be Christ, he was to be put out of the synagogue." The Evangelist's intent is not so much to depict the parents as cowardly in contrast with their courageous, Jesus-confessing son, but rather to show how "the Jews" got caught in their own snares, for whom matters were only made worse by the manner in which the parents answered the questions. Now that the identity of the healed person had been established beyond all doubt, only one question remained: how could anyone still deny the miracle of the healing? Implied, of course, was healing by Jesus, whose name, though not mentioned, was in everyone's thoughts. And this was a question that the Evangelist undoubtedly laid before the consciences of the gainsaying — or self-concealing — believing Jews of his own day (cf. 12:42).

There is great divergence of opinion on the expression "put out of the synagogue."[270] A disciplinary measure by that name is not known to us from the relevant Jewish literature. There was a synagogal ban applied in varying degrees of severity, but apparently it did not include the possibility of exclusion from the synagogal fellowship. It was rather intended to bring the sinner to repentance and to obedience to the law and its official representatives in the fellowship.[271] The rabbinic literature also mentions people who were outside the religious and social fellowship of the synagogue — to whom, therefore, the adjective ἀποσυνάγωγος was applicable — either because they had withdrawn from the synagogue or were thrust from it.[272] The people referred to were held by the Jewish leaders to be apostates and heretics *(minim)*. They were viewed as dangerous opponents against whom one did not act with formal disciplinary procedures but "who were simply excluded from the synagogue by measures that brought home to the simplest Jews that between the synagogue and those circles there existed no form of fellowship."[273]

We know that at a later time, under the influence of the well-known rabbi Gamaliel II, when the separation between church and synagogue assumed definite forms, Christians were officially designated *minim*. The clearest indication

270. ἀποσυνάγωγος γένηται, literally, "become one outside the synagogue" (cf. 12:42). 16:12 has the active: ἀποσυνάγωγον ποιεῖν.

271. So Strack/Billerbeck IV, pp. 329f., as the conclusion of the extensive excursus on pp. 292-333. See also W. Schrage, *TDNT* VII, pp. 848-52; Martyn, *History and Theology,* pp. 37ff., esp. pp. 43f.; see also pp. 156ff.

272. Cf. ποιεῖν in 16:12; see the comments below on vs. 34, in which ἐκβάλλειν is used. See further Strack/Billerbeck IV, p. 331: "The synagogue ban has nothing to do with exclusion from the synagogue"; the three Johannine instances refer to "those separated from the synagogue," that is, expelled from the synagogue. This comes down (according to Strack/Billerbeck) to what in Lk. 6:22 is referred to with ἀφορίσωσιν: one is shut out from fellowship.

273. Strack/Billerbeck, in loc.

of this is perhaps the later insertion of a curse on *minim* (apostates, heretics), especially on the *nazarim* (Jewish Christians), in the Eighteen Benedictions (the Shemoneh Esreh). This insertion took place after the definitive redaction of this prayer toward the end of the first century.[274] Many current interpreters[275] see in Jn. 9:22; 12:42; 16:12 allusions to this curse in the Eighteen Benedictions, the dating of which then has to be set as early as possible, but of course much later than the death of Jesus. The passages in the Fourth Gospel that relate to this "extra-synagogal" position are therefore said in fact to refer to measures with which, not the believing Jews in Jesus' time, but those in "the Johannine community" at the end of the first century, were confronted.

However, aside from the difficulty for dating the Fourth Gospel raised if the Evangelist based his story on the revision of the Shemoneh Esreh,[276] the main objection to this hypothesis is that the curse on the *minim* does not mention expulsion from the synagogue,[277] and certainly not as a measure that only then went into effect against Jewish Christians. Those cursed are people with whom no Jew has had fellowship for a long time, or at least should have had, ought and whose place outside the synagogue did not have to be brought about by decree but was rather assumed ("For the renegades let there be no hope, and may the arrogant kingdom soon be rooted out in our days, and the Nazarenes and the *minim* perish as in a moment and be blotted out from the book of life and with the righteous may they not be inscribed. Blessed art thou, O Lord, who humblest the arrogant").

Some interpreters think that this "benediction" was used to expose as clandestine Christians those who refused to recite it in the synagogue service and thus to expel them.[278] But whatever truth that contains, it would prove only that the purging of Christians perhaps still left in the synagogue was pursued as consistently as possible, not that expulsion of Jewish Christians from the Jewish community had still to begin and was to be effected by the revised Shemoneh Esreh. Furthermore, the notion that this expulsion from the synagogal fellowship was based on one decree issued from a central location in the Judaism of the time seems unrealistic.

Rather, this expulsion was a gradual process shaped by local situations

---

274. See Strack/Billerbeck IV, pp. 208, 212, 330, 331; cf. also Barrett, *Comm.,* p. 360; H. Mulder, *De uitsluiting uit de Synagoge,* 1972, pp. 5ff.

275. So — together with many others — particularly Martyn (*History and Theology,* pp. 18ff.), who attempts to base his two-level theory in large measure on Jn. 9:22 (the "agreement" of the Jews is said to refer to the actions undertaken by Gamaliel II to purge the synagogue of crypto-Christians).

276. See also Martyn, *History and Theology,* p. 54, n. 69, p. 56, n. 75, and his attempt to weaken this challenge.

277. For this objection see already R. A. Hare, *The Theme of Jewish Persecution of Christians in the Gospel according to Matthew,* 1967, pp. 59ff.

278. Martyn, *History and Theology,* pp. 59ff.

and events, which sometimes produced periods of relaxation between church and synagogue and then led to fierce outbursts of hostility and only later brought fixed forms of irreconcilability into the liturgy, as can be inferred from the twelfth of the Eighteen Benedictions. That from the beginning the followers of Jesus were exposed to hatred, persecution, and ostracism not only can be inferred from texts like Lk. 6:22[279] but is also pictured in the book of Acts (cf. 8:1ff.; 9:1ff.). It is hard to imagine that the violent persecution reported there did not also entail isolation and exclusion from the synagogal fellowship.

I do not agree, therefore, that the fear of expulsion of the parents of the man born blind was something inconceivable during Jesus' life and that the agreement mentioned in 9:22 could only have been made some sixty or seventy years later. The Evangelist himself, by using the word "already," clearly indicates the advanced stage that hostility against Jesus and his followers had reached. Such an extreme step was completely consistent with what he has already said about the quickly advancing conflict. Is it so strange that "the Jews," who planned to kill Jesus and looked for ways to arrest him, at the same time did not shrink from intimidating followers who openly acknowledged him as the Messiah and threatening them with expulsion? Already the pressure on the people was so strong that no one spoke of him openly "for fear of the Jews" (7:13). And what "the Jews" thought of those who believed in him becomes nowhere more clear than when they say, in an earlier heated discussion with their officers who have tried in vain to arrest him: "Have any of the authorities or the Pharisees believed in him? But this crowd, who do not know the law, are accursed?" (7:49). In fact the measure referred to in 9:22 (which apparently did not have to assume the form of an official procedure; see the comments on vs. 34) is nothing other than the execution of such a curse.[280]

Hence the "agreement" to which 9:22 refers can hardly be identified with or conceived as a reflex of (what is then viewed as) a general edict of the time of Gamaliel II to expel by a solemn procedure all Christ-believing Jews. As is evident from the Evangelist's wording, the reference here is to an incidental measure adopted by mutual agreement with a view to a specific concrete situation, which in its intent and possible effect was totally shaped by what took place in Jerusalem before the death of Jesus and which, one might hope, would lose its relevance once Jesus had disappeared from the scene.[281] But still

---

279. Cf. also Strack/Billerbeck p. 331, where Lk. 6:22 is cited as parallel to Jn. 16:2: "The connection is most congruent if one takes ἀφορίζειν [in Lk. 6:22], in accord with Ac. 19:9, as 'exclusion from the fellowship' or, in terms of the penal code, 'expulsion from the synagogue.'"

280. So also Pancaro, *Law in the Fourth Gospel*, p. 110: "John 7,49 and 9,34 express the same idea: those who have believed in Jesus do not belong to the Jewish fold any longer; they have been cut off from the community of the Law."

281. "Decide among themselves," BAGD, s.v. συντίθημι (vs. 22), a word that suggests a much more informal decision and hence something of less significance than an order based on

it was a measure in which it became clear how "the true disciples" (cf. 8:31) from the start were and — as the future would teach — remained involved in the hatred and hostility that their Lord evoked in the world. It is undoubtedly part of the Evangelist's purpose, in this masterful account, to describe the man born blind as a shining example, both of true discipleship and of how the faithful were persecuted. His confrontation with "the Jews," which now follows, and the concluding account of his encounter with Jesus will illumine even more clearly both the persecution and the discipleship.

9:24-34

Interrogation and Expulsion of the Man

24   When the Jewish authorities saw that they made no headway with the parents of the man born blind, they again summoned the man himself, this time for the definitive interrogation. The course of the interrogation recalls what Mark and Matthew write about the interrogation of Jesus by the Sanhedrin (Mk. 14:56ff.; Mt. 26:59ff.). For lack of credible incriminating evidence from third parties, the interrogation had to be decisive. The admonition "Give God the praise" is a formula known from other sources (e.g., Josh. 7:19) that in situations like this prompted the person addressed to stand up for the truth.[282] "We know . . ."[283] indicates how the man was to praise God, namely by admitting that "this man," that is, Jesus, was a sinner and hence not a prophet from God. The authorities no longer talk about whether the miracle happened or not. Their concern is to disqualify Jesus.

25, 26   The healed man, however, sticks to what Jesus has done for him. The concessive beginning of his answer, "I do not know whether he is a sinner," is not intended to leave that point open for the moment (cf. vss. 31ff.) but to posit what the healed man knew against what "the Jews" claimed to "know." He knew that though he had been blind he could now see. That was his point, and no other knowledge could tell him otherwise. The Jews (vs. 26), now totally at a loss, could think of nothing better than to ask him again about the facts of

---

an official decision, an understanding that Martyn tries to make plausible (*History and Theology,* pp. 51ff.). According to Martyn the decision of Jn. 9:22 constituted a part of "the series of enactments which were issued . . . by the Jamnia authorities" (pp. 52f.). This interpretation of συνετέθειντο can in no way, in my opinion, square with the text of 9:22; on this see also Mulder, *De uitsluiting uit de Synagoge,* pp. 10ff.

282. On the formula see Strack/Billerbeck II, p. 535; Schlatter (*Comm.,* p. 229) describes it as "laying on the sinner the obligation to acknowledge that in his situation he should be the means by which to honor God." Brown even calls it an "oath formula" (*Comm.* I, p. 374).

283. A recurring term for an unassailable assumption (cf. 3:2; 9:29, 31).

what Jesus — whose name they still did not mention — had done for him. In this way they hoped perhaps to bring him to contradict himself in his testimony.

27-29   But the healed man shifts from the defensive to the offensive. If only they listened better,[284] they would not need to hear again what he has already told them. Why this repeated asking about what they already know? Certainly he must not[285] assume that they wanted "to become his disciples?" The man's mockery does not lay bare the tendentious "thoroughness" of their interrogation but does identify their basic interest, which is to forestall any popular support for Jesus as a result of this spectacular healing. But at hearing the words "his disciples," they explode. They lose their official decorum and rail against the man: "*You*[286] are a disciple of that man, but *we* are disciples of Moses!"[287] The antithesis is intended to expose the utter inferiority of the discipleship to which the man born blind refers.

Again they say what they know: "We know that God spoke to Moses."[288] There lay the beginning of the holy tradition in which they stood and on which their whole religion rested. But "as for this man, we do not know where he comes from." What was the source of his authority on the basis of which he thought he could teach and make disciples for himself? Their statement about Jesus brings out what Jesus has repeatedly referred to as the big difference between him and them (cf. 8:14; 7:27f.). They do not know his origin and therefore deny to him, in the most fundamental way possible, the legitimacy of his right to speak in the name of God.

30-33   The man born blind, undaunted even by this, fights them with their own weapons.[289] He finds it astonishing that they, who so emphatically posit themselves as disciples of Moses, do not know where the man who opened his eyes came from. Echoing their self-assured "we know," he posits another "we know" that casts doubt on their claimed ignorance of Jesus' origin: "We know that God does not listen to sinners" (vs. 31). With this statement the man refers of course to their repeated description of Jesus as a sinner (vs. 24; cf.

284. οὐκ ἠκούσατε must be taken in the sense of "not listen," "not attend to." Some textual witnesses omit οὐκ: "I have already told you and you have heard it," apparently taking ἠκούσατε to mean simply "you have heard."

285. μή expects a negative answer. Here, of course, it is ironic.

286. σὺ . . . ἡμεῖς δέ.

287. On this characteristic self-designation of the rabbis, see K. Rengstorf, *TDNT* IV, p. 443: "Here Moses is regarded as 'our teacher,' as he was often called by the Rabbinate. Those who call themselves his disciples consciously regard themselves as links in the chain which stretches back to Moses and at the beginning of which is the clear and unequivocal revelation to the will of God for the people through him (cf. v. 29a). As compared with Moses, Jesus is unknown and unproved (v. 29b)."

288. Cf., e.g., Nu. 12:2, 8.

289. The γάρ dangles somewhat. It presupposes a preceding (gesture of) contradiction or denial.

vss. 16ff.) and also to ("hear") the miracle, since Jews regarded a miracle as the answer to a miracle-worker's prayer.[290] He does not, however, content himself with this negative statement — to which some of the Pharisees have already spoken in the form of a question (vs. 16b). Leaving no doubt now about what he himself thinks of Jesus' status as a sinner (cf. vs. 25), the man adds the positive side of his "we know," namely that "if any one fears God[291] and does his will, God listens to him" (cf. also 3:2). And this is all the more true where it concerned the unprecedented restoration of sight to one *born* blind (vs. 32). His last word to them is therefore a terse and public confession of Jesus: "If this man were not from God, he could not have done anything" (vs. 33).

34 With that, however, "the Jews" have had enough. Unable to refute the man and unwilling to be lectured by him, they cast into his face their last "argument": "You were born in utter sin!" The expression is reminiscent of texts like Psalm 51. But whereas there the reference is to the sinful condition in which every human being is involved by birth, they are referring to his — now apparently acknowledged! — birth as a blind man. In that, according to their idea of the connection between sin and suffering (cf. comments on vs. 2), he carried the indelible stigma of sin with him, whoever committed the sin (cf. vs. 2). And was he going to lecture them? This last outburst of abuse was the end of anything that might resemble an interrogation or disciplinary consultation. They wanted nothing more to do with the man and so "cast him out."

According to some expositors who believe that expulsion from the synagogue was not yet practiced during Jesus' life (see above), this only meant that they, so to speak, "showed him the door."[292] But most — correctly, I think — see an immediate connection here with vs. 22. By his statements in vss. 31ff. the man unquestionably fell under the verdict of ejection from the synagogal fellowship. The manner in which the verdict is carried out here shows that it did not require an official judicial procedure and a solemn act of excommunication. One may even ask whether such procedures were ever followed since, as mentioned earlier, there is no mention anywhere in Jewish literature of such a formal process of exclusion.[293] Therefore apparently all that is meant in vs. 34 is that after all attempts to change the man's mind had failed, the

---

290. See also 11:41, 42.

291. The word used here, θεοσεβής, does not occur elsewhere in the New Testament. Its sense occurs almost literally in a saying of Rabbi Huna: "Everyone in whom the fear of God is present, that person's words are heard" (Babylonian Talmud *Berakhoth* 6b, cited by Strack/Billerbeck II, p. 535).

292. See, e.g., Brown, *Comm.* I, p. 375. He speaks of a "simple ejection from their presence."

293. See also the quotation from Strack/Billerbeck above ("they simply expelled him from the synagogue").

authorities simply — with no formal judicial process — thrust him from their community[294] or, in the language of John, made him "extra-synagogal,"[295] and he became an "extra-synagogal person,"[296] words that simply indicate the position in which one came to be and that say nothing about how one was sentenced to it.

Thus the man born blind, on account of his brave defense of Jesus, experienced the fate his parents had escaped by their evasive answers: separation from "true" Israelites to be despised and avoided by them. But — as we are about to learn — not by Jesus, who had not lost sight of the man but knew him rather as one "given by the Father," to whom therefore the word applied: "and the one who comes to me I will not cast out" (6:37).

9:35-41

The Man's Confession, "Those Who See" and "Those Who Are Blind"

35 The manner in which Jesus comes back into the picture resembles 5:14. Again Jesus "finds" — certainly not accidentally — the man whom he has healed and enters into conversation with him. However, whereas in ch. 5 he must warn the former paralytic not to fall back into his old life, the man born blind has already passed the test. That Jesus has heard of the man's expulsion places their encounter in a certain light: Jesus is concerned about the excommunicate, seeks out the lost sheep of the house of Israel, and binds him more tightly to himself. That the parable of the good shepherd comes immediately after this story is certainly no accident (see comments on 10:1ff.).

The emphasis with which Jesus asks "Do *you* believe in the Son of man?" undoubtedly refers back to what has happened. The healed man has already evidenced his belief that Jesus is a prophet (vs. 17), one sent and legitimated by God (vs. 33), and, over against "the Jews," has stayed with this conviction to the bitter end. If Jesus now asks concerning the Son of man, his aim is not to bring the man to a "higher level" of belief but rather to disclose to him the "for whom?" and the "what?" of his choice for Jesus, which has made him an excommunicate from the synagogue (cf. Mt. 5:11, 12). The question therefore invites an affirmative answer: "*You* believe in the Son of man, do you not?"

---

294. As excommunication from the Christian fellowship was also described (ἐκβάλλειν, 3 Jn. 10; cf. Mt. 18:17b).

295. ἀποσυνάγωγον ποιεῖν (16:2).

296. ἀποσυνάγωγον γενέσθαι (9:22; 12:42).

36 The man's answer evidences uncertainty: "And who is he, then,[297] Lord, that I may believe in him?" He addresses Jesus with respect ("Lord"; cf. vs. 38) and shows openness to the faith Jesus apparently asks of him. But he does not understand whom Jesus means by "Son of man." Elsewhere in the Fourth Gospel it is also evident that this name was not a current term for the Messiah and hence was not understood (cf. 12:34).[298] For good reason Jesus' question has been called "puzzling."[299] At an early stage copyists substituted "Son of God" for "Son of man" because "believe in the Son of man" occurs nowhere else, unlike the formula "believe in the Son of God," which is, for that very reason, undoubtedly secondary. In any case, for the man born blind, faith in a more or less unidentified figure had to be problematic. There is therefore much difference of opinion on why Jesus posed this question, which he, too, could assume would not be understood.[300] But not only here but repeatedly in the Fourth Gospel Jesus unexpectedly shifts (in the third person) to "the Son of man," even (and especially) when he speaks to people who are not familiar with the title. He thus seeks to make them aware of "greater things" — which he as the divinely Sent One represented — than they had realized (1:51; 3:13ff.; 5:15; 6:27, 62; 8:28).

37 In response to the man's question, "Who then is he [the Son of man]?" Jesus does not for a moment leave him in doubt. In the most concrete way possible he identifies himself with the Son of man: "And you have seen him, and[301] he who speaks with you, it is he!" The perfect tense in the first part indicates that the act of seeing is completed and that its meaning and validity remain: "You have now seen him (the Son of man)," once and for all times. In view of the verb used here for "see,"[302] it is unlikely that Jesus is alluding to the faculty of sight given to the blind man. The whole sentence is designed to establish Jesus' identity as the Son of man as unambiguously as possible: he and no one else is the Son of man (cf. 4:26).

38 On hearing this the healed man abandons all reserve. He answers with a spontaneous cry, "Lord, I believe!" and falls at Jesus' feet. He makes

---

297. καὶ τίς, "who then?"

298. Cf. also de Jonge, *Jesus: Stranger from Heaven and Son of God*, p. 93; idem, *TDNT* IX, pp. 502ff.; C. Colpe, *TDNT* VIII, pp. 433ff. Bultmann thinks that the man born blind was familiar with the title "Son of man" but not with the identity of its bearer (*Comm.*, p. 338; cf. also Brown, *Comm.* I, p. 375: "This question [vs. 35] could reflect the man's ignorance of what the title means but more likely it refers to the identity of the bearer of the title"), but this seems most unlikely in view of the man's social position (as a nontheologian).

299. Schnackenburg, *Comm.* II, p. 321.

300. Cf. Moloney, *Johannine Son of Man*, p. 149.

301. The typically Johannine "And . . . and" is meant to give full emphasis to each part with perhaps a certain climax: "not only . . . but also."

302. θεωρεῖν and not βλέπειν, which together with ἀναβλέπειν is consistently used in the context for the faculty of sight. One should rather think here of 1:14; 6:36, 62; 20:29.

no further inquiry concerning who or what the Son of man is. If the Son of man is Jesus, he is prepared — whatever else this may mean — to believe in the Son of man, to acknowledge him as Lord. His act of falling at Jesus' feet[303] is more than a gesture of respect; it is clearly an answer to the transcendent benefit Jesus has bestowed on the man, an answer the man has in effect already given in his explicit "knowledge" that "this man is of God" but now makes known in the most personal way to Jesus himself as faith in Jesus. With an eye to vs. 24 one might say that now, in his encounter with the one sent by God, he is "giving God the praise" in the true sense of the word. With this he gives his testimony concerning Jesus and then disappears from the scene, but now no longer as an unknown blind man but as one who, in more than one sense, has become one who sees (cf. vss. 39f.).

But we still have the question why this detour concerning the Son of man was necessary to bring the healed man to this confession of faith. It is clear that he worshiped Jesus not because Jesus was worthy of this faith and show of adoration but rather because he had been told that the Son of man was Jesus, namely the one who had first given him sight and now sought to bind him to himself in this way. In view of the entire course of the conversation the answer to this question is twofold: First, by this "detour" Jesus — as throughout his self-revelation — wants the miracle he has performed to be understood within the transcendent ("eschatological") framework of his entire mission. For this the repeated reference to the Son of man clothed with all power (Dn. 7:13ff.) is perhaps the most significant indication. Therefore, as in 5:14, Jesus returns to the healed man to make him conscious of the "greater things" (cf. 1:51) and to place him in a permanent, personal relationship of faith to himself (cf. also 4:50).

Second, it is no less true that the entire course of the conversation proves what it means to "believe" in the Son of man, namely to believe in him who as the Son of man has descended from above, who reveals his glory in "the flesh," who dwells and lives among people, who has been "seen" by them with their own eyes, and who has spoken with them person to person. This man, who has had to sustain himself by begging (vs. 8), undoubtedly did not have such insight into the prophecies of Daniel and the Son of man messianism of *1 Enoch* that on that basis he would worship Jesus as the Son of man. Still it was he who believed in the Son of man, in contrast to the Scripture-trained Pharisees, who "knew" everything so much better. To believe in "the heavenly one" is to fall at his feet as the one who descended from heaven, the incarnate Word. In that faith is realized the separation, the "judgment," which was given to the Son of man (cf. 5:27) and which is mentioned in what follows as the

---

303. προσεκύνησεν αὐτῷ.

grand conclusion to be drawn from the story of the beggar who was born blind, his healing, his being cast out, and of his faith.

39   The conclusion of ch. 9, beginning with vs. 39, opens up the meaning of the preceding story and also serves as a characterization of Jesus' entire public ministry. As indicated in the comments on vss. 35ff., throughout the dispute over this healing Jesus is manifest as the Son of man, the one in whose ministry the distinction of people is realized, what is here called "judgment," for which Jesus came into the world "so that those who do not see may see, and those who see may become blind." The word translated "judgment"[304] refers not so much to the act as to the effect of the judgment realized in Jesus' coming into the world. In 3:19f. the coming of the light is also referred to as a "judgment,"[305] and we are told how the realization of that judgment occurs already in the present world. It is the people themselves who, by how they react to the coming of the light, place themselves on one side or the other of the line of demarcation that the coming of the light into the world establishes. For that reason Jesus can also say that judgment is not the purpose but the effect of his coming into the world (cf. 3:17f.).

Here, of course, reference to those who are "blind" or can "see" is metaphorical. But the idea is not that the miracle has only a figurative meaning and that the healing of the blind man did not belong to the works of God (vs. 3; cf. 5:17ff.).[306] But the purpose of Jesus' coming as the light of the world is not limited to the removal of physical blindness; it calls for a decision that is not given with the miracle itself. For blindness is not limited to the body. One can gain physical sight and still remain blind (cf. 5:14). For that reason the healing miracle belongs to the judgment for which Jesus came into the world. "Not seeing" here describes the general state of a person before the light of the world has illumined him or her. The way to the light lies open before all. Those who do not "see" are those who imagine that they do see. They "become blind"; "not seeing" becomes "the inability to see." They think that they see, they turn from the light, and therefore the coming of the light becomes judgment for them.

40, 41   All this is made even more clear in vss. 40 and 41. Suddenly some Pharisees are back on the scene. One must not ask how or when they came to be there or, still less, regard "who were by him" as an indication that they are allies or supporters of Jesus. They are there to speak once more and to make clear in their person the "judgment" of which Jesus has spoken. Their question means something like "But certainly you do not mean to say that we,

---

304. χρίμα.

305. There χρίσις is used in approximately the same sense as χρίμα is used here.

306. On this see at length (also against Bultmann's understanding of the story) Nicol, *Sēmeia in the Fourth Gospel,* pp. 106-13 and, in regard to ch. 9, pp. 118ff.

too, are blind!"[307] They understand what Jesus means. But the mere thought that merely as Jesus' opponents they are "blind" is so absurd that they throw it, in the form of a question, back at Jesus.

In response Jesus again speaks of "blindness" and "seeing." "If you were blind . . ." means "if you were lacking only in your ability to see, that would not be a sin and would not stand in the way of your being healed" (any more than it was necessary for the man born blind to speak first of his sin, vss. 1ff.). But in their case things are not that simple. They think: "We can see, we need no other light nor anyone to save us from the darkness." That being the case, their sin remains. For the state in which a person exists in this world is certainly one of sin (see the comments on 5:14; 8:24; 3:36; cf. 1 Co. 15:7). But it is not sin that cuts a person off from what Jesus wants to give; it is the illusion that one can manage without Jesus as the light of the world. That is why the sin "remains." If it does not become an object of forgiveness, it remains the object of judgment. It is not sin as such; it is the repudiation of grace that makes a person a lost being (cf. 3:16ff., 36).

10:1-21

The Good Shepherd

John 10 is renowned on account of its depiction of Jesus as the good shepherd and the door of the sheep. Together with Mt. 18:12-14 and Lk. 15:4-7 it is the source and background of what has been throughout the centuries and still is one of the church's most beloved portrayals of Jesus, which, perhaps most often under the familiar image of the young shepherd with the sheep on his shoulders, has from the dawn of Christian art returned again and again as the symbol of Jesus as *Savior*. John 10 has contributed to this because there the good shepherd is contrasted with those who as "strangers" or "thieves and robbers" threaten the flock or who as "hirelings" abandon it. Partly as a result of these polemical and antithetical motifs the construction of this chapter is rather fragmentary and not very transparent in its development.

The starting point — vss. 1-6 — is what is described as a "figure" (a *paroimia* or parable) and is not understood as such by the hearers. Thereupon follow two series of pronouncements in vss. 7-10 and 11-18, in which, in close connection with the parable, Jesus first identifies himself with "the door of the sheep," then with the shepherd himself. All this finds its temporary conclusion in vs. 16, though in vss. 17-18 the thought of vs. 15 is continued, but without the imagery. In vss. 19-21 a reaction again follows from the side of "the Jews,"

---

307. As is clear from the μή with which it begins.

and with this the first main division of ch. 10 ends. In the second division, which begins with vs. 22 and takes us to the Feast of Dedication, the theme of the good shepherd returns (vss. 26ff.), in clear connection with vss. 1-18.

There is much difference of opinion about the link between the beginning of ch. 10 and the end of ch. 9. The thrust of ch. 10 is very polemical, which does link it materially with the conclusion of ch. 9. But must we assume that in the discourse in 10:1-8, beginning with the solemn "truly, truly" of vs. 1, the rather unclear situation of 9:40f. is still presupposed? Not until vs. 21 is there an echo of the story told in ch. 9. Many expositors believe, therefore, that the text has been disordered (here again) and that a rearrangement of the traditional sequence is advisable. In that connection the hypothesis that two pages of the original manuscript have been interchanged has found the most support. The first is said to have contained vss. 19-29, the second vss. 1-18. If one reverses these two pericopes, the sequence becomes: 9:1-41; 10:19-29; 10:1-18; 10:30-39. Important advantages of this arrangement are that the transition between chs. 9 and 10 becomes smoother and that the sayings concerning the good shepherd are kept together and uttered on the same occasion (the Feast of the Dedication).[308] Others go even further in rearranging ch. 10.[309] Although the reversal of vss. 1-18 and 19-29 has much that is attractive, most recent commentators reject it partly because scholars of ancient book manufacturing have advanced objections against such an interchange of pages. Whether the Fourth Gospel was in the form of a codex or of a scroll, such a disordering is considered highly unlikely.[310] Any attempt to explain the supposed confusion of the original sequence in some other way involves an even more difficult hypothetical situation.

Most expositors think, therefore, that we have to be content with the traditional order and must try to understand the chapter before us in its present form.[311] And on closer scrutiny the connection between the end of ch. 9 and the beginning of ch. 10 yields a strong argument for the originality of this transition. Although there is no direct reference back to ch. 9 before 10:21,

---

308. For this hypothesis see, e.g., E. Schweizer, *Ego Eimi,* 1965[2], p. 110. It constitutes part of a more extensive "dislocation theory" that is also applied to other parts of the Gospel. See also A. J. Simonis, *Die Hirtenrede im Johannes-Evangelium,* 1967, pp. 45ff., who rejects the theory in ch. 10 (pp. 59ff.). For the literature see also Schnackenburg, *Comm.* II, pp. 277, 502f.

309. Bultmann, for example. Under the heading "The Light of the World" he brings together as a single unit 8:12; 12:44-50; 8:21-29; and 12:34-36a; of this complex 12:36b and 10:19-21 are said to be the conclusion; after that comes ch. 10 in this order: vss. 22-26, 11-13, 1-10, 14-18, 27-39, 40-42. See his *Comm.,* pp. ix, 312, 358.

310. See, e.g., J. Jeremias, *TDNT* VI, p. 494, who bases himself on an article by C. H. Roberts entitled "The Christian Book and the Greek Papyri." See also K. Aland, *Studien zur Überlieferung des Neuen Testaments und seines Textes,* 1967, pp. 49ff.

311. So, e.g., Jeremias, *TDNT* VI, p. 494; Brown and Schnackenburg in their commentaries; Simonis, *Die Hirtenrede im Johannes-Evangelium,* pp. 38ff.

the new opening ("Truly, truly . . .") in 10:1 need not presuppose a new situation. "Truly, truly . . ." can also be an emphatic continuation of what has just been said, especially of "hard" sayings (cf. 3:3; 6:26, 32; 8:58; 13:38). The retrospective "they"[312] in vs. 6 and the sharply polemical thrust of the parable are in any case the material continuation of the general trend of the preceding chapters, of Jesus' criticism of "the Jews' " spiritual leadership and of their inability and unwillingness to understand him. With the solemn opening in vs. 1, all this is now subsumed under the new and grand theme of "the good Shepherd." That this theme comes up directly after ch. 9 in a sharply antithetical form should not surprise us. For where else in the Gospel is the antithesis between good and bad shepherds clearer than in the conflict around the formerly blind man, who is abused and cast out by "the Jews" but searched out by Jesus as a lost sheep of the house of Israel (cf. 9:35ff.)? Where else is "hearing the voice" of the good Shepherd demonstrated more clearly than in the healed man's clinging to Jesus and his persistent refusal to pay attention to the voice of the Jewish leaders? What at first seems an all too abrupt transition thus proves to be a highly meaningful application of the theme — familiar also from the other Gospels — of Jesus' pastoral care for the sheep who have no shepherd,[313] here undoubtedly (as will be evident later) also determined by Ezekiel 34's prophecy against the false shepherds and promise of the shepherd whom God himself would appoint over his people (Ezk. 34:23).

Undoubtedly the historical situation thus remains less definite than if one puts vss. 1-18 after vss. 19-29 and hence incorporates them into the conversation with the Jews on the Feast of the Dedication. Then, too, the sayings about the shepherd and the sheep in vss. 26ff., plus the parable in vss. 1-6, are uttered on the same occasion. But the vagueness of the historical situation is characteristic for this entire section (cf. 8:21 [after 8:20]; 9:1 [after 8:59]; 9:40 [after 9:35ff.]). And as far as the link between 10:1-6 and 10:26ff. is concerned, the latter can be understood far better after the former, to which it clearly refers, than if, as would be the case if 10:1-18 and 10:19-29 were transposed, it preceded the parable. With the traditional sequence there is a considerable length of time between vss. 1-6 and vss. 26ff.; but, as has been stated earlier, this backward reference by the Evangelist to motifs treated earlier is characteristic for the construction of his Gospel and not a sign of dislocations.

312. See BDF §291.4, 6 on ἐκεῖνοι.

313. Dodd (*Interpretation,* p. 359): "Observe that nowhere in the Gospel, except in chapter IX, are we concerned with the relations between the Jewish authorities and the flock of Israel, which is under their care, as distinct from their relations with Jesus Himself. There is therefore no other place, where the discourse about true and false shepherds could be so fitly introduced."

10:1-6

A Misunderstood Comparison

1-5 As has already been remarked, the sayings — called a "parable" or "comparison" in vs. 6 — about Jesus as the good Shepherd are characterized by their
strongly antithetical nature. At the very beginning of this new section the Evangelist evokes with great and suggestive emphasis the contrast between the image
of the shepherd in his relationship to his sheep and that of the intruder intent on
robbery and theft, a figure alien to the sheep. The details of the depictions fit the
familiar ancient oriental imagery of the shepherd,[314] specifically as we encounter
it in various forms in the Old Testament.[315] There is mention of a sheepfold,[316] an
enclosed[317] space where the sheep were kept at night under the watchful eye of
the "gatekeeper." The combination "thief and robber," though the two words are
not always understood to mean the same thing,[318] probably refers to one and the
same type of intruder (cf. "thief" in vs. 10 as a reference to both). The absence
of the article before "shepherd" in vs. 2 need not mean that the reference is to a
shepherd (among others) with the sheepfold the place in which all the shepherds
have their own sheep. To be sure, vss. 3 and 4 repeatedly mention "his (own)[319]
sheep," but this is not meant to distinguish this shepherd from others but — as vs.
12 clearly intends — to indicate the bond that unites a shepherd with his sheep:
"the sheep that are his." "Hear his voice" in vs. 3 is pregnant: "recognize his
voice," "prick up their ears." That he "called them by name," a picturesque
feature, need not mean that all the sheep were regularly and individually called
by name.[320] With "he goes before them" (vs. 4) one should compare Nu. 27:17
and Ps. 80:1. The "stranger" in vs. 5 need not, of course, be the thief of vs. 1.
There are variations in the imagery to which one need not, on the model of an

---

314. For a summary of Canaanite material see J. C. de Moor, "De goede herder. Oorsprong
en vroege geschiedenis van de herdersmetafoor," in *Bewerken en bewaren. Studies aangeboden
aan prof. dr. K. Runia*, 1982, pp. 36-45.
315. Cf. Jeremias, *TDNT* VI, p. 496: "As regards the origin of the imagery of Jn. 10, the
Palestinian materials, the many Semitisms and the numerous echoes of the OT (esp. Ez. 34) all
point to an OT and Palestinian background."
316. αὐλή.
317. Cf. ἀναβαίνων in vs. 1.
318. λῃστής (cf. Mt. 21:13; Lk. 10:30) can also have a more political meaning: "rebel,"
"terrorist" (cf. Mt. 26:55). In Josephus the Zealots are consistently described as λῃσταί. Cf.
K. Rengstorf, *TDNT* IV, pp. 258-62; Simonis, *Die Hirtenrede im Johannes-Evangelium*, pp. 131ff.,
who thinks of "false messianic adversaries" (p. 139) and believes that "climbing over the wall"
alludes to a recent event (e.g., on the Feast of Tabernacles) when the Zealots, by climbing the
wall of the temple court, gained access to the temple treasury (cf. pp. 150ff.). This conception
seems to me to rest on a far-reaching allegorization of the parable and on an insufficiently based
connection between Jesus' public action and that of the Zealots.
319. τὰ ἴδια might also simply mean "his" (αὐτοῦ).
320. See also Jeremias, *TDNT* VI, p. 490, n. 52.

allegory, ascribe specific metaphorical meanings. The idea is not to identify the thief (etc.) metaphorically but to portray ways in which shepherds distinguish themselves from others in relation to their flocks.

By surveying the whole we can see clearly the focus in the distinction between the shepherd and the thief/robber/stranger. First, the thief and the robber gain access to the sheepfold not by the door but illicitly, but the shepherd enters the sheepfold by the door, the only lawful and normal way. The gatekeeper opens to the shepherd, knowing him as the rightful owner of his sheep, who thus has free access to the flock. Second, between the shepherd and his sheep there is a bond of trust. At the first sound of his voice they prick up their ears and he calls the sheep belonging to him by their familiar name to lead them out. And when he is certain that they have all come out of the sheepfold, he places himself at the head of the flock and they follow him. For they know his voice, and he is familiar to them. But a stranger would not succeed in getting them to follow him. With the same instinctive certainty with which they follow the shepherd they would turn away from a stranger and flee because they did not know his voice. Vss. 7-10 and 11-16 refer back to this twofold distinction of the shepherd from thieves and strangers.

All this finds its provisional conclusion in vs. **6,** where what has been said is called a "comparison" and mention is made of the audience's incomprehension. Much has been written about the meaning of παροιμία ("comparison").[321] The word occurs in the New Testament only here, in 16:25, 29, and in 1 Pt. 2:29. Like παραβολή, which is used most frequently in the Synoptics, and Hebrew *mašal,* it can have several meanings: comparison, proverb, cryptic saying, riddle, and the like. It has often been taken to mean "allegory" here; hence all the features (sheepfold, gatekeeper, etc.) are assumed to have metaphorical meanings. But some commentators regard these verses, rightly I think, as purely parabolic, the point being merely the contrast between the shepherd and the thief/robber.[322] But here, too, a watertight definition of "parable" or "comparison" is not applicable. In any case we are not dealing here with an allegory, even though the history of exegesis is full of allegorical explanations and has led to the most divergent (arbitrary, and partly fantastic) results. Admittedly, the exposition of the parable in vss. 7-18 makes free use of it by gradually enriching it with new features, including the figure of the hireling (vs. 12) and the self-offering of the shepherd for his sheep (vs. 11). Further, in vss. 7-9 a clearly metaphorical meaning is attributed to "the door" as a central motif in the parable (cf. vss. 1 and 2).[323] But

321. See, e.g., Simonis, *Die Hirtenrede im Johannes-Evangelium,* pp. 65-96.
322. Cf. Bultmann, *Comm.,* p. 373.
323. Not so Bultmann, who regards the interpretation of the door in vss. 7ff. as a later addition ("Vv. 7-10 give the impression of being an explanatory gloss on the παροιμία, commenting on the details of vv. 1-5") that lies outside the theme of the parable. See also Jeremias's "difficulty" with "the door," *TDNT* III, pp. 178ff.; elsewhere he calls vss. 7ff. "simply an

this does not mean that we may, apart from this explanation of the parable in John 10 itself, spiritualize elements in the parable or declare them to be metaphors. We are therefore bound to stay within the boundaries of vss. 7-16, which offer a comprehensive elaboration of the parable's twofold thought, without allegorizing all the elements of the parable.

Vs. 6b refers to the audience's incomprehension with respect to the parable. As in other passages (cf. Mt. 13:10ff.; Mk. 4:10-12), this means, not that the imagery was foreign to them, but that they could (or would) not understand that Jesus used it in its sharply antithetical form to describe his mission, in its intent and effect, over against the way in which the Jewish leaders neglected their calling with regard to God's people.

10:7-10

"I Am the Door"

In response to the audience's incomprehension further explanation of the parable is now given in two pericopes, vss. 7-10 and vss. 11-18. In distinction from what Jesus does in corresponding situations in the Synoptic Gospels (cf. Mt. 13:11f., 18, 34; Mk. 4:10ff., 34), he gives this explanation not only to his disciples but in the presence of all who hear him (cf. vss. 19ff.). In the first pericope the focus is on Jesus as the door, in the second on Jesus as the good Shepherd.

7, 8 Again Jesus, with the greatest possible emphasis and openness, removes all doubt about his intent by saying, "Truly, truly, I say to you, I am the door of the sheep." He repeats this saying without "of the sheep" in vs. 9. In light of vss. 1, 2, and 8a, "of the sheep" apparently means the door that gives access to the sheep and by which the shepherd, unlike the thieves and robbers, enters the sheepfold. If one wishes to restrict in that way the meaning of the door in vs. 7, then Jesus is saying that he alone represents lawful access to the sheepfold, the one "who alone mediates the true pastoral office," and hence that those who lack his authorization are thieves and robbers.[324] Hence, in distinction from vs. 9, in vs. 7 (and in vss. 1ff.) Jesus is not himself the shepherd, and the two images are therefore in tension.[325] But vs. 9 shows that

---

allegorising, paraphrasing interpretation controlled by the eastern love of colourful depiction. Two concepts in the parable are now referred to Christ, namely the door (vv. 7-10) and the shepherd of the sheep (vv. 11-18)" (*TDNT* VI, p. 495).

324. So Jeremias, *TDNT* III, p. 180, referring to Jn. 21:15-17; Ep. 4:11; 1 Pt. 5:2-4.

325. So Bultmann, though he goes further in saying that the identification of Jesus with "the door" is a gloss of the Evangelist drawn from a logia source (*Comm.*, pp. 358f., 375). "The image of the shepherd was taken from the Gnostic tradition" and not from the Old Testament (pp.

the meaning is broader: Jesus is also the door *through which the sheep enter the sheepfold.*[326] In vs. 7 the reference is to the first aspect. Jesus calls himself "the door" in order to describe himself over against the thieves, "who climb in from the outside," as the only true shepherd. Because he is "the door of the sheep," he has access to the sheepfold,[327] he exercises pastoral care over the flock, and no one else has the right to manage the flock.

Jesus thus not only ranks himself among trustworthy and good shepherds, in contrast with thieves, but with great emphasis and authority reveals himself as the great Shepherd sent by God to shepherd his people. In this absolute and exclusive sense this saying is on a level with all the great "I am" sayings that proclaim the unique redemptive significance of Jesus' coming and work. But this saying speaks in particular of the special relationship between God and his people, likened throughout salvation history to that between a Shepherd and his sheep (see in particular Ezekiel 34). By calling himself the door of the sheep and (the) (good) Shepherd, Jesus reveals himself as the one in whom this (salvation-historical) relationship has its point of concentration, both from the side of God as Shepherd and from that of Israel as the flock (see further under vs. 14).

In vs. 8 this is brought out in its full, critical, and antithetical significance: "All who came before me are thieves and robbers." The meaning of "all" remains unclear.[328] "Came" points to the pretension with which they appeared in history, as though God had assigned leadership of his people to them, eliminating any need for the (good) Shepherd promised and sent by him. The generalizing "all" need not, of course, exclude the possibility that in his saving action for Israel God also guided his flock by the hands of other true shepherds, who, as such, pointed to the coming of *the* great Shepherd (cf., e.g., Ps. 77:20). The antithesis with "all" refers rather to the general degradation of spiritual leadership in Israel, which is often spoken of in the Old Testament. In, for

---

367ff.). The same is true of the image of "the door," which originally had nothing to do with the parable of the shepherd and was added from a Gnostic context by the Evangelist, though this leads to the confusion of the images in vss. 7-10 (p. 377[7], 378). Others, too, believe there is evidence of another pen in vss. 7-10 (Jeremias, *TDNT* III, p. 179, although he rejects the idea of a Gnostic background to John 10; cf. *TDNT* VI, p. 497). See also Schweizer, *Ego Eimi,* pp. 142ff., who also considers vss. 7-9 secondary, but still thinks "the door" has a Gnostic source, a notion that, as far as John 10 is concerned, is held less and less. See, however, also K. M. Fischer, "Der johanneische Christus und der gnostische Erlöser. Überlegungen auf Grund von Joh. 10," in K.-W. Tröger (ed.), *Gnosis und Neues Testament,* 1973, pp. 245ff.; according to him John 10 works with Gnostic material but is anti-Gnostic in thrust.

326. Cf. the dual subject of εἰσερχέσθαι διά in vss. 1ff. and in vs. 10.

327. Cf. Ezk. 26:2, where Jerusalem as the controlling junction of commercial routes is called "the gate to the nations" (cf. Rv. 3:7; Is. 22:22).

328. Cf. Bultmann, *Comm.:* "It is thus difficult to say whom he had . . . in mind . . ." (p. 377).

example, Ezekiel 34, the prophecy first describes at length the spiritual destruction and misfortune that "the shepherds of Israel" have inflicted on the people and then pictures the coming time of salvation, in which God will "visit" his people and himself assume the shepherd's task. All this is brought out in words and images that are clearly carried over into John 10[329] and other parts of the New Testament.[330] This link with Ezekiel is the more natural because the prophet expressly refers to the Messiah (34:24ff.) for the fulfillment of this promise of God's own shepherding. Hence the resistance Jesus experienced from the Jewish leaders will have to be included in the image here of false shepherds and of the flock they neglected and scattered, just as elsewhere also there is mention of Jesus' compassion for the people "because they were harassed and helpless, like sheep without a shepherd" (Mt. 9:35f.).

The close of vs. 8 adds to this that the false shepherds have also become manifest as such in that "the sheep did not heed them." Jesus thus refers to the bad experience that the people have had with their spiritual leaders and that separated those "sheep" from those "shepherds." At the same time, however, it becomes evident here — as more explicitly in vss. 14ff. — that, just as Jesus speaks of himself as the only lawful Shepherd, so by "the sheep" he also means the true people of God who in their unshepherded state kept hoping that God would "see" them and who on hearing the voice of the good Shepherd, "pricked up their ears."

9, 10   Vs. 9 repeats the saying of vs. 7, now in the absolute form "I am the door." Now the entire focus is on the salvific meaning that this door has for the sheep. We are dealing with two sides of the same matter. The sheep's salvation happens because Jesus has access to the sheep as the one who alone controls the flock: "if any one enters by me, he will be saved." The image and the thing imaged merge. The "entering" is that of the sheep through the door of the sheepfold; but it is also the act of entering into fellowship with Jesus and putting oneself under his protection. Similarly, being "saved" refers both to the security of the sheepfold and to what is portrayed in terms of that security, as in 3:17 (and like, conversely, being "destroyed" in vs. 10; cf. 3:16).

"Come in and go out" in vs. 9b is a general Semitic expression for the course of human life (cf. Dt. 31:2; Ps. 121:8) and does not refer in particular to the sheep going in and out of the sheepfold. Still, these words are directly bound up here with "finding pasture" and are thus incorporated into the image of the Shepherd. Under the Shepherd's guidance they go in and out, are safe, and find food. But we still have to distance ourselves here from the allegorical method of interpretation, which seeks to extract a figurative meaning in every

329. Cf. also Dodd, *Interpretation,* pp. 359, 360, who illumines his statement that "the resemblance [of Ezekiel 34] to John X.1-18 is far-reaching" with an analysis of Ezekiel 34.
330. Cf., e.g., Mt. 9:36; Lk. 15:14ff. with Ezk. 34:5, 16.

element ("entry" is "entry into the church or into eternal life" or, more specifically, is applied to the *vita contemplativa,* and "going out" to the *vita activa*).[331] The Johannine style has a strong bent toward the metaphorical but not the allegorical, and here allegorical interpretation distracts from the main issue, which does not consist in the maximal elaboration of *how,* but in the all-controlling fact *that Jesus* is the door and therefore that in him there is salvation, security, and nourishment for the flock.

Therein also lies the contrast with the thief, who "comes" for no other purpose than to gain control over the sheep, to slaughter them, and thus to destroy them (vs. 10). In this connection one must bear in mind the *tertium comparationis.* Jesus does not picture all those who "came before him" (vs. 8) as bloodthirsty brutes. But what motivates them is not the well-being of the flock but their own desire for profit and power (cf. 5:44). In contrast, the purpose of Jesus' "coming" is that the sheep, for whom he is the door, will have life, in the sense in which he confers life (cf. 5:24; 3:36; 6:40, 50, etc.), and that in abundance.[332] In a sense "abundance" is included in "life," but by making it explicit Jesus makes the image of the shepherd that much more attractive. The relationship between shepherd and sheep is marked by the desire and pleasure of the shepherd to give his sheep not just enough but plenty — a characteristic repeatedly mentioned elsewhere (e.g., Psalm 23, Ezekiel 34). It is this trait that has given the image of the good Shepherd its radiance and glory over against all the unevangelical stinginess and pettiness with which people mete out the salvation of the Lord for themselves and others.

[handwritten: Desire of the Shepherd is not to give the sheep just enough, but plenty.]

10:11-21

"I Am the Good Shepherd"

11a A second application of the parable follows in vss. 11-17, where Jesus twice calls himself the good Shepherd (vss. 11 and 14). It may at first sight seem strange that he first calls himself the door and then the shepherd, but this surprise would be justified only if in vss. 1-5 we were dealing with an allegory. In that case it would be difficult first to apply the door to Jesus, then the shepherd. What happens here, however, is something else: Jesus makes free use of the substance of the comparison.[333] Actually this second application of the comparison flows naturally from the first. As "the door of the sheep" Jesus

---

331. So Bede and Aquinas; see Schnackenburg, *Comm.* II, p. 293, n. 69, p. 507.

332. The last words are lacking in some manuscripts, probably because of homoioteleuton (the two occurrences of ἔχουσιν).

333. See the comments on vs. 6 above.

provides access both to and for the sheep, and now he is the good Shepherd again in both absolute and exclusive senses.[334] Although other passages mention good shepherds, explicitly or implicitly, and also "worthless" or "evil" shepherds (cf. Ezekiel 34; Zc. 11:17, 15),[335] the intent of the saying here is not simply to place Jesus in the category of good and noble shepherds, those who have a real shepherd's heart or the like, or to identify him as "the model shepherd," an example to other shepherds.[336] It is rather, as the repetition in vs. 14 and the associated thought complex (cf. vs. 17) show, to indicate Jesus' *absolute* significance, both christological and soteriological, as the one sent by the Father.[337]

11b-13   This soteriological significance is centered in what follows in the willingness of the good Shepherd to risk his life for the sheep.[338] From here to vs. 17 this forms the ever-expanding theme of the good Shepherd. To be sure, this is first illumined by the practice of the pastoral life in general. But in that, too, the good Shepherd distinguishes himself from the hireling by risking his life for the sheep. Still, the manner in which it is expressed here, "put his life (at risk) for the sheep," points, after vs. 10 ("that they may have life"; cf. also vs. 28), toward the vicarious sacrifice that Jesus will have to make for his own.[339] We thus have here a prelude to the deepest secret of Jesus as the good Shepherd (vss. 15b, 17ff.).

Over against the good Shepherd's readiness to sacrifice himself there is first of all (vss. 12, 13) the image of the hireling. When he sees a wolf coming, he takes to his heels, with fatal consequences for the abandoned sheep, some of whom the wolf "snatches," causing the rest to look for a place of escape and so "scattering" them. These words form a permanent contrast to Jesus' care for his sheep (cf. vs. 28; 11:52). Here again exegesis has allegorized the imagery in all sorts of ways, regarding "the wolf" as the devil and "the hireling" as unfaithful bishops and the like. But these descriptions, however applicable to all sorts of persons of earlier or later times, are intended not to identify persons or groups but to illumine the utterly unique tie between the good Shepherd and his sheep.[340] Hence the description of the hireling as one

334. Cf. Bultmann, *Comm.,* p. 364.

335. See also Strack/Billerbeck II, p. 537.

336. As Brown suggests.

337. As with the "good" wine (2:10), the "true" bread (6:55), and the "true" vine (15:1).

338. That he "puts his life (at risk)" (τὴν ψυχὴν αὐτοῦ τίθησιν) *in the imagery* does not mean that the shepherd must give up his life. Here — in distinction from vs. 15b! — it means "hazard," "risk."

339. Cf. Dodd, *Interpretation:* "This provides the evangelist with the clearest and most explicit statement he has yet permitted himself upon the Passion of Christ as a voluntary and vicarious self-sacrifice" (p. 360). See also G. D. Cloete, *Hemelse Solidariteit, 'n Weg in die relatie tussen christologie en soteriologie in die Vierde Evangelie,* 1980, p. 52.

340. See also Bultmann, *Comm.,* p. 371, n. 3, p. 372.

"who is not a shepherd."[341] For the hireling the essential fact is that "the sheep do not belong to him." The issue is not lack of financial interest since hired hands were subject to severe penalties for losses that they might have prevented, including losses to predators.[342] The issue is, rather (vs. 13), the hireling's lack of will and courage to stay with the flock in its moment of peril.

Verse 14 tells how different the hireling is from the good Shepherd and what the root of that difference is. Here again we encounter an absolute "I am" saying, this one centered in the reciprocal knowledge of Jesus and his own. Although this knowledge is illustrated from the relationship of trust between the shepherd and his sheep (cf. also vss. 3, 4, and 27), it is something deeper. The imagery has a background in Old Testament usage, specifically in descriptions of the relationship of God and his people. God's knowledge means that he adopts people into his fellowship, cares about their lot, chooses them as his own, enters into a personal relationship with them, and calls them to his service.[343] The people's knowledge of God means that they know him as *their* God and themselves as adopted and called by him and, accordingly, that they act in faith, in the consciousness of being called, in obedience.[344] When Jesus, as the good Shepherd, says here that he knows those who are his and that they know him, he represents in his own person that special relationship between God and his people (see the comments on vs. 7 above): *in him* God is concerned about his people as the people of his own possession. In short, in Jesus, God fulfills his promise that he himself will shepherd his people by appointing one shepherd over them (cf. vs. 16; Ezk. 34:15ff., 23ff.), so that in Jesus the sheep of God's flock will know God and hear God's voice.

That Jesus represents this shepherding in an absolute and exclusive way is evident also in vs. 15, where the reciprocal knowledge of Jesus and his own is traced to God's knowledge of him and his knowledge of the Father. "As the Father has known me" has not only a comparative meaning but also a causal meaning: Jesus' knowledge of and by his own is rooted in the mutual knowledge of the Father and the Son. This context of the mutual "knowing" is characteristic for the Johannine kerygma, which repeatedly mentions Jesus' knowledge of the Father (7:29; 8:55; 14:31; 17:25), but the Father's knowledge of Jesus only here. The latter precedes and is the presupposition of the former. The good pleasure of the Father is focused on the Son, who is the object of his love and the one who carries out his work of salvation (3:35; 5:20; 15:9; 17:23ff.). This

---

341. καὶ οὐκ ὢν ποιμήν. Cf. BDF §430.1.

342. See Strack/Billerbeck II, pp. 537ff.

343. Cf., e.g., Gn. 18:19 (God's knowledge of Abraham); Ex. 3:7 (of Israel in Egypt); 33:12, 17 ("I know you by name, and you have found favor in my sight," of Moses); Dt. 34:10; Ho. 13:5 (of Israel in the wilderness); Am. 3:2; Na. 1:7 ("he knows those who take refuge in him").

344. E.g., Ex. 13:13; 1 Sa. 3:17; Jr. 24:7; 31:34; Ho. 5:4; 13:4.

mutual knowledge and love are basic to Jesus' knowledge of his own and confer
on it its unique character. Therefore, whoever knows Jesus also knows the
Father (8:19; 14:7), and the Father loves those who love Jesus and believe in
him (16:27), just as he has loved Jesus (17:23).

Against the background of this knowledge vs. 15b repeats "and put my
life [at risk] for the sheep" from vs. 11. For it is in that self-offering that Jesus'
shepherding finds its culmination. The Son's knowledge of and love for the
Father is directed to that self-offering, in which God's eternal love in Jesus
forces itself into the world (vs. 17; cf. 3:16).

The Gospel has already mentioned Jesus' voluntary self-offering to death
in the enigmatic saying "and the bread that I will give for the life of the world
is my flesh" (6:51). Now the means of this self-offering assumes concrete form,
in such a way that it must have become clear to Jesus' audience, in the price
that the good Shepherd must pay for his sheep if they are not — like sheep
who merely have a hireling watching them — to be snatched from his hand.[345]
Their life is his death, and his death is their life. Not that this explains everything. The full reality of his vicarious self-offering cannot be described within
the scope of this metaphor. The sequel (vss. 17ff.) will show in what respect
and to what extent it transcends the metaphor.

The clear continuation of the thought of vs. 15 in vss. 17 and 18 is
interrupted by vs. **16,** which some consequently think was the work of a later
hand.[346] But the thought of vs. 16 returns in 11:52 and 17:20 and was therefore
not alien to the Evangelist, who may well then have inserted it himself either
as part of the original composition or later.

The question is then what, before continuing this line of thought in vs.
17, he intended by first speaking of Jesus' "other sheep," which can only refer,
according to the majority of interpreters, to believers from among the Gentiles.[347] Some expositors believe that the reference to Jesus' death provided the
occasion for speaking of the Gentiles since it was only by his death that the
Gentiles gained access (cf. 12:20, 23f.).[348] But it seems that the image of the
good Shepherd (which is abandoned after vs. 16) demanded this additional
comment. Shepherd imagery was used of God's covenant with Israel, but with
the coming of the one "good Shepherd" the limits of Israel were exceeded.
The mutual knowledge of the Father and the Son (vs. 15), as the basis of

---

345. See also Dodd, *Interpretation.* He adds: "If that does not tell the whole story, at least
it gives part of the answer to the unanswered question of vi. 52, 'How can this man give us his
flesh to eat?' "

346. E.g., Bultmann. He speaks of a "secondary gloss inserted by the editor . . . prompted
by a specifically ecclesiastical interest, as is shown by its prophecy of the mission and of the
universal church" (*Comm.,* p. 383).

347. For other opinions see below.

348. See, e.g., Schnackenburg, *Comm.* II, pp. 299, 301.

salvation, embraced a broader horizon than just Israel (cf. 4:23). Therefore, Jesus cannot mention "his own," as in vs. 15, without bringing into view the "others." That is why vs. 16 is there between vs. 15 and vss. 17ff.

Jesus speaks of the "other sheep, not of this fold," that belong to him ("I have"), repeating an element (the "sheepfold") from the parable (cf. vs. 1). The "sheepfold" represents the whole of historic Israel, "out of" which Jesus calls *his* sheep. The negative ("not of this fold") means therefore that these others are from the Gentile world. Of these Jesus says that he must "lead" them too, that is, be a shepherd to them. According to some interpreters, the background here is the image of the eschatological gathering of the scattered flock mentioned from time to time in the Old Testament (e.g., Ezk. 37:15ff.; Mi. 2:12), though there it always refers to the lost sheep of Israel. Is. 56:6-8 does speak of bringing foreigners to Mount Zion and of the Lord, who "gathers the outcasts of Israel," gathering yet others to himself.[349] Still, however close this passage is to Jn. 10:16, the latter refers not to gathering scattered sheep but to "leading" (going before) the sheep (in contrast to Jn. 11:52), and does not say that the Gentiles will be *added* to the people of Israel (which has been restored into a gathered flock). What happens here is that "sheep" are placed alongside "sheep" and together, without distinction, form the one flock (cf. again 11:52). Of these "others" it is then said: "and they will hear my voice," namely as sheep who already belong to him, and this "hearing" will, in *this* case, have to be understood of the voice extended to them in Jesus' apostles (cf. 17:20; 20:21ff.).

The closing words, "so there will be[350] one flock and one shepherd," seem to point to a certain expectation or prospect,[351] namely that of the one Shepherd (cf. Ezk. 34:23; 37:24) but also of the flock (cf. Mi. 2:12; Ezk. 37:15ff.). The main thought here is that with the coming of the good Shepherd there will no longer be any scattered sheep of Israel (in accord with the nature of true shepherding; cf. Mt. 12:30 and the Old Testament citations) or any distinction among sheep from whatever "fold" they may have come. The one flock will be as wide as the world. Membership in the people of God will no longer be restricted to one nation or one place of worship but will embrace all who "worship the Father in spirit and in truth" (4:23, 24). But there will be no unity other than that of those who belong to the one Shepherd.

This portrayal of the future is where the comparison (parable) and its

---

349. Cf. O. Hofius, "Die Sammlung der Heiden zur Herde Israëls (Joh. 10,6,11,51f)," *ZNW* 58 (1967), pp. 289-91, who writes of Is. 56:8: "In this saying, which employs the image of Yahweh as shepherd, we have a precise analogy to Jn. 10:16" (p. 290).

350. Alongside γενήσεται, γενήσονται is another often-followed reading (so Nestle-Aland[26, 27]), but it may easily have arisen from the preceding plural (ἀκούσουσιν) and the plural subject as being more natural.

351. Cf. Jeremias, *TDNT* VI: "the promise will be fulfilled" (p. 496).

explanation end. The explanation has increasingly broken out of the boundaries of the parable. In vss. 17 and 18, which now follow, the parable is completely left behind, but the ideas derived from it are developed further in nonmetaphorical terms.

J. L. Martyn gives a totally different explanation of vs. 16. It must be understood, he says, against the background of what occurred in and around "the Johannine community," which is represented by the "sheepfold" of this verse. In place of "lead" (ἀγαγεῖν) one should follow the reading of p⁶⁶, συναγαγεῖν, which Martyn takes as referring to the gathering of what has been scattered (cf. 11:52). This meaning is said to be discoverable from vs. 12, where the sheep are scattered by the wolf. This wolf is said to refer "allegorically" to the Jewish authorities, who because of the cowardice of the "hireling" (secretly believing rulers who at the critical moment abandon the Johannine community) have the opportunity to "scatter" the community. This scattering served as a "Johannine reinterpretation" of the classic motif of the Jewish dispersion among the nations and took the form of the Johannine community's banishment from the synagogue by the introduction of the anti-Christian curse in the Eighteen Benedictions (see the comments above on 9:22). The "other sheep" of vs. 16a are probably other Jewish Christians who have also been scattered as a result of their excommunication from the synagogue. The gathering of the sheep is the vision of the day on which "all of the conventicles of scattered Jewish Christians" will be gathered into one flock under the one good Shepherd, who will be active through the authors of the Johannine Gospel, who despite the threat of martyrdom receive the assurance that the Jewish authorities will never be able to snatch one member of the community from the hands of Jesus and the Father.[352]

This explanation illustrates how the Fourth Gospel becomes one great cryptogram if one regards it as above all a reflection of conditions in the "Johannine community." The main interpretive key must consistently be sought in the highly uncertain exegesis of the word ἀποσυνάγωγος (see the comments above on 9:22, 34). Against this method of interpreting vs. 16 the following objections must be raised: First, the idea that the parable in John 10 is an allegory leads to artificial results. "The wolf," like the "thieves," the "robbers," and the "stranger," becomes the Jewish authorities, and the "hireling" becomes the crypto-Christian Jewish leaders of 12:42, 43. Second, even if one reads συναγαγεῖν in place of ἀγαγεῖν in vs. 16, the verse clearly mentions sheep who, unlike the sheep of "this fold," have not yet heard Jesus' voice and have not been brought to the flock. Hence there can be no question here of gathering Christians dispersed in separate conventicles. Third, the unity under one shepherd mentioned here does not consist in establishing more contact or fellowship among already existing groups of Christians. It comes into being, rather, as appears from vss. 27-29, as all that

352. Martyn, "Glimpses into the History of the Johannine Community," in *l'Évangile de Jean,* ed. M. de Jonge, 1977, pp. 149-75, especially pp. 170-74. See also Brown, *Community,* p. 90, who (though not in his commentary) regards the "other sheep" as Christians (and hence not as Gentiles who still need to be converted), "as J. L. Martyn has argued."

the Father has given the one Shepherd/Son is brought under the protection of that one Shepherd. Therefore, fourth, the "snatching" by the wolf and the scattering that results from it cannot refer to synagogal measures against Christians but (if one views it as a metaphor) can only mean what it is called in vss. 27-29: "snatching" out of "my hand" and the hand of the Father. Not even the curse added to the Eighteen Benedictions could bring that about.

Verse **17** continues the thought of vs. 15. The fact that the Father "loves" the Son keeps coming back in this Gospel (see above). "Love" here is a synonym of "know" in vs. 15. It is not to be understood so much in the sense of an affective relationship between the Father and the Son as of the effective "being" of the Father "with" the Son. He does not leave him (cf. 8:16, 29; 16:32). Because he loves the Son, the Father "gives" everything into the Son's hands (3:35), "shows" him everything (5:20), gives him life in himself (5:26), and gives his own glory (17:24) and name (17:26; cf. 17:12). In his love the Father always and in all things stands behind the Son. Therefore, in "For this reason the Father loves me, because I lay down my life," the idea is not that by giving his life the Son thus gains the Father's love (cf. 17:24). It is rather that in the self-offering of his life the Son follows the Father's mandate (cf. vs. 18) and thus enjoys his approval, which is evident from the fact that he also takes up again the life he lays down.

"I lay down my life, that I may take it again" makes clear to what degree the image of *the* good Shepherd transcends that of all other shepherds, however "good" they may be. "In order that" (ἵνα) does not mean that he would die simply in order to take up his life again in resurrection, as though he would merely give up the lesser for the greater. For he is not taking that road on his own behalf. What causes the love of the Father to go out toward the Son and enables the Son to take up again the life he has laid down is that he goes down that road as the good Shepherd — that is, from unbounded love for his own (cf. 13:1). If they are to have life and abundance (cf. vss. 10, 28ff.), he must offer up his life. The all-controlling idea here is that the driving force and deepest explanation of Jesus' self-offering and resurrection lie in the plan and strategy of the love of the Father for his Son and hence also in the authority that the Father has given the Son with respect to that self-giving and receiving back of life.

It is of that finally that vs. **18** speaks, first of all negatively: "No one takes it from me." This pronouncement is that of one who has power over his own life, not only as *a* good shepherd, as one who manages to give up the last thing he has for his flock before he has to let it go and surrender it to the cruelties of evil powers and people, but as *the* good Shepherd, the one who holds the initiative even when others — human or demonic powers — seemingly decide his fate and that of his flock. Hence the repeated "I have power" — power to lay life down and to take it up.

The expression "lay down"[353] suggests taking off a garment and seems to correspond, not only verbally but also in substance, with what Jesus does in 13:4, 12. There also it is evident how power and love go together: the Lord remains the Lord, but he lays aside everything for his own (cf. 13:6, 12). When he is about to be bound, he has all things in his hands, for he allows himself to be bound in order that his own may go free (cf. 18:6-8). The idea that the suffering and death of Jesus was also an example of his glory and power is characteristic for the Gospel of John. But that power is not the power of one who is so far above suffering and death that they cannot touch him, not that of a god who walks through death on earth, but that of the good Shepherd, of the one who saves the life of his sheep only by giving up his own life, a power qualified, therefore, by the deepest self-denial (cf. ch. 13 again). For that reason one can speak, aside from power, also of the father's *command* or charge (cf. 14:31). It is in that charge and that power that Jesus' shepherding transcends the image of every other "good shepherd." He is the good Shepherd in the absolute sense of that word (see the comments on vs. 11). Or, as we read elsewhere, he is "the great Shepherd of the sheep whom the God of peace brought again from the dead" (Hb. 13:20).

Finally, one may ask what the background of this vicarious self-offering is. Instinctively one's mind goes to the saying of the Baptist: "Behold, the Lamb of God, who takes away the sin of the world" (1:29, 36). Still, in the parable's line of thought it is not the sin-removing or purging power of Jesus' self-offering in death (as in 13:8) that is the dominant motif. It is rather, as becomes clear in vss. 27 and 28, because of the power of the destruction that his own face that he as the good Shepherd must offer up his life in order to save them. And that not as a price he pays to those powers (the devil?) but because he who is from above makes himself one with his own, enters into their distress, and takes it upon himself. This is not in conflict with what shapes the vicarious character of Jesus' suffering and death elsewhere in the Gospel (and in the entire New Testament). It subsumes it, rather, under an aspect that is characteristic of how the Fourth Gospel again and again interprets the descent of the Son of man and the incarnation of the Word in their soteriological significance.

Verses **19-21** describe the divided reaction — the σχίσμα — that the preceding words "again" produced among "the Jews." "Again" might recall 7:43, where σχίσμα was also used. But it is more natural to think of an allusion here to 9:16, which relates not only to the same matter as that to which the "others" appeal (the healing of the man born blind) but also totally corresponds in structure with 10:20, 21. As was discussed earlier, some expositors see in this reflection of ch. 9 an indication that vss. 19ff. originally formed the transition from ch. 9 to ch. 10 and that in the transmission of the text the order of the

---

353. τίθημι.

pericopes was changed. But, apart from what was said earlier against this hypothesis and in favor of the order handed down, the content of vss. 19-21 itself also speaks against such a transposition. The tone and content of the reaction of those who now reject Jesus have become much more fierce than in 9:16, which, after the absolute authority with which Jesus has spoken in vss. 17-18 and that is reflected in vs. 19, is easily explicable and makes more sense than after the concluding passage of ch. 9.

Again "many of them" charge Jesus with being possessed and demented (see the comments on 7:20; 8:48). They ask each other, "Why listen to him any longer?"[354] Others, however, apparently a minority, bring up the issue of the miracle Jesus performed in the life of a blind man (vs. 21). Over and over the absurdity of the charges of Jesus' enemies was recognized within their own circle (cf. 9:16). Again the importance of Jesus' miracles comes powerfully to the fore here.[355] Actually Jesus' words should be enough (cf. 8:14). But if someone does not believe in Jesus on the basis of his words, then that person should still believe on the basis of Jesus' deeds. At the conclusion of the following pericope Jesus confronts "the Jews" with just that thought.

10:22-39

Final Dialogues with "the Jews"

22, 23 These dialogues with "the Jews" take place on the feast of the renewal or dedication of the temple, which lasted eight days and kept alive the memory of the restoration of the temple under Judas Maccabeus on Kislev 25, 165 B.C., after its desecration by the Syrians. The feast was celebrated in the manner of the Feast of Tabernacles.[356] Apparently it did not have the importance of a great pilgrim feast like Passover and Tabernacles.

Apparently, Jesus was still in or near Jerusalem rather than where he was in 7:2ff. Mention of the feast again accentuates the fact that in these chapters the central focus is Jesus' confrontation with the Jews at the center of Jewish life. There is, however, no clear relationship between the feast and the content of the dialogues in vss. 29-39.[357] "It was winter," Kislev 25 falling in December,

---

354. ἀκούετε, durative present.

355. On this see at length Nicol, *Sēmeia in the Fourth Gospel,* pp. 103ff.

356. Cf. Strack/Billerbeck II, pp. 539f.

357. Unless we assume (with A. Guilding, *The Fourth Gospel and Jewish Worship,* 1960) that the feasts featured a three-year cycle of liturgical readings from the Pentateuch and the prophets, including, every three years, a reading from Ezekiel 34 on the Feast of Dedication (cf. pp. 130ff.). There are too many objections against this connection to accept it as a point of departure for exegesis of vss. 22ff.; see, e.g., S. S. Smalley, *John: Evangelist and Interpreter,* 1978, pp. 136-38.

and mention of that fact marks for the reader unfamiliar with this feast the progression of time between the Feast of Tabernacles in ch. 7 and the Passover of Jesus' death. That his confrontation with the Jews is moving to an end is also clear from vs. 24. Some expositors link "it was winter" with the spiritual climate or say that it explains Jesus' stay in Solomon's portico, a walled space on the east side of the temple affording protection against the cold (see, however, Ac. 3:11; 5:12). But both explanations seem far-fetched. Such local and temporal indications, as also in 8:20, etc., furnish proof, rather, of how the memory of certain historical situations was perpetuated in the tradition.

24 Here again it is "the Jews" who come to Jesus and gather around him. Abruptly they ask him the question that has been in the background of all their disputes with Jesus (cf. 7:28, 31, 41ff.; 9:22). Now they demand an answer. They charge that Jesus is keeping them (their "soul") in suspense[358] by letting them guess his intent, namely whether or not he is the Christ. Their question is reminiscent of what the high priest in the Sanhedrin asks Jesus in Mt. 26:63; Lk. 22:67.[359] It is based, both here and there, on the fact that Jesus did not claim publicly to be the Messiah, which corresponds with his refusal in the Synoptic Gospels to allow people to call him the Messiah or make him known as the Messiah (the so-called messianic secret, Mk. 8:30 par.; cf. Mk. 1:34; 5:43; 7:36; 9:9). Such a rumor would have led only to false conclusions and false expectations (cf. Jn. 6:14, 15) because the people and apparently also their leaders had messianic expectations other than those Jesus met (cf. 7:31, 41ff.). Still, the way in which Jesus spoke of his relationship to God as his Father was such that the thought of him being the Messiah, the Redeemer and Ruler promised by God, almost had to take root.

25, 26 Jesus answers that the cause of their negative attitude toward him is not the vagueness of his self-revelation but their own unbelief. "I told you" does not mean that he has in so many words made himself known as the Christ but that he has not left them in doubt as to his true identity and authority to speak to them. "But you remain unbelieving."[360] All that should have convinced them bounced off their stubborn refusal to recognize him for who he was. Again — and toward the end this becomes characteristic for his whole self-witness to the Jews (see below) — Jesus appeals to the works he has done and continues to do[361] "in my Father's name" and that bear witness to him (see the comments on 5:36ff.). These miracles in their all-surpassing power speak for themselves (cf. 9:32, 33). But Jesus, far from performing them as

---

358. τὴν ψυχὴν αἴρειν, literally, "take away our life [ψυχή = breath of life]." Brown, *Comm.* I, pp. 402f., has "keep someone in suspense, place in tension" (cf. BAGD, s.v. αἴρω).

359. See, e.g., Dodd, *Historical Tradition,* pp. 91ff.

360. οὐ πιστεύετε, vss. 25, 26, durative present. Some textual witnesses have the aorist in vs. 25, probably conforming it with εἶπον; others add μοι.

361. ποιῶ.

proof of his own importance (cf. 5:19ff.; 8:28; 14:10, etc.), has consistently done them "in my Father's name," with reference to the Father and his glory. Accordingly, the root of "the Jews' " unbelief is not the ambiguity or vagueness of Jesus' words or actions, by which he has kept them in suspense (vs. 24); it goes deeper: "you do not believe because you do not belong to my sheep" (vs. 26).

Here again (see the comments on 6:44ff.) commentators often refer to "Johannine predestinationism."[362] Undoubtedly the reference here is to the deepest grounds of faith and unbelief. "My sheep," after all, are those whom "the Father has given me" (cf. vs. 29; 6:37ff., etc.). The text speaks of a predetermined situation, but it is rooted not in a divine decree but in "belonging to" and living out of a spiritual field of dynamics other than that in which Jesus' sheep are. Elsewhere this is described as being "born of the flesh," "from below," "of this world" (e.g., 3:7ff.; 8:23). It is this sin-conditioned situation, in its hopelessness and lostness (cf. 8:34ff.), with which Jesus repeatedly confronts his opponents and to which, as here in vss. 27ff., he counterposes his sheep, who listen to his voice and receive eternal life in him.

It is not the case, however — and here lies the permanent meaning of this confrontation — that the situation is closed from God's side, as if Jesus has been sent by the Father merely to note that fact and to proclaim it as immutable. The purpose is, rather, to the bitter end, against the blindness and impotence of unbelief, to pose the miracle of the faith that "hears" the voice of the good Shepherd, not as a humanly impossible possibility whose outcome can only be awaited, but as a permanent road to life proclaimed by Jesus to the end as an *open* road (cf. vs. 37). Faith remains a miracle of God's gift and of the power of the Spirit. It does not disclose its secret (cf. 3:3, 8) and is realized in a person's life only by God. But God does not do so apart from that person but as that person "gives heed," on God's authority and by God's power, to the invitation and command to believe (cf. 5:8, 25).[363] Even though it becomes increasingly clear that the confrontation between Jesus and "the Jews" is moving toward an irreparable break, still to the end the invitation to believe continues to form the basic note of the message he extends to them.

It is against this background that the content of vss. **27-28** must be understood.[364] Over against the impatient ("How long . . . ," vs. 24) and nega-

---

362. E.g., Bultmann, according to whom vs. 26 "expresses the peculiarly Johannine concept of predestination" (*Comm.*, p. 362).

363. For this transition, which is not to be understood within the scope of human possibilities, see the probing essay by J. T. Bakker, "Spiegelbeeld en tegenbeeld. De oude en nieuwe mens bij Schleiermacher en bij Luther," in *Tussen openbaring en ervaring* (Festschrift for G. P. Hartvelt), 1986, pp. 10-22.

364. So also Bultmann: "unbelief can be attacked only by being confronted with the sphere of faith" (*Comm.*, p. 363).

tive attitude of "the Jews" Jesus describes "my sheep," who "hear my voice, and I know them, and they follow me" (cf. vs. 14). These "sheep" are not in doubt about his identity; they know him as he knows them and follow him, their Shepherd, when he goes before them. Full emphasis is laid here on the imperishable and unassailable character of the gift that Jesus, as the good Shepherd, gives the sheep. That gift is described here (as in 5:24) as "eternal life" (undoubtedly again in its present significance). The sheep will never "be lost" (see the comments on vs. 10), not only as a loss to the Shepherd (cf. Lk. 15:4, 6) but also such that they will never be "sheep without a shepherd" (Mt. 9:36). The figurative and the literal meanings of the saying merge (cf. 3:16), as is evident from the addition "forever." The same is true of the words "snatch them out of my hand" in vs. 28b. The imagery stems from vs. 12, where the "wolf" is the subject. "No one" is as broad as possible; it need not be understood particularly of the devil. No power in the world can break the bond between this Shepherd and his sheep (cf. Ro. 8:35ff.).

29 Here Jesus again appeals to his Father. Precisely in what he gives to his own he becomes recognizable in his true identity, namely in his unity with the Father.

The explanation of this text, which comes down to us in many variants, involves considerable difficulties. The reading that many expositors consider original can best be translated "That which the Father has given me [i.e., the sheep; cf. 6:37, 39] is greater than all; and no one can snatch it out of the Father's hand." The text expresses, according to this reading, the all-surpassing value that the flock has for the good Shepherd. It is "greater than all,"[365] "above everything or all,"[366] "the most precious of all."[367] Other commentators believe that such an absolute pronouncement, understood of the flock, could hardly be intended by the Evangelist.[368] They therefore follow a reading according to which the Father is the subject of "is greater." The "soundest" reading that gives expression to this view would be translated "My Father, who has given [them] to me, is greater than all [or "than everything"]." This reading, of course, makes good sense. Moreover, vs. 29b would then fit better with vs. 29a. But it leaves unanswered why this very natural reading was replaced in the textual tradition by another. Everything favors the first reading text-critically, but there is much to be said for the second on the basis of content,[369] which is why I prefer it.

365. NEB note.

366. Grosheide, *Comm.* II, p. 131.

367. Bouma, *Comm.* II^3, 1950, p. 23.

368. "Since, however (in spite of Lagr[ange]), it would not be possible to say of the latter that they were μεῖζον πάντων, the reading must be incorrect" (Bultmann, *Comm.*, p. 386, n. 3).

369. Between the two lies a variety of mixed forms — evidence of the trouble copyists had with the text.

It is clear that vs. 29 seeks to give a further explanation or confirmation of vs. 28. It does so by saying that the Father vouches for what he has charged Jesus to do as the good Shepherd for the sheep and equates himself with Jesus in the preservation of the flock. The "hand" of Jesus is also the hand of the Father.

30 This last reality finds expression in the grand saying with which Jesus' answer to "the Jews' " question ends: "I and the Father are one." Calvin comments on this verse that "the ancients made a wrong use of this passage to prove that Christ is of the same essence with the Father (ὁμοούσιος)." For, he adds, "Christ does not argue about the unity of subtance, but about the agreement that he has with the Father, so that whatever is done by Christ [his "works"] will be confirmed by the power of his Father."[370] By saying this Calvin rightly holds us to the context. In support of the authority with which he speaks, Jesus does not simply appeal to what he is in himself but, in keeping with the whole line of thought in this pericope, to what he is and does for his own: he could not be the good Shepherd or speak thus about his sheep if he did not know himself to be one with the Father in all this.

31, 32 But this last remark again ignites the anger of "the Jews" (as in 5:18; 6:42; 10:20) and makes them, as before (cf. 8:59), take up stones to kill him. Still, a final fierce dispute follows. While they already have the stones in their hands, Jesus confronts them one more time with their blindness and the irrationality of their hatred of him. Again he appeals to his works: "I have shown[371] you many good works[372] from the Father; for which of these do you want to stone[373] me?" The question highlights the dispute in all its sharpness. Jesus had not come to them with claims of his own glory and divinity that they then had to swallow. When he spoke to them of his divine Sonship and his oneness with the Father, he had consistently done so in conjunction with his saving deeds as works done "from the Father" and as a witness to him. For which of these many deeds — which as overwhelming testimony to his having been sent cannot be denied — were they now planning to stone him?

It is remarkable to see how Jesus now lays the entire weight of his having been sent and his oneness with the Father on his works — not only in their supernatural character but rather in their salvific character. Still, as in 7:3, 21,

---

370. "Abusi sunt hoc loco veteres, ut probarent Christum esse Patri ὁμοούσιον. Neque enim Christus de unitate substantiae disputat, sed de consensu quem cum Patre habet: quicquid scilicet geritur a Christo Patris virtute confirmatum iri."

371. ἔδειξα: "By 'showing' them the works, that is, by providing proof that he was sent by God" (Schnackenburg, *Comm.* II, p. 309).

372. ἔργα καλά has a somewhat different meaning here than, e.g., in Mt. 5:16; 1 Pt. 2:12. The emphasis lies on ἔργα as miraculous works (cf. 2:18; 6:30 [τὶ ἐργάζῃ]); καλά refers to their salvific character.

373. λιθάζετε, conative present.

the reference is to his works as miraculous actions. Elsewhere "works" embraces the totality of Jesus' lifework, that is, his words as well as his miracles (cf. 4:34; 17:4), and his words are called "the works" of God (14:10).[374] It is as if, over against people who proved to be deaf to his words, Jesus here makes a final appeal to the undeniable character of his many "good" deeds. Certainly they could not exclude those actions from consideration, even if they could still argue in the abstract about the identity of he who did them!

33 To such reasoning, however, they were not open. Their logic worked differently. If they had to deal only with his deeds, they would not stone him. Even his violation of the sabbath for these deeds was not the most important issue (cf. 5:18). What had them up in arms and what they could no longer tolerate was how he did not cease[375] to equate himself with God. This was conduct for which — whatever else he might do or have done — there was no excuse in their eyes and which deserved no other name than blasphemy and no punishment other than the stipulated death by stoning (cf. Lv. 24:16).

It is certainly no accident that with this statement the final encounter between Jesus and "the Jews" in chs. 5–10 returns to the first. There they brought exactly the same charge against him: "he made himself equal with God" (5:18). The Evangelist could hardly have more effectively clarified where the break lay between Jesus and "the Jews" and why they wanted to kill Jesus (and the basis also for the antithesis between the Christian church and the Jewish synagogue): they rejected as blasphemy his self-revelation as the Son of God.

34, 35 Accordingly, Jesus' answer relates totally to the charge of blasphemy and must be understood as such. His appeal to Scripture is introduced with an established formula: "Is it not written . . . ?" The telling addition "in your law" (see also the comments on 8:12) apparently means: in the law that to uphold, considering your attempt to kill me, is so important to you. This is not to say that this appeal to Scripture is only an ad hominem argument that applied only to them. "It is written" is no less authoritative for Jesus than for them (cf. vs. 35b).

The text on which Jesus bases himself is the divine statement in Ps. 82:6: "I say, 'you are gods.' " Who is addressed here is answered in a number of ways, as is whether Jesus' intent is that of the Psalm or if he deviates from that original idea. Some expositors think that here (as in Psalm 82 itself?)[376] we are dealing with angels, specifically as authorities for and guardian spirits of the

---

374. Cf. Nicol, *Sēmeia in the Fourth Gospel,* p. 116.

375. ποιεῖς, durative present.

376. On this see, e.g., J. Ridderbos, *De Psalmen* II, 1958, p. 326, who himself rejects this view, believing with many others that these "gods" are judges; he adds that this designation in Psalm 82 rests "very specifically on the idea of the special kingship of Yahweh over Israel and not just on the general truth that the government is the vicar of God."

nations. This view has found some support in the Qumran literature.[377] Still, as far as the meaning of our text is concerned — whatever one's view of the original meaning in Psalm 82 — this interpretation has hardly any support.[378] Here the reference is to the relationship between God and *human* beings. Accordingly, as in Psalm 82, the addressees are usually taken to be judges, who are called in the name of God to administer justice and at their appointment are therefore given the honorific title "gods."[379] But nothing in the present context suggests this judicial role.[380] The reference to Psalm 82 seems rather to have a broader import. In Jn. 10:35 the people thus addressed are further defined as those "to whom the word of God came," a formula often also used elsewhere for those called by God to speak or act in his name (cf., e.g., Gn. 5:1; Jr. 1:25; Ho. 1:1; Jl. 1:1; Mi. 1:1; Zp. 1:1; 1 Sa. 15:10; Lk. 3:2). It is in that more general sense (not just applying it to judges) that this oracle of Psalm 82 constitutes the argument here, which begins with "if."[381]

A second point of support follows: "and [if] scripture cannot be broken."[382] Some commentators think that this clause describes the words of Psalm 82 as a promise or a prophecy that is fulfilled in Jesus. The assumption is then that the "gods" in the Psalm are judges, and point to Jesus as the coming world judge, the role in which he often reveals himself in John (as the Son of man; cf. 3:17; 5:22; 8:15, 16; 9:39).[383] But this view is not supported in the text. There is no echo here of the judicial role of those addressed in Psalm 82 and no indication that we are dealing with a fulfillment of a prophetic word of Scripture. The word "broken"[384] means only that because of Scripture's au-

---

377. On this see M. de Jonge and A. S. van der Woude: "11 Q Melchizedek and the New Testament," *NTS* 12 (1966), pp. 301-26.

378. So also de Jonge and van der Woude, "11 Q Melchidezek": "In the Johannine context there is no reason to think of angels." "Moreover, nowhere else in the gospel do heavenly beings like those portrayed in 11 Q Melch. play a role of any importance."

379. So also Morris, *Comm.*, p. 527. See also Brown, *Comm.* I, pp. 403, 410; Lindars, *Comm.*, p. 374. For the view that the people of Israel are meant, see below.

380. Furthermore, the second clause of Ps. 82:6, where after "you are gods" the text continues with "sons of the Most High, all of you," is not cited. This is "surprising" according to Schnackenburg (*Comm.* II, p. 310). One may assume that we are dealing here with an abbreviated manner of citing Scripture in which the context of the quotation, though not mentioned, is also included. It may also be that only Ps. 82:6a is purposely cited as most telling against the indictment of the Jews.

381. εἰ in the sense of *si quidem*.

382. I believe that "and scripture cannot be broken" is still dependent on εἰ and not intended as an interjection or parenthesis.

383. For this view, cf. also Brown (referring to an article by R. Jungkuntz), *Comm.* I, pp. 403, 404, 410, 412.

384. λυθῆναι. The assumption of the view I am arguing against is that here, as in Mt. 5:17f., λύω is used in contrast with πληρόω, so that the translation is: "and the Scripture cannot fail of its fulfillment." But πληρόω is not always used of the fulfillment of a prediction, as is evident from Mt. 5:17 itself; see also my *The Coming of the Kingdom,* 1962, pp. 294ff.

thority the utterance in the Psalm, however strange it may sound, is not to be tampered with.

In vs. **36** follows the conclusion — in the form of a rhetorical question — concerning the charge of blasphemy brought against Jesus. Much emphasis lies on "you": "Do *you* then [in opposition to the words of God and the inviolability of the Scripture] dare to say of him whom the Father has consecrated and sent into the world, 'You are blaspheming,' because I said, 'I am the Son of God'?"

It has sometimes been said that the comparison here is between unlike things (the deity of those addressed in Psalm 82 and the deity of Jesus) and therefore that we have to do with reasoning that is not free from sophistry.[385] Many other expositors have advanced against this that the conclusion here is reached by argument from the lesser to the greater: if this "you are gods" already applies to . . . , etc., then how much more to . . . ," etc. Although the majority believe that there is such an a fortiori argument here,[386] it seems that this transposes the point of the argument. Jesus does consistently put himself in a totally unique relationship to God, one that differs essentially from that of the bearers of the Word of God in the Old Testament (see, e.g., the comments above on 5:19). But still it is remarkable that in vss. 35 and 36 Jesus deliberately refrains from mentioning this difference. The explicit a fortiori element ("how much more . . .") is lacking, and "whom the Father has consecrated and sent into the world" does not describe Jesus over against earlier bearers of the Word of God as "the unique vehicle of God."[387] Precisely such descriptions of the uniqueness of Jesus' mission are lacking in the text. It is the mission of those to whom the Word of God came in the past that is pointed out. It could and indeed was said that they were "consecrated" (set aside and equipped) and "sent," with a worldwide mandate (cf. Jr. 1:2, 5, 7, in which all these ideas come together!). And if in this argument Jesus' purpose was to justify his claim to his unique relationship to God as his Father from Scripture, then would such an argument from the lesser to the greater be compelling? For how could Jesus, for the greater importance of his Sonship, appeal to that which was qualitatively less? Then, certainly, that uniqueness would remain in dispute.

385. A sample of ancient Christian argument from Scripture against the Jews from a time that experienced an increasing need to defend the deity of Christ over against the Jews or a parody on Jewish scriptural theology that fights the Jewish opponents with their own quasi-sophisticated weapons (so Bultmann, *Comm.*, p. 389: he allows for a choice between these two "evils"). See also Strathmann, *Comm.*, pp. 170f.: "He lashes out at these men of the letter with their own weapons," giving, in other words, an ad hominem argument after all!

386. See, e.g., Brown, *Comm.* I, p. 410; but also Calvin.

387. So, e.g., Brown, *Comm.* I, p. 410; Jesus is portrayed as the one in whom the Word of God was "personally present" (so Barrett, *Comm.*, p. 385) or as the one "who transmits God's words and his final and perfect revelation" (Schnackenburg, *Comm.* II, p. 311).

Accordingly, the argumentation in vss. 34-36 has a different point. As in vs. 30, the idea is not to "prove" from Scripture the unique ontological unity of Jesus and the Father or the qualitative distinction between Jesus' mission and the mission of those to whom the Word of God came in the past. It is, rather, to invalidate the charge that, by calling himself the Son of God, he is a blasphemer.[388] The appeal to Psalm 82 was adequate for that purpose even though the reference was not directly to Jesus himself. All that he told "the Jews" is that in their imagined zeal for God's honor they directly contradicted God in his self-revelation. For, as the word of Scripture shows, God himself does not feel diminished in his rights or honor by identifying himself with people to whom his Word comes, nor does he on that account shrink from addressing them as "gods." Evidently God is different from how "the Jews" pictured him. He is not merely God in himself. From of old he extended himself to share himself with people in order thus, in the relationship he established with them and with the authority of the Word with which he invested them, to be known as God.

When Jesus therefore witnessed to his unity with God and called himself the Son of God, this in itself by no means meant that he made himself into God, on his own initiative attributing that honor to himself, and therefore had to be viewed as a blasphemer. All that was at issue between him and his accusers was whether he was credible in what he did and said in God's name. Just as God cannot be known apart from those to whom his Word has come and apart from the mission of his Son, so also Jesus cannot be known in his unity with the Father apart from the effective way in which God acts with him in that relationship and identifies himself with him.[389] How far and how deep that unity goes is not yet in view here.[390] The appeal to Psalm 82 merely points out the line of thought in which that relationship can be understood. If they are ever to understand anything about Jesus, they will first have to understand something of God as he has revealed himself, not merely in his unapproachable oneness and heavenly glory, but also in his self-communicating will to save, in which "his Word came."

---

388. Cf. Calvin on vs. 36 (*Comm.* I, 276): "Christ is not openly and distinctly explaining what He is, as He would have done to His disciples. He is rather concentrating on refuting the slander of His enemies."

389. Cf. ibid.: "Christ is not now discussing what He is in Himself, but what we should acknowledge Him to be from His miracles in human flesh. For we can never apprehend His eternal divinity until we embrace Him as the Redeemer revealed to us by the Father."

390. So also Calvin on vs. 34 (*Comm.* I, 275): "Yet He fits His reply to the persons instead of explaining the matter fully, for He regarded it as sufficient at present to refute their malice. He hints indirectly, rather than expresses plainly, the sense in which He called Himself the Son of God."

Some commentators, appealing to certain rabbinic texts, take "those to whom the Word of God came" to be the people of Israel at Mount Sinai.[391] A. Hanson goes much further by adding that by this Word of God that came to Israel the preexistent Word was meant.[392] On that basis, and with an eye to the further content of Psalm 82, he arrives at an argument from the lesser to the greater. But regardless of this complex elaboration the idea that certain rabbinic theories are in view here is not very plausible. First, the established formula "to whom the Word of God came" refers to the bearers of the Word and not its recipients. There is no evidence that the Evangelist deviated from this use of the formula. Second, in Psalm 82 Israel is not the people to whom the Word of God came. Third, among the rabbinic interpretations of Psalm 82 there are, besides the one cited, others that take the ones "to whom the Word of God came" not as Israel but as Israel's divinely appointed judges.[393] Fourth, the whole notion that the *receiving* the Word of God (except through those who had to *speak* his Word on his behalf) made people "gods," as far as I can see does not occur in any biblical context.

Verses **37-39** continue, elaborate, and clarify the thought of vss. 34-36. The opening statement, "If I am not doing the works of my Father, then do not believe me," again emphasizes — but now in a very radical form — the inviolable unity of Jesus' person and work. He makes the credibility of his person and of his coming into the world dependent on his work, understood as "the works of the Father." Inquiries into his identity (cf. vs. 24) apart from his works are therefore not meaningful, any more than he requires faith in what he is apart from the many-sided witness to what he does (cf. 5:31ff.). That is not to say that Jesus' identity is *based* on what he does. The reverse is the case.[394] But he can be known and believed as Christ, the Son of God, only in answer to whether what he does and says[395] are of God, are "works of the Father," and not a result of abstract thought or talk concerning his person. The believing insight that Jesus and the Father are one, which therefore acknowledges him also as the Son of God and as God, is not the first thing, but in a sense the last thing, that faith can appropriate (cf. 20:28).

Verse 38 takes another step along this line of thought: "but if I do them," that is, these works of the Father, a fact that some of Jesus' opponents apparently cannot deny (cf. 9:16; 10:21), "and you still[396] do not believe in me, then believe the works," that is, as works of God. Jesus does not say that then they will bear

---

391. So Barrett, *Comm.*, pp. 384f.; see also Strack/Billerbeck II, p. 543.

392. "John's Citation of Psalm LXXXII," *NTS* 11 (1965), pp. 158-62; "John's Citation of Psalm LXXXII Reconsidered," *NTS* 13 (1967), pp. 365ff.

393. As noted by Hanson, "John's Citation of Psalm LXXXII Reconsidered," pp. 365f.

394. On this see at length the comments above on 5:19.

395. "The works of the Father" presumably include both: "the total life work of Jesus, the revelation of the Father," as in 14:10 (Nicol, *Sēmeia in the Fourth Gospel*, p. 116).

396. καί: "and still."

no further obligation to believe in him. The apodosis here conveys something quite otherwise. Nevertheless, as the one sent by the Father, Jesus can retreat behind his works. Where faith in his works as works of God breaks through and persists,[397] the way has become open for what he says in the apodosis as his last inviting word to "the Jews": "that you may learn to know and continue to understand[398] that the Father is in me and I am in the Father." Here again, faith in the works is the way to true insight into what is fundamentally realized and becomes visible in the coming of Jesus: his unity with the Father. That is not to say that faith in miracles automatically leads to the belief that Jesus is the Christ, the Son of God, in whom God inaugurates his reign (see the comments on 3:2, 3, where Nicodemus is told that only birth from above can enable a person to see the kingdom of God). But when "faith in the works" (as in the case of the man born blind) does not stop at that which meets the eye but probes further and asks about the "whence," then the way of the new birth opens in seeing Jesus with different eyes and in hearing his voice as that of the good Shepherd.[399]

With these words the last exchange in the great confrontation between Jesus and "the Jews" in chs. 5–10 ends. It ends in a final appeal in which Jesus retreats, as it were, behind his "works," in order yet once more to lay on the conscience of his adversaries the salvific character of his coming as the incontrovertible witness that he has been sent by the Father. But in consequence of this appeal to shed their blindness and to engage in reflection, their aversion to him becomes all the stronger. Again (vs. 39; cf. 7:30) they attempt to lay hold on him and arrest him. But again his hour has not yet come and he escapes from their hands (cf. 8:59).

397. πιστεύετε, durative present.

398. ἵνα γνῶτε καὶ γινώσκητε; the aorist conveys the inchoative of the act, the present its durative form (cf. BDF §318). In place of γινώσκετε some manuscripts have πιστεύ(σ)ητε, perhaps as a correction of a somewhat difficult text.

399. Nicol, *Sēmeia in the Fourth Gospel,* pp. 103ff., speaks of the witness of the miracles in the Fourth Gospel as a "second best." Jesus' word should be enough to persuade people,

> but if that is not the case with some, as a result of their human weakness, Jesus gives the works as second best. This does not mean, however, that the miracles are a weak support for faith because the word ἔργον characterizes them as the works of God (5:17ff.). God knows the weakness of man and gave the miracles along with the Scriptures and John the Baptist as witnesses to Jesus (5:31-40, espec. 5:36). But the theme of testimony also reveals that the miracles are second best because according to 8:14 the testimony of Jesus' word is actually sufficient.

It cannot be denied that the Fourth Gospel regards the meaning of faith in Jesus' miracles ambivalently (cf. the comments on 4:47ff. above). But it is questionable whether the distinction between believing in Jesus and believing in his miracles is a distinction between words and works. At least in 10:38 believing in Jesus means believing in his person, his unity with the Father, etc. Faith in the miracles as witness of and to the Father is no less important than the witness of the Scriptures, the witness of John, and Jesus' self-witness, just as "taken by themselves" none of these is enough to effect faith in Jesus as the Son of God.

10:40-42

Back to the Beginning

The last verses of ch. 10 form a clear break in the construction of the Gospel. They note Jesus' departure to Transjordan, apparently where he could be safe, at least for a time. This also signals the end of Jesus' public ministry until his final journey to take part in the coming Passover celebrations (cf. 11:55f.; 12:1ff.). Only on hearing that his friend Lazarus is sick, and then against his disciples' opposition, will Jesus go once more to Bethany — even then continuing to work while it is day (11:9). Then, after this last great miracle in the circle of his friends, he will again seek out a place where he can be in seclusion (11:54).

Verse 40 tells us that Jesus returned[400] to the Jordan, "to the place where John at first baptized."[401] The Evangelist thus, as we will see, defines this journey as a return to the starting point of Jesus' ministry, that is, to the witness that John the Baptist gave at that place concerning Jesus. What has happened since that beginning is put in the perspective of "how everything began" by this summation, this evaluation of the end in light of the beginning. True, John himself was no longer there to witness to Jesus, but, the Evangelist reports, "many came to him," people who had heard John's testimony and now came to confirm its truth.

The double reference to "many" is striking. Some expositors suspect that this echoes the presence of a Christian community existing in that region at the time of the Evangelist. But the text gives the impression rather that many people from Judea, on hearing that Jesus was residing there again, went there — undoubtedly in sympathy with what happened there in the early days, since John still enjoyed much support among the people (cf. Mt. 21:26; 14:5). Accordingly, the pronouncement they make about Jesus is a confirmation of what John said.[402] No further explication is given of "everything" (that John said . . .). And there was much in John's witness concerning Jesus that still had to be confirmed (cf. 1:29, 33). The point here, however, is the general thrust of John's witness concerning Jesus and his greatness, in the shadow of which John himself could not stand (cf. 1:27, 30; cf. also 3:27ff.). Presumably the concessive introduction to their statement ("John did no sign") means that

---

400. πάλιν is lacking in a number of manuscripts; here it is to be translated "back" rather than "again"; the emphasis does not lie on a repeated going to the same place, but on returning to "where it all began."

401. τὸ πρῶτον can mean "first, for the first time," in distinction from other places where John had baptized, or simply "earlier."

402. This utterance is apparently not directed to Jesus himself. The period before καὶ πολλοί can therefore be placed better after πρὸς αὐτόν; so Bultmann, *Comm.,* p. 394, n. 3.

John's significance as a prophet ("everything John said") was nonetheless powerful for all that. As a rule prophets were expected to do miracles (cf. 9:17; Mk. 6:14ff. par.). But though John's ministry was devoid of miracles (cf. 1:21), the people still held him to be a prophet (cf. Mk. 11:32 par.). Therefore, the pronouncement is not a bit of polemic directed against the later Johannine sect (see the comments on 1:20; 3:26)[403] but rather the unequivocal trust of the many in the prophetic authority of John — even without miracles — which they merely saw confirmed in Jesus' ministry.

The report ends with "and many believed in him there." The intent of this statement (and of this entire conclusion) is clear: despite the hostility against Jesus that was dominant at the center of Jewish life and that already threatened his life, there were nevertheless many in Israel who — in the wilderness where John had called for a "highway" for Jesus — were prepared to come to Jesus and make their decision for him. To be sure, these "many" will not determine the overall picture of the coming events. But there is no reason to think that the Evangelist wanted to cast doubt on their faith (as though it were merely faith in miracles; cf. 2:23; 4:39; 7:31, etc.). The case is rather that they gave to Jesus the faith that he asked for but did not receive from "the Jews" (cf. vss. 37ff.). And they did this with an appeal to John and in the spirit of John. Viewed through the eyes of Jesus' adversaries, his return to where his ministry began might have made of it the very picture of a failed mission. But the Evangelist views things quite differently. He will not write the second main division of his Gospel before placing Jesus once more in the light of his great God-sent witness (1:7). This last word of this first division is at the same time the opening note of the second. For as yet not everything that John said about Jesus had been fulfilled. The truth of it is still to become evident in what follows.

---

403. And put in the mouths of the "many." Cf. Bultmann, *Comm.,* p. 394, n. 4.

11–12

Prelude to the Passion Narrative

Chapters 11 and 12 clearly constitute the transition from the confrontational dialogues between Jesus and "the Jews" (see introduction to chs. 7–10) to the narrative of Jesus' suffering and death, which begins in 13:1. In this interim Jesus withdrew with his disciples to a place across the Jordan. They interrupted their stay when they went to Bethany and Jesus raised Lazarus. But then Jesus again withdrew, now to "a town called Ephraim," where "he remained with the disciples" (11:54). Not until "the Passover of the Jews was near" (vs. 55) does the story take a turn. Then, "six days before the Passover" (12:1), Jesus returned to Bethany and, following his anointing there (vss. 2-7), went into Jerusalem. There his encounter with "some Greeks" present at the festival proved to Jesus that now the decisive hour had struck for him (vss. 20-23). A final dialogue with the crowd, the Evangelist's reflection on Jesus' entire public ministry, and a last word of Jesus himself follow (vss. 33, 34-36, 37-43, 44-50).

This transition to the Passion narrative strongly diverges from this part of the story as we have it in the Synoptics, especially in regard to the place and significance of the raising of Lazarus. While here that event is the climax of Jesus' miracles and of his entire public ministry and is a key factor in the decision of the Sanhedrin to kill Jesus (11:46ff.; 12:10, 18f.), the Synoptics mention nothing of the miracle and thus give it no role in the conflict between Jesus and the Jewish leaders. To many scholars who deny the Fourth Evangelist any direct knowledge of Jesus' life, this is proof that we have in this healing story either a symbolic narrative of the Evangelist's own making or a legend of doubtful historical content that he used in that way. Others are more cautious in their evaluation. They point out that the raising of the dead by Jesus belongs to the undisputed core of the gospel (cf. Mt. 11:5), that Luke also knows of a raising unreported by Matthew and Mark (Lk. 7:11ff.), and that it would certainly be strange if of all Gospel writers John, in whose work salvation is

381

consistently described as "(eternal) life," would not relate a single raising from the dead among the "signs" of Jesus (cf. 20:30, 31). Nevertheless, even for expositors who take this position the historical place that the Evangelist assigns to this miracle remains doubtful. Rather than being based on historical tradition or the Evangelist's own memory, the placing of this miracle at this point is said to be due to the Evangelist himself: not historical but rather "theological" and "pedagogical" motives were decisive for him.[1]

Even from a "theological" point of view the story of the raising of Lazarus does occupy a very important place in the overall structure of the Gospel. But this need not by itself be an argument against the historicity of the sequence of events as it is described here. It is, rather, integral to this order. At this point Jesus has already withdrawn from association with "the Jews" at Jerusalem. When word of Lazarus's illness reaches him and he reveals his intent to go to Judea "again" (the word appears twice in vss. 7 and 8), his disciples object that "the Jews" have "just now" been trying to stone him. Jesus answers that he must "fill up" the twelve hours of daylight (as in 9:4f.). All this presupposes the long prior stay in Judea and Jerusalem and also explains why the uproar caused by this miracle was a sign for the Jewish leaders not to delay any longer but to end Jesus' public appearances by force.

The Synoptics say nothing (at least very little: see below) of this whole development. They give the impression that Jesus went to Jerusalem directly from Galilee, thinking only of the approaching Passover, and that he chose a Transjordanian route and went to Jerusalem via Jericho and Bethany in order to make his "entry" from there. It is only after the entry into Jerusalem that the narratives of John and the Synoptics again flow in the same channel, though subsequently, even in the Passion narrative itself, they again diverge.

Therefore, the question of when Lazarus was raised cannot be answered in isolation but is inextricably bound up with how John as a transmitter of the tradition repeatedly breaks out of the Synoptic geographical and temporal framework and thus demonstrates that he has at his disposal broader knowledge than the tradition enshrined in the Synoptics. However much the Fourth Evangelist was guided in the selection and arrangement of his material by "theological" motives (20:30, 31), so that in many ways his Gospel bears a different character from the other Gospels, this does not mean that the historicity of his compositions can be judged by the degree to which they can be integrated in the narrower framework of the Synoptic tradition.[2]

This is all the more true because the Synoptics themselves are rife with indications that Jesus' ministry outside Galilee and in Jerusalem must have encompassed far more than what they themselves explicitly report. Especially

1. See, e.g., Schnackenburg, *Comm.* II, pp. 345f.; Brown, *Comm.* I, p. 429.
2. See further pp. 4f. above and the comments above on 2:13f. and 4:1f.

relevant to the present text is the statement in Lk. 19:37 (cf. Jn. 12:18) concerning the enthusiasm with which "the whole multitude of the disciples" welcomed Jesus at his entry into Jerusalem "for all the deeds of power that they had seen." This points to more happening in Jerusalem than can be inferred from the Synoptic Gospels themselves, which mention, in fact, no earlier miracles in Jerusalem. It has been suggested that John, not satisfied with this Lukan summary, filled the gap with his story of Lazarus's raising.[3] But this cannot be assumed with any plausibility because we have no proof that the Fourth Evangelist knew the Gospel of Luke and, more importantly, because the scope and diversity of the material peculiar to the Fourth Gospel is such that it cannot be subjected to criteria that would a priori restrict his independence with respect to the Synoptics.

11:1-44

The Raising of Lazarus

In the Lazarus story the miraculous event and Jesus' self-revelation in that event are completely interwoven. Here again all sorts of attempts have been made to distill from the text before us a written or oral source used by the Evangelist (an "original document," "legend," or "tradition"), of which our text is then said to be the Evangelist's "theological redaction." More specifically, some have sought the original locus of this miracle story in the "*sēmeia* source" ("S"),[4] the existence of which has since been accepted by many scholars.[5] It is said that the Evangelist repeatedly interrupts the narrative he has borrowed from "S" with his interpretive remarks and additions and that this can be noted in various ways in the text we have before us.

Most expositors are agreed, however, that the story and the interpretation constitute a unity, so much so that it is impossible on the basis of the text that

---

3. Brown, *Comm.*, in loc.:

"The Fourth Gospel is not satisfied with such a generalization. It is neither sufficiently dramatic nor clear-cut to say that all Jesus' miracles led to enthusiasm on the part of some and hate on the part of others. And so the writer has chosen *one miracle* and to make this the primary representative of all the mighty miracles of which Luke speaks. With a superb sense of development he has chosen a miracle in which Jesus raises a dead man."

4. For the development of this hypothesis see the overview in Haenchen, *Comm.* II, pp. 67ff.

5. Some, however, believe that the narrative (as reconstructed from "S") still contains so many obscurities that even it cannot be regarded as an original report. So Bultmann, *Comm.*, p. 396: "presumably an old narrative had already been edited when it was taken up into the σημεῖα-source, and the Evangelist has further worked over it. We are unable to clear up all the difficulties. . . ."

has been handed down to us to arrive at a credible reconstruction of a miracle story (whether from "S" or some other source) that the Evangelist is assumed to have used.[6] A strong counterargument is the fact that in the style of the story as it lies before us there is nothing suggesting the presence of two distinct original components.[7] Admittedly the structure of the beginning of the story is not entirely clear, but that is already true in vss. 1 and 2 and not just in the "Johannine" vss. 4 and 5.

It is undeniable, however, that a factor for some expositors is the miracle itself standing in the way of taking the story as an original unit as it stands. While in the *sēmeia* source the point is said to be the miracle as such as a tangible supernatural proof of Jesus' messiahship, for the Evangelist the meaning of miracles is said to be only what they symbolize, which is articulated here in vss. 25-27: Jesus is "the resurrection and the life," and all who believe in him will live, even those who, like Lazarus, have died. For those who have arrived at this believing insight — to which Jesus seeks to bring Martha with his "I am" pronouncement — the remainder of the story (the temporary physical revival of Lazarus) is, if not superfluous or even meaningless, then certainly a hindrance to understanding the Evangelist's real intent. Or — in still another interpretation — it was retained by the Evangelist only for his more primitive readers, for whom miracle as such was of paramount interest.

Familiar here is the statement already made by Wellhausen[8] that Jesus' saying in vss. 25f. made the resurrection of Lazarus "completely superfluous" and "robbed the whole event of all meaning." No less radical is the opinion of Becker: "By its thesis John XI 25f. degrades the actual miracle to an absurdity that limps along behind." "To one who takes the 'I am' saying (vs. 25) seriously the miracle is meaningless. To one who marvels at the miracle as theologically significant, the saying is meaningless." Why the Evangelist nevertheless at such great length recorded this miracle (and all the others) is not asked. That he "allows the miracles to live under his roof" is "a decision of the Evangelist that borders on audacity."[9] The manner in which Jesus speaks of himself in his "I am" statement (11:25f.) makes it apparent to what extent the Evangelist

6. Cf., e.g., C. H. Dodd, *Historical Tradition in the Fourth Gospel*, 1965, p. 230: "Nowhere, perhaps, in this gospel have attempts to analyze out a written source, or sources, proved less convincing, and if the evangelist is following a traditional story of fixed pattern, he has covered his tracks." P. 228: "we are dealing with a highly individual composition, a *Musterstück* of its writer's art. The problem of its possible relation to any pre-Johannine strand of tradition is peculiarly difficult, for anything that may have been taken over has been recast in Johannine idiom of speech and thought."

7. See also W. Nicol, himself a proponent of the *sēmeia* source: "There are almost no significant style differences" (*The Semeia in the Fourth Gospel*, 1972, p. 37).

8. *Comm.*, p. 51.

9. J. Becker, "Wunder und Christologie," *NTS* 16 (1969-70), pp. 146, 142.

distanced himself from the miracle christology of the *sēmeia* source and sought to expose it as totally meaningless.

Others, including Haenchen and Bultmann, are more cautious in their treatment of the supposed tension between the christology of the source and that of the Evangelist. According to Haenchen, "the trouble the Fourth Gospel has caused exegetes owes to the fact that the Evangelist has made a 'gospel of miracles' [i.e., "S"] the bearer of his own message." While for the Evangelist the significance of these miracle stories was only that they contained between the lines a "pointer" to a trans-earthly reality, it was his "misfortune" that his readers understood this "gospel of miracles used by him as a pointer," "as a collection of actual miracle stories."[10] Hence the difficulty for the present-day expositor of protecting *his* readers from the danger — apparently still real — of being victimized by this "misfortune."

Bultmann attempts to do justice to both aspects of the narrative. In his view the Evangelist himself thought about the tension between his symbolic approach to the miracle and his source's realistic understanding. He brought these two ways of dealing with the miracle to expression "through the differentiation made between Martha and Mary."[11] Bultmann's idea is that the role of Martha was introduced by the Evangelist himself to express his own understanding of faith and is based on a symbolic interpretation of the miracle. But in the story of Lazarus's real raising the Evangelist leaves room as a second possibility for the more primitive faith in miracles represented in the *sēmeia* source by Mary.

However, of such an inner tension between the Evangelist's symbolic approach to the miracle and the source's realistic understanding there is no evidence whatever in the text. There is not a single indication that the Evangelist identified less with the miracle story that he supposedly edited at such length and with so much realism (still less that he wanted to expose its christology as meaningless!) than with the "I am" sayings of vss. 25f. Everything points rather to the understanding that here, too, the miracle is intended as confirmation of the word of Jesus' self-disclosure spoken earlier.[12] This follows from the overall structure of the story, in which even for the Evangelist the climax is obviously the miracle itself. And it is implied from the beginning in the statements with which the story is introduced, which the critics of the unity of the whole regard as "Johannine." For example, in vs. 4: "This illness does not lead to death. It is, rather, for God's glory, so that the Son of God may be glorified through it." "Glory" and "glorification" obviously refer to the glory manifested in the

10. *Comm.* II, pp. 72, 71.

11. *Comm.*, p. 395.

12. See also, e.g., M. de Jonge, *Jesus: Stranger from Heaven and Son of God,* 1977, p. 125: "This interpretation," that is, that Jesus' conversation with Martha (vss. 22f.) would make the continuing story of the resurrection itself "superfluous," "is clearly wrong; here again the word which calls for faith is followed by the sign which demonstrates the truth and the power of the word."

miracle (as also in the first miracle, 2:11) and not only or primarily to the words of Jesus in vss. 25f. And this is all the more evident in that, in his word to Martha at the time of the miracle itself, Jesus refers back to these earlier words: "Did I not tell you that if you believed, you would see God's glory?" (11:40). So even for the Evangelist, as is evident from these key words, the whole story is involved (see the interpretation below) — not just the issue of belief in Jesus' words but also that of seeing the deeds of his glory (cf. 1:14, 51). The idea of a tension between the event and its interpretation — as if the Johannine message could be abstracted from the reality of the miracle — is in conflict with the pronouncement in 1:14 concerning the incarnation of the Word in its fundamental import for this whole Gospel.[13]

11:1-16
Lazarus's Illness Reported

1-3   The wording of the opening of the story is rather choppy and cumbersome. "Now a certain man was" recalls similar introductions in 5:5; 1 Sa. 1:1; Jb. 1:1. The name Lazarus is an abbreviation of Eleazar ("God helps") and occurs elsewhere in the New Testament only in Lk. 16:19f.[14] The added designation "of Bethany, the village of Mary and her sister Martha" serves not only to distinguish this Bethany from one mentioned earlier (1:28; see also 11:18) but also to bring Mary and Martha into the story. It assumes that the readers know more about these sisters than about their brother, as is evident also from what follows in vs. 2: "Mary was the one who anointed the Lord with perfume." This striking note anticipates 12:1f. but is primarily intended here to alert the readers that the woman prominent in this story is the the one who had become so familiar in the tradition as the one who anointed Jesus. "Whose brother

13. See also Nicol, *Semeia in the Fourth Gospel,* pp. 110f. and the passage he cites from E. C. Hoskyns, *The Fourth Gospel,* 1940, p. 34: "The Gospel stubbornly refuses . . . to be divided into history and interpretation. The history invades the interpretation, and the interpretation pervades the history. . . . Separate the two, and the extremity of violence is done to the text. What Jesus is to the faith of the true Christian believer, he *was* in the flesh: this is the theme of the Fourth Gospel, and it is precisely this unity that constitutes the Problem of the Gospel."

14. On the basis of Lk. 16:30, John 11 has often been linked to the parable in Luke 16. The idea that the latter alludes to our story is in itself meaningful ("The Jews will not believe even if Lazarus rises from the dead"), but it is wrong to conclude that the parable in Luke could already refer back to the story in John 11. Conversely, it is even less acceptable to think that the Fourth Evangelist seized upon the name and person of Lazarus of Bethany in order to historicize the unreal raising of the Lazarus of the parable. There is more support for the assumption that the name Lazarus can be traced to present-day el-Azariyeh (town of Lazarus), situated near the Mount of Olives, close to which there has long been said to have been a tomb. Cf. G. Dalman, *Orte und Wege Jesu,* 1924, pp. 265f.

Lazarus was ill," though it somewhat strangely tags along at the end, is clearly intended to pick up the thread started in vs. 1: "and it was *her* brother Lazarus who was so ill." Vs. 3 then states that these two sisters sent a message to Jesus[15] to inform him of the illness. The words of the message, "Lord, he whom you love is ill," are obviously intended as an urgent appeal from the sisters to Jesus' power and love toward their sick brother. Of the relation of Jesus to Lazarus they say no more than that they were united in human friendship, as was also true of Jesus and Lazarus's sisters (cf. vs. 5). Therefore these words cannot by themselves serve as an argument for the identification of "the disciple whom Jesus loved" as Lazarus.[16]

4 For Jesus the message concerning his friend's illness and the appeal made to him is the signal of great things to come. It does not appear that he knew in advance and at a distance how everything would transpire (cf. vs. 17). We get the impression, rather, that he, too, depended on guidance from God, by which the "what" and the "when" ("the hour," cf. 2:4; 7:6) of what he had to do gradually became clear to him. Even "this illness is not unto death," although it does not constitute a denial that Lazarus would die, by itself says no more than that death would not be the ultimate consequence of this illness, its final word.[17]

The next words are fundamental for the whole story: "It [is] for[18] the glory of God, so that the Son of God may be glorified by means of it[19]" (see also the comments on 9:3b). The glory of God and that of the Son, as elsewhere, are mentioned in a single breath. It is in the sending of the Son that "the glory of God," that is, God's reality in the power and majesty of his presence, manifests itself (cf. 13:31; 14:13; 17:4), and that constitutes the all-controlling motive of the miracle that now follows (see also vs. 40).

Many interpreters believe that these words not only relate to Lazarus's raising but anticipate Jesus' resurrection. The coming miracle would after all occasion Jesus' death and thus his subsequent glorification, which are repeatedly brought to the fore in the chapters that follow (cf. 12:16, 23, 28; 13:1f.; 17:1-4). Accordingly, Jesus' announcement here is said to encompass his own death and resurrection as well and to depict the raising of Lazarus as a prefiguration of his

15. Jesus' name is not mentioned in the original; hence the "him" must refer to the "Lord" of vs. 2, since Jesus is not mentioned in vs. 1 either. This is an argument against the idea that the addition in vs. 2 was not original.

16. Contra, e.g., J. N. Sanders, "Those Whom Jesus Loved," *NTS* 1 (1954-55), p. 33. He takes support for this from the fact that while the Evangelist uses φιλεῖν in the words of the sisters (vs. 3), he uses ἀγαπᾶν in vs. 5, where he is not quoting. It is improbable, however, that the Fourth Gospel makes such an intentional distinction between the two verbs (cf. vs. 3b; 13:23; 20:2; 21:15-17).

17. πρός with the accusative, indicating "purpose, result" (BDF §239.7).

18. ὑπέρ.

19. δι' αὐτῆς.

own resurrection.[20] Linked with this is the idea that when the Fourth Gospel mentions the manifestation of Jesus' glory (as with the first miracle, 2:11), it implies an anticipation of Jesus' resurrection glory and thus attempts to make the glorified Christ in heaven visible in the life of the earthly Jesus.[21]

However, the Fourth Gospel's approach to and presentation of Jesus' glory in his miracles is certainly quite other than this. It aims, instead, and this from the beginning, to make the preexistent glory of God visible and tangible in the earthly existence (the "flesh") of Jesus of Nazareth. Granted, Jesus' future glory is nothing other than a receiving back of what he had with the Father in the beginning before the world existed (cf. 17:5). But between these two states the Son's descent from heaven, as a temporary mission of the Father, has a character of glory totally its own, one that cannot be described as a present intimation of the future glory in heaven. The unique redemptive significance of this descent, of, that is, the incarnation of the Word and of the entrance of God's glory into human life, determines and limits the manifestation of that glory in accordance with its own nature. This is true not only spatially but also temporally, as is clearly evident in, for instance, 11:9. Therefore we must speak of a caesura rather than a link between the raising of Lazarus and the resurrection of Jesus.

5-7 What immediately follows conveys a clear indication of all this. Before the flow of events continues in vss. 6-7 it is noted that "Jesus loved Martha and her sister and Lazarus."[22] This insertion is not — as some have interpreted it — merely a superfluous confirmation of vs. 3b, the result of an unfortunate use of sources. It rather brings to expression that in and alongside the manifestation of God's glory Jesus' human affection for his three friends — again referred to by name — forms another fundamental motive for his conduct, a feature that returns in the sequel. Here, too, this element already plays a part when vs. 6 picks up where vs. 4 left off:[23] "So when he heard that he was ill, he [it is true][24] stayed where he was for two more days. Then [having done that][25] he said to his disciples, 'Let us go back into Judea.' " The whole of vss. 5-7 shows how the human and the divine — his love for his own *and* his regard for the times appointed for him by the Father — are inseparably intertwined in Jesus' conduct and therefore in his glorification as the Son of

20. See, e.g., the commentaries of Bultmann, Schnackenburg, and Brown, in loc.

21. See the lengthy discussions of the proleptic significance of Jesus' manifestation of glory specifically in the miracles in Nicol, *Sēmeia in the Fourth Gospel,* pp. 124-37, especially pp. 128f.

22. It is hard to say why in vs. 5, in contrast with vss. 1f., Martha is mentioned first. The reason is perhaps that of the two sisters she tends to stand in the foreground as the one who takes the initiative (cf. vss. 19ff. and Lk. 10:38b, 40f.).

23. ὡς οὖν ἤκουσαν, vs. 6, after ἀκούσας in vs. 4.

24. The μέν after τότε has no corresponding δέ. Although this is unusual in John, the contrast is easily derived from the context (cf. BDF §447.4). The μέν is more or less concessive.

25. The seemingly superfluous μετὰ τοῦτο therefore marks the first pause Jesus observed.

God (vs. 4). Humanly speaking, Jesus' love would immediately have driven him to take to the road (cf. vss. 21, 32, 36f.) In fact, it *was* his love that made him leave his place of concealment (cf. 10:39, 40). But he also had to wait for the "hour," the "time," appointed for him by the Father (cf. 2:4; 7:6, 8; 8:20; 12:23; 13:1). That this delay served only to enhance the surpassing significance of this miracle — making it not the prevention but the reversal of death — is clear enough from the outcome and runs like a thread through the whole story (cf. vss. 21, 32, 37). But all this ambivalence in Jesus' public conduct — concealing himself one moment and appearing in public the next, which we see again in vss. 54f., knowing himself called to do great deeds but then having to wait for the "hour" and "time" appointed by the Father — characterizes his manifestation of divine glory on earth as that of the one sent by the Father to fulfill his mandate at a time appointed by the Father.

Therefore the idea that Jesus made his decisions here in absolute sovereignty without regard to human feelings — which would then be all the more evidence of the docetic character of this christology[26] — is a denial to Jesus not only of the motive of human love, which is mentioned in vs. 5, but also of the total and constant connection of his conduct to the will of the Father (cf. 4:34; 5:30; 6:38f.), even when it is said of the Son that he gives life to whom he will (5:21; cf. vs. 30). However much the Fourth Gospel stresses the absolute authority with which the Father has clothed the Son and given all things into his hands (3:35; 5:21f., 27 and passim), nevertheless the Son does nothing of himself and can do nothing of himself, but only what he "sees" the Father doing (5:19, 30; 8:28 and elsewhere) in continual fellowship with him and in waiting for his "hour." In that sense there is again (see above) great resemblance between the first miracle (at Cana) and this last miracle. There, too, the appeal to Jesus to act comes from someone who is humanly very close to him; there, too, Jesus refuses to act immediately "on his own" but instead waits until his "hour" has come; and there, too, the miracle is described as the manifestation of his glory (2:14).[27]

26. So E. Käsemann, *The Testament of Jesus: A Study of the Gospel of John in the Light of Chapter 17,* 1968: Jesus "permits Lazarus to lie in the grave for four days in order that the miracle of his resurrection may be more impressive"; with regard to Jesus' absolute and sovereign freedom to act on his own: "almost superfluously the Evangelist notes that this Jesus at all times lies on the bosom of the Father and that to him who is one with the Father the angels descend and from him they again ascend" (p. 9). On Jesus' glorification as Son of God: "One can hardly fail to recognize the danger of his christology of glory, namely, the danger of docetism. It is present in a still naive unreflected form and it has not yet been recognized by the Evangelist or his community" (p. 26, with an appeal to Wellhausen, F. C. Baur, Overbeck, and Hirsch).

27. Cf. H. Giblin, "Suggestion, Negative Response, and Positive Action in St. John's Portrayal of Jesus," *NTS* 26 (1980), p. 209. In addition to 2:1-11 and 11:1-4 Giblin also mentions 4:4b-54 and 7:2-14 as examples of the same literary pattern and analyzes the present pericope at length from that perspective.

8-10 When Jesus then, after two days' delay, invites his disciples to join him on the way back to Judea, he first has to overcome their opposition. Since 9:12 there has been no mention of the disciples. Nor are they mentioned here after 11:16. It is clear from their repeated interventions that their presence — though not always of all twelve (cf. 21:2) — is always to be assumed. But it is obvious that, despite their continuing faithfulness to Jesus, they still consistently allow themselves to be guided by purely human considerations (cf. 4:31f.; 6:7f., 19; 9:2).

Had Jesus informed his disciples of the report he had received from Martha and Mary, and did they therefore understood that he wanted to go to Lazarus in Bethany? Until the announcement of departure in vs. 7, Jesus apparently acts on his own; at least he speaks only of going back to Judea and does not mention "our friend Lazarus" until vs. 11. In any case at first the disciples resist only the idea of returning to Judea. They think only of "the Jews" who "just now"[28] had been seeking to stone him. Did he really want to "go there again"?

Jesus' answer initially focuses only on their reluctance to reenter the danger zone from which he — and they with him — had so recently escaped with their lives. What he says recalls his statement in 9:4, 5 (cf. also 12:35f.), appealing to the general commonsense wisdom that one must take advantage of the light while it shines, though here he speaks directly to the immediate situation. Those who do not "walk during the day" risk all that comes with the darkness. Jesus here speaks further of the "twelve hours of the day" in which one can move without danger (of stumbling) because one can then see "the light of this world," the sun, by the light of which one can find his way.[29] But at nightfall one encounters danger because then "the light is no longer in him." That is, that person no longer has the light of the eye ("the lamp of the body," that is, that by which the body receives light; cf. Mt. 6:2).[30]

The import of this figurative speech is remarkable in more than one respect. The primary thrust is of course directed toward the disciples: as long as Jesus is still with them as "the light of this world" (cf. 9:5), the light is "in them" so that they can see where they are going and are secured against the "stones of stumbling" that (in a variety of ways!) the night brings with it. As long as his "hour" has not come, the Jews have no hold on him (cf. 7:30) and the disciples "walk," in the whole of their existence, in the light of his presence (cf. 8:12). But this saying also indirectly (like vss. 5-7) throws light on the

28. For the meaning of νῦν see, e.g., 21:10.

29. Jews divided the time between dawn and sunset into twelve hours, which did not have the same duration throughout the year (cf. Strack/Billerbeck II, pp. 442, 543), though that plays no role in this text.

30. Elsewhere transferred to the human "heart" as one's internal "eye" and "light" (cf. Ep. 1:18; 1 Jn. 2:11).

character of Jesus' own work and manifestation of glory "in the flesh."[31] It is evident here, as in 9:4, that Jesus' mission is clearly defined and limited temporally.

"Twelve hours" refers primarily to the fullness of the day and the work to be done in it (cf. 9:4; 4:34; 19:30). For that reason Jesus must be available to the last to "do the works of God" and to be "the light of the world" (cf. 9:4, 5), even though the hostility directed at him is taking ever more threatening forms. That he has withdrawn from public view to escape this hostility is not in conflict with this. He has done so because he is conscious that the "twelve hours" of his workday are not yet full and that therefore he must await directions from his Sender. Now that the call comes to him to take to the road again, that is for him evidence that the glory of God was still prepared to manifest itself in him and that his work was not yet finished.

Also included in this reference to "twelve hours," furthermore, is the concern for the approach of the end of day. For that reason, too, the disciples must be on their way, before the night comes and darkness falls for them and for him, with all the risk this entails (vs. 10; cf. 9:5 and 12:35).

This repeated reference to the passage of time and — as the end approaches — to the "little while" still left to Jesus (7:33; 12:35; 13:33; 14:19; 16:16-19) is all the more striking because here (as in 9:3-5) there is no reference to Jesus' future glory, which is mentioned again and again in the sequel (12:18, 23; 17:14). It seems here that what follows the twelve hours of day is only darkness in which no one, including Jesus, can work (9:4). Not that Jesus' future glory is lost from view. But what is unmistakable here is the caesura (already referred to in the comments on vs. 4) between Jesus' earthly manifestation of glory ("in the flesh") and the future glory he is yet to receive (cf. 17:4, 5), a line of demarcation drawn by Jesus' death. This again confirms the core saying in 3:13 that the ascent of the Son of man to heaven to receive all power (cf. Dn. 7:12ff.) can occur only after his descent from heaven (3:14) to be lifted onto and up from the cross.

On this the raising of Lazarus also depends. It is not the prelude to and first installment of Jesus' heavenly glory but rather the transition toward the power and darkness of the world, which is the only means by which the Son of man will be lifted up from the earth to draw his own to him (12:32), that is, as he gives up his flesh and blood for the life of the world (6:51).

11-16 Having thus declared himself on the subject of his return to Judea,[32] Jesus now states its purpose: "Our friend Lazarus has fallen asleep, but I go to awake him out of sleep." That Jesus refers to Lazarus's death under

---

31. Cf. Bultmann: "In the context it is self-evident that this saying (as 9.4) must first be related to Jesus himself, and give the reason for his decision" (*Comm.* p. 399).

32. As the awkward ταῦτα εἶπεν, καὶ μετὰ τοῦτο λέγει can be paraphrased.

the common image of sleep (e.g., Mt. 9:24) brings to expression the power and authority that from the very beginning have filled him with regard to Lazarus's illness (vs. 4) and in which he remains unshaken now that he knows Lazarus has died. We are not told how and when Jesus received this information. Here, too (as in, e.g., 1:47f.; 4:50), he is speaking as one who has supernatural knowledge of the way and will of the Father, the salvific import of which only gradually becomes clear to him (cf. vs. 15).

The disciples, however, do not understand all this (vs. 12). They react (as in, e.g., 4:33; 6:6f.) as persons who, because of their earthly and human manner of thinking, misunderstand Jesus. This recurrent Johannine motif gives Jesus opportunities to explain the matter at hand more fully (e.g., 3:3f.; 6:52f.). This pattern of dialogue is widely termed a literary device.

One can also take the disciples' reaction somewhat more realistically (vs. 13). From the way Jesus speaks of Lazarus "falling asleep" and of "awaking him" they conclude that whatever had come over Lazarus had apparently taken a turn for the better.[33] They see this as all the more reason to persist in their objection to the dangerous trip to Judea.

Jesus puts an end to all misunderstanding by now stating plainly,[34] "Lazarus is dead" (vs. 14). He adds (vs. 15), "and for your sake I am glad that I was not there, so that you may believe." With these words the salvific character of Jesus' manifestation of glory again comes to expression. He starts out on the journey knowing that the time in which he is the light of the world is running out and that his return to Judea will hasten this end. But he goes not for the sake of his own glory but for the sake of the faith of his own. The delay serves to demonstrate that glory in all its splendor to them — once more before the night falls on him and on them and their faith in him is severely tested.

The acute need for this is evident also from the reaction of Thomas[35] to Jesus' new and now definitive proposal to his disciples: "But let us go to him [Lazarus]" (vs. 16). Thomas does not resist. He even urges his fellow disciples "let us also go," but adds significantly: "that we may die with him." His mind has not been changed or put to rest by Jesus' words in vss. 9 and 10. He is certain that to go to Judea means death for them all. Not following Jesus obviously did not occur to him as an option. But his willingness to join Jesus was a matter of accepting the inevitable, clearly without understanding anything of the joy of which Jesus had spoken, to say nothing of being able

33. σῴζεσθαι, here as elsewhere (cf. Mk. 5:23f.) in the sense of becoming well, recovering.
34. παρρησία.
35. The explanation "Didymus" ("twin") is "remarkable" (Schnackenburg, *Comm.* II, p. 515, n. 37) because Thomas was a current Greek name (taken over from the Aramaic and Hellenized), and one may wonder why a translation is added. Is it perhaps that Thomas and others by that name were also known by the Greek equivalent?

to share in it. In what follows (14:5; 20:24f.) Thomas is consistently the one who points out what is unintelligible and unacceptable to the ("sober," "realistic") human mind in what Jesus testified of himself and demanded from his disciples. It is therefore all the more striking and encouraging for those who as a rule follow Jesus in doubt and darkness that it is precisely this ("unbelieving") Thomas who toward the end of this Gospel confesses Jesus in words that before him no one had dared to utter and whose last word can therefore strike the keynote of the entire Gospel of Jesus' glory (cf. 20:28 with 1:1).

11:17-27

Jesus' Journey to Bethany and Conversation with Martha

In vs. **17** the scene of the story changes to Bethany. At his arrival Jesus (apparently with his disciples, vs. 16, though they are not referred to any more) hears that Lazarus has already been in the tomb for four days. This statement, which precedes all else, points to the crucial issue at stake in the story that now follows. Although raising Lazarus from the dead one day after his burial would not have been less of a miracle than after four days, most expositors refer at this point to an idea among the Jews that for three days after death the soul of the deceased returned to the grave, then leaving the body for good, because by then the process of decay became obvious.[36]

18-20 It emerges from the story that Jesus knew of the time of Lazarus's death before he arrived in the village and that his own coming had been announced before he arrived (see vs. 30). The Evangelist first focuses on the situation in the house of the deceased. The short distance Bethany was from Jerusalem,[37] about three kilometers or two miles,[38] explains the presence of the "many Jews" who had come from Jerusalem "to console Martha and Mary[39] concerning their brother," that is, to render a ministry of love to the mourners, an obligation that Jews valued highly and on the fulfillment of which they laid much stress.[40] That "many" came presumably points to the high social standing Lazarus and his sisters had even in Jerusalem and the sympathy that was now extended to the mourning women. At the same time these "Jews" (certainly not meant here in the sense of the authorities who were hostile to

36. See, e.g., Strack/Billerbeck II, pp. 544f.; Schlatter, *Comm.,* pp. 250f.
37. "ἦν is assimilated to the time of the narrative, as v. 6; 18.1; 19.41" (Bultmann, *Comm.,* p. 401, n. 2) and therefore does not point to a situation that changed later.
38. Cf. Strack/Billerbeck II, p. 54.
39. Martha is again mentioned first, as in vs. 5, unlike vs. 45, where Mary alone is referred to.
40. Cf. Strack/Billerbeck IV, pp. 592-607.

Jesus; cf. vss. 45, 46) are also part of the background for the story that now
follows, playing a distinct role in it (cf. vss. 33f.).

In this situation the news that Jesus is on his way reaches Martha (vs.
20). Apparently without involving Mary in her actions (cf. vss. 28, 29) Martha
withdraws from those around her and goes out to meet Jesus. The distinct
roles that Martha and Mary play in this story have often been seen as indicative
of the very different natures of the two women. Martha conveys the impression
that she is an immediately reactive, spontaneous woman unlike her sister who
is perhaps more introverted and certainly more receptive and slower to react
(cf. Lk. 10:38ff.). Martha's prominent role in this story may, as far as she is
concerned, very well point in that direction. She it is who first hears of the
(fervently awaited; cf. vss. 21, 32) arrival of Jesus. Immediately she takes off
to meet him. But still (as, e.g., in 4:7ff.) we must be careful with psychological
explanations. That "Mary persisted in sitting at home" is certainly not intended to be typical for her but is due to her ignorance of Jesus' coming (cf.
vss. 29f.).

There is also the very real danger of turning Mary and Martha into
theological models.[41] According to this view Martha (in John and contrary to
her role in Luke 10), in going out to meet Jesus and in her conversation and
confession in vss. 21-28, gives evidence of a deeper and more self-conscious
faith in Jesus than Mary, who cannot get past her sorrow and can only be
persuaded by the miracle. For some scholars this is proof of the supposed
contradiction in this chapter with regard to the meaning of the miracle (see
above, pp. 383ff. and the comments on vss. 25f. and 32ff.).

21-22 When Martha meets Jesus — everything here is described very
soberly and succinctly — she begins by voicing that which evidently kept her
in a state of utmost tension in the days just prior to Lazarus's death and thereafter
has become a most painful question to her: "Lord, if you had been here, my
brother would not have died!" This motif of the too late arrival returns later
(cf. vs. 32, 37). The Evangelist thus harks back to something Martha and Mary
did not know: Jesus deliberately delayed going to Bethany. What in Jesus'
conduct had to be done for the sake of God's glory has led here to a deeper
trial of faith. But it is precisely in this situation that Martha shows the character
of those who are "in truth his disciples" because they "remain" in Jesus (cf.

---

41. With regard to Martha's questions and answers in this conversation Schnackenburg
writes: "Psychological considerations do not help here"; he believes that "these conversations
must be interpreted in terms of the evangelist's intention as narrator." This applies "without any
doubt" to Martha's mentioning the last day (*Comm.* II, pp. 329f.). But the modern tendency to
render the Gospel figures into theological spokespersons and thereby to dehistoricize these conversations is no less objectionable than the earlier tendency to psychologize and historicize them.
The Evangelist is not writing a theological tract but a story about people of flesh and blood, as
is certainly evident in the present chapter.

8:31f.). Her disappointment was so intense because she believed in Jesus so strongly and expected so much from him.

So on seeing Jesus she not only voices that disappointment but in the same breath brings her faith in him into play as a continuing appeal to his omnipotence as the Son of God: "but[42] even now I know that whatever you ask from God, God will give you." The question arises whether she is, though not in so many words, referring to Jesus' power, even at this stage, to call Lazarus back from the dead. Strictly speaking, if one takes her words by themselves, one could infer this from the unrestricted "whatever you ask."[43] Still, the remainder of the conversation and especially vs. 39 point in another direction. Some have therefore correctly referred to not only the unrestricted nature of "whatever you ask" but also its indefiniteness. It leaves all doors open.[44] But her appeal to Jesus is no less forceful for all that. Even though she herself did not see how at this stage he could still offer help, she does not for that reason release him but by saying "even now I know . . ." she puts the still-unfulfilled answer to her faith in his hands and on the shoulders of him whom God would not refuse whatever he asked. In this respect, too, our story reminds us of that first miracle in which the mother of Jesus, after she too had initially been "put in her place," had nevertheless instructed the servants in charge: "Do whatever he tells you" (2:5).

23 Jesus' answer is not a direct response to the disappointment implied in Martha's words with regard to his "late" arrival but in a sense goes beyond this. "Your brother will rise again" is ambivalent. By these words he is certainly also speaking of what he is about to do (cf. vss. 4, 11). But, as will be evident from vss. 25f., they refer to more than the coming miracle and contain no direct indication — even for Martha — of what Jesus was about to do. But his intention is not to increase the suspense. He continues to delay because, before manifesting his glory, he seeks to unite his disciples to himself on a level deeper than can be achieved by removing their sorrow over Lazarus. Jesus deals pastorally with Martha in a way strongly reminiscent of the course of his earlier encounter with a royal official (4:46ff.). There, too, a person in great personal distress turns to Jesus, and there, too, the miracle is delayed, as it were. At stake in the encounter with Jesus is not just and not primarily that a man gets his deathly ill son back or a woman her dead brother. The "life" and "resurrection" of which Jesus speaks and that he imparts are more than that. It is this that the delay is designed to make us see.

24 Martha, however, is able to hear in Jesus' statement no more than that he is referring her to the great future and the resurrection of the righteous

---

42. The genuineness of ἀλλά is uncertain.

43. ὅσα ἂν αἰτήσῃ.

44. Cf. Schnackenburg, *Comm.* II, p. 329, who speaks of "a form deliberately kept general (ὅσα ἂν) and indefinite" and "a request which leaves all possibilities open" and correctly concludes that "Martha's faith is directed more at Jesus' person than at the nature of the help."

to be expected "on the last day." She has this "knowledge"[45] in common with many of her contemporaries.[46] The Jews who have come to console her have certainly reminded her of it. She therefore immediately assents to Jesus' statement about the resurrection — as she understands it. But "I know" contains a clear undertone of dissatisfaction. Has Jesus come to Bethany only to confirm what she already knows?

25, 26   Jesus' response gives the conversation a turn that is characteristic of the Fourth Gospel. Now he no longer speaks of Lazarus or of the manner of his resurrection, but with great power points to himself as "the resurrection and the life." Here again he does this in the disclosure form of an "I am" statement.[47] Just as that which is truly food and drink, light and life are given only in him and can only be known from him (cf. 4:10, 14; 6:33, 48, 53f.; 8:12, etc.), so also he is "the resurrection and the life"; all who face the recurrent death situations of life and wrestle with questions of death and life can find an answer only through faith in him.

The absolute validity of this statement is emphasized in a pair of artfully combined statements, each of which, in the form of a *mašal,* expresses the same truth in paradoxical manner. The effect is heightened further by the use in both statements of "live" and "die" with dual meanings:

> Whover believes in me, though he dies, yet will live,
> and whoever lives and believes in me will never die.

Vs. 25b refers to death in the natural sense and to living in the sense of eternal life. "Lives" in vs. 26a, on the other hand, refers to natural human existence, while "never die" refers to the eternal life that natural death can neither prevent nor affect. Both statements have the same import,[48] though from different viewpoints: first, that of the deceased believer who will live; second, that of the one who lives in faith and will not die. The common meaning is that everyone who believes in Jesus, in life as in death, participates in the resurrection and the life that Jesus is and that he imparts.

---

45. The reference here, as in, e.g., 3:2; 9:24, 29, 31 and elsewhere, is to "knowing" in the sense of assenting to generally accepted doctrines or religious views.

46. See, e.g., A. Oepke, *TDNT* I, p. 370.

47. On this see at greater length pp. 292, 300.

48. Some interpreters claim that vs. 26 adds another thought to vs. 25, that "live" ("whoever lives," vs. 26) is meant in the sense of vs. 25, and that the whole of vs. 26 teaches the imperishability of the new life (so Calvin, Schlatter, Brown, and others). In that case, however, καὶ πιστεύειν, added under the same definite article as ὁ ζῶν, is then superfluous or has to mean something like "and continues to believe," which in this connection seems forced. It is more natural to assume that ὁ ζῶν in vs. 26 corresponds with κἂν ἀποθάνῃ in vs. 25 and hence refers to natural life: "whoever lives and believes in me," "lives by faith in me." So correctly Bultmann, Schnackenburg, and many others.

Jesus thus, in response to Martha's statement in vs. 24, in a sense reduces the entire resurrection and the resurrection hope to himself and to believing. He thus tells her that resurrection is not only what occurs on "the last day" but an event that has already begun in him and is present, and that believing in the resurrection is therefore a matter of believing in him. This pronouncement — and this whole chapter — is an echo and a realization of what was said in 5:25: "The hour is coming, and now is, when the dead will hear the voice of the Son of God, and those who hear [in faith!] will live." This is not a "spiritualization" of the resurrection — see the sequel! — nor does the resurrection become a timeless datum that is therefore canceled out or meaningless as a future event.[49] It is true both that "the hour is coming and *now is*" and that "whoever believes in me *will* live and never die." Faith in Jesus does not make humans immortal. What it does bring about is that from this moment on they no longer live under the power of death. Resurrection is therefore not a matter of "the last day" but of now, of listening in faith to the Son of God.

Jesus now confronts Martha with this question, before the events of the day take their course: "Do you believe this?" This is why he has come to Bethany after two days' delay: not just to call his friend Lazarus back to life and to restore a brother to his sisters, but to make them realize that what unites him with them and he has to give to them encompasses so much more than what they, in their request for help, have expected of him (see also the comments on vs. 40).

To some interpreters Jesus' manner of speaking about the resurrection and eternal life as an already realized state of affairs, or as a reality recurrently brought about by the power of his word, is proof of the supposed Johannine shift to an eschatology differing from the Jewish future expectation and hope of resurrection, which is voiced by Martha. John makes the future present and thus shows, we are told, the influence of Greek thought. Greek philosophical and religious thought includes resurrection and (eternal) life, but only in the sense of a spiritual deliverance (accomplished by true "knowledge") from the relativity and unreality — experienced as spiritual "death" — of human existence. Terms like "resurrection" and "eternal life" refer either, in idealism, to the opposition between the "higher" and "lower" in humans,[50] or to the more radical dualism of Gnosticism.[51]

But this idea brings Jesus' pronouncement "I am the resurrection and the life" and what follows in vss. 25 and 26 under a viewpoint that is foreign to the Fourth

49. See above, pp. 384f.

50. C. H. Dodd, *The Interpretation of the Fourth Gospel,* 1963, pp. 148f., speaks of "a fluid transition of two kinds of eschatology" in the Fourth Gospel.

51. According to Bultmann, "the future resurrection of Martha's belief becomes irrelevant in face of the present resurrection that faith grasps." In the Fourth Gospel, popular eschatology is set aside (*Comm.,* p. 402).

Gospel and forced on it. When Jesus changes the direction of Martha's faith from a focus on the resurrection on the last day to the resurrection and the life that he represents and grants, this is not a change from or a rejection of an eschatology directed toward the great future in favor of a "realized" eschatology. Jesus himself speaks similarly and most emphatically of a resurrection "at the last day" — in passages that Bultmann and others must regard as coming from a later hand (6:39, 44, 54; cf. 5:28, 29; 12:48).[52] And even here "whoever believes in me, though he dies, yet will live" clearly indicates that the life that Jesus gives continues, preserves its power, and has an ("eschatological") future, even after death.

This does not of course in any way diminish the importance of the totally new emphasis that the Fourth Gospel puts on the presence of the promised salvation — here, of the resurrection. The big question, however, is whether this takes place in accordance with the Hellenistic-Greek understanding, which proceeds from the higher and the lower in humans and places before them the choice between good and evil, light and darkness, so that by gnosis they may arrive at their true "being." When these categories (which are derived from a certain type of anthropology) are introduced into the Gospel, what is lost is the unique character of the Johannine kerygma, which is totally concentrated on the person of Jesus, the Son of God, and therefore in content derivable only from him. It is not a certain "eschatology," however conceived, nor a preexisting "anthropology," of whatever origin, that determines the nature of salvation or the shape of christology in the Fourth Gospel. Rather the reverse is the case — very consistently. The characteristic and remarkable features of the Johannine message of salvation are that it comes to expression in "I am" statements and that the "I" is in effect the predicate: "the light," "the resurrection," etc. — *am I*.[53] That is true here as well. All that Jesus says of "the resurrection and the life" is that it is he who constitutes them and that therefore those who believe in him receive the life that is no longer subject to the power of death. The resurrection and life he grants encompass both present and future because *he* encompasses both as the One in whom the Word reveals itself, the Word that was with God in the beginning and by whom all things were created and who is therefore also the Son of man in whose hands the Father has put the future government over all things, in keeping with the prophecy of Daniel (7:12f.; cf. John 1:51; 3:13; 5:27; 17:2, 5, 24).

This is why there is such emphasis on the "already now" of the resurrection and the life: the Word "*has become flesh* and dwelt among us." And the Son of man did descend from heaven before ascending to heaven to assume his position of power there (3:13). For that reason, too, he did not come to a world that was foreign to him but was made by him (1:9, 10). The resurrection that he is and grants calls the dead not from an inferiority or dichotomy inherent in human existence but from the alienation from God of the life created by him. The "already now" of the resurrection does not consist in being finally or repeatedly released, by the power of his word, from the relativity of time and history. It consists, rather, in communion with God in the relativity of time (which is essential for this temporal life), a communion that cannot be abolished,

---

52. See the comments above on 6:39ff. and 5:28ff.
53. See the comments above on 8:12.

even by death,[54] because nothing and no one can snatch Jesus' own out of his hand (10:28).

But the salvation that has come, including resurrection and life, does not for that reason lose its historical, future character either. In Christ the present and the future are one and do not cease to exist (Hb. 13:8). The Fourth Gospel concentrates everything on the person of Jesus as the Christ and the Son of God and does not say as much about the future perspective of the kingdom of God and of the resurrection from the dead as do the Synoptic Gospels and Paul.[55] But still in this concentration the figure of the Son of man is repeatedly mentioned as the equivalent of the Son of God. How, then, in view of the stress on the incarnation of that Word and the descent from heaven of the Son of man, could the future, in the all-encompassing salvation-historical sense of the word, grow dim, salvation lose its cosmic significance, and the resurrection "at the last day" become "irrelevant"? Because *Jesus* is the resurrection and the resurrection is *he,* the hour *is coming* and *is now,* the barrier has been broken, and union achieved between that which is now and that which is coming.

27 Martha's answer is typical for this phase of the narrative and for the significance that the Evangelist himself clearly attaches to this story. She unambiguously confirms the faith she has already evidenced (vs. 22). And she does this in words that express the content of that faith more fully: "Yes, Lord; I continue to believe[56] that you are the Christ, the Son of God, he who is coming into the world."[57] These words recall Nathanael's confession in 1:49 and express both Israel's messianic hope and the faith of the Christian community (20:30, 31), though Martha speaks as one for whom, as a result of her acquaintance and association with Jesus, the expectation of "him who is coming into the world" had already acquired a meaning uniquely and deeply her own. Still it is striking that in her confession she does not reflect on what Jesus has just said about himself. It is as if she cannot grasp it all at once and react to it. She understands that Jesus is following a different line with her than she has expected and has spoken of the resurrection in a way that is unfamiliar to her as a believing Jew.

Nevertheless, when Jesus confronts her with the question of faith, there is not a hint of hesitation in her words. On his "I am" her spontaneous and uninhibited reply follows: "Yes, Lord, you are," even though for her part she

---

54. The words "though he die" have a concessive meaning; i.e., they do not intend to minimize the reality and power of death but rather to acknowledge them in all their life-threatening significance.

55. For this entire subject and the relevant literature, see the important excursus on "Eschatology in the Fourth Gospel" in Schnackenburg, *Comm.* II, pp. 426-37.

56. The perfect tense of πεπίστευκα expresses the continuation of what has been completed.

57. The present participle does not stress the present but conveys the language of future expectation.

cannot articulate this in any words other than those of her messianic hope. In this respect she reminds us of the man who was blind from birth and who in response to Jesus' word, "he who speaks to you [is the Son of man]," answered, "Lord, I believe," even though he did not know who the Son of man was. It is faith in Jesus that decides everything. For Martha not even the death of Lazarus, which Jesus has not prevented, could detract from this. To the Evangelist and his audience, Martha undoubtedly represented those who believed before they had seen and understood everything of what Jesus' "I am" would come to mean.

11:28-44

The Raising

28-31   Martha goes away with (as vs. 28 makes clear) Jesus' instruction to call Mary. She carries it out by taking her sister aside[58] and telling her the great news, "The teacher is here," significantly adding: "and is calling for you." Some have wondered why Jesus himself did not go to the house of mourning but remained at a distance, outside the village, as it is now stated in vs. 30 to clarify the situation in retrospect. But, as is evident from Martha's private communication to Mary, what mattered to Jesus above all was contact with his friends. The time of his public self-disclosure before "the Jews" was past (cf. 10:39f.; 11:54; 12:3b).

· But even now he could not remain hidden and again came into confrontation with "the Jews" (vss. 33, 42, 45ff.). For when Mary, at Martha's words, arose hastily to go to Jesus outside the village (vss. 20, 30), those who had come to console her followed her, thinking she wanted to return to the tomb to weep there (vs. 31; cf. 20:11; Mt. 28:1; see also 2 Sa. 3:32). And so the entire procession of mourners went again where the dead man had been laid. Martha, too, joined them (cf. vs. 39).

32-37   There has — mistakenly, I believe — been much speculation over Mary's role in the story from this point.[59] According to some, "in her posture of adoration" and in the few sorrowful words with which she meets Jesus, she represents the proper Christian attitude in the face of suffering and death.[60] According to others she and "the Jews" represent — over against Martha — the more "primitive" faith of those who need the external miracle in order to recognize Jesus as the Revealer. This is said to be especially evident in vs. 32,

---

58. λάθρᾳ, "in secret," i.e., without causing a sensation.
59. See above, pp. 393f., and the lengthy discussion of various opinions in Haenchen, *Comm.* II, pp. 65f.
60. So Hirsch, in Haenchen, *Comm.* II, p. 64.

where Mary repeats Martha's words without Martha's second statement (vs. 22). She thus represents "the first step of faith, from which her sister advanced."[61] This last opinion, however, seems far-fetched. The haste (mentioned twice!) with which Mary goes out to Jesus, the reverence with which she falls at his feet,[62] and what she says to him demonstrate that she, no less than her sister, put her trust in him. That no deep personal conversation occurred between her and Jesus, as with Martha, has an obvious explanation in her situation, in which such private conversation between her and Jesus was hardly possible.

Another related point is the striking manner in which Jesus' reaction to the arrival of the "weeping" Mary and the "weeping" Jews who accompanied her is described: he "became grim in spirit and yielded to deep emotion." The first expression denotes anger,[63] the second an accompanying strong emotion that he did not suppress but evidently expressed freely.[64] All this is the more remarkable because Jesus' strong emotions are mentioned again in vss. 35 and 38: First, as he goes where Lazarus has been laid (vs. 34), the text, without comment but all the more emphatically as a fact that needed to be mentioned by itself, states: "Jesus wept." He did so without trying to hide his emotions, as is evident from the reaction of "the Jews," who were struck by the fact: "See how he loved him!" (vs. 36). Then again when he arrives at the tomb Jesus experiences rage mixed with grief (vs. 38): "Then Jesus, again deeply incensed, came to the tomb."

The remarkable stress that the Evangelist puts on Jesus' state of mind has been explained in very different ways. Some say that Jesus' anger (vs. 33) was aroused by the general wailing over Lazarus's death, in which continuing unbelief toward his mission and authority is said to have manifested itself.[65] This seems to contradict Jesus' own weeping (vs. 35).[66] But Jesus' weeping is said — because of Jesus' sense of his own power to raise the dead — to be hardly intelligible except as an expression of grief over so much unbelief, and even to have no other purpose than to provoke an expression of that unbelief by "the Jews" (vss. 36f.).[67]

---

61. So Bultmann, *Comm.*, p. 405.

62. One sees there, positively, also the possible influence of Lk. 10:39; but for a disciple to sit at the master's feet, as in Luke, is something other than to greet someone with prostration, as here.

63. ἐνεβριμήσατο τῷ πνεύματι. The addition τῷ πνεύματι or, in vs. 38, ἐν ἑαυτῷ gives to the verb ἐμβριμᾶσθαι, which elsewhere means something like "rage against" (cf. Mt. 9:30; Mk. 1:43; see also Mk. 14:5), the meaning of an unexpressed but strong sense of vexation, perhaps "be angry at."

64. The active ἐτάραξεν ἑαυτόν is remarkable and is translated by BAGD, p. 805, as "he was troubled or agitated."

65. So, at length, Bultmann, *Comm.*, p. 406.

66. So, rightly, Brown and others.

67. Cf., e.g., Bultmann: "The statement that he wept (v. 35) — where the weeping must be understood as a sign of agitation in the sense of v. 33 — has hardly any other purpose than to

Despite this forced interpretation, the context as a whole makes clear that Jesus' anger is directed not against unbelief (on the part of Mary and those acompanying her) but against that which brought them to this outburst of grief: the death of Lazarus itself. While this is already the obvious implication of vs. 34, it is even more evident in vs. 38, where it is not the weeping people but the tomb that again evokes in Jesus this intense emotion of aversion and sorrow. The emotion is the revulsion of everything that is in him against the power of death. Or as Calvin strikingly comments on vs. 38: "Christ does not come to the sepulchre as an idle spectator, but like a wrestler preparing for the contest. Therefore no wonder that He groans again, for the violent tyranny of death that He had to overcome stands before His eyes."[68]

But for that very reason Jesus' deep inner agitation is not limited to what, in his confrontation with death, applies to himself, but also expresses itself in his solidarity with the grief of those who once more go to the tomb to weep over the loss of their dear brother and friend. He weeps with those who are weeping. When "the Jews" see him as a member of the procession, weeping as he goes, they do not misunderstand him when they say, "See how he loved him!" Jesus allows himself to be caught up in the general grief over Lazarus's death, and there he experiences and participates in the grief of all whose loved ones have gone to the grave. That does not militate against the purpose of his coming to Bethany. As the Son of God he does not come to redeem the world from imaginary grief or to make grief over death imaginary. Therefore he joins the mourning procession for the friend whom he is to raise from the dead, and he weeps.[69]

What "the Jews" do not understand is what some of them formulate as a question — in essence the same question that Martha and Mary asked (vs. 37): "Could not he who opened the eyes of the blind man have kept this man from dying?" They do not understand that the one who is able to do so much has not come too late, even for Lazarus, and that Jesus — precisely by postponing his arrival — wants to teach them once more that for those who believe in him he never comes too late. Nowhere else in the Gospel does the true nature of the entry of God's glory into flesh, of God's identification with the true man Jesus of Nazareth, come more vividly to expression than in Jesus' going — described thus — to the tomb of Lazarus.

Those who failed to see in Jesus' tears anything other than an expression of

---

provoke the utterance of the Jews (vv. 36f.), and so to set in a yet brighter light the motif of faithlessness in the presence of the Revealer" (*Comm.,* p. 407).

68. *Comm.* II, p. 13.

69. Cf. Calvin, *Comm.* II, 11: "Accordingly, when He is about to raise Lazarus, before He grants the cure or help, He shows by His groaning in spirit, by a strong emotion of grief and by tears, that He is as much affected by our ills as if He had suffered them in Himself."

his impotence in the face of the onslaught of death misunderstood him. But the Evangelist's portrayal of Jesus here is not of one who "doth bestride the narrow world like a Colossus," who, elevated far above and incapable of human suffering, does not tolerate tears in his presence. The Evangelist, precisely in the midst of his description of this incomprehensible and inconceivable miracle, includes his strongest expression of Jesus' existence as a human being. He does so to safeguard the sublimity of his message against all idealizing interpretations.[70]

38-40   As described earlier, Jesus' arrival at the tomb is "again" marked by intense agitation, in which, as appears from the word again used,[71] the element of wrath or angry aversion dominates. Here, too, expositors have — among many unconvincing attempts to offer a meaningful interpretation of this passage — tended to see here a reaction to the unbelief of "the Jews," which is said to be expressed in vs. 37.[72] But it is unlikely that the question raised there would have the effect described here. We see here the continuation, rather, of what characterizes the entire passage: Jesus' sharing in the grief of Lazarus's relatives and friends. We also learn that he, as the One sent by the Father, was moved to resist the demonstration of human impotence in the face of death as though it had the last, decisive word in the world. To break this spell he strides to the tomb, not in the sovereign apathy of the great Outsider, but as the One sent into the world by the Father, as the Advocate who has entered human flesh and blood. Accordingly, it is not only from his divine authority but also from his deep human involvement in the death of his friend that, at sight of the large stone that is intended to close off Lazarus's tomb forever, is evoked from him the measured, almost gruff command to the bystanders: "Take away the stone."[73] It is as if in these words a kind of tension is being released. Enough

---

70. This applies not only against the so-called docetic interpretation of Johannine christology but also against certain forms of "orthodoxy" in which, though the true humanity of Jesus is being maintained, it is nevertheless heavily restricted. An example going back to very ancient interpretations is the idea that, since Christ the Son of God was exempt from all passion, he could only have known deep emotion, anger, and grief because and insofar as it seemed good to him as Son of God to adopt these feelings voluntarily, thus, in vs. 33, rousing himself into a state of agitation. It is clear, however, that in this way, on dogmatic grounds, distinctions are carried into the text that deprive the story of its sublime simplicity and natural drama. Here, too, cf. Calvin (*Comm.* II, 12), who rejects this last view (as he found it in Augustine): "But it will, to my mind, be more agreeable to Scripture if we make the simple statement that when the Son of God put on our flesh He also of His own accord put on human feelings, so that He differed in nothing from His brethren, sin only excepted."

71. See the comments above on vs. 33.

72. So Schnackenburg, *Comm.* II, p. 337.

73. ἐπέκειτο ἐπ' αὐτῷ is interpreted variously. Some think of a round stone vertically placed before the opening of the sepulchre, as was evidently the case with Jesus' tomb (cf. Strack/Billerbeck on Mt. 28:2, I, pp. 1059-61); others of a square stone resting horizontally over an opening in the ground (so Schnackenburg, *Comm.* II, pp. 337f.: "what is displayed today as the tomb of Lazarus matches this description").

now of tears and wailing! Enough honor has been bestowed on death! Against the power of death God's glory will now enter the arena!

But for Martha this shift in the course of events is too much. She is introduced here as "the sister of the dead man," certainly, for good reason: as next of kin she more than anyone has the right to speak.[74] When it gets through to her that Jesus is about to open the tomb, she is aroused to opposition. Her extremely realistic language, "Lord, by this time there will be an odor, for he has been dead four days,"[75] expresses her abhorrence at the mere thought that Jesus should expose the body of her brother — in the state in which it must be by this time — to the light of day.

Martha's words, in the nature of the case, are designed to accentuate the utter impossibility and absurdity of the miracle narrated here. One can hardly, in rationalizing fashion, demur at this point and argue that at her first encounter with Jesus she herself said, "Even now I know that whatever you ask from God, God will give you" (vs. 22), and she had answered "Yes" to Jesus' question whether she believed that he was the resurrection and the life (vs. 27). How could she, for all her faith in Jesus as the Messiah come into the world, faith of which she had given evidence, have believed or suspected what Jesus now wanted to show her?

Jesus does not fault Martha for her little faith or demand more faith of her, but asks: "Did I not tell you that if you would believe you would see the glory of God?" He has spoken of himself as "the resurrection and the life." Now he reduces that and everything he has in deeply significant language associated with that saying to the single phrase "the glory of God." It is to reveal God's glory, that is, God himself in his turning to human beings, in all its fullness and truth, including God's power over death, that he has come. And what he is now doing, in the last great work of the twelve hours of his workday, is exhibit that glory before the eyes of Martha and all who have followed her (cf. vs. 4). For he has not come to make faith into miracle faith — as if to make room for the idea that the more a person believes in what God in his omnipotence can do, the greater the hold he or she has on that omnipotence and the more it is at his or her disposal. All that is required of faith is to believe in him who is the light of the world, to let him "go his way," to let him give that

---

74. Some textual witnesses omit "the sister of the dead man," presumably as being superfluous. Some interpreters regard these witnesses as proof that here the Evangelist, following the lengthy passage from his own hand in vss. 20-32, again returns to his "source," where, they say, there was no extensive reference to Martha. But from the very beginning it is evident from the whole story, even in the passages attributed to the "source," that Martha was the sister of Lazarus (vss. 1-3, 19). It seems hard to explain this "redundant" identification of Martha in any way other than I have above. The same phenomenon occurs elsewhere in this Gospel (cf. 6:8; 21:20). Perhaps it is well to repeat Brown's remark (*Comm.* I, p. 426): "The Gospel . . . does show a tendency to reidentify the dramatis personae."

75. For "the *fourth* day," see the comments on vs. 17.

which is not limited by one's own imagination but by the power of God's glory has been manifested in the world in the incarnation of the Word (cf. 1:49-51).

The structure of vss. **41** and **42** is like that of vss. 39 and 40. After Martha's objection and Jesus' response, his command to remove the stone is obeyed without contradiction. Then a new intermezzo follows — this time from Jesus himself — in which, before raising Lazarus, he turns to God: "And Jesus lifted up his eyes and said: Father!" The style is undeniably solemn, marking the grandeur of the moment (cf. 17:1).[76] These last words of Jesus before the miracle, along with those in vs. 40, are all the more significant because the story ends with the accomplishment of the miracle. Thus all attention is concentrated on the miracle as the work of Jesus *together with the Father.*

Jesus gives thanks to the Father for having heard him. No mention has been made of a prior prayer. But the Son can do nothing of himself (5:19, 30; 8:28). He does the works that the Father has given him, and continually gives him, to accomplish (5:36; 4:34). Jesus also expresses his dependence on the Father. One may perhaps even catch here some relief that, after his earlier agitation, now enables him to manifest his unshaken communion with the Father. For in the same breath, as it were, he adds to his thanksgiving that God hears him the words: "I know that you always hear me." As he prays he knows that he is heard as the Son into whose hand the Father has given all things (3:34, 35), granting him to have life in himself as the Father has life in himself (5:26).

The idea that this prayer and thanksgiving do not fit in the relationship between Jesus and the Father and are intended here solely for the benefit of the bystanders, so that they can believe that "you sent me" (vs. 42b), misconstrues the nature of the relationship, which was a living personal interaction (cf. 5:19, 20).[77] This solemn expression of Jesus' thanksgiving, which was seen (and heard?) by all, does find its explanation[78] in the presence of "the Jews." They have come to the grave, fully assured that Lazarus's death is an accomplished fact and that death is invincible, to lament the passing of their friend. Then Jesus lets them take him to the tomb, commands them to open it, and with all eyes focused on him, lifts his eyes to heaven and in full dependence gives thanks to the Father. In this he wants above all else, including the raising of Lazarus, to direct their eyes neither to the grave nor toward himself but to the "whence" of his coming, the secret of his power in words and deeds.

---

76. Looking up to heaven is "mentioned only rarely" as a posture of prayer in Jewish writings (Strack/Billerbeck II, p. 246).

77. So, correctly, Strathmann, *Comm.,* p. 178: "The reason that his prayer is still prayer is that his relation to God is not something static and finished but something personal and dynamic that constantly renews itself," as is evident from the repeated disclosures of Jesus' prayer to God, especially in ch. 17 (cf. also 14:16).

78. διά with accusative and without a following verb.

Because the Son does nothing and is able to do nothing apart from the fact that he is the Son and that the Father loves him, contemplation of the greatest miracle is valueless if it does not bring its witnesses to faith in him as the One sent by the Father (see also the comments on vs. 40). This understanding of miracles characterizes the entire Fourth Gospel and stamps the words and deeds of Jesus from the beginning (1:14, 51). For this same reason Jesus must, as it were, supply this last great miracle with his hallmark and seal before accomplishing it before the eyes of the bystanders.

43-44 With everything said that must first be said, the story of the miracle itself, in all its grandeur, can be extremely brief and sober. Jesus cries out with a loud voice: "Lazarus, come out." Jesus' "crying out" is mentioned elsewhere, but then in the sense of inspired prophetic proclamation (7:28, 37; 12:33; cf. 1:15; Rom. 9:27; Gal. 4:6),[79] sometimes with "with a loud cry" (Lk. 1:42). The reference here, however, is not just to the pneumatic power by which the truth is brought to expression but to the power of God by which the dead are brought to life (cf. 5:28).[80]

In response to that cry the dead man comes out (vs. 44), still bound hand and foot by bandages and with his face wrapped in a cloth — the very picture of humanity subject to the kingdom of death. He is brought out of the half-darkness of the tomb into the full light of the day. This portrays clearly the power and glory of the one who has broken into the "strong man's house" to take his possessions (cf. Is. 49:24f.; Mt. 12:29). Appropriate to this power and glory is the last utterance in the story by which Jesus, as with the sovereign word of the conqueror, commands the bystanders to relieve the newly raised Lazarus of that which keeps him from going out in freedom: "Unbind him, and let him go."

From the beginning commentators have speculated about how Lazarus, wrapped hand and foot in gravecloths, could get out of the tomb. Some have even called this "a miracle within a miracle."[81] Others have seen it as one more proof that what mattered to the Evangelist was "not a report in the historical sense of the word."[82] In our opinion, however, it is legitimate to ask whether this binding of the dead with gravecloths was really intended to tie hands and feet together (so that the dead could not return)[83] and not rather, as with the "wrapping" of the head, to keep the corpse in the proper position (see

---

79. And κράζειν is used in those other places; here κραυγάζειν is used. See also Strack/Billerbeck on Ro. 9:27, II, p. 275.

80. On this "apocalyptic" language, see also Schnackenburg, *Comm.* II, p. 340.

81. So Bultmann, *Comm.*, p. 409; Schnackenburg, *Comm.* II, p. 340.

82. So Schulz, *Comm.*, p. 101.

83. See L. Radermacher, *Neutestamentliche Grammatik*, 1925[2], p. 12; cf. also Bultmann, *Comm.*, p. 409, n. 5.

also the comments on 20:6f.). In any case, this "complex of problems" clearly does not occupy the Evangelist and only detracts from the main issue.

Finally, one may wonder at the abrupt ending of the story. There is not a word about Lazarus or any reaction from Martha, who has played an important role to the very end, or from Mary or even from Thomas. This is often traced back to the "source" that the Evangelist is supposed to have used, which is said to have concluded the miracle story with this last word of Jesus. But here again we need not fall back on a hypothetical unknown for an explanation. This abrupt but significant concluding word is entirely in character for the Johannine kerygma. The people around Jesus are significant to the degree that the grandeur and identity of Jesus are reflected in their lives. That is their enduring significance in the Gospel, not only in a "salvation-historical" sense but also in an exemplaristic sense, that is, in how faith and unbelief are exemplified in them. What matters is not their histories, as in a dictionary of saints. What matters is the identity of Jesus in the signs, which are chosen and documented by the Evangelist for this purpose, Jesus' self-revelation as the Christ, the Son of God (20:30, 31).

11:45-54

The Sanhedrin Takes Counsel, Jesus Withdraws to Ephraim

45-46 The immediate reaction of those who came with Mary and witnessed the miracle was predominantly positive. Many of them "believed" in Jesus. That is, they were now convinced of his divine mission (cf. vs. 42; 3:2). The Evangelist does not further comment on this faith (cf. 7:31; 8:30; 12:42). But "some of them" informed the Pharisees[84] of what had happened, and apparently not in a way that was favorable to Jesus (cf. 5:15; 9:13), at least given the result described in the vss. 47ff.

47-48 The chief priests[85] and Pharisees therefore convene the supreme council — here called the Sanhedrin for the first time[86] — for common deliberation, now that the influence of Jesus among the people has become

---

84. The Evangelist tends to mention especially the Pharisees as the most influential leaders of the people, sometimes in conjunction with the chief priests, sometimes not (7:32, 45, 47; 9:13, 40). Sometimes he mentions just the chief priests as the ruling authority (12:10). The reason is certainly not just that in the days of Jesus the Pharisees already had great influence on the people but that in the Evangelist's day, probably after the fall of Jerusalem, they functioned as the real spiritual leaders. Their name was therefore particularly useful to him as a general term for the Jewish authorities (see also the comments on 7:31 and 12:42).

85. The plural refers to members of the family and officials working together in the Sanhedrin with the high priest.

86. συνέδριον; see at length Strack/Billerbeck I, pp. 997ff.

increasingly disturbing to them (cf. already 7:32ff.). Their question, "What are we to do?"[87] indicates the embarrassment prompted by the "many signs" Jesus has been doing. The reference here, as in 2:23, seems to be especially to the signs Jesus did in Jerusalem and Judea. The Synoptics say little about this, but see also Lk. 19:37. Here again it is evident that the Fourth Gospel has more ample information at its disposal with respect to Jesus' activity.

The members of the Sanhedrin (vs. 48) are afraid that, if they do not intervene, "everyone will believe in him." They thought, that is, that a popular (messianic?) movement was developing around Jesus (cf. 6:15; 12:13; 19:12; see also Ac. 5:35ff.). Such a movement could prompt the Romans to "take from us[88] both the place and the nation." By "place" the city may be intended, but more likely the temple is meant (cf. Ac. 6:13; 21:28). Here, for the first time in the conflict between "the Jews" and Jesus, a political element comes to the fore. Earlier it has always been Jesus' claim, which they regard as blasphemous, that he is the Son of God that has driven them to act against him (cf. 5:18ff.; 10:33, 36; see also 19:7). How justified their fear of Roman intervention because of Jesus was is not clear from what follows. But even if they had no reason to think that Jesus was aiming at political power, they could find occasion in the popular movement around him for acting against him as a claimant to power who would be dangerous to the state.

49-50 At this embarrassed and fearful point in the discussion, Caiaphas takes the floor. To the readers, who were apparently not aware of his dignity, he is introduced simply as "one of them, a certain Caiaphas, who was high priest that year."[89] His intervention in the discussion, however, bears testimony to great political experience and skill. He never refers to Jesus by name. His

---

87. τὶ ποιοῦμεν is probably deliberative, though as a rule the subjunctive is used for that purpose. One can also, of course, translate it as "What [in the world] are we doing?" in the sense of self-criticism.

88. One can, of course, render ἡμῶν simply as a possessive genitive: "take away both our place and our city." But what is obviously at issue is the stake that the Sanhedrin had in all this. For that reason, and also because of the possibility that a pronominal genitive could be placed earlier than its expected position (BDF §473.1), it is better to link ἡμῶν ("us") with the verb in the sense of a so-called "sympathetic dative."

89. Some regard ἀρχιερεὺς ὢν τοῦ ἐνιαυτοῦ ἐκείνου as indicating that the Evangelist thought that Jewish high priests (like their Gentile counterparts in Asia Minor) held office for only one year (so, e.g., Bultman, *Comm.*, pp. 410f., n. 10). Others, however, correctly believe that the Evangelist repeatedly evidences far too much detailed historical knowledge to be charged with such gross ignorance concerning Caiaphas's high priesthood (which extended from A.D. 18 to 36!). Genitive τοῦ ἐνιαυτοῦ ἐκείνου can also very well be understood, especially in view of the indefinite way the Evangelist introduces Caiaphas to his readers, as high priest "of" or "in" that year, namely the year of Jesus' death, meaning "that fateful year in which Jesus died." "John is underlining not the limit of the term but its synchronism" (Brown, *Comm.* I, p. 440, cf. 441f., with an appeal to Bernard, *Comm.* II, p. 404; see also [at length] Schlatter, *Comm.*, p. 248; Morris, *Comm.*, p. 566, and many others).

strategy is, rather, to charge his colleagues in strong language with political incompetence and thus to fault them as leaders of the people: "You don't know anything!" If matters stood as they claimed — and he did not question it — how then could they still be so unsure what they had to do: "You do not understand [or: Do you not understand . . . ?] that it is in your interest for one man to die for the people, and the whole nation not perish."[90] Instead of the somewhat conspicuous "your interest," other manuscripts read "our interest" or, without the personal pronoun, "it is expedient." Even in the reading most often followed, "your interest," Caiaphas seeks to make clear to his fellow council members how simple, and profitable for them as well, the solution of Jesus' case would be if they do not fixate on that one person. For then they will know that sometimes one has to put up with a lesser evil to prevent a larger one, here the death of one for the sake of the nation as a whole. The conclusion of this cynical logic, which Caiaphas does not have to add in so many words, is that the Sanhedrin should now with no further delay attend to the death of that one man. In any case that is their business now that he, as presiding officer of the gathering and leader of the nation as a whole, has so clearly stated the principle according to which they must act.

51 It is precisely on this last point, however, that the Evangelist comments and focuses the entire thrust of the story. With "he did not say this of his own accord" he is not of course relieving Caiaphas of responsibility for his malevolent purpose, but he leaves that purpose aside in order to point his readers to the deep evangelical truth that Caiaphas, despite himself and without realizing it, was expressing in them, namely that Jesus was to die for the salvation of his people, vicariously as the One for the many. And with the next words he is not tracing this "prophecy" back to a charisma inherent in the high priestly office that manifests itself independently of the person of the priest. For although one can cite a few examples of priests being credited with prophetic gifts,[91] prophetic inspiration was not regarded as a privilege automatically belonging to the office of high priest. It is much rather the intent of the Evangelist to say that Caiaphas, as the highest officeholder of that (historic)[92] year, had to give prophetic expression not to his own purpose but to God's

---

90. The words are, successively, λαός ("people," ὑπὲρ τοῦ λαοῦ) and ἔθνος ("nation," ὅλον τὸ ἔθνος), evidently without a distinction in meaning (cf. also vss. 51, 52) — according to some intentionally in order to ignore the distinction (in Jewish ears) between λαός (the Jewish people) and ἔθνος (Gentiles). By itself ὑπὲρ τοῦ λαοῦ could also be omitted, but was added, according to others, to give clearer expression to the element of substitution. The next clause, "and the whole nation not perish," also points to such a substitution. Vs. 52 also mentions Jesus' striving ὑπὲρ τοῦ ἔθνους, but then apparently in the general sense of "on behalf of," as may also be evident from the additional description of the redemptive significance of Jesus' death in vs. 52 (ἀλλ' ἵνα καί).

91. See, e.g., Morris, *Comm.*, p. 568, n. 105.

92. See the comments above on vs. 49.

purpose in the death of Jesus in the words he chose. That this fell to Caiaphas is of course deeply meaningful. One can call it a "tragic irony" that Caiaphas here, "against his knowledge and intention," appears as a prophet.[93] What concerns the Evangelist, above all, however, is that Israel's highest official, with all the authority associated with his office, spoke of Jesus' death as the only way in which the people could be saved. Israel had to hear this from the lips of its own high priest.

Verse **52** adds still another element: "and not for the nation only, but to gather into one the children of God who are scattered abroad." Even here Caiaphas's prophecy is applicable, although in a wider context. For he, too, was concerned about the salvation of the whole nation, the preservation of its unity and thus its deliverance from ruin. The Evangelist points to that unity as the object and binding power of Jesus' death. He does so under a figure he has used before, that of the shepherd who gathers into one flock the scattered children of God.

At the same time he indicates that the issue with Jesus includes more than the people whose unity was of so much concern to Caiaphas. It also concerns, as 10:16 already put it, "other sheep that are not of this fold," here "the children of God who are scattered abroad." The shepherding terminology ("scatter," "gather") clearly alludes to texts like Jr. 23:2ff. and Ezk. 34:12, where the great future salvation is applied to the sheep of God scattered through all nations, who are also described as "God's children" (cf. Is. 43:5, 6: "I will bring your offspring from the east . . . my sons from afar, and my daughters from the end of the earth"). But whereas these Old Testament passages refer to the people of Israel in dispersion (Jr. 23:2ff.: "my flock out of all the countries where I have driven them," etc.), here "God's scattered children" are expressly distinguished from the people of Israel (as in 10:16). The redemptive significance of Jesus' death is universal. He is the Shepherd who gives his life for his sheep wherever they may come from and will therefore "draw all people" to himself and in his elevation on the cross give them the great gathering point and center of their unity (12:20ff., 32, 33). The picture here is no longer that of the Gentiles streaming toward Mount Zion to be incorporated into the people of God. It is, rather, of a new unity of believers from Israel and from the nations and, accordingly, of the new people of God (see the comments on 10:16). Belonging to the flock therefore gains new meaning, that of being known by and knowing the good Shepherd (cf. the comments on 10:14ff.) or, as here, that of being "God's children." This designation, which in passages like Is. 43:5 (see above) refers to Israel's election out of the nations, is here transposed to those known and called by God out of all nations. It thereby gains a somewhat different connotation from what we have in 1:12, the only other place in the

---

93. So Bultmann, *Comm.*, p. 411.

Fourth Gospel where "God's children" are mentioned: there the status of child is the privilege of those who have "received" Jesus.[94]

53-54   Having thus placed the deliberation of the highest Jewish court and the decisive intervention of the high priest with respect to the death of Jesus in this universal redemptive perspective, the Evangelist is content to summarize the result of their deliberation in a single statement. Caiaphas's pronouncement marks a transition, a threshold that is not crossed until now. From that day on their minds are made up and their deliberation exclusively focused on how and when to put Jesus to death. The time they will spend working toward that goal is lengthened (cf. vs. 57) when Jesus eludes their grasp by again retreating from the center of Judea to a less populated area, and not to where he was hiding before the raising of Lazarus (cf. 10:40). He goes to a town called Ephraim, near the wilderness, where he stays with his disciples until the Passover.[95]

11:55–12:8

Jesus' Journey to the Passover Feast and the Anointing at Bethany

55-57   The words "Now the Passover of the Jews was at hand" (vs. 55) finally announce the time in which the gospel story reaches its denouement and which has been referred to repeatedly.[96] They also announce the end of Jesus' stay at Ephraim, the period of rest he has observed with his disciples, undoubtedly with a view to that coming hour. Preceding him to Jerusalem were other pilgrims who had to fulfill certain cultic purification obligations before the day of the feast.[97] That Jesus was known by people who had come from far and wide is evident from what the Evangelist says about the curious looking about for

94. Cf. Schnackenburg, *Comm.* II, pp. 350f. On the relationship between election and faith, being known and knowing, as it repeatedly emerges in the Fourth Gospel, though it is hard for us to express adequately, see above, pp. 232, 368f.

95. There is no absolute certainty on the location of this Ephraim. Usually scholars link it with the present village of et-Taiyibeh, which is about 20 kilometers northeast of Jerusalem; cf. G. Dalman, *Sacred Sites and Ways: Studies in the Topography of the Gospels,* pp. 217f., 268 (also cf. 2 Sa. 13:23; 2 Ch. 13:19). For the trustworthiness of this historical note — against those who credit it with merely "schematic" significance (Bultmann) or view it as a "stylistic device to indicate the explosive atmosphere in and around Jerusalem" (Schnackenburg) — see the interesting (for the entire subject of the geographic accuracy of the Fourth Gospel) essay of B. Schwanck, "Ephraim in Joh. 11:54," in M. de Jonge (ed.), *l'Évangile de Jean,* 1977, pp. 377-84.

96. On "of the Jews" see the comments above on 2:13; 5:1; 6:4; and 7:2.

97. Usually passages like Nu. 9:10, 13 and 2 Ch. 30:17ff. are cited for this practice. For the cultic significance of ἁγνίζειν see also Ac. 21:24ff.; 24:18.

Jesus[98] and about the conversations about him in the temple. The questions the people ask, "What do you think? Certainly he will not come to the feast?" betray both a tense uncertainty and their thought that he would certainly not risk it, the latter because the chief priests and the Pharisees (see the comments on vs. 46) have now issued express orders that anyone knowing where Jesus is should tell them so that they can arrest him. Earlier, too, the conflict between Jesus and the authorities has held the people under a spell of fear and curiosity (7:11ff.; 9:22). But following the recent meeting of the Sanhedrin and the dictum of Caiaphas it is clear to all that nothing less than Jesus' immediate arrest is likely. The tension was therefore all the greater, but was to be discharged differently from how the crowds could anticipate.

12:1-3 With no further reflection on the preceding, we are informed that "Jesus came to Bethany six days before the Passover."[99] Neither the speculations of the people nor the measures taken by his enemies can shape his timing or his itinerary. He does not even, as in 7:20ff., 10, wait and appear at the feast only when it is already in full progress. Rather, he takes ample time to be able to participate also in the preparation for the feast. To that end he goes to Bethany, where then, on the eve of his entry into Jerusalem, his anointing by Mary takes place.

The story of this event is familiar to us also from Mk. 14:3-9 (and Mt. 26:6-13). The account here bears a strong resemblance in outline and in certain details to the Markan account. Nowhere else is it more clear than precisely in these details that the Evangelist depended for his story on a more or less fixed tradition.[100] It is striking in the Johannine version, further, that the woman anoints Jesus' feet and wipes them with her hair (vs. 3). This feature, though lacking in Mark and Matthew, strongly marks the story in Luke of "the woman

---

98. ζητεῖν need not be meant in a hostile sense; cf. 7:11f.

99. For the construction πρὸ ἓξ ἡμερῶν τοῦ πάσχα, see BDF §213. This time indication, however, gives no definite solution to the question of the day on which Jesus arrived in Bethany, since it is not certain whether the day of the Passover is included in the six days. Added to this is the question whether in John the day of Passover started on a Friday evening — as many think — or a day earlier, as the Synoptics clearly assert and is, in our opinion, not excluded in John either (see below on 13:1ff.). Further calculations make it likely that the Passover meal took place on the day before a sabbath.

100. Specifically:

Jn. 12:3:	λίτραν μύρου νάρδου πιστικῆς
Mk. 14:3:	ἀλάβαστρον μύρου νάρδου πιστικῆς πολυτελοῦς
Mt. 26:7:	ἀλάβαστρον μύρου βαρυτίμου
Jn. 12:5:	ἐπράθη τριακοσίων δηναρίων καὶ ἐδόθη πτωχοῖς
Mk. 14:5:	πραθῆναι ἐπάνω δηναρίων τριακοσίων καὶ δοθῆναι τοῖς πτωχοῖς
Mt. 26:9:	πραθῆναι πολλοῦ καὶ δοθῆναι πτωχοῖς

Furthermore, Jn. 12:8 is similar to Mk. 14:8, though it is widely assumed that the form of the statement is original to John.

who was a sinner" at the meal in the house of Simon the Pharisee (Lk. 7:36ff.). John identifies the woman with the Mary of ch. 11 (see also the comments on 11:2). Of another anointing by another woman the Evangelist apparently knows nothing.[101]

It is also clear that the Evangelist goes his own way in this account, not only theologically, as will become evident, but also as a transmitter of the tradition and in editorial differences from the Synoptics.

Those who deny to the author of the Fourth Gospel all independent access to the events recounted are forced to seek an explanation for the uniqueness of this Johannine presentation of the story in the tradition that he has adopted. Thus Schnackenburg, for example, answering how "the Johannine anointing story came into being," opts, from among the "various models" that can be "constructed" for this purpose, for a written "passion narrative" (to be distinguished from the *sēmeia* source) — of which the story of the anointing may very well have been a part. That story is said to have contained all the features that now mark the uniqueness of the Johannine account. But these features individually had different origins, stemmed from different accounts, and were combined at a later stage of the tradition. Thus the anointing of Jesus' feet stems from Luke 7, the presence of Martha and Lazarus from Lk. 10:38-42, and the names of Mary and Judas Iscariot from still other stages in the tradition. Schnackenburg concludes: "For the most part, then, the Evangelist took the story from his source. . . . The pericope contained in the source fitted his theological purposes so well that for the most part he could just take it over. He needed only to place it within the framework of his narrative and add a few emphases."[102]

This "tradition-historical" explanation is based, however, on a series of hypotheses for which no support can be adduced from what we know about the tradition. Furthermore, it is so shaped to the text as we have it that we must conclude that the supposed "source" contained precisely what the Evangelist needed for his theological

---

101. Some interpreters, meanwhile, think that in Jn. 11:2 the woman of Luke 7 is intended, even though two different events are related. From 11:2 it is evident, they say, that the Mary mentioned in John 11 and 12 is no one other than the "sinner" of Luke 7. This is said to explain the admittedly striking conduct of Mary during the dinner at Bethany, namely a repetition of what she has done earlier with her tears as a "sinful woman" accepted by Jesus. Furthermore, it is claimed that she is no one other than Mary Magdalene, out of whom Jesus cast "seven devils" (Lk. 8:2); she now returns as Mary of Bethany, the sister of Lazarus. This is said to explain the link our text forges between her deed and Jesus' burial. In the story of the resurrection, after all, it is Mary Magdalene, not Mary of Bethany, who (along with others) goes to Jesus' grave to complete his burial (cf. Bernard, *Comm.* II, pp. 372ff., 412ff.).

There is no basis, however, for this identification of the "sinful woman" in Luke 7 with Mary Magdalene. The contrary is rather the case: the two are mentioned in close succession but not identified (Lk. 7:37; 8:2). The same applies to the identification of Mary Magdalene ("of Magdala"!) with Mary "of Bethany." In the liturgy of the later church these three women have sometimes been "made into one" (Bernard, *Comm.* II, p. 412; so also Brown, *Comm.* I, p. 452), but in the nature of the case this does not establish any historical connection among them.

102. *Comm.*, II, p. 372.

goals and that this explanation is nothing more than a development of the hypothesis that the Evangelist had no direct knowledge of the details that are characteristic for his account.[103]

In the Synoptics this story comes later, as part of the passion narrative, that is, after Jesus' entry into Jerusalem, but without a more specific time indication. But John has a precise time indication ("six days before the Passover"), and uses the story both to introduce the entry into Jerusalem (vss. 9ff.) and as a sequel to the the raising of Lazarus, in which light it is evidently meant to be understood. This is immediately apparent from "Bethany, where Lazarus was, whom Jesus had raised from the dead." "There," vs. 2 continues with emphasis, "they made him a supper." There, where Jesus had become manifest in all the glory of the One sent by the Father (1:4, 14), doors were opened for him and he sat in the midst of his own as a welcome guest. This is emphasized all the more by the presence of three other guests,[104] who are, unlike in the Synoptics, referred to by name: Martha, in a role characteristic for her, serves the guests. Lazarus is described by the Evangelist in all sobriety as "one of those at table with him," but by his very presence in the flesh demonstrates what has taken place earlier in Bethany. Finally, Mary plays the main role, not, as in the Synoptics, anonymously but, already in 11:2, as the sister of Lazarus and as the one "who anointed the Lord with oil," thus identified within the setting and against the background from which the anointing derives its specific Johannine meaning and interpretation.

Though her actions, given these circumstances, are not inexplicable to the other guests, they are no less sensational and for a woman highly unconventional.[105] She has obviously prepared for the task, having bought a "pound"[106] of fragrant ointment,[107] further described as "pure"[108] and as costly "nard oil" (extracted from the roots of the exotic nard plant). Judas will estimate the price of the oil at three hundred denarii.[109] That she anoints Jesus' feet, not his head,[110] may be explained by Jesus' posture at the table. But that Jesus' feet are mentioned twice is certainly intended to put stress on the deep reverence

103. On this, at greater length, see the comments below on 21:24.
104. We do not get the impression that the meal took place in the house of Lazarus and his sisters itself; cf. vs. 2b; also Mk. 14:3.
105. See, e.g., Schnackenburg, *Comm.* II, p. 522, n. 15.
106. "Pound" = *litra* (the Roman "pound"), equivalent to 12 ounces or 327.45 grams (BAGD, p. 475).
107. μύρον.
108. πιστικῆς, "genuine, pure"; others think of a certain kind of perfume or plant; see BAGD s.v.
109. See the comments above on 6:7.
110. The difference is mentioned explicitly in Lk. 7:46.

and humility with which Mary goes about her act. As though a more direct approach seems immodest to her, she passes behind Jesus as he reclines at the table and pours out the precious ointment over his feet, and that in such quantity that "the whole house was filled with the fragrance of the ointment." The action, thus carried out, can also perhaps explain somewhat the striking[111] gesture by which Mary, evidently with a view to containing the profusely flowing oil and impelled by a sudden rush of deep affection for Jesus, loosens the hair of her head and wipes Jesus' feet with it as if to protect him from any annoyance her act of adoration might cause him.

However all this may have transpired, the scene that the Evangelist depicts is unmistakable. Never did the Son of God dwell more gloriously among humans than at that last banquet, and nowhere else was the response of their faith and love to his presence more vivid and eloquent. Mary's action expresses what she did not have the words to voice, but it "filled the whole house" with the fragrance of her love and as such would continue to spread through the preaching of the gospel in the whole world (cf. Mk. 14:9; Mt. 26:13).

4 The contrast with what follows is, therefore, all the clearer. Here, too, the Evangelist, in more than one respect, goes his own way. Unlike the Synoptics he refers to Judas by name as Mary's counterpart. He does this in almost the same terms as those he used of Judas in 6:71: "one of his disciples (he who was to betray him)."[112] He thus depicts the contrast between Mary and Judas that was now manifesting itself at the meal in all its radical and deadly seriousness. Not only outside the house were the shadows falling to announce the end of the "twelve hours" of Jesus' day: the power of darkness was manifesting itself even in the intimate circle of Jesus' disciples and at the high point of their being together with him.

5, 6 Judas's censure of Mary's act corresponds with that of the "disciples" or "some" mentioned in the Synoptics, who similarly complain about the loss of the oil. Here, however, this attitude cannot be explained as an expression of narrow-mindedness or as understandable but misplaced opposition to so much extravagance in a world full of poor people.[113] The Fourth Evangelist makes it clear that Judas spoke not out of concern for the poor but from the regret of a thief who saw a large sum of money lost to the purse that he administered and from which he enriched himself.[114] Some interpreters believe that this comment can be explained in terms of the tendency, which grew in the course of time, to depict the character of Judas as worse and worse.

---

111. Striking particularly because after an anointing the oil is not normally wiped off. Lk. 7:38 mentions the wiping away of tears, which in the nature of the case is easier to understand.

112. On the name Ἰσκαριώτης see the comments on 6:71.

113. A point of view also much debated by later theologians!

114. βαστάζειν, to be understood here in connection with κλέπτης as "steal" (used in that sense in other connections as well).

They therefore detect a "legendary excrescence" in the motive attributed to him by the Evangelist, which is then said to draw the attention of the reader away from the real point.[115] But from a purely historical viewpoint it is hard to speak here of a false insinuation. That Judas handled the group's money is evident also from 13:29,[116] and that he was greedy and was prepared even to betray Jesus for money is no less established in the tradition.

Closer to the intent of the Evangelist, it seems to us, is the attempt to find in this comment about Judas's motivation a point of contact for a (frequently attempted) psychological interpretation of the figure of Judas, and that with Mary as the counter figure. The two are sharply profiled as contrasting exemplary figures, all the more as their association with Jesus is tested more. In her deep attachment to Jesus, Mary intuits in advance that it is perhaps the last time that she will be at table with Jesus. Therefore, no price is too high and no loss too great to show him what she feels for him. Judas, on account of his disappointed expectations and selfish motives, no less sharply assesses the situation, concluding that Jesus' cause is heading for failure. Jesus' stock is losing its value and Mary's costly display of esteem is money down the drain.

But however meaningful this approach may be (see also below), the real substance of the opposition between Judas and Mary lies deeper. It has more redemptive-historical significance than psychological significance. It brings to the fore the great opposition between light and darkness that dominates the whole Gospel from the beginning and that, as the twelve hours of Jesus' day run out, asserts itself even more clearly. It is the opposition that has already been described in its divisive significance but that, now that final decisions are being made, is depicted to us with great exemplary vividness in the figures of Mary and Judas. "Everyone who does evil hates the light and does not come to the light, so that his deeds will not be exposed. But the one who does what is true comes to the light so that it may be clearly seen that his deeds have been done in God" (3:20, 21).

7-8 In his response to Judas's remark Jesus takes Mary's side. He

---

115. So Bultmann: By putting these words in Judas's mouth (unlike Matthew and Mark) and by saying that Judas was insincere, the Fourth Evangelist "destroyed the real point of the story." And if vs. 8 was a later gloss, then it is clear that the point of the story is in vs. 7: "the anointing of Jesus is an anticipation of the anointing of his dead body" (as in Matthew and Mark).

116. Even Schnackenburg, who speaks of a "legendary excrescence," acknowledges: "On the other hand, the statement that Judas looked after the disciples' common fund is important" (*Comm.* II, p. 368). Brown leaves both possibilities open. On the one hand, he writes, "The picture of Judas' cupidity was naturally painted in darker and darker tones as the story was retold," and even considers it possible that the whole of "the Johannine identification of the disgruntled disciple at Bethany as Judas was part of the popular tendency to present Judas in a hostile light." But he adds: "Yet, neither is it impossible, that precisely because he handled money for the group, Judas was the disciple who did raise a protest at Bethany, and that again the remembrance was lost in the Synoptic tradition" (*Comm.* I, p. 453).

refrains from unmasking Judas's actual intention. That will not be done until Jesus' last meal with his disciples. But in his response here there is something of a final signal of the time that is running out and of the truth that everything depends on interpreting that time.

Jesus' response, as in the Synoptics, consists of two parts, the saying about the poor and the allusion to Jesus' burial. The difference between John and the Synoptics lies in John's reversal of these two parts and the difficult form of the burial saying as he has it.

The manner in which Jesus' burial is mentioned as the event for which Mary anointed his body is striking even in the Synoptics, but the meaning of the saying is clear enough. The burial saying reads very differently in John and can hardly, if at all, be interpreted in the same way as the Synoptic saying. This is still attempted by translating the grammatically difficult but certainly original reading as: "let her be and [let her] keep it for the day of my burial."[117] The crux in this connection, however, is "keep." What is it that Mary must still "keep"? The rest of the ointment, as interpreters usually have it? But everything here, as in the Synoptics (which do not mention "keeping"), suggests that Mary has already poured out all the ointment.[118]

Others, accordingly, rightly judging that Mary could not be preserving any of the ointment, therefore set "leave her alone" apart from what follows, taking the now elliptical next clause[119] as a statement of Mary's purpose in preserving the oil (or to which she was destined by the will of God): reserving it (cf. 2:10) for the day of Jesus' burial. Then the translation reads something like this: "Let her be! She wanted to keep it for the day of my burial"[120] or "had to keep it for the day of my burial."[121] This would imply that in a proleptic sense the day of Jesus' burial had already begun.[122] With this in view Mary had "kept" the oil. The resulting meaning would then be close to that of Mk. 14:8.[123]

---

117. So Bultmann's free rendering: "Leave her! She must keep it for the day of my burial." Though John is "hardly comprehensible" here, his form of the saying "can have no other meaning" than what Bultmann sees in Mk. 14:8; Mt. 26:12 (*Comm.*, p. 416, n. 2).

118. See, among others, the lengthy and convincing refutation of this idea in Brown, *Comm.* I, p. 449.

119. Now nothing precedes the ἵνα to support it, a "brachyology" which occurs frequently in John. On this see at length Schnackenburg, *Comm.* II, p. 369.

120. So also J. Blinzler, *Der Prozeß Jesu*, 1969, pp. 407ff.; cf. also Morris, *Comm.*, pp. 579f.

121. So Schnackenburg, *Comm.*, who therefore translates somewhat less directly: "She had to keep it for the day of my burial" (from the German ed., II, 1971, p. 458); cf. II (in the English ed.), p. 369: "what underlies the action is the will of God."

122. So at length Blinzler: "The expression 'day of my burial' seems to be intended proleptically and to be related to the present. Now already six days before the Passover (12:1), the time of Jesus' passion, the day of death, which among the Jews was at the same time the day of burial, has dawned" (p. 407).

123. Cf. Schnackenburg, *Comm.*, in loc.

But though in the Fourth Gospel Jesus sometimes speaks of the future as present ("the hour is coming and now is," etc.), he never speaks of his death (or burial) as an occurrence that had already begun. Particularly the idea that because of Mary's act Jesus intentionally described the day and the occasion on which he sat at table with his own (see comments on vs. 6) as the day on which he was buried seems to us unduly forced. And no appeal can be made, for an anticipation of this kind, to the burial saying as the Synoptics have it. Mary's anointing of Jesus is called an act that anticipates Jesus burial,[124] but this is not to say that by this act the day of Jesus' burial itself has been advanced. Rather, by the use of "beforehand," that day has been left in place. Furthermore, "the poor you always have with you, but you do not always have me" clearly speaks of the still living Lord and not to the dead Lord who only remains to be buried. It is therefore understandable that various attempts have been made to clear up the concept of "keeping," for instance, by taking its object to be not the oil but something else. This has not, however, led to any illuminating consensus.[125]

A very different light falls on the whole passage if one takes the second clause as an elliptical rhetorical question that Jesus, in defense of Mary, poses to Judas: "Let her alone! Do you suppose she should have kept it [the ointment] until the day of my burial?" This understanding has the great advantage of giving a clear meaning to "keep." In contrast to Judas's (pretended) concern for the poor Jesus traces Mary's act to a different consideration, the urgency of which must have been as obvious to Judas as it was to Mary: the brevity of the time they had to sit at table with Jesus. This Mary had grasped, hence her overwhelming display of esteem and love. Should she have waited and kept the oil till the day on which she could have used it only for Jesus' burial?

And then what follows becomes a weighty allusion to Judas's words: "The poor you always have with you, but you do not always have me." On the day of Jesus' burial they would no longer have him with them. If Mary were to show Jesus her love and respect, she had to do it now, while she still had him with her.

Two objections can be advanced against this understanding — the only one that in our opinion makes sense of "keeping." First, it gives a different significance to the burial motif than what we find in the Synoptics. There it has a positive meaning: Mary's anointing anticipates the gestures of respect due to Jesus at his burial. In John, the

124. προέλαβεν μυρίσαι (Mk. 14:8).
125. Of the many translations offered, two may be mentioned as examples, that of H. Riesenfeld in *TDNT* VIII, p. 145: "Let her alone, she has *observed* (i.e. done) this with a view to my death," and that of the Willibrord version: "She has kept this custom, anticipating the day of my burial."

burial, on this understanding, is when Mary's act of respect will be too late, at least for the living Jesus. Unless we can force John's version to agree with that of the Synoptics, we must accept this divergence of interpretations within the tradition of the same motif, a phenomenon that is not, of course, unusual.

Then which was the original sense of Jesus' saying? In the Synoptics as well as John the saying about the poor appears alongside the burial saying, though in reverse order. The saying about the poor has the same meaning in both John and the Synoptics: Mary is still able to do what she has done: "Unlike the poor, you do not always have me with you." Then, in the Synoptics, comes the burial saying, clearly a new element, one that does not correspond with the first, but stands rather in tension with it. The saying about the poor can hardly be understood as saying that time is running out to serve Jesus with an honorable burial. In the Synoptics the second saying clearly represents a different viewpoint from the first.

In John, however, there is a direct connection between the two sayings, if one takes the second clause of vs. 7 as a question. The burial saying refers to the urgency of the time and the second offers additional motivation. The two sayings constitute a closely integrated unit. But to conclude from this that John conveys the burial saying in its original intent whereas the Synoptics hand down a later interpretation would certainly be premature. One can say that that is how the two sayings impress us, but that proves nothing about the history of the tradition, though there is some argument for this conclusion in noting that, if we take vs. 7b as a question, the Johannine version forms a more clearly defined unit than we have with these two sayings as they are joined in the Synoptics.

The second objection to our understanding of vs. 7b as a question is more important and is doubtless the reason that it is not interpreted as such by most interpreters. This is simply the lack of any interrogative particle.[126] If one rejects any conjectural reconstruction of the text, then one can only argue against this objection that what we have here is a clearly elliptical clause that cannot — at least if one wishes to understand it affirmatively — be clarified in any satisfactory and convincing way and that can more readily be understood as a question, precisely because it is elliptical. If we opt for the interrogative understanding, we do so simply in order to arrive at an intelligible meaning without raising undue difficulties.

If we now survey the entire story we can hardly escape its double meaning. On the one hand, this banquet is a high point at which Jesus' glory in the midst of his own has come to a climax (see above on vss. 1-3). At the same

---

126. The interrogative form is suggested, on the basis of a possible Aramaic background, by C. C. Torrey, *The Aramaic Origin of the Fourth Gospel*, 1922, p. 343: "Should she keep it for the day of my burial?" It can also be found already in Baljon, *Comm.,* who by way of conjecture reads ἵνα τί and translates: "Why should she keep it to the day of my burial?" He adds: "The disappearance of τί from the manuscript was the cause of the difficulties in the other readings" (pp. 214f.). Bultmann reports this translation (as does Morris, *Comm.,* p. 580, n. 27) without adopting it, and notes that "this would give a good sense which could also be obtained through the conjecture ἵνα τί = why?" (Bultmann, *Comm.,* p. 416, n. 2).

time these are the last of the twelve hours of his day (cf. 11:9). Judas is present and in a characteristic manner betrays his secret intentions, intentions known, however, by Jesus. At the same time Jesus also speaks of his own burial, prompted no doubt by the anointing, which was an appropriate gesture of respect before burial. Above all, however, his words disclose the degree to which the approaching end becomes ever more vividly real to him and how intensely and graphically he involves his fellow guests in that end in order to open their eyes to its reality, which is increasingly important for them as well. Mary has an inkling of it. While in Jerusalem the tensions and threats surrounding Jesus grow increasingly more ominous and as Jesus still moves in the fullness of his glory among his own in Bethany and is still "with her," she has grasped the urgency of the moment and has seized the opportunity while it is still available. Thus she gives Jesus the loving response of his own at the appropriate time, doing so vicariously, as it were, for all generations who will remember and honor her for it as long as the gospel is proclaimed (Mk. 14:9).

But for Judas and others who thought that Mary's money could be spent on better causes, the time was no less urgent: time, that is, to believe in the light while it was still with them and thus to escape the darkness of night (cf. 12:35, 36). That is the profound content of the seemingly innocent saying with which the story ends: "but me you do not always have." Again coming to expression in this statement is a motif that is characteristic of the Fourth Gospel and that has gained increasing clarity as the story has progressed:[127] that of the caesura in the manifestation of Jesus' glory, of the temporality and the meaning of his glory "in the flesh."

According to many interpreters, the lines of Jesus' earthly and heavenly glory increasingly merge, especially in these stories involving Lazarus. They claim that Jesus, with Lazarus at his side, already displays features of the Risen One and that his burial is mentioned here as the way of his hidden glory, on account of which his disciples already pay homage to him. But this entails a radical reconstrual of the thrust of these stories. The lines, far from blurring, in fact grow sharper. The Evangelist's intention in this repeated reference to the end of Jesus' manifestation of glory in the flesh — with "the day of his burial" as the point of no return — is to underscore its uniqueness in its controlling significance for the church's faith; at the same time he presents it as the break between faith and unbelief, a separation realized in relation to this end, as that comes most radically and exemplarily to expression in the contrast between Mary and Judas.

---

127. See at length the comments on 9:44; 11:9; 12:35, 36.

12:9-19

Jesus Enters Jerusalem

This pericope has three parts. The first (vss. 9-11) describes the reaction of both the crowd and the leaders to Jesus' return to Bethany and marks the transition to his entry into Jerusalem. The second part (vss. 12-15) conveys in a few bold strokes the story of the entry itself, concluded as in Matthew 21 with a reference to Scripture, namely Zc. 9:9. In the concluding part (vss. 16-19) the Evangelist comments successively on the positions of the disciples, the crowd, and the Pharisees with regard to Jesus' entry into the city. Everything is integrated in the composition — unlike the Synoptics — as the prelude to the passion narrative.

9-11   Vs. 9 connects materially with 11:55ff., where mention is made of the "many" who had come to Jerusalem for the feast and looked for Jesus in vain.[128] They are described here as "the great crowd of the Jews." When they learned that Jesus was in Bethany, they went to the village, "not only on account of Jesus but also to see Lazarus, whom he had raised from the dead." It is already clear, as will be stated emphatically in vss. 17 and 18, that the Evangelist wants his readers to understand Jesus' entry into Jerusalem in the light of the raising of Lazarus. Now the attention of the "chief priests"[129] was focused on Lazarus. They took counsel how they could eliminate him as well as Jesus because, as the Evangelist repeats, "on account of him [Lazarus] many of the Jews were going [to Bethany] and were believing in Jesus," without, however, further commenting on the nature of this faith (cf. 2:23; 4:48; 7:31; 8:30, etc.). The Evangelist's concern now is to point to the miracle as the cause of growing support for Jesus among the people, who no longer allow themselves to be intimidated by the authorities. This support will manifest itself in unprecedented ways in the events of the following day.

12-15   The story of the entry into Jerusalem is familiar, though at somewhat greater length, from the Synoptic Gospels. The biggest difference lies perhaps in the context in which John sets the story (see above). But there are other more or less noticeable differences. Above all there is the brief reference to Jesus' finding "a young donkey," which omits any mention of all the preparations — extensively reported in the Synoptics — leading up to Jesus' acquisition of the animal (Mk. 11:1ff.). There is also the difference in the wording of the welcoming acclamation and of the prophecy of Zc. 9:9 (cf. Mt.

128. Perhaps this connection explains the somewhat striking use here of the article with "crowd." There is doubt about its authenticity and it is already missing in some manuscripts, but omission is much easier to explain than addition.

129. Referred to here as elsewhere — whether in conjunction with the Pharisees or not — as the leading figures in the Sanhedrin (cf. 7:32, 45ff.; 11:47, 57; 18:19, 35; 19:6, 15, 21).

21:5). There can therefore be no question of Johannine dependence on (one of) the Synoptics.[130] But the story is not typically Johannine in style and mode of expression.[131] The desire to trace all this back to "sources" again leads to a mechanism that fundamentally denies to the Evangelist all independence and freedom as a transmitter of the tradition.

What we have before us is the story of an event that has already occupied a fixed place in the tradition and that the Evangelist can assume is known by his readers. This may help explain the extreme conciseness with which he presents it,[132] mentioning only what he needs for his purpose, which is no more than the messianic elucidation of two Bible passages. It is evident from vs. 12 that the Evangelist regarded Jesus' entry as the end point of his earthly self-manifestation as the Messiah of Israel. Immediately after the entry some "Greeks" appear on the scene, the sign for Jesus that the "hour" of his return to the Father has come and with that the end of his presence in the world. Viewed in this light, the Johannine story of the entry is a transitional narrative, marking the caesura between Jesus' earthly and heavenly glory.

12-13   The story begins with a time reference: "the next day." Although the time frame of vss. 9-11 cannot be determined with precision, vs. 12 can best be viewed as a continuation of the story reported in vss. 1-8. If that is correct, the entry took place the day after the anointing at Bethany (whatever day of the week that may have been; see the comments on vs. 1; many think here of "Palm Sunday").

The initiators of the entry were those "who had come to the feast."[133] On hearing of Jesus' coming to Jerusalem, they went out to meet him and prepare for him a royal entry. The Evangelist stresses that it was a royal entry in his brief description: Palm branches[134] were used as symbols for victorious and beneficent rulers;[135] current terminology for reception and "welcoming"[136] of rulers is used (cf. Mt. 8:34; 25:1; 1 Th. 4:17); and Jesus is called "the king of Israel" / "your king."

---

130. Though some argue for it, e.g., E. D. Freed, "The Entry into Jerusalem in the Gospel of John," *JBL* 80 (1961), pp. 329ff. For a contrary view see Dodd, *Historical Tradition,* pp. 152f.

131. On this see, e.g., Nicol, *Sēmeia in the Fourth Gospel,* p. 11.

132. So Bultmann explains the ("supplementary") mention of the ass in vs. 14: "But vv. 14f. so decidedly have the character of an addendum, it must be presumed that the addendum has been anticipated in remembrance of the already well known story" (*Comm.,* p. 418).

133. Is this meant to distinguish them from those in Jerusalem who were less favorably disposed to Jesus (cf. 7:25)?

134. τὰ βαΐα τῶν φοινίκων, literally "the branches of the palm trees." That palm branches were used during the Feast of Tabernacles could perhaps explain the definite article here. Palm branches were not easily available in Jerusalem. Matthew and Mark mention "plucking" but not palm branches.

135. See the lengthy and careful notes in Schnackenburg, *Comm.* II, pp. 373ff.

136. εἰς- or ὑπ-άντησις (see Schnackenburg, *Comm.* II, p. 524, n. 38).

"Hosanna" was typically used as a greeting and blessing.[137] The acclamation that follows is derived from Ps. 118:25, a song in which pilgrims, on entering the temple, wished each other the blessings of salvation.[138] This "coming in the name of the Lord" — applied in the psalm to every pilgrim as an expression of the sacred character of pilgrimage — is applied most eminently to Jesus as the king of Israel, as vs. 13b explicitly adds.[139] This whole of the account of the welcoming of Jesus thus thereby acquires the character of an acclamation by which Israel solemnly welcomes its Messiah into Jerusalem, the city and temple of the great king (cf. Mt. 5:35).

14-15   Only after this are we told that Jesus sits on a donkey that he has "found."[140] While, as stated earlier, the Synoptics give broad attention to the (royal) requisitioning of the animal in preparation for Jesus' entry (Mk. 11:2ff.), that element — in the interest of brevity perhaps — is absent here, but not because the animal was unimportant. Here, too, Jesus acquires a donkey, by whatever means, in order to present himself to the people sitting on the donkey. The Evangelist puts all possible stress on this, as is evident from his comment "as it is written," which in this impersonal form suggests direction from a higher source. For this he appeals to the prophecy of Zechariah, specifically to the words "Behold, your king is coming [to you], sitting on an ass's colt."

This motif of sitting on a donkey, according to many interpreters, makes a fundamental point of the account of the entry, namely rejection of the crowd's nationalistic sentiments, not unlike what the crowd in Galilee had in mind when after the multiplication of the loaves it sought to make Jesus king (6:15).[141] It is questionable, however, whether the intention of the story is to counteract that nationalism. Zechariah's prophecy undoubtedly portrays the "humble" (Mt. 21:5) prince of peace as opposed to a violent monarchy and mentions riding on a donkey as a sign of this humility (9:9f.). When Jesus mounts a donkey, he fulfills not just this element but the entire prophecy. But in the prophecy riding a donkey serves not as a criticism of and warning against nationalistic monarchy but as a message of salvation, the message that from such a king seated on a donkey the people can expect peace and well-being.[142] Hence, in

---

137. Literally, "Please help!" (Schnackenburg, *Comm.* II, p. 375).

138. Especially at the feasts of Passover and Tabernacles (cf. Strack/Billerbeck I, pp. 845f.).

139. καί before "the king" is missing from some manuscripts and has an epexegetical sense; for this addition, see Zp. 3:15.

140. ὀνάριον, a diminutive term ("little donkey"), but by this time no longer understood as such (BDF §111.3).

141. See, e.g., Brown, *Comm.* I, p. 462.

142. Zc. 9:9 reads: "Rejoice greatly, O daughter of Zion! Shout aloud, O daughter of Jerusalem! Lo, your king comes to you; triumphant and victorious is he, humble and riding on an ass." Elsewhere also in prophecy "Fear not!" occurs frequently as a salvific address to Israel as the people of God (cf. Is. 35:4; 48:9 in the Vulgate); it serves in Zp. 3:16 as the parallel to: "Rejoice, O daughter of Zion" (in 3:14).

our text, the words of address, "Fear not, daughter of Zion." Therefore, Jesus' riding a donkey is evidently not experienced by the crowd, in either John or the Synoptics, as an attempt to tone down their festive spirit.[143]

So what the Evangelist has in mind in vss. 14-15 is solely that this riding on a donkey is an expression of the nature of Jesus' kingship. In the Johannine context Jesus' "finding" and mounting the donkey is his direct response to the acclamation of his kingship by the people (vs. 13) and his acceptance of it — in keeping with the salvific kingship of God over Israel pictured in prophecy and the reign of the humble king of peace and justice who, riding on a donkey, makes his royal entry among his people. It is in that form, to which Jesus again gives expression, that he accepts the last stretch of the road on which he must go to receive rule over his people from the hands of God. No one in Jerusalem but Jesus — neither his disciples nor the crowd nor the rulers of Israel — understood that he entered Jerusalem, sitting on a donkey, to receive that kingship and, as the Son of man, to be lifted up on the cross. For that reason the story of the entry, particularly in John's presentation of it, is the story of Jesus' hidden glory, the deep meaning of which only the progress of the events of salvation would disclose. To this the threefold commentary with which the Evangelist concludes this section is directed.

16-18 The first comment on the account of the entry (vs. 16) relates to the fulfillment of prophecy in Jesus riding the donkey (already pointed to in the preceding verses). That (and the words of prophecy relating to it) is what the disciples who were present at the entry did not understand at first; only "when Jesus was glorified," that is, after his resurrection (cf. 2:22), "did they remember that these things had been written about him[144] and that they had done these things to him." The meaning of the last clause is not altogether certain. It is widely assumed that "they" refers to the disciples themselves and that therefore "these things" refers to their involvement with obtaining the donkey, which was not mentioned but assumed to be known. It is also possible that "they" refers to the crowd and that "these things" refers to the royal entry in general. The "things" that "his disciples did not understand" obviously refers to the manner, indicated in the quotation from Zechariah, of Jesus' entry: on the donkey, in which the disciples had a part.[145]

The statement is strongly reminiscent of 2:22 (cf. also 20:9) and evidences the Evangelist's strong historical sense. He is aware that in the way he posits a relation (in vss. 14f.) between Jesus' entry and the prophecy in

---

143. Brown refers to δέ in vs. 14 as an adversative conjunction (*Comm.* I, p. 462). But sometimes δέ is not adversative but merely transitional (BDF §447.7, 8). "A distinction is to be observed between general contrast (δέ) and that which is directly contrary (ἀλλά)" (BDF §447). Thus δέ here means something like "Jesus, on his part . . . ."

144. ἐπ' αὐτῷ, "about" him (BDF §235.5), περὶ αὐτοῦ in D and other manuscripts.

145. The first two ταύτας of the three in vs. 16 refer back, then, to what precedes in vs. 15.

Zechariah 9 he is also writing on the basis of later "remembrance"[146] that came after Jesus' glorification and the sending of the Spirit (14:26). Jesus' entry on a donkey is underscored by the Evangelist's comment, but we are not told how the disciples experienced the entry as a whole. They could not, of course, have insulated themselves from the special — even messianic — character of the event. However, apparently neither they nor the crowd attributed a special meaning to Jesus' initiative in riding into Jerusalem on the back of a donkey. That it was specifically the humility of the donkey-riding king over which his own should rejoice — *that* they would understand only in the light of Scripture. And then they would understood it in the profound sense that Jesus had given to that humility: he was welcomed into the city by the crowd not only as the prince of peace but also as the one to be crucified there as "the king of the Jews."

The second comment (vs. 17) speaks of what moved the crowd to welcome Jesus, namely the powerful impression made on them by the raising of Lazarus. The Evangelist bases this on the still continuing and influential witness[147] of the crowds that were with Jesus "when he called Lazarus out of the tomb and raised him from the dead." This recalls 11:18, 33, 45, which mention the "many" who had come from Jerusalem to console Mary and Martha, heard Jesus' word of power, and witnessed his act of power. It was because of that crowd's testimony that "the crowd" in Jerusalem for the Passover (vs. 18; cf. vs. 12) "went to meet him."[148]

The Evangelist, again after vs. 9, thus emphatically refers to the raising of Lazarus as the cause of the enthusiasm with which the crowd has welcomed Jesus. This underscores anew the meaning that the Evangelist attributes to this great miracle of Jesus as the background of the events by which the crowd, until shortly before Jesus' death, display so much greater openness to Jesus' divine mission than their largely blinded leaders and over and over "believe in him." Still, the emphatic "on account of this" here and the concluding words, "they had heard that he had done this sign," do not point to a permanent conversion but rather to a repetition of what has from the beginning been repeatedly said of the crowd:

146. On this "remembrance" (ἐμνήσθησαν) and the anticipation here of 14:26, see, at greater length, the comments above on 2:22.

147. ἐμαρτύρει, iterative imperfect.

148. As a result of the varying meaning of "the crowd" in vss. 17 and 18 the intent, at first blush, is somewhat unclear. It is perhaps for that reason that some manuscripts read ὅτι in vs. 17 in place of ὅτε (which is what most manuscripts have). The meaning then is "the crowd that had been with Jesus" (at the entry) testified that he had called Lazarus from the grave. Vs. 18 then tells us, again, that the same crowd had gone out to meet Jesus because they had heard, etc. But this makes for a very cumbersome construction. Moreover, the order of first "bearing witness" (vs. 17), then "because they had heard" (vs. 18), said of the same crowd, seems not to be illogical. The textual evidence argues for ὅτε, and the varying meaning of "the crowd" does not constitute an insuperable objection. This is why most interpreters follow this reading.

they believed in Jesus on account of the signs he did (cf. 2:33; 4:45, 48; 6:2; 11:47), that is, where their faith ended, and Jesus knew that on that basis alone he could not trust them (2:24f.; 6:14, 15; 4:48). The Evangelist does not mention this last aspect here, but the crowd, despite the witness they have borne and, as it were, must bear to Jesus at the entry, remains in doubt about him, and this will soon be evident in the only dialogue he has with them after the entry.

Therefore, the comment in vs. 18 suggests that it was "on account of this" *alone* that they "went to meet him." It is as if the Evangelist here refuses to detract from the grandeur of the event, not for the sake of the future and especially not with a view to the Jewish people itself: once Israel had welcomed Jesus and acclaimed him in Jerusalem as the promised king! But they did so because they had heard of the great and undeniable sign he had done. And that is as far as it went (cf. vss. 37f.).

19 The Evangelist's last comment (vs. 19) reports the reaction of the Pharisees. They, too, were deeply impressed by Jesus' action and, in spite of themselves, had to acknowledge his superiority and the ineffectiveness of the measures taken against him thus far. For the moment they were not involved and had nothing better to do than to complain among themselves about the course of events: "You see" (or "Don't you see. . . ?") "that you are not making any gain. The whole world has gone after him." Calvin comments: "This is how desperate men will talk when they are preparing to make their last effort."[149] But the Evangelist could also mean (unlike in vss. 17 and 18) that despite human resistance God's work continues. In their hyperbole ("all the world") the Pharisees, like Caiaphas in 11:49, 50, were saying more than they realized. For the first people to seek contact with Jesus' disciples after the entry were "Greeks" who wanted to see Jesus (vss. 20ff.)

12:20-36

Jesus' Glorification Announced, the Son of Man

This section, although viewed by some as incoherent or as a composite of originally separate pieces,[150] is in content not hard to understand as a unit. The majority of interpreters, accordingly, understand it as an original whole composed by the Evangelist with great care.[151] It consists in the main of a discourse by Jesus

---

149. *Comm.* II, p. 35.

150. E.g., by Bultmann in one of his many radical reconstructions of the — seriously disordered, in his opinion — material of the Gospel.

151. For the literature see, e.g., F. J. Moloney, *The Johannine Son of Man,* 1978, pp. 144ff.; K. Tsychido, "Tradition and Redaction in John 12:1-43," *NTS* 30 (1984), pp. 609-19; L. T. Witkamp, *Jezus van Nazareth in de gemeente van Johannes,* 1986, pp. 194ff.

prompted by a request, passed on to him, from certain "Greeks" who ask to meet him. The historical situation and course of events is unclear: the connection with what precedes is uncertain (see the comments below on vs. 20); the Greeks, having made their request, are not mentioned again; and the entire subsequent discussion (vss. 23-28) is between Jesus and "the crowd." It is clear, however, that the Greeks' request marks the definitive turning point in Jesus' public activity in Israel and by implication in his interaction with the crowd (cf. vss. 35, 36a, and especially 36b). Accordingly, all that follows in vss. 37-43 and 44-50 is a reflection on the negative results of Jesus' public actions in Israel and a summary of the great importance, nonetheless, of those public actions.

20-22   The transition from Jesus' entry into Jerusalem to what now follows, as far as the sequence of events is concerned, is very abrupt. There is not a word here about the elated acclamation of Jesus as the king of Israel at the entry and his own part in it, nor does there seem to be anything left of it among the "crowd" that is present here. In what Jesus is now reported to say one can hardly, if at all, speak of a reaction to the preceding events. All at once, with the coming of the Greeks, everything seems to take a redemptive-historical turn.

There is, however, a connection in that the Greeks are described as being "among those who went up to worship at the feast." The reference is to people of Greek origin,[152] who as proselytes[153] took part in the Jewish Passover.[154] The situation, therefore, is still that of the preceding story. Indeed, the desire of these Greeks to "see" Jesus, that is, to meet and learn to know him (cf. Lk. 9:7; Ac. 28:20, etc.) can be understood very well in light of the preceding events. That for this purpose they turned to Philip and not immediately to Jesus is not strange. They may have done so out of respect for Jesus and because Philip's origin in Transjordanian "Bethsaida of Galilee," reported here for this reason, meant that he could understand Greek.[155] It is more noteworthy that

---

152. Not Greek-speaking Jews (cf. Ac. 6:1) of the diaspora but Greeks. So most interpreters; on this see also H. B. Kossen, "Who Were the Greeks of John XII 20?" in *Studies in John* (Festschrift for J. N. Sevenster), 1970, pp. 97-110.

153. Cf. Ac. 2:11. On proselytes and their varying religious status see, e.g., Strack/Billerbeck II, pp. 715-22, according to whom the reference here is to "half-proselytes" or σεβόμενοι (τὸν θεόν), who without being circumcised accepted Jewish monotheism and observed certain parts of the Mosaic ceremonial law (p. 716; see also p. 548).

154. ἀναβαίνειν and προσκυνεῖν, traditionally used for "going up" to Jerusalem and taking part in cultic activities, in this case in the very limited sense in which this was permitted to Gentiles: "participation in the Passover meal was of course denied them" (Strack/Billerbeck II, p. 549).

155. Cf. G. Dalman, *Sacred Sites and Ways,* p. 165: "St. John (xii, 21) takes it for granted that Philip, being a native of the 'Galilean Bethsaida,' understood Greek, since Galilee had a mixed population and was therefore bilingual." Also, Bethsaida lay across the Jordan, which implies not only knowledge of the language but also association with foreigners and familiarity with Greek culture. It need not surprise us, in view of other examples of this nature (see Dalman, in loc.), that the Evangelist nevertheless considered Bethsaida part of Galilee.

Philip first contacted Andrew, who was also from Bethsaida (1:44), and that together they went to Jesus.[156] For the repeated mention of these two disciples an assortment of explanations has been attempted.[157] The most natural explanation is that the Evangelist, directly or indirectly, had a personal relationship with them that enabled him from time to time to make specific observations about their role as disciples (cf. 1:40, 44; 6:7, 8; 14:8).

23 Jesus' answer does not — at least directly — relate to the Greeks' request. Instead, he announces a decisive transition in his life from this point on, the coming of "the hour" to which repeated reference has been made (cf. 6:62; 7:33; 8:21) and which is now described as "the hour for the Son of man to be glorified." By this is meant the whole of Jesus' passing out of this world to the Father (13:1), which would have its beginning in his now imminent death and its completion in his return to heavenly glory (cf. vss. 24ff.; 17:5, etc.).

It is striking that this glorification is referred to as only beginning now and as until now only a future reality (cf. also 17:1ff., 24). Although Jesus' future glory has been mentioned in this absolute sense before (cf. 7:30, where it is said of Jesus' time on earth that he "was not yet glorified"; see also 12:16), it is no less true that the entire Gospel is full of the revelation of Jesus' glory already during his earthly life, in fact that the manifestation of Jesus' earthly glory "in the flesh" is the Gospel's grand theme (1:14;[158] 2:11; 11:4; cf. 11:46). This glory has not been just proleptically related to Jesus' resurrection and ascension,[159] but has been identified retrospectively as that of the preexistent only-begotten of the Father (1:14) and of the Son of man descended from heaven (1:51; 5:27; 6:27; 9:35f.).[160]

It seems that the glorification of the Son of man is just now "really" beginning and that all that has been said until now about that glory silently becomes mere prelude or preparation. But what actually makes this verse so important for the understanding of the whole Gospel is that it marks a definite break in Jesus' self-revelation as the Son of man. This break can be traced

---

156. On the alternating use of the singular (the second ἔρχεται in vs. 22) and the plural (λέγουσιν), see BDF §135.1d.

157. There is a widespread view, which can be found already in Thomas Aquinas, that the mediation of the two disciples indicates that while Jesus in his own person would proclaim the gospel to the Jews he would do so to the Gentiles by means of the apostles (see, e.g., J. Blank, *Krisis. Untersuchungen zur johanneischer christologie und eschatologie,* 1963, p. 266, and the reference to Thomas given there). However, there is no mention here of an answer of Jesus mediated by the disciples or, therefore, of an implied prediction that from now on the disciples would serve as intermediaries for communicating with Jesus.

158. Cf. Blank, *Krisis,* p. 272: "On this basis [that of 1:14] one may say that according to John the δόξα belongs to the Christ-event as a whole and qualified it in its entirety as revelational event, though it expresses itself in varying ways."

159. Against this "proleptic" view, see pp. 15f., 121, 424f., 634f.

160. For this dual viewpoint (preexistent and redemptive-historical) see the comments above on 5:27 and 9:36-38 and also p. 138, n. 108.

back to and finds its most succinct description in 3:13: "No one has *ascended* into heaven but he who *descended* from heaven, the Son of man."[161] This distinction — others speak of a "descent-ascent schema" — recurs in the Gospel under varying terms.[162] It differs from the familiar (cf. Philippians 2) and much-employed distinction between Jesus' "humiliation" and "exaltation," for the glory of the Son of man is no less central in his descent than in his ascent (cf. 1:50, 51).[163] But basic to it all is the fundamental motif of 3:13: there can be no ascent to heaven, no authority of the Son of man, and no heavenly glory as described in Daniel 7 before the descent from heaven has taken place and has been brought to its conclusion. It is from this perspective that the glorification of the Son of man can be spoken of here in this absolute sense.

Before we can discuss this subject further — in connection with vs. 24 — we must still ask what relationship there is between the coming of the hour of the glorification of the Son of man and the coming of the Greeks. The answer is made more difficult by the disappearance of the Greeks in what follows. The reader is left in the dark as to whether they came into contact with Jesus or not. Some interpreters think they did, and that Jesus' answer must be viewed as a denial of their request: because his hour has come, the time is past for him to enter into new relationships. But that it was specifically "Greeks" that prompted Jesus to make this statement makes this generalizing interpretation implausible. We must rather consider the Pharisees' words at the end of the preceding pericope: "The whole world is going after him!" a statement that is, as it were, illustrated by the approach of the Greeks.[164] In this regard it is also of paramount importance that in vs. 32 Jesus says that when he is lifted up from the earth he will draw *all* people to himself, that is, that it is the universality of Jesus' redemptive significance that characterizes his being lifted up. Now the Greek world is asking for him, and that is the sign for him that the hour of his glorification as the Son of man has come. This need not mean that with this answer to Philip and Andrew he meant that these Greeks must wait to see him until his glorification. Some interpreters believe that something has been lost that stood between vss. 22 and 23.[165] But the Evangelist's concerns were limited. He was evidently interested not in incidental occurrences but in the

---

161. Cf. G. C. Nicholson, *Death as Departure: The Johannine Descent-Ascent Schema,* 1983.

162. "Coming down," "coming," and "being sent" over against "ascending," "returning," "going," and "going away." Apart from 3:13, see also 3:31; 6:38, 62; 7:33; 8:14, 42; 13:1; 16:5; 17:8f.; 20:17.

163. On this see at length Blank, *Krisis,* pp. 80ff., 287; Brown, *Comm.* I, pp. 145f.; Schnackenburg, *Comm.* I, pp. 379ff.

164. So also Bultmann, *Comm.,* p. 423.

165. Cf. Bultmann: "for the suspicion cannot be suppressed that between v. 22 and v. 23 a whole piece has fallen out" (*Comm.,* pp. 420f.).

redemptive-historical transition that announces itself in these occurrences: the arrival of the hour of the glorification of the Son of man.[166]

24 The "hour," thus announced, of Jesus' glorification as the Son of man is characterized by the discussion here, at some length, of Jesus' death as, we might say, the first phase of his glorification. The image used for his death, that of the grain that dying bears much fruit, is variously applied elsewhere (in 1 Co. 15:36ff. of resurrection following death). Here it speaks of the necessity of Jesus' death in relation to his glorification. The strong emphasis in Jesus' words — "Truly, truly, I say to you, *unless* . . ." (cf. the parallel in both structure and content in 6:53 and the "unless" in 1 Co. 15:36) — stresses the seemingly paradoxical, judged by human standards, scandal that Jesus' death as the Christ and the Son of man is the inescapable condition for his glorification as the Son of man. At stake in this is the redemptive significance of this glorification: "unless it dies, it remains alone; if it dies it bears much fruit," a clear reference to the many for whom Jesus gives up his life and who by his death receive eternal life (cf., e.g., 6:51).

The necessity of Jesus' death, thus emphasized, in its redemptive significance for others, is of special importance for the correct understanding of the christology of the Fourth Gospel. To some interpreters the revelation of Jesus' glory as the Son of God in the Fourth Gospel is so dominant that his death must be viewed as necessary only for himself, namely as "departure" to return to the Father.[167] It has no meaning other than as a change of the scene of his glory, a triumphal passage from the earthly to the heavenly, in the single uninterrupted revelation of his glory.[168] But this fails to do justice not only to the soteriological significance of Jesus' death but also to the content of the christological motif in 3:13. Jesus' death is, of course, the presupposition of Jesus' repeated reference to giving up his life for his own (10:15, 17; 15:13),

---

166. Cf. Westcott, *Comm.,* p. 180: "It is not easy to suppose either that the interview preceded v. 23, or that the interview was refused, or that it followed after this scene. On the other hand, St. John has preserved just so much of what was said in reply to their request as gives the permanent interpretation of the incident and no more." See also Schnackenburg, *Comm.* II, p. 383: "Jesus' reply to the two disciples contains no answer to the Greeks, but it is a theological interpretation of their presence." Schnackenburg thinks that the Evangelist avoided a conversation between Jesus and the Greeks "because he had no tradition about one," but adds (on better grounds): "But Jesus' statement that the hour has come for his glorification means more than that."

167. As Nicholson puts it in *Death as Departure,* p. 153: "The departure will be expedited by his death, but this death does not become the focus of attention. It is true that Jesus must depart and that this departure will necessitate his death, so in this sense Jesus is like the grain of wheat which must die to bring life"; p. 128: "For the Fourth Evangelist the death of Jesus is only a means to an end, a stage on the way, that takes him back to the Father" (cf. p. 132).

168. So especially Käsemann: "The one who walks on earth as a stranger, as the messenger sent by the Father, the one who passes through death without turmoil and with jubilation, because he has been called back to the realm of freedom, has fulfilled his mission" (*The Testament of Jesus,* p. 20).

of giving his "flesh" for the life of the world (6:51), of the necessity that he be lifted up as the serpent in the wilderness was, namely, on the tree (the cross). Jesus' death, therefore, is not merely his "departure" from the earthly and his passage to the heavenly regions; it is above all the accomplishment of the necessity laid on him by God, the completion of the work the Father gave him to do (19:30; cf. 17:4), the falling into the earth of the grain that must die first, lest it remain *alone,* and so bear much fruit.[169]

Admittedly, in the Fourth Gospel, more than in the other Gospels, the entire journey of Jesus' descent has been subsumed under the viewpoint of Jesus' glory (1:14, 50, 51, etc.). Special stress is given to Jesus' passion and death as his "power" to lay down his life and to take it up again (10:18). And his crucifixion becomes his "being lifted up" (3:15; 12:32, 34). But this does not mean that his death is not a real death. For Jesus, too, it was true that he had to lose his life to save it (12:25) and that, at the end of the twelve hours of day, night came with its darkness, in which no one can work (9:4f.; 10:9f.). Therefore, laying down his life — however much it was also his deed and not his fate — was also the laying aside of his glory (cf. 13:4, 12f.). "Lift up" is not only a *terminus gloriae* but also a term for the humanly engineered death of shame on the cross (8:28; 18:32).

Jesus' death — we may conclude — is not merely a change of scene that leaves his glory inviolate and that even brings it to a higher stage of development. It rather marks the deep caesura in which the glory of his descent — he who is the light of the world — finds its limitation and its terminus and in which the glory of his ascent begins. It is where the two coincide — in a manner that is utterly paradoxical and scandalous to the human mind (cf. 6:53f.). It therefore also forms the point of division at which faith and unbelief toward Jesus as the Son of man diverge (cf. 6:61f.).[170]

Verses **25** and **26** form an intermezzo in which Jesus, before continuing his consideration of the "hour" that has now begun for him, first involves also the life of his disciples in this law of the grain of wheat. Though these verses somewhat break the flow between vs. 24 and vss. 27ff., such a direct application of Jesus' passion announcement to the life of the disciples also occurs in the Synoptic passion announcement (Mk. 8:31ff.; Mt. 16:21, 24ff.; Lk. 9:22ff.). The historical situation and the terminology in the Synoptics differ sharply from what we have here in John, but that makes it all the more clear that the link Jesus establishes between his course of suffering and what had to be done by and what lay in store for his disciples belonged to the stable nucleus of the tradition that both the Synoptics and John represent. And this is certainly why

169. See also Witkamp, *Jezus van Nazareth,* pp. 212f.
170. See also the valuable reflections on 12:33f. in Blank, *Krisis,* pp. 265f., 270f., where, however, the motif of the caesura does not, in our opinion, come into its own.

the Evangelist inserted these verses before returning to the theme of vss. 23 and 24 in vs. 27.[171]

The statement in vs. 25 is *mašal* with two antithetically parallel lines. A typical *mašal* will use paradox or hyperbole to bring the weight of a matter home to the attentive listener (one who has "ears to hear," Mt. 13:9) as sharply as possible.[172] The meaning of the statement here, though it is worded as a universal truth, is to be understood in the context of what is said in vs. 24 and is further explained in vs. 26: there, too, loss of life is the condition for emergence of new life.

The absolute contrast between loving one's life as the cause of losing it and hating one's life in this world as the way to preserve it for eternal life has been viewed as evidence of dualistic Gnostic thought according to which each person must hate his or her own life because it is part of the cosmos that is hostile to God. But this view fails to take the rhetorical form into account. Elsewhere, too (cf. Luke 14:26), we hear of "hate," but in the sense of self-denial, a willingness for the sake of Jesus to give up things that in themselves are not objectionable but on the contrary very valuable and of which it may be said in another context that one should love them (father, mother, etc.).[173] Furthermore, Jesus says here that one who hates his life in this world will *keep it* for eternal life (cf. Mt. 6:25b).[174] This statement points not to the reprehensible character of this life in itself, but to its destiny in eternity, a goal for which one should be willing to lose it in its transient form.

What is decisive against this Gnostic interpretation of the saying is that here Jesus is putting his disciples on the path of his own surrender of life and departure to the Father. This path is not one of abandoning this world and life in it as inferior and illusory. Instead, he now ends his redemptive work on earth in order, as will be repeatedly shown in chs. 14–17, to continue it in them, with all the risks this entails and with all the promises it offers in keeping with the law of the grain of wheat.[175]

171. Also a reason that here, too, all kinds of tradition-historical hypotheses with respect to shared written sources and conclusions based on such hypotheses with respect to the Johannine redaction remain extremely uncertain. What is clear is the typically Johannine style.

172. See also the comments on 6:27 above.

173. For this opposition — stated in absolute form but intended relatively — between hate and love, see also Mt. 6:24.

174. Cf. Schnackenburg: "φυλάξει (instead of σώσει or εὑρήσει) shows the 'life' to be won not to be merely an eschatological existence in the future, but life in the present which extends into the future" (*Comm.* II, p. 384). Witkamp also writes: "The logion would then [if one had to interpret against a Gnostic background] have to mean: 'One who hates his natural life will keep his spiritual life, that is, his higher self.' John, however, does not know of such Gnostic anthropological dualism; the truth is, he never even says that the believer must hate the κόσμος" (*Jezus van Nazareth*, p. 204).

175. See also the rejection of the Gnostic view (advocated by Bultmann) by Schnackenburg, *Comm.* II, p. 386.

Accordingly, vs. 26 describes discipleship to Jesus as servanthood: one is taken up into the work that Jesus must accomplish, work in which he is Lord and Master and disciples are servants (cf. 13:13, 16; 15:15, 20; Mt. 10:24ff., etc.), entirely in keeping with the position disciples of the rabbis had in relation to their teachers.[176] The emphasis, however, does not lie so much on this servanthood as on the implied obligation: "he must follow me," by itself a general reference to the pupil's permanent presence in the company of a certain rabbi. In this context, where the concern is following *Jesus*,[177] the words "he must follow me" gain a highly charged meaning, implying both the risk entailed in being in the company of this "Lord" and the promise of great reward. For it is in that discipleship that they will experience the paradoxical truth of losing one's life if one loves it and of keeping it forever if one hates it. The first is true because servants are not greater than their Master, and on the road he travels and they follow they will incur the hatred he faces (cf. 15:18ff.; 16:1ff.; 17:14; 1 Jn. 3:13; Mt. 10:21ff., etc.). The second is true because, as Jesus adds, "Where I am, there my servant will also be," a statement referring, as in 14:3 and 17:24, to Jesus' future glory, as also the concluding words: "If anyone serves me, the Father will honor him," namely by letting such a disciple share in the honor and glory of the Son (cf. 14:21, 23; 16:24; 17:22, 23).

Of course, as Jesus' disciples are taken up into the law of the grain of wheat, to which Jesus' mission corresponds, the distinction between him and them, between Master and servants, is not canceled.[178] The discipleship he requires and the outcome of which he predicts do not consist in imitating what he does but in taking the road that he, by giving his life, opens to his own and that he *is* in his own person (14:4ff.).

Finally, it is clear — as emerges prominently also from the concept of serving — that discipleship[179] here "looks ahead to the later missionary activity of the disciples."[180] It is that discipleship, taken up into the continuation of Jesus' work on earth, to which "hating one's life" primarily has reference; in Mk. 8:34 it is called denying oneself and taking up one's cross. Still, John also mentions following Jesus in a more general religious sense (8:12: "he who

---

176. Cf. Strack/Billerbeck I, p. 187: "Being a pupil required personal attachment to the teacher because the pupil learned not merely from the teacher's words but much more from his practical observance of the Torah."

177. Note the double reference to "me" and its emphatic placement (ἐὰν ἐμοί τις διακονῇ, ἐμοὶ ἀκολουθείτω).

178. On this point see at length also Blank, *Krisis,* pp. 274ff.

179. In the New Testament the concept occurs only as a verb, never as a substantive ("discipleship"), and it is exclusively used of following the "historical" Jesus; see further G. Kittel, *TDNT* I, p. 214.

180. So Schnackenburg, *Comm.* II, p. 385.

follows me . . . will have the light of life"). Following Jesus also means acknowledging and choosing him as "the pioneer and perfecter of our faith" (Hb. 12:2) and, though it does not always entail the risk of suffering and death, it remains the radical choice of where to seek and find "life": in self, world, or Jesus. There is no essential difference between the two meanings of "following" Jesus, even though in our text, given the position of the early Christian church, the confrontation with the hate, violence, and threat of death implicit in following Jesus as a direct and contemporary reality certainly occupies the foreground.

27   The verses that now follow resume the thought of vs. 23 and further explain the significance of the "hour" of "glorification" that was announced there. The duality in Jesus' approaching death (see above, on vs. 23) comes strongly to the fore: Jesus' death already belongs to his glorification, but is also the cause of his agitation: "Now is my soul troubled. And what shall I say?" Interpreters who stress only the glory in Jesus' death attempt to explain these words as something other than a person shrinking from the bitterness of death (see also the comments on 11:33, 35).[181] But these words clearly correspond to similar expressions in the Psalms, particularly Ps. 6:4-5 LXX (cf. 41:7 LXX), which, like this Johannine verse, has "my soul is sorely troubled" and "save me." They can, therefore, hardly refer to anything other than the natural human reaction in confrontation with death.

But what is intended is not a sense of dread that suddenly comes over Jesus and from which he will try to free himself in the following words. It is, rather, the realization — which in the progress of his suffering (cf. 13:21) has repeatedly seized him — of the darkness of the path on which he is led by God and of the need to give expression to it. But it is also clear that he not only displayed the image of the suffering devout of the Old Testament but felt called to accomplish his divine mission precisely in his suffering.[182] The following words, "And what shall I say?" are not, as the context indicates, an expression of diffidence and uncertainty about his course of action but an introduction to

---

181. See also Witkamp, *Jezus van Nazareth,* p. 216. He correctly opposes the views of Becker (Jesus is angry because people evidently expected him to try to be saved from this hour) and Nicholson (Jesus is anxious about his disciples in view of the coming events; cf. 14:1). But Witkamp also rejects the idea that the reference could "even" (!) be to "the true humanity of the Johannine Jesus" (as Brown, *Comm.* I, p. 475, has it). Witkamp understands Jesus' agitation (as do other commentators) as "prophetic-pneumatic excitement," "tension before the coming struggle of cosmic proportions of which Jesus in his omniscience is conscious."

182. On the passage as a whole, see also A. T. Wrege, " 'Jesusgeschichte und Jüngergeschick' nach Joh. 12,20-33 und Hebr. 5,7-10," in *Der Ruf der Freiheit und die Antwort der Gemeinde* (Festschrift for J. Jeremias), 1970, pp. 259-88, here pp. 273f.; cf. Schnackenburg, *Comm.* II, p. 384, who also refers to 13:21 and therefore rejects Bultmann's translation "I am afraid"; Schnackenburg paraphrases: "The 'hour' of death and glorification has begun and is experienced by Jesus in its deepest dimension. . . ."

what comes next: Should Jesus — along with the psalmist in his agitation of soul (cf. Ps. 6:3, 4) — say, "Father, save me from this hour"?[183] But this would mean that Jesus still wants to withdraw from what he has understood and has presented to his disciples as the very intent of the hour that has now begun: the glorification of the Son of man in and by his death. Therefore he rejects the question he has posed with the firm assertion: "But[184] for this purpose," namely to take the road of terror and glorification, "I have come to this hour." Here, for all the agreement and solidarity, lies the difference between Jesus and the poet of Psalm 6. His entry into the hour is precisely why others before and after him have not prayed, and will not pray, in vain: "Father, save me from this hour!" Only in Jesus' death lies the security of their life. Only if the grain of wheat dies does it bear much fruit.

28a All that Jesus has to say in turning to the Father is, therefore, "Father, glorify thy name." This reduced to the minimum everything encompassed in the hour that has now come and the path that Jesus must walk: the revelation (the "name") of the glory of the Father. The Son of man is "now" glorified, and therein God is glorified (13:31f.): in, that is, the obedience of the Son to the charge of the Father (10:17), in the power the Son has been given over all flesh (17:1b, 2; 14:13), in the fruit of his death in the life of his own (15:8).

Here some interpreters see the Johannine version of the Synoptic struggle in Gethsemane. The Fourth Evangelist is said to have transposed the Gethsemane scene to Jesus' public activity in Jerusalem for compositional reasons. At the same time he radically refashioned and reinterpreted it in terms of his own theology, especially by stressing Jesus' glory and firm determination over against the Synoptic portrayal of Jesus' inner questioning and prayer that the "cup" might be removed.[185]

But it is doubtful that John should be understood here against the background of the Synoptic Gethsemane tradition and does not rather furnish evidence of proceeding independently of that tradition. The Johannine passage does have strikingly similar features (especially Jesus' agitation) and equally striking differences (not praying for the removal of the cup). But this need not mean that the similarity is based on dependence and that the difference derives from deliberate reinterpretation of the tradition we find in the Synoptics.

In regard to the most obvious similarity, Jesus' agitation, that John need not have depended on the Synoptics is clearly evident from his repeated stress in these chapters

---

183. That we are dealing here with a question and not a prayer to the Father seems to me — as it does to most present-day interpreters — in view of the immediately following "rectification," the explanation that the context itself indicates.

184. Others translate ἀλλά more firmly as a negative: "No!" Cf. BDF §448.4: "after a question to one's self as in classical [Greek]" (ἀλλά = "no"). So also Bultmann.

185. For this hypothesis, see the extensive treatment in Witkamp, *Jezus van Nazareth,* pp. 196ff., 217f.

on Jesus' inner agitation. For instance, 11:33, 35, 38 has no Synoptic parallel. And 13:21 uses the same word as 12:27, unlike the parallel in Mk. 14:18ff. The same is true of the differences: Jesus asks, "And what I shall I say? 'Father, save me from this hour'?" His negative answer to this question is not to be viewed as a negative reflex to the Synoptic tradition (Mk. 14:35). What shapes Jesus' prayer in John is not the Gethsemane prayer but Psalm 6, where the poet *does* add "Save me" to the expression of his inner agitation, which Jesus adopts in John. We see here not a tradition-historical refashioning of the image of Jesus but the voicing of the difference between the Son of God and all other children of God who in times of testing can only cry to be rescued from distress.

This is not to deny that the Fourth Gospel is different from the other Gospels, especially with regard to the hour, so emphatically announced here, of the glorification of the Son of man as *the* issue in Jesus' suffering and death. This will again be evident from the Johannine Gethsemane story (18:1ff.). But we are denying that these differences must be explained either by the Fourth Evangelist's supposed ignorance of the tradition from which he differs or by his need to reinterpret or correct that tradition. The Fourth Evangelist enjoyed much more latitude and freedom than he is allowed when he is considered dependent for all his narrative material on written tradition preceding him. Not only his theology but also his story (the story he tells as a transmitter of the tradition) bears the marks of a greater degree of independence than would be the case were he inclined — positively or negatively — to be shaped in his design and aims by what others wrote before him. The entire story of Jesus' suffering and death that now follows will bear witness to this in ever new ways.

28b The words following Jesus' prayer, "Then a voice came from heaven . . ." describes a mode of revelation that occurs only seldom in Scripture (in the New Testament: Mk. 1:11 par.; 9:7 par.; 2 Pt. 1:17; Ac. 9:4) outside apocalyptic literature (e.g., Rv. 10:4, 8; 11:12; 14:2). Later rabbinic literature frequently mentions the *bat̲ qôl* ("daughter of the voice"), but not, as here, in reference to God's direct speech but in reference to indirect perception or awareness of the voice of God as the echo ("daughter") of the word of God spoken earlier, a "voice" to which no direct authority was attributed but which was a substitute for the earlier direct speech of God through his prophets.[186]

Here the voice is clearly intended as God's direct answer to Jesus' prayer. It is unclear whether this voice was intelligible to people other than Jesus (see the comments on vss. 29 and 30). The content of the divine discourse is expressed tersely, in two verbs used absolutely: "I have glorified it, and I will glorify it again." As the object of this glorification we will, in view of vs. 28a, have to think primarily of the "name" of the Father, but then in the closest possible connection with the path that the Father has walked with his Son until now and will walk from now on. Scholars have occasionally connected "I have

---

186. On this see at length Strack/Billerbeck I, pp. 125-34.

glorified it" with a specific occurrence,[187] either the heavenly voice at Jesus' baptism or the Transfiguration. But John's Gospel does not mention those events. One can also think of Jesus' miracles in general as the witness borne to him by the Father (cf. 5:36, etc.). But the reference here is more likely to the whole of Jesus' earthly activity, in which the Father has glorified his name and Jesus has glorified the Father (cf. 17:4).[188] Similarly, "and I will glorify it again" refers to everything that the hour that has now come will prove to have in it in the way of the glorification of God's name in Jesus. In this answer the Father vouches for Jesus. Just as the Father glorified himself in Jesus' descent as the Son of man, so from now on he will make him known and vindicate him as his Son before the eyes of the world.[189]

29-30 Verse 29 serves as a transition to a broader complex of thought in that the "crowd," which has not been mentioned since vs. 18, reappears with a comment about "the voice from heaven." While for Jesus the voice was a clear answer to his preceding prayer, the crowd heard but did not understand what it said (cf. Ac. 9:8; 21:9). Some thought it was thunder, others the voice of an angel. Many interpreters believe that this is, as elsewhere, a description of the crowd's spiritual "deafness," its remoteness from the revelation event. Jesus, it is then said, takes issue with this posture by saying (vs. 30) that the voice "came for your sake, not for mine" and tries to call the crowd out of their incomprehension to faith.[190]

It is doubtful, however, whether that explanation stands up here. The reference here is not to the understanding of words, but to the sound of the voice. When Jesus says, "for your sake, not for mine," he is not thereby denying that the words were meant for him and is not holding the crowd answerable for what it could not understand. He tells the people, rather, that this "event of the voice" is not merely a matter between him and the Father but concerns his entire mission — now coming to its completion — to the world,[191] a mission in which they are all involved. Of this the voice they had heard was the signal.

31, 32 The all-encompassing event which thus begins now (with emphasis on the "now") is described as "the judgment of the world" and the ejection of "the ruler of the world." The reversal thus announced in eschatological and cosmic terms[192] is of course closely tied in with "the glorification

---

187. In view of the aorist ἐδόξασα.

188. Cf. BDF §332 on the "complexive aorist": "linear actions which (having been completed) are regarded as a whole."

189. Cf. Tsychido, "Tradition and Redaction in John 12:1-43," p. 610.

190. See, e.g., Schnackenburg, *Comm.* II, p. 390; Morris, *Comm.*, p. 597.

191. Cf. Blank, *Krisis*, p. 281: "the decisive act of revelation, in relation to which all that had happened until now was only the prelude."

192. Using the familiar distinction in Jewish eschatology between "this" world/aeon and the "coming" world/aeon.

of the Son of man," into whose hands, according to Daniel 7,[193] God will place dominion over all things, putting an end to the existing world power, which is hostile to him. However much, in the coming and work of Jesus, "this world" is the object of God's love (3:16) and the Son of man is therefore the great bringer of salvation (1:51; 6:27) who gives his life for the life of the world (6:51, 53; cf. 3:17; 12:47), this does not alter the fact that his coming also entails great crisis for the world. Because he has come as the light of the world, he brings out the sin of this world in its aversion and estrangement from God. His coming means judgment for those who love darkness rather than light (cf. 3:19ff.).

In the second part of vs. 31 all this is traced back to the great antithesis in the background of Jesus' coming and work, that of his power struggle with "the ruler of this world,"[194] a struggle that enters its decisive stage with Jesus' glorification as the Son of man. Although there have been allusions to this opposition (cf. 6:70; 8:44), from this point on, with the repeated mention of "the ruler of this world" (14:30; 16:11), it comes powerfully to the fore in its all-determining character. What is realized in Jesus' glorification as the Son of man, as is made evident in vs. 32, is nothing less than the transfer of power over the present God-hating world into the hands of the Son of man. Or, as our text has it, the casting out of this world's ruler.

It has been asked whether in this apocalyptic idiom the expression "being cast out" should be understood in a specific local sense.[195] It is difficult, however, to picture in spatial terms the place of Satan before and after the glorification of the Son of man, and there is legitimate doubt whether "cast out" consistently requires such a spatial conception (cf. 6:37). The real question is in what sense one can speak of the casting out, beginning with Jesus' imminent death, of the ruler of this world. Some scholars think that here, in mythological, cosmic terminology, the absolute and definitive decision is brought to expression, the decision with which the "now" of Jesus' passion and death confronts the human world. This interpretation is said to imply the

193. For this connection see, at greater length, the comments above on 1:50f. and 5:27f.

194. The expression ὁ ἄρχων τοῦ κόσμου, used of Satan, occurs in the New Testament only in John; cf., however, 2 Co. 4:4: ὁ θεὸς τοῦ αἰῶνος, and Ep. 2:2: ἄρχων τῆς ἐξουσίας τοῦ ἀέρος; cf. also 1 Co. 2:6-8. Also to be mentioned are related representations of the powers of darkness and the angel of light in the Qumran texts; see the overview in Schnackenburg, *Comm.* II, p. 391, where he points out the difference: the Qumran texts make an emphatic distinction between "the *now* of a time of war and the *then* of a time of salvation," but in John "the ruler of this world is judged and fundamentally stripped of his power in the eschatological 'hour,'" which has now begun with the exaltation of Jesus.

195. One can mention here those who have been expelled from the circle of disciples and also of Judas (13:30); others, with more justification, think of those who are expelled "from heaven" (cf. Lk. 10:18; Rv. 12:9f.; see also Jb. 1:6f.; Zc. 3:1). On this question see Blank, *Krisis,* pp. 282-84.

elimination of the "traditional eschatology of primitive Christianity."[196] But others believe that the judgment of [the ruler of] the world will only take place in the future and is only anticipated here in a prophetic vision.[197]

Neither position does justice to this statement within the overall context of the Fourth Gospel. One says that nothing "new" can ever follow the "now" of our text and that the Son of man's judgment of the (the ruler of) this world in the present "hour" is the last thing that can be said about it; this implies, as we have repeatedly asserted,[198] a rigorous narrowing of Johannine christology. On the other hand, the judgment of "this world" and the casting out of "this world's ruler" cannot be understood only in an anticipatory sense. The hour that has now begun is also that of "the coming of the ruler of this world" (14:30), that is, for that ruler's decisive assault on Jesus (cf. 13:12, 27; Lk. 22:31, 53); it is also the hour of the world in its unbelief and hostility (cf. 16:32f.). At the same time it is the hour of the world's judgment because by rejecting Jesus it rejects God's only begotten Son (3:18) and crucifies the Son of man (8:28; cf. 6:62; 19:37). And it is the hour for the expulsion of the ruler of this world because he has no grounds for an appeal against Jesus (cf. 14:30); in Jesus' exaltation he loses his claim on the world and is thus driven from the center of his power.

32-33 This last point is further explained in positive terms. The words beginning with "and I" form a double contrast with, and an explanation of, what precedes. In contrast with the expulsion of the ruler of this world, Jesus is lifted up from the earth as the Son of man and clothed with all power by the Father. In him and in the work he has accomplished, the way has been opened to a new rule, that of God's kingdom, in which the world is torn away from the power of Satan. For while judgment passes over this world, "his world," he who is lifted up from the earth draws all people to himself from within this new center of power, that is, by bringing them under his saving rule.

Everything is summed up here in a few key terms. What is at stake is the great reversal of power that determines all that is to come and concerns the entire human world ("all"). The expression "draw to myself" recalls 6:44, where the universal character of this salvific "drawing" of people out of their

---

196. Cf. Bultmann, *Comm.*, p. 431:

The significance of the hour of decision is thus described in the cosmological terminology of the Gnostic myth. If in the Evangelist's mind the myth has lost its mythological content and become historicised, his language on the other hand serves to eliminate the traditional eschatology of primitive Christianity. The turn of the ages results now. . . . Since this "now" the "prince of the world" is judged (16.11); the destiny of man has become definitive. . . . No future in this world's history can bring anything new, and all apocalyptic pictures of the future are empty dreams.

197. This proleptic understanding is held by T. Preiss, *La vie en Christ. La justification dans la pensée johannique,* 1951, pp. 54f.; see also Blank, *Krisis,* pp. 283, 285.

198. See, e.g., pp. 199f., 231.

weakness is also pivotal and where its realization is further explicated. Here the "all" also reflects the coming of the Greeks as the signal of a new dispensation (vs. 23) in which salvation will impart itself to "all" without distinction of people or race and gather them into a new unity (cf. 10:16; 11:52).

To all this the Evangelist adds still one more sentence, one of special significance for an understanding of this great passage and specifically of the nature of Jesus' elevation: "This he said to show[199] by what death[200] he was to die." As in 3:14 and 8:26, he is referring here to Jesus' elevation *on the cross* as the manner and way, as well as the secret and power, of his elevation. The idea that this elevation therefore relates only to Jesus' death on the cross and not to his subsequent glorification[201] is rightly rejected by most interpreters, among other reasons because by this the cross would become too much an isolated event, whereas, as is evident from vss. 23ff., 27ff., it is included in the whole of "the glorification of the Son of man." Moreover, the meaning of "elevation from the earth" (vs. 23) is certainly broader than elevation onto the cross. Jesus' "drawing" all people to himself therefore occurs not only by the attractive power that issues from the cross, however great an element this is (see below). He draws them to himself *from heaven.* Therein lies the transcendence of his person and work as the Son of man who came down from heaven and ascends to heaven (3:14). But it is no less true that the secret and nature of Jesus' elevation, of his victory over "the ruler of this world" as also of his power to draw all people to himself, lies in his elevation *onto the cross,* that is, in his obedience to the Father, which unites heaven and earth, and in his love to his own and all the world. In this, in the spiritual struggle with the transpersonal "worldly" power of alienation and the "slavery" of sin, Jesus overcame the (ruler of this) world (cf. 16:33), opened the way to the Father, and established a new center of power from which, as the crucified Lord, he draws to himself all who believe in him and brings them into this kingdom of love and hope for the future.

Elsewhere in the New Testament as well victory over the hostile powers is related to the death of Christ on the cross: God "reconciled to himself all things, whether on earth or in the heaven, making peace by the blood of his cross" (Col. 1:20); he thus "disarmed the principalities and powers and made a public example of them [in their impotence], triumphing over them [binding them to his triumphal chariot] in him" (Col. 2:14f.); the hostile world power is stripped of every claim that might enable it to subject the world estranged from God to its rule of slavery and death (cf. Ep. 2:14ff.).

199. σημαίνων here means "signifying," "indicating," "announcing" (cf. K. Rengstorff, *TDNT* VII, p. 264).

200. ποίῳ θανάτῳ ἤμελλεν ἀποθνῄσκειν.

201. As is asserted in the important work of W. Thüsing, *Die Erhöhung und Verherrlichung Jesu in Johannesevangelium,* 1960, p. 12.

34 To the crowd, however, the whole idea of a Son of man elevated to, and operating from, heaven is alien. They respond to Jesus' words with an appeal to the law: "The Messiah remains forever." They speak of the Messiah because they assume (rightly) that in speaking of "the Son of man" Jesus is referring to the Messiah that they expect. The figure of the Son of man as an eschatological bringer of salvation is clearly not familiar to them, at least they did not know the object of their messianic expectations under this name.[202] In any case, if Jesus is referring to the Messiah, how can he speak of having to[203] be lifted up? For the content of their objection and the appeal to the law (i.e., Scripture; cf. 10:34; 15:25), scholars usually think[204] of the messianically interpreted words of Ps. 89:36, "his line will endure forever,"[205] which in the eschatology of that time was evidently understood as referring to the permanent presence of the coming Messiah, which was not compatible with being taking up or elevated (to heaven) as Jesus spoke of it. Hence their question: "Who is this Son of man [of whom you speak]?" Or "What kind of Son of man are you speaking of?"[206]

35-36 Jesus' reply is very characteristic of the Fourth Gospel. Again, as in 7:33; 9:4f.; 11:9f.; 12:8; 13:33; 14:19; 16:16ff., he brings up the limited character of his earthly existence and the imminent end of the time in which he is the light of the world. While in 9:4f.; 11:9f. this is a motive for himself and his disciples to do the works of God, here he, in warning ("lest," vs. 35) and encouragement ("that," vs. 36), also speaks to the crowd of the short time that the light still shines among them; and he urges them, as long as they "have" (cf. vs. 8) the light, to

---

202. On this question see at greater length de Jonge, *Jesus: Stranger from Heaven and Son of God*, pp. 94f. Whether the Jews, whose concept of the Messiah was bound up with the expectation of the Davidic king, also linked the Messiah with the (apocalyptic) figure of the Son of Man is very uncertain. With respect to this de Jonge writes: " 'Son of man' is only used by Jesus himself, and to the Jews who refer to it in 12:34 this expression does not convey a clear picture." We do, to be sure, find in Jewish literature a number of cases where "Messiah" and "Son of man" occur together (see also de Jonge in *TDNT* IX, pp. 510ff., and especially Justin Martyr, *Dialogue with Trypho* 32.1), but according to de Jonge "the combination is brought about in different ways and we cannot speak of any fixed concept. . . . It is by no means certain that the Fourth Gospel presupposes the presence of such ideas in the minds of the interlocutors of the crowd. It is only interested in Jesus' singular use of the expression 'Son of Man' and in the fundamental difference between his teaching and current expectations connected with Messiah" (*Jesus: Stranger from Heaven and Son of God*, pp. 95f.). For the identification of the Messiah with the Son of Man see also W. Bittner, "Gott-Menschensohn-Davidsohn. Eine Untersuchung zur Traditionsgeschichte von Daniel 7,13ff.," *Freiburger Zeitschrift für Philosophie und Theologie* 32 (1985), pp. 343-72.

203. In what precedes Jesus has not mentioned this "must." The crowd could rightly speak of this, however, meaning that the Son of man had to fulfill his "program" of salvation. In that sense 3:14 also speaks of the Son of man as he who "must be" lifted up.

204. So especially since W. C. Van Unnik, "The Quotation from the Old Testament in John 12:34," *NovT* 3 (1959), pp. 174-79.

205. τὸ σπέρμα αὐτοῦ μένει εἰς τὸν αἰῶνα (LXX).

206. τίς is not so much an inquiry into the identity of the Son of man — the crowd rightly equated him with the Messiah here — as into his nature.

walk in it, lest the darkness overtake them so that they do not know where they are going. Vs. 36 repeats "while you have the light, walk in the light," but now with a promise: "that you may become [or be] children of the light." All the images and motifs are found earlier (cf. 9:5f.; 10:9f.; 8:12) but here are intended as Jesus' final word to the crowd: "Having said this, Jesus departed and hid himself from them" (cf. 8:59), which concludes this pericope.

It has been said that Jesus fails to answer the crowd's objection (vs. 34) with these words. This is correct in that he says nothing further about his coming elevation as the Son of man but restricts himself to what he still is for the people in the present. Still, this response does contain a reply to their question, in terms of both content and terminology. It can hardly be accidental that while the crowd, appealing to the law, speaks of the Messiah "remaining forever," Jesus puts all possible stress on "the short time" he is still with them as the light of the world and on the necessity of believing in that light now while that is still possible. With that he lays bare, at this moment of the decisive turn in his existence (vs. 23), the great difference between their messianic expectation and his mission as the Son of God. This contrast would assert itself again in the conflict between the church and the synagogue, which is doubtless why the Evangelist stresses it again in this final confrontation between Jesus and the crowd. For what gives Jesus' messiahship its absolute ("remaining forever") significance does not come from the endlessness of his earthly kingship or even his heavenly mode of existence far above all earthly limitation, but the way Israel and all the world must deal with him, the Son of man descended from heaven, life for the world and the light of humanity (1:1; 6:51, etc.). It is on that basis that Jesus, in his final word to the crowd ("while you have the light"), appeals to them. Just as for him there would be no ascent to heaven without the preceding descent from heaven (3:13), so also no one will know the heavenly who has not known and believed the earthly while he is "still among them." This in no way nullifies the word of the law that the Messiah will remain forever; in the revelation of the Son of man it even gains a meaning that far transcends the limits of the Davidic kingship (vss. 49f.). But it is only the incarnation of the Word and the descent of the Son of man in and from which the Messiah's "remaining forever" can be known and understood.

12:37-50

A Retrospective: Israel's Unbelief and Jesus' Self-Revelation

The final section of ch. 12 is divided into two parts. The first (vss. 37-43) recapitulates the unbelief that met Jesus' public activity, the second (vss. 44-50) Jesus' self-revelation as the one sent by the Father, directed not to his own honor but solely to that of the Father and to human salvation.

By itself this double pericope fits very well in the structure of the story
— after Jesus' final words to the crowd (vs. 36b) and before Jesus takes the
initiative to bid farewell to his disciples (13:1). But in another sense these verses
sharply interrupt the ongoing story. The unqualified "they" in vs. 37 may seem
to connect with "the crowd" in vs. 34, but there is an emphatic difference in
content and tone. While Jesus, following his entry into Jerusalem, has urged
the crowd to believe in him and to walk in the light while he is still with them,
vss. 37-43 are limited to a lament over the unbelief of the people and to a
description of the hardening revealed in this unbelief as a fulfillment of prophecy. One gets the impression that the passage was written from a certain
historical distance and added later by the Evangelist, that here, perhaps because
of the increasingly manifest rejection of Jesus as the Messiah of Israel in his
own day, the Evangelist felt the need, at this turning point in his story, to express
the deep seriousness and continuing incongruity of this general unbelief.

As for vss. 44-50, they are also not connected with the historical situation
of vs. 36b. Some scholars do not regard vss. 37-43 and 44-50 as an original
unit but as a later interpolation, originally not intended for this context, that
summarizes Jesus' preaching. Some see another "layer" in the genesis of the
text, discernible by its unique style and attributable to an author other than the
Evangelist.[207] Others believe these verses are displaced from elsewhere in the
Gospel.[208] Our own conclusion is that these two recapitulations do belong
together (see the exegesis below) and were therefore — perhaps later — inserted *together* at this place.

12:37-43

Israel's Unbelief

37-38 Looking back on the result of Jesus' activity among his people, the
Evangelist can only arrive at the conclusion that "they [the people in general]
did not believe in him." That is his concluding judgment about the basic and
lasting[209] negative attitude of the people to Jesus, and that despite Jesus'
revelation of power among them.

Already in the prologue the Evangelist referred to this mysterious negative

---

207. So M. É. Boismard, "Le caractère adventice de Jo. XII,45-50," in *Sacra Pagina II,*
1959, pp. 189ff. Schnackenburg, *Comm.* II, pp. 420f., argues against this position.

208. So, e.g., Bultmann, who regards these verses as part of a longer discourse on the light
consisting of 8:12; 12:44-50; 8:21-29; 12:34-36; and 10:19-21. "Needless to say, there is no real
proof for these ingenious proposals" (Brown, *Comm.* I, p. 490; Brown himself has another
"relocation" proposal).

209. ἐπίστευον, durative imperfect.

reaction to the coming of the light into the world (1:10, 11). Here, at the end, it is especially the many[210] signs Jesus has done "before their eyes"[211] that he brings into play as the great motive that should have prompted them to change their minds (cf. the concluding dialogue of Jesus with the Jewish leaders, 10:37ff.; cf. also 15:24; 20:30, 31).

The Evangelist does not stop with this observation. As in Jesus' coming and work, so also in the unbelief underlying the people's rejection of Jesus, the Evangelist sees fulfillment of prophecy, here the word of the prophet Isaiah (53:1): "Lord, who has believed our report, and to whom has the arm of the Lord been revealed?" The prophet here complains to God[212] that hardly anyone ("who?") has believed what the people (himself included) have heard[213] and what has been revealed to them as proof of God's almighty power ("the arm of the Lord," Dt. 5:15). And, as is evident from the final clause in vs. 38 ("that the word might be fulfilled"), the Evangelist intends not merely to refer to the similarity between unbelief in Isaiah's day and in Jesus' day, but rather places this unbelief in the light of God's ongoing dealings with his backsliding people in the whole history of revelation (cf., e.g., also Dt. 29:3, 4).

Verses **39-40** further elucidate this, first by characterizing this unbelief as inability to believe (cf. 5:44; 8:43; also 6:44, 65). For this latter point the Evangelist appeals[214] to another statement by the same prophet, Is. 6:10, which is repeatedly cited in the New Testament (Mt. 13:13ff.; cf. Mk. 4:12; Lk. 8:10; Ac. 28:26f.; Ro. 11:18). Here we have an abbreviated version of the original[215] that emphasizes that the blinding of eyes and the hardening of hearts are a work of God himself.[216] Unbelief is not thereby blamed on God in a predestinarian sense, but is rather described as a punishment from God: he abandons unbelieving people to themselves, thus confirming them in their evil, blinding their eyes

210. τοσαῦτα.
211. ἔμπροσθεν αὐτῶν.
212. κύριε, at least in the LXX. Not in the Masoretic Text.
213. τῇ ἀκοῇ ἡμῶν is difficult to translate. It is clear that what is meant is not "hearing" but "what was heard." Some simply translate "preaching" (e.g., Bultmann, *Comm.,* p. 453). But the reference in this connection (see vs. 40, as also the words ἔμπροσθεν αὐτῶν) is particularly to the revelation of God as that which could be heard and seen by all. "Our," then, refers not to the subject of the preaching but to those who heard the Word of God and to the prophet as the "pioneer" listener; see also the commentaries on Is. 53:1 and Ro. 10:16 (e.g., my *Aan de Romeinen,* 1977, pp. 241ff.).
214. διὰ τοῦτο is explicated by the following ὅτι clause (cf. 5:16, 18; 8:47; 10:17; 12:18).
215. Both of the Masoretic Text and of the LXX. Some scholars say it cannot therefore be from the same author as vs. 38, which is entirely in conformity with the LXX. But the freedom with which the Evangelist cites the original in cases like vs. 40 can hardly serve as proof that elsewhere he could not quote a text entirely in conformity with the LXX, and conversely.
216. Specifically by the use of the active voice: "He [God] has blinded. . . ," where the LXX has the less direct passive: "[the heart of the people] has become hardened." The Masoretic Text has the imperative (directed to the prophet): "Make the heart of this people insensitive."

and hardening their hearts, as a result of which whatever God gives them to see and hear can no longer lead to salvation, that is, to repentance and healing.

That all this is in direct fulfillment of the words of Isaiah is made evident in vs. **41**: "This the prophet said because[217] he saw his glory and spoke of him." "His" refers to Christ — it is "his glory" — as the concluding words of vs. 41 confirm: "spoke of him." The Evangelist does not mean that Isaiah already foresaw Jesus' (later) glory, but that the glory of God as the prophet foresaw it in his vision was no other than that which the Son of God had with the Father before the world was and that was to be manifested before the eyes of all in the incarnation of the Word (17:4; 1:14, 18). For that reason ("because") the prophetic judgment of hardening on account of the unbelief of the people was fully applicable to the rejection of Jesus by Israel, and even came to fulfillment therein.

By placing the controversy between Jesus and the people in the light of prophecy, the Evangelist traces the glory of Christ back to its ultimate preexistent state and reduces the blinding of the people to its final seriousness, to the divinely ordained judgment on the rejection of his Son (cf. 3:18f.). He allows this judgment to stand in all its severity without adding to it or subtracting from it. But he does this as an Evangelist. He does not present this judgment to his readers as the unalterable end of the decree that lies behind it. He rather cites from Scripture a prophetic oracle that has not lost its meaning but rather comes to its full significance and supreme relevance precisely in the rejection of Jesus. It does so in accordance with the nature of prophecy as the word of God that permanently goes out to the world, a word that, even when it announces God's judgment on the world that has become estranged from him, is never his final word, by which he would be turning definitively from the world and leaving it no future. He seeks to picture before the world's eyes, and cause it to experience, the futurelessness of its existence apart from him — as a final call to return to him (cf. Is. 6:11-13). The Evangelist could not have conveyed to Israel a more severe judgment or made a stronger appeal than by thus calling to mind these words from the heart of Israel's prophecy.

42-43 But all that is not the whole story. In vs. 37 the Evangelist speaks in general of the people's failure to believe in Jesus. In vs. 42 he returns to the issue of belief with a "nevertheless,"[218] which may at first seem to be a correction but is actually a comment that does not relativize the preceding but rather completes it: despite the general judgment in vs. 37, "many, even of the

---

217. Some textual witnesses have ὅτε in place of ὅτι, probably because ὅτε is easier to explain. Precisely for that reason, however, and because it has the better manuscript support, ὅτι should be considered original. But interpretation of it is rather difficult.

218. ὅμως, "all the same, nevertheless, yet," used rarely in this sense in the New Testament, reinforced here by the adversative (frequent in John) μέντοι, "all the same, however."

authorities, believed in him." The Evangelist thus undoubtedly also responds to the positive reactions of the people to Jesus' public ministry — reactions repeatedly mentioned in the Gospel and frequently (as here) described as "faith" responses (2:23; 7:31; 8:30; 10:42; 11:45; 12:11), usually evoked by Jesus' miracles but also by the impresssion that his words made on many people (e.g., 8:30). Among these "many" he specifically mentions "authorities," by which are meant Jewish authorities in general and, we may assume, members of the Sanhedrin in particular (cf., e.g., 3:1; 7:45, 50).[219] But he immediately adds that "for fear of the Pharisees they did not confess it, lest they should be put out of the synagogue."

This ties in closely with what has been related in 7:31f., 45ff.; 9:32. There, too, "many believed in Jesus," and measures were taken at the initiative of the Pharisees by "the chief priests and Pharisees" (the Sanhedrin) against Jesus, culminating in the agreement that anyone confessing him as Christ was to be (declared) an excommunicate from the synagogue (see the comments above on 9:22).[220] The reference is not to an established disciplinary measure to be applied to members of the synagogue to bring them to orthodoxy. Such an excommunicate was, rather, in the position of those who lived outside the synagogue community (Gentiles, heretics, and apostates) and were denied all recognition as Jews (9:34;

219. καὶ ἐκ τῶν ἀρχόντων πολλοί does not limit the "many" to the authorities but includes them "also."

220. In conjunction with the "chief priests" the Pharisees over and again function as the highest Jewish authority in the Fourth Gospel (7:32, 45; 11:47, 57; 18:3). Formally speaking, Pharisees did not belong to the Sanhedrin as Pharisees but as members of the class of scribes. But this distinction, here and elsewhere, is not always observed. Unlike the Synoptics, John consistently speaks of Pharisees and never of scribes.

The frequent mention of the Pharisees in the Fourth Gospel is often viewed as an argument (among others) that the picture given, for example, here and in chs. 7 and 9 does not convey the historical situation at the time of Jesus but rather that of, on the one hand, the Pharisaic rabbinate as it developed in Jamnia in the years 70-100 and asserted itself as the spiritual leadership of the Jewish people and, on the other, of the measures taken against the Christian church (see also the next note). The power attributed to the Pharisees in the Johannine texts is said to be clearly anachronistic and to project later developments back into the life of Jesus. Witkamp, for example, writes in connection with this text: "The idea that ἄρχοντες would be afraid of being expelled from the synagogue by Pharisees is inconceivable at the time of the second temple" (Jezus van Nazareth, pp. 343f.).

But here (cf. 7:32) the Pharisees act primarily in their capacity as custodians of Jewish orthodoxy, which explains why people were afraid of them when it came to confessing Jesus as the Messiah. Admittedly they also functioned as the executive authorities in the Sanhedrin, but they did so in conjunction with the chief priests. But how could they do that at any time other than when the second temple still existed? And where, then, is the anachronism? This is not to deny that the frequent mention of the Pharisees (and not of the Sadducees, for example) may be linked with their predominant position in the synagogue Judaism of the time when John wrote his Gospel. But this evidently did not prevent him from writing in the correct historical perspective about the Pharisees of Jesus' time in regard to, for example, their constant cooperation with the chief priests.

cf. also Lk. 6:22).[221] In the expanding conflict between the Jews and Jesus, therefore, much was already at stake (cf. 9:22), not only for him but also for those who confessed him as the Messiah, which kept many from openly taking their stand with him (cf. 7:13, 32; 9:22, 23). This situation was to repeat itself over and over in the future and could potentially cost a disciple of Jesus his or her life (cf. 16:2; Mt. 10:21, 22; Ac. 5:33; 8:1ff.; 9:1ff., etc.).

It is against this background that one must understand the severe verdict that the Evangelist pronounces over those who "for fear of the Pharisees" refused to align themselves openly with Jesus: "for they loved human praise more than God's praise."[222] Still the words in which this verdict is couched also indicate that more is at issue here than the traumatic experiences of the church with the later rabbinic synagogue and the moral half-heartedness of crypto-believers. In fact the Evangelist merely repeats the words that Jesus addressed to his opponents from the beginning: "How can you believe when you accept glory from one another and do not seek the glory that comes from the only God?" (5:44). These words do not illumine just a particular historical situation. They give expression, rather, to the radical view of humanity — the anthropological antithesis — that governs Jesus' confrontation with the Jews — the crowd as well as the authorities — from the beginning (cf. 2:24ff.; 3:3).[223] But this antithesis is no more than the counterpart of the absolute manner in which Jesus by his coming into the world represents the salvation revealed to Israel (4:22). He not only placed a radical choice before people but also pointed to the source of that choice, the reality "from above" that transcends the human inability and unwillingness to believe. The last word here, then, is not that of Israel's unbelief but of Jesus' self-witness as the one sent by the Father (vss. 44-50).

12:44-50

The Nature of Jesus' Self-Revelation

Jesus' summary of the witness concerning himself is introduced by these solemn words: "Jesus, however, cried out and said. . . ." This refers less to the volume

---

221. The word ἀποσυνάγωγος, which is attested only in John, refers to an already existing position that confessors of Jesus might get into (γένεσθαι, 9:22; 12:42) or be brought into (ποιεῖν, 16:2) and says nothing about the way in which this was effected. See Strack/Billerbeck IV, p. 331. Against the conception of J. L. Martyn and others that this decision refers in reality to much later measures taken by the Jewish leadership in Jamnia to arrive at a definitive split between church and synagogue, see the objections in the comments above on 9:22. For the ongoing discussion, in which other objections are advanced against this hypothesis, see also D. M. Smith, "Judaism and the Gospel of John," in *Jews and Christians,* ed. J. H. Charlesworth, 1990, pp. 76-99, particularly pp. 83ff.

222. τοῦ θεοῦ, subjective genitive; cf. 5:44: παρὰ τοῦ μόνου θεοῦ.

223. On this antithesis see at length pp. 287-330 above.

of his voice than to his act of openly testifying within the hearing of all (cf.
1:15; 7:28, 37).[224] The "however" ties this to what precedes: whatever Jesus'
opponents may say about him, there can be no uncertainty, given Jesus' own
witness, about who he is and why he has come.

This connection is also clear from the content of the summary. It contains
nothing that has not been said earlier.[225] But the tone and the selection of
material, from beginning to end, clearly intend to resist any misunderstanding
of Jesus' person and the purpose of his coming (vss. 47, 49: "I did not come
to . . . but to . . . ," "I have not spoken on my own authority"). The specific
idea resisted is that his coming took place at his own initiative, was based on
his own authority, and was directed toward his own glory. Over against this
Jesus sets his subjection to the command of his Father and his sole motive: the
salvation of the world.

Verse **44** sums this up at the outset. With "whoever believes in me,
believes not in me but in him who sent me," Jesus means that when he asks
people to believe, he is not thinking of himself and his own authority but rather
that of the one who sent him.[226] Similarly vs. **45**: "whoever sees me [in the
miracles I performed] sees [the glory of] him who sent me," whose agent is
all that I am.

Verse **46** also makes the point that the purpose of Jesus' coming does not
lie within himself, but is tied to his relation to the world. "As for me ["I" in
an emphatic position], I have come as light into the world with the purpose
[and no other] that everyone who believes in me should not remain in darkness"
(cf. 8:12). Again, this is for "whoever believes in me," but the reason for the
saying is not Jesus but the person who walks in darkness.

47   Therefore if anyone hears Jesus' sayings but does not "keep" (or
"observe") them, then Jesus[227] is not the one who judges that person, "for I
did not come to judge the world but to save the world." These last words again
repeat a point made earlier on several occasions (cf. 3:17; 8:15). Jesus is thus
perhaps responding to the charge that his preaching was harsh and rigorous,
hence arrogant. Still, he came into the world, even if he pronounces judgment
on the negative attitude his opponents are adopting toward him, not to condemn
them but to lead them from darkness to light (cf. 8:12, 15). That is the grand
premise of this entire Gospel (cf. 3:16).

48   Nonetheless, one who rejects Jesus and does not receive his sayings

224. "The verb χράζειν . . . is best rendered as crying in the sense of proclamation"
(W. Grundmann, *TDNT* III, p. 901).

225. See, e.g., the parallels noted in the margin in Nestle-Aland.

226. In the nature of the case the antithetical construction "believes not in me but . . ." is
not absolute (cf. 14:1) but a rhetorical device (a *mašal*) that powerfully stresses the point at issue
(cf. the comments on 6:27; see also BDF §448.1).

227. ἐγώ, again emphatic.

cannot do so with impunity: such a person "has a judge," namely in "the word that I have spoken," which will "in the last day," when judgment will be rendered, testify against that person. Elsewhere where the Gospel mentions the resurrection from the dead and the judgment, it does say that the Father has given all judgment to the Son (5:22) because he is the Son of man (5:27). But Jesus' coming into the world has a different purpose. Before ascending to heaven and receiving power over all things from the Father, the Son of man must first descend from heaven to save the world from judgment.

49 Therefore again we hear: "I have not spoken on my own authority." This statement indicates that Jesus' word, as the Father's word, will mean condemnation for those who reject it (cf. 5:45). Stated positively, "the Father, who sent me, has himself commanded me what to say."[228] It is not Jesus but the Father himself who defines the purpose of Jesus' mission and the content of his message.

50 And Jesus "knows" (in virtue of his union with the Father and of what he has "heard" from him; cf. 5:30; 8:20, 40; 15:15; 3:22) that that commandment "is eternal life,"[229] that it seeks to create life out of death and cause light to arise in darkness. That and no other is the commandment, the charge, he has received from the Father and with which he has complied: "What I say, therefore, I say as the Father has bidden me."

Basic to this entire self-witness are Jesus' absolute mission-consciousness and his oneness with the Father. But whereas elsewhere — against those who accuse him of blasphemy — he speaks at length of that Son-to-Father relationship (see especially 5:19-30), here he deliberately subordinates his person to his message in order to cut off any notion that in asking people to believe his words he is seeking to gratify his own ego, claiming something beyond the authority that the Father has given him, or seeking for himself something other than to be the light of the world.

In that emphasis on the message lies the connection with vss. 37-43. The summary of Jesus' witness concerning himself in vss. 44-50 is written from a specific perspective and is clearly defined by that perspective, which is that of Jesus' self-vindication over against the unbelief described in vss. 37-43. What offended "the Jews" and caused them to reject him as Israel's Messiah and God's Son (and was to remain the main issue in the continuing conflict of the church with Judaism and the world) was the absolute authority with which he proclaimed to them the Word of God as the only way to life. When in reaction

---

228. For this recurrent "not of myself" motif and its implications, see at length the comments above on 5:19.

229. The equation of "commandment" and "life" established by the copula is "Johannine and certainly Semitizing, style (cf. 3:19; 17:3; 1 Jn. 3:23; 4:10; 5:9, 11, 14)" (Schnackenburg, *Comm.* II, p. 424; cf. also Dt. 32:47).

to their unbelief Jesus steps back in favor of his words and deeds (cf. 10:34ff.), he does not thereby cancel himself out to make the way of faith easier for them. He confronts them, rather, all the more forcefully with the truth of his words and of his whole mission as that of the light of the world (cf. 7:17ff.). And he does this not because the significance of his person only consists in or is based on his words and works but because as the Son of God, in his union with the Father, he can only be known from his divinely originated words (6:68) and from his works as the embodiment, the incarnation, of God's love for the world (3:16).

The Last Supper Conversations
with the Disciples

13:1

Transition

13:1 forms a clear transition to a new section of the Gospel. Chs. 11 and 12 increasing lead into the Passion narrative, especially from 12:23 on, and here the narrative reaches the meal on the evening prior to the day of Jesus' death. The focus is, at last, on Jesus' relation to his disciples, in regard to both what is about to happen (ch. 13) and the time following his departure (chs. 14–17). Thus, as in the Synoptics, the meal referred to in 13:2 is the opening act of the story of Jesus' death (see the comments on 13:2ff.), but, unlike the Synoptics, John has five chapters of Jesus' farewell conversations with his disciples during the meal. These conversations are, in ch. 13, occasioned first by the footwashing and then by the identification and dismissal of the betrayer. But they continue and come to focus (chs. 14–17) on Jesus' departure and the time thereafter. These chapters, as Jesus' testament to his disciples, form a clearly distinct whole in the Gospel, the composition of which again calls for further discussion. Only in 18:1 does the narrative of Jesus' death, begun in 13:1, continue.

13:1-3 provides a double introduction, which is given a solemn tone by its shaping in two parallel sentences. Here the Evangelist indicates the framework within which he wants us to interpret this entire story, beginning with the footwashing. A number of the Gospel's themes reach their point of culmination in ch. 13.[1] The two parts of this introduction have been seen as proof that

---

1. See G. D. Cloete, *Hemelse Solidariteit. In Weg in die relasie tussen christologie en soteriologie in die Vierde Evangelie,* 1980, p. 104, cf. p. 114.

various redactors have been at work here. But however closely connected the two parts are, the import of vs. 1 is broader than that of vss. 2f.: the first sentence ("having loved . . . he loved them to the end") relates to the whole of Jesus' suffering and death, which is about to be described, while "Jesus, knowing . . ." in vs. 3 relates especially to the last meal, referring to it as a symbolic overture to and anticipation of the chain of events announced in vs. 1.

"Before the feast of the Passover" resumes the story interrupted in 12:37-40; the repeated reference to the approaching feast (cf. 11:55; 12:1) now indicates that the story has entered its decisive phase.[2] Although the sentence construction is somewhat unclear, the reference to the feast is clearly not intended to date Jesus' love for his disciples to the time before the Passover[3] but to point to Jesus' foreknowledge of what awaits him at the Passover. When we are told next that he (then) "loved his own to the end," the reference is only to the fullness of Jesus' love as it manifested itself from that moment:[4] it was love to the last breath and love in its highest intensity.[5]

The dominant thought in this overture is that of the Son sent by the Father into the world and now returning to him. The Son is the focus of the Passion story, the one into whose hands the Father has given all things. He knows his own "hour." He is not caught by surprise or driven off course by it; for him it is rather the sign to take the initiative, to break through the boundaries of this world, and thus to return to the place he came from and to the Father who sent him. A grander opening of the story of Jesus' death is hardly imaginable.

At the same time — and this is no less remarkable for an understanding of the Johannine Passion story — 13:1 places all that follows in the perspective of Jesus' love for his own. This is all the more striking because until now Jesus' love has not been so emphatically identified as the fundamental motive for his actions. That it always has been cannot be doubted (cf. ch. 10). Still, it is the Passion story of which this love is the great theme; there it is seen as the progressive and cumulative motive, that is, as love *to the end* and *to the limit*.

---

2. πρό here does not imply indeterminate duration or stress that the feast had not yet occurred. It emphasizes, rather, the feast's imminence.

3. Bultmann even writes: "to date ἀγαπήσας . . . εἰς τὸ τέλος ἠγάπησεν would be absurd." He thinks, however, that this objection remains even when one links, as we have, πρὸ τῆς ἑορτῆς τοῦ πάσχα with εἰδώς because — though this link would be meaningful in the subordinate clause — the connection with the main verb would indirectly persist (it "would come back in the end to a dating of εἰς τέλος ἠγάπησεν"). For that reason he wants — by a complicated surgical procedure — to break open the entire text as we have it in 13:1-3 (*Comm.,* p. 403). But ἠγάπησεν does not coincide temporally with πρὸ τῆς ἑορτῆς but speaks rather of progression in Jesus' display of love, based on the starting point indicated in εἰδώς.

4. ἠγάπησεν refers not only to Jesus' love as a state of mind but also to the concrete expression of this love in the footwashing and in his self-giving "to the end"; on the whole matter, see also W. K. Grossouw, "A Note on John XIII 1-3," *NovT* 8 (1966), pp. 124-31.

5. εἰς τέλος has both temporal and intensive meaning.

Though this motive of love does not compete with the motive of glory — one can speak of the glory and power of Jesus' love in his suffering and death — it does significantly qualify it.

Some have thought that in John's Gospel Jesus' glory receives so much stress, including in the Passion story, that the Gospel can hardly be said to be free of a kind of Docetism, that is, that Jesus' suffering is not real suffering in John, that the cross is not Jesus' humiliation but only his exaltation, and that therefore his "going out of this world" consisted merely in a triumphal departure to where he was before.[6] But this is a one-sided rendering of the concept of glory, one that sharply curtails the meaning of the Gospel as a whole and of its Passion story in particular. Precisely when Jesus knows that his hour has come and when he becomes more acutely conscious of his departure out of this world, his love goes out, as never before, to "his own who are *in* the world." His hour was also their hour, the hour of decision for them as well. Soteriology — Jesus' death — is completely joined with christology — with glory — and gives that glory its ambivalence (as we have pointed out)[7] as elevation onto the cross, as the ascent of him who desended to the very depths of this world (cf. 3:13).[8]

The story that follows, the footwashing, is characteristic and revelatory of this complex of themes in vss. 1-3.

13:2-38

The Final Meal

Much has been written about the origin and the literary and material unity of this story.[9] It occurs only here in the Gospels. Those who deny to the Fourth Evangelist all independent knowledge of Jesus' life trace this story to the tradition, whether oral or fixed in one or more written sources, on which the Evangelist is said to have been dependent for his Passion narrative. The narrative as we have it before us is further said to be the Johannine rendering of that tradition. But because evidence is lacking, discussion of this issue remains no more than a working with unknowns. Of more importance is the similarity, noted by many interpreters, between this narrative and certain pronouncements of Jesus in the story of the last meal in Lk. 22:24ff. There, too, Jesus admonishes his disciples not to elevate themselves above each other

6. See the comments above on 12:24f. (on the views of Käsemann, Nicholson, and others).

7. See the comments on 12:23ff. above.

8. See Cloete, *Hemelse Solidariteit.*

9. On the history of exegesis, see especially the important work by G. Richter, *Die Fußwaschung im Johannesevangelium. Geschichte ihrer Deutung,* 1967.

and makes himself an example of one who serves: "For who is greater, one seated at the table or one who serves? Is it not the one seated at the table? But I am among you as one who serves" (Lk. 22:27). This is all the more remarkable because the word "serve" expressly marks Jesus' servanthood among his own as a slave's service *at table,* as in Lk. 12:37; 17:8, where, as in Jn. 13:4, we also read of the servant at the table "girding himself." Some therefore believe that Lk. 22:24ff. underlies the entire narrative of the foot-washing.[10] Most interpreters, however, reject such a genetic link.[11] The service at table that Jesus speaks of is not footwashing but waiting on guests (cf. Lk. 17:8; 12:37). The Johannine story has no reference to serving at table, and Jesus acts first and explains his action only later.[12] Accordingly, everything points rather to the presence of an original story of a footwashing *during* (or after) the meal (vs. 4), which was certainly unusual.

A more difficult question concerns the unity of the narrative: Do Jesus' dispute with Peter (vss. 6ff.) and Jesus' interpretation of the footwashing (vss. 12ff.) belong together? Many interpreters regard these two parts of the story as giving two different meanings to the footwashing (see further below).

Another preliminary question we cannot ignore at this point is that of the character and date of the meal mentioned in vs. 2, a question that coincides with the still unresolved controversy over the dating of Jesus' death in the Fourth Gospel. It is certain that this meal occurred on the Thursday evening that preceded the day of Jesus' death, Friday, and was therefore the meal that the Synoptic Gospels place on the eve of Jesus' death. This is clear, despite all the differences between John and the Synoptics, from a compassion of Jn. 13:26; 18:30 with Mk. 14:18-21 par. and of Jn. 18:1 with Mk. 14:28 par. One may therefore assume that this meal was generally known in the tradition (cf. also 21:20, which mentions simply "the meal"). So what is at issue is not the day but the date of that day — "the most disputed calendric question in the N.T."[13]

The Synoptics identify this meal with the Passover meal, held at the beginning of Nisan 15, what we would call the evening of Nisan 14, assuming that the day of Jesus' death occurred on the first day of Passover. But John 13 does not call its meal a Passover meal, which is evidence enough for many interpreters that it could not have been the Passover meal and therefore that Jesus' death on the following day did not

10. So, for example, Bultmann, according to whom this story must be counted in its original form (later developed into its present form by the Evangelist) as belonging to the form-critical genre of the apophthegm, in which sayings of Jesus are set into the context of specific situations at a later stage of the tradition than the saying itself; see Bultmann, *The History of the Synoptic Tradition,* 1963, pp. 11, 48, 61ff.

11. See, e.g., Brown, *Comm.* II, p. 568; Cloete, *Hemelse Solidariteit,* in loc.

12. Bultmann concedes that the form in John 13, which he characterizes as an apophthegm, is a "relatively late" instance of that genre "since Jesus' own action here constitutes the occasion for his saying" and not vice versa (*Comm.,* pp. 47f.).

13. So Brown, *Comm.* II, pp. 555f.

occur on the Passover. Everything is said to have occurred a day earlier: the meal on the evening of Nisan 13 and Jesus' death on the 14th, so that "only after Jesus' body was in the tomb did sunset mark the opening of the feast when the Passover meal could be eaten."[14]

This conclusion is by no means obvious from John 13 itself, which in fact supports the opposite view. We have noted that "before the feast of the Passover" in vs. 1 means that the concluding phase of Jesus' earthly life was about to begin, with the celebration of the feast. "During supper" immediately follows in vs. 2, and it is natural to understand this as referring to the Passover meal.[15] Admittedly the Evangelist does not mention the Passover meal in so many words, but this need not mean any more than that the viewpoint from which he intended to regard this farewell meal was not the Passover meal but the footwashing. The argument from silence cannot be decisive, especially because the story is marked by indirect references to the Passover meal: it was a festal meal taking place in Jerusalem at a late hour, and the disciples assumed that Judas went out to distribute alms, which was commonly done the night of Passover.[16] John not only does not speak of this last meal as the Passover meal but also refrains from mentioning the institution of the Last Supper, which, according to the tradition (in the Synoptics and in 1 Co. 11:23), took place in the same night ("the night in which he was betrayed"). It is certainly likely that John knew of this institution and that in not mentioning it he was guided by other than negative considerations.[17] What comes out in both "omissions" is John's unique and characteristic purpose and manner of working, both as a transmitter of the tradition and as an Evangelist, that is, his selective use of the material available to him.[18] In leaving out references to the Passover and the Last Supper, he clearly worked within the perspective from which, according to the the opening verses of the chapter, he wanted his readers to see the significance of Jesus' death, and he characteristically omitted what he could assume was generally known among his readers.[19]

While therefore ch. 13 does not argue against the meal there being the Passover, many interpreters nevertheless believe that chs. 18 and 19 clearly support the Nisan 14 dating of Jesus' death and conclude that the meal is not intended to be the Passover.

14. Ibid.

15. Some therefore translate: "and when the (familiar) meal had come" or "during supper"; see also E. Behm, *TDNT* II, p. 34.

16. This is also recognized by, for example, Brown: "That there are Passover characteristics in the meal even in John is undeniable" (*Comm.* II, p. 556; similarly Lindars, *Comm.,* pp. 445ff.). J. Jeremias, *The Eucharistic Words of Jesus,* 1966, pp. 41ff., 79ff., regards 18:28 as decisive against viewing the meal of 13:2 as a Passover meal and concludes that "the Johannine report is therefore not uniform" (p. 82); on this, see further below. Cf. also R. Schippers, *Jezus Christus en het historisch ouderzoek* I, 1969, pp. 53ff.

17. For the different views about this "omission," see, e.g., at length Lindars, *Comm.,* pp. 442ff.

18. For this "reduction" see at greater length pp. 7f. above.

19. In the case of the Last Supper he had all the more reason for this assumption because he has already spoken at length about the saving significance of Jesus' death as the giving of his flesh and blood as food and drink for eternal life, words that are foundational to the Supper (6:51ff.).

This support comes in the form of indirect historical references and theological indications.[20] Others even think that John, contrary to the tradition of Jesus' death on Nisan 15, of which his own story clearly bears the marks, adapted the day of Jesus' death to Nisan 14 for the sake of his own theology.[21]

For this viewpoint scholars appeal especially to 19:14: "Now it was the day of preparation of the Passover,[22] about the sixth hour. He [Pilate] said to the Jews, 'Here is your king!' " The first time indication is said to refer to the day before Passover, and "the sixth hour" is said to be a clear reference to noon on that day, the moment at which the priests killed the Passover lambs in the temple. This would be, on this understanding, an implicit statement that Jesus was slain as the lamb of God at just that time on the day preceding the great memorial feast of Israel's liberation.

The main objection to this interpretation, however, is that "preparation" (παρασκευή) is a technical term for the day preceding the *sabbath,* also called "the day before the sabbath" (Mk. 15:42). It is used absolutely in Jn. 19:31 and with "of the Jews" in 19:42. Use of it for the day before Passover is not known.[23] Therefore the phrase in 19:14 must refer to the "preparation" before the sabbath at Passover and not to the day preceding Passover — especially since 19:31 calls the sabbath following this day of preparation a "great day,"[24] in accord with a rabbinical custom of calling a sabbath falling on Nisan 16 "the great sabbath" since on that day the firstfruits were presented (cf. Lv. 23:11). Thus we have another indirect but important argument that the day of Jesus' death was Nisan 15, the first day of Passover.[25]

Consequently there is no ground whatever for the view that the Evangelist, in the precise time reference in 19:14, was implicitly ("theologically") saying that Jesus was the true Passover lamb, a view that is in any case improbable because in the entire context not a word is said about such an interpretation of Jesus' death.[26] The point of

20. Cf. Brown, *Comm.* II, pp. 556, 895.

21. So, very pronouncedly, Lindars, *Comm.,* p. 446: "It is difficult to eradicate the impression that the death of Jesus on the eve of Passover is a purely Johannine invention, dictated by his theological interest, regardless of the tradition which he was actually handling."

22. παρασκευὴ τοῦ πάσχα.

23. According to Strack/Billerbeck II, pp. 812ff., we have before us here a translation of the rabbinic term ʿerebֹ pesaḥֹ. But ʿerebֹ means "evening," which can hardly coincide with "the sixth hour," while παρασκευή means "preparation" and refers to the whole of Friday. On this see at length J. van Bruggen, *Christus op Aarde,* 1987, pp. 190ff.

24. ἦν γὰρ μεγάλη ἡμέρα ἐκείνου τοῦ σαββάτου.

25. Bultmann comments on 19:31 as follows (*Comm.,* p. 676):

Certainly it is surprising that no mention is made of the Passover, unlike 18:28; 19:14. That may well be due to the fact that this story is derived from a tradition according to which Jesus was crucified on the 15th Nisan, as in the Synoptics. According to the source the μεγάλη ἡμέρα was the sabbath of the Passover week, which in this case fell together with the 16th Nisan; the day could be called "great," because on it (according to Pharisaic tradition) the omer offering (Lev. 23:1) was made.

The question is whether all this can be so easily eliminated from the discussion by referring to another source.

26. Cf. also C. H. Dodd, *The Interpretation of the Fourth Gospel,* 1963, p. 234: If the Evangelist had wanted to make that connection, it is "somewhat strange that he has not said

this time reference is, rather, that precisely on this Friday of Passover, the day of Israel's historic liberation, Pilate mockingly confronted the Jews with Jesus' kingship, just as in 18:39, using the same title, he attempted to release Jesus as a political favor, something he customarily did "at the Passover."

In light of all this, therefore, the appeal to 18:28, which many regard as the clearest argument that John followed a unique dating of the crucifixion, can no longer be regarded as decisive. This verse by itself, and in view of texts like Mk. 14:12, 14; Lk. 22:15, does seem to refer to eating the Passover lamb on the evening of the same day, in which case 13:2 would have to refer to another meal. Many interpreters even think that no other interpretation is possible.[27] But even some who argue for a unique Johannine dating concede that "eating the Passover," though usually understood in this way, can also, when the context suggests it, be taken in a broader sense, as referring to a festive meal on the day(s) following Passover itself.[28] Taking all the data in John 13, 18, and 19 together, one can only say, in my opinion, that the context does suggest this broader sense and that in any case 18:28 is not an incontrovertible veto of the Johannine dating of Jesus' death on Nisan 15.[29]

What position one takes with regard to this continuing issue is unimportant for the interpretation of the pericope before.[30] The key to the pericope is, rather, as stated above, the entirely unique manner in which the Evangelist delivers his story of the last meal and frames it within the whole of his Gospel.

13:2-11

The Footwashing

2-3   As the story of the footwashing begins, the situation is described in three ways: First, "during the meal." The Evangelist refrains from more precisely

---

anything to call attention to this synchronism." And this all the more because the Evangelist repeatedly shows that he realizes that his readers were not familiar with all the details and fine points of the earlier Jewish temple service. The same is true of the appeal to 19:36. Not only does the diction suggest Ps. 34:20 rather than Ex. 12:46, but in 19:31-37 Jesus' death is nowhere related to the Passover, "which would have been so natural" (Bultmann, *Comm.*, p. 677). See further in the comments below on 19:36.

27. Jeremias speaks of "the dating of the Last Supper on the eve of the Passover — actually only unambiguously stated in John 18:28" (*Eucharistic Words*, p. 82).

28. Cf. Strack/Billerbeck II, p. 837.

29. Others advance as an objection to such an understanding of 18:28 that there would have been time enough for the chief priests to purify themselves since the Passover meal would not have taken place until the evening of that day. But this raises the troublesome question of what precisely is meant by "defilement"; for this discussion, see, e.g., Lindars, *Comm.*, p. 545; J. van Bruggen, *Christus op aarde*, 1987, p. 191, who, on the basis of this purification, concludes that the reference in 18:28 *cannot* be to the eating of the Passover lamb.

30. See also Bultmann's overall judgment: "Nor is the historical question, which of the two datings is correct (perhaps the Johannine), of any importance for the interpretation of John" (*Comm.* p. 465, n. 1).

describing this meal although, as we have seen, the time reference in vs. 1 and a number of indirect indications clearly point, in our opinion, to the Passover meal. In any case this was the last meal of Jesus with his disciples and the setting for his "final" words to them — "final" in more than one sense. As such it was to enter history as "the" meal (21:20) and as "the night when he took bread and was betrayed" (cf. 1 Co. 11:23).

Second, "the devil had already put it into the heart of Judas Iscariot,[31] Simon's son, to betray him." Jesus' departure from this world (vs. 1) was also the hour of his great contest with "the ruler of this world" (see the comments on 12:31), which now had to be fought to the finish (cf. 14:30). In this respect as well there is now no longer any delay. The devil had already taken position, deep in the intimate circle of Jesus' disciples, in the heart of Judas Iscariot, by nudging him to the decision to "betray" Jesus. How he would do this is sufficiently well known and not described here, but the word used is the key word in the entire Passion narrative for Jesus' being *"handed over* into human hands." Here it is the demonic starting point in the process that pervades the entire story from start to finish as a chain of faithlessness.[32]

Third, Jesus' knowledge is here expressed a second time (cf. vs. 1), "that the Father had given all things into his hands, and that he had come from God and was going to God." When the decisive hour came he knew what he had to do, as the one who came from and returned to God, by taking into his hands the task the Father had authorized him to perform: laying down his life and taking it up again (cf. 10:17). The initiative to accomplish this was now for him to take.

4-5 The first thing that strikes us in this connection is that Jesus' care and attention is now focused above all on his disciples, "his own" (vs. 1), whom he, in "departing from this world" (vs. 4), had to leave behind in the world. All the conversations in the following chapters are devoted to this coming time, but in the symbolic action of the footwashing he first lays down the foundation on which alone their future fellowship as the church in the world could rest.

The gradual unfolding of the setting in the the subordinate clause and participial clause in vss. 2 and 3, then finally the verbs of the main clause, "he rose from the meal and laid aside his garments," suggest something of a turning point. Most interpreters correctly see in this statement and in Jesus' replacement of his garments in vs. 12 an allusion to the repeated use of the same words in 10:17, 18. Jesus lays aside his garments to take on the slave's job of footwash-

---

31. On the name see the comments above on 6:71; 12:4.

32. From Judas to the Sanhedrin, from the Sanhedrin to Pilate, and from Pilate to the executioners (cf. 18:5, 30, 35; 19:6; and in the Synoptics passim); the word is also used of the path Jesus had to follow under God's direction as the Son of Man (cf. Mt. 17:22 par.).

ing, which is then described in detail: he girds himself with a towel, pours water into a basin, and washes the disciples' feet, drying them with the towel. But there is also in his conduct an element of undeniable grandeur. He does not act as a slave who must do his work inconspicuously and then disappear from the scene before the meal. Only after he has reclined at the table with his disciples and eaten and drunk with them does he suddenly (certainly to the amazement of all) take the initiative to wash their feet.[33] And with the same "power" (cf. 10:18) with which he "lays aside" his garments does he later put them on again to resume his place among the disciples and to ask them: "Do you know what I have done to you?" (vs. 12).

6-9 But before he asks that question we have an interruption that is highly remarkable for the thrust of the whole story. When it is Simon Peter's[34] turn to let Jesus wash his feet, Jesus encounters strong resistance: "*Lord, are you* going to wash *my* feet?" What prompts Peter to say this is clear enough from the way he puts it. He considers Jesus' action completely incompatible with their mutual relationship ("you . . . me"), incompatible above all with Jesus' glory as he, speaking on behalf of all the disciples who have let Jesus wash their feet, have confessed it (6:68). As the story develops, Peter will express this resistance in increasingly stronger language (and deeds! vs. 37; 18:10, 15, 25). His present argument therefore touches on a dimension in the story that he will only learn to understand over a long period and in a way that is painful.

Jesus' reply (vs. 7) anticipates this, but in a hidden way that is characteristic for the historical situation. He neither explains nor justifies his conduct to Peter but, tying in with Peter's own "you . . . me" and on the basis of the difference between them, corrects Peter with "What *I* am doing *you* do not understand now." The idea that Jesus thus refers to the explanation he gives immediately after the footwashing (as though he said, "Have a moment's patience. I will explain it to you in a minute")[35] is now almost universally rejected and seems contradicted by vs. 8. "Later"[36] is to be understood rather as an allusion to the idea in texts like 12:16 (cf. 2:22), which refer to the time after Jesus' resurrection: then, by the light of Scripture and under the guidance of the Spirit, the light will dawn for the disciples in general and for Peter in a most personal way on what now appears perplexing and unacceptable.

---

33. ἐκ τοῦ δείπνου is probably best translated "*after* the meal"; cf. A. Friedrichsen, "Bemerkungen zur Fußwaschung Joh 13," *ZNW* 38 (1939), p. 94. He, too, sees here a description of a surprising aspect of the footwashing, "since the footwashing certainly had its natural place before the meal" (cf. Lk. 7:14).

34. Here referred to by his double name, as elsewhere when his most striking and characteristic interventions are described (6:68; 13:9, 24, 36; 18:10, 15, 25; 21:3f.).

35. See below.

36. μετὰ ταῦτα; cf. ὕστερον in vs. 36.

The exchange that follows (vs. 8) shows how profound this misunderstanding was and how much was at issue. Peter no longer asks questions but most vehemently ("not in all eternity"; see the Greek) rejects the idea that Jesus will wash *his* feet.

Jesus' reply is no less absolute. He no longer speaks of "understanding later," but now confronts Peter with a choice between all or nothing: "If I do not wash you, you have no part in me." The expression is Semitic and describes not so much the personal relationship but the solidarity in destiny of the two men.[37] Only by humbling himself before his own as a servant could Jesus come to glory and make his disciples participants in that glory. If Peter stands by his refusal, their ways will part and he will lose all that he thinks he has found in Jesus. Or, in Calvin's words, "in refusing such a service, he rejects the principal part of his own salvation."[38]

At hearing these words (vs. 9), Peter at once changes his mind and tone. Despite what Jesus has said about "understanding later" Peter now thinks he has already understood Jesus' intention, namely that by washing his feet Jesus seeks to bring home to him, and to remove, his impurity. And now of course the issue is different and the roles of "you" and "me" are correctly assigned. Again Peter's spontaneity is in evidence: if it is a matter of his impurity, then it is not enough just to wash his feet. Then also his hands and head — he needs a complete bath from Jesus!

10-11 The truth is that Peter has not understood Jesus any better than the first time. Jesus is only concerned about the feet, that is, about performing a slave's duty. There not Peter but Jesus is the lesser figure. Jesus' concern is therefore not to induce Peter to understand himself better (as a sinner) but in one symbolic act to present himself to his disciples, as he leaves them, for all time to come in the form of a servant. That it must be so and not otherwise Peter will not understand until later. Jesus therefore rejects Peter's spontaneous statement and insists that washing Peter's feet is all that matters: "He who has bathed does not need to wash, except for his feet, for he is clean all over." This statement reflects the situation in which the disciples find themselves with Jesus. Guests were hardly expected to take a complete bath. They did so in advance in order to come to the table "completely clean." All they needed was a slave who on their arrival would wash their feet to remove the dust they had collected on the way. It is that general truth that Jesus now applies in a spiritual sense to his disciples: "and you are clean, but not all of you." They sit at table with Jesus as his disciples, clean not because they have purified themselves and made themselves worthy of this privilege but because of the word he has

---

37. Cf. Bultmann: "The meaning was originally: to have a share with a person in something" (*Comm.*, p. 468).

38. "Atqui tale officium repellens, quod praecipium est in salute sua repudiat."

spoken to them (15:3), because he knows them and has taken them into the fellowship of his love (cf. 10:27f.; 15:1ff., 9, 16-17; 17:6; Lk. 22:28f.).

That they sit at table with him is proof of that, though not for all of them. In his oblique reference to the betrayer Jesus anticipates something that will come up again later during the meal (vss. 18f.). By saying that "not all" are clean, Jesus makes it all the more clear that he intends with the footwashing to confront them not with their impurity, an impurity he must deal with before going away, but rather with the image and example of their Lord as he is with them at that last meal and lays aside his garments to wash their feet. The significance of this act constitutes the focus of what follows.

From ancient times to the present interpreters have strongly differed on the interpretation of vs. 10 and therefore on the significance of the footwashing.[39] This difference of opinion is already reflected in the varying transmission of the text. Most of the important manuscripts have the reading we have followed above: "one who has bathed does not need to wash, except for the feet." One important manuscript lacks "except for the feet,"[40] which then yields the translation: "one who has bathed does not need to wash (or to be washed)."[41]

Of crucial importance for the whole interpretation are the words "one who has bathed."[42] Many interpreters understand them as referring to the footwashing itself and regard "bathe" as representing the purifying power of Jesus' death.[43] The idea could be that by this footwashing the disciples would be taken up into the purifying event of Jesus' death in such an all-embracing way that any additional washing (such as Peter has mentioned) would become redundant.[44] In such a view "except for the feet" would of course make no sense and would have to be explained as an insertion by copyists who no longer understood that: "one who has bathed" refers to the footwashing itself.[45]

But this interpretation — however frequently followed — corresponds neither

---

39. Cf. Schnackenburg: "Jesus' reply to Peter in this verse is one of the places in the fourth gospel that is most disputed by exegetes. It has been interpreted in very many different ways and this divergence of interpretation has played the most important part in the extreme variety of views concerning the meaning of the washing of the disciples' feet" (*Comm.* III, p. 20). Still very important for this topic is Richter's *Die Fußwaschung,* which offers a survey of interpretation from the church fathers up into modern times. See also F. F. Segovia, "John 13:1-20: The Footwashing in the Johannine Tradition," *ZNW* 73 (1982), pp. 32f.

40. εἰ μὴ τοὺς πόδας.

41. ℵ, some editions of the Vulgate, and some patristic citations.

42. ὁ λελουμένος.

43. See, e.g., Brown, *Comm.* II, pp. 566f.; Schnackenburg, *Comm.* III, p. 21.

44. Many interpreters think that this reading — apparently apart from the historical context — also involves a theological rejection of certain ritual washings. Some have applied this interpretation in a sacramental sense (see, e.g., the lengthy discussion by Bultmann, *Comm.,* p. 471). But the text offers not a single material point of contact for such an interpretation. See also Grosheide, *Comm.* II, p. 256, which has an extensive bibliography of older literature.

45. Cf. Brown, *Comm.* II, p. 568.

terminologically nor in content to the text's train of thought. The meaning of the footwashing is greatly blurred if not totally lost. It is made clear throughout the passage that the footwashing was a *partial* purification by the use of the verb νίπτειν. The verb used in "one who has bathed" is λούειν, which, if it referred to the footwashing, would at least have to be regarded as a forced transition.[46] And this metaphorical interpretation of vs. 10 fails to fit into the content of the text. Apart from whether there is in this Gospel any point of contact for a portrayal of Jesus' death as a water purification (let alone that a partial *foot*washing could represent that portrayal metaphorically), the image used here — "one who has bathed" — clearly refers not to a purification that the disciples must still undergo (i.e., in the event of the cross) but rather to the purity that they have already received as Jesus' disciples, as is evident from the emphatic observation that follows: "and you are clean, but not all of you" (see the exegesis above).

And finally, there is a no less weighty objection: By thus making the footwashing into (a symbol of) a total bath of purification, one changes the specific meaning of Jesus' symbolic act. As *foot*washing, it represents Jesus' servanthood and not the disciples' impurity. If we take it otherwise, we break up the unity of the story. According to Jesus' explanation (see below), the footwashing that the disciples must render to each other is not washing but self-denial and mutual service.

That Jesus washes *feet* is the key. "Except for the feet" must not be deleted as redundant or meaningless. It constitutes the point of the statement and of the entire story. Some interpreters proceed from the longer text but take the idea of purification as their point of departure and have regarded "Except for the feet" as representing an additional washing that the disciples, because of their continuing contacts with the world, need over and over, even though they are fundamentally clean because they belong to Jesus.[47] But even if one tries in this way to do more justice to the text as handed down and to "one who has bathed does not need to wash," our principal objection still stands: the actual and exclusive *tertium comparationis* of Jesus' symbolic action is not the purification of the disciples but the servanthood of Jesus himself.[48]

---

46. Schnackenburg (*Comm.* III, p. 21) also admits this: "λούεσθαι, however, cannot simply point to the washing of the feet that had just taken place. Almost always, this verb is used to indicate a complete bath, whereas νίπτεσθαι is employed in the case of partial washing." Later, however, he writes that λούεσθαι must be "factually" understood as referring to the footwashing (in view of the theological meaning of the statement that he favors; see n. 43 above).

47. So, at length, Calvin, *Comm.* II, p. 59:

For, as Christ washes from head to foot those whom He admits to be His disciples, so the lower part remains to be daily cleansed in those whom He has cleansed. The children of God are not totally regenerated on the first day so that they only live a heavenly life. On the contrary, the remnants of the flesh remain in them, and they have a continual struggle all through their lives. *Feet*, therefore, is a metaphor for all the passions and cares by which we are brought into contact with the world. . . . What is spoken of here is not the forgiveness of sins, but the renewal by which Christ gradually and continually delivers His followers completely from the desires of the flesh.

48. Irrespective of the certainly very far-fetched sense one has to assign to the symbolic significance of "the feet" in this interpretation; see the quotation from Calvin in n. 47.

13:12-17

Jesus' Interpretation of the Footwashing

Verse **12** picks up the thread of the story interrupted by vss. 6-11. After Jesus has completed the footwashing — including of the now apparently no longer recalcitrant Peter — and again "put on" the garments he had earlier laid aside (see the comments on vs. 4), he resumes his place at the table and, as teacher, takes up again the conduct of the conversation by confronting his disciples with a question: "Do you know what I have done to you?" He is thus evidently — though not directly — acting on the "later understanding" he has promised Peter (vs. 7). Only later will the disciples receive the full answer to this question, which is related to the laying aside of Jesus' glory. He has washed their feet to portray to them the nature of the fellowship that not only unites them with him but must also be the permanent measure and source of their mutual relations when he is gone from them.

13-15   Jesus expresses this with, "You call me Teacher and Lord, and you are right, for so I am." Their bond to him is not merely one of personal affection and respect. It has been shaped above all by the fact that he has bound himself to them and they to him in a fellowship of life and learning in which he is their teacher *(rabbi)* and master *(mari)*[49] and in which they understand themselves to be subject to his authority and instructions. Hence also (vs. 14) their obligation to wash one another's feet. For in being bound to him they are also bound to each other and therefore can only appeal to him as master and teacher if they are prepared to do as he, at his farewell from the world, has done for them.

For thus (vs. 15) "I have given you once for all[50] an example, so that you also might do as I have done for you." By the word "example" Jesus describes his deed as "a rule of life"[51] for their future association with each other. In this and similar statements (13:34; 15:9, 12; 17:11, 23) the conjunction "as"[52] indicates not only similarity and adherence to a standard but also the ground on which this discipleship rests and the source from which it gains its strength. "As I have done for you" does not mean that in their contacts with each other the disciples can or should equal Jesus' love for them. It directs them, rather, to Jesus' self-sacrificial love for them as the source and driving force for their love for each other — "just as" his love for them has its source and ground in the Father's love for him (15:9).

---

49. On the analogy of titles that defined the relationship between Jewish teachers of the Torah and their followers.

50. ἔδωκα; cf. BDF §333: "An act valid for all time can be expressed by the aorist."

51. In this connection Bultmann speaks of "the last testament of the departing Revealer" (*Comm.*, p. 475).

52. καθώς.

Verses **16** and **17** again place a heavy emphasis on the imperatives involved in discipleship and on the salutary effect they have when they are carried out. The obligations come first, introduced by heavily charged words that are characteristic of Jesus' self-revelation: "Truly, truly, I say to you." "If anywhere" — so we may paraphrase — "the rule here is: The disciple is not greater than the Teacher, nor the emissary than the one who sent him" (cf. Mt. 10:24; Lk. 6:40). The statement is very general and is sometimes thought of as a proverbial saying. But here, of course, we must understand it in light of what precedes, though from the second clause it is evident that it does not just speak of the disciples' mutual relations. The force of the statement is clearly that they must not take too lightly the prospect that awaits them as disciples and emissaries of Jesus in the world. The "truly, truly" carries a warning. The disciples still do not realize where Jesus' self-surrender for their sake and the sake of the world is to take him, or therefore what following him as their Teacher will mean for them. This he will discuss further, including how it concerns the *difference* between them and him (vss. 36f.). But with increasing clarity Jesus places the future of their discipleship in the light of the events he is now initiating. And that (vs. 17) not just as a warning to prepare them for it but also as a promise: "If you know these things, blessed are you if you do them." Knowledge calls for performance and cannot be isolated from it. But when what is known is done, those who have accepted Jesus as their Lord will also participate in the prospect and actuality of his glory. That is the beatitude for those who in *their conduct* demonstrate that they are truly his disciples (cf. 12:26).

The Unity of the Footwashing Story

I have attempted to interpret the story of the footwashing and its interpretation in vss. 12ff., including the interruption in vss. 6-11, as a coherent whole. In the history of interpretation this unity has recurrently been a subject of much discussion and dispute. This discussion has continued into recent exegesis and has led to a multiplicity of views concerning the meaning of the footwashing that is so great as to defy summarizing.[53] The real crux of the story is said to lie in the fact that the manner in which Jesus speaks about the footwashing in his conversation with Peter is quite different from the answer he gives in vs. 12ff. to the question that he himself poses. In the latter everything hinges on the footwashing serving as an example. But in his confrontation with Peter Jesus is said to mean something much deeper, or at least very different, something Peter does not understand but without which he will "have no part" in Jesus. What Jesus says to Peter about purification makes the footwashing a symbol for Jesus' act of total purification in his surrender for his own on the cross (see the comments on vs. 10). On this

---

53. See Richter, *Die Fußwaschung.*

basis commentators frequently refer to the "double meaning" of the footwashing: in vss. 12ff. a "parenetic" ("moral," "pastoral") meaning, in vss. 7-10 a christological (or "soteriological") meaning. These meanings contradict each other at essential points,[54] and could not have formed an original unity.[55]

As a rule scholars judge that vss. 6-10, because of their "christological-soteriological" approach, are more typically Johannine than the "parenetic" interpretation in vss. 12ff. The latter is said to rest on a broader base in the tradition (cf., e.g., vs. 13 with Mt. 10:24, 25; Lk. 6:40; 1 Tm. 5:10). Therefore, although the *account* of the footwashing occurs only in John, the version of the story represented in Jesus' explanation in vss. 12ff. led a life of its own in the tradition. This version of the story (further edited or not) gained a secondary position in John's story alongside the version represented in vss. 6-10. According to some, this combination was the work of the Evangelist himself, who incorporated the "example" motif into his story in order to furnish it with a new grounding by means of vss. 6-10.[56] Others, however, think that not the Evangelist but a later redactor inserted vss. 12ff. for reasons that interpreters understand in diverse ways.[57]

It is our conviction, however, that the whole idea that we are dealing with two competing interpretations is based on a failure to appreciate the fundamental motif that controls the entire story from beginning to end, which is that of the footwashing as symbol of servitude and of readiness to deny oneself in the service of others. That is no less true for Jesus' conversation with Peter than for the explanation in vss. 12ff. It is undoubtedly true that in his conversation with Peter Jesus has in mind more than Peter was able to understand at that moment. There Jesus partly unveils the deeper messianic dimension of what he is "doing." But he does not pursue the point and again limits himself — even when Peter asks for a total purification — to washing *feet* as the one thing Peter "needed."

Interpretation is derailed when it is not restricted to *foot*washing and to the motif of the servant, when, that is, it seeks to impart to the footwashing a soteriological meaning applicable only to Jesus and not to the disciples, namely the all-embracing purification from sin. Thus the connection with vs. 12 is blocked and the story is broken up into two "interpretations."

The story has only one interpretation, the one given in vss. 12ff. The deeper (salvation-historical) background is referred to, but remains unexplained. The shadows of the cross peep through again and again. But what is happening is still veiled. In so relating the story the Evangelist respects the boundaries of the historical situation in which the events occur. He does not write the story of Jesus going to the cross as

---

54. So, e.g., elaborately, Richter, *Die Fußwaschung*, p 306.

55. So, e.g., Bultmann (with many others), who, though holding the view that we are dealing with two competing "interpretations," nevertheless states: "It is the task of the exegesis to demonstrate the inner unity of the two interpretations" (*Comm.*, p. 462).

56. So Bultmann, *Comm.,* in loc.

57. Cf. Schnackenburg, *Comm.* III, p. 24; Richter, *Die Fußwaschung*, pp. 309f. See also Brown, *Comm.* II, pp. 559ff., and the tradition-historical reconstructions of other authors mentioned there, among them M. E. Boismard, "Le lavement des pieds (Jn XIII,1-17)," *Revue Biblique* 71 (1964), pp. 5-24.

historicized theology, but repeatedly stresses that the events preceded the disciples' understanding of the events and would be understood in their deep divine sense only "afterward," with the aid of the Spirit's witness. Consequently vs. 10 — like other statements in which Jesus encounters and reacts to his hearers' incomprehension (cf. vs. 36; 6:52; 2:19, etc.) — acquires an air of mystery. The time for "understanding" it has not yet come. For that reason, too, the interpretation in vss. 12ff. is restricted to the "example" character of the footwashing.

However — and this is the no-less important other side of the issue — this "parenetic" thrust of the footwashing did not exist without the deeper dimension it gets in John 13. It did not first lead a moral life of its own to be given, only later, a "christological" background (by some "church" theologian) and thus gain a place in the Passion narrative. The degree to which the two parts of the story — not only compositionally and stylistically but also in content — form an unbreakable unity is evident from vss. 12ff. themselves, where the ground for and inspiration of what Jesus asks of his disciples is precisely pointed out in the conjunction "as," in that which he "has done" for them (see the exegesis above). But there is more. The dual interpretation view of 13:1-17 breaks apart that which, in the whole of Jesus' farewell in chs. 13–17, is constantly interconnected and described as an inseparable unity: Jesus' love for his own, culminating in the all-determining exclusive salvific significance of his suffering and death, *and* the love he asks of his own as the new commandment to be fulfilled on the basis of his love for them. What Jesus here both "does" for his own and asks of them has its place in the whole context of God's love for the world in giving up his Son (3:16). As the Father has loved the Son, so the Son loves his own (15:9) so that they may also love one another (13:34; 15:12). The commandment to mutual love is a commandment to "remain" in the love of the one who sends the disciples. For just "as" the Son kept the commandments of his Father and remains in his love, so they will keep his commandments when they — taken up into the oneness of the Father and the Son (17:21, 23, 26) — remain in his love (15:10).

13:18-30

The Betrayal Predicted, Judas Dismissed

Verses **18-20** form a transition to the identification and dismissal of Judas as the betrayer. They link up with vss. 10b-11, which have already alluded to Judas. Vs. 18 echoes the "not all" of vs. 11, and Jesus' foreknowledge of his betrayer returns with "I know whom I have chosen," though one can argue whether Judas is included in that category or whether "chosen" refers to those whom Jesus has truly bound to himself and appropriated for himself, in which case Judas has not been included from the beginning. In 6:70 ("Did I not choose you, the Twelve, and one of you is a devil?") the choice is of all twelve; it is likely that Judas is among the "chosen" here.

Jesus adds: "but that the Scripture may be fulfilled." The "that" does not link up with a preceding verb and therefore hangs somewhat in the air (cf. 9:3). One cannot therefore say that Jesus chose Judas to fulfill Scripture; we must read the clause more generally in the sense that "this happened/had to happen, so that. . . ." The citation is from Ps. 41:9. It is not certain if we should read "my bread" or "bread with me." The first agrees with Psalm 41 and could refer to Jesus as the host who hands out the bread. Some take "has lifted his heel against me" to mean "has shown the bottom of his foot as a gesture of contempt"; others take it to mean simply "has kicked me." The citation not only confirms that what Judas was about to do was foretold in Scripture but no less brings out the treacherous and faithless nature of his deed: he was about to abandon one whose bread he ate and in whose intimate fellowship he had spent time.

In vs. 19 Jesus tells why he is already (literally "from now on") informing his disciples that "not all" would remain faithful to him and that therefore "not all" of them could count on the promise of salvation given to them (vss. 10, 17). He does this so that Judas's betrayal will not shake their faith in Jesus but rather confirm them in the knowledge that, even with regard to Judas, Jesus is not surprised by developments but knows what awaits him (cf. vs. 18). This motif recurs in what follows in statements (14:29; 16:1, 4, 32, 33) that recall similar utterances in the Old Testament in which fulfilled prophecies are identified as proof of God's omnipotence (Ezk. 24:24; Is. 43:10; 46:10). Here, in the Johannine Passion story, such statements are above all intended to make Jesus' power and authority indisputable, even in his suffering and death (cf. 13:1, 3). They are also made with a view to the temptation inherent, for the disciples and (later) the church, in Jesus' suffering and death, not to believe "that I am he," that is, that Jesus is the Christ, the Son of God (20:31). Similarly Jesus, in his earlier dispute with "the Jews," has pointed to the future to establish his identity (8:28): "When you have lifted up the Son of man, then you will know that I am he."

Verses 18-20, as a transition between the story of the footwashing and the identification of Judas as the betrayer, thus have a clearly apologetic intent. This focus must be understood also against the background of the continuing conflict between the church and the synagogue with regard to the suffering Messiah. Vs. 20 does not seem to fit with this concern, but it can be understood as an encouragement to Jesus' disciples not to waver in their work in the service and name of Jesus by whatever opposition or contradiction they might encounter.[58]

---

58. Others understand vs. 20 in the context of vss. 12ff., and it does tie in well with vs. 16; the content of vss. 16 and 20 is linked elsewhere in the tradition (cf. Mt. 10:24, 40). In connection with vs. 16 it would be the intent of vs. 20 to say that though the emissary is inferior to the one who has sent him, he may not for that reason be treated with contempt. If one wishes to draw vs. 17 into this context as well, the meaning would be: "Blessed are you when you show love to one another. For this love is regarded as having been shown to me." But in that case one has to view vss. 18 and 19 as a later insertion, forcing vs. 20 to limp along behind. However, it is also quite possible to understand vs. 20 in connection with vss. 18 and 19.

21   The transition to a new pericope and a new phase in the story is evident from the introductory expression,[59] from the report of Jesus' agitation, and from the following lengthy and solemn phrasing: "and he testified, saying 'Truly, truly, I say to you: one of you will betray me.'" The betrayal is not announced here for the first time; on the contrary, it has been repeatedly prepared for (6:64, 70, 71; 12:4; 13:2, 11, 18ff.).[60] Now, however, Jesus knows that the time has come when the break between him and Judas will become reality. For as long as possible he has tolerated Judas as the hidden traitor in the circle of his disciples, right up into the footwashing. Now that the meal is almost finished and Jesus has begun to prepare the disciples for the time of separation, there is no longer any room for Judas. Again Jesus takes the initiative, now by exposing Judas and sending him away. Nevertheless, Jesus himself experiences the weight of the moment in a state of profound agitation (see the comments on 12:27; 11:33, 38). The authority with which he speaks ("Truly, truly . . .") and the veiled way in which he tells his disciples of his knowledge that he will be handed over to his enemies by one of them[61] do not, in the Fourth Gospel, exclude the deep human emotions that repeatedly come over him on the way to the cross and in which he makes himself one with the ancient psalmists whose utterances he repeats (cf. comments on 12:27; 13:18).[62]

22-24   The disciples, affirmed and addressed by Jesus in their profound union with him only a moment earlier, are deeply embarrassed and look at each other disturbed and speechless. In the Synoptics the betrayer's identity remains a secret: Judas asks, "Is it I, rabbi?" and the answer is apparently intended for his ears alone (Mt. 26:25). But in John the story of the exposure and dismissal of Judas is told in greater detail. This is closely linked with the role played in the story by the disciple "whom Jesus loved."[63]

Of immediate importance for this unnamed disciple's identity is his introduction as "one of Jesus' disciples," which here means one of the Twelve, not only because according to the whole tradition known to us it was the Twelve who

59. ταῦτα εἰπών; cf. 7:9; 9:6; 11:28; 18:1.

60. For all the similarity with the corresponding stories in the Synoptics (Mt. 26:21ff.; Mk. 14:18ff.; Lk. 22:21ff.), John goes his own way here. Therefore, no conclusions can be drawn about how and to what degree he was dependent on existing tradition, if at all. This is all the more true with respect to the hypothetical sources with which the tradition-historical method operates in order to understand the independence and uniqueness of the Johannine story. For a survey of the studies of this pericope according to this method — and the very divergent results it has led to — see, e.g., L. T. Witkamp, *Jezus van Nazareth in de gemeente van Johannes,* 1986, pp. 231ff. For an understanding of the text before us, however, that sort of study contributes hardly anything certain.

61. See here, too, the striking use of ἐμαρτύρηθεν.

62. For that reason it seems to us that the idea that ἐταράχθη τῷ πνεύματι describes "not Jesus' emotional crisis, but his speaking in the spirit," as Bultmann puts it (*Comm.,* p. 481, n. 2), poses a false contrast.

63. On this disciple see 19:26, 35; 20:2ff.; 21:7, 20-25.

were with Jesus at the last Supper (Mt. 26:20; Mk. 14:17; Lk. 22:14, 30) but also because "one of you" in vs. 21 is used emphatically of "the Twelve" in 6:70, with that identification repeated in 6:71. No less telling, then, is the place this disciple occupies at the table: "at the breast of Jesus." This description assumes the custom of the time of reclining at table on special occasions.[64] Each guest leaned on his left arm with his elbow on a cushion so that his head would be near the chest of the person to his left.[65] "At the breast of Jesus" therefore means not only that this disciple was in the place of honor to the right of Jesus, the host, but also that he had opportunity to conduct the tête-à-tête with Jesus described in vs. 25 without being overheard by the others at the table. Many interpreters see in "at the breast of Jesus" an allusion to 1:18: "As the Son is in the bosom of the Father, so this disciple is in the bosom of Jesus."[66] 21:20 refers back to the beloved disciple's place at "the" meal, though not with the word used in 1:18.[67] The idea that the Evangelist intended such an allusion to 1:18 is certainly possible, but it would certainly be very indirect.

This disciple's place in the seat of honor is explained by the note that he was the one "whom Jesus loved." He is identified as such for the first time here.[68] While this identification conceals his identity, certainly for a reason, it also emphasizes his special relationship with Jesus. What that relationship amounted to is not said. Jesus loved the other disciples (cf. 13:1; 15:9, etc.) and called them his "friends," but always with an eye to the fellowship he maintained with them as his *disciples* and to their destiny as his *apostles* (cf. 15:15, 16). What distinguished this disciple from the others must therefore have been a more personal relationship of friendship (cf. 11:5), possibly also of kinship (see the comments on 19:25f.). The relationship does not come up again in the story (but see also 19:26, 27). The reference here to this disciple is evidently intended to stress the role he plays in the unfolding events, which is shaped by that personal relationship to Jesus.

The relationship (and this disciple's proximity to Jesus at the table) plays a role here in that Peter, who, as so often, reacts first amid the confusion created

---

64. On this, in connection with the character of this last meal (whether it was a Passover meal or not), see at length, Jeremias, *Eucharistic Words*, pp. 48f.

65. On this arrangement at table, see at length Strack/Billerbeck IV, p. 618.

66. So Schnackenburg, *Comm.* (German ed., III, 1975, p. 34; this is omitted from the English translation); cf. also Brown, *Comm.* II, p. 577: "In other words, the Disciple is as intimate with Jesus as Jesus is with the Father." So also M. de Jonge, *Jesus: Stranger from Heaven and Son of God*, 1977, p. 212: "His unique position of trust towards Jesus somehow reflects Jesus' unique relationship with the Father." Witkamp, *Jezus van Nazareth in de gemeente van Johannes*, pp. 340ff., goes much further: see below.

67. In 21:20 not κόλπος but στῆθος is used, as also further on in the present text (vs. 25).

68. But see also the comments on 1:37ff. "The other disciple" in 18:15; "the other disciple, the one whom Jesus loved," in 20:2. On this designation see further the discussion of authorship after the comments on ch. 21.

by Jesus' statement and gestures specifically to the beloved disciple, asking him to find out whom Jesus is speaking of.[69] Without attaching far-reaching ("theological") conclusions to this event, we must still say that it is typical for the place of these two disciples in the circle around Jesus and reflects other incidents in this Gospel:[70] here and elsewhere Peter and the beloved disciple act in close conjunction (cf. 18:15ff.; 20:3ff.), especially in ch. 21, where they are expressly placed side-by-side in their permanent significance for the later church. Peter, as in the other Gospels, occupies a central place among the disciples (see especially 6:68; 1:42). There is no evidence of competition between the two (cf. 20:3ff.) or of subjection by Jesus of one to the other (cf. 21:15ff., 20ff.). But the beloved disciple has a priority of his own in that circle, not in opposition to but alongside that of Peter, a priority that proves to be a determining factor in the origination and character of the Fourth Gospel (see the comments on 21:24).

25-27 The real importance of this disciple's action, however, lies in the manner in which Jesus involves him in the sequence of events. When, at Peter's prompting,[71] he asks, "Lord, who is it?" Jesus answers: "It is he to whom I will give this morsel[72] when I have dipped it." The answer is significant not only because it discloses the identity of the betrayer, but also because it makes the beloved disciple a witness to that identification. As Jesus dips the morsel and, as the host, presents it to Judas he not only unmasks Judas as the betrayer to the beloved disciple but also sets in motion a sequence of events in which Judas will play a decisive role. With the morsel, Satan enters into Judas.[73] Everything that until now has awaited fulfillment becomes real: the bread prophecy of Psalm 41 (cf. vs. 18), the Satan-inspired plan to "betray" Jesus

---

69. πυθέσθαι τίς ἂν εἴη περὶ οὗ λέγει. The text is uncertain; some manuscripts read καὶ λέγει αὐτῷ εἰπὲ τίς ἐστιν περὶ οὗ λέγει, in which case the first λέγει (with Peter as the subject) would mean something like "let him know" or "whisper" and εἰπέ would mean "ask (him)." Still other manuscripts add these words to the text we are following (with λέγει becoming ἔλεγεν). At first sight, at least, the text we are following is clearer and is therefore generally regarded as secondary.

70. See the comments above on 1:39.

71. οὕτως in vs. 25 is somewhat hard to translate; it is, perhaps for that reason, missing from some manuscripts, but is as a rule interpreted as we have taken it here: "in keeping with Peter's signal," "accordingly."

72. Usually scholars take the rare word ψωμίον to refer to a piece of bread that was dipped in a fruit purée (or in wine; cf. Ruth 2:14). But because bread was probably not presented particularly by the host, some think it refers to meat (but cf., again, Ruth 2:14). This passage also plays a role in the discussion concerning the date and character of the Last Supper. The "morsel" is also said possibly to refer to the bitter herbs that at a certain phase of the Passover meal were dipped in the charoseth sauce (cf. Jeremias, *Eucharistic Words*). But, of course, this cannot be proven.

73. To see tension here with the "already" in vs. 2 is hypercritical. Vs. 2 refers to the plan, "already" here to its execution. The emphatic τότε aims merely to draw attention to the significance of the moment. "This was the moment in which. . . !" (Bultmann, *Comm.*, p. 482, n. 5).

(vs. 2), Satan himself moving into action. All these things have awaited the signal that Jesus — into whose hands the Father has put all things — had to give. He now gives that signal expressly to Judas: "What you are going to do, do quickly!"[74]

28-29   Again the unique role that the beloved disciple plays in the story is made evident, now by what is said about the other disciples: "No one at the table knew why he [Jesus] said this." Evidently they could not understand the whispered exchange between Jesus and the beloved disciple. They could hear the dismissal of Judas, but could only guess at its purpose. Therefore, "some" of them connected it with Judas's role as administrator of the common fund (cf. 12:6), either that he was sent to buy necessities for the feast or that he should give alms to the poor.[75] They thought all this apparently without further reflection on the matter. The intentional mention of the disciples' not understanding what was happening in their very midst is proof of how little they suspected Judas as Jesus' potential betrayer. As a result — and this is surely the intention of the Evangelist — the beloved disciple's position of trust is highlighted, for he is the only one to know what Jesus' dismissal of Judas really meant.

In recent exegesis we frequently encounter the idea that this — from now on recurrent — special involvement of the beloved disciple in the closing events of Jesus' life on earth must be understood as symbolic, not historical. Even though most scholars who entertain this view regard the beloved disciple as a historical figure (the founder or leader of the "Johannine community"), the actions ascribed to him in the Gospel, both here and elsewhere, are said to have a merely, or at least predominantly, symbolic meaning. As the ideal disciple or apostolic witness, he is said to represent, in the midst of the not-yet-understanding disciples before Easter, the faith of the later church (or the theology of the "Johannine school") and thus to shed proleptically on the life of Jesus the light that had dawned on the church after Easter and under the guidance of the Spirit. From this vantage point, we are told, his role at the last meal is to be understood. Appeal is made to vs. 23 (understood in the light of 1:18): "One of his disciples, whom Jesus loved, was lying close to the the breast of Jesus."[76]

---

74. τάχιον, which has the same meaning here as, e.g., in Hb. 13:23.

75. On the possible link between almsgiving and Passover night, see above, p. 455.

76. This view has been very explicitly developed by Witkamp in *Jezus van Nazareth*. In distinction from "scholars who first inquire into historicity and then possibly into theology," he explains vs. 23 as follows (pp. 340f.):

> The beloved disciple relates to Jesus as Jesus relates to the Father. During the Last Supper he lies ἐν τῷ κόλπῳ τοῦ 'Ιησοῦ (13:23), just as Jesus lay in the bosom of the Father. In Jesus' case this meant he was thereby enabled to reveal God. For the beloved disciple it means the same. His intimacy with Jesus, his being beloved, had *revelational relevance*. . . . When it is said of him alone that he reclined at Jesus' breast, this suggests a unique position that, like that of Jesus with the Father, is not transferable. He alone is the disciple who has direct access to Jesus. This implies that the others had to rely on his witness.

After the exposition of ch. 21 we will summarize everything that is continually at issue in the interpretation of the beloved disciple passages and that is consequently of special importance for the interpretation of the Fourth Gospel. But because the above-mentioned view is based particularly on the present passage, we must say now that this passage offers no support whatever for such an idealizing and ahistorical interpretation of the role of the beloved disciple and is, rather, totally at odds with it. What distinguishes the beloved disciple from his fellow disciples is not only that Jesus made him privy to his foreknowledge that Judas was the betrayer but also that he made him a witness of his dismissal of Judas, thus offering proof that he was not taken by surprise by Judas's betrayal.

Accordingly, what Jesus said to all his disciples a few moments earlier ("one of you"), so that when it took place they might "believe that I am he" (vss. 18, 19, 21), he now — now that it was beginning to happen — makes clear in word and deed to this one disciple. This disciple's special significance as a witness to Jesus stands out as a motif that, as we will see, returns in the later passages that mention him (see the comments on 18:15ff.; 19:35; 20:5ff.), which is why at the end of ch. 21 so much stress is laid on the reliability of *his* testimony (21:24; cf. vs. 20). But this does not make him the ideal post-Easter disciple who thus here already represents "proleptically" (and therefore unhistorically) the insight, faith, or theology of the later "Johannine community." What makes his witness so important and gives him a certain priority among the disciples next to Peter is his intimate relationship with the *earthly* Jesus, whose glory *in the flesh* he observed and experienced at such close range that he could well be called its witness par excellence.

But he was not this in an exclusive sense but, as at the first time he is mentioned (vs. 23), as "one of the disciples." They were all witnesses of the same glory, which is why the content of the whole Gospel can be summed up as the account of the signs (of Jesus' glory) that Jesus had done "in the presence of the disciples" (20:30, 31).[77] *In this respect* one must make a sharp distinction between the Evangelist and the disciple whom Jesus loved. According to 21:24 they were one and the same person (on this point we see at length the discussion after the comments on ch. 21). The Evangelist interprets and explains in the light of the Scriptures and appeals ("post-Easter") to the assistance of the Spirit. But the Evangelist portrays the beloved disciple with the utmost sobriety and restraint. He is, if you please, the great *receptive* witness who was involved *as such* in revelation history and for whom the salvation-historical ("theological") understanding and interpretation of the events *still had to come,* just as it did for the other disciples (see the comments on 20:9; 19:36; cf. 2:22; 12:16; 14:26). All this does not detract from his special significance as the disciple and witness beloved by Jesus, but it does keep us from depriving him (as a symbolic figure) of his historic place among Jesus' disciples.

77. The idea that one should understand the words of vs. 23, "who reclined at the breast of Jesus," "theologically" in the light of 1:18 as a description of the unique and exclusive revelational position of the beloved disciple, as he who alone had direct access to Jesus and on whose witness the others were dependent (see n. 76), therefore seems very far removed from the significance that the Evangelist ascribes to all the disciples, who "were with Jesus from the beginning" as the church-founding witnesses of Jesus' glory (cf., e.g., 15:27; 20:30, 31).

30 Judas's departure is described with utmost sobriety, but in a very telling way. No sooner had he received the bread of fellowship from Jesus' own hand than "he left immediately." He was in no less a hurry than Jesus. The dark power that had already taken possession of his heart now drove him to carry out his (long-cherished?) plan. "And it was night" is surely more than a temporal reference. It was "the night of the betrayal" (cf. 1 Co. 11:23), of "the power of darkness." It was the night against which Jesus had repeatedly warned both the crowd and his disciples, that they should believe in the light before it was too late (cf. 9:4; 11:10; 12:35). Into that night Judas vanished to do what he had to do (vs. 27). We are not told where or to whom he went. The outcome will be evident soon enough (cf. 18:2ff.). With his departure the die was cast and the separation between light and darkness was final.

13:31-38

The Approaching Farewell, Peter's Denial Foretold

Verses 31-38 form a fluid transition between 13:1-30 and ch. 14. They directly continue vs. 30 and the Last Supper conversation as we know it also from the Synoptics (cf. vss. 36-38 with Mt. 26:33ff. par.). And they also anticipate the great themes of chs. 14–17, which are lengthy monologues with only one further reference to the meal of ch. 13 (14:31).

Verses **31-32** depict the situation beginning with the departure of Judas from the viewpoint of Jesus' glory. This glory will come up again and again in the following chapters, especially in the prayer in ch. 17 (14:13; 15:8; 16:14; 17:1-5, 10, 22, 24).[78] Typically, here again Jesus identifies himself as the bearer of the divine glory with the Son of man (cf. 12:23; 1:51), the self-designation that is associated with the absolutely transcendent character of Jesus' messiahship and that also serves as an alternative for the title Son of God.[79] Accordingly, the change from one to the other of the two titles of majesty does not create tension (cf., e.g., 13:31 with 17:1ff.),[80] with this difference, however, that (the glory of) "the Son of God" refers specifically to Christ's (preexistent) personal relation to God, while "the Son of man" refers to the ("eschatological") salvation-historical function and mandate Christ has been given by God. Both of these realities emerge here. When Jesus dismisses Judas, he says, "now is the Son of man glorified," and this bears on the fulfillment of the mandate

---

78. On this see at length G. B. Caird, "The Glory of God in the Fourth Gospel: An Exercise in Biblical Semantics," *NTS* 15 (1968-69), pp. 265-77.

79. See further in the comments on 1:51; cf. also p. 138, n. 108, and p. 200.

80. Cf. also 11:4, where in place of δοξασθῇ ὁ υἱὸς τοῦ θεοῦ is also found the reading . . . τοῦ ἀνθρώπου.

given him by God as the Son of man on earth, which is now reaching its culmination; for the "night" into which Judas disappears also marks the end of the "day" in which Jesus must do the "work" that the Father had given him to do, which is to be the light of the world (cf. 9:4, 5; 11:9f.; 12:35) as the Son of man descended from heaven (cf. 3:13). For that reason we read next, "and in him God is glorified": God is glorified in the fulfillment of the mandate for which God has sent Jesus (cf. 17:4).

The end of the descent of the Son of man is also the beginning of his ascent. This we learn in vs. 32: "if" — as vs. 31 intended — "God was glorified in him, God will also glorify him in himself" in answer to his own glorification in the Son of man (cf. Ph. 2:9ff.),[81] in his return to where he was before (6:62), to his glory as the Son with the Father before the world was (17:5, 24; 1:1). It is that glory to which Jesus now directs himself, in distinction from the stage of glory he is (as it were) leaving behind. That return still lies before him, and he is still to pray for it with urgency (17:1ff.). Between the two still lie the night and the cross as the place at which and the way in which the Son of man "must be lifted up" (3:14). But that hour is now at hand: "he will glorify him [the Son of man] at once." There is no gap between the Son of man's descent and ascent or between the glory of the one and the glory of the other. But the glory of the descent from heaven is not the same as the glory of the ascent to and into heaven: the two are "worlds" apart. Hence the disciples still need to be given extensive instruction, and Jesus will still pray at length before he leaves.

33   The second great theme that is struck in vss. 31-38 and that returns again and again in what follows is that Jesus' imminent glorification is also his departure and separation from the disciples. In the term of address "little children," which occurs only here in this Gospel (but frequently in the Johannine epistles), we are certainly permitted to hear an assertion of deep emotional attachment, especially in view of this final farewell and departure, though the rabbis commonly used such a form of address in speaking to their pupils.[82] Now that he is departing and they must stay behind, Jesus' concern embraces them in a particular way. Admittedly, he does express himself in the same words as he has used in speaking to "the Jews" (7:33ff.; cf. 8:21ff.; 12:35), and he reminds the disciples of that: "Yet a little while I am with you. You will seek me, and, as I said to the Jews, so now I say to you. . . ." For "the Jews" this

---

81. Basic to the transition here is not — as in Philippians — a humiliation-exaltation scheme but a descent-ascent motif. But this does not exclude the fact that in John Jesus' exaltation by the Father also has the character of God's answer to (or reward for) the doing of his will by the earthly Jesus — *pace* E. Käsemann, *The Testament of Jesus,* 1968, p. 18; see also the comments above on 12:23. Schnackenburg speaks correctly of the "response-character of [God's] activity" (*Comm.,* German ed., III, p. 56; English ed., III, p. 50, has "correspondence").

82. Though apparently not in this diminutive form; cf. Strack/Billerbeck II, p. 559.

was a warning to believe in him before it was too late. For the disciples it certainly means something else (cf. 14:19; 16:16ff.). But Jesus still stresses that he is going away, and following him is no less impossible for the disciples than for the others. For him and therefore for them his departure leads to another mode of existence. Until now he has participated in their mode of existence (1:14) and they have been able to see his glory with their own eyes and touch it (as it were) with their own hands. But all that will now come to an end. Their faith in him will have to face very different demands than before.

Here, too, we are struck by the strong salvation-historical discontinuity that is posited in the Fourth Gospel between the modes of existence of the earthly and the heavenly Jesus. Jesus' work and fellowship with his own are not merely transferred from earth to heaven in order to go on there as usual.[83] It is precisely this difference that will be the subject of lengthy discourse in what follows but to which Jesus now already wishes to alert the disciples, who are now largely groping in the dark.

Bceause the transition from vs. 33 to vss. 34 and 35 seems at first rather abrupt and because vs. 36 seems to link up with vs. 33 better than with vss. 34 and 35, some expositors regard vss. 34 and 35 as an insertion by a later redactor.[84] The question is, then, what moved the redactor thus to break the connection between vss. 33 and 36 and whether this is not an oversimple shifting of the problem. Others understand vss. 31-35 to be a unit that originally served as the introduction to ch. 15, after which ch. 16 then followed. In that reconstruction, ch. 14, joined with 13:36-38, is said to have formed the conclusion of the whole and at the same time the transition to 18:1ff.[85] Most expositors reject this radical reconstruction and consider the text before us as original, granting that the transitions between vss. 31-32, 33, and 34-35 are not smooth.[86] We abide by the idea expressed earlier that this closing section of ch. 13 anticipates, from varying vantage points, that which is further elaborated in the cycle of chapters beginning with ch. 14, a structure for conceptual development that is not foreign to the Fourth Gospel (found also in ch. 14 and in chs. 15–16; see below).[87]

34 After the glorification of Jesus (vss. 31-32) and the disciples' consequent remaining behind on earth (vs. 33) follows, as the third vantage point of the approaching time, the "new commandment" as the basic rule for their

---

83. On this see at length the comments above on 9:4ff. and 11:9ff.

84. So Schnackenburg, though he recognizes that the insertion of the love commandment is "very much in the spirit of the Evangelist and fits in very well" (*Comm.* III, p. 53).

85. Bultmann, *Comm.,* pp. 523ff., 595ff.

86. Brown (following Loisy) writes that the parts are "more juxtaposed than connected." But he adds: "Nevertheless, one can trace the logic that led to the union of these disparate elements" (*Comm.,* p. 609).

87. On this see also p. 262, n. 27.

emerging community. Only in the fulfillment of this rule is fellowship with their glorified Lord maintained and the ground and meaning of their existence indicated to the church that remains behind. This theme has already been presented to the disciples in its paramount importance for the future in the footwashing. And it will come up again in the following chapters (e.g., 15:9ff.). Hence this verse, like vss. 31-32 and vs. 33, also anticipates a coming theme.

The sentence construction of vs. 34 is not entirely clear, but the second half of the sentence is clearly designed to elucidate the first part, so that the translation must read approximately as follows: "I [herewith] give you a new commandment: that[88] you love one another and that, as I have loved you, you also love one another."

The expression "a new commandment," which also occurs in 1 Jn. 2:8, is striking and much debated. It cannot mean that Jesus was the first to posit the obligation to love one another. It was, after all, also the fundamental rule of life in the Old Testament (cf. Lv. 19:18; Lk. 10:25ff.)[89] and held as an ideal in pagan antiquity, whether in the general sense of philanthropy or in the sense of political solidarity.[90] Scholars have explained this newness of the Christian love-commandment in various ways — for example, in terms of degree and intensity or scope — but, in view of what love is able to do also from purely humanitarian motives (cf. Ro. 5:7), not always convincingly.

As translated above, the new commandment of which Jesus speaks is given further definition and explanation in the words "as I have loved you" (cf. 15:12). In Jesus' love the commandment comes into play in a new salvation-historical way[91] and receives a new grounding and, by his Spirit, a new possibility of fulfillment (cf. Ro. 8:3, 4) and, in content, a characteristic definition (cf. 15:13). Already in the footwashing Jesus gave his disciples the "example" of that love. And that not only in the ethical command, imperative sense of the word, but above all in the indicative sense of how he, as the One sent by God, represents his love to the world. For as "his own" must love one another "as" Jesus has loved them, so he has loved them "as" the Father has loved him (cf. 15:9), that is, as he revealed God's love to the world in his

---

88. The first ἵνα indicates epexegetically (cf. BDF §394) the content of ἐντολήν; the second ties in with the following καθὼς ἠγάπησα ὑμᾶς, which clarifies vs. 34a. According to other expositors, the second ἵνα clause is not parallel to the first but states the purpose of the καθώς clause (cf. Bultmann, *Comm.,* p. 525, n. 5). The second clause then gains a more independent place next to the first with its new beginning: "as I have loved you, that you may also love one another." But in my view καθώς should be seen as further explication of ἐντολὴν καινήν, not as a new rationale for ἀγαπᾶτε ἀλλήλους.

89. For the rabbinic view see Strack/Billerbeck I, p. 353 on Mt. 5:43, but also II, p. 559 on Jn. 13:34.

90. See Bultmann, *Comm.,* p. 527, n. 2.

91. Cf. J. Behm, *TDNT* III, pp. 449f.

self-abandonment for his own and for the life of the world (cf. 3:16; 10:17; 15:12, 13; 6:51; 1 Jn. 4:10; Ro. 5:8).

Accordingly, the "newness" in the commandment lies fundamentally in the new possibility that the commandment has acquired because God has, as it were, set the sending of his Son behind the commandment, thus making it fulfillable, as Paul puts it in Ro. 8:3ff. For that reason the new commandment can also be described in 1 Jn. 2:8 as that which "is true in him [Christ] and in you, because the darkness is passing away and the true light is already shining." The newness of the commandment lies in its "truth," that is, in the effect in which it proves itself in Christ as "true," as answering to its purpose. It is therefore known as "new" and "true" from its fruits, just as Christ can also be called the "true" vine because whoever remains in his fellowship also remains in his love, by doing his "commandments" (15:9ff.).

35 It is noteworthy that Jesus repeatedly speaks in vss. 34-35 of "love *for one another.*" This certainly does not mean that in their acts of love the disciples are to restrict themselves to their own circle. Jesus refers precisely to what the disciples in their mutual relations can and should mean for the world: "By this will all know . . ." (cf. 17:21). Everything will depend on whether as disciples they love one another. In this mutual love lies the criterion of the identity by which they will be known to the world, not in order to win the world's admiration by their irreproachable conduct as a separatist group, but so that, by their mutual acts of service and self-denial (cf. vs. 15), they may evoke the image of Jesus in his self-sacrificial love for sinful humanity. Again and again everything is referred to *his* love as the great underlying secret from which the church not only derives its unity (17:20-23) but also as that which alone can redeem the world from its lostness, for God and for one another (3:16).

36-38 Before all this is elaborated in depth and breadth in the following chapters, we encounter the dialogue with Peter in vss. 36-38.[92] Peter's question, "Lord, where are you going?" clearly picks up on vs. 33.[93] Peter asks the question because he cannot imagine Jesus going where his disciples cannot follow or will not want to follow. Jesus has, to be sure, already spoken thus to "the Jews" (7:33), but — as Peter evidently tries to say — certainly he and the other disciples are not to be equated with "the Jews!"

---

92. This passage occurs in Luke in the conversations of the Last Supper, in Matthew and Mark on the way to the Mount of Olives. While John's account agrees with the Synoptics in this regard, the independence of its tradition is again clearly evident from its structure and from various details as compared with the other Gospels; for the comparison, see, e.g., Brown, *Comm.* II, pp. 614ff.

93. Hence vs. 36 reaches back past vs. 34. The idea that vs. 34 breaks up the contextual flow and must therefore be a later insertion (see above) evidently poses different demands on sequence than the Evangelist does; for a similar resumption of something not immediately preceding, see, e.g., 10:15-17.

Jesus' reply is in the main a repetition of his statement in vs. 33, with the important difference that he now limits this inability to "follow" to the present ("now") and adds: "but you shall follow afterward." Again Jesus speaks in words that Peter will understand only "later." Thus the dialogue is parallel with the dialogue during the footwashing, again Peter is not satisfied afterward (cf. 13:7), and again no language is too strong to convince Jesus that Peter means what he says. What can possibly prevent him from following Jesus now? He is prepared to risk everything and "lay down his life" for Jesus. He is prepared to match Jesus' willingness to give his life for his own (10:15ff.).

Jesus' answer (again, cf. vs. 8b) is striking in its extraordinary sharpness. Almost contemptuously he hurls Peter's words back at him: "Will *you* lay down your life for *me*?" In the same breath, with the solemnity of a revelational saying, he announces to Peter the role he will actually play, now, in this very night: "Truly, truly, I say to you, the cock will — before the night elapses[94] — not crow until you have denied me three times." The severity with which Jesus repulses Peter is not to be explained solely as a rebuke of Peter's spontaneous overconfidence, the disgraceful outcome of which Jesus foresees; the solemn, prophetic seriousness of "truly, truly, I say to you" rather concerns Peter's opposition to and indeed encroachment on the utterly unique character of Jesus' departure. The problem is not only that Jesus, in being "lifted up from the earth," is going where his disciples cannot follow him but also, and especially, that Peter is trying to hold him back from going the way that the Father has ordered for him, from drinking the cup the Father has given him to drink, from entering into confrontation with the power of darkness. This Jesus must find most profoundly painful in Peter's opposition. For this very reason his earlier statement to all the disciples, "you cannot follow me now," is of such scarcely fathomable depth.[95]

But for that reason Peter's attempt to divert him from that path or to protect him from himself on it (cf. 18:10) is not only an assault on Jesus' obedience to the Father but as such also a way of adding to the bitterness of his suffering, as will be evident before the night is over. Peter will disown Jesus

---

94. For this designation of early morning in the rabbinic literature, see, e.g., Strack/Biller-beck I, p. 993.

95. Or, J. C. Sikkel puts it in *Zie het lam Gods,* 1965, pp. 89ff.:

We are not able. . . . Jesus has to go forward alone. We cannot go with him in that battle of faith, in that clinging to the Scriptures as he enters the deep waters, the swirling maelstrom of death. We cannot go where sin is to be atoned for, where the debt is to be paid, where, in submitting to the suffering of death and curse, the soul of Jesus has to pour itself out. . . . It is one single life that is in him and in us, and therefore Jesus' way is our way. We go along with him. Where he is, there we will also be. We will suffer with him, and we will also be glorified with him. . . . But he *goes on ahead* — we *follow.* He goes forward alone. *In that way we cannot follow him.*

three times, not for lack of courage, but because he is unwilling and powerless to be considered a disciple of a Lord in fetters on his way to a cross.

This last word of Jesus to Peter also demonstrates in a striking way what following Jesus really is. "You will deny me three times" does not undo "you will follow afterward." But it does put all the stress on "afterward": Afterward, when Jesus by the power of his self-surrender has overcome the power of the world, when Peter has turned from his way to the way of his Lord (cf. Lk. 22:32). Then the disciples will follow Jesus in his going to the Father. For where the Lord will be, there his servants will also be (12:26).[96] But "afterward" they will also follow him on earth, when he has departed and it will prove true of them that "a servant is not greater than his master" (vs. 16) and that "if anyone serves me, he must follow me" (12:26). But even then their following will only take them on a road that Jesus has first traveled alone and has thus made passable for them.

---

96. Cf. also Bultmann, *Comm.*, p. 598:

Ὕστερον ["afterward"] is to be understood as equally fundamental as μετὰ ταῦτα in 13:7: Jesus must first have gone and have conquered the world; or: in the light of Jesus' death, by becoming aware of his own powerlessness, Peter must first become convinced of Jesus' victory before he can follow him. His following will then consist, as will be stated in 14:1-4, in Jesus fetching him; what is required of him, on his side, is not an act of heroism, but expectant preparedness.

14–17

The Farewell Discourses

With 14:1 begins Jesus' great farewell discourse in chs. 14–16, which culminates and is concluded in the so-called high-priestly prayer of ch. 17. Although in 13:31ff. we have already encountered anticipations of themes that are variously elaborated in the farewell discourse, still chs. 14–17 clearly constitute a single distinct composition that forms the fifth part of this Gospel and a unique chapter in Jesus' self-revelation in it.

For the literary character of this discourse, scholars have correctly referred to the genre of the farewell discourse or testament, which was very popular in antiquity, both in the Greco-Roman and in the Jewish world (e.g., in the Old Testament, Gn. 27:1-40; 47:29–50:14; 50:22-26; Deuteronomy 31–34; in the New Testament, Acts 20:18ff.; 2 Timothy 4; and of course the Synoptic farewell discourse, Mark 13 par.).[1] Three elements are dominant in this genre — in keeping with the nature of testamentary farewell discourse: review of the past, giving of instructions, and a look forward to the future, usually combined with words of consolation and admonition.[2]

It is not hard to recognize these elements in Jesus' farewell discourse, as the exegesis will show, but John 14–17 is not simply a typical "farewell discourse." "A testament in the mouth of the Prince of Life is, however, most unusual and we can hardly suppose that the Evangelist failed to reflect on this paradox."[3] We cannot speak here, therefore, of a "farewell" or "last will and

---

1. See especially the extensive examination of the relevant Old Testament, apocryphal, and pseudepigraphal texts in M. Winter, *Die Abschiedsworte der Väter und das Vermächtnis Jesu. Gattungsgeschichtliche Untersuchungen der Vermächtnisrede im Blick auf Joh. 13–17,* 1988.

2. Cf. the summary in Winter, *Abschiedsworte der Väter und das Vermächtnis Jesu,* p. 244.

3. So E. Käsemann, *The Testament of Jesus,* 1968, pp. 4f. Whereas Winter speaks of John's formal and material dependence on Old Testament and later Jewish "testamentary discourses," he also recognizes "the unparalleled position of John in the history of the genre," which finds its

testament" in the true sense of these words. The *continuing* fellowship of Jesus with his own after he "goes to the Father" constitutes the real theme of this discourse. The connection with the traditional literary genre serves to bring out the turning point in the great curve of Jesus' self-revelation in the Fourth Gospel (the Gospel's "christology"), which is the point at which the Son of man's descent from heaven passes over into his ascent back to where he came from (cf. 3:13; 12:23ff.).[4]

All this is dealt with in regard to its bearing on Jesus' disciples, who remain behind on earth. In this respect the line begun in 13:1 is continued. Jesus' attention is not wholly focused on his departure to the Father, his own glorification, but above all on the salvation implied in it for his disciples in the world.

Thus this discourse is distinguished from the great farewell discourse in the Synoptic Gospels (Mark 13 par.). There the disciples' future is framed within a series of apocalyptic events that encompass heaven and earth. Not a trace of that appears in the Johannine farewell discourse. Here everything is concentrated on the continuing *spiritual* fellowship of Jesus as the heavenly Lord with his disciples on earth. There is no clear historical future perspective, no explicit mention of the formation of the coming church as an institution, and no mention of the church's future development in history. The relationship of church and world comes up only in terms of antithesis. The present and coming kingdom of God, the worldwide missionary continuation of Jesus' work on earth, and the self-understanding of the church in the world in light of this mission do not come up.

Scholars have viewed this as one of the many surprising marks of the Fourth Gospel, perhaps even the most surprising of all, and have proposed a variety of material and historical explanations — for example, that the church is considered in John only in terms of its individual members or that the Johannine community, because of its sectarian nature, was marginal to the general development of the churches and led a strongly introverted life.[5]

Regardless, however, of the many important and unanswered questions regarding the future and life of the coming church in the world, this must not seduce us into an individualizing or sectarianizing reduction of the message of the Fourth Gospel. The disciples are clearly addressed in terms of their apostolic calling as those who will continue Jesus' work on earth (14:12ff. and passim),

---

explanation in John's christology and about which there can therefore be no doubt. "For in John both the understanding of the past and admonitions and pronouncements about the future are totally centered in Jesus" (*Abschiedsworte der Väter und das Vermächtnis Jesu,* p. 245).

4. On this basic motif see at greater length the comments above on 12:23ff.

5. Käsemann has especially raised this problem and has attempted to explain it at length in this manner; see his chapter on "The Community under the Word," pp. 27-55 in *The Testament of Jesus.*

and their joint witness, as those who have been with Jesus from the beginning, is too emphatically characterized as fundamental for the entire coming church (14:26, 27; 15:16; 20:30, 31) for this to be valid. But all this is subsumed under the perspective of the continuing fellowship of the ascended Jesus with his disciples on earth and of the coming church that will believe in Jesus through their word. Their common future is grounded in that fellowship. That is the "eschatological" dimension of 14:1ff., as well as the conclusion of the end of ch. 17. But Jesus is also the way who leads to that future. And all the ethical admonition, comfort, and power that radiate from this farewell have no other purpose than that the church on earth should understand itself as belonging to him in heaven and that it should abide in him as he abides in its members. In this the church, together with Jesus — in accordance with an ancient depiction of the people of God — appears as the vine and the branches in which he, responding to the church's faith and prayer, its life under his word, its affliction, and its calling in the world, will prove himself to be the Living One.

A second and closely related perspective here is that for their future Jesus refers his disciples to the "other Paraclete." He himself will still have many things to tell them, but they will not be able to bear them now. Therefore he must speak to them mainly in "figures" (16:12, 25). But he will send them his Spirit as the great "helper" who will show them the way to the future, will further explain Jesus' words to them, and, in the great continuing conflict between the church and the world, will vouch for the truth and make it plain (cf. 16:7ff.).

In saying this Jesus is not taking leave and referring the disciples exclusively to the Spirit for their future. He is going away, and they will see him no more. But he will also "come," after "a short while," to manifest himself to them as the Living One (14:9ff.) and, with the Father, to make his home with them (14:23), just as at some time he will "come again" to take them to himself in his Father's "rooms" (14:3). But the Spirit "dwells with" them and will "be in" them (14:17) in order to maintain their fellowship with their heavenly Lord. How all this is to be understood theologically in its unity and diversity is not part of Jesus' focus in his farewell. The truth here is that between the Lord and the Spirit the church will find in this field of interaction and power the ground of its existence, its way to the future, and its calling in the world.

The many things that the church will have to face in the future — in regard to both its relation to the world and its own organization — recede into the background. But one cannot conclude from this silence that the Fourth Gospel has little ecclesiological content. All one can say is that this farewell discourse directs the coming church toward ongoing fellowship with its Lord and guidance by the Spirit as the only possible and permanent point of orientation to enable it to manifest itself in the world as the church of Christ. In theological terms, in the Fourth Gospel eschatology and ecclesiology are totally under the sway of christology.

There is considerable difference of opinion concerning the composition of the farewell discourse. Again questions are raised with respect to the original unity of the text we have before us, now mainly in chs. 14–16.

The much-debated but unresolved problem of the transition between chs. 14 and 15 plays an important role here. At the end of ch. 14 (in vs. 31) Jesus invites his disciples to join him in leaving the scene of their meal and seems to indicate a desire to break off his conversations with them. But in 15:1ff. the discourse is continued at great length and with no explanation why. From ancient times it has been concluded that the remainder of the discourse and the prayer in ch. 17 were uttered by Jesus on the way to the Mount of Olives. In the same way, in Mark and Matthew Jesus' prediction of Peter's denial occurs not in the "upper room" but on the road to Gethsemane (Mt. 26:30ff.; Mk. 14:26ff.). But it is hard to imagine that all that is in chs. 15–17 was said during the walk at night to Gethsemane. Not until 18:1, it seems, do we read of the departure[6] from the house where the last meal took place.

Accordingly, two other explanations are offered. The first is that the text has fallen into disarray, and part or all of ch. 14, including vs. 31, ended up in the wrong place and thus lost its natural link with 18:1.[7] But an acceptable reconstruction of the putative original order is hard to give. For that reason most recent interpreters have stopped trying to find one. Lifting the conclusion of ch. 14 from its context, in which it fits perfectly well, is already most objectionable. If therefore one transposes the whole of ch. 14 to the end of the discourse, one runs into the very real objection that ch. 14 is basic to the whole of chs. 14–16. The most important objection to this transposition of part or all of ch. 14 to the end of chs. 14–17 is ch. 17 itself, which is so clearly the conclusion and culmination of the whole discourse[8] that to put it back at the beginning[9] seems far too forced.

Others therefore think that in the text before us we have not an original unit but a later combination, from either the Evangelist or other "redactors," of a number of compositions of words of Jesus that originated earlier. Ch. 14 (possibly 13:31–14:31) is generally considered the "original" farewell discourse, to which chs. 15–17 are said to have been added later.[10] Others stay

6. ἐξῆλθεν.

7. For the various reconstructions see, e.g., J. Schneider, "Die Abschiedsrede Jesu. Ein Beitrag zur Frage der Composition von Johannes 13,31–17,26," in *Gott und die Götter* (Festschrift for E. Fascher), 1958, pp. 103-12, esp. p. 104. Also Brown, *Comm.* II, pp. 583ff.

8. Cf. Schneider, "Die Abschiedsrede Jesu," pp. 104ff.: "The prayer can only form the conclusion of the farewell discourse. It is its culmination. After Jesus has said to his disciples everything he has to say in his hour of farewell, he turns, already totally removed inwardly from events on earth, toward God."

9. So Bultmann, who exchanges the order of chs. 14 and 17. See his *Comm.*, pp. 461ff.

10. See, e.g., Schnackenburg. With regard to 13:31–14:31 he writes: "The evangelist's authorship of this clear conception cannot be disputed, with the result that this section is for the

more closely to the text as it has been handed down to us and believe that in chs. 14 (or 13:31–14:31) and 15–16 we have two independent farewell discourses, one more concise and one more elaborate. Both were incorporated into the Gospel, unchanged and in succession, out of respect for their author, by the final redactors (cf. 21:24ff.).[11]

Others go much further and think that underlying chapters 15–16 (or 15–17) is a much more complicated tradition history. This view has prompted a variety of widely divergent tradition-historical explanations.[12] Some think that the material incorporated here comes mostly from the Evangelist and has been added to ch. 14 later by a redactor.[13] Others think this is all the work of later redactors and believe they can discern not only distinct "layers" but also very different "unharmonized" theologies.[14] All this is said to be a clear reflection of the different phases the Johannine community passed through in its confrontation with the synagogue and then later with the hostile world around it (cf., e.g., 15:18ff.).[15]

But however we judge the formal break between ch. 14 and chs. 15–17, we must take our starting point in the unity of content in chs. 14–17. Chs. 15 and 16 are expansions of ch. 14, which ends provisionally with vs. 31. The idea that in ch. 15 we have the beginning of a "second" farewell discourse is hard to accept. The parable of the true vine, which begins abruptly in 15:1, gives from the outset no sign that a new discourse is beginning. Neither the parable nor the explication in 15:9-17 alludes to a farewell situation. They can only be

---

most part not called into question by literary critics" (*Comm.* III, p. 48). Others, however, want to reckon with "redactional revisions and expansions in several places" in 13:31–14:31 (Winter, *Die Abschiedsworte der Väter und das Vermächtnis Jesu,* p. 176; so also Becker).

11. See Schneider, "Die Abschiedsrede Jesu," p. 115, who refers for this idea to a similar view of Strathmann, *Comm.* (6th ed., 1951), p. 213.

12. See, e.g., the lengthy analysis of Brown, *Comm.* II, pp. 586ff. and the outline on pp. 545-47. He speaks of "several independent last discourses, eventually combined into the Last Discourse, as we know it" (p. 586) and arranges the material in three "divisions": 13:31–14:31; chs. 15–16, and ch. 17. Chs. 15–16 he then divides into three "subdivisions" in which are found "last discourses" independent of 13:31–14:31. For Schnackenburg's view of the origin of chs. 15 and 16, see his *Comm.* III, pp. 89ff.

13. So, e.g., Brown, *Comm.* II, p. 586: "The material in these added discourses [i.e., what appears after ch. 14] is not necessarily inferior to or later than the material of Division 1 [i.e., 13:31–14:31]." The final redactor incorporated "genuinely Johannine material."

14. See, e.g., Becker, "Die Abschiedsreden Jesu im Johannesevangelium," *ZNW* 61 (1970), pp. 215-46. Becker finds in chs. 15–16 three distinct "supplements" from three different authors, each with his own theological "concern" (pp. 229ff.).

15. See J. Painter, "The Farewell Discourses and the History of Johannine Christianity," *NTS* 27 (1981), pp. 525-43. Also Winter, *Die Abschiedsworte der Väter und das Vermächtnis Jesu,* pp. 211ff., who thinks, however, that "these chapters do not contain sufficient information to permit the reconstruction of a 'historical' development of the Johannine community."

understood as such against the background of ch. 14. Furthermore, 15:1-17 is materially closely related with ch. 14 in that the image of the vine elaborates at length an important motif in ch. 14 — the continuing fellowship between Jesus and his own (cf. 14:2ff., 23).

The same is true for the long section from 15:18 to 16:12 (or 16:15), in which the time of Jesus' departure is further unfolded, now admittedly from a new perspective, that of "hatred of the world," but again in close connection with ch. 14. For what is said about the Spirit's assistance clearly forms an expansion of the brief announcement of "another[16] Paraclete" made earlier in 14:16. The relative clause "whom I will send to you from the Father, even the Spirit of truth, who proceeds from the Father" in 15:26 clearly refers back to the main sentence of the earlier announcement, as does 16:13: "When the Spirit of truth comes."

The conclusion of chs. 15–16 in 16:12-33 is in content nothing other than a return to and expansion of (the conclusion of) ch. 14. It picks up the dialogue form of the beginning of ch. 14. Everything is focused, as in ch. 14, on the concrete farewell situation, and again we have a transition to events that are about to happen, as in 14:31. The transition in 16:12-15 is also clearly linked with the transition in 14:25-26 (cf. vs. 30). At the same time 16:12-33 expands on the ideas in ch. 14: Jesus speaks more fully than in 14:19 about the "short time" of his absence and the new dispensation to come (16:19-28) and prepares his disciples for events that are now immediately at hand (vss. 29-33).

Surveying the whole, one clearly sees the extent to which ch. 14 is foundational to chs. 15 and 16 in content and sometimes even verbally. There is no indication whatever that a second discourse begins in ch. 15. We get the impression rather that the themes advanced in ch. 14, which are already linked with 13:31ff., return in the following chapters, in the usual manner of the Fourth Gospel, more expansively and in terms of new viewpoints, and receive a new conclusion in 16:16-33, one that is again oriented to the end of ch. 14. How and when the new start marked by 15:1 came into being can hardly be ascertained with any degree of assurance. In any case the unity in content and style of this section militates against the idea that the author (or "redactor[s]") destroyed the original conjunction of ch. 14 and ch. 18 to make room for a number of additional themes of diverse origin without apparently worrying about or giving thought to the result of such a intrusion into the existing structure.[17]

16. Consistently described in chs. 15 and 16 as *the* Paraclete, that is, the one mentioned in 14:16.

17. Cf. Becker, *Comm.* I, p. 35, where he speaks (inter alia) of chs. 15–17: "These block-like insertions fail totally to fit the recognizable structure, and their literary oddity contains the most theological changes in viewpoint." See also Winter, *Abschiedsworte der Väter und das Vermächtnis Jesu,* pp. 174f.

Others, viewing things more historically, have seen in the new viewpoints in chs. 15 and 16 (e.g., "hatred of the world," 15:18ff.) and in supposed contradictions and differences of nuance in the different parts of chs. 14–16 an indication of the different historical "phases" and "layers" by which the Gospel is thought to have been built up and in which theological developments in the "Johannine community" are thought to be reflected.[18] But the resourcefulness displayed in this method is often greater than its power to persuade, and it does not solve "the problem of 14:31." This is not to deny of course that the expansion of ch. 14 in chs. 15 and 16 shows conceptual development. But the question is whether one must try to discover from that development "phases" in the continuing fortunes and theology of the later community[19] or whether it is more natural to think — in view of the unity in content of the whole — that the author himself, who had more resources at his disposal than he used in ch. 14, felt the need at some time to illumine or enrich what he had written. That he did not remove the end of ch. 14 or adapt it to the section he added may seem strange. But this is no more inexplicable than that those who were responsible for the final redaction of the Gospel left the text that came down to them in this way as they found it.

14:1-31

Jesus' Departure: A Reason for Joy, Not Sadness

Ch. 14 forms a distinct unit provisionally concluded by vs. 31 (cf. vss. 1 and 27). The composition as a whole is a continuous explication, from various angles, of the salvific character of Jesus' departure, summarized in the end by the statement that the disciples' love for him must not express itself in sadness and fear but in joy (vss. 27ff.).

Further division of the chapter is difficult. One can discern a number of clear perspectives in terms of which the main idea is unfolded, but the transitions are vague. One must keep in mind the merely relative importance of even a cautious grouping of related verses (as we will attempt for the sake of clarity below).[20]

---

18. See specifically Painter, "Farewell Discourses."

19. On the application of this method in general and on the farewell discourse in particular, see also the exposition in M. de Jonge, *Jesus, Stranger from Heaven and Son of God,* 1977, pp. 97-102, 199, which rejects this approach.

20. On the internal organization of ch. 14 and the various proposals for subdividing the material, see also Brown, *Comm.* II, pp. 623ff. and his own "hesitant" proposal. In the same spirit Schnackenburg, *Comm.,* III, pp. 57f.

14:1-3

No Final Farewell

1, 2 Although following 13:38 the abruptly introduced saying "Let not your hearts be troubled" constitutes the opening statement of a new section, this admonition clearly relates to the situation described in the preceding, in particular to the announcement — which the disciples have not understood — of Jesus' departure and of their inability to follow him (13:33). With increasing clarity it has dawned on them that things are heading toward a separation, a prospect that not only disturbs their feelings of love for him but also in no way fits the images they have formed of their following him. It therefore was a direct challenge to their faith in him (cf. Lk. 22:31ff.).

Jesus responds to both issues. His statement is first of all a pastoral word of comfort by which he seeks to quiet their inner dejection and agitation — feelings that were not foreign to Jesus himself.[21] In the same breath, however, he appeals to them to continue to believe in him,[22] a motif carried through in what follows (cf. vss. 10ff.). But here this appeal is meant especially as a request to *trust* that he will not permanently leave them behind but will keep his promise that they will follow him later (13:36).

To this end he appeals to their faith in God as the basis for their faith in him: "Surely you believe in God! Then believe also in me!" (Or "If you believe in God, then believe also in me!").[23] Jesus will not be setting out for an unfamiliar destination. He is going to the Father, and this is the guarantee of the disciples' future. He has spoken to them of his Father as their Father. With this appeal in mind he immediately adds: "In my Father's house are many dwellings." Not only is he, the Son of that household, expected at the place where he was "at home," but also those he has made his own (cf. 17:6, 10).

The last part of vs. 2, "if it were not so . . . ," is hard to translate.[24] In view of the context, however, the meaning can hardly be other than: "If matters stood otherwise with my going away and if it were only my business and not yours as well, then would I have spoken to you about it as I have? For I am going away precisely for the purpose of preparing a place for you." With "would I have told you . . . ?" Jesus is evidently referring to his "going away" and their "following afterward" (13:36); he now explains that he is going away

---

21. μὴ ταρασσέσθω ὑμῶν ἡ καρδία, using the verb also used in 12:27 of Jesus' own inner agitation, there echoing Ps. 6:3.

22. εἰς ἐμὲ πιστεύετε, durative present.

23. The chiastically structured pronouncement coordinates two clauses ("believe in God," "believe in me") and makes the second (imperative) clause dependent on the first (indicative).

24. "However it is turned, it still does not give a satisfactory meaning" (Schnackenburg, *Comm.* III, p. 59).

"to prepare a place" for them, imagery that fits the earlier mention of "my Father's house."[25]

3 Still, this goal of going away, however full of promise and encouragement for the disciples it is, does not cancel out the separation itself. What now follows therefore, though it does not yet involve the intervening time, expresses the full significance of what his going away and preparing a place means for them: "I will come again and will take you to myself, so that where I am you may also be." His departure will mean the definitive cancellation of the separation and will give to their "following later" unimagined content. He himself will return for them and will thus make good his promise to them: "Where I am, there will my servant be also"; "if anyone serves me, the Father will honor him" (12:26; cf. 17:24).

These statements are of characteristic significance for the Fourth Gospel for more than one reason. In the first place, right at the beginning of the farewell discourse they place the whole of the disciples' coming time on earth in the perspective of Jesus' final return to take them to where he is. The same thought comes back at the end of ch. 17. All that lies between the beginning and the end of chs. 14–17 is devoted to Jesus' concern for them in the interim before his final coming, which thus gets by far the most attention. But this interim is bounded by a future that is determinative for the whole road that they have to travel. Their life on earth finds its direction, goal, and power in their belonging to him who is in heaven. From now on that will mark the secret and the ambivalence of their existence on earth (cf. 16:33).

These statements are also characteristic for the Fourth Gospel because this future is not portrayed to the disciples in the language of traditional eschatology but in that of Jesus' self-consciousness as the one sent by the Father. We encounter here what we have already noted[26] about the church's learning to understand itself in terms of its union with Christ. Jesus describes the future abode of the church not only as "where he is going" and "where he is" but also as his "Father's house," in which there are many "rooms" and in which he will "prepare a place" for his own. "House" as a term for the place where

25. Popular for a long time was the translation "I would have told you," that is, "I would have told you [that there would not be a place for you in my Father's house]" (e.g., NIV). But such a statement would not only be very businesslike (others call it "trivial" or "banal") but really redundant. Most recent interpreters therefore reject it, and rightly. It is better to think here of a question (see also Nestle-Aland). Some then extend the question to the end of vs. 2 — "Would I have told you that I am going away to prepare a place for you?" — and refer to passages such as 12:26, 32. But there the striking expression "prepare a place" (which fits so well with vs. 14:2a!) is not used. Accordingly, we will have to limit the question to the first words (εἰ δὲ μή, εἶπον ἄν) and expand it somewhat: "If the situation were otherwise — that is, with my going away — would I have spoken to you about it in that manner?" (see, e.g., Schnackenburg, *Comm.* III, pp. 57ff.). But the translation remains somewhat conjectural.

26. See above, pp. 482f.

God resides conveys an idea found frequently in both the Old Testament and in Jewish and Hellenistic writings of the time of Jesus. But in these writings "house of God" is normally used of the temple, not heaven.[27] In any case, the focus of the expression here is that it is "my Father's" house, the place where Jesus goes because he is at home there.

Similarly, "dwellings" or "rooms" as a term for the place where people will be after this life was certainly known in the religious world of Jesus' day. Still, the way in which it is used here is certainly not explained by this religio-historical background.[28] It flows, rather, directly from Jesus' self-consciousness and his understanding of heaven as *his* Father's house. In *that* house there is room in abundance. That is what makes it his Father's house. With "preparing a place" we again have a concept that has clear parallels in the New Testament (Mt. 25:34; Mk. 10:40; 1 Co. 2:9; Hb. 11:16; 1 Pt. 1:4) and elsewhere.[29] But here the concept is subject to the imagery in vs. 2a. Jesus is returning as the Son of the house (cf. 8:35)[30] who has completed his task and who can therefore assign all the rooms available in the house to the many who believe in his name. The church's future is completely determined by its union with Christ, and this gives the eschatological depiction of the church this graphic and sober character (see further the comments on 17:24).

Many interpreters have serious objections to this explanation, especially of Jesus' "return." The difficulty arises out of the Fourth Gospel's supposed "present eschatology," the idea that this Gospel consistently represents the salvation that appeared in Jesus' coming as the inauguration and realization in the present of the great future. This is thought to contradict, and therefore make unacceptable, the explanation of Jesus' "return" in the sense of the parousia referred to elsewhere in the New Testament.

In keeping with this "present eschatology" some interpreters have interpreted vss. 2-3 as referring to a *spiritual* reunion of Jesus with his disciples. 14:22ff. also mentions Jesus' "coming," but not then in the eschatological sense, but in the sense of his "coming" after his resurrection and of his permanent fellowship with his disciples on earth. This plays a large role in this spiritual interpretation of 14:2f., in which the "Father's house" with its "many rooms" in a spiritual sense is "the spaces of God's

---

27. Cf. BAGD, s.v.

28. On all this see at length G. Fischer, *Die himmlischen Wohnungen. Untersuchungen zu Joh. 14,2f.,* 1975. Fischer notes (p. 290) that his studies have clearly shown that "though ideas occur in certain religious currents that are reminiscent of the imagery in Jn. 14:2a, the elements of correspondence are never so conclusive as to establish religio-historical dependence."

29. Cf. Fischer, *Die himmlischen Wohnungen,* p. 86, where he speaks of "the apocalyptic motif that the eschatological riches of salvation, created already at the beginning of time and lying ready in secret for the elect, will be revealed at the end of time."

30. For the link with 8:35, see also Schnackenburg, *Comm.* III, p. 62.

love" in which Jesus causes his disciples to share by "taking them to himself," that is, by making them spiritually one with himself.[31] In a somewhat more nuanced way others say that Jesus' spiritual "return" after Easter finds its completion for his disciples in the "place of consummation" described in vs. 2. They add, however, that we cannot link to this last act of Jesus' coming the idea of his appearance in glory, the parousia. They stress that the whole passage reinterprets the tradition of the parousia.[32] Becker's judgment is more radical. He admits that vss. 2 and 3 can only be understood as referring to the parousia (Hb. 9:28 is "close both in time and content") and speak of Christ's exaltation and communion with his disciples in the same sense as "the early Christian tradition in 1 Co. 16:22ff.; 1 Th. 1:9, etc." But the Fourth Evangelist used an older apocalyptic revelatory saying that he "explains and decisively reinterprets in what follows (vss. 4ff., 18ff.)."[33] Still others believe that Jesus' "return" and his taking his disciples to himself refer to his bringing his disciples to himself when they die.[34]

All these forced understandings of vss. 2 and 3 are based on the view (repeatedly combated in this commentary) that because of the "presence" statements in John there is no room for a still to be expected "coming" of Jesus that has dimensions of glory that are not or cannot be manifested in this earthly dispensation. The earthly future of the disciples, as it is spoken of in this farewell discourse, is set in a framework of pronouncements about the future (14:2, 3 and 17:24ff.), which proves that there is room for such a still future "coming" of Jesus — in agreement with passages like 5:27f.; 6:39f., not to mention 1 Jn. 2:28, which explicitly refers to Jesus' parousia. Jn 3:2 describes the parousia over against the "not yet" of the present: "We are God's children now. It does not yet appear what we will be, but we know that when he appears we will be like him, for we shall see him as he is."

Still it is true — and characteristic for John's Gospel (but cf. 5:28) — that

31. For these ideas, which again take various forms, see the lengthy overview in Fischer, *Die himmlischen Wohnungen,* pp. 299-304. In this sense see also C. H. Dodd, the well-known exponent of "realized eschatology," though he does acknowledge that in Jn. 14:2 we have "the closest approach to the traditional language of the Church's eschatology" (*The Interpretation of the Fourth Gospel,* 1963, pp. 404ff.).

32. So, in a very lengthy argument, Schnackenburg, *Comm.* III, p. 62: Jesus's words that he is coming back and will take his disciples to himself "should not . . . be in any way interpreted as referring to the parousia since this would be in contradiction to the evangelist's present eschatology."

33. Becker, *Comm.,* pp. 460f.

34. So Bultmann, who thinks that here the Evangelist uses the language of Gnostic mythology: The souls of initiates are taken up after death into the world of light, where they will see the glory of the Revealer (*Comm.,* pp. 599ff.) But apart from the gnosticizing character of this explanation, the "coming again" mentioned in vs. 3 too clearly refers to a single grand event for us to think here of Jesus coming back over and over at the deaths of his disciples. Cf. also Käsemann: "Of course, John 14,2f. does not mean that in the hour of death Jesus brings his own to himself" (*The Testament of Jesus,* p. 72).

the description of this future revelation, of Jesus' coming again, is devoid of apocalyptic imagery and cosmic dimensions and limits itself to the salvation contained in it for the disciples. There is thus a remarkable difference between John and Paul. The latter also speaks, in virtually the same words, of believers being "taken up" and of "being always with the Lord" (1 Th. 4:16ff.). But whereas Paul, especially in 1 Thessalonians, pulls out all the stops on his apocalyptic organ ("the voice of the archangel," "the trumpet of God," "being caught up together in the clouds to meet the Lord in the air"), John expresses the same thing in the language of his christology, of Jesus' union with the Father and of the disciples' participation in that union by dwelling with him in "the house of his Father," so that "where I am, you may be also" (cf. 17:23ff.). If one wishes to speak of a reinterpretation, then this relates not to the substance of the parousia as the revelation of future glory but to the way in which this event is identified with and interpreted in terms of the person and work of Jesus as the Son of man and the Son of God, totally in keeping with the thrust of the entire Gospel. This implies a sobering of the apocalyptic picture, and the Evangelist no doubt had his reasons for that. The inconceivable "something" takes a back seat to "he" and "I" ("I am he . . . ," 8:28) and explains why the future becomes present, for Jesus *is* the coming one.

But this is not to deprive his "coming" of the dimension of glory, which still lies in the future. As the Son of God he is also the Son of man, in whose hands the Father has put all things (3:35; 5:20). Accordingly, Jesus' farewell not only contains the promise of his permanent presence in and for the church in a timeless sense, but also opens up for the church the way it must go, the command it must fulfill, and the prospect of his return, when the church will see him as he is, in the revelation of his all-encompassing glory and power, for which the Father predestined him before the foundation of the world (cf. 17:24).

14:4-11

"You Know the Way"

In direct connection with the preceding Jesus now speaks further about the life of his disciples on earth after his departure. This becomes the topic of the farewell discourse until Jesus returns at the end of ch. 17 to what he spoke of in 14:1-3.

The internal structure of vss. 4-11 becomes clear only on close scrutiny. Jesus begins by saying that the disciples know the *way* he is going.[35] The theme

---

35. At first sight the sentence construction is somewhat unclear. Strictly speaking it refers only to *his* way, though the way of the disciples is clearly intended as well (vs. 6). Some scholars

is still that of encouragement with a view to the approaching separation (vs. 1), but now not on the basis of his return but on the basis of the disciples' knowledge of where he is going as he leaves and hence also of the place where from now on they will be moving toward, the Father's house (cf. vs. 6). With "you know the way" Jesus is telling them that, however much they may regret his leaving, they need not be in doubt about the destination of their own way on earth. By his departure they are given a clear indication of that goal.

5 Thomas's radical objection to Jesus' statement, though expressed with all respect, is not only characteristic of his own role in the Gospel (see the comments on 11:16; 20:24f.) but also conveys the uncertainty of his fellow disciples ("*we* do not know"). They have no idea what this "going away" is all about if it means the end of their following Jesus as the Messiah of Israel and Son of God confessed by them. How then can they know "the way" of which Jesus is speaking and to which they are apparently reduced as his disciples?

6 Jesus' answer — with good reason called the core statement of this entire Gospel — is striking because in this last and all-encompassing "I am" statement he, as the departing one, calls himself the *way*. It is a way he not only points to but *is*, the only way that gives access to the Father. And it is in that function that he is also *"the truth and the life."* He is the truth as the reliable one, the one who is what he says he is and does what he says he will do, just as he is the "true" vine who will in fact yield fruit (cf. Jr. 2:21). For that reason he is also the life that is from God and that imparts itself as "the light of humans" (1:4) so that they can know the Father as the only true God and Jesus Christ, whom the Father has sent (17:3). In all these core sayings Jesus posits himself in his exclusivity as the one sent by the Father and hence as the only way: "No one comes to the Father *but by me*."[36] Other ways present themselves, but they do not prove to be true in accordance with "God is light and in him there is no darkness at all" (1 Jn. 1:5).

7 In vss. 7-11 the entire focus is once more on this significance of Jesus as the only access to the Father and the guarantee for the ongoing life of the disciples in the world, first in the pronouncement of vs. 7a: "If you have known me, you will know my Father also." Jesus connects their knowledge of the Father and their life in fellowship with the Father not only to the future but above all to the faith experience they have received in their earthly contact with

---

try to bring this out in translation by relating οἴδατε to both ὅπου ἐγὼ ὑπάγω and τὴν ὁδόν ("You know where I am going, and you know the way to it as well"). This undoubtedly conveys the sense, but it is more a clarification than a translation. Some manuscripts insert καί after οἴδατε and repeat οἴδατε after τὸν ὁδον, clearly also as a clarification. But this addition is not necessary for an understanding of the text, especially because the whole emphasis is on "the way," which is certainly not intended only as the way of Jesus.

36. εἰ μὴ δι' ἐμοῦ.

him.[37] In knowing Jesus, that is, in their faith in Jesus as he has revealed himself on earth, lies the secret and certainty for the coming church of its continuing knowledge of God as the Father of Jesus Christ. Because Jesus has kindled that knowledge in the hearts of his own, he cannot be separated from them. In the time that now exists with Jesus' departure[38] they will not be reduced to their own resources or forced to find their own way. Living on the way to the future is living out of faith — knowledge of the God whom Jesus had revealed to them as his Father before their very eyes.

Since the textual witnesses supporting either of the two readings of vs. 7a are nearly equal in value, we must decide between them on the basis of which version of the statement seems more likely in context. Apart from minor differences, they are: "If you had known me, you would have known my Father also" (RSV) and "If you have known me, you will know my Father also." The subjunctive in the first denies the disciples true knowledge of Jesus, while the second assumes just such knowledge and regards it as the necessary condition for knowledge of the Father. Although the disciples — Thomas as well as Philip in vs. 8 — repeatedly give evidence of their incomprehension and "not knowing" (cf. vs. 9), the second reading seems much preferable to us. That Jesus would deny to his disciples knowledge of him and of the Father (like the unbelieving Jews in 8:19) does not seem possible because of vs. 7b[39] and, more generally, because of the bond that united Jesus with his disciples.

8 The last statement, "and you have seen him," again encounters resistance, voiced this time by Philip in a brief but pithy reaction in which he interrupts Jesus: "Lord, show us the Father, and we will be satisfied." Earlier Philip, responding to a "test" question of Jesus, showed that he did not understand the scope of Jesus' authority (6:7).[40] But it is certainly not the Evangelist's

---

37. The "if" is not meant conditionally but rather causally as denoting a reality: "since" (BDF §372.1). For another reading see below.

38. ἀπ' ἄρτι usually means "from now on" and is often so translated here. But as, e.g., in 13:19 (note perfect ἑωράκατε), it evidently refers not to the future that is at that moment being inaugurated but to a situation that has existed (see also Bultmann, *Comm.,* pp. 608, n. 1, 478, n. 4). Other interpreters admittedly think that here, too, the phrase should be translated "from now on (you know him)." In that case they have in mind the coming revelation of Jesus in his suffering and departure to the Father, in which the Father will make himself known in him, or the coming of the Spirit, who will teach them and remind them of all things (vss. 26; 16:13). But both the present "you know him" and the perfect "you have seen him," which is further explained in vss. 9ff., point in another direction.

39. Accordingly, expositors who opt for the first reading are forced to consider whether vs. 7b is an ameliorating addition to the "hard" saying in vs. 7a (e.g., Brown, *Comm.* II, p. 621, who opts for the first reading and declares vs. 7b "suspect as an amelioration of a difficulty").

40. There also commenting on the (in)sufficiency of something; see also Schnackenburg, *Comm.* III, p. 68.

intent to expose Philip in particular as a person lacking in faith. He wants, rather, in conveying the reaction of Philip, a disciple from the beginning (1:43ff.), and Jesus' answer to it, to display both the ultimate basis of the church's faith — which is the revelation — and the contemplation by Jesus' disciples of his glory in the flesh (1:18). Later Jesus will speak of the mission of "another Paraclete" and of his own "coming" again after his departure. But first he must repeat what he has said before in much the same language: that all this can only be, and can only be understood, on the basis of the work he has already accomplished in *this* world (cf. vss. 10, 11).

9-11 Jesus confronts Philip with an appeal to his own dwelling among them, a reality that is now coming to an end: "Have I been with you so long, and yet you have not known[41] me, Philip?" Philip has been one of Jesus' chosen disciples from the beginning (1:43; 15:16, 27). Jesus holds him accountable for that, undoubtedly with a view to the faith of the church whose existence will be based on Philip's witness as well. It was true for Philip in particular — and this is Jesus' accusation — that "the one who has seen me has seen the Father." How then can he still say, "Show us the Father"?

Jesus explicates this anew (see the comments on 10:38; cf. also 14:20; 17:21) in a reciprocal formula of immanence in which he gives expression to his unity with the Father: "Do you not believe[42] that I am in the Father and that the Father is in me?" For "I am in the Father" he appeals to the fact that he does not speak the words he addresses to them "on my own" but solely from within his unity with the Father (cf. 12:49; 6:17; 8:28);[43] and for "the Father is in me" to the fact that the Father does his works in uninterrupted communion with him.[44] Of course, with *"my* words" and *"the Father's* works" Jesus is not setting out a contrast. It is true as well of the works that he does not do them on his own (cf. 5:19), and among the works that God does in him are his words as well (cf. 4:34; 17:4). For that reason "the Father's works" are often interpreted as including Jesus' words and miracles.[45]

Still, there is something to be said, with a view to vs. 11b (cf. 10:38; 15:22, 23), for thinking especially of miracles in "the works" in vs. 10b. It is clear that, from the perspective of Jesus' mission, his words and works are equally revelatory of his unity with the Father, but also that from a human point of view his miracles had more revelatory value than his words.[46] Jesus therefore

41. ἔγνωκας, perfect, refers to a lasting and real acquaintance.

42. οὐ πιστεύεις expects an affirmative answer.

43. On this see at length the comments above on 5:19.

44. ἐν ἐμοὶ μένων.

45. For the understanding and use of ἔργον in John see at length W. Nicol, *The Semeia in the Fourth Gospel,* 1972, pp. 116f.

46. Cf. Brown, *Comm.* II, p. 622, on this text. Brown speaks of "greater confirmatory value."

begins by saying that the words he spoke testified to his unity with the Father. "Believe me that I am in the Father and the Father in me" in vs. 11 means in this context that Jesus' words should also have been enough for his disciples (vs. 8). But when he adds, "but if not, then believe me for the sake of the works themselves," this clearly relates to the effect — visible to all — of Jesus' unity with the Father: the miracles are here, in distinction from his words, "the works themselves." Of course in view of the entire context this is not to say (anymore than in 10:38) that faith in Jesus and in his Father has been reduced to faith in miracles. But in speaking thus at the time of his departure and in response to Philip's "Show us the Father," Jesus does point to the glory of his Father that is visible and tangible in his own coming in the flesh. Under the Father's reign, so manifested, his disciples will be granted life as his followers and witnesses in the world.[47] This simultaneously leads into vss. 12 and 13.

14:12-24

The Continuation of Jesus' Work and Continuing Fellowship with His Own, the Assistance of the Spirit

This section is transitional in that from here on everything is focused on the time — beginning with Jesus' departure — when the disciples will be left behind on earth, the time of the church in the interim between Jesus' departure and his return. Three focal points are prominent here: the progress of Jesus' work and the involvement of his disciples in it, as well as doing this work and keeping his commandments (vss. 12-15); the assistance of the Spirit as the "other Paraclete" (vss. 16-17); and Jesus' ongoing fellowship with his own (vss. 18-24). Here again the thoughts flow into each other and their progression is not sharply demarcated. Thus vss. 12-15 anticipate vss. 18-24. Still there is a clearly discernible structure.

---

47. See also Schnackenburg, *Comm.* III, p. 70: The admonition in the farewell discourse is "clear evidence of the evangelist's deep and radical reflection about the words and works of Jesus as well as his entire activity on earth and his appearance among men."

According to Bultmann, who throughout his commentary relativizes the significance of Jesus' miracles in the Fourth Gospel and in fact regards them as superfluous (see my comments on 11:32ff. above), the statement "and if not, believe me for the sake of the works themselves" refers exclusively to the *words* of Jesus: "Jesus' word . . . discloses a man's reality. If he tries to understand himself by subjecting his existence to this word then he will experience the work of the Father on him" (*Comm.*, pp. 609f.); see also his *Theology of the New Testament* II, 1955, p. 61: "the 'works' of v. 11 are neither more nor less than the 'words' of v. 10"; cf. further his *Comm.*, pp. 388 and 390. But how could the alternative (εἰ μή) to faith in Jesus' word (that is, his saying that he and the Father are one and that the disciples have seen the Father in him) lie in faith in that same word? Against this view see also Schnackenburg, Brown, and other commentators, as also Nicol, *Semeia in the Fourth Gospel,* p. 119.

12 The disciples have been witnesses of Jesus' works while he has been with them (so the preceding verses), and this is the permanent basis not only for their faith (and through them that of the coming church, 20:30, 31) but also for their involvement in the progress of his works on earth after he has gone from them. The new solemn opening ("Truly, truly, I say to you") places a particularly heavy emphasis on the connection between faith and the disciples' involvement in his works.[48] The statement, thus introduced, that "the one who believes in me will also do the works that I do; and even[49] greater works than these will that person do" thus gains the character of an authoritative promise to the disciples, the fulfillment of which will even surpass what they have been seeing him do.

Exegetes have always wondered what is signified by "and even greater than these." Surely the disciples will not do greater works than the raising of Lazarus or the healing of a man blind from birth? The end of vs. 12, "because I go to the Father," points in a different direction. "Greater" does not mean that their works will surpass those of Jesus but that the works that Jesus has done on earth are merely the beginnings and signs of the all-encompassing power and glory with which he as the heavenly Lord will be clothed and in the exercise of which the disciples will be involved in this dispensation of redemptive history. Twice earlier Jesus has spoken of "greater things" than those that he has shown to his disciples and other spectators (1:50; 5:20), and in both cases he refers to the Son of man, the apocalyptic figure clothed with all power (Dn. 7:13-14) with whom he identifies himself. In the farewell discourse Jesus does not speak (as, e.g., in 3:13; 6:62; 8:28; 12:23, 31ff.) of the Son of man. Nor does he portray the future task and position of the disciples in apocalyptic language, as in Lk. 22:29f., where, in his final dialogues with them, he appoints for them a kingdom as the Father has appointed it for him (cf. Mt. 28:18). And here (as in vss. 13-14) he puts the missionary mandate of his disciples in a grand perspective, but limits himself to that general promise — as he does elsewhere when he calls the disciples the "reapers" of what others (including himself) have "sown" (4:37f.) — the concrete and still unsuspected fulfillment of which will be manifest only later (cf. 16:12, 13).

13, 14 But the extent to which Jesus holds himself responsible and accountable for this fulfillment — at the same time and in the same act further explaining the real secret of these "greater works" — is evident from the answers to prayer he promises, a motif that recurs in the following chapters in various forms (15:16; 16:23, 24, 26; see also 15:7; 1 Jn. 3:21, 22; 5:14, 15). "Ask in my name" occurs only in John (but cf. Mt. 18:19, 20). It means something like "ask with an appeal to me." But here Jesus is not only the one

---

48. For a similar effect of the ἀμὴν ἀμὴν λέγω ὑμῖν, see the comments above on 10:1.
49. καί here has an ascensive sense: "even." See BDF §442.12.

in whose name the disciples will pray but also the one to whom they will address their prayers[50] and who will himself answer them — unlike 15:16; 16:23, where the Father is the one addressed and the one who answers. Consequently, the text adds, "that the Father may be glorified in the Son." The glorification of the Father in the Son will continue on earth even after Jesus has gone to the Father. But the works are still his, and he continues to bear responsibility for them, even though he has involved and authorized his disciples to assist therein as his apostles. Therefore, when they pray for the performance of those works with an appeal to his name, they can count on him to hear them. That is the pledge repeated with all due clarity and emphasis in vs. 14.[51]

Most remarkable in this pronouncement of course is the unqualified and unconditional nature of Jesus' promise: "*whatever*[52] you ask in my name," "if you ask anything in my name." Other similar promises of answered prayer add conditions such as doing the commandments, prayer in accordance with the will of God, or the agreement of two or more believers in what is asked (1 Jn. 3:21, 22; 5:14, 15; Mt. 18:19). It is often said that these conditions "may have been dictated by the realistic experience in the life of the community that not all requests were granted."[53] It is usually concluded that the unconditional forms of the sayings are therefore "more original" and that "in the Johannine tradition the conditioned forms are not attributed to Jesus."[54]

Regardless of whether the sayings with conditions are understood as accommodations to experience, the saying here is not intended as an unconditional pledge that every believing prayer, of whatever content, will be heard. The saying must be understood in immediate connection with what precedes: it ties in with "for I go to the Father" and explains the "for" by suggesting that from his position in heaven Jesus will do whatever the disciples ask with a view to the glorification of the Father in the Son.[55] This saying must always, in fact, be understood anew in this context, with regard to both what Jesus' disciples may ask of him, the Exalted One, and what they may expect as answers in this earthly dispensation. The main point is that, by putting so much stress here and in what follows on prayer in his name, Jesus is pledging to his disciples

50. At least according to the most commonly followed reading, με, in vs. 14. Although in vs. 13 με is lacking after αἰτήσητε, it is also — as ποιήσω proves — presupposed there.

51. Despite the omission of this verse as redundant in some manuscripts and the fact that it is "disputed and omitted by many recent literary critics" (Schnackenburg, *Comm.* III, p. 73).

52. ὅ τι ἄν.

53. So Brown, *Comm.* II, p. 635.

54. Ibid.

55. Cf. M. de Jonge, *Jesus: Stranger from Heaven and Son of God,* p. 178: "vs. 12 gives the assurance that 'whoever believes in me, the works that I do he shall do also, and greater works than these shall he do.' Why? Because Jesus is going to the Father and will do whatever the believers shall ask 'in his name.' "

that he is not withdrawing from them by his departure but will be able, because of his heavenly glory, to give them everything they will need for the continuation of his work on earth, and he refers them to prayer as the way of his continuing fellowship with them.

After what was said first in vss. 9-11 and then in vss. 12-14 to encourage the perplexed disciples, vss. **15-24** further explicate the promise of Jesus' continuing fellowship from two very important perspectives: that of the sending of "another Paraclete" (vss. 16-17) and that of Jesus' own coming to them (vss. 18-24). The starting point of the whole passage is "keep my commandments" (vs. 15), to which there is recurrent reference in vss. 21, 23, and 24 (which is why vss. 15-24 belong together and why vs. 18 must not, as some interpreters think, be taken as the beginning of a new topic and a new pericope).

Verse **15** furnishes a further specification of what the disciples must do on the road ahead: "keep my commandments." In this Jesus appeals to their love for him, partly because now that he is leaving them they are clearly showing it (cf. 13:36).[56] But he asks them to show that love in keeping the commandments later when he is gone. For that reason we must not think here primarily of moral precepts but of what Jesus has earlier revealed to them and taught them, that is, what vss. 23 and 25 (referring back to vs. 15) call his "word" (cf. 8:51f.; 15:20; 17:6). On the road ahead that will count above all in the keeping (not just in the sense of a precious possession but in the sense of a command to be carried out) of Jesus' commandments. In so doing they will be revealed in the world as his disciples.

Verses **16-17** speak of how in this practice Jesus will demonstrate to them his permanent help and fellowship. To that end he first promises them that, on his request, the Father "will give you another Paraclete to be with you forever," a promise only stated generally in this first announcement of the sending of the Paraclete; further explication of this promise will follow later. But at this point we must take a closer look at the general significance of the Paraclete as it is conveyed in these chapters of the Fourth Gospel and in the New Testament as a whole.[57]

The (Other) Paraclete

Here we have the first of five most remarkable pronouncements on the Paraclete (see further 14:26; 15:26; 16:7-11, 12-15). He will be *another* Paraclete, that is, someone other than the one the disciples have until now possessed in the person of Jesus

---

56. ἐάν has the meaning of εἴ where it introduces a causal indicative (cf. BDF §373): "if you truly love me, as I know you do." The following τηρήσετε is close in intent to the indicative (which some manuscripts have), but then in the form of the expression of trust.

57. Leaving aside 1 Jn. 2:1, which speaks of Jesus himself.

himself.[58] This Paraclete will take Jesus' place after Jesus' departure (cf. 16:7) and in his activity as Paraclete will do nothing other than what Jesus has been doing,[59] except that in doing it he will continue and advance Jesus' work. He is further described as "the Spirit of truth" (vs. 17; 15:26; 16:13) or simply "the Holy Spirit." It is striking that these "Spirit" designations are further descriptions of the Paraclete and not, as one might expect, the reverse. There can be no doubt that with these further characterizations the Evangelist is speaking of the Spirit of God as he is mentioned repeatedly throughout the Gospel in his absolute divine mode of existence and life-conferring power. Accordingly, as further characterizations of the other Paraclete, these names do not point to a conceptual universe in which a variety of spirits, both good and evil, act individually and make themselves felt in the world; the reference here is to nothing other than the Spirit of God as he manifests himself in the Paraclete, the Spirit of God who leads the church into the truth, the Holy Spirit who keeps the church close to God and distinguishes it from the world.

This does not of course explain the uniqueness of this name "Paraclete" for the Spirit, which is found only in the Fourth Gospel. In the history of exegesis, especially in recent years, much attention has been devoted to the name,[60] without leading to a consensus. Two main issues are at stake. First, what is the specific meaning of the word παράκλητος as a designation for the work of the Holy Spirit? Second, does this use of the word have its background in similar ideas in the Old Testament, in Jewish writings, or outside Judaism and, if so, to what degree?

As to the first of these questions, the consensus is that in John 14–16 παράκλητος does not have the meaning in Greek and Hellenistic usage of "advocate, professional legal adviser, defender, or representative before a court."[61] In 1 Jn. 2:1 Jesus himself is very clearly called "an advocate with the Father," and this function is attributed to the Spirit elsewhere in the New Testament (cf. Ro. 8:27), though without the title παράκλητος. But in John 14–16 no such function of the Spirit as advocate of the disciples and defender before God is mentioned. Some Greek and Latin patristic writers did understand and translate the term in the juridical sense in these chapters, but also understood the Paraclete as "Comforter," a meaning derivable from the active sense of the verb παρακαλέω,[62] clear proof that even then exegetes were not satisfied with the translation "advocate." But it is clear from what is said in the five statements in chs. 14–16 about the work of the Paraclete as the "Spirit of truth" who will lead the disciples into all truth, stand by them in their witness to Jesus and in their confrontation

---

58. This is certainly the intent. It is not, as only a few translate, "another, a Paraclete," a translation that excludes the idea of a preceding Paraclete. Against this view, see, e.g., J. Behm, *TDNT* V, 800.

59. See the summary and comparison in Bultmann, *Comm.,* pp. 566f.

60. See J. Behm, *TDNT* V, pp. 800-814; O. Betz, *Der Paraklet,* 1963; R. Brown, "The Paraclete in the Fourth Gospel," *NTS* 13 (1967), pp. 113-32; G. Johnston, *The Spirit-Paraclete in the Gospel of John,* 1970; U. B. Müller, "Die Parakletenvorstellung im Johannesevangelium," *ZTK* 71 (1974), pp. 31-77; J. Veenhof, *De Parakleet,* 1974. See also the excursuses in Bultmann, *Comm.,* pp. 566-72; Schnackenburg, *Comm.* III, pp. 138-54; Becker, *Comm.,* pp. 470-75 (with extensive bibliography, p. 470).

61. For the material see, e.g., J. Behm, *TDNT* V, pp. 800ff.

62. Ibid., p. 803.

with "the world," and show them the way to the future[63] that the translation "Comforter" is also inadequate.

If the special use of παράκλητος in John 14–16 cannot be ascertained on the basis of the ancient usage known to us, then we are led to the second question we have asked, which has been posed especially in more recent studies: Can we point to concepts or figures belonging to the religious environment of the New Testament that served as background for the figure of the Paraclete in John? Functions attributed in John to the Paraclete (like "guiding into truth," "bringing to remembrance," etc.) are widely ascribed to other God-given spirits, angels, wisdom, and the like.[64] This shows that in his descriptions of the work of the Spirit John was not speaking in a vacuum but could in all sorts of ways make terminological connections with expressions from the Old Testament and other religious literature. But it does not explain the specific use he makes of the word παράκλητος.

Others, therefore, have adopted as their starting point the concept — prevalent in the environment of the New Testament — of persons or angels or the Spirit (or even sacrifices and the like) that serve as advocates with God on behalf of the people.[65] With a view to the context of John 14–16 emphasis is given to the broader understanding of advocacy in the passages in question: the advocate with God is also God's witness to humans (like Moses). Thus the Spirit is said not only to be the Advocate speaking to God on behalf of people but also one who speaks to people on behalf of God.[66]

While all these extensive studies have cast much light on the figure of the advocate in the Old Testament and early Jewish literature, they do not solve the real problem: in John 14–16 the Spirit is not an (or the) advocate for the disciples; therefore this title cannot have been borrowed from the advocate figures of the Old Testament

---

63. Not so H. Riesenfeld, who persists in translating "Comforter," appealing to the Old Testament figure of Wisdom, specifically as it appears in Pr. 8:4ff. While "comforter" and "comfort" have an eschatological sense in other Old Testament passages as well, such as Isaiah 40ff., in Pr. 8:4 — as is evident from the Septuagint translation — Wisdom is said to assume the role of the eschatological Comforter, and in view of the functions further attributed to Wisdom in Proverbs, these instances have given rise both to the *idea and the name* of the Paraclete, the one who is the Spirit of Truth, as this is manifest in John 14–16. So Riesenfeld in "A Probable Background to the Johannine Paraclete," in *Ex orbe religionum* (Festschrift for G. Widengren) I, 1972, pp. 266-74, specifically pp. 272f.

But the Septuagint translation in Pr. 8:4, παρακαλῶ need not mean "comfort" (instead of "call") and seems in any case a weak ground for the view that Wisdom in Proverbs 8 produced both the name and the idea for "the eschatological Comforter" as the background of John 14–16.

64. On this general background see at length Brown, "The Paraclete in the Fourth Gospel," and his *Comm.* II, pp. 1135-39. He refers to "the basic elements, scattered in Jewish thought, that appear in the Johannine picture of the Paraclete" (p. 1139). For a summary of these more general features see also J. Behm, *TDNT* V, pp. 806-12.

65. For the texts in question see Strack/Billerbeck II, pp. 560f., and, at length, N. Johansson, *"Parakletoi." Vorstellungen von Fürsprechern für die Menschen vor God in der alttestamentlichen Religion, im Spätjudentum und im Urchristentum,* 1940.

66. A position already defended by S. Mowinckel in "Die Vorstellungen des Spätjudentums vom heiligen Geist als Fürsprecher," *ZNW* 52 (1933), pp. 97-130; in the same line, see Johansson, *"Parakletoi,"* pp. 157ff. Also J. Behm, *TDNT* V, pp. 806ff., despite questions that he raises and difficulties that attend this view, which he does not consider insuperable (p. 812).

or other sources. Such "advocates" are, in isolated and disparate statements, credited with functions that sometimes echo, though not exactly, what is said about the Paraclete in John. But such functions are always closely linked with their advocacy functions as result or accompanying function, while in John it is precisely advocacy that is lacking in the work of the Spirit as Paraclete.[67]

O. Betz locates the Johannine Paraclete concept much more specifically in Jewish writings, in what he calls the "heretical" Qumran literature.[68] Betz does start by assuming an advocacy function for the Paraclete. In the theology of the Qumran sect, he says, this function developed in a very specific and characteristic fashion, namely in the dualistic notion of the two opposimg principles of the present age, "the spirit of truth" and "the spirit of deception," Michael and Belial, the teacher of righteousness and his opponents. It is within the framework of this cosmic-dualistic judicial struggle that Betz understands the Johannine Paraclete, who as "the Spirit of truth" enters the arena against the deceptive spirit of the world as the great Advocate of the church and Accuser of the world.

However many incidental points of agreement may be demonstrable here,[69] the differences in content are far too great for us to be able to find the background for the Johannine "Spirit of truth" in Qumran's dualistic struggle of the spirits. Decisive here is first of all the context in which the Paraclete of John 14–16 is introduced and receives his place in the history of redemption. Jesus calls him "another Paraclete," obviously as one in addition to himself. He makes it clear that all that this Paraclete does is related to the continuation of his own work and is determined in content by his work. The Paraclete as "Spirit of truth" no more finds his background in angel or spirit figures of the Old Testament or the contemporary religious thought world than Jesus as the Son of God sent by the Father finds his background as Paraclete in those figures.[70] The Holy Spirit as Paraclete is not an alien figure in the Gospel, a being or spirit whose origin and identity must be more precisely established. He is rather specifically called "the Spirit of truth" or simply "the Holy Spirit," and is no other than the Spirit of whom the Gospel speaks regularly (cf. 3:5f., 34; 4:23; 6:63; 7:39; 20:22).

As for the antithetical element in the work of the Spirit, the antithesis with "the world," which plays such a large role in the Fourth Gospel as a whole, comes to clear expression in the sayings about the Paraclete. This occurs already with the first introduction of "the Spirit of truth," which, in contrast with the disciples, "the world cannot

---

67. Accordingly, most of the more recent commentaries see little of value in this (temporarily popular) explanation; see, e.g., Schnackenburg, Becker, and Bultmann. Bultmann writes: "there is no point in going back to Jewish ideas to discover the origin of the figure of the Paraclete, because the interpretation of this figure as Spirit is secondary" (*Comm.,* p. 570). Bultmann himself looks for the religio-historical background in Gnostic (and other) writings in which certain mythological figures are described as "helpers" and guides, ideas that show much more correspondence with the functions of the Paraclete in John 14–16. But here, too, the distance is very great (see the comments below on the view of O. Betz).

68. Betz, *Der Paraklet.*

69. Ibid., pp. 176-202.

70. Cf. Becker, *Comm.,* p. 472: "It is hardly the case that personal-angelological concepts stood godfather to the Johannine Spirit-Paraclete concept, and a direct derivation of the Johannine Spirit of truth from Qumran is impossible on religio-historical grounds."

receive." And in 15:18–16:15, which refers to the "hatred of the world" against the disciples, the help they will receive from the Spirit is said in 16:8-11 to consist in the fact that in three ways the Spirit will put the world in the wrong. Nevertheless, in all this we are not dealing with a still undecided "dualistic power struggle," nor is the picture in 16:8-11 that of a legal trial (before God) in which the Spirit as advocate argues the rights of the church against a spirit of deception.[71] It is, rather, of the accomplished fact of Christ's victory (16:33), whose truth and consequences the Spirit will forever make plain and thus assist the church on its way into the future. Here again it is evident that the designation "Paraclete" does not find its origin from the Spirit being an advocate in a still undecided trial but in the reality of the Spirit positively guiding the church into all truth, bringing to the church's remembrance all the words of Jesus.

Therefore, for the specific use and meaning of the name "Paraclete" in John 14–16 we are dependent on the texts themselves and cannot base our conclusions on representations and figures in other sources. Some, perhaps most,[72] scholars think that the title, so understood, already existed in the Christian tradition with which John was in contact. Even if this is true, it does not help us interpret and translate the term, since texts to establish this are lacking. An argument to the contrary is that this qualification of the Spirit is used exclusively in chs. 14–16 and that in 14:16, where it occurs for the first time, it has no definite article (so that it is "another Paraclete") and so is clearly not a term for the Spirit with which the readers are assumed to be familiar. It is only in the later sayings that we read of *the* Paraclete, namely the one referred to in 14:16, and that the designation thus acquires the status of a title. All this supports the thesis that Jesus uses the term here ad hoc, referring thus to an understanding of the Spirit specific to this context.[73] The function of the Spirit as described here is clearly defined by the situation of the approaching farewell, that is, by what the disciples would especially need once Jesus had left.[74] The Spirit is therefore the one "who will be with you forever," whom "you know because he remains with you and will be in you"; that is, he will make himself known to them in the permanent assistance and fellowship that he will give to them. And that in contrast with "the world," which "cannot receive him" because it lacks the proper spiritual organ needed to perceive him and hence will not know him either. "Paraclete" — we may conclude — here has a specific meaning that can hardly be conveyed in one word in our language (and many others) but of which the dominant idea is of someone who offers assistance in a situation in which help is needed.[75]

---

71. See the exegesis below, pp. 531f.

72. According to Schnackenburg, *Comm.* III, p. 148.

73. Cf. Becker, *Comm.,* pp. 473f.

74. It has been correctly remarked that other "very fundamental functions of the Holy Spirit [e.g., those mentioned in ch. 3] are not mentioned here" (L. Floor, *Persoon en werk van de Heilige Geest,* 1988, p. 33).

75. Cf., e.g., Brown, "The Paraclete in the Fourth Gospel," pp. 118ff.:

No one translation (like "witness," "spokesman," "counsellor," "helper") captures the complexity of these functions. In rendering this word into Latin for the Vulgate, Jerome had a choice among such Old Latin renderings as *advocatus* and *consolator* and the custom

In that sense, too, he is the "*other* Paraclete" besides Jesus. This proves that Jesus does not equate himself with the Spirit.[76] Even with respect to his heavenly existence and his future, Jesus is not the Spirit, and what is said elsewhere of the Spirit is not all true of Jesus. This distinction of persons and work will be maintained every time that we read of the unique activity of the Spirit over against Jesus and of Jesus' activity over against the Spirit (e.g., 15:26; 16:7). Highly characteristic for the Fourth Gospel, on the other hand, is how closely the work of the Spirit as Paraclete of the church in the interim is bound up with that of Jesus himself and must be understood completely in its light — proof, if further proof is needed, that the Fourth Gospel's christology is its all-controlling motif. The paraclete is another (*the* other) Paraclete besides Jesus, the one whom the Father will send at Jesus' request, in the service of true insight into what Jesus has said (cf. vs. 26). He will not speak from himself but will glorify Jesus and take all that he has to say "from me" (Jesus). Thus all his work will go back to that of Jesus (cf. 16:13ff.). Hence the striking resemblance of the work of the Spirit and Jesus' own work.[77] Sometimes their activities even totally coincide, as in 14:23, where it is said that Jesus, with the Father, will "make our home" with the person who keeps his word, which is said in virtually identical words[78] of the Spirit as well (cf. 14:16, 17).[79]

18-20 Vs. 18, with a fresh start, continues the line of thought begun in vss. 12ff. Regardless of what has been said of the sending of the Spirit, it is also

---

of transliterating the term simply as *paracletus*. In the Gospel he took the latter expedient (*advocatus* appears in 1 John), a course also followed in the Syriac and Coptic traditions.

Brown recommends that we do the same and use "Paraclete, a near transliteration that at least preserves the uniqueness of the title and does not emphasize one of the aspects of the concept to the detriment of others." In his translation Schnackenburg also lets the original word stand (*Comm.* III, pp. 138-54). Bultmann writes: "The meaning of the term here is 'helper,' not 'advocate' as it is in I Jn. 2:1" (*Theology* II, p. 88 n.).

76. On this see also Floor, *Persoon en werk van de Heilige Geest,* pp. 32f.

77. For a complete list of corresponding statements about the Spirit and about Jesus, see Bultmann, *Comm.,* p. 567. Cf. also his *Theology* II, pp. 88f.

78. Cf. μονή in vs. 23 with μένειν in vs. 17.

79. Bultmann speaks of the Paraclete as "a parallel figure to Jesus himself" (*Comm.,* p. 567). He claims that the Evangelist has taken over the motif of "two successive sendings of two Paracletes" ("the duplication of the figure of the Revealer") from his Gnostic source as an "appropriate form" for expressing his conception of the Holy Spirit (*Comm.,* p. 567). Elsewhere Bultmann speaks of a "two-fold designation" that is solely intended to make certain the progress and power of the revelation, "the power of the proclamation in the community" (pp. 553ff.).

Still, however strong the parallelism between the work of the Spirit in the church and the work of Jesus, it is hard to think that the Evangelist needed a mythological figure stemming from the thought-world of Gnosticism to give expression to this concurrence. The Holy Spirit is not a new figure imported into this context. What unites the person of the Spirit as "the other Paraclete" so closely with that of the glorified Christ and makes their respective activities one is the care of the church, which is given as a task to Jesus by the Father (cf. 17:6ff.) in the new dispensation of salvation inaugurated with Jesus' glorification.

true of Jesus himself as the departing one that "I will not leave you behind as orphans." The idea of "orphans" is evoked by his farewell and refers to the relation between Jesus and his own as teacher and pupils.[80] In 13:33 Jesus, admittedly, calls his disciples "children," but Jesus is nowhere called their father.

Then, very simply, follows the statement "I will come to you." Over the years this "coming" has been interpreted in close connection with vs. 3, whether, as in the exegesis of the ancient Latin fathers, by applying the content of vss. 19 and 20 totally to Jesus' parousia, or, as some moderns do, by taking everything that occurs after Jesus' departure (resurrection, ascension, Pentecost, and second coming) as a single "coming" in which successive phases are not temporally distinguished.[81] But though "I will come to you" as such is non-specific, it is clear from what immediately follows that this "coming" and the disciples' soon-to-be expected seeing again of Jesus[82] can only be the self-revelation visible to the disciples of Jesus of the risen one in his appearing to them.[83] Also what follows, "because I live, you will live also" and "in that day you will know," points in that direction, though obviously "you will live also" does not apply only to those who have "seen" Jesus as the risen one (20:29).

"In that day" marks the great transition to be effected by Jesus' resurrection.[84] For the world Jesus' going away represents the end of the time in which the light was present (12:35). "Yet a little while" is a heavily charged phrase

80. Cf. Strack/Billerbeck II, p. 563, for the use of the same imagery in rabbinic literature. The idea that "orphans" here has the same sense as "the poor" (οἱ πτωχοί) has in Mt. 5:3; 11:5; Lk. 4:18; 6:20, etc., which would then characterize the role of the Paraclete as that of the great advocate of the oppressed people of God in the trial between God and Satan taking shape in the coming of God's Kingdom (a thesis that D. E. Holwerda defends at length in his dissertation, *The Holy Spirit and Eschatology in the Gospel of John,* 1959), is hard to make plausible in the context of chs. 14–16 and is therefore certainly not to be accepted as "a key to the understanding of the Farewell Discourses" (proposition 2 in Holwerda's dissertation; see also p. 38).

81. See, e.g., Bultmann, *Comm.,* p. 620; see also p. 580.

82. 16:16 reads "A little while, and you will see me no more; again a little while, and you will see me," and therefore even more clearly pinpoints the meaning of "yet a little while" in 14:19. Cf. also Brown, *Comm.,* ad loc.: "the statement in vs. 19 that the world will not see Jesus does not fit the parousia at all."

83. For this θεωρεῖν, alternating with ὁρᾶν, as terminology that bears exclusively on the visible appearance of Jesus, see 20:14, 20, 25, 27, 29; Schnackenburg: "The Easter experience is the subject of reflection in this statement" (*Comm.* III, p. 78).

84. Some scholars, appealing to 16:23, interpret "day" more broadly as "time," which then applies also to "coming" and "seeing" (e.g., Fischer, *Die himmlischen Wohnungen,* pp. 318ff.). θεωρεῖν would then denote in general the continuing "new experience of the Lord" and not "a once-for-all event" (Fischer, p. 316). But θεωρεῖν, like ὁρᾶν, is used exclusively for the appearances and in this connection also shapes the meaning of "in that day," even though that phrase taken alone can, in fact, denote a longer period. Cf. Schnackenburg on 14:20: "On 'that day,' that is, the day of Easter, that true knowing . . . begins" (*Comm.* III, p. 79).

familiar from the Old Testament (Is. 10:25; 29:17; Jr. 28:17 LXX; Ho. 1:4; Ps. 36:10 LXX) that indicates a state of being left alone and "seeking in vain" (7:33, 34). For the disciples, however, "yet a little while . . . and you will see me." His coming to them will not be long delayed and will deliver them from the uncertainty in which now they are still caught up. With "because I live, you will live also" Jesus does not mean that this life will not be theirs until later or that faith in it will be based on this "seeing." For Jesus' entire self-revelation has already consisted in the reality that he is the Resurrection and the Life; everyone who now believes in him, even if he or she dies, will yet live (11:25; cf. 5:26, 27; 10:18). The saying "because I live, you will live also" rather means that in Jesus' coming and their "seeing" him it will become overpoweringly clear that just as death has no power over him, so no one will be able to snatch them out of his hand, and all this because of his unity with the Father (cf. 10:28-30).

For, as vs. 20 tells us, "in that day," that is, the day of his resurrection, "you will know that I am in my Father, and you in me, and I in you." It is that unbreakable unity of the Father and the Son that will effect the resurrection and into which from now on the disciples will be incorporated — a unity of life between him and them that will be expressed in the same "reciprocal formula of immanence" as that of the unity of the Father and the Son (cf. 17:21ff.), what Paul refers to when he speaks of dying with Christ and of being raised with him (Ro. 6:3ff.; Col. 2:12; 3:1ff.) and which will be further unfolded in what follows.

21 In a way that is typical for the Fourth Gospel, vs. 21 harks back to vs. 15 in order to place the meaning of what was said there in a broader context and a clearer light. Again Jesus speaks of having and doing[85] his commandments (in the broad sense of "my word"; cf. vss. 23f. and see the comments on vs. 15) as the indispensable (vs. 15) and unmistakable (vs. 21) evidence of his disciples' love for him. While earlier, in vss. 16 and 17, Jesus has already pledged to them the assistance of the Spirit, he now returns to it as the great principle of the continuing fellowship he will maintain with them in his "coming" to them in and after the resurrection. Thus one can say that vs. 21 further interprets the immediately preceding words "you in me, and I in you." But here — and here again the power of the resurrection proves itself — the love of the Father is included and given prominence: "He who loves me will be loved by my Father." At the same time we learn the real and final goal of Jesus' departure. Not that the Father will only be moved to that love by the return of his Son and the completion of his task (cf. 3:16). But the Father's love only comes fully into its own and finds its dwelling place (cf. vs. 23) in those who

---

85. ἔχειν and τηρεῖν "are parallel and correspond in the same way as ἀκούω and φυλάσσω (12:47) or ἀκούω and πιστεύω (5:24)" (H. Riesenfeld, *TDNT* VIII, p. 144).

have received Jesus as the one sent by him (3:16; cf. 16:27) and have been moved by Jesus to faith in the love of God.

But this leaves untouched what the disciples may still expect from Jesus himself, as is evident from the end of vs. 21. However much in his departure to be with the Father there is an element of "stepping back" behind the Father (cf. vs. 28; 16:26f.), still the love existing between Jesus and the disciples remains the lasting foundation of their fellowship; from their side, in keeping his commandments and doing his word; from his side, in "I will love him and manifest myself to him."

The word translated "manifest"[86] occurs only here in John's Gospel and can have several meanings.[87] By itself it could very well refer to Jesus' appearances after his resurrection (Mt. 27:53, though in the rest of the New Testament it is not used for this purpose; see also Ac. 10:43 and Mk. 16:9),[88] and the choice of this striking word can certainly be explained in part in terms of the influence of contexts in which the appearances are clearly in view. Still, here it is clear from the context that the self-manifestation of Jesus mentioned in vs. 21 is not restricted to those appearances. The transition from the second to the third person in vss. 20 and 21 by itself points to a more general meaning. But it is evident especially from the further explanation Jesus gives in vs. 20 that we are here dealing with his progressive self-revelation after his departure.[89] Admittedly, as stated above, the transitions are fluid. The different stages of Jesus' coming in ch. 14 (vss. 3, 19, 23), however undeniable, are not sharply demarcated from each other in their temporal succession. The intent of the structure of the discourse is clearly not to describe the stages of the redemptive dispensation beginning after Jesus' death, but rather, with the reserve with which Jesus speaks before his resurrection, referring his disciples to the other Paraclete for what is to come (16:12ff.), to bring home to them one thing: Jesus will not leave them behind as orphans but will, also after his first "coming" (vs.18), manifest himself to them again and again as the Living One (cf. vs. 23).

22-24 However, it is this "self-revelation" promised by Jesus to his disciples, in contrast to the world's failure to see, which he has predicted, which

86. ἐμφανίζω.

87. See R. Bultmann and D. Lührmann, *TDNT* IX, pp. 7f.

88. Where words having the same stem are used for the appearances: ἐμφανὴ γενέσθαι (Ac. 10:43), ἐφάνη (Mk. 16:9), and ἐφανερώθη (Jn. 21:14).

89. For some interpreters this is a reason for believing that in vss. 19f. as well the reference is not to the resurrection and to "seeing" the appearances but to Jesus' fellowship with his own in a general and lasting sense (cf. the comments on vss. 19f.). Others even think that in vs. 21 the aim of the saying is to reinterpret the entire traditional view of "the appearances of the Risen One," as in Mk. 16:9 — where the related word ἐφάνη is used — and that in the sense of vs. 23 (cf. R. Bultmann and D. Lührmann, *TDNT* IX, p. 7; Becker, *Comm.*, p. 468). However, in our opinion, the import of vss. 19 and 20 too clearly proves the opposite.

causes Judas[90] to ask, "Why?"[91] According to some scholars, the question is prompted by the thought that showing himself demonstratively to the world would serve Jesus' cause better than merely revealing himself to the disciples, a consideration that will later be used by unbelieving critics of Jesus' resurrection and that the Evangelist puts in Judas's mouth here. But even without this last item of information, the question attributed to Judas is not at all hard to understand: Why must the world be excluded? Would not the world, on seeing Jesus again, be much more willing to believe in him?

Jesus' answer (vs. 23) contains nothing other than what Jesus has already said in vs. 21. His self-revelation after his departure will only be open to those who will keep his word as the word of the one sent by the Father and thus give proof of their love for him. It is they, therefore, who are loved by God and may count on his continuing fellowship. This fellowship is described here, and this new element further qualifies Jesus' self-revelation: "and we will come to him and make our home with him."[92]

The idea of God dwelling with his people is a frequent motif in the Old Testament and is used there in both cultic and eschatological senses (e.g., Ex. 25:8; Ezk. 37:26f.; Zc. 2:10 LXX[93]). The reference here is to the new spiritual presence — prepared by Jesus — of God in the hearts of people (cf. 4:23, 24), to be understood of course in close connection with the ongoing indwelling of the Spirit (vs. 17). Again Jesus mentions "coming," as in vs. 18 (and vs. 3), but now in the plural, the "we" of Jesus with the Father, which is repeatedly stressed (vs. 21; 16:27). Again it is expressed — and here in the image of indwelling — that only with Jesus' departure will the real purpose of his coming and dwelling on earth (1:14) be achieved. That purpose is the restoration of human fellowship with God himself (cf. vs. 28). Jesus no longer comes alone, as the one sent by the Father, to pave the way for God's love in the world and to create a dwelling place for that love in the hearts of his own. He comes, rather, together with the Father, "for the Father himself loves you, because you have loved me and have believed that I came from the Father" (16:27).

90. Expressly distinguished from Judas Iscariot (cf. Lk. 6:16; Ac. 1:13), later also identified with the Thaddaeus mentioned in Mk. 3:18 and the Lebbaeus of Mt. 10:3. Syriac manuscripts read, in place of "Judas," either "Thomas" (sy[S]) or "Judas Thomas" (sy[C]). For the implications of this reading, which is generally considered secondary, see A. F. J. Klijn, "John XIV and the Name Judas Thomas," in *Studies in John* (Festschrift for J. N. Sevenster), 1970, pp. 88-96.

91. καί (lacking in some manuscripts but not unusual in questions; cf. BDF §442.8) τί (= διὰ τί) γέγονεν ὅτι (= δι' ὅτι), literally "And for what reason is it? Why?"

92. μονὴν . . . ποιησόμεθα. The difference between this and the more customary μένειν (1:38; cf. 14:17) is that it gives expression to the initiatory act: "take up residence."

93. Where the daughter of Zion is exhorted to rejoice, "For lo, I come and I will pitch my tent (κατασκηνώσω) among you."

But still remarkable is the parallelism with the act of "preparing a place" in vss. 1, 2. There, too, the reference is to occupying "dwellings," but there the concern is with places in heaven "in my Father's house," whence Jesus "comes" to take his own to himself in the dwellings prepared for them there. In this pre-Easter discourse Jesus always refers to the whole of his future fellowship with his own with the one word "come," and the succession of different redemptive-historical phases in this coming is largely veiled. Nevertheless in this strikingly diverse use of the same image there is additional proof of the differences in this "coming" and therefore of the untenability of the view that in John the resurrection and the parousia coincide, with no mention of a clearly distinguishable interim between the two of them.[94]

Finally (vs. 24), in response to Judas's question why Jesus does not reveal himself to the world, Jesus says only, "Whoever does not love me does not keep my words." At this point he draws no further conclusions but the intent is clear. Again the point is that keeping Jesus' words is the criterion of loving and belonging to him.

Accordingly, when Jesus said of the world that it will "see him no more" (vs. 19), this is not because he has excluded it in advance. "No more" tells us that the world has "seen" and especially heard Jesus while he has been among them as the light and has said to them, "While you have the light, believe in the light" (12:35, 36). From all this — contracted here into "my words" — no one is excluded; but one who does not keep Jesus' words — this is the unspoken conclusion — excludes himself or herself from seeing the Risen One and from lasting fellowship with him and the Father. All this is so because of the decisive significance of the *word,* of which Jesus finally (also, significantly, in answer to Judas) once more says: "and the word that you hear is not mine but that of the Father who sent me." Therefore, "the world will see me no more" does not mean that after Jesus' departure there is no future left other than the "darkness" against which Jesus has warned but — and this is the dominant thrust throughout the Fourth Gospel — that there is no fellowship with the heavenly Jesus for those who think they can escape the decision confronting them in the word of the earthly Jesus, the one sent by the Father.

---

94. As two representations of the same thing, namely that faith in Jesus means being transposed into "eternal life" as "eschatological existence." Cf. Bultmann, *Comm.,* pp. 622f.; Becker, *Comm.,* pp. 468f.; also Schnackenburg writes: "The statement in v. 2 about the 'many dwellings in the Father's house' is now fulfilled, but with a paradoxical change of emphasis. . . . The disciples are now 'where Jesus is' (see v. 3), in the sphere of God's love." Though "John has not lost sight of physical death . . . he also clearly expects that the final revelation and sight of glory will take place in the heavenly world. . . ."

14:25-31

A Provisional Ending

25, 26   In the Farewell Discourse "These things I have spoken to you" is a frequently recurring phrase (15:11; 16:1 [cf. vs. 4], 6, 25, 33), with which the instruction that precedes is held up before the disciples as words of farewell that are not to be forgotten, often with a purpose clause ("so that") in which Jesus makes known the intent of the instruction. Here Jesus adds, "while I am still with you," thus indicating that his instruction to his disciples is coming to an end, certainly one more reason for them not to forget while he is still with them what he is imparting to them as his farewell gift. But this phrase serves especially — as vs. 26 expressly indicates — to refer them again to the "other" Paraclete, who will continue Jesus' work among them.

Here the Paraclete is called by the customary name "the Holy Spirit" (see the comments on vs. 16) and is further described as the one "whom the Father will send in my name." Until now Jesus has always been the one referred to as sent by the Father. That mission is now coming to an end and will soon be completed. Jesus' future "coming" to his disciples will have another character. That is not to say that the Spirit will come in the place of Jesus or that Jesus will not be involved in the Spirit's mission (which until now has been his mission). For the Father, the great director of the mission, will send the Spirit "in my name," which here means "at my initiative" (vs. 16: "at my request"). Elsewhere the same thing is said with "the Paraclete, whom I will send to you from[95] the Father" (15:26; cf. 16:7). Accordingly, however hard it may be for us to put all that is said in the Farewell Discourse about the Father, the Son, and the Holy Spirit into a well-integrated trinitarian context, the picture here is not unclear: The work that the Spirit is sent out to do as the other Paraclete remains the work of Jesus; the work is being continued by the Spirit, but Jesus, in his heavenly mode of existence and position of power, is and remains the great sponsor of that work.

The main point is the nature of the work that is here assigned to the Spirit as the one who assists the disciples: "He will teach you all things, and bring to your remembrance all that I have said to you." The need for this among the disciples was acute, as is evident from the questions that they ask Jesus during this farewell, which prove their incomprehension. But the Spirit's work will relate to their understanding of all of Jesus' coming and work, the mode of his going to the Father, and everything in his speech and conduct that has seemed puzzling and incomprehensible. The Spirit will "teach" them "all," as "the Spirit of truth" (vs. 17; 15:26; 16:13). Therefore, the statement about "teaching

---

95. παρά with genitive.

all things" is explained by "and bring to your remembrance all that I have said to you," which obviously relates not just to the disciples' capacity to remember but also to the process of learning to understand that which lay hidden,[96] as an undiscovered treasure, in their memories and tradition concerning Jesus (see also the comments on 15:26; 16:13f.). It is clear from the terms of this Paraclete saying, as well as that of 16:13, that these sayings relate mostly to the disciples as the eyewitnesses whom Jesus has chosen and called, who have been with him from the beginning (15:27), and in whose minds the Spirit can therefore bring to remembrance Jesus' words. It is also clear that the Evangelist thus indirectly gives an important clue to the character of his own Gospel.[97]

27-29 The conclusion of the whole of ch. 14 begins with the customary shalom greeting, here expressly intended as farewell: "Peace I leave with you," reinforced by the emphatic statement "*my* peace I give to you." The possessive pronoun "my" and the words "I give" are further explained in what follows: "not as the world gives do I give to you." The "world" — here, presumably, meaning "people in general" — extends shalom as a wish, pious or otherwise, sincerely or perhaps superficially, but always without the ability to give what is wished for the other. Jesus' "shalom" is not a cheap wish. He is now at the point of going away on a journey in which he will have to fight for that peace against the powers of darkness and violence (vs. 30; 16:33), a peace that he will have to bring back from the depths of death (cf. 20:19, 26). But he also knows where and to whom he is going, and his "shalom" is therefore a benediction full of grace and divine power. For that reason he now repeats the word with which he began: "Let not your hearts be troubled, neither let them be afraid" (vs. 1; cf. 16:33).[98]

Indeed, still more than that (vs. 28): "You certainly heard me say to you, 'I go away, and I will come to you.' Now then, if[99] you love me and believe in my word, you must certainly *rejoice* that I am going to the Father." Then follows Jesus' final "argument," in which he, as though his own words were not enough, steps back to appeal to the weak and vacillating faith of his disciples, an argument that should convince them of the reliability of his farewell shalom: "for the Father is greater than I." This is the same motif that he began his words of encouragement with: "if you believe in God, then believe also in me." But this time he says it with all the force of his being sent by the Father: not to seek his own glory but that of his Sender (cf. 5:19, 30; 7:17f.; 8:38; 14:10).

---

96. Cf. pp. 15f. above and the comments on 2:22; 12:16; and 20:9.

97. Cf. L. T. Witkamp, *Jezus van Nazareth in de gemeente van Johannes,* 1986, p. 305: "What is meant is again clearly indicated by John's Gospel itself: what we find in it is not a complete overview of the history and words of Jesus (cf. 20:30), but an interpretive reminder that attempts to lay bare the essence, the interior, of the tradition."

98. μὴ ταρασσέσθω ὑμῶν ἡ καρδία μηδὲ δειλιάτω. δειλάω means "be disheartened in a cowardly manner"; it appears with ταράσσεσθαι also in Is. 13:7. Cf. BAGD s.v.

99. For this use of εἰ with perfect indicative, see the comments on vs. 7.

This strange form of argument,[100] "the Father is greater than I," has over the years occasioned an assortment of profound dogmatic discussions of the intratrinitarian ontological relationship between the Son and the Father and of the relationship between Jesus' divine and human "natures."[101] But in the process these words have all too often been abstracted from the line of thought pursued in the text, where Jesus is obviously not concerned to teach his disciples about the nature of his divine personhood or the distinction between his human and his divine nature — or to detract from the glory in which he participated as the Son of God (cf. 5:20f.). All that is at issue here is what is "more," "greater," or "more profitable" (cf. 16:7) for the disciples: Jesus' remaining with them on earth or his going away to the Father? In the context everything is focused on his departure. That the Father is "more" than Jesus means only that his return to the Father is the beginning of a new dispensation of grace, one based in heaven and therefore coming down from the Father. This new dispensation will exceed the limitations of the dispensation represented by Jesus' presence on earth (cf. vs. 12), just as the glory that Jesus will receive as the Son who returns to the Father will be greater than his earthly glory (17:5, 24), even though both issue from his oneness with the Father. Jesus is not excluded from that "greater" reality that the Father will confer on the disciples after Jesus' departure (cf. 17:11-13). He will, in fact, have a hand in it, as is evident from everything that has been said so far, especially about his "coming" to them. Therefore, his disciples, instead of wanting to keep him with them, should extend their vision to a higher plane than what they have thus far been capable of, so that, when these things happen, they will not remain behind in despair and unbelief but be in a state of joy and expectancy.

This last point is expressed in vs. 29: "And now I have told you before it happens, so that, when it does, you may believe" (cf. 13:19; 16:4, 32f.). They are to "believe," not simply "be prepared for" or "be warned against" the moment at which they must give him up. They are to believe in the "greater" reality with which he will return.[102]

---

100. So Bultmann, *Comm.,* p. 629.

101. Specifically in the ancient christological conflicts, but also in later popular and scholarly discussion of the divine sonship of Christ. This led both to a subordinationist christology like that of Arius and — on the orthodox side — to the view that 14:28 referred to the irreversible *order* in trinitarian relationships (the Father begets the Son and not vice versa and so is "greater" in that sense). Others have sought a solution in the fact that Jesus speaks here from within his human nature as a "servant" and not from within his divine nature (e.g., Schnackenburg, *Comm.* II, pp. 85f.).

102. Cf. Calvin, though he puts less stress than we have on Jesus' departure and change of scene. He, too, rejects the christological interpretation: "In these words He shows, not in what respect He differs in Himself from the Father, but why He descended to us; which was, to unite us to God. For, until we have reached that point, we stand so to say in mid-course. We also imagine only a semi-Christ and a mutilated Christ unless He leads us to God" (*Comm.* II, p. 89).

30-31 From this point on the time is short: Jesus will no longer talk "much"[103] with his disciples, because the enemy is already on his way. Again he calls this enemy "the ruler of this world" (see the comments on 12:31; 16:11). For what is taking place is not just what people are devising against him and have already brought about (cf. 18:3). It bears the eschatological stamp of the conflict between the kingdom of God and the domain of Satan, the power of darkness (cf. Lk. 22:53). This transcendent background becomes visible again and again throughout the story of Jesus' suffering and death (cf. 6:70; 8:44; 13:2, 27).

Jesus immediately adds: "but he has no hold on me."[104] Jesus does not belong to the "world" of which Satan is the ruler and on which Satan can make claims. Rather, the crisis, the judgment that is now being passed on the world, will furnish proof of what Jesus earlier called the casting out of the ruler of this world (12:31; cf. 16:33). But he also makes it known that for him what is about to take place is not an imaginary struggle, not merely a "triumphant" departure from this world, which conceals itself behind the screen of his suffering and dying.[105] It is, rather, "so that the world will know that I love the Father."[106]

This love is further explicated in the very emphatic concluding statement: "And as the Father has commanded me, so I do" (cf. 12:49, 50). Jesus is commanded to lay down his life in order to take it up again (cf. 10:17f.), in keeping with the great rule of his coming, which is that "no one has ascended into heaven but he who descended from heaven" (3:13). This means that he will not avoid the confrontation with the ruler of this world, who is coming to meet him with everything that is at his disposal in this world: betrayal, denial, violence, and injustice, but will step forward to meet him. And Jesus will do that so that the world may know that for him this is the

103. The word "much" is lacking in a Syriac version (sy^{sin}), which some commentators regard as giving the original text. The word was added, according to this view, because of all that follows in chs. 15–17. But in view of the otherwise unanimous manuscript and version witness it is hard to regard the single exception as the original text, which does not mean, of course, that chs. 15–17 are thereby disqualified as "not much." It is rather an additional argument for the thesis that ch. 14 forms an original unit that was later augmented with chs. 15–17.

104. Various translations are possible. Usually scholars have in mind a Semitic expression meaning "he has no claim on me." But one can also proceed from the sense of ἔχειν, "have power to, be capable of," and translate: "in my case (as it concerns me) he is not capable of anything," or, more simply, "against me he is powerless."

105. For this interpretation of Jesus' going away, see above, pp. 430f.

106. The ἵνα clause seems to be dependent on no main clause. To take "Rise, let us go hence" as the clause on which it is dependent, as has been suggested, seems — if not "unreasonable" (so Bultmann) — forced, a too abrupt stylistic transition from the farewell discourse to a proposal to take to the road (though in content it would yield good sense). Usually, therefore, the ἵνα is taken to be elliptical (as in 13:18; cf. 9:3), indicating why Jesus' words must now end. The translation could therefore be: "but (or "because") the world must know. . . .'"

direction and the manner in which the Father has commanded him to go. It will "know" this when in the near future it sees him walk through the streets of Jerusalem, condemned to die, and then hanging on a cross; it will "know," if it wants to or not, if it understands it or not, that that is the way and the manner in which he will overcome the ruler of this world, and in him the world, not by might or violence, but by the power of his love for the Father and of the Father's love.

Again it is evident that "the world" is the embodiment of the power of unbelief and opposition to God and therefore the designation of the great antithesis in which Jesus finds himself. But the world also remains the object of Jesus' claim to faith and conversion (cf. 17:21) and is included in Jesus' self-surrender in death (cf. 6:51). For precisely when he delivers himself up, the world must learn to know him as the Other and the Greater in whom judgment (cf. 12:31) passes over the mode of existence to which it is subject and shows it the only way in which it can be delivered from judgment.

With this the climax of Jesus' discourse has been reached. "Rise, let us go from here" gives the signal that Jesus will fulfill the "so I do." Although, in light of all that still follows, various attempts have been made to interpret the end of vs. 31 metaphorically, the words "from here" point clearly to a literal change of location (cf. 18:1). The problem of the continuing farewell discourse demands another explanation (see above, pp. 485ff.).

15:1-8

"I Am the True Vine"

1 Now begins, without any transitional formula or connection with the preceding but with the emphatic thematic saying "I am the true vine," a new line of thought that, under another key word ("love"), is continued in vss. 9-17. This is clearly a first addition introduced into the text later than ch. 14.[107] In a way that is characteristic for the Fourth Gospel it offers a further explication of themes that have been introduced earlier. Vss. 1-8 contain a graphic elaboration of the spiritual fellowship Jesus has promised in ch. 14, a fellowship that he will maintain with his disciples after his departure (cf. 14:23). In vss. 9-17, similarly in close connection with 14:15, 21f., this fellowship is further explicated and developed in terms of *remaining* in one another's *love*.

At the outset the idea of fellowship between Jesus and his own is centrally expressed, in a highly characteristic way, in the image of the vine. As in ch. 10, so here one can speak of a "similitude" (10:6) with allegorical features (15:2, 6),

107. See above, pp. 486f.

which is therefore difficult to define precisely according to genre.[108] Of more importance for the meaning is that in this opening statement "I am the true vine" we have an "I am" saying in which "the true" emphasizes distinction from or even the contrast with persons or things that have received the same predicate[109] — like "the true bread" in distinction from the bread in the wilderness and "the good shepherd" in contrast to robbers and hirelings (6:32ff.; 10:11; cf. 2:10). In all these sayings, the designation is to be understood in a redemptive-historical sense, that is, in the light of the Old Testament and Jewish writings in which Israel is referred to as the vine planted by God (e.g., Ps. 80:9-12, 15f.; Ho. 11:1; Ezekiel 15; 19:10f., Jr. 2:21 [LXX ἄμπελον . . . ἀληθινήν]).[110]

But the imagery also occurs in more varied form, in particular in the familiar song of the vineyard in Isaiah 5.[111] In the context of our text there is no clear indication that the opening statement in vs. 1 and its elaboration are linked with a specific Old Testament passage.[112] The main thing, however, is that Jesus, by calling himself the true vine and, in immediate association therewith, his Father the planter and keeper of the vineyard,[113] applies to himself this redemptive-historical description of the people of God. He thus becomes the one who represents or embodies the people. As in ch. 10 he is called the true Shepherd of God's flock (in contrast to the false shepherds, in accordance with Ezekiel 34), so here he is the vine, God's "planting" of the people who

108. See also the comments above on 10:6.

109. Bultmann calls the "I am" formula as it is used here a "recognition formula" (*Comm.,* pp. 225f.; see pp. 292f., n. 121 above).

110. Here, too, scholars have sought the religio-historical background elsewhere, namely in the myth of "the tree of life" as it occurs in the — very late! — Mandaean-Gnostic writings, where the imagery is elaborated in such a way that it is sometimes clearly reminiscent of certain phrases in John 15. For this view, see Bultmann, *Comm.,* pp. 530ff.; he regards ἀληθινός and καλός as "the language of (Gnostic) dualism" (p. 530). And see especially E. Schweizer, *Ego Eimi,* 1939, pp. 37f. But this interpretation is clearly in retreat (Schweizer later altered his views significantly; see the second edition of *Ego eimi,* 1963, pp. 3ff.; also his *Neotestamentica,* 1963, pp. 77ff.). The Old Testament connection is much more plausible and, considering the recurring application in the Fourth Gospel of Old Testament concepts and motifs to the person and work of Jesus ("lamb of God," "bread from heaven," "temple," fulfiller of "the Sabbath," "good Shepherd," 1:29; 6:32f.; 2:21; 7:23; 10:11), can be understood much more readily as the background of John 15 than can the use made in late Gnostic writings of a pagan myth. Apart from commentaries like those of Barrett, Brown, and Schnackenburg, see also the lengthy refutation by R. Borig, *Der wahre Weinstock,* 1967, pp. 135-98.

111. See at length Borig, *Der wahre Weinstock,* pp. 84-128; A. Joubert, "L'image de la Vigne (Jean 15)," in *Oikonomia. Heilsgeschichte als Theme der Theologie,* ed. F. Christ (Festschrift for O. Cullmann), 1967, pp. 93-99.

112. Though Dodd, *Interpretation of the Fourth Gospel,* p. 411, argues for a link with Psalm 80.

113. It is hard to explain why God is designated with the general word γεωργός, "farmer, one who tills the ground," and not with the obvious and more speciifc word ἀμπελουργός (cf. Lk. 13:7). But this need not have a special reason (cf. Mk. 12:1-9, which repeatedly refers to vineyard workers — not the vineyard owner — as γεωργοί).

belong to him in the world. This implies that the disciples' belonging to Jesus as the "branches" of the vine (vs. 5) denotes not only a personal relationship but also their incorporation into the great community of the people God has appropriated for himself out of the world (cf. 17:6).[114] In distinction from ch. 10, the contrast between the "true" and the "false" or the "true" and the "useless" vine is not further specified (as in Ezk. 15:1-8; 19:10; see also ch. 17); by speaking of "the true vine" this verse refers to the vine's positive purpose-fulfilling and fruit-bearing character (cf. Jr. 2:21).

2-3 Accordingly, as the primary qualification of the "true" vine Jesus, we are immediately told, "Every branch in me that bears no fruit he cuts away. And every branch that does bear fruit he prunes[115] so that it may bear more fruit." Often, as with the parable of the good shepherd,[116] the intent of these words is sidetracked because "cutting away" and "cleaning" are given an allegorical meaning that is not in the text. For example "cutting away" is associated with excommunication,[117] and "cleaning" is associated with church discipline[118] or with the purifying effect of a trial of faith or the like. But "cutting away" is further explained in vs. 6, and there is a clear indication in vs. 3 of the meaning of "cleaning": "You are already clean *by the word* that I have spoken to you."

Accordingly, the special care that the Father bestows on the vine as planter and vinedresser and his making it the "true" vine does not consist of an assortment of secondary actions that support the mission of his Son, but in this mission itself, in the dividing and purifying power of Jesus' word of authority, which is the word of God himself (and is therefore introduced into the metaphor as God's own action). What makes Jesus the true vine is that, as the one sent by God, he gathers a community, a fellowship of life, in which his word exerts a redeeming, life-creating, continually purifying, and dividing effect (cf. 14:23f.). For that reason he can say to his disciples, "You are already clean,"

114. Contrary to E. Käsemann, *The Testament of Jesus,* p. 28: "Just as the concept 'Church' is absent, so are the titles of honour such as the 'family' or the 'people of God,' the 'heavenly building' or the 'Body of Christ.' Correspondingly, the disciples seem to come into focus only as individuals . . ."; also pp. 30f.: "It becomes evident that the community is viewed primarily not from the aspect of its corporateness, but rather from the aspect of its individual members." On this "ecclesiological" aspect, see at length Borig, *Der wahre Weinstock,* pp. 250ff.: "zur Ekklesi-ologie der Weinstockrede."

115. On the phenomenon of the concurrence of the two different but similar-sounding verbs αἴρειν and καθαίρειν, see BDF §488.2. καθαίρειν in the sense intended here of pruning and so "cleansing" a vine is rare; see Borig, *Der wahre Weinstock,* p. 38. It clearly functions here in part in connection with καθαροί in vs. 3.

116. See pp. 355, 358, 363f. above.

117. Cf. 1 Co. 5:13 (ἐξάρατε), Dt. 17:7 (ἐξάρετε).

118. See also Bultmann, *Comm.,* p. 533, n. 4 (cf. n. 2): "Nor of course does καθαίρειν stand for the church's disciplinary action," but church discipline "may be able to undertake the task of καθ. in certain circumstances." But Bultmann does support Loisy's view, according to which καθαίρειν is realized "through the action of the Spirit and the practice of charity."

which does not mean they have already attained a degree of spiritual or moral perfection, but that he has so deeply bound them to himself by his word that in virtue of that fellowship they are able and ready to do his word and to bear fruit (cf. vss. 7f.; see also the comments on 13:10).[119]

4-5   Therefore everything depends on remaining in him, in order, on the basis of that new purity in him, to bear much fruit. For "As the branch cannot bear fruit *by itself* unless it remains in the vine, neither can you unless you remain in me." The same thought returns in vs. 5 in the form of a promise, with another characteristic "I am" saying,[120] and with an additional admonition: "apart from me you can do nothing."

This motif of "remaining" is characteristic of the Fourth Gospel and recurs in all sorts of expressions,[121] but here it occurs more often (seven times) and with greater emphasis than elsewhere. This is explained by the farewell situation, in which Jesus is urging his disciples to remain faithful to him after his departure. The necessity and nature of this "remaining" are advanced here, more clearly than anywhere else, with the image of the vine as the only possibility of continuing to bear fruit. Therefore, "remaining in him" is not a state of rest, an adherence to what the disciples have already received in Jesus solely to conserve it (cf. Mt. 25:24f.), but an adherence to *him* as the vital source of help and strength, in order to bear much fruit.

Hence the imperative: "Remain in me!" But joined to this imperative in the frequently repeated "reciprocal formula of immanence" is "and I in you," a phrase to be understood from just as much an active "remaining" by the propulsive effect of his word and Spirit. "For apart from me you can do nothing," that is, nothing that corresponds to the new life that he bestows and the new commandment that he gives. For without this reciprocal remaining in him and him in them they will fall back on themselves, either in total unfruitfulness or lapsing into the wild growth that is no longer shaped by his word, into activism or idealism that is neither derived from nor directed to him.

6   The uselessness and hopelessness of this prospect is once more (cf. vs. 2) brought out with great clarity and seriousness: "Whoever does not remain in me is cast out as a branch and withers."[122] Again it is evident that "remaining in him" does not consist in a self-sufficient and settled state. There is a sort of

---

119. Partly on the basis of 13:10 some have thought that vs. 2a refers, or at least alludes, to Judas. With this one might consider whether vs. 2b does not then, in view of the situation, portray Peter as the example of a branch who in order to bear more fruit had to be radically purified and pruned by the great Vinedresser. Although in these two men we may see striking illustrations of the saying in vs. 2, the formulation and intent of that verse are too general to allow us to say that the reference is specifically to them.

120. Cf. 6:35, 48, 51; 10:11, 14.

121. See also the comments above on 8:31.

122. The aorists ἐβλήθη and ἐξηράνθη are usually taken to be gnomic or as pointing to the future; see BDF §333; see also Borig, *Der wahre Weinstock,* p. 51.

fellowship with Jesus, a temporary faith and fruitbearing (6:66ff.; 8:31ff.; cf. Mt. 13:19 [and vs. 21!]), that is comparable to withered or unpruned wild branches and, in its outcome, to what happens to such branches. Here the image and the thing signified run together: the one who "does not remain in me" is "cast out," a metaphorical reference to judgment that is used elsewhere apart from the imagery of the vine and the branches (cf. 6:37). But what comes next, "as a branch and withers; and people[123] gather the branches and throw them into the fire, and they are burned," is not an allegorical reference to the way in which judgment is realized in the lives of humans (see again on vs. 2). It refers, rather — within the framework of the vine imagery — to what is useless for the purpose for which the vinedresser planted his vine, the purpose, that is, for which the Father sent his Son into the world, and the judgment implied therein (cf. 3:16ff.; Mt. 3:10; Ezk. 15:1-8).

Verse **7** continues the thought in a positive direction. "And my words remain in you" stands in place of and explains the "I in you" of vss. 4 and 5, referring to the permanent impact of Jesus' words on his own.[124] If they remain in him and he in them, then the promise in 14:13 applies to them: their prayers will be heard. For prayer is one of the most important forms of "remaining in him." Here again their prayers and the answers to those prayers will be related especially to "the works" that they will do as Jesus' disciples and that will thereby be qualified as "the fruit of the vine."

Verse **8** forms a kind of conclusion, one that returns to the beginning and summarizes the purpose of all that has preceded. The glorification of the Father, which consists in their "bearing much fruit" and thus shows that they are "my disciples" (cf. 17:10).[125] At the same time these words, which conclude the "similitude," bring the passage as a whole back into the atmosphere of farewell. For with this assignment and promise Jesus sends them into the future.

15:9-17

"Remain in My Love"

Verses 9-17 are linked closely with vss. 1-8 and need to be understood completely within that context. The vine is not mentioned again apart from an

---

123. The passive that has become customary here in translations conceals the active voice of the original. One may supply οἱ ἄνθρωποι as the subject; cf. BDF §130.2.

124. The "words" (ῥήματα) remaining in believers is the same as the believers' keeping the commandments (vss. 10, 20) and adds nothing to the believers' remaining in Jesus, though it "highlights the element of obedience that is contained in the idea of loyalty of faith" (Bultmann, *Comm.*, p. 538, n. 5).

125. καὶ γένησθε ἐμοὶ μαθηταί: "and you will be my disciples."

allusion in vs. 16, but with the aid of the vine imagery vss. 1-8 have described a framework that is filled in in vss. 9-17.

This is immediately clear in vs. **9**, where the theme "remain *in me*" from vss. 1-8 becomes "remain *in my love.*" The fellowship described in vss. 1-8 is thus further defined as a fellowship of love, specifically as a fellowship of the love that is represented by *Jesus,* which the disciples must "remain" as branches that find the source of their vitality in the vine. Moreover, just as vs. 1 refers to the one who planted the vine, so here the opening statement is "As[126] the Father has loved me, so have I loved you." The love in which the disciples must remain does not begin with Jesus but has its source and energy in the love with which the Father has loved his Son by "giving" him for the salvation of the world (3:16).

10   What applies to the origin of the love described here applies also to what it means to "remain in my love": "If you *keep my commandments,* you will remain in my love." This saying virtually repeats 14:15, 21, but here it is further conditioned by, and finds its deepest grounding in, the obedience of the Son himself to the Father in the fulfillment of his mission in the world.

11   But before discussing this reality, Jesus recapitulates what he has just said, beginning with the customary "These things I have spoken to you" (see the comments on 14:25). The recapitulation is simultaneously a climax: "that my joy may be in you, and that your joy may be full." To remain in Jesus' love is at the same time to share in his joy, a joy Jesus finds in being loved and sent by the Father and in carrying out the Father's commandments. What Jesus elsewhere calls his food and drink, namely "to do the will of him who sent me and to accomplish his work" (4:34), he here calls the joy that fills his life. It is the prospect of that joy that Jesus also offers his disciples now that *he* is sending *them* into the world. What now fills them with sadness will later prove to be the way that leads them to the highest fulfillment of their lives (cf. 14:28; 16:22) and to the honor that the Father bestows on those who seek to follow Jesus as servants (cf. 12:26). The expression "that your joy may be full" is a typically Johannine description of the highest implication of Jesus' self-revelation to his own (cf. 3:29; 16:24; 17:13; 1 Jn. 1:4).[127] Here all the stress lies on the disciples' being absorbed into the joy of their Lord in fulfilling God's work on earth, if they remain in his love.

12-14   Following this high point vs. 12 returns to vs. 10 as the beginning

---

126. This "as" is foundational for what follows. See the comments above on 13:15; see also 13:34; 15:12; 17:11, 21.

127. The use of the word "joy" for divine salvation has its background in much of the Old Testament. "Fullness of joy" occurs also in the rabbinic literature as a designation for the salvation that will be realized and revealed in the great future. See H. Conzelmann, *TDNT* IX, pp. 359-72; Strack/Billerbeck II, pp. 429, 566; for non-Jewish sources see Bultmann, *Comm.,* p. 505, n. 4, where he strongly stresses the cultic character of this joy.

of a further explication of "my commandments." For the first time in this passage the content of Jesus' commandment is described as the disciples' love for each other. Again, however — and here the main idea of the pericope is continued — Jesus adds, "as I have loved you." To make this clear Jesus refers to the greatest sacrifice friends can make for each other, the sacrifice of their lives. In the formulation given here, "No one has greater love than this: that someone lay down[128] his life for his friends," no consideration is given to the position that it would even be a greater love to lay down one's life for his enemies (cf. Mt. 5:44; Ro. 5:6f.). But throughout this passage the reference is to mutual relations among the disciples (cf. vss. 12, 17). It is also clear that Jesus is speaking here from the concrete situation of farewell, in which he interprets his departure to go to the Father, the voluntary laying down of his life, as the demonstration and example of his love for the disciples as his friends.

Therefore, with "You are my friends if you do what I command you," that is, when you love each other (vs. 14), Jesus does not mean that he makes his friendship with them dependent on their obedience to his commandments. He means, rather, that in their love for each other they will be recognizable as those whom he has made his friends by taking them up into his love. Some interpreters believe that vs. 13 gives expression to the lengths to which the disciples' love for each other should go if they love just as Jesus has loved them: they, too, should be prepared to die for each other. Appeal is made to 1 Jn. 3:16, where this link is expressly made.[129] That verse speaks of the extremity of love required of Christians for each other. But the point here and in the "as" in vs. 12 is the uniqueness of Jesus' part in the community of love that unites him and Christians: he unites himself to them as a friend among friends, and he makes for them the greatest sacrifice that friends can make for each other.[130]

Accordingly, vs. **15** (with vs. 16) further pursues the theme of the uniqueness of Jesus' kindness to his friends as their Lord: "No longer do I call you servants, for the servant does not know what his master is doing." A servant's duty is simply to obey without asking questions. All that matters is the command. "But I have called you friends, for all that I have heard from my Father I have made known to you." Not that their subordinate position as pupils in relation to their teacher and servants in relation to their master was abolished by this (cf. 13:13, 16); rather, their servant status solely under the commandment

---

128. τίθεναι τὴν ψυχὴν αὐτοῦ by itself need not mean more than "risk his life" (cf. the comments above on 10:11). Here, where it is used of Jesus, it has the full meaning of "lay down his life" (cf. 10:15b, 17f.; 3:16).

129. E.g., Schnackenburg, *Comm.* III, p. 109.

130. Cf. Bultmann, *Comm.,* p. 542: "the only thing that is specifically Christian is the grounding of this command and, in line with this, its realization"; see also the comments above on 13:34f.

has now made way for their initiation into the purposes of their Lord — into the secret of his own coming and mission in the world, which Jesus refers to as "all that I have heard from my Father" (cf. 5:19, 20, 30; 3:11, 32; 8:26, 40). This is the Father's means of redeeming the world. By the sacrifice of his Son he will gather a new people in the world, a fellowship of love, men and women living in the freedom of the children of God and brought under the regime of the Son of his love (cf. 1:13; 8:31, 32, 35; Ro. 8:34-36).

16, 17   For that reason the relation in which the disciples stand to Jesus is not based on their initiative: "You have not chosen me" as leader to give shape to your moral and social ideals, but "I have chosen you." This saying speaks of Christ's sovereign freedom to choose whom and what he will — and of the privilege of being called out of the world (vs. 19) to be Jesus' disciples and friends. The purpose Jesus has for those so chosen is that they are "appointed"[131] to "go and bear fruit," a statement that recalls the nature of their communion with him as branches of the vine. Similarly, the words that follow, "and that your fruit should remain," continue the thought of "remaining" in Jesus (vss. 1-8), in his love (vss. 9ff.). With that, Jesus again attaches to this reality the certainty that their prayers will be heard by the Father in everything they may ask in Jesus' name (cf. 14:30f.).[132] For in the fulfillment of their task as Jesus' disciples the way to the Father lies open for them so that with an appeal to Jesus' name they may ask of the Father everything he has commanded them.

Interpreters differ on whether "go and bear fruit" refers particularly to the missionary mandate.[133] "Go" could, at first sight, point in that direction, as in, for example, Lk. 10:3. But it is questionable whether this word by itself can prove that this intent is present. It may rather serve, as elsewhere, to place greater stress on the second verb ("bear fruit"), with which it forms a unit.[134] In this passage fruitbearing represents the disciples' love for one another, and this argues against a specifically missionary intent here, so that few have

---

131. ἔθηκα ὑμᾶς ἵνα: "appoint you to"; cf. BAGD s.v.: for this meaning see also Ac. 20:28; 1 Co. 12:18, 28.

132. The ἵνα in vs. 16b does not mean that fruitbearing has as its goal the answering of prayer and that the answer therefore depends on the bearing of fruit. This ἵνα is rather the continuation of the ἵνα in vs. 16a and links the answering of the disciples' prayer to their election and appointment by Jesus.

133. On this see at length Borig, *Der wahre Weinstock,* pp. 237ff. He mentions two basic interpretations, one taking the fruitbearing to be "missionary activity," the other (more commonly followed) taking it to be "the moral-religious activity of the disciples within the Christian community." For the first view, see, e.g., Schlatter, *Comm.,* p. 305; W. Thüsing, *Die Erhöhung und Verherrlichung Jesu in Johannesevangelium,* 1960, pp. 107f.

134. G. Delling, *TDNT* VIII, p. 505: "the prior imperative not only makes the expression more vivid but also prepares the ground for the second imperative." See also Schnackenburg, *Comm.* III, p. 422, n. 71.

followed that interpretation. This is not to deny, however, that the proclamation of the gospel in the world constitutes part of the fruitbearing of the disciples, nor that the mutual love of the disciples has a "missionary" meaning (cf. 13:35).

Verse 17 concludes the passage by again referring to the disciples' mutual love (thus forming an *inclusio*) as the great content of Jesus' commandment (cf. vs. 12), now for the first time without "as I have loved you." "One another" thereby gets all the emphasis, obviously not in an exclusive sense but in order — within the context of and as a summary of all that precedes in vss. 1-16 — to point to love as the great principle in the building and maintaining of *communion* and as the criterion of God's *community* in the world, the "vine" he has planted.

In sum, just as 1 Corinthians 13 has been called the New Testament's "ode to love," so also Jn. 15:1-17 is the magna carta of the Christian love commandment. In 1 Corinthians 13 Paul describes love as the greatest of the triad of faith, hope, and love in the rich plurality of its manifestations. So here John, by placing the "similitude" of the true vine first, indicates the great redemption-historical connections within which Jesus taught his disciples to understand the "new commandment" that he gave them. For the love that Jesus asked of his own is no other than that love ("just as") with which the Father had loved him, the love that moved the Father to send his Son into the world and to unite in him, the true vine, his people in the world, a new community. For the disciples this love consists in remaining in the love of the Son who, by giving his life for them, his friends, provided the new foundation and the new criterion for their love for one another. By the fruits of this love of the disciples for each other, the Father glorifies himself in this new community, the vine he has planted.

It is by this grand conception of being taken up by faith in Jesus into the love of the Father and the Son that the church can understand itself in its uniqueness in and for the world. It is also therein that the church receives the essential criterion for its belonging to the community of the true vine.

15:18–16:15

The Hostility of the World and the Witness of the Paraclete

The transition from the end of 15:17 to this new pericope is rather abrupt. Throughout vss. 1-17 the focus is on the close fellowship that unites Jesus with the disciples as his friends. But now the overriding emphasis is on the hostility that will be directed against the disciples after Jesus' departure. However, in this very contrast lies the connection between the two sections, as is specifically clear from the reference in vs. 19 back to Jesus' election of the disciples, which was mentioned in vs. 16. It is the privilege of being chosen by Jesus out of the world that is the world's reason for hating them (vss. 18-21). The motif of hostility remains central in what follows, first in its inexcusable character (vss. 21-25), then, as a warning to the disciples, in its quality as a lethal threat (in 16:1ff.). This section is also marked by the repeated and explained promise of the Holy Spirit, first in 15:26-27, where the reference is to the witnessing function of the Spirit together with that of the disciples; then in 16:7-11, where the character of this witness as directed against the world stands outs. 16:12-15 concludes this section with Jesus' statement that he must now restrict himself to what he has just said, but that the Paraclete, as the Spirit of truth and the guide for the future, will continue Jesus' work on earth and provide his disciples with everything that they will need for that future.

18-19 The opening words, "If the world hates you," present this hatred to the disciples not only as a possibility but as a reality that they cannot avoid because they belong to Jesus: "Know that it has hated me before it hated you."[135] Although this hostility is presented here (especially in vs. 19) as an essential characteristic of the world, this is no proof that this Johannine understanding is rooted in a Gnostic dualism proceeding from an original opposition between God and the world.[136] Passages such as 3:16; 4:40; 6:51; 1 Jn. 4:14 could certainly not be harmonized with such a background.

The coming of Jesus, especially the authority with which he conducted himself in the world as the Son of God, encounters radical and, as it were, monolithic opposition (cf. 3:19ff.; 7:7; 10:33, etc.), the real cause and culpable character of which is further pointed out in vss. 21ff. That hatred will also be directed at the disciples. If they were "of the world" (vs. 19), that is, if they let their conduct be conditioned by their belonging to the world,[137] the world would not hate them (7:7), but would love them, regard them as its own, and deal with them as such. The disciples, however, as persons who have been called out of the world by Jesus and made his possession and friends (cf. vss. 14-16), do not belong to the world. For that reason the world hates them as killjoys — as followers of the one who constantly finds fault with the world and consigns it to God's judgment because of its estrangement from God.

20, 21 Again Jesus reminds his disciples of the rule he impressed on them at the meal: "A servant is not greater than his master" (cf. 13:16). In

---

135. πρῶτον ὑμῶν, comparative (cf. BDF §62).

136. On this see the comments above on 3:3. This view (advanced by the school of Bultmann) is especially defended by L. Schrottroff in *Der Glaubende und die feindliche Welt: Beobachtungen zum gnostischen Dualismus und seiner Bedeutung für Paulus und das Johannesevangelium,* 1970.

137. For this use of ἐx see the comments above on 3:31.

speaking of a "servant" (i.e., a slave), he is not contradicting what he said in vs. 15. Because he has taken them into his confidence as his servants and involved them so closely in his mission, it is all the more true that as his servants they are "not greater" than he, that is, not above what he, in carrying out his mission, must endure. Jesus then proceeds to speak of "persecution." The world's hatred will not limit itself to spiritual resistance but will also threaten their safety and their lives (cf. 16:1ff.), as was also true for him. What follows is striking: "If they kept my word, they will keep yours also," words that in this context, where the subject is the world's hatred, do not seem to fit (cf. also vs. 21). For this reason some interpreters take the "if" as "to the degree that," which, they say, has a purely negative meaning.[138] But perhaps the intent of the parallelism in vs. 20b is to interpret "A disciple is not greater than his master" in the general sense that the disciples must share the bad with their master no less than the good, which, for Jesus' disciples would, in fact, mean something predominantly negative.

Verse 21 again refers to the close tie between Jesus and the disciples as the real cause of the world's hatred. With "on my account" (= "because of me"; cf. Mk. 13:13; Mt. 10:22) Jesus links everything that will happen to them to himself. He puts it down on his own account, as it were. The disciples are not responsible for it.

Before he enters on a discussion of this in 16:1, Jesus once more discloses the deepest cause and the real character of the world's hatred. He does this in the same words with which he has repeatedly told "the Jews" the real reason for their unbelief and hostility toward him: they thereby gave proof that they did not "know him who sent me," and that in the deep existential sense of the word "know": they were estranged from, and did not let themselves be appropriated by, the God of whom Jesus spoke and for whom he, as the one sent by the Father, sought to win them by his words and works.[139]

22-25 The deep seriousness of this is now expressed with stringent reasoning and brought to its ultimate conclusion. "If I had not *come* and *spoken* to them, they would have no sin; but now they have no excuse (πρόφασις)." Here Jesus speaks of sin in absolute terms. He does not mean, naturally, that if he had not come there would have been no sin in the world. But he measures the excusable character of sin — yes or no — by the world's response to his coming and his word. If Jesus had not come and had not spoken of God as he has, then God would not yet have spoken his final word of love to the world and the world would not yet have given God its final answer. But now that the world has not "known" the Father in the mission of his Son, no reservations

---

138. So, e.g., Brown, *Comm.* II, p. 687: "They will keep your word to the extent they have kept mine (and they have not kept mine)."

139. On this failure to "know" God, see also the comments on 7:28f.; 8:19, 51.

or excuses remain with respect to sin. Sin — even previously committed sin — stands in its full significance as sin (cf. 9:41).

On that basis the awesome saying of vs. 23 can now follow: "Whoever hates me hates my Father also." "Hate" shares in the absoluteness of Jesus' words about sin and bears not a moral or affective sense but the most objective sense it can. To hate is to turn away from the way that God has opened for salvation. This hatred is the human "no" to the divine "yes" expressed in the mission of his Son. And this all the more because the power and authority that God has given the Son to speak and act in his name was so unmistakable that it should have convinced the world. For — here vs. 24 again picks up the argument of vs. 22 but now in a heightened sense — "if I had not done among them the works that no one else did, they would not have sin. But now they have both seen and hated both me and my Father." The two "both . . . and" constructions have a cumulative effect of bringing to expression in a single loaded sentence both the mystery and guilt of "seeing" the works and neverthe-less "hating me and my Father."[140] Here, too (see the comments on 14:10f.), Jesus first speaks of his words (vs. 22), then in vs. 24 of his works (i.e., his miracles) as the most undeniable proofs of his divine mission (see also the comments on 10:37f.). The works are proofs not only because he has in them given evidence of his supernatural ability but above all because he has demon-strated in them the saving Word of God that has become incarnate in him.

To all this — in an elliptical construction[141] — vs. 25 adds that however mysterious and culpable the world's hatred may be, it occurs in fulfillment of a word "written in their law: 'They hated me without a cause.' " The appeal to what is "written" occurs frequently in rabbinic literature and is no less characteristic for the Fourth Gospel than for the other Gospels (cf. 6:31, 45; 10:34; 12:14, 16), further proof of the extent to which its entire presentation of Jesus' self-revelation has its roots in the Old Testament to the same degree. Therefore the reference here to "their" law is clearly intended not to distance the reader from the law as belonging exclusively to "Judaism" but to place the Jews' hatred in the perspective of a law that they themselves regarded as holy and inviolable (cf. 5:39).[142]

Here again "law" is to be understood in the broad sense of "Scripture," as in 10:34. The quotation is from the Psalms, but it is not certain which. The reference may be to Ps. 35:19 or to Ps. 69:4 (and Ps. 109:3 and Ps. 119:161 also speak of "attacking" or

---

140. Cf. BDF §444.3: νῦν δὲ καὶ ἑωράκασιν καὶ ("and still") μεμισήκασιν καὶ ("both") ἐμὲ καὶ ("as well as") τὸν πατέρα μου (who to them seemed separate).

141. Cf. BDF §448.7: Elliptical ἀλλ' ἵνα: "But this occurred that . . . ," "but it had to be that."

142. See also the comments above on 8:12.

"persecuting without cause"). Perhaps "the word" here is not a specific text but the recurrent Old Testament motif of the innocent but persecuted righteous. Some interpreters, not without reason, think especially of Ps. 69:4, since elsewhere in the New Testament Psalm 69 is applied to Jesus (2:17; 19:28 [?]; Mt. 27:34; Ro. 15:35).

It is specifically this element of hate "without cause" that Jesus applies to himself and by which the psalmist asserts his innocence before God and people and laments the unfounded, irrational,[143] and mysterious character of the hatred he must endure at the hands of his enemies. This is proof again (cf. 12:27; 13:18) of how deeply Jesus in his suffering understood himself to be one with the true people of God as it comes to expression in Israel's holy tradition. At the same time it is he against whom this hatred without cause comes to its fulfillment, that is, where it becomes manifest in its final ("eschatological") seriousness as the attitude of not wanting to "know" the Messiah of Israel, the one sent by the Father. It becomes manifest as well in its impotence (cf. 12:31; 14:30), but in this connection especially in its essentially inexplicable and mysterious character (cf. 1;10, 11).

26, 27   Over against this refusal to acknowledge him Jesus now posits as the great counterweight that will vindicate him against the world, the coming and work of the Paraclete, the Spirit of truth (cf. 14:17).

In distinction from 14:16, 26, where the Father is the one who sends the Paraclete, here Jesus is the sender (as in 16:7), with the addition, however, of "from the Father,"[144] and "who proceeds from the Father." The terminology varies and is unsystematized. In 14:26 we read that the Father will send the Spirit, but with the addition of "in my name." Admittedly, the "procession" of the Spirit is only described as occurring "from the Father," just as Jesus "proceeded from the Father" (8:42; 16:27, etc.). The Father — we may say — is primary in these relations, the source and origin of all life and salvation. All that the glorified Son is empowered to do and does occurs in fellowship with the Father (cf. 17:21, 23), but the Father puts everything at the disposal of the Son, including the sending of the Spirit (cf. Ac. 2:33).

When, after all the negative things he has said, Jesus now promises the coming of the Paraclete as the one who will bear witness to him, this is naturally intended to reassure the disciples that in the enormous opposition they encounter in the world they will not stand alone. The Paraclete's witness to Jesus is the assistance that the Spirit will give the disciples in the great controversy between

---

143. δωρεάν can have several meanings; here, however, it is clearly that which is "undeserved" (cf. BAGD s.v.).

144. παρὰ τοῦ πατρός.

the church and the world with regard to the truth concerning Jesus, that is, the trustworthiness of his self-revelation in word and deed as the one sent by the Father. The earthly Jesus not only bore witness to himself but could also appeal to the testimony of others, namely John the Baptist and, above all, the Father, who bore witness to Jesus in Jesus' works, as also to the witness of the Scriptures (see 5:31f., 36f., 39). In the same way, in his heavenly life, Jesus will have the Spirit as his permanent witness on earth, a witness who will forever keep Jesus' name and cause alive in their imperishable significance in Jesus' community of disciples and through them in the world.

Jesus will speak at length about the content of the Paraclete's witness. For now the Evangelist is content to state the promise — and immediately adds (vs. 27), "but you also are witnesses." The Spirit not only enables them to stand against the world's resistance but above all stands by them as they continue Jesus' work on earth (cf. 14:12f.). Hence the addition "because you have been with me from the beginning," words that clearly refer to the original apostolic eyewitness of the disciples as the foundation of the coming church (cf. 1:14; 20:30, 31; 21:24). "The beginning," as frequently in the New Testament, is the beginning of Jesus' public ministry, when he attached his disciples to himself so that, as is clear here, they might be witnesses of his works and words (cf. Mk. 1:1; Lk. 1:2). It is so that they can bear that witness that the Spirit will inspire and enable them (cf. 14:26). The Spirit will not "speak of himself" but will "take of mine" and so lead the disciples in, and keep them faithful to, Jesus' own words and works (see the comments on 16:13-15).[145]

Some interpreters think that "because you *are* [present tense] with me from the beginning" also refers to the disciples' ongoing fellowship with the exalted Christ, on which their witness concerning Jesus is therefore also grounded ("because"). From this they conclude that the witness concerning Jesus (and hence that of the Fourth Gospel) repeatedly referred to here is not just (or not at all) to the earthly Jesus but also to the exalted Christ.[146]

But "you are with me" clearly refers to the disciples' association with the earthly Jesus that has continued from the beginning to the present moment of Jesus' farewell,

---

145. The reference here is evidently — in distinction, say, from Ro. 8:16 — to what in theology is called the *external testimony of the Holy Spirit* in distinction from the *internal testimony.*

146. So, e.g., Bultmann: "Their witness is not, therefore, a historical account of that which was, but — however much it is based on that which was — it is "repetition," "a calling to mind," in the light of their present relationship with him (*Comm.*, p. 554). Witkamp, who follows Bultmann in this last point, writes: "The witness is something other than a repetition of the past; it is *witness concerning the glorified Christ.* Because as the glorified one he is identical with the earthly Jesus, historical continuity is necessary to *adequately describe the glorified Jesus*" (*Jezus van Nazareth,* p. 311, italics added).

an association that is expressly distinguished from the time to come (14:25; 16:2, 12f.).[147] It is therefore not to be understood as referring proleptically to their association with the glorified Christ. Furthermore, although the disciples' witness concerning Jesus will be dependent on the Spirit, who will enable them to understand the coming and significance of the earthly Jesus, this does not mean that the object of their witness — and hence the very concept of "witness" itself — will shift from the earthly Jesus to the heavenly Jesus, in connection with which the former will only enable them to speak correctly of the latter. The disciples are — in keeping with the meaning of the word "witness" — witnesses of that which they have seen and heard from the beginning. Of that the Holy Spirit will bring the true meaning "to their remembrance," namely the glory of Jesus as he *was* and not as he became by his going away.

This is why the subject matter of the Fourth Gospel is not witness concerning the presence of the glorified Christ in the church but witness concerning the antecedent incarnation of the Word as the foundation of the faith of the coming church (20:30, 31). This is not, of course, to detract one iota from the ontological identity of the earthly and heavenly Jesus, but it is in keeping with the nature of the gospel as historical kerygma.[148]

16:1-4a   With "I have said this to you," words that are characteristic for these chapters, Jesus returns both to his warning against the world's hatred and to the immediately preceding promise of the Spirit. Both the warning and the promise are intended to keep the disciples from "falling," that is, from letting themselves be drawn away from faith[149] in Jesus.

From the verses that follow it becomes especially clear that when the Fourth Gospel mentions "the world" and its hate it is referring to Jews that do not believe in Christ. In their unbelief they manifest themselves as the world that is alienated from God (cf. 8:21, 23). For "they" (continuing the "they" in 15:21ff.) "will put you out of the synagogues" (vs. 2),[150] which, as in 9:22, refers not to an official synagogue disciplinary measure but to a decision to

---

147. See also Brown, *Comm.* II, p. 690.

148. Clearer and more correct, in our opinion, is what Witkamp writes on 14:25 (*Jezus van Nazareth,* p. 306): "The church is permanently united with the earthly Jesus; therefore, the memory that the meaning of history discloses to the present is of central significance in the work of the Paraclete." But later (p. 355) he writes that "in John the upward connection has priority over the connection with the past; the two belong together but the lived relationship with the glorified Christ is more important than their being eyewitnesses." However, according to John, the lived relationship is *based on* what Jesus has done in the presence of his disciples, the eyewitnesses (cf. 20:30f.), and therefore the "connection with the past" has priority.

149. σκανδαλίζειν, "give offense," "cause to fall," on account of the σκάνδαλον (the "stumbling block") placed in their path; the New Testament uses the middle voice (as here) especially of stumbling resulting from hatred and persecution (cf. Mt. 24:10; Mk. 4:17) or from the nature of the gospel (Jn. 6:6; 1 Co. 1:22; Gl. 5:11; Mt. 16:23).

150. ἀποσυναγώγους ποιήσουσιν, literally "make extra-synagogal." On this expression and the controversy linked with it see the comments above on 9:22.

regard and treat a person as no longer belonging to the Jewish community.[151] This manifestation of the world's hatred had apparently already occurred and in fact was no longer unusual (cf. 9:22; 12:42). With "indeed,[152] the hour is coming" Jesus tells his disciples that the hatred will escalate: "whoever kills you will think he is offering service to God." This probably refers to actions on the part of Jews who are no longer content to eject believers in Jesus from the synagogue but who persecute Christians and threaten their lives from religious motives, either on their own (Ac. 7:58; 14:19; 2 Co. 11:24f.) or through Jewish or Gentile rulers (Ac. 9:14; 12:1f.; 14:5f.; 18:12, etc.).

Verse 3 repeats what has been said in 15:21,[153] but this time with the addition (vs. 4a) that when that time comes the disciples will remember Jesus' words, that he has foretold all this to prepare them for it (cf. 13:19; 14:29).

4b-6   Again Jesus tells his disciples that they must not think of his departure as only a source of sadness and loss and not of advantage. He "did not say these things" to them "from the beginning," not to conceal these matters but "because I was with you": in his presence they were safe and secure (cf. 11:9). "But now," he continues, "I am going to him who sent me," and everything will therefore be different from what it has been. With "yet none of you asks me, 'Where are you going?' " he is, if not making an accusation, at least expressing astonishment that they apparently lack interest in that question. He himself says why they have not asked: "Because I have said these things to you, sorrow has filled your hearts." Their minds are still so fixed on "these things," his departure and their remaining behind, that they cannot think of anything else, such as the salvific purpose of his departure. That is what they should focus their thoughts on, which he will again forcefully point out to them (vs. 7).

It has repeatedly been asked how vs. 5b can agree with 13:36 and 14:5, where the question where Jesus was going has already been raised. For some interpreters this is just one more proof that the order of the chapters was disturbed (see pp. 484f. above).[154] Others say, correctly in our opinion, that 16:5 only expresses in a different way what

---

151. Like the synagogue "curse," designed to lead to repentance. Cf. 9:22 (34); 12:42; Lk. 6:22.

152. ἀλλά in the sense of "indeed" (the time will come); see BDF §448.6. For this heightening see also Bultmann: "ἀλλ' ἔρχεται ὥρα clearly contrasts that which is already familiar and no longer a matter of astonishment with something new and astounding: it will come to martyrdom!" (*Comm.*, p. 556). This is one more reason for not thinking of expulsion from the synagogue as a measure applied only at the end of the first century, as many interpreters, following esp. J. L. Martyn, think today — and even find therein their main argument for positing the anachronistic character of John 9 and similar stories (see the comments above on 9:22; 12:42).

153. It is lacking (for that reason?) in some manuscripts.

154. See Bultmann, *Comm.*, pp. 459f.

was intended in 13:36 and 14:5, namely that the disciples did not understand where Jesus was going.[155] Literally, "Where are you going?" has been asked before,[156] but only as an expression of incomprehension of what was going to happen to Jesus (and to the disciples). Apparently the disciples, even after Jesus has told them of the salvific character of his departure, have not reached the point where they want further information from him about his departure *from that perspective* (cf. 16:17f.). "In asking, they did not lift up their minds to trust as they should above all have done, and this was the chief duty that they were bound to perform. And so the meaning is, 'As soon as you hear of my departure, you become alarmed and do not consider whither or for what purpose I go away' " (Calvin).[157]

7 In the face of this negative reaction to his departure Jesus now states with great emphasis: "But I tell you *the truth*" — what follows has the status of a revelatory saying — "it is to your advantage that I go away." For why it is to their advantage he cites the promise of the Paraclete in 15:26 and affirms that they will only experience the blessing of that promise after he has gone to the Father and has sent the Spirit to them. Earlier Jesus has pointed out to his disciples the "advantage" of his departure — an announcement that should have made them joyful — on that occasion with the motivation: "for the Father is greater than I" (14:28; cf. 14:12).

These passages make it clear how Jesus' coming into and departure from the world (cf. 13:1, 3) can only be understood in the broader redemptive-historical context of God's work of salvation. Jesus' coming as the incarnation of the Word is the fulfilling culmination of this work of salvation. But as such it is temporary (cf. 9:4; 11:9f.; 12:35). He descends in order to ascend back to where he was (3:13). But this return does not mean the end of his work on earth but rather a new beginning that will by the sending of the Spirit bring Jesus' work to full manifestation. It is not enough to say that the disciples will fully understand the true identity of Jesus only through the internal presence of the Spirit.[158] For Jesus' earthly interaction with his disciples has already been based on the internal bond between him and them (cf. 13:10; 15:3, 9ff.). Accordingly, when in 7:39, with a view to the expected coming of the Spirit, Jesus says: "He who believes in me, out of his heart will flow rivers of living water," this undoubtedly refers to the outpouring of the Spirit into the hearts of believers, which will lead them to a better understanding, but it also has to do with the continuation of Jesus' work on earth and the new power that the

155. So Brown, *Comm.* II, p. 710, a conclusion with which he then, however, connects the hypothesis of different "layers" in the Fourth Gospel.

156. Some therefore believe that Jesus refers back here to those occasions by saying, "*Now* (unlike in 13:36) you no longer ask me." So M. J. Lagrange, *Comm.*, p. 418.

157. Calvin, *Comm.* II, p. 115.

158. So Brown, *Comm.* II, p. 711.

Spirit will inject into it. The disciples, with the assistance of the Spirit, will play an important role in this (15:26, 27). Therefore, when Jesus says that his departure is to their advantage because thereby he will prepare the way for the Spirit's coming, it is not of course their personal interest he has in view. Their existence in the security of Jesus' presence will come to an end. But only by the coming of the Spirit will they become that for which Jesus has called and loved them. By the Spirit they will become Jesus' apostles in the full sense of the word (20:22f.); the *Spirit* will teach them not to remain fixed on what they have experienced during their time with Jesus (cf. Lk. 22:35ff.), will lead them into the future, and will incorporate them into the "greater works" that still lie ahead (14:12f.), though still under Jesus' ongoing control and protection (14:13, 14; 15:16).

Verses 8-15 further explicate that ongoing work of the Spirit for the disciples' benefit. In keeping with the dominant theme of this entire pericope the assistance of the Spirit relates first of all to the world's spiritual opposition (vss. **8-11**). The difficulty of these verses is evident from the divergence here among commentaries and monographs on this passage.[159]

8-11 Verse 8 begins with a summary of what is explicated in vss. 9-11: "And he [the Paraclete], by his coming, will prove the world guilty[160] with respect to[161] sin, righteousness, and judgment." Others translate ἐλέγξει as "convince" rather than as "prove guilty."[162] "Sin," "righteousness," and "judgment" are what the world will be convinced of by the Paraclete. But unlike 8:46, this translation does not fit here, because the world being (subjectively) convinced would clash with 14:17.[163] The reference here is rather to the world being objectively proved wrong in its inexcusable unbelief. "Sin," "righteousness," and "judgment" are perspectives in terms of which the world's wrong and guilt will be proven. How, then, should we understand this activity of the Spirit against the world? According to some interpreters, this refers to a cosmic trial taking place before God. The Paraclete, as advocate of the believing community, represents the cause of Jesus against the world and thus helps the church achieve victory. For similar conceptions of the final judgment scholars refer to contemporary Jewish apocalyptic literature in which especially the

---

159. See, e.g., E. Bammel, "Jesus und der Paraklet in Johannes 16," in *Christ and Spirit in the New Testament* (Festschrift for C. F. D. Moule), 1973, pp. 199f.; D. A. Carson, "The Function of the Paraclete in John 16:7-11," *JBL* 98 (1979), pp. 547-66, with extensive discussion of the literature; at length also Witkamp, *Jezus van Nazareth,* pp. 281, 312-27.

160. ἐλέγξει is used of the introduction of evidence by which the truth is brought to light and falsehood is unmasked.

161. περί with genitive identifying the substance of the argument; cf. 8:46; Jude 15; BAGD s.v. ἐλέγχω.

162. Cf., e.g., RSV in contrast to NRSV.

163. So, correctly, also Brown, *Comm.* II, p. 711, with an appeal to Mowinckel.

figure of Enoch, as accuser of the ungodly, is said to resemble the Johannine Paraclete.[164]

It is clear that the Fourth Gospel's antithesis between Jesus and hostile Jews, described as "the world," and the conflict with the "ruler of this world," which lies behind it, is repeatedly described in forensic terms and portrayed as a trial (e.g., 5:31ff., 36f.; 8:13f., 17f.) in which God will one day pronounce judgment (5:45; cf. 3:18f.; 5:24; 12:31, 48). These forensic features return in our immediate context with the description of the disciples and the Paraclete as witnesses (cf. 15:26; 16:11). But it is another question whether in vss. 8-11 all this has the form of a legal trial in which the Paraclete plays the role of advocate and does so on the analogy of a figure like Enoch in Jewish apocalyptic. Even apart from the fact that Enoch's role in the final judgment has a totally different meaning from that of the Paraclete, here the Paraclete does not act before God as prosecutor or public defender in a trial that is still undecided, but as one who brings the truth to light with respect to a settled issue (cf. vs. 11). The idea, as has already been stated in general terms in 15:26,[165] is rather that in his witness vis-à-vis the world the Spirit acts as (helper-)Paraclete to the disciples in their ongoing witness concerning Jesus by portraying to *them* the true nature of the world, of Jesus' departure, and of his victory over the world.[166]

Verses 9-11 go on by explicating[167] how the Spirit proves the world guilty: "with respect to sin, that they do not believe in me" (vs. 9), "with respect to righteousness, that I go to the Father and you will see me no more" (vs. 10), and "with respect to judgment, that the ruler of this world is judged" (vs. 11). For the first the Evangelist refers back to 15:21ff. (cf. 9:41). What makes the

---

164. So in particular O. Betz, *Der Paraklet,* but also Schnackenburg, *Comm.* III, p. 146, though he is more cautious in his formulations and rejects Betz's idea that the "teacher of righteousness" in the Qumran literature played a similar role.

165. See also Bultmann, *Comm.,* in loc.

166. Not in the sense, however, that the mind or spirit of the disciples is the "internal" forum before which the Spirit testifies. For it is the disciples' task to be not the forum of the truth but its witnesses. For this view see Brown, *Comm.* II, p. 712, who correctly rejects the notion that "the trial" takes place before God, i.e., in the final judgment. But then he goes on: "The forum is internal. In Johannine realized eschatology elements of world judgement are incorporated here; yet the courtroom is not in some apocalyptic Valley of Jehoshaphat (Joel iii 2, 12) but in the mind and understanding of the disciples." Brown appeals here to M.-F. Berrouard, "Le Paraclet, défendeur du Christ devant la conscience du croyant (Jean XVI 8-11)," *RSPT* 13 (1949), pp. 351-89. Against this too limited view of the work of the Paraclete, see also Witkamp, *Jezus van Nazareth,* p. 316.

167. The repeated "ὅτι" is not causal ("because") but explicative. It refers not to knowledge people already possess but introduces a further explanation; cf. Bultmann, *Comm.,* p. 563, n. 3: "Of course in vss. 9-11 ὅτι has in each case the purpose of expounding, not substantiating what has been said"; similarly Schnackenburg, who writes about these parallel ὅτι clauses as "explicative clauses" (*Comm.,* ad loc.), against, among others, Zahn and Morris.

world culpable is its conflict with Jesus. Its real sin is that "they do not believe in me." As in 3:18, they have not believed in the name of the only begotten Son of God, despite the full authority of his self-revelation. The Fourth Gospel consistently stresses the religious character of sin. It is not blind to sin as moral corruption (cf. 3:19, 20) or to the enslaving character of sin (cf. 8:34ff.). But it reaches behind these characteristics of sin by stressing that the world's deepest misery and lostness does not consist in its moral imperfection but in its estrangement from God and its refusal to allow itself to be called out of that condition by the one whom God has sent for that purpose (9:41).

The witness of the Spirit, thus described, is not — any more than that of the Son himself — aimed at the condemnation and destruction of the world in the judgment of God (cf. 3:17). But vs. 9 does heavily underscore where, in this "contest" with the world, the Spirit draws the line of demarcation and on what his witness — and that of the believing community that is shaped by his assistance — is concentrated: on faith in Jesus, in whom God has spoken his decisive word in the world, both to save and to judge (3:36).

Over against "sin" stands "righteousness" (vs. 10).[168] Neither term has an article or a genitive modifier. In their essential nature, sin and righteousness are absolute opposites.[169] But both are defined in the controversy over Jesus. For just as sin is explicated as unbelief that is anti-Jesus, so righteousness is explicated as Jesus' going to the Father, an event in which, against those who reject him as the one sent by the Father, he is unmistakably vindicated, proven righteous. Elsewhere also Jesus' vindication as the Son of God is attributed to the Spirit, but then by the Spirit's part in Jesus' resurrection and ascension to glory (1 Tm. 3:16; cf. Ro. 1:4; 8:11).[170] The kinship among these passages in undeniable because here as well the vindication implicit in Jesus' departure is in his resurrection and glorification. Here, however, the vindication of Jesus is a dominant element in the ongoing witness of the Spirit and thereby a basis for the witness of the believing community against the world, which sees Jesus' death as his ultimate powerlessness and hence as a stumbling block in the way of faith in him (cf. 1 Co. 1:18, 23f.).

The meaning of vs. 10b, "and you will see me no more," is hard to establish. That the disciples will not see Jesus again is, of course, inherent in

168. μὲν . . . δέ.

169. See also B. Lindars, "Δικαιοσύνη in Jn. 16:8 and 10," in *Mélanges Bibliques* (Festschrift for B. Rigaux), 1970, pp. 275-85. Differently, W. Stenger, "Δικαιοσύνη in Jo. XVI 8:10," *NovT* 21 (1979), pp. 2-10. The latter speaks of Jesus' righteousness as "a basic righteousness he possesses in virtue of his origin." But in vss. 8 and 10 the reference is to the concept of righteousness as such (with no subjective genitive). Elsewhere, too, the idea of Jesus' ultimate vindication against his enemies repeatedly emerges more or less explicitly in the Fourth Gospel (e.g., 8:50, 54). On this see at length Schnackenburg, *Comm.* III, p. 131.

170. See also my *De Pastorale Brieven,* 1967, pp. 104f., and *Aan de Romeinen,* 1977², pp. 25, 178.

his departure. Perhaps these words intend nothing more than to mark his departure as his passage to another world, to his glorified mode of existence. Some interpreters want to go further and think that this clause involves the disciples in Jesus' vindication by his departure. But despite all attempts to the contrary it is extremely difficult to assign a meaning that is advantageous to the disciples to this negative statement — unless it refers to the advantage of not seeing over the seeing that has until now conditioned their association with him (cf. vs. 7). But if that is the meaning, it has been conveyed in an extremely subtle manner.[171]

The third point with respect to which the Spirit will prove the wrong and culpability of the world is "judgment," which is further explicated with the statement that "the ruler of this world is judged" (vs. 11). These words clearly refer back to 12:31ff. (cf. 14:30). What Jesus announced there will return, in the witness of the Spirit, as an accomplished event: God's condemnation, on the cross, once and for all, of "the ruler of this world," the power of sin and unbelief that has held the world in thrall. Here this is stated as the counterpart of what has just been said about "righteousness," that is, about the vindication of Jesus by God in the highest exercise of his authority, as the regime of love and self-surrender. For it is in one and the same event that both "judgment" and "righteousness" are realized in their once for all eschatological significance.

One can hardly fail to notice the antithetical sharpness with which this witness of the Spirit against and to the world is described. Frequently this is explained in terms of the historical situation in which these words were spoken, or in terms of the threatened position in which the Johannine community is said to have found itself. But it is of no less importance that this antithesis concerns the nature of the choice with which Jesus' mission, specifically his death and resurrection, always confronts the world, and which therefore always shapes the witness of the Spirit and the witness — dependent thereon — of the believing community in the world.

Still, even here this antithesis is not just directed *against* the world. Here, too,[172] the positive significance of the proclamation of judgment in the Word of God that continues to go out to the world remains in force. As long as that Word goes out, judgment is not God's final and definitive word. Therefore, in

---

171. For the ongoing discussion of this difficult clause see, aside from the commentaries (esp. Schnackenburg, *Comm.* III, pp. 130f.), the above-mentioned monographs. For the last-mentioned view 20:29 is referred to; cf. Brown, *Comm.* II, p. 713: "Until Jesus returns to take them with him to his heavenly dwelling place (XIV,2-3, XVII,24), believers shall not see him physically but only in and through his Spirit, the Paraclete. They come under the rubric of those fortunate ones 'who have not seen him and yet they have believed' (XX,29)." But "not having seen" is not put on a level higher than "having seen" in 20:29.

172. See also the comments above on 12:37-43.

announcing the witness against the world, Jesus is not taking his leave from the world in order from now on to go on only with his disciples. What determines the nature of this antithesis is Jesus' absolute and unremitting claim on the world, the claim with which he was sent into the world by the Father and which he, even as he returns to the Father, asserts over the world with undiminished vigor by the sending of his Spirit, not to condemn the world but to save it.

All this, in keeping with the character of the Fourth Gospel, is not laid out in a meticulously balanced system of teachings. That will be immediately apparent from the following verses. What is true, above all else here — and in this respect the "world" also undoubtedly reflects the historical situation — is Jesus' promise that the Spirit of truth will triumph over the power of the world, even when that power surrounds the disciples in all its dark menace, as in this moment of farewell, as Jesus is about to go away and leave them behind in the world.

12-15　　By thus speaking of the Spirit Jesus clarifies the Spirit's "help" to his disciples at a point where that help is essential for them. At the same time he also tells them that there is still much he must tell them about the future, but they "cannot bear that now." The "now" is the same as that of 13:7, the "now" that Jesus mentioned to Peter along with a "later." Like "not understand" in 13:7, the disciples' inability to "bear" referred to here[173] undoubtedly refers to the opaque character of the events that are taking shape as Jesus speaks. Despite his words of consolation and his promise to "come back" so that they can see him again, Jesus cannot unpack for them the full meaning of these events; that would be too much for them (cf. vss. 31, 32). Only the overpowering surprise of seeing him again after his resurrection will explain the riddle — partly in the light of the Scriptures (cf. 20:9) and above all through the assistance of the Spirit.

It is on the coming of the Spirit of truth[174] that Jesus now again focuses all their attention (vss. 13f.). "He will guide you into all the truth," like "walk in the truth," occurs repeatedly in the Psalms (e.g., Pss. 25:5; 86:11) in reference to the true knowledge of God that believers desire of him so as to be able to "walk" in its light. In that truth the Spirit will from now on guide the disciples, and fully ("*all*" truth"). But the Spirit will not speak "of himself"[175] but of "whatever he will hear,"[176] just as Jesus has not spoken "of himself," but of what he heard and saw of the Father (see the comments on 15:19f.;[177] 3:32; 8:26, 28, 40; 14:10; 15:15). The issue here is the continuity of the Spirit's word

---

173. βαστάζειν, "of divine mysteries" (cf. BAGD s.v.).
174. ὅταν δὲ ἔλθῃ ἐκεῖνος.
175. ἀφ' ἑαυτοῦ.
176. Also transmitted as "hears" (cf. 5:20).
177. See at greater length pp. 191ff. above.

in relation to that of Jesus as revelation that goes back to the Father. Accordingly, "the Spirit's word is not something new, to be contrasted with what Jesus said . . . the Spirit only states the latter afresh. The Spirit will not bring new illumination, or disclose new mysteries; on the contrary, in the proclamation effected by him, the word that Jesus spoke continues to be efficacious."[178] Therefore, "and declare to you the things that are to come" should be understood not in a specifically apocalyptic sense but in more general terms: the Spirit will lead the believing community on its way into the future "into all truth" as it will need it then.

Verses 14 and 15 again reinforce the preceding promise with other words. The stress on the work of the Spirit in glorifying Jesus is explicated with "he will take what is mine and declare it to you." The Spirit will totally adhere to what Jesus calls "what is mine," that is, the word Jesus has spoken and the work he has done on the Father's command and in fellowship with him (cf. vs. 15). This does not mean that the Spirit merely repeats Jesus' words. He takes "what is mine," bringing forth the treasure entrusted to Jesus, in order to redistribute it in his own way, "bringing it to remembrance" (cf. 14:26), and thus is the permanent mediator between Jesus and those who belong to Jesus. All this is twice summed up in the general word "declare,"[179] which elsewhere as well has a referential sense, indicating a reannouncement of what has been communicated before.[180]

Vs. 15, in conclusion, picks up the expression "what is mine" from vs. 14 as referring to "all that the Father has" (cf. 17:10) and of which the Father has given to Jesus full disposal as the Son (cf. 3:35). Because the Father has given it to Jesus, the Spirit will take from "what is mine." He will declare nothing other than God's own Word as God has revealed it in the coming and work of Jesus Christ.

I have already noted at some length that these sayings, along with those in 14:26 and 15:26, are of special importance for the evaluation of the unique character of the Fourth Gospel.[181] It is the Spirit who thus witnesses along with the disciples and makes their witness into a vehicle of his own (cf. 14:26, 27). The Spirit does this because they were with Jesus "from the beginning." Accordingly, however much the working of the Spirit as described in chs. 14–16 involves the entire church to come and is not restricted to the disciples whom Jesus addresses in his words of farewell, one cannot simply characterize this discourse as a general address to the coming community (cf. 17:20). The reference here is above all to the apostolic witness effected by the Spirit, which forms the foundation of the coming church's faith (20:30, 31). It is the disciples

---

178. Bultmann, *Comm.*, p. 575.
179. ἀναγγέλειν.
180. See, e.g., Brown, *Comm.* II, p. 708, which refers to Joüon's 1938 study.
181. See pp. 3, 15f. above.

whom Jesus himself has chosen, who, despite their grief over his imminent departure, are called, as the first ones to be called in this way, to give that foundational witness. As such they are distinguished in the Fourth Gospel from the coming church (see also the comments on 14:26).

16:16-33

"You Will See Me Again," "Sorrow Will Become Joy"

This section forms the conclusion of the farewell discourse. In content it is closely linked with ch. 14. The great middle part of the discourse (15:1–16:15) distances itself somewhat from the concrete situation of the story by relating primarily to the future existence of the believing community as God's (new) planting, its life in a world that is hostile to it, and the assistance of the Paraclete that comes to its aid in that hostile world. But 16:16ff. take us back totally into the atmosphere of the imminent separation and the things that will face and threaten the disciples immediately afterward. It is remarkable for this close connection with ch. 14 that the disciples' interventions, which were characteristic for the first section and lacking in 15:1–16:15, now return.

Nonetheless duplications suggesting two distinct farewell discourses are not present here. The motif of the "little while" in 14:19, though it recurs here, does so from a new perspective (see the comments on vs. 16). Furthermore, the incomprehension of the disciples, which came to expression in 14:5 and 8, returns, but in heightened form (vss. 17-18). After the lengthy answer Jesus gives in vss. 19-28, there is a shift in the disciples' mood such that Jesus must now warn them against the danger of underestimating what still awaits them (vss. 29-33). Hence in both respects one can speak here of a supplementation of ch. 14; as a result the situation of farewell and the readiness of the disciples to comply with the words "rise, let us go from here" come to stand in a clearer light. Therefore, the idea that in all this there is evidence of the work of different authors is hard to render plausible. One matter remains: the composition of the entire discourse fails to meet the criteria modern authors would want to apply to a farewell discourse. But it is hard to see why the responsibility for this should be attributed to one or more later "redactors" (who would then have given themselves that degree of license) and not to the original author himself.

One might say that vs. **16** refers back to 14:19 (cf. 13:33). Both texts speak of "a little while" and refer to "not seeing again" and "seeing." However, whereas in ch. 14 the disciples' imminent seeing again is taken up into the discussion of the ongoing fellowship of love between Jesus and the disciples (cf. also 13:33, 34), here the entire focus is again on his imminent departure as the great stumbling block for the disciples' being at peace. But here again with the "little while" the Evangelist refers to Jesus' imminent death and resurrection (and assumes that his readers so understand). Nevertheless, it is entirely in keeping with the historical situation ("pre-Easter") that Jesus here again uses the much less specific word "see" without indicating how or where they will see him.

17, 18 The disciples' striking and elaborate repetition of Jesus' words,[182] first in the private reaction of some of them (vs. 17; cf. 4:27; 6:52) and then in vs. 18, further underscores the incomprehension spoken of in these words. The "little while" within which from now on everything will take place and that they will not see him again and then see him again are totally unclear to them. Also the whole idea of his departure to the Father, despite all he has said about it earlier in response to their questions (cf. 14:2, 3, 5f.; 16:5), remains opaque to them.[183] Hence (vs. 18) the question that lay unanswered on everyone's tongue[184] but that no one — out of respect or fear of revealing their irresoluteness again — dared put to Jesus directly: "What does he mean by 'a little while'? We do not know what he means."

19-22 Again, because he knows his disciples (cf. 6:61; see also the comments on 1:47ff.; 2:24f.), Jesus knows what they are talking about among themselves. In his response, in which he repeats his saying of vs. 16,[185] there is an element of amazement that they are still in doubt[186] about the meaning of his words, which they should understand by now. With great prophetic emphasis he now portrays to them the answer as a reality that they must no longer deny or evade: "Truly, truly, I say to you, you will weep and lament, but the world will rejoice." That speaks of the (short) time in which, by (and by the manner of) his departure, everything that they have believed of him and hoped for will seem lost and in which the world will think that it has succeeded in its schemes against him and is rid of him for good. Jesus portrays this to his disciples in unvarnished words, undoubtedly "so that when their hour comes you may remember that I told you about them" (16:4; cf. 13:19). The secret of his suffering and death is no less strange to his disciples than that of his resurrection and ascension (cf. 13:37f.; 16:31). Therefore he tells them again, "You will be sorrowful," but this time adding, with no less emphasis, "your sorrow will turn into joy" (20b).

Jesus then proceeds directly (vs. 21) to the ever-new image of the woman giving birth, who experiences pain "because her hour has come," and then joy,

---

182. Though such repetitions are "typical of simple narrative, esp. in the Near East" (Brown, *Comm.* II, p. 720).

183. The ὅτι before ὑπάγω in the question in direct discourse in vs. 17 can best be taken as recitative.

184. ἔλεγον, imperfect of duration.

185. Again alternating between θεωρεῖν (in "not see") and ὁρᾶν (of the future "seeing"). We will see this alternation again in the resurrection narrative (θεωρεῖν in 20:6, 12, 14; ὁρᾶν in 20:8, 18, 20, 25, 27, 29).

186. Ζητεῖτε: "asking yourselves about," "wondering about" (cf. BAGD s.v.), durative present.

which makes her forget the pain, because "a child has been born into the world." The image is used often, with an assortment of applications, in biblical and Jewish writings (cf. Is. 26:17f.; 66:7f.; Mi. 4:9f., etc.), and there is no reason to think that its use here refers back to a single specific text.[187] The *tertium comparationis* lies not only in the conversion of sorrow into joy but also in the fact that without this sorrow no joy is possible and that the joy is "brought forth," as it were, by the sorrow.[188] That is also how it will be for the disciples: "So you have sorrow now," as inevitably as a woman in labor. "But I will see you again" as the Living One (cf. 14:19), the one who will disclose himself to them and change their sorrow into joy, a joy that "no one will take from you." For in his return "out of" his going away, in his life "out of" death, lies the certainty that nothing and no one will ever be able to separate them from his love.

23, 24   As in 14:20, after the promise that they will see him again, Jesus gives a further explication of the salvation that attends the promise, introducing it with "on that day," words to be repeated in vs. 26. He does not thereby shift the perspective to the parousia, since what he describes in vss. 23-24 clearly precedes what comes with the parousia.[189] Nor does "on that day" fix all that follows on the day when they see him again. It rather designates the day of the general resurrection as the beginning of a new dispensation characterized above all by the fact that "you will no longer ask anything of me." Jesus thus undoubtedly refers to questions like those the disciples have been asking (cf. 14:5; 16:18, 19).[190] The great joy of seeing him again will put an end to the torment of uncertainty. In place of uncertainty Jesus again emphatically holds out to them the prospect of the Father granting them all that they will ask of

187. Unless "and your hearts will rejoice" in v. 22 refers back to Is. 66:14, where the same words — at some distance — follow the image of a woman giving birth in 66:7-11.

188. Other (especially Catholic) interpreters, appealing to Gn. 3:16; 4:1, see here an allusion to Eve and her progeny, which will destroy the head of the serpent. The woman of Rv. 12:1ff. is mentioned in this connection as well. There as here the woman who gives birth to the child is said to be Mary. A connection is also made with Jn. 19:25-27, where Jesus addresses Mary as "woman" and designates her as "mother" of the disciple "whom Jesus loved," which is taken to refer to her position as "mother of the church." The word θλῖψις ("sorrow") in 16:21 is then said to be an allusion to the eschatological "woes" that are to precede the coming of the Messiah, thus indicating allegorically the Messiah's birth. For all the details, assembled from a wide range of sources, see esp. Brown, *Comm.* II, pp. 721f., 731f., who appeals to A. Feuillet, "L'heure de la femme (Jn 16,21) et l'heure de la Mère de Jésus (Jn 19,25-27)," *Biblica* 47 (1966), pp. 169-84, 361-80, 557-73. This mariological interpretation has been rightly rejected by other (including Catholic) commentators as far-fetched and based too much on fragmentary evidence; see, e.g., Schnackenburg, *Comm.* III, pp. 158f. See also above on the "mariological" links assumed in 2:3ff. and, below, the comments on 19:25-27.

189. See also Schnackenburg's lucid exposition of 14:20 and 16:23.

190. Though ἐρωτᾶν can also refer to asking in the the sense of prayer (cf. vs. 2b; 14:16). In this connection, however, "ask questions" seems, in view of what precedes, more likely than "pray" since up to this point the disciples have not "prayed" to Jesus, and αἰτεῖν is used for prayer in what follows.

him in Jesus' name (cf. 15:7, 16). Apparently, the intent of this passage is that seeing Jesus again as the one glorified by God will not only silence the questions that still assault them but will also open for them the way to the Father, enabling them from this point on to pray to *their* Father in Jesus' name in the certainty of being heard.

The comment in vs. 24, "Hitherto you have asked nothing in my name," thus marks the change of dispensations: though Jesus has from the beginning pointed out to them the way to the Father and has himself *been* that way, up until now he has been with them on earth, the place from which their prayers have gone up. He has not yet been in heaven, the place from which the prayers are answered. Accordingly, "praying in my name," in the sense of making an appeal to Jesus' power and authority as the one glorified by the Father in heaven, marks the difference between "hitherto" and "from now on."[191] On the basis of the approaching transition Jesus urges and promises his disciples: "Pray and you will receive," again with the addition found in 15:11 (cf. 17:13): "so that your joy may be complete," that is, so that they may have the joy of seeing him again, which no one will be able to take away from them (cf. vs. 22).

25 Once more the Evangelist employs the concluding formula, "I have said this to you" (cf. 14:25; 15:11; 16:1), but this time with the remarkable addition "in veiled language" (ἐν παροιμίαις), which is then repeated in the following clause with its opposite, "openly, in plain words" (παρρησίᾳ), both referring to Jesus' words "concerning the Father." παροιμία has a range of meanings including "parable," "riddle," and "cryptic saying."[192] The key question here is what Jesus refers to with "this" or "these things." He does not refer thus to the image in vs. 21, which clarifies and does not conceal. More likely he refers to the words in vs. 18 that tripped the disciples up ("We do not know what he is saying"). But evidently he has a broader meaning. In vs. 25b he refers more generally to his speaking "about the Father" and points the disciples to the future, when he will no longer speak "in veiled language" but will "tell you about the Father in plain words."[193]

Jesus has in mind here what he has called (in vs. 12) the "many things" that he cannot tell them now (because they "cannot bear them" now) but that the Spirit

---

191. The idea is somewhat different if one does not, with other important manuscripts, link "in my name" with "what you ask" but with "will give it to you" (so many interpreters, including Bultmann, Schnackenburg, Barrett, and Lindars). The following words, "Hitherto you have asked nothing in my name," argue for the reading that we (with Nestle) have followed and may have led to the other reading. The choice is difficult, but in the interpretation given above it makes little difference.

192. See the comments above on 10:6.

193. Cf. T. Zahn, *Comm.,* 600: "In this connection one must not think only of 13:8, 10; 14:2, 23; 15:1-6; 16:21; on the contrary, the character of παροιμία, which conceals as well as reveals the truth, more or less marks all that Jesus has taught. The well-meaning in particular would not understand the naked truth."

of truth will teach them. Here, by contrast with the future clarity, Jesus' earthly message and self-revelation, which the Evangelist has been describing, are characterized as provisional. For, although in his witness to Jesus' coming and work on earth the Evangelist is conscious of being allowed to share in the Paraclete's witness (see the comments on 13:26; 14:26), his whole presentation of Jesus' self-revelation is no less characterized by this use of images and allusions, the full meaning of which must remain hidden to Jesus' hearers, both the disciples and "the Jews." Indeed, it must often have sounded puzzling to their ears.

Admittedly, some interpreters think that the reason for this incomprehension was not Jesus' manner of speaking but unbelief (in the case of "the Jews") or failure to achieve believing insight (in the case of the disciples). According to this view Jesus' saying in vs. 25a should be understood in a subjective sense: "I have spoken in language that was mysterious *to you*."[194] But we must make some careful distinctions here. The entire Gospel aims to bring out the undeniable grandeur and majesty of Jesus' self-revelation as the glory of the incarnate Word and to expose the inexcusable character of unbelief in the face of this revelation (cf. the concluding sayings in 12:37-42; 15:22-24). This applies primarily of course to Jews who are hostile to Jesus. When they finally say, "How long will you keep us in suspense? If you are the Christ, tell us plainly (παρρησίᾳ)," Jesus answers with "I told you and you do not believe" and as a final ground appeals to his works (10:24, 25, 37, 38). But in some situations he also faults the disciples, who amid all opposition have been faithful to him, for their lack of faith: "Have I been with you so long, and yet you do not know me" (14:8; cf. vs. 16; see also 20:27)? Therefore in 16:25 Jesus does not want in any way to detract from the fundamental clarity of his earlier self-revelation or to explain or excuse the inadequate reaction of his disciples.[195]

194. See, e.g., Becker, *Comm.* II, p. 503, who speaks of "subjective readiness to take it in" on the part of the disciples, who changed after the resurrection, while the "pre-Easter" and "post-Easter" statements of Jesus remained the same. See, however, vs. 25b: "then I shall no longer speak to you in figures but tell you plainly of the Father." Bultmann, too, subjectizes (*Comm.*, p. 584):

> It is possible to understand the words of Jesus only in the reality of believing existence. . . . Not that he will say anything new; not even that the meaning of what has already been said will gradually become comprehensible to the mind; for Jesus had never imparted theoretical knowledge. Rather, what was once said will become clear in the eschatological existence, for which it was spoken from the beginning.

See also Calvin on vs. 25 (*Comm.* II, 128): "The fact, however, clearly shows that Christ was not speaking allegorically, but using a simple and even elementary way of speaking to His disciples; but such was their ignorance, that they hearkened to Him with astonishment. The obscurity therefore did not lie so much in the teaching as in their minds."

195. For that reason the translation of ἐν παροιμίας as "in riddles" ("as if the early Jesus generally spoke only in riddles," Becker, *Comm.*, in loc.) is to be rejected. Even though such a description may be applied to certain sayings of Jesus, it is utterly inappropriate as a description of the general character of his preaching.

But this does not alter the fact of the veiled character of Jesus' words and actions — that in their deepest meaning they are often neither understood nor understandable (cf. 13:7). And this is true not only of what the Evangelist explicitly says would be understood only after Jesus' resurrection or at the parousia of the Son of man (cf. 2:22; 6:61, 62; 7:39; 8:28; 12:16, 32, 33; 13:7); this element in Jesus' pre-Easter words and deeds, this reference to a later horizon of understanding, characterizes the whole of his preaching, as can be demonstrated from several core sayings and high points in Jesus' self-revelation (e.g., 1:51; 3:13f.; 4:13f., 21f.; 5:21f., 25f.; 6:33f., 48, 51; 7:33f., 37f.; 8:21f., 56f.; 9:4f., 35f.; 10:6, 17f.; 11:9f.; 12:23f., 35f.; 13:31f.). It is also evident from the reactions of those who hear but do not understand, which cannot be charged solely to their unbelief (e.g., 4:11f.; 6:30f., 41f., 52, 60; 7:35f., 41; 8:52; 10:24; 12:34; 14:5f., 8, 22).[196] It is nowhere more clear than in this veiled language that the Evangelist, though he stands in the full light of fulfillment, is nevertheless, as a transmitter of Jesus' words and works, fully conscious of the pre-Easter redemption-historical situation in which they were spoken and done.[197]

It is against this background that the "plain proclamation[198] concerning the Father" Jesus holds in prospect is to be understood. The reference here cannot only be to the few words the Evangelist records of the resurrected Jesus in chs. 20 and 21 but must also include the character of the preaching of salvation that begins in that "hour" (cf. 16:14, 15). What gives this preaching its "open" character and removes the veil from the preceding παροιμίαι is the great event of Jesus' death and resurrection, an event that to the disciples is still veiled during the farewell discourse. Until now Jesus has been able to speak of the necessity and deep mystery of this event only in veiled language and "parables" (cf. 2:20; 3:13, 14; 6:51f.; 12:24f.). Only the realization of that event, or complex of events, as it was now about to occur in his going to the Father, would enable them to "see" and understand all his preaching concerning the Father and himself as the only way, truth, and life.

26, 27 Jesus now guides the disciples' thinking in that direction by adding to the preceding announcement: "On that day you will pray to the Father in my name; but I do not say to you that I will [still] pray to the Father for you," that is, that he will speak to the Father on their behalf that their prayers

---

196. Scholars have pointed, correctly, to the analogy with the so-called "messianic secret" in Mark and the other Synoptic Gospels; see my *Zelfopenbaring en Zelfverberging*, 1946, pp. 66-69.

197. Bultmann, too, speaks of the "basic provisionality also of believing knowledge," "which will only become true understanding through the tests it will have to undergo again and again in the future" (*Comm.*, p. 576, n. 2), but of course he understands this not in a redemption-historical sense but in an "existentialist" sense.

198. ἀπαγγέλλω occurs only here in John (cf. 1 Jn. 1:2, 3 as an alternate for ἀναγγέλλω in vs. 5; on ἀναγγέλλω see the comments above on 16:4 and Schnackenburg, *Comm.* III, p. 161).

might be answered. Here Jesus gives expression to the real and ultimate goal of his entire mission and the task he was to fulfill on earth, which was to restore people to fellowship with God. For that reason his preaching was fundamentally a proclamation of the Father and he had to walk to the end the way of love in a world estranged from God and hostile to himself. But also for that reason there would be a time when, because that task had been completed, his intercession would no longer be needed. It has been rightly said[199] that this does not contradict the idea of the heavenly intercession of the Son (Ro. 8:34; Hb. 7:25) because that intercession is not concerned with the ongoing answering of prayer but with the Christian's status before God, which is grounded on the priestly work of Christ. For his own Jesus is the way to the Father and will remain that in their prayers "in his name," and his return to the Father means that in him they have one who prepares a place for them in heaven and acts there as their advocate (cf. 14:2; 12:26; 17:24). But his departure also implies that "the true worshipers will worship the Father in spirit and in truth, for such the Father himself seeks to worship him" (4:23, 24; cf. 6:45). Here this is expressed in the words of vs. 27: "for the Father himself loves you, because you have loved me and have believed that I came from the Father." Love for Jesus restores direct access to God. In that love the Father recognizes his own (cf. 14:21, 23; 1:13; 17:9f.). It is the one great love by which God loved the world in his Son and which returns to him in those who, in the name of his Son, turn to him as their Father (cf. 17:20-23).[200]

The concluding chiasm in vs. **28** is magnificent in both its harmonious simplicity and the consciousness of power and authority that it conveys. Jesus once more portrays to his disciples the way he must go in order, as the one sent by the Father, to fulfill his task. As a summary of his entire self-revelation this saying is reminiscent of the fundamental saying in 3:13 regarding the descent and ascent of the Son of man in their mutual determination and inseparable unity. "I came from the Father" echoes the conclusion of vs. 27. The disciples have learned to believe in Jesus as the one from the Father.[201] "I have come into the world" does not just say the same thing in different words but explicates "coming from" as "going into the world," here undoubtedly intended in the pregnant sense of "descending" with all its consequences. But Jesus did not come into the world to remain there indefinitely and to go down into its history but "to leave the world and to go to the Father" as the continuation of his coming from the Father, which has been his aim from the

199. Brown, *Comm.* II, p. 735.

200. Cf., in this sense, Calvin's lengthy and eloquent exposition ending with: "This is a remarkable passage, by which we are taught that we have the heart of God as soon as we place before Him the name of His Son."

201. In some manuscripts the first half of the verse is lacking, perhaps because of homoioteleuton. Most interpreters adhere to the text we have followed.

beginning.[202] In contrast with 3:13, here the emphasis is on this latter part. It is Jesus' departure that disturbed the disciples.

29, 30   The disciples' response here is strikingly different from their earlier reactions to Jesus' words. It is as if all at once they feel the need to place themselves unconditionally behind him and seek to remove the impression that he can no longer count on them. Against his saying in vs. 25, "the hour is coming," they twice set the word "now," as if they are already in the situation in which they need not ask him any questions (vs. 23).[203] For this they base themselves on his words and say, "Now you are speaking plainly, no longer in any way in obscure language." What has impressed them is the continuing authority and power with which Jesus speaks to them of the Father: "Now we know that you know all things, and need no one to question you." By this they mean not only that he has again demonstrated that he knows their questions before they ask them (vs. 19) but also that he has all the answers to their questions and therefore needs no one to put these questions to him. "For this reason,"[204] they conclude, despite all their earlier questions, they do not doubt ("we believe") that he has come from God.

This witness of the disciples is striking for the great loyalty that comes through in it, evidence that they are clinging in faith to Jesus as the one sent by the Father. But the manner in which they reject the idea that only the future will give the answers they need as Jesus' disciples is clearly reminiscent of 13:36ff., where Peter opposes Jesus' restrained way of speaking of the future. This is evident from the answer Jesus now gives them, though it is less sharp than his earlier response to Peter's overbearing self-confidence.

31-33   Jesus places a provocative question mark over the disciples' "by this we believe": "Do you now believe?"[205] It is the same question he put to Peter in 13:38 and in the same way echoes the words of the previous speaker.[206] Not that he thereby questions their sincerity, but he does let them know that the time ("now") to speak so confidently has not yet arrived. An "hour" other than the one they think they can anticipate must come first and is indeed already presenting itself, the hour in which the world's hostility will so powerfully press down on them that they will abandon him and seek their refuge elsewhere: "The hour is coming, indeed it has come, when you will be scattered, every man to his home, and will leave me alone." Most commentators correctly refer to Mt. 26:31; Mk. 14:27, where Jesus, similarly at the Last Supper, announces the flight of the disciples ("You will all fall away"), which is interpreted as fulfillment of Zc. 13:7 ("I will strike the shepherd, and the sheep will be

---

202. πάλιν here denotes not a repetition but the converse of the first half of the saying.
203. χρείαν ἔχειν ἵνα is typically Johannine (cf. 2:25; BDF §393.5).
204. ἐν τούτῳ; see BDF §219.2.
205. ἄρτι picks up the νῦν in vss. 29f.; cf. 13:36f.
206. For this connection with 13:36ff., see also Schnackenburg, *Comm.* III, p. 164.

scattered"). Here, too, there is mention of "being scattered," undoubtedly also as an image of sheep without a shepherd. But the Evangelist proves his independence from the Synoptic tradition, for the background of the saying is not only in Zechariah 13 but also in 1 Kg. 22:17, which mentions not only scattering of sheep but also "everyone returning to his home in peace." There the idea is that when in the battle the captain (the "shepherd") has been put out of action the enemy will stop fighting against the scattered army. They can then all return to their home *in peace.*[207] In our text we have the same idea: in the hour that is now dawning Jesus will have to bear the full burden of the world's hostility to him alone, while the disciples go free, each to his home, and abandon Jesus. The disciples will not be the ones abandoned (like sheep); Jesus will be abandoned (as the shepherd). "And will leave me alone" need not therefore imply an accusation of disloyalty or cowardice (cf. 18:10) but states rather that there will be a time when the disciples cannot follow Jesus (cf. 13:36) and Jesus must walk the road alone, and can do so as the good Shepherd who gives his life for his sheep so that not one of them is lost (cf. 18:9; 10:11, 15, 28). For that reason we then read: "but I am not alone, for the Father is with me" (cf. 8:16, 29). He goes his way as one sent by the Father, to whom the Father's love goes out precisely because he lays down his life in order to take it up again (10:17) and who therefore knows himself to be "with the Father" when all others abandon him.

Jesus thus does not unreservedly accept the disciples' confession of faith. Instead, he confronts them with the reality that is now coming toward them. But he does so not to take from them the confidence of faith that possesses them but to make them understand that their faith will be severely tested. That is undoubtedly the import of his final statement in vs. 33. Again — and with it this entire last great "addition" in 16:15-33 returns to the conclusion of ch. 14 — Jesus speaks to them of *peace,*[208] "peace in me," now identified as the content and import of all his preceding words. Here, too, as in 14:27, he sets that "peace" over against "the world," but here the world in its permanent hostility against the disciples. However great that threat may be — and it will undoubtedly come to them! — they must not be afraid: "Be of good cheer, I have overcome the world" (see the comments on 12:31; 14:30; 16:11). With this final exhortation and assertion of his power Jesus concludes his farewell discourse, as a word that they should always and again call to mind (cf. 13:19; 14:26), not only in the "hour" that is now coming and has come, but throughout their entire permanently embattled existence as the believing community in the world.

---

207. Cf. C. van Gelderen, *De boeken der Koningen* II, 1950[2], p. 303.

208. The allusion to 1 Kg. 22:27, in which there is similar mention of "peace," may still be in effect here.

17:1-26

The Farewell Prayer

Jesus' farewell discourse shades off into and is concluded[209] by a farewell prayer. For centuries this prayer has also been called the "high priestly prayer."[210] This name is appropriate when we view this prayer as an intercession for the coming church (cf. vss. 9, 20), and the sacrifice to which Jesus refers (vss. 17, 19) can serve as an argument for this description. But this characterization cannot be derived from the text, neither here, while Jesus is still on earth when he makes his intercession, nor from the farewell discourse, which mentions his future intercession in heaven (16:26). In substance this prayer is very closely linked with the farewell discourse,[211] which is why we choose the designation "farewell prayer."

As with the farewell discourse, so for this final prayer scholars have referred to similar farewell prayers by well-known figures in the Old Testament and in Jewish writings. The degree to which one can speak here of a specific literary genre that might have served as a model for Jesus' farewell prayer seems doubtful. One can, it is true, point to common elements in Jesus' prayer and in other similar "testamentary" farewell prayers, specifically the review of the past, the associated element of giving an account, and the intercession for the future of those who remain behind, which dominates this prayer structurally.[212] These similarities to other farewell prayers are important, but they tend in large part to flow naturally from the farewell situation as such.

Expositors agree that the unique character of the person and work of Christ as attested throughout the farewell discourse determines the content, form, and diction of the farewell prayer. As in all the preceding discourses of Jesus,[213] so in this prayer we have not a document taken verbatim from the lips of Jesus but a composition of the Evangelist, who, conscious of sharing in Jesus' mandate and authorization to the apostles to be his witnesses, shaped Jesus' farewell within the framework and in the language in which he presents Jesus' earthly self-revelation as a whole (cf. 1:1-18).[214] One must therefore not

---

209. Cf. vs. 1: ταῦτα ἐλάλησεν . . . καὶ ἐπάρας . . . εἶπεν. . . . Bultmann's view, according to which this prayer was originally placed before the farewell discourse (*Comm.*, pp. 460ff.), has not been followed by others.

210. According to Schnackenburg the expression goes back to D. Chytraeus (d. 1600), but the idea that Jesus here intercedes as high priest for the people can already be found in Cyril of Alexandria (Schnackenburg, *Comm.* III, p. 433).

211. See, e.g., the thirteen points of contact M. Winter lists in *Die Abschiedsworte der Väter und das Vermächtnis Jesu,* pp. 208f.

212. Cf. Winter, *Die Abschiedsworte der Väter und das Vermächtnis Jesu,* pp. 209f.

213. See also pp. 324ff. above.

214. See the comments on vs. 3, which refers to Jesus in the third person.

look for the historical in the specific phraseology of this prayer, as though the Spirit "brought to" the apostles' "remembrance" and thus by inspiration conveyed the very words of Jesus. The prayer is, rather, a portrayal of the sovereign way in which Jesus, as the one sent by the Father, returns to his Sender, asking to be discharged from the work that he has completed, but also praying for its continuation by the Father himself. Thus the Evangelist not only interprets his own faith, or that of the believing community, but also functions as a witness to and transmitter of Jesus' self-revelation, which was to form the foundation for that faith (20:30, 31; 21:24).

The prayer begins with Jesus' petition for his glorification by the Father on the basis of his completed work (vss. 1-5) and goes on, in close connection with this, to intercession for the maintenance and consummation of this work in Jesus' disciples and the coming community (vss. 6-26). Expositors have attempted to further divide the prayer in a variety of ways and on the basis of a number of methods and criteria. Some proceed from the structure of representatives of the farewell prayer genre, others from the rhythmic cadence that the prayer is said to show or from the recurrent transitional formula "and now" and the use of certain transitional keywords.[215] The majority, however, attempt to lay bare the structural outline on the basis of the content of the prayer.[216] But neither form nor content has thus far led to a consensus. We must ask, therefore, whether the Evangelist actually went to work as schematically as commentators have supposed. In our opinion the structure is not severe enough and the transitions are too fluid for us to speak of a detailed and sharply delineated thought scheme.

This is not to deny, however, that, on the basis of the opening petition (vss. 1-5), which dominates the whole, the intercession for the disciples in vss. 6-26 shows a clearly progressive movement of thought that can be summed up in a few main points: Jesus' intercession for his own as those given to him by the Father concerns in succession their preservation and sanctification in the world (vss. 11-19) and their unity as those shaped by these realities (vss. 20-23). The prayer as a whole is concluded by Jesus' petition that his own may share in the eternal glory that has been given to the Son by the Father (vss. 24-26).

---

215. For these views see further Schnackenburg, *Comm.* III, p. 169.

216. On these classifications see Becker's ample overview in "Aufbau, Schichtung und theologie-geschichtliche Stellung des Gebetes in Johannes 17," *ZNW* 60 (1969), pp. 54-83, here pp. 57-60; Becker, *Comm.*, pp. 508-17.

17:1-5

Jesus' Petition for His Glorification
on the Basis of His Completed Work

1, 2 In close connection with his words of farewell to his disciples Jesus now turns his eyes to heaven with this petition: "Father, the hour has come; glorify your Son that the Son may glorify you." In this form of address and the subsequent words the unique character of this prayer immediately stands out. It cannot be compared with any other prayer uttered in a situation of farewell. It is certainly a prayer, being addressed from start to finish to God. But it can also be called a farewell prayer, since Jesus utters it in the hearing of his disciples and lays before God the completion of his work on earth, so that from this time on God himself will assume responsibility for that work. But it is also clear that Jesus remains the crucially involved partner in that work. Without his presence in heaven the continuation of his work by the Father is inconceivable. This is evident not only in the last part of this prayer (cf. vss. 21ff., 24ff.) but also at the beginning: when he says "glorify your Son that the Son may glorify you," he is not praying for a new relationship to the Father or for a glory that will from now on be mutually realized between him and the Father ("intertrin-itarianly") away from the earth and in heaven. The reference is, rather, to no other glory than the glory he already possesses on earth, the glory pronounced over him by the voice from heaven (12:28), the glory in which he as the incarnate Word has become manifest and been seen (1:14; 2:11, etc.) and in which he as the Son has consistently glorified the Father (cf. 11:4, 40; 9:3).

Verse 2 speaks of this explicitly: Jesus, by way of motivation,[217] imme-diately adds, "since you have given him power over all flesh" (cf. 3:35; 13:3). We have repeatedly referred to the parallel pronouncements in 13:31, 32, which in identical terms mention the reciprocal glorification of the Father and the Son of man.[218] It is in the function and power[219] of the figure of the eschatological Son of man that the Son of God came down from heaven, in order thus (cf. 3:13), from heaven, to exercise that power in an unrestricted sense (cf. 7:39), an exercise to which he was predestined by the Father and for which he now prays. This glorification is then further described with the Semitic term (cf., e.g., Jr. 32:27) "over all flesh," that is, over all (human) life, created by God, in its impermanence, mentioned here presumably because of the end for which the Father has clothed Jesus with that power, namely to grant eternal life to humans, who do not possess this life in themselves (cf. 3:16; 5:26f., etc.) —

---

217. For the causative sense of καθώς, see the comments above on 13:15; 15:9f.; cf. also 17:21ff.

218. See the comments above on 1:51; 3:14, 16; 5:27.

219. ἐξουσία; cf. Mt. 28:18.

specifically "to all whom [*or* that] the Father has given him" (cf. 6:39, 44), a further qualification of the power and mandate given to Jesus by the Father that recurs in what follows and receives special attention in vss. 6-10 (see below).

3, 4 Verse 3 interrupts the connection with vs. 4 and further explicates the meaning of "eternal life": "And this is eternal life, that they know you, the only true God, and Jesus Christ, whom you have sent." It is most striking that this explanation takes place in prayer to God and that Jesus speaks of himself in the third person as "Jesus Christ," a designation that occurs only one other time in the entire Gospel, not in a quotation (1:17). Accordingly, this verse is usually viewed as an insertion by a later hand.[220] It is questionable, however, whether this striking addition must be explained as a disturbing "alien body" inserted by a later hand. In the presentation of Jesus' prayer of farewell by the Evangelist it may be intended as an indication of the extent to which Jesus from the beginning involved the overhearing disciples in his prayer by once more depicting before their eyes the power given him by the Father in its full salvific meaning, as it concerned them. When in this connection the Evangelist (possibly) uses formulations used in the later community, he does not substitute the confession of the community for his witness as apostle and interpreter of Jesus but rather confirms the extent to which the confession of the one true God and of Jesus Christ whom he sent forms the interpretation of the heart of Jesus' self-revelation right into his farewell prayer.

At the same time these words, however much they were added with an eye to the disciples and as a link between vss. 2 and 4, contain one more motive for God to hear Jesus' prayer for his glorification. For by granting eternal life to his disciples, life consisting in the fact that they have again learned to know the Father as the one true God and Jesus Christ as the one whom he has sent, Jesus has glorified the Father on earth (vs. 4) and has attained the full goal of the mandate (the "work") that the Father has given him to fulfill.

5 Therefore he can now ("and now") pray for his glorification, a state he then proceeds to describe as "the glory that I had with you before the world was made." These words speak of the preexistent,[221] original glory of the Son with the Father that Jesus, now that as Son he is returning to the house of the Father (cf. 16:28; 14:1), presently requests of the Father as the

220. Schnackenburg calls Jesus' self-designation as "Jesus Christ" in the prayer "unsuitable and contrary to the style of the prayer as a whole" (*Comm.* III, p. 172). Also, the use of this name must be understood, it is said, as a traditional formula of professing one's faith just as the attributes "only and true" (God) are said to be traditional attributes added to God's name (see Bultmann, *Comm.*, p. 494, n. 7).

221. πρὸ τοῦ τὸν κόσμον εἶναι, expressed in vs. 24 by πρὸ καταβολῆς κόσμου, in 1:1 by ἐν ἀρχῇ; cf. also 6:62.

glory due to him there. It is the unique glory of the Son "with" the Father,[222] of the Word that was "with God[223] and was God" (1:1), a glory antecedent to the power with which he was clothed as the Son of man by God when he descended from heaven. But it is not an absolute state of glory, uninvolved in any revelation, but a divine glory that transcends the temporal world *in its relatedness to "all things,"* for it is the glory of the divine Word, by whom all things were made and in whom was life and the light of life of humans (1:4, 5) as he has made it known in the incarnation of the Word. Therefore, if Jesus is here, on the boundary between two worlds, praying to be permitted to return to the glory he had with the Father, he is thinking not just of himself with a view to rediscovering himself and withdrawing to the "eternal" glory due to himself alone, but rather of that glory in its ongoing relatedness to his work on earth.

For that reason the petition for his glorification now passes into prayer for his own, in a multiplicity of aspects, having as its final object that in their way they might also share in his glory, the glory that the Father gave him, because to that end the Father has loved him and destined him from before the foundation of the world (vs. 24; cf. 3:16, 35; 5:20; 10:17; 15:9).

17:6-10

Jesus' Intercession for Those Given to Him by the Father

6-8 The transition to Jesus' intercession for the disciples occurs in vs. 6. Before giving explicit content to this intercession (vss. 11ff.), Jesus first (vss. 6-10) renders an account — certainly as support for his intercession — to the effect that he has completed his work entirely in keeping with the will of his Father. This has consisted, first, in that he has manifested (nothing other than) "God's name,"[224] which alternates with "your word" (or "words") and with "everything that you have given me." That "everything" is all that Jesus has said and done and also, and this is no less characteristic for this entire passage (cf. vs. 2), those to whom Jesus has revealed God's name, those "whom you gave me out of the world," to which is added, as if to put full emphasis on this last element: "they were yours,[225] and you gave them to me."

These last expressions have (again) elicited the charge of "determinism,"

---

222. παρὰ σοί.

223. πρὸς τὸν θεόν.

224. By God's "name" is meant God as he reveals and makes himself known in action (cf. 12:28). On the significance of God's "name," see at length C. A. van Peursen, *De Naam die geschiedenis maakt. Het geheim van de bijbelse godsnamen,* 1991, pp. 31ff. and passim.

225. σοὶ ἦσαν.

here specifically God's exclusive election by grace before all times.[226] But the reference here to "yours" and to "those whom you have given me" does not refer to a pretemporal election and still less is meant in a deterministic sense. It has, rather, a salvation-historical (or "eschatological") sense.

The best commentary on this is 6:37, 39, 44ff. There also we read of "everything that the Father has given me," which is qualified as what "the Father draws" so that it "will come to me." "It will come" in keeping with fulfillment of the ("eschatological") prophecy of salvation of those who are drawn. That prophecy reads, "All will be taught by God." As a result of it "Everyone who has heard and learned from the Father comes to me" (6:45). Jesus did not manifest God's name to those who had no knowledge of it but rather to those who were among the people to whom God had from of old revealed "his name" and to whom he had obligated himself to reveal his name in the future (cf. Is. 52:6; Ezk. 39:7).[227] The addition "out of the world" does indicate that God has given them to Jesus out of the alienation from God that has surrounded them (cf. 1:9, 10) by "drawing" them out of it (cf. 6:44, 45) so that they might "come" to Jesus (6:37). At the same time the entire passage stresses that this "giving" of "his own" to Jesus by the Father must not be understood in a deterministic sense (which would render talk of "faith" superfluous) but took place precisely in the way of Jesus' manifestation of God's name and by way of the faith of the persons thus addressed by Jesus.

This connection comes immediately to expression in 17:6 and continues with almost monotonous repetition in vss. 7 and 8. "They were yours, and you gave them to me, and they have *kept* your word," that is, they observed and appropriated the word (vs. 6).[228] "Now they know/acknowledge that everything you have given me is from you" (vs. 7).[229] "Now" refers to the result of Jesus' entire work ("everything") as this is being manifested among those with whom Jesus enters into this prayer before the Father. "For the words that you gave to me I have given to them, and they have *received* them in the — ever deepening[230] — awareness that I came from you; and they have *believed* that you

226. See Becker, *Comm.*, p. 521. On p. 519 he writes: "This determinism, which conditions history and the ecclesiasticized dualism of cosmos and church, not only comes out in vs. 2 but permeates the entire prayer, as no other Johannine passage, so repetitively and so stereotypically. The language of divine giving stresses this determinism such that it has become superfluous to speak of faith."

227. On this and on the link between "being drawn by the Father" and "believing in Jesus" see at length pp. 232ff. above.

228. For this (Johannine) meaning of τηρεῖν, see BAGD s.v.; Bultmann, *Comm.*, p. 498, n. 2.

229. παρὰ σοῦ εἰσιν.

230. ἔγνωσαν ἀληθῶς. The preceding ἔγνωκαν in vs. 7 refers to the ultimate result. The aorists ἔλαβον and ἔγνωσαν refer to the way in which that result is obtained.

sent me" (vs. 8). As is evident from the faith they display *as God's people,* they have recognized in Jesus the one who sent Jesus.

Jesus, we may conclude, traces everything back to God himself: all his public actions as the manifestation of God's name, all his words and works as given[231] to him by the Father, his entire coming from God,[232] and those with whom he now appears before God and for whom he prays as those whom the Father has given[233] him, as is evident from their faith in him. In all this one can see the element of Jesus' "account" of what he has done, which characterizes other prayers as well.[234] But here it functions above all as ground for his intercession for his own. It is the Father's own work, the Father's own people, with whom he is returning to the Father and for whom he now further requests the Father's preservation.

This last point is forcefully and sharply brought out a second time in vss. **9-10**: "I am praying for them; I am not praying for the world but for those whom you gave me, because they are yours." "I am not praying for the world" has caused consternation, but it does not characterize Jesus' attitude to "the world" in general (cf. vs. 18; 6:51). It must be understood in the context we have mentioned: Jesus is giving an accounting for his now-completed work. Just as in being sent by the Father Jesus did not go his own way (cf. 6:38, 39) and did not seek glory from people (cf. 5:41f.; 7:18), so here he comes in prayer before the Father with the outcome of that work and not with other people, nor does he here pray for others, but for those who have been given to him by the Father and in whom he has found room for the words of the Father. For that reason he can finally say: "All mine are yours," all that he can call his own as a result of the realization of his mandate had been given him by the Father, and nothing less than that. But here, too, this is the case in the mutuality based on his unity with the Father: "and yours are mine," his own for whom he now prays as those who believe in him and who belong to him, with the certainty that the Father will hear him. The conclusion of vs. 10, "And I am glorified in them," ties in with the preceding and at the same time leads to what follows. For it is the glory of the work completed *for and in his own,* the continuation and consummation of which Jesus now asks and desires from the Father.

---

231. ἔδωκας, δέδωκας, vss. 6f.
232. παρὰ σοῦ, twice. παρὰ σοῦ ἐξῆλθον is not to be understood "trinitarianly" but as synonymous with σύ με ἀπέστειλας.
233. ἔδωκας twice, δέδωκας in vs. 9.
234. See p. 516 above.

17:11-19

Jesus' Petition for the Preservation and Sanctification of His Own in the World

11-13 Now begins the actual *intercession* (vs. 11b) in a slowly unfolding train of thought and constant recalling of the same motifs.

The focus of this intercession is the preservation of the disciples in the world and is motivated by Jesus' departure from the world while[235] his disciples stay in it. This prompts him to use a repeated solemn form of address and prayer: "Holy Father,[236] keep them in your name, which you have given me."[237] The preservation has in view the threatening character of the world surrounding them (vss. 14, 15; cf. 15:18ff.). Here again the means to that end is the name entrusted to Jesus by the Father (vs. 6; cf. vs. 12), understood as the efficacious working of the word of God addressed to them, the goal and result being that within that word they may be one, "as we are one." This last phrase introduces a motif that helps to shape the entire prayer and, while not coming to its full development until vss. 20ff., serves here to define the unity of the disciples as their being taken together into the fellowship of the Father and the Son. In that fellowship they are safe from that which threatens them in the world.

Vs. 12 speaks of the preservation "in your name" as that which Jesus has been doing "while I was with them," and further describes it with "I guarded them," probably, in view of vs. 12b ("lost"), to be understood in terms of the image of the shepherd watching over his flock (cf. 10:12, 28, 29). The result has been that "none of them [the flock] was lost," however much the enemy has been against them. As in 13:10, the exception — Judas — is mentioned and described here as "the son of destruction," a model of what it means to be "lost,"[238] the fate from which Jesus has protected his own. "That the Scripture might be fulfilled" is not meant in a deterministic sense as making what was once predicted and decided in the name of God necessary. It refers, as does 13:18, to texts like Ps. 41:9 to point out that Jesus knew himself to be one with, and had to go the way of, the threatened people of God in the world

---

235. The second καί in vs. 11 is adversative.

236. This formula of address, which is imbued with a sense of God's majesty and individuality, occurs also elsewhere in Jewish and Christian writings, though rarely in Christian writings (as in Rv. 6:10; see O. Procksch and K. G. Kuhn, *TDNT* I, pp. 88ff.).

237. In place of ᾧ δέδωκας several manuscripts have οὓς δέδωκας and therefore make the disciples, rather than the "name," what has been given to Jesus. But the reading followed above has strong evidence, is accepted as original by most interpreters, and fits very well in the context.

238. ὁ υἱὸς ἀπολείας refers back to the preceding (οὐδεὶς) ἀπώλετο. υἱός with a genitive noun is a frequently occurring Semitic combination meaning "one who belongs to" or "one who is controlled by" (cf. BAGD s.v. υἱός). The expression is used for the Antichrist in 2 Th. 2:3 and elsewhere in apocalyptic literature of Satan himself.

to fulfill their God-given task. This appeal to Scripture is striking in the prayer of the Son to the Father (see the comments on vs. 2). But the Evangelist includes it in his reproduction of the prayer as proof to fellow hearers of the prayer that Judas's lostness, far from being unconnected with Jesus' mission from the Father, was one of the elements shaping its content.

With "but now" (vs. 13), which contrasts with "while I was with them" in vs. 12, Jesus expands the thought of vss. 11 and 12: his departure to the Father and the necessity of surrendering his care for his own into the hand of the Father is no loss for the disciples, but instead a cause of joy (cf. 14:28): "But now I am coming to you; and I say this [in their hearing] in the world so that they may have my joy made complete in themselves." Again we encounter the typically Johannine expression "fullness of joy," which Jesus applies to himself and to his disciples as a term for complete salvation (see the comments on 3:19; 15:11; 16:24) and uses here of the joy that they who remain in the world may share with him in his departure: "my joy in them." They could not wish for themselves a better preservation and a more certain future than what Jesus, as his last word and deed in the world, places in the hands of his Father.

According to some interpreters this passage reflects a very different view of the disciples' future than what appears in chs. 14–16, in which Jesus speaks with so much emphasis of his own continuing care for his disciples ("I will not leave you desolate," etc.) and of the Spirit's care for them. According to these interpreters this proves that ch. 17 is the work of a different redactor than the preceding chapters.[239] But this seems to be an all too narrow view of the varied manner in which the Evangelist does his work by again and again expatiating on what he has already said from new angles. Here, moreover, he describes Jesus' prayer *to the Father;* all the emphasis therefore falls on the work of the latter. That no other "understanding" needs to underlie this material is also clear from the conclusion of ch. 14, which in vs. 28 is strongly reminiscent of 17:14; there, too, the disciples are exhorted to rejoice over Jesus' departure, and in terms of the motif that is all-controlling here as well: "because the Father is greater than I" (14:28).

14-16 Verse 14 again picks up the thought of vs. 12a and, in a mode of reasoning that is most typical for John, gradually, by the addition of new viewpoints, works it out. In this connection special attention is devoted to the disciples' relation to "the world," which is mentioned first in its antithetic character: "I have given them your word, and the world has hated them." The

---

239. So, e.g., Becker, *Comm.,* p. 523. He speaks of another "understanding" in ch. 17 from what is seen in 14:2ff., 18ff.: "With Jesus' mission his mandate with repect to the community on earth runs out as well. Now God takes care of the community that has been left behind. The shift from christology to the doctrine of God is undeniable."

world is hostile because, as in 15:19, the disciples "are not of the world, as I am not of the world" (see the comments on 8:23 and 3:31). The world "hates" (see the comments on 15:18) that which is not "of the world"; it does not tolerate that which is foreign to it because that thing runs counter to the world's starting point and pattern of life (cf. 3:19, 20; 7:7ff.).

Verse 15, however, besides making an important addition to what has just been said, offers further explanation of it and gives it a certain twist. The motif of preservation is continued, but when Jesus says, "I am not asking you to take them out of the world, but I ask you to protect them from the evil one,"[240] he is also making known in what respect the disciples must be protected in the world. He is not thus distinguishing between "the world" and "the evil one." What is called "the evil one" here is elsewhere called "the ruler of this world" (12:31; 14:30; 16:11), and the world is accordingly seen as his domain. For that reason we read next:[241] "They are not of the world, even as I am not of the world." Even so, the disciples' place and mandate are *in* the world. Therefore, "I am not asking you to take them out of the world" is not concessive ("Even though . . ."), as though that would be better for the disciples. For that reason Jesus does not ask just that God protect them but introduces another viewpoint that controls the thought: "Sanctify them in the truth" (vs. 17).

17-19 "To sanctify" is tantamount to separating, to preparing the disciples for service to God. The idea of preservation is continued in sanctification (note the structural parallelism between vs. 11 and vss. 16 and 17), but, as the transition to vs. 18 shows, the stress is now completely on the positive aspect of sanctification, on consecration for the sacred service of God in the world. "In the truth" again refers to the realm in which that consecration is realized, that of the truth of God's word and of his name (cf. vs. 11). Within that realm the disciples are not only safe in the world but also capable of continuing the work for which Jesus has destined them, their mission in the world.

Verses 18 and 19 speak of that mission. With "as you have sent me into the world" Jesus appeals to the agreement of the mandate he has given his disciples with his own mission from the Father and to the fact that their mission is based on his own and therefore serves to continue *the Father's* work. The content and purpose of the disciples' consecration are thus placed in a clear perspective. They do not consecrate themselves to service for God *away from* the world, but rather in the act of entering *into* the world. Again we encounter here the nuanced use of the word "world" in the Fourth Gospel.

---

240. τηρεῖν ἐκ, "protect them lest they fall into the hands of." τοῦ πονηροῦ can be translated "evil" but here certainly refers to the personal "evil one" (cf. 1 Jn. 2:13; 4:4; 5:16). But the boundaries are fluid (cf. 1 Jn. 5:18f.).

241. In some manuscripts this has (for that very reason?) been omitted.

Although it frequently means nothing other than the domain of "the ruler of the world" and as such the sum total of human life in its alienation from and independence of God, here again the usage clearly shows how the world cannot be abandoned by God (cf. 3:16) or by Jesus (cf. 6:51) or, therefore, by the disciples.

We read here of the disciples' being sent into the world, but their mission mandate does not come up until 20:21. This does not mean that in this regard, too, ch. 17 can only be explained in terms of the Evangelist's postresurrection perspective. The disciples' mission only acquires its full relevance after the resurrection, but their appointment as Jesus' witnesses and apostles in the world is still the great presupposition of their call to follow Jesus (e.g., 4:36ff.; 6:12; 15:27; 17:20). What is new here is that Jesus — still in the world (vs. 13) — prays to the Father that the disciples may be equipped for this purpose. This points to Jesus' own share in that consecration: "For their sake I consecrate myself [present tense], so that they may also be truly consecrated."

10:36 also mentions Jesus' "consecration," but in connection with his having been sent by the Father (and hence in the sense found in 17:17). Here Jesus' active self-consecration on behalf of his own is undoubtedly his self-surrender on their behalf. He consecrates himself as a *sacrifice* for his own. This meaning of "consecrate" goes back to Old Testament usage (e.g., Ex. 13:2; Dt. 15:19),[242] and the preposition "for"[243] ("on behalf of" or "in place of") is used in several New Testament statements concerning Jesus' sacrificial death for his own (or "for the world," cf. 6:51; Mk. 14:24; 1 Co. 11:24; Hb. 2:9, etc.).[244]

It is on account of the atoning, sin-removing power of Jesus' sacrifice (cf. 1:29, 35) that the disciples will also be "truly consecrated" to the sacred ministry for which Jesus has appointed them to speak in his name. The use of "truly" refers to the uniqueness of this consecration, a consecration by which every other atonement ritual or priestly mediation designed to give them access to that ministry is rendered inadequate and superfluous.[245]

---

242. For the frequent use of ἁγιάζειν in the terminology of sacrifice, see also BAGD s.v.
243. ὑπέρ.
244. See also Bultmann, *Comm.*, p. 235, n. 1. Accordingly, the view that Jesus' self-consecration on behalf of his own relates not to his sacrifice but to his consecration in heaven on behalf of his disciples seems to be in conflict with the thrust of this whole pericope, which places all the emphasis precisely on what Jesus is now doing on earth for the consecration of his disciples with a view to their coming ministry on earth.
245. ἐν ἀληθείᾳ, here, in distinction from vs. 17, without the article and therefore to be taken adverbially. Others think it refers back to vs. 17 and therefore has to be understood in the same sense: "in the truth." Although an assortment of meaningful ideas can be associated with this translation, the fact is that vs. 19 understands the consecration of the disciples under another viewpoint than vs. 17 does, namely that of Jesus' self-offering alongside that of the realm of the truth of the word of God (see also 13:10; 15:3).

Several commentaries justifiably refer to the great distance between the "openness to the world" frequently recommended today also in Christian circles and the apparent world-avoiding attitude of the Johannine community, as seen in the farewell discourses and prayer. An example is Schnackenburg, who does not, however, regard this attitude as normative for a Christian worldview. While he recognizes that the evil one continues to threaten our world and that "the community which is on its guard against that evil power and prays (the Lord's Prayer!) to be kept from it is performing a positive and provocative task on behalf of mankind," he explains the attitude toward the world emerging here as originating "in a fundamentally dualistic way of thinking and in the situation in which an oppressed and inward-looking community was placed."[246]

Brown's judgment is much less critical. He, too, writes that the attitude described in John 17 "strikes many Christians as strange and even as a distortion of the true Christian apostolate": "In an age of involvement where men are considering the role of the church in the modern world, the refusal of the Johannine Jesus to pray for the world is a scandal." He points out, however, that hostility to the world is not peculiar to John but is reflected also in Ja. 4:4 and Gl. 1:4. But there are also many passages in the New Testament that "inculcate involvement in the world" and that become especially important when the church is tending to sequester itself from the world. But, he thinks, if Christians believe that "Scripture has a certain power to judge and correct," then passages such as we find here in John "have a message for an era that is naively optimistic about changing the world or even about affirming its values without change."[247]

In our opinion the idea of "Johannine dualism" is not at all helpful in theological interpretation if it refers to something more or other than the break, caused by sin, between God and the world created by him and belonging to him. That the world, even in its state of subjection to an alien power, remains the object of God's saving will, expressed in his Son's mission, belongs to the core content of the Gospel (1:3, 9ff.; 3:16). For that reason the undeniable difference between the assessment of the world that emerges here in Jesus' prayer and the "openness" to "solidarity" with a predominantly non-Christian society so often advocated in our day can hardly be explained in terms of the Johannine community's supposed dualistic view of life. How could that community also, and in the same breath, have Jesus say, "As you have sent me into the world, so I have sent them into the world" (vs. 18)? What could dissuade that community from worrying about self-preservation and from withdrawing from the world more than the consciousness of having been sent into the world *as Jesus had been sent,* and had let himself be sent, into the world by the Father? The difference between Jesus' farewell prayer in John and contemporary ideas of "openness" and "solidarity" vis-à-vis the world does not consist in the stronger mission-consciousness of the latter — the contrary is rather the case! — or in greater compassion toward the world's distress. It lies rather in a radically different assessment of the nature of that distress and of the ongoing crisis in which the world is caught up. What "moves" Jesus, in this prayer and in his entire mission in the world, is, negatively, the world's estrange-

---

246. Schnackenburg, *Comm.* III, p. 184.
247. Brown, *Comm.* II, p. 764.

ment from and lostness before God its creator and, positively, Jesus' struggle and willingness to offer himself up for the world (6:51) in order to restore it to the love of God, that is, to his own fellowship and unity with the Father. This difference in approach to the "distress" of the world cannot be traced back to dualistic cultural or religious elements that crept into the Gospel and that have been overcome in modern consciousness. It must be traced, rather, to the absolute character of Jesus' self-revelation as the One sent by the Father, as the way, the truth, and the life as articulated in the Gospel.

In the light of this both parts of Jesus' petition "I am not asking you to take them out of the world, but I ask you to protect them from the evil one" are equally fundamental. The first is not to be construed as relating concessively to the second. The disciples' place in the world is not something that they can give up because the world is not something that God can give up. The watchword for their future and their self-preservation (their "identity") cannot, therefore, be that they must position themselves as much as possible outside the world. They may be forced out because of the world's hostility, but the essential nature of the church is not that of a conventicle. Precisely for that reason God must "protect" the church from "the evil one," not only from open or violent hostility and "hatred" but also from the world's desire to squeeze the church into its secular patterns of life and to seduce it into solidarity, a process that goes beyond the "distress" of the world.

17:20-23

"That They May Be One, Even As We Are One"

20   The transition to this section brings "those who believe in me through their world"[248] into Jesus' intercession, with vs. 18 clearly in the background. Jesus sends the disciples into the world to continue his work in the world by means of "the words" he "gives" them, just as the Father, when he sent Jesus into the world, gave him "his words" (cf. vs. 8).

That such a clear distinction is made here between Jesus' disciples and future believers ("not only . . . but also") does not mean that the whole preceding section concerned only the former. The "they" of whom Jesus has repeatedly spoken are not only the apostles, the founders of the future community, but also represent that community itself. Still it is again made clear how much Jesus lodged the preaching of the gospel above all in the apostolate of the disciples he himself called and empowered (see the comments on 15:26). But here "those who will believe in me through their word" are expressly mentioned in Jesus' intercession along with the disciples themselves, undoubtedly because in the following verses everything is concentrated on the

---

248. As spoken at the Last Supper, the present participle πιστευόντων undoubtedly refers to the future (for this usage see BDF §339.2b). Accordingly, several textual witnesses have the future participle.

ultimate goal of Jesus' entire work, the work he has begun on earth and will continue in heaven. And that goal is that *all* who believe in him may be one as he and the Father are one.

21   Verses 21-23 form a clear unit consisting of two strophes, as is evident not only from the repeated reciprocal formula of immanence but also from the repetition in the two concluding purpose clauses: "that the world may believe."[249] The first question that confronts us in vs. 21 is whether this verse describes the content of the prayer mentioned in vs. 20 ("I pray . . . that they may all be one") or whether the opening clause is a purpose clause ("I pray . . . in order that they may all be one"). If the first, then, after praying for the preservation and consecration of the disciples present, Jesus now prays for the unity of "all," both the disciples and the future church. But one can also understand vs. 20 ("I do not pray for these only . . .") as referring to the preceding petitions: "I do not pray [all this] for them but also . . . ," then adding in a purpose clause: "that they may all be one." In this way "those who will believe in me through their word" are brought into not only the petition for unity but also the preceding petitions, which is undoubtedly a more likely construal. This translation also commends itself in the light of vs. 11, where the subject of unity comes up in the same way: "that they may be one, even as we are one," there also clearly as the goal of the preceding petition: "Father, protect them in your name." We may conclude, therefore, that the unity intended here is not an additional and separate blessing Jesus asks of the Father but the great object that Jesus aimed for during his life on earth and now desires from the Father for the future as well: "in order that

---

249. This unity of composition is even more striking if, with Holwerda ("Punten in komma's," *Opbouw* 3 [34], 1990, pp. 52ff.), we join the first half of vs. 22 to what precedes so that it is dependent on (the first) "that the world may believe. . . ." Then "that they may be one" in vs. 22 repeats "that they all may be one" in vs. 21 and is therefore still dependent on "I pray" in vs. 21, while the conclusion of vs. 22, "even as we are one" (in keeping with "even as . . ." in vs. 21), together with vs. 23, forms the second strophe. So, beginning with vs. 22b, one must then read: "(I pray) that they may be one; even as we are one, I in them and you in me, so that they may become perfectly one, so that the world may know. . . ." There is thus a consistently applied parallelism between the second strophe and the first ("I pray . . . that they may all be one even as you, Father, are in me, and I in you, so they in us, that the world . . ."), especially in the concluding purpose clauses.

Holwerda provides a totally consistent schematic ordering of the material. But however attractive and sagacious this transposition of periods and commas may be, objections can be made: First, the division of vs. 22 into three parts is oversubtle (especially the comma placed between ἕν and καθώς) and therefore hard to recognize as the intent of the Evangelist. Second, on grounds of subject matter there is good reason to take vs. 22a (in keeping with the traditional division of the verses) as the beginning of the second cycle and not as the conclusion of the first (see the comments above). Finally, Holwerda's entire reconstruction stands or falls with the idea that the ἵνα in vs. 21a (which is then said to be picked up in the middle of vs. 22) introduces not a purpose clause ("in order that") but the content of the prayer introduced in vs. 20 ("I pray that"), a view that in my opinion does not deserve preference (see again the comments above).

they may all be one [a clause appearing in vss. 11, 21, 22, and 23],[250] even as we are one."

On the meaning of this passage, which is often cited and discussed in ecumenical literature because of its ecclesiological significance,[251] opinions strongly diverge. What seems to be of fundamental importance for its interpretation is the repeated description of this unity: "as you, Father, are in me, and I am in you, may they also be [one] in us" (vs. 21), "as we are one" (vs. 22), and "I in them, and you in me," with the addition "that they may become completely one" (vs. 23). The church's final goal is not unity as such, however it is understood, but "unity *in us*," being one *"as we are one,"* where "even as"[252] not only indicates a resemblance between the church's unity and the unity between the Father and the Son, but also gives the church's unity its ground and character. Accordingly, the theme of this passage can only be "that they may all be one *in us*."

Käsemann,[253] who strongly stresses this linkage as well, even thinks that the unity of the Christian community is vindicated here on the basis of its participation in the ontological unity of the Father and the Son.[254] But there can be no misunderstanding the fact that when Jesus here repeatedly makes his unity with the Father foundational to his unity with his own and to their unity with each other, he has in mind not the ontological unity of the Father and the Son but the unity and reciprocal immanence between him and the Father as it comes to light *in the performance of the divine work of salvation.*[255] It is *this* unity that surfaces in the Gospel again and again, not only with "the Son can do nothing on his own, but only what he sees the Father doing" (5:19) and "what he has heard from him" (cf. 8:26), but also where the same "reciprocal formula of immanence" is used (see the comments on 10:38; 14:10) and where Jesus explicitly states, "I and the Father are one" (10:30).[256] That this sort of

250. ἕν in vs. 21b is lacking before ὦσιν, at least in the reading that most follow. It is so obviously intended after καθώς that it could be omitted.

251. See, e.g., the extensive summary in Brown, *Comm.* II, pp 775ff., 782.

252. On this use of καθώς, see the comments above on 13:15; 15:10ff.; and 17:18.

253. In his lengthy critical discussion of "Christian unity" in *The Testament of Jesus*, pp. 56ff., which includes his rejection of the ethical, personalistic, and mystical views of this unity.

254. Ibid., pp. 70f. He refers to far-reaching Gnostic influence, namely the idea of emanation, according to which the divine imparts itself through a series of stages to the earthly. "This almost frightening understanding of the Johannine community must be called gnosticizing. Here one perceives most clearly John's naive docetism, which extends to his ecclesiology also" (p. 70). For this understanding of the Fourth Gospel as naively docetic, see p. 49, n. 99 above.

255. See also Calvin on 17:21 (*Comm* II, p. 148): "Many of the fathers interpreted these words absolutely, as meaning that Christ is one with the Father because He is the eternal God. But the Arian controversy made them seize on detached passages and twist them to a foreign sense." Christ speaks here, rather, of that unity in terms of his office as Mediator and as Head of the church.

256. See p. 371 above.

unity is also meant here is evident from everything that precedes, where Jesus in a number of expressions emphasizes the complete harmony and concurrence between the Father and the Son in carrying out the work of salvation assigned to him by the Father (vss. 2-4, 6-13; cf. vs. 10!).

All this gives us the thrust of Jesus' prayer for his own. What is described with "even as you, Father, are in me, and I am in you" and "may they also be in us" as determinative for the church's unity is the church's participation and incorporation in the work accomplished by Christ in unity with the Father. The church's participation is meant to take place in keeping with its nature as the one flock belonging to the one Shepherd (10:7), who knows his own as the Father knows him and as he knows the Father (10:14-16), and as branches engrafted in the one true vine, of which the Father is the "vinegrower" (15:1, 4f., 9f.). This has already been explicitly expressed in 17:11, 12, where Jesus prays that the Father may protect his disciples in the name that the Father has given him so that "they may be one as we are one" and then adds that he himself has guarded them in the name given to him by the Father so that "not one of them was lost" from that bond of unity, except "the son of perdition" (cf. 6:39).

Accordingly, what constitutes and qualifies this unity of the coming community and its incorporation into the fellowship of the Father and the Son is its having been brought and kept under the rule of the word and name of God, which the Father has given to his Son, and the Son has revealed to his own (vss. 6-8, 11-12). Therefore, too, the commandment that matches this prayer for unity is, as was stated earlier, "remain in my love," that is, in Jesus' commandments, "just as I have kept my Father's commandments and abide in his love" (15:9-10).

It is evident from all this that the unity of the coming community is not considered here from the viewpoint of "being with each other" and still less from that of their calling and willingness to *form* a united group with each other and to organize and shape it in the most efficient manner. That, too, undoubtedly belongs directly or in a more derivative sense to Jesus' care for his church, even in his farewell discourse (cf. 13:12ff.). But here the dominant thought of Jesus' prayer is that the church's unity may be controlled by, and find its criterion in, its unity with the Father and the Son, that is, in Jesus' coming into the world and his work in the world in keeping with *his* unity with the Father.

This is apparent also from the concluding clause of vs. 21: "so that the world may believe that you have sent me" (cf. vs. 23). What must engender this belief on the part of the world is not the church's unity as such or the degree to which it asserts itself in the world as a unified movement (alongside similar movements!), but the liberating power of Jesus' word and Spirit as it comes to expression in the church. *This* is what must bring the world to believe that Jesus did not come of his own accord and did not appoint himself as Savior but was sent by God himself. In several ways this places before the church the responsibility of its congruence with the mission and example of its Lord (cf. 13:15, 35; 15:16; 1 Jn. 2:19, 23, 24; 2 Jn. 8f.).[257] But it is not this ecclesiastical responsibility, still less church problems (as in the Johannine letters), that controls the perspective of Jesus' farewell prayer for unity. That perspective comes, rather, from the christological farewell, so that the prayer asks the Father to guard the work that Jesus has accomplished in the pursuit of his mandate and in agreement with the Father's will and to vindicate him against the world: "that the world may believe that *you* have sent *me.*"

This is not to say that the statement "that the world may believe" has only a negative incriminating sense — "believe despite itself" — that then supposedly comes to clearer expression in vs. 23 with "(be compelled to) recognize" (cf. 8:28).[258] It is clear from vs. 18 that the believing community has its positive mandate to fulfill in the world. But it is clear from the context that in this prayer Jesus is directly concerned about the continuation of his work and that of the Father *in his own,*[259] and only indirectly about the world's faith. The idea of the vindication of Jesus' work against the world's hostility (cf. 16:10) is no less at work here than that of the appeal to the world to recognize and confess Jesus as the one sent by the Father (see the comments below on vs. 25).

22-23   As in vss. 12-19, so here, along with praying to the Father for his own, Jesus appeals to what he himself has done for them during his earthly ministry:[260] "The glory that you have given me I have given them, so that they may be one, as we are one." This describes what Jesus gave to his own in the

257. See also Brown, *Comm.* II, p. 778.

258. So Calvin on vs. 21 (*Comm.* II, p. 148): "Believe" is "imprecisely used by the Evangelist for 'to know'; that is, when unbelievers, convicted by their own experience, perceive the heavenly and divine glory of Christ. Hence, believing they do not believe; for this feeling does not penetrate into the inward attitude of the heart." Becker acknowledges that "believe" in vs. 21b is more "liberal-minded" toward the world than "recognize" in vs. 23, which refers not to "recognition leading to salvation" but to "insight into one's own lostness," while vs. 21b assumes "the possibility that the world might come to believe." This difference then again suggests to Becker that there are two different editorial hands at work here (*Comm.*, p. 526). Following Käsemann, Becker writes that Christian mission is "not directed to the world as such" but only to those in the world whom the Father gave to Christ, "hence the elect, those who have been called to faith" (Becker, *Comm.*, p. 527).

259. ἵνα in vs. 21b is no longer dependent on "I pray" in vs. 20 (as are the two preceding ἵναs), "but states the purpose or result of ἕν . . . εἶναι" (Bultmann, *Comm.*, p. 514, n. 4; see also Brown, *Comm.* II, p. 770).

260. Cf. Schnackenburg: "This statement and that of vs. 22a can be grouped among a series of statements in which Jesus refers, in this discourse, to what he has done for the disciples: he has kept them in the Father's name (v. 12); he has given them the word of the Father (v. 14); he has sent them into the world (v. 18) and he has sanctified himself for them (v. 19)" (*Comm.* III, p. 192). For the view that vs. 22a is to be understood with vs. 21 and is therefore dependent on "that the world may believe," see n. 249 above.

most exalted terms. Jesus has already said, "I have given them all that you have given me," which was more precisely defined as "eternal life" (vss. 2-3).[261] By speaking now of giving his "glory" Jesus brings out how deep the foundation of their unity is and how far it reaches. For that reason "that they may all be one as we are one" is again followed in vs. 23 by "I in them, and you in me" to indicate that by his indwelling of the community ("I in them") the community shares in the glory that the Father has given him ("you in me"). Jesus says all this to highlight the total and inviolable unity for which he has destined his own: "that[262] they may become perfectly one."[263]

The meaning of this "glory," as Jesus' gift to his own and the basis for their perfected unity, is hard to describe in a single word.[264] In vss. 24f. we again read of Jesus' "glory," but then as Jesus' *heavenly* glory, the glory he had before the foundation of the world and that the disciples may one day contemplate in heaven. In vs. 22, however, the reference is not to this preexistent (and postexistent) glory of Jesus, which at his departure he still had to receive (vs. 2), but to the glory with which the Father clothed and equipped him as the Son of man for his mission in the world (cf. vs. 2a; 3:34, 35; 5:20, 27; 10:17). "Glory," therefore, refers here not to a single, all-surpassing gift but to Jesus' all-embracing *authority* and *power* and its manifestation during the performance of his task in the world (cf. 1:50, 51; 2:11; 11:4, 40ff.).

So when Jesus speaks here of the glory given to him by the Father as something he then gives to the disciples, this can hardly refer to anything other than that in their association with him they will be involved in the performance of that task, and not only for their own salvation but also as fellow agents in carrying out Jesus' task, already during his life on earth (cf. 9:4; 4:38; 6:5, 12) but above all as those who will continue his work after his departure. Not only has Jesus given them charge to that end, but he has also promised his assistance, hearing all their prayers, even given them the prospect of doing "greater works" than those he himself has done (14:12-14, etc.; cf. also 20:21-23).

Verse 23, finally, also refers to this in virtually the same words as vs. 21:[265] "that the world may recognize that you have sent me," here, however,

---

261. "He had nothing for Himself alone but rather was rich to enrich His believers" (Calvin, *Comm.* II, p. 149).

262. ἵνα repeats the ἵνα in vs. 22 and introduces a final clause that is parallel with the final clause in vs. 22.

263. ἵνα ὦσιν τετελειμένοι is hard to translate and is therefore usually viewed as a further description of the unity: "that they may attain perfect unity" (cf. BAGD s.v. τελειόω). τελειόω refers here not to inner moral perfection but to being brought to the highest possible point, the attainment of the highest degree, here the highest degree of unity.

264. For various descriptions, see Schnackenburg, *Comm.* III, p. 192.

265. In place of πιστεύῃ in vs. 21, vs. 23 has γινώσκῃ, but with no plausible difference in meaning (e.g., Bultmann: "without distinction"). For the reading πιστεύσῃ and the conclusions to be drawn from it, see Brown, *Comm.* II, p. 776.

with the addition, "and have loved them as you have loved me." God's "love" for Jesus is closely tied with Jesus' mission as the agent of God's saving work in the world (cf. 3:35; 5:20; 10:17), and the same is true of God's love for the disciples. This love is manifest in the fact that the Father not only protects the disciples but also wants to incorporate them in his work in the world and make them serviceable to that work (vss. 15ff.). Therefore, "that the world may recognize that you have loved them" means that in the disciples' comings and goings in the world not only their unity with Jesus as the one sent by the Father (see the comments on vs. 21) but also the love of the Father himself for the world in and through their ministry will come to expression as an appeal to the world.

17:24-26

Prayer for the Future Union of His Own with Himself

24 Though vss. 24-26 are linked closely with the preceding, they also clearly form the conclusion of the prayer as a whole, starting with the new address "Father." The content of these verses goes beyond what has preceded: Jesus now speaks of his disciples' sharing in his future glory. One can therefore say that Jesus asks here for the culmination of everything he has prayed for on behalf of "those whom you have given me," as he once more describes his disciples, commending them to his Father (cf. vss. 2, 6f.).

The new address "Father" (cf. vss. 1, 13), expanded in vs. 25 to "righteous Father," again brings out the urgent and just character of what Jesus asks of the Father, as does the striking phrase "I desire," with which he presents his petition to the Father. Jesus does not pray here as a claimant, but as *the Son,* as one who knew he could rightly assume ownership over the many rooms in the Father's house (cf. 14:2, 3), a subject with which the end of the farewell prayer clearly returns to the opening word of the farewell discourse! "I desire," spoken in the disciples' hearing, is certainly intended therefore to tell them how much their future, no less than his own (vs. 1), concerns him and how certain they can be of sharing in its glory.

"That those also . . . may be with me where I am" undoubtedly, as in 13:36 and 14:3, refers to the great future in which Jesus will come again (14:3; elsewhere in Johannine writings called his "parousia"; cf. 1 Jn. 2:28; 3:2) and take his own to himself to be with him where he is, in the place of his heavenly glory.[266] On the "where," "when," and "how" of this new mode of being, the Evangelist characteristically says nothing more. All that matters is the certainty

266. On this see at length the comments on 14:2f.

of that future[267] and "with me" as its content (cf. also Ph. 1:23; 1 Th. 4:17; Lk. 23:43; Rv. 3:4, 21, etc.).

This content is then further described as "seeing my glory that you have given me." Even during his time on earth Jesus shared with his own the glory given to him by the Father (vs. 22; cf. 1:14), thus incorporating them into the perfection of the unity of the Father and the Son (vs. 23). But this presence — inaugurated with Jesus' coming on earth — of the salvation promised by God does not take away the prospect of future glory, either for Jesus or for his own. Not until then, when Jesus will have departed and prepared for them a place in the Father's house, will they see his full, no longer limited, glory and in seeing it be freed from what now obscures or blocks its realization. Or, as it is said in 1 Jn. 3:2: "Beloved, we are God's children now. What we shall be does not yet appear, but we know that when he appears we will be like him, because we will see him as he is" (cf. also Col. 3:4).[268] What is then said in vs. 24c,

---

267. Käsemann: "The fact that this futurist hope is simply taken for granted in John, that it is expressed almost incidentally and emphasized only at the end of chapter 17, makes his hope all the more significant" (*The Testament of Jesus*, p. 72). The eschatology of the Fourth Gospel is thus limited to "the final unification of the community in heaven" and the glorification of the children of God. The old apocalyptic tradition in which a cosmic revolution was expected has been spiritualized under Gnostic influence.

But one may ask whether this self-evident character that Käsemann assumes with respect to the eschatologized hope of the community (even though it is expressed only "incidentally") does not apply also to the future of the entire created world, however remarkable it may be that no separate mention is made of this in the Fourth Gospel (unlike the Synoptics). But apart from texts like 5:25, see, in general, the important role played by the Son of man in the Fourth Gospel (with clear reference in 5:27 to its cosmic-apocalyptic background in Daniel 7; cf. also Jn. 1:51; 3:13; 6:27, 62; 8:28). When Jesus' glorification is described as the glorification of the Son of man (cf. 12:23; 13:31), this diction is hard to understand if one does not take into account "all power in heaven and earth" (Mt. 28:18), which is typical for Son of man eschatology (cf. also Jn. 17:2). Here, too, one must again ask about the Evangelist's unique purpose and not draw far-reaching conclusions from his silences.

268. Here Bultmann, *Comm.*, p. 520, is very much on target:

But nothing positive [*anschaulich*, i.e., "concrete"] can be said about it in explanation; for what is said in 1 John 3:2 is just as relevant here; οὔπω ἐφανερώθη τί ἐσόμεθα. . . . The only thing that is clear is that an existence for the believers with the Revealer beyond death is requested, and thus promised. Death has become insignificant for them (11.25f.); but not in the sense that they can ignore it because their earthly life is now complete and meaningful in itself; but because their life is not enclosed within the limits of temporal-historical existence. The reality of the revelation does not lie in the inward superiority of light over darkness, enabling the believer to stand outside the battle, safe in the knowledge of the eternal values and inward union with them. On the contrary, meaning is given to the temporal event in that it is determined by powers which have their reality beyond the reality it has, yet without being eternal in the sense of idealist thought. History is not a symphony in which everything is woven harmoniously into a whole; no, in history judgment is carried through. But this holds out a promise at the same time: what happens can achieve its purpose. History runs its course before the judgement-seat of God. Thus it is also true of the believer that his participation in life is not exhausted in his historical existence within

"because you loved me before the foundation of the world," bases this coming glory of God's eternal love on, that is, the good pleasure of the Father to cause his own to share in the glory given to the Son from all eternity (cf. Ep. 1:4).

25-26   Verse 25 ties in immediately with the preceding with an appeal to God's justice. This appeal gives the preceding "I desire" its motivation and the whole prayer its final ground, its foundation in God's good pleasure. To that end Jesus again points to his unity with the Father in carrying out this saving will and to the faith in it he has found in his own. And this in contrast with the world, so that by this appeal he seeks the answer to his prayer with all the more urgency as the vindication of himself and his own over against the world. It is in that sense also that "while the world . . . ," which is hard to place in the context, can best be understood: Jesus thus contrasts the world's ignorance of the Father (cf. 7:28; 8:19, 55; 15:21) with his own knowledge of the Father,[269] that is, with his fidelity to the task and word given to him by the Father, completely along the lines of 8:55. But in the same breath he adds: "and these have recognized that you sent me," referring thus to the ones whom he now concretely introduces to the Father as those who have recognized him as sent by the Father, for whom he therefore now pleads in the same manner as for himself.

The conclusion in vs. 26 again sums up the entire purpose of Jesus' mission: "I have made your name known to them." That was his life and his "food" (4:32): to make the Father known as he wanted to be known, to teach them the "name" by which the Father wants to be invoked. To this Jesus adds: "and I will make it known." His work on earth has not yet been completed. His passion still lies ahead of him, the suffering in which that "name" will still be at issue in the most far-reaching way. But here the reference is more to Jesus' continuing work in heaven. This is also clear from the last words: "so that the love with which you have loved me may be in them, and I in them." With these words Jesus again places his entire mission in the vast context in which the Evangelist put it from the beginning (1:1ff.) and traces the salvation he brings to its ultimate source, the love that existed "before the foundation of the world" and proceeded from the Father to the Son, as the Word that was in the beginning with God and was God. In him

---

time, even though nothing positive can be said about the "then" beyond death. The Evangelist avoids all speculation about any heavenly journey of the soul, and refrains from any description of conditions of another world, such as form part of Gnostic mythology. But the fact that he has seen that "the view beyond has been barred" from us, does not make him fall back on the opinion that human life can find its completeness in this world; he knows the double possibility: that it falls to pieces in condemnation, or that it is eternal in faith.

269. δέ, vs. 25b.

that love went out to the world, because in the Word was life and the life was the light of all people (1:1-4). In the consciousness of being the bearer and mediator of that eternal love, Jesus prays that the love with which the Father has loved him may be in his disciples as what redeems and shapes their lives. But he himself will be the one who will keep them in that love (cf. 15:7ff.). Therefore once more he adds the words "and I in them" as the final and all-decisive word of the Savior.

18–19

Jesus' Suffering and Death

Now, after lengthy preparatory chapters, follows the actual story of Jesus' passion and death. The main outline of this story is the same as in the Synoptic Gospels: Jesus' goes to Gethsemane, he is arrested after a sign given by Judas, he is tried first by the Jewish authorities and then by the Roman governor Pontius Pilate, Pilate sentences him to death by crucifixion, and Jesus is crucified, dies, and, on the same day and before the beginning of the sabbath, is buried by Joseph of Arimathea. In this course of events we have the oral tradition concerning Jesus' passion and death, which, there is reason to assume, achieved a more or less fixed form at an early stage and formed the starting point for the whole tradition of the life of Jesus as that tradition functioned in the church.

But for all the commonality in the main outline, the passion narrative shows great diversity in its written forms in both the selection and the presentation of the material (cf. Lk. 1:1ff.). One can see this already in the Synoptic Gospels, where it can be traced in part to the Evangelists' differing redactions of the same material and in part no less to the richness and diversity of the traditions they have drawn on in pursuing their goals in writing their Gospels.

And, again, though the general outline is clearly visible even in John, the unique character of John in both selection and presentation sets it apart from the Synoptics. Still, early study of the Gospel traditions saw the general similarities of the passion narratives as important evidence that John was in part dependent on the Synoptics.[1] More recently scholars largely abandoned this viewpoint and have assumed the unique character of the Johannine passion

---

1. Many recent exegetes remain faithful to this position (see below); for its proponents and opponents see, e.g., the bibliographies in F. Neirynck, "John and the Synoptics," in *l'Évangile de Jean*, ed. M. de Jonge, 1977, pp. 7ff.

narrative as a starting point.[2] The striking resemblance in certain details between John and the Synoptics continues to be of interest, as we have seen in the description of events outside the passion narrative (see the comments on 6:1-13; 12:1-8) and as is the case in the passion narratives. But these resemblances can hardly be decisive. One can hardly picture John with the Synoptic Gospels before him sometimes taking over a phrase or detail from them, but more often showing no interest in them at all.

Scholars have therefore searched for other written accounts on which John is assumed to have been dependent. The main arguments for the existence of one or more such sources are that the Fourth Evangelist was too distant in time from the events he describes to have possessed direct knowledge of those events and that a distinction must be made in his Gospel between what is is typically Johannine in theology and what is not. The conclusion is that John's passion narrative is a theological redaction of an already existing document, which is said to be clearly evident in "non-Johannine" parts of the narrative.[3]

Some have tried by detailed investigation to understand more throroughly this source and possibly the events behind it. Attempts have also been made to establish connections with sources of Luke that might explain certain striking similarities between John and Luke.[4] These subtle studies have led to complex reconstructions of the development of written sources that supposedly preceded the passion narratives that have come down to us.[5] These studies have received widely varied assessments.[6] Adherents of the theory of direct dependence of John on the Synoptics — in opposition to this ever more subjective application of the tradition-historical method — stay with the verifiable material before us (the four existing Gospels) though with more reserve than was formerly the case with that basic approach.[7] They do not think necessarily of literary

---

2. For a lengthy account of this reversal, see, e.g., J. Blinzler, *Johannes und die Synoptiker. Ein Forschungsbericht,* 1965, pp. 16-60.

3. See, e.g., Bultmann, *Comm.,* p. 635; Schnackenburg, *Comm.* III, p. 219. The circular nature of this argument is clear. First one establishes (on the basis of the Gospel itself, of course) what is typically Johannine, in order then to use that as the criterion of what belongs to the pre-Johannine "passion narrative" and how John used that pre-Johannine material.

4. See, e.g., A. Dauer, *Die Passionsgeschichte im Johannesevangelium. Eine traditionsgeschichtliche Untersuchung zu Joh 18,1–19,3,* 1972. See also F. Hahn, *Der Prozeß Jesu nach dem Johannesevangelium,* 1970, pp. 23f. For a critical discussion of this issue see P. Borgen, "John and the Synoptics: Can Paul Offer Help?" in *Tradition and Interpretation in the New Testament* (Festschrift for E. E. Ellis), 1987, pp. 80ff.

5. See, e.g., the constructions in Becker, *Comm.,* pp. 532ff.

6. One can read the interesting report of the discussions held on this subject at the twenty-sixth session of the Journées Bibliques de Louvain, held August 20-22, 1975, by M. de Jonge in his "Introduction" in *l'Évangile de Jean,* 1977, pp. 15ff.

7. So Neirynck, "John and the Synoptics," pp. 72-106. See also M. Sabbe's critique of Dauer's hypothesis in "The Arrest of Jesus in Jn 18,1-11 and its Relation to the Synoptic Gospels," in *l'Évangile de Jean,* pp. 203f.

use of the Synoptics by John or of deliberate borrowing, supplementation, correction, or interpretation of the Synoptic documents. Johannine use of the Synoptics could also have amounted to familiarity with one or more of the Synoptic Gospels, used then "from memory," probably Mark for the general sequence of the passion narrative and possibly Luke as well, considering the occasional verbal similarities.[8]

The important question is whether these attempts to trace the origin of the Johannine passion narrative to (ever deepening "layers" of) written sources do justice to the unique character of the Gospel as we have it and to the author's own witness. Was the author of the Fourth Gospel — whoever he was — necessarily dependent for his knowledge of the general course of Jesus' final journey to the cross either on the Synoptics (above all Mark) or, when that theory fails, on an earlier foundational "passion narrative," after the apostolic witness had already been preached and taught in the church for decades and had, in the manner of Near Eastern traditions, assumed more or less fixed forms?[9] The mere fact that the Evangelist — as we have seen again and again — assumes that his readers know in general terms about the events that he narrates points in a very different direction from that of a primarily *literary* development. Furthermore, and this touches on the unique character of the Fourth Gospel, we must question the correctness of what stands as a kind of dogma in some modern studies, namely that the Fourth Evangelist had no substantial personal knowledge of the events that he narrates and that therefore the value of his writing is not in his transmission of the tradition but only in the distinctive way in which he, as a theologian, edited and interpreted the written sources at his disposal.

It is clear that this tears apart what for the Evangelist himself was an unbreakable unity, that of event and interpretation. For him one does not exist without the other. This is clear from the manner in which he intentionally, throughout the Gospel, including the passion narrative, stresses the factual character of what he narrates. It is also evident from the Gospel's literary structure, in which event and interpretation are presented as an original unity. Not just the remarkable unity of style, which has been repeatedly emphasized by many scholars, but also the Gospel's integration of form and content, of historical material and interpretation, is too natural and organic to permit any surgical separation, the attribution of some components to the Evangelist and of others to his "source," a process in which no single "source" ever proves to be enough.

Certainly the Evangelist was conscious of the twofold nature of his

8. Neirynck, "John and the Synoptics," pp. 80f.

9. For the importance of oral tradition, see C. H. Dodd, *Historical Tradition in the Fourth Gospel*, 1963. See also Borgen, "John and the Synoptics," p. 93.

undertaking. As a transmitter of the tradition it was certainly not his purpose (cf. 20:30) to put everything down in writing for an audience ignorant of the core of the gospel tradition. He sought, rather, to confirm the community in its faith-knowledge by giving its members a purer foundation for their faith. He does this — as we have seen — in the awareness of the assistance of the Holy Spirit, promised by Jesus to his disciples for their witness. This explains in part the freedom with which the Evangelist varies his method as a transmitter of the tradition, relating what was important for his purposes and ignoring other important matters. But it is also clear that he numbers himself among those to whom Jesus promised this cooperation of the Spirit, those who had been with Jesus "from the beginning" (15:27). Therefore his knowledge of what he writes about is in part direct.

This does not mean that he wrote completely from his own memory and without the help of others. In the passion narrative we must deal especially with the role of the "beloved disciple," to whose direct eyewitness involvement the Evangelist appeals with so much emphasis (19:35). That issue will further engage us later when we ask the question of authorship.[10] But in more general terms it is true here as throughout the Gospel that the Evangelist writes from within the community of those who were witnesses with him of the glory of the incarnate Word (1:14; 1 Jn. 1:1ff.), on the basis of what Jesus revealed of his glory in their presence (20:30, 31), and on the basis of the deeper insight into what they had experienced in their dealings with Jesus that they gained after his resurrection (2:22; 12:16; cf. also 14:26). It is in terms of this common witness, the witness of those who were with Jesus and with some of whom the Evangelist may have had close ties (note the references to them in 1:40, 43, 46; 6:5, 8; 12:22) that he presents his Gospel and wanted it to be understood and believed. With this witness he, in his way and with his special intentions, represents the apostolic tradition.

All this, of course, does not solve all the problems that come up especially in comparing the Johannine and the Synoptic traditions of Jesus' passion and death. But it does cut through the great presupposition that exegesis of the Johannine narrative must assume that the factual foundations underlying it lay outside the Evangelist's personal observation and field of vision and can only be found in written sources that he utilized. It is my conviction that the Fourth Gospel, including its passion narrative, has a much more personal and wider background than that, a background that cannot be precisely described in all its parts, and that it therefore calls for a much more open-minded approach than what arises from the presuppositions of the tradition-historical method.[11]

---

10. See below.

11. Cf., to cite just one example, Brown's critique of Richter's view that the narrative of Jesus' arrest is simply a "theological elaboration of the Synoptic or pre-Synoptic account," one

Chapters 18 and 19 are clearly divided into three nearly equal sections: Jesus' arrest and trial in 18:1-27, his trial before Pilate in 18:28–19:16, and his crucifixion, death, and burial in 19:17-42. The first and third sections contain successions of events that make possible further division. The second section, which is completely devoted to Jesus' trial before and condemnation by Pilate, is especially detailed. Some scholars regard it as a composition of seven parts, a grouping that is said to be discernible also in the other two sections. We will restrict ourselves here to the more obvious scheme.

18:1-12

The Arrest

1 The first words of vs. 1 may very well have been originally intended — before chs. 15–17 were inserted — as the continuation of 14:31. The narrative that follows is in more than one respect a striking illustration of Jesus' words in 14:30, 31.

Jesus and his disciples go to a "garden"[12] across the Kidron brook from where they have been during their meal and at the foot of the Mount of Olives. Unlike the Synoptics, John mentions neither the Mount of Olives nor the name of the garden. And the Synoptics do not mention the Kidron brook in their description of the place. Of course they are referring to the same place, but from the start John's presentation is independent of the Synoptics.

2 This independence is even more evident from the narrative of Jesus' arrest. John does not mention Jesus' agony in Gethsemane before the arrest (cf. Jesus' agitation of spirit in 12:23, 27f. and see comments there). Only the word "cup" in vs. 11 is clearly reminiscent of the Synoptic prayer in Gethsemane. This is undoubtedly linked with the perspective from which the Evangelist wants the reader to understand the narrative, that of Jesus' authority and power with which he, in obedience to the Father, now surrenders himself into the hands of humans (cf. also 13:1-3; 14:30, 31).

The narrative in John is extremely concise. The focus is on a few high points in a story with which his readers were undoubtedly familiar. There is no attempt to give a comprehensive account of the course of events. The moments highlighted are those in which Jesus most clearly manifests his glory. The light falls successively on Judas, the band of soldiers, the disciples, and Peter.

---

in which numerous details are ignored: "In our judgment, in order to do justice to all the complexities of the Johannine account one must allow for both a reliable independent tradition and a highly theological elaboration" (*Comm.* II, p. 817).

12. κῆπος.

Of immediate interest is the role of Judas, an indispensable link in the narrative, but here reduced to the essentials. Judas is described as Jesus' betrayer, as in every mention of him in the Fourth Gospel, but here twice, and as the betrayer in action.[13] As one of Jesus' disciples he "knew the place where Jesus often met with[14] his disciples" and therefore where Jesus might be on a night like this one.

3 "So Judas" — the narrative plunges forward — "went there with[15] a detachment of soldiers." This is all we are told of Judas's activity. It is not reported what he did after Jesus dismissed him (13:27-30), how he made common cause with the Jewish leaders, or that he identified Jesus to the soldiers with a kiss. In John's narrative this identification is controlled by Jesus himself. Later, in vs. 5, it is said of Judas only that he "was standing with them," namely with those to whom Jesus was identifying himself. He "was standing," that is, on their side over against Jesus as the one who had removed the mask he had been hiding behind but who had then lost the initiative and no longer had any role left to play. And that is where the Evangelist leaves him. There is not a word of Judas's repentance or death, nor any reflection on his mysterious role in the Gospel. However important the often attempted reflection on that subject might be, what matters for the Evangelist is only that Judas disappeared into the power of this world as it came out against Jesus, in clear correspondence with the word with which Jesus had gone on his way with his own (14:30, 31).

The Evangelist's description of the composition and equipment of the force sent out against Jesus is undoubtedly intended to bring out all the more clearly Jesus' authority in every step of the course of events. There were two groups of armed men, the "detachment" of soldiers or police under the direction of the chiliarch mentioned in vs. 12 and "officers from the chief priests and the Pharisees" ("the Jews" in vs. 12),[16] that is, servants of the Sanhedrin (cf. 7:32, 45; 18:22).[17] Together, equipped appropriately for a nightly ambush of a band of criminals — "with lanterns,[18] torches, and weapons" — they went to the place that Judas was to show them.

There is much difference of opinion as to who are meant by the "detachment" (σπεῖρα). Often the word is used for the Roman cohort, a detachment of soldiers of about 600 men, or some part of a cohort. The reference would, then, be to the Roman garrison

13. ὁ παραδιδοὺς αὐτόν.
14. συνήχθη. For this meaning cf. Ac. 11:26.
15. λαβών = "with" (BDF §419.1), not as their commander but as their guide.
16. For the "chief priests and scribes" as a term for the highest Jewish authority, the Sanhedrin, see the comments on 7:48.
17. On these "servants" of the Sanhedrin see at length J. Blinzler, *Der Prozeß Jesu*, 1969[4], pp. 87ff., 126-28.
18. φάνος here (with λάμπας, "torch") means "lantern."

quartered in Jerusalem, and this might suggest that Pilate had already been approached for his cooperation in arresting Jesus.

Some scholars, however, think that such a joint operation of Roman soldiers and Jewish law enforcement officers is virtually inconceivable, especially the handing over of Jesus, with the cooperation with a Roman commander, to Jewish authorities (and not to the Antonia fortress, the headquarters of the Roman occupation forces in Jerusalem). The report is therefore regarded as unhistorical. For theological reasons, it is said, John has Roman and Jewish forces join in a common action, thus giving a universal meaning to the power moving against Jesus — and to Jesus' superiority over them all.[19]

More credence should be accorded to the view, defined at length by Blinzler, that by this "detachment" is not a Roman but a Jewish armed force, the temple guard or police, known from other passages. As in the Septuagint and Josephus, this guard is, like its captain (the "chiliarch" in vs. 12), given Roman military names.[20] John calls these temple police "*the* σπεῖρα," that is, the only qualified armed group, under the circumstances, at the Sanhedrin's disposal, along with the Sanhedrin's own court officers. This view is certainly not unattractive, but whether the application of Roman military usage to Jewish forces was familiar to the Evangelist and his readers cannot be answered with certainty.

Some expositors do not deem Roman participation in this operation impossible.[21] Such a joint venture between Jews and Romans was certainly not customary and probably hardly conceivable under normal circumstances. But at this time the situation in Jerusalem was not normal (cf. 12:19), and Roman fear of a possible pretender to the Jewish throne could prompt unusual actions. That such a joint undertaking was far from unthinkable is clearly evident from Mt. 28:6ff., which also refers to "soldiers" made available, under the authority of "the governor," to the Sanhedrin, who, when that for which they were loaned had got out of hand, gave the chief priests a report of what had happened. We cannot easily establish today what could or could not be done in Jerusalem in those days.

4-6 Jesus' reaction to the appearance of Judas and the armed men is the key moment of the story. In it, Jesus manifests his glory just as he is being deprived of his freedom. Here again the Evangelist appeals to Jesus' foreknowledge, which for Jesus always means action (see the comments on 13:1-3). "Jesus, knowing everything that would happen to him, came forward and said to them, 'Whom are

---

19. See, e.g., Bultmann, *Comm.*, p. 637, according to whom this combination is based on John's interest in the opposition between Jesus and the Roman state. See also Schnackenburg, who thinks that in the "source" from which the Evangelist drew his material the "detachment" referred to the Jewish police, while the Evangelist here clearly has in mind Roman soldiers, so representing the joint operation of Jews and Gentiles as the "whole unbelieving cosmos." So his report becomes a "theological representation," in connection with which "a verdict such as 'mistake' or 'deception' is quite out of place" (*Comm.* III, p. 223).

20. Blinzler, *Prozeß*, pp. 95f.

21. E.g., F. F. Bruce, "The Trial of Jesus in the Fourth Gospel," in *Gospel Perspectives* I, ed. R. T. France and David Wenham, 1980, p. 9. See also Brown, *Comm.* II, pp. 799, 808, 815f.

you looking for?' "[22] He is not, of course, asking them what he does not already know. The question has its place in a situation of apparently complete inequality of power, but it is not they but he who takes charge and asks for clarification. Clearly impressed, they promptly answer: "Jesus of Nazareth,"[23] a name that needed no further explanation since it was on everyone's lips. Jesus' response is simply "I am he," by which Jesus seems simply to be identifying himself as that much-discussed person,[24] though he thus also expresses his full self-understanding as the one sent by God with absolute authority, just as on numerous other occasions he has made himself known with these two words (see, e.g., the comments on 8:24).[25] And that not only in the salvific sense of the "I am" (the true bread, the true vine, the good Shepherd, etc.), but also as the "I am," as he would one day reveal himself before the eyes of those who now threaten his life. At this point in the story the Evangelist once more (see the comments on vs. 2) refers to "Judas, who betrayed him," here simply as one standing with those who had come out to arrest Jesus. This not only suggests that Judas's task of identifying Jesus had been taken out of his hands, but also that Jesus' "I am he" — in this highly significant and revealing sense — is also directed to Judas.

Immediately thereafter follows the effect of Jesus' self-identification on his opponents, which as a word of power took them totally by surprise: "they shrank back and fell to the ground." The authority with which he came toward them and which they experienced as superhuman (cf. 7:46) caused them to step back and fall down. These actions, as is evident from what follows in vs. 7, must not be construed spatially, as is sometimes done. They convey, rather, the transcendent ("eschatological," cf. 8:28) character of the confrontation between Jesus and the power of darkness that came out against him (cf. 14:30; 12:31).[26]

7-9 Now follows, without any further reference to the situation, the repetition of Jesus' question "Whom are you looking for?" and the response of the still inert team sent out to arrest him. The characteristic feature here — the third key moment of the Johannine narrative — now no longer concerns Jesus himself but the care that he shows in this decisive moment for his disciples. Jesus

22. ἐξῆλθεν, which others take as "stepped outside the garden." But Jesus apparently did not remove himself from his disciples (vss. 8f.).

23. Here Ναζωραῖον (cf. Mt. 2:23), elsewhere also Ναζαρηνός. The name Nazareth comes through more clearly in the latter. For the origin of the first spelling and the different meanings assigned to it (again with a view to Matthew 2), see the lengthy analysis in Brown, *Comm.* II, pp. 809f. On its meaning here there can be no uncertainty.

24. So Bultmann: "We have here the profane formula of recognition" (*Comm.*, p. 639, n. 4; cf. p. 225, n. 3).

25. See also Brown: "The Johannine scene illustrates that Jesus has God's power over the forces of darkness because he has the divine name" (*Comm.* II, p. 818). However, against the latter point ("the divine name") see the comments above on 8:24.

26. See, e.g., passages like Pss. 27:1-3; 56:(7-)10 in which the superior power of God over his enemies is similarly described.

disposes of the first issue by saying: "I have told you (haven't I?) that I am he." There need be no further uncertainty on that; the armed men should know what their duty is with respect to him. But he immediately adds: "If, then, you are looking for *me,* let these men go." Again it is Jesus who determines the course of events. With the same superiority with which he has spoken of himself he now negotiates the free withdrawal of his own. The Evangelist brings this element to the fore to establish the truth and fulfillment of something Jesus has said earlier: "I have not lost a single one of those you gave me" (cf. 17:12; 6:37). These words thus allude to the care of the good Shepherd for the sheep entrusted to him, care that achieves its full meaning (its "fulfillment") precisely here now that he is giving up his own life (on "let them go" see also 16:32 and its allusion to 1 Kg. 22:17). It is also remarkable that the formula "this was to fulfill the word," which elsewhere always refers to fulfillment of Scripture, here refers to Jesus' own words, which suggests that Jesus' words are thus being afforded no less authority than the Old Testament Scriptures.[27]

10-12 No further mention is made of the withdrawal of the disciples, and their confusion and attempts at resistance, matters on which the Synoptics focus, are absent here. Again one is struck by the clearly selective narrative method of the Evangelist, who highlights only a few, to him significant, key moments in what happened, a method in which he certainly assumes familiarity with the general course of events among his readers. Contrasting with this again is the fact that he alone reports that it was Peter who cut off the right ear of the high priest's slave and that the slave's name was Malchus (Lk. 22:50 has the incident without those details), thus exhibiting a knowledge of particulars that may be related to what the Fourth Evangelist (again alone) tells us later about Peter and some servants of the high priest (vss. 15ff., 26).

Peter resists Jesus' self-humiliation and self-offering, which are completely unacceptable in one whom Peter has acknowledged as the Holy One of God (6:69) and whom he now sees being given up into the hands of his enemies. Indeed, this resistance runs through the whole Johannine passion narrative (13:6ff., 24, 36ff.; 18:17ff., 25ff.). Here again the Evangelist's interest is not in Peter as a person or as a psychological type but in the unacceptable — to human understanding (and to Peter before his "conversion," Lk. 22:32; cf. Jn. 21:15ff.) — "offense" and "folly" of the suffering and execution of the Son of God. This time Peter does not stop at using only words. He has, like others (cf. Lk. 22:38, 49), taken along a sword, and Jesus' earlier manifestations of power may have reinforced thoughts that the moment has come for his disciples to fight for him. But the Evangelist leaves all that aside. He confines himself to mentioning Jesus' final admonition to his disciple, the disciple who now

---

27. Cf. Brown, *Comm.* II, p. 811, who views this as the beginning "of an attitude that would lead toward the recognition of canonical Christian writings alongside the Jewish ones."

stands in his way by resorting to violence: "Put your sword back into its sheath! Should I not drink the cup that the Father has given me?"

This word about the cup, the last key moment of the narrative, in direct succession to "I am he," is the core of John's entire passion narrative and passion interpretation. Jesus is not departing as the victim of Judas's betrayal and the superior might of his enemies. He has the power to lay down his life before taking it up again, and no one takes it from him (10:18).[28] What he does and suffers he does and suffers out of love for and obedience to the Father (cf. 14:21). But his suffering is not for that reason any less real, and Jesus does not pass through it as if he were inviolable. The "cup" symbolizes, rather, the bitterness of the suffering and death he must endure (cf. Mt. 26:39 par.). It is the surrender of his life, which he must give for his own (17:19) and for the life of the world (6:51) as the Lamb of God who thus carries away the world's sin (1:29, 36). The sin of the world constitutes the inexpressible bitterness of the cup that he, and he alone, must drink. But the cup is still what the Father has given him to drink. Jesus' power consists in his obedience to do "as the Father has commanded" him (14:31) to the bitter end.

Here, with this last word about the cup, the Evangelist breaks off. Vs. 12 follows with the statement of the arrest and removal of Jesus.

18:13-27

Jesus before Annas, Peter's Denial

13, 14 The narrative in 18:13-27 interweaves Annas's interrogation of Jesus and Peter's denial of Jesus and begins with the statement that "they" (see vs. 12) "first took him to Annas." "First," because after this arraignment there will be a second (vs. 24). Annas was the father-in-law of Caiaphas, the high priest "of that year."[29] Apparently Annas derived from that relationship the right or at least the freedom to summon Jesus to come before him for questioning before cross-examination by Caiaphas himself, who as high priest was the Sanhedrin's presiding officer. Annas is known from extrabiblical sources as a dominant figure in the priestly aristocracy, who was himself appointed high priest in A.D. 5.[30] That he retained great influence even after his deposition by the Romans in A.D. 16 can be inferred from the fact that five of his sons held the office of high priest and that he is mentioned elsewhere alongside (or even before) Caiaphas (Lk. 3:2; Ac. 4:6). Here he will even be called "the high

28. On this passage see also pp. 365ff. above.
29. On "of that year" see the comments above on 11:49.
30. Josephus, *Antiquities* 18.1.2.

priest" (vs. 19), but this only means that he (like other former high priests)[31] was known by this title even after he left office. The readers would not misunderstand since Caiaphas is named as high priest in vs. 13 and in 11:49.[32] Anticipating the transfer of Jesus from Annas to Caiaphas, the text here says of Caiaphas that he was the person who had advised the Jews that "it is better to have one man die for the people" (vs. 14; cf. 11:49f.).

The historicity of this encounter with Annas is strongly doubted, if not completely rejected, by some of the scholars who deny to John all independent knowledge of the events in question. These scholars point to the lack of any trace of such a hearing before Annas in the Synoptics and the lack in John of any word about the official session of the Sanhedrin and the sentence pronounced there. The conclusion is that various versions of the same hearing were in circulation in the tradition and that John's narrative can be somehow explained on that basis. Other scholars who consider a hearing before Annas improbable alongside one before the Sanhedrin see here (as in vss. 3f.) a presentation inspired by Johannine theology from which no historical conclusions can be drawn.[33]

But to our mind there is no reason to think of this narrative as a tradition that has gone astray or as the Evangelist's composition that, whichever it is, displaced the trial of Jesus conducted by the Sanhedrin under the guidance of Caiaphas,[34] especially because it appears in a section in which the Evangelist gives evidence of special knowledge of the situation (see vss. 15ff.). The interrogation by Annas does not have the character of an official trial, a court session convened by someone in authority, leading to an appropriate verdict; it is rather a preliminary examination (note "first" in vs. 13; also vs. 24), undertaken at Annas's own initiative (see the comments). It is remarkable that the Evangelist does not say a word about the trial under Caiaphas, though the account of the trial before Pilate alludes to the trial before Caiaphas (19:7). The idea that the Evangelist did not know of the trial before Caiaphas is, solely in view of his narrative itself, hard to accept. We have here a manifestation of the selective method of the Evangelist, whose aim is not to give as complete a report as possible of the events and who could therefore skip certain events, even very important and undoubtedly generally known events, either because he had already conveyed their significance in another way (e.g., the institution of the Lord's Supper and Jesus' agony

31. For the evidence see Brown, *Comm.* II, p. 820.

32. Admittedly, some copyists understood the high priest in vs. 19 as Caiaphas and therefore placed vs. 24 directly after vs. 13, interpreting the whole of vss. 19-23 as referring to Caiaphas. But in that case Annas's sole role would have consisted in immediately sending Jesus on to Caiaphas, in effect making vs. 13 virtually superfluous. If that had been the original sequence, moreover, it would be much harder to explain why later copyists would have made Annas Jesus' interrogator in place of Caiaphas.

33. So also Schnackenburg on this passage. He decides against the overly complicated tradition-historical reconstructions of Dauer and Hahn (see pp. 570f. above) and in favor of the "theological" option. He considers it possible that the Evangelist himself "saw things in this way," but adds that "one can hardly draw historical conclusions from his *presentation*" (*Comm.* III, p. 233).

34. Against this see also Blinzler, *Prozeß*, pp. 134-36.

in Gethsemane) or because he did not need them for his kerygmatic ("theological") purposes (e.g., the small number of miracle stories [20:30, 31] and the brief description of what took place on Golgotha [see the comments on 19:17ff.]). And he does report a number of events or details that we do not find elsewhere, such as this interrogation before Annas, simply because it serves his purposes.

The omission of Jesus' trial before Caiaphas and the Sanhedrin is easily explicable on the basis of the Evangelist's mention of an earlier Sanhedrin session (11:47ff.), to which the Evangelist expressly alludes in 18:14. There he has already clearly portrayed the Sanhedrin's view of Jesus and its members' firm decision to kill him, on Caiaphas's recommendation (cf. 11:57; 12:10 [note "also"]). And it is not hard to understand why the Evangelist includes the hearing before Annas: Jesus' reply to Annas makes clear the falsehood of the Jewish case against Jesus. Therefore, after what has been reported in 11:47, the further development of that falsehood does not need to be described again. This also explains why in John the real "trial of Jesus" occurs before Pilate, in connection with which the decisive part played by "the Jews" is reported at length.

15, 16 Before describing Jesus' interrogation by Annas, the Evangelist first inserts part of the story of Peter's denial (vss. 15-18). Only after Jesus has been interrogated and led away to Caiaphas do we hear Peter's second and third denials (vss. 25-27). Peter is in the high priest's courtyard while Jesus is being interrogated by Annas, and he apparently remains there until early morning (vs. 27), when, after the trial before the Sanhedrin, Jesus is taken to Pilate (cf. vs. 28). This arrangement of the events undoubtedly sets before the reader the contrast during that long night between Jesus and Peter.

The narrative begins — significantly (cf. 13:36ff.) — by speaking of Peter following Jesus. Even after what happened in Gethsemane, Peter was not willing to stop following Jesus (see also Mk. 14:53 par.). In the Synoptics only Peter follows ("from a distance"), but here "another disciple" goes with him. Some manuscripts read "*the* other disciple," which would identify this disciple with the one similarly described in 20:2, "the one whom Jesus loved" (cf. 13:23). Many expositors have thought that even without the article that disciple is meant here, and with good reason. Here for the first time in John's Gospel "another disciple" is mentioned, and then 20:2 mentions "the other disciple," "the other" referring back to 18:15. In favor of this identification is that the "other disciple" of 18:15 accompanies Peter, which is characteristic of "the disciple whom Jesus loved" (cf. 13:23-26; 20:2-10; 21:7, 21ff.). That the disciple here is not explicitly identified with the beloved disciple may seem strange after 13:23ff.[35] But up to 21:21ff. an atmosphere of restraint and anonymity hangs over the figure of "the beloved disciple."

---

35. Schnackenburg calls this "incomprehensible" and refers for this otherwise "unknown figure" to John's "source" (*Comm.* III, p. 235).

This disciple was "known to"[36] ("an acquaintance of")[37] the high priest, which some find incompatible with the disciple whom Jesus loved. It would be better, we are told, to think here of someone from Jerusalem who was less closely connected with Jesus — for example, a secret disciple like Joseph of Arimathea (19:38; cf. also 12:42) or Nicodemus. But it is hard to draw any compelling conclusions from this more or less casual comment. How seriously must we take this acquaintance? All that is implied is that this disciple had access to the high priest's dwelling and was acquainted with some of the servants there. He was undoubtedly a member of the circle of Jesus' close disciples. With Peter he followed Jesus immediately after Jesus' arrest in the garden, an event at which he was apparently present and from which he made his way with Peter to the place where Jesus was being taken.

The detailed description of the two disciples' entry into the courtyard[38] is remarkable and anticipates their journey to Jesus' tomb (20:2ff.). Here, as in 20:3, Peter is mentioned first, but the other disciple is apparently ahead of Peter. While he has already gone inside after Jesus, Peter is still standing outside at the gate, apparently lacking his companion's free access. So the other disciple goes out and talks with "the woman who guarded the gate" to admit Peter. But as the two pass, the woman, the first to do so, asks Peter the question that will dominate the entire story. Why was it important to the Evangelist to convey such a detailed picture of the role of the "other disciple"? Certainly not just to explain how Peter managed to get past the woman at the gate. He did it, rather, to focus on the other disciple as the one before whose eyes and with whose cooperation all this took place. The "other disciple" is not mentioned again in this story. But it can hardly be accidental that his role of eyewitness is significant for the disciple whom Jesus loved, as we have seen in our discussion of 13:23ff. This role is stressed in 19:35, continues in 20:2, and sums up his entire significance in 21:24. That the disciple who is so strikingly depicted in 18:15, 16 was no other than "the disciple whom Jesus loved" is, therefore, for all the restraint the Evangelist observes with regard to his identity, hard to dispute.

---

36. γνωστὸς τῷ, vs. 15.

37. γνωστὸς τοῦ, vs. 16.

38. αὐλή in the first place denotes a courtyard, an uncovered enclosed space adjoining a building. It may also refer to the house or palace to which the courtyard belongs (see BAGD s.v.). Here it apparently refers to the courtyard, the place outside in the cold where the servants were. By "the courtyard of the high priest" some scholars understand the courtyard of Annas's house. This, then, would imply that Annas had a separate residence. But although in vs. 19 he is also described as "the high priest," after vs. 13 the article (used twice) rather suggests Caiaphas. One must therefore picture the examination by Annas as taking place in the halls of the official high-priestly palace, in the courtyard of which, according to other reports, Peter's denial took place. Accordingly, Jesus' transfer from Annas to Caiaphas must not then be understood as his removal from one palace to another.

Peter's first "denial" of Jesus directly follows in vs. **17** in the presence of the same gatekeeper[39] who has just given him access. She addresses Peter in words that clearly betray doubt:[40] "You are not also[41] one of this man's disciples, are you?" We are not told what prompts the woman to ask the question or what she plans to do if Peter gives an affirmative answer. She apparently did not have a high opinion of Jesus ("this man"). How dangerous in fact it would be for Peter (and the other disciple) to be identified as disciples of Jesus is hard for us to say. In any case Peter does not want to be so identified. He denies it as tersely as possible: "I am not." And that, remarkably enough in the narrative of the Fourth Gospel (cf. vss. 25, 27), is all he will say. But he thereby takes the first step on the road against which Jesus has warned him (see further in the comments on vs. 27).

Verse **18** describes how Peter joined the little clusters of servants[42] who because of the night's cold had started a charcoal fire and stood around it warming themselves. The idea is clearly that Peter sought to be as inconspicuous as possible but still observe what was happening.

19-21   Meanwhile — and here the Evangelist again picks up the thread of the story begun in vss. 13 and 14 — Jesus has been taken to Annas for questioning. That we are dealing here not with a formal trial before the Sanhedrin[43] but with a hearing arranged solely on the personal authority of Annas is clear not only from the context (see the comments on vs. 3) but also from the way in which the facts are reported here. There is no charge or witnesses, only an extremely general question about Jesus' "disciples and his teaching." Some have seen in this the opening question of what was intended to be a more detailed interrogation. However that may be, Jesus' answer puts a stop to any further attempt. He refuses to reply to Annas's question because it concerns

---

39. Here expressly called ἡ παιδίσκη ἡ θυρωρός. The Synoptics also mention a παιδίσκη in connection with the first denial, but not as gatekeeper. Some scholars find the idea of a female gatekeeper at night hard to imagine and regard this female gatekeeper as a later adaptation to the Synoptic tradition. But then it is precisely this passage that gives evidence of the Evangelist's original knowledge (see above). In any case the text that has come down to us has no trace of a later adaptation. Admittedly, the Sinaitic Syriac refers in vs. 16 to a male gatekeeper and in vs. 17 to "the maidservant of the gatekeeper." But this reading is too isolated to be original.

40. A question beginning with μή usually expects a negative answer. But in some cases this combination has a doubting or deliberative meaning (cf. 4:28; see BDF §427.2).

41. "Also" *could* mean "like your companion." In that case the other disciple would have been known as a disciple of Jesus, at least by this servant. But this again evokes new and troublesome questions. And it might simply mean "like all the others" (so Mk. 14:69; Mt. 26:69).

42. A distinction is made between δοῦλοι and ὑπηρέται; the first probably denotes the domestic servants of the high priest (cf. vss. 10, 26), the latter officers of the Sanhedrin (cf. vs. 3; 7:32, 45).

43. Of which the Evangelist is said to have taken over a report, in a very brief form, from his "source"; so Bultmann, *Comm.*, p. 644.

what Annas already knows. Jesus has spoken openly, not just before his disciples, but before whoever has wanted to listen ("the world"). Over and over Jesus has taught "in the synagogue (cf. 6:59ff.) and in the temple (cf. 5:14ff.; 7:14ff.; 10:23), where all the Jews come together," in spiritual confrontation with the leaders of Israel, situations in which the question "Who are you?" have been posed with increasing urgency and in which that question has been answered with increasing clarity (cf. 10:24, 33). That is where the real decisions have already been made. Not without irony Jesus adds: "Why then are you still interrogating me?" If you still feel a need to do this, ask these people who have heard me and you will see that they know very well what I said!

Jesus' answer was designed to destroy the illusion that between him and the Jewish authorities, of whom Annas was one of the most important, there was still something that needed to be cleared up and that a trial was needed to achieve that clarification. The die had been cast long before in his relations with them, and the judicial process they were organizing against him and the supposed objectivity with which his interrogator was approaching him were a farce that Jesus exposed by his answer.

This explains why the Evangelist confines himself to this interrogation by Annas and omits (especially after what he has already said about it in 11:49), the trial before the Sanhedrin. And this for all the more reason because a trial before the secular judge was still to come, the trial in which the real issue between Jesus and the Jews would again come to light (cf. 19:7) and in which Jesus would speak.

22-24 Of Annas's reaction we hear no more than that he sends Jesus bound to Caiaphas, the incumbent high priest (see the comments on vss. 13, 14). But someone there does respond to Jesus' words, one of the officers (cf. vss. 3, 12), who, on hearing Jesus response to the high priest, strikes him on the face, saying: "Is that how you answer the high priest?" He evidently considers Jesus' answer a violation of the respect due to the high priest (cf. Ex. 22:28).

Jesus' answer to this maltreatment is filled with self-control and dignity. But he does not turn the other cheek (cf. Mt 5:39). At stake in this moment is more than love of one's enemy. It is a question of truth and justice in this final contest between Jesus and the Judaism represented by the high priest. Accordingly, *Jesus'* final question — presumably formulated in connection with what the law said was owed rulers[44] — is: "If I have spoken wrongly, prove[45] it; but if I have spoken rightly, why do you strike me?"

With this blow struck by the high priest's servant and Jesus' unanswered

---

44. Cf. Ex. 22:28 in the Septuagint: ἄρχοντας τοῦ λαοῦ σου οὐ κακῶς ἐρεῖς.

45. For this meaning of μαρτυρεῖν, see BAGD s.v. 1a: "furnish proof"; Bultmann: "synonymous with ἐλέγχειν" (*Comm.*, p. 647).

question not only Jesus' hearing before Annas but also the confrontation between Jesus and official Judaism — described at such length by John — is
brought to a close in an unmistakable, highly telling way. From this point on
Jesus is in the hands of Pilate.

25-27 But Peter must still deal with the high priest's servants. Here
again the connection that the Evangelist fashions between what is happening
with Jesus and what is happening with Peter is most revealing. Vs. 25 picks
up the thread of vs. 18. While Peter is warming himself by the fire, he is again
confronted with the same question: "You are not[46] also one of his disciples,
are you?" He denies it with the same terse response: "I am not."

Then, without any direct connection, follows the third question (vs. 26),
but now more directly and more threateningly and from a member of the high
priest's staff, a man related to the servant whose ear Peter has cut off. His
questions sound as if there is hardly any doubt at all: "Did I not[47] see you in
the garden with him?" It is not made clear whether the speaker in vs. 26 reacts
directly to Peter's denial in vs. 25 or whether, as in the Synoptics, the third
question surfaces later ("after a little while," Mk. 14:70; Mt. 26:73; "about an
hour later," Lk. 22:59); in the Synoptics the questioner is not identified as a
relative of Malchus but as one of those who recognized Peter by his speech.
This question made things very hot for Peter, but we are not told in what words
he responded. The Evangelist confines himself solely to Peter's denial, this
time with the telling addition, "and at once the cock crowed."

This is the fulfillment of 13:38, perhaps more clearly in John than in the
Synoptics. Comparison of the four reports brings out, apart from the differences
and discrepancies in detail among them,[48] the restraint with which John describes Peter's answers. John has no trace of the increasing emphasis and
vehemence with which Peter denies that he knew Jesus ("that man"), culminating in oaths (Mk. 14:71), and nothing about Peter's contrition and bitter
tears when the cockcrow brought him to his senses.

According to some expositors this story had no particular "theological"
significance for the Evangelist and was merely borrowed from his "source"
because he needed it in connection with 13:36-38.[49] But this narrative constitutes the dramatic climax of Peter's recurrent (in this Gospel) resistance to

---

46. On μή at the beginning of the question, see the comments on vs. 17 above.

47. οὐ at the beginning of the question expects an affirmative answer.

48. For a survey and discussion of the sometimes very negative conclusions that some
expositors have drawn from this, see Brown, *Comm.* II, pp. 836f. An attempt to harmonize
"everything" in the four Gospels and to turn it into a single coherent narrative is made, for
instance, by J. van Bruggen, *Christus op aarde. Zijn levensbeschijving door leerlingen en tijde-
noten*, 1987, pp. 222-24.

49. So Bultmann: The story belongs to the reports from the Evangelist's "source," which
he did not utilize to support his own theology (*Comm.*, pp. 642-48).

Jesus' self-humiliation (13:6ff.) and self-offering in death (13:24, 36f.; 18:10). It is in part precisely in the extreme restraint of Peter's repeated "I am not" that the point of the Johannine narrative is to be found. The Evangelist abstains from making any psychological or moral assessment of Peter's threefold denial, whether in his fear or his cowardice or his collapsing overconfidence.

Peter is not brought on the scene here, as is often said, as an admonitory example for the church, which, in following Jesus, can be all too unreliable. In the extreme restraint of the repeated "I am not"[50] the Evangelist is rather echoing the repeated "I am"[51] with which Jesus answers his interrogators (vss. 5, 8). With this contrast the Evangelist lays bare the deeper meaning of Peter's denial. Peter's threefold denial affirms the loneliness of Jesus' suffering and death: Jesus goes alone on a road from which no one can keep him and on which no one, not even Peter, can join him or follow him (13:36; cf. 13:33). Peter tries to follow Jesus, and that only plunges him into denying Jesus. Jesus had foretold this. The cock crows "at once" into Peter's ears when for the third time he must say of himself: "I am not."

With this the story ends. But, unlike Judas, Peter returns "afterward" (cf. 13:7, 36), when Jesus summons Peter to "follow" him on the road on which he has "once for all" preceded Peter and all his own and which he has made traversable for them only by "going to the Father" (cf. 21:15ff.).

18:28–19:16a

Jesus before Pilate

The account of Jesus' trial and sentencing before Pilate takes up an important segment of the Johannine passion narrative, made all the more striking because the preceding trial before the Sanhedrin is not mentioned (see above). What makes this pericope so inordinately important is first of all the length at which the Evangelist describes the role — and hence the responsibility — of both Pilate and "the Jews" in the drama of Jesus' condemnation to death on the cross. It is undeniable that Jesus was condemned to death by the representative of the Roman Empire and on the basis of Roman law, and the sentence of death by crucifixion was carried out as a Roman penalty. But it is no less clear that in this account "the Jews" drove Pilate to this resolution of the matter. Without this pressure Jesus would never have been condemned by Pilate.

Second, as the account unfolds it becomes progressively more clear that although the issue in this trial is Jesus' alleged political aspirations (as "king

---

50. οὐκ εἰμί.
51. ἐγώ εἰμι.

of the Jews") the Jews' actual grievance is the way in which he has spoken of his unity with the Father. This they consider pure blasphemy. This ambiguity makes the whole trial a farce from the start. But it also explains the stubbornness with which the Jews demand Jesus' death and consider no method too reprehensible to force their will on the governor.

In modern times, especially after what happened to the Jews in World War II, scholars have viewed this division of roles as extremely biased in favor of Pilate and against the Jews. The "almost incredible impudence" with which the Jews try to pressure Pilate is seen as an attempt on the part of John (or the tradition he followed) "to fasten the full guilt of the condemnation of Jesus firmly on the Jews and to exonerate the Romans."[52] There is also the well-known statement of Winter: "From John 18,29 onward the Fourth Gospel contains nothing of any value for the assessment of historical facts."[53] And Lapide writes of John 18: "The Jewish New Testament scholar is strongly tempted to answer Pilate's question 'What is truth' by saying: 'In any case not this account of the Roman trial.' "[54] This shift of responsibility from the truly guilty — Pilate and the Romans — to the Jews must be explained primarily, according to Lapide, not from hatred of the Jews but from fear of the Romans, because they would feel insulted if the responsibility were too emphatically ascribed to them or because, if the "true" facts of the case were known — namely that Pilate, for political reasons, took the initiative to have Jesus put to death — the Christian faith ran the risk of being declared an illicit religion in other places as well.[55]

Against this approach, however, a number of objections can be advanced. Pilate does not come out that much more favorably than the Jews in this account. He does say more than once that, as judge, he thinks Jesus is innocent. But the repetition of this finding takes nothing from the unprincipled character and above all the injustice of his condemnation of Jesus to the cross, but rather emphasizes it. Accordingly, it is hard to see how the assignment of roles could exonerate or placate the Romans at the expense of the Jews. On the contrary, one may well ask whether more damage could be done to the majesty of Roman justice than by Pilate's representation of it in the trial of Jesus.

Furthermore, the Evangelist does not know which side was more culpable, Pilate or the Jews. The construction of his account brings out in a masterly way

---

52. So, e.g., E. Haenchen, *Gott und Mensch,* 1965, p. 151: "The narrator's sole aim is to show that the Jews were (almost) solely responsible for the death of Jesus."

53. P. Winter, *On the Trial of Jesus,* 1961, p. 89.

54. P. Lapide, *Wie waren schuldig aan de dood van Jesus*? 1988, p. 81; after he had first written concerning the conversation between Jesus and Pilate that preceded the question: "Now, within the court, follows what can only be called a philosophical dialogue between two intimate friends," p. 80.

55. Cf. Lapide, *Wie waren schuldig,* p. 86.

that the deep hostility between Pilate and the Jews did not prevent them from finally uniting into a single front against Jesus. Both parties had to do violence to their own positions — Pilate by allowing himself to be blackmailed as "a friend of the emperor" by the despised Jews, the Jews by passing themselves off to him as those who recognized no other king than the emperor and therefore wanted nothing to do with a "king of the Jews." The carefully planned structure of the account of Pilate's repeated going in and coming out, of the progressively more vehement dispute between him and the Jews, is not intended, therefore, to measure the relative guilt of the two parties but to exhibit the paradoxical outcome of the whole process — how they found each other in a single unprincipled alliance against Jesus (cf. Acts 4:27).

To what degree does the structure of the account give a historically precise reflection of what happened? Scholars have at times viewed the entire presentation of the trial before Pilate in the Fourth Gospel as historically untrustworthy and have had difficulty finding words strong enough to condemn it as inferior.[56] By and large scholars have given up this negative approach, among other reasons because we cannot apply to John's account of the trial criteria that apply to a legal report. We must rather ask what the Evangelist wanted his readers to understand by means of this account.[57] Granted, mention is then made of "the thoroughly *theological* shaping of the events of the trial," while for the interpretation "the *historical question* will be allowed to recede."[58] Undoubtedly contained in this statement is the truth that here, too, the Evangelist's aim is not to convey a report of the events that is as objectively "neutral" and complete as possible, but as *Evangelist* to depict before the eyes of his readers the essential features of the events in their inevitable development and outcome. And this undoubtedly in a very summarizing and selective way, a method that can hardly be conceived in any other way in view of the time-consuming (cf. vs. 28; 19:14) and increasingly chaotic character of the events. In that sense one can undoubtedly speak of an independent and free presentation of the narrative.[59]

But this does not mean that the Evangelist so lost sight of the actual course of events (or was so ill-informed about it) that the section before us can still

---

56. See Haenchen's discussion of what authors like J. Wellhausen and E. Schwarz (1908) wrote about the Fourth Gospel and this pericope in particular in "Jesus vor Pilatus (Joh. 18,28–19,16)," in *Gott und Mensch*, pp. 144ff.

57. See, e.g., Haenchen, "Jesus vor Pilatus," pp. 147f., 155.

58. So Schnackenburg, *Comm.* III, p. 241.

59. Admittedly, scholars have attempted here, too, to go back to an underlying written source, said to have been "theologically" rewritten by the Evangelist. But even authors who tend to speak of this source with a high degree of assurance recognize the difficulty of applying this ("tradition-historical") method to the text before us. See, e.g., Bultmann, *Comm.*, pp. 649f.; Schnackenburg, *Comm.* III, p. 242; Becker, *Comm.* II, pp. 556f. An exception is A. Dauer, *Die Passionsgeschichte im Johannesevangelium*, pp. 119f.

only be judged and evaluated on the basis of its theological characteristics and no longer on the basis of its historical qualities. Militating against this is not only the strong historical sense underlying the whole Gospel but also the Evangelist's repeatedly emerging — here also — knowledge of historical and local details (cf. 18:31; 19:13, 14).[60] But clearly this does not relieve our exegesis of the task of dealing with historical questions (see, e.g., the comments on vss. 29 and 31).

This finally brings us to the *division* of the material. Although it is always difficult to determine whether a division of the material that is acceptable to us is also intended as such by the author, in regard to this pericope there is a clear consensus. It distinguishes seven phases in the trial linked to successive initiatives of Pilate and in part with his "going in" and "going out of" the praetorium, a division that we follow for the most part below.

18:28-32

Jesus Handed Over to Pilate

Verse **28**, along with vs. 24, tells us that Jesus, who, bound by Annas, had been taken to the high priest Caiaphas, was sent by the latter to the Roman praetorium. The account is very general, devoid of any details about the situation as such. Those who led Jesus to Pilate ("Then they") remain anonymous. One must think in the first place of the high priest's officers (cf. 19:6), but from vss. 28b, 29ff. it is immediately evident that the Jewish authorities are themselves present from the start. Later on there is mention of "the Jews" (vs. 38; 19:7, 12, 14), particularly of the chief priests (19:6, 15) acting as representatives of the Jewish people (cf. 18:35; 19:7), which does not of course mean that the Evangelist holds the whole Jewish nation responsible for Jesus' death. The case is rather that in John's account "the crowd" is kept firmly in the background (see below).

By "praetorium" is meant Pilate's residence, which was also the place where he administered justice. Its location is uncertain. Some scholars identify it with the fortress Antonia situated on the northwest side of the temple square,[61] others with Herod's palace in the western part of the city near the present-day Jaffa gate.[62] "It was early" places the events at about 6 a.m., not an unusual

---

60. See, e.g., Brown, *Comm.* II, p. 861; Blinzler, *Prozeß*, p. 274.

61. At the beginning of the present-day Via Dolorosa, in the convent of the Sisters of Zion, one is shown the Lithostrotos (19:13), a large stone floor laid bare by excavations. In the immediate neighborhood is also the so-called Ecce Homo Arch, which may date back to the time of Agrippa I (reigned A.D. 37-44).

62. So Blinzler, *Prozeß*, pp. 250f.

time for initiating official actions. 19:14 will mention the "sixth hour" as the time when the trial was drawing to a close, which gives us a period of six hours for the trial as a whole.

While "they," that is, "the Jews," brought Jesus to the entrance of the praetorium, "they themselves" did not enter so that they could eat the Passover.[63] This comment is meant primarily to explain why the scene keeps changing in what follows (in and out of the praetorium), though one may also read in it the ambivalence of "the Jews": while they do not shrink from persuading Pilate with all the means at their disposal to sentence Jesus to death, they are most scrupulous in the observation of their formal religious duties. Some commentators see in "that they might eat the Passover" a more specific sense: it was of the utmost importance to them to be able to eat the Passover, but they rejected the true Passover lamb.[64] But it is questionable whether the Fourth Gospel views Jesus' death as the death of "the true Passover lamb" (see comments on 1:29ff.; 19:36).

29 Only now the name of Pilate, the Roman prefect of Judea in A.D. 26-36, is mentioned. He is brought on the scene without any further introductory comments. Since Christians knew him as the principal figure in the trial of Jesus (cf. 1 Tm. 6:13), there was no need for the Evangelist to describe him further. Pilate first came out of the praetorium to ask what accusation the Jews had against "this man." They had evidently taken Jesus to the praetorium without a specific accusation, hoping that Pilate would ratify the death sentence they had already pronounced (cf. vs. 31). But he was not of a mind to act on that intent. Although he was undoubtedly familiar with the controversial figure of Jesus (see the comments on vss. 3 and 33), he took a purely juridical view and wanted to hear the "accusation."[65] And since on religious grounds the Jews refused to enter the praetorium and he was apparently well aware of the explosive nature of the issue, he himself came outside to compel them to pursue a more regular judicial procedure than they apparently had in mind.

---

63. Whether this refers to the meal on the eve of the fifteenth of Nisan or should be taken more broadly is important in relation to the broader question of the date of the Passover in John (see the comments above on 13:1). But for the present context this issue is not especially important. The issue here is the cultic purity that Jews would lose if they entered a Gentile dwelling — like the Roman courthouse — and which, when lost, would prevent them from participating in any religious meal.

64. See, e.g., H. Schlier, "Jesus und Pilatus," in his *Die Zeit der Kirche*, 1956, pp. 56-74, esp. p. 58; but also more recent ones like Schnackenburg, *Comm.* III, p. 244; Becker, *Comm.*, p. 562.

65. κατηγορία: "in the technical juridical sense of the word, the accusation by means of which a trial was begun. Pilate wants to start the discussion" (P. J. Verdam, *Sanhedrin en Gabbatha*, 1959, p. 33).

Some interpreters deem it historically inconceivable that Pilate should — not once but several times[66] — have gone outside the courthouse and in that way conducted the trial. In this some see proof of the total ignorance of the Evangelist concerning what happened,[67] others the simplification of his narrative style[68] or his ridicule of the embattled governor.[69] But such judgments are questionable given the unusual mass appearance of the Jews at the courthouse — and on a feast day! Accordingly, most interpreters judge differently.[70] In Pilate's repeated going in and out one may undoubtedly see not so much a precise account of the proceedings as the Evangelist's presentation of the unfolding events. But considering the six-hour length of the trial and that Pilate twice showed Jesus to the Jews as "king" in his totally pitiable and non-dangerous condition, this movement can hardly be described as the nervous pacing of a caricatured Pilate.

30 The Jews refuse to deal with Pilate's demand and are even indignant that he makes it: "If this man were not a criminal, we would not have handed him over to you." The meaning of this reply is variously understood. Two factors seem important: first, the Jews' aversion to any Roman meddling in their judicial affairs and their endeavor, where it was imposed, to keep it to a minimum[71] and, second, the fact that their real accusation against Jesus — that by making himself out to be the Messiah and the Son of God he was guilty of blasphemy — would fail to convince Pilate that Jesus was a threat to the public order and deserved the death penalty. In the course of the trial they will be forced to state their real complaint against Jesus (19:7). But then it will also become clear how unamenable Pilate is to that point of view. Accordingly, they now speak of "this criminal," a description by means of which they seek both

---

66. ἐξῆλθαν in vss. 18:29, 38; 19:4; see also 19:14; εἰσῆλθεν in 18:33; 19:9; see also 19:1.

67. So Lapide, who speaks of the "sensitivity and astonishing conciliatoriness of the tyrant" assumed by the Evangelist, *Wie waren schuldig,* pp. 78ff.

68. So Haenchen, *Gott und Mensch,* p. 148, who first states, "We know enough of Roman governors to be certain that it would never have occurred to Pilate to appear in person"; "he was not a messenger boy." But then Haenchen adds: "But how little this correct objection actually says! Here speaks a narrator who simplifies things down to what is essential to him."

69. So Becker, *Comm.* II, p. 558.

70. So, e.g., Brown with regard to the argument that a Roman governor would never have lowered himself to go out to the Jewish authorities if they refused to enter the praetorium: "How can one be so sure? Were there never moments when Pilate, like other politicians, had to swallow his pride in order to avert worse troubles?" (*Comm.* II, p. 859; see also Schlatter, *Comm.,* p. 337); cf. also Blinzler, who thinks Pilate went out to give consideration to the religious objections of the Jews and who offers "a series of proofs" for such a course of conduct on the part of Roman officials (*Prozeß,* p. 276, n. 2).

71. See on this at greater length Verdam, *Sanhedrin en Gabbatha,* pp. 32f.: "Pilate wants to start the proceedings. But this does not suit the accusers. They think the issue is clear; they have come not for a trial but for a signature," that is, the *exequatur.*

to impress on Pilate the danger Jesus presents to the public order and at the same time to avoid a concrete charge.

31 But Pilate knows the weakness of their position and takes the opportunity to make them feel it to the full. As if he was agreeing with them, he invites them to try Jesus in accordance with their own law as they understand it, saying, in effect, "If you think your accusation against 'this man' does not concern me, then why do you come here?" The Jews cannot respond other than by acknowledging that they lack such jurisdiction: "We are not permitted to put anyone to death." They allude thus to the rule, known from other contemporary sources and adopted by the Romans with a view to the imperial interest, that death sentences were not to be carried out apart from duly empowered Roman authority. The Jews also thus let Pilate know that they want nothing less than the death of Jesus. Though they have reached this decision behind closed doors, Pilate is of course already aware of it. The Evangelist reflects on this last point in vs. 32.

This interpretation, the one most often followed in the history of exegesis, assumes that the Jews were right — historically speaking — in saying that this rule of Roman law applied to them. Against this interpretation it has been argued that the Sanhedrin as the supreme Jewish judicial authority did have the right to impose the death penalty (the *ius gladii et necis*) and that the presentation in John 18 cannot be historically correct. Scholars appeal for this opinion to a number of instances in which Jews did carry out the death penalty without the consent of the Roman authorities (e.g., Ac. 7:58-60 [Stephen]; 12:1ff. [James]) or where it is assumed that they could (Ac. 25:9-11; Jn. 8:5ff.; 16:1, 2; Ac. 9:1, 2; 22:4).[72]

Others have pointed out, on the basis of extensive studies of the administration of law in the Roman provinces, that, however multiform and complex this legislation may have been in the subject provinces, the Romans, with an eye to their imperial self-interest, saw to keeping the death penalty in their own hands.[73] The supposed counterexamples are regarded on closer scrutiny as open to more than one interpretation[74] or as at most exceptions that cannot negate the general rule.[75] Although there is no consensus on this issue, most commentators are inclined to follow the judgment of

---

72. This viewpoint had already been argued in an influential essay by H. Lietzmann, "Der Prozeß Jesu" (1931), in *Kleine Schriften* II, 1958, 251ff., and was later defended at length by, among others, P. Winter in *On the Trial of Jesus.*

73. See A. N. Sherwin-White, *Roman Society and Roman Law in the New Testament,* 1963, p. 36; Verdam, *Sanhedrin en Gabbatha,* pp. 14ff., who speaks of the "iron rule" in Roman provinces that death sentences could not be carried out in isolation from the Romans (pp. 28f.). The turbulent province of Judea would have been the last place for the Romans to make an exception to that rule.

74. See, e.g., the summaries in Brown, *Comm.* II, pp. 849f.; E. Lohse, *TDNT* VII, pp. 865ff.

75. So also Lohse, *TDNT* VII, 866: "If the Romans did not stop lynch law or grant free protection to the Jews, their consent was by no means the rule."

those scholars who see in the statement of the Jews in Jn. 18:31 a rule to which they were in fact subject under the Roman administration and which furnishes the historical reason that (according to the whole New Testament tradition) the Sanhedrin handed Jesus over to Pilate.[76]

Another view is that the Jews could, as far as the Romans were concerned, legally carry out the death sentence but that their own law prohibited them from doing so on the Passover.[77] Against this view, which can already be found in Augustine, there is the weighty and, I believe, conclusive objection that there is not a shred of evidence that the proscription that the text speaks of was limited to feast days or of an appeal to the Jews' own law.[78] That interpreters of vs. 31 have often inserted the word "today"[79] cannot alter the fact that it is not there.

32   As in vs. 9, so also here, the Evangelist interrupts his account by mentioning the "fulfillment" (elsewhere used of Scripture texts) of a saying by Jesus, here with regard to the manner of his death. The reference is to his repeated description of his death as "elevation" (8:28; 12:32, 33; 3:14). He is now moving toward that death now that the Jews must place him in the hands of Pilate, death by crucifixion being a Roman practice. The Evangelist thus implies that this transfer of the case to Pilate does not happen by chance. Not only has Jesus foreseen and foretold the form of death that is to ensue from this, but it is also integral to the divine plan of salvation. As Moses lifted up the serpent in the wilderness, so also the Son of man "must" be lifted up (3:14). The way in which he will be "elevated" by the Father is also the manner of his ignominious death, death as effected by the Romans. It is in this light that the Evangelist portrays to his readers the now following unfolding of the trial, thus prefacing his account of the actual trial with this preliminary demarcation of the respective "powers."

18:33-38

The First Interrogation: Jesus' Kingship

Pilate has won the first battle. He will conduct his own judicial inquiry, and to that end he goes back into the praetorium. The hearing that follows is

---

76. See also J. Jeremias, "Zur Geschichtlichkeit des Verhörs Jesu vor dem Hohen-Rat," *ZNW* 43 (1950), p. 51; Blinzler, *Prozeß,* pp. 229-44.

77. Defended at length by J. van Bruggen, *Christus op aarde,* 1987, pp. 193-200.

78. See also Brown, with the same argument. He speaks of a "not particularly successful [attempt] to circumvent the difficulty by interpreting John's statement in a limited way." Other attempts of that kind have been made as well. "However," his conclusion reads, "the Johannine text gives no hint of limitation or qualification as regards time" (*Comm.* II, p. 850).

79. As by Van Bruggen, *Christus op aarde,* pp. 193f.

particularly interesting because it takes place exclusively between Pilate and Jesus: neither the accusers nor, evidently, anyone else (except possibly some of Pilate's officers) are present. Here again the Evangelist departs from the Synoptics (Mt. 27:12; Mk. 15:3; Lk. 23:2). After summoning Jesus to appear before him, Pilate does begin with the question that, according to the Synoptics as well, dominated the entire trial: "Are you the King of the Jews?" But Jesus' reply in John is not limited, as in the Synoptics, to a mere "You say so," but is more extensive, followed by a dialogue about Jesus' kingship, and totally Johannine (cf. vss. 36ff.). Here as well John does not follow an existing tradition but presents Jesus before Pilate in accordance with his self-revelation in this Gospel as a whole.

With this opening question Pilate, though earlier he has asked the Jews for a formal complaint, proves he knows very well what has prompted "the Jews" to want to rid themselves of Jesus: his messianic claims. But Pilate approaches the issue totally as a Roman. As a non-Jew he speaks of "the king of the Jews," not "the king of Israel," as Jews would (cf. Mk. 15:32).[80] And when he says "king," he has in mind the political sense of the word. What else in Jesus' supposed kingship could be of interest to him as Roman governor? One may indeed wonder whether, as he sees Jesus bound before him and can for the first time form an impresssion of him, his question does not immediately convey a sense of disbelief and astonishment. Is *this* the man who is claiming to be the king of the Jews?

34, 35 Before answering Pilate's question Jesus asks whether he is speaking on his own, that is, whether Jesus' public conduct itself has prompted the question or whether he is acting on the instigation of others. With this counterquestion Jesus obviously seeks to establish that the initiative for this hearing comes not from Pilate but from the Jews. Pilate's response betrays — at the best — some irritation: "I am not a Jew, am I?"[81] This conveys not so much contempt for Jews as the fact that Pilate does not want to be associated in what he regarded as a purely Jewish affair, as is made clear by what follows ("your own nation and chief priests have handed you over to me"). Pilate refuses to be questioned by Jesus or diverted from the issue at hand. He immediately continues the hearing with a question: "What have you done?" That is, what is Jesus' crime such that the chief priests, the authorities of Jesus' people, have found it necessary to hand him over to Pilate?

36 Jesus now answers Pilate's initial question by speaking of his kingship in the affirmative but at the same time qualifying it in a sense that removes it from what Pilate had in mind. This is the only place in the Fourth Gospel that expressly mentions Jesus' kingship, and it is here mainly to distinguish

---

80. On this differentiation of usage, see the comments above on 1:19.
81. μήτι ἐγὼ Ἰουδαῖός εἰμι.

Jesus' kingship from what Pilate has referred to.[82] When Jesus counters that his kingship (or "kingdom") "is not from this world," he describes it thereby as being in origin and nature of another order than the kingship of which Pilate has spoken. Elsewhere Jesus says the same thing with terms like "not from below," "not of this world" (8:23), "not from here" (vs. 38), or, positively, "from heaven" or "from above." If it were "from this world," then his servants,[83] that is, the troops that would in that case be at his disposal, would fight to prevent him from falling into the hands of the Jews. The words undoubtedly contain an allusion to Jesus' arrest, about which Pilate certainly knows (cf. vs. 3).[84] Jesus reiterates:[85] "but as it is, my kingdom is not from here,"[86] as the situation in which he finds himself all too clearly demonstrates.

The history of exegesis and of the church has again and again asked what this pronouncement means for the relationship of those under Jesus' lordship to worldly governments and the means of power it uses.[87] The passage does not, in fact, discuss this question. Most commentators have correctly stressed that Jesus' pronouncement in 18:36 and everything in this pericope that is connected with it (see also the comments on 19:11) do not portray a confrontation of Jesus' kingdom with the state,[88] but indicate, rather, that his kingdom is distinct from "the kingdom of this world" at a point of immediate interest: it is not based on force. Although the text does not discuss it further, this implies that the Christian community as well, since it is subject to the rule of Christ, must seek power for its existence and worldly task not in external means but, in Paul's words, in the "sword" and the "armor" of the Spirit.

This is not to say that the kingdom of Christ and the kingdom of the world, since they are distinct in origin and character, exclude each other or bear no relation to each other.[89] When Jesus says that his kingdom is "not of this world" as also he and his own are "not of this world" (17:16), he does not thereby deny the positive task that the disciples have *in* this world (see the comments on 17:15f.) or that the world in its present form ("this world") is devoid of powers and agencies that uphold it in a positive

82. On 3:3, 5 ("entering the kingdom of God") see the comments there.
83. ὑπήρεται, as in 18:3, 22; 19:6.
84. So, correctly, Schnackenburg.
85. In keeping with the Johannine manner; cf. Bultmann, *Comm.*, p. 654, n. 1.
86. ἐντεῦθεν, here synonymous with ἐκ τοῦ κόσμου τούτου.
87. On this see, e.g., Schlier, "Jesus und Pilatus" and several of the commentaries.
88. As asserted by Bultmann, "For the Evangelist the interest in the trial of Jesus is wholly transferred to the encounter with the Roman state" (*Comm.*, p. 644; cf. pp. 637f. and passim). Later Bultmann backed away from this view of John 18, which he had apparently defined when he was strongly affected by political relations during the Nazi regime. See Bultmann's *Das Evangelium des Johannes. Ergänzungsheft*, 1957, pp. 52f. Important for this entire question (including among other things Karl Barth's exegesis of John 18–19) is D. Luhrmann, "Der Staat und die Verkündigung, Rudolf Bultmanns Auslegung von Joh 18,28 bis 19,16," in *Theologia Crucia — Signum Crucis* (Festschrift for E. Dinkler), 1979, pp. 358-75.
89. See also Schlier, "Jesus und Pilatus."

sense, for example, to establish justice in it against the destructive powers of injustice and oppression — and this also for the benefit of the cause of Christ in the world. Other books of the New Testament (e.g., Ro. 13:1ff.; 2:15; 1 Pt. 2:13f., Tit. 3:1) develop this viewpoint, but the Fourth Gospel does not, though the present pericope contains a clear though indirect proof of this in the position and conduct of Pilate. Even though he handed Jesus over to be crucified and thus committed the gravest possible injustice, his repeated attempts to release Jesus show that as a judge he was aware of his duty to acquit Jesus.

Accordingly, when Jesus contrasts his heavenly kingship with the world's kingship, he does not thereby portray every worldly regime as totally subject to "the ruler of this world." Nor does he see no ground for appeal to earthly government on his own behalf or that of his own. Not only does Nicodemus appeal to the existing Jewish legal order on behalf of Jesus (7:51), but Jesus himself, when he is struck by the high priest's servant, protests and appeals to the rules for a just trial ("bear witness to the wrong," 18:23).

We cannot therefore draw from Jesus' rejection of any defense by violence during his arrest the conclusion that he would also demand the total defenselessness of his disciples in times of oppression and that he would reject all use of worldly power for their benefit as incompatible with his kingdom. What is at issue in vs. 36b is that Jesus' kingdom is based on something other than such power or protection. It is based on his self-surrender, on his offering of himself for the sin of the world.[90] For that reason, when his "hour" has come, his disciples are not allowed to try to prevent his arrest. And he himself eventually quits trying to answer the charges advanced against him. In distinction from all worldly government, it is only by the power of his Spirit that he establishes his rule in the hearts of humans and admits them to his kingdom (cf. 3:3, 5f.). However much worldly government might want to serve justice, peace, and liberation, it cannot remove the sin of the world, because it has no power over the hearts of human beings.

Accordingly, the place and the calling of the Christian community in the world are determined by its differentness. As citizens not only of this world but also of Jesus' kingdom, Christians are concerned with the struggle for justice and righteousness, even in the political and social senses of those words, and that not only for the benefit of the church but also for the well-being of the world. But the meaning of their existence as the church in the world does not lie there. The primary focus of their attention and message is otherwise. It is not found in what unites it with "the world" but in what distinguishes it from the world. It is found in what Jesus now (vs. 37) positively describes as the content of his kingship: testimony to the truth as he has heard and received it from the Father.[91]

---

90. See ibid., pp. 62f.

91. In his exposition of vs. 36 Calvin discusses whether "it is lawful to defend the kingdom of Christ by arms" (*Comm.* II, pp. 166f.): "I reply: First, those who draw the conclusion that the teaching of the Gospel and the pure worship of God should not defended by arms are wrong and ignorant. For Christ argues only from the facts of the present case how frivolous were the calumnies of the Jews." He goes on to argue that the kingdom of Christ, being spiritual, must be founded on the doctrine and power of the Spirit, "for neither the laws and edicts of men nor their

37 Pilate concludes — correctly, though still in the form of a question: "So you are in fact a king?" This time Jesus' reply is unqualifiedly positive: "As you say I am," that is, yes, I am a king.[92] Jesus then explains this further, strongly emphasizing his function: "For this I was born, and for this I came into the world: to testify to the truth." Jesus' kingship consists in the utterly unique authority with which he represents the truth in the world. His birth and coming had no other purpose than to "bear witness to the truth," in the absolute sense in which the Fourth Gospel continually speaks of the truth: Jesus testifies to what "he has seen and heard of the Father" (cf. 3:31-36), indeed to the truth that he himself is (14:6) and for which he answers with his life, person, and work. By speaking of himself as "witness," Jesus — standing before the judgment seat of Pilate — is using the language of the courtroom (cf. 1 Tm. 6:13), but not as the accused testifying on his own behalf but as the one who, in the suit that God brings against the world, has come to testify against the rule of the lie and for "the truth," that is, for God and for God's claim on the world. In that testimony Jesus kingship consists. All who are "of the truth" and "from above" listen to his voice and heed it as God's people, as those who recognize the voice of the good Shepherd and give evidence of belonging to "his own" (cf. 10:3f.; 16:27; 17:6ff.).

From these last words of vs. 37 it is clear that Jesus has reversed the roles in the trial with his answer to Pilate's question. He makes no attempt to refute the charge brought against him or to persuade Pilate that he is not a public danger. Instead he is in this trial — indirectly but not for that reason any less clearly — posing the questions that will really bring out the truth. And that for "everyone," including Pilate. When it comes to the truth, where does Pilate stand as a judge?

38 Pilate's reaction to Jesus' words is remarkable. Shrugging his shoulders, in effect, he asks Jesus, "What is truth?" Then ("after he had said this") he goes outside to the Jews and says to *them:* "I find no crime in him whatever." Pilate's question has been interpreted in a number of ways. Sometimes it is viewed as an expression of philosophical skepticism. But it is doubtful that we can assume such depth — that which would give expression to the futility of a search for truth — in a person like Pilate. Bultmann believes that

---

punishments reach into consciences, yet this does not prevent princes from incidentally defending Christ's kingdom, partly by establishing external discipline and partly by lending their protection to the Church against the ungodly." "But," he concludes, "the depravity of the world causes the kingdom of Christ to be established more by the blood of martyrs than by the aid of arms."

92. σὺ λέγεις (cf. Mt. 26:25, 64 — with Mk. 14:62!). The idea, therefore, is not that Jesus leaves it open for Pilate to judge. See also Strack/Billerbeck I, p. 990; similarly, on the basis of *Roman* law, Lapide (who refers for this to Mommsen), *Wie waren schuldig,* p. 76. Bultmann correctly remarks that the immediately following statement is senseless "if one attempts to understand it otherwise" (*Comm.,* p. 654, n. 6).

Pilate here again expresses the neutrality of the state, which can have nothing to do with questions like those that Jesus apparently has in mind.[93] But what matters in this pericope, as we have seen, is certainly not a confrontation with the (Roman) state. We therefore prefer to adopt the increasingly accepted view that Pilate chose not to comment on Jesus' reference — unintelligible to Pilate — to the truth, but in so acting indicated at the same time that he saw no reason in whatever Jesus might mean to take him seriously or even to condemn him for his royal claims.

For the Evangelist Pilate's question amounts to a rejection of Jesus' witness.[94] Still, having heard Jesus, Pilate understands at least enough of the truth to realize that he cannot condemn "this man" to death as a revolutionary. And with this message he now returns to the Jews: "I find no crime in him." The occasion of the Passover evidently suggests to him that some better arrangement might be made between him and them, the release, that is, of a Jewish prisoner on this day. This might offer a way out of the impasse without too much loss of face for either party. In any case he now presents this solution to the Jews.

18:39-40

Jesus or Barabbas?

39 This part of the passion narrative is in all four Gospels and is characterized in John by summarizing brevity. At some points the Johannine account differs from the presentation in the other Gospels (which also differ from each other in certain details).[95] In John it is Pilate himself who brings up an existing custom,[96] conciliatory to the Jews, of releasing a prisoner at the Passover, so that he can release Jesus. So that they will go along with them, he presents this as a favor to them rather than as doing right to Jesus. He calls Jesus "the king of the Jews," a title suggesting the mockery that Pilate has expressed and will

---

93. The state "which as such is not interested in the question that moves man as to the determining reality of his life" (*Comm.*, p. 656, n. 2).

94. The idea that we must go further and may assume that the Evangelist intends to give the answer to Pilate's unanswered question in the following narrative of Jesus' death and resurrection and that this reality shapes the entire concept of truth in the Fourth Gospel (cf. Morris, *Comm.*, pp. 770 and 294f.) seems to be a conclusion drawn rather too generally from the context.

95. For a "Comparative Chart for the Barabbas Incident" see Brown, *Comm.* II, pp. 870f.

96. ἔστιν δὲ συνήθεια ὑμῖν. In the Jewish sources no clear examples or proofs exist of such a Passover custom (what is in later literature called the *privilegium paschale*), though some scholars believe that Mishnah *Pesaḥim* 8:6 is a point of contact. In the history of the Roman legal administration of the day one does find clear examples of such acts of mercy toward convicts on certain occasions. For both of these matters see Blinzler, *Prozeß*, pp. 317ff. and 303ff. respectively.

continue to express to the end (cf. 19:14, 15, 19f.) and expressing what he regards as the absurd nature of the charge made by the Jews. But he is prepared, if they agree, not to offend them by completely exonerating Jesus on his own. For that reason he proposes to them the opportunity to extend to their "king" the privilege of release at the Passover. Thus — he apparently reasons — he might spare them the necessity of a humiliating retreat and himself the condemnation of an innocent man.

That in thinking this he is totally misjudging the situation will be evident soon enough. Here, too, however, the Evangelist refrains from commenting on Pilate's strategic or psychological considerations. What matters for the Evangelist is that on that day and in that way the Jews were confronted with Jesus as "their king." And indirectly but very tellingly he brings the deeper meaning of this to expression by mention of both the Passover and of Jesus as "the king of the Jews." The connection can hardly be accidental. The Passover was the ancient festival of Israel's liberation, and it was on that day that Pilate kept confronting the Jews with the decision of what to do with Jesus, their king. Nowhere more sharply than here does it become apparent that the messianic kingship of Jesus was "foolishness" to the Romans and an "offense" to the Jews (cf. 1 Co. 1:23), nor does the redemptive-historical character of Jesus' suffering and death come to the fore anywhere more clearly in its decision-demanding significance than in the choice for or against Jesus on this day of the great feast of Israel's liberation.

40 But the Jews do not allow themselves to be sidetracked by Pilate's proposed solution. The Evangelist needs only one sentence to put their reaction into words: "They cried out again: 'Not this man, but Barabbas!'" It has not been said before that they "cried out"; from now on (cf. 19:6, 12, 15) their words become simply an emotional demonstration of resistance to Pilate's attempts to release Jesus. Arguments no longer play a role. "The Jews" increase the pressure on Pilate. It is likely that the growing crowd also plays a role, as one can infer from the Synoptics' accounts. Still, in John, the subject remains "they," "the Jews" (19:12, 15) or "the chief priests and their officers" (19:6). Pilate has mentioned their "nation" already in 18:35, and the Evangelist refers to "many of the Jews" as later spectators in 19:20.

Of Barabbas, apart from what is said in vs. 40b, we know only what we are told in Mk. 15:7 (cf. Lk. 20:19), which is that he was in prison with other insurgents who had "committed murder during the insurrection."[97] The word we have translated as "insurgent"[98] can also mean something like "robber"

---

97. There has been much speculation about his name "son of Abbas" (father), in some manuscripts spelled Bar-rabbas ("son of rabban," "son of our master") or as Jesus Barabbas (particularly in Matthew). See the overview in Brown, *Comm.* II, pp. 856f. However, the name also frequently occurs elsewhere as an ordinary personal name (cf. Strack/Billerbeck I, p. 1031).

98. ληστής.

or "thief" (cf. 10:2). But in view of Mk. 15:7 the meaning "revolutionary" or "rebel" against the existing order, which also occurs elsewhere, is more likely (cf. Mt. 26:55). Some suggest that Barabbas may therefore have been a member or even a leader[99] of the party of the Zealots, who repeatedly committed acts of terrorism.[100] In the end Jesus was to be nailed to the cross as "king of the Jews" between two such revolutionaries (Mt. 27:38; Mk. 15:27).

But John brings out none of this, not even in 19:18. The name of Barabbas comes from nowhere as an opposing candidate against Jesus for release on the Passover. The only thing the Evangelist adds, and this in conclusion to the Barabbas scene, is: "Now Barabbas was an insurgent." And with that one comment he discloses in a dramatic way the point at which all those who were involved in this "trial of Jesus" had arrived: the Jewish leaders, by choosing a violent revolutionary over Jesus, discard all pretense that their indictment against Jesus arose from concern for maintaining the political and social order. Now Pilate knows that his ambivalent attitude to Jesus has gained almost nothing. Jesus also, drinking the bitter cup that the Father has given him to drink, hears the shouts of the leaders of the people from outside the praetorium: "Not this man, but Barabbas!"

19:1-5

"Here Is the Man!"

1-3 Pilate, seeing that by this route he is not achieving his goal, seizes on another method: he has Jesus scourged. Roman citizens could be scourged only after a verdict, but scourging could be used as a means of interrogation of noncitizens. But Jesus has already "confessed" that he is a king, so Pilate has him scourged to satisfy his accusers, which was also permitted.[101] The scourging is followed by the soldiers' mockery of Jesus (vss. 2, 3).[102] Although the location of these events is not altogether clear, one may infer from vs. 4 that the mockery took place in the praetorium.

99. In connection with the adjective ἐπίσημος (δέσμος) in Mt. 27:16.
100. So, e.g., A. Schlatter, *Der Evangelist Matthäus,* 1957[4], 756f. (on Mt. 26:55); see also the full treatment of λῃστής by K. H. Rengstorf in *TDNT* IV, pp. 257-62, especially p. 261.
101. So Verdam, *Sanhedrin en Gabbatha,* p. 28. While in Matthew and Mark the scourging takes place as punishment prior to the crucifixion (Mt. 27:26; Mk. 15:15), in Luke, as in John, it is an attempt on the part of Pilate to satisfy the Jews in order then to release Jesus (Lk. 23:16, 22). Scourgings were applied in varying degrees of severity depending on the goal pursued (cf. Brown, *Comm.* II, p. 874).
102. The words ἐμαστίγωσεν (vs. 1) and ῥαπίσματα (vs. 3), occurring in conjunction, recall the prophecy of the Servant of the Lord in Isaiah 50, where vs. 6 (in the Septuagint) also mentions scourging (μάστιγας) and blows (ῥαπίσματα).

Again, the account of the mockery by the soldiers is very brief in comparison with that in Matthew and Mark. The thorns that the soldiers twisted into a wreath and placed on Jesus' head are clearly intended as mockery of Jesus' royal dignity. That the thorns were also meant to injure Jesus is not evident here.[103] The purple robe, also worn by the Roman military,[104] served together with the wreath of thorns to represent royal garments in the cruel game played by the soldiers.

4, 5 In the present context, however, the scourging and mockery function in particular as part of Pilate's overall tactics. The scourging is meant to give some satisfaction to the Jews, and the sight of the grotesquely dressed Jesus should do even more to convince them how absurd their accusation against Jesus is. Consequently, Pilate goes outside and announces Jesus' appearance: "Look, I am bringing him out to you to let you know [or "that you may understand"] that I find no crime in him."

Then follows the dramatic statement: "And Jesus came out, wearing the crown of thorns and the purple robe." Pilate did not have to add anything other than a sentence that in all its brevity has become immortal: "Here is[105] the man!" By itself this does nothing more than call attention to the figure of Jesus, who is here and elsewhere called "the [or "that"] man." But here, in the charged scene in which he must now display himself, it means: the man in all his ludicrous unworthiness and wretchedness. Must the Roman governor and the Jewish Sanhedrin continue to quarrel about him as though this man were a threat to the empire?

Some commentators believe that Pilate is trying at this point to arouse the Jews' compassion.[106] It is doubtful, however, whether he can assume that much humanity in this moment or whether he himself is led by such a motive. He attempts to sway the Jews by presenting Jesus not as pitiable but as worthless. At the same time — and this is clearly the main thrust of the successive phases of the narrative — to save himself from having to make a decision he plunges Jesus deeper into physical and mental degradation. Accordingly, it can hardly be made more clear that the Evangelist does not present Jesus' suffering simply as a triumphant passage to his exaltation. However great Jesus' dignity and spiritual inviolability are in standing up to Pilate (cf. also vss. 9ff.), this in no way detracts from the reality of Jesus' course of suffering. It is therefore

---

103. Mt. 27:29f. mentions a reed — the "scepter" that the soldiers placed in Jesus' hands and with which they then struck him on his head.

104. For these and other particulars, see R. Delbrueck, "Antiquarisches zu den Verspottungen Jesu," *ZNW* 41 (1942), p. 132.

105. ἰδού, like ἴδε, both originally imperatives, is used as a demonstrative particle to focus the attention of the listener (or reader); here it is linked with the nominative in the sense of "here is" or "here comes" (cf. BAGD s.v. ἰδού).

106. So Schlatter, *Comm.* in loc.

not amiss that *ecce homo* has been taken over in Christian tradition as the catchword for this suffering Messiah.

Some commentators do see *ecce homo* as a reference to the glory of Jesus. According to this view, Pilate — like Caiaphas in 11:50ff., without realizing it — by using the word "man" (ἄνθρωπος), was identifying Jesus as "the Son of man," the judge of the world clothed by God with all power.[107] Others see in "the man" an allusion to the incarnation, which is said to have "become visible [here] in its extremest consequence."[108] The text itself has no trace of all this — unlike Caiaphas's statement, that is, in the reference to his high priesthood (11:51). It is hard to imagine on what ground the Evangelist could have attributed such a prophetic gift to Pilate.

19:6-11

The Second Interrogation: The Heart of the Issue

6, 7 On "the chief priests and the officers," however, this entire display makes no impression in Jesus' favor at all. Rather, the spectacle ("when they saw him") of Jesus ravaged by scourging and mockery becomes an incentive to risk everything. Now they demand Jesus' death, and that by way of the death penalty as the Romans applied it to a hardened criminal: death on a cross.

It can hardly be accidental that the Evangelist no longer speaks in general of "the Jews" but of "the chief priests," who, along with "the officers" under their command, are the first to cry out, "Crucify him!" Thus the most aristocratic representatives of the Sanhedrin press their demand. As the Evangelist has repeatedly shown, opposition to Jesus lay not with the people but with these leaders. The true nature of their motives can no longer remain hidden. When Pilate once more attests Jesus' innocence and seeks to shift responsibility for Jesus' crucifixion to them ("Take him yourselves and crucify him"), the members of the Sanhedrin reach for their last device: the appeal to their own law. Undoubtedly they do this with great reluctance since it exposes their real motives to Pilate. For now it is clear that their real complaint against Jesus is what they have accused him of, namely the political danger he poses, but that, according to their own law, by "making himself the Son of God" he deserves the death penalty as a blasphemer.

The Evangelist's narrative comes to a head with this new accusation. And

---

107. So Barrett, *Comm.*, p. 541. For these and related views, see also Brown, *Comm.* II, p. 876, who himself speaks of "an exalted title" (p. 890).

108. So Bultmann, *Comm.*, p. 659.

now, in the final conversation between Pilate and Jesus (vss. 9-11), everything is concentrated. The key redemptive-historical issue in this trial is not whether Jesus is being indicted and condemned under false pretenses, but whether he is who he claims to be: the Son of God, the Messiah sent to Israel, and therefore whether the Jews can rightly, on the basis of their own law, demand his death (cf. Lv. 24:16). This charge has been behind the Jews' confrontation with Jesus from the beginning (cf. 5:18; 10:33, 36), and for this they now demand the death penalty from Pilate.

8 "When Pilate heard this, he was the more afraid." Some commentators read this as an indication of Pilate's dread of the supernatural in the figure of Jesus.[109] The idea is that in his first conversation with Jesus he was already impressed by Jesus' supernatural dignity and that now, hearing the Jews speaking of "the Son of God," he is restrained all the more from convicting Jesus. But of such fear in his earlier conversation with Jesus — to which "more" would refer — there is no evidence (cf. 18:38),[110] nor is there evidence of such fear in what follows (cf. vs. 20). For that reason we far prefer the view according to which Pilate's fear arose from his increasing uneasiness at being driven by the Jews into a position from which he had less and less of a way of extricating himself.[111] He knows, after all, their fanaticism when things concern "their law," and especially in an issue that so deeply touches them as the present one.

9-11 Even now he tries to escape the decision. Instead of ruling that this accusation is outside his jurisdiction, he again (as in 18:33) withdraws with Jesus into the praetorium. He addresses the accusation by asking Jesus, "Where are you from?" That was the fundamental question not only in the conflict between Jesus and the Jews but for the whole world's understanding of people. Jesus no longer answers Pilate's question. Earlier, when Pilate was questioning him about kingship, Jesus has already told of his origin (18:36). He has not left Pilate in the dark about what motivates him and has in Pilate's presence appealed to the Truth that he represents. But now he is silent. He does not recognize Pilate as a judge in this new matter. Pilate, incensed at this silence, says, "Don't you understand that I have power to release you, and power to crucify you?" Jesus makes one final statement and lays bare the actual situation of the moment: "You would have no power over me unless it had been given to you from above."

---

109. Schnackenburg speaks of "the numinous terror before the divine," "fear by the judge of the accused, who appears to him as a higher being" (*Comm.* III, p. 200). Bultmann speaks of "numinous fear" of "the superhuman" that Pilate encounters in Jesus (*Comm.,* p. 661; see also Barrett, *Comm.,* p. 542).

110. Some proponents of this view therefore wish to translate μᾶλλον by "very," an unlikely translation.

111. See, e.g., Becker, *Comm.* II, p. 575.

Commentators both ancient[112] and modern[113] have understood this statement to refer to the divine institution of government as it is spoken of in Romans 13. But in more recent exegesis this has been replaced, correctly we think, by the view that it relates to the concrete situation, that is, to Pilate's power to release Jesus or to crucify him.[114] For that reason the divine background of Pilate's power is described as "given from above." Jesus' kingdom has just been described as "not from this world" (18:36), and Jesus has repeatedly described the origin of his own coming and work as "from above." It is "from above" that Pilate also has received his power and in that context that he plays his divinely given role.[115] By saying this Jesus not only explains Pilate's position but also his own. In that providential arrangement, "given from above," Pilate's interrogation of Jesus is a stage in the process in which Pilate himself must fulfill the will of God. Therefore, Jesus is in God's hands and not in Pilate's. He keeps silent because he must drink the cup that the Father has given him to drink. Part of that cup is the necessity of submitting to Pilate's arbitrary use of power and letting himself be crucified as a criminal, thus bearing "the sin of the world" (1:29), being "made to be sin" by God (2 Co. 5:21).

This does not of course exculpate Pilate as an unjust judge. But in saying this Jesus does point to the larger contexts that help shape and limit Pilate's guilt. "Therefore," he continues, "he who delivered me to you has the greater sin." Striking here is the use of the singular. Some scholars have thought of Caiaphas; others of Judas or Satan. But Judas no longer plays any role at this point, Caiaphas is no longer the dominant figure, and Pilate's sin can hardly be compared with that of Satan. The reference is clearly to the Jews who have handed Jesus over to Pilate.[116] Their sin is greater than that of Pilate because they are much more deeply involved than he is in what is now taking place at his judgment seat. And this not only because they have instigated the trial but much more because it was in their midst that Jesus spoke his word and did his

---

112. Schnackenburg refers to Augustine. Calvin mentions the view of those who explain "you would have no power" in a general sense, saying, that is, "that nothing is done in the world save by God's permission." Calvin himself prefers the opinion of those who "restrict this passage to the office of the magistrate" (*Comm.* II, p. 174).

113. E.g., Bultmann (so his *Comm.* but differently in his *Ergänzungsheft!*); Schlier, "Jesus und Pilatus," p. 71, and numerous others.

114. Hence the striking neuter with which the feminine ἐξουσία (i.e., the concrete power to release or to crucify) is continued in the subordinate clause: εἰ μὴ ἦν δεδομένον σοι: "unless it"; a feminine could be understood more easily if the antecedent referred to the power of government in general.

115. Cf. also Blinzler, *Prozeß*, p. 333: "What has given him power over Jesus is not the rights and means belonging to him as the bearer of state power but a dispensation from above, namely the mysterious will of God."

116. The singular, however, remains striking. Some scholars speak of the "general singular" and point to a usage like that in Lk. 17:1.

signs and because their law contained everything by which they could and should have recognized Jesus as the one sent by the Father.

In this light we can again see the shallowness of the view that to exonerate the Romans the Evangelist, in this statement, lays the blame for Jesus' death so much less on Pilate and so much more on the Jews.[117] What the Evangelist is expressing in this often-cited passage is not a political but a redemptive-historical judgment upon the Jewish leaders. And even as he makes this judgment, his portrayal of Pilate makes it clear that means no compliment to the Romans.

19:12-16a

Jesus Condemned

12 From this point on everything presses toward a denouement. After the final exchange (vss. 9-11) Pilate no longer considers further examination necessary and now makes every effort[118] to release Jesus. The word "tried," meanwhile, indicates that he was conscious of resistance.

Suddenly, however, "the Jews" are also on the scene. It is not clear how one must picture this transition. They were outside and so have not witnessed the conversation between Jesus and Pilate and do not know of Pilate's intentions. But somehow they understand that what has gone on inside is in danger of taking the wrong turn and that they must play their last cards against Pilate. With Pilate still in the praetorium with Jesus (cf. vs. 13), "the Jews" air their impatience by raising an outcry, focused no longer on Jesus but on Pilate's political position, specifically the support he enjoys in Rome: "If you release this man, you are no longer Caesar's friend. Everyone who claims to be a king sets himself against the emperor."[119]

Nowadays scholars assume that "Caesar's friend" refers not simply to the emperor's favor but is a formal title of honor (*amicus Caesari*) that is said to have been accorded to Pilate and that obviously was very valuable to him.[120] The emperor of that time, Tiberius, was inclined to be suspicious of anything that could threaten his hegemony. So, whether or not the words represent a title,[121] it is clear how strong a weapon they were against Pilate.

---

117. Vs. 11 "also exhibits an apologetic tendency as is more and more noticeable in early Christianity. . . . The blame is taken from the Roman at the cost of the Jews, he is almost 'excused.' But John does not go so far as to clear him of guilt . . ." (Schnackenburg, *Comm.* III, p. 262).

118. ἐζήτει, iterative imperfect.

119. ἀντιλέγειν, besides "contradict," can also mean "resist" (cf. Rm. 10:21; Tit. 2:9).

120. Specifically on the basis of E. Bammel, "φίλος τοῦ Καίσαρος," *TLZ* 77 (1952), pp. 205ff.

121. For objections against this view of "Caesar's friend," see, e.g., Brown, *Comm.* II, p. 879.

13, 14a From Pilate's conduct it is immediately evident how effective this ploy is. He understands all too well that this was not an empty threat. "The Jews" would know how to find their way to Rome to hurt his political career. At once matters take a turn: "When Pilate heard *these words,* he brought Jesus out and sat down on the judgment seat." He knew the decision now had to be made, and he proceeded to bring it about in accordance with the judicial pattern given for that purpose:[122] indictment first (vs. 14b), then request of penalty (vs. 15), then finally the verdict (vs. 16). The text does not describe this process in formal judicial formulas but in terms of the continued dialogue between Pilate and the Jews. Pilate again pours out his scorn on the Jews and depicts the absurdity of their indictment and demand. But in the end he sees no way out other than to condemn Jesus.

According to another interpretation of vss. 12-16, ἐκάθισεν ("he sat") should be translated transitively and in connection with the preceding clause: "He brought Jesus out and sat *him* down on the judgment seat" to present him to the Jews, as in vs. 5, as the mock king.[123] Some see in this the even deeper meaning that as the Son of man Jesus is the last and highest Judge and that, without knowing it, Pilate gives Jesus the place that is due him.[124]

Still, the transitive interpretation of ἐκάθισεν, with however much talent it is defended, is certainly incorrect. The idea that Pilate, as though Jesus had not yet been sufficiently presented to the Jews as mock king, should to that end have used his judgment seat, the symbol of his own dignity as the emperor's representative (cf. "Caesar's tribunal" in Ac. 25:10), is totally implausible. What would the emperor, whose favor so much concerned Pilate, have thought of that? How, under these circumstances, could the trial be brought to an end? With Jesus on the judgment seat while Pilate, standing alongside, gave the verdict? The whole procedure itself would have become a laughingstock. That was certainly not Pilate's intent, nor that of the Evangelist, as the following words show.

The Evangelist marks the historical significance of the condemnation of Jesus by expressly establishing the location of Pilate's judgment seat and hence of the trial and the time. The place is called "Lithostrotos" or "Gabbatha" in "Hebrew" (i.e., Aramaic); the former means something like "tiled place," but the meaning of the latter is uncertain because of disagreement about the Semitic word or stem from which "Gabbatha" is derived.[125]

---

122. Cf. Blinzler, *Prozeß,* pp. 349ff.
123. For this view see at length ibid., pp. 346-56.
124. See also Barrett, *Comm.,* in loc., though he states this with some reservation.
125. Some opt for the metaphorical "place of the bare forehead," which is said to lead to the meaning of "elevated place" or "hump."

Because of uncertainty concerning the location of the praetorium (see the comments on vs. 28), the place meant here can no longer be identified with certainty.

There is also a significant difference of opinion, connected with the dating of the Passover in John, concerning the time reference in vs. 14: "Now it was the day of Preparation for the Passover." We take "preparation" (παρασκευή) to be the fixed name for the day before the sabbath, hence "Friday." The addition of "Passover" then makes this a reference to the Friday during Passover. Accordingly, Pilate's sentencing of Jesus fell on the Friday of the great feast of liberation itself and is meant to be understood in that context (see the comments on vs. 39; 13:1).[126]

14b-16 Pilate's first words from the judgment seat are, "Here is your king." Now that the verdict has been given, the court must first decide what crime the accused has committed. To this end Pilate traces everything to Jesus' kingship and therefore presents Jesus to the Jews under the heading of their own accusation. But by calling the abused and degraded Jesus "your king" he is again confronting the Jews — with undisguised mockery — with the absurdity of their accusation: "Here, then, is your king whose claims you take so seriously that even the emperor in Rome has to be on his guard!"

But the Jews (vs. 15), now that they have come so far — with Pilate on the judgment seat! — no longer allow themselves to be put off by his mockery and anger. They have not another word to say for Jesus or his kingship except this one thing that in *their* anger they shout at Pilate: "Away with him, away with him, crucify him!"

Pilate already knows he has lost the battle. But he does not capitulate before once more deeply offending their national pride: "Must I then crucify your king?" — plunge the king of the Jews into the deepest disgrace? But the chief priests catch Pilate in his own words and reverse the roles. He may make light of it, but they cannot regard those who make themselves out to be kings as so unimportant. So, as though he has fallen behind them in loyalty to the only legitimate king, they answer, "*We* have no king but the emperor."

That the members of the Sanhedrin could hardly have struck a more cynical pose than that of loyal subjects of the emperor could not have escaped them. But there was no more effective way than this to outmaneuver Pilate in the game he played with the one he calls their king. Though he knew from long experience with the Jews the hypocrisy of this sudden loyalty to the emperor, he understood from this renewed mention of the emperor that all further delay was futile and could even get him into trouble. For that reason

---

126. Many of the more recent commentators translate "preparation for Passover," taking this to refer to the day preceding the celebration of Passover, i.e., the fourteenth of Nisan. For the arguments see above on 13:1ff.

vs. 16 simply reports: "Then he handed him over to them to be crucified." This means not that he literally placed Jesus in their hands (see the comments on vss. 16b, 23) but that by judicial pronouncement he granted the Jews what they had asked for.

One can only admire the masterly way in which the Evangelist has described the stages, all leading to this climax, of the power struggle between Pilate and the Jews. What has been at stake from the beginning is Jesus' condemnation to death by crucifixion. It is neither the intrigue on both sides, nor Pilate's unprincipled conduct, nor the Sanhedrin's fanaticism, with however much dramatic and psychological talent they are depicted, that constitute the actual subject of the Evangelist. Nor is his concern to give a new answer to who was to blame for the decision to crucify Jesus. Striking, rather, is the fact that in this account every sign of moral, psychological, or juridical disqualification is absent. The Evangelist's aim is to describe the way Jesus had to go in obedience to the Father and the cup the Father gave him to drink. That is what Jesus himself impresses on Pilate: "You would have no power over me if it was not given to you from above." Viewed in that light, the cruel and disgraceful way in which Pilate and the Jews played their game with Jesus is not a farce or a sham in which human guilt and responsibility hardly count any more (see vs. 11b!) or one describable as a *felix culpa*. It is rather the depth of the incarnation of the Word and the descent of the Son of man in its most extreme consequences that the Evangelist depicts in this sober and realistic narrative. But he does this to portray not a powerless victim given over to human caprice but the one who in his obedience to the Father has the "power" to lay down his life, the Lamb of God who takes the sin of the world on himself and bears it away (cf. 1:29, 36).

19:16b-27

"Crucified . . ."

The last part of the passion narrative (19:16b-42) opens with the account of Jesus' crucifixion. In contrast with the lengthy account of the trial before Pilate (18:28–19:12) and with the Synoptic account of the crucifixion, this last part is very concise. Here again John's selective independence comes to the fore. John lacks various passages known from the Synoptics,[127] but also includes features and information that we find in none of the other Gospels — specifically, the dispute between the Jews and Pilate over the inscription, Jesus' last

---

127. For a complete list and comparison see Brown, *Comm.* II, pp. 914ff.; earlier also in Dodd, *Historical Tradition in the Fourth Gospel.*

will with respect to his mother, and the lengthy account of his death in vss. 31-37. Even where John and the Synoptics agree, the differences in how John conveys it are striking. Especially striking, finally, are John's appeal to eyewitness testimony (vs. 35) and his mention of the disciple whom Jesus loved (vs. 26). These are, in my opinion, indications that can shed more light on the origin and independence of the Johannine tradition than attempts, made here also, to determine the difference between the wording of the Evangelist himself and his (hypothetical) written source(s).

16b-18 Immediately after Pilate's decision, it is carried out. The anonymous "they" who take the initiative in this regard can only be the Roman soldiers (cf. vs. 23). From this moment on Jesus is completely in their hands, and the Jews can only watch (vs. 21). Jesus, carrying his own cross,[128] goes out of the city to "The Place of the Skull,"[129] which is called "Golgotha" in "Hebrew" (i.e., Aramaic), apparently an elevated location with a round, bare shape[130] that today is usually pointed out in the Church of the Sepulchre, not far outside the city wall of that day (the "second" wall; cf. vs. 20).

"There they crucified him" (vs. 18). The execution itself, an extremely cruel procedure, is not described.[131] The manner in which it was carried out was not always equally cruel. Some victims were tied to the upright pole, but Jesus is nailed to the cross (cf. 20:27). The Evangelists abstain from any attempt to describe this barbaric procedure, which could not be used against Roman citizens. The New Testament has no trace of any passion mysticism oriented to the physical torture of Jesus.[132] "Two others" were also crucified, men not here described as criminals, "one on either side, with Jesus between them." This last point indicates that Jesus was the most prominent of the three. He, after all, was "the king of the Jews."

19-22 Pilate has an inscription placed on the cross stating the reason for Jesus' execution. A sign indicating the crime would be hung around the neck of a criminal on the way to execution. It was probably this sign that Pilate had the soldiers attach to the cross, so that Jesus' crime could be known to all.

This matter occasioned still another conflict between Pilate and the chief

128. The dative ἑαυτῷ is probably intended simply to indicate the custom that someone convicted to die by crucifixion had to carry his own cross.

129. κρανίου is, then, an epexegetical or appositional genitive; cf. BDF §412.2; Mt. 27:33; Mk. 15:22. Others translate: "to the place called 'the skull' "; cf. Lk. 23:33.

130. And therefore not so called on account of the executions performed there, which would suggest decapitation, not the customary punishment in Palestine.

131. On the application of this penalty see at length Blinzler, *Prozeß,* pp. 357-86.

132. Nor is Gl. 3:1 (οἷς κατ' ὀφθαλμοὺς Ἰησοῦς Χριστὸς προεγράφη ἐν ὑμῖν ἐσταυρωμένος) to be understood in the sense of an actual description. For this restraint in describing it, which was also observed in contemporary ancient literature, see also Becker, *Comm.,* p. 586.

priests. The inscription Pilate ordered read: "Jesus the Nazarene, the King of the Jews."[133] Because of the proximity of the place of execution to Jerusalem "many of the Jews" in the city, which was filled with visitors for the Passover, read the inscription. Here "the Jews" are obviously not those who were hostile to Jesus but rather the masses, who were by and large ignorant of what had taken place inside and around Pilate's praetorium and who were thus all at once confronted not only with Jesus' execution but also with the disgraceful way (for him and for them) in which he was displayed as their king. Pilated added to the offense by, in order to give the matter the widest possible publicity, having the inscription written up in three languages: "Hebrew" (Aramaic), Latin, and Greek: the local vernacular, the official language, and the language of common international communication.

Pilate had given the matter careful thought and thus paid back the Jews for forcing him to act against his will. If Jesus, with his royal pretensions, was indeed so dangerous that he deserved to die on the cross, then the whole world would know what his crime was. No wonder that the chief priests (vs. 21) came to Pilate to protest this. Now it seemed that Jesus would indeed be displayed before the whole world as *their* king and go down in history as such. They asked, therefore, that the inscription be changed to say that Jesus only *claimed* to be the king of the Jews. But Pilate (vs. 22) was no longer interested in being conciliatory. They should have thought of this matter when he told them he could not take Jesus' kingship seriously. So his last word, brief and to the point, was: "What I have written I have written."[134] Having said that he left them with their "king."

In this remarkable detail, which occurs only in John, we see the continuation of the line that runs through the entire trial before Pilate: he can still not exercise any power other than what has been "given from above" (vs. 11). What he was unwilling to undo — let the crucified Jesus of Nazareth be identified as the Messiah, the king of Israel — is, in fact, the pivotal issue in the entire passion narrative. And this is so in what follows, as Pilate and "the Jews" recede to the background and the focus is shifted to the crucified Jesus himself. For the Scriptures had not yet been fulfilled in him (vss. 23-25), and he had not yet said and done everything that he would say and do before he knew that "all was now completed" (vss. 25-27, 28).

23, 24 The soldiers are mentioned explicitly here again for the first time since vs. 2. After they have crucified Jesus, then, as their last item of business, they divide his garments among themselves, which they are entitled

133. It occurs in all four Evangelists, though in somewhat varying form. All have "the king of the Jews," Matthew with "Jesus." Only John has "the Nazarene" (cf. 18:7).
134. ὁ γέγραφα, γέγραφα: the double perfect cumulatively indicates the completed action.
135. χιτών, in distinction from ἱμάτιον (outer garment).

to as those who have carried out the crucifixion. Jesus' inner garment[135] is mentioned separately because it was "seamless, woven in one piece from the top."[136] The soldiers decide to leave it intact and to cast lots for it. The Synoptic Gospels mention neither this detail nor the fulfillment of Scripture,[137] which the Fourth Evangelist is concerned to stress and one of the few particulars that he includes in his account of the crucifixion. He cites for this purpose Ps. 22:19, entirely in conformity with the Septuagint.[138] In the Psalm the poet graphically depicts his hopeless situation: his enemies, into whose hands he has fallen, are already at work dividing and casting lots for his clothes — which are all he has left to him — before leaving him behind half dead. The Evangelist uses the formula "this was to fulfill the Scripture" to indicate that the divine work of salvation anticipated by the suffering and (temporary) redemption of Old Testament believers[139] has its final and imperishable fulfillment in Jesus' descent, including his suffering on the cross, and in his exaltation.

The closing words, "and that is what the soldiers did," are judged by some interpreters to be superfluous, but taken by others as a meaningful contrast to what follows regarding the women standing by the cross.[140] But these words are rather meant to underscore the importance of the preceding passage, which the Evangelist, skipping over several other key moments in Jesus' suffering on the cross, includes in his narrative before describing its last phase. What these four unknown Roman soldiers did was nothing other and nothing less than to fulfill what was written about Jesus, that is, about the last thing that anyone could do to him before he died. "And *that* is what the soldiers did." All that follows is what Jesus himself must still bring to fulfillment before he knows that "all is accomplished" and can bow his head (vss. 28, 30).

25-27 This last deed is Jesus' testamentary disposition with respect to

---

136. Commentators have speculated at length about the possible deeper meaning of "the tunic without seam" in connection with, among other things, the seamless robe said by Josephus to be worn by the high priest. On these speculations see, at length, Bultmann, *Comm.,* p. 671, n. 2, who, however — correctly I think — does nothing with them. In this Gospel this detail seems to have no other significance than to explain what was done with one specific garment, which is clearly distinguished from the "division" of the rest of Jesus' clothes.

137. Though they do use the words of Psalm 22.

138. Although there is no express mention there, or in the Masoretic Text, of the inner garment. Whether in the Psalm τὸν ἱματισμόν (in the second clause) is meant to be a synonym of τὰ ἱμάτια (in the first clause) or a reference to a different garment, as here in John, is yet another question (see N. H. Ridderbos, *De Psalmen* I, 1962, p. 240).

139. The conclusion of Psalm 22, where the poet speaks of the answer to his prayer, is also understood in Talmudic literature "in a universal messianic-eschatological sense, but nowhere is there mention of the person of the Messiah" (Strack/Billerbeck II, p. 574).

140. The latter point to the μὲν . . . δέ in vss. 24b-25a as well as to the *four* women mentioned in vs. 25. But the meaning of the suggested contrast is not obvious.

his mother and the disciple whom he loves. The presence of a number of women is also reported in the Synoptics (though after Jesus' death has been reported). The four named here are Jesus' mother, her sister, Mary the wife (or mother or daughter) of Clopas,[141] and Mary Magdalene. [142]

The Synoptics agree, with certainty, only with respect to Mary Magdalene. But it is possible that Matthew's "the mother of the sons of Zebedee" ("Salome" in Mark) was the sister of Jesus' mother mentioned in John. In this case, John the son of Zebedee would be a cousin of Jesus, which would be an important datum in the ongoing discussion of the identity of "the disciple whom Jesus loved" and would offer a ready explanation why Jesus entrusted his mother to this disciple. Although we cannot speak with certainty here, and some scholars do advance objections to this identification,[143] it was and is defended by some, precisely with a view to the authorship of the Fourth Gospel.[144]

These women "were standing by the cross." In the Synoptics we read that they were "looking on from a distance" to see what was happening. Of course, this does not exclude the possibility that before Jesus died they came closer (cf. also vs. 35). We are only told that Jesus "saw his mother" — along with "the disciple whom he loved," who was apparently with the women. Jesus once more speaks to these two, first to his mother, "Woman, here is your son," then to the disciple, "Here is your mother."

Many — particularly Protestant — interpreters restrict the significance of

141. Μαρία ἡ τοῦ Κλωπᾶ has also been read in apposition to ἡ ἀδελφὴ τῆς μητρὸς αὐτοῦ. In that case John mentions only three women, but then the two sisters would have the same name. Most recent scholarship assumes that we are dealing with two pairs of women. The first pair are not named but are identified as "his mother" and "her sister." The second pair are both named Mary and further identified as ἡ τοῦ Κλωπᾶ and ἡ Μαγδαληνή. We do not have any more information about the first of these two Marys. According to later tradition (Eusebius, *Historia Ecclesiastica* 3.11) Clopas was a brother of Mary's husband Joseph. In that case ἡ τοῦ Κλωπᾶ would probably have to be translated "the wife of Clopas," and this Mary would be a sister-in-law of Jesus' mother. Sometimes Clopas is also linked with the Cleopas of Lk. 24:18, but the names are not interchangeable.

142. The possibility that other women were also present can be deduced from Mk. 15:40; Mt. 27:56.

143. E.g., J. van Bruggen, with an argument from silence: "This seems very improbable, since all trace of family kinship both in and outside the Gospels is lacking" (*Christus op aarde,* p. 267). In the same vein see also Schnackenburg, who objects especially to a combination of the Synoptic lists of women with Jn. 19:25 because John proceeds from a different (written) tradition. But the fact that John is not dependent on the Synoptics does not exclude the possibility that with other words ("his mother's sister") he refers to the same person as the one the Synoptics call "the mother of the sons of Zebedee" or "Salome."

144. Of the older commentaries see, e.g., Westcott and Zahn; of the more recent, e.g., Morris; at length and positively, Brown, *Comm.* I, p. xcvii; II, p. 906.

this passage to Jesus personally caring for his mother;[145] an interpretation sometimes combined with lengthy statements on the example of Jesus' love as, in obedience to the Father, he forgets himself and does not neglect his obligations to his mother.[146] (Of course, the words of this text have prompted many others to make the figure of Mary the subject of deeply devout meditation: *Stabat mater dolorosa.* . . .) And commentators have often sought some explanation for Jesus' statement to "the disciple whom he loved" in the negative attitude of Jesus' own brothers (cf. 7:5), who are said to have prompted him to designate this disciple as the future caretaker of his mother.[147]

It is doubtful, however, that the meaning of this narrative is limited to this personal dimension — however much that aspect is present. The Evangelist's focus is elsewhere.[148] However deep the sorrow in which Jesus sees his mother standing by the cross (cf. Lk. 2:35), that is not what he speaks to her about. All he says, with extreme brevity, is: "Woman, here is your son." He refrains from calling her "mother," he asks her to relinquish him as son, and he refers her to the disciple standing by her as the one who will take his place. All this recalls 2:4 — the only other context in which Mary appears in John's Gospel — where Jesus rebuffs his mother with the same form of address because his "hour" (the "hour" of the manifestation of his glory, 2:11) has not yet come, the hour she has anticipated.[149] Now again they face an "hour" that is decisive for both (vs. 27),[150] an hour in which as Jesus' mother she must again step back in submission to the law of life that the Father has set for her son and in which she, like every other disciple of Jesus, must also know her place (cf. 12:25f.; 13:16).

At the same time this seemingly detached incident implies that the bond that Mary has had with Jesus, though from now on it will be terminated, will be continued in another way. Jesus chooses his words with the utmost care and economy, so charging them with all the more meaning. What Mary gives up and what she receives are expressed in one and the same statement: "Here is your son." "Here is your mother" does not mean — as has been asserted over and over in the history of interpretation — that from now on Mary will exercise

---

145. Strikingly characterized by Barclay: "There is something infinitely moving in the fact that Jesus in the agony of the Cross, in the moment when the salvation of the world hung in the balance, thought of the loneliness of His mother in the days when He was taken away" (quoted in Morris, *Comm.,* p. 611).

146. So, at length, Calvin, *Comm.* II, pp. 180f.

147. See, e.g., Zahn, *Comm.,* pp. 658f.; Grosheide, *Comm.* II, pp. 501f.; Morris, *Comm.,* p. 812.

148. Schnackenburg, *Comm.* III, p. 280, counts against the interpretation that "sees in the scene nothing more than Jesus' childlike concern for his mother" the "unmistakable theological interest of the Evangelist."

149. See p. 105 above.

150. ἀπ' ἐκείνης τῆς ὥρας.

her motherhood over this disciple, but rather that this disciple will from now on be a son to her, showing her the care that a mother needs from her son. As Jesus dies, he replaces himself with the disciple whom he loves, and that in accordance with the apostolic rule "he who receives you receives me" (cf. 13:20; Mt. 10:40), which in this extreme situation he applies to both Mary and that disciple. He does not name this disciple as son to his own mother because Mary otherwise will lack friends or relatives to give her a loving welcome. People whose names are given are standing around her. He does it rather because this disciple is the one with whom he can identify himself as son of his mother and in whom Mary can find her son back.

What gives unique significance to this passage in the Fourth Gospel is not, therefore, that Jesus still regulates his family relations in an act in which the disciple whom Jesus loves is introduced from outside in order, for lack of a better, to assume a leading role in it. It is, rather, that in these two persons, in this final moment, Jesus' love is extended in a much deeper and wider way to those whom he has loved in the world (cf. 13:1ff.), in a way that will be determinative for their entire future fellowship. For in the relationship that the dying Jesus establishes between these two persons, who of all of them were the closest to him, he paradigmatically contracts the image of the coming community that he is leaving behind on earth, but also bringing under the care that in his time on earth he has provided, and through which in the new dispensation after his death he himself will continue his work. Both Mary his mother and the disciple whom he loves represent in the most authentic manner this new community: Mary will from this moment on step back as his mother and uniquely reflect the image of the community that remains behind on earth. The disciple whom Jesus loves no less significantly represents those whom Jesus has bound to himself from the beginning to be his witnesses and to continue his work on earth. This disciple was the one in whom Jesus, when the hour of their separation had come, had confided in particular, who alone had followed him until this very moment, and who was to be the witness par excellence of Jesus' death and on account of this special bond was destined by Jesus to occupy a permanent place in the coming community (cf. 1:37ff.; 13:23ff.; 18:15; 19:26; 21:20, 23, 24).

It is in this light that we must view Jesus' final statements to these two and the words with which the Evangelist concludes this passage: "And from that hour the disciple took her into his own home."[151] This is not merely a

---

151. εἰς τὰ ἴδια is hard to render with precision. It denotes more than simply "house" as building or residence, also describing its uniqueness, a uniqueness conferred by the inhabitant. See also Schnackenburg, *Comm.,* in loc., and the article cited by him on John 19:27b by J. de la Potterie, "Das Wort Jesu, 'Siehe deine Mutter' und die Annahme der Mutter durch den Jünger (Joh. 19,27b)," in *Neues Testament und Kirche* (Festschrift for Schnackenburg), 1974, pp. 191-219: "From that hour the disciple took her (in)to his own home" (p. 216). Schnackenburg speaks of "the spiritual area, as it were, into which the disciple receives Jesus' mother" (*Comm.* III, p. 279).

historical note pertaining to Mary's place of residence after Jesus' death but a salvation-historical reference — in the manner of the Fourth Gospel — to the new "family of God" that from that hour took form as a result of Jesus' final testamentary disposition. In this manner alone can we fully understand why the Evangelist has this particular incident as the final act of the redemptive event of Jesus' suffering and death. "After this" — after Jesus had uttered those words — "Jesus knew that all was *now* finished" (vs. 28).

With this explanation we distance ourselves from two other interpretations that — with a number of variations — have sought the point of this passage either in an idealized understanding of Mary or in the disciple whom Jesus loved as symbolic ideal figure of the later ("Johannine") community.

Attempts have been made in a vast literature to find support in this passage for the understanding of Mary as the mother of the church, which has developed since the twelfth century. This support has been sought specifically in Jesus' statement to the disciple, "here is your mother," and in what follows: "And from that hour he took her into his own home." This is taken to mean that Mary's motherhood continues in the church, which is symbolically represented by the place she occupies in the disciple's house. On this foundation widely varying attempts have been made to define the nature of this motherhood in terms of these statements or, more precisely, to link a variety of mariological conceptions to these statements.[152] Discussion of these suggestions and speculations comes to have little meaning when one recognizes that the mariological interpretation of "this is your mother" is contradicted by the entire situation. Mary is placed *in the care of* the beloved disciple, as is evident also from the concluding statement in vs. 27b.[153] Mary does not take the disciple into *her* house; he takes her into *his*.

Some commentators who reject the mariological interpretation prefer to connect the deeper meaning of this passage with the significance of the beloved disciple for the coming community. Here, too, as elsewhere (see the comments on 13:23ff.), however, they ascribe to his conduct not historical but merely symbolic significance. This occurs most radically, of course, when the whole figure of the beloved disciple is viewed as a symbol and denied all historicity. For example, Bultmann regards this disciple as the symbolic representation of Gentile Christianity. In this incident at the cross, then, Mary symbolizes Jewish Christianity that overcomes the offense of the cross. The Gentile Christianity represented by the beloved disciple is charged to honor this Jewish Christianity as its mother from whom it has come, while Jewish Christianity is charged to let itself be taken up and integrated into the "home" of Gentile Christianity, that is, into the membership of the one great fellowship of the church.[154] But this view has

152. On this see, at length, Brown, *Comm.* II, pp. 922ff., who himself presents a "mariological" interpretation as well.

153. Schnackenburg, a Catholic, writes: "Finally the scene beneath the cross is also unable to carry the burden of proof [of Mary's motherhood of the church]; for the main point remains that Mary is entrusted to the disciple and he receives her as his own" (*Comm.* III, p. 280).

154. So Bultmann, *Comm.*, p. 673.

found virtually no support because neither here nor elsewhere in the text can one find any point of contact for this supposed typically Gentile Christian character of the beloved disciple. The contrary, we daresay, is the case.[155]

Others also see in the disciple whom Jesus loved, here as in 13:23ff., a figure from the later (Johannine) community, its founder perhaps, but one who *in the Gospel* plays a nonhistorical, symbolic role, that of the ideal disciple projected back into the life of Jesus — all this, of course, to confirm his authority and the significance of the community he represents. In this passage he is that "ideal disciple"; he, with the community he founded ("his house"), already have this significance, which is normative also for other Christians. On the significance ("symbolic," of course) to be accorded to Mary in this connection, opinions again vary widely.[156]

Even apart from the problems that occur in connection with this last point,[157] this idealistic-symbolic interpretation meets with what we regard as insuperable objections, as it has already in connection with 13:23ff. First, the arguments against the historicity of this passage are so unconvincing that they cannot bear the weight of the symbolic view.[158] Second, this abrupt transition of genre from historical narrative to symbolic narrative is a significant exegetical problem, particularly since the immediately following verses lay so much stress on the eyewitness report of the same disciple (vs. 35). And third, this symbolization is also a radical *theological* shift in the point of the story. Mary and the beloved disciple symbolize — in the final act of the dying Jesus in his love for his own to the end — the ideal disciple and the community he founded. The christological perspective is thus no longer primary and dominant but receives its content from ecclesiology, a reversal that may well be called crucial in the interpretation of the whole Gospel.

---

155. On this see, at greater length, the comments below on 21:24ff.

156. According to some, she is here the symbol of believers from the time of Jesus' earthly revelation who were taken into the house of the beloved disciples (the later community led by him) to be further instructed in the ongoing work of the exalted Lord. These, conversely, would then preserve and strengthen the ties of the community to "pre-Easter" tradition. Hence the double saying, "Here is your son" and "Here is your mother." For this construction, see at length T. Witkamp, *Jezus van Nazareth in de gemeente van Johannes,* 1986, pp. 335, 346ff., with mention of other authors, like B. Lindars, who think along these lines.

157. Schnackenburg, a Catholic author, thinks that more content (than "not a few" Protestant exegetes give it) needs to be given to the *active* motherhood of Mary, which he hears in the words "Here is your mother." He thinks the intent of the saying may also be to remind the Christian community of the "material womb" from which Jesus himself has sprung, that is, the Judaism represented by Mary (*Comm.* III, pp. 278-82).

158. Witkamp *(Jezus van Nazareth)* mentions three such arguments and refers in this connection to the work of Dauer *(Die Passionsgeschichte im Johannesevangelium)*: a) There is no Synoptic parallel (which, however, cannot be a criterion for historicity); b) there is said to be a contradiction with 16:32 (but if one takes a strict view of 16:32, then 18:15ff., 25ff., which do have Synoptic parallels, would have to be unhistorical); and c) it would be unlikely for Jesus to have waited until this moment before making provision for his mother (but according to the Evangelist this act of caring derives its meaning precisely from its character as last act before the statement that "all was now finished," vs. 28).

19:28-37
". . . Died . . ."

28   As already noted in our comments on vss. 26f., it is clear from the introductory words of this new pericope how much meaning the Evangelist attaches to Jesus' words of farewell to Mary and his beloved disciple in the framework of the work of salvation that Jesus has been sent to accomplish. This has been the concluding act of that work, and it leaves nothing more to do for the completion of that work.[159]

Nevertheless, between the reference to Jesus knowing that "all was finished" (vs. 28a; cf. 13:1; 18:4) and his statement "it is finished" in vs. 30 is inserted the passage about his thirst. Mark and Matthew also mention Jesus' thirst, but with no words from Jesus or reference to Scripture. Here it is the reference to Scripture that stands in the foreground as the motive of Jesus' complaint about thirst: "that Scripture should come to its (final) fulfillment."[160] The intent is not to add something to the preceding "all was now finished" but to show how Jesus, even in his final moments when there was nothing more left for him "to do," still in his thirst, one of the most terrible torments of death by crucifixion, fulfilled Scripture. Although Ps. 69:21 is clearly in mind here (see the comments on vs. 29), it is not quoted. This may suggest that the reference is not to fulfillment of a specific detail but to the entire picture of the suffering righteous one in Psalm 69, which John repeatedly cites (cf. 2:17; 15:25; see, however, also Ps. 22:15).

In describing the depth of Jesus' suffering the Fourth Gospel nowhere comes closer to the final word on the cross in Matthew and Mark, Ps. 22:1, than he does here.[161] Although it is probably characteristic for the Fourth Gospel that the word of extreme forsakenness in Psalm 22 is lacking, from vs. 28 it is again evident (cf., e.g., 18:11) that the regal power and authority — so prominent in John — with which Jesus accepts his suffering and goes out to meet his enemies in no way means that he is fundamentally immune to that suffering and passes through it unaffected. "I thirst" is not a proof of how strictly Jesus

---

159. This is indicated by the word ἤδη, which we have translated "now," but also carries the meaning "now already." The phrase μετὰ τοῦτο also points in this direction.

160. τελειωθῇ. In every other case πληρόω is used for fulfillment of Scripture. Some scholars (e.g., Bultmann) regard the word used here as synonymous. Still, the exception to the rule seems not to be without meaning. The reference here is to that which is final and definitive; see also the translation of BAGD (p. 809): "in order that the scripture might receive its final fulfillment."

161. This in contrast with the view of Loisy and others that in John the death of Jesus is not a portrayal of suffering, shame, or total abandonment — as in the Synoptics — but that there is a cry of victory in the last word ("it is finished") — as a substitute for the "defeat" in Matthew and Mark. Against this see also Brown, *Comm.* II, p. 931.

fulfilled Scripture but a lament wrung from him out of the depth of his suffering in which his solidarity with those who had lamented their suffering in Scripture consists above all in the fact that he and they took their suffering to God and laid it out before him (e.g., Pss. 69:19; 63:1). That Jesus knew, better than anyone else before or after him, that in his suffering he was fulfilling a divine calling is evident from his last word on the cross (vs. 30). But this in no way detracts from the deep reality of his suffering and solidarity with his own. It is rather the very foundation of Jesus' last word.[162]

29 The details described here, specifically the "sour wine"[163] offered to Jesus, refer to Ps. 69:21 ("For my thirst they gave me vinegar to drink").[164] In Psalm 69 the presentation of this drink is an act of hostility to aggravate suffering (possibly because of its effect; "poison for food, vinegar for my thirst"). Here it evidently does not have that connotation. All the stress is on Jesus' thirst and the soldiers' response.[165] Admittedly, the manner in which the drink is offered does depict the extremity of Jesus' situation. A sponge soaked in sour wine is attached to the top of a stalk of hyssop[166] and so held to Jesus' mouth as the only way to give him a drink.

30 With this, however, the end came for Jesus. After saying "It is finished," "he bowed his head and gave up his spirit." This whole scene typifies his death as a final *act* of self-offering done after he had finished the work that God had given him to do (17:4; cf. 4:34; 13:3; 10:18; 14:31). It is also to this act that the "all" of vs. 28 refers. Accordingly, we cannot weaken "It is finished" by hearing in it only a sigh of relief that the end had been reached or as an indication of the personal completion that Jesus is said to have reached on his journey.[167] It is precisely as a reference to the task the

162. Others, to bring out the "deeper" meaning of "I thirst," relate it to the cup saying in 18:11: "Jesus intends to drink the cup of suffering and death to the last dregs. Therefore, he also 'takes' the drink presented to him" (Schnackenburg, *Comm.* III, pp. 283f.; cf. also Brown, *Comm.* II, p. 930). The comparison with the "last drops" is striking, but the image in 18:11 is *symbolically* hard to connect with the words "I thirst."

163. ὄξος, sour wine or vinegar, a cheap diluted sort of wine favored by the poor (cf. BAGD s.v.).

164. In the Septuagint, εἰς τὴν δίψαν μου ἐπότισάν με ὄξος.

165. On this see at length Blinzler, *Prozeß,* p. 370, n. 50.

166. ὑσσώπῳ. Precisely what is meant is not clear because the hyssop plant does not develop stalks, which is what is apparently intended here. In Matthew and Mark the reference is more generally to a reed (see, however, Blinzler, *Prozeß,* p. 370, n. 51). Some therefore follow the ancient conjecture: ὑσσῷ = javelin, which is very attractive but without foundation in the manuscripts. Others believe that the reference here is to (a) hyssop (stalk) because of the use of hyssop in purification — according to Ex. 12:22 especially around Passover. The Evangelist is thought to have chosen this word as an allusion to the blood of the Passover lamb, which was applied to lintels and doorposts with a bundle of hyssop leaves — here in relation to Jesus as Passover lamb. But this is far-fetched, especially because it is by no means certain that the Fourth Gospel thinks of Jesus as the Passover lamb.

167. Against this "Gnostic" explanation, see also Becker, *Comm.* II, pp. 594f.

Father gave Jesus to perform that this cry indicated for him not only the end of the road that he had to travel but also the completed work of salvation that he had accomplished for his own as the new foundation laid once for all for the life of the world.[168]

31 The now following section, which is continued in the narrative of the burial in vss. 38-42, is devoted to the question: "What happened to Jesus' body?"[169] First it is the Jews in their request to Pilate, then the soldiers at Pilate's behest, and finally Joseph of Arimathea and Nicodemus who, each in their own way, play a role in what happened to Jesus' body.

First, then, "the Jews," that is, here again, the leaders of the people, who had closely followed the course of events (cf. vs. 21). What caused them concern — since it was the day of preparation (Friday) and the sabbath was at hand — was that the bodies of those who had been crucified would remain on the crosses on the Sabbath. And since "the day of *that* sabbath"[170] was "great" — a designation that was especially applied to the sabbath on which the firstfruits were brought (Lv. 23:11; see below), they again turned to Pilate, this time with the respectable request that "the legs[171] of the crucified men might be broken and their bodies removed [from the crosses]." The custom was to break the legs with a heavy mallet (the *crurifragium*) to thus — however horribly — end their suffering, but the Romans did not always do this. Sometimes, as a deterrent to other malefactors, they left those they had crucified hanging on the cross until they had died, and after. For "the Jews" apparently only respect for the coming great sabbath played a role. According to the law of Moses, to which the practice of crucifixion is not known, a hanged person, regardless of the day, could not be left hanging into the night (Dt. 21:22). We are not told whether the Jews, in making their request to Pilate, explicitly referred to the sabbath. In any case Pilate acceded to their request.

Indirectly vs. 31, as stated earlier (see the comments on 13:1ff.), contains an important indication that Jesus died on the fifteenth of Nisan. If the day on which the firstfruits were dedicated — according to the Pharisaic tradition, the sixteenth of Nisan — coincided with the sabbath, then people spoke of "the great sabbath." Therefore the day that preceded this sabbath, the day on which Jesus was crucified must have been the fifteenth of Nisan.

---

168. For other understandings — meaningful as such but not rooted in the text — of "it is finished," see, e.g., Brown, *Comm.* II, pp. 907f.; Dauer, *Passionsgeschichte,* pp. 211f. For example, the eternal sabbath rest now — on this Friday — begins for Jesus as well as the completion of the work which until now he has had to do, even on the sabbath (cf. 5:17).

169. So Becker, *Comm.* II, p. 596.

170. ἡ ἡμέρα ἐκείνου τοῦ σαββάτου.

171. τὰ σκέλη, "leg bones" (cf. BAGD s.v.).

32-34 But Jesus, unlike the other men who had been crucified with him, had already died. The soldiers who were charged to carry out the Jews' request, observing this, did not break Jesus' legs. Before further commenting on this fact, the Evangelist first mentions something that was no less important to him, namely that one of the soldiers, apparently to be sure Jesus was dead, thrust his spear into Jesus' side, and "at once blood and water came out."

These last words are interpreted in very different ways. Some regard the occurrence as a miracle of profound significance: the streams of blood and water that flowed from Jesus' dead body are said to indicate supernaturally the two sacraments of baptism and eucharist.[173] But there is no reason for thinking of a miracle here. What we are told need not mean any more than that a bloody and watery substance came out of the spear wound, which to those present confirmed that Jesus was dead. It is doubtful that the occurrence conceals any deeper meaning. A connection with 7:38[174] does not establish this deeper meaning because the words used there ("out of his belly will flow") refer not to Jesus but to the operation of the Spirit in believers.[175] A connection with 1 Jn. 5:6,[176] which mentions blood and water (though in reverse order), or with other passages in which water or the blood of Jesus appear in metaphors for redemption is too often made only on the basis of a similarity in the sounds of the words. And when the Evangelist comes to explain the redemptive significance of what occurred with the body of Jesus in the light of Scripture and as seen by an eyewitness (vss. 36f.), he mentions only that Jesus' body was pierced and that his bones were not broken; there is no reference to blood and water. Accordingly, it is most arbitrary, as all too often exegetes have done,[177] to relate

---

172. καταγνύναι τὰ σκέλη. For the form of the aorist subjunctive κατεαγῶσιν, see BDF §§66.2; 101 (s.v. ἀγνύναι). ἀρθῶσιν (grammatically connected incorrectly with τὰ σκέλη) obviously refers to the removal of the dead bodies from the cross.

173. So, e.g., Bultmann, *Comm.*, pp. 677f. The Church Fathers, including Origen, and later authors, including Thomas Aquinas, and later Lagrange, Godet, and Loisy took this event to be a miracle.

174. So, e.g., Schnackenburg: The promise in 7:38 "now finds its fulfillment: Out of Jesus' body (κοιλία!) flow blood and water, a life-giving river" (*Comm.* III, p. 294). More generally (with no reference to 7:38) also Morris: The Fourth Gospel makes "consistent reference in the use of both terms [blood and water] to the life that Christ gives. We conclude, then, that John is reminding us that life, real life, comes through Christ's death" (*Comm.* p. 820); so also Barrett, *Comm.*, p. 556.

175. On this see at length pp. 274f. above.

176. So, e.g., Calvin. He rejects the idea of a miracle, but believes that the Evangelist intended with this precise description of the natural occurrence to point believers, in keeping with 1 Jn. 5:6, to "the true atonement" and "the true washing" brought by the death of Jesus, in the same way as occurs through the sacraments. "For this reason I do not object to Augustine writing that our sacraments have flowed from Christ's side" (*Comm.* II, p. 186).

177. For the history of exposition in the ancient church see the very competent treatment of this passage — still convincing in its refutation of the symbolic view — in Zahn, *Comm.*, pp. 663f.

vs. 35 ("he who saw it . . .") in particular to vs. 34c ("blood and water") and
not to the whole of vss. 32-34. That the reference is to the whole appears clearly
from the beginning of vs. 36: "These things [plural] occurred. . . ."[178]

Admittedly, this still does not tell us what moved the Evangelist to discuss
these particular physical details — "water and blood" — so realistically and
at such length. Some commentators see here the rejection of a docetic view,[179]
one that teaches that as the Son of God Jesus did not have a real physical body
and therefore did not really die.[180] But the intent of this passage is clearly
positive (cf. vs. 35c), and other parts of this Gospel make it hard to demonstrate
a deliberately anti-Gnostic intent. Therefore, this last part of vs. 34 can best be
understood generally as one more proof of the trustworthiness — attested with
so much emphasis in vs. 35 — of the person who with his own eyes saw the
things related in vss. 32-34 and could therefore testify of them in detail.[181]

35 Verses 35f. speak further and in a more intentional and concrete
manner about the eyewitness testimony underlying the narrative of Jesus' death
and about the readers' interest therein. That "he who saw this" is "the disciple
whom Jesus loved" is generally agreed. Vss. 26f. readily suggest this identification. The witness is identified as male, and no other acquaintances or disciples
are mentioned as standing at the cross. The idea that one of the soldiers is this
eyewitness is very unlikely. Moreover, 21:24 is important for the identification
of this witness as the beloved disciple, for there, in similar words, it is said of
this disciple: "This is the disciple who is testifying to these things . . . and we
know that his testimony is true." Everything, then, suggests that the eyewitness
of 19:35 and the disciple intended in 21:24 are one and the same person.

After "and his testimony is true" we then read, "and he knows that he
is telling the truth — that you also may believe." The much discussed question
here is: Who is meant by this second "he"[182] who knows that the first speaks
the truth? Some think that this climactic "he" can only refer to Jesus or God.[183]
But, although such use of "he" occurs elsewhere in John, it always appears in
contexts that provide an immediate point of contact for it, without which it
could not be understood in that sense. Scholars therefore usually assume that
this "he" is the narrator.[184] Thus the Evangelist, with an appeal to himself,
seeks to confirm the trustworthiness of the narrative as emphatically as possible.

---

178. ταῦτα, not τοῦτο.

179. See also 1 Jn. 4:2f.; 5:6.

180. For this antithetical view of vs. 34 see, e.g., Zahn, *Comm.,* pp. 663f.; and especially
the lengthy defense in G. Richter, *Studien zum Johannesevangelium,* 1977, pp. 120-42. Against
this view is Schnackenburg, *Comm.* III, pp. 462f., nn. 85, 89.

181. For this interpretation see also Becker, *Comm.,* pp. 599f.

182. ἐκεῖνος.

183. So especially older interpreters like Erasmus but also Lagrange, Zahn, Grosheide, and
Hoskyns; also Bultmann, who believes, however, that the text is corrupt; see below.

184. Cf. BDF §291.6.

Still it remains remarkable that the Evangelist, having first established the "objective" trustworthiness of what the beloved disciple has attested (perfect), then adds that he himself ("subjectively") knows that what the disciple "is saying" (present) is true. How can the Evangelist thus "swear," as it were, that this witness is reliable unless he himself is this witness, the beloved disciple? This last conclusion is therefore the most plausible. The Evangelist himself then indirectly says of himself what others testify of him directly, and with the same words, in 21:24: "he is the disciple" (the one loved by Jesus) "who is testifying to these things" and of whom "we know that his testimony is true."[185] In the same way, the purpose he attributes to the beloved disciple in 19:35 ("so that you may believe") is the same as the purpose he has for writing his Gospel (20:31) and is expressed in the same words.

In this way, one can also understand the transition in vs. 35 from the perfect ("has testified") to the present ("knows," "is telling"). First the Evangelist speaks as the person who at one time stood by the cross, saw with his own eyes what has just been related, and testified to it — not only after many years but from the moment he saw it; "and that testimony is [and was] true" to the present day. Then he speaks of the present in the following words: "and [therefore] *that* [witness] knows that he is telling the truth" — now that as Evangelist he writes of it to his readers. "And he" marks the shift from eyewitness to Evangelist, so "he knows that he is telling the truth" is not a superfluous repetition but has a new and permanent relevance for the readers now being addressed: "so that you also may believe." Finally, that the Evangelist speaks so anonymously and in the third person about himself is of course striking but entirely in keeping with the anonymous and sometimes allusive way in which the beloved disciple is spoken of (cf. 18:15 and 1:37, 40). His person remains hidden behind his testimony (see at greater length the comments following 21:24).

The closing words, "so that you also may believe," as stated earlier,

---

185. Bultmann (*Comm.*, p. 679) follows the same reasoning, with the fundamental difference that he regards 19:35, like 21:24, as the product of a later redactor who sought to enhance the authority of the Fourth Gospel by attributing it to the beloved disciple. Bultmann regards this attribution as impossible, regarding the beloved disciple as an unhistorical ideal figure and the Fourth Gospel as clearly not the work of an eyewitness. See further in the comments below on 21:24.

Others as well, such as Schnackenburg, regard 19:35 as a later insertion, not the work of the Evangelist, since the Evangelist normally introduces his comments differently. But Schnackenburg's real objections obviously arise from the idea that this entire identification of the author with the beloved disciple is solely based on the later tendency, said to be manifest also in 21:24, to give greater weight by this means to the authority of this Gospel.

The context, however, gives a clear indication of the originality of 19:35: without it, vs. 36 would have to connect with vs. 34; but the "for" of vs. 36 clearly reflects on the conclusion of vs. 35 and hangs in the air without vs. 35.

strongly resemble vss. 20:30, 31 and are to be understood in the same way. The church's faith[186] rests on the eyewitness account of the disciples, who were called and destined for that purpose (cf. 17:21; 15:27) so that the members of the community along with these disciples may by faith be fellow participants in the eternal life revealed in that account (cf. 1 Jn. 1:3; Jn. 20:31). The purpose clause introduced by "so that" is intended not only to confirm the church's faith in the historicity of Jesus' death on the cross or of the details mentioned here but to direct its attention to the fulfillment of prophecy in those details as proof of the degree to which God's involvement with and saving counsel for his Son is manifest in the particular manner of Jesus' dying. Of this, finally, vss. 36 and 37 speak.

36, 37   That "so that you may believe" in vs. 35 is thus focused on the fulfillment of prophecy is proven by the causal "for" with which vs. 36 begins. It is because of that divine dispensation and intent that the death of Jesus — an offense and folly to the natural mind — is for the Christian community the ground and confirmation of its belief that Jesus is the Christ, the Son of God.

In support of this belief the Evangelist cites two Scripture texts.[187] The first relates to what was narrated in vs. 33. The Evangelist presumably has in mind Ps. 34:20, where as proof of God's special care for the righteous it is said: "He keeps all his bones; not one of them is broken."[188] Many expositors see here, instead, the Mosaic law that all the bones of the Passover lamb must be intact (Ex. 12:46;[189] Nu. 9:12[190]). Thus Jesus is described as the true Passover lamb, which would be especially striking if Jesus died on the fourteenth of Nisan, the day on which the Passover lambs were presented in the temple and killed. But this view is certainly doubtful. Jesus was killed not on the fourteenth of Nisan but on the fifteenth, the day of the Passover feast itself, not the day when the lambs were presented and killed. Furthermore, this pericope contains no allusion to Passover,[191] and Jesus' death is not related to Passover or the Passover lamb anywhere else in this Gospel.[192] Further, a citation from the

---

186. As in 20:31, so here, too, the reading πιστεύητε is to be preferred over πιστεύσητε; see, e.g., Schnackenburg, *Comm.* III, p. 463, n. 88: "An instant of 'coming to believe' is hardly intended." The present tense points to the continuation and reinforcement of the faith of the existing community, entirely in keeping with the aim of the Fourth Gospel (see the comments below on 20:30f.).

187. Very clearly intended by γραφή here; witness the words "And again another Scripture says" (vs. 37).

188. Septuagint: ἕν ἐξ αὐτῶν οὐ συντριβήσεται.

189. Septuagint: καὶ ὀστοῦν οὐ συντρίψετε ἀπ᾽ αὐτοῦ.

190. Septuagint: καὶ ὀστοῦν οὐ συντρίψουσιν ἀπ᾽ αὐτοῦ.

191. "Which nevertheless would have been so natural" (Bultmann, *Comm.*, p. 677, n. 1) if the Passover lamb were intended here.

192. Not even in 1:29 (see at greater length pp. 71f. above, with reference to Dodd, *Interpretation of the Fourth Gospel*, p. 233).

Psalms is more in line with the preceding references to Scripture than a precept from the Pentateuch, a body of writings that is cited nowhere else in John.

If, then, Psalm 34 is being cited, then the Evangelist thus refers (as with the next citation) to the turning point, begun with the death of Jesus, in God's dealings with his Son. The Son is no longer the object of the world's hostility. From now on, now that he has accomplished his task, he is the object of God's special care. This care is extended even to his body, which is no longer subject to the cruel insolence of his enemies but kept from further mutilation and about to be returned to his friends. The following citation, from the prophecy in Zc. 12:10-14, speaks of the same reversal: great mourning is predicted over "him whom they have pierced," a figure strongly reminiscent of the man of sorrows in Isaiah 53.[193]

The connection between the words of this citation of Zc. 12:11 ("they shall look on him whom they have pierced") and what is meant in the Old Testament text is not certain.[194] It *is* clear — and in agreement with the intent of Zechariah 12 — that "they shall look on him" is to be understood here as: look with contrition, reverence, awe, and (possibly) horror at the one whom they have treated with violence (cf. Rv. 1:7; Mt. 24:30). In the prophecy this contrition is the result of "the outpouring of the spirit of compassion and supplication," which in the time of salvation announced by the prophet will bring the people at all levels to repentance with respect to "him whom they have pierced" (Zc. 12:10a). In John this redemptive significance of "looking on" does not come to explicit expression. One can also take it as a threat of what awaits those who have pierced Jesus (Rv. 1:7; cf. Jn. 8:27). But in the way in which "looking on" emerges here we are not dealing first of all with salvation or disaster but with *the one who is pierced* appearing before the eyes of all as the one lifted up by God. "The one lifted up ... is not to be overlooked by mankind. They will and must look to him whom they have pierced, for their salvation or destruction."[195]

At the same time this says that the fulfillment of the prophecy intended by the Evangelist is not limited to the piercing of Jesus' side. The fulfillment concerns the reversal that Jesus, precisely as the one who was pierced, will bring about among those who have inflicted this violence on him; a reversal that in Zc. 13:1 is described in its saving significance: "On that day a fountain

---

193. On the possibility of identifying this figure in the time of the prophet, see, e.g., J. Ridderbos, *De kleine Profeten* III, 1968, p. 170.

194. The translation of Zc. 12:11 is difficult. The most obvious rendering, "they will look on me [i.e., God], whom they have pierced," hardly makes good sense. Some, assuming corruption of the text, propose as a conjecture "on him" in place of "on me," which would completely agree with our text. Others place a period behind "on me" and then continue: "He whom they have pierced — they will mourn over him" (see J. Ridderbos, *De kleine Profeten*, p. 169).

195. Schnackenburg, *Comm.* III, p. 294.

will be opened for the house of David . . . to cleanse them from sin and impurity." Accordingly, in Jn. 19:37, more than in the first citation of Scripture (vs. 36), the reversal begun with Jesus' death is described in its all-encompassing character. The reversal consists in the fact that from now on, because of Jesus' self-offering in death, he is the one whom no one seeking salvation can bypass. In the one who was pierced (Zechariah 12) God places everyone before the great decision, just as that occurs in the man of sorrows of Isaiah 53 (cf. Jn. 12:38) and in the Son of man who had to be lifted up on the cross as Moses lifted up the serpent in the wilderness (3:14). Thus this last double "fulfillment" of Scripture shows that the manner of Jesus' death has heralded the great reversal that is in effect from now on as the response of God and of people to the "It is finished" of the Son of God.

In that light, finally, we can also understand why precisely for "these things" the Evangelist so emphatically appeals to the irrefutable testimony of him "who saw this" (vs. 35): so that the readers will not only be informed about the "that" and "how" of Jesus' death but so that they will "believe" in these things as the way in which Jesus was *lifted up* by the Father on the cross, so that everyone who believes in him may have eternal life.

19:38-42
". . . and Was Buried"

With the words "after these things" the account of Jesus' burial begins. This account concludes the passion narrative and forms the transition to and preparation for the resurrection narrative. What stands out here is the special care devoted to Jesus' body, along with the honorable character of the burial. The description in vss. 32-37, especially in the citations of Scripture there, of the reversal that had its beginning immediately with Jesus' death is continued in the account of the burial. But we can also already detect in this account points of contact for what follows (cf. vs. 40 with 20:5; vs. 41 with 20:15).

John's report largely agrees with that of the Synoptics: the initiative of Joseph of Arimathea, the burial in an as-yet-unused tomb, the background of the imminent Sabbath. But there are also important differences: the involvement of Nicodemus alongside Joseph, the use of a large amount of myrrh and aloes by the two men, and that no women are mentioned as witnesses at the entombment. But even in what John has in common with the Synoptics, as for example in the mention of Joseph, the details are different and John's complete independence of the Synoptic tradition and his own kerygmatic purpose stand out.

38 Joseph's request to Pilate for permission to dispose of Jesus' body is reported first, as in the Synoptics. "Of Arimathea"[196] evidently refers to his place of origin and not to his place of residence. Mark and Luke mention his membership in the Sanhedrin (cf. Lk. 23:51). That Jesus was buried in Joseph's own tomb (Mt. 27:60) suggests that Joseph was a resident of Jerusalem. His influential position meant that he could risk approaching Pilate with this request (cf. Mk. 15:43). John does not stress Joseph's prominent position but describes him as "a disciple of Jesus, though a secret one, for fear of the Jews." According to some interpreters, one must therefore view Joseph's conduct in the light of 12:42, 43, which also mentions secret believers among the rulers of the Jews who "loved human glory more than the glory that comes from God" and so remained, even with their "belief" in Jesus, in the wrong camp. The same is said to be true of Nicodemus (see the comments on vs. 39). That they now, after Jesus' death, come forward is said to indicate that they showed their colors too late, had reached a dead end, and "were unable to look beyond the grave."[197]

The context, however, points in another direction. Joseph's activity is rather to be seen in the light of the reversal pointed out above, the reversal that came into effect when Jesus died. Many interpreters[198] therefore point with more justification to 12:32: "When I am lifted up from the earth, I will draw all people to myself," though that seems to relate especially to Jesus' future activity from heaven. But here the reference is still to Jesus lifted up on the cross or, as vs. 37 has it, to "looking on him whom they have pierced." As we have said on vs. 37, this "looking on" and the reversal inherent in it is not limited to a threat from Jesus' immediate enemies ("the Jews") but is intended, at least in the light of Zechariah 12, as proof of a reversal in the attitude of all Israel as they "see him whom they have pierced," that is, as they become aware of what they have done to him, to the one sent by God. That at this stage Joseph of Arimathea (and soon also Nicodemus) come forward as such — as representatives of the true Israel — illustrates the nature of this reversal all the more strikingly. The report — perhaps also the sight — of Jesus' death gives Joseph the courage he lacked earlier to stand up for Jesus as his disciple — proof that Jesus' power as the one pierced extends into the Sanhedrin and that the inscription on his cross will from now on make itself felt in its true, divinely intended meaning. Therefore, while Jesus' closest disciples are still powerlessly looking on at what is happening or are not to be found because of their still unconquered fear of "the Jews" (cf. 20:19), Joseph comes forward first. He knows how to

---

196. Arimathea is usually identified with Ramathaim-zophim, mentioned in 1 Sa. 1:1 (Ramah in vs. 19). On the probable location see Brown, *Comm.* II, p. 938; Schnackenburg, *Comm.* III, p. 464, n. 105, and the literature mentioned there.

197. For this view see at length pp. 282-85 above.

198. Such as Calvin (see also below on vs. 39) and also more recent commentators such as Brown.

reach Pilate and takes the initiative to pay the dead Jesus the respect due to him, regardless of what this will cost him in "human glory" (12:43).

Pilate consents (after summoning the centurion to reassure himself that Jesus is dead, Mk. 15:44). Until the end he holds life and death power over Jesus. But all his power is subject to the great provison of Jesus' last word to him (19:11). Then, with the road clear for Joseph, Joseph no longer hesitates and before the eyes of anyone who wants to see it he makes his way to Golgotha "and to the body." Some important manuscripts have the verbs in the plural, probably because of an assumption that Joseph could not do what was needed unaided. But it was he who took on himself the responsibility for all.

39, 40   That Joseph did not have to face the task alone is clear from the new appearance of Nicodemus. Nicodemus was also a member of the Sanhedrin (3:1; 7:50f.). That he accompanied Joseph therefore reinforces what we have said about vs. 38. The Evangelist introduces Nicodemus's involvement, as he did Joseph's, with a reference to his earlier involvement with Jesus: "who had at first come to him by night." We have seen that we cannot include him with Joseph among the crypto-believers referred to in 12:40.[199] Still, in this reference to "by night" and "at first" there is an indication of the big difference between that past and the present. Seeing Jesus' miracles (3:2) could not bring Nicodemus to openly join Jesus' disciples, but Jesus' death can. Nicodemus thus continues the line of his earlier public action on behalf of Jesus in the Sanhedrin (7:50ff.), this time not merely as a judge taking a stand in support of Jesus' civil rights but now, like Joseph, as one driven by the impact of Jesus' death.[200] There is no longer any possibility of misunderstanding Nicodemus's intentions or his assessment of Jesus. He comes, bringing "a mixture of myrrh and aloes, a hundred [Roman] pounds in weight," as though to extend to Jesus the royal honor due to him.

"Myrrh" is a fragrant resin, "aloes" a quickly drying aromatic tree sap. Some interpreters think that the mixture of the two was for embalming,[201] others that it was for anointing.[202] There is no mention here of embalming or anointing

---

199. In 3:1ff. he is not a believer (cf. vss. 10f.), and in 7:50 he is not among the secret believers. On these secret believers (according to the two-level theory, they were projected back into the Gospel from within the later community) see at length pp. 282ff. above.

200. Calvin, commenting on 19:38, asks (*Comm.* II, p. 188): "Where do they suddenly get such heroic courage from, that in the last straits they boldly come out into the open?" He answers: "It is . . . certain that this was done by a heavenly impulse, so that those who were afraid to give Him due honour while He was alive now hasten to His dead body as if they were new men." "This shows," he continues, "the truth of what Christ Himself said, 'Except a grain of wheat die, it abideth alone; but if it die, it beareth much fruit' (John 12:24). Here we have an outstanding proof that His death was even more quickening than His life."

201. So, e.g., BAGD s.v. ἀλόη, μίγμα, and σμύρνα.

202. Cf. Strack/Billerbeck II, p. 53: embalming was not customary among Jews, as it was among Egyptians.

(cf. Mk. 16:2). It says only that "they bound [Jesus' body] in linen cloths with the spices": the powdered mixture was spread between the cloths as a pleasant-smelling antidote against the stench of the corpse.[203] The binding presumably relates to the wrapping of Jesus' hands and feet (cf. 11:44, which also mentions the separate napkin, as in 20:7).[204] "As is the burial custom of the Jews" is added for the benefit of readers not familiar with Jewish customs.

With that, apparently, the disposal of Jesus' body is completed for the Fourth Evangelist. It is carried out by Joseph and Nicodemus and possibly others, who would be included in the plural verbs in vss. 40 and 42. From Mark and Luke, though not from Matthew, we get the impression that this entombment was temporary: on the third day the women go to the tomb with spices to anoint Jesus' body (Mk. 16:1). Several proposals have been made to harmonize the accounts: for example, the women were not present and so did not know that Joseph and Nicodemus had prepared the body for the tomb. But the story is told from clearly different viewpoints in John and the Synoptics. In John, the abundance of spices is proof of the reversal not only in the conduct of Joseph and Nicodemus but also in the way in which the Father deals with his Son after the "It is finished." In Mark and Luke the spices — on the third day — serve rather as proof, along with the women's astonished questions, from the other side: "Why do you seek the living among the dead?" In John the linen cloths play a clear role, in view of 20:5f., that the Synoptics' shroud does not play.

Did these differing details work their way through the tradition to land in different places and then begin to function in those places? Or is this another proof that the Fourth Evangelist was more precisely informed about some matters than his fellow Evangelists before him? In a case like the one under discussion it seems harder to believe that the Fourth Evangelist slanted the details to suit his theological interests — or even created them — than that the Synoptics (witness also that they differ among themselves in the details of the story) had less precise and consistent information than John.

41, 42   In the account of the burial proper the same line is continued. When the special care of Jesus' friends for his body is completed, there is for

---

203. So, e.g., Schnackenburg, with an appeal to Blinzler's description of Jesus' burial (*Comm.* III, p. 349).

204. ὀθονίοις; cf. 20:5f.; Lk. 24:12. The Synoptics mention a "linen shroud" (σινδών) that Joseph purchased and wrapped Jesus' body in, which gives a somewhat different picture. Among Catholic interpreters there is much discussion of the difference because of the shroud of Turin. An assortment of unconvincing attempts have been made to argue that ὀθόνια in John and σινδών in the Synoptics represent the same burial garment (see at length Brown and Schnackenburg). It is clear that John (with a view to 20:5f.) was especially interested in the burial cloths (cf. Lk. 24:12), from which also the risen Lazarus had to be freed (cf. 11:44). But it is doubtful that these burial cloths were the only covering for bodies thus buried. In the case of Lazarus there is mention only of the bandages in which his hands and feet were wrapped. But this seems to assume rather than exclude the presence of a shroud.

him, close to where he was crucified, a tomb, one that lay ready to receive him. And it is not a tomb fitting for a crucified criminal, for whom even a mass grave would do. It is, rather, in the shadowed isolation of a supervised (20:15) garden. That the tomb has never been used also fits the providential, sacred character of what now takes place there. When Jesus has completed his task on earth, everything in the immediate surroundings proves to be available to him as though it has long been reserved and made ready for him (cf. Mk. 11:2).

But the story of the earthly Jesus is also determined to the end by human factors and considerations. There was — one must admit — little time for any other choice. It was already Friday evening. People had to hurry their work to get it done before the sabbath began. Again the Evangelist mentions "the Jewish day of preparation"[205] as the time within which the action had to be completed if a violation of the Jewish law was to be avoided, the same reason that "the Jews" wanted to hasten the death of the crucified (vs. 31). Joseph and Nicodemus had to get Jesus buried in time. It is hard to say whether the Evangelist, in this repeated reference to the approaching sabbath, has in mind a divine providence giving rest to Jesus after he had completed his task on the sixth day. It is clear in any case that the time between Jesus' death and his resurrection is in the Fourth Gospel a transitional period. The descent of the Son of man reaches its lowest point in a human tomb, but also finds there its passage and transition to his ascent to glory, though the signs that point out this transition in Jesus' entombment only become visible in the light that is still to come, "on the first day of the week," the first words of the next chapter.

---

205. παρασκευή; see above on vs. 14. There is no question of a Passover preparation. The reference is only to Friday. John is in complete agreement with the Synoptics here (cf. Mk. 15:42; Lk. 23:54; see also Bultmann, *Comm.*, in loc.).

20

The Empty Tomb and
the Appearances of the Risen One

20:1-10

Two Disciples Visit the Tomb

From the manner in which the Fourth Evangelist describes events on "the first day of the week" (20:1ff.) and thereafter we again see the extent to which, as a transmitter and interpreter of the tradition and as a narrator, he goes his own way, one that differs from that of the Synoptics. To some degree he describes the same events (Jesus' appearance to Mary Magdalene, vss. 11-18; to the assembled disciples, vss. 19-23), but does so in a way uniquely his own. And he relates other events not found elsewhere, in which Peter and "the disciple whom Jesus loved" appear (vss. 1-10; ch. 21).

This independent presentation is immediately recognized from the opening of the resurrection narrative. Like the Synoptics the Fourth Evangelist begins in vs. 1 with the report of the women going to the tomb early on that first day of the week, but here it is only one woman, Mary Magdalene. Before Jesus appears to her (vss. 11ff.) she goes to the two disciples because she has discovered that the stone has been removed from the tomb. The report of the two disciples going to the tomb (vss. 3-10) is thus an interlude in which the Evangelist lets his readers know that, within the general framework of the events of that morning, which were undoubtedly familiar to them, something else took place that, as the sequel will show (see comments on vss. 9, 10), is of special significance for an understanding of everything that happened that morning. This interlude is characteristically graphic (vss. 3-6) and realistically precise (vss. 6-7), as is the case whenever "the disciple whom Jesus loved" is present as a witness (cf. 1:37-39; 13:23-25; 18:15, 16; 19:35; 21:7). All this clearly indicates the independent knowledge — knowledge closely associated with the disciple whom Jesus loved (cf. 19:35) — of the author in the presentation and structure of his narrative.

Those who deny to the author of the Fourth Gospel all independent knowledge of what he writes about, particularly those who ascribe to the conduct of the beloved disciple a nonhistorical, symbolic meaning, can only view this narrative as a theological redaction of a written source. "The historical question must recede into the background."[1] Bultmann, for example, believes that the Evangelist has inserted the narrative of the two disciples, by means of vs. 2, into a report, known to him from elsewhere, of Mary going to the tomb. The intention of this insertion is to represent Peter and the beloved disciple, the symbolic representatives of Jewish and Gentile Christianity, in a competitive relationship: though Peter, the Jew, enters first, the beloved disciple, a Gentile, shows the greatest readiness to believe.[2] Most proponents of the symbolic interpretation reject this interpretation as unprovable and limit the symbolism to the figure of the beloved disciple. In his race with Peter, he leaves Peter behind and is thus the first to believe and therefore, again, the "ideal disciple."[3] This symbolic role of the figure of the beloved disciple is said to have been introduced by the Evangelist into the resurrection narrative as he received it from his sources.[4]

1. Schackenburg, *Comm.* III, p. 310.

2. So Bultmann, *Comm.,* p. 685. For his hypothesis of the Jewish and Gentile Christianity represented respectively by Peter and the beloved disciple, see the comments above on 13:23ff.; 19:26f.

3. As in 13:23; 19:26 (see the comments there).

4. See, e.g., Schnackenburg, *Comm.* III, p. 304ff.

As for the origin of this narrative in vss. 1-10 itself, which the Evangelist took over from his "source," some scholars believe that behind it again lies concealed a more deeply layered development. They suggest that we must assume the existence in an earlier stage of two narratives, one that described Mary's visit to the tomb and another in which Peter was the main figure. The two narratives later merged in the source from which John drew his material. But even behind these two narratives tradition-historical research continues, in a most detailed fashion, e.g., in Becker, *Comm.,* pp. 605-12.

On the origin(s) of 20:1-20 see also Brown, *Comm.* II, pp. 966f., who, however, with more of a concern for what is historical, sees in these verses a combination of *three* basic narratives. And G. Hartmann, in "Die Vorlage der Osterberichte in John 20," *ZNW* 55 (1964), pp. 197-220, sees in Jn. 20:1-18 the Johannine reworking of a single continuous narrative, a written source that represented an "independent" development of the traditions concerning the Easter event.

All these hypotheses clearly rest on extremely detailed text analyses, of which no two are the same and all of which therefore offer little certainty, even for those who deny to the author all independent knowledge of the events in question. This is admitted — specifically in this case — by the most convinced and experienced practitioners of this method. Schnackenburg recognizes that the assumption of a "source" used by the Evangelist is only "a working hypothesis" and that the distinction between the source and its Johannine reworking remains uncertain in many ways (*Comm.* III, pp. 304, 307). Becker himself labels his far-reaching and extremely hypothetical reconstruction of the prehistory of Jn. 20:18 as "this laborious walk through tradition history" (*Comm.,* p. 612; cf. pp. 605ff.).

Even apart from the dubious character of the view that the activity of the beloved disciple in the Gospel has no historical basis but only symbolic meaning, this view cannot be applied to the present narrative. As will be evident from what follows, this disciple does not represent true post-Easter discipleship *over against* Peter (the "race" with Peter) but rather acts in conjunction with Peter as a fellow witness of the empty tomb before Jesus has appeared to anyone and before even these two disciples have come to understand that Jesus must rise from the dead. The narrative here is a preliminary and therefore a "not-yet" narrative (cf. vs. 9). It is the narrative of the empty tomb and as such the basis for what follows. The real resurrection narrative is still to come. In it the first post-Easter testimony is accorded not to the beloved ("ideal") disciple but to Mary Magdalene, while the beloved disciple and Peter were still "at home" (vs. 10).[5]

Therefore, along with many other interpreters, we believe that the narrative in 20:1-10 as we have it is an independent and original unit. The Evangelist tells what happened that morning, on the basis of his own knowledge, but links it with the familiar story of the women who went to the tomb. His own account is of how, before any appearance of Jesus, two supremely reliable witnesses went to the tomb. He tells of this to establish that the tomb was empty, what state it was in, and to make clear that not the empty tomb but only the appearance of the risen Lord is the basis of the church's faith.[6]

1, 2   The Johannine resurrection narrative begins with traditional material: the women walking to the tomb. The Evangelist took for granted that his readers knew of this story. He mentions only one woman, but has her speak in the plural: "we do not know . . ." (vs. 2). He focuses completely, nonetheless, on the special role that Mary Magdalene plays in all the events of that morning of "the first day of the week" (of which we find a weak but clear echo in Mk. 16:9). He does not say why she went to the tomb (see the comments on 19:40). All attention is immediately focused on the fact that when she arrived she found the stone, which was there to seal off the tomb, removed. This discovery is reported also by the other Gospels, but they have the women come closer and encounter angels. Here Mary immediately — apparently without entering the

5. Cf. ἀγγέλλουσα in vs. 18.

6. See, beside many others, R. Mahoney, *Two Disciples at the Tomb: The Background and Message of John 20,1-10,* 1974. Mahoney critically discusses hypotheses like those of Bultmann, Brown, and Hartmann (see above) and concludes that it is impossible to reconstruct precisely the source(s) of John, in fact that there is no proof whatever that the narrative we have before us in 20:1-10 is based on an original narrative of comparable length. The contrary is, rather, the case, and the Johannine narrative, he says, has a much more independent character. In this connection Mahoney thinks of Lk. 24:24 as the starting point and further of the use of elements from the "first narrative" of the women at the tomb (pp. 171ff.). B. Lindars, "The Composition of John XX," *NTS* (1960/61), pp. 142-47, expresses a similar view; Lindars believes that as possible sources of John 20 only those can be considered that are also used by one or more of the Synoptics and, further, that "the entirely Johannine vocabulary" of all the remainder makes unlikely the possibility of other sources (p. 147).

open tomb or looking inside — concludes that Jesus' body has been taken away and runs off to Peter and the beloved disciple to tell them this shocking news. She says more than she can prove; her entire conduct betrays the special ties she has with Jesus (cf. also vs. 17; Mk. 16:9; Lk. 8:2). What she has seen makes her fear that some have not been able to leave Jesus' dead body alone but have removed it from the care of his own.

She goes to Peter and to "the other disciple" (cf. 18:15), "the one whom Jesus loved" (cf. 13:23),[7] undoubtedly on account of their special position among the disciples. Some think that the repetition of the preposition ("*to* Peter and *to* . . .") might already indicate that the activity of the beloved disciple has been inserted into the narrative (see above) others, on better grounds, that Peter and the other disciple were not together and that Mary ran first to Peter and then to the other disciple. We are not told where they went after 18:15, 27; 19:27. But they went to the tomb together.[8]

3-8 It is, indeed, remarkable how graphically the Evangelist describes the two disciples going together and then being together at the tomb. Recent exegetes have made much of this, especially focusing on the difference between the two disciples' approach to the tomb. "The other disciple ran ahead of Peter and reached the tomb first" (vs. 4); this is said to indicate his "priority" in the narrative and, especially in connection with the conclusion in vs. 8 ("he saw and believed"), to mark him here as well as the ideal disciple.[9] This does not take into account that Peter is the first to enter the tomb and takes careful note of the situation there (vss. 5-7), which is of no less importance for the intent of the narrative. Perhaps the "other disciple" even waited for Peter to give him the priority or at least not to enter the tomb without him. Something is repeated here that can be observed over and over in the relationship between the two men: the beloved disciple has a unique position alongside that of Peter, and in some respects he stays a step ahead of him, but without in any way diminishing Peter's special place among the disciples.[10]

However one wants to judge this matter, here the dominant emphasis is not on the differences in the conduct of the two men[11] but — and this was of far greater importance for the church — on what they saw together as two important witnesses (cf. 8:17) that early that morning Jesus' tomb was empty. For that reason, after "they went toward the tomb" (vs. 3) we read the emphatic

7. Here ἐφίλει, with no difference in meaning from ἠγάπα in 13:23; 19:26; 21:20.

8. On this "together" (ὁμοῦ) in vs. 4a (cf. 21:2), see also BAGD s.v., which translates "at the same time (as), in company (with) . . . the two were running together."

9. See, e.g., Schnackenburg, who sees in this "the point of the narrative" (*Comm.* III, p. 310).

10. On this see further the comments on 1:39 and 21:20ff.

11. Which on closer scrutiny can hardly be established as being of any essential importance at all.

addition: "and those two went together" (vs. 4). The statement that the other disciple walked faster (perhaps he was in a greater hurry?) may be striking, but it can hardly mean that already (before he had seen anything, vs. 8) he knew or suspected more than Peter. The detailed manner in which they went to the tomb is described (it was not a "race") is rather designed to put all the stress on the reliability of their testimony.

The same precision also applies to their observation of the linen cloths.[12] The "other disciple" came first, stooped down, and saw them lying in the tomb, but he did not enter. Peter, on the other hand, immediately — in character! — went in and saw not only the linen cloths lying there but also "the cloth[13] that had been on Jesus' head," though it was "not lying with the linen cloths but rolled up in a place by itself."[14] At the entombment these cloths served to keep the hands and feet of the body together and to hold the head in the desired position. Now they lay there, left behind in good order, each in its own place, as discarded attributes that were no longer of any use and also, with the stone that had been rolled away, as silent witnesses of Jesus' victory not only over death but also over the grave in which his body had been laid.

Of no less importance for the understanding of the whole, further, is the manner in which the Evangelist, in just a few sober words, describes and judges the reaction of the beloved disciples. After Peter had gone in and carefully surveyed everything, "Then [the beloved disciple] also went in, and he saw and believed." Not only the emptiness of the grave but above all the sight of the cloths and the witness borne by this whole scene aroused faith in him. The form of the verb[15] indicates the breakthrough of a new beginning. Unlike Mary, who from the removal of the stone and the open tomb could only conclude that "people" had taken Jesus away, in the beloved disciple, at sight of all this, a sense arose that something else must have happened with Jesus' body, that another hand, God's hand, had been at work here. With this one sober statement the Evangelist leaves the matter. He does not define this faith. It was like a new certainty that took hold of this disciple while understanding was still lacking. One cannot, therefore, speak of the "clear and strong faith of the beloved disciple," marking him as the ideal disciple.[16] The way in which the Evangelist arranges and continues the narrative contradicts this. It is striking here (unlike 21:7) that this disciple does not say a word about his faith to Peter.[17]

---

12. τὰ ὀθόνια; see the comments above on 19:40.
13. τὸ σουδάριον; cf. 11:44.
14. χωρίς: "by itself" (cf. BDF §216.2).
15. ἐπίστευσεν, ingressive aorist.
16. So Schnackenburg, *Comm.* III, p. 312; also Brown, *Comm.* II, p. 1005.
17. This is noted by others such as M. de Jonge, "The Beloved Disciple and the Date of the Gospel of John," in *Text and Interpretation* (Festschrift for M. Black, ed. E. Best and R. M. Wilson), 1979, pp. 99-114, here pp. 102, 107.

The Evangelist does not speak at all of Peter's reaction to the discovery, which was, though, shocking to him as well (cf. Lk. 24:12). Some interpreters regard this as an indication that his experience was the same as that of the other disciple and that he too "believed."[18] Others hold to precisely the opposite opinion.[19] Neither view has sufficient support. The Evangelist intentionally keeps silent on the subject in order to describe a situation that is unclear to both disciples. And he concludes his narrative by stressing what the two had in common: he explains their conduct ("for") by saying that they did not yet understand the Scripture and adds, "Then the disciples went back to their homes." Evidently they saw no alternative to being by themselves again.

9, 10   With this last point we have in a sense been given the point of the narrative. The two disciples have seen the empty tomb with their own eyes and, unlike Mary, have understood that it was not the hands of desecrators but the hand of Another that has been at work there. At the same time they have not yet understood the essence of the matter, namely that Jesus "had to rise from the dead." Often this statement has been interpreted as finding fault with them.[20] But though this motif, which comes to the fore elsewhere (cf. Lk. 24:25ff.), may also be a factor here, the emphasis here lies rather on the words (which appear here for the first time) "rise from the dead" as a description of the manner of Jesus' being lifted up. Jesus has repeatedly spoken of "going" to the Father and of "returning" to his own. And he added: "because I live, you also will live" (14:19). But that this departure could occur by way of his death and grave and that he would come back to them not only as the Living One but as the Living One who had risen from the dead and the grave — that had remained foreign to them, and now the two disciples have yet to understand it.

The Evangelist, from his post-Easter viewpoint, refers to "the Scripture" as the recorded redemptive promise and counsel of God that it had to happen that way.[21] Here again the reference is clearly not to a specific text that the disciples had not yet thought of but rather (as in 1 Co. 15:3, 4) to the whole of Scripture, against the background of which Jesus *had to* rise from the dead if God's saving counsel with the sending of his Son, the Messiah of Israel and the Savior of the world, was to be fully realized. Peter and the other disciple "did not *yet* understand," as they would later, when the Spirit would guide them into all the truth (cf. 2:22; 16:12ff., etc.). At Pentecost Peter, as the spokesman for Jesus' apostles, would, in the light of the Scriptures, explain that God had raised Jesus from the dead "because it was impossible for him to be held by it [death], for him to be abandoned to Hades, or for his flesh to see corruption" (Ac. 2:24-31). The church

---

18. So, e.g., Zahn, *Comm.,* p. 674; Bultmann, *Comm.,* in loc.
19. So, e.g., Brown, *Comm.,* in loc.
20. See, e.g., Calvin's comments.
21. Although the words "the Scripture" are lacking in some Latin manuscripts.

would learn to see with increasing clarity that in his suffering and death Jesus had taken on himself the distress and death of his own, which from ancient times they had plaintively voiced to God in their psalms and prayers. Thus Jesus fulfilled the Scriptures. He did not suffer his own suffering and did not die his own death. Therefore, he also "had to" rise from the dead, according to the Scriptures, thus fulfilling all God's promises to his people. In the same way, in his words to Mary in vs. 17, he would now ascend, in that same solidarity with his brothers, to his Father and their Father, to his God and their God — or, in Paul's words, as the firstborn from the dead (Col. 1:18) and as the firstfruits of those who had fallen asleep (1 Co. 15:20, 23).

Accordingly, what the Evangelist has in mind with this interlude about the two disciples, which precedes all the appearances of the resurrected Jesus, is to highlight this unique character of the Easter event in the whole framework of Jesus' departure and ascension to his Father (cf. vs. 17). One cannot, as many do, eliminate the empty tomb and what the tomb did contain from the resurrection narrative as unessential elements. It is precisely the emptiness of the tomb in which the specific meaning of Easter *as Jesus' rising from the dead* manifests itself most unambiguously and constitutes the (negative) presupposition of everything that will occur from this point on. This is what these two reliable witnesses first had to ascertain before the actual narrative of Jesus' return and self-revelation as the Living One could begin. The Evangelist hands us the key to understanding this with "for they did not yet understand the Scripture." Of course we are not told what happened to Jesus' body in the tomb. That belongs, as part of the absolutely unique resurrection event itself, among the unwritten and indescribable components in all the canonical resurrection narratives. Jesus' resurrection — unlike the raising of Lazarus, for example — was not a return to Jesus' earlier earthly life but an "ascent" (vs. 17) to a heavenly mode of existence veiled from the earthly eyes, ears, and imaginations even of the most reliable witnesses. Of this, in close conjunction with vss. 1-10, the next pericope speaks. Here again the Evangelist tells his story from step to step, not in a series of narratives that are originally unrelated to each other but in a masterfully selected succession of "signs that Jesus did in the presence of his disciples" (20:30, 31).

20:11-18

Jesus Appears to Mary Magdalene

11-13 The narrative that began with Mary Magdalene in vs. 1 but was interrupted in vss. 3-10 is from this point on focused on her experiences at the tomb. The transition is somewhat abrupt in that her return to the tomb with, or at some distance from, the two disciples is not mentioned but simply assumed. The opening words of vs. 11, "But Mary stood[22] . . . outside the tomb," do, however, clearly tie in with what precedes. She did not go home, as the two disciples did. In her grief — twice expressed here by her continued weeping[23] — she could not take leave, however purposelessly she might seem to be walking around. Everything here points to the special ties that bound her to Jesus (cf. Mark 16:9).

In that state she (again?) bent forward to look into the tomb and saw two angels clothed in white,[24] one sitting at the head and the other at the foot of the place where Jesus' body had been, again, as in vs. 7, to mark the emptiness of that space. The other Gospels also mention Mary encountering angels at the tomb (Mk. 16:1, 5; Mt. 28:1, 5). But there, as messengers of salvation, they play a central role. Here the role they play is totally subordinate to the appearance of Jesus himself. They do ask Mary, "Why are you weeping?" This is the question posed again and again "from above," from the perspective of the resurrection, to those who in their grief and uncertainty still judge everything from the perspective of death.[25] But Mary's grief is so intense that even the presence of angels in the tomb can spark no other answer than the complaint with which she earlier turned to the two disciples, this time — with Mary speaking to figures who were unfamiliar to her — entirely in the first person: "They have taken away *my* Lord, and *I* do not know where they have laid him." Could they perhaps tell her more about this?

14, 15 But all at once Jesus himself is there. He, as it were, takes over the angels' side in the conversation. How he came to be there is not described. Suddenly Mary is conscious of the presence of someone behind her. Without waiting for the angels to speak she "turned around and saw Jesus standing," without, however, recognizing him. Her failure to recognize him has been explained in a number of ways: it was still somewhat dark (?) or, given her state of mind, she could not have expected him there. But the real reason is that she thought she was still dealing with someone else, perhaps the gardener, who could answer her question: "If you have taken him away, tell me where you have laid him, and I will take him away" (vs. 15).

All this is designed to bring out something more than Mary's state of mind as still groping in the dark. We should rather think of the supernatural character of Jesus' coming as the Risen One, as a result of which contact with him was unlike a natural encounter with the senses. So it was with the disciples going to

22. εἰστήκει, pluperfect.

23. κλαίουσα, ἔκλαιεν.

24. ἐν λευκοῖς, elliptical as in Mt. 11:8. Celestial figures always appear in white (cf. Mt. 17:2 par.; 28:3 par.; Ac. 1:10; Dn. 7:9, etc.).

25. Which on the angels' part sometimes again leads to astonishment over the lack of understanding for *their* situation and so to a dialogue of mutual astonishment (cf. Lk. 24:17-25).

Emmaus (Luke 24), who also failed to recognize Jesus in the traveler who joined them on the road, and in the story of the miraculous catch of fish, in which the disciples standing on the shore "did not know that it was Jesus" (Jn. 21:4).[26]

Mary does recognize Jesus until he calls her out of the spell of her confused cares over his dead body by simply but emphatically addressing her by name: "Mary."[27] He approaches her as one who knows her and wants her to recognize him (cf. 10:3, 4). The Risen One is none other than the earthly Jesus, who has known her and whom she has known. At the sound of *his* voice calling *her* name she recognizes him, now turning to him with the name in which her belonging to him finds expression: "Rabbouni." The Evangelist puts that "Hebrew" (Aramaic) name on her lips as the name of her past connection with Jesus, explaining it for his Greek readers as "Teacher." "Rabbouni" literally means "*my* teacher" or "*my* master," but it is used elsewhere simply as an equivalent to the common word "Rabbi."[28] Nevertheless, in this description of Jesus' appearance to Mary there is undeniably something very personal. Unlike his other resurrection appearances, here Jesus simply calls her by name and she recognizes him as she hears him. So the way in which she turns to him and answers him with "Rabbouni" does have a strong personal and affective component (see also "my Lord" in vs. 13). All this is easy to link with her prehistory as a woman saved by Jesus from great distress (Mk. 16:9), but the Evangelist does not mention this. Jesus reveals himself first to her, but then distances himself somewhat in what he says to her (vs. 17), from which we may perhaps infer that even in this encounter with Mary we are shown that with Jesus' resurrection a new era and another kind of relationship between Jesus and his own were inaugurated. In this respect, then, this reunion with Mary Magdalene, the woman who felt so much personal affection for Jesus, is strongly reminiscent of Jesus' farewell to his mother (19:26). For what was true when Jesus addressed his last word to his mother from the cross is also true for Mary Magdalene when he appears to her first: from now on everything will be different.

17   That everything has changed is also conveyed by what Jesus says to Mary next: "Do not hold on to me because I have not yet ascended to the Father." Both parts of this statement have given interpreters considerable trouble, as is evident from the multiplicity of explanations it has received.[29]

---

26. The same words as in 20:14.

27. Here only spelled Μαριάμ.

28. Some interpreters have, admittedly, seen in it a diminutive term of endearment with a strong charitable sound ("my dear Rabbi"). It has been proven, however, that in the usage of those days "Rabbouni" need not have had any other meaning than the customary "Rabbi" (see E. Lohse, *TDNT* VI, pp. 964f.; Schnackenburg, *Comm.* III, p. 317 with n. 50 on p. 470). Accordingly, the Evangelist translates it with the same Greek word with which in 1:38 he translates "Rabbi," not including "my" in the translation.

29. See, e.g., Brown, who with respect to the first part alone mentions no less than twelve "different types of explanations," which he discusses in part (*Comm.* II, pp. 992f.).

The two clauses must be understood in close connection with each other. For that reason the common translation "do not touch me" is not satisfactory. Certainly the meaning cannot be that Jesus not yet having ascended stands in the way of touching him or that one could touch him only after he had ascended. What is referred to is not touching but "clutching at" (with the intent or result of) "holding onto," "holding back" (cf. Lk. 7:14). The "for" linking the second clause to the first leads to a natural explanation why Jesus rejects such "holding on" by Mary: he has not yet arrived at his goal; his "ascent to the Father" has not yet been completed. While he is on that journey Mary must not hold him back or want to keep him with herself. The next statement is entirely congruent with this understanding: "But go to my brothers and tell them, 'I am ascending to my Father and your Father, to my God and your God.'"

These statements refer twice to Jesus' ascent to his Father. One is inclined to think here of the ascension, forty days after his resurrection, described in Acts 1. But as is evident in vs. 17b, John uses the word in a broader sense. The present tense ("I am ascending") indicates that Jesus' ascent to the Father, his "departure from this world" (13:1), has begun and is still being accomplished as an ongoing and still uncompleted event.[30] This manner of speaking implies a close link with Jesus' statements about being "on the way" and going "to the Father" in his farewell discourse, which are also in the present tense (e.g., 14:4, 12, 28; 16:5, 28). Now, however, this "going away" has reached the stage of "ascending," Jesus' departure from this earth. Everything is thus rooted in the fundamental statement in 3:13, where Jesus' entire coming and work is summed up and described as the double movement of the Son of man's descent from and ascent to heaven.

This is not to say, however, that in the Fourth Gospel Easter and Ascension (and Pentecost; see the comments on vs. 22) coincide. All one can say is that in the one word "ascending" everything is summed up that belongs to Jesus' passage from this world to the Father (13:1), his resurrection from the dead and his enthronement as the Son of man. But from 20:17 it is clear that this entire salvific process is realized in *phases,* each with its own meaning. Jesus "is ascending," but for a long time "has not yet ascended."

And each phase has its own part in Jesus' self-revelation. From now on, as the Risen One, Jesus is no longer with his own on earth as before. But at this point the stage of the Spirit's indwelling in Jesus' own after his ascension is completed has not yet begun (cf. 14:19f. with 14:23). In the same way, the glory that Jesus exhibited to his own during his earthly life differs from the

---

30. ἀναβαίνω. Some speak here of a durative present, others of a futuristic use of the present as we see in verbs of coming and going so that the present here means "I am in the process of going/coming up," with the point of arrival still in the future (cf. BDF §323.3).

contemplation that he requests from the Father for their future existence "with him" (17:24; see further below on 20:20).

It is quite another question whether this temporal (and spatial) distinction of the phases in which the one great salvific event of Jesus' ascent is presented and in which Jesus successively reveals himself ("appears") to his own can also give us insight into the nature of Jesus' *mode of existence* during that ascent. Does Jesus' statements "I am ascending" and "I have not yet ascended" mean that he is on the boundary between two worlds, no longer on earth and not yet in heaven? Or, to take it another step farther, are there, in the manner in which Jesus revealed himself to his own in that intermediate period (as one who had been crucified and pierced; cf. vss. 20, 27), any indications concerning his mode of existence in the time before his final ascension? We will return to this question in vss. 20 and 27. But here, in Jesus' self-revelation to Mary, it is already evident that clear boundaries are set around our imagination. Not only is all further description of Jesus' "coming" and "going" lacking in John (see also the comments on vss. 19, 26, and 30), not only does the manner in which he reveals himself to Mary (calling her by name) differ from what he does later with his disciples (showing them his pierced hands and side), but insight into the nature of Jesus' mode of existence and the actions belonging to it is also, in the nature of the case, denied to us. Such insight belongs, like Jesus' resurrection, to another reality and order of communication than those "of this world" (13:1).

Accordingly, 20:17 mentions the phase of Jesus' (as yet uncompleted) ascent to the Father, but not in an abstract christological sense but in direct connection with what this ascent means in all of its facets for his own — what it means for the process of their coming to understand the great salvific event of Jesus' resurrection and what it means for Mary as she and through her Jesus' disciples become aware of their involvement in Jesus' ascent to the Father and as they are thus prepared for the task Jesus will give them in this involvement. "I have not yet ascended" therefore means something like: My *earthly task* with respect to you is not yet complete at this stage prior to when I will have permanent fellowship with you from heaven.[31]

This, then, is how we must also understand the message that Mary is to convey to Jesus' disciples ("I am ascending to my Father and your Father, to my God and your God"): it is the good news of his resurrection and a signal

---

31. Among the lengthy disquisitions that interpreters of this passage ("not easy to understand, as all kinds of speculation show," Schnackenburg, *Comm.* III, p. 318) devote to it, certain statements of Brown seem, in my estimation, to point in the right direction. On the relation between vs. 17a and 17b he writes (*Comm.* II, pp. 1014f.):

> In our opinion, the statement "I am ascending to my Father" in 17b is not an exact determination of time and has no implication for the state of the risen Jesus previous to that statement. It is a theological statement contrasting the passing nature of Jesus' presence in his post-resurrectional appearances and the permanent nature of his presence in the Spirit.

of their ongoing involvement in it, a signal that will soon be followed by further manifestations (vss. 19ff.). This meaning also comes out in the remarkable designation of Jesus' disciples as "my brothers," which is clearly not a reference to Jesus' natural brothers and thus occurs only here in the Gospel of John (cf., however, Mt. 28:10), undoubtedly in close connection with the elaborate "to my Father and your Father, to my God and your God." Here again we pick up the note — recurrent in Jesus' farewell words — that his departure is to the advantage of his disciples (14:2; 16:7). It brings them into the closest possible fellowship with the Father (14:28; 16:26f.). Hence the repeated "to my and to your" emphasizes not the difference between Jesus and his disciples but what they have in common. Because God is Jesus' Father, he is also their Father; because he is Jesus' God, he is also their God. They are taken up into the fellowship that unites Jesus and the Father (cf. 17:21, 22). Everything he has told and promised them earlier returns, but now in the present reality of his ascent to the Father. Just as the power of his ascent to heaven is his descent from heaven (3:13), so also the secret and basis of their participation in his fellowship with God are the work he has accomplished for them in his descent.

18 The conclusion is typically Johannine, sober as always. We must focus on the core words. Jesus' departure from Mary is not described, any more than his coming or his miraculous appearance to her. Mary's full name is given just as at the beginning in vs. 1. Again she seeks out the disciples (cf. vs. 2), but now not in desperation but as the messenger[32] of good news. As such, even before she conveys Jesus' words to his disciples, she speaks of her own liberating experience: "I have seen the Lord!"[33] With that the story ends. Now the word is out. It has been spoken not by Peter or by the beloved disciple but by Mary Magdalene. And with that she disappears from the Gospel. The disciples' reaction is not reported. This is not yet their story. Evening must first come, the evening of that first day of the week, before it becomes also their story.

20:19-23

Jesus Appears to the Disciples

Between this narrative and the preceding there is no verbal connection. But in content there is a very close connection in that the disciples' involvement in Jesus' ascent (indicated in vs. 17) is further explicated. While vs. 18 speaks vaguely of

---

32. ἀγγέλουσα.

33. The construction involves a mingling of direct and indirect speech that is hard to convey in translation, in which one would very much like to preserve the lively directness of the statement, "I have seen the Lord!"

"the disciples," here they have — evidently as the Twelve (cf. vs. 24) — reestablished contact with each other, except of course for Judas and, as vs. 24 tells us, Thomas. The manner in which Jesus now reveals himself to them and as the Risen One gives them directions for the future of the church gives special meaning to this first appearance to them on that first day.[34] We also read of this appearance in Lk. 24:36ff. (cf. Mk. 16:14). But for all the agreement in substance, John conveys the story in a form and wording uniquely his own. He does this in a strongly summarizing manner, first by briefly describing the appearance itself (vss. 19b, 20) and then by speaking of, in three main points, the instructions and powers Jesus gives to his disciples (elsewhere distributed over various resurrection stories): their mission (vs. 21), the inspiration of the Holy Spirit (vs. 22), and their authorization to forgive and retain sins (vs. 23).

19 The story begins with a clear time reference that marks the (salvation-)historical character of Jesus' first meeting with his disciples: "On the evening of that day, the first day of the week. . . ." That "the doors were shut where the disciples were staying" is explained in part by "their fear of the Jews." As well-known followers of Jesus they still felt threatened, so that at Jesus' arrest they all fled and sought shelter, each on his own (cf. 16:32; 18:8, 15). Now they are all together again, but not without taking precautions. Still, the prominent mention of the "closed doors" is undoubtedly also (and primarily; cf. vs. 26) intended to indicate the miraculous character of Jesus' coming to them. All at once, despite the closed doors, Jesus "came" into their midst and addressed them with his — in these circumstances particularly powerful (cf. 14:7ff.) — greeting: "Peace be with you."

20 After he greets them Jesus shows his hands and side as a means of self-identification. He has returned to them in his identity as the historic person who before his death gave them the promise of that return ("after a little while"). And to prove who he is he shows them the scars of his suffering and violent death, not just as signs by which to recognize him but also as signs of victory. He shows himself to them as the triumphant one, the one "whom they have pierced," in keeping with what 19:37 has said about the prophetic-messianic significance of his pierced side. Now he returns to them to enable them to share in his victory over death and the grave and thus to give them the sign by which they will be allowed to continue his work on earth as the secret of their power and the content of their message.

After what we have said about vs. 17 concerning the nature of Jesus' self-revelation as the Risen One in this period of his ascent, there is nothing here to enable us to draw any further conclusions. It is clear that in rising from the dead Jesus did not return in his earthly corporeal existence. The involvement

---

34. Cf. Schnackenburg: "It is the appearance which is of decisive importance for the Easter faith, for the life and future of the church" (*Comm.* III, p. 321).

of his body in the event of resurrection, to which vss. 6ff. give such clear witness, points precisely to the transition to the heavenly body (which Paul describes as "the body of his glory," Ph. 3:21; cf. 1 Co. 15:44, 49, 53). It is on the basis of this ascent, which began with the resurrection, that here he makes himself known to his own in his victory as the one who was pierced on the cross; just as he made himself known to Mary by calling her by name, to the disciples going to Emmaus by breaking bread (Lk. 24:35; cf. Jn. 21:12), and finally as the one who from then on takes his leave from the earth at his ascension to heaven (Luke 24; Acts 1). Any idea that before his final ascension Jesus still returned for a time in his earthly body in the injured state described here and, unobserved by people, still spent some forty days in that body, only leads to unacceptable speculations. All the text here allows us to say is that during the time of Jesus' ascent he "revealed" himself and "appeared" to his disciples as they had known him in his earthly body, but no longer as a participant in general human interaction or as one accessible to common human experience (cf. 14:19). We lack adequate words and ideas for this manner of self-revelation. But the Evangelist (immediately after relating Jesus' appearance to Thomas) mentions this manner of Jesus' self-revelation after his resurrection among the "signs" that "Jesus did in the presence of his disciples" and that form the content of the apostolic witness and the faith of the community based on that witness (vss. 30f.).

Of the disciples it is then said — and this is their only reaction here — that "they rejoiced when they saw him." This is not merely a comment in passing but clearly a reflection of "the fulfillment of joy" Jesus promised them especially in 16:20-24 (cf. 15:11; 17:13), where he spoke of the joy of seeing one another again in contrast with the sorrow of farewell.

21 It is that joy of reunion that in part determines and gives content to the repeated benediction, "Peace be with you" (cf. 14:27f.), which in turn forms the transition to the three core statements in vss. 21-23, a summary that is strongly reminiscent of Jesus' word of farewell in Mt. 28:18-20.

This summary first of all concerns the disciples' mission, which Jesus has spoken of in his farewell prayer (17:18) but now directly addresses to the disciples. As there, so here, he speaks of their mission in immediate connection with his own mission from the Father, which is again related to the unity of the Father and the Son, a unity in which the disciples participate (cf. 17:21ff.). As the Father, in sending his Son, continues to stand behind him and to take part in his work (cf., e.g., 8:16, 29), so also Jesus' being sent by the Father remains in force in the mission of his disciples, who continue his work on earth (cf. 14:12ff.). He gives them a part in that work in the sense that — in keeping

---

35. ἀποστέλλειν, here alternating with πέμπειν, which is to be understood as having the same sense (cf. 17:18).

with the meaning of the Greek word[35] — they represent him, according to the rule that "Whoever receives you receives me, and whoever receives me receives the one who sent me" (Mt. 10:40; cf. Jn. 13:20).[36]

The content of their mission is not spelled out here. Also lacking are the words added in 17:18: "into the world." All the stress here falls on the idea of authorization, not on their being sent into the world.[37] Although this last component is undoubtedly included in the calling that the disciples, as apostles of Jesus, must fulfill, their authorization is not limited to their missionary activity, that is, to their activity outside the church. This is also evident from what follows, where this mission coincides with the bestowal of the Holy Spirit and the authorization to forgive and retain sins, which clearly relates also to the ongoing activity of the disciples in the community that takes shape as a result of their labors (cf. 21:15bff.).

Verse **22** speaks of this giving of the Spirit as empowerment for the disciples' "mission": "He breathed on them,[38] and said to them: 'Receive the Holy Spirit.'" This breathing on the disciples recalls texts like Gn. 2:7; Ezk. 37:5f.; Wis. 17:11 that mention God's life-giving breath. If the reference to these texts were direct, then the meaning would be that just as in the beginning God breathed a living spirit into humankind, so in this moment of the new creation Jesus breathes the Holy Spirit into the disciples and so grants them eternal life.[39] But this expression can also refer to the transmission of the working of the Spirit in a broader sense, which in the present context, that of the mission and authorization of the disciples, is much more natural. The giving of the Spirit is therefore to be understood as Jesus' equipping of the disciples for the work assigned to them.

Others see here a reference to the Holy Spirit *in general,* as in 7:39, which speaks of the "coming" of the Spirit as it is imparted to all believers. This leads to the view that in John Easter and Pentecost coincide. There is nothing in this Gospel to suggest a later outpouring of the Spirit to be distinguished from the one spoken of here.[40] But in view of the entire context it is hard to deny that the bestowal of the Spirit referred to here is related particularly to the equipping of Jesus' disciples for their task as continuers of Jesus' work and must therefore be distinguished from the outpouring of the Spirit on "all flesh" without distinction that was to take place at Pentecost. Jn. 7:39 speaks of Pentecost, and in a much more general and more exuberant manner than 20:22 speaks of this more limited

---

36. On this see at length my study in *De apostolische Kerk,* 1954, pp. 39-97, and my *Redemptive History and the New Testament Scriptures* (revised ed., 1988), pp. 12ff.

37. Cf. *De apostolische Kerk,* pp. 61ff.

38. It is not certain whether the αὐτοῖς that follows λέγει also goes with ἐνεφύσησεν or that the latter is used absolutely.

39. So, e.g., Brown, with reference to vss. 1-5 of the Prologue (*Comm.* II, p. 1037).

40. So Schnackenburg, *Comm.* III, p. 325.

giving of the Spirit.[41] This Gospel is restricted — as are all the others! — to the story of the redemptive dispensation determined by Jesus' coming on earth. Of that story Easter is the great turning point and end point. But neither that whole story nor the narrative of this appearance excludes any of what could yet be expected from the exalted Lord and the Spirit *on the basis of Easter.*

23 The last words of Jesus' address to his disciples are also to be understood in close connection with what precedes: "If you forgive the sins of any, they are forgiven; if you retain the sins of any, they are retained." This clearly recalls Mt. 16:19 and 18:18. But while those Matthean texts show strong kinship with rabbinic formulations and must be interpreted in that light,[42] the meaning of Jesus' words here is direct and is focused exclusively on the authority given to the disciples by Jesus to forgive or retain sins.[43] This saying also conveys the central content of the disciples' mission, referred to in vs. 21, namely to proclaim with authority, as representatives of the exalted Lord, the remission of sins as the real goal of his mission from the Father and therefore also of their mission from him. In this connection some scholars — with a view to passages like Mt. 28:16ff. and Mk. 16:16 — think here of baptism. But the general proclamation of the gospel is no less intended by the second part of the saying ("to retain").

The main point, however, is the authority given to his disciples: "they *are* forgiven, they *are* retained," that is, by God. Often this is understood as referring to the pronouncement God will make in the final judgment.[44] And that is undoubtedly included in these passive expressions (which here as elsewhere are used of God's actions). Still, "forgiven, retained" cannot be speaking solely of the final judgment. In the proclamation of the gospel in the name and in accordance with the instructions of Jesus, he himself is the speaker. And he came to earth to forgive sins (cf. Mt. 9:6 par.). That forgiveness goes into effect with his word. Here also the disciples are permitted to continue his work.

For that reason it is undoubtedly important that the authority to forgive sins is closely associated here with the reception of the Holy Spirit. By the Spirit, whom Jesus bestows on the apostles for the fulfillment of their task, he shows himself to be present in them as the living Lord who forgives sins on earth.[45]

---

41. See also J. Jeremias, *TDNT* III, p. 753.

42. On these texts see at length my *The Coming of the Kingdom,* 1962, pp. 359ff.

43. κρατεῖν is not used elsewhere in this sense (cf. BAGD s.v.), but here clearly is meant as the opposite of ἀφιέναι.

44. The passive perfects ἀφέωνται (other manuscripts have the present ἀφίονται) and κεκράτηνται have a future significance (cf. BDF §323.1); see also J. Jeremias, *TDNT* III, p. 753: " 'God will forgive them,' i.e. He will confirm the promised remission at the Last Day." On the future significance of these verbs and their theological implications, see also Brown, *Comm.* II, pp. 1023ff.

45. See also Jeremias, *TDNT* III, p. 753: "Through the Spirit whom he sends as his authorising messenger, Christ himself is directly at work as the One who forgives."

This description of the task of the disciples as remission and retention of sins is remarkable as the Fourth Gospel's only mention of the forgiveness of sins (which makes the Gospel different from 1 John). With this the Evangelist summarizes the content of the preaching of the gospel in traditional terms (cf., e.g., Lk. 24:47; Ac. 2:38; 5:31). In the Fourth Gospel the concept of sin is defined christologically (9:41; 15:22ff.; 16:9), as is doing "the work of God" (6:29). Accordingly, the forgiveness and permanent retention of sins comes as one of an array of images for the saving significance of Jesus' coming and work: "The Lamb of God, who takes away sin" (1:29), redemption from "the slavery of sin" (8:34-36), movement "from darkness to light" (3:19ff.), not perishing but having "eternal life" (3:16), and "the privilege of becoming children of God" (1:12) — as opposed to "remaining under God's wrath," "dying in sin," or "sin remaining" (8:21, 24; 9:41). Therefore the authority to forgive and to retain the sins of others that Jesus gives his disciples does not consist in the application of moral standards but in placing people before the decisive choice to accept in faith the grace of God manifest in the sending of his Son or to remain in sin and to fall under divine judgment (cf. 1:18; 3:18, 19).

Still left, finally, is the important question whether the powers Jesus confers on his disciples are exclusively or at least primarily for the narrow circle of the twelve chosen disciples (cf. vs. 24; 6:70, 71; 15:16) or apply without distinction to all who believe in Jesus as the Christ, the Son of God. Many contemporary interpreters assume that the latter is self-evident.[46] It is true that John does not draw a sharp line of demarcation between what applies to the Twelve and what applies to the church to come, which is by anticipation represented by the Twelve, as that number symbolizes. But this does not alter the fact that throughout the Gospel the appointment and authorization of these first twelve are foundational for the faith of the church.[47] Accordingly, a clear distinction is repeatedly made between the two, as in the statement of this Gospel's purpose in 20:30, 31 (on the one hand, Jesus' disciples, vs. 30; on the other, the "you" of the church, vs. 31; cf. "we" and "you" in 1 Jn. 1:1ff.; cf. also Jn. 15:27; 16:4; 17:20; see also the comments on 20:29). This is not to say that the threefold mandate in 20:22 and 23 exclusively concerns the ones Jesus has "sent" (the "apostles," although this word occurs in this specific sense only in 13:16) and that their powers will find an exclusively hierarchical continuation in the church (cf. Mt. 16:18, 19 with 18:15-18). The work of the

46. Cf. Bultmann: "It is self-evident that it is not a special apostolic authority that is imparted here, but that the community as such is equipped with this authority: for as in chs. 13–16 the μαθηταί represent the community" (*Comm.*, p. 693). Schnackenburg, less forcefully but with equal certainty, writes: "Any restriction to the disciples who are present is not apparent and scarcely intended; John nowhere calls them 'apostles' in the specific sense. They represent for him the entire community of believers" (*Comm.* III, p. 324).

47. See the comments on the history of their calling, pp. 15f. above.

apostles will be continued in the church under the banner of the *ongoing* promises of the Risen One and the Spirit sent by him. But it will continue only on the foundation of those who have been his witnesses from the beginning and in accordance with their standard. In that sense they have a unique standing in the history of the church.

All this, however, gets no further attention in this very brief account of the Risen One's last disposition. The coming outpouring of the Spirit and questions about the "apostolic church" that arose in history fall outside the boundaries of the Johannine Gospel and its purpose. Negative conclusions drawn from this regarding John's understanding of the church have no foundation or point of contact in the Gospel itself. Continuation on the road that Jesus points out is subject to the dispensation and guidance of the promised Paraclete, who will announce "the things that are to come" to the disciples, "lead them into all truth," and "take from what is mine."

20:24-29

Jesus Appears Again to the Disciples, This Time with Thomas among Them

24, 25 The narrative that begins here is closely tied in with what has preceded in that Jesus appears again under much the same circumstances. But this time he appears in the presence of Thomas and particularly addresses Thomas, who is also called Didymus ("the Twin"; cf. 11:16). Thomas again comes on the scene in a way that can be called characteristic for him, as the disciple who, though evidently genuinely loyal to Jesus, repeatedly gives evidence of his resistance to Jesus' departure to the Father and his lack of understanding of that departure (11:16; 14:5). That he, though one of the Twelve, was *for that very reason* not in their company "when Jesus came" is an obvious inference, though not said in so many words. In any case, when the others told him the great news, "We have seen the Lord!" (cf. vs. 18), and apparently spoke to him of Jesus' pierced hands and feet, he not only did not believe it but did not even take their words seriously. His reaction, "Unless I see in his hands the print of the nails, place my finger in the mark[48] of the nails, and place my hand in his side, I will not believe" is undoubtedly not intended to lay down a serious condition for belief but to expose the

---

48. In the manuscripts there is much confusion over whether vs. 25 has in both cases τύπος ("mark") or τόπος ("place") or whether one and then the other. As a rule τύπος is considered original in the first place. In the second place τόπος could be original, with certain later manuscripts adapting it to the preceding τύπος. Certainty, in any case, is hard to achieve.

absurdity of what they tell him: "before I would believe *that,* I would first . . ." (cf. 6:52).

Accordingly, Thomas's unbelief (about which there is much debate in the commentaries) does not mean that he — like the people in Cana (4:48) — wants to see signs and wonders before he believes. It means, rather, that he rejects as impossible the whole idea of the miracle of which his fellow disciples are talking. So it is not as a miracle-hungry Thomas but as the skeptical Thomas that he appears on the scene here again.

26, 27 Verse 26 ties in closely with vs. 19. Eight days later, hence again on the first day of the week, the day of the resurrection, Jesus' disciples were again together in a closed room,[49] but this time with Thomas, who, despite himself, had sought out their company. Again Jesus came "while the doors were shut." This time that the doors were closed is noted without the explanation "for fear of the Jews" and, therefore, more clearly than in vs. 19, to indicate the miraculous and irresistible character of Jesus' coming. Again he thus presents himself in their midst with his "peace" greeting.

But then he immediately turns to Thomas and responds directly to the manner in which Thomas has expressed his disbelief: "*Put* your finger here, and *see* my hands; *reach out* your hand, and *put*[50] it in my side; and be no longer unbelieving but believing." Many interpreters think that Jesus' "invitation" is intended literally and that Thomas literally complies before making his confession. But it seems rather that Jesus' offer is meant to shame Thomas with his own words. It certainly seems unlikely that Thomas comes to his confession only on the basis of an examination of Jesus' body. The confession sounds more like a direct and spontaneous reaction to Jesus' appearance and words, which totally overwhelm Thomas.

28 The confession "My Lord and my God!" conveys Thomas's deep shame and reverence at seeing Jesus' divine glory, a glory surpassing all human standards. It also reflects the strong personal sense with which Thomas yields to Jesus. In the combination of these two titles (sometimes with the addition of the personal pronoun) some scholars refer to passages in which the psalmist similarly turns to God (e.g., Ps. 35:24). Others have viewed the two predicates as descriptive of Jesus' human and divine modes of being.[51] But in Thomas's spontaneous exclamation we do not have a liturgical or dogmatic formulation. The case was rather that the usual address of respect, "my lord" (cf. 13:13), was not sufficient. For what, at the sight of Jesus, filled Thomas with awe he

---

49. πάλιν ἦσαν ἔσω, "again they were inside," with no further determination of place that might furnish a geographical connection among the various appearances.

50. For these interjections, "standard imperatives" like ἴδε, φέρε, and βάλε, as also for the adverbs δεῦτε and ὧδε, see BDF §§107; 336.

51. See the citations from Augustine and Aquinas in Schnackenburg, *Comm.* III, p. 475, n. 106.

had only one word left: "my God." For who could do what Jesus did and thus as the one who was pierced appear in omnipotence but he with whom God had united himself in this manner?

But this does not alter the remarkable fact that here, for the first time in this Gospel, Jesus is addressed in the absolute sense as "my God" and that this lofty word at the end of the Gospel comes from the lips of "unbelieving" Thomas. Here is an important clue to the origin of the high character of the entire Johannine witness to Jesus as the Christ, the Son of God (the character of Johannine "christology," if you will). In this confession of Thomas, however personally it is formulated, the Fourth Gospel reaches its climax and returns to its starting point in the Prologue: the coming and work of Jesus the Christ, the Word that was from the beginning with God and was God has become flesh and has dwelled among us. Thomas himself is a paradigm for the fact that only the superiority of Jesus' historical self-revelation, with many a fall, brought the disciples to the confession of Jesus as Lord and God. This constitutes the foundation of the high ("christological") stakes in this entire Gospel.[52] Jesus' resurrection is the end and climax of that historical self-revelation. It is only in the light of the resurrection and on seeing the Risen One that Thomas surrenders and that the disciples begin to understand who in truth Jesus was in the authority with which he has spoken to them and in the works he has done. This understanding will from now on be deepened by the coming of the Paraclete, who was promised them in order to witness with them to this reality. But all this does not mean that faith in the risen heavenly Lord will cause the image of the earthly Jesus to grow dim and transform it into that of the heavenly Lord. For just as no one ascended to heaven but he who descended from heaven, the Son of man (3:13), so also no one will know the heavenly Lord and Son of God other than in his descent, in the glory of the incarnate Word of God.[53] To this Jesus' last word to Thomas testifies, as do the words with which the Evangelist provisionally concludes his Gospel (vss. 29ff.).

29 Jesus accepts Thomas's confession: "Because you have seen, you believe."[54] And he also pronounces a blessing on "those who believe without having seen." Some view this blessing as a timeless statement: faith need not or even ought not to be based on sight.[55] This is then said to be directed against Thomas, whose faith did rest on sight and was therefore inferior to that of others. But Jesus is speaking here of a transition that will come into effect from

---

52. For this linkage see also p. 35 above.

53. On this see at length pp. 15f. above.

54. The statement is sometimes construed as a question, as in 16:31 (so RSV, NRSV, Nestle-Aland). But there is here no doubt concerning the reliability of Thomas's faith (unlike 16:31). The perfect πεπίστευκας indicates, rather, that Thomas's unbelief has now been definitively overcome (as is also evident from his inspired confession).

55. The aorists must in that case be taken as gnomic.

this point on. From now on — at least after Jesus' final departure to the Father — people will have to believe without seeing, simply on the basis of the apostles' witness (cf. 17:18, 20). And such people — the church of the future — Jesus addresses here, over Thomas's head as it were, with his last word, a beatitude for them all!

There is undoubtedly present in the contrast here a gentle reproach to Thomas. He has not believed the testimony of his fellow disciples that they have "seen the Lord." He has dismissed it as absurd, even though as one of Jesus' designated witnesses he himself will soon have to ask others to have faith without seeing. But believing on the basis of seeing is not thereby degraded as a concession Jesus makes to the weakness of some, a concession that ought not be needed. If it were, all the appearances and miracles in which he has revealed himself in the presence of his disciples (vs. 30) would fall under the same judgment, which is indeed the case according to some interpreters of this last word of Jesus.[56] But such a view not only rests on a spiritualizing denial of the reality of the resurrection narratives as signs of Jesus' glory but also conflicts with the entire import of the Gospel, as is very clear from the summarizing epilogue to the Gospel that now follows.[57]

56. So, specifically, Bultmann. He writes (*Comm.,* p. 696) that Thomas's doubt described here is

> representative of the common attitude of men, who cannot believe without seeing miracles (4.48). As the miracle is a concession to the weakness of man, so is the appearance of the Risen Jesus a concession to the weakness of the disciples. Fundamentally they ought not to need it! Fundamentally it ought not to be the sight of the Risen Lord that first moves the disciples to believe "the word that Jesus spoke" (2.22), for this word alone should have the power to convince them.
>
> . . . There is embedded in the narrative of Thomas also a peculiar critique concerning the value of the Easter stories; they can claim only a relative worth. And if this critical saying of Jesus forms the conclusion of the Easter narratives, the hearer or reader is warned not to take them to be more than they can be: not as narrations of events . . . but as proclaimed word, in which the recounted events have become symbolic pictures for the fellowship which the Lord, who has ascended to the Father, holds with his own.

See also what Bultmann writes about the "superfluity" of the resurrection of Lazarus.

57. Against Bultmann see, among others, Brown, *Comm.* II, pp. 1050-51. He writes (quoting the first edition of Barrett, *Comm.* [1955], p. 477) that a really adequate type of belief

> does not discard the sign or the appearance of the risen Jesus, for the use of the visible is an indispensable condition of the Word's have become flesh. As long as Jesus stood among men, one had to come to faith through the visible. Now, at the end of the Gospel, another attitude becomes possible and necessary. This is the era of the Spirit or the invisible presence of Jesus (xiv 17), and the era of signs or appearances is passing away. The transition from 29a to 29b is not merely that one era precedes the other, but that one leads to the other. "But for the fact that Thomas and the other apostles saw the incarnate Christ there would have been no Christian faith at all." Or as the Evangelist himself phrases it in xx 30-31, he has narrated signs so that people may believe — certainly not a rejection of the value of signs for faith.

20:30, 31

Epilogue

30   Along with vs. 29 (see above), this verse forms the provisional conclusion of the entire Gospel. In this epilogue the Evangelist accounts for his selection of material. "Jesus did many other signs"[58] indicates the wealth of materials available to the author and represents a conventional sort of statement used in various forms at the end of many other writings of the time.[59] But the reference to "signs" not only has literary or rhetorical significance but also conveys that the Evangelist's choices of material fit together closely with the purpose of his Gospel (vs. 31). One factor in his sometimes very striking selectivity is the general knowledge of the life of Jesus that he repeatedly presupposes in his readers, though he does not mention that here.[60]

It is remarkable that the Evangelist summarizes all that precedes as "signs" that "Jesus did" (cf. 12:37). Here again we see the great significance that the Evangelist — unlike many of his interpreters[61] — attaches to Jesus' miracles, both with a view to the culpable unbelief of the Jews (10:37ff.), the "they" of 12:37ff., and as the basis of the church's faith, as here. This Gospel firmly rejects a sensationalist desire for miracles and a superficial faith in miracles (cf. 2:23ff.; 4:48; 6:14, 15). But miracles as media of revelation very clearly belong to the essential content of the Johannine message of salvation,[62] not only "spiritually" interpreted, as they often are, but also as signs that Jesus was sent by the Father. In the present passage (vss. 29, 30) this is certainly very clear.

Some scholars have weakened the significance of this statement by assuming that it was taken over from the so-called sēmeia source, from which the Evangelist is also said to have borrowed his miracle stories and which is supposed to have contained a much more positive evaluation of miracles than that of the Evangelist himself.[63] But this argument is clearly meant only to save the hypothesis and cannot in any case weaken the Evangelist's *own* view as it is expressed in this concluding core statement, or make it a matter of indifference.[64] And this the less because he speaks of these "signs" in direct connection

58. πολλὰ μὲν οὖν καὶ ἄλλα corresponds with ταῦτα δέ in vs. 31; καί here has a more or less pleonastic sense (cf. BDF §442.11).

59. See examples in Bultmann, *Comm.*, p. 697, n. 2.

60. See at length pp. 7f. above.

61. See, e.g., the comments on vs. 29 and on ch. 11.

62. See the far-reaching discussion of the significance of Jesus' *sēmeia* by W. Nicol, *The Sēmeia in the Fourth Gospel,* 1972, esp. pp. 105ff.

63. See above, e.g., on ch. 11.

64. For example, Becker, who writes that it is "utterly inexplicable" how the Evangelist can summarize his Gospel with the word "signs." The conclusion, therefore, is that the summary

with Jesus' appearances and undoubtedly includes their miraculous character in these words.

Accordingly, the word "signs" refers not only to certain miraculous acts but to any event in which Jesus' divine glory is manifest (cf. 2:11).[65] In that sense we can understand that the word "signs" is used here as a summarizing characterization of Jesus' self-revelation, which was sometimes experienced and commented on as "no longer human" in his *words* by those who heard him (cf. 7:46; 18:6). As such the signs eminently belong to the manifestations of Jesus' "glory in the flesh," which is posited as central in 1:14.

This is why it is specified here that Jesus did the signs "before" or "in the presence of" his disciples.[66] Here again we see the distinction made in vs. 29 between those who have "seen" and those who have not. The disciples constitute the salvation-historical link between Jesus and those who will believe in him through their word, which they speak as those authorized by Jesus to speak it. The Evangelist ascribes this undeniable *apostolic* character to their witness and thus also to his own reporting. This also comes to expression in the solemn formulas with which he makes his report foundational for the faith of his readers as that which has been written down once for all.[67]

Verse **31** then further states for what purpose the Evangelist wrote down (precisely) these signs: "that you may believe that Jesus is the Christ, the Son of God." One may say that all the Evangelists pursued this goal in their writing. But the Fourth Evangelist, more than the others, concentrates everything on

---

was borrowed from the *sēmeia* source. Thus it was "a matter of indifference to the Evangelist" whether his Gospel could be summarized under the heading of "signs." What attracted him in the conclusion of the *sēmeia* source was that by means of it "a literary conclusion was marked, christology was given theological prominence, and the demand of faith . . . was accentuated" (*Comm.*, pp. 632f.). But the unique significance attributed in this core statement to Jesus' "signs" can hardly be eliminated from the discussion as a "certain indifference toward such externals."

65. Nicol speaks of a "widening" of the *sēmeion* concept "to include the appearances." He adds: "John never directly says the resurrection is also a *sēmeion* in 2:18, he answers by referring to his resurrection. . . . The concept *sēmeion* has acquired striking elasticity" (*Sēmeia,* p. 115). Schnackenburg takes over this idea (*Comm.* III, p. 337), but not where Nicol "in the last analysis" wants to extend the words ποιεῖν σημεῖα to "all that the Gospel of John preaches about Jesus, both the works and the words" (*Sēmeia,* p. 115).

66. ἐνώπιον τῶν μαθητῶν: "before the eyes of" or "in the presence of" (cf. BAGD s.v. ἐνώπιον).

67. ταῦτα δὲ γέγραπται; cf. G. Schrenk, *TDNT* I, p. 745: "When quoting the OT, John almost always uses the introductory γεγραμμένον . . . and in 20:31, when speaking of the aim of his own writing, i.e., to awaken faith, he can use a word which elsewhere he reserves for OT Scripture, namely γέγραπται. Indeed, in the previous verse (v. 30) we already find the expression: ὃ οὐκ ἔστιν γεγραμμένα ἐν τῷ βιβλίῳ τούτῳ." See also my *Redemptive History and the New Testament Scriptures,* 1988, pp. 22ff.

the person of Jesus as the Messiah and Son of God and omits much other material that also belongs to the core of the gospel.[68] Therefore, when he says that he has written about "these [signs]" "so that you may believe . . . ," this means that in the way in which he has narrated and interpreted the signs the utterly unique character of Jesus' mission as Messiah and Son of God comes to the fore, both christologically and soteriologically. The signs thus constitute the content and foundation of the church's faith.

Among interpreters there is much disagreement — partly as a result of the variant readings of the original text[69] — concerning the readership whom the Evangelist addresses with "so that you may believe." Is this those who do not yet believe, whom he seeks to bring them to faith and who, some think, were Jews, either Jews in general[70] or specifically Hellenistic Jews living in the Diaspora?[71] Or does the Evangelist address people who already believe, with the purpose of strengthening their faith?[72] The latter view undoubtedly deserves preference. Even though the text as we now have it cannot settle the issue, the Evangelist elsewhere clearly includes his readers among the "we" who believe (1:16). And the impression made by his Gospel as a whole is certainly not that of a book for beginners[73] but rather that of a deeper discussion of the meaning of Jesus' self-revelation for readers in whom he assumes a long acquaintance with the general picture of the course of Jesus' life. The Evangelist does, admittedly, strongly stress the signs Jesus did in the presence of "the Jews" and "the multitude," but he does this especially to demonstrate the incomprehensible character of their unbelief (cf. 12:37-43). The positive manner in which he now addresses his readers with an appeal to Jesus' signs definitely does not suggest that he has in mind Jews who do not believe in Jesus. It all fits better in a situation of ongoing and deepening confrontation between the church and non-Christian Jews over the person of Jesus, in which the Evangelist seeks to lead the church more fully into the saving significance of Jesus' coming and work to confirm the faith of Jewish and Gentile Christians alike.

It is hard to say whether some of vs. 31 (and how much) is drawn from a confessional statement, as some interpreters think. It does very succinctly

68. On this see at length pp. 7ff. above.

69. πιστεύσητε, which as ingressive aorist could mean "begin to believe," versus present tense πιστεύητε, which points rather to the reinforcement and confirmation of faith. Both readings have support in important textual witnesses, though perhaps the latter has stronger support than the former.

70. Cf. K. Bornhäuser, *Das Johannesevangelism. Eine Missionsschrift für Israel,* 1928.

71. See especially W. C. van Unnik, "The Purpose of St. John's Gospel," in *The Gospels Reconsidered,* 1960, pp. 166-69; J. A. T. Robinson, "The Destination and Purpose of St. John's Gospel," *NTS* 6 (1959/60), pp. 117-31.

72. So most recent interpreters.

73. The aorist tense of πιστεύειν need not always point to a beginning (cf. 11:40).

convey the christological content of the Fourth Gospel. The premise of all the narratives is the confession — already uttered by the first disciples — that Jesus is "the Messiah" of Israel (1:41),[74] "of whom Moses and the prophets wrote" (1:45), "the Son of God, the king of Israel" (1:49). Jesus accepts that confession but immediately holds out to them the promise of seeing "greater things," placing his entire mission in the transcendent light of an opened heaven and the Son of man clothed with all power (1:50, 51). As a result the messianic title "Son of God" used in 1:45 acquires a transcendent meaning as that which indicates the preexistent ontological relation to God that underlies this all-embracing function of the Son of man (see the comments on 1:51; 3:13f., 16f.; 5:26, 27).[75] One cannot, therefore, simply view "Son of God" in 20:31 as synonymous with "Messiah," as proof (for the Jews) that Jesus was their promised messianic king. But it is no less true that "the Christ" neither loses its original messianic significance nor is completely overshadowed by "the Son of God."[76] Jesus is the Messiah of Israel, but in a way that can no longer be expressed in the traditional messianic categories and far exceeds them in content. It is that content that prompts "the Jews" to charge Jesus with blasphemy (5:18; 10:33, 36; 19:7), that caused Thomas to confess him as "my God," and that the Evangelist in his Prologue ascribed to the Word who was in the beginning with God.

Finally, as the object and fruit of that faith the Evangelist mentions: "that believing you may have *life* in his name," that is, that all-embracing salvation — which keeps coming back in the Gospel — to which faith in Jesus as the only-begotten of the Father gives access (cf. 3:15, 16, 36; 6:40; 5:24). With that we have a highly concentrated summary of the content and purpose of the Fourth Gospel that, at least initially, concludes all that has preceded. The question that now confronts us is how we must understand the addition of ch. 21, which again begins with "After these things . . ." (cf. 3:22; 5:1; 6:1; 7:1; 19:38).

74. On this see at greater length pp. 84f. above.
75. Cf. above pp. 92ff., 137ff., and 200 above.
76. Against this position see at length van Unnik, "Purpose of St. John's Gospel," pp. 174f.

21

Jesus' Appearance at the Sea of Tiberias and the Conclusion of the Gospel

Of the many questions that ch. 21 poses, certainly the first is whether this chapter belonged to the Fourth Gospel from the beginning or was added later. The primary facts are that it is nowhere lacking in the text tradition and that, if it was added later, what existed before was only the Evangelist's original unpublished composition. Was ch. 21 a part of this or was it added afterward, either by the Evangelist himself or by a later hand?

The occasion for this question is obvious. Following the epilogue in 20:30, 31, in which the Evangelist, in stating his purpose, clearly limits himself to the "signs" recorded in the preceding chapters, one does not expect that after a repetition of the transition formula "after these things" he will simply go on to tell us of still another resurrection appearance of Jesus. Furthermore, at the end of ch. 21 people other than the author speak ("and we know that his testimony is true," vs. 24b) and conclude the book in a different way (vs. 25). The obvious question is whether these others added the whole of ch. 21, and this question is now generally answered in the affirmative.[1] Still, there are also many who continue to ascribe ch. 21 to the Evangelist and regard only vss. 24 (or 24b) and 25 as an addition by, say, his pupils.[2] The main argument favoring this view is that ch. 21 too clearly, both as to style and content, betrays the hand of the Evangelist than what we would have to attribute it to others.

But opinions are divided on the style of ch. 21. Besides typically Johannine characteristics, ch. 21 also contains a number of words and expressions

---

1. For an overview see, e.g., W. G. Kümmel, *Introduction to the New Testament,* 1975, p. 208.

2. Ibid., p. 208, n. 47.

that do not occur elsewhere in the Gospel, that one cannot simply ascribe to the special nature of the material, and that to some scholars are proof that in ch. 21 we are dealing with an unknown redactor.[3]

Though, then, style can probably not settle the issue, the case is stronger if one looks at content. Both directly and indirectly, 21:1 and 14 refer back to what precedes in speaking of Peter and the beloved disciple together. Also very striking is Jesus' threefold question to Peter in the light of 13:38 and 18:16ff. All this suggests that this final chapter is intended to bring into sharper profile the figures of Peter and the beloved disciple in the resurrection drama, especially in connection with the role they were to play in the church. Although one could say that this last point crosses the limit of what the Evangelist clearly meant to do (20:31), it also means the prolongation of a line demanded by what precedes, without which especially Peter would have been left in a questionable light (18:27; 20:10). From this perspective there is much that argues for ascribing the majority of ch. 21 to the Evangelist, as the completion of his narrative, albeit as a striking — also with a view to developments in the community (cf. vs. 23) — addition to a provisionally concluded whole.

That others as well had a hand in this completion is clear from vss. 24 and 25, where they themselves speak. The extent of their part in the conclusion is uncertain and will demand our further attention. At any rate, a clear decision between the two views we have described is difficult. If, with many contemporary interpreters, one concludes that all of ch. 21 was added by a later author, then one must also say that ch. 21 is made up of material that is closely connected with all that goes before and that completes that earlier material.

Chapter 21 is divided readily into two nearly equal parts (vss. 1-14 and 15-23), which together tell of Jesus' third appearance to his disciples as the Risen One, this time at the Sea of Tiberias. Jesus appears in the presence of seven of his closest disciples during a miraculous catch of fish and a subsequent meal (vss. 1-14). Here already the beloved disciple and Peter come to the fore in characteristic ways. In the second part Jesus first speaks at length with Peter (vss. 15-29), and then, prompted by a question from Peter, makes a significant statement about the continuation of his work by the beloved disciple (vss. 20-22). After the narrator's correction of a misunderstanding of this last state-

---

3. M. É. Boismard has pointed out the differences and infers an "anonymous redactor," whom he relates to the Gospel of Luke ("Le Chapitre XXI de Saint Jean. Essai de Critique Littérairé," _Revue Biblique_ 54 [1947], pp. 473ff.). E. Ruckstuhl (_Die litterarische Einheit des Johannesevangeliums_, 1951, pp. 146ff.) and R. Mahoney (_Two Disciples at the Tomb: The Background and Message of John 20:1-10_, 1974, pp. 17f.) come to a very different conclusion, as does Schlatter, who even writes: "The attribution of the new narrative to another author is impossible, however, since the identical linguistic conventions have been fully maintained" (_Comm._, p. 363). Bultmann, though denying that the Evangelist is the author of this chapter, judges: "Language and style admittedly afford no sure proof" (_Comm._ p. 700).

ment, we have the "editorial" conclusion, identifying the beloved disciple as the trustworthy witness and author of the Gospel (vss. 23f.).

Hence one cannot say that ch. 21 deals exclusively with these two figures and their place in the coming community. The self-revelation of Jesus in the presence of seven disciples, especially in light of the miraculous catch of fish, has an important purpose and significance of its own. Still, against the background of this event, the beloved disciple and Peter do play a special role. Jesus' self-revelation is focused on these two,[4] and the entire Gospel, by referring to their futures, finds its completion.

Many contemporary interpreters believe that a variety of material of diverse origins has been brought together in ch. 21. Although discussion of this subject extends to a number of details, the main concerns are whether vss. 1-13 form an original unit and whether the two main parts of the narrative (vss. 1-13 and 14-23) originally belonged together or were joined later. We will limit ourselves to the most important views.

According to some interpreters, the author of vss. 1-13 has incorporated a resurrection appearance story into the story of a miraculous catch of fish. The two interwoven narratives can be separated and reconstructed by means of analysis of the text.[5] The main argument for this view is that the obscurity and gaps in the narrative as we have it are traceable to the differing situations of the two narratives.

The text does pose certain difficulties, but the objections to this proposal are formidable. Aside from the fact that the attempts to separate the two stories have not led to any consensus,[6] the following arguments can be adduced. First, the beginning of the miraculous catch story is completely conditioned also by resurrection appearance motifs (see the exegesis below), and its further development cannot be separated from its intent as a resurrection appearance narrative. Second, if one tries to separate the two stories, one has too little left of the resurrection narrative to speak of a conceivable, situated narrative, and its significance is sharply reduced. Into what sort of situation does Jesus appear in vs. 4 if the story of the disciples who have gone out to fish is taken away? Did the entire

---

4. See also E. Ruckstuhl, "Zur Aussage und Botschaft von Johannes 21," in *Die Kirche des Anfangs* (Festschrift for H. Schürmann), 1978, pp. 339-62: "In both sections these figures, along with the risen Jesus, are the main actors. The difference between their respective charisms, their relation to each other, and the relation to them of the Johannine community are the primary themes in vss. 1-14 and in 15-23(24)" (p. 340).

5. See specifically R. Pesch, *Der reiche Fischfang Lk 5,1-11, Joh 21:1-14. Wundergeschichte — Berufungsgeschichte — Erscheinungsbericht,* 1969, whose reconstruction is taken over with several modifications by Schnackenburg, *Comm.* III, p. 345. But see also Bultmann, *Comm.,* pp. 703f.

6. Schnackenburg, too, acknowledges: "The separation between tradition and what is editorial in Jn 21:2-13 is especially difficult and has not yet led to a satisfactory solution" (*Comm.* III, p. 345).

appearance consist of a meal arranged by Jesus at which no one said a word? Does not this third and final revelation of the Risen One derive its meaning solely from the authority demonstrated by him in the miracle of the catch of fish and from the renewed assignment to his disciples to continue his work on earth? It is no wonder that even proponents of this two-narratives hypothesis suggest that one reason the two narratives were joined was that the story of the great catch of fish could show more forcefully the fullness of the power of the Risen One, whose appearance was the author's primary interest here.[7]

With regard to the original unity of the two main parts of ch. 21, the closing statement in vs. 14 describes the appearance of Jesus in vss. 1-14 as a unit in itself. This seems to be reinforced by the correspondence between "he revealed himself" in vs. 1 and "he was revealed" in vs. 14. But vs. 15 forges a clear link between vss. 1-13 and vss. 15-23, and the other disciples remain present (cf. vs. 15) in this second part of the chapter, which focuses first on Peter and then on the beloved disciple. That these two disciples are mentioned separately and emphatically in vss. 1-14 is another argument for unity. Vss. 1-13 leave the relationship between Jesus and Peter unresolved. Furthermore, and more importantly, both parts of the chapter together constitute the explanation for the addition of this chapter to the Gospel: it was added to describe the passage from Jesus' work on earth to its continuation through his disciples. Therefore, we encounter first Jesus' demonstrative promise and assignment of a task to his disciples *in general,* then, in close association with this, Jesus' assignments to Peter and the beloved disciple in their special significance for the church of the future.[8]

21:1-14

The Miraculous Catch of Fish

1 The words "after this" continue the narrative in John's customary way (cf. 3:22; 5:1; 6:1; 7:1). With "Jesus again revealed himself" they explicitly label the following as a resurrection narrative (cf. vs. 14). This revelation took place "by the Sea of Tiberias" (cf. 6:1), that is, in Galilee, mentioned elsewhere as where Jesus told his disciples to meet him after his resurrection (cf. Mk. 14:27; 16:7; Mt. 28:7, 10; 28:16).

2, 3 The beginning of the story, however brief, clearly assumes the resurrection situation. Against the background of vs. 1, that Simon Peter and six other disciples "were together" obviously does not just refer to an undefined "once upon a time" when the disciples decided to go fishing but to the con-

---

7. Cf. Schnackenburg, *Comm.* III, p. 347.
8. See Ruckstuhl, "Zur Aussage und Botschaft von Johannes 21."

tinuation of the unity they recovered after Jesus' resurrection. The listing of some of their names undoubtedly serves to "verify" the resurrection (cf. 1 Co. 15:5f.), something lacking, as a rule, in the miracle stories.

Successively mentioned, after Simon Peter, are Thomas and Nathanael (this time, unlike 1:45f., with his place of origin, Cana of Galilee), the sons of Zebedee (also from Galilee), here mentioned in the Fourth Gospel for the first and only time as such — a notice of some importance with regard to identification of "the disciple whom Jesus loved," who appears in the narrative but is not mentioned in this list as such. The beloved disciple, identified in vs. 24 as the writer of all this, could have been one of these two brothers — namely John, in view of James's early death. "Two other disciples" are mentioned next, and the beloved disciple could have been one of them. Why they remain anonymous is not clear. Some interpreters point out that they complete the number seven, under which number these disciples could represent the church to come.[9] But in the roles played in relation to the church of the future both by these seven (vss. 1-14) and by Peter and the beloved disciple (vss. 15-25) the disciples lay the foundations for the church rather than represent it. And the determinative number for the disciples was not seven but twelve. The number seven is not mentioned and has no symbolic significance here.

What moves the disciples — again at the instigation of Peter — to go fishing is not reported. One can, of course, speculate.[10] All one can say with any certainty is that fishing was unusual for this group as disciples of Jesus. That "they caught nothing" is not unusual. But here this notice clearly functions as a transition to what begins in vs. 4.

4 "Just as day was breaking," so that everything was becoming visible, "Jesus was standing on the beach." The same verb is used of Jesus' sudden and unexplained "standing" in 20:14, 19, and 26. This time he is standing "on the beach." With the same words as in 20:14, it is said that "the disciples did not know that it was Jesus."[11]

---

9. So, e.g., Schnackenburg, who refers to the seven churches in Revelation 2–3; cf. Resch, *Der reiche Fischfang,* p. 148 and (somewhat more reserved) Ruckstuhl, "Zur Aussage und Botschaft von Johannes 21," p. 342.

10. So, e.g., Grosheide, *Comm.,* p. 553: By saying "I am going fishing" Peter is announcing "his return to his earlier occupation. He sees no point in preaching; it does not help." Grosheide speaks of Peter's "discouragement, which places all the apostolic work at risk, the more so now that the other apostles think about it in the same way," which necessitates a new appearance. Grosheide refers to Hoskyns, who views this attitude of the disciples as the fulfillment of 16:32.

11. According to the two-narratives hypothesis (see above), vs. 4a came from one story (the "fishing" story) and vs. 4b from the other. But, apart from the highly artificial character of such weaving together of two stories by the author, vs. 4a in combination with vs. 4b is clearly the language of an appearance. Besides, the sudden presence of Jesus on the beach at dawn in a narrative whose sole focus is a catch of fish is hard to explain. As a description of Jesus' "appearance" this inexplicable element is characteristic.

5, 6   The miracle is introduced by the manner in which Jesus, standing on the beach, makes contact with the disciples nearby (cf. vs. 8). The address "children" — some expositors translate "boys" or "lads"[12] — contains a suggestion of the paternal familiarity and attitude present in teacher-pupil relationships. Jesus' question about their fishing expects a negative answer: "You haven't caught any fish,[13] have you?" Jesus knows the answer either because the disciples were still fishing at the break of day or perhaps because of his omniscience. With no sign that they recognize him, the disciples respond with a mere "no." Jesus' word of power follows: "Cast the net to the right side of the boat, and you will find [some]."[14] When the disciples follow this instruction, they are then unable to haul the net in because there are so many fish.

It is clear at the outset (see further on vs. 11) that the fish are not just intended for a meal. In vs. 10 Jesus does tell his disciples to bring some of the freshly caught fish for a meal. But in view of the small number of those present, we must clearly not think here of a feeding miracle like that in ch. 6. The story rather symbolizes the effective authorization and promise of the Risen One to fulfill the missionary mandate that he has given to his disciples. The miracle of the catch of fish thus gives to this resurrection appearance, and to the meal that the disciples once more have with Jesus, their own specific meaning. Lk. 5:1-11 places a similar miracle story before the resurrection, which though it is different in many ways and is not to be equated with the story here,[15] is also interpreted symbolically with a view to Peter's future activity. This Johannine story has a distinct setting as a resurrection narrative and in close conjunction with two earlier resurrection narratives (20:19ff.). In that setting the meal that follows also has its specific meaning and finds its continuation, as we will see in what follows.

7   Before all that unfolds, the reactions to the astonishing catch of fish on the part of the beloved disciple and Peter are reported. Again they act in conjunction, as in 13:23ff.; 18:15f.; 20:3ff., 8ff., and in ways characteristic for each of them and for their relationship. The beloved disciple, though not mentioned as such in the list of vs. 2 but known to the readers as "that" disciple,[16] first understands the meaning of what has happened and in that respect is again a step ahead of Peter. He voices it in the word of recognition that is typical in the resurrection appearances: "It is the Lord!" (cf. 20:18, 25; 21:12). Peter reacts immediately, in a way that is no less characteristic for him.

---

12. See Brown, *Comm.* II, p. 1070, who refers to Bernard's well-known commentary.
13. προσφάγιον, literally "side dish," usually referred to as fish eaten with bread.
14. Why it had to be the right side is hard to say. The right side was considered the favorable side (Mt. 5:29f.; 25:33; cf. Mk. 16:15; Lk. 1:11).
15. See Schnackenburg, *Comm.* III, p. 355.
16. ἐκεῖνος, "the well-known one," "the one previously named" (cf. BDF §291.3).

He tucks in his outer garment[17] — the only thing he had on — and plunges into the sea, leaving behind his companions, the boat, and the sea in order to be the first to reach Jesus. That he had a special reason for this is clear and will emerge later.

The Evangelist thus again sketches the relationship between the two disciples and at the same time anticipates the second part of the narrative (vss. 15ff.). Some scholars have again sought to view the beloved disciple here as the "ideal disciple," on whose post-Easter witness the other disciples were dependent.[18] But, though in relation to Peter this disciple is here again the first, he is in this regard by no means the first and only post-Easter witness among the disciples. He is a witness in the Gospel only here in the added ch. 21. And the other disciples are not at all dependent on him for their witness (cf. vs. 12; 20:18, 25).

Peter's role here of leader and spokesman of the disciples is no less characteristic, also in his relationship with the beloved disciple (cf. 20:6). It is remarkable here that this role is initially limited to jumping into the sea. Not a word is said about his arrival on the beach or that he is the first to meet Jesus. Peter only, rather unexpectedly, "surfaces" again in vs. 11, which is proof to some of the incoherent and composite character of the narrative.[19] But the author responsible for this narrative is clearly not interested in giving a complete report but only in describing the main moments significant for his purpose. Peter only returns when he again plays a leading role, in vs. 11 and particularly in vss. 15ff., where Jesus, echoing Peter's love of primacy ("more than these"), addresses him individually. But first the fishing story must be continued.

8-10 "The other disciples" — perhaps more intent on saving the boat and the catch than Peter was — "came in the boat, dragging the net full of fish" behind the boat (cf. vs. 6). The comment that "they were not far from the land, but about a hundred yards[20] off" explains how all this could have taken place as told: the distance they had to drag the net behind the boat (and that Peter had to swim) was not long.

Compared with this detailed precision the extreme conciseness of what follows is striking. When the disciples had gone ashore, they saw a charcoal fire

---

17. ἐπεδύτης appears only here in the New Testament and denotes a garment worn over another garment. The nakedness here is interpreted in a number of ways. Some think it means that he has been wearing only an inner garment and now for his meeting with Jesus puts on a more appropriate outer garment; others, that he has been completely unclothed and now puts on the outer garment. Still others think that all he does is to tuck up and tie in with a cincture the garment he wore over his otherwise naked body (διεζώσατο), so as to have freedom of movement in the water. In our opinion this last view deserves preference.

18. On this see at length the comments on 13:23ff. above.

19. See Bultmann, *Comm.*, pp. 702f.; Schnackenburg, *Comm*, III, pp. 343f.

20. πῆχυς, "about 18 inches, or .462 of a meter" (BAGD s.v.).

with fish[21] on it and bread, evidently intended as preparation for a meal (vs. 9). All this, arranged by Jesus himself, is not striking in a resurrection appearance story, but it is in a fishing story. The Evangelist says not a word about it, but immediately goes on to Jesus' words to his disciples: "Bring some of the fish that you have just caught." Why does Jesus, who has fish for the meal on the fire, tell the disciples to bring fish from those they have caught?[22] The connections here do not seem as unclear as that question might suggest. Only as the disciples bring fish that have just been caught does the meal prepared by Jesus achieve its full significance. Jesus makes the usual meal of bread and fish, which the disciples have so often shared with him, into a resurrection meal, not only by sitting down with them as the Risen One, but also by involving them in it as those who share in his resurrection power and as those who will continue his work on earth. Therefore some of the fish that they have just caught from the abundance he showed them when the net was hauled ashore must be put on the table. Hence his earlier question in vs. 5 and hence his instructions here, as signs of the time of salvation inaugurated with his ascent. The unity of the narrative is not artificial but is present from its beginning.

11 At Jesus' word Peter is again the first to carry out the command. He goes aboard the now unmanned boat and, however he did it, pulled the net ashore.[23] Only then is it revealed what occurred in the depth of the sea after Jesus' said, "Cast the net on the right side of the boat": one hundred fifty-three fish in one net, and without tearing the net!

Aside from the power and authority of the Risen One symbolized in general in this description, attempts have been made also to interpret the details allegorically. From early times on commentators have focused on the number one hundred fifty-three to find a deeper meaning in it. Attempts to that end are being

---

21. ὀψάριον, vss. 9, 10, 13 (as in 6:9, 11), is fish as food. ἰχθύς, vss. 6, 8, 11, is fish as a living animal (cf. BDF §111.3).

22. It is particularly this point that interpreters regard as proof that two stories have been woven together. Here, they say, we see the "seam": On the one hand, there is the appearance story with its premise in the arranged meal and the fish and its continuation in vss. 12ff. On the other hand, there is the fishing story in vss. 2ff., for which vss. 10f. are the denouement. See, e.g., following Pesch, the highly complicated tradition-historical analyses and reconstructions in Schnackenburg, *Comm.* III, pp. 345ff., 356ff. Ruckstuhl, who otherwise has much more appreciation for the inner unity of this pericope, thinks that one cannot avoid Pesch's two-narrative hypothesis (cf. his exegesis of vss. 5 and 10 in "Zur Aussage und Botschaft von Johannes 21," pp. 347-49). Against this separation into two stories, see above, pp. 657f.

23. ἀπέβησαν in vs. 9 and then ἀνέβη here are used of getting off the boat and then reboarding. Apparently the idea is that the net was attached to the stern of the boat (cf. vss. 6, 8), so that to get to the net one first had to board the boat. The precise course of events cannot, in view of the extremely sober description, be pictured in detail. Was Peter able to haul the net ashore all by himself? In any case counting the fish was not a job for one. The Evangelist leaves some detail to the imagination of the reader. For the explanation given here, see also Brown, *Comm.* II, pp. 1073f.

made to this day — without, however, arriving at any credible result, to say nothing of one that has become generally accepted. What is at stake in this number in the text is the huge quantity, as is evident from the immediately following statement: "and though there were so many, the net was not torn." The unqualified number means something like "no fewer than one hundred fifty-three." Carefully counting the fish after a catch was probably never done. But the astonishing quantity of fish in that one net was so unusual that there was reason to count them and, with that, reason for this number to gain a fixed place in the tradition. Many interpreters, even today,[24] however critical they may be of theological interpretations from the past, nevertheless see in the details here a characteristic sign of the church. The large number is said at least to represent the all-embracing character of the community to be won by the disciples for Jesus, while the unbroken net is thought to symbolize the church's unbreakable unity (as the fruit of Jesus' prayer in ch. 17). However attractive this interpretation may seem at first sight, on closer scrutiny it cannot be maintained. Even in general, the great multitude of large fish hauled ashore by Peter can hardly serve as a picture of the church that then, as the result of the labor of all the apostles, is brought to Jesus by Peter as the head of the mission;[25] especially not if one remembers that Peter did this at Jesus' command in order — with a view to a *meal* — to "bring some of the fish you have just caught." Nor can the large number be explained in terms of the universality of the community,[26] since the catch consisted exclusively of "big" fish. And the unbroken net does not symbolize the discipline that the church needs in order to preserve its unity. The unbroken net refers, rather, to the element — referred to elsewhere — of "not letting any be lost," which the disciples are to observe always in their missionary practice (cf. 6:12).[27] This is not to say that the perspective of the church is missing in the narrative. The whole of Jesus' command and power symbolized in the catch of fish is undoubtedly directed toward bringing in the church,[28] but then certainly in the specific sense of Jesus' apostolic mandate and promise to his disciples.

12, 13 In keeping with this is the fact that when Jesus invites his disciples

---

24. See Ruckstuhl, "Zur Aussage und Botschaft von Johannes 21," pp. 345f.; Bultmann, *Comm.*, p. 709; Becker, *Comm.*, p. 642; Brown, *Comm.* II, p. 1097; Schnackenburg, *Comm.* III, pp. 357f.

25. Despite Ruckstuhl ("Zur Aussage und Botschaft von Johannes 21," pp. 345ff.). Others also appeal to "draw" (εἵλκυειν), which is said to echo 12:34 (cf. Brown, *Comm.* II, p. 1097: "the risen Jesus accomplishes his prophecy of drawing all men to himself through the apostolic ministry symbolized by the catch of fish and the hauling ashore").

26. So Schnackenburg.

27. For this motif see the comments above on 6:12ff.

28. Grosheide apparently rejects even this: "It seems that even a moderately allegorical explanation to the effect that the large number of fish symbolizes the large number of people that will be won for Christ by the preaching of the apostles (Alford) is inappropriate" (*Comm.* II, p. 557). The whole story "has no symbolic significance" (p. 559, n. 1).

to the meal, nothing further needs to be said. The entire focus is rather on the mysterious and overwhelming character of his presence and the disciples' being together with him. After everything that has happened and in view of the size of their catch they are no longer uncertain who they are with; "None of the disciples dared ask him, 'Who are you?' " Repeated here is what forces itself on them in all the resurrection appearances: the miracle of the "wholly-otherness" of his presence and of their "knowing" him, as compared to their experience of him before his death and resurrection, so that now they are kept from speaking to him. Knowing it was *he,* they shrink from entering into the mystery of his presence.

But Jesus "came" (vs. 13, here again indicative of his appearance) not only to show himself to them as the Living One but, on the basis of the new reality of his existence, to continue his fellowship with them as those called and sent out by him and to cause them to share in the gifts at his disposal as the living Lord. And so he invited them to sit at table with him, took the bread, and also the fish of the miracle, and gave them of it as provision from his hands for the journey that now lay before them and as heavenly equipment for the ministry on earth to which he had called them and for which he had destined them.[29]

14 This appearance ("revelation"), as far as it concerns the disciples as a group, is concluded in vs. 14. By speaking of "the third time" the author clearly incorporates this story into the preceding narrative. That the appearance to Mary Magdalene is not counted is further proof that when the author speaks of Jesus' "disciples" he has in mind the "apostolic" witness represented by them (see the comments on 20:21ff., 30). The word "now" suggests that Jesus' self-revelation became all the more undeniable for having occurred this third time. "After he was raised from the dead" is an expression that in its passive form is used only here in the Fourth Gospel (cf., however, 20:9).

21:15-23

Jesus' Farewell to Peter and to the Disciple That He Loved

15-17 The conversation of Jesus with Peter that now follows is focused especially on Peter's continuation of Jesus' work in the church and, in close conjunction with that, on the future of the beloved disciple.

---

29. There has been considerable discussion, also in connection with ch. 6, of whether the meal in ch. 21 is sacramental, especially among Catholic interpreters, but see also O. Cullmann, *Les Sacraments dans l'Évangile johannique,* 1951. See also at length Brown, *Comm.* II, pp. 1098ff. and the works referred to there. If one rejects a sacramental understanding of John 6 (cf. pp. 214ff., 236ff. above), then such an interpretation seems even more far-fetched here. Some Catholic authors are restrained, though not totally averse to such ideas, e.g., Ruckstuhl, "Zur Aussage und Botschaft von Johannes 21," p. 347; Schnackenburg, *Comm.* III, p. 359.

Jesus' thrice-repeated question, "Simon, son of John,[30] do you love me . . . ?" reflects Peter's threefold denial of Jesus and the dialogue preceding it at the Last Supper (19:16ff., 25ff.; 13:36ff.). The words of address also recall those spoken at Jesus' first encounter with Peter (1:42): "You are Simon, son of John; you shall be called Cephas." In this use of Peter's original name some scholars see Jesus taking a certain distance from Peter.[31] It seems that Jesus wants to make Peter feel that, before going further with him, he must first make a fresh beginning with him.

The repeated question presumably, in view of what follows in vs. 18, relates not only to Peter's attitude toward Jesus but also and especially to his readiness to serve and follow Jesus. The words added the first time Jesus asks the question, "more than these," might refer to the way in which Peter has until now taken the lead in comparison to the other disciples,[32] to Peter's earlier statement that he was willing to give Jesus his all (13:37; Mk. 14:29), and to what Peter will experience in the future (vss. 18, 19). In any case, thus formulated, this question is designed to let Peter know that loving and following Jesus can have more implications for him than he perhaps has thought and practiced in the past (cf. vs. 18a).

Peter's affirmative answer is without hesitation and appeals to Jesus' knowledge of him. The appeal does not have the sense of "Why ask me? You know me, don't you?" Jesus' knowledge is, rather, the last thing on which Peter can base an appeal before Jesus. His own actions have witnessed against him, and "more than these" seems to mock him more than justify him. All that is left to Peter is, "You know that I love you," an appeal to Jesus' knowledge of him as one of his own (10:14; cf. Lk. 22:32).

Some scholars think that the word "love" with which Peter replies,[33] which is different from the word used in Jesus' first two questions,[34] contains something more than a mere affirmation on Peter's part. The love of which Jesus speaks (ἀγάπη) is said to be higher and more spiritual than the more natural, emotional love (φίλη) Peter had the

---

30. For this name see the comments above on 1:42.

31. "Jesus is treating him less familiarly and thus challenging his friendship" (Brown, *Comm.* II, p. 1102).

32. The obvious meaning is "Do you love me more than these people love me?" not "Do you love me more than you love these people." The latter understanding has hardly any grounds in the context, and it sidetracks the train of thought. Some scholars have understood τούτων to be neuter, "more than these things," which is said to refer to the nets and the fishing business, Peter's old way of life. But for such a question Peter's conduct hardly gives any ground. One can hardly accept the notion that in asking this question Jesus was reproaching Peter for having gone fishing again.

33. φιλεῖν.

34. ἀγαπᾶν.

courage to ascribe to himself. The different words are then said to suggest the distance that is bridged in Jesus' third question, where he uses the same word as Peter (φιλεῖν, vs. 17). Though in the course of time much has been made of this supposed difference, scholars have become increasingly convinced that it plays no role here. φιλεῖν is used where it says that Jesus asked the same question the third time. And when Jesus finally takes over the word Peter has used in his answers, Peter does not feel relieved by it. Rather, he feels sad that Jesus has now asked him the same question a third time. And it is no less significant that the Evangelist himself uses the two words interchangeably when he speaks of Jesus' love for his disciples (15:9; 16:27; 11:3, 5) and for the beloved disciple (20:2; 13:23) and of the disciples' love for him (8:42; 16:27).[35]

In response to Peter's repeated assertion of his love for Jesus, Jesus answers with "Feed my lambs" (vs. 15), "Tend my sheep" (vs. 16), and "Feed my sheep" (vs. 17). The differences ("lambs" and "sheep," "feed" and "tend") can, taken strictly, express the shepherd's total care for the whole flock. But one thing is pivotal here: Jesus attests — again three times and in the presence of the other disciples as in 13:38 — his full confidence in Peter as future shepherd of his church.

Shepherding is one of the most frequent and characteristic images for leadership and care of the church. It is rooted in the portrayal of God as shepherd of his people (e.g., Pss. 23; 77:20; Ezekiel 34) and of Jesus as the good shepherd (10:1ff., 26ff.; Hb. 13:20; 1 Pt. 2:25, etc.). As such it is not typically "apostolic" but rather characteristic of every task or ministry in the church (cf. Ac. 20:28; Ep. 4:11; 1 Pt. 5:1ff.). Accordingly, there is in Jesus' repeated designation of Peter as shepherd nothing unique. Peter is not charged with the care of the entire flock as Jesus' earthly vicar, and he is not the chief shepherd to whom all the other shepherds are subordinate.[36] Peter's commissioning here is not different from that of all the disciples in 20:21-23.[37] This

35. An additional complication is the view that ἀγαπᾶν, of which Jesus first speaks (twice), would not have been too high a concept for Peter but, conversely, too distant and cool an expression for his intensely warm feelings for Jesus. In that case, Jesus' question is translated, "Are you really devoted to me?" and Peter's answer, "I tenderly love you." Only in his third question Jesus is said to have expressed himself in warmer emotional terms. Against this view (expressed by, among others, Trench) see the lengthy evaluation of the terms in Morris, *Comm.*, pp. 871f.; also Schnackenburg, *Comm.* III, pp. 362f.: "the two verbs are used . . . synonymously in John's gospel."

36. Cf. Schnackenburg: "It is unique that in Jn. 21:15-17 Peter is given the pastoral office over all Jesus' 'lambs' or 'sheep'; in this connection, he has a prominent position which is also confirmed by Mt. 16:18f." He speaks of Peter's ministry "as an office and in relation to Jesus as an earthly representation." But he acknowledges that "the interpretation represented by the exegesis of the Fathers and later of Catholic theologians, that in this passage, not only all believers, but, especially, the other disciples are subordinated to Peter, is not to be read into the text" (*Comm.* III, pp. 365f.).

37. The same is true of Mt. 16:18f. (cf. Mt. 18:18).

charge to Peter is so emphatic because of his earlier threefold denial and Jesus' thrice-attested willingness to continue to entrust to him the care of his church, as well as because Peter is the "Cephas" (1:42) on whom Jesus will build his church (Mt. 16:18; cf. Jn. 6:68). But "you will be called Cephas" will apply to him not only as spokesman and as the first-mentioned of the disciples, as until now he (with ups and downs) has acted, but no less or even especially as a follower, for which Jesus had destined him, as is evident in the transition to vss. 17-19.

Peter is grieved because Jesus asks him the third time, "Simon, do you love me?" Does Jesus have a reason for asking again? Peter answers, more firmly than the previous times, with, "Lord, you know *all things;* you know that I love you." Jesus does not specifically respond to this statement but merely repeats what he has said before: "Feed my sheep."

18-19a   What Jesus now adds with great prophetic power ("Truly, truly, I say to you") in a sense explains all that precedes. Jesus has sought not so much Peter's triple retraction of his denial, and even less to embarrass him again before the other disciples; it is rather what awaits Peter in the future that prompts Jesus to reinforce his ties with him as never before. To that end Jesus now applies to Peter the image of one who in the strength of youth can walk and stand where he pleases but in the weakness of old age must depend not only on the help of others (so that he need only "stretch out his hands") but also on their will, even if they take him where he does not want to go. In Peter's case this will not be occasioned by the infirmities of old age, which he will not be spared, but by the need to submit to powers that will take him "where you did not wish to go," and that in a highly charged sense, further explained by the Evangelist: "This he said to indicate the kind of death by which he would glorify God," namely as a martyr in the service of his Lord (cf. 1 Pt. 4:16).

A fair number of interpreters understand the statement of vs. 18 in a more specific sense. They believe that "stretch out your hands" refers to Peter's crucifixion, and "another will gird you" to binding with a rope before crucifixion. An immediate objection is that "stretch out your hands" is *followed* by the "binding" and leading away of Peter. Others, therefore, view the stretching out of Peter's hands as voluntary submission to handcuffing. But can "gird" be used of handcuffing? Therefore, along with many others, we prefer the view that "the kind of death by which he would die" does not refer to a specific mode of execution but more generally to Peter's death as that of a martyr.

19b   The specific meaning in this context of Jesus' next words to Peter, "Follow me," is not totally clear. It seems most likely with a view to vss. 15f. that this is an allusion to the conversation that took place on the eve of Jesus' death (13:36ff.), when Peter's following of Jesus was also discussed in a profound way. Then Jesus said: "Where I am going you cannot follow me now; but you will follow afterward." Peter contradicted him: "Lord, why can I not follow you now? I will lay down my life for you." All this comes back now but is viewed from the perspective of the "afterward" of 13:36 (cf. 13:7), that is, of what has happened since. Following Jesus — to which Jesus now calls Peter — has been placed on another foundation than that of Peter "girding himself" and his willingness to assume the risks entailed. He is now asked to follow Jesus on a road that Jesus has traveled first and alone and on which he, as the great Shepherd of the sheep, has given his life. Now the time has come for Peter to tend the sheep. The risks of following have not diminished. But the way Peter must go has been pioneered; as his Lord's follower and as shepherd of his Lord's sheep he will be not only a participant in his Lord's death but also a witness to and participant in his Lord's resurrection.

20, 21 It is remarkable that Jesus' farewell to Peter does not take place apart from the involvement of the beloved disciple. A line visible throughout the Gospel is extended here that clearly tends to bring into the foreground, along with the well-known figure of Peter, this other disciple, not to compete with Peter or to detract from his authority but as one who, among the disciples of Jesus, has assumed and will assume a place no less important than that of Peter. The depiction of the situation in vs. 20a is not altogether clear[38] and is therefore understood by some scholars as an artificial connection created by the author to make room here for the well-known saying in vs. 22. But it is precisely in relation to the preceding dialogue that Peter's question ("Lord, what about this man?") gains its significance.

It is striking that the author — differently than in vs. 7 — once more expressly identifies this disciple as the one who had reclined next to Jesus at "the" supper and had said: "Lord, who is it that is going to betray you?" (13:23f.). Evidently the intent is once more to put the spotlight on him as Jesus' confidante, next to Peter (cf. 13:24!), and on his continuing followership of Jesus. What matters in this passage is the future of *both* disciples, and that in their interconnectedness.

22, 23 Jesus urges Peter not to meddle with what he has in mind for the other disciple, even if it differs from what he has predicted for Peter. Jesus' answer suggests, in fact, that it will be different. The emphasis here is on Jesus' authority and power — "if it is my will" — not in a vague potential sense ("supposing it was my will that he should remain . . .") but rather as

---

38. "When Peter turned he saw the disciple whom Jesus loved following" (in some manuscripts the last word is lacking). Apparently the event occurs after the meal, when Peter takes to the road, along with Jesus, and turns to see the other disciple also detaching himself from the others and following Jesus.

an indication that what Jesus has in mind[39] is not involved between him and Peter.

This, then, is how we must view the much-discussed vs. 23. The author tells how Jesus' saying[40] was received in the church ("among the brothers") as the word that the disciple would not die.[41] He immediately adds, however, that Jesus did not at all speak of the disciple's death but said: "*If it is my will* that he remain until I come." To substantiate this he again cites Jesus' words, which speak not of "not dying" but of "continuing." Thus he suggests that, while Peter's destiny lay in the God-glorifying significance of his death, Jesus' purpose with the other disciple lay rather in his *continuing,* though not in the sense — as the Evangelist expressly states — that this disciple could not die before the coming of Jesus. Instead, by continuing, he would serve Jesus as his disciple throughout his life. Undoubtedly the full meaning of Jesus' saying about this disciple — like the saying about Peter in vss. 18-19 — would come out only later. But for that very reason it was Jesus' prerogative to will and to know all this ("if it is my will"), not Peter's. What applies to both disciples is the call to follow Jesus, each with his own destiny. For Peter it means that he will complete his life like the "good Shepherd" in self-offering for Jesus' flock. For the beloved disciple this means his continuing witness[42] until the coming of his Lord in glory (cf. vs. 24).[43]

With this interpretation we are distancing ourselves from the widespread view that in repeating Jesus' saying the author sought solely to stress the conditional character of Jesus' statement and thus to invalidate the appeal of James and John to the saying. With "*if* it is my will" Jesus is said only to leave open the possibility that this disciple would

---

39. ἐὰν θέλω, indicative (see below).

40. There is some uncertainty whether οὗτος ὁ λόγος refers back to vs. 22 or to the saying or rumor that had spread among the disciples that "that disciple will not die" (cf. Schnackenburg: "the saying spread abroad among the brethren that this disciple was not to die," *Comm.* III, p. 367; similarly RSV and NRSV). Although οὗτος ὁ λόγος, which immediately follows vs. 22, naturally makes us think of Jesus' own saying, it offers a different version of it, which is explicitly corrected by the author. Therefore, though the transitions are very fluid here, there is much to be said, in substance, in favor of this view.

41. This misunderstanding, according to some scholars, occasioned confusion and uncertainty, either because the beloved disciple had already died or, on account of his advanced age, his death seemed imminent. Others even speak of a crisis occasioned by the delay of Jesus' parousia while more and more of the apostles, even the beloved disciple, died. Our passage, then, coming from the leaders of the community (the "we" of vs. 24), served to respond to this crisis. On this see at length Thyen, "Entwicklungen der johanneischen Theologie," in *L'Évangile de Jean,* ed. M. de Jonge, 1977, pp. 259-99, here pp. 268-73; cf. Becker, *Comm.* II, pp. 648f. This understanding is based on presuppositions for which one can in part appeal to passages like 1 Th. 4;13ff. but which cannot be substantiated from the Fourth Gospel.

42. ὁ μαρτυρῶν, present participle, vs. 24.

43. For this "guidance of the text," see Thyen, "Entwicklungen der johanneischen Theologie," pp. 272f.

not die. Hence, if this disciple should die, that would only prove that Jesus in his sovereign authority had not willed that he should remain alive.[44]

Others, however, correctly state that, given this interpretation, the passage about the future importance of the beloved disciple, which concludes the whole Gospel, has little to say and is merely negative. It evidently makes no distinction — any more than James and John would have — between "not dying" and "remaining," whereas the author makes a point of stressing this difference, first in his own statement and then by repeating Jesus' saying. But it is hard to believe that Jesus would correct Peter by presenting him with a possibility that he had no intention to realize, instead of asking Peter not to interfere in that for which he in his sovereign authority had *actually* destined the disciple whom he loved. And vs. 24 makes it clear that the protasis of vs. 22 contains an indicative verb, not a subjunctive.[45]

Finally, one can ask whether already in vs. 23 the "we" of vs. 24 are speaking, that is, those who before bringing the Gospel to a close wish to correct the misunderstanding over Jesus' answer to Peter that has arisen among "the brothers." If that is the case, Jesus' last word to Peter is the original end of ch. 21. Although that is possible, there is more reason, in our estimate, to ascribe vss. 22 and 23 to the same author, namely the author of the preceding narrative. Not until vs. 24 do the "we" begin to speak.

21:24-25

Conclusion

24 Here a "we" takes the floor to place all possible stress on the permanent significance of the beloved disciple with reference to the content of the Gospel ("these things") as the "we" received it. These people are evidently those who by adding these words are putting the finishing touch on ch. 21 and are thereby presenting the whole Gospel to its readers as the work of the beloved disciple.

---

44. So many older commentaries, but among more recent ones, see also Bultmann: "Now v. 23 of course affirms that the saying of Jesus was not a prophecy but only a hypothetical statement" (*Comm.* p. 715); so also Schulz, *Comm.,* and others.

45. For this latter interpretation see, e.g., Schnackenburg, *Comm.* III, p. 371; M. de Jonge, "The Beloved Disciple and the Date of the Gospel of John," in *Text and Interpretation* (Festschrift for M. Black, ed. E. Best and R. M. Wilson), 1979, pp. 99-114; and especially Thyen, who calls the potential view ("if it is my will") "a barely tolerable triviality" within which "instead of closing with the expected enlightenment about the fate and significance of the disciple whom Jesus loved whose authority up until this point had been carefully built up, the Gospel would end with a correction of a banal misunderstanding" and "the purposeful and pointed differentiation of 'remaining' and 'not dying' becomes a disconnected appendix" ("Entwicklungen der johanneischen Theologie," pp. 270f.).

This "we" is understood to be the community that formed around the beloved disciple, to which he left his Gospel as his legacy.[46]

But the main point of this statement is its description of the real and permanent significance of this disciple as the one "who testifies concerning these things and has written them." Some have identified "these things" solely in relation to the immediately preceding narrative in this chapter.[47] But since "these things" is also the object of "he has written," it can hardly be understood as anything other than a description of the whole Gospel (cf. also vs. 25), as by far the majority of interpreters assume.[48] "Who testifies to these things" refers primarily to this disciple's permanent significance as an eyewitness (and earwitness) of the things described in the Gospel.[49] "And who has written these things" serves to reinforce the preceding "testimony": the beloved disciple has written down his testimony and made it into Scripture (see also the comments on 20:30, 31) so that it is no longer dependent on his presence. As the continuation of vs. 23 all this therefore shows what Jesus meant with "If it is my will that he remain. . . ."

This statement thus points to the beloved disciple as witness and author of the entire preceding narrative. There has naturally been much discussion (with varying conclusions) of the "beloved disciple" passages and, with that, of the character and content of the entire Gospel. How all this bears on the statement in 21:24 requires a separate, summarizing discussion (see below). We can note here only that the words "testifying" and "has written" are not open to misunderstanding and relate above all to the person of the beloved disciple and that one cannot therefore weaken his "writing" by viewing it as "nonliteral"[50] or "causative" (in the sense of 19:22).[51]

46. See further on this "we," below, pp. 677f.

47. See, e.g., C. H. Dodd, *Historical Tradition in the Fourth Gospel,* 1965, p. 15, which refers to an earlier article by Dodd.

48. See, e.g., Schnackenburg, *Comm.* III, p. 373.

49. ὁ μαρτυρῶν, present participle; cf. μεμαρτύρηκεν in 19:35, which similarly refers to his permanent significance.

50. T. Witkamp, for example, writes that it is "not necessary to take these words in a modern sense, as though the beloved disciple were the author in a literal sense" (*Jezus van Nazareth in de gemeente van Johannes,* 1986, p. 350), in order thus to create room for a role of the beloved disciple in the Fourth Gospel that is largely detached from the written witness of this Gospel.

51. For the right understanding of ὁ γράψας ταῦτα ("the one who has written these things"), aside from the commentaries by Barrett, Morris, and others, see also de Jonge, "The Beloved Disciple and the Date of the Gospel of John," pp. 101f.:

Opinions may differ as to whether ὁ γράψας should be interpreted as a causative (cf. XIX,22) or not; the important thing is, however, that the "we" who wrote vs. 24 regard this anonymous Beloved Disciple as the author of the Gospel and claim his authority for it, the authority of an eye-witness and a direct follower of Jesus.

See also de Jonge's *Jesus: Stranger from Heaven and Son of God,* 1977, p. 221: "The participle γράψας ταῦτα is sometimes taken as a causative (cf. 19:2), but in the context it means certainly more. What the disciple witnesses all along stands now on paper."

"And we know" once more confirms the "truth" and hence the trustworthiness of "his witness." They clearly recall 19:35. But there the author of the Gospel himself, on the basis of his own testimony, calls for faith in the church (cf. 20:31). Here the "we" of the church itself places beyond all doubt the reliability and authority of this disciple. After the apostle's witness comes the church's confession, a clear additional proof of how roles are divided when the "we" is speaking in the Fourth Gospel (cf. 1:14 and comments there).

25 The final (second) ending once more surveys the whole Gospel. It speaks hyperbolically of all "the things Jesus did." This statement is again from another hand than vs. 24 ("I suppose"). It has been said that such an exaggerated way of glorifying Jesus' deeds is not in the spirit of the Evangelist himself.[52] Still, these words also hint at what, in his way and indeed much more soberly, the Evangelist himself has expressed in 20:30-31: that this Gospel has made no attempt at completeness and that its content must be judged accordingly.

The Beloved Disciple

The statement with which the "we" of 21:24 concludes what precedes, precisely as concluding statement, is naturally of particular interest with regard to identification of the beloved disciple. This, then, is the place for us to summarize what we have mentioned only fragmentarily so far, though all that we have noted must be taken into account to assess the true value and intent of the "we" ending. Here both that the disciple "gives witness" and that he "has written" are important. The two issues are intertwined, but we will take the first as our starting point.

The Beloved Disciple as Witness

Nowhere more clearly than in 21:24 is the beloved disciple referred to as a historical person and not a symbolic figure.[53] Furthermore, this disciple is not referred to primarily here as one who lived in the midst of the church but as the disciple as mentioned *in this context* ("This is"), along with Peter, that is, as a member of the circle of Jesus' closest disciples and as such beloved by Jesus (cf. vs. 20). The concern of the statement is to characterize the role and importance of this disciple as that of eyewitness (and earwitness) of "these things" and to describe him, therefore, as most reliable in his witness (vs. 24c). This qualification — we can now observe — agrees completely with the role that earlier passages that speak of him have given to him. This, therefore, is

52. "Who is interested in the deeper significance of Jesus works." So Schnackenburg, *Comm.* III, p. 374, who offers a highly critical assessment of the ending.
53. This is also acknowledged by Bultmann (cf. *Comm.*, pp. 483, 716f.); for him, however, this is proof that the author of 21:24 identified a later authority in the church with the figure of the beloved disciple (whom Bultmann apparently does not understand as symbolic) in order thus to make the Gospel more authoritative (p. 716).

further proof that all attempts to interpret his activity in a nonhistorical, symbolic sense (that of the "ideal disciple") bring about a fundamental change in his significance and turn it in a completely different direction (see the comments on 13:23ff.; 18:15; 19:26f., 35[!]; 20:2ff.).

But it is also clear, in light of the Gospel as a whole, that 21:24 cannot be intended to characterize all of the preceding material as the personal memoirs of the beloved disciple. Not only does the Gospel contain more than a factual report of what happened but it also is based on a broader witness than that of just the beloved disciple. In his concluding recapitulation of his work in 20:30, 31, the Evangelist himself describes his work as that of recording the signs Jesus did in his disciples' presence, thus revealing his glory as the Christ and the Son of God. The Evangelist's aim is not to furnish, as the foundation for the church's faith, anything other or more than this broad apostolic witness, however much he includes his own part as an eyewitness (1:14; 15:26, 27) and however much he appeals specifically to the beloved disciple's eyewitness report (cf. 19:35).

In that sense there is undoubtedly a difference in point of view between the witness of the "we" in 21:24 and the Evangelist's testimony concerning his writing. What comes to the fore in the "we" statement is a special bond with the beloved disciple; he is their witness par excellence. Naturally they do not write that he is the only witness, but they do, by their statement, publish the Gospel under his authority as their permanent witness.

In the Gospel itself, viewed now as a whole, this disciple remains much more in the background in the redemptive events he experiences along with the other disciples. There is good reason in the framework of the Gospel to recognize the beloved disciple in the anonymous disciple of 1:35ff. But he appears as the beloved disciple only in the passion narrative, beginning with ch. 13, and only at a few points, though they are key points. In Jesus' lengthy farewell discourse in chs. 14-17 and in the appearance stories and the commissioning of the disciples in ch. 20, this disciple is not mentioned separately. Only in ch. 21 does he, along with Peter, come to the fore in the full light of the resurrection and receive from the Risen One his permanent role in the coming church. So it is with this earlier material in ch. 21 that the "we" in vs. 24 refer to (*"This* is the disciple").

On the basis of this limited but prominent role, some scholars believe that the passages relating to the beloved disciple do not constitute an original unity with the rest of the Gospel. These scholars claim that the figure of the beloved disciple, in the sense in which the "we" of 21:24 speak of him, was only later inserted into an already existing textual unit (a "basic document") in order to give the book greater authority. The notion of the "ideal disciple" again plays an important role in this hypothesis.[54]

But as long as one takes the figure of the beloved disciple — however special it is in itself — for what it is and as he is described by the "we" of 21:24, namely as an eyewitness and not a "theological" ideal figure, then there is no reason that he should

---

54. So especially Thyen, "Entwicklungen der johanneischen Theologie." See also T. Lorenzen, *Der Lieblingsjünger im Johannesevangelium,* 1971, and, with more restraint ("possibly but not necessarily"), de Jonge, "The Beloved Disciple and the Date of the Gospel of John," pp. 105f.; Schnackenburg, *Comm.* III, pp. 380ff.

not at the same time function in the entire Gospel as "disciple among the disciples" and why his special witness should not be subsumed under the general heading of the apostolic witness in the sense spoken of in 20:30 (cf. 1:14). Nor can his late appearance on the Gospel's stage serve as an argument against this. The Gospel is, after all, constructed so that the disciples (after the graphic narrative of their calling in 1:35-51) are referred to only in general terms and mentioned by name in only a few cases. Not until 13:1 does Jesus address them in particular and does their part in the progression of the narrative get full attention. Only after 1:41f. do Peter and the beloved disciple play special roles in the passion narrative (of which 6:68 is undoubtedly part of the background). And this argument is all the more compelling because during the passion the two disciples repeatedly act in conjunction, though each in his own way: Peter in his prominent role as spokesman for the disciples and in his continuing opposition to Jesus' journey to the cross, the "other" disciple in his special relationship of trust to Jesus (cf. 13:23ff.; 19:26). Thus these two are the only disciples who follow Jesus after his arrest (each for his own reasons and despite Jesus' saying in 16:32!). Thus, following Peter's denial, in a highly characteristic way, the "other" is the only disciple left to hear Jesus' last words, together with Jesus' mother, and to witness the circumstances of Jesus' death (19:26f., 33-35).

The mere fact of this conjunction of the activities of the two disciples — intended perhaps already in 1:40f. and continued and deepened in the resurrection narrative (20:2ff.; 21) — makes it extremely difficult to abstract the beloved disciple from this context and to take him as a figure later inserted into an existing narrative. The integral manner in which the passages concerning him are incorporated into the Gospel resists this construction, and one also faces the difficult question whether and to what degree the undeniably historical figure of Peter was taken up into this symbolization process. Finally, and no less important, the settings in which the beloved disciple plays a role, with Peter or not, are always ones to which only he can give testimony because of the special bond he has with Jesus: either he participates in events that remain hidden to others (13:23, 26) or he follows Jesus when the others have disappeared (18:15f.; 19:26, 35; cf. 1:39). That bond materializes in his special role as a witness and explains the limitations of that role.

Attempts to Identify the Disciple

Since, therefore, the historicity of the beloved disciple's role in the Gospel can hardly be denied, it is natural to ask whether we can identify him among the disciples of Jesus known to us. All the data point in one direction. In 13:1-23 he is explicitly called "one of his disciples," by whom are meant, here as so often, the narrow circle of men whom Jesus chose and with whom he formed special ties (cf. 13:18), those who are called the Twelve, with whom, according to the whole tradition, Jesus observed the Last Supper. Among these, according to 13:23, this one disciple was the one "whom Jesus loved," an expression describing personal friendship (cf. 11:5; or also kinship? see the comments on 19:25). These criteria exclude some who have been identified as this disciple, such as Lazarus[55] or John Mark. Everything tends to confirm the ecclesiastical

---

55. See the comments above on 11:3.

tradition that, in part on the basis of patristic testimonies,[56] has linked the name of John, son of Zebedee, with the Fourth Gospel. Favoring this identification, of course, is the special place that this disciple has in the other Gospels, in particular his being frequently in the company of Peter (e.g., Lk. 22:8, where John and Peter are appointed to prepare the Last Supper; see also Ac. 3:1; 4:13, 19; 8:14; Gl. 2:9). Arguments from silence, though they are always to be handled with care, are also of importance here. How else can one explain that the central figure of John is not mentioned by name in the Fourth Gospel?[57] And can one imagine that in the period in which the Gospel was written a church community (known or unknown) could demand and acquire for its chief pastor such ("canonical") authority as that of an intimate of Jesus and the equal of Peter if this person had not himself belonged to the circle of Jesus' first disciples (the apostles)?[58]

Meanwhile this — one might say rather obvious — identification of the beloved disciple with John the son of Zebedee is rejected by others on the ground of the strictly observed anonymity in which the beloved disciple appears in the Gospel. Various interpreters — even when they more or less freely concede that the beloved disciple must have stood in a very personal relationship if not to Jesus himself then certainly to people from his immediate circle — regard this anonymity as the strongest argument that this disciple cannot be identified with the apostle John or someone from the immediate circle of Jesus' first disciples. The reasoning is that if the beloved disciple had belonged to the circle of the apostles or had at least been one of the familiar figures in primitive Christianity, he would certainly have been mentioned as such by the Johannine circle, for whom it was of the greatest importance to gain recognition in the larger church for the witness to Christ that they held in such high esteem.[59]

This "strongest" argument is only compelling, however, if one assumes that the Gospel's author was not the apostle John (or someone else from Jesus' closest circle). If the author was in fact someone else, it is certainly hard to explain why he consistently refers to the anonymous "beloved disciple" and not explicitly to "John," since he refers to Peter, Andrew, Thomas, and others by name. But if the beloved disciple was the author himself, as 21:24 emphatically states, and if he was a figure of the first rank in the church, as we have tried to show, then the case is very different

---

56. For these (variously assessed) testimonies see the various introductions to the New Testament.

57. See also the comments above on 21:2.

58. Not even Schnackenburg, in the extensive apology for his revised position, can completely avoid this question: "The question is not unimportant whether John's gospel is an anonymous, obscure work of doubtful origin, or whether it does have a connection with that original generation of witnesses from the time of Jesus which the later church called upon for 'its apostolic tradition' " (*Comm.* III, p. 385). But he refrains from drawing any conclusions from this observation.

59. So, e.g., Schnackenburg: "The anonymity of the beloved disciple becomes immediately understandable if he really was a relatively unknown man in primitive Christianity. . . ." This he regards as "the strongest argument for the apostle John not to be identified with the beloved disciple." That identification was, admittedly, made at an early date. But "the Johannine circle did not in any way want to insinuate this falsely" (*Comm.* III, p. 384). See also de Jonge, "The Beloved Disciple and the Date of the Gospel of John," p. 109, with an appeal to Thyen.

and the argument from anonymity works the other direction. Who other than such a prominent author, the beloved disciple himself, could have better reason for not referring to the beloved disciple by name? He did not do this, of course, to keep that identity a secret (which he could never do successfully!) but to subordinate his own role in the narrative to the goal he has set for himself, which is to record what Jesus revealed of his glory in the presence of his disciples (20:30, 31). When the "we" in 21:24 refrain from revealing his name, they do so neither out of ignorance of his name nor to introduce as authoritative their unknown (to the outside world) founder and leader under the honorific title of disciple but to respect the anonymity that the author himself has observed.

It has been said that such authorial reserve is hard to reconcile with the "name of honor" that "the disciple whom Jesus loved" indirectly attributes to himself. But "name of honor" is hardly an appropriate term, and the translation "favorite disciple" is certainly wrong. Inconsistent with such a interpretation are the extremely down-to-earth and unelaborated sobriety with which the author uses this designation, his alternation of it with other more impersonal designations (as in 18:15; 19:35; cf. also 20:2), the absence of any attempt as "beloved disciple" to assert himself in competition with his fellow disciples, especially Peter, and most of all the atmosphere of restraint — sometimes called "mysterious" — that he observes with respect to his person from beginning to end, especially when the reference is directly to himself (21:21). What compels him to refer to himself with this term is to some degree pragmatic: it explains, as in 13:23 and 19:26, 27, the special confidence that Jesus has in him. But the primary reason is that the designation brings out the trustworthiness and apostolic authority of his witness. This is undoubtedly also why in 21:20, in introducing Jesus' saying concerning his "remaining" and in the statement of the "we" in vs. 24 that refers back to it, this trustworthiness is expressly accentuated.

The Authorship of the Gospel

With this last statement we have arrived at the subject of the authorship ascribed to the beloved disciple in 21:24. Assessment of this authorship is naturally closely tied in with the first part of the statement in that verse. If one assigns to the beloved disciple not the role of eyewitness but that of a (more or less) symbolic figure, one will also have greater difficulty seeing him as the author who reliably recorded "these things" that we have before us. Accordingly, the degree to which this disciple's role as eyewitness is not fully recognized corresponds to the degree that his authorship (in the sense of 21:24) becomes nebulous.[60] Those who deem it impossible that the Fourth Gospel was written by an intimate disciple and eyewitness of Jesus are more inclined (or compelled!) to declare the beloved disciple a fiction or an ideal figure.

Still, even if one sees the beloved disciple's activity in the Fourth Gospel as really reflecting the eyewitness testimony spoken of in 21:24, one cannot simply conclude that he was the author of the Gospel as we have it. As stated earlier, "who

---

60. As in the case of the "nonliteral" and "causative" interpretations of the words "has written"; see the comments above on the verse.

has written these things" is not a disclosure, added at the last minute, of who in fact wrote the book. It is, rather, in all its brevity, a further description of the beloved disciple's witness as recorded in writing[61] and therefore the more reliable and "true" (see the closing words of the verse). If, however, one further views these words in the light of the whole Gospel, then it is clear that the authorship of the Gospel encompasses much more than mere recording of what the beloved disciple as transmitter of the tradition heard and saw. Its extensive theological interpretation dominates the book, and we must factor that component into the issue of authorship.

A "Johannine Circle"?

This last point has led some scholars who want to give due weight to the eyewitness role of the beloved disciple (whoever he was) to conclude that the Gospel as we have it was written by not just one person but as the result of an advanced "theology" of the person of Jesus that developed in a certain "school" or "circle" of which that one person was the spiritual father or leader.

A point of contact for this hypothesis could be the fact that the Fourth Gospel clearly did not come to us from the hand of the author-Evangelist himself, but is presented to us by the "we" of 21:24. That verse does occasion a range of questions: Why did not the Evangelist publish the book himself? Who are the "we"? Were they coworkers or pupils of the beloved disciple?[62] Did they perhaps have more of a hand in the origination of the Gospel as we have it than merely its publication? That would point to the existence of the widely accepted Johannine "school" or "circle,"[63] from which the Gospel as we have it is said to have emerged as the end product of a theological development that is itself reflected in the Gospel. The point of departure for this hypothesis is indeed the spiritual paternity of the beloved disciple, who is said to have laid the first historical foundation, which related especially to the life of Jesus, either from his own memory or from tradition available to him. From this, under the influence of his direction, there gradually developed a deeper insight into the life of Jesus. This process, it is said, can be demonstrated from the various "levels" or "strata" of the book. The process came to an end in ch. 21, which was added by the "we."[64] The different "phases" are said to be recognizable from certain irregularities, abrupt transitions, repetitions, and the like, for example, in the farewell discourse,[65] in which revisions by the author himself or later redactors are said to be clearly discernible. Pursuing this line of thought, some think they are able to trace in these different redactions not merely the progression of Johannine theology but also the changing circumstances of the Johannine community, to which the content of the Gospel was

61. Cf. G. Schrenk, *TDNT* I, p. 745, who points to "the emphatic equation of μαρτυρεῖν and γράφειν in John 21:24" as the documentation of the witness.

62. For the view that the author describes himself as (or includes himself in) the "we," see, e.g., the lengthy discussion (which rightly rejects this view) of Brown, *Comm.* II, pp. 1124-25.

63. See O. Cullmann, *The Johannine Circle*, 1976.

64. So, in the main, Brown's reconstruction in his *Comm.* I, pp. xxxiv-xxxix; see also his analysis of the Farewell Discourse (II, pp. 586ff.) and his interpretation of 21:24 (II, p. 1125).

65. See the exegesis above.

adapted.[66] It is clear that in this way "who has written these things" is taken in a very broad sense to refer to a collective authorship strongly conditioned by the Johannine school or the whole community.

Now it is undoubtedly true that with respect to the manner and form in which the Fourth Gospel has come down to us we face a number of questions for which there are no simple answers. It cannot be denied that the author was unable or disinclined to publish his writing himself. It is most likely that he had already died and that the "we" in 21:24, his pupils or spiritual kin, had received it as part of his legacy. It is also clear that, whether on instructions from him or not, they knew themselves authorized to publish it in this form and on his authority. One can further see in this verse an indication that earlier they had been involved in some way in the work of the beloved disciple. We simply know too little of the way in which this grandly conceived work came into being, of the possibilities at the author's disposal, and of the assistance he may have needed from others — too little to make responsible pronouncements on these issues. The simple expression "has written," coming in the same breath as "bearing witness," opens a space we cannot precisely measure.

It is no less clear that the Gospel as we have it is the result of long and profound reflection on the meaning of the coming and work of Jesus of Nazareth. The Evangelist himself describes it as the fruit of the Spirit's co-witness (14:26; cf. 15:26; 16:13). In this respect there is undoubtedly no small difference between the beloved disciple as eyewitness and the beloved disciple as author of the Gospel, in the sense that the true meaning and deep sense of what he heard and saw still had to be disclosed, to him as well as the other disciples, by the light of Scripture (cf. 20:9, 10; 2:22; 12:16; 14:25f.; 16:12). For that reason "testimony" in 21:24 (cf. 19:35), which stresses the reliability of what was written — "the factuality of his history,"[67] is not the last and most characteristic thing that can be said of the content and thrust of the Fourth Gospel. The author's aim, both as transmitter of the tradition and as Evangelist, is above all to unfold for the community the revelatory significance — oriented to faith and ever more deeply understood by the author himself — of what Jesus said and did in the presence of the disciples.[68]

But can such a development be demonstrated from supposed "levels" and "strata" that are said to be distinguishable in the Gospel but about the details of which no two scholars are in agreement? We have seen over and over how problematic all sorts of interpretations are that see the hand of a later redactor in every real or imagined irregularity in the structure of the book. It could certainly be that the author had not yet produced the final draft and that the "we" of 21:24, out of respect for him, published it in the form in which they received it, that the author followed standards different from those of his modern critics and was therefore less troubled by a transition like that from 14:31 to 15:1, and therefore that those interpreters are right who apply the

---

66. So, following Brown, J. Painter, who sees a reflection of the ongoing deterioration between the Johannine community and the "world" surrounding it in the various "stages" discernible in the Farewell Discourse ("The Farewell Discourses and the History of Johannine Christianity," *NTS* 27 [1981], pp. 525-43).

67. G. Strathmann, *TDNT* IV, p. 498.

68. See at length pp. 7ff. above.

rule that when differences or irregularities occur in a piece of writing they are to be consistently viewed as irregularities within the framework of that writing and not immediately attributed to secondary authors.[69]

And this is all the more true when frequently far-reaching conclusions are drawn from these supposed findings with respect to the changing historical circumstances in which the readers found themselves.[70] The image of Jesus as it is described in the Fourth Gospel is then in fact that of "Jesus of Nazareth" *in the Johannine community,* and increasingly shows less of the features of Jesus' historical self-revelation and more of the circumstances and the theology of that community.[71] This is not to deny that in its aim, selection of the material, and form, this Gospel is also shaped by the needs of the readers of the time in which it was written, specifically by the deepening conflict between the Christian community and the Jewish synagogue over Jesus (cf. 15:18f.; 16:1f.; 20:30, 31, etc.). But this certainly occurs in such a general way that on the basis of the Gospel as we have it one cannot form any concrete image of a specific "Johannine" community, let alone of recognizable social or theological developments in such a community.

What must most of all restrain us from entering on such particularization and sectarianizing of the Fourth Gospel is the undeniable general apostolic and catholic consciousness evidenced by the Evangelist and by the corresponding presentation of the Gospel by the "we" in 21:24. It is *generally* apostolic in that, even as the disciple whom Jesus loved, the author refrains from saying anything that could indicate a confessional direction of his own or a particular insight — developed in his own school or circle — into the person and work of Jesus as the Christ and the Son of God. In his summary of the Gospel (20:30, 31) he appeals to the revelation of Jesus' glory *in the presence of his disciples.* He anonymously includes himself among those who have beheld the glory of the incarnate Word (1:14) and who from the very beginning as Jesus' disciples have received for their testimony the assurance of the Spirit's joint witness (15:26, 27; 20:22f.).[72] And it is *catholic* because thus the author presents himself

---

69. For this rule see also de Jonge's insightful essay, "Variety and Development in Johannine Christology," in his *Jesus: Stranger from Heaven and Son of God,* pp. 193-222, in which he also discusses the Johannine letters (p. 199).

70. On this see de Jonge, *Jesus: Stranger from Heaven and Son of God,* pp. 198f. He writes about the need to observe "great circumspection" in employing the Gospel as a historical source for the community situation, caution which is "all the more necessary when we deal with reconstructed sources and earlier stages of redaction. In fact no author escapes reasoning in a circle" (p. 199).

71. See at greater length pp. 282f., 364 on the "two-level" theory of J. L. Martyn.

72. On the apostolic character, which is integral with eyewitness origin, see the comments above on 1:14. Bultmann writes (*Comm.,* p. 484): "While there is no doubt that the Evangelist includes himself in the circle of those who utter the ἐθεασάμεθα of 1.14, it is equally certain that he cannot have been an eyewitness in the sense of one who gives first-hand testimony." But in his interpretation of 1:14 Bultmann clearly indicates that though ἐθεασάμεθα not only refers to a sensory seeing but to "the sight of faith," still every new generation is dependent on these eyewitnesses. The church, after all, is constituted not by an "idea" but by "a concrete history and its tradition," from which it cannot free itself if it is to have faith (cf. *Comm.,* pp. 69f.). It is therefore hard to see how the Evangelist can include himself in the circle of 1:14 without himself being a historical eyewitness.

to his readers, not as the interpreter of their particular "Johannine" faith or as the spokesman for their theology, but as a permanent witness, appointed by Jesus and placed in his service, for the whole community to come (cf. 19:27; 20:31), in the most comprehensive sense in which time after time Jesus had spoken of it (cf. 17:20; 20:29; see also 4:35-38 ["the Savior of the world," vs. 42]).

Accordingly, it is only in that sense that the "we" in 21:24 are able to speak, not as jointly responsible with the author for the content of the Gospel, nor as included in the "we" of 1:14, but as spokespersons for the community who receives the Gospel, who accepts the writing that lies before them as the codification — valid for the entire church community — of the beloved disciple's apostolic witness.[73]

Negative Assumptions

A much more radical viewpoint with respect to 21:24 is adopted by those scholars who, on the basis of the entire content of the Fourth Gospel, think that it cannot have been written by an eyewitness and certainly not by the apostle John. Since the first half of the nineteenth century Johannine authorship — little challenged until then — was increasingly called into question. A range of motives, arising partly from worldview and partly from related methods of approach, have played a role in this. Thus, the high self-revelation in word and deed attributed to Jesus is said to represent a christology too advanced to be attributed to eyewitnesses or contemporaries of Jesus. Therefore it points to a much later time, perhaps the middle of the second century. Other scholars have abandoned the idea of an eyewitness because they claim that the Fourth Gospel's entire image of Jesus was not *intended* to be historical but only depicts graphically the high spiritual significance that the author attributed to the person of Jesus. In any case, the author's profundity as a "theologian," sometimes described as "idealistic" and then again as "Gnostic," was said to be simply inconceivable in the case of a simple fisherman from Galilee. On top of this the terminology — not terribly Jewish — and the conceptual world were said to suggest a clearly Hellenistic and syncretistic background.

Much of this criticism, meanwhile, has made way for a much less radical approach. The discovery of early second-century papryi containing fragments of the Fourth Gospel constitutes proof of a much earlier origin than critics had assumed until then. According to the religio-historical method, which had long been applied to the Fourth Gospel, the Gospel can only be understood against the background of certain

---

73. Brown (appealing to an article by F. W. Grosheide, *Gereformeerd theologisch tijdschrift* 53 [1953], pp. 117f.) rightly speaks of ch. 21 as possibly representing "the threshold of the period of canon formation." "With the passing of the apostolic generation, of which the Beloved Disciple may have been one of the last prominent members, there seems to have arisen in the Church a desire to preserve a witness that would never again be given." Brown emphasizes that the Evangelist's "insistence that the work reflects the testimony of an eyewitness of Jesus' ministry exemplifies the mentality behind canon formation" (*Comm.* II, p. 1128). Also Thyen, though very critical with respect to the testimony of an eyewitness, writes: "In the figure of the beloved disciple the criterion [used in the later canonization process] of apostolicity and eyewitness origin has been anticipated" ("Entwicklungen der johanneischen Theologie," p. 292).

Gnostic systems. But that has been proven unsound as a result of the discovery of genuinely (Christian-)Gnostic writings at Nag Hammadi whose content is worlds apart from that of the Fourth Gospel. As for Judaism, the Qumran scrolls have shown that the Jewish intellectual world of that time had a much more varied character than was previously believed and that the Fourth Gospel is by no means alien to it.

Still, rejection of Johannine authorship, which has become a kind of tradition, has maintained itself at one point in the work of many scholars, namely the idea that underlying the Fourth Gospel there are older written sources from which the author is said to have derived his knowledge of the life of Jesus and of which his book is said to be the "Johannine" redaction. The author himself, they say, had no direct access to what is narrated and therefore no direct knowledge of it. But while some scholars view the linking of the Fourth Gospel with the beloved disciple as nothing more than an attempt to give it more authority and regard this disciple's authorship as a mere fiction,[74] others attempt to do more justice to 21:24. According to them, the author may very well have been in contact with the highly esteemed figure of the beloved disciple and may even have been subject to that disciple's theological influence. For that reason the disciple is named as the book's "causative" author. But even the disciple was not an eyewitness of Jesus himself but at most someone who had contact with persons from the earliest period and received from them firsthand information about Jesus, traces of which can still be pointed out in the Gospel.[75] But for by far the biggest part the author was dependent on earlier written sources. The originality of his work is said to lie in the grand manner in which he "theologically" processed the material he took from his sources.

At several salient points of the exegesis we have already dealt with this persistent distinction between traditional material taken over from the sources and its theological reworking by the author. We stumbled time after time on the utterly hypothetical, basically circular, and not infrequently forced character of this method. That it is such is undoubtedly why it leads to the most divergent results and is viewed by many other scholars with strong reserve and not infrequently with outright skepticism.[76] Naturally, this is not to say that the author, even if he himself was one of the eyewitnesses, cannot have made use of information supplied by others whom he held to be authentic witnesses. Just that his concluding summary describes the content of his writing as

74. See the construction of Bultmann described earlier, pp. 672f. above.

75. For these possible connections between the author and "the disciple whom Jesus loved" see the suggestions of Schnackenburg (*Comm.* III., pp. 373, 381ff.), which is considered authoritative for this whole view.

76. See, e.g., the lengthy, critical discussion of "Theories of Multiple Sources" (specifically Bultmann's) by Brown, *Comm.* I, pp. xxviii-xxxii. Thyen also speaks, though from a different perspective from ours, of the "vague hypothesis" of "written sources still open to reconstruction" such as Bultmann's "revelatory discourse source" and the sign source and passion source of others ("Entwicklungen der johanneischen Theologie," p. 282); elsewhere Thyen speaks against the idea of the "outright slavish use of sources by the Evangelist" (p. 267). He himself, however, does accept *Grundschrift* underlying the Gospel as we now have it (p. 283). See also de Jonge's very reserved attitude toward attempts "to dissect pericopes in order to assign sentences and clauses to various sources, traditions, and redaction layers" ("The Beloved Disciple and the Date of the Gospel of John," p. 107).

"signs that Jesus did in the presence of his disciples" means that he bases his narrative on more than his own testimony. And when in more than one incident or miraculous event he mentions the names of fellow disciples who were especially or even solely involved (cf. 1:43ff.; 6:5ff.; 12:21ff.), this indicates that there he was dependent on the knowledge of others. Here, too, in 21:24 we have to do with a statement that makes the beloved disciple above all the guarantor of the reliability of "these things" but that does not intend to be a comprehensive and exclusive formula with respect to his "testimony" or to the writing of his Gospel.

The heart of our objection to the above *view*, therefore, lies in the dependence on the sources *systematically* attributed to the author and the related "history-of-religions" approach that takes no, or hardly any, account of his status as eyewitness and limits the author's independence to his "theological" interpretation of the material furnished him beforehand. Inimical to such a position is the dominant unity of style and the carefully crafted structure and design that marks this Gospel, but it also falls utterly short the moment one takes into consideration the great diversity and freedom of presentation of all its narrative material. One can imagine — though it is hard to prove! — that for his miracle stories the Evangelist (also?) drew materials from a so-called Sign Source and that for his passion narrative he made use of an already existing older summary statement of Jesus' suffering and death. But what are we to think of the lengthy "dialogue stories," of the frequently lively question-and-answer "games" like those between Jesus and the Samaritan woman (ch. 4), between the man blind from birth and the Pharisees (ch. 9), between Jesus and Pilate (chs. 18, 19), to say nothing about the long disputational dialogues between Jesus and "the Jews" (chs. 5–8)?

Can we assume for all these stories — written, on the one hand, with great freedom and furnished, on the other, with numerous precise historical details[77] — that there were as many written sources because the author himself had nothing to contribute, since he had no independent access to what took place? Does not all this point to a much more general and closer historical involvement of the author in what he describes? And so, for the assessment of the whole, is there not a much more trustworthy starting point in the "testimony" of this disciple — strongly attested in 21:24 and clearly demonstrated in passages that concern the role of the beloved disciple — than in the hypothesis that replaces it, a hypothesis that works with hypothetical sources as though we had them lying on the table in front of us?

Conclusion

But regardless of what can be said in justified criticism against this systematic division of the Gospel into material from "sources" and the author's theological interpretation of that material, what is decisive is the fundamental objection that scholars have thus,

---

77. Cf. Westcott's detailed and still important argument with respect to this "indirect evidence" of Johannine authorship: "a) The author was a Jew; b) a Jew of Palestine"; a wide range of arguments from silence (that what the Evangelist does not describe he does not know) are therefore irrelevant (*Comm.*, pp. v-xviii). On the latter point see also Schnackenburg, *Comm.* I, p. 93.

in determining the unique character of the Fourth Gospel and the identity of its author, made an a priori separation in what for the author and for the Gospel he wrote was inseparable. What moves the Evangelist to write is not his theological ability to construct a grand christology from traditional material that he could not — and we certainly cannot — verify. It was, rather, the profound awareness and inspiration of having been a witness to revelation. In his writing he traces this awareness to — and articulates it as — the overwhelming personal experience of what he himself — in the great theme of the book — calls *beholding* the glory of God in *the flesh,* Jesus of Nazareth, *and* the intimately related awareness of being permitted and compelled to be the witness — sent by Jesus himself and led by the Spirit — to that glory.

It is these two elements, the personal experience and the call to be a witness, that determine not only the content of his book, but also his identity and credibility. That he is the apostle John, the son of Zebedee, is nowhere stated. It is rather deliberately concealed. The secret of the authority with which he points out and confirms to the church the foundation of its faith (20:30, 31) does not lie in his personal qualities but in the events whose glory he "beheld" and later, by the Spirit, learned to understand. The secret of his authority is perpetuated in the permanent and life-giving power of that witness for all who believe (20:30; 21:24).

Therefore, his book, as it emphatically attests and graphically tells of the entry of God's glory into our human reality, confronts us with questions to which we, from within our modern experience of reality, cannot give adequate answers any more than the first witnesses could from within their experience (cf. 11:40; 20:25). That is clear. We cannot change that by retreating from the "story" — as "of course" not original with the Evangelist himself — to the "safe haven" of his theology, as though the whole could thus retain some meaning within the boundaries of our thinking. What we are confronted with in this Gospel, as a matter of faith, is the salvific breaking down from above of the boundaries by which our thinking and acting are circumscribed (cf. 3:5). This confrontation, however, is not with a "higher reality" as such, one that would merely relativize our reality. The confrontation is with the entry into our reality of the glory ("the name," 17:6, 26, etc.) of God and with the "signs" of the "life" for which God once created and still continues to destine the world (1:4) — just as he who was "in the bosom of the Father" revealed that name and that life to us by his words and deeds (1:18)[78] so that "by believing in that name" we may have life (20:31).

---

78. See also C. A. van Peursen, *De Naam die geschiedenis maakt,* 1991, for his views, inter alia, of what he calls "the surrealism of the miracles" (pp. 106-16).

Index of Names

Index of Subjects

Index of Scripture References